AA

B&B Guide 2013

AA Lifestyle Guides

43rd edition
© AA Media Limited 2012.
AA Media Limited retains the copyright in the current edition
© 2012 and in all subsequent editions, reprints and amendments to editions.
The information contained in this directory is sourced from the AA's establishment database.

Please contact:
The Editor, AA B&B Guide, AA Media Limited, Fanum House, Basing View, Basingstoke, Hampshire RG21 4EA
Advertising Sales Department: advertisingsales@theAA.com
Editorial Department: lifestyleguides@theAA.com
AA Hotel Scheme Enquiries: 01256 844455

AA Media Limited would like to thank the following photographers, companies and picture libraries for their assistance in the preparation of this book.

Typeset by Servis Filmsetting Ltd, Stockport
Printed in Italy by Printer Trento SRL, Trento
Directory compiled by the AA Lifestyle Guides Department and managed in the Librios Information Management System and generated from the AA establishment database system.

Published by AA Publishing, which is a trading name of AA Media Limited whose registered office is: Fanum House, Basing View, Basingstoke, Hampshire RG21 4EA
Registered number 06112600

A CIP catalogue record for this book is available from the British Library.
ISBN: 978-0-7495-7360-7
A04891

Maps prepared by the
Mapping Services Department of
AA Publishing.

Maps © AA Media Limited 2012.

Contains Ordnance Survey data
© Crown copyright and database right 2012.
Licence number 100021153.

 Land & Property Services. This is based upon Crown Copyright and is reproduced with the permission of Land & Property Services under delegated authority from the Controller of Her Majesty's Stationery Office.
© Crown copyright and database rights 2012
Licence number 100,363.
Permit number 110096

 Ordnance Survey Ireland Ireland's National Mapping Agency
Republic of Ireland mapping based on © Ordnance Survey Ireland/ Government of Ireland Copyright
Permit number MP000611

Information on National Parks in England provided by the Countryside Agency (Natural England).

Information on National Parks in Scotland provided by Scottish Natural Heritage.

Information on National Parks in Wales provided by The Countryside Council for Wales.

Contents

How to Use the Guide

1 LOCATION, MAP REFERENCE & NAME

Each country is listed in alphabetical order by county then town/village. The Channel Islands and Isle of Man follow the England section and the Scottish islands follow the rest of Scotland. Establishments are listed alphabetically in descending order of Stars with any Gold Stars first in each rating.

The map page number refers to the atlas at the back of the guide and is followed by the National Grid Reference. To find the town/village, read the first figure across and the second figure vertically within the lettered square. You can find routes at **theAA.com** or **www.AAbookings.ie**. Farmhouse entries also have a six-figure National Grid Reference, which can be used with Ordnance Survey maps or **www.ordnancesurvey.co.uk**.

We also show the name of the proprietors, as often farms are known locally by their name.

London has its own Plans (see end of atlas), and London establishments have Plan number based on these.

2 CLASSIFICATION & DESIGNATOR

See pages 6 and 7.

Five Star establishments are highlighted as Premier Collection, and they are listed on page 20.

If the establishment's name is shown in *italics*, then details have not been confirmed by the proprietor for this edition.

⊛ **Rosettes** The AA's food award, see page 10.

🥚 **Egg cups and** 🥧 **pies** These symbols indicate that, in the experience of the inspector, either breakfast or dinner (or both) are really special, and have an emphasis on freshly prepared local ingredients.

3 E-MAIL ADDRESS & WEBSITE

E-mail and website addresses are included where they have been specified by the establishment. Such websites are not under the control of AA Media Limited, who cannot accept any responsibility or liability in respect

---

1 | **CORTON DENHAM** Map 4 ST62 | **1**

2 **The Queens Arms**
★★★★ ⊛ INN

DT9 4LR
☎ **01963 220317** 🖨 **01963 220797**
3 **e-mail:** relax@thequeensarms.com
web: www.thequeensarms.com
4 **dir:** *A303 exit Chapel Cross signed South Cadbury & Corton Denham. Follow signs to South Cadbury. Through village, after 0.25m turn left up hill signed Sherborne & Corton Denham. Left at top of hill, pub at end of village on right*

6 This is a proper inn located in peaceful countryside and complete with roaring log fire, a friendly welcome from the staff and a labrador in the bar. Bedrooms and bathrooms come in a range of shapes and sizes, and all are well decorated and comfortably furnished. In addition to a very good selection of real ales, this is a paradise for bottled beer lovers with a great choice from around the world. Excellent, quality local produce is utilised to provide a choice of delicious dinners which may be enjoyed in the traditional bar or character restaurant.

7 **Rooms** 5 en suite 3 annexe en suite (1 GF) S £80-£85; D £95-£120* **Facilities** FTV DVD iPod docking station Lounge tea/coffee Dinner available Direct Dial Cen ht **9** Wi-fi ⛵ 18 Riding 🏌 **Extras** Speciality toiletries, robes/slippers some rooms **Conf** Max 35 Thtr 35 Class 25 Board 35 **Parking** 20 **Notes** LB **8**

10 **11**

---

of any and all matters whatsoever relating to such websites.

4 DIRECTIONS & DISTANCES

Distances in **directions** are given in miles (m) and yards (yds), or kilometres (km) and metres (mtrs) in the Republic of Ireland.

5 PHOTOGRAPHS

Establishments may choose to include a photograph.

---

6 DESCRIPTION

Written by the inspector at the time of his or her visit.

7 ROOMS

The number of letting bedrooms (rms), or rooms with a bath or shower en suite are shown. Bedrooms that have a private bathroom (pri facs) adjacent are indicated.

The number of bedrooms in an annexe of equivalent standard are also shown. Facilities may not be the same as in the main building.

Charges are per night:

S bed and breakfast per person

D bed and breakfast for two people sharing a room. If an asterisk (∗) follows the prices this indicates 2012 prices.

The euro € is the currency of the Republic of Ireland.

Prices are indications only, so check before booking. Some places may offer free accommodation to children provided they share their parents' room.

8 FACILITIES

Most bedrooms will have TV. If this is important to you, please check when booking. If **TV4B** appears, this means that there are TVs in four bedrooms.

If **Dinner** is shown, you may have to order in advance. Please check when booking. For other abbreviations and symbols, see the table on the right.

9 EXTRAS

Anything the establishment offers in rooms that are more than expected e.g. specialist toiletries, trouser press, home-made biscuits etc.

10 PARKING

Parking is usually followed by the number of spaces. Motorists should be aware that some establishments may charge for parking. Please check when booking.

Key to Symbols and abbreviations

★☆	Classification (see page 6)
⊛	AA Rosette award (see page 10)
A	Associate entry (see page 7)
U	Unclassified rating (see page 7)
☎	Phone number
▤	Fax number
▤	A very special breakfast, with an emphasis on freshly prepared local ingredients
⊜	A very special dinner, with an emphasis on freshly prepared local ingredients
S	Single room
D	Double room (2 people sharing)
pri fac	Private facilities
fmly	Family bedroom
GF	Ground floor bedroom
LB	Short/Leisure breaks
✳	2012 prices
Cen ht	Full central heating
ch fac	Special facilities for children
TVL	Lounge with television
Lounge	Lounge without television
TV4B	Television in four bedrooms
STV	Satellite television
FTV	Freeview television
Wi-fi	Wireless internet
⊛	Credit/debit cards not accepted
tea/coffee	Tea and coffee-making facilities
Conf	Conference facilities
rms	Bedrooms in main building
Etr	Easter
fr	From
RS	Restricted service
⌀	Secure storage
⊗	No dogs
⊡	Indoor swimming pool
⊡	Heated indoor swimming pool
⊰	Outdoor swimming pool
⊰	Heated outdoor swimming pool
⅏	Croquet lawn
⊝	Tennis court
⌀	Golf (followed by number of holes)

11 NOTES

Although many establishments allow dogs, they may be excluded from some areas of the accommodation and some breeds, particularly those requiring an exceptional license, may not be acceptable at all. Under the Disability Discrimination Act 1995 access should be allowed to guide dogs and assistance dogs. Please check the establishment's policy when making your booking.

No children - children cannot be accommodated, or a minimum age may be specified, e.g. No Children 4yrs means no children under four years old.

Establishments with special facilities for children (**ch fac**) may include a babysitting service or baby-intercom system, playroom or playground, laundry facilities, drying and ironing facilities, cots, high chairs and special meals. If you have very young children, check before booking.

No coaches is published in good faith from details supplied by the establishment. Inns have well-defined legal obligations towards travellers; in the event of a query the customer should contact the proprietor or local licensing authority.

Additional facilities such as lifts or any leisure activities available are also listed.

LB indicates that Short or Leisure Breaks are available. Contact the establishment for details.

Establishments are open all year unless **Closed** days/dates/months are shown. Some places are open all year but offer a restricted service (**RS**) in low season. If the text does not say what the restricted services are you should check before booking.

Civ Wed 50 The establishment is licensed for civil weddings and can accommodate 50 guests for the ceremony.

⊛ shows that **credit/debit cards are not accepted**, but check when booking. Where credit cards are accepted there may be an extra charge.

Smoking Since July 1st 2007 smoking is banned in all public places in the United Kingdom and Ireland. The proprietor can designate one or more bedrooms with ventilation systems where the occupants can smoke, but communal areas must be smoke-free. Communal areas include the interior bars and restaurants in pubs and inns. We indicate number of smoking rooms (if any).

Conference facilities Conf indicates that facilities are available. Total number of delegates that can be accommodated is shown, plus maximum numbers in various settings.

AA Inspected Guest Accommodation

The AA inspects and classifies more than 2,600 guest houses, farmhouses, inns and restaurants with rooms for its Guest Accommodation Scheme, under common quality standards agreed between the AA, VisitBritain, VisitScotland and VisitWales. AA recognised establishments pay an annual fee according to the classification and the number of bedrooms. The classification is not transferable if an establishment changes hands.

The AA presents several awards within the Guest Accommodation scheme, including the **AA Friendliest B&B of the Year**, which showcases the very finest hospitality in the country, **Guest Accommodation of the Year Awards**, presented to establishments in Scotland, Ireland, Wales and England, **AA London B&B of the Year**, and **AA Funkiest B&B of the Year**. See pages 12 to 15 for this year's winners.

Stars

AA Stars classify guest accommodation at five levels of quality, from one at the simplest, to five offering the highest quality. In order to achieve a one Star rating an establishment must meet certain minimum entry requirements, including:

- A cooked breakfast, or substantial continental option is provided.
- The proprietor and/or staff are available for your arrival, departure and at all meal times.
- Once registered, you have access to the establishment at all times unless previously notified.
- All areas of operation meet minimum quality requirements for cleanliness, maintenance and hospitality as well as facilities and the delivery of services.
- A dining room or similar eating area is available unless meals are only served in bedrooms.

Our research shows that quality is very important to visitors. To obtain a higher Star rating, an establishment must provide increased quality standards across all areas, with particular emphasis in four key areas:

- Cleanliness and housekeeping
- Hospitality and service
- Quality and condition of bedrooms, bathrooms and public rooms
- Food quality

There are also particular requirements in order for an establishment to achieve three, four or five Stars, for example:

Three Stars and above
- access to both sides of all beds for double occupancy
- bathrooms/shower rooms cannot be used by the proprietor
- there is a washbasin in every guest bedroom (either in the bedrooms or the en suite/private facility)

Four Stars
- half of bedrooms must be en suite or have private facilities

Five Stars
- all bedrooms must be en suite or have private facilities

Establishments applying for AA recognition are visited by one of the AA's qualified accommodation inspectors as a mystery guest. Inspectors stay overnight to make a thorough test of the accommodation, food, and hospitality. After paying the bill the following morning they identify themselves and ask to be shown round the premises. The inspector completes a full report, resulting in a recommendation for the appropriate Star rating. After this first visit, the establishment will receive an annual visit to check that standards are maintained. If it changes hands, the new owners must re-apply for classification, as standards can change.

Guests can expect to find the following minimum standards at all levels:

- Pleasant and helpful welcome and service, and sound standards of housekeeping and maintenance
- Comfortable accommodation equipped to modern standards
- Bedding and towels changed for each new guest, and at least weekly if the room is taken for a long stay
- Adequate storage, heating, lighting and comfortable seating
- A sufficient hot water supply at reasonable times
- A full cooked breakfast. (If this is not provided, the fact must be advertised and a substantial continental breakfast must be offered)

When an AA inspector has visited a property, and evaluated all the aspects of the accommodation for comfort, facilities, attention to detail and presentation, you can be confident the Star rating will allow you to make the right choice for an enjoyable stay.

★ Highly Commended

Gold Stars indicate that an accommodation is in the top ten percent of its Star rating. Gold Stars only apply to 3, 4 or 5 Star establishments.

Accommodation Designators

Along with the Star ratings, six designators have been introduced. The proprietors, in discussion with our inspectors, choose which designator best describes their establishment:

BED & BREAKFAST

A private house run by the owner with accommodation for no more than six paying guests.

GUEST HOUSE

Run on a more commercial basis than a B&B, the accommodation provides for more than six paying guests and there are usually more services; for example staff as well as the owner may provide dinner.

FARMHOUSE

The B&B or guest house accommodation is part of a working farm or smallholding.

INN

The accommodation is provided in a fully licensed establishment. The bar will be open to non-residents and can provide food in the evenings.

RESTAURANT WITH ROOMS

This is a destination restaurant offering overnight accommodation, with dining being the main business and open to non-residents. The restaurant should offer a high standard of food and restaurant service at least five nights a week. A liquor licence is necessary and there is a maximum of 12 bedrooms.

GUEST ACCOMMODATION

Any establishment that meets the minimum entry requirements is eligible for this general category.

⊍ Unclassified entries

A small number of establishments in this guide have this symbol because their Star classification was not confirmed at the time of going to press. This may be due to a change of ownership or because the establishment has only recently joined the AA rating scheme. For up-to-date information on these and other new establishments check **theAA.com.**

⚠ Associate entries

These establishments have been inspected and rated by VisitBritain, VisitScotland or VisitWales, and have joined the AA scheme on a marketing-only basis. A limited entry for these places appears in the guide, while descriptions for these establishments appear on **theAA.com.**

Guesthouse Insurance

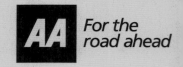

For the road ahead

We could **save you £££'s** on your insurance.

PRICE MATCH FACILITY *Now Available**

Our fantastic Guesthouse Insurance Package includes the following:

- ✔ Buildings and Contents, including frozen foods, wines & spirit
- ✔ Generous seasonal increases in stock cover
- ✔ Guests Effects
- ✔ Public Liability & Employers Liability
- ✔ Loss of Licence
- ✔ Business Interruption covered
- ✔ Money with personal accident & assault benefits

WHY CHOOSE US?

- • Highly Competitive Rates
- • Quick Quotes and Instant Cover
- • Over 40 years experience in commercial insurance
- • Pay in Instalments

- • Winner of numerous industry awards
- • Live Entertainment Covered
- • Friendly, experienced team waiting to take your calls

Call us on
0800 107 9787

There may be restricted access to some establishments, particularly in the late morning and the afternoon, so do check when booking.

London prices tend to be higher than outside the capital, and normally only bed and breakfast is provided, although some establishments do provide a full meal service.

Farmhouses: Sometimes the land has been sold and only the house remains, but many are working farms and some farmers are happy to allow visitors to look around, or even to help feed the animals. However, you should always exercise care and never leave children unsupervised. Although the directory entry states the acreage and the type of farming, do check when booking to make sure that it matches your expectations. The farmhouses are listed under towns or villages, but do ask for directions when booking.

Inns: Traditional inns often have a cosy bar, convivial atmosphere, and good beer and pub food. Those listed in the guide will provide breakfast in a suitable room, and should also serve light meals during licensing hours. The character of the properties vary according to whether they are country inns or town establishments. Check before you book, including arrival times as these may be restricted to opening hours.

Booking

Book as early as possible, particularly for the peak holiday period (early June to the end of September) and for Easter and other public holidays. In some parts of Scotland the skiing season is also a peak holiday period. Some establishments only accept weekly bookings from Saturday, and some require a deposit on booking.

Prices

Minimum and maximum prices are shown for one (S) and two people (D) per night and include a full breakfast. If dinner is also included this is indicated in brackets (incl dinner). Where prices are for the room only, this is indicated.

Useful Information *continued*

Prices in the guide include VAT (and service where applicable), except the Channel Islands where VAT does not apply.

Where proprietors have been unable to provide us with their 2013 charges we publish the 2012 price as a rough guide (shown by an asterisk *). Where no prices are given, please make enquiries direct.

Cancellation

If you have to cancel a booking, let the proprietor know at once. If the room cannot be re-let you may be held legally responsible for partial payment; you could lose your deposit or be liable for compensation, so consider taking out cancellation insurance.

Food and drink

Some guest accommodation provides evening meals, ranging from a set meal to a full menu. Some even have their own restaurant. You may have to arrange dinner in advance, at breakfast, or on the previous day, so do ask when booking.

If you book on bed, breakfast and evening meal terms, you may find that the tariff includes only the set menu. If there is a carte you may be able to order from this and pay a supplement.

On Sundays, many establishments serve the main meal at midday, and provide only a cold supper in the evening. In some parts of Britain, particularly in Scotland, high tea (i.e. a savoury dish followed by bread and butter, scones and cakes) is sometimes served instead of, or as an alternative to, dinner.

Facilities for Disabled Guests

The Equality Act 2010 provides legal rights for disabled people including access to goods, services and facilities, and means that service providers may have to consider making adjustments to their premises. For more information about the Act see www.direct.gov.uk/en/DisabledPeople/RightsAndObligations/DisabilityRights/DG_4001068 or www.equalities.gov.uk.

The establishments in this guide should be aware of their obligations under the Act. We recommend that you always telephone in advance to ensure that the establishment you have chosen has appropriate facilities.

Please note: AA inspectors are not accredited to make inspections under the National Accessibility Scheme. We indicate in entries if an establishment has ground floor rooms; and if a B&B tells us they have disabled facilities this is included in the description.

AA Rosette Awards
The AA awards Rosettes to over 2,000 restaurants as the best in the UK.

Excellent local restaurants serving food prepared with care, understanding and skill, using good quality ingredients.

The best local restaurants, which aim for and achieve higher standards and better consistency, and where a greater precision is apparent in the cooking. There will be obvious attention to the selection of quality ingredients.

Outstanding restaurants that demand recognition well beyond their local area.

Among the very best restaurants in the British Isles, where the cooking demands national recognition.

The finest restaurants in the British Isles, where the cooking compares with the best in the world.

AA B&B Awards

Each year the AA likes to celebrate the cream of the Guest Accommodation scheme crop. Held this year at The Royal Horseguards Hotel, London, the event recognised and rewarded more than 30 very deserving finalists, for demonstrating all-round excellence and unfailing standards, and for providing outstanding service to their guests. All finalists were treated to a champagne reception followed by a formal four-course celebratory luncheon. They also received a personalised certificate and an engraved Villeroy & Boch decanter, as well as a goody bag to take home with them.

Above: Alistair Sandall, AA Key Account Manager (left) presenting Lorraine with her award, accompanied by Michele Fitzpatrick (right) CEO of eviivo.

FRIENDLIEST B&B OF THE YEAR

Sponsored by **eviivo**

RAINS FARM ★★★★
Allerston, North Yorkshire Page 332

Rains Farm is a 17th-century farmhouse on the edge of the North Yorkshire Moors, and Lorraine Allanson has been part of the operation since it opened as a B&B in the 1980s. More than that, she was actually born here, on the farm. This means she not only knows the area like the back of her hand, but her pride in the farm and her ambition to make it a fulfilling and memorable place to stay are second to none. From the excellent local produce served at breakfast, to the lovely views from the attractive and well equipped bedrooms, everything is as good as Lorraine and her team can make it. As well as the B&B operation there are self-catering cottages available, and a good deal of wildlife can be observed in the area. Read more about Lorraine on page 16.

FUNKIEST B&B OF THE YEAR

DRAGONFLY ★★★★★

Chester, Cheshire Page 44

Dragonfly is an exclusive boutique townhouse in the heart of Chester city centre, where "hip meets history", effectively blending contemporary furnishings with an opulent Georgian setting. Individually designed rooms are modern and minimalist, but far from getting a cool reception, guests are treated as friends coming to stay. Each room is fully equipped with "dreamy beds", flat screen TV, floating workspaces with Wi-fi, and iPod docking station. Each room also has a quarry slate bathroom with a massive shower. The Dragonfly is distinctive and memorable in so many ways. An interview with Lucie Shipp is on page 20 of this guide.

GUEST ACCOMMODATION OF THE YEAR FOR LONDON

MARBLE ARCH BY MONTCALM
London W1 Page 207

Just a short walk from the bustle of Oxford St, Marble Arch by Montcalm is an oasis of calm and comfort, as well as being wonderfully opulent. In the lobby the spiral staircase is lit by a chandelier which is some twenty plus feet in length. The stylishly appointed bedrooms are equipped with everything the modern businessman or tourist could wish for; media hubs, mini-bars, air conditioning and many other notable extras. Bathrooms have a choice of baths or monsoon showers with quality towels and toiletries. All this combined with warm, friendly and helpful staff, who are on hand at every occasion to assist guests.

AA Guest Accommodation of the Year

Every year we ask our inspectors to nominate those establishments they feel come closest to the ideal of what a B&B should be. They consider location, food standards and quality of furniture and fittings, as well as charm and hospitality. From a shortlist of around 20, one is selected from each country in the guide.

ENGLAND

EAST HOUSE
Broadway, Worcestershire page 327

This stunning Cotswold stone property is at the top of the upper High Street, set in its own beautifully manicured garden, with stunning views over the local countryside. The proprietors moved here from London and have invested love and care into developing the house. Two new bedrooms and all public areas have recently been refurbished. There are four bedrooms in total, offering every luxury and comfort. The bathrooms are even better and are equipped with Bulgari toiletries. There are two lounges and a bijou dining room. Champange (or tea if preferred) is offered to guests on arrival.

SCOTLAND

ARDEN COUNTRY HOUSE

Linlithgow, West Lothian page 384

Set in 105 acres of wooded sheep farm, with stunning panoramic views, this delightful country house enjoys a peaceful location within easy reach of Edinburgh. Owner Beth Cruickshank ensures that guests can expect friendly hospitality and attentive service. The three en suite bedrooms are spacious, beautifully appointed and equipped with many thoughtful extras. A delightful breakfast room overlooks lovely landscaped gardens and breakfasts are indeed really special; Scottish specialities freshly cooked to order.

WALES
CRUG-GLAS COUNTRY HOUSE

Solva, Pembrokeshire page 408

This fine house is on a farm of approximately 600 acres, situated about a mile inland from the coast of St Davids Peninsula. It has high levels of comfort and relaxation, along with flawless attention to detail provided by charming host, Janet Evans. Each individually designed bedroom has well-chosen fabrics, grand furnishings and luxury bathrooms. The top floor suite has spectacular views. The restaurant is committed to using the best in local Pembrokeshire produce, while afternoon tea is served between 2 and 5pm.

REPUBLIC OF IRELAND
THE HERON'S COVE ★★★★ ◎ ⌂
Goleen, County Cork page 424

The Heron's Cove is a little gem that could easily be missed, tucked away on a side street in a delightful tidal cove, frequented by wildlife. Proprietor Sue Hill established the business in 1985, and now offers five very comfortable bedrooms that are smartly decorated and furnished, with good big beds and balconies. The traditional white washed house includes a restaurant and wine bar with an open turf fire.

The Warmest Welcome

Julia Hynard talks to Lorraine Allanson, from the AA's Friendliest B&B of the Year 2012-13, Rains Farm, Allerston, near Pickering in North Yorkshire

Lorraine Allanson was invited to the annual Bed and Breakfast of the Year awards as one of 25 finalists in the Friendliest B&B category. It never crossed her mind that she would win.

She attended the event at The Royal Horseguards Hotel in the heart of Whitehall in May, along with her mother and their respective partners. It is a magnificent hotel and Lorraine said how much they all enjoyed their stay there and the chance to explore and enjoy the sights of London. It was "a very special couple of days".

The 25 finalists came forward in turn to receive their crystal decanters, and she was among the last to be called. Realisation dawned, and she was "blown away" to be announced the winner.

"It's wonderful to win a competition that you haven't entered but been nominated for," she says, describing the AA as "an iconic brand – a brand you can definitely trust", which makes the award all the more significant to her.

A Life-long tenant at Rains Farm

Lorraine has lived all her life in the farmhouse where today she welcomes B&B guests. "I was born in this house,' she says, 'and I absolutely love it."

It's not hard to see why – the farmhouse and old stone barns, converted into five AA-rated self-catering cottages, are beautifully situated in a rural location with stunning views and "seven acres of wildlife heaven" with plenty of cover for local birds and animals to make their homes.

Lorraine's parents Ray and Jean Allanson came to the farm as a young couple in 1959, occupying half the main house at Rains Farm where Ray worked

"I am always delighted when someone comes to stay with me."

as a labourer. The couple's four children grew up there and after years of hard work, the family took over the tenancy. As a child aged five or six, Lorraine recalls helping out on the farm before school.

As a school-leaver, Lorraine worked on the farm full time, but went on to have a variety of other jobs, including a career as a semi-professional singer and stints of working in hotels and restaurants.

The family started the B&B as tenant farmers in the 1980s, and then had the chance to buy the farm in 1990 – a huge leap of faith with interest rates at 16%. The family agreed that half the mortgage payments would come from the farm and half from the B&B business.

Sadly, Ray died in 1994 and while they couldn't manage the farm, Jean and Lorraine were determined to keep their beloved home and develop their B&B business. The outbuildings were in a poor state, but they redesigned them as attractive self-catering cottages and refurbished the B&B accommodation. Out went the 1980s shared bathrooms and in came modern en suites. Lorraine explains that her mother had both ambition and a strong work ethic, which she has instilled in Lorraine. They were determined that the accommodation would provide the maximum comfort and that this was worth investing in – a policy they have stuck to through subsequent refurbishments.

Jean and Lorraine were also ahead of the times in their commitment to running an environmentally friendly business, designing their accommodation to include recycling facilities, for which they won an award from the local council. They still produce little waste, as they are avid recyclers and composters.

These days Lorraine does most of the work of the business herself, though mum Jean, now in her 70s, helps with the washing and when it gets really busy Lorraine's partner Andy (a landscape gardener) helps with the beds, but not often in the garden!

Life in this rural idyll could be quite isolating, – it's around a mile from the nearest village – particularly as Lorraine loves to be with people. So the business is a perfect fit for her personality. She gets to meet people every day and welcome them into the home of which she is so proud.

Lorraine provides a "relaxed and joyful environment". She says, "I try to judge just how much interaction my guests would like from me so that my service is attentive but not intrusive."

"Many guests like a good laugh or a chat; some want someone to listen to them, particularly if they are having a tough time in their lives, while others have their own agenda!"

The show must go on

Lorraine's years as a singer help her to maintain friendly and considerate service during her own tough times. She recalls when her father was very ill and passed out, hitting his head in the fall. She left her mother to call for assistance and literally stepped over him to go into the dining room with a big smile and a warm 'good morning' – the skills of professional hostess and seasoned performer.

She feels strongly that "the best memories for guests are those imprinted by the hosts. No matter how appealing the accommodation might be, if the warmth of the welcome falls short it will detract from the guest's experience and they may never return."

Good food is also integral to a stay at Rains Farm. Lorraine aims to give her guests "perfection on a plate" with breakfasts created from the best of local produce. She bakes her own bread and "takes great care over any food that leaves my kitchen". For other meals Lorraine has devised a food trail for her guests, including the best of local farm shops, cafés, bistros, pubs and fine dining restaurants.

Her guests are predominantly people who enjoy the peace of the countryside and the wild beauty of the area, including the North York Moors, the Heritage Coast, the Yorkshire Wolds and the area's many attractions. Lorraine says she has many guests who return year after year until it is like welcoming old friends back into your home.

For Lorraine, her ultimate ambition is for her guests to be happy. As she says, "I am always delighted when someone comes to stay with me. They could have stayed anywhere but they chose to come here and that's wonderful."

It is clear from talking to Lorraine that those who make that decision will not be disappointed.

The dining room at Dragonfly

A Dragonfly's Tale

The co-owners of Dragonfly in Chester were thrilled to pick up the AA's Funkiest B&B Award for 2012-13, and it's fair to say that the cool, stylish look blending Georgian charm with modish contemporary touches came about by design rather than chance.

Lucie Shipp and Kelvin Elliot met in 2006 when she was working as a Virgin air stewardess and he was in sales for Foxton estate agents. Both were business-minded but "we didn't know what we wanted to do for our first venture, so went to work in Australia for a year to look for inspiration," explains Lucie. Once there, they worked for Merivale – the Sydney-based hotel company and, having enjoyed setting up new boutique hotels, returned to the UK and took over Lucie's mum's fairly traditional 20-bedroomed B&B in Carlisle for a year. Here they gained some valuable experience, started saving "every penny we could" and, vitally, checked that they enjoyed running somewhere together. It was at that early stage that they started thinking about the design aspect. "We wanted to create a stylish, chic look, so everywhere we went

we collected pieces that fitted our image. For example, we went to the Lake District and found some retro 50s phones which we bought. We went to lots of antiques fairs and still do. It's definitely a work in progress". By this stage, the bits and pieces were piling up and her mum was asking where they were going to put them.

Knowing what they wanted to create, the couple then started to scout out the ideal location. "After lots of research, travelling around, and checking out websites, we looked for a gap in the market for our idea, somewhere that was busy all year round and didn't have anywhere like us." Chester fitted the bill and, having "looked at loads of properties", they saw the beautiful Georgian townhouse that is now Dragonfly. It was love at first sight. On the practical side, "it's very central

and right opposite the racecourse, so a great location" adds Lucie. The name Dragonfly, incidentally appealed to Lucie because in Japan, where she travelled in her previous air stewardess life, it stands for "success and prosperity".

All the basics were there in the Grade II listed property, but Lucie and Kelvin got stuck in to make sure their dream Bed & Breakfast became a reality. It took eight months to do everything, from replastering the walls to designing the rooms and finding the right place for all of their treasures (which include Eames and Barcelona chairs, as well as an old typewriter found languishing in the basement and now lovingly displayed) and they finished this massive undertaking on Christmas Eve 2009.

Lucie says that rather than being influenced by a particular designer,

they were "inspired by the vibe and atmosphere of places I'd seen in Brighton, plus we love Soho House, in fact we love all of the group's places. They're relaxed but a bit special with an eclectic feel."

Links with a local art gallery means there's a fresh display of pictures on the walls which guests can also buy if the fancy takes them. "It's quite modern, there's some amazing stuff similar to Banksy, we pick pieces we like that are in keeping with the design of the place." Farrow & Ball paint graces the walls and the five rooms feature all mod cons of flat screen TV, iPod dock and Wi-fi, along with en suite quarry slate bathrooms with massive showers. "No expense was spared" on superbly comfortable beds either, so it's far from a case of 'all style and no substance'.

The breakfast room "is such a lovely room. People love the Georgian features, and the patio doors open out onto the courtyard in the summer. Amazing mirrors reflect the light and make the huge room seem even bigger and Jazz FM plays away in the background." A detail not lost on their appreciative guests, as one gushed on the website comments, "even the radio was tuned to a trendy, funky station to enhance the mood."

Indeed many guests enjoy their stay so much they return time and again, such as the ones who came on the first day Dragonfly opened and now "book every year. It's perfect location-wise, you can pop in, freshen up then go straight out into town." Race days are understandably big business: "it's great for us, but there are only five meetings a year so we can't rely solely on that". Locals make up the

Left: A bedroom at Dragonfly

Right: A bathroom at Dragonfly

lion's share of the business, booking nights away for birthdays, weddings and anniversaries, and a few Americans make up the numbers. So enamoured are many of the guests that Lucie and Kelvin receive many dragonfly-themed gifts by way of thanks for a memorable stay.

Lucie believes that the old image of a chintzy B&B is out-of-date now in what's an increasingly competitive marketplace. "People expect a lot more, they're looking for personal service and some nice touches. When the likes of chain hotels such as Travelodge and Premier Inn are slashing their prices and there are so many B&Bs in the area we have to provide something special."

One of the ways they keep costs competitive is, in another non-traditional twist, not to insist guests take the breakfast element of the deal. "It's only £9.95 for everything and probably 75% of guests do take it, but then again we're so central that if people want to go to a café in Chester for breakfast they can do, though it'll probably cost more." It is however, Lucie adds, "part of the experience" and allows the hosts to demonstrate some of their notable hospitality. "We treat our guests as friends and strike up a good rapport with them" which also involves recommending places to dine out and remembering to ask about their meal the next day. Although Lucie and Kelvin aren't there 24 hours a day now, thanks to a new addition to the family, standards are met by manager Sam Giles, and the couple remain hands-on juggling childcare and their first baby.

"…even the radio was tuned to a trendy, funky station…"

When it comes to the future, the Shipps are understandably cautious of rapid expansion in the current market. "We've got a niche product, guests love the personal service and this is ultimately manageable, plus it gives us the space for family time". However, Lucie concedes "Possibly in a couple of years we might do some more research and open a second Dragonfly, maybe in York. It means starting all over again but we quite like the setting up, and we've been really lucky with Chester so who knows?"

★★★★★ Premier Collection

ENGLAND

BERKSHIRE
HURLEY
The Olde Bell Inn
WINDSOR
Magna Carta

BUCKINGHAMSHIRE
BEACONSFIELD
Crazy Bear Beaconsfield

CAMBRIDGESHIRE
ELTON
The Crown Inn

CHESHIRE
BURWARDSLEY
The Pheasant Inn
CHESTER
Dragonfly
Mitchell's of Chester Guest House
Oddfellows
Stone Villa Chester
MALPAS
Tilston Lodge
WARMINGHAM
The Bear's Paw

CORNWALL & ISLES OF SCILLY
LAUNCESTON
Primrose Cottage
LOOE
The Beach House
PADSTOW
The Seafood Restaurant
PENZANCE
Camilla House
Ennys
The Summer House
PERRANUTHNOE
Ednovean Farm
POLPERRO
Trenderway Farm
ST AUSTELL
Anchorage House
Highland Court Lodge
Lower Barn

ST BLAZEY
Nanscawen Manor House
Penarwyn House

CUMBRIA
AMBLESIDE
Drunken Duck Inn
BORROWDALE
Hazel Bank Country House
BRAMPTON
Lanercost Bed and Breakfast
CARTMEL
L'enclume
CONISTON
Wheelgate Country Guest House
CROSTHWAITE
The Punchbowl Inn at Crosthwaite
GRASMERE
Moss Grove Organic
KESWICK
The Grange Country Guest House
KIRKBY LONSDALE
Hipping Hall
Plato's
The Sun Inn
LORTON
The Old Vicarage
LUPTON
The Plough Inn Lupton
NEAR SAWREY
Ees Wyke Country House
NEWBY BRIDGE
The Knoll Country House
PENRITH
Brooklands Guest House
TROUTBECK
Broadoaks Country House
WINDERMERE
Applegarth Villa & Restaurant
The Cranleigh
The Howbeck
Newstead
Oakbank House
Windermere Suites
The Woodlands

DERBYSHIRE
ASHBOURNE
Turlow Bank
BELPER
Chevin Green Farm
Dannah Farm Country House
BRADWELL
The Samuel Fox Country Inn
BUXTON
Buxton's Victorian Guest House
HOPE
Underleigh House
MATLOCK
Holmefield Guest House
NEWHAVEN
The Smithy
WESTON UNDERWOOD
Park View Farm

DEVON
ASHWATER
Blagdon Manor
AXMINSTER
Kerrington House
BUDLEIGH SALTERTON
Heath Close
CHAGFORD
Parford Well
CHILLATON
Tor Cottage
DARTMOUTH
Nonsuch House
Strete Barton House
HORNS CROSS
The Round House
LUSTLEIGH
Eastwrey Barton
Woodley House
LYDFORD
Moor View House
LYNMOUTH
The Heatherville
LYNTON
Victoria Lodge
ROUSDON
The Dower House
SIDMOUTH
The Salty Monk

TEDBURN ST MARY
Frogmill Bed & Breakfast
TEIGNMOUTH
Thomas Luny House
TORQUAY
Linden House
The Marstan

DORSET

BRIDPORT
The Roundham House
The Shave Cross Inn
CHRISTCHURCH
Druid House
The Lord Bute & Restaurant
DORCHESTER
Little Court
FARNHAM
Farnham Farm House
SHAFTESBURY
The Old Chapel
SHERBORNE
The Kings Arms
Munden House
WAREHAM
Kemps Country House
WIMBORNE MINSTER
Les Bouviers Restaurant with Rooms

ESSEX

CHIPPING ONGAR
Diggins Farm
WIX
Dairy House Farm

GLOUCESTERSHIRE

BLOCKLEY
Lower Brook House
CHELTENHAM
Beaumont House
Cleeve Hill House
Georgian House
Lypiatt House
CHIPPING CAMPDEN
The Malt House
Staddlestones
CIRENCESTER
The Fleece at Cirencester

COLN ST ALDWYNS
The New Inn at Coln
NETHER WESTCOTE
The Feathered Nest Inn

HAMPSHIRE

ALTON
The Anchor Inn
BARTON-ON-SEA
Pebble Beach
BROCKENHURST
The Cottage Lodge
MILFORD ON SEA
Ha'penny House
SOUTHAMPTON
White Star Tavern, Dining and Rooms
WINCHESTER
Giffard House
Orchard House
29 Christchurch Road

HEREFORDSHIRE

HEREFORD
Somerville House
LEINTWARDINE
The Lion
LEOMINSTER
Hills Farm
The Old Rectory Pembridge
ROSS-ON-WYE
Orles Barn
Wilton Court Restaurant with Rooms

HERTFORDSHIRE

HERTFORD
Rigsbys Guest House
HERTFORD HEATH
Brides Farm
Rushen

KENT

CANTERBURY
Magnolia House
CRANBROOK
Waters End
DEAL
Sutherland House
DODDINGTON
The Old Vicarage

DOVER
The Marquis at Alkham
FOLKESTONE
The Relish
HAWKHURST
Southgate-Little Fowlers
IVYCHURCH
Olde Moat House
MARDEN
Merzie Meadows
ROYAL TUNBRIDGE WELLS
Danehurst House

LANCASHIRE

WHITEWELL
The Inn at Whitewell

LEICESTERSHIRE

KEGWORTH
Kegworth House

LINCOLNSHIRE

HEMSWELL
Hemswell Court
HOUGH-ON-THE-HILL
The Brownlow Arms
LINCOLN
Minster Lodge
MARKET RASEN
The Advocate Arms
STAMFORD
Meadow View
WINTERINGHAM
Winteringham Fields

LONDON POSTAL DISTRICTS

LONDON SW3
San Domenico House
LONDON W1
The Marble Arch by Montcalm

NORFOLK

BLAKENEY
Blakeney House
CLEY NEXT THE SEA
Old Town Hall House
GREAT HOCKHAM
Home Hall Organic B&B

★ ★ ★ ★ ★ Premier Collection *continued*

GREAT YARMOUTH
Andover House
3 Norfolk Square
HINDRINGHAM
Field House
NORWICH
Brasteds
SHERINGHAM
Ashbourne House
The Eiders Bed & Breakfast
The Eight Acres
THURSFORD
Holly Lodge

NORTHUMBERLAND
MORPETH
Eshott Hall
WOOLER
The Old Manse

NOTTINGHAMSHIRE
ELTON
The Grange
HOLBECK
Browns
NOTTINGHAM
Restaurant Sat Bains with Rooms

OXFORDSHIRE
ABINGDON-ON-THAMES
B&B Rafters
BANBURY
Tree Tops Guest House
BURFORD
Burford House
FARINGDON
Buscot Manor B&B
OXFORD
The Bocardo
Burlington House
STADHAMPTON
The Crazy Bear
WANTAGE
Brook Barn Country House
WITNEY
Old Swan & Minster Mill

SHROPSHIRE
BRIDGNORTH
The Albynes
CHURCH STRETTON
Field House
Willowfield Guest House
IRONBRIDGE
The Library House
LUDLOW
The Clive Bar & Restaurant with Rooms
De Greys of Ludlow
MARKET DRAYTON
Ternhill Farm House
& The Cottage Restaurant
OSWESTRY
Greystones
SHREWSBURY
Drapers Hall
Mad Jack's Restaurant & Bar

SOMERSET
BATH
Apsley House
The Ayrlington
Cheriton House
Chestnuts House
Dorian House
One Three Nine
Paradise House
Tasburgh House
DULVERTON
Tarr Farm Inn
FROME
Lullington House
HOLCOMBE
Holcombe Inn
NORTON ST PHILIP
Bath Lodge Castle
TAUNTON
Elm Villa
WELLS
Beaconsfield Farm
WESTON-SUPER-MARE
Church House
9 The Park
WITHYPOOL
Kings Farm
YEOVIL
Little Barwick House

STAFFORDSHIRE
LICHFIELD
Pipe Hill House
St Johns House
RUGELEY
Colton House
TAMWORTH
Oak Tree Farm

SUFFOLK
BURY ST EDMUNDS
Clarice House
HOLTON
Valley Farm
LAVENHAM
Lavenham Great House
'Restaurant With Rooms'
Lavenham Old Rectory
Lavenham Priory
SOUTHWOLD
Sutherland House
STOWMARKET
Bays Farm
YAXLEY
The Auberge

SURREY
CHIDDINGFOLD
The Crown Inn

SUSSEX, EAST
DITCHLING
Tovey Lodge
EASTBOURNE
The Berkeley
The Manse B&B
Ocklynge Manor
HASTINGS & ST LEONARDS
Barn House Seaview B&B
The Cloudesley
The Laindons
Stream House
HERSTMONCEUX
Wartling Place
RYE
Jeake's House
Manor Farm Oast
White Vine House

SUSSEX, WEST
CHICHESTER
Rooks Hill
The Royal Oak Inn
ROGATE
Mizzards Farm
SIDLESHAM
The Crab & Lobster
Lockgate Dairy
WEST MARDEN
West Marden Farmhouse

TYNE & WEAR
SUNNISIDE
Hedley Hall Country House

WARWICKSHIRE
ATHERSTONE
Chapel House Restaurant With Rooms
ETTINGTON
Fulready Manor
STRATFORD-UPON-AVON
Cherry Trees

WEST MIDLANDS
BIRMINGHAM
Westbourne Lodge

WIGHT, ISLE OF
GODSHILL
Godshill Park Farm House
Koala Cottage
NITON
Enchanted Manor
TOTLAND BAY
Sentry Mead
VENTNOR
The Hambrough
The Leconfield

WILTSHIRE
BOX
The Northey Arms
BURTON
The Old House at Home
CORSHAM
The Methuen Arms
DEVIZES
Blounts Court Farm

EDINGTON
The Three Daggers
SALISBURY
Quidhampton Mill

WORCESTERSHIRE
BEWDLEY
Kateshill House
Number Thirty
BROADWAY
Abbots Grange
East House
Mill Hay House
Russell's

YORKSHIRE, EAST RIDING OF
BEVERLEY
Burton Mount Country House
BRIDLINGTON
Marton Grange

YORKSHIRE, NORTH
AMPLEFORTH
Shallowdale House
APPLETREEWICK
Knowles Lodge
ASENBY
Crab Manor
BAINBRIDGE
Yorebridge House
BOROUGHBRIDGE
The Crown Inn
GOLDSBOROUGH
Goldsborough Hall
GRASSINGTON
Ashfield House
Grassington House
HETTON
The Angel Inn
KIRKBY FLEETHAM
The Black Horse
KNARESBOROUGH
General Tarleton Inn
LEYBURN
Capple Bank Farm
OLDSTEAD
The Black Swan at Oldstead
PICKERING
17 Burgate

RIPON
Mallard Grange
THIRSK
Spital Hill
THORNTON WATLASS
Thornton Watlass Hall

YORKSHIRE, WEST
HAWORTH
Ashmount Country House
HUDDERSFIELD
315 Bar and Restaurant

CHANNEL ISLANDS

JERSEY
ST AUBIN
The Panorama

ISLE OF MAN

ISLE OF MAN
PORT ST MARY
Aaron House

SCOTLAND

ARGYLL & BUTE
CONNEL
Ards House
OBAN
Blarcreen House

DUMFRIES & GALLOWAY
THORNHILL
Gillbank House

EDINBURGH, CITY OF
EDINBURGH
Elmview
Kew House
23 Mayfield
21212
The Witchery by the Castle

★★★★★ Premier Collection *continued*

FIFE
PEAT INN
The Peat Inn
ST ANDREWS
The Paddock

HIGHLAND
AVIEMORE
The Old Minister's House
BRACHLA
Loch Ness Lodge
DORNOCH
2 Quail
INVERNESS
Daviot Lodge
Trafford Bank
KINGUSSIE
The Cross at Kingussie
POOLEWE
Pool House

PERTH & KINROSS
ALYTH
Tigh Na Leigh Guesthouse

SCOTTISH BORDERS
MELROSE
Fauhope House

SOUTH AYRSHIRE
AYR
26 The Crescent

STIRLING
STRATHYRE
Creagan House

WEST LOTHIAN
LINLITHGOW
Arden Country House
LIVINGSTON
Ashcroft Farmhouse

SKYE, ISLE OF
STRUAN
Ullinish Country Lodge

WALES

ANGLESEY, ISLE OF
BEAUMARIS
Ye Olde Bulls Head Inn

CARMARTHENSHIRE
LLANWRDA
Tyllwyd Hir Bed & Breakfast
ST CLEARS
Coedllys Country House

CEREDIGION
ABERAERON
Feathers Royal
Ty Mawr Mansion
ABERYSTWYTH
Awel-Deg

CONWY
ABERGELE
The Kinmel Arms
BETWS-Y-COED
Penmachno Hall
Tan-y-Foel Country House
CONWY
The Groes Inn
The Old Rectory Country House
LLANDUDNO
Bryn Derwen
LLANRWST
Plas Maenan Country House
RHOS-ON-SEA
Plas Rhos

DENBIGHSHIRE
LLANDRILLO
Tyddyn Llan Restaurant
LLANDYRNOG
Pentre Mawr Country House
RUTHIN
Firgrove Country House B&B
ST ASAPH
Tan-Yr-Onnen Guest House

GWYNEDD
CAERNARFON
Plas Dinas Country House
DOLGELLAU
Tyddynmawr Farmhouse

MONMOUTHSHIRE
SKENFRITH
The Bell at Skenfrith
WHITEBROOK
The Crown at Whitebrook

PEMBROKESHIRE
FISHGUARD
Erw-Lon Farm
NARBERTH
The Grove
NEWPORT
Y Garth Boutique B&B
ST DAVIDS
Ramsey House
SOLVA
Crug-Glas Country House
Lochmeyler Farm Guest House

POWYS
BRECON
Canal Bank
The Coach House
Peterstone Court
CAERSWS
The Talkhouse
CRICKHOWELL
Glangrwyney Court
LLANDRINDOD WELLS
Guidfa House
WELSHPOOL
Moors Farm B&B

SWANSEA
MUMBLES
Little Langland
PARKMILL
Maes-Yr-Haf Restaurant with Rooms
REYNOLDSTON
Fairyhill

NORTHERN IRELAND

CO ANTRIM
BUSHMILLS
Causeway Lodge
Whitepark House

CO DOWN
HOLYWOOD
Rayanne House

CO LONDONDERRY
COLERAINE
Greenhill House

CO TYRONE
DUNGANNON
Grange Lodge

REPUBLIC OF IRELAND

CO CLARE
LAHINCH
Moy House

CO CORK
BLARNEY
Ashlee Lodge
KINSALE
Friar's Lodge
The Old Bank House
Rivermount House
SHANAGARRY
Ballymaloe House
YOUGHAL
Ahernes

DUBLIN
DUBLIN
Butlers Town House
Glenogra Town House
Harrington Hall

CO KERRY
DINGLE
Emlagh House
Gormans Clifftop House & Restaurant
KILLARNEY
Fairview Guest House
Foleys Town House
Old Weir Lodge
KILLORGLIN
Carrig House Country House & Restaurant

CO KILDARE
ATHY
Coursetown Country House

CO MEATH
SLANE
Tankardstown

CO MONAGHAN
GLASLOUGH
The Castle at Castle Leslie Estate

CO TIPPERARY
THURLES
The Castle
Inch House Country House & Restaurant

CO WATERFORD
BALLYMACARBRY
Hanoras Cottage
WATERFORD
Sion Hill House & Gardens

CO WEXFORD
CAMPILE
Kilmokea Country Manor & Gardens

England

View over Ashdown Forest

BEDFORDSHIRE

DUNSTABLE   Map 11 TL02

The Highwayman

★★★ INN

London Rd LU6 3DX
☎ 01582 601122 ▤ 01582 603812
e-mail: 6466@greeneking.co.uk
web: www.oldenglish.co.uk
dir: N'bound: M1 junct 9, A5, 6m on right. S'bound: M1
junct 11, A505, left on A5 towards London. Property on
left

This establishment continues to prove popular with
business guests, partly due to its convenient location just
south of the town, and also for its ample parking space.
The accommodation is comfortable, well equipped and
cheerfully decorated. The public areas include a large
public bar where meals are available.

Rooms 52 en suite (3 fmly) (24 GF) S £20–£70;
D £30–£90 (room only)* Facilities STV TVL tea/coffee
Dinner available Direct Dial Cen ht Wi-fi Parking 76
Notes LB ⊗

MILTON ERNEST   Map 11 TL05

The Queens Head

★★★ INN

2 Rushden Rd MK44 1RU
☎ 01234 822412 ▤ 01234 822337
e-mail: 6495@greeneking.co.uk
dir: From Bedford follow A6 towards Kettering, on left
entering Milton Ernest

This character inn provides good accommodation together
with a wide range of dishes from the imaginative menu,
and real ales from the cosy bar. Staff are friendly and
polite. Ample parking is available.

Rooms 13 en suite (4 GF) Facilities tea/coffee Direct
Dial Wi-fi Parking

WOBURN   Map 11 SP93

The Bell

★★★★ INN

21 Bedford St MK17 9QB
☎ 01525 290280 ▤ 01525 290017
e-mail: bell.woburn@oldenglishinns.co.uk
dir: M1 junct 13/A507 to Woburn Sands. Take 1st left,
then next left. At T-junct turn right

The bar, restaurant and some of the bedrooms are housed
in this charming inn, which has retained many original
features. The rest of the bedrooms, together with a
comfortable lounge, are located in a Georgian building
directly opposite. Ample parking is provided behind both
buildings.

Rooms 24 en suite (4 GF) Facilities tea/coffee Direct
Dial Parking 50

BERKSHIRE

BEENHAM   Map 5 SU56

The Six Bells

★★★★ ⇔ INN

The Green RG7 5NX
☎ 0118 971 3368
e-mail: info@thesixbells.co.uk
web: www.thesixbells.co.uk
dir: Exit A4 between Reading & Newbury, follow signs for
Beenham

The Six Bells is a traditional village pub with a good
atmosphere, friendly service and comfortable, well-
appointed bedrooms. The restaurant offers a good choice
of well-prepared and tasty dishes. The establishment is
convenient for Thatcham and Newbury.

Rooms 4 en suite Facilities FTV tea/coffee Dinner
available Cen ht Conf Max 40 Thtr 40 Class 40 Board 25
Parking 20 Notes ⊗ No Children 16yrs No coaches

BOXFORD   Map 5 SU47

High Street Farm Barn Bed &
Breakfast (SU424714)

★★★★ FARMHOUSE

RG20 8DD
☎ 01488 608783 & 07768 324707   Mr & Mrs Boden
e-mail: nboden@uk2.net
dir: 0.5m W of village centre. Off B4000 to Boxford, farm
1st on left opposite pub

A converted barn situated on a small holding in the
Berkshire village of Boxford. Bedrooms are smartly
furnished and a comfortable lounge is available for
guests use. Breakfast, which is served at one table,
includes free-range eggs from the farm and home-made
breads and marmalades.

Rooms 2 en suite (2 GF) S fr £55; D fr £75* Facilities FTV
tea/coffee Cen ht Parking 4 Notes ⊗ ⊜ 15 acres sheep

White Hart Cottage

★★★ BED AND BREAKFAST

Westbrook RG20 8DN
☎ 01488 608410
e-mail: gillian@jones-parry.orangehome.co.uk
dir: 0.3m NW of Boxford. Off B4000 to Boxford, left for
Westbrook, premises on right

Guests are ensured of a friendly welcome at this pretty
cottage, peacefully located in the delightful village of
Boxford. Newbury and the M4 are both just a short drive
away. Bedrooms are attractively appointed and guests
have access to a small TV lounge. A hearty breakfast is
served at the large kitchen table.

Rooms 3 rms (1 en suite) (2 pri facs) Facilities TVL TV2B
tea/coffee Cen ht Parking 6 Notes ⊗ No Children Closed
12 Dec-12 Jan ⊜

Bell @ Boxford

★★★ ◪ INN

Lambourn Rd RG20 8DD
☎ 01488 608721 ▤ 01488 608502
e-mail: paul@bellatboxford.com
dir: M4 junct 14, A338 towards Wantage. Right onto
B4000 to x-rds signed Boxford

Rooms 10 en suite (4 GF) S £45–£80; D £55–£90*
Facilities FTV DVD tea/coffee Dinner available Direct Dial
Cen ht Wi-fi Pool table Conf Max 12 Board 12 Parking 35

CHIEVELEY   Map 5 SU47

The Crab at Chieveley

★★★★★ ◉◉ GUEST ACCOMMODATION

Wantage Rd RG20 8UE
☎ 01635 247550 ▤ 01635 247440
e-mail: info@crabatchieveley.com
dir: 1.5m W of Chieveley on B4494

The individually themed bedrooms at this former pub
have been appointed to a very high standard and include
a full range of modern amenities. Ground-floor rooms
have a small private patio area complete with a hot tub.
The warm and cosy restaurant offers an extensive and
award-winning range of fish and seafood dishes.

Rooms 8 en suite 5 annexe en suite (7 GF) D £85–£105*
(incl.dinner) Facilities FTV DVD tea/coffee Dinner
available Direct Dial Cen ht Licensed Wi-fi Hot tub
Japanese spa suite Conf Max 14 Thtr 14 Class 14 Board
14 Parking 80 Notes LB

EAST GARSTON   Map 5 SU37

Queens Arms

★★★★ INN

RG17 7ET
☎ 01488 648757
e-mail: info@queenshotel.co.uk
dir: From A338 into Shefford, then follow signs to East
Garston. On right as you enter village

The perfect location for lovers of country pursuits, the
Queens Arms is located in the beautiful Lambourn Valley.
The individually themed bedrooms are well appointed and
offer sumptuous beds, flat screen TVs and Wi-fi. The bar
is well stocked, and the restaurant serves great British
food that is based on local produce.

Rooms 8 en suite (1 fmly) (1 GF) S £70–£90; D £80–£145
Facilities FTV DVD tea/coffee Dinner available Direct Dial
Cen ht Wi-fi ⅃ 18 Fishing Riding Parking 30 Notes LB
Closed 25 Dec

HUNGERFORD
Map 5 SU36

The Crown & Garter
★★★★ 🍽 INN

Great Common, Inkpen RG17 9QR
☎ **01488 668325**
e-mail: gill.hern@btopenworld.com
web: www.crownandgarter.co.uk
dir: *4m SE of Hungerford. Exit A4 into Kintbury, opposite corner stores into Inkpen Rd, straight on for 2m*

Peacefully located in the attractive village of Inkpen, this charming 17th-century inn has a bar with large inglenook log fire, where interesting well-prepared dishes are offered. The bedrooms surround a pretty garden, and are comprehensively equipped and attractively decorated in a country cottage style.

Rooms 9 annexe en suite (9 GF) **Facilities** FTV tea/coffee Dinner available Cen ht Wi-fi **Parking** 40 **Notes** LB ⊗ No Children 7yrs RS No lunch Mon/Tue No coaches

The Pheasant Inn
★★★★ 🍽 INN

Ermin St, Shefford Woodlands RG17 7AA
☎ **01488 648284** 🖷 **01488 648971**
e-mail: enquiries@thepheasant-inn.co.uk
web: www.thepheasant-inn.co.uk
dir: *M4 junct 14, A338, left onto B4000 towards Lambourn*

The Pheasant Inn is a friendly, traditional property conveniently located 400 yards from the M4 and close to the racing centre of Lambourn and also Newbury Racecourse. The horseracing theme runs throughout the traditional pub and restaurant where lunch and dinner are served daily. Bedrooms in contrast are contemporary in style providing guests with comfortable accommodation; all feature flat screen TVs, free Wi-fi and in-room beverage making facilities.

Rooms 11 en suite (4 GF) **Facilities** FTV TVL tea/coffee Dinner available Cen ht Wi-fi Shooting & fishing by arrangement **Conf** Max 14 Board 14 **Parking** 100

The Swan Inn
★★★★ 🍷 🍽 INN

Craven Rd, Inkpen RG17 9DX
☎ **01488 668326** 🖷 **01488 668306**
e-mail: enquiries@theswaninn-organics.co.uk
web: www.theswaninn-organics.co.uk
dir: *3.5m SE of Hungerford. S on Hungerford High St past rail bridge, left to Hungerford Common, right signed Inkpen*

This delightful village inn dates back to the 17th century, has open fires and beams in the bar, and the bonus of a smart restaurant. Bedrooms are generally spacious and well equipped. Organic produce is available from the on-site farm shop, so the bar, restaurant and breakfast menus all feature local organic produce too.

Rooms 10 en suite (2 fmly) S £70-£80; D £85-£105* **Facilities** FTV tea/coffee Dinner available Direct Dial Cen ht Wi-fi 🛁 **Extras** Trouser press **Conf** Max 40 Thtr 40 Class 40 Board 12 **Parking** 50 **Notes** ⊗ Closed 25-26 Dec

HURLEY
Map 5 SU88

The Olde Bell Inn
★★★★★ 🍽🍽 🍷 INN

High St SL6 5LX
☎ **01628 825881** 🖷 **01628 825939**
e-mail: oldebellreception@coachinginn.co.uk
dir: *M4 junct 8/9 follow signs for Henley. At rdbt take A4130 to Hurley, turn right to Hurley Village, 800yds on right*

Originally built in 1135, this charming coaching inn has lots of original features, and the cosy bar and lounge are warm and welcoming. There is a range of individually styled bedrooms, each with a modern well-equipped bathroom. The Olde Bell Inn has an award-winning restaurant and extensive landscaped gardens. The Tighe Barn and Malt House cater for functions and private parties, and there are a range of business facilities.

Rooms 11 en suite 37 annexe en suite (19 fmly) (21 GF) D £109-£400* **Facilities** FTV tea/coffee Dinner available Direct Dial Cen ht Wi-fi 🛁 🥾 **Conf** Max 130 Thtr 130 Class 50 Board 40 **Parking** 60 **Notes** Civ Wed 130

Black Boys Inn
★★★★ 🍽🍽 RESTAURANT WITH ROOMS

Henley Rd SL6 5NQ
☎ **01628 824212**
e-mail: info@blackboysinn.co.uk
web: www.blackboysinn.co.uk
dir: *1m W of Hurley on A4130*

Just a short drive from Henley, the traditional exterior of this friendly establishment is a contrast to the smart modernity within. Popular with locals, the restaurant is the stage for Simon Bonwick's imaginative cuisine, and has a buzzing atmosphere. The well-appointed bedrooms are situated in converted barns close by.

Rooms 8 annexe en suite (5 GF) S £75-£87.50; D £87.50-£120* **Facilities** FTV tea/coffee Dinner available Cen ht Wi-fi **Conf** Max 8 Board 8 **Parking** 40 **Notes** No coaches

KNOWL HILL
Map 5 SU87

Bird in Hand Country Inn
★★★★ 🅰 INN

Bath Rd RG10 9UP
☎ **01628 826622 & 822781** 🖷 **01628 826748**
e-mail: info@birdinhand.co.uk
dir: *M4 junct 8/9, A404 towards Henley. At junct 9b onto A4 towards Reading, 3m, Knowl Hill on right after BP garage*

Rooms 3 en suite 12 annexe en suite (1 fmly) (6 GF) S £40-£110; D £60-£120* **Facilities** FTV tea/coffee Dinner available Direct Dial Cen ht Wi-fi **Conf** Max 50 Thtr 50 Class 30 Board 40 **Parking** 80 **Notes** LB

NEWBURY   Map 5 SU46

Pilgrims Guest House

★★★★ GUEST ACCOMMODATION

Oxford Rd RG14 1XB
☎ 01635 40694 📠 01635 44873
e-mail: office@pilgrimsgh.co.uk
web: www.pilgrimsnewbury.co.uk
dir: *In Newbury exit A4 at Waitrose rdbt onto B4494 towards Wantage, 0.5m on left*

Located close to the town centre, this smartly presented house has comfortable bedrooms with modern bathrooms; some rooms are located in a new annexe. Wi-fi is provided throughout the property and breakfast is served in the bright dining room. Parking is available.

Rooms 13 rms (9 en suite) 4 annexe en suite (1 fmly) (3 GF) S £43-£56.50; D £56-£65* **Facilities** FTV Lounge tea/coffee Cen ht Wi-fi 🔒 **Parking** 17 **Notes** ⊗ Closed 24 Dec-2 Jan

Rookwood Farm House

★★★★ GUEST ACCOMMODATION

Stockcross RG20 8JX
☎ 01488 608676 📠 01488 657961
e-mail: charlotte@rookwoodfarmhouse.co.uk
dir: *2m W of Newbury, at junct A4 & A34 onto B4000, 0.75m to Stockcross, 1st right signed Woodspeen, bear left, 1st on right*

This farmhouse enjoys wonderful views and is very much a family home. Bedrooms are attractively presented and feature fine pieces of furniture. Breakfast is served on one large table in the kitchen. The coach house has a kitchen and sitting room and, during the summer, visitors can enjoy the beautiful gardens and outdoor pool.

Rooms 2 rms (1 en suite) (1 pri facs) 2 annexe en suite (1 fmly) S £55-£65; D £80-£90* **Facilities** TVL tea/coffee Cen ht Wi-fi ↝ 🌂 ⚲ 9 **Conf** Max 16 Board 16 **Parking** 4 **Notes** ⊗

The Limes Guest House

★★★ GUEST HOUSE

368 London Rd RG14 2QH
☎ 01635 33082 📠 01635 580023
e-mail: s.j.sweeney@btinternet.com
web: www.limesguesthouse.co.uk
dir: *M4 junct 13, 3m S towards Newbury. Take A4 to towards Thatcham/Reading, 400yds past Newbury Business Park on left*

Built in 1910, this Edwardian house is convenient for Newbury and Thatcham, and Newbury Racecourse is only a mile away. The en suite bedrooms are individually decorated. Wi-fi internet access and ample parking are available. Breakfast is served in the light dining room overlooking the well-kept rear garden.

Rooms 17 en suite (2 fmly) (9 GF) S £58-£68; D £78-£98* **Facilities** FTV TVL tea/coffee Dinner available Direct Dial Cen ht Licensed Wi-fi 🔒 **Parking** 20 **Notes** ⊗

PANGBOURNE   Map 5 SU67

Weir View House

★★★★ GUEST ACCOMMODATION

9 Shooters Hill RG8 7DZ
☎ 0118 984 2120 📠 0118 984 3777
e-mail: info@weirview.co.uk
web: www.weirview.co.uk
dir: *A329 N from Pangbourne, after mini-rdbt under rail bridge, opposite The Swan pub*

A warm welcome is guaranteed at this delightful house, situated in the village of Pangbourne overlooking the River Thames. The spacious modern bedrooms have been finished to a very high standard and the thoughtful extras include a well-stocked mini-bar. A continental breakfast is served in the bright and airy dining room, and freshly cooked meals can be delivered to your room from the pub across the road.

Rooms 9 en suite (6 fmly) (3 GF) **Facilities** FTV DVD TVL tea/coffee Direct Dial Cen ht Wi-fi 🔒 **Extras** Mini-bar - chargeable, robes/slippers in some rooms **Conf** Max 10 Board 10 **Parking** 10 **Notes** ⊗

See advert on opposite page

READING   Map 5 SU77

Chestnuts Bed & Breakfast

★★★ BED AND BREAKFAST

Basingstoke Rd, Spencers Wood RG7 1AA
☎ 0118 988 6171 & 07903 956397
e-mail: chestnuts4bb@hotmail.com
dir: *M4 junct 11, A33 for Basingstoke, next rdbt onto B3349 (Three Mile Cross), over white-spot rdbt. Chestnuts 1m on left between chemist & bakery*

This detached Georgian house is convenient for the business parks of Reading, just 1.5 miles from the M4 and with easy access to the M3. The house provides spacious bedrooms, warm hospitality, a good breakfast, and off-road parking.

Rooms 2 rms 2 annexe en suite S £35-£45; D £50-£55* **Facilities** FTV tea/coffee Cen ht Wi-fi **Parking** 4 **Notes** ⊗ No Children 16yrs 🚭

The Wee Waif

★★★ INN

Old Bath Rd, Charvil RG10 9RJ
☎ 0118 944 0066 📠 0118 969 1525

Located on the outskirts of Reading with easy access to popular transport networks. Bedrooms provide lodge style accommodation with guest comfort in mind. All day dining is available from the popular Hungry Horse restaurant and bar, where breakfast is also served. Ample parking is available.

Rooms 42 en suite **Parking**

La Baguette Reading

★★ GUEST ACCOMMODATION

7 Blagrave St RG1 1PJ
☎ 0118 956 0882 & 07966 263843 📠 0118 957 4650
e-mail: bookings@labaguettes.co.uk

Located a short walk from Reading town centre, and close to the main train station. Bedrooms vary in size and provide comfortable accommodation for the traveller. A varied choice of breakfast is served in the popular 'La Baguette' sandwich shop below.

Rooms 6 rms (6 pri facs) (2 fmly) S £55-£95; D £75-£135* **Facilities** STV FTV tea/coffee Cen ht Wi-fi **Notes** LB

SLOUGH   Map 6 SU97

Furnival Lodge

★★★★ 🄰 GUEST HOUSE

53-55 Furnival Av SL2 1DH
☎ 01753 570333 📠 01753 670038
e-mail: info@furnival-lodge.co.uk
web: www.furnival-lodge.co.uk
dir: *Just off A355 (Farnham Rd), adjacent to BP garage*

Rooms 10 en suite (1 fmly) (3 GF) **Facilities** TVL Cen ht Wi-fi **Parking** 7 **Notes** ⊗

Save on B&Bs and Hotels. Book at **theAA.com/hotel**

BERKSHIRE 35 **ENGLAN**

WINDSOR
Map 6 SU97

PREMIER COLLECTION

Magna Carta
★★★★★ 🏛 GUEST ACCOMMODATION

Thames Side SL4 1QN
☎ 07836 551912
e-mail: dominic@magna-carta.co.uk
web: www.magna-carta.co.uk
dir: *M4 junct 5 follow signs to Datchet, then Windsor. At Windsor & Eton riverside station turn right & down to river*

A most exciting way to experience life-afloat, this superbly equipped barge offers bed and breakfast between charter cruising on the Thames. Accommodation is particularly comfortable and pleasantly spacious. The lounge and deck space is notable too, not only for the river views, but for the wealth of facilities, there is a hot tub on deck, and an impressive range of books, DVDs and music, but also a well stocked bar, from where the large picture windows look on to the tranquil river. Breakfast cooked in the galley, is super, offering an excellent choice from local suppliers.

Rooms 4 en suite S £120-£130; D £150-£170*
Facilities DVD Lounge tea/coffee Cen ht Licensed Wi-fi Hot tub **Conf** Max 8 Board 8 **Notes** LB ⊗ RS pre-booked cruises

Innkeeper's Lodge Old Windsor
★★★★ INN

Staright Rd, Old Winsdor SL4 2RR
☎ 0845 112 6104
e-mail: info@innkeeperslodge.com
web: www.innkeeperslodge.com

At Innkeeper's Lodge you'll find accommodation with comfort and character in equal measure, and everything needed for a relaxing stay, from easy check-in and free parking to complimentary breakfast and a cosy pub serving great value food and drink on the doorstep. Each Lodge has quality rooms, and there are Lodges in a variety of locations from towns and cities to countryside settings across the UK.

Rooms 15 en suite (2 fmly) (7 GF) **Facilities** FTV tea/coffee Dinner available Direct Dial Wi-fi **Parking**

Park Farm
★★★★ GUEST ACCOMMODATION

St Leonards Rd SL4 3EA
☎ 01753 866823
e-mail: stay@parkfarm.com
dir: *M4 junct 6, at end of dual-carriageway take 3rd exit. At T-junct, turn right, Park Farm on left*

Ideally situated between Windsor and Legoland, Park Farm offers a warm welcome and traditionally styled accommodation. Each bedroom has a range of useful facilities. Some rooms also have romantic wrought-iron beds. The owners aim to offer guests a friendly and personal service including advice and information on where to eat or what to do in the area. Bunk beds can be added for children.

Rooms 4 rms (3 en suite) (1 pri facs) (2 fmly) (2 GF) S £65-£85; D £85-£95* **Facilities** FTV DVD iPod docking station tea/coffee Cen ht Wi-fi **Parking** 8 **Notes** ⊗ ⚙

Clarence Guest House
★★★ GUEST HOUSE

9 Clarence Rd SL4 5AE
☎ 01753 864436 📠 01753 857060
e-mail: clarence.hotel@btconnect.com
web: www.clarencehotelwindsor.co.uk
dir: *M4 junct 6, dual carriageway to Windsor, left at 1st rdbt into Clarence Rd*

This Grade II listed Victorian house is in the heart of Windsor. Space in some rooms is limited, but all are well maintained and offer excellent value for money. Facilities include a lounge with a well-stocked bar, and a steam room. Breakfast is served in the dining room overlooking attractive gardens.

Rooms 20 en suite (6 fmly) (2 GF) (15 smoking) S £45-£84; D £49-£94 **Facilities** FTV DVD TVL tea/coffee Cen ht Licensed Wi-fi Sauna Steam room **Parking** 4 **Notes** LB

WINDSOR *continued*

The Windsor Trooper

★★★ INN

97 St Leonards Rd SL4 3BZ
☎ 01753 670123
e-mail: thewindsortrooper@live.co.uk
dir: *M4 junct 6, at rdbt follow signs for Windsor, then straight over next 2 rdbts signed Staines-on-Thames, take 1st road on left*

Located close to many local attractions and in walking distance of the town centre, this traditional inn provides comfortable annexed accommodation with some rooms suitable for families. Dinner is available in the bright and airy conservatory, where a range of daily specials are often available. A freshly prepared breakfast is served and limited secure car parking is available.

Rooms 4 en suite 5 annexe en suite (3 fmly) (5 GF)
Facilities FTV tea/coffee Dinner available Cen ht Wi-fi
Parking 9 **Notes** ⊗

WOKINGHAM   Map 5 SU86

Quarters

★★★★ GUEST ACCOMMODATION

14 Milton Rd RG40 1DB
☎ 0118 979 7071 📠 0118 977 0057
e-mail: elaineizod@hotmail.com
dir: *From town centre on A321 towards Henley & Twyford. Left at 1st mini-rdbt into Milton Rd*

Located just a short walk from the town centre, a warm welcome is assured here. Stylishly decorated bedrooms are well equipped and spacious. A hearty breakfast is served around the communal dining table.

Rooms 3 en suite S £45-£50; D £65-£70* **Facilities** FTV DVD iPod docking station tea/coffee Cen ht Wi-fi **Notes** ⊗ No Children ✉

BRISTOL

BRISTOL   Map 4 ST57

Westfield House

★★★★ ➾ BED AND BREAKFAST

37 Stoke Hill, Stoke Bishop BS9 1LQ
☎ 0117 962 6119 📠 0117 325 9965
e-mail: admin@westfieldhouse.net
dir: *1.8m NW of city centre in Stoke Bishop*

A genuine welcome is assured at this friendly, family-run B&B in a quiet location on the edge of Durdham Downs. The very well-equipped bedrooms offer high levels of quality and comfort. Home-cooked dinners are available by arrangement, and in summer these can be enjoyed on the patio overlooking the large rear garden.

Rooms 3 en suite S £65-£98; D £85-£120* **Facilities** FTV DVD TVL tea/coffee Dinner available Direct Dial Cen ht Wi-fi ✱ **Conf** Max 10 Board 10 **Parking** 5 **Notes** LB ⊗ No Children 11yrs

---

Downs Edge

★★★★ GUEST HOUSE

Saville Rd, Stoke Bishop BS9 1JA
☎ 0117 968 3264 & 07885 866463 📠 0117 968 7063
e-mail: welcome@downsedge.com
web: www.downsedge.com
dir: *M5 junct 17, A4018, at 4th rdbt right onto B4054 (Parrys Ln), 1st left into Saville Rd, 3rd right into Hollybush Ln, left after 2nd speed ramp into Downs Edge Drive*

This attractive country house has a quiet parkland setting in the heart of the city, on the edge of Durdham Downs. It stands in glorious gardens and is furnished with period pieces and paintings. The pleasant, well-equipped bedrooms have en suite facilities and the added bonus of sweeping views across the Downs. A nice finishing touch to each room is a basket of life's little necessities. Breakfast is an impressive variety of hot and cold dishes. There is a drawing room with an open fire, and a library containing many books about Bristol.

Downs Edge

Rooms 4 en suite 3 annexe en suite S £59-£69;
D £79-£88* **Facilities** FTV Lounge tea/coffee Cen ht Wi-fi
Conf Board 12 **Parking** 8 **Notes** ⊗ No Children 6yrs
Closed Xmas & New Year

See advert on opposite page

Greenlands *(ST597636)*

★★★★ FARMHOUSE

BS39 4ES
☎ 01275 333487 📄 01275 331211 **Mrs J Cleverley**

(For full entry see Stanton Drew (Somerset))

Valley Farm

★★★★ BED AND BREAKFAST

Sandy Ln BS39 4EL
☎ 01275 332723 & 07799 768161
e-mail: valleyfarm2010@btinternet.com

(For full entry see Stanton Drew (Somerset))

Westbury Park Guest House

★★★★ GUEST HOUSE

37 Westbury Rd, Westbury-on-Trym BS9 3AU
☎ 0117 962 0465
e-mail: westburypark@btconnect.com
dir: *M5 junct 17, A4018, 3.5m opposite gates of Badminton School*

On the edge of Durdham Downs, this detached guest house is ideally located for many of Bristol's attractions. Breakfast is served in the spacious dining room overlooking the front garden. Bedrooms and bathrooms come in a range of shapes and sizes, including one room on the ground floor.

Rooms 8 en suite (1 fmly) (1 GF) **Facilities** tea/coffee
Cen ht Wi-fi **Parking** 3 **Notes** ⊗ No Children 5yrs

Mayfair Lodge

★★★ GUEST HOUSE

5 Henleaze Rd, Westbury-on-Trym BS9 4EX
☎ 0117 962 2008 📄 0117 962 2008
e-mail: enquiries@mayfairlodge.co.uk
dir: *M5 junct 17, A4018, after 3rd rdbt into Henleaze Rd. Lodge 50yds on left*

This charming Victorian house is in a residential area close to Durdham Downs and Bristol Zoo. Mayfair Lodge has well-equipped bedrooms of varying sizes and a relaxed, friendly atmosphere. Breakfast is served at separate tables in the bright dining room. Off-road parking is available behind the property.

Rooms 9 rms (6 en suite) **Facilities** FTV tea/coffee Cen ht
Wi-fi **Parking** 6 **Notes** ⊗ No Children 10yrs Closed Xmas
& New Year

The Washington

★★★ GUEST HOUSE

11-15 St Pauls Rd, Clifton BS8 1LX
☎ 0117 973 3980 📄 0117 973 4740
e-mail: washington@cliftonhotels.com
dir: *A4018 into city, right at lights opposite BBC, house 200yds on left*

This large terraced house is within walking distance of the city centre and Clifton Village. The bedrooms are well equipped for business guests. Public areas include a modern reception lounge and a bright basement breakfast room. The property has secure parking and a rear patio garden.

Rooms 46 rms (40 en suite) (4 fmly) (10 GF) S £42-£73;
D £59-£91* **Facilities** FTV tea/coffee Direct Dial Cen ht
Licensed Wi-fi Reduced rate pass for local health club
Extras Fresh fruit **Parking** 16 **Notes** Closed 23 Dec-3 Jan

BUCKINGHAMSHIRE

AMERSHAM   Map 6 SU99

Wildhatch

★★★★ BED AND BREAKFAST

Coleshill Ln, Winchmore Hill HP7 0NT
☎ 01494 722611 & 07736 713636 📄 01494 722611
e-mail: di.john.wildhatch@btinternet.com
dir: *M40 junct 2 N on A355, after 1.5m left at Harte & Magpies public house. Fork left at Coleshill & continue to Winchmore Hill, house 2nd on left after 30mph sign*

This beautifully presented modern house offers well-equipped bedrooms and comfortable public rooms. Hospitality is a major strength. Delicious, freshly cooked breakfasts are served in the dining room overlooking the gardens and surrounding countryside. Weather permitting breakfast may be taken on the terrace. Close to major motorway links.

Rooms 2 en suite (1 fmly) S £45-£50; D £65-£75
Facilities FTV DVD TVL tea/coffee Dinner available Cen ht
Wi-fi ⚓ 18 🔦 cycle hire **Parking** 4 **Notes** LB ⊗ Closed 23
Dec-17 Jan ⊛

ASTON CLINTON   Map 5 SP81

Innkeeper's Lodge Aylesbury (East)

★★★★ INN

London Rd HP22 5HP
☎ 0845 112 6094
e-mail: info@innkeeperslodge.com
web: www.innkeeperslodge.com

At Innkeeper's Lodge you'll find accommodation with comfort and character in equal measure, and everything needed for a relaxing stay, from easy check-in and free parking to complimentary breakfast and a cosy pub serving great value food and drink on the doorstep. Each Lodge has quality rooms, and there are Lodges in a variety of locations from towns and cities to countryside settings across the UK.

Rooms 11 en suite (4 fmly) (3 GF) **Facilities** FTV tea/
coffee Dinner available Direct Dial Wi-fi **Parking**

AYLESBURY   Map 11 SP81

Innkeeper's Lodge Aylesbury (South)

★★★★ 🍽 INN

40 Main St, Weston Turville HP22 5RW
☎ 0845 112 6095
e-mail: info@innkeeperslodge.com
web: www. innkeeperslodge.com

At Innkeeper's Lodge you'll find accommodation with comfort and character in equal measure, and everything needed for a relaxing stay, from easy check-in and free parking to complimentary breakfast and a cosy pub serving great value food and drink on the doorstep. Each Lodge has quality rooms, and there are Lodges in a variety of locations from towns and cities to countryside settings across the UK.

Rooms 16 en suite (5 GF) **Facilities** FTV tea/coffee Dinner available Direct Dial Wi-fi **Parking**

BEACONSFIELD Map 6 SU99

PREMIER COLLECTION

Crazy Bear Beaconsfield

★★★★★ ❀ GUEST ACCOMMODATION

75 Wycombe End, Old Town HP9 1LX
☎ 01494 673086 📠 01494 730183
e-mail: enquiries@crazybear-beaconsfield.co.uk
dir: M40 junct 2, 3rd exit from rdbt, next rdbt 1st exit.
Over 2 mini-rdbts, on right

Located in the heart of the old town, this former inn
dating from Tudor times has been completely restored
to create an exciting and vibrant environment. Good
food in both the Thai and the English restaurants,
classic cocktails and an extensive wine list can be
enjoyed. The rooms are individually appointed with
unusual fabrics and dazzling colours.

Rooms 6 en suite 4 annexe en suite (2 GF)
Facilities STV Dinner available Direct Dial Cen ht
Licensed Wi-fi ⚓ Jacuzzi **Conf** Max 40 Board 22
Parking 12 **Notes** ⊗

BRILL Map 11 SP61

Poletrees Farm *(SP660160)*

★★★★ FARMHOUSE

Ludgershall Rd HP18 9TZ
☎ 01844 238276 📠 01844 238276 Mrs A Cooper
e-mail: poletrees.farm@btinternet.com
dir: Exit S from A41 signed Ludgershall/Brill, after railway
bridge 0.5m on left

Located between the villages of Ludgershall and Brill,
this 16th-century farmhouse retains many original
features including a wealth of exposed beams. The
bedrooms are in converted outbuildings, and the cosy
dining room is the setting for a wholesome breakfast.

Rooms 4 annexe en suite (4 GF) S £40-£60; D £80*
Facilities FTV TVL tea/coffee Cen ht **Parking** 6 **Notes** LB
⊗ No Children 10yrs 110 acres beef/sheep

CHALFONT ST GILES Map 6 SU99

The White Hart

★★★ INN

Three Households HP8 4LP
☎ 01494 872441 & 0845 608 6040
e-mail: 5630@greeneking.co.uk

At the heart of this beautiful village, is located this
popular inn. The bedrooms are modern and well equipped,
while public areas feature a spacious lounge bar and a
relaxed dining/conservatory area where a varied selection
of dishes is available. Public parking is adjacent to the
inn and there are also pleasant grounds.

Rooms 11 en suite (5 GF) **Facilities** FTV tea/coffee Dinner
available Cen ht Wi-fi **Conf** Max 50 Thtr 50 Class 20
Board 20 **Parking** 34

DENHAM Map 6 TQ08

The Falcon Inn

★★★★ ➰ INN

Village Rd UB9 5BE
☎ 01895 832125
e-mail: mail@falcondenham.com
web: www.falcondenham.com
dir: M40 junct 1, follow A40 & Gerrards Cross signs.
Approx 200yds, right into Old Mill Rd, pub opposite
village green

This 18th-century inn stands in the heart of the
picturesque village of Denham, opposite the green. The
bedrooms, with smart shower rooms en suite, are well
equipped and display original features. Carefully
prepared dishes and a good selection of wines are
available for lunch and dinner in the cosy restaurant.

Rooms 4 en suite S £78; D £90 (room only)*
Facilities FTV DVD tea/coffee Dinner available Cen ht
Wi-fi 🔒 **Extras** Fresh fruit **Notes** LB No Children 10yrs

FORD Map 5 SP70

Dinton Hermit

★★★ INN

Water Ln HP17 8XH
☎ 01296 747473 📠 01296 748819
e-mail: relax@dintonhermit.co.uk
dir: 2m from A418

A restored 400-year-old, Grade II listed property that now
provides a smart restaurant and atmospheric bedrooms in
both the old inn and in the 200-year-old barn conversion.
Bedrooms are well equipped and comfortable, and the
restaurant is popular with locals and guests alike.

Rooms 7 rms (5 en suite) (2 pri facs) 6 annexe en suite
(8 GF) S £92.50; D £92.50* **Facilities** FTV tea/coffee
Dinner available Cen ht Wi-fi **Extras** Mineral water
Parking 40 **Notes** LB

GREAT MISSENDEN Map 6 SP80

Nags Head Inn & Restaurant

★★★★ ❀ INN

London Rd HP16 0DG
☎ 01494 862200 📠 01494 862685
e-mail: goodfood@nagsheadbucks.com
web: www.nagsheadbucks.com
dir: N of Amersham on A413, left at Chiltern hospital into
London Rd signed Great Missenden

This delightful 15th-century inn located in the
picturesque Chiltern Hills, has a popular reputation
locally thanks to its extensive menu with local produce
and carefully prepared dishes. Individually designed
bedrooms are comfortable with a modern twist ensuring a
home-from-home feel. Ample parking is available.

Rooms 5 en suite (1 fmly) S £75-£115; D £95-£115*
Facilities FTV tea/coffee Dinner available Cen ht Wi-fi 🔒
Extras Speciality toiletries **Conf** Max 50 **Parking** 40

See advert on opposite page

HAMBLEDEN
Map 5 SU78

The Stag & Huntsman
[U]

RG9 6RP
☎ 01491 571227
e-mail: enquiries@thestagandhuntsman.co.uk

Currently the rating for this establishment is not confirmed. This may be due to a change of ownership or because it has only recently joined the AA rating scheme.

Rooms 9 en suite S £80–£110; D £90–£140*

HIGH WYCOMBE
Map 5 SU89

Clifton Lodge
★★★ GUEST HOUSE

210 West Wycombe Rd HP12 3AR
☎ 01494 440095 ◻ 01494 536322
e-mail: mail@cliftonlodgehotel.com
web: www.cliftonlodgehotel.com
dir: A40 from town centre towards Aylesbury, on right after BP station & opposite phone box

Located west of the town centre, this long-established, owner-managed establishment provides a range of bedrooms, popular with a regular commercial clientele. Public areas include an attractive conservatory-dining room and a cosy lounge. Ample parking behind the property.

Rooms 32 rms (20 en suite) (1 fmly) (7 GF) **Facilities** FTV Lounge tea/coffee Dinner available Cen ht Licensed Wi-fi **Conf** Max 25 Thtr 25 Class 20 Board 15 **Parking** 28 **Notes** LB ⊗

IVINGHOE
Map 11 SP91

The Brownlow B&B
★★★★ GUEST ACCOMMODATION

LU7 9DY
☎ 01296 668787
e-mail: info@thebrownlow.com
dir: A41 to Tring then A488 to Ivinghoe/Dunstable. Follow Leighton Buzzard signs

The Brownlow at Ivinghoe was built in the early 1800s to serve the newly finished Grand Union Canal, and it has remained in the same family ever since. The old stables have now been converted into well-appointed bedrooms, which offer plenty of modern amenities. Breakfast is served at the communal table overlooking the canal. The Brownlow was a Finalist in the AA Friendliest B&B of the Year Award 2012-13.

Rooms 5 en suite (5 GF) **Facilities** FTV TVL tea/coffee Cen ht Wi-fi **Parking** 6 **Notes** ⊗ No Children 6yrs

MILTON KEYNES
Map 11 SP83

The Cock
★★★ INN

72-74 High St, Stony Stratford MK11 1AH
☎ 01908 567733 ◻ 01908 562109
e-mail: 6432@greeneking.co.uk
dir: In village centre

This historic 15th-century coaching inn is situated in the picturesque market town of Stony Stratford with the Silverstone ace Circuit nearby. The bedrooms are en suite and equipped with modern amenities, food is served all day whilst the function room is the perfect venue for all occasions. Parking is available.

Rooms 31 en suite (4 fmly) (7 GF) **Facilities** tea/coffee Dinner available Direct Dial Cen ht Wi-fi **Conf** Max 100 Thtr 100 Class 50 Board 45 **Parking** **Notes** ⊗ Civ Wed 100

WADDESDON
Map 11 SP71

The Five Arrows
★★★★ ⊖ RESTAURANT WITH ROOMS

High St HP18 0JE
☎ 01296 651727 ◻ 01296 655716
e-mail: five.arrows@nationaltrust.org.uk
dir: On A41 in Waddesdon. Into Baker St for car park

This Grade II listed building with elaborate Elizabethan chimney stacks, stands at the gates of Waddesdon Manor and was named after the Rothschild family emblem. Individually styled en suite bedrooms are comfortable and well appointed. Friendly staff are on hand to offer a warm welcome. Alfresco dining is possible in the warmer months.

Rooms 11 en suite (3 GF) **Facilities** FTV tea/coffee Dinner available Direct Dial Cen ht Wi-fi **Conf** Max 20 Thtr 20 Class 20 Board 20 **Parking** 40 **Notes** Civ Wed 60

CAMBRIDGESHIRE

BOXWORTH
Map 12 TL36

The Golden Ball Inn
★★★★ INN

High St CB23 4LY
☎ 01954 267397 ◻ 01954 267497
e-mail: info@goldenballhotel.co.uk
dir: In village centre

The Golden Ball is a delightful 17th-century thatched inn with modern accommodation. The bedrooms are well appointed and each bathroom has a bath and power shower. The inn is very popular for its restaurant, pub meals and real ales, and service is helpful and friendly.

Rooms 11 en suite (1 fmly) (9 GF) **Facilities** FTV tea/coffee Dinner available Direct Dial Cen ht Wi-fi **Parking** 75

CAMBRIDGE
Map 12 TL45

Benson House
★★★★ GUEST HOUSE

24 Huntingdon Rd CB3 0HH
☎ 01223 311594 📠 01223 311594
e-mail: bensonhouse@btconnect.com
web: www.bensonhouse.co.uk
dir: *0.5m NW of city centre on A604*

This popular guest house is well placed for the city centre and New Hall and Fitzwilliam colleges. Its pleasant bedrooms vary in size and style and are well equipped. There is limited private parking behind the property.

Benson House

Rooms 6 en suite (1 GF) **Facilities** FTV tea/coffee Cen ht Wi-fi **Parking** 5 **Notes** ⊗ No Children 12yrs Closed 31 Dec

Rose Corner
★★★★ BED AND BREAKFAST

42 Woodcock Close, Impington CB24 9LD
☎ 01223 563136 & 07733 027581
e-mail: enquiries@rose-corner.co.uk
web: www.rose-corner.co.uk
dir: *4m N of Cambridge. A14 junct 32, B1049 N into Impington, exit Milton Rd into Woodcock Close*

Rose Corner is a detached property in a quiet cul-de-sac in the popular village of Impington, north of the city. Its spacious bedrooms are carefully furnished and thoughtfully equipped, and breakfast is served in the comfortable lounge/dining room overlooking the rear gardens.

Rooms 5 rms (3 en suite) S £35; D £70 **Facilities** FTV TVL tea/coffee Cen ht Wi-fi **Parking** 5 **Notes** ⊗ No Children 11yrs

The Alpha Milton Guest House
★★★ GUEST ACCOMMODATION

61-63 Milton Rd CB4 1XA
☎ 01223 311625 📠 01223 565100
e-mail: info@alphamilton.com
dir: *0.5m NE of city centre*

The Alpha Milton is in a residential area just a short walk from the city centre. The attractive lounge-dining room overlooks the rear garden, and the pleasant bedrooms all have a good range of facilities.

Rooms 8 rms (7 en suite) (1 pri facs) (2 fmly) (2 GF) S £50-£70; D £70-£90 (room only)* **Facilities** DVD TVL tea/coffee Dinner available Cen ht Wi-fi **Parking** 8 **Notes** ⊗

Hamden Guest House
★★★ GUEST HOUSE

89 High St, Cherry Hinton CB1 9LU
☎ 01223 413263 📠 01223 245960
e-mail: info@hamdenguesthouse.co.uk
web: www.hamdenguesthouse.co.uk
dir: *3m SE of city centre. From M11 exit A1134 to Cherry Hinton; from A14 exit N on A1303 signed Cambridge & Cherry Hinton*

Expect a warm welcome at this small, family-run guest house, which is just a short drive from the city centre. The

Save on B&Bs and Hotels. Book at theAA.com/hotel

CAMBRIDGESHIRE 41 ENGLAND

pleasant bedrooms are generally quite spacious and equipped with many thoughtful extras. Public rooms include a large kitchen-dining room where breakfast is served at individual tables.

Hamden Guest House

Rooms 3 en suite (2 fmly) (1 GF) S £40-£50; D £60-£70 **Facilities** FTV tea/coffee Direct Dial Cen ht Wi-fi **Parking** 6 **Notes** LB ⊗ No Children 5yrs

See advert on opposite page

Southampton Guest House

★★★ GUEST HOUSE

7 Elizabeth Way CB4 1DE
☎ 01223 357780 📠 01223 314297
e-mail: southamptonhouse@btinternet.com
web: www.southamptonguesthouse.com
dir: 0.5m E of city centre

The proprietors provide a friendly service at their terraced guest house, which is on the inner ring road, just a short walk from the Grafton Centre. The property has well-equipped bedrooms, and a comprehensive English breakfast is served.

Southampton Guest House

Rooms 5 en suite (3 fmly) (1 GF) S £35-£50; D £45-£58 **Facilities** tea/coffee Direct Dial Cen ht Wi-fi **Parking** 8 **Notes** ⊗ 🚭

ELTON	Map 12 TL09

PREMIER COLLECTION

The Crown Inn

★★★★★ INN

8 Duck St PE8 6RQ
☎ 01832 280232
e-mail: inncrown@googlemail.com
web: www.thecrowninn.org
dir: A1 junct 17, A605 W. In 3.5m right signed Elton, 0.9m, left signed Nassington. On village green

Expect a warm welcome at this delightful village pub, situated opposite the village green. The property dates back to the 16th century, and has undergone major refurbishment in the last few years, yet retains many of its original features, such as a large inglenook fireplace and oak-beamed ceilings. The smartly decorated bedrooms are tastefully appointed and thoughtfully equipped. Public rooms include a large open-plan lounge bar, a small relaxed dining area to the front, and a tastefully appointed circular restaurant.

The Crown Inn

Rooms 3 en suite 2 annexe en suite (2 fmly) (2 GF) **Facilities** FTV DVD tea/coffee Dinner available Direct Dial Cen ht Wi-fi ♿ **Conf** Max 40 Thtr 25 Class 40 Board 25 **Parking** 15 **Notes** RS Sun eve & Mon (ex BH) Restaurant only closed No coaches

See advert on page 42

ELY	Map 12 TL58

The Anchor Inn

★★★★ ⊛ 🍴 RESTAURANT WITH ROOMS
- -
Sutton Gault CB6 2BD
☎ 01353 778537 📠 01353 776180
e-mail: anchorinn@popmail.bta.com
dir: W of Ely. Sutton Gault signed from B1381 at S end of Sutton

Located beside the New Bedford River with stunning country views, this 17th-century inn has a wealth of original features enhanced by period furniture. The spacious bedrooms are tastefully appointed and equipped with many thoughtful touches. The friendly team of staff offer helpful and attentive service.

Rooms 4 en suite (2 fmly) **Facilities** FTV tea/coffee Dinner available Direct Dial Cen ht Wi-fi **Parking** 16 **Notes** ⊗ No coaches

The Nyton

★★★★ 🍴 GUEST ACCOMMODATION
- -
7 Barton Rd CB7 4HZ
☎ 01353 662459 📠 01353 666217
e-mail: nytonhotel@yahoo.co.uk
dir: From S, A10 into Ely on Cambridge Rd, pass golf course, 1st right

Set in two acres of mature gardens, this family-run establishment offers comfortable bedrooms in a range of sizes and styles. The pleasant public rooms include a wood-panelled restaurant, a smart bar, and a conservatory-lounge overlooking the gardens. Meals are available in the dining room and informal light meals are served in the lounge bar.

Rooms 9 en suite (3 fmly) (2 GF) **Facilities** FTV TVL tea/coffee Dinner available Direct Dial Cen ht Licensed Wi-fi ♿ 18 **Conf** Max 40 Thtr 40 Class 20 Board 40 **Parking** 25 **Notes** ⊗ Civ Wed 100

ELY *continued*

The Three Pickerels

★★★★ INN

19 Bridge Rd, Mepal CB6 2AR
☎ 01353 777777 ▤ 01353 777891
e-mail: info@thethreepickerels.co.uk
web: www.thethreepickerels.co.uk

Situated in the tranquil village of Mepal on the outskirts of Ely, this property sits on the banks of the New Bedford River and has views of the surrounding grassland. Public rooms include a smart bar, a dining room and a lovely lounge overlooking the river. The smartly appointed bedrooms are comfortable and well equipped.

Rooms 4 en suite (1 fmly) S fr £50; D fr £85*
Facilities FTV TVL tea/coffee Dinner available Cen ht Wi-fi Fishing Pool table **Parking** 40 **Notes** LB ⊗

HILTON   Map 12 TL26

The Prince of Wales

★★★ INN

Potton Rd PE28 9NG
☎ 01480 830257 ▤ 01480 830257
e-mail: simon@thehiltonpow.co.uk
dir: *A14 onto B1040 towards Biggleswade, 2m into village, Prince of Wales on left*

This popular village inn offers a choice of cosy traditional bars serving good food and real ales. The pleasantly decorated bedrooms are equipped with modern facilities. A hearty breakfast is served in the dining room at individual tables.

Rooms 4 en suite S £39-£49; D £65-£75 **Facilities** FTV DVD tea/coffee Dinner available Direct Dial Cen ht Wi-fi Pool table **Parking** 12 **Notes** No Children 5yrs

---

HINXTON   Map 12 TL44

The Red Lion Inn

★★★★ ◉ INN

32 High St CB10 1QY
☎ 01799 530601 ▤ 01799 252601
e-mail: info@redlionhinxton.co.uk
dir: *Nbound only: M11 junct 9, towards A11, left onto A1301. Left to Hinxton. Or M11 junct 10, A505 towards A11/Newmarket. At rdbt 3rd exit onto A1301, right to Hinxton*

The Red Lion Inn is a 16th-century free house pub-restaurant, with high quality purpose-built accommodation, set in the pretty conservation village of Hinxton. In the winter guests can relax by the well-stoked fire, while in summer they can relax in the attractive walled garden, overlooked by a dovecote and the village church.

Rooms 8 annexe en suite (2 fmly) (8 GF) S £90; D £115-£135* **Facilities** FTV DVD tea/coffee Dinner available Direct Dial Cen ht Wi-fi **Parking** 43 **Notes** LB

HOLYWELL   Map 12 TL37

The Old Ferryboat Inn

★★★ INN

Back Ln PE27 4TG
☎ 01480 463227 ▤ 01480 463245
e-mail: 8638@greeneking.co.uk

This delightful thatched inn sits in a tranquil setting beside the Great Ouse river, on the periphery of the village of Holywell. Said to be the oldest inn in England, with foundations dating back to 560AD, the inn retains much original character and charm. Bedrooms are soundly appointed, and the open-plan public rooms have a pleasing relaxed atmosphere: the extensive gardens, with views of the river, are a popular attraction in the summer months.

Rooms 7 en suite **Facilities** tea/coffee Dinner available Cen ht Wi-fi **Conf** Max 60 Thtr 60 Class 32 Board 24 **Parking** 70

HUNTINGDON   Map 12 TL27

Cheriton House

★★★★★ ☒ BED AND BREAKFAST

Mill St, Houghton PE28 2AZ
☎ 01480 464004 ▤ 01480 496960
e-mail: sales@cheritonhousecambs.co.uk
dir: *In village of Houghton, through village square, signed to river & mill*

Rooms 2 en suite 3 annexe en suite (3 GF) S £72-£75; D £75-£88* **Facilities** FTV DVD Lounge tea/coffee Cen ht Wi-fi ⊁ ♨ ♪ 12 🔒 **Parking** 7 **Notes** LB ⊗ No Children 14yrs

---

PETERBOROUGH Map 12 TL19

Aaron Park

★★★★ GUEST ACCOMMODATION

109 Park Rd PE1 2TR
☎ 01733 564849 🖹 01733 564855
e-mail: aaronparkhotel@yahoo.co.uk
dir: A1 onto A1139 to junct 5, to city centre on Boongate, over rdbt into Crawthorne Rd, over lights, next left

Family service is both friendly and helpful at this Victorian house, which is situated in a tree-lined avenue just a short walk from the city centre and cathedral. Bedrooms come in a variety of styles and sizes; each room is nicely presented and has a good range of modern facilities. Freshly cooked breakfasts are carefully presented and provide a good start to the day.

Rooms 10 en suite (3 fmly) (2 GF) S £48; D £75*
Facilities FTV tea/coffee Cen ht Wi-fi **Parking** 8 **Notes** ⊗ Closed Xmas

STETCHWORTH Map 12 TL65

The Old Mill

★★★★ BED AND BREAKFAST

Mill Ln CB8 9TR
☎ 01638 507839 & 07831 179948
e-mail: gbell839@aol.com
dir: In village centre off Tea Kettle Ln

Situated in a delightful village, the Old Mill consists of a thoughtfully equipped self-contained flat sleeping four, with a small kitchen, quality pine furniture and a DVD player. Access is via a private staircase leading to a sun terrace overlooking mature gardens. Breakfast is served at a large communal table in the main house.

Rooms 1 annexe en suite **Facilities** FTV TVL tea/coffee Cen ht Wi-fi 🐾 **Parking** 2 **Notes** ⊗

UFFORD Map 12 TF00

The White Hart

★★★★ 🍽 INN

Main St PE9 3BH
☎ 01780 740250 🖹 01780 740927
e-mail: info@whitehartufford.co.uk

Just five miles from Stamford and ten miles from Peterborough, this charming 17th-century inn is home to Ufford Ales which are served in the bar. The property is built from local stone and retains many of its original features. The delightful bedrooms are tastefully furnished and thoughtfully equipped. Public rooms include a lounge bar, conservatory and restaurant.

Rooms 6 en suite (2 GF) **Facilities** tea/coffee Dinner available Cen ht Wi-fi **Conf** Max 30 Thtr 30 Class 20 Board 20 **Parking** 30 **Notes** Civ Wed 30

WILLINGHAM Map 12 TL47

Willingham House

★★★★ 🍽 GUEST ACCOMMODATION

50 Church St CB4 5HT
☎ 01954 260606 🖹 01954 260603
e-mail: willinghamhouse@hotmail.com
web: www.cambridgewillinghamhouse.com
dir: A14 junct 29 onto B1050 to Willingham

A former rectory, this elegant Victorian house has been sympathetically renovated and extended to provide high standards of comfort and facilities. Bedrooms are thoughtfully furnished, and imaginative dinners are served in an attractive dining room. Extensive conference facilities and pretty mature grounds are additional features.

Rooms 16 en suite 6 annexe en suite (7 GF) **Facilities** TVL tea/coffee Dinner available Cen ht Licensed Wi-fi Pool table **Conf** Max 40 Thtr 40 Class 23 Board 24 **Parking** 40 **Notes** ⊗ Closed 25-27 Dec

CHESHIRE

ALDERLEY EDGE Map 16 SJ87

Innkeeper's Lodge Alderley Edge

★★★★ INN

5-9 Wilmslow Rd SK9 7QN
☎ 0845 112 6020
e-mail: info@innkeeperslodge.com
web: www.innkeeperslodge.com

At Innkeeper's Lodge you'll find accommodation with comfort and character in equal measure, and everything needed for a relaxing stay, from easy check-in and free parking to complimentary breakfast and a cosy pub serving great value food and drink on the doorstep. Each Lodge has quality rooms, and there are Lodges in a variety of locations from towns and cities to countryside settings across the UK.

Rooms 10 en suite (2 fmly) **Facilities** FTV tea/coffee Dinner available Direct Dial Wi-fi **Parking** 50

AUDLEM Map 15 SJ64

Little Heath Farm (SJ663455)

★★★★ FARMHOUSE

CW3 0HE
☎ 01270 811324 Mrs H M Bennion
e-mail: littleheath.farm@gmail.com
dir: Exit A525 in village onto A529 towards Nantwich for 0.3m. Farm opposite village green

The 200-year-old brick farmhouse retains much original character, including low beamed ceilings. The traditionally furnished public areas include a cosy sitting room and a dining room where guests dine family style. The bedrooms are stylish, and the friendly proprietors create a relaxing atmosphere.

Rooms 3 en suite (1 fmly) **Facilities** TVL tea/coffee Cen ht **Conf** Max 10 Board 10 **Parking** 6 **Notes** ⊗ 50 acres mixed

BURWARDSLEY Map 15 SJ55

PREMIER COLLECTION

The Pheasant Inn

★★★★★ 🍽 INN

Higher Burwardsley CH3 9PF
☎ 01829 770434 🖹 01829 771097
e-mail: info@thepheasantinn.co.uk
web: www.thepheasantinn.co.uk
dir: From A41, left to Tattenhall, right at 1st junct & left at 2nd Higher Burwardsley. At post office left, signed

This delightful 300-year-old inn sits high on the Peckforton Hills and enjoys spectacular views over the Cheshire Plain. Well-equipped, comfortable bedrooms are housed in an adjacent converted barn. Creative dishes are served either in the stylish restaurant or in the traditional, beamed bar. Real fires are lit in the winter months.

Rooms 2 en suite 10 annexe en suite (2 fmly) (5 GF) S £55-£130; D £75-£140* **Facilities** FTV Lounge tea/coffee Dinner available Direct Dial Cen ht Wi-fi ♿ 18 **Parking** 80

Cheshire Cheese Cottage

★★★★ BED AND BREAKFAST

Burwardsley Rd CH3 9NS
☎ 01829 770887 🖹 01829 770887
e-mail: r.rosney@yahoo.co.uk

A very warm welcome awaits at this delightful little cottage, which is set in its own extensive grounds and colourful gardens on the outskirts of the village. The

continued

BURWARDSLEY *continued*

accommodation consists of two modern bedrooms on the ground floor. There is also a conservatory which doubles as both lounge and breakfast room; breakfasts are freshly cooked and hearty. Owner Rose Rosney is a qualified masseur and guests can book treatments if they wish.

Rooms 2 en suite (2 GF) **Facilities** FTV TVL tea/coffee Direct Dial Cen ht Wi-fi ⅃ 18 Riding **Parking** 4 **Notes** ⊗ No Children 🕭

CHESTER
Map 15 SJ46

See also Malpas

PREMIER COLLECTION

Mitchell's of Chester Guest House
★★★★★ GUEST HOUSE

28 Hough Green CH4 8JQ
☎ 01244 679004 📠 01244 659567
e-mail: mitoches@dialstart.net
web: www.mitchellsofchester.com
dir: *1m SW of city centre. A483 onto A5104, 300yds on right in Hough Green*

A warm welcome is assured at this delightfully restored and elegant Victorian house, located on the south side of the Dee and the city. Bedrooms are very well equipped and delightfully furnished, and there is a comfortable guests' lounge where an open fire burns on colder days. Substantial breakfasts are served in the bright, south-facing dining room, and special diets can be catered for.

Rooms 7 en suite (1 fmly) (1 GF) S £36-£55; D £67-£97 **Facilities** FTV DVD TVL tea/coffee Cen ht Licensed Wi-fi **Parking** 5 **Notes** LB ⊗ No Children 8yrs Closed 21-29 Dec

PREMIER COLLECTION

Oddfellows
★★★★★ ◉ 🍴 RESTAURANT WITH ROOMS

20 Lower Bridge St CH1 1RS
☎ 01244 400001
e-mail: reception@oddfellows.biz

Surrounded by designer shops and only a few minutes' walk from the Chester Rows, old meets new at this stylish Georgian mansion. The upper ground floor comprises a walled garden with ornamental moat, Arabian tents, a roofed patio, a cocktail bar with an excellent wine selection, a bustling brasserie and an Alice in Wonderland tea room. Fine dining, featuring local produce, is skilfully prepared in the brasserie restaurant and a sumptuous 'members' lounge is also available to diners and resident guests. Bedrooms have the wow factor with super beds and every conceivable guest extra. Conference facilities are also available.

Rooms 4 en suite **Facilities** FTV tea/coffee Dinner available Direct Dial Cen ht Wi-fi **Conf** Max 40 Thtr 40 **Parking** 4 **Notes** ⊗ No coaches Civ Wed 60

AA FUNKIEST B&B OF THE YEAR

PREMIER COLLECTION

Dragonfly
★★★★★ GUEST ACCOMMODATION

94 Watergate St CH1 2LF
☎ 01244 346740 📠 01244 346740
e-mail: sleep@hoteldragonfly.com
dir: *M53 junct 12, A56 signed Chester. 2nd exit from rdbt into St Oswalds Way, at next rdbt 1st exit into St Martin's Way. At lights right into New Crane St*

Located a stone's throw from the racecourse and within easy walking distance of the city centre and its attractions, this elegant Georgian terraced house has been sympathetically restored to provide high standards of comfort and facilities. Stylish and vibrant decor and furnishing schemes throughout the interior are matched by the many period features; hospitality is natural and caring. Dragonfly is the winner of the AA Funkiest B&B of the Year Award 2012-13.

Rooms 5 en suite D £115-£150 (room only) **Facilities** FTV tea/coffee Cen ht Wi-fi **Parking** 2 **Notes** ⊗ No Children 14yrs

PREMIER COLLECTION

Stone Villa Chester
★★★★★ GUEST ACCOMMODATION

Stone Place, Hoole Rd CH2 3NR
☎ 01244 345014 📠 01244 345015
e-mail: info@stonevillachester.co.uk
dir: *0.5m NE of city on A56 Hoole Rd*

Stone Villa Chester is a family-run establishment tucked away in a quiet cul-de-sac, 50 yards from the main approach road into Chester. The guest bedrooms are well equipped and delightfully furnished. Hearty breakfasts are served in the pleasant rear dining room and special diets can be catered for. Private off-road parking is available.

Rooms 10 en suite (4 fmly) (3 GF) **Facilities** FTV tea/coffee Direct Dial Cen ht Wi-fi ⅃ 18 **Parking** 10 **Notes** ⊗

Coach House Restaurant with Rooms
★★★★ RESTAURANT WITH ROOMS

29 Northgate St CH1 2HQ
☎ 01244 251900 📠 01244 351436
web: www.coachhousechester.co.uk
dir: *Telephone for detailed directions*

Ideally located in the centre of the city, this restaurant with rooms has been appointed to provide high standards of comfort and facilities. Its sumptuous bedrooms have a wealth of thoughtful extras, and imaginative food is available in the bistro-style restaurant or in the cosy bar area. A warm welcome is assured.

Rooms 9 en suite (3 fmly) **Facilities** FTV tea/coffee Dinner available Direct Dial Wi-fi **Notes** ⊗ Closed 25 Dec

Cheltenham Lodge
★★★★ GUEST ACCOMMODATION

58 Hoole Rd, Hoole CH2 3NL
☎ 01244 346767
e-mail: cheltenhamlodge@btinternet.com
web: www.cheltenhamlodge.co.uk
dir: *1m NE of city centre on A56*

This personally-run guest accommodation lies midway between the city centre and the M53. The attractive bedrooms are well appointed and equipped with a wealth of extras. Family rooms and rooms on the ground floor are available. Substantial breakfasts are served in the smart dining room.

Rooms 5 en suite (2 fmly) (2 GF) **Facilities** FTV tea/coffee Cen ht **Parking** 5 **Notes** ⊗ Closed 23 Dec-7 Jan 🕭

Save on B&Bs and Hotels. Book at **theAA.com/hotel**

CHESHIRE 45 ENGLAND

Green Gables

★★★ GUEST HOUSE

11 Eversley Park CH2 2AJ
☎ 01244 372243 🖷 01244 376352
e-mail: perruzza_d@hotmail.com
dir: *Off A5116 Liverpool Rd signed Countess of Chester Hospital, right at 3rd pedestrian lights to Eversley Park*

Green Gables is an attractive Victorian house, set in pretty gardens, in a quiet residential area close to the city centre. The well-equipped bedrooms include a family room, and there is a choice of sitting rooms. The bright breakfast room is strikingly decorated.

Rooms 2 en suite (1 fmly) S £44-£65; D £70-£90*
Facilities FTV DVD TVL tea/coffee Cen ht Wi-fi 🔌 **Parking** 8 **Notes** ⊗ ⊜

Lavender Lodge

★★★★ GUEST ACCOMMODATION

46 Hoole Rd CH2 3NL
☎ 01244 323204 🖷 01244 329821
e-mail: bookings@lavenderlodgechester.co.uk
web: www.lavenderlodgechester.co.uk
dir: *1m NE of city centre on A56, opposite All Saints Church*

A warm welcome is assured at this smart, late Victorian house located within easy walking distance of central attractions. The comfortable bedrooms are equipped with thoughtful extras and have modern bathrooms. Hearty breakfasts are served in the attractive dining room.

Rooms 5 rms (4 en suite) (1 pri facs) (2 fmly) S £35-£50; D £70-£80* **Facilities** FTV tea/coffee Cen ht Wi-fi 🔌 **Parking** 7 **Notes** LB ⊗ Closed 24 Dec-2 Jan

The Old Farmhouse B&B

★★★★ BED AND BREAKFAST

9 Eggbridge Ln, Waverton CH3 7PE
☎ 01244 332124 & 07949 820119
e-mail: jmitchellgreenwalls@hotmail.com
web: www.chestereggbridgefarm.co.uk
dir: *From A41 at Waverton left into Moor Ln, left into Eggbridge Ln, over canal bridge, house on right*

A warm welcome is assured at this 18th-century former farmhouse, located in a village community three miles south of the city centre. Cosy bedrooms are equipped with a wealth of thoughtful extras, and hearty breakfasts feature local or home-made produce.

Rooms 2 rms (1 en suite) (1 pri facs) S £35-£45; D £70-£75* **Facilities** FTV TVL tea/coffee Cen ht Wi-fi 🔌 **Parking** 5 **Notes** LB ⊗ No Children 10yrs Closed 13-28 Feb RS Xmas continental breakfast only

Summerhill Guest House

★★★★ GUEST HOUSE

4 Greenfield Ln, Hoole Village CH2 2PA
☎ 01244 400020 & 400334
e-mail: summerhill10@sky.com
dir: *1.5m NE of city centre. A56 onto A41, 1st right*

Summerhill is a converted Edwardian house with comfortable, well-equipped accommodation. All bedrooms include flat screen TV, and free Wi-fi is available throughout. The helpful owners create a friendly atmosphere, and provide hearty breakfasts in the attractive dining room that overlooks the well maintained gardens.

Rooms 4 en suite (1 fmly) S £30-£45; D £60-£80*
Facilities FTV TVL tea/coffee Cen ht Wi-fi **Parking** 4 **Notes** LB ⊗ No Children 8yrs

The Limes

★★★★ 🅰 GUEST ACCOMMODATION

12 Hoole Rd CH2 3NJ
☎ 01244 328239
e-mail: bookings@limes-chester.co.uk
Rooms 9 en suite (2 fmly) (2 GF) **Facilities** FTV tea/coffee Direct Dial Cen ht **Parking** 10 **Notes** ⊗ Closed Xmas-1 Jan

George & Dragon

★★★ INN

1 Liverpool Rd CH2 1AA
☎ 01244 380714 🖷 01244 378461
e-mail: 7783@greeneking.co.uk

This former old coaching inn with its black and white Tudor façade is situated just five minutes from the city centre. A traditional inn with sports viewing, cask ales, dining and weekly entertainment, with a late bar until midnight. Bedrooms vary in size. Parking is available on-site.

Rooms 14 en suite (2 fmly) **Facilities** FTV tea/coffee Dinner available Cen ht Wi-fi **Parking** 20 **Notes** ⊗ No coaches

Glen Garth

★★★ GUEST ACCOMMODATION

59 Hoole Rd CH2 3NJ
☎ 01244 310260 🖷 01244 559073
e-mail: glengarthguesthouse@btconnect.com
dir: *Exit M53 onto A56, 0.5m E of city*

Situated within easy walking distance of the city, family-run Glen Garth provides well-equipped bedrooms, and hearty breakfasts served in the pleasant rear dining room. Friendly, attentive service is a strength here.

Rooms 5 rms (3 en suite) (2 pri facs) (3 fmly) S £35-£40; D £70-£90* **Facilities** FTV DVD tea/coffee Cen ht Wi-fi ⚿ 18 **Parking** 5 **Notes** LB ⊗

Innkeeper's Lodge Chester Christleton

★★★ INN

Whitchurch Rd CH3 6AE
☎ 0845 112 6022
e-mail: info@innkeeperslodge.com
web: www.innkeeperslodge.com

At Innkeeper's Lodge you'll find accommodation with comfort and character in equal measure, and everything needed for a relaxing stay, from easy check-in and free parking to complimentary breakfast and a cosy pub serving great value food and drink on the doorstep. Each Lodge has quality rooms, and there are Lodges in a variety of locations from towns and cities to countryside settings across the UK.

Rooms 14 en suite (3 fmly) (4 GF) **Facilities** FTV tea/coffee Dinner available Direct Dial Wi-fi **Parking**

The Oaklands

★★ INN

93 Hoole Rd, Hoole CH2 3NB
☎ 01244 345528
e-mail: 7878@greeneking.co.uk

This busy and popular public house is conveniently located for access to both the city centre and the M56. A wide range of food is available in the stylish open-plan bar and dining area. Bedrooms vary in size, and service is friendly and attentive.

Rooms 14 rms (13 en suite) (1 pri facs) (2 fmly) (4 GF) **Facilities** FTV TVL tea/coffee Dinner available Cen ht Wi-fi **Parking** 30 **Notes** ⊗

Edgar House

Ⓤ

22 City Walls CH1 1SB
☎ 01244 347007
e-mail: enquiries@edgarhouse.co.uk
web: www.edgarhouse.co.uk
dir: *From city centre ring road (A5268) S on Lower Bridge St towards river. Last left into Duke St*

Currently the rating for this establishment is not confirmed. This may be due to a change of ownership or because it has only recently joined the AA rating scheme.

Rooms 8 en suite (3 GF) **Facilities** FTV DVD Lounge TVL tea/coffee Cen ht Licensed Wi-fi **Parking** 8 **Notes** ⊗ No Children 14yrs

CONGLETON — Map 16 SJ86

Egerton Arms Country Inn

★★★★ INN

Astbury Village CW12 4RQ
☎ 01260 273946 📠 01260 277273
e-mail: egertonastbury@totalise.co.uk
dir: 1.5m SW of Congleton off A34, by St Mary's Church Astbury

This traditional country inn stands opposite the church in the pretty village of Astbury. The creative, good-value menus in the bars and restaurant attract a strong local following, and the bedrooms have been appointed to provide high standards of comfort and facilities.

Rooms 6 en suite (1 fmly) S £50-£60; D £70-£80*
Facilities FTV DVD tea/coffee Dinner available Cen ht Wi-fi ♿ **Conf** Max 40 Thtr 40 Class 30 Board 20 **Parking** 100 **Notes** LB ⊗ No coaches

The Plough At Eaton

★★★★ INN

Macclesfield Rd, Eaton CW12 2NH
☎ 01260 280207 📠 01260 298458
e-mail: theploughinn@hotmail.co.uk
web: www.theploughinnateaton.com
dir: On A536 (Congleton to Macclesfield road), 1.5m from Congleton town centre

A renovated traditional inn offering high quality meals and very comfortable bedrooms in an adjacent building. The rooms vary in style with some contemporary and others more traditionally furnished, all have very good en suite bathrooms. The spacious bar is appealing and there are also attractive outdoor seating areas.

Rooms 17 annexe en suite (2 fmly) (8 GF) **Facilities** tea/coffee Dinner available Direct Dial Cen ht Wi-fi **Parking** 78 **Notes** RS 25-26 Dec & 1 Jan Close at 6pm Civ Wed 60

Sandhole Farm

★★★★ Ⓐ GUEST ACCOMMODATION

Hulme Walfield CW12 2JH
☎ 01260 224419 📠 01260 224766
e-mail: veronica@sandholefarm.co.uk
dir: 2m N of Congleton. Off A34 down driveway

Rooms 16 annexe en suite (3 fmly) (7 GF) S fr £60; D fr £90* **Facilities** FTV TVL tea/coffee Direct Dial Cen ht Wi-fi **Conf** Thtr 80 Class 80 Board 50 **Parking** 50 **Notes** ⊗ RS Xmas wk Self-catering only Civ Wed 150

FARNDON — Map 15 SJ45

The Farndon

★★★★ ⬅ INN

High St CH3 6PU
☎ 01829 270570 📠 01829 272060
e-mail: enquiries@thefarndon.co.uk
web: www.thefarndon.co.uk
dir: Just off A534 in village on main street

Located close to Chester and the north Wales coast, The Farndon is a family-run, traditional, 16th-century coaching inn with a modern twist. The attractive bedrooms are well equipped, and downstairs the bar offers open log fires and a selection of real ales and fine wines, together with a wide range of imaginative dishes.

Rooms 5 en suite S £65-£75; D £85-£95 **Facilities** FTV Lounge tea/coffee Dinner available Direct Dial Cen ht Wi-fi **Parking** 15 **Notes** LB ⊗ No coaches

KNUTSFORD — Map 15 SJ77

The Hinton Guest House

★★★★ GUEST HOUSE

Town Ln, Mobberley WA16 7HH
☎ 01565 873484 📠 01565 873484
e-mail: the.hinton@virgin.net
dir: 1m NE on B5085 in Mobberley

The Hinton Guest House is a spacious, family-run, detached house in the village of Mobberley, close to historic Knutsford. There is a range of comfortable bedrooms, all well furnished and thoughtfully equipped. Complimentary Wi-fi access is provided. Comprehensive breakfasts are served in the attractive dining room, and a lounge is also available.

Rooms 6 en suite (1 fmly) **Facilities** FTV DVD TVL tea/coffee Cen ht Licensed Wi-fi ♿ **Parking** 8 **Notes** ⊗

The Cottage Restaurant & Lodge

★★★★ GUEST ACCOMMODATION

London Rd, Allostock WA16 9LU
☎ 01565 722470 📠 01565 722749
e-mail: reception@thecottageknutsford.co.uk
dir: M6 junct 18/19 onto A50, between Holmes Chapel & Knutsford

This well presented family-run establishment enjoys a peaceful location on the A50 between Knutsford and Holmes Chapel. Smart, spacious lodge-style bedrooms complement an attractive open-plan restaurant and bar lounge. Bedrooms are thoughtfully equipped and offer good levels of comfort. Conference and meeting facilities, as well as ample parking, are available.

Rooms 11 annexe en suite (4 fmly) (5 GF) S £50-£89; D £60-£95* **Facilities** FTV tea/coffee Dinner available Direct Dial Cen ht Licensed Wi-fi **Conf** Max 40 Thtr 40 Class 25 Board 25 **Parking** 40 **Notes** LB ⊗

The Dog Inn

★★★★ INN

Well Bank Ln, Over Peover WA16 8UP
☎ 01625 861421 📠 01625 864800
e-mail: thedoginnpeover@btconnect.com
web: www.doginn-overpeover.co.uk
dir: 4m SE of Knutsford. Off A50 at Whipping Stocks 2m to Peover Heath

Set in delightful Cheshire countryside, the front of this popular 18th-century inn is adorned with hanging baskets and tubs. The attractive bedrooms have many extras, while the lounge bar and restaurant offer a wide selection of ales and an extensive all-day menu using local produce.

Rooms 6 en suite **Facilities** FTV tea/coffee Dinner available Direct Dial Cen ht Wi-fi Pool table **Parking** 80

Save on B&Bs and Hotels. Book at **theAA.com/hotel**

CHESHIRE 47 ENGLAND

LOWER WITHINGTON — Map 15 SJ86

Holly Tree Farm (SJ802709)

★★★★ FARMHOUSE

Holmes Chapel Rd SK11 9DT
☎ 01477 571257 & 07979 910800
🖷 01477 571257 Mrs Venables
e-mail: davidathollies@aol.com
web: www.hollytreefarm.org
dir: *On A535 Holmes Chapel Rd in front of Jodrell Bank*

Located close to Jodrell Bank, Holly Tree Farm offers a good base for the business person or for touring the local attractions. Rooms are located in the house adjacent to the farm and are attractive and well equipped. Hearty breakfasts are taken in the farmhouse, and the emphasis is on local produce from the farm's own shop.

Rooms 4 en suite (1 fmly) (1 GF) S £30-£35; D £65-£70 **Facilities** FTV TVL tea/coffee Cen ht Wi-fi 🔒 **Extras** Mini-fridge **Parking** 3 **Notes** LB ⊗ 100 acres beef/sheep/poultry

MALPAS — Map 15 SJ44

PREMIER COLLECTION

Tilston Lodge

★★★★★ 🏠 GUEST ACCOMMODATION

Tilston SY14 7DR
☎ 01829 250223 🖷 01829 250223
e-mail: kathie.ritchie@yahoo.co.uk
dir: *A41 S from Chester for 10m, turn right for Tilston. Left at T-junct. Lodge 200yds on right*

A former hunting lodge, this impressive Victorian house stands in 16 acres of rolling orchards and pasture, which are home to rare breeds of sheep and poultry. The spacious bedrooms are furnished with fine period pieces and a wealth of thoughtful extras. Ground-floor areas overlook immaculate gardens, and a choice of lounges is available in addition to the elegant dining room, the setting for memorable breakfasts.

Rooms 3 en suite (1 fmly) S £50-£55; D £80-£90* **Facilities** FTV Lounge TVL tea/coffee Cen ht Wi-fi 🐾 Hot tub **Extras** Chocolate, fruit **Parking** 8 **Notes** LB ⊗

Hampton House Farm (SJ505496)

★★★★ FARMHOUSE

Stevensons Ln, Hampton SY14 8JS
☎ 01948 820588 Mrs E H Sarginson
e-mail: enquiries@hamptonhousefarm.co.uk
dir: *2m NE of Malpas. Exit A41 into Cholmondeley Rd, next left*

Parts of this house are reputed to date from 1600, and quality furnishing styles highlight the many retained period features including a wealth of exposed beams. It is located on a quiet dairy farm and offers thoughtfully appointed accommodation and a warm welcome.

Rooms 2 en suite S £45; D £65* **Facilities** TVL tea/coffee Cen ht Wi-fi 🔒 **Parking** 12 **Notes** ⊗ No Children 12yrs 🐾 180 acres mixed

The Paddock

★★★★ BED AND BREAKFAST

Malpas Rd, Tilston SY14 7DR
☎ 01829 250569 & 07754 857057
e-mail: info@thepaddocktilston.com
web: www.thepaddocktilston.com
dir: *Turn off A4, on entering Tilston, left at T-junct, 200mtrs on left, 1st drive after 40mph speed limit sign, with lamp-post at bottom of drive*

The Paddock is set in the small village of Tilston, with easy access to Chester and Wrexham, and is just a short distance from 10 golf courses. A warm welcome is assured at this family home which offers guests the choice of three comfortable, well-equipped bedrooms, all

with excellent bathroom facilities. There is a large summer house at the bottom of the garden where hosts Gail and Steve offer afternoon tea to arriving guests on warmer days. Well cooked breakfasts feature locally sourced ingredients. Wi-fi is available, and the property has its own parking.

Rooms 3 rms (2 en suite) (1 pri facs) (1 fmly) S £35-£60; D £70-£100 **Facilities** FTV DVD iPod docking station Lounge tea/coffee Cen ht Wi-fi 🔒 **Parking** 3 **Notes** ⊗

MIDDLEWICH — Map 15 SJ76

The Sandhurst

★★★★ 🍽 GUEST ACCOMMODATION

69 Chester Rd CW10 9EU
☎ 01606 834125 🖷 0870 928 1111
e-mail: sandhursthotel@aol.com
dir: *M6 junct 18 towards Middlewich, over rdbt, straight ahead at lights. At junct take 2nd turn (Chester Rd), on left after mini-rdbt*

You will find a quintessential English atmosphere at this Edwardian-themed family-run guest accommodation. Rooms are comfortable, the first floor rooms more traditional with the top floor rooms being of a modern style. The elegant dining room is the setting for imaginative dinners and a comfortable lounge/bar is also available. Car parking is available along with picturesque gardens at the rear. Theme nights are a speciality.

Rooms 7 en suite 5 annexe rms 3 annexe en suite (4 fmly) (3 GF) S £57.50-£59.50; D £65* **Facilities** FTV Lounge tea/coffee Dinner available Cen ht Licensed Wi-fi 🔒 **Parking** 20 **Notes** ⊗ Civ Wed 55

NANTWICH — Map 15 SJ65

See also Wybunbury

Henhull Hall (SJ641536)

★★★★ FARMHOUSE

Welshmans Ln CW5 6AD
☎ 01270 624158 🖷 01270 624158 Mr & Mrs Percival
e-mail: philippercival@hotmail.com
dir: *M6 junct 16, A500 towards Nantwich, then A51 past Reaseheath, left into Welshmans Ln, 0.25m on left*

Expect a warm welcome at Henhull Hall, which has been in the Percival family since 1924. The Hall stands on the site of the Battle of Nantwich fought in 1644. The farmhouse is amidst acres of farmland with beautiful grounds and gardens surrounding the house. Bedrooms are spacious and individually decorated; breakfast is served in the attractive dining room and features fresh farm produce.

Rooms 2 rms (1 en suite) (1 pri facs) (1 fmly) S £40-£45; D £80-£90 **Facilities** DVD Lounge TVL TV1B tea/coffee Cen ht Wi-fi 🐾 🔒 **Conf** Max 10 Thtr 10 Class 10 Board 10 **Parking** 4 **Notes** 🐾 345 acres dairy/arable

NANTWICH *continued*

Oakland House

★★★★ GUEST ACCOMMODATION

252 Newcastle Rd, Blakelow, Shavington CW5 7ET
☎ 01270 567134
e-mail: enquiries@oaklandhouseonline.co.uk
dir: *2m E of Nantwich. Off A500 into Shavington, house 0.5m W of village*

Oakland House offers a friendly and relaxed atmosphere. Bedrooms, some of which are in a separate chalet, are attractively furnished and well equipped. There is a spacious sitting room, and a modern conservatory overlooks the pretty garden and the Cheshire countryside beyond. Substantial breakfasts are served either around one large table or at separate tables.

Rooms 3 en suite 6 annexe en suite (1 fmly) (6 GF)
Facilities FTV TVL tea/coffee Cen ht Wi-fi **Parking** 13
Notes LB Closed 31 Dec

The Cheshire Cat

[U]

26 Welsh Row CW5 5ED
☎ 01270 623020 📠 01270 613350
e-mail: hello@thecatatnantwich.com
web: www.thecat.com
dir: *Left off B5341 onto Welsh Row*

Currently the rating for this establishment is not confirmed. This may be due to a change of ownership or because it has only recently joined the AA rating scheme.

Rooms 11 en suite 1 annexe en suite (1 fmly) (5 GF)
S £60-£180; D £85-£180* **Facilities** FTV TVL tea/coffee
Dinner available Direct Dial Cen ht Licensed Wi-fi
Parking 20 **Notes** LB ⊗

NORTHWICH — Map 15 SJ67

The Red Lion

★★★ INN

277 Chester Rd, Hartford CW8 1QL
☎ 01606 74597
e-mail: cathy.iglesias@tesco.net
web: www.redlionhartford.com
dir: *From A556 take Hartford exit. Red Lion at 1st junct on left next to church*

Located in the community of Hartford opposite the parish church, this popular inn provides a range of real ales and traditional pub food in the cosy public areas or neat beer garden. Smart bedrooms feature many thoughtful extras in addition to efficient en suite shower rooms.

Rooms 3 en suite (1 fmly) S £40-£44.95; D £50-£60*
Facilities FTV DVD tea/coffee Dinner available Cen ht
Wi-fi Pool table 🎱 **Parking** 6 **Notes** No coaches

PRESTBURY — Map 16 SJ87

Hilltop Country House

★★★★ GUEST ACCOMMODATION

Hill top, Flash Ln SK10 4ED
☎ 01625 829940
e-mail: enquiries@hilltopcountryhouse.co.uk
web: www.hilltopcountryhouse.co.uk
dir: *A523 from Macclesfield to Stockport. At 3rd rdbt turn right to Bollington. In 40mtrs turn left & follow signs*

Hilltop Country House is a hidden gem, set in rural Cheshire, with easy access to motorway and rail links. The four en suite bedrooms are very comfortable, with luxurious beds and good accessories. Breakfasts are served in the 17th-century dining room and guarantee a hearty start to the day.

Rooms 4 en suite (2 GF) S £60; D £84 **Facilities** FTV tea/coffee Dinner available Cen ht Wi-fi **Extras** Speciality toiletries **Conf** Max 40 Thtr 40 Board 18 **Parking** 50
Notes LB ⊗ ⊜ Civ Wed 62

RAINOW — Map 16 SJ97

Common Barn Farm B&B *(SJ965764)*

★★★★ FARMHOUSE

Smith Ln SK10 5XJ
☎ 01625 574878 & 07779 816098   Mrs R Cooper
e-mail: g_greengrass@hotmail.com
web: www.cottages-with-a-view.co.uk
dir: *B5470 through Rainow towards Whaley Bridge, right into Smith Ln, 0.5m on right down drive*

Located high in the Pennines and straddling the border of Cheshire and the Peak District, this barn conversion provides a popular destination for walkers. Bedrooms are spacious and stylish, and all bathrooms offer modern power showers. A conservatory lounge is ideal for relaxation while enjoying stunning views. Hearty breakfasts are as memorable as the warmth of welcome. A coffee shop during the day provides light snacks and home-baked fare.

Rooms 5 annexe en suite (1 fmly) (3 GF) S £45; D £65*
Facilities FTV TVL tea/coffee Cen ht Wi-fi Fishing 🐟
Conf Max 25 **Parking** 40 **Notes** LB ⊗ 250 acres sheep

SANDBACH — Map 15 SJ76

Innkeeper's Lodge Sandbach, Holmes Chapel

★★★ INN

Brereton Green CW11 1RS
☎ 0845 112 6026
e-mail: enquiries@innkeeperslodge.com
web: www.innkeeperslodge.com

At Innkeeper's Lodge you'll find accommodation with comfort and character in equal measure, and everything needed for a relaxing stay, from easy check-in and free parking to complimentary breakfast and a cosy pub

serving great value food and drink on the doorstep. Each Lodge has quality rooms, and there are Lodges in a variety of locations from towns and cities to countryside settings across the UK.

Rooms 25 en suite (6 fmly) (10 GF) **Facilities** FTV tea/coffee Dinner available Direct Dial Wi-fi **Parking**

TARPORLEY — Map 15 SJ56

New Farm

★★★★ GUEST ACCOMMODATION

Long Ln, Wettenhall CW7 4DW
☎ 01270 528213
e-mail: info@newfarmcheshire.com
dir: *M6 junct 16, A51 (signed Nantwich/Chester), pass NWF feedmill, over railway bridge. In Alphram right signed New Farm*

Set in the peaceful and picturesque Cheshire countryside, this family-run business provides comfortable, modern facilities in a converted milking parlour. All bedrooms are on the ground floor and complimentary Wi-fi is provided. Hearty breakfasts are served in the contemporary dining room. Coarse fishing and a caravan park are available on site.

Rooms 5 en suite (5 GF) **Facilities** FTV TVL tea/coffee
Cen ht Wi-fi ♨ 18 Fishing **Conf** Max 10 **Parking** 7
Notes ⊗

Alvanley Arms Inn

★★★★ ⊜ INN

Forest Rd, Cotebrook CW6 9DS
☎ 01829 760200
e-mail: info@alvanleyarms.co.uk
dir: *2m NE of Tarporley on A49 in Cotebrook*

This historic inn dates back to the 17th century so the bar and dining areas feature exposed original beams alongside a wide choice of home-cooked meals that utilise local produce. Bedrooms are well equipped with complimentary Wi-fi access. The adjoining Shire Horse Centre and Countryside Park is popular with families. Delamere Forest Park and Oulton Park race circuit are nearby.

Rooms 7 en suite S £29.50-£57.50; D £39.50-£105*
Facilities FTV tea/coffee Dinner available Cen ht Wi-fi 🛎
Free entry to adjacent Shire Horse Centre **Parking** 60
Notes ⊗ Closed 25 Dec & 26 Dec eve, 1 Jan eve No coaches

WARMINGHAM
Map 15 SJ76

PREMIER COLLECTION

The Bear's Paw
★★★★★ INN

School Ln CW11 3QN
☎ 01270 526317
e-mail: info@thebearspaw.co.uk
web: www.thebearspaw.co.uk
dir: M6 junct 17, A534, A533 signed Middlewich & Northwich. Continue on A533, left into Mill Ln, left into Warmingham Ln. Right into Plant Ln, left into Green Ln

Located beside a small river in a rural Cheshire village, this 19th-century inn provides very comfortable and well equipped boutique bedrooms with a wealth of thoughtful and practical extras. A friendly team deliver imaginative food, utilising quality seasonal produce, in an attractive open-plan dining room, and a choice of sumptuous lounge areas is also available.

Rooms 17 en suite (4 fmly) S £95-£125; D £105-£140*
Facilities STV FTV iPod docking station Lounge tea/coffee Dinner available Direct Dial Cen ht Wi-fi
Extras Apple TV (deposit required) **Parking** 75
Notes LB

WYBUNBURY
Map 15 SJ64

Lea Farm (SJ717489)
★★★ FARMHOUSE

Wrinehill Rd CW5 7NS
☎ 01270 841429 Mrs J E Callwood
e-mail: leafarm@hotmail.co.uk
dir: 1m E of Wybunbury church on unclassified road

This working dairy farm is surrounded by delightful gardens and beautiful Cheshire countryside. The spacious bedrooms have modern facilities and there is a cosy lounge. Hearty breakfasts are served in the attractive dining room, which looks out over the garden with its resident peacocks.

Rooms 3 rms (2 en suite) (1 fmly) S £30-£36;
D £50-£60* **Facilities** FTV Lounge TVL tea/coffee Cen ht Wi-fi Fishing Pool table 🛎 **Extras** Home-made biscuits
Parking 24 **Notes** LB ⊜ 150 acres dairy/beef

CORNWALL & ISLES OF SCILLY

BODMIN
Map 2 SX06

Castle Canyke Farm
★★★★ BED AND BREAKFAST

Priors Barn Rd PL31 1HG
☎ 01208 79109
e-mail: bookings@castlecanykefarm.co.uk
web: www.castlecanykefarm.co.uk
dir: On A389/A38 Priory Rd between church & Carminow Cross rdbt

A traditional bed and breakfast operation with very friendly hosts offering comfortable, well appointed rooms in a very handy location, with off-street parking. Hearty breakfasts are served in the conservatory, guests have their own lounge, and there is also a pretty garden to the rear.

Rooms 3 en suite (1 fmly) **Facilities** FTV TVL tea/coffee Cen ht Wi-fi **Parking** 3 **Notes** ⊗ No Children 8yrs ⊜

Mennabroom Farm (SX161703)
★★★★ 🏠 ⊜ FARMHOUSE

Warleggan PL30 4HE
☎ 01208 821272 Mr Barrett
e-mail: enquiries@mennabroom.com
web: www.mennabroom.co.uk
dir: A30 take exit signed Colliford Lake. After 2.8m turn right signed Mennabroom Cottages, turn right into Mennabroom

Set in the midst of Bodmin Moor this extremely comfortable farmhouse offers a haven of peace and tranquility for visitors to the beautiful West Country. Rooms are well appointed with quality furnishings and very comfortable beds. Guests are welcomed with afternoon tea, dinner is available upon request and breakfast uses the farm's home-produced eggs, bacon and sausage. Self-catering cottages are also available.

Rooms 2 en suite S £40-£45; D £70-£80* **Facilities** FTV DVD Lounge TVL tea/coffee Dinner available Cen ht Wi-fi ch fac 🛎 **Extras** Speciality toiletries - complimentary **Parking** 6 **Notes** LB 40 acres sheep/pigs

---

Roscrea
★★★★ 🏠 BED AND BREAKFAST

18 Saint Nicholas' St PL31 1AD
☎ 01208 74400
e-mail: roscrea@btconnect.com
dir: From Bodmin take B3268 to Lostwithiel. Roscrea 0.25m on left

Dating back to 1805, this fascinating house was once the home of a celebrated local schoolmaster. Now sympathetically restored to its former glory, this is an excellent location for anyone wishing to explore all that Cornwall has to offer. Comfort and quality are evident throughout all areas, matched by the warmth of the welcome. Breakfast is a treat here, featuring local produce and eggs from the resident hens. Dinner is also available by prior arrangement.

Rooms 3 rms (2 en suite) (1 pri facs) S £39-£49;
D £70-£78* **Facilities** FTV DVD TVL tea/coffee Dinner available Cen ht Wi-fi 🛎 Facilities for drying **Parking** 2
Notes LB ⊗ ⊜

BODMIN *continued*

Mount Pleasant Farm

★★★ GUEST ACCOMMODATION

Mount PL30 4EX
☎ 01208 821342
e-mail: info@mountpleasantcottages.co.uk
dir: *A30 from Bodmin towards Launceston for 4m, right signed Millpool, continue 3m*

Set in 10 acres, this is a wonderfully peaceful base from which to explore the delights of Cornwall. Originally a farmhouse dating back to the 17th century, there is something here for all the family with extensive facilities including a games barn and heated swimming pool. Cosy bedrooms are well furnished, while public areas include a spacious sun lounge and extensive gardens. Breakfast, served in the well-appointed dining room, features local produce and is a highlight of any stay; home-cooked evening meals are available by prior arrangement.

Rooms 6 en suite (3 fmly) S £32-£42; D £54-£74*
Facilities FTV TVL tea/coffee Dinner available Cen ht ⊙
Pool table Games barn **Parking** 8 **Notes** LB ⊛

Bangors Organic

★★★★ 🍽 GUEST HOUSE

Poundstock EX23 0DP
☎ 01288 361297
e-mail: info@bangorsorganic.co.uk
dir: *4m S of Bude. On A39 in Poundstock*

Situated a few miles south of Bude, this renovated Victorian establishment offers elegant accommodation with a good level of comfort. Bedrooms are furnished to a high standard and are located in the main house or an adjacent coach house; the latter being more contemporary in style. The bathrooms are a particular feature here, being impressively spacious and luxurious. Breakfast and dinner, featuring organic, local and home-made produce, are served in the pleasant dining room. The establishment is certified as being organic by the Soil Association. Bangors Organic was a Finalist in the AA Friendliest B&B of the Year Award 2012-13.

Rooms 2 en suite 2 annexe en suite (1 GF) **Facilities** FTV TVL tea/coffee Dinner available Cen ht Licensed Wi-fi Badminton **Parking** 10 **Notes** ⊛ No Children 12yrs

Dylan's Guest House

★★★★ GUEST HOUSE

12 Downs View EX23 8RF
☎ 01288 354705
e-mail: dylansbude@tiscali.co.uk
dir: *From A39 onto A3073 at Stratton, at 2nd rdbt right to town centre, through town centre, signed Downs View*

Appointed to a high standard, this late Victorian house overlooks the golf course and is just a five-minute walk from the beach. There is a refreshing and appealing style here, derived from a combination of original features and a crisp, contemporary decor. The well-equipped bedrooms are light and airy with impressive levels of comfort. Plenty of choice is offered at breakfast, which is carefully prepared from quality produce and served in the attractive dining room.

Rooms 4 rms (3 en suite) (1 pri facs) (1 fmly) S £45-£50; D £50-£70 **Facilities** FTV TVL tea/coffee Cen ht **Notes** LB ⊛ ⊛

Fairway House

★★★★ GUEST HOUSE

8 Downs View EX23 8RF
☎ 01288 355059
e-mail: enquiries@fairwayguesthouse.co.uk
dir: *N through town to Flexbury, follow brown tourist signs to Downs View from golf course*

Genuine hospitality and attentive service await at this delightful Victorian terrace property, which overlooks the golf course and is close to the beach, the South West Coastal Footpath and the town centre. The comfortable bedrooms are of a high standard and have many thoughtful extra facilities. Breakfast uses local produce, including free range local farm eggs and extra thick back bacon, and is served at separate tables. Full English, omelettes, kippers or continental options are available.

Rooms 7 rms (5 en suite) (2 pri facs) (1 fmly) S £34-£50; D £58-£70* **Facilities** FTV Lounge tea/coffee Cen ht Wi-fi 🔒 **Notes** LB ⊛ Closed Dec-Jan ⊛

Bude Haven

★★★★ GUEST ACCOMMODATION

Flexbury Av EX23 8NS
☎ 01288 352305 📠 01288 352662
e-mail: enquiries@budehavenhotel.com
dir: *0.5m N of Bude in Flexbury centre*

Quietly located within a short stroll of the town and beaches, this welcoming establishment is an ideal base from which to explore the spectacular North Cornish coast. Bedrooms provide good levels of space and comfort with all the expected little extras. Public areas include the bar/lounge and restaurant, where a selection of dishes is offered most nights of the week. Additional facilities include a hot tub for a relaxing soak at the end of the day.

Rooms 10 en suite (1 fmly) **Facilities** FTV tea/coffee Dinner available Cen ht Licensed Wi-fi Hot tub **Parking** 4 **Notes** ⊛

Pencarrol Guest House

★★★★ GUEST HOUSE

21 Downs View EX23 8RF
☎ 01288 352478
e-mail: pencarrolbude@aol.com
dir: *0.5m N of Bude. N from Bude into Flexbury village*

This cosy guest house is only a short walk from Bude centre and Crooklets Beach, and has glorious views over the golf course. Bedrooms are attractively furnished and there is a first-floor lounge. Breakfast is served at separate tables in the dining room.

Rooms 5 rms (3 en suite) (2 pri facs) (2 fmly) (1 GF) S £33-£36; D £68-£76 **Facilities** FTV TVL tea/coffee Cen ht 🔒 **Notes** LB ⊛ Closed Nov-Feb ⊛

Save on B&Bs and Hotels. Book at theAA.com/hotel

CORNWALL & ISLES OF SCILLY 51 **ENGLAND**

Surf Haven Guest House

★★★★ 🅰 GUEST HOUSE

31 Downs View EX23 8RG
☎ 01288 353923 & 07835 852205
e-mail: info@surfhaven.co.uk
web: www.surfhaven.co.uk
dir: From A3072 follow signs to Bude town centre then follow sign for Crooklets Beach

Rooms 8 rms (7 en suite) (1 pri facs) (4 fmly) (1 GF) S £33-£45; D £54-£70* **Facilities** FTV TVL tea/coffee Cen ht Wi-fi **Parking** 8 **Notes** LB

Sea Jade Guest House

★★★ GUEST ACCOMMODATION

15 Burn View EX23 8BZ
☎ 01288 353404 & 07737 541540
e-mail: seajadeguesthouse@yahoo.co.uk
dir: A39 turn right follow signs for Bude & golf course

A warm welcome awaits at this popular establishment which is well located within a few minutes' walk of both the town and beaches. Bedrooms are light and airy with a simple, contemporary styling; some have views across the golf course. Breakfast is a generous offering and guaranteed to get the day off to a satisfying start.

Rooms 8 rms (7 en suite) (1 pri facs) (4 fmly) (2 GF) **Facilities** FTV TVL tea/coffee Cen ht Wi-fi ⚿ 18 **Notes** LB ⊗ 🚭

Woodpeckers

★★★★ GUEST HOUSE

Rilla Mill PL17 7NT
☎ 01579 363717
e-mail: alisonmerchant@virgin.net
dir: 5m NW of Callington. Exit B3254 at Upton Cross x-rds for Rilla Mill

Set in a conservation village, in a wooded valley, by a tumbling stream, this modern, detached house offers cosy, well-equipped bedrooms with numerous, thoughtful extras. Home-cooked dinners, using the best of local ingredients, are available by prior arrangement. The hot tub in the garden is an additional feature.

Rooms 3 en suite **Facilities** STV FTV tea/coffee Dinner available Cen ht Gym Spa/Hot tub **Parking** 7 **Notes** LB ⊗ 🚭

Lower Tresmorn Farm (SX164975)

★★★★ FARMHOUSE

EX23 0NU
☎ 01840 230667 & 07786 227437   Ms R Crocker
e-mail: rachel.crocker@talk21.com
web: www.lowertresmorn.co.uk
dir: Take Tresmorn turn off coast road, 2m N of Crackington Haven

Set in North Cornwall's heritage coast area, parts of this charming farmhouse date back to medieval times. The welcome is warm and genuine with a reviving cup of tea and piece of cake always on offer. Bedrooms are located in the main house and an adjacent converted barn; all provide plenty of comfort. Breakfast makes use of local and farm produce.

Rooms 3 rms (2 en suite) (1 pri facs) 3 annexe en suite (2 fmly) (2 GF) S £40-£55; D £60-£82* **Facilities** FTV TVL TV4B tea/coffee Wi-fi 🔒 **Parking** 6 **Notes** ⊗ No Children 8yrs RS 20 Dec-5 Jan B&B only 222 acres beef/sheep

Bears & Boxes Country Guest House

★★★★ 🍴 🛏 GUEST HOUSE

Penrose, Dizzard EX23 0NX
☎ 01840 230318
e-mail: rwfrh@btinternet.com
web: www.bearsandboxes.com
dir: 1.5m NE of St Gennys in Dizzard

Dating in part from the mid 17th century, Bears & Boxes is a small, family-run guest house situated 500 yards from the coastal path. Guests are welcomed with a tray of tea and home-made cake, and the caring owners are always around to give advice on the local area. The cosy bedrooms have numerous thoughtful extras, and evening meals, using the very best of local ingredients and cooked with flair, are served by arrangement.

Rooms 2 en suite S £37; D £74 **Facilities** FTV DVD TVL tea/coffee Dinner available Cen ht Wi-fi 🔒 **Parking** 6

The Liscawn

★★★★ GUEST ACCOMMODATION

PL11 3BD
☎ 01503 230863
e-mail: enquiries@liscawn.co.uk
web: www.liscawn.co.uk
dir: A374 onto B3247 to Crafthole, through village, left at rdbt, 0.3m on left

A well established, friendly, family-run guest accommodation with comfortable rooms. Serving food every night of the week, The Liscawn sits in mature grounds and is a few minutes from the coastal path and Whitsand Bay.

Rooms 8 en suite 5 annexe en suite (3 fmly) (2 GF) S £45-£55; D £60-£90* **Facilities** FTV tea/coffee Dinner available Cen ht Licensed Children's play area **Conf** Max 60 Thtr 60 Class 40 Board 35 **Parking** 50 **Notes** Civ Wed 70

Carrek Woth

★★★ GUEST ACCOMMODATION

West Pentire Rd TR8 5SA
☎ 01637 830530
web: www.carrekwoth.co.uk
dir: W from Crantock towards West Pentire

Many guests return to this friendly, family-run house where hospitality and service are noteworthy. Carrek Woth takes its name from the Cornish for Goose Rock, which can be seen in Crantock Bay. All the rooms are ground floor and neatly furnished, and some have good views. The lounge looks toward Newquay and the sea. Breakfast is served in the attractive dining room; Sunday lunch is also available.

Rooms 6 en suite (1 fmly) (6 GF) S fr £48; D fr £74 **Facilities** FTV TVL tea/coffee Cen ht **Parking** 6 **Notes** LB Closed mid Oct-mid Nov 🚭

FALMOUTH   Map 2 SW83

Bosanneth Guest House

★★★★ 🍴 GUEST HOUSE

Gyllyngvase Hill TR11 4DW
☎ 01326 314649 📠 01326 314649
e-mail: stay@bosanneth.co.uk
web: www.bosanneth.co.uk
dir: *From Truro on A39 follow signs for beaches/docks, 3rd right mini-rdbt Melvil Rd, 3rd right into Gyllyngvase Hill*

Well situated property with comfortable and stylish bedrooms and very friendly hosts. Some rooms have a sea view and dinner is served nightly. A full Cornish breakfast is served in the dining room.

Rooms 8 en suite S £45-£59* **Facilities** FTV Lounge tea/coffee Dinner available Cen ht Licensed Wi-fi **Extras** Speciality toiletries, robes **Parking** 7 **Notes** LB ⊗ No Children 15yrs Closed Nov

Prospect House

★★★★ GUEST ACCOMMODATION

1 Church Rd, Penryn TR10 8DA
☎ 01326 373198 📠 01326 373198
e-mail: stay@prospecthouse-penryn.co.uk
web: www.prospecthouse-penryn.co.uk
dir: *Exit A39 at Treluswell rdbt onto B3292, right at Penryn town centre sign. Left at junct to town hall, left into Saint Gluivas St, at bottom on left*

Situated close to the waterside, Prospect House is an attractive building, built for a ship's captain around 1820. The original charm of the house has been carefully maintained and the attractive bedrooms are well equipped. A comfortable lounge is available, and freshly cooked breakfasts are served in the elegant dining room.

Rooms 3 en suite S £45-£50; D £75-£80* **Facilities** FTV Lounge tea/coffee Cen ht Wi-fi **Conf** Max 6 **Parking** 4 **Notes** ⊗

The Rosemary

★★★★ GUEST ACCOMMODATION

22 Gyllyngvase Ter TR11 4DL
☎ 01326 314669
e-mail: stay@therosemary.co.uk
web: www.therosemary.co.uk
dir: *A39 Melvill Rd signed to beaches & seafront, right onto Gyllyngvase Rd, 1st left*

Just a short walk from the beach, this welcoming establishment is conveniently located for exploring the local area. The well-equipped bedrooms all provide impressive levels of comfort and quality, with many having the added bonus of wonderful views across Falmouth Bay. Breakfast is a generous and tasty start to the day, and is served in the light and airy dining room. Other facilities include a bar and guest lounge, while outside a decked area and rear garden are also available for guests.

Rooms 8 en suite (2 fmly) S £48-£53; D £77-£105* **Facilities** FTV DVD Lounge tea/coffee Cen ht Licensed Wi-fi ⚓ **Extras** Speciality toiletries **Parking** 2 **Notes** LB ⊗ Closed end Oct-9 Feb

See advert on opposite page

Anacapri

★★★★ GUEST ACCOMMODATION

Gyllyngvase Rd TR11 4DJ
☎ 01326 311454 📠 01326 311474
e-mail: anacapri@btconnect.com
web: www.hotelanacapri.co.uk
dir: *A39 (Truro to Falmouth), straight on at lights. Over next 2 rdbts into Melvill Rd, down hill, 2nd right into Gyllyngvase Rd, Anacapri on right*

In an elevated position overlooking Gyllyngvase Beach with views of Falmouth Bay beyond, this family-run establishment extends a warm welcome to all. Bedrooms have similar standards of comfort and quality, and the majority have sea views. Public areas include a convivial bar, a lounge and the smart breakfast room with views out to sea.

Rooms 16 en suite S £40-£70; D £60-£125* **Facilities** FTV Lounge TVL tea/coffee Cen ht Licensed Wi-fi **Parking** 16 **Notes** ⊗ No Children 10yrs Closed mid Dec-mid Jan

Melvill House

★★★★ GUEST ACCOMMODATION

52 Melvill Rd TR11 4DQ
☎ 01326 316645 📠 01326 211608
e-mail: melvillhouse@btconnect.com
dir: *On A39 near town centre & docks*

Well situated for the beach, the town centre and the National Maritime Museum on the harbour, Melvill House is a family-run establishment with a relaxed atmosphere. Some bedrooms have four-poster beds, and breakfast is served in the smart dining room. Ample parking.

Rooms 7 en suite (2 fmly) (1 GF) S £35-£45; D £70-£85 **Facilities** FTV TVL tea/coffee Cen ht Wi-fi **Parking** 8 **Notes** LB ⊗

The Rathgowry

★★★★ GUEST HOUSE

Gyllyngvase Hill TR11 4DN
☎ 01326 313482
e-mail: enquiries@rathgowry.co.uk
web: www.rathgowry.co.uk
dir: *A39 into Falmouth, follow signs for docks & beaches. A39 becomes Melvill Rd. Cross bridge over rail line, 2nd right into Gyllyngvase Hill*

Located in a quieter residential area yet only a few minutes' stroll from the beach and 15 minutes from the town centre, this traditionally styled property offers a range of differently sized, well-equipped bedrooms and bathrooms. Extras include home-made biscuits and Wi-fi in all rooms. A varied menu is offered at breakfast including American pancakes with maple syrup and bacon, a full continental and a complete English cooked option.

Rooms 9 rms (7 en suite) (2 pri facs) (5 fmly) **Facilities** FTV tea/coffee Cen ht Wi-fi ⚓ 18 **Parking** 7 **Notes** LB ⊗

Save on B&Bs and Hotels. Book at **theAA.com/hotel**

CORNWALL & ISLES OF SCILLY 53 **ENGLAND**

Rosemullion

★★★★ GUEST ACCOMMODATION

Gyllyngvase Hill TR11 4DF
☎ 01326 314690 🖹 01326 210098
e-mail: gail@rosemullionhotel.demon.co.uk
web: www.rosemullionhotel.co.uk

Recognisable by its mock-Tudor exterior, this friendly establishment is well situated for both the town centre and the beach. Some of the comfortable bedrooms are on the ground floor, while a few rooms on the top floor have views to Falmouth Bay. Hospitality and service are strengths. Breakfast, served in the panelled dining room, is freshly cooked and there is a well appointed lounge.

Rooms 13 rms (11 en suite) (2 pri facs) (3 GF)
D £70-£88* **Facilities** FTV Lounge tea/coffee Cen ht Wi-fi
Parking 18 **Notes** LB ⊗ No Children Closed 23-31 Dec

The Westcott

★★★★ 🅐 GUEST ACCOMMODATION

Gyllyngvase Hill TR11 4DN
☎ 01326 311309 🖹 01326 330222
e-mail: westcotthotel@btinternet.com
web: www.westcotthotelfalmouth.co.uk
dir: A39 from Truro to Falmouth. Gyllyngvase Hill on right 600yds before Princess Pavillion

Rooms 9 en suite **Facilities** FTV TVL tea/coffee Cen ht
Wi-fi **Parking** 7 **Notes** ⊗ No Children 5yrs

The Observatory Guest House

★★★ GUEST HOUSE

27 Western Ter TR11 4QL
☎ 01326 314509
e-mail: theobservatory@talktalk.net
dir: On A39, Dracaena Ave into Western Terrace

This interesting house is in a pleasant location, close to the town and harbour. The proprietors are very friendly hosts. Bedrooms come in a range of sizes, and freshly cooked breakfasts, with vegetarian options, are served in the dining room. On-site parking is an added bonus.

Rooms 6 en suite (2 fmly) (3 GF) S £35-£40; D £60*
Facilities FTV DVD tea/coffee Cen ht Wi-fi 🔒 **Parking** 6
Notes LB ⊗

Trevoil Guest House

★★★ GUEST HOUSE

25 Avenue Rd TR11 4AY
☎ 01326 314145 & 07966 409782 🖹 01326 314145
e-mail: alan.jewel@btconnect.com
dir: Exit A39 (Melvill Rd) left into Avenue Rd, 150yds from Maritime Museum

Located within walking distance of the town centre, the friendly Trevoil is a comfortable and relaxed environment. Breakfast is enjoyed in the light, pleasant dining room.

Rooms 8 rms (4 en suite) (3 fmly) (1 GF) **Facilities** FTV
tea/coffee Cen ht Wi-fi **Parking** 6

The Tudor Court

★★★ GUEST HOUSE

55 Melvill Rd TR11 4DF
☎ 01326 312807
e-mail: enquiries@tudorcourthotel.com
dir: A39 to Falmouth straight through Dracaena Ave, into Melvill Rd. Tudor Court 300yds on right

This mock Tudor establishment offers bright, well-equipped bedrooms, some having the benefit of distant sea views. A comfortable bar/lounge is available for guests and in the dining room, which overlooks the attractive garden, a freshly cooked, full English breakfast is served.

Rooms 10 rms (9 en suite) (1 pri facs) (1 fmly)
S £30-£45; D £60-£82 **Facilities** FTV TVL tea/coffee
Cen ht Licensed Wi-fi **Parking** 10 **Notes** LB

FALMOUTH *continued*

Eden Lodge

★★ GUEST HOUSE

54 Melvill Rd TR11 4DQ
☎ 01326 212989 & 07715 696218
e-mail: edenlodge@hotmail.com
dir: *On A39, on left 200yds past Fox Rosehill Gardens*

Very well located on Melvill Road with off-road parking, Eden Lodge boasts comfortable rooms and a swimming pool. The friendly hosts serve dinner by arrangement and do all they can to ensure a comfortable stay.

Rooms 5 rms (4 en suite) (2 fmly) (1 GF) **Facilities** FTV TVL tea/coffee Dinner available Cen ht Licensed Wi-fi ⊙ Gym Massage & aromatherapy by appointment **Parking** 9 **Notes** ⊛

FLUSHING   Map 2 SW83

Trefusis Barton Farmhouse

B&B *(SW815341)*

★★★ FARMHOUSE

TR11 5TD
☎ 01326 374257 & 07866 045646
▤ 01326 374257 Mrs J Laity
e-mail: trefusisbarton@aol.com
dir: *Exit A39 towards Carclew, follow signs to Mylor Bridge, left at mini-rdbt, 0.5m, straight over at x-rds*

This working farm is easily reached high above the village of Flushing. It is convenient for a relaxing break or for touring, and the comfortable bedrooms have many thoughtful extras. Breakfast is served at the farmhouse kitchen table, fresh from the Aga.

Rooms 3 en suite (1 GF) D £68-£70* **Facilities** FTV tea/coffee Cen ht Wi-fi **Parking** 6 **Notes** ⊛ ⊛ 400 acres arable/beef

---

FOWEY   Map 2 SX15

Trevanion Guest House

★★★★ GUEST ACCOMMODATION

70 Lostwithiel St PL23 1BQ
☎ 01726 832602
e-mail: alisteve@trevanionguesthouse.co.uk
web: www.trevanionguesthouse.co.uk
dir: *A3082 into Fowey, down hill, left into Lostwithiel St. Trevanion on left*

This 16th-century merchant's house provides friendly, comfortable accommodation within easy walking distance of the historic town of Fowey and is also convenient for visiting the Eden Project. A hearty farmhouse-style, cooked breakfast, using local produce, is served in the attractive dining room; other menu options are available.

Rooms 5 rms (4 en suite) (1 pri facs) (2 fmly) (1 GF) S £40-£50; D £60-£75* **Facilities** FTV DVD tea/coffee Dinner available Cen ht Wi-fi **Parking** 6 **Notes** LB ⊛

GORRAN HAVEN   Map 2 SX04

The Mead

★ ★ ★ ★ BED AND BREAKFAST

PL26 6HU
☎ 01726 842981
e-mail: maureengoff@tiscali.co.uk
dir: *A30 signed to St Austell continue towards Mevagissey. Signed for Gorran Haven, 1st right Wansford Meadows*

Guests are welcomed at this new, comfortable home with a complimentary cream tea. Peacefully situated in Gorran Haven, within a ten-minute walk of the sandy beach, Heligan and the Eden Project are a short drive away. The bedrooms feature larger than average beds and numerous extra facilities. Hearty breakfasts are served in the ground-floor dining room and include free-range eggs from the owner's hens, whenever possible.

Rooms 2 en suite S £50; D £70* **Facilities** FTV DVD Lounge tea/coffee Cen ht Wi-fi ⊜ **Parking** 2 **Notes** ⊛ No Children Closed Xmas ⊛

GWEEK   Map 2 SW72

Black Swan

Ⓤ

TR12 6TU
☎ 01326 221502

Currently the rating for this establishment is not confirmed. This may be due to a change of ownership or because it has only recently joined the AA rating scheme.

Rooms 4 en suite **Facilities** tea/coffee Dinner available Wi-fi **Parking** 15

HAYLE   Map 2 SW53

Calize Country House

★ ★ ★ ★ ⌂ GUEST ACCOMMODATION

Prosper Hill, Gwithian TR27 5BW
☎ 01736 753268
e-mail: jilly@calize.co.uk
dir: *2m NE of Hayle. B3301 in Gwithian at Red River Inn, house 350yds up hill on left*

This refurbished establishment has superb views of the sea and countryside, and is well located for the beaches and coves of West Penwith, walking, birdwatching, and the many gardens in the area. The attentive proprietors provide a most welcoming environment and invite you to share their comfortable lounge, which has a log-burning fire during colder months. Enjoyable breakfasts featuring delicious home-made fare are served around a communal table with sea views.

Rooms 4 en suite **Facilities** FTV TVL tea/coffee Cen ht Wi-fi **Parking** 6 **Notes** ⊛ No Children 12yrs ⊛

HELFORD   Map 2 SW72

Prince of Wales

★★★★ INN

Newtown, St Martin TR12 6DP
☎ 01326 231247
e-mail: webmail@princeofwalesnewtown.co.uk

A traditional pub in a quiet village setting, privately owned and run with care and much pride. The bedrooms are bright, comfortable and well furnished and include such extras as iPod docking stations. Dinner is served every evening and breakfast features locally sourced, quality produce.

Rooms 3 en suite (2 fmly) **Facilities** FTV TVL tea/coffee Dinner available Direct Dial Cen ht Wi-fi ⌓ 18 **Parking** 70 **Notes** No coaches

---

HELSTON   Map 2 SW62

See also St Keverne

The Queens Arms

★ ★ ★ INN

Breage TR13 9PD
☎ 01326 573485
e-mail: chris-brazier@btconnect.com

A traditional inn in a quiet village location near to Helston, serving home-cooked food every night of the week. The bedrooms are bright, comfortable and well appointed, and the cosy bar is a great meeting place for locals and guests alike. Good food and good beer, coupled with commendable hospitality, make The Queens Arms a popular venue.

Rooms 2 en suite D £75-£85* **Facilities** FTV tea/coffee Dinner available Cen ht Wi-fi Pool table **Parking** 15 **Notes** LB No Children No coaches

Save on B&Bs and Hotels. Book at **theAA.com/hotel**

CORNWALL & ISLES OF SCILLY 55 ENGLAND

The Crown Inn

★★★ INN

PL30 5BT
☎ 01208 872707 ▤ 01208 871208
e-mail: thecrown@wagtailinns.com
web: www.wagtailinns.com
dir: Signed from A390, 2m W of Lostwithiel. Inn 0.5m down lane into village, opposite church

This character inn has a long history, reflected in its worn flagstone floors, aged beams, open fireplaces and an ancient well. Dating in part from the 12th century, The Crown has undergone a faithful restoration. Dining is a feature and menus offer a wide choice of fresh fish, local produce and interesting dishes. The attractive bedrooms are more contemporary and are impressively appointed. The garden is a delight.

Rooms 2 en suite 7 annexe en suite (1 fmly) (7 GF) D £39.95–£89.95* **Facilities** FTV tea/coffee Dinner available Cen ht Wi-fi ⚓ **Parking** 50

PREMIER COLLECTION

Primrose Cottage

★★★★★ ⚐ ⚐ BED AND BREAKFAST

Lawhitton PL15 9PE
☎ 01566 773645
e-mail: enquiry@primrosecottagesuites.co.uk
web: www.primrosecottagesuites.co.uk
dir: Exit A30 Tavistock, follow A388 through Launceston for Plymouth then B3362, Tavistock 2.5m

Originally a cottage, this impressive property has been imaginatively developed to provide stylish accommodation. From its elevated position, views across the lush countryside are wonderful. All bedrooms provide high levels of comfort with separate seating areas; two of the spacious suites have external entrances. Breakfast makes use of excellent local produce, and a guest lounge is also available. Outside, guests can enjoy the garden, or perhaps take a stroll down to the River Tamar for a spot of fishing.

Rooms 2 en suite 1 annexe en suite (1 GF) S £70–£90; D £90–£130 **Facilities** FTV tea/coffee Dinner available Cen ht Wi-fi Fishing ⚓ **Extras** Wine, home-made cakes - complimentary **Parking** 5 **Notes** ⊗ No Children 12yrs Closed 23-28 Dec

Hurdon Farm (SX333828)

★★★★ ⚐ FARMHOUSE

PL15 9LS
☎ 01566 772955 Mrs M Smith
e-mail: hurdonfarm@hotmail.co.uk
dir: A30 onto A388 to Launceston, at rdbt exit for hospital, 2nd right signed Trebullett, premises 1st on right

Genuine hospitality is assured at this delightful 18th-century granite farmhouse. The bedrooms are individually furnished and decorated, and equipped with numerous extras. The delicious dinners, by arrangement, use only the best local produce, and include home-made puddings and the farm's own clotted cream.

Rooms 6 en suite (1 fmly) (1 GF) S £34–£38; D £56–£70* **Facilities** FTV TVL tea/coffee Dinner available Cen ht Wi-fi **Parking** 10 **Notes** LB ⊗ Closed Nov-Apr ⊕ 400 acres mixed

Bradridge Farm (SX328938)

★★★★ FARMHOUSE

PL15 9RL
☎ 01409 271264 & 07748 253346
▤ 01409 271331 Mrs A Strout
e-mail: angela@bradridgefarm.co.uk
dir: 5.5m N of Launceston. Exit B3254 at Ladycross sign for Boyton, Bradridge 2nd farm on right after Boyton school

The late Victorian farmhouse stands in glorious countryside on the border of Devon and Cornwall. The well-presented bedrooms have numerous thoughtful extras, and the Aga-cooked breakfasts feature farm-fresh eggs.

Rooms 4 rms (3 en suite) (1 fmly) **Facilities** FTV Lounge TVL tea/coffee Cen ht Fishing **Parking** 6 **Notes** LB Closed Nov-Feb ⊕ 250 acres arable/beef/sheep/hens

Tyne Wells House

★★★★ BED AND BREAKFAST

Pennygillam PL15 7EE
☎ 01566 775810
e-mail: btucker@talktalk.net
web: www.tynewells.co.uk
dir: 0.6m SW of town centre. Exit A30 onto Pennygillam rdbt, house off rdbt

Situated on the outskirts of town, Tyne Wells House has panoramic views over the countryside. There's a relaxed and friendly atmosphere and the bedrooms are neatly furnished. A hearty breakfast is served in the dining room, which overlooks the garden.

Rooms 3 rms (2 en suite) (1 pri facs) (1 fmly) S £35–£45; D £54–£68 **Facilities** FTV DVD tea/coffee Cen ht Wi-fi ⚓ **Parking** 4 **Notes** LB ⊗ ⊕

B&B @ Rose Cottage

★★★ BED AND BREAKFAST

Rose Cottage, 5 Lower Cleaverfield PL15 8ED
☎ 01566 779292
e-mail: info@rosecottagecornwall.co.uk
dir: Exit A30 at Launceston onto A388. Lower Cleaverfield 200yds on left after 2nd mini-rdbt

A warm and genuine welcome is extended to all guests at this charming cottage, parts of which date back several hundred years. A homely atmosphere ensures a relaxing and enjoyable stay, and every effort is made to assist with any local information required. The bedrooms are very comfortable, and breakfast is served in the attractive dining room which has lovely views across the valley. Wi-fi access is also available.

Rooms 3 rms (2 en suite) (1 pri facs) S £28–£39; D £56–£78* **Facilities** FTV tea/coffee Cen ht Wi-fi ⚓ **Parking** 4 **Notes** LB ⊗ No Children 12yrs

LISKEARD
Map 2 SX26

See also Callington

Redgate Smithy

★★★★ 🏠 BED AND BREAKFAST

Redgate, St Cleer PL14 6RU
☎ 01579 321578
e-mail: enquiries@redgatesmithy.co.uk
web: www.redgatesmithy.co.uk
dir: *3m NW of Liskeard. Exit A30 at Bolventor/Jamaica Inn into St Cleer Rd for 7m, B&B just past x-rds*

This 200-year-old converted smithy is on the southern fringe of Bodmin Moor near Golitha Falls. The friendly accommodation offers smartly furnished, cottage-style bedrooms with many extra facilities. There are several dining options nearby, and a wide choice of freshly cooked breakfasts is served in the conservatory.

Rooms 3 rms (2 en suite) (1 pri facs) S £49; D £78*
Facilities FTV tea/coffee Cen ht Wi-fi **Parking** 3 **Notes** LB
No Children 12yrs Closed Dec-Jan

Trecarne House

★★★★ GUEST ACCOMMODATION

Penhale Grange, St Cleer PL14 5EB
☎ 01579 343543 📠 01579 343543
e-mail: trish@trecarnehouse.co.uk
dir: *B3254 N from Liskeard to St Cleer. Right at Post Office, 3rd left after church, 2nd right, house on right*

A warm welcome awaits at this large family home, peacefully located on the edge of the village. The stylish and spacious bedrooms, which have magnificent country views, feature pine floors and have many thoughtful extras. The buffet-style breakfast offers a wide choice, which can be enjoyed in the dining room or bright conservatory overlooking rolling countryside.

Rooms 3 en suite (2 fmly) **Facilities** TVL tea/coffee Cen ht Table tennis Trampoline **Conf** Max 12 **Parking** 6 **Notes** ⊗

Elnor Guest House

★★★ GUEST HOUSE

1 Russell St PL14 4BP
☎ 01579 342472 📠 01579 345673
e-mail: infoelnorguesthouse@talktalk.net
dir: *Exit A38 from Plymouth into town centre, house on right opposite florist on road to railway station, pass British Legion & The Railway pub*

Elnor is a well-established, friendly guest house, close to the town centre and railway station, and just a short drive from Bodmin Moor and other places of interest. Bedrooms are neatly presented and well equipped, and some are on the ground floor. A cosy lounge is available.

Rooms 6 rms (4 en suite) 3 annexe en suite (3 fmly) (4 GF) S £30-£35; D £65* **Facilities** FTV TVL tea/coffee Direct Dial Cen ht Wi-fi 🛁 **Parking** 7 **Notes** ⊗ 🐾

LOOE
Map 2 SX25

PREMIER COLLECTION

The Beach House

★★★★★ 🏠 GUEST ACCOMMODATION

Marine Dr, Hannafore PL13 2DH
☎ 01503 262598 📠 01503 262298
e-mail: enquiries@thebeachhouselooe.co.uk
web: www.thebeachhouselooe.co.uk
dir: *From Looe W over bridge, left to Hannafore & Marine Drive, on right after Tom Sawyer Tavern*

This peaceful property has panoramic sea views and is just a short walk from the harbour, restaurants and town. Some rooms have stylish hand-made furniture, and the bedrooms are well equipped and have many extras. Hearty breakfasts are served in the first-floor dining room, a good start for walking the South West Coast Path which passes right by the house.

Rooms 5 en suite (4 GF) S £60-£130; D £80-£130*
Facilities FTV tea/coffee Cen ht Wi-fi Beauty treatment room **Parking** 6 **Notes** LB ⊗ No Children 16yrs Closed Xmas

Barclay House

★★★★ ◉◉ GUEST ACCOMMODATION

St Martin's Rd PL13 1LP
☎ 01503 262929 📠 01503 262632
e-mail: reception@barclayhouse.co.uk
web: www.barclayhouse.co.uk
dir: *1st house on left on entering Looe from A38*

This establishment stands in six acres of grounds overlooking Looe Harbour, and is within walking distance of the town. The thoughtfully furnished bedrooms have modern facilities, and there are a sitting room, a spacious bar, and a terrace where guests can enjoy an aperitif in the summer months. Enjoyable freshly prepared dinners are served in the light and airy restaurant that proves popular with locals and tourists alike. A heated swimming pool is also available.

Rooms 11 en suite 1 annexe en suite (1 fmly) (1 GF) S £55-£145; D £115-£195* **Facilities** FTV Lounge tea/coffee Dinner available Direct Dial Cen ht Licensed Wi-fi ch fac ⚡ ♿ 18 Sauna Gym ⚱ Hair salon massage & beauty treatments **Extras** Speciality toiletries, chocolates, water - complimentary **Conf** Max 40 Thtr 20 Class 10 Board 18 **Parking** 25 **Notes** LB ⊗ Civ Wed 70

Bay View Farm (SX282548)

★★★★ ⌐ FARMHOUSE

St Martins PL13 1NZ
☎ 01503 265922 📠 01503 265922 Mrs E Elford
e-mail: mike@looebaycaravans.co.uk
web: www.looedirectory.co.uk/bay-view-farm.htm
dir: 2m NE of Looe. Off B3253 for Monkey Sanctuary, farm signed

Bay View Farm is a renovated and extended bungalow, which has a truly spectacular location with ever-changing views across Looe Bay. The spacious bedrooms have many thoughtful extras. Add a genuine Cornish welcome, tranquillity and great food, and it's easy to see why guests are drawn back again and again to this special place.

Rooms 3 en suite (3 GF) S £35-£38; D £60-£65 **Facilities** TVL tea/coffee Dinner available Cen ht **Parking** 3 **Notes** LB ⊗ No Children 5yrs ⊜ 56 acres mixed/shire horses

Bucklawren Farm (SX278540)

★★★★ FARMHOUSE

St Martin-by-Looe PL13 1NZ
☎ 01503 240738 📠 01503 240481 Mrs J Henly
e-mail: bucklawren@btopenworld.com
web: www.bucklawren.co.uk
dir: 2m NE of Looe. Off B3253 to Monkey Sanctuary, 0.5m right to Bucklawren, farmhouse 0.5m on left

This spacious 19th-century farmhouse stands in 400 acres of farmland just a mile from the beach. The attractive bedrooms, including one on the ground floor, are well equipped, and the front-facing rooms have spectacular views across fields to the sea. Breakfast is served in the dining room, and tempting home-cooked evening meals are available at the Granary Restaurant which is in a converted barn.

Rooms 6 en suite 1 annexe rm (1 pri facs) (3 fmly) (1 GF) S £40-£55; D £66-£80 **Facilities** FTV Lounge TVL tea/coffee Cen ht Wi-fi ⬇ **Parking** 7 **Notes** LB ⊗ No Children 5yrs Closed Nov-Feb 400 acres arable/beef

Polgover Farm (SX277586)

★★★★ FARMHOUSE

Widegates PL13 1PY
☎ 01503 240248 Mrs L Wills
e-mail: enquiries@polgoverfarm.co.uk
dir: 4m NE of Looe. A38 S onto B3251 & B3252, 0.5m on right

This attractive house stands in peaceful farmland with fine views. The welcoming proprietors ensure guests feel at home. Comfortable bedrooms are tastefully decorated with numerous thoughtful extras, and hearty breakfasts are served in the very pleasant lounge.

Rooms 3 rms (2 en suite) (1 pri facs) D £66-£78 **Facilities** FTV Lounge tea/coffee Cen ht Wi-fi **Extras** Bottled water **Parking** 9 **Notes** LB ⊗ No Children 12yrs Closed Nov-Feb 93 acres arable/sheep

Polraen Country House

★★★★ ⚑ ⌐ GUEST ACCOMMODATION

Sandplace PL13 1PJ
☎ 01503 263956
e-mail: enquiries@polraen.co.uk
web: www.polraen.co.uk
dir: 2m N of Looe at junct A387 & B3254

This 18th-century stone house, formerly a coaching inn, sits in the peaceful Looe Valley. The charming hosts provide friendly service in a relaxed atmosphere, and the bedrooms and public areas are stylishly co-ordinated and well equipped. The licensed bar, lounge and dining room overlook the garden, and there are facilities for children. The excellent evening meals feature local produce.

Rooms 5 en suite (2 fmly) D £80-£106* **Facilities** FTV TVL tea/coffee Dinner available Cen ht Licensed Wi-fi ♿ 18 ⚱ **Conf** Max 20 Thtr 16 Class 16 Board 16 **Parking** 20 **Notes** LB ⊗ Closed 23-28 Dec RS Nov-Feb dinner by prior arrangement

Trehaven Manor

★★★★ ⚑ ⌐ GUEST ACCOMMODATION

Station Rd PL13 1HN
☎ 01503 262028 📠 01503 265613
e-mail: enquiries@trehavenhotel.co.uk
web: www.trehavenhotel.co.uk
dir: In East Looe between railway station & bridge. Trehaven's drive adjacent to The Globe public house

Run by a charming family, this former rectory has a stunning location with magnificent views of the estuary. Many of the attractive bedrooms have views, and all are particularly well equipped. There is also a cosy lounge bar. Dinner, by arrangement, specialises in Oriental cuisine, and breakfast features traditional fare; the meals are memorable.

Rooms 7 en suite (1 fmly) (1 GF) **Facilities** TVL tea/coffee Dinner available Cen ht Licensed **Parking** 8 **Notes** ⊗

LOOE *continued*

Tremaine Farm *(SX194558)*

★ ★ ★ ★ FARMHOUSE

Pelynt PL13 2LT
☎ 01503 220417 **Mrs R Philp**
e-mail: tremainefarm@tiscali.co.uk
web: www.tremainefarm.co.uk
dir: *5m NW of Looe. B3359 N from Pelynt, left at x-rds*

Convenient for Fowey, Looe and Polperro, this pleasant
working farm offers a comfortable stay. The proprietors
provide friendly hospitality and attentive service, and the
spacious bedrooms are well equipped with impressive
bathrooms. A hearty breakfast is served in the dining
room and there is a particularly pleasant guest lounge.

Rooms 2 rms (1 en suite) (1 pri facs) (1 fmly)
Facilities FTV TVL tea/coffee Cen ht Wi-fi **Parking** 6
Notes LB ⊗ ⊜ 300 acres arable/sheep/potatoes

Coombe Farm

★ ★ ★ ★ GUEST ACCOMMODATION

Widegates PL13 1QN
☎ 01503 240223
e-mail: coombe_farm@hotmail.com
web: www.coombefarmhotel.co.uk
dir: *3.5m E of Looe on B3253 just S of Widegates*

Set in ten acres of grounds and gardens, Coombe Farm
has a friendly atmosphere. The bedrooms are in a
converted stone barn, and are comfortable and spacious.
Each has a dining area, with breakfast delivered to your
room.

Rooms 3 annexe en suite (1 fmly) (3 GF) **Facilities** STV
FTV tea/coffee Direct Dial ⌁ ⚲ 18 **Parking** 20
Notes Closed 15 Dec-5 Jan

Down Ende

★ ★ ★ ★ ⟶ GUEST ACCOMMODATION

Widegates PL13 1QN
☎ 01503 240213 🖷 01503 240213
e-mail: teresa@downende.com
web: www.downende.com
dir: *A374 towards Looe, right A387 road becomes B3253
on left after Coombe Farm*

Set in its own grounds, guests are assured of a warm
welcome at this young family's home. Bedrooms are
comfortable and well equipped, the majority overlooking
the gardens to the front of the property. Home-cooked
evening meals are a highlight and use the best of local
produce, prepared with care and skill.

Rooms 7 en suite 1 annexe en suite (1 fmly) (2 GF) S £55;
D £70-£80 **Facilities** Lounge tea/coffee Dinner available
Cen ht Licensed Wi-fi ⚲ 18 ⚲ **Conf** Max 20 **Parking** 9
Notes LB ⊗

Shutta House

★ ★ ★ ★ GUEST ACCOMMODATION

Shutta PL13 1LS
☎ 01503 264233
e-mail: enquiries@shuttahouse.co.uk
web: www.shuttahouse.co.uk
dir: *From A58 Liskeard, follow A387 to Looe, opposite
railway station*

This fine Victorian house was once the vicarage and the
current owners have created appealing and contemporary
accommodation. All the bedrooms offer high standards of
comfort with elegant styling and original character.
Breakfasts, served in the light and airy dining room,
utilise locally-sourced produce whenever possible. Guests
are also welcome to use the garden which overlooks the
East Looe River.

Rooms 3 en suite S £38-£50; D £56-£85* **Facilities** FTV
tea/coffee Cen ht Wi-fi ⚲ **Conf** Max 6 Thtr 6 Class 6 Board
6 **Parking** 1 **Notes** ⊗ No Children 11yrs

Little Harbour

★ ★ ★ GUEST HOUSE

Church St PL13 2EX
☎ 01503 262474
e-mail: littleharbour@btinternet.com
web: www.looedirectory.co.uk
dir: *From harbour West Looe, right into Princess Sq, guest
house on left*

Little Harbour is situated almost on Looe's harbourside in
the historic old town; it has a pleasant and convenient
location and parking is available. The proprietors are
friendly and attentive, and bedrooms are well appointed
and attractively decorated. Breakfast is served freshly
cooked in the dining room.

Rooms 5 en suite (1 fmly) S £15-£35; D £30-£85*
Facilities FTV Lounge tea/coffee Cen ht Wi-fi **Parking** 3
Notes LB No Children 5yrs

The Old Malt House

★ ★ ★ BED AND BREAKFAST

West Looe Hill PL13 2HE
☎ 01503 264976
e-mail: stay@oldmalthouselooe.com
web: www.oldmalthouselooe.com
dir: *A387 to Looe, 1st left after bridge, right behind fire
station, 100yds on left*

A short, level stroll from the harbour front, The Old Malt
House dates back to 1650 and is very conveniently
situated for all of Looe's amenities. The cosy bedrooms
are well equipped and are approached via an external
stone staircase, while a hearty breakfast using local
produce, is served in the ground floor dining room.

Rooms 3 en suite S £30-£50; D £50-£65* **Facilities** FTV
DVD tea/coffee Cen ht Wi-fi **Parking** 3 **Notes** LB ⊗ No
Children

Save on B&Bs and Hotels. Book at **theAA.com/hotel**

CORNWALL & ISLES OF SCILLY   59   ENGLAND

St Johns Court

★★★ BED AND BREAKFAST

East Cliff PL13 1DE
☎ 01503 263792
e-mail: stay@stjohnscourtlooe.co.uk
dir: *300yds S of Looe bridge. Through Fore St, left at Ship Inn, 200yds on left*

With stunning views over Looe, the estuary and the beach, this late Victorian, stone-built property offers comfortable accommodation. Guests are assured of a very friendly, relaxed and informal atmosphere, along with a hearty breakfast each morning.

Rooms 3 en suite D £65-£80* **Facilities** FTV TVL tea/coffee Cen ht Wi-fi ⅃ 18 **Parking** 2 **Notes** LB ⊗ Closed Oct-Mar 🐾

The Ship Inn

★★★ INN

Fore St PL13 1AD
☎ 01503 263124 🖨 01503 263624
e-mail: reservations@smallandfriendly.co.uk
web: www.smallandfriendly.co.uk

This lively family pub is located in the very heart of bustling East Looe and has a local following. The bedrooms are comfortable and equipped with all the expected facilities. A wide range of popular dishes is served at lunch times and during the evenings, with light refreshments available throughout the day.

Rooms 8 en suite (1 fmly) S £35; D £70 **Facilities** FTV tea/coffee Dinner available Cen ht Wi-fi Pool table **Notes** LB

Penrose B&B

★★★★ GUEST ACCOMMODATION

1 The Terrace PL22 0DT
☎ 01208 871417 & 07766 900179 🖨 01208 871101
e-mail: enquiries@penrosebb.co.uk
web: www.penrosebb.co.uk
dir: *In Lostwithiel on A390 (Edgcumbe Rd) into Scrations Ln, turn 1st right for parking*

Just a short walk from the town centre, this grand Victorian house offers comfortable accommodation and a genuine homely atmosphere. Many of the bedrooms have the original fireplaces and all are equipped with thoughtful extras. Breakfast is a generous offering and is served in the elegant dining room, with views over the garden. Wi-fi access is also available.

Rooms 7 en suite (3 fmly) (2 GF) S £30-£70; D £40-£100 **Facilities** FTV DVD TVL tea/coffee Cen ht Wi-fi 🔒 **Parking** 8 **Notes** LB 🐾

Hartswell Farm (SX119597)

★★★ FARMHOUSE

St Winnow PL22 0RB
☎ 01208 873419 Mrs W Jordan
e-mail: hartswell@connexions.co.uk
web: www.connexions.co.uk/hartswell
dir: *1m E of Lostwithiel. S off A390 at Downend Garage, farm 0.25m up hill on left*

This 17th-century farmhouse has a wonderfully peaceful setting, and offers generous hospitality and a homely atmosphere. The cosy bedrooms look across rolling countryside, and breakfast includes tasty eggs fresh from the farm. A self-catering barn conversion is available. Hartswell Farm boasts a small herd of Red Poll cattle.

Rooms 2 rms (1 en suite) (1 pri facs) S £35-£45; D £60-£80 **Facilities** STV TVL TV1B tea/coffee Cen ht Wi-fi 🔒 Sailing days for 5 night stays **Parking** 3 **Notes** LB ⊗ No Children 6yrs 🐾 52 acres rare breed cattle

Glenleigh

★★★ GUEST HOUSE

Higher Fore St TR17 0BQ
☎ 01736 710308
e-mail: info@marazionhotels.com
dir: *A394 to Penzance, opposite Fire Engine Inn*

This proud granite house has an elevated position with wonderful views towards St Michael's Mount. Built in the late 19th century, it is an ideal mix of Victorian charm and modern amenities. The welcoming proprietors have been here for more than 25 years and many guests return. A full English or continental breakfast is available.

Rooms 9 en suite (1 fmly) (1 GF) S £37-£38; D £74-£76* **Facilities** FTV TVL tea/coffee Cen ht Licensed Wi-fi **Parking** 9 **Notes** LB ⊗ No Children 3yrs Closed Nov-Mar 🐾

Kerryanna Country House

★★★★ BED AND BREAKFAST

Treleaven Farm, Valley Rd PL26 6SA
☎ 01726 843558 🖨 01726 843558
e-mail: enquiries@kerryanna.co.uk
dir: *B3273 St Austell to Mevagissey road, right at bottom of hill, next to playground*

Located on the peaceful outskirts of this fishing village, Kerryanna stands in two acres of gardens and looks across the countryside to the sea. The attractive bedrooms are comfortably furnished. There are three cosy lounges and a swimming pool.

Rooms 3 en suite D £72-£73* **Facilities** FTV tea/coffee Cen ht ⤳ **Parking** 6 **Notes** LB ⊗ No Children 15yrs Closed Oct-Apr 🐾

The Plume of Feathers

★★★★ INN

TR8 5AX
☎ 01872 510387 & 511122 🖨 01872 511124
e-mail: enquiries@theplume.info
dir: *Just off A30 & A3076, follow signs*

A very popular inn with origins dating back to 16th century, situated close to Newquay and the beaches. The restaurant offers a varied menu which relies heavily on local produce. The stylish bedrooms are decorated in neutral colours and have wrought-iron beds with quality linens. The garden makes an ideal place to enjoy a meal or a Cornish tea. Staff are very friendly.

Rooms 7 annexe en suite (1 fmly) (5 GF) **Facilities** FTV tea/coffee Dinner available Cen ht Wi-fi **Parking** 40 **Notes** LB No coaches

West Point B&B

★★★★ BED AND BREAKFAST

West Point, Crimp EX23 9PB
☎ 01288 331594
e-mail: bramhill@hotmail.co.uk
dir: *A361 to Barnstaple onto A39 towards Bude. 7m after Clovelly rdbt on right*

Ideally placed for exploring the beautiful countryside and coasts of north Cornwall and north Devon, this smartly appointed establishment is surrounded by colourful gardens with far-reaching views to the rear. Guests are assured of a genuine welcome plus the freedom of all-day access. Both bedrooms are comfortable, light and airy; one has a four-poster bed and patio doors leading to the garden. Additional facilities include a guest lounge and dining room where local farm produce is on offer whenever possible.

Rooms 2 en suite (1 fmly) (2 GF) S £35; D £60 **Facilities** FTV TVL tea/coffee Cen ht Wi-fi 🛁 **Extras** Speciality toiletries **Parking** 4 **Notes** LB ⊗ Closed 22 Dec-2 Jan ⊛

| MOUSEHOLE | Map 2 SW42 |

The Cornish Range Restaurant with Rooms

★★★★ ⊛ RESTAURANT WITH ROOMS

6 Chapel St TR19 6BD
☎ 01736 731488
e-mail: info@cornishrange.co.uk
dir: *From Penzance take B3315, through Newlyn to Mousehole. Along harbour, past Ship Inn, sharp right, left, establishment on right*

This is a memorable place to eat and stay. Stylish rooms, with delightful Cornish home-made furnishings, and attentive, friendly service create a relaxing environment. Interesting and accurate cuisine relies heavily on freshly-landed, local fish and shellfish, as well as local meat and poultry, and the freshest fruit and vegetables.

The Cornish Range Restaurant with Rooms

Rooms 3 en suite **Facilities** FTV tea/coffee Dinner available Cen ht Wi-fi **Notes** ⊗ RS evenings only in winter months No coaches

| MULLION | Map 2 SW61 |

Colvennor Farmhouse

★★★★ BED AND BREAKFAST

Cury TR12 7BJ
☎ 01326 241208 📠 01326 241208
e-mail: colvennor@btinternet.com
web: www.colvennorfarmhouse.com
dir: *A3083 (Helston-Lizard), over rdbt at end of airfield, next right to Cury/Poldhu Cove, farm 1.4m on right at top of hill*

Peacefully located, this Grade II listed former farmhouse is a wonderfully relaxing base from which to explore the picturesque delights of The Lizard. Parts of the house date back to the 17th century, but fortunately modern comforts are now in place with bedrooms and bathrooms offering high levels of quality and character. Breakfast utilises excellent local produce and is served in the attractive dining room. Guests also have a lovely lounge at their disposal that has a log burner to keep the chill off in cooler months; there is also a large garden.

Rooms 3 en suite (1 GF) S £49-£50; D £65-£70* **Facilities** FTV DVD TVL tea/coffee Cen ht Wi-fi ⚲ 18 🛁 **Parking** 3 **Notes** ⊗ No Children 10yrs ⊛

| NEWQUAY | Map 2 SW86 |

The Windward

★★★★ GUEST ACCOMMODATION

Alexandra Rd, Porth Bay TR7 3NB
☎ 01637 873185 📠 01637 851400
e-mail: enquiries@windwardhotel.co.uk
dir: *1.5m NE of town centre. A3508 towards Newquay, right onto B3276 (Padstow road), 1m on right*

Windward is pleasantly located almost on Porth Beach and is also convenient for the airport. It offers spectacular views, friendly hospitality, and a pleasant bar and terrace for relaxing. The spacious bedrooms, some with balconies, and many with sea views, are well equipped. Breakfast is served in the restaurant overlooking the beach.

Rooms 13 en suite (3 fmly) (3 GF) S £50-£76; D £88-£98* **Facilities** FTV DVD TVL tea/coffee Cen ht Licensed Wi-fi 🛁 **Conf** Max 30 Thtr 30 Class 30 Board 30 **Parking** 15 **Notes** LB ⊗

Meadow View

★★★ GUEST ACCOMMODATION

135 Mount Wise TR7 1QR
☎ 01637 873132
e-mail: meadowview135@hotmail.com
web: www.meadowviewnewquay.co.uk
dir: *A392 into Newquay to Mountwise, Meadow View on left before rdbt to Pentire*

Expect a warm welcome at this detached property which is ideally located just a short walk from Newquay, and the famous Fistral Beach which is renowned for surfing. Waterworld, the Eden Project, and the Pentire Peninsular with its rolling green coastline are all just a short drive away. The bedrooms are comfortable and some have countryside views. A hearty breakfast is served in the pleasant dining room and there is a cosy sun lounge to relax in.

Rooms 7 en suite (2 fmly) **Facilities** tea/coffee Cen ht **Parking** 7 **Notes** ⊗ No Children 5yrs Closed 7 Nov-mid Feb ⊛

The Three Tees

★★★ GUEST ACCOMMODATION

21 Carminow Way TR7 3AY
☎ 01637 872055 📠 01637 872055
e-mail: greg@3tees.co.uk
web: www.3tees.co.uk
dir: *A30 onto A392 signed Newquay. Right at Quintrell Downs rdbt signed Porth, over x-rds, 3rd right*

Located in a quiet residential area just a short walk from the town and beach, this friendly family-run accommodation is comfortable and well equipped. There is a lounge, a bar and a sun lounge for the use of guests. Breakfast is served in the dining room, where snacks are available throughout the day. The bar serves light snacks in the evenings. In addition to bedrooms in the main house, a family annexe is also available, newly built within the garden and offering flexible, level-access accommodation.

Rooms 8 rms (7 en suite) (1 pri facs) 1 annexe en suite (4 fmly) (2 GF) D £68-£76* **Facilities** FTV DVD TVL tea/coffee Cen ht Licensed Wi-fi 🛁 **Parking** 11 **Notes** LB Closed Nov-Feb

Tregarthen Guest House

★★★ GUEST ACCOMMODATION

1 Arundel Way TR7 3BB
☎ 01637 873554 📄 01637 873554
e-mail: info@tregarthen.co.uk
web: www.tregarthen.co.uk
dir: *A30 onto A392, at Quintrell onto A3058 (Henver Rd), Arundel Way 4th right*

Tregarthen is located in a quiet residential area just a short walk from the beaches and town centre. The owners of this delightful detached property provide warm hospitality along with comfortable accommodation which is smartly furnished and well-equipped. Hearty breakfasts are served at individual tables in the spacious ground-floor dining room. Ample parking is available.

Rooms 6 en suite 1 annexe en suite (1 fmly) (6 GF)
D £50-£75* **Facilities** FTV tea/coffee Cen ht Wi-fi 🛁
Parking 7 **Notes** LB ⊗ Closed Xmas

Wenden Guest House

★★★ GUEST HOUSE

11 Berry Rd TR7 1AU
☎ 01637 872604 📄 01637 872604
e-mail: wenden@newquay-holidays.co.uk
web: www.newquay-holidays.co.uk
dir: *In town centre off seafront Cliff Rd, near station*

This family-run guest house offers bright, modern accommodation near the beach and the town centre. Bedrooms have been carefully designed to make best use of space, and each is individually styled. Breakfast, served in the stylish dining room, is a filling start to the day.

Rooms 7 en suite D £50-£70* **Facilities** FTV DVD tea/coffee Cen ht Wi-fi 🛁 **Extras** Mini-fridge **Parking** 7
Notes LB ⊗ No Children 16yrs Closed 1wk Xmas RS Nov-Feb 2 nights stay minimum

Avalon

★★★ GUEST ACCOMMODATION

4 Edgcumbe Gardens TR7 2QD
☎ 01637 877522 & 07870 320346
e-mail: enquiries@avalonnewquay.co.uk
dir: *From A30 at Quintrell Downs rdbt onto A3058 signed St Columb Minor. Left in 1m opposite Rocklands*

Conveniently situated within walking distance of the town centre and the beaches, in a quiet residential area, Avalon provides comfortable accommodation, and enjoys the benefit of on-site parking. Guests may enjoy the front-facing sun terrace during summer months. Golfing holiday offers are available.

Rooms 6 rms (5 en suite) (1 pri facs) (1 fmly) S £26-£35;
D £52-£70* **Facilities** FTV tea/coffee Wi-fi **Parking** 6
Notes LB

The Croft

★★★ GUEST ACCOMMODATION

37 Mount Wise TR7 2BL
☎ 01637 871520 📄 01637 871520
e-mail: info@the-crofthotel.co.uk
web: www.the-crofthotel.co.uk
dir: *In town centre nr Towan Beach, junct Mount Wise & Mayfield Rd*

Located just minutes away from the town centre and beach, The Croft is comfortable and the friendly hosts create a homely atmosphere. A full English breakfast is served in the informal bar-dining room.

Rooms 8 rms (6 en suite) (2 pri facs) (4 fmly)
D £50-£70* **Facilities** FTV tea/coffee Cen ht Licensed 🛁
Parking 7 **Notes** LB ⊗

Dewolf Guest House

★★★ GUEST HOUSE

100 Henver Rd TR7 3BL
☎ 01637 874746
e-mail: holidays@dewolfguesthouse.com
dir: *A392 onto A3058 at Quintrell Downs rdbt, guest house on left just past mini-rdbts, before crossing*

Making guests feel welcome and at home is the priority here. The bedrooms in the main house are bright and well equipped, and there are two more in a separate single storey building at the rear. The guest house is just a short walk from Porth Beach and all the local attractions.

Rooms 4 en suite 2 annexe en suite (1 fmly) (3 GF)
S £30-£45; D £60-£90 **Facilities** FTV tea/coffee Cen ht
Licensed **Extras** Mini-fridges **Parking** 6 **Notes** LB

Milber Guest House

★★★ GUEST HOUSE

11 Michell Av TR7 1BN
☎ 01637 872825
e-mail: suemilber@aol.com
dir: *A392 to Newquay. From Quintrell rdbt onto A3058 (Quintrell Rd then Henver Rd) left into Narrowcliffe, becomes Cliff Rd. Left into Berry Rd, right into Mount Wise. 2nd right into Michell Ave, house on left*

This small and friendly guest house is situated in the centre of Newquay. Bedrooms are comfortable and offer lots of useful facilities. The bar is open most reasonable times, and guests are given their own keys so they can come and go as they please.

Rooms 6 rms (4 en suite) (6 fmly) (1 GF) S £25-£30;
D £40-£60* **Facilities** FTV tea/coffee Cen ht Licensed 🛁
Notes LB ⊗ 🐾

Pencrebar

★★★ GUEST ACCOMMODATION

4 Berry Rd TR7 1AT
☎ 01637 872037
e-mail: enquiries@pencrebar.com
web: www.pencrebar.com
dir: *A30 onto A392, right at boating lake on entering Newquay*

This friendly family-run house is a short walk from Newquay's popular beaches and the town centre. Bedrooms are all spacious and well planned. Delicious breakfasts are served in the attractive dining room. Secure car parking is available for guests.

Rooms 7 en suite (2 fmly) D £48-£64* **Facilities** FTV DVD tea/coffee Cen ht Wi-fi 🛁 Off site parking - charged all year **Extras** Mini-fridge **Notes** LB ⊗

Porth Lodge

★★★ INN

Porth Bean Rd TR7 3LT
☎ 01637 874483
e-mail: info@porthlodgehotel.co.uk

Porth Lodge is a popular venue with its own bowling alley. The property has been appointed to provide bedrooms that are very comfortable and well equipped. Food is served daily, and the team are friendly and helpful.

Rooms 16 en suite (1 fmly) S £35-£50; D £65-£90*
Facilities FTV tea/coffee Dinner available Cen ht Wi-fi
🎱 18 Pool table 🛁 Ten pin bowling alley **Conf** Thtr 40
Class 30 Board 20 **Parking** 20 **Notes** LB

Rolling Waves

★★★ GUEST HOUSE

Alexandra Rd, Porth TR7 3NB
☎ 01637 873236 📄 01637 873236
e-mail: enquiries@rollingwaves.co.uk
dir: *A30 onto A392, A3058 towards Newquay. B3276 to Porth, pass Mermaid public house*

Rolling Waves is a family-owned and run guest house with great views across the bay. The bedrooms are comfortable, the hosts friendly and welcoming, and dinner is available on request.

Rooms 7 rms (6 en suite) (1 pri facs) (2 fmly) (3 GF)
S £30-£38; D £60-£76 **Facilities** FTV TVL tea/coffee
Dinner available Cen ht Licensed **Parking** 7 **Notes** LB ⊗

NEWQUAY *continued*

St Breca

★★★ GUEST HOUSE

22 Mount Wise TR7 2BG
☎ 01637 872745
e-mail: enquiries@stbreca.co.uk
dir: *A30 onto A392. Follow signs to Newquay, then to Mount Wise*

This friendly guest house is conveniently located a few minutes' walk from the town centre, beaches and other amenities. It provides soundly maintained, modern bedrooms, and separate tables are provided in the attractive breakfast room.

Rooms 10 rms (8 en suite) (2 pri facs) (3 fmly) (2 GF)
Facilities tea/coffee Cen ht **Parking** 8 **Notes** ⊗

The Silver Jubilee

★★★ GUEST HOUSE

13 Berry Rd TR7 1AU
☎ 01637 874544 & 07779 518484
e-mail: andrew.hatton@talktalk.net
dir: *Follow A3058 into Newquay. After railway station, left at lights, 3rd house on left*

Silver Jubilee is a small establishment situated on the level in the heart of Newquay. All amenities including shopping centre and beaches are about three minutes' walk away. Breakfast (and dinner Easter to September) are served in the dining room. There is also a bar/lounge for a pre-dinner drink or post-meal relaxation.

Rooms 7 en suite (3 fmly) S £40-£50; D £60-£80*
Facilities FTV Lounge tea/coffee Dinner available Cen ht Licensed Wi-fi 🔒 **Parking** 4 **Notes** LB ⊗

Summer Breeze

★★★ GUEST HOUSE

20 Mount Wise TR7 2BG
☎ 01637 871518 & 07800 584681
e-mail: summer-breeze@sky.com
web: www.summer-breeze.info
dir: *A30 onto A392 signed to Newquay. Right at Pentire rdbt, house 0.5m on left*

Guests are assured of a warm welcome at this centrally located guest house; just a couple of minutes from the town centre and not much further from the beaches. The bedrooms are neatly furnished and decorated, and equipped with modern facilities. Freshly cooked, hearty breakfasts are served each morning in the sunny breakfast room; prior notice is appreciated for the vegetarian option.

Rooms 6 en suite (3 fmly) (1 GF) S £30-£60; D £50-£80*
Facilities FTV tea/coffee Cen ht Wi-fi **Parking** 4 **Notes** LB ⊗

Tir Chonaill

★★★ GUEST ACCOMMODATION

106 Mount Wise TR7 1QP
☎ 01637 876492
e-mail: tirchonailhotel@talk21.com
web: www.tirchonaill.co.uk
dir: *A392 into Newquay, at last rdbt right into Mount Wise, signed*

Expect a warm welcome at the long-established and family-owned Tir Chonaill, situated close to the beaches and the town centre. Some of the neat bedrooms have wonderful views across town to the sea, and the hearty breakfasts are sure to satisfy.

Rooms 9 en suite (9 fmly) (1 GF) S £37.50-£60; D £60-£85* **Facilities** FTV TVL tea/coffee Cen ht Wi-fi ⛷ 18 **Parking** 10 **Notes** LB

PADSTOW | Map 2 SW97

The Seafood Restaurant

★★★★★ ◉◉◉ 🏠 RESTAURANT WITH ROOMS

Riverside PL28 8BY
☎ 01841 532700 📠 01841 532942
e-mail: reservations@rickstein.com
dir: *Into town centre down hill, follow round sharp bend, restaurant on left*

Food lovers continue to beat a well-trodden path to this legendary establishment. Situated on the edge of the harbour, just a stone's throw from the shops, The Seafood Restaurant offers stylish and comfortable bedrooms that boast numerous thoughtful extras; some have views of the estuary and a couple have stunning private balconies. Service is relaxed and friendly; booking is essential for both accommodation and a table in the restaurant.

Rooms 14 en suite 6 annexe en suite (6 fmly) (3 GF) D £97-£325* **Facilities** FTV DVD tea/coffee Dinner available Direct Dial Cen ht Lift Wi-fi 🔒 Cookery School **Extras** Mini-bar - chargeable **Parking** 12 **Notes** LB Closed 24-26 Dec RS 1 May restaurant closed No coaches

The Old Mill House

★★★★ 🏠 GUEST HOUSE

PL27 7QT
☎ 01841 540388 📠 01841 540406
e-mail: enquiries@theoldmillhouse.com
web: www.theoldmillhouse.com
dir: *2m S of Padstow. In centre of Little Petherick on A389*

Situated in an Area of Outstanding Natural Beauty, The Old Mill House is a 16th-century corn mill with attractive secluded gardens beside a gentle stream. Guests enjoy an English breakfast in the room where the mill wheel still turns.

Rooms 7 en suite S £65-£85; D £80-£120* **Facilities** FTV Lounge TVL tea/coffee Direct Dial Cen ht Licensed Wi-fi **Parking** 20 **Notes** ⊗ No Children 14yrs Closed Nov-Feb

Penjoly Guest House

★★★★ 🏠 GUEST HOUSE

Padstow Rd PL28 8LB
☎ 01841 533535
e-mail: penjoly.padstow@btopenworld.com
dir: *1m S of Padstow. Off A389 near Padstow Holiday Park*

A very professionally run establishment, where attention to detail and quality are noteworthy throughout. Bedrooms are delightfully decorated and complemented by an impressive range of extras. Breakfast is served in the attractive breakfast room or in the conservatory, and a guest lounge is also available. This is a perfect base for exploring the West Country's delights, and for seeking out the gastronomic restaurants of Cornwall. Guests have the convenience of off-road parking.

Rooms 3 en suite (3 GF) S £76.50–£81; D £85–£90 **Facilities** STV FTV DVD TVL tea/coffee Cen ht Wi-fi **Extras** Robes **Parking** 10 **Notes** ⊗ No Children 16yrs 🌐

Rick Stein's Café

★★★★ BED AND BREAKFAST

10 Middle St PL28 8AP
☎ 01841 532700 📠 01841 532942
e-mail: reservations@rickstein.com
dir: *A389 into town, one way past church, 3rd right*

Another Rick Stein success story, this lively café by day, restaurant by night, offers good food, quality accommodation, and is just a short walk from the harbour. Three bedrooms are available - each is quite different but have high standards of cosseting comfort. Friendly and personable staff are always on hand.

Rooms 3 en suite (1 fmly) D £97–£145* **Facilities** FTV DVD tea/coffee Dinner available Direct Dial Cen ht Licensed Wi-fi ♿ Cookery school **Extras** Mini-bar **Notes** LB Closed 1 May BH RS 24–26 Dec

Roselyn

★★★★ BED AND BREAKFAST

20 Grenville Rd PL28 8EX
☎ 01841 532756
e-mail: padstowbbroselyn@bushinternet.com
web: www.padstowbbroselyn.co.uk
dir: *After blue 'Welcome to Padstow' sign, Grenville Rd 2nd left*

This charming, small establishment is in a quiet residential area just a 10-minute walk from the centre of the delightful fishing port. Guests are assured of warm hospitality, and smartly furnished, well-equipped bedrooms. A good choice of breakfast options is available.

Rooms 3 en suite S £50–£80; D £70–£80* **Facilities** FTV tea/coffee Cen ht Wi-fi ♿ **Parking** 4 **Notes** LB ⊗ Closed Xmas & New Year

Little Pentyre

★★ BED AND BREAKFAST

6 Moyle Rd PL28 8DG
☎ 01841 532246
e-mail: JujuLloyd@aol.com
dir: *From A389, right into Sarahs Ln, bear right into Moyle Rd*

Within easy, level walking distance of the town centre, Little Pentyre is situated in a quiet residential area, adjacent to the Camel Estuary and Trail. The comfortable bedrooms are well equipped and guests enjoy a freshly cooked breakfast, featuring eggs from the hens in the rear garden.

Rooms 2 en suite (2 GF) D £55* **Facilities** FTV tea/coffee Cen ht ♿ **Parking** 2 **Notes** No Children 10yrs 🌐

Wingfield House

★★ BED AND BREAKFAST

Dennis Ln PL28 8DP
☎ 01841 532617
e-mail: besidetheseaside@btinternet.com
dir: *Into Padstow on A389, 1st right into Sarahs Ln. At bottom of hill, right into Dennis Ln, 3rd entrance on right*

A very friendly, traditional bed and breakfast a few minutes' walk from Padstow town centre. The comfortable bedrooms are well appointed and have shared facilities. Hearty breakfasts are served at a large table in the dining room, and guests have the use of a TV lounge. There is off-road parking.

Rooms 3 rms (1 pri facs) (2 fmly) **Facilities** FTV TVL tea/coffee Cen ht Wi-fi **Parking** 5 **Notes** LB 🌐

PAR   **Map 2 SX05**

The Britannia Inn & Restaurant

★★★★ INN

St Austell Rd PL24 2SL
☎ 01726 812889 & 815796 📠 01726 812089
e-mail: info@britanniainn.com
web: www.britanniainn.com
dir: *On A390 between Par & St Austell, next to Cornish Market World*

This long established inn is situated between Par and St Austell and is just a five-minute drive from The Eden Project. There is a very genuine welcome here and a collective effort to ensure guests are well looked after and leave happy. A choice of bars is available, together with attractive gardens, function room and range of dining options. The extensive menu features plenty of Cornish produce with a range of daily specials also offered. Bedrooms have been recently built and offer contemporary style and comfort with impressive, high quality bathrooms.

Rooms 5 en suite (4 fmly) S £60–£80; D £70–£110* **Facilities** FTV tea/coffee Dinner available Direct Dial Cen ht Wi-fi **Conf** Max 75 Thtr 60 Class 45 Board 50 **Parking** 105

Elmswood House

★★★★ GUEST ACCOMMODATION

73 Tehidy Rd, Tywardreath PL24 2QD
☎ 01726 814221
e-mail: enquiries@elmswoodhousehotel.co.uk
web: www.elmswoodhousehotel.co.uk
dir: *Right from Par station, then 1st left to top of hill, opposite village church*

Elmswood is a fine Victorian house set in the middle of the village opposite the church, and many guests return for the warm welcome. Bedrooms have quality furnishings and many extra facilities, and the attractive dining room, lounge and bar overlook a beautiful garden.

Rooms 6 en suite (1 fmly) (1 GF) D £65–£80* **Facilities** FTV Lounge TVL tea/coffee Cen ht Licensed Wi-fi **Parking** 6 **Notes** ⊗ No Children 10yrs Closed Jan

The Royal Inn

★★★★ INN

66 Eastcliffe Rd, Tywardreath PL24 2AJ
☎ 01726 815601 📠 01726 816415
e-mail: info@royal-inn.co.uk
dir: *Adjacent to Par railway station*

Situated next to the local railway station, on the edge of Tywardreath, this free house provides high standards of comfort and quality. Only five minutes from Par Sands and four miles from the Eden Project, it is an ideal base for exploring Cornwall. The open-plan bar area has slate floors and a large open fire; the atmosphere is relaxed and diners can choose from the bar menu or can dine more formally in the restaurant or conservatory. All bedrooms have TV, clock radio, direct-dial telephone, hairdryer and refreshment tray. All twin rooms have sofa beds (suitable for children under 14), and the family suite is suitable for families of 4 or 5.

Rooms 15 en suite (8 fmly) (4 GF) **Facilities** STV FTV tea/coffee Dinner available Direct Dial Cen ht Wi-fi ♿ Pool table **Conf** Max 20 Thtr 8 Class 8 Board 20 **Parking** 17 **Notes** LB Closed 23–26 Dec & 30 Dec–1 Jan

PENZANCE   Map 2 SW43

PREMIER COLLECTION

Camilla House

★★★★★ 🏠 GUEST HOUSE

12 Regent Ter TR18 4DW
☎ 01736 363771 📠 01736 363771
e-mail: enquiries@camillahouse.co.uk
web: www.camillahouse.co.uk
dir: *A30 to Penzance, at rail station follow road along harbourfront into Promenade Rd. Opposite Jubilee Bathing Pool, Regent Terrace 2nd right*

The friendly proprietors at this attractive Grade II listed terrace house do their utmost to ensure a comfortable stay. Wi-fi is available throughout the house, and there is also access to computers in the lounge. The bedrooms and bathrooms are attractive, and provide many added extras. Some bedrooms and the dining room have delightful sea views.

Rooms 8 rms (7 en suite) (1 pri facs) (1 GF) S £35-£40; D £70-£95* **Facilities** FTV DVD TVL tea/coffee Dinner available Cen ht Licensed Wi-fi 🛁 **Parking** 6 **Notes** LB ⊗

PREMIER COLLECTION

Ednovean Farm (SW538295)

★★★★★ 🏠 FARMHOUSE

TR20 9LZ
☎ 01736 711883 Mr & Mrs C Taylor
e-mail: info@ednoveanfarm.co.uk
web: www.ednoveanfarm.co.uk

(For full entry see Perranuthnoe)

PREMIER COLLECTION

Ennys

★★★★★ 🏠 GUEST ACCOMMODATION

Trewhella Ln TR20 9BZ
☎ 01736 740262 📠 01736 740055
e-mail: ennys@ennys.co.uk
web: www.ennys.co.uk

(For full entry see St Hilary)

PREMIER COLLECTION

The Summer House

★★★★★ 🏠 GUEST ACCOMMODATION

Cornwall Ter TR18 4HL
☎ 01736 363744 📠 01736 360959
e-mail: reception@summerhouse-cornwall.com
web: www.summerhouse-cornwall.com
dir: *A30 to Penzance, at rail station follow along harbour onto Promenade, pass Jubilee Pool, right after Queens Hotel. Summer House 30yds on left*

This house, in a delightful residential location close to the seafront and harbour, is decorated in a Mediterranean style. The walled garden also reflects the theme, with sub-tropical plantings and attractive blue tables and chairs; dinner and drinks are served here on summer evenings. Expect warm hospitality and attentive service in tastefully furnished surroundings.

Rooms 5 en suite **Facilities** FTV TVL tea/coffee Dinner available Cen ht Licensed Wi-fi **Parking** 6 **Notes** ⊗ No Children 13yrs Closed Nov-Mar

Chy-an-Mor

★★★★ GUEST ACCOMMODATION

15 Regent Ter TR18 4DW
☎ 01736 363441
e-mail: reception@chyanmor.co.uk
dir: *A30 to Penzance, at rail station, follow harbour front into Promenade Rd. Pass Jubilee Pool, right at Stanley Guest House*

This elegant Grade II listed Georgian house has been appointed to provide high standards throughout. Bedrooms are individually designed and equipped with thoughtful extras, and many have spectacular views over Mount's Bay. The spacious lounge has similar views and tasty and satisfying breakfasts are served in the dining room. Ample off-street parking is available.

Rooms 9 en suite S £45; D £70-£90* **Facilities** FTV Lounge tea/coffee Cen ht Wi-fi Beauty treatments available **Parking** 16 **Notes** LB ⊗ No Children 14yrs Closed 15 Nov-15 Mar

The Dunedin

★★★★ GUEST ACCOMMODATION

Alexandra Rd TR18 4LZ
☎ 01736 362652 📠 01736 360497
e-mail: info@dunedinhotel.co.uk
web: www.dunedinhotel.co.uk
dir: *A30 to Penzance, at rail station along harbour front onto Promenade Rd, right onto Alexandra Rd, Dunedin on right*

The house is in a tree-lined avenue just a stroll from the promenade and town centre. The friendly proprietors provide a relaxed atmosphere. Bedrooms are well equipped and smartly decorated to a high standard.

There is a cosy lounge and hearty breakfasts are served in the dining room.

Rooms 8 rms (8 pri facs) (2 fmly) (2 GF) S £40-£50; D £62-£80 **Facilities** FTV DVD TVL tea/coffee Cen ht Wi-fi ♨ **Notes** LB ⊗ No Children 5yrs Closed 12 Dec-2 Jan ⊜

Mount Royal

★★★★ GUEST ACCOMMODATION

Chyandour Cliff TR18 3LQ
☎ 01736 362233 📠 01736 362233
e-mail: mountroyal@btconnect.com
dir: From A30 onto coast road into town

Part Georgian and part Victorian, the spacious Mount Royal has splendid views over Mount's Bay and is convenient for the town's attractions. There's a gracious elegance throughout with the impressive dining room retaining its original fireplace and ornate sideboard. Parking available to the rear of the property.

Rooms 6 en suite (1 fmly) (1 GF) S £75-£100; D £90-£110 **Facilities** Lounge tea/coffee Cen ht Wi-fi ♨ **Parking** 8 **Notes** LB ⊗ Closed Oct-May ⊜

The Old Vicarage

★★★★ BED AND BREAKFAST

Churchtown, St Hilary TR20 9DQ
☎ 01736 711508 & 07736 101230 📠 01736 711508
e-mail: johnbd524@aol.com
dir: 5m E of Penzance. Off B3280 in St Hilary

Guests will certainly feel very much at home with the friendly welcome they'll receive on arrival. The spacious bedrooms are thoughtfully equipped, and there is a snooker room, a comfortable lounge and extensive gardens. Guests can also take advantage of the trekking and riding school, run by the proprietors who own a small stud farm.

Rooms 4 en suite (2 fmly) (1 GF) D £65-£75* **Facilities** FTV TVL tea/coffee Cen ht Wi-fi Riding **Parking** 8 **Notes** LB

The Carlton

★★★ GUEST HOUSE

Promenade TR18 4NW
☎ 01736 362081 📠 01736 362081
e-mail: carltonhotelpenzance@talk21.com
dir: From A30 signs for harbour & Newlyn, on right after rdbt

Situated on the pleasant promenade and having sea views from some of its rooms, The Carlton is an easy stroll from the town centre and amenities. Bedrooms are traditionally styled. There is a guest lounge and spacious dining room, both sea facing.

Rooms 12 rms (9 en suite) (3 smoking) S £27-£30; D £50-£60* **Facilities** FTV TVL tea/coffee **Notes** ⊗

The Coldstreamer Inn

★★★ ⑤ INN

Gulval TR18 3BB
☎ 01736 362072 📠 01736 322072
e-mail: info@coldstreamer-penzance.co.uk
dir: 1m NE of Penzance on B3311, right into School Ln in Gulval, opposite church

Standing opposite the picturesque church in the pretty village of Gulval, this is very much the local hostelry with plenty of atmosphere and banter. Public areas have homely charm and the restaurant is the venue for impressive cuisine, prepared with skill, passion and excellent produce. After a relaxing evening, comfortable bedrooms await for a good night's sleep in preparation for a tasty, freshly cooked breakfast.

Rooms 3 en suite S £60-£75; D £70-£85 **Facilities** FTV tea/coffee Dinner available Cen ht Wi-fi ♨

The Dolphin Tavern

★★★ INN

Quay St TR18 4BD
☎ 01736 364106
e-mail: dolphintavern@tiscali.co.uk
dir: Opposite Penzance harbour

A traditional inn just a few yards away from Penzance Harbour, usefully located for the Scillonian Ferry. Rooms are comfortable and well presented, staff are friendly and attentive, and food is available in the bar and restaurant daily from a wide menu with daily-changing specials.

Rooms 2 en suite **Facilities** FTV tea/coffee Dinner available Cen ht Wi-fi Pool table in winter only **Notes** ⊗ No coaches

Mount View

★★★ INN

Longrock TR20 8JJ
☎ 01736 710416 📠 01736 710416
dir: Exit A30 at Marazion/Penzance rdbt, 3rd exit signed Longrock. On right after pelican crossing

This Victorian inn, just a short walk from the beach and half a mile from the Isles of Scilly heliport, is a good base for exploring West Cornwall. Bedrooms are well equipped, including a hospitality tray, and the bar is popular with locals. Breakfast is served in the dining room, and a dinner menu is available.

Mount View

Rooms 5 rms (3 en suite) (2 fmly) (2 smoking) **Facilities** FTV tea/coffee Dinner available Wi-fi Pool table **Conf** Max 20 **Parking** 8 **Notes** RS Sun closed 4.30pm-7pm

Penmorvah

★★★ GUEST ACCOMMODATION

61 Alexandra Rd TR18 4LZ
☎ 01736 363711
e-mail: penmorvah_penzance@talktalk.net
dir: A30 to Penzance, at railway station follow road along harbourfront, pass Jubilee pool. At mini-rdbt, right into Alexandra Rd

A well situated property offering comfortable rooms, all of which are en suite. Penmorvah is just a few minutes' walk from the seafront with convenient on-street parking nearby.

Rooms 7 en suite (1 fmly) (3 GF) **Facilities** FTV tea/coffee Cen ht ♨ **Notes** LB No Children 5yrs ⊜

The Swordfish Inn

★★★ INN

The Strand, Newlyn TR18 5HN
☎ 01736 362830
e-mail: info@swordfishinn.co.uk
dir: 1m SW of Penzance

Situated in the very heart of the fishing village of Newlyn, The Swordfish has been totally renovated to provide modern comforts within a traditional and convivial environment. The spacious, comfortable bedrooms are well appointed, as are the en suite shower rooms. This establishment is a popular venue for locals and tourists alike.

Rooms 4 en suite (1 smoking) S £30; D £60* **Facilities** FTV tea/coffee Cen ht Wi-fi **Notes** LB ⊗ No coaches

PERRANARWORTHAL — Map 2 SW73

Blankednick Farm

★ ★ ★ ★ BED AND BREAKFAST

Ponsanooth TR3 7JN
☎ 01872 863784 & 07799 054771
dir: *A39 Truro to Falmouth road, at Perranarworthal, 2nd right turn after Norway Inn. B&B signed*

This traditional bed and breakfast has very high standards throughout plus a very warm welcome from experienced hosts. Blankednick Farm is in a quiet yet accessible location and sits in 16 acres of grounds and gardens. The bedrooms are very well appointed, and hearty Aga-cooked breakfasts are served at a large table in the dining room.

Rooms 2 en suite **Facilities** FTV tea/coffee Cen ht Wi-fi **Parking** 10 **Notes** ⊛

PERRANPORTH — Map 2 SW75

St Georges Country House

★ ★ ★ ★ GUEST ACCOMMODATION

St Georges Hill TR6 0ED
☎ 01872 572184
e-mail: info@stgeorgescountryhouse.co.uk
web: www.stgeorgescountryhouse.co.uk

Situated in an elevated position above Perranporth, St Georges is a very friendly and comfortable establishment. The owners and staff are attentive and very welcoming. Food is served most evenings and there is also a bar and large sitting room with comfy sofas and lots of books.

Rooms 7 en suite (2 fmly) **Facilities** FTV TVL tea/coffee Dinner available Cen ht Licensed Wi-fi **Conf** Max 20 Board 20 **Parking** 10 **Notes** Closed 23-30 Dec

PERRANUTHNOE — Map 2 SW52

PREMIER COLLECTION

Ednovean Farm *(SW538295)*

★ ★ ★ ★ ★ ⌂ FARMHOUSE

TR20 9LZ
☎ 01736 711883 **Mr & Mrs C Taylor**
e-mail: info@ednoveanfarm.co.uk
web: www.ednoveanfarm.co.uk
dir: *Off A394 towards Perranuthnoe at Dynasty Restaurant, farm drive on left on bend by post box*

Tranquillity is guaranteed at this 17th-century farmhouse, which looks across the countryside towards St Michael's Mount. The bedrooms are individually styled and are very comfortable. The impressive, Mediterranean-style gardens are ideal for relaxing and taking in the superb views. In addition to the sitting room, there is also a garden room and several patios. Breakfast is served at a magnificent oak table.

Rooms 3 en suite (3 GF) S fr £110; D fr £120 **Facilities** FTV DVD iPod docking station Lounge tea/coffee Cen ht Wi-fi **Extras** Speciality toiletries **Parking** 4 **Notes** LB ⊛ No Children 16yrs Closed 24-28 Dec 22 acres grassland/stud

The Victoria Inn

★ ★ ★ ⊛ INN

TR20 9NP
☎ 01736 710309
e-mail: enquiries@victoriainn-penzance.co.uk
dir: *Off A394 into village*

This attractive and friendly inn, popular with locals and visitors alike, reputedly originates from the Middle Ages. The food on offer should not be missed. The skilled kitchen team produces consistently impressive dishes which are served either in the cosy bar or the restaurant. The menus feature great local produce, including excellent, locally landed fish. The bedrooms are well presented and provide good levels of comfort.

Rooms 2 en suite S £50-£75; D £75* **Facilities** FTV DVD tea/coffee Dinner available Wi-fi **Extras** Fruit, magazines **Parking** 10 **Notes** No Children 18yrs Closed 1wk Jan No coaches

POLPERRO — Map 2 SX25

PREMIER COLLECTION

Trenderway Farm *(SX214533)*

★ ★ ★ ★ ★ ⌂ FARMHOUSE

Pelynt PL13 2LY
☎ 01503 272214 ▤ 0870 705 9998 **Messrs Peled & Harris**
e-mail: stay@trenderwayfarm.com
web: www.trenderwayfarm.co.uk
dir: *Take A387 from Looe to Polperro, right at signpost to Pelynt. 3rd left at signed junct to farm. Continue down lane to gravel car park*

Set in 200 acres on a working farm, warm hospitality is offered in this delightful 16th-century farmhouse. Stylish bedrooms, both in the farmhouse and in the adjacent barns, offer high levels of comfort and include Wi-fi access. Hearty breakfasts are served in the conservatory overlooking the lake, and free-range eggs from the farm, as well as high quality local produce, are served.

Rooms 2 en suite 5 annexe en suite (2 GF) D £95-£200* **Facilities** FTV DVD Lounge tea/coffee Cen ht Wi-fi ⚓ Lakes Falconry school **Extras** Speciality toiletries **Conf** Max 100 Thtr 100 Class 50 Board 15 **Parking** 8 **Notes** LB ⊛ No Children Civ Wed 150 200 acres beef/sheep/orchards

Trenake Manor Farm (SX190555)

★★★★ FARMHOUSE

Pelynt PL13 2LT
☎ 01503 220835 📠 01503 220835 Mrs L Philp
e-mail: lorraine@cornishfarmhouse.co.uk
dir: 3.5m N of Polperro. A390 onto B3359 for Looe, 5m left at small x-rds

The welcoming 15th-century farmhouse is surrounded by countryside and is a good base for touring Cornwall. Bedrooms have considerate finishing touches and there is a comfortable lounge. Breakfast, using local produce, is enjoyed in the cosy dining room (you may just spot the milking cows quietly passing the end of the garden).

Rooms 3 en suite (1 fmly) **Facilities** FTV TVL tea/coffee Cen ht Wi-fi **Parking** 10 **Notes** LB 🐾 1000 acres dairy/beef/arable

Penryn House

★★★★ GUEST ACCOMMODATION

The Coombes PL13 2RQ
☎ 01503 272157 📠 01503 273055
e-mail: enquiries@penrynhouse.co.uk
web: www.penrynhouse.co.uk
dir: A387 to Polperro, at mini-rdbt left down hill into village (ignore restricted access). 200yds on left

Penryn House has a relaxed atmosphere and offers a warm welcome. Every effort is made to ensure a memorable stay. Bedrooms are neatly presented and reflect the character of the building. After a day exploring, enjoy a drink at the bar and relax in the comfortable lounge.

Rooms 12 en suite (3 fmly) S £41-£61; D £72-£102* **Facilities** FTV Lounge tea/coffee Licensed Wi-fi 🐾 **Parking** 13 **Notes** LB

PORTHLEVEN   Map 2 SW62

Kota Restaurant with Rooms

★★★ 🍴 RESTAURANT WITH ROOMS

Harbour Head TR13 9JA
☎ 01326 562407 📠 01326 562407
e-mail: kota@btconnect.com
dir: B3304 from Helston into Porthleven. Kota on harbour opposite slipway

Overlooking the water, this 300-year-old building is the home of Kota Restaurant (Kota being the Maori word for shellfish). The bedrooms are approached from a granite stairway to the side of the building. The family room is spacious and has the benefit of harbour views, while the smaller, double room is at the rear of the property. The enthusiastic young owners ensure guests enjoy their stay here, and a meal in the restaurant should not be missed. Breakfast features the best local produce.

Rooms 2 annexe en suite (1 fmly) S £50-£70; D £60-£95* **Facilities** FTV DVD tea/coffee Dinner available Wi-fi ⚓ 18 🚲 **Parking** 1 **Notes** 🐾 Closed 24-26 Dec & Jan No coaches

---

PORTLOE   Map 2 SW93

Carradale

★★★★ BED AND BREAKFAST

TR2 5RB
☎ 01872 501508
e-mail: barbara495@btinternet.com
dir: Off A3078 into Portloe, B&B 200yds from Ship Inn

Carradale lies on the outskirts of this picturesque fishing village, a short walk from the South West Coast Path. It provides warm hospitality, a good level of comfort and well equipped bedrooms. There is an upper-floor lounge with a TV, and breakfast is served around a communal table in the pleasant dining room.

Rooms 2 en suite (1 fmly) (1 GF) **Facilities** TVL tea/coffee Cen ht **Parking** 5 **Notes** 🐾 🐾

REDRUTH   Map 2 SW64

Old Railway Yard

★★★★ BED AND BREAKFAST

Lanner Hill TR16 5SZ
☎ 01209 314514 & 07970 595598
e-mail: g.s.collier@btinternet.com
dir: A393 Redruth/Falmouth road, at brow of hill before Lanner village, turn right, 125mtrs

The Old Railway Yard is a traditional bed and breakfast situated off Lanner Hill, with easy access to the A30. The hosts are friendly and attentive and make their guests really feel at home. The bedrooms are very well appointed; there is a small guest lounge and a conservatory, as well as the garden for guests to enjoy.

Rooms 3 rms (2 en suite) (1 pri facs) S £40-£60; D £40-£70* **Facilities** FTV DVD TVL tea/coffee Dinner available Cen ht Wi-fi 🐾 **Parking** 8 **Notes** LB 🐾 No Children 6yrs

---

Lanner Inn

★★ INN

The Square, Lanner TR16 6EH
☎ 01209 215611 📠 01209 214065
e-mail: info@lannerinn.co.uk
web: www.lannerinn.co.uk
dir: 2m SE of Redruth. In Lanner on A393

Conveniently situated for access to Redruth and the A30, this traditional inn is situated in the centre of Lanner and has a good local following. Recent refurbishment has created a new bar and dining room to go along with the comfortable bedrooms. This inn is owner-run and managed, and the team of staff are very friendly.

Rooms 5 en suite 1 annexe en suite (3 fmly) (1 GF) **Facilities** FTV tea/coffee Dinner available Cen ht Wi-fi Pool table **Parking** 16

RUAN HIGH LANES   Map 2 SW93

Treswithian Barn

Ⓤ

TR2 5JT
☎ 01872 501274

Currently the rating for this establishment is not confirmed. This may be due to a change of ownership or because it has only recently joined the AA rating scheme.

Rooms 2 en suite D £65-£70* **Facilities** FTV tea/coffee Cen ht 🐾 **Extras** Snacks, bottled water - complimentary **Parking** 4 **Notes** 🐾 Closed 31 Oct-Mar 🐾

The Coach House

★★★★ GUEST ACCOMMODATION

Kuggar TR12 7LY
☎ 01326 291044
e-mail: mjanmakin@aol.com
dir: *1m N of Ruan Minor in Kuggar*

This 17th-century house is close to Kennack Sands and Goonhilly Downs National Nature Reserve. The friendly proprietors provide a warm welcome and their guests can relax in the spacious lounge-dining room where a fire burns in colder months. Breakfast provides a tasty start to the day before setting off to explore this beautiful area.

Rooms 3 en suite S £41; D £72* **Facilities** FTV TVL tea/coffee Cen ht Wi-fi **Parking** 10 **Notes** LB ⊗ Closed Xmas ⊗

Driftwood Spars

★★★★ ⊜ GUEST ACCOMMODATION

Trevaunance Cove TR5 0RT
☎ 01872 552428
e-mail: info@driftwoodspars.co.uk
web: www.driftwoodspars.co.uk
dir: *A30 to Chiverton rdbt, right onto B3277, through village. Driftwood Spars 200yds before beach*

Partly built from shipwreck timbers, this 18th-century inn attracts locals and visitors alike. The attractive bedrooms, some in an annexe, are decorated in a bright, seaside style with many interesting features. Local produce, including delicious seafood, is served in the informal pub dining room and in the restaurant, together with a range from hand-pulled beers.

Rooms 9 en suite 6 annexe en suite (4 fmly) (5 GF) S £50-£70; D £86-£102* **Facilities** tea/coffee Dinner available Direct Dial Cen ht Licensed Wi-fi Pool table

Table football **Conf** Max 50 Thtr 50 Class 25 Board 20 **Parking** 40 **Notes** LB RS 25 Dec no lunch/dinner, no bar in evening Civ Wed 80

Penkerris

★★ GUEST HOUSE

Penwinnick Rd TR5 0PA
☎ 01872 552262 ▤ 01872 552262
e-mail: penkerris@gmail.com
web: www.penkerris.co.uk
dir: *A30 onto B3277 to village, Penkerris on right after village sign*

Set in gardens on the edge of the village, this Edwardian house is an engaging place to stay with a relaxed and welcoming atmosphere. Period features abound with character elements at every turn. The best possible use is made of space in the bedrooms, and home-cooked evening meals, using local produce, are served by prior arrangement. Breakfast provides a wonderful start to the day with the resident hens happily contributing the eggs. Ample parking is available.

Rooms 7 rms (4 en suite) (3 fmly) S £22.50-£45; D £40-£70 **Facilities** FTV TVL tea/coffee Dinner available Licensed Wi-fi Badminton Volleyball **Parking** 9 **Notes** LB

See also Gorran Haven & St Blazey

Anchorage House

★★★★★ ⊜ ⊜ GUEST ACCOMMODATION

Nettles Corner, Tregrehan Mills PL25 3RH
☎ 01726 814071 ▤ 01726 814071
e-mail: info@anchoragehouse.co.uk
web: www.anchoragehouse.co.uk
dir: *2 m E of town centre off A390, opposite St Austell Garden Centre*

This Georgian-style house is set in an acre of carefully landscaped gardens at the end of a private lane. Guests are met upon arrival with afternoon tea, often served on the patio, and dinner is served in the evening by arrangement. The luxurious bedrooms are equipped to the highest standard and include satellite TV, fresh fruit, magazines, bottled water and chocolates. Guests also have use of the pool, hot tub, gym and sauna. The house is a short distance from the Eden Project, the Lost Gardens of Heligan, Carlyon Bay and Charlestown Harbour.

Rooms 4 en suite 1 annexe en suite (1 GF) S £75-£80; D £105-£130* **Facilities** STV FTV DVD Lounge tea/coffee Dinner available Cen ht Wi-fi ⓣ Sauna Gym ⓑ Hot tub **Parking** 6 **Notes** ⊗ No Children 16yrs Closed Dec-Feb

Penarwyn House

★★★★★ ⊜ GUEST ACCOMMODATION

PL24 2DS
☎ 01726 814224 ▤ 01726 814224
e-mail: stay@penarwyn.co.uk
web: www.penarwyn.co.uk

(For full entry see St Blazey)

Highland Court Lodge

★★★★★ ⊜ GUEST ACCOMMODATION

Biscovey Rd, Biscovey, Par PL24 2HW
☎ 01726 813320 ▤ 01726 813320
e-mail: enquiries@highlandcourt.co.uk
web: www.highlandcourt.co.uk
dir: *2m E of St Austell. A390 E to St Blazey Gate, right into Biscovey Rd, 300yds on right*

This is an extremely well presented and maintained contemporary building with stunning views over St Austell Bay, and is just over one mile from the Eden Project. Its impressive en suite bedrooms have luxurious fabrics and each room opens onto a private patio. There is a lounge with deep sofas, and the terrace shares the fine views. Breakfasts are served in the attractive dining area, and include porridge, the Full Cornish (with Cornish hogs puddings) and kippers. A spa and treatment room is available.

Rooms 3 en suite (2 fmly) (3 GF) S £90-£125; D £120-£190* **Facilities** FTV DVD TVL tea/coffee Cen ht Licensed Wi-fi ⓑ **Extras** Mini-bar, speciality toiletries, bath robes **Conf** Max 12 Class 12 Board 12 **Parking** 10 **Notes** LB ⊗

Lower Barn

★★★★★ ⊜ GUEST ACCOMMODATION

Bosue, St Ewe PL26 6ET
☎ 01726 844881
e-mail: janie@bosue.co.uk
web: www.bosue.co.uk
dir: *3.5m SW of St Austell. Off B3273 at x-rds signed Lost Gardens of Heligan, Lower Barn signed 1m on right*

This converted barn, tucked away in countryside with easy access to local attractions, has huge appeal. Warm colours create a Mediterranean feel, complemented by informal and genuine hospitality. Bedrooms have a host of extras. Breakfast is served around a large table or on the patio deck overlooking the garden, which also has a hot tub.

Rooms 3 en suite (1 fmly) (1 GF) **Facilities** tea/coffee Dinner available Cen ht Sauna Hot tub Spa treatments **Parking** 7 **Notes** ⊗ Closed Jan

PREMIER COLLECTION

Nanscawen Manor House

★★★★★ GUEST ACCOMMODATION

Prideaux Rd, Luxulyan Valley PL24 2SR
☎ 01726 814488 & 07811 022423
e-mail: keith@nanscawen.com
web: www.nanscawen.com

(For full entry see St Blazey)

Hunter's Moon

★★★★ GUEST HOUSE

Chapel Hill, Polgooth PL26 7BU
☎ 01726 66445
e-mail: enquiries@huntersmooncornwall.co.uk
dir: *1.5m SW of town centre. Off B3273 into Polgooth, pass village shop on left, 1st right*

Hunter's Moon lies in a quiet village just a few miles from Heligan and within easy reach of the Eden Project. Service is friendly and attentive and the bedrooms are well equipped for business or leisure. There is a conservatory-lounge and a pretty garden to enjoy during warmer weather. Breakfast is served in the cosy dining room and the nearby village inn serves freshly prepared meals.

Rooms 4 en suite (2 fmly) S £54-£56; D £76-£78* **Facilities** FTV Lounge tea/coffee Cen ht Wi-fi 🔋 **Extras** Fridge for guest use **Parking** 5 **Notes** ⊗ No Children 14yrs 🚭

Sunnyvale Bed & Breakfast

★★★★ BED AND BREAKFAST

Hewas Water PL26 7JF
☎ 01726 882572
e-mail: jm.uden@hotmail.com
dir: *4m SW of St Austell. Exit A390 in Hewas Water*

This house has pleasant gardens in a peaceful location, and the very friendly proprietor makes you feel most welcome. Both the bedrooms, with an extensive range of facilities, are on the ground floor; one is specifically designed for the less able guests. Breakfast is either taken in the main house at separate tables, or in the bedroom by prior arrangement.

Rooms 2 annexe en suite (2 GF) S £45; D £70* **Facilities** FTV DVD tea/coffee Cen ht Wi-fi **Parking** 4 **Notes** ⊗ No Children 16yrs 🚭

The Elms

★★★★ BED AND BREAKFAST

14 Penwinnick Rd PL25 5DW
☎ 01726 74981 ▤ 01726 74981
e-mail: pete@edenbb.co.uk
web: www.edenbb.co.uk
dir: *0.5m SW of town centre. On A390 at junct with Pondhu Rd*

Well located for the Eden Project or for touring Cornwall, this bed and breakfast offers a relaxed and friendly environment for leisure and business guests. Bedrooms, one with a four-poster bed, are well equipped and there is an inviting lounge. Breakfast is served in the conservatory dining room.

Rooms 3 en suite 1 annexe en suite (1 GF) S £35-£36; D £60-£80* **Facilities** FTV Lounge TVL tea/coffee Cen ht Wi-fi ⟂ 18 🔋 **Parking** 4 **Notes** LB ⊗

Elmswood House

★★★★ GUEST ACCOMMODATION

73 Tehidy Rd, Tywardreath PL24 2QD
☎ 01726 814221
e-mail: enquiries@elmswoodhousehotel.co.uk
web: www.elmswoodhousehotel.co.uk

(For full entry see Par)

Langdale House

★★★★ BED AND BREAKFAST

1A Southbourne Rd PL25 4RU
☎ 01726 71404 & 07764 531050 ▤ 01726 63798
e-mail: stay@langdalehousecornwall.co.uk
web: www.langdalehousecornwall.co.uk
dir: *On A390 St Austell bypass, 0.5m S of town centre*

Handily placed for the town centre, this is an ideal choice for both business and leisure guests and a great place to relax, unwind and re-charge the batteries. Quality and comfort levels are high throughout, both within the elegant bedrooms and the impressive bathrooms. The welcome is warm and friendly with every effort made to ensure an enjoyable and rewarding stay. Breakfast is served in the attractive dining room, with a good range of dishes offered. Super-fast Wi-fi is provided.

Rooms 3 en suite S £45-£70; D £55-£80* **Facilities** FTV tea/coffee Cen ht Wi-fi **Parking** 3 **Notes** LB ⊗ No Children 5yrs

---

Polgreen Farm *(SX008503)*

★★★★ FARMHOUSE

London Apprentice PL26 7AP
☎ 01726 75151　Mr Berryman
e-mail: polgreen.farm@btinternet.com
web: www.polgreenfarm.co.uk
dir: *1.5m S of St Austell. Exit B3273, left on entering London Apprentice & signed*

Guests return regularly for the friendly welcome at this peaceful establishment located just south of St Austell. The spacious and well-equipped bedrooms are divided between the main house and an adjoining property, and each building has a comfortable lounge. Breakfast is served in a pleasant conservatory overlooking the garden.

Rooms 3 rms (2 en suite) (1 pri facs) 4 annexe en suite (1 fmly) (1 GF) S £30-£45; D £64-£72 **Facilities** FTV Lounge TVL tea/coffee Cen ht **Parking** 8 **Notes** LB ⊗ 🚭 64 acres livestock

ST AUSTELL *continued*

Sunnycroft

★★★★ GUEST ACCOMMODATION

28 Penwinnick Rd PL25 5DS
☎ 01726 216247 📠 01726 879409
e-mail: enquiries@accommodationstaustell.co.uk
web: www.accommodationstaustell.co.uk
dir: *600yds SW of town centre on A390*

Just a short walk from the town centre, this 1930s house is conveniently situated for the Eden Project. The bright bedrooms offer good levels of comfort. Tasty and substantial breakfasts are served in the light and airy conservatory dining room. Ample off-road, secure parking is available too.

Rooms 5 en suite **Facilities** FTV tea/coffee Dinner available Cen ht Wi-fi ⅃ 18 **Parking** 10 **Notes** No Children 7yrs Closed 24-26 Dec

T'Gallants

★★★★ GUEST HOUSE

6 Charlestown Rd, Charlestown PL25 3NJ
☎ 01726 70203 📠 01726 70203
e-mail: enquiries@tgallants.co.uk
dir: *0.5m SE of town off A390 rdbt signed Charlestown*

The fine Georgian house partly dates from 1630, and overlooks the historic port of Charlestown, with its fleet of square-rigged sailing ships. The bedrooms are well presented and spacious, and one has a four-poster bed and views of the port. Breakfast is served in the attractive dining room with a choice of traditional or continental offered. A guest lounge is also available.

Rooms 7 en suite S £50; D £70-£100* **Facilities** FTV TVL tea/coffee Cen ht Wi-fi 🔔 **Notes** ⊗

ST BLAZEY   Map 2 SX05

PREMIER COLLECTION

Penarwyn House

★★★★★ 🔔 GUEST ACCOMMODATION

PL24 2DS
☎ 01726 814224 📠 01726 814224
e-mail: stay@penarwyn.co.uk
web: www.penarwyn.co.uk
dir: *A390 W through St Blazey, left before 2nd speed camera into Doubletrees School, Penarwyn straight ahead*

This large impressive Victorian house stands in tranquil surroundings close to main routes, with the Eden Project, The Lost Gardens of Heligan, Fowey, the coastal footpath and National Trust properties all close by. Painstakingly restored, the spacious house offers a host of facilities, and the bedrooms are particularly comfortable and delightfully appointed. On arrival, guests are welcomed with afternoon tea and cake, and breakfast is always a highlight. Jan and Mike offer very welcoming hospitality and place a great emphasis upon service.

Rooms 4 en suite (1 fmly) S £60-£75; D £80-£150 **Facilities** FTV Lounge tea/coffee Cen ht Wi-fi 3/4 size snooker table **Parking** 6 **Notes** LB ⊗ No Children 10yrs

PREMIER COLLECTION

Nanscawen Manor House

★★★★★ GUEST ACCOMMODATION

Prideaux Rd, Luxulyan Valley PL24 2SR
☎ 01726 814488 & 07811 022423
e-mail: keith@nanscawen.com
web: www.nanscawen.com
dir: *A390 W to St Blazey, right after railway, Nanscawen 0.75m on right*

This renovated manor house originates from the 14th century and provides a high standard of accommodation, with elegant bedrooms and bathrooms with spa baths. There are extra pampering touches throughout, a spacious lounge with a well-stocked honesty bar, and five acres of pleasant gardens with splendid woodland views. Breakfast, served in the conservatory, features fresh local produce.

Rooms 3 en suite (3 fmly) S £60-£88; D £78-£120* **Facilities** STV FTV DVD Lounge tea/coffee Direct Dial Cen ht Wi-fi 🎣 🔔 Hot tub **Parking** 8 **Notes** ⊗ No Children 12yrs

ST BURYAN   Map 2 SW42

Tregurnow Farm *(SW444242)*

★★★★ FARMHOUSE

TR19 6BL
☎ 01736 810255 Mr G Jeffery
e-mail: tregurnow@lamorna.biz

Tucked away near St Buryan, Tregurnow Farm offers traditional, quality farmhouse bed and breakfast and self-catering facilities. Peace and quiet, stunning views and hearty breakfasts are hallmarks of a stay here. Close to Mousehole, Minnack Theatre and Penzance, this is a good base for touring the far south-west of the county.

Rooms 3 en suite **Notes** Closed Oct-Apr

ST HILARY   Map 2 SW53

PREMIER COLLECTION

Ennys

★★★★★ GUEST ACCOMMODATION

Trewhella Ln TR20 9BZ
☎ 01736 740262 ▤ 01736 740055
e-mail: ennys@ennys.co.uk
web: www.ennys.co.uk
dir: 1m N of B3280 Leedstown-Goldsithney road at end of Trewhella Ln

Set off the beaten track, this 17th-century manor house is a perfect place to unwind. A friendly welcome awaits, and a complimentary afternoon tea is laid out in the kitchen. Ennys retains much original character and the rooms are impressively furnished. A delightful Cornish breakfast is served in the dining room, using a wealth of fresh local ingredients and home-produced fresh eggs. Three self-catering cottages are available.

Rooms 3 en suite 2 annexe en suite (1 GF) S £80-£135; D £105-£155* **Facilities** FTV DVD iPod docking station Lounge tea/coffee Cen ht Wi-fi ⊹ ☒ ▤ Yoga studio & classes **Extras** Speciality toiletries **Parking** 8 **Notes** ⊗ No Children 16yrs Closed Nov-28 Mar

ST IVES   Map 2 SW54

Lamorna Lodge

★★★★ GUEST ACCOMMODATION

Boskerris Rd, Carbis Bay TR26 2NG
☎ 01736 795967
e-mail: lamorna@tr26.wanadoo.co.uk
dir: A30 onto A3074, right after playground in Carbis Bay, establishment 200yds on right

A truly genuine welcome is assured at this quietly situated establishment which is just a short walk from Carbis Bay beach. Wonderful views over St Ives Bay to Godrevy Lighthouse can be enjoyed from the spacious lounge, a view also shared by some of the stylish bedrooms. Breakfast utilises local Cornish produce and is served in the elegant surroundings of the dining room. A stylish terrace has recently been added with lovely sea views.

Rooms 9 en suite (2 fmly) (2 GF) S £55-£65; D £90-£110* **Facilities** FTV DVD Lounge tea/coffee Cen ht Wi-fi ☖ **Conf** Max 18 Thtr 18 Class 18 Board 18 **Parking** 9 **Notes** LB ⊗ Closed 5 Nov-10 Mar

The Nook

★★★★ GUEST ACCOMMODATION

Ayr TR26 1EQ
☎ 01736 795913
e-mail: info@nookstives.co.uk
web: www.nookstives.co.uk
dir: A30 to St Ives left at NatWest, right at rdbt & left at top of hill

Having undergone an extensive refurbishment, The Nook is an ideal base for exploring Cornwall's spectacular coastline, gardens and countryside. The comfortable bedrooms are furnished in a contemporary style and are equipped with numerous facilities. There is a wide variety on offer at breakfast, from full English or continental, to scrambled eggs with smoked salmon.

Rooms 11 en suite (1 fmly) (1 GF) **Facilities** FTV TVL tea/coffee Cen ht Wi-fi **Parking** 10 **Notes** ⊗

Treliska

★★★★ GUEST ACCOMMODATION

3 Bedford Rd TR26 1SP
☎ 01736 797678 ▤ 01736 797678
e-mail: info@treliska.com
web: www.treliska.com
dir: A3074 to St Ives, fork at Porthminster Hotel into town, at T-junct facing Barclays Bank left into Bedford Rd, house on right

This stylish, friendly and relaxed home is close to the seafront, restaurants and galleries. There is a refreshing approach here with a contemporary feel throughout. Impressive bathrooms have invigorating showers, while the attractive bedrooms are configured to maximise comfort. Enjoyable, freshly cooked Cornish breakfasts are served in the lounge-dining room with a choice of coffee available at all times to guests. Additional facilities include internet and Wi-fi connections.

Rooms 5 en suite **Facilities** FTV tea/coffee Cen ht Wi-fi **Notes** ⊗ No Children 10yrs ⊜

Wheal-e-Mine Bed & Breakfast

★★★★ ⌂ BED AND BREAKFAST

9 Belmont Ter TR26 1DZ
☎ 01736 795051 & 07523 332018 ▤ 01736 795051
e-mail: whealemine@btinternet.com
web: www.stivesbedandbreakfast.com
dir: A3074 into town, left at x-rds onto B3306, right at rdbt, left at top of hill

Guests are assured of a warm, friendly welcome at this Victorian terraced property, which over the last few years has been fully upgraded with style and flair. Bedrooms are well appointed and each boasts distant sea views. A hearty breakfast is served each morning in the attractive dining room. On-site parking at the rear of the property is an added bonus.

Rooms 3 en suite D £82-£95* **Facilities** FTV DVD tea/coffee Cen ht ☖ Free membership to local gym/swimming pool **Parking** 3 **Notes** LB ⊗ No Children 18yrs Closed Oct-Mar

Borthalan

★★★★ GUEST ACCOMMODATION

Off Boskerris Rd, Carbis Bay TR26 2NQ
☎ 01736 795946 ▤ 01736 795946
e-mail: borthalanhotel@btconnect.com
dir: A3074 into Carbis Bay, right onto Boskerris Rd, 1st left onto cul-de-sac

Quietly situated, this welcoming establishment is just a short walk from Carbis Bay station; from here it's a 3-minute journey to St Ives which avoids the hassle of parking the car. The friendly proprietors provide a relaxing environment, with every effort made to ensure an enjoyable stay. Bedrooms are well equipped and smartly presented - some have lovely sea views. There is a cosy lounge and an attractive garden, and breakfast is served in the bright dining room.

Rooms 7 en suite **Facilities** TVL tea/coffee Cen ht Licensed **Parking** 7 **Notes** ⊗ No Children 12yrs Closed Xmas

Chy Conyn

★★★★ BED AND BREAKFAST

8 Ayr Ter TR26 1ED
☎ 01736 798068
e-mail: mail@chyconyn.co.uk

Located in a pleasant residential area, just above the town, this comfortable bed and breakfast offers accommodation in a range of sizes; all rooms have plenty of useful extras. Breakfast is served in the relaxing and well-presented dining room. Wi-fi is available. There is a car park is to the rear of the property.

Rooms 3 en suite (1 fmly) D £65-£85* **Facilities** FTV DVD tea/coffee Cen ht Wi-fi **Parking** 2 **Notes** ⊗

ST IVES *continued*

Coombe Farmhouse

★★★★ BED AND BREAKFAST

TR27 6NW
☎ 01736 740843
e-mail: coombefarmhouse@aol.com
web: www.coombefarmhouse.com
dir: *1.5m W of Lelant. Exit A3074 to Lelant Downs*

Built of sturdy granite, this early 19th-century farmhouse is in a delightful location tucked away at the southern foot of Trencrom Hill, yet convenient for St Ives. The comfortable bedrooms are attractively decorated. There is a cosy lounge, and substantial breakfasts, featuring farm-fresh eggs, are served in the dining room overlooking the garden.

Rooms 3 rms (2 en suite) (1 pri facs) S £45; D £78-£84*
Facilities FTV TVL TV2B tea/coffee Cen ht **Extras** Bottled water - complimentary **Parking** 3 **Notes** ⊗ No Children 12yrs Closed Dec ⊛

Edgar's

★★★★ GUEST ACCOMMODATION

Chy-an-Creet, Higher Stennack TR26 2HA
☎ 01736 796559 📠 01736 796559
e-mail: stay@edgarshotel.co.uk
web: www.edgarshotel.co.uk
dir: *0.5m W of town centre on B3306, opposite Leach Pottery*

High standards of comfort are provided at this friendly, family-run property. Public areas are spacious and include a comfortable guest lounge, and bedrooms, some on the ground floor, are well equipped. Breakfast, served in the dining room, includes home-made preserves and makes good use of local produce. Good off-road parking available.

Rooms 5 en suite (2 fmly) (1 GF) S £55-£80; D £70-£95*
Facilities FTV TVL tea/coffee Cen ht Wi-fi ⬛ **Parking** 7
Notes LB Closed Nov-Feb

Little Leaf Guest House

★★★★ GUEST ACCOMMODATION

16 Park Av TR26 2DN
☎ 01736 795427 & 07855 490831
e-mail: hello@littleleafguesthouse.co.uk
dir: *A3074 through Lelant into St Ives, right at Porthminster Hotel. Left into Gabriel St, Park Av on left*

There's an engaging, fresh and contemporary style at Little Leaf, which boasts stunning views over the roof tops of St Ives to the harbour and sea beyond. Bedrooms are light, bright and individually designed with plenty of comfort; one has a sea-facing balcony. The tasty breakfasts, featuring daily specials, are served in the attractive dining room, which incorporates a small guest lounge area.

Rooms 5 en suite (1 fmly) S £45-£95; D £60-£115*
Facilities FTV DVD iPod docking station Lounge tea/coffee

Cen ht Licensed Wi-fi Easel hire for painters, iPad for guest use **Notes** LB ⊗ No Children 7yrs Closed Dec-29 Mar

The Mustard Tree

★★★★ GUEST HOUSE

Sea View Meadows, St Ives Rd, Carbis Bay TR26 2JX
☎ 01736 795677 & 07840 072323
e-mail: enquiries@mustard-tree.co.uk
dir: *A3074 to Carbis Bay, The Mustard Tree on right opposite Methodist church*

Set in delightful gardens and with sea views, this attractive house is just a short drive from the centre of St Ives, and the coastal path that leads from Carbis Bay to St Ives. The pleasant bedrooms are very comfortable and have many extra facilities. A splendid choice is offered at breakfast, with vegetarian and continental options; a range of 'lite bites' is available in the early evening.

Rooms 9 rms (8 en suite) (1 pri facs) (2 fmly) (4 GF) S £34-£42; D £68-£90* **Facilities** FTV DVD TVL tea/coffee Dinner available Cen ht Wi-fi **Extras** Guest PC available **Conf** Max 20 **Parking** 9 **Notes** ⊗

The Old Count House

★★★★ GUEST HOUSE

1 Trenwith Square TR26 1DQ
☎ 01736 795369 & 07853 844777 📠 01736 799109
e-mail: counthouse@btconnect.com
web: www.theoldcounthouse-stives.co.uk
dir: *Follow signs to St Ives, house between leisure centre & school*

Situated in a quiet residential area with on-site parking, The Old Count House is a granite stone house, where Victorian mine workers collected their wages. Guests are assured of a warm welcome and an extensive choice at breakfast. Bedrooms vary in size, with all rooms being well equipped. The town centre and all its restaurants is only a five-minute walk away.

The Old Count House

Rooms 10 rms (9 en suite) (1 pri facs) (2 GF) S £45-£50; D £80-£95* **Facilities** FTV DVD Lounge TVL tea/coffee Cen ht Wi-fi Sauna ⬛ **Parking** 9 **Notes** ⊗ No Children Closed Nov & 20-29 Dec

Old Vicarage

★★★★ GUEST HOUSE

Parc-an-Creet TR26 2ES
☎ 01736 796124
e-mail: stay@oldvicarage.com
web: www.oldvicarage.com
dir: *From A3074 in town centre take B3306, 0.5m right into Parc-an-Creet*

This former Victorian rectory stands in secluded gardens in a quiet part of St Ives and is convenient for the seaside, town and Tate St Ives. The bedrooms are enhanced by modern facilities. A good choice of local produce is offered at breakfast, plus home-made yoghurt and preserves.

Rooms 6 en suite (4 fmly) S £66-£71; D £88-£98*
Facilities FTV TVL tea/coffee Cen ht Licensed Wi-fi **Parking** 12 **Notes** LB Closed Dec-Jan Civ Wed 40

The Queens

★★★★ ⊛ INN

High St TR26 1RR
☎ 01736 796468 📠 01736 799953
e-mail: info@queenshotelstives.com
dir: *A3074 to town centre*

Handily placed in the centre of town, just a short stroll from the harbour, this is an ideal location for exploring the charms of St Ives. Newly refurbished bedrooms offer style and comfort with local Cornish artwork and lovely comfy beds. Bathrooms are also light, bright and modern. The relaxing bar and lounge is the venue for very enjoyable cuisine with excellent local produce utilised within simple and effective dishes.

Rooms 8 en suite (2 fmly) S £60-£120; D £70-£140*
Facilities FTV tea/coffee Dinner available Cen ht Wi-fi Pool table **Notes** LB

The Regent

★★★★ GUEST ACCOMMODATION

Fernlea Ter TR26 2BH
☎ 01736 796195 📠 01736 794641
e-mail: keith@regenthotel.com
web: www.regenthotel.com
dir: In town centre, near bus & railway station

This popular and attractive property stands on an elevated position convenient for the town centre and seafront. The Regent has well-equipped bedrooms, some with spectacular sea vistas, and the comfortable lounge also has great views. The breakfast choices, including vegetarian, are excellent.

Rooms 10 rms (8 en suite) (1 fmly) Facilities TVL tea/coffee Cen ht Wi-fi Parking 12 Notes ⊗ No Children 16yrs

Rivendell Guest House

★★★★ GUEST HOUSE

7 Porthminster Ter TR26 2DQ
☎ 01736 794923 & 07837 468875
e-mail: rivendellstives@aol.com
web: www.rivendell-stives.co.uk
dir: A3074 to St Ives, left at junct, left again, up hill, over road, 50yds on right

Just a short walk from the town centre and harbour, this friendly and welcoming establishment has much to offer those visiting this lovely area. Bedrooms are all well appointed with contemporary comforts; some also have the benefit of sea views. Breakfast is served in the attractive dining room, which leads through to the guest lounge.

Rooms 7 rms (6 en suite) (1 pri facs) S £33-£35; D £74-£88* Facilities FTV TVL tea/coffee Cen ht Wi-fi Parking 5 Notes LB ⊗ Closed 23-27 Dec

The Rookery

★★★★ GUEST ACCOMMODATION

8 The Terrace TR26 2BL
☎ 01736 799401
e-mail: therookerystives@hotmail.com
dir: A3074 through Carbis Bay, right fork at Porthminster Hotel, The Rookery 500yds on left

This friendly establishment stands on an elevated position overlooking the town and sandy beach. The attractive bedrooms include one on the ground floor and a luxurious suite, all of which are well equipped and offer a good level of comfort. Breakfast is served in the first-floor dining room at separate tables.

Rooms 7 en suite (2 fmly) (1 GF) Facilities FTV tea/coffee Cen ht Wi-fi 🔥 Parking 7 Notes ⊗ No Children 7yrs

St Dennis

★★★★ 🏠 BED AND BREAKFAST

6 Albany Ter TR26 2BS
☎ 01736 795027
e-mail: info@staystives.co.uk
dir: A3074 to St Ives, pass St Ives Motor Co on right, continue down hill, Albany Ter 1st left, signed Edward Hain Hospital

St Dennis is a friendly and comfortable place to stay and is within walking distance of the town and beaches. Breakfast is a real treat with an emphasis on excellent local organic produce; the comprehensive menu includes choices for vegetarians and lighter, healthier options. The bedrooms are attractively decorated and have many thoughtful touches. Ample parking is available.

Rooms 3 en suite D £82-£96* Facilities FTV DVD iPod docking station tea/coffee Cen ht Wi-fi Parking 5 Notes ⊗ No Children 12yrs Closed Oct-Mar

Thurlestone Guest House

★★★★ GUEST ACCOMMODATION

St Ives Rd, Carbis Bay TR26 2RT
☎ 01736 796369
e-mail: thurlestoneguesthouse@yahoo.co.uk
dir: A3074 to Carbis Bay, pass convenience store on left, 0.25m on left next to Carbis Bay Holidays Office

This former granite chapel, built in 1843, now offers stylish, comfortable accommodation. The welcoming proprietors provide a relaxed environment, and many guests return regularly. Now totally upgraded, the property offers a cosy lounge bar and well-equipped bedrooms, some with sea views.

Rooms 7 en suite (1 fmly) (1 GF) S £37-£45; D £64-£88* Facilities FTV DVD TVL tea/coffee Cen ht Licensed Wi-fi Extras Safe Parking 5 Notes ⊗ Closed Nov-Mar

Portarlington

★★★ GUEST ACCOMMODATION

11 Parc Bean TR26 1EA
☎ 01736 797278 📠 01736 797278
e-mail: info@portarlington.co.uk
web: www.portarlington.co.uk

This pleasant home is convenient for the town, beaches and Tate St Ives. The friendly proprietors have long welcomed guests to their home and many return regularly. Bedrooms are well furnished and some have sea views. There is a comfortable lounge, and enjoyable breakfasts are served in the attractive dining room.

Rooms 4 en suite (3 fmly) Facilities FTV TVL tea/coffee Cen ht 🔥 Extras Fridges in all bedrooms Parking 4 Notes LB ⊗ No Children 3yrs Closed Nov-Jan 🐾

The Sloop Inn

★★★ INN

The Wharf TR26 1LP
☎ 01736 796584 📠 01736 793322
e-mail: sloopinn@btinternet.com
web: www.sloop-inn.co.uk
dir: On St Ives harbour by middle slipway

This attractive, historic inn has an imposing position on the harbour. Each of the guest rooms has a nautical name, many enjoy pleasant views, and all have impressive modern facilities. A good choice of dishes is offered at lunch and dinner in the atmospheric restaurant-bar.

Rooms 18 en suite (6 fmly) (3 GF) (3 smoking) Facilities FTV tea/coffee Dinner available Cen ht Wi-fi Parking 6 Notes LB No coaches

ST JUST (NEAR LAND'S END)   Map 2 SW33

The Wellington

★★ INN

Market Square TR19 7HD
☎ 01736 787319 📠 01736 787906
e-mail: wellingtonhotel@msn.com
dir: 6m W of Penzance

This friendly inn, situated in the busy market square, offers comfortable accommodation and is popular with locals and visitors alike. The bedrooms are spacious and well equipped. Home-cooked food and local ales from the well-stocked bar make for a pleasant stay.

Rooms 5 en suite 6 annexe en suite (4 fmly) (3 GF) S £45-£50; D £75-£80* Facilities FTV tea/coffee Dinner available Direct Dial Cen ht Wi-fi ♨ 18 Pool table 🎱 Conf Max 20 Notes LB

ST KEVERNE — Map 2 SW72

Gallen-Treath Guest House

★★★ GUEST HOUSE

Porthallow TR12 6PL
☎ 01326 280400 & 07579 967836
e-mail: gallentreath@btclick.com
dir: 1.5m SE of St Keverne in Porthallow

Gallen-Treath has super views over the countryside and sea from its elevated position above Porthallow. Bedrooms are individually decorated and feature many personal touches. Guests can relax in the large, comfortable lounge complete with balcony. Hearty breakfasts and dinners (by arrangement) are served in the bright dining room.

Rooms 5 rms (4 en suite) (1 pri facs) (1 fmly) (1 GF) S £29-£36; D £58-£72* **Facilities** FTV TVL tea/coffee Dinner available Cen ht Licensed **Parking** 6

The Three Tuns

U

The Square TR12 6NA
☎ 01326 280949

Currently the rating for this establishment is not confirmed. This may be due to a change of ownership or because it has only recently joined the AA rating scheme.

Rooms 5 en suite (1 fmly) **Facilities** tea/coffee Dinner available Wi-fi **Parking** 15

ST MAWGAN — Map 2 SW86

The Falcon Inn

★★★★ INN

TR8 4EP
☎ 01637 860225
e-mail: thefalconinnstmawgan@gmail.com
dir: A30 towards Newquay airport, follow signs for St Mawgan. Turn right, signed, Falcon Inn at bottom of hill

A traditional village pub serving good food and drink along with two well presented and comfortable en suite bedrooms. The owners and friendly staff create a pleasant atmosphere. The quiet location, along with plenty of off-street parking, make this a popular venue. Please note that the pub is closed between 3-6pm - access for the accommodation can be arranged for these times.

Rooms 2 en suite **Facilities** FTV tea/coffee Dinner available Direct Dial Cen ht Wi-fi ⅃ 18 ⌕ **Conf** Thtr 30 Class 20 Board 20 **Parking** 20 **Notes** LB RS 25-26 Dec

SALTASH — Map 3 SX45

Smeaton Farm (SX387634)

★★★★★ 🏠 🚜 FARMHOUSE

PL12 6RZ
☎ 01579 351833 🖅 01579 351833 Mr & Mrs Jones
e-mail: info@smeatonfarm.co.uk
web: www.smeatonfarm.co.uk
dir: 1m N of Hatt & 1m S of St Mellion just off A388

This elegant Georgian farmhouse is surrounded by 450 acres of rolling Cornish farmland, providing a wonderfully peaceful place to stay. Home to the Jones family, the atmosphere is relaxed and hospitable, with every effort made to ensure a comfortable and rewarding break. Bedrooms are spacious, light and airy. Enjoyable dinners often feature home-reared meats and the sausages at breakfast come highly recommended.

Rooms 3 en suite (1 fmly) **Facilities** FTV TVL tea/coffee Dinner available Cen ht Licensed Wi-fi ⅃ Riding Cornish maze Guided farm tours **Conf** Board 10 **Parking** 8 **Notes** LB ⊗ 450 acres arable/beef/sheep/organic

Crooked Inn

★★★★ INN

Stoketon Cross, Trematon PL12 4RZ
☎ 01752 848177 🖅 01752 843203
e-mail: info@crooked-inn.co.uk
dir: 1.5m NW of Saltash. A38 W from Saltash, 2nd left to Trematon, sharp right

The friendly animals that freely roam the courtyard add to the relaxed country style of this delightful property. The spacious bedrooms are well equipped, and freshly cooked dinners are available in the bar and conservatory. Breakfast is served in the cottage-style dining room.

Rooms 18 annexe rms 15 annexe en suite (5 fmly) (7 GF) **Facilities** tea/coffee Dinner available Cen ht ⅃ **Conf** Max 60 **Parking** 45 **Notes** Closed 25 Dec

ISLES OF SCILLY

ST MARY'S — Map 2 SV91

Crebinick House

★★★★ GUEST HOUSE

Church St TR21 0JT
☎ 01720 422968
e-mail: aa@crebinick.co.uk
web: www.crebinick.co.uk
dir: House 500yds from quay through Hugh Town; (airport bus to house)

Many guests return time and again to this friendly, family-run house close to the town centre and the seafront. The granite-built property dates from 1760 and has smart, well-equipped bedrooms; two are on the ground floor. There is a quiet lounge for relaxing.

Rooms 6 en suite (2 GF) S £50-£65; D £76-£96* **Facilities** FTV TVL tea/coffee Cen ht Wi-fi **Notes** ⊗ No Children 10yrs Closed Nov-Mar 🐾

TRESCO — Map 2 SV81

New Inn

★★★★ 🍴 INN

TR24 0QQ
☎ 01720 422844 & 423006 🖅 01720 423200
e-mail: newinn@tresco.co.uk
web: www.tresco.co.uk
dir: By New Grimsby Quay

This friendly, popular inn is located at the island's centre point and offers bright, attractive and well-equipped bedrooms, many with splendid sea views. Guests have an extensive choice from the menu at both lunch and dinner and can also choose where they take their meals - either in the airy bistro-style Pavilion, the popular bar which serves real ales, or the elegant restaurant. A heated outdoor pool is also available.

Rooms 16 en suite (2 GF) S £55-£120; D £110-£240* **Facilities** FTV DVD Lounge tea/coffee Dinner available Direct Dial Cen ht Wi-fi ⅃ 🎣 Fishing Pool table **Notes** LB ⊗ No coaches

SENNEN · Map 2 SW32

Mayon Farmhouse

★★★★ BED AND BREAKFAST

TR19 7AD
☎ **01736 871757**
e-mail: mayonfarmhouse@hotmail.co.uk
web: www.mayonfarmhouse.co.uk
dir: *A30 to Sennen, driveway opposite Post Office*

Guests receive a genuine welcome and a cream tea at this 19th-century, granite former farmhouse. About one mile from Land's End, and conveniently situated for visiting the Minack Theatre, it has country and distant coastal views. The attractive bedrooms are comfortable and well equipped, and an imaginative choice is offered at breakfast.

Rooms 4 rms (3 en suite) (1 pri facs) (1 fmly) D fr £85*
Facilities FTV DVD TVL tea/coffee Cen ht Wi-fi ♨
Extras Fruit, chocolates, home-made biscuits **Parking** 30
Notes LB ⊗ No Children 14yrs

TINTAGEL · Map 2 SX08

Pendrin House

★★★★ GUEST HOUSE

Atlantic Rd PL34 0DE
☎ **01840 770560**
e-mail: info@pendrintintagel.co.uk
dir: *Through village, pass entrance to Tintagel Castle, last house on right before Headlands Caravan Park*

Located close to coastal walks, the castle and the town centre, this Victorian house provides comfortable accommodation with most rooms having sea or country views. Additional facilities include a cosy lounge and ample off-road parking.

Rooms 9 rms (5 en suite) (4 pri facs) S £30-£35;
D £60-£70* **Facilities** FTV TVL tea/coffee Cen ht
Parking 6 **Notes** ⊗ No Children 12yrs

Reevescott

★★★ BED AND BREAKFAST

Trethevy PL34 0BG
☎ **01840 770533 & 07814 503034**
e-mail: fenann@live.co.uk

Situated between Boscastle and Tintagel, this is a great location for exploring the stunning coast and countryside of north Cornwall. The welcome here is warm and genuine, and the atmosphere is relaxed and homely - it's the perfect place to de-stress. Bedrooms have all the expected comforts, and one is on the ground floor. Breakfast is a treat for the taste buds, and also the eyes as there are breathtaking views from the dining room across the fields to Bossiney Cove.

Rooms 2 en suite (1 GF) **Facilities** TVL tea/coffee Cen ht
Wi-fi **Parking** 2 **Notes** ⊗ Closed Oct-Etr ⊛

TRURO · Map 2 SW84

Bissick Old Mill

★★★★ GUEST HOUSE

Ladock TR2 4PG
☎ **01726 882557**
e-mail: enquiries@bissickoldmill.plus.com
web: www.bissickoldmill.co.uk
dir: *6m NE of Truro. Exit B3275 in Ladock centre by Falmouth Arms pub*

This charming family-run mill, dates back some 300 years. Low ceilings, beams, stone walls and an impressive fireplace all contribute to its character. Equally inviting is the hospitality extended to guests, who are instantly made welcome. The breakfast is a memorable aspect of any stay with the menu offering a range of freshly prepared hot dishes.

Rooms 3 en suite 1 annexe en suite (1 fmly) (1 GF)
S £50-£60; D £60-£87.50* **Facilities** FTV TVL tea/coffee
Direct Dial Cen ht Wi-fi **Parking** 6 **Notes** LB

Bodrean Manor Farm *(SW851480)*

★★★★ FARMHOUSE

Trispen TR4 9AG
☎ **07970 955857 Mrs M Marsh**
e-mail: bodrean@hotmail.co.uk
web: www.bodreanmanorfarm.co.uk
dir: *3m NE of Truro. A30 onto A39 towards Truro, left after Trispen signed Frogmore & Trehane, farm drive 100yds*

This friendly farmhouse is located in peaceful countryside, convenient for Truro or as a touring base. It has all the charm of an historic house but is styled and fitted with modern facilities. Bedrooms are thoughtfully and extensively equipped, and the bathrooms are well provisioned with soft towels and a host of toiletries. The home-cooked breakfast served in the smartly appointed dining room, around a large communal table, is a feature. Storage for motorbikes and cycles is available.

Rooms 3 rms (2 en suite) (1 pri facs) (1 fmly)
Facilities FTV TVL tea/coffee Cen ht Wi-fi **Parking** 6
Notes ⊗ ⊛ 220 acres mixed

The Haven

★★★★ BED AND BREAKFAST

Truro Vean Ter TR1 1HA
☎ **01872 264197 & 07977 815177**
e-mail: thehaven7@btinternet.com
dir: *Entering Truro from A39 or A390, right at 1st rdbt, through 2 sets of lights, next right then immediately left. On left (no through road)*

A warm and genuine welcome is assured at this extended property within a few minutes' walk of the city centre. Bedrooms are bright and well furnished; beds are very comfortable and bathrooms well equipped. Freshly cooked, hearty breakfasts are served at a large table, in either the separate breakfast room or new conservatory, which leads on to a balcony. The Haven benefits from off-street parking and views of the cathedral.

Rooms 3 rms (2 en suite) (1 pri facs) (3 GF) D £70-£75*
Facilities FTV Lounge tea/coffee Cen ht Wi-fi **Parking** 3
Notes ⊗ No Children 7yrs Closed Nov-Jan ⊛

Manor Cottage

★★★★ GUEST ACCOMMODATION

Tresillian TR2 4BN
☎ **01872 520212**
e-mail: manorcottage@live.co.uk
dir: *3m E of Truro on A390, on left opposite river*

Located just a few minutes drive from Truro this well-run Regency house is friendly and comfortable. The owners do their utmost to make guests feel at home. Breakfast is served in the conservatory. Dogs are not allowed as there is a resident cat, by the name of Rufus.

Rooms 3 rms (2 en suite) (1 pri facs) (2 fmly) S £38-£65;
D £68-£78* **Facilities** FTV Lounge tea/coffee Wi-fi ♨
Extras Bottled water **Parking** 8 **Notes** LB ⊗

Oxturn House

★★★★ BED AND BREAKFAST

Ladock TR2 4NQ
☎ **01726 884348**
e-mail: oxturnhouse@hotmail.com
web: www.oxturnhouse.co.uk
dir: *6m NE of Truro. B3275 into Ladock, take lane opposite Falmouth Arms, up hill 200yds, 1st right after end 30mph sign, Oxturn on right*

A friendly welcome is assured at this large family house, set slightly above the village and close to a pub and several dining venues. Bedrooms are spacious and a pleasant lounge is available. In summer you can enjoy the country views from the patio. Hearty breakfasts are served in the dining room.

Rooms 2 rms (1 en suite) (1 pri facs) D £66-£78*
Facilities TVL tea/coffee Cen ht Wi-fi **Parking** 4 **Notes** ⊗
No Children 12yrs Closed Dec-Feb ⊛

TRURO *continued*

Coronation Guest House

★★★ BED AND BREAKFAST

2 Coronation Ter TR1 3HJ
☎ 01872 274514
e-mail: email@coronationguesthouse.com
dir: *Opposite railway station*

Located just a short distance from the city centre and close to the railway station, this Victorian accommodation is attentively cared for. Bedrooms, although not spacious, are clean and bright. A freshly prepared traditional English breakfast is taken in the pleasant dining room at the rear of the house.

Rooms 3 rms (2 pri facs) S £30-£35; D £60*
Facilities FTV tea/coffee Cen ht Wi-fi **Notes** ⊗ No Children 8yrs ⊜

Donnington Guest House

★★★ GUEST ACCOMMODATION

43 Treyew Rd TR1 2BY
☎ 01872 222552 & 07787 555475
e-mail: info@donnington-guesthouse.co.uk

A well located property within a 12-minute walk of the city centre, Donnington Guest House is actually two houses operating as one, with breakfast being taken in the breakfast room of one of them. Well-appointed bedrooms, a friendly host and good off-road parking make this a very popular venue.

Rooms 14 rms (12 en suite) (2 pri facs) (5 fmly) (3 GF) S £25-£35; D £50-£70* **Facilities** FTV DVD tea/coffee Cen ht Lift Wi-fi ♨ 18 ♠ **Extras** Fridges in all bedrooms **Conf** Class 14 **Parking** 11 **Notes** ⊜

The Laurels

★★★ BED AND BREAKFAST

Penwethers TR3 6EA
☎ 07794 472171
e-mail: annie.toms@hotmail.com
dir: *From A39 onto A390 (Tregolls Rd), through 3 rdbts. Take exit towards Redruth (Treyew Rd) next left to Penwethers*

A traditional bed and breakfast operation offering comfortable accommodation in a home-from-home environment. It is ideally located in a quiet location, yet is just minutes from the cathedral city of Truro. Off-road parking is available.

Rooms 3 rms (1 en suite) (1 pri facs) (2 fmly) S £45; D £65* **Facilities** FTV TV2B tea/coffee Wi-fi **Parking** 3 **Notes** ⊗ ⊜

Polsue Manor Farm *(SW858462)*

★★★ FARMHOUSE

Tresillian TR2 4BP
☎ 01872 520234 Mrs G Holliday
e-mail: geraldineholliday@hotmail.com
dir: *2m NE of Truro. Farm entrance on A390 at S end of Tresillian*

Polsue Manor Farm is a 190-acre sheep farm in peaceful countryside, a short drive from Truro. The farmhouse provides a relaxing break from the city, with hearty breakfasts and warm hospitality. The spacious dining room has pleasant views and three large communal tables. Bedrooms do not offer televisions but there is a homely lounge equipped with a television and video recorder with a selection of videos for viewing.

Rooms 5 rms (2 en suite) (3 fmly) (1 GF) **Facilities** TVL tea/coffee **Parking** 5 **Notes** Closed 21 Dec-2 Jan 190 acres mixed/sheep/horses

Resparveth Farm *(SW914499)*

★★★ FARMHOUSE

Grampound Rd TR2 4EF
☎ 01726 882382 🖷 01726 882382 Ms L Willey
e-mail: lisawilley83@hotmail.com

The new owners of this traditional farmhouse bed and breakfast do all they can to make a stay as comfortable as possible. It's a handy location for St Austell, the Eden Project and Truro, offering comfortable rooms and freshly cooked breakfasts at one large table in the breakfast room featuring an original Cornish Range.

Rooms 3 en suite **Facilities** FTV TVL tea/coffee Cen ht Wi-fi **Parking** 4 **Notes** 65 acres dairy

The Bay Tree

★★ GUEST ACCOMMODATION

28 Ferris Town TR1 3JH
☎ 01872 240274

A well established, friendly property within a few minutes' walk of the railway station and the city centre. The bedrooms are comfortable and have shared facilities, and breakfast is served at large tables in the dining room.

Rooms 3 rms (2 fmly) S £40-£50; D £55-£65* **Facilities** tea/coffee Cen ht Wi-fi **Notes** RS Proprietors' holidays ⊜

Elerkey Guest House

★★★★ GUEST HOUSE

Elerkey House TR2 5QA
☎ 01872 501261 & 501160
e-mail: enquiries@elerkey.co.uk
web: www.elerkey.co.uk
dir: *In village, 1st left after church & water gardens*

This peaceful home is surrounded by attractive gardens in a tranquil village. The proprietors and their family provide exemplary hospitality and many guests return time and again. The pleasantly appointed bedrooms have many considerate extras.

Rooms 4 en suite (1 fmly) S £50-£80; D £60-£80 **Facilities** FTV DVD tea/coffee Direct Dial Cen ht Wi-fi Art gallery & gift shop **Parking** 4 **Notes** LB ⊗ Closed Dec-Feb

The Gurnard's Head

★★★ ◉ INN

Treen TR26 3DE
☎ 01736 796928
e-mail: enquiries@gurnardshead.co.uk
dir: *5m from St Ives on B3306, 4.5m from Penzance via New Mill*

This inn is ideally located for enjoying the beautiful coastline, and is very popular with walkers keen to rest their weary legs. The style is relaxed with a log fire in the bar providing a warm welcome on colder days, and outside seating ideal for enjoying the sun. Lunch and dinner are available either in the bar or the adjoining restaurant area. The dinner menu is not extensive but there are interesting choices and everything is home-made, including the bread. Breakfast is also a treat with newspapers on the bar to peruse whilst easing into the day.

Rooms 7 en suite **Facilities** tea/coffee Dinner available Wi-fi **Parking** 40 **Notes** Closed 25 Dec & 4 days mid Jan No coaches

CUMBRIA

ALSTON   Map 18 NY74

See also Cowshill (Co Durham)

Alston House

★★★★ ⸺ RESTAURANT WITH ROOMS

Townfoot CA9 3RN
☎ 01434 382200 📄 01434 382493
e-mail: alstonhouse@fsmail.net
web: www.alstonhouse.co.uk
dir: On A686 opposite Spar garage

Located at the foot of the town, this family-owned restaurant with rooms provides well-equipped, stylish and comfortable accommodation. The kitchen serves both modern and traditional dishes with flair and creativity. Alston House runs a café during the day serving light meals and afternoon teas.

Rooms 7 en suite (3 fmly) **Facilities** tea/coffee Dinner available Cen ht Wi-fi ch fac ⚓ 9 Fishing **Conf** Max 70 Thtr 70 Class 30 Board 30 **Parking** 20 **Notes** Civ Wed

Lowbyer Manor Country House

★★★★ ▦ GUEST HOUSE

Hexham Rd CA9 3JX
☎ 01434 381230 📄 01434 381425
e-mail: stay@lowbyer.com
web: www.lowbyer.com
dir: 250yds N of village centre on A686. Pass South Tynedale Railway on left, turn right

Located on the edge of the village, this Grade II listed Georgian building retains many original features, which are highlighted by the furnishings and decor. Cosy bedrooms are filled with a wealth of thoughtful extras and day rooms include an elegant dining room, a comfortable lounge and bar equipped with lots of historical artefacts.

Rooms 9 en suite (1 fmly) S £36-£60; D £72-£86 **Facilities** FTV Lounge tea/coffee Cen ht Licensed Wi-fi ⚓ **Parking** 9 **Notes** LB

AMBLESIDE   Map 18 NY30

PREMIER COLLECTION

Drunken Duck Inn

★★★★★ ◎◎ ▦ INN

Barngates LA22 0NG
☎ 015394 36347 📄 015394 36781
e-mail: info@drunkenduckinn.co.uk
web: www.drunkenduckinn.co.uk
dir: B5286, S from Ambleside towards Hawkshead, 2.5m signed right, 0.5m up hill

This 400-year-old, traditional coaching inn has been stylishly modernised to offer a high standard of accommodation. Superior rooms are in a courtyard house looking out over private gardens and a tarn. The bar retains its original character and is the hub of the inn. Fresh, local produce features on the imaginative menus served there and in the cosy restaurant. The on-site brewery ensures a fine selection of award-winning ales.

Rooms 8 en suite 9 annexe en suite (5 GF) S £71.25-£221.25; D £95-£295* **Facilities** FTV Lounge Dinner available Direct Dial Cen ht Wi-fi Fishing ⚓ **Parking** 40 **Notes** Closed 25 Dec No coaches

High Grassings Country House

★★★★ GUEST ACCOMMODATION

Outgate LA22 0PU
☎ 015394 36484
e-mail: info@highgrassings.com
dir: M6 junct 36, A590, A591, through Kendal & Windermere to Ambleside. Take A593 towards Coniston. Left at Clappersgate. Right in 1m signed Coniston/Tarn Hows. Pass Drunken Duck pub on right, house 1m on right

This delightful property is nestled between Ambleside and Hawkshead, close to Tarn Hows. Situated within 20 acres

of grounds leading up to the fells, this property boasts attractive views from each bedroom. Each room comprises of stylish yet simply decorated furnishings, and the barn conversion provides high quality accommodation. A good quality breakfast can be enjoyed from the conservatory overlooking the mountains.

Rooms 3 en suite (2 fmly) (1 GF) S £70-£120; D £75-£155* **Facilities** FTV Lounge tea/coffee Cen ht Wi-fi Complimentary use of local leisure spa **Extras** Fruit **Parking** 8 **Notes** LB ⊗

Riverside

★★★★ ▦ GUEST HOUSE

Under Loughrigg LA22 9LJ
☎ 015394 32395 📄 015394 32440
e-mail: info@riverside-at-ambleside.co.uk
web: www.riverside-at-ambleside.co.uk
dir: A593 from Ambleside to Coniston, over stone bridge, right into Under Loughrigg Ln, Riverside 150yds left

A friendly atmosphere prevails at this Victorian house, situated on a quiet lane by the River Rothay, below Loughrigg Fell. Bedrooms, all with lovely views, are very comfortable, stylishly furnished and feature homely extras; some have spa baths. A log-burning stove warms the lounge in winter. Guests can use the garden, which has seating for morning and evening sun.

Rooms 6 en suite (1 fmly) **Facilities** TVL tea/coffee Cen ht Licensed Fishing Jacuzzi **Parking** 15 **Notes** ⊗ No Children 5yrs Closed Xmas & New Year

AMBLESIDE *continued*

Wateredge Inn

☆☆☆☆☆ INN

Waterhead Bay LA22 0EP
☎ 015394 32332 📠 015394 31878
e-mail: rec@wateredgeinn.co.uk
web: www.wateredgeinn.co.uk
dir: *On A59, at Waterhead, 1m S of Ambleside. Inn at end of promenade by lake*

This modern inn has an idyllic location on the shore of Windermere at Waterhead Bay. The pretty bedrooms are particularly smart and generally spacious, and all offer a high standard of quality and comfort. The airy bar-restaurant opens onto attractive gardens, which have magnificent lake views. There is also a comfortable lounge, bar and dining area.

Rooms 15 en suite 7 annexe en suite (4 fmly) (3 GF) S £40-£62; D £75-£175* **Facilities** Lounge tea/coffee Dinner available Cen ht Wi-fi Complimentary membership of nearby leisure club **Parking** 40 **Notes** LB Closed 25-26 Dec No coaches

Ambleside Lodge

★★★★ GUEST HOUSE

Rothay Rd LA22 0EJ
☎ 015394 31681 📠 015394 34547
e-mail: enquiries@ambleside-lodge.com
web: www.ambleside-lodge.com

Located close to the centre of this historic market town, this Grade II listed 18th-century residence has a peaceful atmosphere. The stylishly decorated, elegant accommodation includes attractive bedrooms with antique and contemporary pieces, including four-poster beds. Attentive, personal service is provided.

Rooms 18 en suite (2 fmly) (1 GF) **Facilities** FTV tea/coffee Cen ht Wi-fi **Parking** 20

Broadview Guest House

★★★★ 🏠 GUEST HOUSE

Lake Rd LA22 0DN
☎ 015394 32431
e-mail: enquiries@broadviewguesthouse.co.uk
web: www.broadviewguesthouse.co.uk
dir: *On A591 S side of Ambleside, on Lake Rd opposite Garden Centre*

Just a short walk from the centre of Ambleside a warm welcome is assured at this popular guest house, where regular improvements enhance the guest experience. Bedrooms are thoughtfully furnished and comprehensive breakfasts provide an excellent start to the day.

Rooms 6 rms (3 en suite) (1 pri facs) **Facilities** FTV tea/coffee Cen ht Wi-fi Access to nearby leisure club **Notes** ⊗

Cherry Garth

★★★ GUEST HOUSE

Old Lake Rd LA22 0DH
☎ 015394 33128 📠 015394 33885
e-mail: reception@cherrygarth.com
web: www.cherrygarth.com
dir: *M6 junct 36, follow signs for Windermere, A591 N into Ambleside, over lights, 800yds on right*

Set on the southern approach to the town, this detached house sits in well-landscaped gardens giving views of Loughrigg Fell and Wetherlam. Bedrooms offer a range of styles, are spacious and have modern fittings with all of the expected facilities. Traditional Lakeland breakfasts are served in the lounge-breakfast room overlooking the front garden.

Rooms 11 en suite (2 fmly) (3 GF) S £40-£67.50; D £80-£135* **Facilities** STV DVD tea/coffee Cen ht Licensed Wi-fi 🔒 **Parking** 14 **Notes** LB

Kent House

★★★★ GUEST HOUSE

Lake Rd LA22 0AD
☎ 015394 33279
e-mail: mail@kent-house.com
web: www.kent-house.com
dir: *From town centre, pass Post Office on one-way system 300mtrs on left on terrace above main road*

From an elevated location overlooking the town, this traditional Lakeland house offers comfortable, well-equipped accommodation with attractive bedrooms. Traditional breakfasts featuring the best of local produce are served at individual tables in the elegant dining room.

Rooms 5 rms (4 en suite) (1 pri facs) (2 fmly) **Facilities** FTV tea/coffee Cen ht Wi-fi **Parking** 2

Lake House

★★★★ GUEST ACCOMMODATION

Waterhead Bay LA22 0HD
☎ 015394 32360 📠 015394 31474
e-mail: info@lakehousehotel.co.uk
dir: *From S: M6 junct 36, A590, then A591 towards Kendal & Windermere. House 3m N of Windermere. From N: M6 junct 40, A66 to Keswick, then A591 to Ambleside. House just S of town*

Set on a hillside with lake views, this delightful house has very stylish accommodation and a homely atmosphere. The bedrooms are all individual in style and include many homely extras. Dinner is available at the nearby sister property with complimentary transport, and leisure facilities are available there too. Breakfast is an interesting and substantial cold buffet.

Rooms 12 en suite 7 annexe en suite (3 fmly) (4 GF) S £59-£89; D £69-£119 **Facilities** FTV TVL tea/coffee Cen ht Licensed Wi-fi **Parking** 19 **Notes** LB No Children 14yrs

Lakes Lodge

★★★★ GUEST ACCOMMODATION

Lake Rd LA22 0DB
☎ 015394 33240 📠 015394 31474
e-mail: info@lakeslodge.co.uk
dir: *Enter Ambleside on A59, right around one-way system, on exiting town turn right onto Lake Rd*

Lakes Lodge is located in the centre of Ambleside. Friendly service and simply furnished, contemporary bedrooms in a range of sizes are offered, and wine, beer and champagne can be served to bedrooms during the day and evening, until 9pm. A continental breakfast buffet is served in the café-style breakfast room. Guests can arrange use of an indoor pool at a nearby hotel.

Rooms 16 en suite (4 fmly) (6 GF) S £55-£85; D £59-£99 **Facilities** FTV DVD Lounge tea/coffee Cen ht Licensed Wi-fi **Parking** 14 **Notes** LB Closed 23-27 Dec

The Log House

★★★★ ⑩ RESTAURANT WITH ROOMS

Lake Rd LA22 0DN
☎ 015394 31077
e-mail: info@loghouse.co.uk
web: www.loghouse.co.uk
dir: *From Windermere into Ambleside on A591. On left after Hayes Garden Centre*

This charming and historic Norwegian building is located midway between the town centre and the shore of Lake Windermere, just five minutes' walk to each. Guests can enjoy delicious meals in the attractive restaurant, which also has a bar area. There are three comfortable bedrooms, each equipped with thoughtful accessories such as DVD/VCR players and hairdryers. Wi-fi is also available.

Rooms 3 en suite S £40-£92.75; D £60-£92.75*
Facilities FTV DVD iPod docking station Lounge tea/coffee
Dinner available Cen ht Wi-fi Leisure facilities at nearby
hotel **Extras** Speciality toiletries - complimentary
Parking 3 **Notes** LB ⊗ No coaches

Rysdale Guesthouse

★★★★ GUEST ACCOMMODATION

Rothay Rd LA22 0EE
☎ 015394 32140 ▤ 015394 33999
e-mail: info@rysdalehotel.co.uk
dir: A591 into Ambleside, one-way system to A593,
Rysdale on right facing church

This Edwardian house is only a stroll from the village
centre and overlooks the church and the park. The friendly
proprietors offer attractive, well-equipped bedrooms,
carefully decorated throughout with co-ordinated soft
fabrics. Some have period furniture and most enjoy
superb mountain views, as does the smart dining room.
There is also a cosy lounge with an inglenook fire place.

Rooms 9 rms (7 en suite) (2 pri facs) (2 fmly)
Facilities DVD Lounge tea/coffee Cen ht Wi-fi 🛁
Complimentary pass to Lanedale Country Club **Parking** 2
Notes ⊗ No Children 4yrs Closed 23-26 Dec RS Jan
wknds only 🕭

Wanslea Guest House

★★★★ GUEST HOUSE

Low Fold, Lake Rd LA22 0DN
☎ 015394 33884 ▤ 015394 33884
e-mail: information@wanslea.co.uk
dir: On S side of town, opposite garden centre

Located between town centre and lakeside pier, this
Victorian house provides a range of thoughtfully
furnished bedrooms, some of which are individually
themed and equipped with spa baths. Comprehensive
breakfasts are served in the spacious dining room and a
cosy lounge is available.

Rooms 8 en suite (1 fmly) S £30-£50; D £60-£90
Facilities FTV Lounge tea/coffee Cen ht Wi-fi 🕭 **Notes** LB
⊗ No Children 6yrs Closed 23-26 Dec

The Old Vicarage

★★★★ 🅰 GUEST ACCOMMODATION

Vicarage Rd LA22 9DH
☎ 015394 33364 ▤ 015394 34734
e-mail: info@oldvicarageambleside.co.uk
web: www.oldvicarageambleside.co.uk
dir: In town centre. Exit Compston Rd into Vicarage Rd
Rooms 15 en suite (4 fmly) (2 GF) D £74-£134*
Facilities FTV Lounge tea/coffee Cen ht Wi-fi 🐾 🛁
Riding Sauna Pool table 🛁 Hot tub **Extras** Mini-fridge
Parking 17 **Notes** LB Closed 23-28 Dec

APPLEBY-IN-WESTMORLAND   Map 18 NY62

Hall Croft

★★★★ 🛏 BED AND BREAKFAST

Dufton CA16 6DB
☎ 017683 52902
e-mail: hallcroft@phonecoop.coop
dir: 3m N of Appleby. In Dufton by village green

Standing at the end of a lime-tree avenue, Hall Croft,
built in 1882, has been restored to its original glory.
Bedrooms are comfortably proportioned, traditionally
furnished and well equipped. Breakfasts, served in the
lounge-dining room, are substantial and include a range
of home-made produce. Guests can enjoy the lovely
garden, which has views of the Pennines.

Rooms 3 rms (2 en suite) (1 pri facs) S £36; D £62*
Facilities FTV DVD tea/coffee Cen ht Wi-fi **Parking** 3
Notes Closed 24-26 Dec 🕭

BOOT   Map 18 NY10

Brook House Inn

★★★★ 🍽 INN

CA19 1TG
☎ 01946 723288 ▤ 01946 723160
e-mail: stay@brookhouseinn.co.uk
web: www.brookhouseinn.co.uk
dir: In village centre. 0.5m NE of Dalegarth station

Located in the heart of Eskdale, this impressive inn dates
from the early 18th century and has been renovated to
offer comfortable accommodation with smart, modern
bathrooms for weary walkers and travellers. Wholesome
meals using local produce are served in the traditionally
furnished dining room or attractive bar, the latter
featuring real ales and country memorabilia.

Rooms 8 en suite (2 fmly) **Facilities** FTV tea/coffee Dinner
available Cen ht Wi-fi **Conf** Max 35 **Parking** 24 **Notes** LB
Closed 25 Dec

BORROWDALE   Map 18 NY21

PREMIER COLLECTION

Hazel Bank Country House

GUEST ACCOMMODATION

Rosthwaite CA12 5XB
☎ 017687 77248 ▤ 017687 77373
e-mail: info@hazelbankhotel.co.uk
web: www.hazelbankcountryhouse.co.uk
dir: B5289 from Keswick towards Borrowdale, left after
sign for Rosthwaite

Arrival at this grand Victorian house is impressive,
reached via a picturesque hump back bridge and
winding drive. Set on an elevated position surrounded
by four acres of gardens and woodland, Hazel Bank
enjoys magnificent views of Borrowdale. Carefully
cooked dishes are served in the elegant dining room;
the daily-changing, four-course dinner menu features
fresh, local ingredients. There is a friendly atmosphere
here and the proprietors are very welcoming.

Rooms 8 en suite (2 GF) **Facilities** FTV tea/coffee
Dinner available Cen ht Licensed Wi-fi 🖐 **Parking** 8
Notes ⊗ No Children 10yrs

BOWNESS-ON-WINDERMERE

See Windermere

BRAITHWAITE — Map 18 NY22

The Cottage in the Wood

★★★★ ◉◉ ⌂ RESTAURANT WITH ROOMS

Whinlatter Pass CA12 5TW
☎ 017687 78409
e-mail: relax@thecottageinthewood.co.uk
dir: M6 junct 40, A66 W. After Keswick exit for Braithwaite via Whinlatter Pass (B5292), establishment at top of pass

This charming property sits on wooded hills with striking views of Skiddaw, and is conveniently placed for Keswick. The professional owners provide excellent hospitality in a relaxed manner. The award-winning food, freshly prepared and locally sourced, is served in the bright and welcoming conservatory restaurant that has stunning views. The comfortable bedrooms are well appointed and have many useful extras.

Rooms 9 en suite (1 GF) D £88–£220 Facilities FTV Lounge tea/coffee Dinner available Direct Dial Cen ht Wi-fi ♨ Parking 15 Notes LB ⊗ No Children 10yrs Closed Jan RS Mon closed No coaches

The Royal Oak

★★★ INN

CA12 5SY
☎ 017687 78533 🖷 017687 78533
e-mail: info@royaloak-braithwaite.co.uk
web: www.royaloak-braithwaite.co.uk
dir: In village centre

The Royal Oak, in the pretty village of Braithwaite, has delightful views of Skiddaw and Barrow, and is a good base for tourists and walkers. Some of the well-equipped bedrooms are furnished with four-poster beds. Hearty meals and traditional Cumbrian breakfasts are served in the restaurant, and there is an atmospheric, well-stocked bar.

Rooms 10 en suite (1 fmly) Facilities STV FTV tea/coffee Dinner available Cen ht Wi-fi ♨ Parking 20 Notes LB

BRAMPTON — Map 21 NY56

PREMIER COLLECTION

Lanercost Bed and Breakfast

★★★★★ ⌂ GUEST ACCOMMODATION

Lanercost CA8 2HQ
☎ 016977 42589 & 07976 977204
e-mail: info@lanercostbedandbreakfast.co.uk
web: www.lanercostbedandbreakfast.co.uk
dir: Follow signs to Lanercost Priory

Built in 1840 in the grounds of Lanercost Priory which is close to Hadrian's Wall, this property offers individually designed bedrooms of a good size with quality fixtures and fittings. Public areas are welcoming and enhanced with artwork and objets d'art. The hearty, award-winning breakfasts use local produce and make a wonderful start to the day. Lanercost B&B was a Finalist in the AA Friendliest B&B of the Year Award 2012-13.

Rooms 4 en suite Facilities FTV tea/coffee Dinner available Cen ht Wi-fi ♨ 18 Fishing Riding Conf Max 10 Thtr 10 Class 10 Board 10 Parking 6 Notes ⊛

The Blacksmiths Arms

★★★★ INN

Talkin Village CA8 1LE
☎ 016977 3452 & 42111 🖷 016977 3396
e-mail: blacksmithsarmstalkin@yahoo.co.uk
web: www.blacksmithstalkin.co.uk
dir: B6413 from Brampton to Castle Carrock, after level crossing 2nd left signed Talkin

Dating from the early 19th century and used as a smithy until the 1950s, this friendly village inn offers good home-cooked fare and real ales, with two Cumbrian cask beers always available. Bedrooms are well equipped, and three are particularly smart. An extensive menu and daily specials are offered in the cosy bar lounges or the smart, panelled Old Forge Restaurant.

Rooms 5 en suite 3 annexe en suite (2 fmly) (3 GF) S £55–£60; D £75–£85 Facilities FTV tea/coffee Dinner available Direct Dial Cen ht Wi-fi ♨ 18 ♨ Parking 20 Notes ⊗ No coaches

CALDBECK — Map 18 NY34

Swaledale Watch Farm

★★★★ GUEST ACCOMMODATION

Whelpo CA7 8HQ
☎ 016974 78409 🖷 016974 78409
e-mail: nan.savage@talk21.com
web: www.swaledale-watch.co.uk
dir: 1m SW of Caldbeck on B5299

This attractive farmhouse, set in its own nature reserve, is in a peaceful location with a backdrop of picturesque fells. The en suite bedrooms are spacious and well equipped. Two rooms are in an adjacent converted farm building and share a comfortable sitting room. Traditional hearty breakfasts are served in the attractive dining room overlooking the garden, with views of the fells.

Rooms 2 en suite 2 annexe en suite (2 fmly) (4 GF) S £30–£35; D £60–£64* Facilities FTV DVD TVL tea/coffee Cen ht Wi-fi ♨ 100 acre Nature Reserve, badger watching evenings Parking 8 Notes Closed 24-26 Dec

CARLISLE — Map 18 NY35

See also Brampton

Cambro House

★★★★ GUEST ACCOMMODATION

173 Warwick Rd CA1 1LP
☎ 01228 543094
e-mail: davidcambro@aol.com
dir: M6 junct 43, into Warwick Rd, 1m on right before St Aidan's Church

This smart Victorian house is close to the town centre and motorway. The spacious bedrooms are brightly decorated, smartly appointed and thoughtfully equipped. A hearty Cumbrian breakfast is served in the cosy morning room.

Rooms 3 en suite (1 GF) S £40; D £55–£60 Facilities FTV tea/coffee Cen ht Wi-fi Parking 2 Notes LB ⊗ No Children 5yrs

No1 Guest House

★★★★ BED AND BREAKFAST

1 Etterby St CA3 9JB
☎ 01228 547285 & 07899 948711
e-mail: sheila@carlislebandb.co.uk
dir: M6 junct 44 onto A7, right at 7th lights onto Etterby St, house 1st on left

This small friendly house is on the north side of the city within walking distance of the centre. The attractive, well-equipped en suite bedrooms consist of a double, a twin and a single room. Hearty traditional breakfasts featuring the best of local produce, are served in the ground-floor dining room.

Rooms 3 en suite Facilities FTV tea/coffee Dinner available Cen ht Wi-fi Parking 1 Notes LB ⊗

Save on B&Bs and Hotels. Book at theAA.com/hotel

CUMBRIA 81 ENGLAND

Angus House & Almonds Restaurant

★★★ 👄 GUEST ACCOMMODATION

14-16 Scotland Rd CA3 9DG
☎ 01228 523546 📠 01228 531895
e-mail: hotel@angus-hotel.co.uk
web: www.angus-hotel.co.uk
dir: 0.5m N of city centre on A7

Situated just north of the city, this family-run establishment is ideal for business and leisure. A warm welcome is assured and the accommodation is well equipped. Almonds Restaurant provides enjoyable food and home baking, and there is also a lounge and a large meeting room.

Rooms 10 en suite (2 fmly) **Facilities** FTV Lounge tea/coffee Dinner available Direct Dial Cen ht Licensed Wi-fi 🔊 **Conf** Max 25 Thtr 25 Class 16 Board 16 **Notes** LB

CARTMEL   Map 18 SD37

PREMIER COLLECTION

L'enclume

★★★★★★ 🍴🍴🍴🍴🍴 RESTAURANT WITH ROOMS

Cavendish St LA11 6PZ
☎ 015395 36362
e-mail: info@lenclume.co.uk
dir: From A590 turn left for Cartmel before Newby Bridge

L'enclume is a delightful 13th-century property in the heart of a lovely village offering 21st-century cooking that is more than worth travelling some distance for. Simon Rogan cooks imaginative and adventurous food in this stylish restaurant. Individually designed, modern, en suite rooms vary in size and style, and are either in the main property or dotted about the village only a few moments' walk from the restaurant.

Rooms 7 en suite 5 annexe en suite (3 fmly) (3 GF) S £69-£169; D £99-£199* **Facilities** STV DVD tea/coffee Dinner available Direct Dial Cen ht **Parking** 11 **Notes** ⊗ No coaches

---

CONISTON   Map 18 SD39

PREMIER COLLECTION

Wheelgate Country Guest House

★★★★★ 🏠 GUEST HOUSE

Little Arrow LA21 8AU
☎ 015394 41418
e-mail: enquiry@wheelgate.co.uk
dir: 1.5m S of Coniston, on W side of road

Linda and Steve Abbott invite their guests to relax and unwind in the friendly atmosphere of their 17th-century country house. Enjoy an award winning breakfast, individually designed en suite bedrooms, and perhaps a drink in the cosy bar. Situated in a peaceful rural location amidst the breathtaking lake and mountain scenery of Coniston, Wheelgate is the ideal location for exploring the beautiful Lake District.

Rooms 4 en suite 1 annexe en suite (1 GF) S £33-£38; D £60-£76* **Facilities** FTV Lounge tea/coffee Cen ht Licensed 🔊 **Parking** 5 **Notes** LB ⊗ No Children 8yrs Closed Nov-Apr

---

CROSTHWAITE   Map 18 SD49

PREMIER COLLECTION

The Punchbowl Inn at Crosthwaite

★★★★★ 🍴🍴 INN

Lyth Valley LA8 8HR
☎ 015395 68237 📠 015397 68875
e-mail: info@the-punchbowl.co.uk
dir: M6 junct 36 signed Barrow, on A5074 towards Windermere, turn right for Crosthwaite. At E end of village beside church

Located in the stunning Lyth Valley alongside the village church, this historic inn has been renovated to provide excellent standards of comfort and facilities. Its sumptuous bedrooms have a wealth of thoughtful extras, and imaginative food is available in the elegant restaurant or in the rustic-style bar with open fires. A warm welcome and professional service is assured.

Rooms 9 en suite S £95-£160; D £95-£165* **Facilities** FTV Dinner available Direct Dial Cen ht Wi-fi 🔊 **Extras** Speciality toiletries, jam & scones **Parking** 25 **Notes** No coaches Civ Wed 50

Crosthwaite House

★★★★ GUEST HOUSE

LA8 8BP
☎ 015395 68264 📠 015395 68264
e-mail: bookings@crosthwaitehouse.co.uk
web: www.crosthwaitehouse.co.uk
dir: A590 onto A5074, 4m right to Crosthwaite, 0.5m turn left

Enjoying stunning views across the Lyth Valley, this friendly Georgian house is a haven of tranquillity. Bedrooms are spacious and offer a host of thoughtful extras. The reception rooms include a comfortable lounge and a pleasant dining room with polished floorboards and individual tables.

Rooms 6 en suite S £35-£40; D £70-£80* **Facilities** FTV TVL tea/coffee Cen ht Wi-fi 🔊 **Extras** Home-made biscuits - complimentary **Parking** 10 **Notes** Closed mid Nov-Mar

---

Tarnside Farmhouse

★★★★ BED AND BREAKFAST

LA8 8BU
☎ 015395 68640
e-mail: tarnsidefarmhouse@hotmail.co.uk
dir: M6 junct 36, A590 for 5m. Take A5074 signed Bowness & Windermere, establishment in 5m on right

Situated within the Lyth Valley this B&B offers quiet and tranquil surroundings with stunning views across the fells and mountains. Sole use of a large and comfortable lounge is available complete with log wood burner, wide screen digital TV, and Wi-fi.

Rooms 1 rm (1 pri facs) S £50; D £70-£80* **Facilities** TVL Cen ht Wi-fi 🛏️ 🔊 **Parking** 1 **Notes** No Children RS Closed Wed

---

GRANGE-OVER-SANDS   Map 18 SD47

Corner Beech House

★★★★ 🏛️ GUEST ACCOMMODATION

Methven Ter, Kents Bank Rd LA11 7DP
☎ 015395 33088
e-mail: info@cornerbeech.co.uk
web: www.cornerbeech.co.uk
dir: M6 junct 36, A590, left onto B5277 to Grange-over-Sands. Main road becomes Esplanade, then Park Rd, then Methven Terrace

Overlooking Morecambe Bay, this Edwardian house is well maintained and offers a friendly atmosphere. Hearty breakfasts featuring home-made and local produce are served in the attractive dining room. All bedrooms are en suite and well equipped with sitting area, widescreen digital TV and DVD player.

Rooms 3 en suite S £49; D £72-£80 **Facilities** FTV DVD tea/coffee Cen ht Wi-fi 🔊 **Extras** Mineral water - complimentary **Parking** 5 **Notes** ⊗ No Children 16yrs

GRANGE-OVER-SANDS *continued*

Greenacres Country Guest House

★★★★ ⚠ GUEST HOUSE

Lindale LA11 6LP
☎ 015395 34578 & 07776 211616 🖷 015395 34578
e-mail: greenacres.lindale@gmail.com
web: www.greenacres-lindale.co.uk
dir: *M6 junct 36, A590 signed Kendal/Barrow. After 3m 1st exit at rdbt, continue on A590, 1st exit at rdbt onto B5277, house on right before mini-rdbt*

Rooms 4 en suite 1 annexe en suite S £53; D £72-£82*
Facilities FTV iPod docking station TVL TV4B tea/coffee Cen ht Packed lunches available, drying facilities
Parking 5 Notes LB ⊗ No Children 12yrs

GRASMERE	Map 18 NY30

PREMIER COLLECTION

Moss Grove Organic

☆☆☆☆☆ 🛏 GUEST ACCOMMODATION

LA22 9SW
☎ 015394 35251 🖷 015394 35306
e-mail: enquiries@mossgrove.com
web: www.mossgrove.com
dir: *From S: M6 junct 36 onto A591 signed Keswick. From N: M6 junct 40 onto A591 signed Windermere*

Located in the centre of Grasmere, this impressive Victorian house has been appointed using as many natural products as possible with ongoing dedication to causing minimal environmental impact. The stylish bedrooms are decorated with beautiful wallpaper and natural clay paints, featuring hand-made beds and furnishings. Bose home entertainment systems, flat screen TVs and luxury bathrooms add further comfort. Extensive continental breakfasts are served in the spacious kitchen, where guests can help themselves and dine at the large wooden dining table.

Rooms 11 en suite (2 GF) S £99-£244; D £114-£259
Facilities STV tea/coffee Cen ht Licensed Wi-fi
Parking 11 Notes LB No Children 14yrs Closed 24-25 Dec

Silver Lea Guest House

★★★★ GUEST HOUSE

Easedale Rd LA22 9QE
☎ 015394 35657 & 07818 678109 🖷 015394 35657
e-mail: info@silverlea.com
dir: *Easedale Rd opposite village green, Silver Lea 300yds on right*

A friendly welcome is assured at this ivy-clad Lakeland-stone house, just a short walk from the village. Delicious, freshly cooked breakfasts are served in the cosy cottage dining room. Bedrooms, some having their own sitting area, are fresh in appearance and very comfortable. Silver Lea is an ideal base for walking and exploring the Lake District.

Rooms 4 en suite D £84-£98* Facilities FTV tea/coffee Cen ht Wi-fi Parking 4 Notes LB ⊗ No Children 11yrs

White Moss House

★★★★ 🛏 GUEST HOUSE

Rydal Water LA22 9SE
☎ 015394 35295 🖷 015394 35516
e-mail: sue@whitemoss.com
web: www.whitemoss.com
dir: *On A591 1m S of Grasmere, 2m N of Ambleside*

This traditional Lakeland house was once bought by Wordsworth for his son. It benefits from a central location and has a loyal following. The individually styled bedrooms are comfortable and thoughtfully equipped. There is also a two-room suite in a cottage on the hillside above the house. Afternoon tea is served in the inviting lounge. It is possible to book all five rooms for a private 'house party', dinner is then available by arrangement.

Rooms 5 en suite S £69-£99; D £78-£130* Facilities FTV DVD tea/coffee Direct Dial Cen ht Licensed Wi-fi Fishing Free use of local leisure club & fishing permits
Extras Speciality toiletries, home-made cakes on arrival
Parking 10 Notes LB ⊗ Closed Dec-Jan

GRIZEDALE	Map 18 SD39

Grizedale Lodge

★★★★ GUEST HOUSE

LA22 0QL
☎ 015394 36532
e-mail: enquiries@grizedale-lodge.com
web: www.grizedale-lodge.com
dir: *From Hawkshead follow signs S to Grizedale. Lodge 2m on right*

Set in the heart of Grizedale Forest Park, close to the Go Ape centre and two miles away from the village of Hawkshead, this lovely property offers quiet and tranquil surroundings ideal for a relaxing break away. Hospitality is key here and Richard and Debs will be keen to welcome you into their home. The comfortable lounge with open log fire and views of the forest, makes this an ideal place to relax. All the rooms are well decorated and some offer four poster beds. Good home cooked dinners and appetising breakfasts. Mountain bike storage also available.

Rooms 8 en suite (1 fmly) (2 GF) D £63-£110*
Facilities FTV DVD Lounge tea/coffee Dinner available Cen ht Licensed Wi-fi 🛁 Extras Speciality toiletries
Parking 12

HAWKSHEAD	Map 18 SD39

See also Near Sawrey

PREMIER COLLECTION

Ees Wyke Country House

★★★★★ ⚘ 🛏 GUEST HOUSE

LA22 0JZ
☎ 015394 36393
e-mail: mail@eeswyke.co.uk
web: www.eeswyke.co.uk

(For full entry see Near Sawrey)

The Queen's Head Inn & Restaurant

★★★★ 🍽 INN

Main St LA22 0NS
☎ 015394 36271 🖷 015394 36722
e-mail: info@queensheadhawkshead.co.uk
web: www.queensheadhawkshead.co.uk
dir: *M6 junct 36, then A590 to Newby Bridge. Over rdbt, 1st right into Hawkshead*

This 16th-century inn features a wood-panelled bar with low, oak-beamed ceilings and an open log fire; and the elegant dining area serves an excellent selection of quality dishes. The bedrooms are all comfortable, and the rooms in the adjacent cottage have benefited from recent refurbishment and now all modern and attractively furnished.

Rooms 10 en suite 3 annexe en suite (1 fmly) (2 GF) S £50-£70; D £75-£100* Facilities FTV DVD tea/coffee Dinner available Cen ht Wi-fi

Sawrey Ground

★★★★ 🛏 GUEST ACCOMMODATION

Hawkshead Hill LA22 0PP
☎ 015394 36683
e-mail: mail@sawreyground.com
dir: *B5285 from Hawkshead, 1m to Hawkshead Hill, sharp right after Baptist chapel, signs to Tarn Hows for 0.25m. Sawrey Ground on right*

Set in the heart of the Lake District, this charming 17th-century farmhouse has a superb setting on the doorstep of Tarn Hows. The flagstone entrance hall leads to a sitting room with a beamed ceiling, where an open fire burns on winter nights. Hearty breakfasts featuring fresh fruit and home-baked bread are served in the dining

Save on B&Bs and Hotels. Book at **theAA.com/hotel**

CUMBRIA   83   ENGLAND

room. The traditional bedrooms are furnished in pine and oak.

Sawrey Ground

Rooms 2 en suite **Facilities** FTV tea/coffee Cen ht Wi-fi **Parking** 6 **Notes** ⊗ No Children 8yrs Closed mid Nov-beg Mar 🏖

The Sun Inn

★★★★ INN

Main St LA22 0NT
☎ 015394 36236 📠 015394 36155
e-mail: rooms@suninn.co.uk
web: www.suninn.co.uk

Situated in the popular village of Hawkshead, The Sun Inn is full of character. Dating from the 16th-century it features a wood-panelled bar with low, oak-beamed ceilings. Substantial, carefully prepared meals are served in the bar and dining room. The bedrooms are modern in style, attractively furnished and include a four-poster room.

Rooms 8 en suite (1 fmly) S £45-£60; D £75-£100 **Facilities** FTV tea/coffee Dinner available Cen ht Wi-fi Fishing Pool table 🔒 **Notes** LB

Kings Arms

★★★ INN

LA22 0NZ
☎ 015394 36372 📠 015394 36006
e-mail: info@kingsarmshawkshead.co.uk
web: www.kingsarmshawkshead.co.uk
dir: M6 junct 36, A591, left onto A593 at Waterhead. 1m, onto B5286 to Hawkshead, Kings Arms in main square

A traditional Lakeland inn in the heart of a conservation area. The cosy, thoughtfully equipped bedrooms retain much character and are traditionally furnished. A good choice of freshly prepared food is available in the lounge bar and the neatly presented dining room.

Rooms 8 en suite (3 fmly) S £55-£65; D £80-£96* **Facilities** FTV DVD tea/coffee Dinner available Direct Dial Cen ht Wi-fi 🎣 ⚓ 18 Fishing Riding 🔒 Bowling green **Notes** LB Closed 25 Dec

---

HOLMROOK   Map 18 SD09

The Lutwidge Arms

★★★ INN

CA19 1UH
☎ 019467 24230 📠 019467 24100
e-mail: mail@lutwidgearms.co.uk
dir: M6 junct 36, A590 towards Barrow. Follow A595 towards Whitehaven & Workington, property in village centre

This Victorian roadside inn is family run and offers a welcoming atmosphere. Its name comes from the Lutwidge family of Holmrook Hall, who included Charles Lutwidge Dodgson, better known as Lewis Carroll. The bar and restaurant offer a wide range of meals during the evening. Bedrooms are comfortably equipped.

Rooms 11 en suite 5 annexe en suite (5 fmly) (5 GF) S fr £60; D £70-£95* **Facilities** FTV TVL tea/coffee Dinner available Cen ht Wi-fi Pool table **Parking** 30 **Notes** LB ⊗

IREBY   Map 18 NY23

Woodlands Country House

★★★★ 🏠 🍽 GUEST HOUSE

CA7 1EX
☎ 016973 71791 📠 016973 71482
e-mail: stay@woodlandsatireby.co.uk
web: www.woodlandsatireby.co.uk
dir: M6 junct 40, A66, pass Keswick, at rdbt right onto A591. At Castle Inn right signed Ireby, 2nd left signed Ireby. Pass church on left, last house in village

Previously a vicarage, this lovely Victorian home is set in well tended gardens that attract lots of wildlife. Guests are given a warm welcome by the friendly owners and delicious home-cooked evening meals are available by prior arrangement. A peaceful lounge and cosy bar with snug are also available. Bedrooms are attractively furnished and thoughtfully equipped.

Rooms 4 en suite 3 annexe en suite (3 fmly) (3 GF) **Facilities** FTV TVL tea/coffee Dinner available Cen ht Licensed Wi-fi **Parking** 11

KESWICK   Map 18 NY22

See also Lorton

The Grange Country Guest House

★★★★★ 🏠 GUEST HOUSE

Manor Brow, Ambleside Rd CA12 4BA
☎ 017687 72500 📠 0707 500 4885
e-mail: info@grangekeswick.com
web: www.grangekeswick.com
dir: M6 junct 40, A66, 15m. Onto A591, 1m, right into Manor Brow

This stylish Victorian residence stands in beautiful gardens just a stroll from the town centre and offers a relaxed atmosphere and professional service. The spacious bedrooms are well equipped and some have beams and mountain views. Spacious lounges and ample parking are available. The proprietors are keen to give advice on walks and local activities.

Rooms 10 en suite (1 GF) S £78-£80; D £100-£124* **Facilities** FTV Lounge tea/coffee Direct Dial Cen ht Licensed Wi-fi **Extras** Speciality toiletries **Parking** 10 **Notes** LB ⊗ No Children 10yrs Closed Jan

---

Amble House

★★★★ 🏠 GUEST HOUSE

23 Eskin St CA12 4DQ
☎ 017687 73288
e-mail: info@amblehouse.co.uk
web: www.amblehouse.co.uk
dir: 400yds SE of town centre. Exit A5271 (Penrith Rd) into Greta St & Eskin St

An enthusiastic welcome awaits you at this Victorian mid-terrace house, close to the town centre. The thoughtfully equipped bedrooms have co-ordinated decor and are furnished in pine. Healthy breakfasts are served in the attractive dining room.

Rooms 5 en suite S £40-£50; D £66-£80* **Facilities** tea/coffee Cen ht Wi-fi 🔒 **Notes** LB ⊗ No Children 16yrs Closed 24-26 Dec

KESWICK *continued*

Badgers Wood

★★★★ GUEST HOUSE

30 Stanger St CA12 5JU
☎ 017687 72621 📄 017687 72621
e-mail: enquiries@badgers-wood.co.uk
web: www.badgers-wood.co.uk
dir: *In town centre off A5271(main street)*

A warm welcome awaits guests at this delightful
Victorian terrace house, located in a quiet area close to
the town centre. The smart bedrooms are furnished to a
high standard and are well equipped; the attractive
breakfast room at the front of the house overlooks the
fells. Off-road parking is an added benefit.

Rooms 6 en suite S £39-£44; D £74-£79* **Facilities** FTV
DVD tea/coffee Cen ht Wi-fi 🔒 **Parking** 4 **Notes** ⊗ No
Children 12yrs Closed Nov-Jan ☺

Dalegarth House

★★★★ 🍴 GUEST ACCOMMODATION

Portinscale CA12 5RQ
☎ 017687 72817
e-mail: allerdalechef@aol.com
dir: *Off A66 to Portinscale, pass Farmers Arms, 500yds
on left*

The friendly family-run establishment stands on an
elevated position in the village of Portinscale, and has
fine views from the well-tended garden. The attractive
bedrooms are well equipped, and there is a peaceful
lounge, a well-stocked bar, and a spacious dining room
where the resident owner-chef produces hearty breakfasts
and delicious evening meals.

Rooms 8 en suite 2 annexe en suite (1 fmly) (2 GF)
S £62-£65; D £124-£140* (incl.dinner) **Facilities** FTV
Lounge tea/coffee Dinner available Cen ht Licensed Wi-fi 🔒
Extras Home-made cakes - complimentary **Parking** 10
Notes LB ⊗ No Children 12yrs Closed 24 Dec-13 Feb

The Edwardene

★★★★ 🏠 GUEST ACCOMMODATION

26 Southey St CA12 4EF
☎ 017687 73586
e-mail: info@edwardenehotel.com
dir: *M6 junct 40, A66 follow 1st sign to Keswick, right
into Penrith Rd. Sharp left by war memorial into Southey
St, 150mtrs on right*

Located close to the heart of the town centre, this
Victorian Lakeland stone building retains many of its
original features. Bedrooms are well equipped with many
thoughtful extras provided throughout. A comfortable
lounge is available, and the generous Cumbrian
breakfast is served in the stylish dining room.

Rooms 11 en suite (1 fmly) S £45-£46; D £84-£98*
Facilities FTV TVL tea/coffee Cen ht Licensed Wi-fi 🔒
Parking 2 **Notes** LB ⊗

Lakeside House

★★★★ GUEST ACCOMMODATION

40 Lake Rd CA12 5ES
☎ 017687 72868
e-mail: enquiries@lakesidehouse.co.uk
web: www.lakesidehouse.co.uk
dir: *At mini-rdbt in town centre follow signs for
Borrowdale/Derwentwater signs onto B5271. 0.4m, right
into The Heads. Left at end, Lakeside House on left*

Offering commanding views overlooking the park, this
period building was totally refurbished a few years ago,
and now boasts a mix of original and contemporary styled
bedrooms. Comfortable beds and high quality fixtures
and fittings are used to good effect. A hearty Cumbrian
breakfast is served in a bright and welcoming breakfast
room. Hospitality is wonderful and service is attentive.

Rooms 14 en suite (2 fmly) **Facilities** FTV iPod docking
station Lounge tea/coffee Cen ht Licensed Wi-fi ⚡ 🔒
Notes LB ⊗ Closed 23-27 Dec

Rooms 36

★★★★ GUEST ACCOMMODATION

36 Lake Rd CA12 5DQ
☎ 017687 72764 & 74416
e-mail: andy@rooms36.co.uk
web: www.rooms36.co.uk
dir: *M6 junct 40, A66 to Keswick. From Main St in Keswick
follow Borrowdale (B5289) signs. Right at next mini-rdbt
into Heads Rd (B5289), 4th right into The Heads, left at
end into Lake Rd*

Refurbished to a high standard and renamed, Rooms 36
overlooks Hope Park at the end of Lake Road. Modern
bedrooms feature iPod docking stations, Tassimo coffee
machines, comfortable beds and Herdwick wool carpets
as standard. En suites are well appointed and public
area decor is enhanced with wonderful artwork by local
artist Tessa Kennedy.

Rooms 36

Rooms 6 en suite (4 fmly) S £60-£70; D £70-£140*
Facilities STV FTV iPod docking station Lounge TVL tea/
coffee Cen ht Wi-fi 🔒 **Parking** 2

Sunnyside Guest House

★★★★ GUEST HOUSE

25 Southey St CA12 4EF
☎ 017687 72446
e-mail: enquiries@sunnysideguesthouse.com
web: www.sunnysideguesthouse.com
dir: *200yds E of town centre. Exit A5271 (Penrith Rd) into
Southey St. Sunnyside on left*

This stylish guest house is in a quiet area close to the
town centre. Bedrooms have been appointed to a high
standard and are comfortably furnished and well
equipped. There is a spacious and comfortable lounge
with plenty of books and magazines. Breakfast is served
at individual tables in the airy and attractive dining
room, and private parking is available.

Rooms 7 en suite D £75-£80* **Facilities** FTV Lounge tea/
coffee Cen ht Wi-fi 🔒 **Parking** 8 **Notes** LB ⊗ No Children
12yrs Closed 3 Jan-10 Feb

Claremont House

★★★★ GUEST ACCOMMODATION

Chestnut Hill CA12 4LT
☎ 017687 72089
e-mail: claremontkeswick@btinternet.com
web: www.claremonthousekeswick.co.uk
dir: *A591 N into Chestnut Hill. Pass Manor Brow on left,
Claremont House 100yds on right*

This impressive 19th-century house is set in mature
grounds where red squirrels regularly visit and has
commanding views over Keswick and beyond. It is within
walking distance of the town and is ideal for walkers.
Guests can expect comfortable bedrooms, a hearty
breakfast and friendly service. The resident owners also
offer a hot drink and cake on your arrival. The current
owners took over in August 2011 so Claremont House has
undergone extensive refurbishment. Free Wi-fi is also
available.

Rooms 6 en suite (1 fmly) (1 GF) **Facilities** FTV tea/coffee Cen ht Wi-fi ▲ **Extras** Flowers, wine, chocolate - chargeable **Parking** 7 **Notes** LB ⊗ No Children 8yrs

Craglands Guest House

★★★★ GUEST ACCOMMODATION

Penrith Rd CA12 4LJ
☎ 017687 74406
e-mail: craglands@msn.com
dir: 0.5m E of Keswick centre on A5271 (Penrith Rd) at junct A591

This Victorian house occupies an elevated position within walking distance of the town centre. The good value accommodation provides attractive, well equipped bedrooms. Pauline and Mark offer a warm welcome and serve delicious breakfasts with local produce and home-made breads.

Rooms 7 rms (5 en suite) **Facilities** FTV tea/coffee Dinner available Cen ht Wi-fi **Parking** 6 **Notes** ⊗ No Children 8yrs

Cragside

★★★★ GUEST ACCOMMODATION

39 Blencathra St CA12 4HX
☎ 017687 73344 📠 017687 73344
e-mail: cragside-keswick@hotmail.com
dir: A591 Penrith Rd into Keswick, under rail bridge, 2nd left

Expect warm hospitality at this establishment, located within easy walking distance of the town centre. The attractive bedrooms are well equipped, and many have fine views of the fells. Hearty Cumbrian breakfasts are served in the breakfast room, which overlooks the small front garden. Visually or hearing impaired guests are catered for, with Braille information, televisions with teletext, and a loop system installed in the dining room.

Rooms 4 en suite (1 fmly) S £50-£60; D £55-£70 **Facilities** FTV DVD tea/coffee Cen ht Wi-fi **Notes** No Children 5yrs

Dorchester House

★★★★ GUEST ACCOMMODATION

17 Southey St CA12 4EG
☎ 017687 73256
e-mail: dennis@dorchesterhouse.co.uk
dir: 200yds E of town centre. Exit A5271 (Penrith Rd) into Southey St, 150yds on left

A warm welcome awaits you at this property, just a stroll from the town centre and its amenities. The comfortably proportioned, well-maintained bedrooms offer pleasing co-ordinated decor. Hearty breakfasts are served in the attractive ground-floor dining room.

Rooms 8 rms (7 en suite) (1 pri facs) (2 fmly) **Facilities** FTV tea/coffee Cen ht Wi-fi **Notes** ⊗ No Children 6yrs

Eden Green Guest House

★★★★ GUEST HOUSE

20 Blencathra St CA12 4HP
☎ 017687 72077 📠 017687 80870
e-mail: enquiries@edengreenguesthouse.com
web: www.edengreenguesthouse.com
dir: A591 Penrith Rd into Keswick, under railway bridge, 2nd left, house 500yds on left

This mid-terrace house, faced with local stone, offers well-decorated and furnished bedrooms, some suitable for families and some with fine views of Skiddaw. Traditional English and vegetarian breakfasts are served in the neat breakfast room, and packed lunches can be provided on request.

Rooms 5 en suite (1 fmly) (1 GF) **Facilities** tea/coffee Cen ht Wi-fi **Notes** ⊗ No Children 8yrs

Elm Tree Lodge

★★★★ GUEST ACCOMMODATION

16 Leonard St CA12 4EL
☎ 017687 71050 & 07980 521079
e-mail: info@elmtreelodge-keswick.co.uk
dir: Exit A66, pass ambulance depot, left before pedestrian crossing, left into Southey St. 3rd left into Helvellyn St, 1st right into Leonard St, property 3rd on right

Close to the town centre, this tastefully decorated Victorian house offers a variety of room sizes, bedrooms feature stripped pine, period furniture, crisp white linen and modern en suites or private shower room. Hearty breakfasts are served in the charming dining room and feature local produce. A friendly welcome is guaranteed.

Rooms 4 rms (3 en suite) (1 pri facs) S £46-£50; D £60-£75 **Facilities** FTV tea/coffee Cen ht Wi-fi **Parking** 2 **Notes** LB ⊗ No Children 8yrs

Hazelmere

★★★★ GUEST ACCOMMODATION

Crosthwaite Rd CA12 5PG
☎ 017687 72445
e-mail: info@hazelmerekeswick.co.uk
web: www.hazelmerekeswick.co.uk
dir: Exit A66 at Crosthwaite rdbt (A591 junct) for Keswick, Hazelmere 400yds on right

Hazelmere is peacefully located overlooking the River Greta and perfect for walking in the surrounding fells or to the shores of Derwentwater. The market place is only a short stroll away. The house has benefited from complete refurbishment by the friendly owners who can offer advice on local walks and cycle routes. All bedrooms feature stunning views and are well equipped. Guests can also enjoy watching the birds and other wildlife visiting the garden.

Rooms 6 en suite (1 fmly) S £38-£45; D £70-£85 **Facilities** FTV DVD tea/coffee Cen ht Wi-fi ▲ **Parking** 7 **Notes** No Children 8yrs

Hedgehog Hill Guest House

★★★★ GUEST HOUSE

18 Blencathra St CA12 4HP
☎ 017687 80654
e-mail: keith@hedgehoghill.co.uk
dir: M6 junct 40, A66 to Keswick. Left into Blencathra St

Expect warm hospitality at this Victorian terrace house. Hedgehog Hill is convenient for the town centre, local attractions and many walks. Bedrooms are comfortably equipped and offer thoughtful extras. Hearty breakfasts are served in the light and airy dining room with vegetarians well catered for.

Rooms 6 rms (4 en suite) S £30-£33; D £64-£78* **Facilities** FTV tea/coffee Cen ht Wi-fi ▲ **Extras** Fairtrade snacks **Notes** ⊗ No Children 12yrs Closed 23-26 Dec

The Hollies

★★★★ GUEST HOUSE

Threlkeld CA12 4RX
☎ 017687 79216
e-mail: info@theholliesinlakeland.co.uk
dir: M6 junct 40 W on A66 towards Keswick. Turn right into Threlkeld, on main village road opposite village hall

The Hollies is located in the picturesque village of Threlkeld with commanding views up to Blencathra and across to the Helvellyn range. A warm and genuine welcome awaits, along with refreshments and home baking. Bedrooms are well appointed and comfortable with thoughtful extras provided as standard. Quality breakfasts are served on individual tables.

Rooms 4 en suite S £43-£58; D £66-£86* **Facilities** FTV DVD tea/coffee Cen ht Wi-fi ▲ **Parking** 6 **Notes** Closed 25 Dec

Honister House

★★★★ 🛏 BED AND BREAKFAST

1 Borrowdale Rd CA12 5DD
☎ 017687 73181
e-mail: honisterhouse@btconnect.com
web: www.honisterhouse.co.uk
dir: 100yds S of town centre, exit Market Sq into Borrowdale Rd

This charming family home is one of the oldest properties in Keswick, dating from the 18th century, and has attractive and well-equipped bedrooms. John and Susie Stakes are the friendly proprietors, who offer a warm welcome and serve hearty breakfasts utilising high quality local, organic and Fair Trade produce wherever possible.

Rooms 3 en suite D £75-£77* **Facilities** FTV DVD tea/coffee Cen ht Wi-fi ▲ **Extras** Speciality toiletries, home-made biscuits **Notes** LB ⊗

KESWICK *continued*

The Inn at Keswick

★★★★ INN

Main St CA12 5HZ
☎ 017687 74584
e-mail: relax@keswicklodge.co.uk
dir: *M6 junct 40, A66 to Keswick town centre to war memorial x-rds. Left into Station St. Inn 100yds*

Located on the corner of the vibrant market square this large, friendly 18th-century coaching inn offers a wide range of meals throughout the day and evening. There is a fully stocked bar complete with well-kept cask ales. Bedrooms vary in size but all are contemporary, smartly presented and feature quality accessories such as LCD TVs. There is also a drying room.

Rooms 19 en suite (2 fmly) **Facilities** FTV tea/coffee Dinner available Cen ht

Keswick Park

★★★★ GUEST ACCOMMODATION

33 Station Rd CA12 4NA
☎ 017687 72072 🖷 017687 74816
e-mail: reservations@keswickparkhotel.com
web: www.keswickparkhotel.com
dir: *200yds NE of town centre. Exit A5271 Penrith Rd into Station Rd*

A friendly welcome awaits at this comfortable Victorian house, situated within a short walking distance of the town centre. Bedrooms are mostly of a good size, and have homely extras. The breakfast room is divided into two sections and there is also is a cosy bar. Guests might like to sit on the front garden patio while enjoying refreshments.

Rooms 16 en suite (2 fmly) **Facilities** FTV TVL tea/coffee Direct Dial Cen ht Licensed Wi-fi **Parking** 8 **Notes** ⊗

Avondale Guest House

★★★★ 🅰 GUEST ACCOMMODATION

20 Southey St CA12 4EF
☎ 017687 72735
e-mail: enquiries@avondaleguesthouse.com
dir: *A66 to Keswick. A591 towards town centre, left at war memorial into Station St. Sharp left into Southey St, 100yds on right*

Rooms 6 en suite S £36-£42; D £72-£84* **Facilities** FTV Lounge tea/coffee Cen ht Wi-fi 🔒 **Notes** ⊗ No Children 12yrs

Portland House

★★★★ 🅰 GUEST ACCOMMODATION

19 Leonard St CA12 4EL
☎ 017687 74230
e-mail: stay@portlandhouse.net
dir: *A66 onto A591 towards town, left at war memorial into Station St. Sharp left into Southey St, 4th left into Church St. On left hand corner at next junct with Leonard St*

Rooms 6 en suite (1 GF) S £37-£40; D £74-£90* **Facilities** FTV Cen ht Wi-fi **Notes** ⊗ No Children 12yrs

Sandon Guesthouse

★★★★ 🅰 GUEST HOUSE

13 Southey St CA12 4EG
☎ 017687 73648
e-mail: enquiries@sandonguesthouse.com
dir: *200yds E of town centre. Exit A5271 (Penrith Rd) into Southey St*

Rooms 6 rms (5 en suite) (1 pri facs) S £40-£45; D £80-£90 **Facilities** FTV DVD tea/coffee Cen ht 🔒 **Notes** ⊗ No Children 4yrs Closed 24 Dec (day), 25-26 Dec

The George

★★★ 🍽 INN

Saint Johns St CA12 5AZ
☎ 017687 72076 🖷 017687 75968
e-mail: rooms@thegeorgekeswick.co.uk
dir: *M6 junct 40, A66, take left filter road signed Keswick, pass pub on left. At x-rds left into Station St, 150yds on left*

Located in the centre of town this property is Keswick's oldest coaching inn. There is an abundance of character with wooden beamed bar, cosy seating areas and an atmospheric, candle-lit dining room. Food is a highlight with a wide choice of freshly prepared dishes. Bedrooms are simply presented and comfortable. Parking permits and storage for cycles are available.

Rooms 12 en suite (2 fmly) S £60-£100; D £100* **Facilities** FTV tea/coffee Dinner available Cen ht 🔒 **Parking** 4 **Notes** No coaches

Springs Farm B&B (NY274227)

★★★ FARMHOUSE

Springs Farm, Springs Rd CA12 4AN
☎ 017687 72144 & 07816 824253   Ms H Hutton
e-mail: springsfarm@fwi.co.uk
dir: *A66 into Keswick, left at T-junct onto Chestnut Hill. After 200yds right on Manor Brow, then left into Springs Road. 0.5m at end of road*

Part of a working diary farm, the farmhouse was built around 150 years ago. Guests can expect comfortable accommodation and a well-cooked breakfast with eggs from the farm's own hens that will be seen walking around the gardens. Springs Farm B&B is ideally located in the heart of the countryside but surprising close to the town centre, which is an easy 10 minutes walk away.

Rooms 3 en suite S £42-£48; D £73-£78* **Facilities** STV FTV TVL tea/coffee Cen ht Wi-fi **Parking** 6 **Notes** LB Closed 19-29 Dec 180 acres dairy

KIRKBY LONSDALE	Map 18 SD67

PREMIER COLLECTION

Hipping Hall

★★★★★ 🟠🟠🟠 🍴 RESTAURANT WITH ROOMS

Cowan Bridge LA6 2JJ
☎ 015242 71187 🖷 015242 72452
e-mail: info@hippinghall.com
dir: *M6 junct 36, A65 through Kirkby Lonsdale towards Skipton. On right after Cowan Bridge*

Close to the market town of Kirkby Lonsdale, Hipping Hall offers spacious, feature bedrooms, designed in soft shades with sumptuous textures and fabrics; the bathrooms use natural stone, slate and limestone to great effect. There are also three spacious cottage suites that create a real hideaway experience. The sitting room, with large, comfortable sofas has a traditional feel. The restaurant is a 15th-century hall with tapestries and a minstrels' gallery that is as impressive as it is intimate.

Rooms 6 en suite 3 annexe en suite (1 GF) **Facilities** Dinner available Direct Dial Cen ht 🔖 **Parking** 30 **Notes** No Children 12yrs Closed 3-8 Jan No coaches Civ Wed 42

PREMIER COLLECTION

Plato's

★★★★★ 　 RESTAURANT WITH ROOMS

2 Mill Brow LA6 2AT
☎ **01524 274180**
e-mail: sally@platoskirkby.co.uk
dir: *M6 junct 36, A65 Kirkby Lonsdale, after 5m at rdbt take 1st exit, onto one-way system*

Tucked away in the heart of the popular market town, Plato's is steeped in history. Sumptuous bedrooms have a wealth of thoughtful extras, and imaginative food is available in the elegant restaurant with its open-plan kitchen. The lounge bar is more rustic in style with fires to relax by. A warm welcome and professional service is assured.

Rooms 8 en suite **Facilities** FTV TVL tea/coffee Dinner available Cen ht Wi-fi ch fac 🏊 🎿 18 **Notes** No coaches

PREMIER COLLECTION

The Sun Inn

★★★★★ ◉ RESTAURANT WITH ROOMS

6 Market St LA6 2AU
☎ **015242 71965** 📠 **015242 72485**
e-mail: email@sun-inn.info
web: www.sun-inn.info
dir: *From A65 follow signs to town centre. Inn on main street*

The Sun is a 17th-century inn situated in a historic market town, overlooking St Mary's Church. The atmospheric bar features stone walls, wooden beams and log fires with real ales available. Delicious meals are served in the bar and more formal, modern restaurant. Traditional and modern styles are blended together in the beautifully appointed rooms with excellent en suites.

Rooms 11 en suite (1 fmly) S £76-£109; D £110-£162*
Facilities FTV tea/coffee Dinner available Cen ht Wi-fi 🏊 🎿 18 **Extras** Bath robes, speciality toiletries
Notes LB No coaches

The Copper Kettle

★★★ 🄰 GUEST ACCOMMODATION

3-5 Market St LA6 2AU
☎ **015242 71714** 📠 **015242 71714**
e-mail: gamble_p@btconnect.com
dir: *In town centre, down lane by Post Office*
Rooms 5 en suite (2 fmly) **Facilities** FTV tea/coffee Dinner available Licensed **Parking** 3 **Notes** LB

KIRKBY STEPHEN　　　　　　Map 18 NY70

Brownber Hall Country House

★★★★ GUEST ACCOMMODATION

Newbiggin-on-Lune CA17 4NX
☎ **015396 23208**
e-mail: enquiries@brownberhall.co.uk
web: www.brownberhall.co.uk
dir: *5m from M6 junct 38 along A685 towards Kirkby Stephen*

Having an elevated position with superb views of the surrounding countryside, Brownber Hall, built in 1860, has been restored to its original glory. The en suite bedrooms are comfortably proportioned, attractively decorated and well equipped. The ground floor has two lovely reception rooms, which retain many original features, and a charming dining room where traditional breakfasts are served.

Rooms 10 rms (8 en suite) (2 pri facs) (1 fmly) (1 GF) S £35-£50; D £70-£85* **Facilities** FTV TVL tea/coffee Cen ht Lift Licensed Wi-fi 🎿 18 **Parking** 8 **Notes** LB No Children 7yrs Closed 22-28 Dec

---

LITTLE LANGDALE　　　　　　Map 18 NY30

Three Shires Inn

★★★★ 　 INN

LA22 9NZ
☎ **015394 37215** 📠 **015394 37127**
e-mail: enquiry@threeshiresinn.co.uk
dir: *Exit A593, 3m from Ambleside at 2nd junct signed Langdales. 1st left after 0.5m, 1m along lane*

Enjoying an outstanding rural location, this family-run inn was built in 1872. The brightly decorated bedrooms are individual in style and many offer panoramic views. The attractive lounge features a roaring fire in the cooler months and there is a traditional style bar with a great selection of local ales. Meals can be taken in either the bar or cosy restaurant.

Rooms 10 en suite (1 fmly) S £50-£110; D £88-£126
Facilities FTV Lounge TVL tea/coffee Dinner available Cen ht Wi-fi 🅿 Use of local country club **Parking** 15 **Notes** LB Closed 25 Dec RS Dec & Jan wknds & New Year only No coaches

---

LORTON　　　　　　Map 18 NY12

PREMIER COLLECTION

The Old Vicarage

★★★★★ 🏠 　 GUEST HOUSE

Church Ln CA13 9UN
☎ **01900 85656**
e-mail: info@oldvicarage.co.uk
web: www.oldvicarage.co.uk
dir: *B5292 onto B5289 N of Lorton. 1st left signed Church. House 1st on right*

This delightful Victorian house offers spacious accommodation in the peaceful Lorton Vale, at the heart of the Lake District National Park. A converted coach-house offers two rooms with exposed stone walls, and is ideal for families with older children. Bedrooms in the main house are well equipped and have excellent views of the distant mountains. Delicious home cooking is served in the bright dining room.

Rooms 6 en suite 2 annexe en suite (1 GF) S £96-£104; D £120-£140* **Facilities** FTV DVD Lounge tea/coffee Dinner available Cen ht Licensed Wi-fi 🅿 **Parking** 10 **Notes** ⊗ No Children 8yrs

LOWESWATER · Map 18 NY12

Kirkstile Inn

★★★★ 😊 INN

CA13 0RU
☎ 01900 85219
e-mail: info@kirkstile.com
web: www.kirkstile.com
dir: A66 onto B5292 into Lorton, left signed Buttermere.
Follow signs to Loweswater, left signed Kirkstile Inn

This historic 16th-century inn lies in a valley surrounded
by mountains. Serving great food and ale, its rustic bar
and adjoining rooms are a mecca for walkers. There is
also a cosy restaurant offering a quieter ambiance.
Bedrooms retain their original character. There is a
spacious family suite in an annexe, with two bedrooms, a
lounge and a bathroom.

Rooms 7 en suite 3 annexe en suite (1 fmly) (2 GF)
S £63.50–£90; D £99–£109* **Facilities** TVL TV3B tea/
coffee Dinner available Cen ht Wi-fi **Parking** 30 **Notes** LB
Closed 25 Dec No coaches

LUPTON · Map 18 SD58

PREMIER COLLECTION

The Plough Inn Lupton

★★★★★ 😊 INN

Cow Brow LA6 1PJ
☎ 015395 67700
e-mail: info@theploughatlupton.co.uk
dir: M6 junct 36 onto A65 towards Kirkby Lonsdale.
Through Nook, up hill, inn on right

This delightful inn's interior is open plan and a real
delight; modern but with a rustic farmhouse
appearance. There are large beams, and a log-burning
stove surrounded by large comfortable sofas so you can
relax and read the papers. The bedrooms are well
proportioned and reflect the inn's high standards; all
have feature bathrooms with roll-top baths and walk-in
showers. The staff are excellent and guests are made
to feel like part of the family. The inn is open all year
and serves food every day.

Rooms 5 en suite (1 fmly) S £85–£165; D £95–£195*
Facilities FTV DVD Dinner available Cen ht Wi-fi ⚿ 18
⚿ **Extras** Speciality toiletries, botted water **Conf** Max 8
Thtr 8 Board 8 **Parking** 50 **Notes** No coaches

NEAR SAWREY · Map 18 SD39

PREMIER COLLECTION

Ees Wyke Country House

★★★★★ 😊 🏠 GUEST HOUSE

LA22 0JZ
☎ 015394 36393
e-mail: mail@eeswyke.co.uk
web: www.eeswyke.co.uk
dir: On B5285 on W side of village

A warm welcome awaits at this elegant Georgian
country house with views over Esthwaite Water and the
surrounding countryside. The thoughtfully equipped
bedrooms have been decorated and furnished with
care. There is a charming lounge with an open fire, and
a splendid dining room where a carefully prepared five-
course dinner is served. Breakfasts have a fine
reputation due to the skilful use of local produce.

Rooms 8 en suite (1 GF) S £59–£73; D £89–£138
Facilities FTV Lounge tea/coffee Dinner available
Cen ht Licensed Wi-fi ⚿ **Extras** Sherry, peanuts
Parking 12 **Notes** LB ⊗ No Children 12yrs

NEWBY BRIDGE · Map 18 SD38

PREMIER COLLECTION

The Knoll Country House

★★★★★ 🏠 🌿 GUEST ACCOMMODATION

Lakeside LA12 8AU
☎ 015395 31347 📠 015395 30850
e-mail: info@theknoll-lakeside.co.uk
dir: A590 W to Newby Bridge, over rdbt, signed right for
Lake Steamers, house 0.5m on left

This delightful Edwardian villa stands in a leafy dell on
the western side of Windermere. Public areas have
many original features, including an open fire in the
cosy lounge and dining room. The attractive bedrooms
vary in style and outlook, but are all very stylish. Jenny
and her enthusiastic team extend a very caring and
natural welcome. Jenny also prepares a very good range
of excellent dishes at breakfast and dinner.

Rooms 8 en suite 1 annexe rm (1 pri facs) S £75–£105;
D £85–£155 **Facilities** STV FTV DVD iPod docking
station Lounge TVL tea/coffee Dinner available Direct
Dial Cen ht Licensed Wi-fi ⚿ Use of nearby hotel leisure
spa **Extras** Fruit & wine in one room **Conf** Max 30 Thtr
30 Class 18 Board 12 **Parking** 9 **Notes** LB ⊗ No
Children 16yrs Closed 24-26 Dec Civ Wed 40

Lakes End Guest House

★★★★ GUEST HOUSE

LA12 8ND
☎ 015395 31260 📠 015395 31260
e-mail: info@lakes-end.co.uk
web: www.lakes-end.co.uk
dir: On A590 in Newby Bridge, 100yds from rdbt

In a sheltered, wooded setting away from the road, Lakes
End is convenient for the coast and the lakes. The
bedrooms have been thoughtfully furnished and
equipped. Traditional English breakfasts are served, and
delicious home-cooked evening meals can be provided by
arrangement.

Rooms 4 en suite (1 fmly) (1 GF) S £40–£50; D £65–£80*
Facilities STV FTV tea/coffee Dinner available Cen ht
Licensed Wi-fi ⚿ Membership to local hotel spa **Parking** 6
Notes LB ⊗

Lyndhurst Country House

★★★★ 🏠 GUEST HOUSE

LA12 8ND
☎ 015395 31245
e-mail: chris@lyndhurstcountryhouse.co.uk
dir: On junct of A590 & A592 at Newby Bridge rdbt

This 1920s house is situated close to the southern tip of
Lake Windermere. Accommodation consists of three
comfortable, tastefully decorated bedrooms, each with en
suite shower room. Hearty breakfasts feature local
produce and are served in the pleasant dining room,
which also has a lounge area opening onto the garden.

Rooms 3 en suite S £55–£70; D £70–£80* **Facilities** FTV Lounge tea/coffee Cen ht Wi-fi **Parking** 3 **Notes** ⊗ No Children 8yrs Closed 23–28 Dec

The Coach House

★★★★ BED AND BREAKFAST

Hollow Oak LA12 8AD
☎ 015395 31622
e-mail: coachho@talk21.com
web: www.coachho.com
dir: 2.5m SW of Newby Bridge. A590 onto B5278 signed Cark, 1st left into rear of white house

This converted coach house stands in delightful gardens south of Lake Windermere. The hosts offer a warm welcome and are a good source of local knowledge. The modern bedrooms are light and airy, and there is a cosy lounge. Breakfast is served in a converted stable.

Rooms 3 rms (2 en suite) (1 pri facs) S £31.50–£40; D £49.50–£60* **Facilities** FTV DVD iPod docking station TVL tea/coffee Cen ht Wi-fi ⊛ **Parking** 3 **Notes** LB ⊗ No Children 10yrs

PENRITH	Map 18 NY53

PREMIER COLLECTION

Brooklands Guest House

★★★★★ ⌂ GUEST HOUSE

2 Portland Place CA11 7QN
☎ 01768 863395 ▤ 01768 863395
e-mail: enquiries@brooklandsguesthouse.com
web: www.brooklandsguesthouse.com
dir: M6 junct 40, follow sign for TIC, left at town hall, 50yds on left

In the bustling market town of Penrith this beautifully appointed house offers individually furnished bedrooms with high quality accessories and some luxury touches. Nothing seems to be too much trouble for the friendly owners, and from romantic breaks to excellent storage for cyclists, all guests are very well looked after. Delicious breakfasts featuring Cumbrian produce are served in the attractive dining room.

Rooms 6 en suite (1 fmly) S £40–£60; D £75–£85* **Facilities** FTV DVD iPod docking station tea/coffee Cen ht Wi-fi ⊛ **Extras** Speciality toiletries, fresh fruit **Parking** 2 **Notes** LB ⊗ Closed 24 Dec–4 Jan

Albany House

★★★★ GUEST HOUSE

5 Portland Place CA11 7QN
☎ 01768 863072
e-mail: info@albany-house.org.uk
dir: Left at town hall into Portland Place. 30yds on left

A well maintained Victorian house located close to Penrith town centre. Bedrooms are spacious, comfortable and thoughtfully equipped. Wholesome breakfasts utilising local ingredients are served in the attractive breakfast room.

Rooms 5 rms (3 en suite) (2 pri facs) (1 fmly) D £60–£75 **Facilities** FTV tea/coffee Dinner available Cen ht Wi-fi ⌂ **Notes** LB ⊗

Brandelhow Guest House

★★★★ ⌂ GUEST HOUSE

1 Portland Place CA11 7QN
☎ 01768 864470
e-mail: enquiries@brandelhowguesthouse.co.uk
web: www.brandelhowguesthouse.co.uk
dir: In town centre on one-way system, left at town hall

Situated within easy walking distance of central amenities, this friendly guest house is also convenient for the Lakes and M6. The bedrooms are thoughtfully furnished and some are suitable for families. Breakfasts, utilising quality local produce, are served in a Cumbria-themed dining room overlooking the pretty courtyard garden. Afternoon and high teas are available by arrangement.

Rooms 5 rms (4 en suite) (1 pri facs) (2 fmly) **Facilities** FTV tea/coffee Cen ht Wi-fi **Notes** ⊗ Closed 31 Dec & 1 Jan

Acorn Guest House

★★★★ GUEST HOUSE

Scotland Rd CA11 9HL
☎ 01768 868696
e-mail: acornguesthouse@fsmail.net
web: www.acorn-guesthouse.co.uk

This house is on the edge of the town and is popular with walkers and cyclists. Bedrooms are generally spacious and a substantial, freshly cooked breakfast made with local produce is served. Drying facilities and safe storage for bikes are available. High teas can be provided by arrangement.

Rooms 8 en suite (2 fmly) S £49–£55; D £70–£74* **Facilities** FTV tea/coffee Cen ht Wi-fi **Parking** 8 **Notes** ⊗

Glendale Guest House

★★★★ GUEST HOUSE

4 Portland Place CA11 7QN
☎ 01768 210061
e-mail: glendaleguesthouse@yahoo.co.uk
web: www.glendaleguesthouse.com
dir: M6 junct 40, follow town centre signs. Pass castle, turn left before town hall

This friendly family-run guest house is part of a Victorian terrace only a stroll from the town centre and convenient for the lakes and Eden Valley. Drying facilities are available. Bedrooms vary in size, but all are attractive, and well equipped and presented. Hearty breakfasts are served at individual tables in the charming ground-floor dining room.

Rooms 7 en suite (3 fmly) **Facilities** FTV tea/coffee Cen ht Wi-fi

RAVENSTONEDALE	Map 18 NY70

The Black Swan

★★★★ ⌂ ⊜ INN

CA17 4NG
☎ 015396 23204 ▤ 015396 23204
e-mail: enquiries@blackswanhotel.com
dir: M6 junct 38. Black Swan on A685, W of Kirkby Stephen

Set in the heart of this quiet village, the inn is popular with visitors and locals and offers a very friendly welcome. Bedrooms are individually styled and comfortably equipped. There is an informal atmosphere in the bar areas and home-made meals can be taken in the bar or the stylish dining room. Relax by the fire in the cooler months and enjoy the riverside garden in the summer. The Black Swan is the AA Pub of the Year for England 2012-2013.

Rooms 10 en suite 4 annexe en suite (3 fmly) (4 GF) S fr £55; D £75–£125* **Facilities** FTV Lounge tea/coffee Dinner available Cen ht Wi-fi ch fac ⌕ ⌖ 9 Fishing Riding Snooker ⌂ **Extras** Speciality toiletries, snacks, water **Conf** Max 14 Thtr 14 Class 14 Board 14 **Parking** 20 **Notes** LB

RAVENSTONEDALE *continued*

The Fat Lamb

★★★★ INN

Crossbank CA17 4LL
☎ 015396 23242
e-mail: enquiries@fatlamb.co.uk
dir: *On A683, between Kirkby Stephen & Sedbergh*

Solid stone walls and open fires feature at this 17th-century inn. Recently refurbished bedrooms and en suites are comfortable. A ground floor accessible room with en suite wet room is available. Guests can enjoy a choice of dining options serving well-cooked dishes using local produce in either the traditional bar or the more formal dining room. There is also a beer garden.

Rooms 12 en suite (4 fmly) (5 GF) S £53-£59; D £90-£98 **Facilities** tea/coffee Dinner available Wi-fi ch fac Private 5-acre nature reserve **Conf** Thtr 60 Class 30 Board 30 **Parking** 60

RYDAL

See Ambleside

SEASCALE   Map 18 NY00

Cumbrian Lodge

★★★★ ⊛ RESTAURANT WITH ROOMS

Gosforth Rd CA20 1JG
☎ 019467 27309 ≣ 019467 27158
e-mail: cumbrianlodge@btconnect.com
web: www.cumbrianlodge.com
dir: *Exit A595 at Gosforth onto B5344 signed Seascale, 2m on left*

This well-run restaurant with rooms enjoys a relaxed and friendly atmosphere, and tasty, well-prepared dinners prove popular locally. The decor and fixtures are modern throughout, and the bedrooms are well-equipped for both business and leisure guests. The thatched garden buildings provide a delightful opportunity for eating alfresco under canvas panels, for up to 12 diners.

Rooms 6 en suite (1 fmly) S £79.50; D £90* **Facilities** FTV tea/coffee Dinner available Direct Dial Cen ht Wi-fi ⌕ ♪ 18 **Extras** Speciality toiletries **Parking** 15 **Notes** ⊗ No coaches

SHAP   Map 18 NY51

Brookfield Guest House

★★★★ GUEST HOUSE

CA10 3PZ
☎ 01931 716397 ≣ 01931 716397
e-mail: info@brookfieldshap.co.uk
dir: *M6 junct 39, A6 towards Shap, 1st accommodation off motorway, on right*

Having a quiet rural location within easy reach of the M6, this inviting house stands in well-tended gardens. Bedrooms are thoughtfully appointed and well

maintained. There is a comfortable lounge, and a small bar area next to the traditional dining room where substantial, home-cooked breakfasts are served at individual tables.

Rooms 4 rms (3 en suite) (1 pri facs) S £40-£50; D £75-£80 **Facilities** FTV TVL tea/coffee Cen ht Licensed Wi-fi ♿ **Conf** Max 20 **Parking** 20 **Notes** ⊗ No Children 12yrs Closed Nov-1 Mar 🐾

TEMPLE SOWERBY   Map 18 NY62

The Kings Arms

★★★★ ⇔ INN

CA10 1SB
☎ 017683 62944
e-mail: enquiries@kingsarmstemplesowerby.co.uk
dir: *M6 junct 40, E on A66 to Temple Sowerby, Kings Arms in village*

The Kings Arms is located in the peaceful village of Temple Sowerby just a couple of minutes from the A66 bypass and a short drive from Centre Parcs. An historical property dating back over 400 years with a good deal of charm and character, it has benefited from a large refurbishment programme. Quality food is served in the small restaurant or in the bar itself close to the open fire. Comfortable, well-appointed accommodation makes this property an ideal location to tour the surrounding areas.

Rooms 8 en suite (5 fmly) S £50; D £80* **Facilities** FTV Lounge tea/coffee Dinner available Cen ht Wi-fi Fishing ♿ **Parking** 20 **Notes** LB

Skygarth Farm *(NY612261)*

★★★ FARMHOUSE

CA10 1SS
☎ 017683 61300 ≣ 017683 61300 **Mrs Robinson**
e-mail: enquire@skygarth.co.uk
dir: *Off A66 at Temple Sowerby for Morland, Skygarth 500yds on right, follow signs*

Skygarth is just south of the village, half a mile from the busy main road. The house stands in a cobbled courtyard surrounded by cowsheds, with gardens to the rear, where red squirrels feed. There are two well-proportioned bedrooms and an attractive lounge where tasty breakfasts are served.

Rooms 2 rms (2 fmly) S £30-£35; D £50-£60* **Facilities** FTV TVL tea/coffee Cen ht Wi-fi ♿ **Extras** Robes **Parking** 4 **Notes** ⊗ Closed Dec-Jan 🐾 200 acres mixed

TROUTBECK (NEAR KESWICK)   Map 18 NY32

Lane Head Farm Country Guest House

★★★★ ⌂ GUEST HOUSE

CA11 0SY
☎ 017687 79220
e-mail: info@laneheadfarm.co.uk
web: www.laneheadfarm.co.uk
dir: *On A66 between Penrith & Keswick, 1m W of Troutbeck*

Built around 1750 and surrounded by rolling fells with great road links to the rest of the lakes, Lane Head Farm offers well-presented gardens and seating so guests can enjoy the lovely location. Good-sized bedrooms are well appointed with many useful extras provided as standard. There is a peaceful lounge with books and games, and breakfast is served on individual tables in the large dining room.

Rooms 7 en suite (1 GF) S £50-£84; D £60-£168* **Facilities** FTV iPod docking station Lounge tea/coffee Cen ht Wi-fi ♿ **Extras** Home-made biscuits, mini-fridge - some rooms **Parking** 9 **Notes** LB No Children 10yrs Closed 24-26 Dec

TROUTBECK (NEAR WINDERMERE) Map 18 NY40

PREMIER COLLECTION

Broadoaks Country House

★★★★★ ⇔ GUEST ACCOMMODATION

Bridge Ln LA23 1LA
☎ 015394 45566 ≣ 015394 88766
e-mail: enquiries@broadoakscountryhouse.co.uk
web: www.broadoakscountryhouse.co.uk
dir: *Exit A591 junct 36 pass Windermere. Filing station on left, 1st right 0.5m*

This impressive Lakeland stone house has been restored to its original Victorian grandeur and is set in seven acres of landscaped grounds with stunning views of the Troutbeck Valley. Individually furnished bedrooms are well appointed and en suite bathrooms feature either whirlpool or Victorian roll top baths. Spacious day rooms include the music room, featuring a Bechstein piano. Meals are served by friendly and attentive staff in the elegant dining room.

Rooms 12 en suite 7 annexe en suite (8 fmly) (7 GF) S £99-£250; D £99-£250* **Facilities** STV FTV DVD iPod docking station tea/coffee Dinner available Direct Dial Cen ht Licensed Wi-fi 🐾 Fishing Arrangement with local leisure facility **Extras** Speciality toiletries **Conf** Max 62 Thtr 40 Class 45 Board 45 **Parking** 40 **Notes** LB Civ Wed 64

The Queen's Head

★★★★ ⌕ INN

Townhead LA23 1PW
☎ 015394 32174 ▯ 015394 31938
e-mail: reservations@queensheadtroutbeck.co.uk
web: www.queensheadtroutbeck.co.uk
dir: *M6 junct 36 onto A591, past Windermere towards Ambleside. At mini-rdbt, right onto A592 for Ullswater, 3m on left*

This 17th-century coaching inn has stunning views of the Troutbeck valley. The delightful bedrooms, several with four-poster beds, are traditionally furnished and equipped with modern facilities. Beams, flagstone floors, and a bar that was once an Elizabethan four-poster, provide a wonderful setting in which to enjoy imaginative food, real ales and fine wines.

Rooms 10 en suite 5 annexe en suite (1 fmly) (2 GF) S £75; D £120-£150* **Facilities** FTV tea/coffee Dinner available Cen ht Wi-fi ▯ **Conf** Max 30 **Parking** 65 **Notes** LB RS 25 Dec pre-booked lunch only & 31 Dec pre-booked dinner only

ULVERSTON   Map 18 SD27

Church Walk House

★★★★ BED AND BREAKFAST

Church Walk LA12 7EW
☎ 01229 582211 & 07774 368331
e-mail: martinchadd@btinternet.com
dir: *In town centre opposite Stables furniture shop on corner of Fountain St & Church Walk*

This Grade II listed 18th-century residence stands in the heart of the historic market town. Stylishly decorated, the accommodation includes attractive bedrooms with a mix of antiques and contemporary pieces. Service is attentive and there is a small herbal garden and patio.

Rooms 3 rms (2 en suite) (1 pri facs) **Facilities** TVL tea/coffee Cen ht

WASDALE HEAD   Map 18 NY10

Wasdale Head Inn

★★★ INN

CA20 1EX
☎ 019467 26229 ▯ 019647 26334
e-mail: reception@wasdale.com
dir: *Leave A595 at Santon Bridge or Gosforth if travelling S. Follow signs for Wasdale*

Wasdale Head is known as the birthplace of British climbing for good reason. The setting is breathtaking, surrounded by the fells with the brooding Wast Water close by. Inside, the decor is enhanced with objets d'art and photos of climbers and mountains. Bedrooms and public areas are comfortable, and the service is relaxed and informal. Real ales and good food are served in the rustic bar while a separate restaurant is available for residents.

Rooms 9 en suite 3 annexe en suite (2 fmly) (1 GF) S £59; D £118-£130* **Facilities** FTV Lounge tea/coffee Dinner available Direct Dial Cen ht Wi-fi ▯ **Extras** Bath salts **Conf** Max 20 Thtr 20 Class 20 Board 20 **Parking** 30 **Notes** LB No coaches

WHITEHAVEN   Map 18 NX91

Glenfield Guest House

★★★★ GUEST HOUSE

Back Corkickle CA28 7TS
☎ 01946 691911 & 07810 632890 ▯ 01946 694060
e-mail: glenfieldgh@gmail.com
web: www.glenfield-whitehaven.co.uk
dir: *0.5m SE of town centre on A5094*

The imposing, family-run Victorian house is in a conservation area close to the historic town centre and harbour. Margaret and Andrew provide a relaxed environment with friendly but unobtrusive service, and this is a good start point for the Sea to Sea (C2C) cycle ride.

Rooms 6 en suite (2 fmly) S £50; D £80* **Facilities** FTV DVD TVL tea/coffee Dinner available Cen ht Licensed Wi-fi ▯ **Notes** ⊗

WINDERMERE   Map 18 SD49

The Cranleigh

★★★★★ GUEST HOUSE

Kendal Rd, Bowness LA23 3EW
☎ 015394 43293 ▯ 015394 47283
e-mail: enquiries@thecranleigh.com
dir: *From Lake Rd into Kendal Rd, house 150yds on right*

Just a short walk from Lake Windermere this smartly appointed period property has been transformed to provide stylish accommodation. Bedrooms are divided between the main house and adjacent building. Luxury and superior rooms are impressive, featuring spa baths, illuminated showers and an excellent range of accessories. The new Sanctuary Suite comes with its own hot tub. Guests have complimentary use of leisure facilities at a nearby hotel.

Rooms 11 en suite 6 annexe en suite (3 GF) **Facilities** FTV DVD iPod docking station tea/coffee Direct Dial Cen ht Licensed Wi-fi ⊙ Snooker Sauna Gym Complimentary use of off-site leisure facilities **Parking** 13 **Notes** LB ⊗ No Children 16yrs

The Howbeck

★★★★★ ⌕ GUEST HOUSE

New Rd LA23 2LA
☎ 015394 44739
e-mail: relax@howbeck.co.uk
dir: *A591 through Windermere town centre, left towards Bowness*

Howbeck is a delightful Victorian villa, convenient for the village and the lake. Bedrooms are well appointed and feature lovely soft furnishings, along with luxurious spa baths in some cases. There is a bright lounge with internet access and an attractive dining room where home-prepared hearty Cumbrian breakfasts are served at individual tables.

Rooms 10 en suite 1 annexe en suite (3 GF) S £75-£150; D £110-£250* **Facilities** STV FTV TVL tea/coffee Cen ht Licensed Wi-fi Free membership to spa & leisure club 0.5m **Parking** 12 **Notes** LB ⊗ Closed 24-25 Dec

Windermere Suites

★★★★★ ⌕ BED AND BREAKFAST

New Rd LA23 2LA
☎ 015394 47672 & 43356
e-mail: reservations@windermeresuites.co.uk
dir: *Through village on one-way system towards Bowness-on-Windermere. 50mtrs past The Ellerthwaite*

Close to Windermere and Bowness, Windermere Suites is a very special boutique town house which offers eight individual suites, all combining contemporary designer furniture with cutting edge entertainment technology and sheer elegance. Each suite has its own lounge area, and the bathrooms have large spa baths complete with TV, mood lighting and power showers. Rooms also have mini-bars and room service up to 10pm. An unusual feature is the 'living showroom' element, if you like an item of furniture or decoration you can order it at a discount.

Rooms 8 en suite (3 GF) S £150-£200; D £180-£300 **Facilities** STV FTV DVD iPod docking station TVL tea/coffee Cen ht Licensed Wi-fi Free use of spa & leisure club 0.5m **Extras** Mini-bar, safe **Parking** 9 **Notes** LB ⊗

WINDERMERE *continued*

PREMIER COLLECTION

Applegarth Villa & Restaurant

★★★★★ GUEST ACCOMMODATION

College Rd LA23 1BU
☎ 015394 43206 📠 015394 46636
e-mail: info@lakesapplegarth.co.uk
web: www.lakesapplegarth.co.uk
dir: *M6 junct 36, A591 towards Windermere. On entering town left after NatWest Bank into Elleray Rd. 1st right into College Rd, Applegarth on right*

This period building set in the heart of Windermere, offers elegantly furnished accommodation with luxurious bathrooms. The attractive conservatory dining room offers stunning views of the mountains and serves locally sourced produce. The oak-panelled bar with fire is a perfect retreat on a winters evening. Private off-road parking and spa facilities are a bonus.

Rooms 14 en suite S £90-£130; D £130-£290
Facilities FTV iPod docking station tea/coffee Dinner available Direct Dial Cen ht Licensed Wi-fi 🦶 Complimentary leisure facilities at nearby hotel
Parking 16 Notes LB ⊗ No Children 18yrs

PREMIER COLLECTION

Newstead

★★★★★ GUEST HOUSE

New Rd LA23 2EE
☎ 015394 44485 📠 015394 88904
e-mail: info@newstead-guesthouse.co.uk
dir: *0.5m from A591 between Windermere & Bowness*

A family home set in landscaped gardens, this spacious Victorian house offers very comfortable well-equipped accommodation. The attractive bedrooms are very individual and retain original features such as fireplaces as well as many thoughtful extra touches. There is an elegant lounge and a smart dining room where freshly cooked breakfasts are served at individual tables.

Rooms 9 en suite (1 fmly) Facilities FTV TV7B tea/coffee Cen ht Wi-fi Free use of Parklands Leisure Club
Parking 10 Notes ⊗ No Children 7yrs ✉

PREMIER COLLECTION

Oakbank House

★★★★★ GUEST HOUSE

Helm Rd LA23 3BU
☎ 015394 43386 📠 015394 47965
e-mail: enquiries@oakbankhousehotel.co.uk
web: www.oakbankhousehotel.co.uk
dir: *Exit A591 through town centre into Bowness. Helm Rd 100yds on left after cinema*

Oakbank House is just off the main street in Bowness village, overlooking Windermere and the fells beyond. Bedrooms are individually styled, attractive and very well equipped; most have stunning lake views. There is an elegant lounge with a perpetual coffee pot, and delicious breakfasts are served at individual tables in the dining room.

Rooms 12 rms (11 en suite) (1 pri facs) (3 GF) S £55-£90; D £50-£120* Facilities FTV Lounge tea/coffee Cen ht Wi-fi Free membership of local country club Extras Speciality toiletries Parking 14 Notes LB ⊗ RS 20-26 Dec

PREMIER COLLECTION

The Woodlands

★★★★★ GUEST HOUSE

New Rd LA23 2EE
☎ 015394 43915 📠 015394 43915
e-mail: enquiries@woodlands-windermere.co.uk
web: www.woodlands-windermere.co.uk
dir: *One-way system through town down New Rd towards lake, premises by war memorial clock*

Just a short walk from Lake Windermere, guests can expect stylish accommodation and friendly, attentive service. Bedrooms (including two contemporary 4-poster rooms) have been individually decorated and feature quality furnishings and accessories, such as flat screen TVs. Guests are welcome to relax in the comfortable lounge where there is also a well stocked bar offering beers, wine, champagnes and rich Italian coffees. A wide choice is offered at breakfast which is served in the spacious dining room.

Rooms 14 en suite (2 fmly) (3 GF) Facilities tea/coffee Dinner available Cen ht Licensed Free facilities at local leisure/sports club Parking 17

The Cottage

★★★★ 🏠 GUEST ACCOMMODATION

Elleray Rd LA23 1AG
☎ 015394 44796
e-mail: enquiries@thecottageguesthouse.com
dir: *A591, past Windermere Hotel, in 150yds left into Elleray Rd. The Cottage 150yds on left*

Built in 1847, this attractive house offers a blend of modern and traditional styles. The tastefully furnished bedrooms are well equipped and comfortable. A wide choice of freshly cooked breakfasts is served in the spacious dining room at individual tables.

Rooms 8 en suite (2 GF) S £28-£44; D £56-£90
Facilities FTV tea/coffee Cen ht Parking 8 Notes ⊗ No Children 11yrs Closed Nov-Jan

Dene House

★★★★ GUEST ACCOMMODATION

Kendal Rd LA23 3EW
☎ 015394 48236 📠 015394 48236
e-mail: denehouse@ignetics.co.uk
dir: *0.2m S of Bowness centre on A5074, next to Burnside Hotel*

A friendly welcome awaits you at this smart Victorian house, in a peaceful location just a short walk from the centre of Bowness. The elegant bedrooms are generally spacious, individually decorated and are particularly well equipped. Afternoon tea is served on the patio, which overlooks a well-tended garden. A car park is available.

Rooms 7 rms (6 en suite) (1 pri facs) (1 GF) S £37-£45; D £74-£96* Facilities FTV iPod docking station tea/coffee Cen ht Wi-fi Nearby leisure centre facilities available Parking 7 Notes LB ⊗ No Children 10yrs

Fairfield House and Gardens

★★★★ 🏠 GUEST HOUSE

Brantfell Rd, Bowness-on-Windermere LA23 3AE
☎ 015394 46565 📠 015394 46564
e-mail: tonyandliz@the-fairfield.co.uk
web: www.the-fairfield.co.uk
dir: *Into Bowness town centre, turn opposite St Martin's Church & sharp left by Spinnery restaurant, house 200mtrs on right*

Situated just above Bowness and Lake Windermere this Lakeland country house is tucked away in a half acre of secluded, peaceful gardens. The house has been beautifully appointed to combine Georgian and Victorian features with stylish, contemporary design. Guests are shown warm hospitality and can relax in the delightful lounge. Bedrooms are well furnished, varying in size and style with some featuring luxurious bathrooms. Delicious breakfasts are served in the attractive dining room or on the terrace in warmer weather.

Fairfield House and Gardens

Rooms 10 en suite (2 fmly) (3 GF) S £80–£90; D £80–£130* **Facilities** Lounge tea/coffee Cen ht Licensed Wi-fi ⬥ ♨ 18 ⬥ **Conf** Max 20 Thtr 20 Class 10 Board 12 **Parking** 10 **Notes** LB No Children 10yrs

Glenville House

★★★★ GUEST HOUSE

Lake Rd LA23 2EQ
☎ 015394 43371 ▤ 015394 48457
e-mail: mail@glenvillehouse.co.uk
dir: *Off A591 into Windermere, B5074 to Bowness, Glenville 0.5m on right next to St John's Church*

This traditional Lakeland stone house has a relaxing and friendly atmosphere, and is just a short walk from the town centre and Lake Windermere. Breakfast, including a wide choice of cooked dishes, is served in the pleasant dining room. Bedrooms are attractively decorated and furnished with good quality en suite bathrooms.

Rooms 7 en suite (1 GF) **Facilities** STV tea/coffee Cen ht Wi-fi **Parking** 7 **Notes** LB ⊗ No Children

The Hideaway at Windermere

★★★★ ⊛⊛ RESTAURANT WITH ROOMS

Phoenix Way LA23 1DB
☎ 015394 43070
e-mail: eatandstay@thehideawayatwindermere.co.uk
web: www.thehideawayatwindermere.co.uk
dir: *Exit A591 at Ravensworth B&B, into Phoenix Way, The Hideaway 100mtrs on right*

Quietly tucked away, this beautiful Victorian Lakeland house is personally-run by owners Richard and Lisa. Delicious food, individually designed bedrooms and warm hospitality ensure an enjoyable stay. There is a beautifully appointed lounge looking out to the garden, and the restaurant is split between two light and airy rooms; here guests will find the emphasis is on fresh, local ingredients and attentive, yet friendly service. Bedrooms vary in size and style - the larger rooms feature luxury bathrooms.

Rooms 10 en suite 1 annexe en suite D £90–£190 **Facilities** FTV Lounge tea/coffee Dinner available Direct Dial Cen ht Wi-fi ⬥ Off-site spa facilities available **Parking** 15 **Notes** LB ⊗ No Children 12yrs Closed Jan-mid Feb RS Mon & Tue Rest closed for dinner (ex New Year) No coaches

Jerichos

★★★★★ ⊛⊛ RESTAURANT WITH ROOMS

College Rd LA23 1BX
☎ 015394 42522 ▤ 015394 88899
e-mail: info@jerichos.co.uk
dir: *A591 to Windermere, 2nd left into Elleray Rd then 1st right into College Rd*

Dating back to around 1870, this centrally located property has been lovingly restored by its current owners. All the elegantly furnished bedrooms are en suite and the top floor rooms have views of the fells. Breakfast is served in the Restaurant Room, and the comfortable lounge has a real fire to relax by on chillier days. The chef/proprietor has established a strong reputation for his creative menus that use the best local and seasonal produce. The restaurant is always busy so booking is essential. Wi-fi is available.

Rooms 10 en suite S £45–£55; D £75–£125* **Facilities** FTV iPod docking station Lounge tea/coffee Dinner available Cen ht Wi-fi ⬥ **Extras** Speciality toiletries **Parking** 12 **Notes** LB ⊗ No Children 12yrs Closed 20 Nov-10 Dec & 3wks from 8 Jan No coaches

The Wild Boar

★★★★ INN

Crook LA23 3NF
☎ 015394 45225 ▤ 015394 42498
e-mail: thewildboar@englishlakes.co.uk
dir: *2.5m S of Windermere on B5284. From Crook 3.5m, on right*

Steeped in history this former coaching inn enjoys a peaceful rural location close to Windermere. Public areas include a welcoming lounge and a cosy bar where an extensive choice of wines, ales and whiskies are served. The Grill and recent addition of a Smokehouse feature quality local and seasonal ingredients. Bedrooms, some with four-poster beds, vary in style and size. Leisure facilities are available close by.

Rooms 33 en suite (2 fmly) (9 GF) **Facilities** FTV tea/coffee Dinner available Direct Dial Cen ht **Conf** Thtr 40 Class 10 Board 20 **Parking** 60 **Notes** LB

Annisgarth B&B

★★★★ ⌂ BED AND BREAKFAST

48 Craig Walk LA23 2JT
☎ 015394 43866 ▤ 015394 43866
e-mail: stayannisgarth@ymail.com
dir: *After police station turn left onto Beresford Rd, left again at top of road, Annisgarth on left*

This friendly B&B is located in a quiet location just a short stroll away from Bowness-on-Windermere. The bedrooms offer a good level of comfort and are all thoughtfully equipped. A good quality breakfast with fresh ingredients can be enjoyed in the morning, and warm hospitality is a strength here.

Rooms 3 rms (2 en suite) (1 pri facs) (1 fmly) **Facilities** FTV tea/coffee Cen ht Wi-fi **Notes** ⊗ No Children 10yrs ⊛

Blenheim Lodge

★★★★ GUEST ACCOMMODATION

Brantfell Rd, Bowness-on-Windermere LA23 3AE
☎ 015394 43440
e-mail: enquiries@blenheim-lodge.com
dir: *From Windermere to Bowness village, left at mini-rdbt, up to top of Brantfell Rd & turn right*

From a peaceful position above the town of Bowness, Blenheim Lodge has some stunning panoramic views of Lake Windermere. Bedrooms are well equipped featuring antique furnishings and pocket-sprung mattresses. Most beds are antiques themselves and include two William IV four-posters and three Louis XV beds. There is a comfortable lounge and a beautifully decorated dining room.

Rooms 11 rms (10 en suite) (1 pri facs) (2 fmly) (2 GF) S £55.75–£63; D £88–£150* **Facilities** FTV TVL tea/coffee Licensed ⬥ 2 free fishing permits/free country club membership **Parking** 11 **Notes** LB ⊗ Closed 25 Dec RS 20-27 Dec may open, phone for details

The Coach House

★★★★ GUEST ACCOMMODATION

Lake Rd LA23 2EQ
☎ 015394 44494
e-mail: enquiries@lakedistrictbandb.com
web: www.lakedistrictbandb.com
dir: *A591 to Windermere, house 0.5m on right opposite St Herbert's Church*

Expect a relaxed and welcoming atmosphere at this stylish house, which has a minimalist interior with bright decor and cosmopolitan furnishings. The attractive bedrooms are well equipped. There is a reception lounge, and a breakfast room where freshly prepared breakfasts feature the best of local produce.

Rooms 5 en suite D £50-£85 **Facilities** FTV tea/coffee Cen ht Wi-fi Use of local health & leisure club **Parking** 5 **Notes** LB ⊗ No Children 12yrs Closed 24-26 Dec

WINDERMERE *continued*

The Coppice

★★★★ 🏠 🍴 GUEST HOUSE

Brook Rd LA23 2ED
☎ 015394 88501 📠 015394 42148
e-mail: chris@thecoppice.co.uk
web: www.thecoppice.co.uk
dir: *0.25m S of village centre on A5074*

This attractive detached house lies between Windermere and Bowness. There are colourful public rooms and bedrooms, and a restaurant serving freshly prepared local produce. The bedrooms vary in size and style and have good facilities.

Rooms 9 en suite (2 fmly) (1 GF) **Facilities** tea/coffee Dinner available Cen ht Licensed Wi-fi Private leisure club membership **Parking** 10

Fir Trees

★★★★ GUEST HOUSE

Lake Rd LA23 2EQ
☎ 015394 42272 📠 015394 42512
e-mail: enquiries@fir-trees.co.uk
web: www.fir-trees.co.uk
dir: *Exit A591 through town, Lake Rd in 0.5m, Fir Trees on left after clock tower*

Located halfway between Windermere town and the lake, this spacious Victorian house offers attractive and well equipped accommodation. Bedrooms are generously proportioned and have many thoughtful extra touches. Breakfasts, featuring the best of local produce, are served at individual tables in the smart dining room.

Rooms 9 en suite (2 fmly) (3 GF) S £55-£66; D £68-£76 **Facilities** tea/coffee Dinner available Cen ht Wi-fi Fishing **Parking** 9 **Notes** LB ⊗ No Children 5yrs

Glencree

★★★★ GUEST HOUSE

Lake Rd LA23 2EQ
☎ 015394 45822 & 07974 697114 📠 05603 420040
e-mail: h.butterworth@btinternet.com
web: www.glencreelakes.co.uk
dir: *From town centre signs for Bowness & The Lake, Glencree on right after large wooded area on right*

Colourful hanging baskets and floral displays adorn the car park and entrance to Glencree, which lies between Windermere and Bowness. Bedrooms are brightly decorated and individually furnished. The attractive lounge, with an honesty bar, is next to the dining room, where breakfasts are served at individual tables.

Rooms 6 en suite (1 fmly) (1 GF) **Facilities** FTV TVL tea/coffee Dinner available Cen ht Licensed Wi-fi **Parking** 6 **Notes** ⊗

The Haven

★★★★ BED AND BREAKFAST

10 Birch St LA23 1EG
☎ 015394 44017
e-mail: thehaven.windermere@btopenworld.com
dir: *On A5074 enter one-way system, 3rd left into Birch St*

Built from Lakeland slate and stone, this Victorian house is just a stroll from the town centre and shops. The bright, spacious bedrooms offer en suite or private facilities, and one has a Victorian brass bed. A hearty Cumbrian breakfast is served in the well-appointed dining room that doubles as a lounge.

Rooms 3 en suite (1 fmly) D £56-£80* **Facilities** FTV DVD Lounge tea/coffee Cen ht Wi-fi 🔒 **Parking** 3 **Notes** LB ⊗ No Children 7yrs

Holly-Wood Guest House

★★★★ GUEST HOUSE

Holly Rd LA23 2AF
☎ 015394 42219
e-mail: info@hollywoodguesthouse.co.uk
web: www.hollywoodguesthouse.co.uk
dir: *M6 junct 36 left onto A590 signed Kendal then A591 towards Windermere, left into town, left again into Ellerthwaite Rd, next left into Holly Rd*

This attractive Victorian end terrace is located in a quiet residential area just a few minutes' walk from the town centre. Guests are offered a friendly welcome, comfortable, well equipped bedrooms and a freshly prepared breakfast. Limited off-street parking is also available.

Rooms 6 en suite (1 fmly) S £37.50-£42.50; D £65-£82 **Facilities** FTV iPod docking station tea/coffee Cen ht Wi-fi 🔒 **Extras** Speciality toiletries **Parking** 3 **Notes** ⊗ No Children 10yrs Closed 23-27 Dec

Save on B&Bs and Hotels. Book at theAA.com/hotel

CUMBRIA 95 ENGLAND

Invergarry Guest House

★★★ GUEST HOUSE

3 Thornbarrow Rd LA23 2EW
☎ **015394 44561**
e-mail: invergarryguesthouse@btinternet.com
dir: *From Kendal follow signs to Windermere, take 1st left in town. Around one-way system into New Rd, then Lake Rd towards lake, 1st left after zebra crossing*

Invergarry is a small traditional Lakeland guest house. The bedrooms are comfortable and have flat screen TVs as well as some traditional pieces of furniture; all are en suite with good sized shower rooms. Garden rooms are spacious and well-behaved dogs are welcome here. The location of the house is ideal for touring the Lakes or visiting local attractions such as the Beatrix Potter World. Wi-fi is also available.

Rooms 4 en suite 1 annexe en suite (1 GF) S £60-£99; D £77-£99* **Facilities** FTV tea/coffee Cen ht Wi-fi ⬧ **Extras** Home-made cake, marmalade & jam **Parking** 1 **Notes** LB No Children 18yrs Closed Nov-Mar

The Old Court House

★★★★ GUEST HOUSE

Lake Rd LA23 3AP
☎ **015394 45096**
e-mail: alison@theoch.co.uk
dir: *On Windermere-Bowness road at junct Longlands Rd*

Guests are given a warm welcome at this attractive former Victorian police station and courthouse, located in the centre of Bowness. Comfortable, pine-furnished bedrooms offer a good range of extra facilities. Freshly prepared breakfasts are served in the bright ground-floor dining room.

Rooms 6 en suite (2 GF) S £35-£60; D £60-£90* **Facilities** tea/coffee Cen ht Wi-fi **Parking** 6 **Notes** LB ⊗ No Children 10yrs

The Willowsmere

★★★★ ⬧ GUEST HOUSE

Ambleside Rd LA23 1ES
☎ **015394 43575** ▤ **015394 44962**
e-mail: info@thewillowsmere.com
web: www.thewillowsmere.com
dir: *On A591, 500yds on left after Windermere station, towards Ambleside*

The Willowsmere is a friendly, family-run establishment within easy walking distance of the town centre. It stands in a colourful, well-tended garden, with a patio and water feature to the rear. The attractive bedrooms are spacious, and there is a choice of inviting lounges and a well-stocked bar. Delicious breakfasts are served at individual tables in the stylish dining room.

Rooms 12 en suite (1 GF) **Facilities** TVL tea/coffee Cen ht Licensed Wi-fi Free use of pool, sauna and gym at local hotel **Parking** 15 **Notes** ⊗ No Children 12yrs

Rockside Guest House

★★★★ 🅰 GUEST HOUSE

25 Church St LA23 1AQ
☎ **015394 45343**
e-mail: enquiries@rockside-guesthouse.co.uk
Rooms 9 en suite D £60-£90*

Broadlands Guest House

★★★ GUEST HOUSE

19 Broad St LA23 2AB
☎ **015394 46532**
e-mail: enquiries@broadlandsbandb.co.uk
dir: *From A591 follow one-way system, left into Broad St after pedestrian crossing*

Warm and genuine hospitality is offered at this attractive house opposite the park and library, convenient for central amenities. Bedrooms are pleasantly co-ordinated and comfortably furnished. Freshly prepared breakfasts featuring local and home-made produce are served in the attractive ground floor dining room.

Rooms 3 en suite S £35-£40; D £65-£75* **Facilities** FTV tea/coffee Cen ht Wi-fi ⬧ 36 **Notes** LB ⊗ No Children Closed Dec-Feb

Brook House

★★★ GUEST HOUSE

30 Ellerthwaite Rd LA23 2AH
☎ **015394 44932**
e-mail: stay@brookhouselakes.co.uk
web: www.brookhouselakes.co.uk
dir: *M6 junct 36, A591, through one-way system. Ellerthwaite Rd 2nd left, 200yds on right*

Brook House is a Lakeland stone Victorian guest house located in a quiet part of Windermere and offers a very relaxed friendly atmosphere. Accessible with or without a car and close to all amenities, it is a perfect base for exploring the Lake District. Private parking and a guest lounge are also available. Whisky warmer weekends are run through winter.

Brook House

Rooms 5 en suite (1 fmly) **Facilities** FTV tea/coffee Cen ht **Parking** 5 **Notes** ⊗

Adam Place Guest House

★★★ GUEST HOUSE

1 Park Av LA23 2AR
☎ **015394 44600 & 07879 640757** ▤ **015394 44600**
e-mail: adamplacewindermere@yahoo.com
web: www.adam-place.co.uk
dir: *Exit A591 into Windermere, through town centre, left into Ellerthwaite Rd & Park Av*

Located in a mainly residential area within easy walking distance of lake and town centre, this stone Victorian house has been renovated to provide comfortable and homely bedrooms. Comprehensive breakfasts are served in the cosy dining room and there is a pretty patio garden.

Rooms 5 en suite (2 fmly) S £38-£48; D £76-£96 **Facilities** FTV tea/coffee Cen ht ⬧ **Notes** LB ⊗ No Children 6yrs

Green Gables Guest House

★★★ GUEST HOUSE

37 Broad St LA23 2AB
☎ **015394 43886**
e-mail: info@greengablesguesthouse.co.uk
dir: *A591 into Windermere, 1st left after pelican crossing, opposite car park*

Aptly named, Green Gables is a friendly guest house looking onto Elleray Gardens. Just a short walk from the centre, the house is attractively furnished and offers bright, fresh and well appointed bedrooms. There is a comfortable bar-lounge, and substantial breakfasts are served in the spacious dining room.

Rooms 7 rms (4 en suite) (3 pri facs) (3 fmly) (1 GF) **Facilities** TVL tea/coffee Cen ht Licensed **Notes** ⊗ Closed 23-27 Dec

The Sleepwell Inn

★★★ GUEST ACCOMMODATION

Washington St CA14 3AY
☎ 01900 65772 🗎 01900 68770
e-mail: kawildwchotel@aol.com
dir: M6 junct 40, W on A66. At bottom of Ramsay Brow
left into Washington St, 300yds on left opposite church

Comfortable and well appointed accommodation situated
just 100 meters from sister property, the Washington
Central Hotel. Guests have full use of these facilities and
this is where breakfast is served. Limited off-road car
parking is available to the rear. Rooms differ in size and
styles with some inter-connecting rooms available.

Rooms 24 en suite (4 fmly) (12 GF) S £50; D £70 (room
only)* **Facilities** FTV Lounge TVL tea/coffee Dinner
available Direct Dial Cen ht Licensed Wi-fi 🔒 Facilities
available at Washington Central Hotel **Parking** 32
Notes LB ⊗ Civ Wed 300

DERBYSHIRE

PREMIER COLLECTION

Turlow Bank

★★★★★ 🏠 BED AND BREAKFAST

Hognaston DE6 1PW
☎ 01335 370299 🗎 01335 370299
e-mail: turlowbank@w3z.co.uk
web: www.turlowbank.co.uk
dir: Off B5035 to Hognaston (signed Hognaston only),
through village towards Hulland Ward, Turlow Bank
0.5m, look for clock tower

Set in delightful gardens on a superb elevated position
close to Carsington Water, this extended 19th-century
farmhouse provides high levels of comfort with
excellent facilities. Bedrooms are equipped with many
thoughtful extras and feature quality modern
bathrooms. Comprehensive breakfasts, which include
free-range chicken or duck eggs, are served at a family
table in the cosy dining room. A spacious lounge is
available. Hospitality is memorable.

Rooms 2 en suite D £76-£90* **Facilities** TVL tea/coffee
Cen ht Wi-fi 🥄 🔒 **Parking** 6 **Notes** ⊗ No Children 12yrs
Closed 25-27 Dec 📧

Compton House

★★★★ GUEST ACCOMMODATION

27-31 Compton DE6 1BX
☎ 01335 343100
e-mail: jane@comptonhouse.co.uk
web: www.comptonhouse.co.uk
dir: A52 from Derby into Ashbourne, over lights at bottom
of hill, house 100yds on left opposite garage

Within easy walking distance of the central attractions,
this conversion of three cottages has resulted in a house
with good standards of comfort and facilities. Bedrooms
are filled with homely extras and comprehensive
breakfasts are served in the cottage-style dining room.

Rooms 5 en suite (2 fmly) (1 GF) **Facilities** TVL tea/coffee
Cen ht Wi-fi **Parking** 6

Mercaston Hall (SK279419)

★★★★ FARMHOUSE

Mercaston DE6 3BL
☎ 01335 360263 & 07836 648102   Mr & Mrs A Haddon
e-mail: mercastonhall@btinternet.com
dir: Exit A52 in Brailsford into Luke Ln, 1m, right at 1st
x-rds, house 1m on right

Located in a pretty hamlet, this medieval building retains
many original features. Bedrooms are homely, and
additional facilities include an all-weather tennis court
and a livery service. Wi-fi access is also available. This is
a good base for visiting local stately homes, the Derwent
Valley mills and Dovedale.

Rooms 3 en suite S £55; D £80* **Facilities** FTV DVD
Lounge tea/coffee Cen ht Wi-fi 🌳 🔒 **Extras** Fridges in all
rooms **Parking** 3 **Notes** No Children 5yrs Closed Xmas 📧
60 acres mixed

The Wheel House

★★★★ 🏠 BED AND BREAKFAST

Belper Rd, Hulland Ward DE6 3EE
☎ 01335 372837 🗎 01335 372837
e-mail: thewheelhouse@btinternet.com
dir: Between Ashbourne & Belper on A517

This comfortably furnished house is set in open
countryside on the main road between Ashbourne and
Belper. The bedrooms are well furnished and a cosy
lounge is also available. Breakfasts are hearty, and
guests can expect friendly and attentive service.

Rooms 3 en suite S £45-£50; D £65-£75 **Facilities** FTV
TVL tea/coffee Dinner available Cen ht Wi-fi 🔒
Extras Bottled water, jar of sweets **Parking** 5 **Notes** LB ⊗

Homesclose House

★★★ BED AND BREAKFAST

DE6 2DA
☎ 01335 324475
e-mail: gilltomlinson@tiscali.co.uk
dir: Off A52 into village centre

Stunning views of the surrounding countryside and
manicured gardens are a feature of this beautifully
maintained dormer bungalow. Bedrooms are filled with
homely extras, and an attractive dining room with one
family table is the setting for breakfast.

Rooms 3 rms (2 en suite) (1 fmly) (1 GF) S £28-£30;
D £50-£55* **Facilities** FTV tea/coffee Cen ht Wi-fi 🔒
Parking 4 **Notes** LB Closed Dec-Jan 📧

Avenue House

★★★★ GUEST ACCOMMODATION

The Avenue DE45 1EQ
☎ 01629 812467
dir: Exit A6 onto The Avenue, 1st house on right

Located a short walk from the town centre, this
impressive Victorian house has original features
complemented by the decor and furnishings. Bedrooms
have many thoughtful extras and the modern bathrooms
contain power showers. Hearty English breakfasts are
served in the traditionally furnished dining room.

Rooms 3 en suite **Facilities** FTV tea/coffee Cen ht
Parking 3 **Notes** ⊗ 📧

Wyedale Bed & Breakfast

★★★★ BED AND BREAKFAST

Wyedale House, 25 Holywell DE45 1BA
☎ 01629 812845
dir: 500yds SE of town centre, off A6 (Haddon Rd)

Wyedale is close to the town centre and is ideal for
relaxing or touring. Bedrooms, one of which is on the
ground floor, are spacious and freshly decorated.
Breakfast is served in the attractive dining room, which
overlooks the rear patio.

Rooms 4 en suite (1 fmly) (1 GF) S fr £45; D fr £60*
Facilities tea/coffee Cen ht Wi-fi 🌳 Fishing 🔒 **Parking** 5
Notes ⊗ Closed 31 Dec RS 24 Dec

Wyeclose

★★★ BED AND BREAKFAST

5 Granby Croft DE45 1ET
☎ 01629 813702
e-mail: h.wilson@talk21.com
dir: Exit A6 (Matlock St) into Granby Rd & Granby Croft

Located in a quiet cul-de-sac in the town centre, this
Edwardian house provides thoughtfully furnished
bedroom accommodation with smart modern bathrooms
and an attractive dining room, the setting for

comprehensive breakfasts. Original family art is a feature in the ground-floor areas.

Rooms 2 rms (1 en suite) (1 pri facs) S fr £40; D £60 **Facilities** FTV DVD tea/coffee Cen ht Wi-fi 🅿 **Parking** 3 **Notes** ⊗ No Children 8yrs Closed Xmas & New Year ⊜

Everton

★★★ GUEST HOUSE

Haddon Rd DE45 1AW
☎ 01629 815028
e-mail: trish@evertonbandb.co.uk
dir: S of Bakewell on A6

Ideally located opposite a public park and a few minutes walk from central attractions, this large semi-detached house provides comfortable homely bedrooms. Delicious cooked breakfasts are served in an attractive pine-furnished dining room.

Rooms 3 rms (2 en suite) (1 pri facs) (1 fmly) **Facilities** tea/coffee Cen ht **Parking** 6 **Notes** ⊗ Closed 24-26 Dec RS 30-31 Dec ⊜

BAMFORD   Map 16 SK28

Thornhill View

★★★ GUEST ACCOMMODATION

Hope Rd, Bamford S33 0AL
☎ 01433 651823 & 07792 782565
e-mail: thornhill4bb@aol.com
dir: 0.5m SW of Bamford. On A6187 pass Thornhill Ln junct

Comfortable accommodation in a secluded location, set back from the main road running through the Hope Valley near to the Rising Sun Inn. Compact bedrooms are well equipped, and Jo Fairbairn is a caring hostess.

Rooms 3 rms (2 en suite) (1 pri facs) (2 GF) S £40-£50; D £64* **Facilities** FTV DVD tea/coffee Cen ht Wi-fi **Parking** 3 **Notes** LB ⊗ ⊜

BEELEY   Map 16 SK26

The Devonshire Arms at Beeley

★★★★★ ⊛⊛ INN

Devonshire Square DE4 2NR
☎ 01629 733259 & 01756 718111 📠 01629 734542
e-mail: enquiries@devonshirebeeley.co.uk
web: www.devonshirebeeley.co.uk
dir: B6012 towards Matlock, pass Chatsworth House. After 1.5m turn left, 2nd entrance to Beeley

The Devonshire Arms is a picturesque country inn at the heart of village life. It offers all the charm and character of a historic inn with a warm and comfortable interior, full of oak beams and stone crannies, but venture inside a little further and the decor is the startlingly different; the brasserie has contemporary bar, glass-fronted wine store and colourful furnishings. For the ultimate escape, there are four stylish cottage bedrooms.

Rooms 4 en suite 4 annexe en suite (1 fmly) (2 GF) S £109-£189; D £129-£219* **Facilities** STV tea/coffee Dinner available Direct Dial Cen ht Wi-fi **Parking** 40 **Notes** No coaches

---

BELPER   Map 11 SK34

PREMIER COLLECTION

Dannah Farm Country House

★★★★★ 🌂 GUEST ACCOMMODATION

Bowmans Ln, Shottle DE56 2DR
☎ 01773 550273 & 550630 📠 01773 550590
e-mail: slack@dannah.co.uk
web: www.dannah.co.uk
dir: A517 from Belper towards Ashbourne, 1.5m right into Shottle after Hanging Gate pub on right, over x-rds & right

Part of the Chatsworth Estates at Shottle, on an elevated position with stunning views, this impressive Georgian house and its outbuildings have been renovated to provide luxurious, individually styled bedrooms. Two have private hot tubs, one has a sauna, and there is a Spa Cabin that can be booked separately. The elegant dining room is the setting for memorable breakfasts, which make use of the finest local produce.

Rooms 8 en suite (1 fmly) (2 GF) S £85-£150; D £165-£275* **Facilities** FTV DVD iPod docking station Lounge tea/coffee Cen ht Licensed Wi-fi Sauna Leisure cabin, hot tub **Extras** Bath robes **Parking** 20 **Notes** LB ⊗ Closed 24-26 Dec

---

PREMIER COLLECTION

Chevin Green Farm

★★★★★ GUEST ACCOMMODATION

Chevin Rd DE56 2UN
☎ 01773 822328 📠 01773 822328
e-mail: chevingreenfarm@btinternet.com
dir: Exit A6 opposite Strutt Arms at Milford into Chevin Rd, 1.5m on left

Mr and Mrs Marley welcome guests to this beautiful stone building, appointed to a high standard with original beams, lovely finishing touches and stunning views of the Derwent Valley and beyond. Bedrooms are individually styled, featuring high quality furnishings and excellent bathrooms. Breakfast focuses on home-made and local ingredients. The lounge and wonderful gardens also provide additional space for guests to relax.

Rooms 5 en suite (1 fmly) (1 GF) S £39-£70; D £78-£140* **Facilities** FTV DVD TVL tea/coffee Cen ht Wi-fi **Extras** Bottled water **Parking** 5 **Notes** LB ⊗ No Children 16yrs Closed Xmas & New Year

---

BONSALL   Map 16 SK25

Pig of Lead

★★★★ GUEST ACCOMMODATION

Via Gellia Rd DE4 2AJ
☎ 01629 820040 📠 01629 820040
e-mail: pigoflead@aol.com
dir: 0.5m SE of Bonsall on A5012

This delightful property dating back over two hundred years was once an inn named after a measurement of lead, which used to be mined locally. Only five minutes from Matlock Bath, this is a good base for exploring the area. Individually styled bedrooms are comfortable and well appointed. A warm welcome and hearty breakfasts featuring local produce can be assured here.

Rooms 3 en suite S £45-£60; D £65-£90* **Facilities** FTV DVD Lounge tea/coffee Cen ht Wi-fi **Parking** 3 **Notes** ⊗ No Children 14yrs ⊜

BRADWELL   Map 16 SK18

PREMIER COLLECTION

The Samuel Fox Country Inn

★★★★★ ⊛⊛ INN

Stretfield Rd S33 9JT
☎ 01433 621562 📠 01433 623770
e-mail: thesamuelfox@hotmail.co.uk
dir: M1 junct 29, A617 towards Chesterfield, A619 signed Baslow & Buxton, 2nd rdbt A623 for 7m, take B6049 to Bradwell, through village on left

Recently renamed after Bradwell's most famous son, industrial magnate Samuel Fox, who built the steelworks at Stocksbridge, The Samuel Fox has undergone a full refurbishment and is modern and stylish while retaining its rustic charm. Bedrooms are both immaculately presented and extensively equipped. Service is highly attentive. Modern British cuisine is served in the restaurant with breathtaking views over Bradwell.

Rooms 4 en suite S £85; D £125* **Facilities** FTV tea/coffee Dinner available Direct Dial Cen ht Wi-fi 🅿 **Parking** 15 **Notes** LB ⊗

BUXTON   Map 16 SK07

PREMIER COLLECTION

Buxton's Victorian Guest House

★★★★★ GUEST HOUSE

3A Broad Walk SK17 6JE
☎ 01298 78759 ▤ 01298 74732
e-mail: buxtonvictorian@btconnect.com
web: www.buxtonvictorian.co.uk
dir: *Follow signs to Opera House, proceed to Old Hall Hotel, right into Hartington Rd, car park 100yds on right*

Standing in a prime position overlooking the Pavilion Gardens, this delightfully furnished house has an interesting Victorian style. Bedrooms are individually themed and have many thoughtful extras. A comfortable lounge is available. Excellent breakfasts are served in the Oriental breakfast room and hospitality is first class. Complimentary Wi-fi access is provided. Buxton's Victorian Guest House was a Finalist in the AA Friendliest B&B of the Year Award 2012-13.

Rooms 7 en suite (2 fmly) (1 GF) S £54-£80; D £78-£100* **Facilities** FTV Lounge tea/coffee Cen ht Wi-fi ⌁ 18 Riding ⓐ **Extras** Speciality toiletries - complimentary **Parking** 9 **Notes** LB ⊗ No Children 4yrs Closed 22 Dec-12 Jan

Oldfield Guest House

★★★★ GUEST HOUSE

8 Macclesfield Rd SK17 9AH
☎ 01298 78264
e-mail: avril@oldfieldhousebuxton.co.uk
web: www.oldfieldhousebuxton.co.uk
dir: *On B5059 0.5m SW of town centre*

Located within easy walking distance of the centre, this impressive Victorian house provides spacious bedrooms with modern en suites. Comprehensive breakfasts are served in the bright dining room, and a cosy lounge is available.

Rooms 5 en suite (1 GF) D £80-£90* **Facilities** FTV DVD TVL tea/coffee Cen ht ⌁ 18 **Extras** Speciality toiletries, bottled water **Parking** 7 **Notes** LB ⊗ No Children 8yrs Closed Xmas

Grosvenor House

★★★★ GUEST HOUSE

1 Broad Walk SK17 6JE
☎ 01298 72439
e-mail: grosvenor.buxton@btopenworld.com
dir: *In town centre*

This Victorian house is centrally located overlooking the Pavilion Gardens and Opera House. Bedrooms are carefully furnished and have many thoughtful extras. There is a comfortable period-style sitting room, and freshly prepared imaginative breakfasts are served in the cosy dining room.

Rooms 8 en suite (1 fmly) S £50; D £65-£85* **Facilities** FTV DVD Lounge tea/coffee Cen ht Wi-fi ⌁ **Extras** Fridges in 4 rooms **Parking** 2 **Notes** ⊗ Closed Xmas-New Year

Roseleigh

★★★★ GUEST HOUSE

19 Broad Walk SK17 6JR
☎ 01298 24904 ▤ 01298 24904
e-mail: enquiries@roseleighhotel.co.uk
web: www.roseleighhotel.co.uk
dir: *A6 to Morrisons rdbt, into Dale Rd, right at lights, 100yds left by Swan pub, down hill, right into Hartington Rd*

This elegant property has a prime location overlooking Pavilion Gardens, and the quality furnishings and decor highlight the many original features. The thoughtfully furnished bedrooms have smart modern shower rooms, and a comfortable lounge is also available.

Rooms 14 rms (12 en suite) (2 pri facs) (1 GF) S £40-£92; D £78-£92* **Facilities** Lounge tea/coffee Cen ht Wi-fi **Parking** 9 **Notes** ⊗ No Children 6yrs Closed 16 Dec-16 Jan

CASTLETON   Map 16 SK18

Innkeeper's Lodge Castleton, Peak District

★★★ INN

Castle St S33 8WG
☎ 0845 112 6046
e-mail: info@innkeeperslodge.com
web: www.innkeeperslodge.com

At Innkeeper's Lodge you'll find accommodation with comfort and character in equal measure, and everything needed for a relaxing stay, from easy check-in and free parking to complimentary breakfast and a cosy pub serving great value food and drink on the doorstep. Each Lodge has quality rooms, and there are Lodges in a variety of locations from towns and cities to countryside settings across the UK.

Rooms 15 en suite (4 fmly) (3 GF) **Facilities** FTV tea/coffee Dinner available Direct Dial Wi-fi **Parking**

CHINLEY   Map 16 SK08

The Old Hall Inn

★★★★ INN

Whitehough SK23 6EJ
☎ 01663 750529
e-mail: info@old-hall-inn.co.uk
Rooms 4 en suite S £65-£69; D £69-£95 **Facilities** FTV DVD tea/coffee Dinner available Cen ht Wi-fi ⓐ **Parking** 20 **Notes** LB

CROMFORD   Map 16 SK25

Alison House

★★★★ GUEST ACCOMMODATION

Intake Ln DE4 3RH
☎ 01629 822211 ▤ 01629 822316
e-mail: info@alison-house-hotel.co.uk
web: www.alison-house-hotel.co.uk
dir: *From A6, SE of Cromford, right into Intake Ln*

This very well furnished and spacious 18th-century house stands in seven acres of grounds just a short walk from the village. Public rooms are comfortable and bedrooms are mostly very spacious.

Rooms 16 en suite (1 fmly) (4 GF) **Facilities** tea/coffee Dinner available Direct Dial Cen ht Licensed Wi-fi ⌁ **Conf** Max 40 Thtr 40 Class 40 Board 40 **Parking** 30 **Notes** Civ Wed 50

DERBY   Map 11 SK33

See also Belper & Melbourne

The Derby Conference Centre

★★★★ GUEST ACCOMMODATION

London Rd DE24 8UX
☎ 0845 880 8101 📠 0870 890 0030
e-mail: reservations@thederbyconferencecentre.com
web: www.thederbyconferencecentre.com
dir: *M1 junct 25, A52 towards Derby. Filter left onto
A5111 signed Ring Road. At Raynesway Park rdbt 3rd exit
signed Ring Road/Alvaston. At next rdbt A6 towards Derby
centre. Pass Wickes, left into entrance*

Formerly a railway training centre, this Grade II-listed art
deco building has undergone major refurbishment to
modernise the public areas, meeting rooms and
accommodation, yet it still retains original features such
as the wall paintings by Norman Wilkinson. Extensive
conference facilities include a lecture theatre, and the
grounds are perfect for team building events or wedding
photos. Complimentary Wi-fi access is provided.

Rooms 50 en suite (10 GF) Facilities FTV TVL tea/coffee
Dinner available Cen ht Licensed Wi-fi Pool table
Conf Max 1000 Thtr 400 Class 80 Board 50 Parking 250
Notes ⊗ Closed 24 Dec-4 Jan Civ Wed 400

FENNY BENTLEY   Map 16 SK14

Bentley Brook Inn

★★★ INN

DE6 1LF
☎ 01335 350278 📠 01335 350422
e-mail: all@bentleybrookinn.co.uk
dir: *2m N of Ashbourne at junct of A515 & B5056*

This popular inn is located in the Peak District National
Park, just north of Ashbourne. It is a charming building
with an attractive terrace, sweeping lawns, and nursery
gardens. A well-appointed family restaurant dominates
the ground floor, where a wide range of dishes is
available all day. The character bar serves beer from its
own micro-brewery. Bedrooms are well appointed and
thoughtfully equipped.

Rooms 11 en suite (1 fmly) (2 GF) Facilities TVL tea/
coffee Dinner available Direct Dial Cen ht Wi-fi Conf Max
11 Thtr 11 Class 11 Board 11 Parking 100 Notes Civ Wed
40

FOOLOW   Map 16 SK17

The Bulls Head Inn

★★★★ INN

S32 5QR
☎ 01433 630873 📠 01433 631738
e-mail: wilbnd@aol.com
dir: *Off A623 into Foolow*

Located in the village centre, this popular inn retains
many original features and offers comfortable, well-
equipped bedrooms. Extensive and imaginative bar meals
are served in the traditionally furnished dining room or in
the cosy bar areas. The inn welcomes well-behaved dogs
in the bar (and even muddy boots on the flagstone areas).

Rooms 3 en suite (1 fmly) Facilities tea/coffee Dinner
available Cen ht ♿ 18 Parking 20

FROGGATT   Map 16 SK27

The Chequers Inn

★★★★ ⊛ INN

S32 3ZJ
☎ 01433 630231 📠 01433 631072
e-mail: info@chequers-froggatt.com
dir: *On A625 between Sheffield & Bakewell, 0.75m from
Calver*

A very popular 16th-century inn offering an extensive
range of well-cooked food. The bedrooms are
comprehensively equipped with all modern comforts and
the hospitality is professional and sincere. A good
location for touring Derbyshire, the Peak Park, and
visiting Chatsworth.

Rooms 6 en suite S £85-£115; D £85-£115*
Facilities FTV tea/coffee Dinner available Cen ht Wi-fi
Parking 45 Notes LB ⊗ Closed 25 Dec No coaches

GLOSSOP   Map 16 SK09

Allmans Heath Cottage Bed & Breakfast

★★★★ 🏠 BED AND BREAKFAST

Woodhead Rd SK13 7QE
☎ 01457 857867 & 07783 842900
e-mail: julie@allmansheathcottage.co.uk
dir: *From Glossop town centre lights, proceed up Norfolk
St towards Woodhead for 1m. Continue through tunnel of
trees, on left turning in at farm gate*

Just one mile from Glossop, this converted farm cottage
has beamed ceilings, open fires and many original
features. All the rooms command spectacular views over
open countryside, and hospitality is warm and friendly.

Rooms 2 rms (1 en suite) (1 pri facs) S fr £45; D fr £70*
Facilities FTV TVL tea/coffee Cen ht Wi-fi ♿ Parking 6
Notes ⊗

Woodlands

★★★★ BED AND BREAKFAST

Woodseats Ln, Charlesworth SK13 5DP
☎ 01457 866568 & 07817 595786
e-mail: brian.mairs@sky.com
dir: *3m SW of Glossop. Off A626, 0.5m from Charlesworth
towards Marple*

This delightful Victorian house stands in well-tended
grounds and offers very well-equipped and delightfully
furnished bedrooms. There is a comfy lounge and a
conservatory serving very good breakfasts and lunch.
There is also an award-winning tea room.

Rooms 3 rms (2 en suite) (1 pri facs) S £45-£50;
D £65-£75 Facilities FTV DVD Lounge TVL tea/coffee
Cen ht Licensed Wi-fi ♿ Extras Bath robes, bottled water -
complimentary Parking 6 Notes LB ⊗ No Children 12yrs

GREAT HUCKLOW   Map 16 SK17

The Queen Anne

★★★ 🍴 INN

SK17 8RF
☎ 01298 871246 📠 01298 873504
e-mail: angelaryan100@aol.com
web: www.queenanneinn.co.uk
dir: *Exit A623 onto B6049 to Great Hucklow*

Set in the heart of this pretty village, The Queen Anne has
been a licensed inn for over 300 years and the public
areas retain many original features. The bedrooms are in
a separate building with direct access, and have modern
shower rooms en suite.

Rooms 2 annexe en suite (2 GF) Facilities TVL tea/coffee
Dinner available Cen ht Parking 20 Notes ⊗ No Children
10yrs Closed Xmas & New Year

HARDSTOFT   Map 16 SK46

The Shoulder at Hardstoft

★★★★ ⊛⊛ 🍴 INN

Deep Ln S45 8AF
☎ 01246 850276
e-mail: info@thefamousshoulder.co.uk
dir: *B6039 follow signs for Hardwick Hall, 1st right after
turning off B6039*

This 300-year-old country pub has been carefully
refurbished and there is a friendly atmosphere along with
real ales and log fires. Delicious, home-cooked meals are
skilfully prepared and served throughout the informal bar
and restaurant. Bedrooms vary in size but all are well
furnished and complimentary Wi-fi is provided. There is
also a function room available.

Rooms 4 en suite (1 fmly) Facilities FTV tea/coffee Dinner
available Cen ht Wi-fi Extras Bottled water, home-made
biscuits Conf Max 80 Thtr 80 Class 40 Board 40
Parking 50

HARTINGTON
Map 16 SK16

Bank House Guest House

★★★★ GUEST ACCOMMODATION

Market Place SK17 0AL
☎ 01298 84465
dir: *B5054 into village centre*

Bank House is a very well-maintained Grade II listed Georgian building that stands in the main square of this delightful village. Bedrooms are neat and fresh in appearance, and there is a comfortable television lounge. A hearty breakfast is served in the ground-floor cottage-style dining room.

Rooms 5 rms (3 en suite) (3 fmly) S £30-£38; D £55-£62 **Facilities** FTV TVL tea/coffee Cen ht Wi-fi 🐾 **Parking** 2 **Notes** LB ⊗ Closed Xmas RS 22-28 Dec ⊜

HARTSHORNE
Map 10 SK32

The Mill Wheel

★★★★ ⚜ INN

Ticknall Rd DE11 7AS
☎ 01283 550335 📠 01283 552833
e-mail: info@themillwheel.co.uk
web: www.themillwheel.co.uk
dir: *M42 junct 2, A511 to Woodville, left onto A514 towards Derby to Hartshorne*

This popular inn and restaurant provides a wide range of well-prepared food and has a large mill wheel in the bar. Bedrooms are modern and well-equipped while friendly and attentive service is provided.

Rooms 4 en suite (2 GF) D £56-£60* **Facilities** FTV tea/coffee Dinner available Cen ht Wi-fi **Conf** Max 24 Thtr 24 Board 12 **Parking** 55 **Notes** ⊗

HATHERSAGE
Map 16 SK28

The Plough Inn

★★★★ ⚜ INN

Leadmill Bridge S32 1BA
☎ 01433 650319 📠 01433 651049
e-mail: sales@theploughinn-hathersage.co.uk
web: www.theploughinn-hathersage.co.uk
dir: *1m SE of Hathersage on B6001. Over bridge, 150yds beyond at Leadmill*

This delightful 16th-century inn with beer garden has an idyllic location by the River Derwent. A selection of real ales and imaginative food is served in the spacious public areas, and original fireplaces and exposed beams have been preserved. The attractive, well equipped bedrooms include several refurbished luxury rooms, and Wi-fi access is available throughout.

The Plough Inn

Rooms 3 en suite 2 annexe en suite (1 GF) S £70-£95; D £95-£130* **Facilities** FTV DVD iPod docking station tea/coffee Dinner available Direct Dial Cen ht Wi-fi ⚽ 18 🐾 **Extras** Fruit - complimentary **Parking** 50 **Notes** LB Closed 25 Dec No coaches

The Millstone Inn

★★★★ ⚞ INN

Sheffield Rd S32 1DA
☎ 01433 650258 📠 01433 651664
e-mail: jerry@millstoneinn.co.uk
web: www.millstoneinn.co.uk
dir: *0.5m SE of village on A6187*

This timber and stone inn has a stunning view overlooking the Hope Valley. Real ales, an open fire and friendly service add to the welcoming atmosphere in the bar. Food is served all day, with emphasis on local ingredients and the Terrace Tea Room is open from 8am to 5pm, Monday to Saturday. Bedrooms are spacious, and complimentary Wi-fi is provided.

Rooms 8 en suite (3 fmly) **Facilities** tea/coffee Dinner available Direct Dial Cen ht Wi-fi Gym membership free to guests **Conf** Max 40 Thtr 40 Class 40 Board 40 **Parking** 80

The Scotsman's Pack Inn

★★★★ INN

School Ln S32 1BZ
☎ 01433 650253 📠 01433 650712
e-mail: scotsmans.pack@btinternet.com
dir: *A625 into Hathersage, right into School Ln towards church. Scotsman's Pack 100yds on right*

This comfortable inn on the edge of the village provides a wide range of well-prepared food. The bedrooms are compact, well-furnished and thoughtfully equipped, while the bar, which contains 'Little John's chair', is a great place to meet the locals. Hearty breakfasts are served in the separate dining room, and the staff are very friendly.

Rooms 5 en suite **Facilities** tea/coffee Dinner available Cen ht **Conf** Max 20 **Parking** 17 **Notes** LB ⊗ RS 25 Dec eve no food served

HOPE
Map 16 SK18

PREMIER COLLECTION

Underleigh House

★★★★★ ⚞ GUEST ACCOMMODATION

Lose Hill Ln S33 6AF
☎ 01433 621372 📠 01433 621324
e-mail: info@underleighhouse.co.uk
web: www.underleighhouse.co.uk
dir: *From village church on A6187 into Edale Rd, 1m left into Lose Hill Ln*

Situated at the end of a private lane, surrounded by glorious scenery, Underleigh House was converted from a barn and cottage that dates from 1873, and now offers carefully furnished and attractively decorated bedrooms with modern facilities. One room has a private lounge and others have access to the gardens. There is a very spacious lounge with comfortable chairs and a welcoming log fire. Memorable breakfasts are served at one large table in the dining room.

Rooms 5 en suite (2 GF) S £70-£85; D £90-£105* **Facilities** DVD TVL tea/coffee Direct Dial Cen ht Licensed Wi-fi 🐾 **Extras** Speciality toiletries, fruit, sweets - complimentary **Parking** 6 **Notes** LB No Children 12yrs Closed Xmas, New Year & 6-31 Jan

Stoney Ridge

★★★★ ⚞ GUEST ACCOMMODATION

Granby Rd, Bradwell S33 9HU
☎ 01433 620538
e-mail: info@stoneyridge.org.uk
web: www.stoneyridge.org.uk
dir: *From N end of Bradwell on B6049 into Gore Ln, uphill, pass Ye Olde Bowling Green Inn, left into Granby Rd*

This large, split-level bungalow stands in attractive mature gardens at the highest part of the village and has extensive views. Hens roam freely in the landscaped garden, and their fresh eggs add to the hearty breakfasts. Bedrooms are attractively furnished and thoughtfully equipped, and there is a spacious comfortable lounge and a superb indoor swimming pool.

Rooms 4 rms (3 en suite) (1 pri facs) S £48-£56; D £60-£76 **Facilities** STV FTV TVL tea/coffee Cen ht Wi-fi 🕾 🏐 **Parking** 3 **Notes** LB No Children 10yrs RS Winter Pool may be closed for maintenance

Poachers Arms

★★★★ Ⓐ INN

95 Castleton Rd S33 6SB
☎ 01433 620380
e-mail: btissington95@aol.com
web: www.poachersarms.co.uk
dir: On A625/A6187 between Hope & Castleton

Rooms 4 en suite **Facilities** tea/coffee Dinner available Cen ht Wi-fi **Parking** 30 **Notes** ⊗ No coaches

Round Meadow Barn

★★★ BED AND BREAKFAST

Parsons Ln S33 6RB
☎ 01433 621347 & 07836 689422 📠 01433 621347
e-mail: geof@harrisrmb.freeserve.co.uk
dir: Exit A625 (Hope Rd) N onto Parsons Ln, over rail bridge, in 200yds right into hay barnyard, through gates, across 3 fields, house on left

This converted barn, with original stone walls and exposed timbers, stands in open fields in the picturesque Hope Valley. The bedrooms are large enough for families and there are two modern bathrooms. Breakfast is served at one large table adjoining the family kitchen.

Rooms 3 rms (1 en suite) (2 pri facs) (1 fmly) S £38-£45; D £66-£72* **Facilities** FTV tea/coffee Cen ht 🏐 **Parking** 8 **Notes** LB ⊗

MATLOCK   Map 16 SK35

Holmefield Guest House

★★★★★ 🚪 GUEST HOUSE

Dale Road North, Darley Dale DE4 2HY
☎ 01629 735347
e-mail: holmefieldguesthouse@btinternet.com
web: www.holmefieldguesthouse.co.uk
dir: Between Bakewell & Matlock on A6. 1m from Rowsley & Chatsworth Estate, 0.5m from Peak Rail

Standing in mature grounds between Matlock and Bakewell, this elegant Victorian house has been furnished with flair to offer good levels of comfort and facilities. Imaginative dinners feature seasonal local produce, including some from the Chatsworth Estate. Warm hospitality and attentive service are assured.

Rooms 4 en suite 3 annexe en suite (1 fmly) (2 GF) **Facilities** tea/coffee Dinner available Direct Dial Cen ht Wi-fi Pool table **Parking** 10 **Notes** ⊗

Hearthstone Farm (SK308583)

★★★★ 🏠 FARMHOUSE

Hearthstone Ln, Riber DE4 5JW
☎ 01629 534304 Mrs Gilman
e-mail: enquiries@hearthstonefarm.co.uk
web: www.hearthstonefarm.co.uk
dir: A615 at Tansley (2m E of Matlock), turn opposite Royal Oak towards Riber, at gates to Riber Hall left into Riber Rd, 1st left into Hearthstone Ln, farmhouse on left

Situated on a stunning elevated location, this traditional stone farmhouse retains many original features and is stylishly decorated throughout. Bedrooms are equipped with a wealth of homely extras and comprehensive breakfasts feature the farm's organic produce. There is a very comfortable lounge, and the farm animals in the grounds are an attraction.

Rooms 3 en suite S £50-£55; D £70-£75* **Facilities** FTV TVL tea/coffee Cen ht **Parking** 6 **Notes** LB Closed Xmas & New Year 🐾 150 acres beef/lamb

Hodgkinsons

★★★★ 🚪 GUEST ACCOMMODATION

150 South Pde, Matlock Bath DE4 3NR
☎ 01629 582170 📠 01629 584891
e-mail: enquiries@hodgkinsons-hotel.co.uk
dir: On A6 in village centre, corner of Waterloo Rd & South Parade

This fine Georgian building was renovated in the Victorian era and has many interesting and unusual features. Bedrooms are equipped with fine antique furniture and a wealth of thoughtful extras. The elegant dining room is the setting for imaginative dinners. Hodgkinsons was a Finalist in the AA Friendliest B&B of the Year Award 2012-13.

Rooms 8 en suite (1 fmly) S £45-£85; D £89-£155* **Facilities** FTV tea/coffee Dinner available Direct Dial Cen ht Licensed Wi-fi garden **Conf** Max 12 Thtr 12 Class 12 Board 12 **Parking** 5 **Notes** LB Closed 24-26 Dec

The Pines

★★★★ BED AND BREAKFAST

12 Eversleigh Rd, Darley Bridge DE4 2JW
☎ 01629 732646
e-mail: info@thepinesbandb.co.uk
dir: From Bakewell or Matlock take A6 to Darley Dale. Turn at Whitworth Hotel onto B5057, pass Square & Compass pub & The 3 Stags Heads, The Pines on right

Dating from the 1820s this home as been authentically restored. Standing in a secluded and pretty garden, The Pines makes an ideal location for visiting the Peak District. Three spacious en suite bedrooms are stylishly furnished using rich fabrics. Comprehensive breakfasts, utilising quality local produce, offer a hearty start to the day.

Rooms 3 en suite S £40-£50; D £65-£75 **Facilities** FTV tea/coffee Dinner available Cen ht Wi-fi **Parking** 5 **Notes** LB 🐾

Yew Tree Cottage

★★★★ 🏠 BED AND BREAKFAST

The Knoll, Tansley DE4 5FP
☎ 01629 583862 & 07799 541903
e-mail: enquiries@ytcbb.co.uk
dir: 1.2m E of Matlock. Off A615 into Tansley centre

This 18th-century cottage has been renovated to provide high standards of comfort while retaining original character. Memorable breakfasts are served in the elegant dining room, and a cosy lounge is available. A warm welcome and attentive service are assured. Yew Tree Cottage was a Finalist in the AA Friendliest B&B of the Year Award 2012-13.

Rooms 3 en suite D £75-£95 **Facilities** FTV DVD TVL tea/coffee Cen ht Wi-fi Sauna 🏐 **Parking** 3 **Notes** LB ⊗ No Children 12yrs

Woodside

★★★★ BED AND BREAKFAST

Stanton Lees DE4 2LQ
☎ 01629 734320 📠 01629 734320
e-mail: kmptr21@googlemail.com
web: www.woodsidestantonlees.co.uk
dir: 4m NW of Matlock. A6 onto B5057 into Darley Bridge, right opposite pub to Stanton Lees, right fork in village

Located on an elevated position with stunning views of the surrounding countryside, this mellow stone house has been renovated to provide high standards of comfort and facilities. Carefully decorated bedrooms come with a wealth of thoughtful extras, and ground floor areas include a comfortable lounge and conservatory overlooking the garden, which is home to a variety of wild birds.

Rooms 3 en suite S £40-£42; D £62-£72 **Facilities** FTV TVL tea/coffee Cen ht **Parking** 3 **Notes** ⊗ No Children 3yrs 🐾

MATLOCK *continued*

The Red Lion

★ ★ ★ INN

Matlock Green DE4 3BT
☎ **01629 584888**
dir: *500yds SE of town centre on A632*

This comfortable free house is a good base for exploring Matlock and the surrounding Derbyshire countryside. Each bedroom is comfortably furnished, and one comes complete with a four-poster. Public areas include a games area with open fires, and a restaurant where a wide selection of meals is on offer. Private parking is a bonus.

Rooms 6 en suite **Facilities** tea/coffee Dinner available Cen ht Pool table **Parking** 20 **Notes** ⊗

Farley Farm (SK294622)

★ ★ ★ FARMHOUSE

Farley DE4 5LR
☎ **01629 582533 & 07801 756409**
🖹 **01629 584856 Mrs Brailsford**
e-mail: eric.brailsford@btconnect.com
web: www.farleyfarm.co.uk
dir: *1m N of Matlock. From A6 rdbt towards Bakewell, 1st right, right at top of hill, left up Farley Hill, 2nd farm on left*

Guests can expect a warm welcome at this traditional stone farmhouse. In addition to farming, the proprietors also breed dogs and horses. The bedrooms are pleasantly decorated and equipped with many useful extras. A hearty farmhouse breakfast offers a good start to any day.

Rooms 2 en suite (3 fmly) D £60* **Facilities** FTV TVL tea/coffee Cen ht Riding 🐴 **Parking** 8 **Notes** LB ⊛ 165 acres arable/beef/dairy

Red House Carriage Museum

★ ★ ★ GUEST ACCOMMODATION

Old Rd, Darley Dale DE4 2ER
☎ **01629 733583** 🖹 **01629 733583**
e-mail: redhousestables@hotmail.co.uk
dir: *2m N of Matlock, left from A6, 200yds on left*

Located in a famous working carriage-driving school and museum, this detached house provides homely and thoughtfully equipped bedrooms, including one on the ground floor and two in a former stable. Comprehensive breakfasts are served at a family table in an attractive dining room, and the comfortable lounge area overlooks the spacious gardens.

Rooms 2 rms (1 en suite) 2 annexe en suite (1 fmly) (1 GF) S £30-£40; D £70-£75* **Facilities** tea/coffee Cen ht Horse & carriage trips **Parking** 5 **Notes** ⊗ RS Nov-Mar Mon-Sat 10-4 & Sun 10-2 ⊛

MELBOURNE   Map 11 SK32

The Coach House

★★★★ GUEST HOUSE

69 Derby Rd DE73 8FE
☎ 01332 862338 📠 01332 695281
e-mail: enquiries@coachhouse-hotel.co.uk
web: www.coachhouse-hotel.co.uk
dir: *Off B587 in village centre*

Located in the heart of a conservation area and close to Donington Park and East Midlands Airport, this traditional cottage has been restored to provide good standards of comfort and facilities. Bedrooms are thoughtfully furnished, and two are in converted stables. A lounge and secure parking are available.

Rooms 6 en suite (1 fmly) (3 GF) S £37-£42; D £54-£68*
Facilities FTV TVL tea/coffee Cen ht Wi-fi ⬤ **Parking** 6
Notes LB ⊗

The Paddock

★★★★ ⊛⊛ INN

222 Station Rd DE73 8BQ
☎ 01332 864716 📠 01332 694607
e-mail: reception@paddockmelbourne.com

Formerly known as The Railway due to the track that runs along the rear of the property, The Paddock is popular with locals and residents alike. The fine dining restaurant provides a contemporary backdrop to imaginative dishes; the older inn building has a more traditional feel, with local real ales and hearty meals. The contemporary bedrooms provide comfortable accommodation with modern amenities.

Rooms 8 en suite (1 fmly) (2 GF) S £50-£70;
D £70-£200* **Facilities** FTV Lounge TVL tea/coffee Dinner available Cen ht Wi-fi ⬤ **Extras** Trouser press **Conf** Max 20 Thtr 20 Class 20 Board 20 **Parking** 20 **Notes** LB

The Melbourne Arms

★★★ INN

92 Ashby Rd DE73 8ES
☎ 01332 864949 📠 01332 865525
e-mail: info@melbournearms.co.uk
web: www.melbournearms.co.uk
dir: *3m from East Midlands Airport*

Well located for the airport and Donington Park, this Grade-II listed inn provides modern, thoughtfully equipped bedrooms, one of which is in a converted outbuilding. Ground floor areas include two bars, a coffee shop and an elegant Indian restaurant.

Rooms 10 en suite (1 fmly) (3 GF) S £35-£45;
D £50-£100 **Facilities** FTV Lounge TVL tea/coffee Dinner available Cen ht Wi-fi Fishing Riding Bouncy Castle for children (weather permitting) **Extras** Fridges in some rooms **Conf** Max 25 Thtr 15 Class 15 Board 15 **Parking** 52 **Notes** Closed 26 Dec

See advert on opposite page

NEWHAVEN   Map 16 SK16

PREMIER COLLECTION

The Smithy

★★★★★ 🏠 GUEST ACCOMMODATION

SK17 0DT
☎ 01298 84548
e-mail: lynnandgary@thesmithybedandbreakfast.co.uk
web: www.thesmithybedandbreakfast.co.uk
dir: *0.5m S of Newhaven on A515. Adjacent to Biggin Ln, private driveway opposite Ivy House*

Set in a peaceful location close to the Tissington and High Peak trails, the 17th-century drovers' inn and blacksmith's workshop have been carefully renovated. Bedrooms, which are in a former barn, are well equipped. Enjoyable breakfasts, which include free-range eggs and home-made preserves, are served in the forge, which features the original bellows on the vast open hearth.

Rooms 4 en suite (2 GF) S £45-£50; D £72-£90*
Facilities FTV DVD TVL tea/coffee Cen ht Wi-fi ⬤
Conf Max 20 Thtr 15 Board 10 **Parking** 8 **Notes** LB ⊗
No Children 🐾

NEW MILLS   Map 16 SK08

Pack Horse Inn

★★★★ 🅰 INN

Mellor Rd SK22 4QQ
☎ 01663 742365 📠 01663 741674
e-mail: info@packhorseinn.co.uk
dir: *A6 onto A6015, left at lights. Right at rdbt, 0.5m, left into Mellor Rd*
Rooms 7 en suite 5 annexe en suite (1 fmly) (2 GF)
Facilities tea/coffee Dinner available Cen ht Wi-fi
Parking 50 **Notes** ⊗ No coaches

PILSLEY
Map 16 SK27

Holly Cottage

★★★★ 🏠 BED AND BREAKFAST

DE45 1UH

☎ 01246 582245

e-mail: hollycottagebandb@btinternet.com

dir: *Follow brown tourist signs for Chatsworth & Pilsley. Holly Cottage next to post office in Pilsley*

A warm welcome is assured at this mellow stone cottage, part of a combined Post Office and shop in the conservation area of Pilsley, which is owned by the adjacent Chatsworth Estate. The cosy bedrooms feature a wealth of thoughtful extras, and comprehensive breakfasts, utilising quality local produce, are taken in an attractive pine-furnished dining room.

Rooms 3 en suite **Facilities** tea/coffee Cen ht Wi-fi **Notes** LB ⊗ No Children 10yrs

----

Devonshire Arms Pilsley

★★★ INN

The High St DE45 1UL

☎ 01246 583258

e-mail: res@devonshirehotels.co.uk

dir: *From A619, in Baslow, at rdbt take 1st exit onto B6012. Follow signs to Chatsworth, 2nd right to Pilsley*

The newest addition to the Devonshire Hotels and Restaurant group, The Devonshire Arms at Pilsley is just two miles from Chatsworth House, and also a minute's walk from the Chatsworth farm shop which provides much of the food served. All rooms are en suite, quite individual in design and offer very impressive quality and comfort.

Rooms 7 en suite (1 fmly) **Facilities** tea/coffee Dinner available Cen ht **Parking** 10 **Notes** ⊗ No coaches

ROWSLEY
Map 16 SK26

The Grouse and Claret

★★★★ INN

Station Rd DE4 2EB

☎ 01629 733233 📠 01629 735194

e-mail: grouseandclaret.matlock@marstons.co.uk

dir: *M1 junct 28, A6 5m from Matlock, 3m from Bakewell*

A busy inn with a wide range of dishes available in the spacious bars. Bedrooms are pleasantly furnished and staff are friendly and attentive.

Rooms 8 en suite (2 fmly) **Facilities** STV tea/coffee Dinner available Cen ht Wi-fi **Parking** 78 **Notes** ⊗ No coaches

SWADLINCOTE
Map 10 SK21

Overseale House

★★★ BED AND BREAKFAST

Acresford Rd, Overseal DE12 6HX

☎ 01283 763741

e-mail: oversealehouse@hotmail.com

web: www.oversealehouse.co.uk

dir: *On A444 between Burton upon Trent & M42 junct 11*

Located in the village, this well-proportioned Georgian mansion, built for a renowned industrialist, retains many original features including a magnificent dining room decorated with ornate mouldings. The period-furnished ground floor areas include a cosy sitting room, and bedrooms contain many thoughtful extras.

Rooms 4 en suite 1 annexe en suite (3 fmly) (2 GF) **Facilities** tea/coffee Cen ht Wi-fi **Conf** Max 14 Board 14 **Parking** 6 **Notes** ⊛

TIDESWELL
Map 16 SK17

Poppies

★★★ GUEST ACCOMMODATION

Bank Square SK17 8LA

☎ 01298 871083

e-mail: poptidza@dialstart.net

dir: *On B6049 in village centre opposite NatWest bank*

A friendly welcome is assured at this non-smoking house, located in the heart of a former lead-mining and textile community, a short walk from the 14th-century parish church. The two bedrooms are homely and practical. There is a third room presented as a comfortable lounge, which is also available as an additional bedroom if needed.

Rooms 2 rms (1 en suite) (1 pri facs) (1 fmly) S £27-£39.50; D £54-£59 **Facilities** FTV DVD tea/coffee Cen ht Wi-fi ⓓ **Notes** ⊛

WESTON UNDERWOOD
Map 10 SK24

PREMIER COLLECTION

Park View Farm (SK293425)

★★★★★ FARMHOUSE

DE6 4PA

☎ 01335 360352 & 07771 573057

📠 01335 360352 Mrs Adams

e-mail: enquiries@parkviewfarm.co.uk

web: www.parkviewfarm.co.uk

dir: *From A52/A38 rdbt W of Derby, take A38 N, 1st left to Kedleston Hall. Continue for 1.5m past the Hall, farm on left as you enter the village*

This impressive, vine-covered, Victorian farmhouse is surrounded by beautiful gardens, and forms part of a working organic sheep farm. Each bedroom has an antique four-poster bed, attractive decor, period furniture and pleasant touches such as flowers and books. Breakfasts come straight from the Aga and include home-made bread, fresh fruit compotes, and fresh eggs from the farm's own chickens. Guests have use of a drawing room. There are also two self-catering cottages on the farm.

Rooms 3 en suite **Facilities** FTV TVL tea/coffee Cen ht Wi-fi **Parking** 10 **Notes** ⊗ No Children 8yrs Closed Xmas ⊛ 370 acres organic arable/sheep

WINSTER
Map 16 SK26

Brae Cottage

★★★★ 🅐 GUEST ACCOMMODATION

East Bank DE4 2DT

☎ 01629 650375

dir: *A6 onto B5057, driveway on right past pub*

Rooms 2 annexe en suite (1 fmly) (2 GF) S £45-£60; D £60-£70 **Facilities** tea/coffee Cen ht 🍴 **Parking** 2 **Notes** ⊗ No Children 11yrs ⊛

YOULGREAVE
Map 16 SK26

The George

★★★ INN

Church St DE45 1UW

☎ 01629 636292 📠 01632 636292

dir: *3m S of Bakewell in Youlgreave, opposite church*

The public bars of the 17th-century George are popular with locals and tourists. Bedroom styles vary, and all have shower rooms en suite. Breakfast is served in the lounge bar, and a range of bar meals and snacks is available.

Rooms 3 en suite (1 fmly) **Facilities** tea/coffee Dinner available Cen ht Fishing **Parking** 12 **Notes** ⊛

Save on B&Bs and Hotels. Book at **theAA.com/hotel**

DEVON 105 ENGLAND

DEVON

APPLEDORE
Map 3 SS43

Appledore House

★★★★ GUEST ACCOMMODATION

Meeting St EX39 1RJ
☎ 01237 421471 & 07825 141459
e-mail: info@appledore-house.co.uk
web: www.appledore-house.co.uk
dir: *A361 N Devon Link Road, follow signs to Bideford, then Appledore*

An imposing house set on the hill overlooking the town and across the water towards Instow with a number of rooms having impressive views. A house with high standards and proprietors with a genuine concern for their guests' comfort and wellbeing.

Rooms 5 en suite (1 fmly) (1 GF) S £60-£65; D £80-£115* **Facilities** FTV tea/coffee Cen ht Wi-fi 🔒 **Extras** Cream teas **Conf** Max 20 Thtr 20 Class 20 Board 12 **Parking** 3 **Notes** LB ⊗

ASHBURTON
Map 3 SX77

Greencott

★★★★ GUEST HOUSE

Landscove TQ13 7LZ
☎ 01803 762649
dir: *3m SE of Ashburton. Exit A38 at Peartree junct, Landscove signed on slip road, village green 2m on right, opposite village hall*

Greencott has a peaceful village location and superb country views. Your hosts extend a very warm welcome and there is a relaxed home-from-home atmosphere. Service is attentive and caring and many guests return time and again. Bedrooms are attractive, comfortable and very well equipped. Delicious breakfasts are served around an oak dining table.

Rooms 2 en suite S £25; D £50* **Facilities** TVL tea/coffee Cen ht **Parking** 3 **Notes** LB ⊗ Closed 25-26 Dec ⊛

Gages Mill Country Guest House

★★★★ GUEST ACCOMMODATION

Buckfastleigh Rd TQ13 7JW
☎ 01364 652391
e-mail: katestone@gagesmill.co.uk
web: www.gagesmill.co.uk
dir: *Off A38 at Peartree junct, turn right then left at fuel station, Gages Mill 500yds on left*

Conveniently situated within easy access of the A38, this Grade II listed building was formerly a woollen mill. Very much a family home, there is a relaxed and welcoming style here with every effort made to ensure a rewarding and memorable stay. The bedrooms provide good standards of comfort and many have lovely views across the surrounding fields. Breakfast provides a substantial and enjoyable start to the day with plenty of choice for all appetites.

Rooms 7 en suite (1 fmly) (1 GF) S £60-£65; D £75-£85* **Facilities** TVL tea/coffee Cen ht Licensed Wi-fi 🔒 **Parking** 7 **Notes** ⊗ Closed Nov-Feb ⊛

Sladesdown Farm (SX765684)

★★★★ FARMHOUSE

Landscove TQ13 7ND
☎ 01364 653973 📠 01364 653973 Mr & Mrs Mason
e-mail: sue@sladesdown.co.uk
web: www.sladesdownfarm.co.uk
dir: *2m S of Ashburton. Off A38 at Peartree junct, Landscove signed on slip road, left at 2nd x-rds, farm 100yds right*

Surrounded by lush green fields, woodland and rolling hills, Sladesdown is a picturesque choice for anyone looking for a peaceful, rural hideaway that has easy access to the A38. This modern farmhouse offers spacious, attractive and homely accommodation with a natural and genuine welcome assured. Bedrooms provide impressive levels of comfort with lovely views being an added bonus. A hearty breakfast, featuring delicious local and home-made produce, is the perfect start to the day.

Rooms 4 rms (2 en suite) (2 pri facs) (1 fmly) S £35-£40; D £60-£70* **Facilities** tea/coffee Cen ht **Parking** 8 **Notes** ⊗ No Children 10yrs ⊛ 40 acres beef/turkeys/chickens

ASHWATER   Map 3 SX39

PREMIER COLLECTION

Blagdon Manor

☆☆☆☆☆ ◎◎ 🍽 RESTAURANT WITH ROOMS

EX21 5DF
☎ **01409 211224** 📠 **01409 211634**
e-mail: stay@blagdon.com
web: www. blagdon.com
dir: A388 towards Launceston/Holsworthy. Approx 2m
N of Chapman's Well take 2nd right for Ashwater. Next
right beside Blagdon Lodge, 0.25m to manor

Located on the borders of Devon and Cornwall within
easy reach of the coast, and set in its own beautifully
kept natural gardens, this small and friendly
restaurant with rooms offers a charming home-from-
home atmosphere. The tranquillity of the secluded
setting, the character and charm of the house and its
unhurried pace ensure calm and relaxation. High levels
of service, personal touches and thoughtful extras are
all part of a stay here. Steve Morey cooks with passion
and his commitment to using only the finest local
ingredients speaks volumes.

Rooms 7 en suite S £90; D £145-£205* **Facilities** FTV
Lounge tea/coffee Dinner available Direct Dial Cen ht
Wi-fi 🦢 ♨ Giant chess **Parking** 13 **Notes** No Children
12yrs Closed Jan RS Mon & Tue closed No coaches

ATHERINGTON   Map 3 SS52

West Down (SS582228)

★★★★ 🍽 FARMHOUSE

Little Eastacombe EX37 9HP
☎ **01769 560551** 📠 **01769 560551** Mr & Mrs Savery
e-mail: info@westdown.co.uk
dir: 0.5m from Atherington on B3227 to Torrington, turn
right, 100yds on left

Set within 25 acres of lush Devon countryside, this
establishment makes a good base for exploring the area.
A peaceful atmosphere and caring hospitality are
assured. Bedrooms are equipped with a host of
thoughtful extras, and every effort is made to ensure an
enjoyable stay. A choice of homely lounges is available;
breakfast and scrumptious dinners are served in the sun
lounge.

Rooms 2 en suite 2 annexe en suite (2 GF) S £45-£50;
D £72-£90* **Facilities** TVL tea/coffee Dinner available
Cen ht Wi-fi **Parking** 8 **Notes** LB ⊗ ⊛ 25 acres sheep/
chickens

AXMINSTER   Map 4 SY29

PREMIER COLLECTION

Kerrington House

☆☆☆☆☆ 🍽 ⊜ GUEST ACCOMMODATION

Musbury Rd EX13 5JR
☎ **01297 35333** 📠 **01297 35345**
e-mail: info@kerringtonhouse.com
dir: 0.5m from Axminster on A358 towards Seaton,
house on left

This former Victorian gentleman's residence has been
decorated and furnished to very high standards to
make guests comfortable throughout their visit.
Bedrooms and bathrooms include a range of welcome
extras. Afternoon tea may be enjoyed in the comfortably
furnished lounge, or in the warmer months, outside
overlooking the landscaped gardens. Locally sourced
produce is used both at breakfast and at dinner which
is available by prior arrangement.

Rooms 5 en suite (1 fmly) S £80; D £115*
Facilities FTV tea/coffee Dinner available Cen ht
Licensed Wi-fi 🌐 **Conf** Max 12 Board 12 **Parking** 6
Notes LB ⊗

BAMPTON   Map 3 SS92

The Bark House

★★★★ ⊜ GUEST ACCOMMODATION

Oakfordbridge EX16 9HZ
☎ **01398 351236**
dir: A361 to rdbt at Tiverton onto A396 for Dulverton, then
onto Oakfordbridge. House on right

Located in the stunning Exe Valley and surrounded by
wonderful unspoilt countryside, this is a perfect place to
relax and unwind. Hospitality is the hallmark here and a
cup of tea by the fireside is always on offer. Both
breakfast and dinner make use of the excellent local
produce, and are served in the attractive dining room,
overlooking fields and the river. Bedrooms have a homely,
cottage-style feel with comfy beds to ensure a peaceful
night's sleep.

Rooms 6 rms (5 en suite) (1 pri facs) (1 fmly) **Facilities**
tea/coffee Dinner available Cen ht Licensed **Parking** 6

Newhouse Farm (SS892228)

★★★★ ⊜ FARMHOUSE

EX16 9JE
☎ **01398 351347** Mrs A Boldry
e-mail: anne.boldry@btconnect.com
web: www.newhouse-farm-holidays.co.uk
dir: 5m W of Bampton on B3227

Set in 42 acres of rolling farmland, this delightful
farmhouse provides a friendly and informal atmosphere.
The smart, rustic-style bedrooms are well equipped with
modern facilities, and imaginative and delicious home-
cooked dinners, using the best local produce, are

available by arrangement. Home-made bread and
preserves feature at breakfast which can be enjoyed
outside on the patio in the summer months.

Rooms 3 en suite (1 GF) D £65-£75* **Facilities** FTV tea/
coffee Dinner available Cen ht Fishing **Parking** 3
Notes LB ⊗ No Children 10yrs Closed Xmas & New Year
42 acres beef/sheep

The Quarrymans Rest

★★★★ ◎ INN

Briton St EX16 9LN
☎ **01398 331480**
e-mail: info@thequarrymansrest.co.uk
dir: M5 junct 27 towards Tiverton on A361, at rdbt right
signed Bampton. At next rdbt take 2nd exit signed
Bampton, on right

This popular and atmospheric inn is located in the
bustling town of Bampton, a perfect location for exploring
the beautiful scenery of the Exmoor National Park. There's
always plenty of good natured banter around the bar
which features a range of local ales. Bedrooms are varied
in size, but all have a number of thoughtful extras, as do
the bathrooms with fluffy towels and quality toiletries.
Local produce is very much to the fore in well executed
dishes ranging from pub classics to more creative
offerings.

Rooms 3 en suite **Facilities** STV tea/coffee Dinner
available Cen ht Wi-fi ♿ 18 Pool table **Parking** 6 **Notes** No
coaches

Exeter Inn

[U]

Tiverton Rd EX16 9DY
☎ 01398 331345

Currently the rating for this establishment is not confirmed. This may be due to a change of ownership or because it has only recently joined the AA rating scheme.

Rooms 12 en suite (2 fmly) **Facilities** FTV tea/coffee Dinner available Wi-fi **Parking** 50

The Swan

[U]

Station Rd EX16 9NG
☎ 01398 332248
e-mail: info@theswan.co

Currently the rating for this establishment is not confirmed. This may be due to a change of ownership or because it has only recently joined the AA rating scheme.

Rooms 3 en suite S £60; D £85* **Notes** Closed 25-26 Dec

BARNSTAPLE   Map 3 SS53

Cedars Lodge

★★★★ INN

Bickington Rd EX31 2HP
☎ 01271 371784 ▤ 01271 325733
e-mail: cedars.barnstaple@oldenglishinns.co.uk

Once a private country house, this popular establishment stands in three-acre gardens, situated just outside Barnstaple and within easy reach of the M5 and major roads. Bedrooms are located in the adjacent lodge which is set around a courtyard facing the main house; all rooms offer generous levels of comfort and modern facilities. The popular conservatory restaurant serves a wide choice of dishes.

Rooms 2 en suite 32 annexe en suite (7 fmly) **Facilities** FTV TVL tea/coffee Dinner available Direct Dial Cen ht Wi-fi ⅃ 18 **Conf** Max 250 Thtr 250 Class 100 Board 100 **Parking** 200 **Notes** Civ Wed

Lower Yelland Farm Guest House

★★★★ GUEST HOUSE

Fremington EX31 3EN
☎ 01231 860101
e-mail: peterday@loweryellandfarm.co.uk
web: www.loweryellandfarm.co.uk
dir: Approaching Barnstaple on A361, at 1st rdbt take 1st exit A39 (Bideford). Straight over next 2 rdbts, at 3rd rdbt take 3rd exit. Over 2 mini-rdbts, at 3rd take 1st exit onto B3233. Through Fremington, 1st turn on right

A well established property close to Instow and within easy reach of Barnstaple and North Devon. Peter Day does all he can to make his guests welcome and serves a high quality traditional farmhouse breakfast including home-made jams, marmalades and even home-made bread in the attractive breakfast room. En suite bedrooms are well presented and appointed, and there is ample off-road parking for guests.

Rooms 7 en suite (1 fmly) (1 GF) S £37.50-£40; D £60-£80 **Facilities** FTV Lounge tea/coffee Cen ht Wi-fi ⌃ ⅃ 18 ☝ **Parking** 7 **Notes** LB

Cresta Guest House

★★★ GUEST HOUSE

26 Sticklepath Hill EX31 2BU
☎ 01271 374022
e-mail: contact@crestaguesthouse.co.uk
web: www.crestaguesthouse.co.uk
dir: On A3215, 0.6m W of town centre, top of hill on right

A warm welcome is assured at this family-run establishment, situated on the western outskirts of Barnstaple. The well-equipped, individually styled bedrooms are smartly appointed and include ground-floor rooms. A hearty breakfast is served in the modern and comfortable dining room.

Rooms 6 rms (4 en suite) (2 pri facs) 2 annexe en suite (2 fmly) (2 GF) S £25; D £50* **Facilities** FTV tea/coffee Cen ht Wi-fi ☝ **Parking** 6 **Notes** ⊗ Closed 2wks Xmas

BEER   Map 4 SY28

Anchor Inn

★★★★ INN

Fore St EX12 3ET
☎ 01297 20386 ▤ 01297 24474
e-mail: 6403@greeneking.co.uk
dir: A3052 at Hangmans Stone onto B3174 into Beer, located on slipway

Overlooking the sea in the idyllic village of Beer, this perennially popular inn has a well deserved reputation for the warmth of its welcome and convivial atmosphere. A number of the well appointed bedrooms have the added bonus of sea views. The menu makes plentiful use of the excellent local fish, much of which is landed just yards away. The cliff-top beer garden is a wonderful spot in summer months to soak up some sun whilst enjoying freshly barbecued food.

Rooms 6 rms (5 en suite) (1 pri facs) D £40-£95* **Facilities** STV FTV tea/coffee Dinner available Cen ht Wi-fi **Notes** LB

BEESANDS   Map 3 SX84

The Cricket Inn

★★★★ ◉ INN

TQ7 2EN
☎ 01548 580215
e-mail: enquiries@thecricketinn.com
web: www.thecricketinn.com
dir: From Kingsbridge follow A379 towards Dartmouth, at Stokenham mini-rdbt turn right for Beesands

Dating back to 1867 this charming seaside inn is situated almost on the beach at Start Bay. The well-appointed bedrooms have fantastic views, comfortable beds and flat screen TVs. The daily-changing fish menu includes locally-caught crabs, lobster and perhaps hand-dived scallops.

Rooms 8 en suite (1 fmly) **Facilities** FTV tea/coffee Dinner available Cen ht Wi-fi **Parking** 30 **Notes** No coaches

See advert on page 108

"THE INN ON THE SHORE"

The Cricket Inn opened its doors in 1867 to serve the thirsty fishermen of this sleepy beachside South Hams village, although there are only a few working fishermen left, the village still retains its charm, and the Cricket serves both locals and tourist alike.

A refurbishment in the spring of 2010 consisted of a new restaurant and 4 extra rooms, making 8 rooms in total, 5 with glorious sea views of Start Bay, including twins and family rooms. All rooms are en-suite with 4ft x 3ft walk-in showers, flat screen TVs (some with DVD players), and all the doubles are king size.

The Restaurant specialises in fresh seafood brought straight out the bay in front of the Inn, including diver caught scallops, lobster and crab plus locally reared beef for those steak lovers. There is something for everyone, including the kids.

The Cricket Inn, Beesands, Kingsbridge, South Devon, TQ7 2EN

01548 580215

enquiries@thecricketinn.com   www.thecricketinn.com

LAT. 50 15.0573N   LONG. 003 39.3197W

BERRYNARBOR Map 3 SS54

Berry Mill House

★★★★ 🍽 GUEST ACCOMMODATION

Mill Ln EX34 9SH
☎ **01271 882990**
e-mail: enquiries@berrymillhouse.co.uk
web: www.berrymillhouse.co.uk
dir: *500yds NW of village centre. A399 W through Combe Martin, 2nd left at bottom of the hill, house on left*

In a wooded valley on the edge of the village, this former grain mill is a 5-minute walk on the coastal path. Guests are assured of a warm reception from the owners, who enjoy welcoming guests to their home. The freshly cooked breakfast provides a substantial start to the day while home-cooked evening meals are available by arrangement.

Rooms 3 en suite **Facilities** FTV TVL tea/coffee Dinner available Cen ht Licensed Wi-fi 🔌 **Parking** 6 **Notes** ⊗ No Children 12yrs Closed Nov-1 Mar 🐾

BIDEFORD Map 3 SS42

The Pines at Eastleigh

★★★★ 🏡 GUEST ACCOMMODATION

The Pines, Eastleigh EX39 4PA
☎ **01271 860561** 📠 **01271 861689**
e-mail: pirrie@thepinesateastleigh.co.uk
dir: *A39 onto A386 signed East-the-Water. 1st left signed Eastleigh, 500yds next left, 1.5m to village, house on right*

Friendly hospitality is assured at this Georgian house, set in seven acres of hilltop grounds. Two of the comfortable bedrooms are located in the main house, the remainder in converted barns around a charming courtyard that has a pretty pond and well. A delicious breakfast, featuring local and home-made produce, is served in the dining room, and a lounge and honesty bar are also available.

Rooms 6 en suite (1 fmly) (4 GF) S £35-£45; D £75-£89 **Facilities** FTV DVD Lounge tea/coffee Direct Dial Cen ht Licensed Wi-fi 🔌 🔌 Archery, Air rifle target shooting **Conf** Max 25 Thtr 20 Board 20 **Parking** 20 **Notes** LB No Children 9yrs

BITTADON Map 3 SS54

Centery Farm

★★★★ BED AND BREAKFAST

EX31 4HN
☎ **01271 879603**
e-mail: stay@centeryfarm.co.uk
dir: *From Barnstaple on A39, left onto B3230 signed Ilfracombe. Pass through Muddiford & Bittadon, at 1st staggered x-rds on right*

Well situated just outside Ilfracombe set back from the main road with easy access to the town and Barnstaple. The very friendly hosts offer a genuinely warm welcome with home-made scones and local jam and clotted cream.

Bedrooms are well appointed, beds are very comfortable and en suites are well appointed. Breakfast offers quality, locally sourced ingredients and makes a great start to the day. Centery Farm was a Runner-up for the AA Friendliest B&B of the Year Award 2012-13.

Rooms 4 rms (3 en suite) (1 pri facs) S £45-£50; D £72-£80* **Facilities** STV TVL tea/coffee Cen ht Wi-fi 🔌 **Parking** 20 **Notes** LB ⊗ No Children 16yrs Closed Dec-1 Mar

BOVEY TRACEY Map 3 SX87

The Cromwell Arms

★★★★ INN

Fore St TQ13 9AE
☎ **01626 833473** 📠 **01626 836873**
e-mail: info@thecromwellarms.co.uk
dir: *From A38 from Exeter towards Plymouth take A382 at Drumbridges rdbt & follow Bovey Tracey signs. At mini-rdbt take 2nd exit, follow town centre signs. At next rdbt take 3rd exit into Station Rd (B3344) & up hill*

A traditional country inn situated in the heart of Bovey Tracey, on the southern edge of Dartmoor and approximately three miles from Newton Abbot, The Cromwell dates back from the 1600s, is full of original charm and has been enhanced with 21st-century facilities. This is an atmospheric, friendly pub with lots of character, which is suitable for all ages and is open all day every day.

Rooms 12 en suite (2 fmly) S fr £37.50; D £75-£80* **Facilities** STV FTV DVD tea/coffee Dinner available Direct Dial Cen ht Wi-fi 🔌 Beauty therapy **Extras** Wine, champagne, flowers, chocolates - chargeable **Conf** Max 40 Thtr 40 Class 25 Board 25 **Parking** 25

BRIXHAM Map 3 SX95

Anchorage Guest House

★★★★ GUEST HOUSE

170 New Rd TQ5 8DA
☎ **01803 852960 & 07950 536362**
e-mail: enquiries@brixham-anchorage.co.uk
dir: *A3022, enter Brixham, left at lights at junct with Monksbridge Rd. Pass Toll House immediately on right*

Conveniently located within walking distance of the town centre and harbour, this is an excellent choice for anyone looking to explore the many attractions of this popular holiday area. The dining room and the bedrooms have a light, bright contemporary style with many extra facilities provided to ensure a comfortable stay. Guests are welcome to use the delightful garden and ample parking is also a bonus.

Rooms 7 rms (6 en suite) (1 pri facs) (1 fmly) (4 GF) S £28-£36; D £52-£66* **Facilities** FTV tea/coffee Cen ht Wi-fi 🔌 **Parking** 6 **Notes** ⊗

BUCKFAST Map 3 SX76

Furzeleigh Mill

★★★ GUEST ACCOMMODATION

Old Ashburton Rd TQ11 0JP
☎ **01364 643476**
e-mail: enquiries@furzeleigh.co.uk
web: www.furzeleigh.co.uk
dir: *Exit A38 at Dartbridge junct, right at end slip road, right signed Ashburton/Prince Town (NB do not cross River Dart bridge), 200yds right*

This Grade II listed, 16th-century converted corn mill stands in its own grounds and is a good base for touring Dartmoor. Spacious family rooms are available as well as a lounge and a bar. All meals are served in the dining room and use local produce.

Rooms 14 en suite (2 fmly) S £44-£55; D £68-£85* **Facilities** FTV TVL tea/coffee Dinner available Cen ht Licensed Wi-fi **Conf** Max 20 Thtr 20 **Parking** 32 **Notes** LB Closed 23 Dec-2 Jan

BUCKFASTLEIGH Map 3 SX76

Kilbury Manor

★★★★ 🏡 GUEST ACCOMMODATION

Colston Rd TQ11 0LN
☎ **01364 644079**
e-mail: info@kilburymanor.co.uk
web: www.kilburymanor.co.uk
dir: *Off A38 onto B3380 to Buckfastleigh, left onto Old Totnes Rd, at bottom turn right, Kilbury Manor on left*

Dating back to the 17th century, this charming Devon longhouse is situated in the tranquil surroundings of the Dart Valley with access to the river across the meadow. Bedrooms have an abundance of character and are located in the main house and in adjacent converted barns; all provide high levels of comfort. The stylish bathrooms are also appointed to impressive standards. Breakfast is served in the elegant dining room with local produce very much in evidence.

Rooms 4 rms (3 en suite) (1 pri facs) (1 GF) S £65-£70; D £75-£95* **Facilities** FTV DVD tea/coffee Cen ht Wi-fi **Parking** 5 **Notes** No Children 7yrs 🐾

Dartbridge Inn

★★★ 🅰 INN

Totnes Rd TQ11 0JR
☎ **01364 642214** 📠 **01364 643839**
e-mail: dartbridgeinn@oldenglishinns.co.uk
web: www.oldenglishinns.co.uk
dir: *0.5m NE of town centre. A38 onto A384, 250yds on left*

Rooms 10 en suite (1 fmly) **Facilities** tea/coffee Direct Dial **Conf** Max 150 Thtr 150 Class 75 Board 40 **Parking** 100 **Notes** LB

BUCKLAND MONACHORUM — Map 3 SX46

Drake Manor

[U]

The Village PL20 7NA
☎ 01822 853892

Currently the rating for this establishment is not confirmed. This may be due to a change of ownership or because it has only recently joined the AA rating scheme.

Rooms 4 en suite **Facilities** FTV tea/coffee Dinner available **Parking** 4

BUDLEIGH SALTERTON — Map 3 SY08

PREMIER COLLECTION

Heath Close

★★★★★ GUEST ACCOMMODATION

Lansdowne Rd EX9 6AH
☎ 01395 444337
e-mail: info@heathclose.com
web: www.heathclose.com

On the outskirts of picturesque Budleigh Salterton and just a short walk from the South West Coastal Path which follows the Jurassic Coast, this delightful house offers high quality accommodation and a generous welcome from owners Eileen and Graham. Bedrooms are located both in the main house and an adjacent self-contained cottage, all providing an engaging blend of style, comfort and luxury. A light and airy lounge opens onto the garden, and breakfast can be served either in the attractive dining room or on the terrace in summer months. The terrace is also the ideal location for a Devon cream tea.

Rooms 5 en suite (1 fmly) (2 GF) S £75-£79; D £95-£105* **Facilities** FTV TVL TV4B tea/coffee Cen ht Wi-fi **Parking** 12 **Notes** LB ⊗ No Children 16yrs

Hansard House

★★★★ GUEST ACCOMMODATION

3 Northview Rd EX9 6BY
☎ 01395 442773 📠 01395 442475
e-mail: enquiries@hansardhousehotel.co.uk
web: www.hansardhousehotel.co.uk
dir: 500yds W of town centre

Hansard House is quietly situated a short walk from the town centre. Many of the well-presented bedrooms have commanding views across the town to the countryside and estuary beyond. Several are located on the ground floor and have easier access. Guests enjoy a varied selection at breakfast including a range of healthy options. The dining room and lounge are both comfortably furnished.

Rooms 12 en suite (1 fmly) (3 GF) S £42-£60; D £85-£98* **Facilities** STV TVL tea/coffee Direct Dial Cen ht Lift Licensed Wi-fi **Parking** 11 **Notes** LB

CHAGFORD — Map 3 SX78

PREMIER COLLECTION

Parford Well

★★★★★ BED AND BREAKFAST

Sandy Park TQ13 8JW
☎ 01647 433353
e-mail: tim@parfordwell.co.uk
web: www.parfordwell.co.uk
dir: A30 onto A382, after 3m left at Sandy Park towards Drewsteignton, house 50yds on left

Set in delightful grounds on the edge of Dartmoor, this attractive house is a restful and friendly home. Quality and style combine in the comfortable bedrooms; the lounge overlooks the well-tended gardens and breakfast is served at tables laid with crisp linen and silverware in one of two dining rooms. Carefully cooked, top local ingredients are hallmarks of a breakfast that makes the perfect start to a day exploring the moors.

Rooms 3 rms (2 en suite) (1 pri facs) S £45-£95; D £80-£95* **Facilities** TVL tea/coffee Cen ht Wi-fi **Extras** Speciality toiletries **Parking** 4 **Notes** ⊗ No Children 8yrs 🐾

Easton Court

★★★★ GUEST ACCOMMODATION

Easton Cross TQ13 8JL
☎ 01647 433469
e-mail: stay@easton.co.uk
web: www.easton.co.uk
dir: *1m E of Chagford at junct A382 & B3206*

Set in Dartmoor National Park, the age of this picturesque house is evident in the oak beams and thick granite walls. Guests can come and go via a separate entrance. Relaxation is obligatory, either in the lovely garden or in the snug surroundings of the lounge. The delightful bedrooms all have country views.

Rooms 5 en suite (2 GF) S £45-£60; D £70-£85* **Facilities** STV FTV DVD iPod docking station tea/coffee Cen ht Wi-fi ⬧ 18 ⬧ **Parking** 5 **Notes** ⊗ No Children 10yrs

---

CHILLATON   Map 3 SX48

PREMIER COLLECTION

Tor Cottage

★★★★★ GUEST ACCOMMODATION

PL16 0JE
☎ 01822 860248 ⬧ 01822 860126
e-mail: info@torcottage.co.uk
web: www.torcottage.co.uk
dir: *A30 Lewdown exit through Chillaton towards Tavistock, 300yds after Post Office right signed 'Bridlepath No Public Vehicular Access' to end*

Tor Cottage, located in its own valley with 18 acres of grounds, is a welcome antidote to the fast pace of everyday life. Rooms are spacious and elegant; the cottage-wing bedroom has a separate sitting room, and the garden rooms have their own wood burners. The gardens are delightful, with a stream and heated outdoor pool. An exceptional range of dishes is offered at breakfast, which can be enjoyed either in the conservatory dining room or on the terrace.

Rooms 1 en suite 3 annexe en suite (3 GF) S £98; D £150-£155* **Facilities** FTV TVL tea/coffee Cen ht Wi-fi ⬧ **Parking** 8 **Notes** LB ⊗ No Children 14yrs Closed mid Dec-beg Feb

---

CHULMLEIGH   Map 3 SS61

The Old Bakehouse

★★★★ GUEST HOUSE

South Molton St EX18 7BW
☎ 01769 580074 & 580137 ⬧ 01769 580074
e-mail: oldbakehouse@colinandholly.co.uk
web: www.colinandholly.co.uk
dir: *A377 onto B3096 into village centre, left into South Molton St, 100yds on left*

This 16th-century, thatched house is situated in the centre of Chulmleigh, a hilltop town which stands above

a beautiful river valley. The charming bedrooms are equipped with many extras such as DVD players (library available) and are located across a pretty, secluded courtyard garden in the former village bakery. A wealth of beams, thick cob walls and wood-burning stove all contribute to the character and comfort. A generous choice is offered at breakfast with an emphasis on excellent local produce.

Rooms 3 en suite (1 GF) S £50; D £65-£75 **Facilities** FTV DVD Lounge tea/coffee Cen ht Wi-fi ⬧ 18 ⬧ **Extras** Home-made biscuits **Notes** LB ⊗ No Children 11yrs

---

CLOVELLY   Map 3 SS32

East Dyke Farmhouse *(SS312235)*

★★★★ FARMHOUSE

East Dyke Farm, Higher Clovelly EX39 5RU
☎ 01237 431216 **Mrs H Goaman**
e-mail: steve.goaman@virgin.net
web: www.bedbreakfastclovelly.co.uk
dir: *A39 onto B3237 at Clovelly Cross rdbt, farm 500yds on left*

Adjoining an Iron Age hill fort, this working farm has glorious views of Bideford Bay in the distance. The farmhouse has a friendly atmosphere and offers attractively co-ordinated bedrooms. A key feature here are the breakfasts - local produce and delicious home-made preserves are served around one large table.

Rooms 3 rms (2 en suite) (1 pri facs) (1 fmly) S £40-£45; D £60-£70 **Facilities** FTV TVL tea/coffee Cen ht Wi-fi ⬧ **Extras** Fridges **Parking** 6 **Notes** ⊗ Closed 24-26 Dec ⬧ 350 acres beef/arable

---

COLEFORD   Map 3 SS70

The New Inn

★★★★ INN

EX17 5BZ
☎ 01363 84242 ⬧ 01363 85044
e-mail: enquiries@thenewinncoleford.co.uk
dir: *Exit A377 into Coleford, 1.5m to inn*

Originally dating back to the 13th century, this charming thatched village inn has much to offer, and provides a relaxing base from which to explore this beautiful corner of Devon. Bedrooms are spacious, comfortable and well appointed with lovely beds and lots of period features retained. Roaring fires, flagged floors and Captain, the resident parrot, all combine to create an engaging atmosphere. A choice of carefully prepared dishes is on offer in the restaurant and bar lounges, with local produce strongly featured.

Rooms 6 en suite (4 fmly) (1 GF) S £60-£70; D £80-£95 **Facilities** DVD tea/coffee Dinner available Direct Dial Cen ht Wi-fi ⬧ 18 ⬧ **Extras** Bottled water - complimentary **Parking** 50 **Notes** LB Closed 25-26 Dec No coaches

---

CROYDE   Map 3 SS43

The Whiteleaf

★★★★ ⬧ GUEST HOUSE

Croyde Rd EX33 1PN
☎ 01271 890266
dir: *On B3231 entering Croyde, on left at 'Road Narrows' sign*

A warm, family welcome awaits guests at this attractive house within easy walking distance of the pretty village and the sandy beach. Each of the well-equipped bedrooms has its own charm, and three rooms have decked balconies. Ambitious and imaginative dinners, using fresh seasonal produce, are served in the elegant restaurant.

Rooms 5 en suite (2 fmly) S £63-£68; D £82-£94* **Facilities** FTV Lounge tea/coffee Dinner available Direct Dial Cen ht Licensed ⬧ **Extras** Mini-bar **Parking** 10 **Notes** LB ⊗ Closed 24-26 Dec

---

Denham House

★★★★ ⬧ BED AND BREAKFAST

North Buckland EX33 1HY
☎ 01271 890297
e-mail: info@denhamhouse.co.uk
web: www.denhamhouse.co.uk
dir: *From Barnstaple A361, 2nd left after Knowle, follow lane into North Buckland, house on right*

Rooms 6 en suite (2 fmly) D £60-£70 **Facilities** FTV DVD Lounge TVL tea/coffee Cen ht Licensed Snooker Pool table ⬧ Table tennis Skittle Alley Games Room **Parking** 7 **Notes** LB ⊗

CULLOMPTON   Map 3 ST00

Lower Ford Farm *(SS978095)*

★★★★ FARMHOUSE

EX15 1LX
☎ 01884 252354 **Ms D Pring**
e-mail: lowerfordfarm@hotmail.com
dir: *M5 junct 28 Cullompton, take road by HSBC bank. At Whitedown x-rds turn left then 1st left*

A peacefully located 15th-century farmhouse offering naturally welcoming hospitality with a real home-from-home atmosphere. Surrounded by delightful countryside, this working farm provides a peaceful retreat. Bedrooms are comfortably furnished and equipped with some welcome extras to add to guest comfort. A spacious lounge is also available. In addition to the large, farmhouse breakfast, the wonderful home-cooked dinners (available by prior arrangement) should not be missed.

Rooms 3 en suite (1 fmly) **Facilities** FTV TVL tea/coffee Dinner available Wi-fi **Parking** 6 **Notes** ⊗ Closed Nov-Jan ⬧ 350 acres beef/sheep/arable

CULLOMPTON *continued*

Weir Mill Farm *(ST040108)*

★★★★ FARMHOUSE

Jaycroft, Willand EX15 2RE
☎ 01884 820803 Mrs R Parish
e-mail: rita@weirmill-devon.co.uk
dir: *2m N of Cullompton. M5 junct 27, B3181 to Willand, left at rdbt onto B3340 signed Uffculme, 50yds right into Willand Moor Rd, after Lupin Way left into lane*

Set in extensive farmland, this charming 19th-century farmhouse offers comfortable accommodation with a relaxed and homely atmosphere. The spacious bedrooms are attractively decorated and equipped with an impressive range of thoughtful extras. A good choice is offered at breakfast in the well-appointed dining room.

Rooms 3 en suite (1 fmly) S £37-£40; D £64-£70*
Facilities FTV TVL tea/coffee Cen ht Wi-fi ⬛ **Parking** 5
Notes ⊗ ⊛ 100 acres arable/beef

Wishay Farm *(SS994056)*

★★★ FARMHOUSE

Trinity EX15 1PE
☎ 01884 33223 ≡ 01884 33223 Mrs Baker
e-mail: wishayfarm@btopenworld.com
dir: *2m SW of Cullompton. From town centre into Colbrook Ln, 1.5m to junct, continue straight on, farm 200yds on left*

This is a 280-acre, working arable and beef farm with a modernised Grade II listed farmhouse. The house has a peaceful location with pleasant country views. The two bedrooms are spacious and comfortably furnished. A traditional farmhouse breakfast is served in the dining room, and a separate guest lounge is also available.

Rooms 2 rms (1 en suite) (1 pri facs) (2 fmly) S £35; D £56-£60* **Facilities** FTV TVL tea/coffee Cen ht Wi-fi **Parking** 3 **Notes** LB ⊗ ⊛ 280 acres arable/beef

---

Brimpts Farm

★★★ GUEST ACCOMMODATION

PL20 6SG
☎ 01364 631450
e-mail: info@brimptsfarm.co.uk
web: www.brimptsfarm.co.uk
dir: *Dartmeet at E end of B3357, establishment signed on right at top of hill*

A popular venue for walkers and lovers of the great outdoors, Brimpts is peacefully situated in the heart of Dartmoor and has been a Duchy of Cornwall farm since 1307. Bedrooms are simply furnished and many have wonderful views across Dartmoor. Dinner is served by arrangement. Additional facilities include a sauna and spa, and a children's play area. Brimpts is also home to the Dartmoor Pony Heritage Trust.

Rooms 10 en suite (2 fmly) (7 GF) S £32.50; D £55-£65*
Facilities Lounge TVL TV1B tea/coffee Dinner available Cen ht Licensed Wi-fi Sauna Pool table ⬛ Farm walks & trails, Hot tub **Conf** Max 60 Thtr 60 Class 40 Board 25 **Parking** 50 **Notes** LB

PREMIER COLLECTION

Nonsuch House

★★★★★ ⬛ 🞕 GUEST ACCOMMODATION

Church Hill, Kingswear TQ6 0BX
☎ 01803 752829 ≡ 01803 752357
e-mail: enquiries@nonsuch-house.co.uk
web: www.nonsuch-house.co.uk
dir: *A3022 onto A379 2m before Brixham. Fork left onto B3205. Left up Higher Contour Rd, down Ridley Hill, house on bend on left at top of Church Hill*

This delightful Edwardian property has fabulous views across the Dart estuary. The marvellous hosts combine friendliness with unobtrusive service. Bedrooms are spacious and superbly appointed, each with a spectacular panorama of the harbour. Fresh, local ingredients are served at dinner, including top-quality meat, fish, and farmhouse cheeses. Breakfast, on the patio in good weather, features freshly squeezed juice, local sausages and home-baked bread.

Rooms 4 en suite (2 GF) **Facilities** FTV tea/coffee Dinner available Cen ht Wi-fi Membership of local spa **Parking** 4 **Notes** ⊗ No Children 12yrs RS Sat & Tue-Wed no dinner available

PREMIER COLLECTION

Strete Barton House

★★★★★ GUEST HOUSE

Totnes Rd TQ6 0RU
☎ 01803 770364 ≡ 01803 771182
e-mail: info@stretebarton.co.uk
web: www.stretebarton.co.uk

(For full entry see Strete)

See advert on opposite page

Angélique Rooms

★★★★ RESTAURANT WITH ROOMS

51 Victoria Rd TQ6 9RT
☎ 01803 839425 ≡ 01803 839505
e-mail: info@angeliquedartmouth.co.uk
dir: *In Dartmouth take one-way system, 1st left at NatWest Bank*

This terrace property offers very comfortable, contemporary, stylish accommodation, equipped with numerous extra facilities. Breakfast includes freshly squeezed orange juice; specials such as eggs Benedict and scrambled eggs with smoked salmon should not be missed.

Rooms 7 en suite (2 fmly) (1 GF) S fr £85; D £85-£299*
Facilities FTV DVD tea/coffee Dinner available Cen ht Wi-fi ♪ 18 **Extras** Mineral water - complimentary
Notes LB ⊗ Closed Xmas No coaches

Save on B&Bs and Hotels. Book at **theAA.com/hotel**

DEVON 113 ENGLAND

Cherub's Nest

★★★★ GUEST ACCOMMODATION

15 Higher St TQ6 9RB
☎ 01803 832482
e-mail: cherubsnest4bb@aol.com
web: www.cherubsnest.co.uk
dir: *From Lower Dartmouth ferry along Lower St, left onto Smith St, left onto Higher St, Cherub's Nest 50yds on left*

Dating from 1710, this former merchant's house, bedecked with flowers during the summer, is located in the very heart of historic Dartmouth. Full of character, the individually decorated bedrooms vary in size, but all are attractive and well equipped. A choice of breakfasts is served in the cosy dining room.

Rooms 3 en suite **Facilities** FTV tea/coffee Cen ht Wi-fi **Notes** ⊗ No Children 10yrs

DAWLISH   Map 3 SX97

Manor Farm *(SX952749)*

★★★★ 🅰 FARMHOUSE

Holcombe EX7 0JT
☎ 01626 863020 Mr & Mrs Clemens
e-mail: humphreyclem@aol.com
dir: *A379 through Dawlish, after 1.5m turn right into Fordens Ln. Entrance opposite Castle Inn*
Rooms 3 rms (2 en suite) (1 pri facs) (1 fmly) D £64-£66 **Facilities** FTV DVD tea/coffee Cen ht Wi-fi Riding Pool table ⚓ **Parking** 6 **Notes** ⊗ 🐾 135 acres beef/livery

DODDISCOMBSLEIGH   Map 3 SX88

The Nobody Inn

★★★★ 🍽 INN

EX6 7PS
☎ 01647 252394 📠 01647 252978
e-mail: info@nobodyinn.co.uk
web: www.nobodyinn.co.uk
dir: *From A38 turn off at top of Haldon Hill, follow signs to Doddiscombsleigh*

Dating back to the 16th century, this fascinating inn is something of a Mecca for lovers of wine, whisky and local ale - the choices are extensive. Of course, that's not forgetting the impressive food, much of which is sourced locally including an extensive cheese selection. Bedrooms and bathrooms have been appointed to provide high levels of quality, comfort and individuality. Reassuringly, the bars and lounges remain unchanged with charmingly mis-matched furniture, age-darkened beams and an inglenook fireplace.

Rooms 5 rms (4 en suite) (1 pri facs) (1 fmly) S £45-£65; D £60-£95* **Facilities** FTV DVD tea/coffee Dinner available Direct Dial Wi-fi ⚓ **Conf** Max 24 **Parking** 50 **Notes** No Children 5yrs No coaches

EXETER   Map 3 SX99

Chi Restaurant & Bar with Accommodation

★★★★ 🍽 RESTAURANT WITH ROOMS

Fore St, Kenton EX6 8LD
☎ 01626 890213 📠 01626 891678
e-mail: enquiries@chi-restaurant.co.uk
web: www.chi-restaurant.co.uk
dir: *5m S of Exeter. M5 junct 30, A379 towards Dawlish, in village centre*

This former pub has been spectacularly transformed into a chic and contemporary bar, allied with a stylish Chinese restaurant. Dishes are beautifully presented with an emphasis on quality produce and authenticity, resulting in a memorable dining experience. Bedrooms are well equipped and all provide good levels of space and comfort, along with modern bathrooms.

Rooms 5 en suite (2 fmly) S £37.80-£42; D £52.20-£58 (room only)* **Facilities** FTV DVD TVL tea/coffee Dinner available Direct Dial Cen ht Wi-fi ⚓ **Parking** 26 **Notes** ⊗ No coaches

Strete Barton House - South Hams Luxury Coastal Guest House

16th Century Manor House set in the picturesque village of Strete, near Dartmouth. Panoramic sea views. Only one mile from award winning beaches of Blackpool Sands and Slapton Sands. The South West Coast Path a mere 50 metres away. Contemporary interior; Egyptian cotton sheets; fluffy white towels; feather-down pillows; luxury toiletries; beverage tray; flat screen TV and DVD/CD player.

T: 01803 770364   F: 01803 771182   E: info@stretebarton.co.uk   W: www.stretebarton.co.uk

AA ★★★★★ Guest House

B&B GUIDE 2013

EXETER *continued*

Mill Farm (SX959839)

★★★★ FARMHOUSE

Kenton EX6 8JR
☎ 01392 832471 **Mrs D Lambert**
e-mail: info@millfarmstay.co.uk
dir: *A379 from Exeter towards Dawlish, over mini-rdbt by Swans Nest, farm 1.75m on right*

Located just a short drive from the Powderham Estate, this imposing farmhouse is surrounded by pasture. Each of the spacious bedrooms (single, twin, double and family) is stylishly co-ordinated and comfortably furnished; all rooms have countryside views. Breakfast (including vegetarian options) is served in the sunny dining room and a lounge is also provided. A packed breakfast can be prepared if a very early start is required.

Rooms 5 en suite (3 fmly) **Facilities** FTV TVL tea/coffee Cen ht Wi-fi **Parking** 12 **Notes** ⊗ No Children 6yrs Closed Xmas 30 acres horses

Innkeeper's Lodge Exeter, Clyst St George

★★★ INN

Clyst St George EX3 0QJ
☎ 0845 112 6086
e-mail: info@innkeeperslodge.com
web: www.innkeeperslodge.com

At Innkeeper's Lodge you'll find accommodation with comfort and character in equal measure, and everything needed for a relaxing stay, from easy check-in and free parking to complimentary breakfast and a cosy pub serving great value food and drink on the doorstep. Each Lodge has quality rooms, and there are Lodges in a variety of locations from towns and cities to countryside settings across the UK.

Rooms 21 en suite (6 fmly) (8 GF) **Facilities** FTV tea/coffee Dinner available Direct Dial Wi-fi **Parking**

Barn

★★★★ GUEST ACCOMMODATION

Foxholes Hill, Marine Dr EX8 2DF
☎ 01395 224411 🖷 01395 225445
e-mail: exmouthbarn@gmail.com
web: www.barnhotel.co.uk
dir: *From M5 junct 30 take A376 to Exmouth, then follow signs to seafront. At rdbt last exit into Foxholes Hill. Located on right*

This Grade II listed establishment has a prime location, close to miles of sandy beaches. Equally pleasant is the immaculate rear garden, which is sea-facing and features a terrace and swimming pool for use during the summer. Service is attentive and friendly, and spectacular sea views are enjoyed from most of the well-

equipped bedrooms and public rooms. Breakfast is served in the elegant surroundings of the dining room.

Rooms 11 en suite (4 fmly) S £39-£50; D £59-£105* **Facilities** FTV DVD Lounge tea/coffee Direct Dial Cen ht Licensed ⚲ **Parking** 30 **Notes** LB Closed 23 Dec-10 Jan

The Devoncourt

★★★★ GUEST ACCOMMODATION

16 Douglas Av EX8 2EX
☎ 01395 272277 🖷 01395 269315
e-mail: enquiries@devoncourt.com
web: www.devoncourthotel.com
dir: *M5/A376 to Exmouth, follow seafront to Maer Rd, right at T-junct*

The Devoncourt stands in four acres of mature, subtropical gardens, sloping gently towards the sea and overlooking two miles of sandy beaches. It offers extensive leisure facilities, and the smartly furnished bedrooms are exceptionally well equipped. The spacious public areas are available to timeshare owners as well as guests. For meals there is a choice between the informal bar and the restaurant.

Rooms 52 en suite 2 annexe en suite (35 fmly) (8 GF) (49 smoking) S £68-£84; D £100-£120* **Facilities** FTV DVD TVL tea/coffee Dinner available Direct Dial Cen ht Lift Licensed Wi-fi ⊕ ⚲ ⟆ Snooker Sauna Gym Sun shower, jacuzzi **Parking** 50 **Notes** LB ⊗ Civ Wed 100

Locksbeam Farm (SS483205)

★★★★ FARMHOUSE

EX38 7EZ
☎ 01805 623213 **Mrs T Martin**
e-mail: tracey@locksbeamfarm.co.uk

A traditional working dairy farm offering warm hospitality and good quality accommodation. The en suite rooms are thoughtfully appointed with comfortable beds. Breakfast offers quality local produce such as sausages, eggs and bacon, and local jams and marmalades are also offered.

Rooms 5 en suite **Notes** Closed Nov-Feb dairy/arable

Stanborough Farm (SX767527)

★★★★ FARMHOUSE

Halwell TQ9 7JQ
☎ 01548 821306 & 07807 787327 **Ms H Reeve**
e-mail: stanboroughfarm@hotmail.com
web: www.stanboroughfarm.co.uk
dir: *From Halwell turn right signed Moreleigh, farm on left*

A warm welcome is received on arrival on this working dairy farm, and after a comfortable night's sleep a freshly cooked farmhouse breakfast, using produce from the farm whenever possible, is served in the attractive breakfast room overlooking the garden. Both en suite bedrooms have been appointed to a high standard and offer all the comforts required by the modern traveller. An ideal location for exploring the South Hams. There are two country pubs within walking distance.

Rooms 2 en suite S £40-£50; D £65-£80* **Facilities** FTV tea/coffee Cen ht Wi-fi **Parking** 3 **Notes** ⊗ ⊜ 130 acres dairy/poultry

See advert on opposite page

Save on B&Bs and Hotels. Book at **theAA.com/hotel**

DEVON 115 **ENGLAND**

HAYTOR VALE	Map 3 SX77

Rock Inn

★★★★ ⚫ INN

TQ13 9XP

☎ 01364 661305 & 661465 📠 01364 661242

e-mail: inn@rock-inn.co.uk

dir: *A38 onto 382 to Bovey Tracey, in 0.5m left onto B3387 to Haytor*

Dating back to the 1750s, this former coaching inn is in a pretty hamlet on the edge of Dartmoor. Each named after a Grand National winner, the individually decorated bedrooms have some nice extra touches. Bars are full of character, with flagstone floors and old beams, and offer a wide range of dishes, cooked with imagination.

Rooms 9 en suite S £79-£99; D £89-£139* **Facilities** STV Dinner available **Notes** Closed 25-26 Dec

HEASLEY MILL	Map 3 SS73

Tabor Hill Farm B&B - Livery Yard

★★★★ BED AND BREAKFAST

EX36 3LQ

☎ 01598 740528

e-mail: taborhillfarm@btinternet.com

dir: *Situated between North Molton & Sandyway*

Tabor Hill Farm and Livery is set in the Exmoor National Park with superb views and peace and quiet, ideal for a relaxing stay. Rooms are tastefully appointed with excellent beds and power showers. A hearty Rayburn cooked breakfast is served at one table and uses local, quality produce including eggs from the resident flock of hens. Livery is also a part of the package here if needed and excellent stabling is available at a modest charge.

Rooms 2 en suite D £80 **Facilities** FTV tea/coffee Cen ht Wi-fi Fishing Stabling available **Parking** 8 **Notes** LB No Children 12yrs ⊛

HOLSWORTHY	Map 3 SS30

The Hollies Farm Guest House (SS371001)

★★★★ FARMHOUSE

Clawton EX22 6PN

☎ 01409 253770 & 07972 510014   Mr & Mrs G Colwill

e-mail: theholliesfarm@hotmail.com

web: www.theholliesfarm.co.uk

dir: *Exit A388 at Clawton signed vineyard, left in 2m, The Hollies in lane on left after T-junct, signed. At end of farm lane, fork right*

This sheep and beef farm offers comfortable, modern accommodation with a family atmosphere. There are pleasant views across the countryside from most bedrooms; all are well appointed. Breakfast is served in the conservatory, and dinner is available by arrangement. There is also a barbecue area with a gazebo.

Rooms 3 en suite (2 fmly) S £30-£40; D £58-£65 **Facilities** TVL tea/coffee Dinner available Cen ht ⚓ ⚲ Outdoor hot tub **Parking** 6 **Notes** LB ⊛ Closed 24-25 Dec ⊛ 25 acres beef/sheep

HONITON	Map 4 ST10

Monkton Court

★★★★ ⚫⚫ RESTAURANT WITH ROOMS

Monkton EX14 9QH

☎ 01404 42309

e-mail: enquiries@monktoncourthotel.co.uk

dir: *2m E A30 from Honiton*

Located on the A30 near Honiton and on the edge of the ancient Blackdown Hills, Monkton Court is a former vicarage steeped in history. There is a range of well-equipped and comfortably furnished bedrooms and bathrooms in addition to a relaxing lounge and spacious restaurant. Dinner should not be missed with a range of skilful and flavoursome dishes showcasing local produce and creativity.

Rooms 7 en suite (1 fmly) (1 GF) **Facilities** FTV tea/coffee Dinner available Direct Dial Cen ht Wi-fi **Conf** Max 75 Thtr 50 Class 30 Board 50 **Parking** 19 **Notes** ⊛

Ridgeway Farm

★★★★ GUEST ACCOMMODATION

Awliscombe EX14 3PY

☎ 01404 841331 📠 01404 841119

e-mail: jessica@ridgewayfarm.co.uk

dir: *3m NW of Honiton. A30 onto A373, through Awliscombe to near end of 40mph zone, right opposite Godford Farm, farm 500mtrs up narrow lane, sign at entrance*

This 18th-century farmhouse has a peaceful location on the slopes of Hembury Hill, and is a good base for exploring nearby Honiton and the east Devon coast. Renovations have brought the cosy accommodation to a high standard and the atmosphere is relaxed and homely. The proprietors and their family pets assure a warm welcome.

Rooms 2 en suite S £36-£38; D £58-£64 **Facilities** FTV TVL tea/coffee Dinner available Cen ht Wi-fi **Parking** 4 **Notes** LB ⊛

HONITON *continued*

Threshays

★★★ BED AND BREAKFAST

Awliscombe EX14 3QB
☎ 01404 43551 & 07811 675800 📠 01404 43551
e-mail: threshays@btinternet.com
dir: 2.5m NW of Honiton on A373

A converted threshing barn, situated on a non-working farm, Threshays has wonderful views over open countryside. With tea and cake offered on arrival, this family-run establishment provides comfortable accommodation in a friendly atmosphere. The lounge-dining room is a light and airy setting for the enjoying the good breakfasts. Ample parking is a bonus.

Rooms 2 rms (1 fmly) S £30; D £56 **Facilities** TVL tea/coffee Cen ht Wi-fi **Parking** 4 **Notes** ⊗ ⊜

HOPE COVE   Map 3 SX64

Cottage

★★★★ GUEST ACCOMMODATION

TQ7 3HJ
☎ 01548 561555 📠 01548 561455
e-mail: info@hopecove.com
dir: From Kingsbridge on A381 to Salcombe. 2nd right at Marlborough, left for Inner Hope

Glorious sunsets can be seen over the attractive bay from this popular accommodation. Friendly and attentive service from the staff and management mean many guests return here. Bedrooms, many with sea views and some with balconies, are well equipped. The restaurant offers an enjoyable dining experience.

Rooms 34 rms (31 en suite) (3 pri facs) (5 fmly) (7 GF) S £51.95-£105; D £103.90-£190* (incl.dinner) **Facilities** FTV DVD Lounge TVL tea/coffee Dinner available Direct Dial Licensed Wi-fi ch fac ⚓ 18 🔑 Table tennis **Conf** Max 70 Thtr 60 Class 60 Board 30 **Parking** 50 **Notes** LB Closed early Jan-early Feb

HORNS CROSS   Map 3 SS32

PREMIER COLLECTION

The Round House

★★★★★ GUEST HOUSE

EX39 5DN
☎ 01237 451687
e-mail: michael.m.clifford@btinternet.com
web: www.the-round-house.co.uk
dir: 1m W of Horns Cross on A39, 0.5m past Hoops Inn towards Bude

This charming converted barn stands in landscaped gardens within easy reach of Clovelly. Guests receive a warm welcome and a complimentary cream tea on arrival, which may be served in the lounge with its exposed beams and inglenook fireplace. Bedrooms are comfortable with numerous thoughtful extra facilities. A varied choice is offered at breakfast.

Rooms 3 en suite (1 fmly) (1 GF) S fr £40; D fr £65* **Facilities** FTV TVL tea/coffee Cen ht Wi-fi **Parking** 8 **Notes** ⊗ No Children 12yrs

The Hoops Inn

★★★★ GUEST ACCOMMODATION

The Hoops EX39 5DL
☎ 01237 451222
e-mail: sales@hoopsinn.co.uk
web: www.hoopsinn.co.uk

The Hoops, with its whitewashed walls, thatched roof and real fires, has been welcoming guests for many centuries. Bedrooms have plenty of character and include a number with four-poster or half-tester beds. Guests have the use of a quiet lounge and a pleasant seating area in the delightful rear garden. A fine selection of home-cooked meals can be enjoyed in the bar or restaurant.

Rooms 13 en suite **Facilities** Dinner available Licensed

ILFRACOMBE   Map 3 SS54

Strathmore

★★★★ GUEST ACCOMMODATION

57 St Brannock's Rd EX34 8EQ
☎ 01271 862248 📠 01271 862248
e-mail: info@the-strathmore.co.uk
web: www.the-strathmore.co.uk
dir: A361 from Barnstaple to Ilfracombe, Strathmore 1.5m from Mullacot Cross entering Ilfracombe

Situated within walking distance of the town centre and beach, this charming Victorian property offers a very warm welcome. The attractive bedrooms are comfortably furnished, while public areas include a well-stocked bar, an attractive terraced garden, and an elegant breakfast room.

Rooms 8 en suite (3 fmly) S £40; D £70-£76* **Facilities** FTV DVD Lounge tea/coffee Cen ht Licensed Wi-fi 🔑 **Parking** 7 **Notes** LB

Collingdale Guest House

★★★★ GUEST HOUSE

13 Larkstone Ter EX34 9NU
☎ 01271 863770
e-mail: thecollingdale@gmail.com
web: www.thecollingdale.co.uk
dir: Take A399 E through Ilfracombe, on left past B3230 turning

Overlooking the harbour, this Victorian guest house is within easy walking distance of the town centre and seafront. The well-presented bedrooms, many with sweeping sea views, are furnished to a high standard with many thoughtful extras. The comfortable lounge and elegant dining room share the magnificent views. A cosy bar is also available for a tipple before bedtime.

Rooms 9 rms (8 en suite) (1 pri facs) (3 fmly) S fr £45* **Facilities** FTV TVL tea/coffee Licensed Wi-fi ⚓ 18 **Notes** LB ⊗ No Children 8yrs Closed Nov-Feb

Marine Court

★★★★ GUEST HOUSE

Hillsborough Rd EX34 9QQ
☎ 01271 862920 & 07791 051778
e-mail: info@marinecourthoteldevon.co.uk
dir: M5 junct 27, A361 to Barnstaple, continue to Ilfracombe

Marine Court is a well-established guest house offering comfortable, well appointed rooms in a handy location. Guests are assured a very warm welcome from the hosts who do all they can to ensure a comfortable stay. Guests have use of a small bar lounge where drinks can be served, and off-road parking is a bonus.

Rooms 8 en suite (2 fmly) S £42.50-£45; D £62-£78*
Facilities FTV DVD Lounge tea/coffee Cen ht Licensed
Parking 5 **Notes** ⊗ No Children 8yrs Closed Nov-Mar

Norbury House

★★★★ GUEST HOUSE

Torrs Park EX34 8AZ
☎ 01271 863888
e-mail: info@norburyhouse.co.uk
dir: From A399 to end of High St/Church St. At mini-rdbt after lights take 1st exit into Church Rd. Bear left into Osbourne Rd. At T-junct left into Torrs Park. House at top of hill on right

This detached Victorian residence has a refreshingly different, contemporary style, and the genuinely warm welcome is allied with a helpful and attentive approach. A variety of bedroom styles is offered but all provide impressive levels of comfort and quality. An elegant lounge leads through to a conservatory which has an honesty bar. Outside, the peaceful terraced gardens have lovely views. Cuisine is taken seriously here, with breakfast featuring quality, local produce.

Rooms 6 en suite (2 fmly) **Facilities** FTV tea/coffee Cen ht Licensed Wi-fi **Conf** Max 18 Thtr 14 Class 14 Board 12 **Parking** 6 **Notes** ⊗

Avalon

★★★ GUEST HOUSE

6 Capstone Crescent EX34 9BT
☎ 01271 863325 📠 01271 866543
e-mail: avalon_ilfracombe@yahoo.co.uk
web: www.avalon-hotel.co.uk
dir: A361 to Ilfracombe, left at 1st lights, straight on 2nd lights, left at end of one-way system, left again

Conveniently located near the centre of Ilfracombe, this well-established guest house has magnificent sea views from the bedrooms and dining room. Avalon offers well-equipped bedrooms, one of which is located on the ground floor. Breakfast is served at separate tables in the well-appointed dining room and parking is available free of charge nearby.

Rooms 9 en suite (3 fmly) (1 GF) S £33-£43; D £56-£64*
Facilities FTV tea/coffee Wi-fi 🛁 **Parking** 7 **Notes** LB ⊗ No Children 6yrs Closed Xmas & New Year

KENTISBEARE   Map 3 ST00

Orway Crescent Farm Bed & Breakfast

★★★★ BED AND BREAKFAST

Orway Crescent Farm, Orway EX15 2EX
☎ 01884 266876 & 0845 658 8472 📠 01884 266876
e-mail: orway.crescentfarm@btinternet.com
dir: M5 junct 28, A373 towards Honiton. 5m, Keepers Cottage pub on right, next left for Sheldon & Broad Rd. 3rd left to Orway, farm at bottom of hill

Located in a sleepy rural hamlet, this welcoming home has appointed to an impressive standard and is just five miles from the M5. Bedrooms combine comfort and quality in equal measure, and have numerous useful extras which typify the caring and helpful approach here. The stylish modern bathrooms are simply superb, either for an invigorating shower or relaxing soak in the bath. The dining room is the venue for substantial breakfasts with lovely views across the fields to woodland beyond.

Rooms 3 en suite (1 fmly) (1 GF) **Facilities** STV FTV tea/coffee Cen ht Wi-fi **Parking** 3 **Notes** ⊗

KENTISBURY   Map 3 SS64

Night In Gails

★★★★ 🏠 GUEST ACCOMMODATION

Kentisbury Mill EX31 4NF
☎ 01271 883545
e-mail: info@kentisburymill.co.uk
dir: M5 junct 27, A361 towards Barnstaple, then A399 to Blackmoor Gate. Left at Blackmoor Gate onto A39, right onto B3229 at Kentisbury Ford, 1m on right

Originally consisting of an 18th-century cottage and mill, this relaxing hideaway has been sympathetically renovated to provide impressive levels of comfort, allied with caring hospitality. Bedrooms offer an appealing blend of old and new, with views over the extensive gardens. A guest lounge is also provided with plenty of local information for those wanting to explore the dramatic coast and countryside. Breakfast is Aga-cooked and includes superb eggs laid by the resident hens, together with other wonderful local produce - a perfect start to the day.

Rooms 4 en suite **Facilities** FTV tea/coffee Cen ht Wi-fi **Parking** 6 **Notes** ⊗ Closed Xmas

LEWDOWN   Map 3 SX48

Lobhill Accommodation

★★★★ BED AND BREAKFAST

Lewdown EX20 4DT
☎ 01566 783542 & 07817 244687
e-mail: jane.colwill@btopenworld.com
web: www.lobhillbedandbreakfast.co.uk
dir: Exit A30 at Sourton Cross, follow signs for Lewdown onto old A30. Lobhill 1m before Lewdown

Ideally situated for easy access to moorland and the Devon and Cornwall coasts, this stone farmhouse dates back some 130 years. Peacefully located, its renovation has resulted in impressive levels of quality, while still retaining a reassuringly traditional and homely feel. Bedrooms (including one on the ground floor with separate access) have free Wi-fi and views of the countryside. Tasty and satisfying breakfasts are cooked on the Aga and served either in the dining room or at the kitchen table. Guests are welcome to make use of the lovely gardens and summerhouse, or explore the woodland walks.

Rooms 3 en suite (1 fmly) (1 GF) **Facilities** FTV tea/coffee Cen ht Wi-fi **Parking** 8

LIFTON   Map 3 SX38

Tinhay Mill Guest House and Restaurant

★★★★ 🍴 RESTAURANT WITH ROOMS

Tinhay PL16 0AJ
☎ 01566 784201 📠 01566 784201
e-mail: tinhay.mill@talk21.com
web: www.tinhaymillrestaurant.co.uk
dir: A30/A388 approach Lifton, establishment at bottom of village on right

These former mill cottages are now a delightful restaurant with charming rooms. Beams and open fireplaces set the scene, and everything is geared to ensure a relaxed and comfortable stay. Bedrooms are spacious and well equipped, with many thoughtful extras. Cuisine is taken seriously here, using the best of local produce.

Rooms 6 en suite (1 GF) S £50-£75; D £80-£103*
Facilities FTV DVD TVL tea/coffee Dinner available Cen ht Wi-fi 🛁 **Parking** 13 **Notes** LB ⊗ No Children 14yrs Closed Dec-Jan No coaches

LUSTLEIGH   Map 3 SX78

PREMIER COLLECTION

Eastwrey Barton

★★★★★ 🍴 GUEST ACCOMMODATION

Moretonhampstead Rd TQ13 9SN
☎ 01647 277338 📠 01647 277133
e-mail: info@eastwreybarton.co.uk
web: www.eastwreybarton.co.uk
dir: *On A382 between Bovey Tracey &
Moretonhampstead, 6m from A38 (Drumbridges junct)*

Warm hospitality and a genuine welcome are hallmarks
at this family-run establishment, situated inside the
Dartmoor National Park. Built in the 18th century, the
house retains many original features and has views
across the Wray Valley. Bedrooms are spacious and
well equipped, while public areas include a snug
lounge warmed by a crackling log fire. Breakfast and
dinner showcase local produce with an impressive wine
list to accompany the latter.

Rooms 5 en suite (1 fmly) S £75-£95; D £100-£120*
Facilities FTV Lounge tea/coffee Dinner available
Cen ht Licensed Wi-fi 🅿 **Parking** 18 **Notes** ⊗ No
Children 10yrs

PREMIER COLLECTION

Woodley House

★★★★★ 🍴 GUEST ACCOMMODATION

Caseley Hill TQ13 9TN
☎ 01647 277214 📠 01647 277126
dir: *Exit A382 into village, at T-junct right to Caseley,
house 2nd on left*

Set just a stroll from the village pub, church and tea
room, Woodley House is a peaceful and tranquil retreat,
with super views over the rolling countryside. A hearty
breakfast, featuring as many as 12 home-made
preserves, home-baked bread and a vast range of
cooked breakfast options, can be enjoyed in the
charming dining room. A good base for walkers, and
dogs are welcome too.

Rooms 1 en suite S £50; D £70-£72* **Facilities** FTV TVL
tea/coffee Cen ht 🅿 **Parking** 3 **Notes** No Children 10yrs
🐾

LYDFORD   Map 3 SX58

PREMIER COLLECTION

Moor View House

★★★★★ 🍴 GUEST ACCOMMODATION

Vale Down EX20 4BB
☎ 01822 820220 📠 01822 820220
dir: *4m from Sourton A30/A386, signed Tavistock, NE
of Lydford*

Built around 1870, this charming house once changed
hands over a game of cards. The elegant bedrooms are
furnished with interesting pieces and retain many
original features. Breakfast, and dinner by
arrangement, are served house-party style at a large
oak table. The two acres of moorland gardens give
access to Dartmoor.

Rooms 4 en suite 1 annexe rm (1 pri facs) S £45-£55;
D £70-£85* **Facilities** FTV Lounge TVL tea/coffee
Dinner available Cen ht Licensed ⚓ 🅿 **Extras** Fruit -
complimentary **Parking** 15 **Notes** LB ⊗ No Children
12yrs Closed 23 Dec-2 Jan 🐾

LYNMOUTH   Map 3 SS74

PREMIER COLLECTION

The Heatherville

★★★★★ 🍴 🍴 GUEST ACCOMMODATION

Tors Park EX35 6NB
☎ 01598 752327 & 753893 📠 01598 753893
e-mail: theheatherville@aol.com
dir: *Exit A39 into Tors Rd, 1st left fork into Tors Park*

This wonderful Victorian establishment stands high
above Lynmouth, from where the views across the
wooded valley are quite superb. There is an abundance
of charm and quality here with each bedroom
individually styled with both comfort and character.
Public rooms are also inviting with an elegant lounge
and snug bar, whilst the dining room is the attractive
venue for skilfully prepared dinners and substantial
breakfasts.

Rooms 6 en suite D £95-£120 **Facilities** FTV DVD
Lounge tea/coffee Dinner available Cen ht Licensed
Wi-fi 🅿 **Parking** 6 **Notes** LB ⊗ No Children 16yrs Closed
Nov-Mar

Rock House

★★★★ GUEST ACCOMMODATION

Manor Green EX35 6EN
☎ 01598 753508 📠 0800 7566964
e-mail: enquiries@rock-house.co.uk
dir: *From A39, at foot of Countisbury Hill right into drive,
pass Manor Green (play area) to Rock House*

Located next to the river with wonderful views of the
harbour and out to sea, this enchanting establishment
dates back to the 18th century and has much to offer.
Bedrooms are well appointed, and many have the benefit
of wonderful views of the rolling waves. A choice of
menus is offered, either in the spacious lounge/bar or in
the smart dining room. The garden is a popular venue for
cream teas in the summer.

Rooms 8 en suite (1 GF) **Facilities** TVL tea/coffee Dinner
available Cen ht Licensed Wi-fi **Parking** 8 **Notes** Closed
24-25 Dec

Save on B&Bs and Hotels. Book at **theAA.com/hotel**

DEVON 119 ENGLAND

LYNTON — Map 3 SS74

PREMIER COLLECTION

Victoria Lodge

★★★★★ 🏡 GUEST ACCOMMODATION

30-31 Lee Rd EX35 6BS
☎ 01598 753203
e-mail: info@victorialodge.co.uk
web: www.victorialodge.co.uk
dir: *Exit A39 in village centre opposite post office*

A warm welcome awaits at this elegant villa, built in the 1880s and located in the heart of Lynton. Named after Queen Victoria's children and grandchildren, and reflecting the style of the period, bedrooms are decorated in rich colours and feature coronets, half-tester and four-poster beds.

Rooms 8 en suite S £64-£128; D £75-£150 **Facilities** FTV DVD iPod docking station Lounge tea/coffee Cen ht Licensed Wi-fi 🅿 **Parking** 6 **Notes** ⊗ No Children 11yrs Closed Nov-23 Mar

---

Pine Lodge Guest House

[U]

Lynway EX35 6AX
☎ 01598 753230
e-mail: info@pinelodgelynton.co.uk

Currently the rating for this establishment is not confirmed. This may be due to a change of ownership or because it has only recently joined the AA rating scheme.

Rooms 5 en suite D £70-£80*

MODBURY — Map 3 SX65

The Exeter Inn

[U]

Church St PL21 0QR
☎ 01548 831225

Currently the rating for this establishment is not confirmed. This may be due to a change of ownership or because it has only recently joined the AA rating scheme.

Rooms 6 en suite (1 fmly) **Facilities** FTV tea/coffee Dinner available Wi-fi

---

MORETONHAMPSTEAD — Map 3 SX78

Great Sloncombe Farm (SX737864)

★★★★ 🅰 FARMHOUSE

TQ13 8QF
☎ 01647 440595 📠 01647 440595 Mrs T Merchant
e-mail: hmerchant@sloncombe.freeserve.co.uk
dir: *A382 from Moretonhampstead towards Chagford, 1.5m left at sharp double bend & farm 0.5m up lane*

Rooms 3 en suite **Facilities** FTV tea/coffee Cen ht Wi-fi **Parking** 3 **Notes** 170 acres beef/horses

---

NEWTON ABBOT — Map 3 SX87

See also Widecombe in the Moor

Bulleigh Park Farm (SX860660)

★★★★ 🏡 FARMHOUSE

Ipplepen TQ12 5UA
☎ 01803 872254 📠 01803 872254 Mrs A Dallyn
e-mail: bulleigh@lineone.net
dir: *3.5m S of Newton Abbot. Exit A381 at Parkhill Cross, by petrol station, for Compton, 1m, signed*

Bulleigh Park is a working farm, producing award-winning Aberdeen Angus beef. The owners have also won an award for green tourism by reducing the impact of the business on the environment. Expect a friendly welcome at this family home set in glorious countryside, where breakfasts are notable for the wealth of fresh, local and home-made produce, and the porridge is cooked using a secret recipe.

Rooms 2 en suite 1 annexe en suite (1 fmly) S £45-£48; D £74-£90 **Facilities** FTV Lounge TVL tea/coffee Cen ht Wi-fi **Parking** 6 **Notes** LB Closed Dec-1 Feb 60 acres beef/sheep/hens

---

NEWTON POPPLEFORD — Map 3 SY08

Moores' Restaurant & Rooms

★★★ 🍴🍴 RESTAURANT WITH ROOMS

6 Greenbank, High St EX10 0EB
☎ 01395 568100
e-mail: info.moores@btconnect.com
dir: *On A3052 in village centre, 3m from Sidmouth*

Centrally located in the village, this small restaurant offers very comfortable, practically furnished bedrooms. Guests are assured of a friendly welcome and relaxed, efficient service. Good quality, locally sourced ingredients are used to produce imaginative dishes full of natural flavours.

Rooms 3 rms (1 en suite) (2 fmly) **Facilities** FTV tea/coffee Dinner available Cen ht ch fac **Conf** Max 12 Board 12 **Notes** ⊗ Closed 1st 2wks Jan No coaches

---

OTTERY ST MARY — Map 3 SY19

Fluxton Farm

★★ BED AND BREAKFAST

Fluxton EX11 1RJ
☎ 01404 812818 📠 01404 814843
web: www.fluxtonfarm.co.uk
dir: *2m SW of Ottery St Mary. B3174, W from Ottery over river, left, next left to Fluxton*

A haven for cat lovers, Fluxton Farm offers comfortable accommodation with a choice of lounges and a large garden, complete with pond and ducks. Set in peaceful farmland four miles from the coast, this 16th-century longhouse has a wealth of beams and open fireplaces.

Rooms 7 en suite S £27.50-£32.50; D £55-£65* **Facilities** FTV TVL tea/coffee Cen ht Wi-fi 🅿 **Parking** 15 **Notes** LB No Children 8yrs RS Nov-Apr pre-booked & wknds only 🐾

The Clydesdale

★★★★ GUEST HOUSE

5 Polsham Park TQ3 2AD
☎ 01803 558402 📠 01803 558402
e-mail: theclydesdale@hotmail.co.uk
web: www.theclydesdale.co.uk
dir: *Exit A3022 (Torquay Rd) into Lower Polsham Rd, 2nd right into Polsham Park*

Tucked away in a quiet residential area, this is an ideal location from which to explore the varied attractions of Paignton and the wider Torbay area. The welcome is warm and genuine with every effort made to ensure a relaxed and rewarding stay. The bedrooms are well appointed and provide all the expected modern comforts. Breakfasts, and dinner by arrangement, are served in the dining room; a separate guest lounge is also available.

Rooms 7 en suite (1 fmly) (2 GF) **Facilities** FTV TVL tea/coffee Dinner available Cen ht Wi-fi 🛝 **Parking** 6 **Notes** LB ⊗ Closed Xmas & New Year

Merritt House B&B

★★★★ 🏠 GUEST ACCOMMODATION

7 Queens Rd TQ4 6AT
☎ 01803 528959
e-mail: bookings@merritthouse.co.uk
dir: *From Paignton seafront, right into Torbay Rd, 1st left into Queens Rd, house on right*

Just a five-minute stroll from the seafront and town centre, this elegant Victorian property is ideally situated to make the most of this traditional resort. The owners take understandable pride in their establishment and will assist in any way possible to ensure a relaxed and rewarding stay. Bedrooms and bathrooms are thoughtfully furnished and generously equipped, and breakfast is a real treat with plenty of choice, and an emphasis on local and home-made produce.

Rooms 7 en suite (3 GF) S £28-£45; D £50-£74
Facilities FTV DVD tea/coffee ht Wi-fi 🛝 Drying room
Extras Fruit - complimentary **Conf** Max 7 Board 7
Parking 4 **Notes** No Children 14yrs Closed 20 Dec-7 Jan

The Wentworth Guest House

★★★★ GUEST HOUSE

18 Youngs Park Rd, Goodrington TQ4 6BU
☎ 01803 557843
e-mail: enquiries@wentworthguesthouse.co.uk
dir: *Through Paignton on A378, 1m left at rdbt, sharp right onto Roundham Rd, right & right again onto Youngs Park Rd*

Quietly located opposite a pretty park, this is an ideal location for exploring the many and varied attractions of the English Riviera. Goodrington's lovely beaches are just a short stroll away and the town centre is a 10-15 minute walk away. The caring owners make every effort to ensure guests enjoy a relaxing break, and are always on hand to assist with local information. Bedrooms offer good levels of comfort and include both a dog-friendly room and family rooms. Breakfast is served in the informal dining room with a cosy guest lounge also provided.

Rooms 10 en suite (1 fmly) S £27-£30; D £54-£70*
Facilities FTV TVL tea/coffee Cen ht Licensed Wi-fi
Parking 5 **Notes** LB Closed 16 Dec-2 Jan

Bay Cottage

★★★ GUEST ACCOMMODATION

4 Beach Rd TQ4 6AY
☎ 01803 525729
web: www.baycottagepaignton.co.uk
dir: *Along B3201 Esplanade Rd past Paignton Pier, Beach Rd 2nd right*

Quietly located in a level terrace, the seafront, park, harbour and shops are all just a short stroll away. Run in a friendly and relaxed manner, Bay Cottage offers a range of bedrooms of various shapes and sizes, with a guest lounge also made available. Dinner is offered by prior arrangement and includes enjoyable home cooking in hearty portions.

Rooms 8 en suite (3 fmly) S £22-£25; D £44-£50
Facilities FTV TVL tea/coffee Dinner available Cen ht Wi-fi
Notes LB ⊗

The Park

★★★ GUEST ACCOMMODATION

Esplanade Rd TQ4 6BQ
☎ 01803 557856 📠 01803 555626
e-mail: stay@theparkhotel.net
web: www.theparkhotel.net
dir: *On Paignton seafront, nearly opposite pier*

This large establishment has a prominent position on the seafront with excellent views of Torbay. The pleasant bedrooms are spacious and available in a number of options, and several have sea views. Entertainment is provided on some evenings in the lounge. Dinner and breakfast are served in the spacious dining room, which overlooks the attractive front garden.

Rooms 47 en suite (5 fmly) (3 GF) S £25-£43; D £50-£86
Facilities tea/coffee Dinner available Cen ht Lift Licensed Wi-fi Pool table 🛝 Games room with 3/4 snooker table & table tennis **Conf** Max 120 Thtr 80 Class 120 Board 40 **Parking** 38 **Notes** LB

Berkeley's of St James

★★★★ GUEST ACCOMMODATION

4 St James Place East, The Hoe PL1 3AS
☎ 01752 221654 📠 01752 221654
e-mail: enquiry@onthehoe.co.uk
dir: *Exit A38 towards city centre, left at The Hoe sign, straight on at 7 sets of lights, left into Athenaeum St, right into Crescent Av, 1st left*

Located in a quiet square close to The Hoe and just a short walk from the city centre, this is a good choice for business or leisure. Bedrooms are comfortable and attractive, and come equipped with a number of thoughtful extras. An enjoyable breakfast using organic and local produce, whenever possible, is served in the dining room.

Rooms 5 en suite (1 fmly) (1 GF) S £45-£55; D £65-£75 **Facilities** FTV tea/coffee Cen ht Wi-fi ⚓ **Parking** 3 **Notes** LB ⊗ Closed 23 Dec-1 Jan

Brittany Guest House
★★★★ GUEST ACCOMMODATION

28 Athenaeum St, The Hoe PL1 2RQ
☎ 01752 262247
e-mail: thebrittanyguesthouse@btconnect.com
dir: *A38/City Centre follow signs for Pavillions, left at mini-rdbt, left at lights into Athenaeum St*

Situated in a pleasant street, within walking distance of Plymouth's many attractions, this well presented house offers comfortable and well-equipped accommodation. The proprietors provide friendly hospitality, and many guests return frequently. Freshly cooked breakfast is served in the attractive dining room. Parking available.

Rooms 10 en suite (3 fmly) (1 GF) **Facilities** FTV tea/coffee Cen ht Wi-fi **Parking** 6 **Notes** ⊗ No Children 5yrs Closed 20 Dec-2 Jan

Jewell's
★★★★ GUEST ACCOMMODATION

220 Citadel Rd, The Hoe PL1 3BB
☎ 01752 254760 ⎙ 01752 254760
e-mail: jewellsguest@btconnect.com
dir: *A38 towards city centre, follow sign for The Barbican, then The Hoe. Left at lights, right at top of road into Citadel Rd. Jewell's 0.25m*

This smart, comfortable, family-run establishment is only a short walk from The Hoe and is convenient for the city centre and The Barbican. Bedrooms come with a wide range of extra facilities, and breakfast is served in the pleasant dining room. Some secure parking is available.

Rooms 10 rms (7 en suite) (5 fmly) **Facilities** FTV tea/coffee Cen ht Wi-fi **Parking** 3 **Notes** LB ⊗

Rainbow Lodge Guest House
★★★★ GUEST HOUSE

29 Athenaeum St, The Hoe PL1 2RQ
☎ 01752 229699
e-mail: info@rainbowlodgeplymouth.co.uk
web: www.rainbowlodgeplymouth.co.uk
dir: *A38 onto A374. Follow City Centre signs for 3m, into Exeter St. Bear left into Breton Side at lights, follow road, left into Athenaeum St at Walrus pub*

Just a short stroll from The Hoe, this small and friendly establishment is well placed for exploring the city. Bedrooms are varied in size and style, some of which are suitable for family use. Substantial breakfasts are served in the homely dining room.

Rooms 11 rms (7 en suite) (1 pri facs) (2 fmly) (1 GF) S £32-£48; D £49-£65* **Facilities** FTV tea/coffee Cen ht Wi-fi **Extras** Speciality toiletries **Parking** 6 **Notes** LB ⊗ No Children 5yrs Closed 22 Dec-5 Jan

Ashgrove House
★★★ GUEST ACCOMMODATION

218 Citadel Rd, The Hoe PL1 3BB
☎ 01752 664046 ⎙ 01752 252112
e-mail: ashgroveho@aol.com
dir: *Follow signs for The Hoe*

Conveniently situated within walking distance of all the city's attractions, this personally-run establishment offers well-presented accommodation; ideal for commercial visitors and also welcoming to children. Freshly-cooked breakfasts are provided and a comfortable lounge is available for guests.

Rooms 10 en suite (5 fmly) **Facilities** FTV TVL tea/coffee Cen ht Wi-fi **Notes** ⊗

Devonshire Guest House
★★★ GUEST ACCOMMODATION

22 Lockyer Rd, Mannamead PL3 4RL
☎ 01752 220726 ⎙ 01752 220766
e-mail: devonshiregh@blueyonder.co.uk
dir: *At Hyde Park pub on traffic island turn left into Wilderness Rd. After 60yds left into Lockyer Rd*

This comfortable Victorian house is located in a residential area close to Mutley Plain high street, from where there is a regular bus service to the city centre. The well-proportioned bedrooms are bright and attractive, and guests can use the comfy lounge. Parking is available.

Rooms 10 rms (5 en suite) (4 fmly) (3 GF) **Facilities** FTV TVL tea/coffee Cen ht Licensed Wi-fi **Parking** 6 **Notes** ⊗

The Firs Guest Accommodation
★★★ GUEST ACCOMMODATION

13 Pier St, West Hoe PL1 3BS
☎ 01752 262870 & 300010
e-mail: thefirsguesthouse@hotmail.co.uk

A well located and well established house on the West Hoe with convenient on-street parking. Friendly owners and comfortable rooms make it a popular destination.

Rooms 7 rms (2 en suite) (2 fmly) (1 GF) **Facilities** FTV tea/coffee Dinner available Cen ht Wi-fi ⚓ Fishing trips can be arranged **Notes** LB

The Lamplighter
★★★ GUEST ACCOMMODATION

103 Citadel Rd, The Hoe PL1 2RN
☎ 01752 663855 & 07793 360815
e-mail: stay@lamplighterplymouth.co.uk
web: www.lamplighterplymouth.co.uk
dir: *Near war memorial*

With easy access to The Hoe, The Barbican and the city centre, this comfortable house provides a good base for leisure or business. Bedrooms, including family rooms, are light and airy and furnished to a consistent standard.

Breakfast is served in the dining room, which has an adjoining lounge area.

Rooms 9 rms (7 en suite) (2 pri facs) (2 fmly) S £35-£55; D £50-£60* **Facilities** FTV TVL tea/coffee Cen ht Wi-fi ⚓ **Parking** 4

ROUSDON   Map 4 SY29

PREMIER COLLECTION

The Dower House
★★★★★ ⊜ GUEST ACCOMMODATION

DT7 3RB
☎ 01297 21047 ⎙ 01428 661387
e-mail: info@dhhotel.com
dir: *Off A3052, 3m W of Lyme Regis*

Handily placed, a short drive from Lyme Regis and the coast, this fine old Victorian building has an interesting and varied history. The atmosphere is warm and welcoming, with all bedrooms offering lots of comfort and character. The friendly bar lounge has doors opening onto a decked area with wonderful views across the rolling countryside. Local produce, including excellent fish, features on the daily-changing menu, and is served in the elegant dining room. There is a heated outdoor swimming pool.

Rooms 10 en suite (2 fmly) (1 GF) **Facilities** FTV tea/coffee Dinner available Direct Dial Cen ht Licensed Wi-fi **Conf** Max 45 Thtr 45 Class 20 Board 20 **Parking** 25 **Notes** Closed 2-31 Jan Civ Wed 140

SEATON   Map 4 SY29

Mariners
★★★★ ⚓ ⊜ GUEST ACCOMMODATION

East Walk Esplanade EX12 2NP
☎ 01297 20560
web: www.marinershotelseaton.co.uk
dir: *Off A3052 signed Seaton, Mariners on seafront*

Located just yards from the beach and cliff paths, this comfortable establishment has a friendly and relaxed atmosphere. Bedrooms, some with sea views, are well equipped, and public rooms are light and airy. The dining room is the venue for enjoyable breakfasts that utilise quality local produce; afternoon teas are also available on the seafront terrace.

Rooms 10 en suite (1 fmly) (2 GF) **Facilities** tea/coffee Dinner available Cen ht Licensed **Parking** 10 **Notes** ⊗ No Children 5yrs RS Nov-Jan Closed at certain times

SEATON *continued*

Holmleigh House Bed and Breakfast

★★★★ 🄰 GUEST ACCOMMODATION

Sea Hill EX12 2QT
☎ 01297 625671
e-mail: contact@holmleighhouse.com
Rooms 3 en suite S £48-£55; D £70-£80 **Facilities** DVD
iPod docking station TVL tea/coffee Cen ht Wi-fi 🍷
Extras Speciality toiletries, robes, mini-fridge **Notes** LB
🚫 Closed 23-28 Dec 🐾

SHALDON

See Teignmouth

SIDMOUTH   Map 3 SY18

See also Ottery St Mary

PREMIER COLLECTION

The Salty Monk

★★★★★ ◉◉ 🍴 RESTAURANT WITH ROOMS

Church St, Sidford EX10 9QP
☎ 01395 513174
e-mail: saltymonk@btconnect.com
web: www.saltymonk.co.uk
dir: *On A3052 opposite church in Sidford*

Set in the village of Sidford, this attractive property
dates from the 16th century. There's oodles of style and
appeal here and each bedroom has a unique identity.
Bathrooms are equally special with multi-jet showers,
spa baths and cosseting robes and towels. The output
from the kitchen is impressive with excellent local
produce very much in evidence, served in the elegant
surroundings of the restaurant. A mini spa facility is
available.

Rooms 5 en suite 1 annexe en suite (3 GF) S £75-£150;
D £120-£180* **Facilities** FTV DVD Lounge tea/coffee
Dinner available Cen ht Wi-fi 🍷 18 Sauna Gym 🍷 Hot tub
Extras Speciality toiletries etc - complimentary
Conf Max 14 Board 14 **Parking** 20 **Notes** LB Closed
1wk Nov & 3wks Jan No coaches

Blue Ball Inn

★★★★★ INN

Stevens Cross, Sidford EX10 9QL
☎ 01395 514062 📠 01395 519584
e-mail: rogernewton@blueballinn.net
dir: *On A3052, at Sidford straight over lights. Inn 600yds*

Ideally placed for exploring the many delights of east
Devon, this long established inn has been overseen by
five generations of the Newton family since 1912, and
can trace its history back to 1385. After a devastating fire
in 2006, the inn has been lovingly rebuilt and now
provides impressive levels of comfort and quality. The
bedrooms and stylish bathrooms provide an appealing
blend of old and new. The extensive bars have cosy nooks

in which to enjoy the food and drink on offer, with an
attractive garden also available.

Rooms 9 en suite (2 fmly) (1 GF) S £60; D £95*
Facilities FTV Lounge tea/coffee Dinner available Cen ht
Wi-fi 🍷 18 🍷 **Conf** Max 65 Thtr 30 Class 50 Board 30
Parking 80 **Notes** LB 🚫

The Groveside

★★★★ GUEST HOUSE

Vicarage Rd EX10 8UQ
☎ 01395 513406
e-mail: info@thegroveside.co.uk
web: www.thegroveside.co.uk
dir: *0.5m N of seafront on A375*

Conveniently situated a short, level walking distance
from the town centre, The Groveside offers boutique-style
accommodation. A number of influences, such as Art
Deco, have been used to impressive effect in the
bedrooms, while bathrooms also show individuality and
flair. Guests are assured of attentive service and a
relaxed and friendly atmosphere. Home-cooked evening
meals are served by prior arrangement. On-site parking is
an added bonus.

Rooms 9 en suite S £37-£40; D £74-£80* **Facilities** FTV
TVL tea/coffee Dinner available Cen ht Wi-fi Pamper
wknds in Nov **Conf** Max 14 Class 14 Board 14 **Parking** 9
Notes LB 🚫 No Children 12yrs

The Old Farmhouse

★★★★ GUEST ACCOMMODATION

Hillside Rd EX10 8JG
☎ 01395 512284
web: www.theoldfarmhousesidmouth.co.uk
dir: *A3052 from Exeter to Sidmouth, right at Bowd x-rds,
2m left at rdbt, left at mini-rdbt, next right, over hump-
back bridge, bear right on the corner*

This beautiful 16th-century thatched farmhouse, in a
quiet residential area just a stroll from the Esplanade
and shops, has been lovingly restored. Bedrooms are
attractively decorated and the charming public rooms
feature beams and an inglenook fireplace. The welcoming
proprietors provide memorable dinners using traditional
recipes and fresh local ingredients.

The Old Farmhouse

Rooms 3 en suite 3 annexe en suite (1 fmly) (1 GF)
D £64-£76* **Facilities** TVL TV3B tea/coffee Dinner
available Cen ht Licensed Wi-fi **Parking** 4 **Notes** LB 🚫 No
Children 12yrs Closed Nov-Feb 🐾

Cheriton Guest House

★★★★ GUEST ACCOMMODATION

Vicarage Rd EX10 8UQ
☎ 01395 513810 & 07899 793314
e-mail: info@cheriton-guesthouse.co.uk

Located just a 10-minute stroll from the seafront, this is
a convenient location for exploring the charming appeal
of Sidmouth. A flexible approach to guest requirements is
adopted here, and every effort is made to ensure a relaxed
and rewarding experience. Bedrooms provide good levels
of comfort with all the expected extras; public rooms
include a stylish lounge and airy breakfast room.

Rooms 8 en suite **Facilities** FTV Lounge tea/coffee Cen ht
Wi-fi **Parking** 7 **Notes** LB 🚫

Dukes

★★★★ 🍺 INN

The Esplanade EX10 8AR
☎ 01395 513320 📠 01395 519318
e-mail: dukes@sidmouthinn.co.uk
web: www.dukessidmouth.co.uk
dir: *Exit A3052 to Sidmouth, left onto Esplanade*

Situated in the heart of Sidmouth, this stylish inn offers a
relaxed and convivial atmosphere created by a great
team of attentive staff. Bedrooms provide good levels of
comfort and a number have the benefit of sea views. The
menu utilises the seasonal produce that this area has to
offer. A choice of dining areas is available including the
patio garden - perfect for soaking up the sun.

Rooms 13 en suite (5 fmly) S £40-£51; D £90-£132*
Facilities FTV DVD iPod docking station tea/coffee Dinner
available Direct Dial Cen ht Wi-fi **Parking** 9 **Notes** LB RS
25 Dec Bar & rest for residents only

Glendevon

★★★★ GUEST HOUSE

Cotmaton Rd EX10 8QX
☎ 01395 514028
e-mail: enquiries@glendevon-hotel.co.uk
web: www.glendevon-hotel.co.uk
dir: A3052 onto B3176 to mini-rdbt. Right, house 100yds
on right

Located in a quiet residential area just a short walk from
the town centre and beaches, this stylish Victorian house
offers neat, comfortable bedrooms. Guests are assured of
a warm welcome from the resident owners, who provide
attentive service and wholesome home-cooked evening
meals by arrangement. A lounge is also available.

Rooms 8 en suite **Facilities** FTV tea/coffee Dinner
available Cen ht Licensed **Notes** ⊗ No Children ⊜

Bramley Lodge Guest House

★★★ GUEST HOUSE

Vicarage Rd EX10 8UQ
☎ 01395 515710
e-mail: bramleyowner@btinternet.com
dir: 0.5m N of seafront on A375

Guests are assured of a warm and friendly welcome at
this family-run, small guest house, located about a half
mile from the sea. The neatly furnished bedrooms vary in
size, and all are equipped to a good standard. Home-
cooked evening meals are available, by prior
arrangement, with special diets on request.

Rooms 6 rms (5 en suite) (1 fmly) S £33-£39; D £66-£80
Facilities FTV Lounge tea/coffee Dinner available Cen ht
Parking 6 **Notes** ⊗ Closed mid Nov-mid Feb RS 1st wk
Aug week-long bookings only ⊜

Bearslake Inn

★★★★ ⊜ INN

Lake EX20 4HQ
☎ 01837 861334 ▨ 01837 861108
e-mail: enquiries@bearslakeinn.com
dir: A30 from Exeter onto A386 signed Sourton &
Tavistock, 2m on left from junct

Situated on the edge of the Dartmoor National Park, this
thatched inn is believed to date back to the 13th century
and was originally part of a working farm. There is
character in abundance here with beams, flagstone floors
and low ceilings, all of which contribute to an engaging
atmosphere. Bedrooms have great individuality and
provide period features combined with contemporary
comforts. Local produce is very much in evidence on the
menu with dinner served in the attractive Stable
Restaurant. The beer garden is bordered by a moorland
stream with wonderful views across open countryside.

Rooms 6 en suite (3 fmly) (1 GF) S £68; D £96*
Facilities FTV DVD tea/coffee Dinner available Cen ht
Wi-fi **Parking** 35 **Notes** LB No coaches

Glazebrook House

★★★★ ◉ GUEST ACCOMMODATION

TQ10 9JE
☎ 01364 73322 ▨ 01364 72350
e-mail: enquiries@glazebrookhouse.com
web: www.glazebrookhouse.com
dir: From A38 follow brown signs

Enjoying a tranquil and convenient location next to the
Dartmoor National Park and set within four acres of
gardens, this 18th-century former gentleman's residence
offers a friendly welcome and comfortable
accommodation. Elegant public areas provide ample
space to relax and enjoy the atmosphere, whilst bedrooms
are well appointed and include a number with four-poster
beds. The dishes on the menus are created from
interesting combinations of fresh, locally-sourced
produce.

Rooms 10 en suite S £50-£55; D £80-£135*
Facilities FTV Lounge tea/coffee Dinner available Direct
Dial Cen ht Licensed Wi-fi ♨ 18 ♨ Reflexology & reiki
Extras Speciality toiletries **Conf** Max 80 Thtr 80 Class 60
Board 40 **Parking** 40 **Notes** LB Closed 1st 2wks Jan RS
1st wk Aug restaurant closed Civ Wed

The Coaching Inn

★★★ INN

Queen St EX36 3BJ
☎ 01769 572526
dir: In town centre

This long established, former coaching inn, has been
providing a warm welcome for weary travellers for many
years. Situated in the heart of this bustling town, guests
are assured of a relaxing stay with a genuine, family-run
atmosphere. Bedrooms provide good levels of comfort. An
extensive menu is provided with an emphasis on quality
and value for money.

Rooms 10 en suite (2 fmly) **Facilities** tea/coffee Dinner
available Cen ht Wi-fi Pool table **Conf** Max 100 Thtr 40
Class 40 Board 40 **Parking** 40 **Notes** ⊗

West Down Guest House & Farm

★★★ 🄰 GUEST ACCOMMODATION

Whitechapel, Bishops Nympton EX36 3EQ
☎ 01769 550839
e-mail: westdown@btinternet.com
web: www.westdown-devon.co.uk
dir: M5 junct 27 onto A361 towards Barnstaple. At 2nd
rdbt, 3rd exit & 150yds over bridge, immediate right
Rooms 5 en suite S £35; D £65*

PREMIER COLLECTION

Strete Barton House

★★★★★ GUEST HOUSE

Totnes Rd TQ6 0RU
☎ 01803 770364 ▨ 01803 771182
e-mail: info@stretebarton.co.uk
web: www.stretebarton.co.uk
dir: Off A379 coastal road into village, just below
church

This delightful 16th-century former farmhouse blends
stylish accommodation with its original character. The
bedrooms are very comfortably furnished and well
equipped with useful extras. Breakfast utilises quality
local produce and is served in the spacious dining
room. Guests are also welcome to use the very
comfortable lounge, complete with log-burning stove lit
in the cooler months. The village lies between
Dartmouth and Kingsbridge and has easy access to the
natural beauty of the South Hams as well as local pubs
and restaurants.

Rooms 5 rms (4 en suite) (1 pri facs) 1 annexe en suite
D £105-£160* **Facilities** FTV DVD Lounge tea/coffee
Cen ht Wi-fi ♨ 18 ♨ **Extras** Speciality toiletries, guest
fridge **Parking** 4 **Notes** LB No Children 8yrs

See advert on page 113

TAVISTOCK — Map 3 SX47

PREMIER COLLECTION

Tor Cottage

⌂ GUEST ACCOMMODATION

PL16 0JE
☎ 01822 860248 📠 01822 860126
e-mail: info@torcottage.co.uk
web: www.torcottage.co.uk

(For full entry see Chillaton)

The Coach House

★★★ GUEST ACCOMMODATION

Ottery PL19 8NS
☎ 01822 617515 📠 01822 617515
e-mail: estevens255@aol.com
web: www.thecoachousehotel.co.uk
dir: *2.5m NW of Tavistock. A390 from Tavistock to Gulworthy Cross, at rdbt take 3rd exit towards Chipshop Inn turn right to Ottery, 1st building in village*

Dating from 1857, this building was constructed for the Duke of Bedford and converted by the current owners. Some bedrooms are on the ground floor and in an adjacent barn conversion. Dinner is available in the cosy dining room or the restaurant, which leads onto the south-facing garden.

Rooms 6 en suite 3 annexe en suite (4 GF) S £40-£49; D £65-£90* **Facilities** FTV Lounge tea/coffee Dinner available Direct Dial Cen ht Licensed Wi-fi **Parking** 24 **Notes** LB No Children 5yrs

---

Sampford Manor

★★★ BED AND BREAKFAST

Sampford Spiney PL20 6LH
☎ 01822 853442
e-mail: manor@sampford-spiney.fsnet.co.uk
web: www.sampford-spiney.fsnet.co.uk
dir: *B3357 towards Princetown, right at 1st x-rds. Next x-rds Warren Cross left for Sampford Spiney. 2nd right, house below church*

Once owned by Sir Francis Drake, this manor house is tucked away in a tranquil corner of Dartmoor National Park. The family home is full of character, with exposed beams and slate floors, while outside, a herd of award-winning alpacas graze in the fields. Genuine hospitality is assured together with scrumptious breakfasts featuring home-produced eggs. Children, horses (stabling available) and dogs are all equally welcome.

Rooms 3 rms (2 pri facs) (1 fmly) **Facilities** FTV tea/coffee Cen ht **Parking** 3 **Notes** Closed Xmas 🐾

Tavistock Inn

ⓤ

19 Brook St PL19 0HD
☎ 01822 615736

Currently the rating for this establishment is not confirmed. This may be due to a change of ownership or because it has only recently joined the AA rating scheme.

Rooms 4 en suite (2 fmly) **Facilities** FTV tea/coffee Dinner available Wi-fi

---

TEDBURN ST MARY — Map 3 SX89

PREMIER COLLECTION

Frogmill Bed & Breakfast

★★★★★ ⌂ ⇔ BED AND BREAKFAST

Frogmill EX6 6ES
☎ 01647 272727 📠 01647 24088
e-mail: frogmillbandb@btinternet.com
web: www.frogmillbandb.co.uk
dir: *From A30 take exit signed Cheriton Bishop. Take Tedburn road, then left towards Credition. After 1m left to Froggy Mill, 1m on left*

Situated in the heart of Devon, this former mill house is as picturesque as could be, complete with thatch and babbling brook. The grounds are spectacular with around 10 acres of woodland and pasture, and the welcome is as impressive as the location with a cream tea in the garden being the perfect way to start the stay. Bedrooms offer comfort, quality and individuality and include a separate, self-contained suite, away from the main building. Bathrooms offer soft towels and invigorating showers. Food is a treat here with eggs for breakfast contributed by the resident hens, and accomplished dinners available by prior arrangement. In addition to the elegant dining room, a guest lounge is provided with deep leather sofas and woodburner.

Rooms 2 en suite 1 annexe en suite (1 fmly) (1 GF) S £50-£60; D £80-£95* **Facilities** STV FTV iPod docking station Lounge tea/coffee Dinner available Cen ht Wi-fi 🔒 **Extras** Fruit, robes, chocolates - complimentary **Parking** 6

TEIGNMOUTH — Map 3 SX97

PREMIER COLLECTION

Thomas Luny House

⌂ GUEST ACCOMMODATION

Teign St TQ14 8EG
☎ 01626 772976
e-mail: alisonandjohn@thomas-luny-house.co.uk
web: www.thomas-luny-house.co.uk
dir: *A381 to Teignmouth, at 3rd lights right to quay, 50yds left into Teign St, after 60yds right through white archway*

Built in the late 18th century by marine artist Thomas Luny, this charming house offers unique and comfortable accommodation in the old quarter of Teignmouth. Bedrooms are individually decorated and furnished, and all are well equipped with a good range of extras. An elegant drawing room with French windows leads into a walled garden with a terraced sitting area. A superb breakfast, featuring local produce, is served in the attractive dining room.

Rooms 4 en suite S £65-£75; D £80-£102* **Facilities** FTV Lounge tea/coffee Direct Dial Cen ht Licensed Wi-fi **Parking** 8 **Notes** LB ⊗ No Children 12yrs

Save on B&Bs and Hotels. Book at **theAA.com/hotel**

DEVON 125 ENGLAND

Potters Mooring

★★★★ GUEST ACCOMMODATION

30 The Green, Shaldon TQ14 0DN
☎ 01626 873225 📠 01626 872909
e-mail: mail@pottersmooring.co.uk
web: www.pottersmooring.co.uk
dir: *A38 onto A380 signed Torquay, B3192 to Teignmouth & Shaldon, over river, follow signs to Potters Mooring*

A former sea captain's residence dating from 1625, Potters Mooring has been appointed to provide charming accommodation of a very high standard, including a four-poster room. The friendly proprietors make every effort to ensure an enjoyable stay and the Captain Potter's breakfast features tasty local produce.

Rooms 5 rms (4 en suite) (1 pri facs) (1 fmly)
Facilities FTV tea/coffee Cen ht Wi-fi **Parking** 8

TIVERTON   Map 3 SS91

Hornhill Farmhouse (SS965117)

★★★★ 🏠 FARMHOUSE

Exeter Hill EX16 4PL
☎ 01884 253352 Mrs B Pugsley
e-mail: hornhill@tinyworld.co.uk
web: www.hornhill-farmhouse.co.uk
dir: *Signs to Grand Western Canal, right fork up Exeter Hill. Farmhouse on left at top of hill*

Hornhill has a peaceful hilltop setting with panoramic views of the town and the Exe Valley. Elegant decor and furnishings enhance the character of the farmhouse, which in part dates from the 18th century. Bedrooms are beautifully equipped with modern facilities and there is a lovely sitting room with a log fire. Breakfast is served at one large table in the spacious dining room.

Rooms 3 rms (1 en suite) (2 pri facs) (1 GF) S £35-£45; D £65-£75 **Facilities** FTV Lounge tea/coffee Wi-fi 🍴 **Parking** 5 **Notes** ⊗ No Children 12yrs 🐄 75 acres beef/sheep

Quoit-At-Cross (ST923188)

★★★ FARMHOUSE

Stoodleigh EX16 9PJ
☎ 01398 351280 Mrs L Hill
e-mail: quoit-at-cross@hotmail.co.uk
dir: *M5 junct 27 for Tiverton. A396 N for Bampton, after 3.5m turn left over bridge for Stoodleigh, farmhouse on 1st junct in village centre*

This delightful, stone-built farmhouse commands lovely views over rolling Devonshire countryside and is a great place from which to explore this picturesque area. A warm and genuine welcome is assured with a homely and relaxed atmosphere. The comfortable, attractive bedrooms are well furnished and have many extra facilities. A crackling fire keeps the lounge snug and warm during colder nights, whilst in the summer, the pretty garden is available to guests.

Rooms 4 en suite (2 fmly) S £40; D £66-£76
Facilities FTV DVD TVL tea/coffee Dinner available Cen ht Fishing Riding Pool table Wildlife garden & farm wildlife trail **Extras** Speciality toiletries, snacks, fridge available **Conf** Max 15 **Parking** 4 **Notes** LB Closed Xmas 🐄 160 acres organic/mixed

---

TORBAY

See Brixham, Paignton and Torquay

TORQUAY   Map 3 SX96

PREMIER COLLECTION

Linden House

★★★★★ GUEST ACCOMMODATION

31 Bampfylde Rd TQ2 5AY
☎ 01803 212281
e-mail: lindenhouse.torquay@virgin.net
dir: *To Torquay on A3022, follow seafront/Riveria Centre signs. Filter right at Torre railway station, straight on at lights. After next lights, 1st left into Bampfylde Rd. House 1st on left*

This elegant Victorian building has been appointed in a classic style with soft neutral colours providing charm and elegance. An especially warm welcome is provided by the enthusiastic proprietors. Bedrooms and bathrooms provide a range of welcome extras and include a garden room with its own patio. Gluten-free breakfasts can be provided.

Linden House

Rooms 7 en suite (1 GF) S £55-£65; D £70-£90*
Facilities FTV TVL tea/coffee Cen ht Wi-fi **Parking** 7 **Notes** LB ⊗ No Children 16yrs Closed 24 Dec-2 Jan

PREMIER COLLECTION

The Marstan

★★★★★ GUEST HOUSE

Meadfoot Sea Rd TQ1 2LQ
☎ 01803 292837 📠 01803 299202
e-mail: enquiries@marstanhotel.co.uk
dir: *A3022 to seafront, left onto A379 Torbay Rd & Babbacombe Rd, right onto Meadfoot Rd, Marstan on right*

This elegant mid 19th-century villa provides high levels of comfort and quality throughout. The hospitality and service are excellent, and every effort is made to create a relaxed and enjoyable atmosphere. Public areas include an impressive dining room, a bar and a comfortable lounge. Outdoors, guests can enjoy a heated swimming pool and hot tub in the secluded garden.

Rooms 9 en suite (1 fmly) (2 GF) S £55-£75; D £75-£155* **Facilities** FTV iPod docking station Lounge tea/coffee Direct Dial Cen ht Licensed Wi-fi 🍴 Hot tub **Parking** 8 **Notes** LB ⊗

Meadfoot Bay Guest House

★★★★ GUEST ACCOMMODATION

Meadfoot Sea Rd TQ1 2LQ
☎ 01803 294722 📠 01803 214473
e-mail: stay@meadfoot.com
web: www.meadfoot.com
dir: *A3022 to seafront, onto A379, right into Meadfoot Rd, 0.5m on right*

The Meadfoot Bay is a family-run guest house situated in the Meadfoot conservation area, just north of Torquay harbour, and only 200 metres from a delightful Blue Flag beach. Rooms vary in size and facilities, and include standard, superior, superior deluxe and The St Andrews Suite. Free parking is available in the private car park, and free Wi-fi is a bonus. Meadfoot Bay is completely non-smoking.

Rooms 18 en suite (2 GF) S £36.40-£52; D £72.80-£104* **Facilities** FTV Lounge TVL tea/coffee Cen ht Licensed Wi-fi 🏋 18 Access to nearby health club **Parking** 16 **Notes** LB ⊗ No Children 14yrs

TORQUAY *continued*

Ashfield Guest House

★★★★ GUEST ACCOMMODATION

9 Scarborough Rd TQ2 5UJ
☎ **01803 293537**
e-mail: enquiries@ashfieldguesthouse.co.uk
dir: *From seafront into Belgrave Rd, in 300mtrs right into Scarborough Rd, house 100mtrs on left*

On a quiet side street, and just a short walk from the bustling town centre, this fine mid-terrace property offers comfortable bedrooms. The house has been sympathetically restored in recent years and guests have the sole use of the large lounge. Breakfasts are served at individual tables in the bright airy dining room.

Rooms 6 en suite (2 fmly) (2 GF) **Facilities** FTV TVL tea/coffee Cen ht Wi-fi **Parking** 3 **Notes** ⊗ Closed Dec-Mar

Aveland House

★★★★ 🏠 GUEST ACCOMMODATION

Aveland Rd, Babbacombe TQ1 3PT
☎ **01803 326622 & 328940**
e-mail: avelandhouse@aol.com
web: www.avelandhouse.co.uk
dir: *A3022 to Torquay, left onto B3199 (Hele Rd) into Westhill Rd. Then Warbro Rd, 2nd left into Aveland Rd*

Set in well-tended gardens in a peaceful area of Babbacombe, close to the South West Coastal Path, beaches, shops and attractions, Aveland House is within easy walking distance of Torquay harbour and town. This family-run house offers warm and attentive service. The attractive bedrooms are well equipped, with free Wi-fi throughout. A pleasant bar and two comfortable TV lounges are available. Hearing-impaired visitors are especially welcome, as both the proprietors are OCSL signers. Evening meals and bar snacks are available by arrangement. Coeliacs and special diets can be catered for.

Rooms 10 en suite (1 fmly) S £36-£38; D £72-£86*
Facilities Lounge TVL tea/coffee Dinner available Cen ht Licensed Wi-fi Licensed bar **Extras** Chocolate **Parking** 10 **Notes** LB ⊗ No Children 2yrs RS Sun no evening meals

Barclay Court

★★★★ GUEST ACCOMMODATION

29 Castle Rd TQ1 3BB
☎ **01803 292791**
e-mail: enquiries@barclaycourthotel.co.uk
dir: *M5 onto A38 then A380 to Torquay. A3022 Newton Rd left onto Upton Rd, right towards Lymington Rd. Right to Castle Circus, Castle Rd on left*

The delightful, personally-run Barclay Court is within easy walking distance of Torquay's attractions and offers a friendly, relaxed atmosphere. Individually decorated rooms vary in size, but all are en suite and well equipped. There is a games room on the lower-ground floor and the

garden is a quiet retreat especially in the summer months.

Rooms 4 en suite 6 annexe en suite (1 fmly) (1 GF) **Facilities** FTV TVL tea/coffee Games room **Parking** 7 **Notes** ⊗ Closed 25 Dec & New Year RS Nov-Mar Limited rooms available 🐾

Blue Conifer

★★★★ GUEST ACCOMMODATION

Higher Downs Rd, The Seafront, Babbacombe TQ1 3LD
☎ **01803 327637**
dir: *Follow signs for Babbacombe & seafront, premises 500yds from model village, opposite cliff railway*

Surrounded by neat gardens with splendid views across beaches to the bay, this attractive property provides a relaxed and friendly atmosphere. Bedrooms, many with sea views, are well equipped and one is on the ground floor. A relaxing lounge and spacious car park are welcome additions.

Rooms 7 en suite (3 fmly) (1 GF) **Facilities** FTV tea/coffee Cen ht **Parking** 9 **Notes** Closed Nov-Feb 🐾

Brooklands

★★★★ GUEST HOUSE

5 Scarborough Rd TQ2 5UJ
☎ **01803 296696 & 07900 417855** 📠 **01803 296696**
e-mail: enquiries@brooklandsguesthousetorquay.com
dir: *From seafront into Belgrave Rd. Scarborough Rd 300mtrs on right*

This Victorian, personally-run terraced property is in a convenient location for both the seafront and town centre, and is an ideal base for visiting the attractions of the English Riviera. Bedrooms have good facilities with a thoughtful range of extras. The attractive breakfast room has separate tables, and there is also a separate lounge. Dinner is available during the summer season. On-street parking is available, or at the rear on request.

Rooms 5 en suite (1 fmly) S £30-£40; D £50-£60*
Facilities FTV TVL tea/coffee Dinner available Cen ht Wi-fi Use of nearby health and fitness centre **Extras** Snacks, beverages - complimentary **Parking** 1 **Notes** LB ⊗ No Children 2yrs

The Coppice

★★★★ GUEST ACCOMMODATION

Barrington Rd TQ1 2QJ
☎ **01803 297786 & 211085** 📠 **01803 211085**
e-mail: reservations@coppicehotel.co.uk
web: www.coppicehotel.co.uk
dir: *1m from harbour on Babbacombe Rd, opposite St Matthias Church*

Friendly and comfortable, The Coppice is a popular choice and provides a convenient location that is within walking distance of the beaches and shops. In addition to the indoor and outdoor swimming pools, evening

entertainment is often provided in the spacious bar. Bedrooms are bright and airy with modern amenities.

Rooms 39 en suite (10 fmly) (28 GF) S £25-£55; D £50-£110 **Facilities** FTV Lounge tea/coffee Dinner available Cen ht Licensed Wi-fi 🕸 🐾 ♨ 9 Sauna Gym Pool table **Conf** Max 60 Thtr 60 Class 60 Board 60 **Parking** 34 **Notes** LB ⊗

Court Prior

★★★★ GUEST HOUSE

St Lukes Road South TQ2 5NZ
☎ **01803 292766**
e-mail: courtprior@btconnect.com
dir: *A380 to Torquay, at Halfords right at lights onto Avenue Rd to seafront, left at next lights up Sheddon Hill, 2nd right onto St Lukes Rd*

Located in a quiet residential area within walking distance of the seafront and town centre, this charming house, built in 1860, offers comfortable accommodation. The bedrooms are spacious, well decorated and pleasantly furnished throughout. There is also a large comfortable lounge.

Rooms 9 en suite (3 fmly) (1 GF) **Facilities** FTV TVL tea/coffee Cen ht Wi-fi **Parking** 9 **Notes** ⊗ No Children 12yrs

The Downs, Babbacombe

★★★★ GUEST ACCOMMODATION

41-43 Babbacombe Downs Rd, Babbacombe TQ1 3LN
☎ **01803 328543**
e-mail: manager@downshotel.co.uk
dir: *From Torquay, A329 to Babbacombe. Off Babbacombe road turn left into Princes St. Left into Babbacombe Downs Rd, 20mtrs on left*

Originally built in the 1850s, this elegant building forms part of a seafront terrace with direct access to the promenade and Babbacombe Downs. The warmth of welcome is matched by attentive service, with every effort made to ensure a rewarding and relaxing stay. Bedrooms offer impressive levels of comfort and most have spectacular views across Lyme Bay with balconies being an added bonus. For guests with limited mobility, assisted access is available to the first floor. Additional facilities include the convivial lounge/bar and spacious restaurant where enjoyable dinners and breakfasts are offered.

Rooms 12 en suite (4 fmly) S £50-£65; D £65-£80*
Facilities FTV TVL tea/coffee Dinner available Direct Dial Cen ht Licensed Wi-fi **Parking** 8 **Notes** LB

Save on B&Bs and Hotels. Book at **theAA.com/hotel**

DEVON 127 ENGLAND

The Elmington

★★★★ GUEST ACCOMMODATION

St Anges Ln, Chelston TQ2 6QE
☎ 01803 605192 📠 01803 690489
e-mail: mail@elmimgton.co.uk
web: www.elmington.co.uk
dir: At rear of rail station

Set in sub-tropical gardens with views over the bay, this splendid Victorian villa has been lovingly restored. The comfortable bedrooms are brightly decorated and vary in size and style. There is a spacious lounge, bar and dining room. Additional facilities include an outdoor pool and terrace.

Rooms 19 en suite **Facilities** FTV TVL tea/coffee Dinner available Cen ht Licensed Wi-fi ⚲ ♨ ♪ Pool table **Parking** 24 **Notes** ✕ Closed Nov-Mar

Glenorleigh

★★★★ GUEST ACCOMMODATION

26 Cleveland Rd TQ2 5BE
☎ 01803 292135 📠 01803 213717
e-mail: glenorleighhotel@btinternet.com
web: www.glenorleigh.co.uk
dir: A380 from Newton Abbot onto A3022, at Torre station lights right into Avenue Rd, 1st left, across 1st junct, 200yds on right

Located in a residential area, the Glenorleigh provides a range of smart bedrooms with some on ground floor level. Offering guests a solarium, a heated outdoor pool with terrace and a convivial bar, this family-run establishment is ideal for both leisure or business guests. Breakfast provides a hearty start to the day, and dinner is available with prior notice.

Rooms 15 rms (14 en suite) (6 fmly) (7 GF) S £30-£40; D £60-£80* **Facilities** FTV TVL tea/coffee Dinner available Cen ht Licensed Wi-fi ⚲ Pool table ♨ **Parking** 10 **Notes** LB ✕

Grosvenor House

★★★★ GUEST HOUSE

Falkland Rd TQ2 5JP
☎ 01803 294110
e-mail: stay@grosvenorhousehotel.co.uk
dir: From Newton Abbot to Torquay, at Torre station right by Halfords, left at 2nd lights onto Falkland Rd

This long established guest house is ideally situated being just a short walk from the town centre and seafront. Run by a Christian couple, Nigel and Angela make every effort to ensure guests have a relaxing and enjoyable stay and are always on hand to offer helpful local information. The bedrooms are well appointed and comfortably furnished whilst public areas include a guest lounge, bar and attractive dining room where tasty dinners and breakfasts are served.

Rooms 8 en suite (4 fmly) (3 GF) D fr £120 **Facilities** FTV TVL tea/coffee Dinner available Cen ht Licensed Wi-fi **Parking** 7 **Notes** LB ✕ Closed Oct-Etr

Headland View

★★★★ GUEST HOUSE

37 Babbacombe Downs Rd, Babbacombe TQ1 3LN
☎ 01803 312612 & 07762 960230
e-mail: reception@headlandview.com
dir: A379 S to Babbacombe. Exit Babbacombe Rd left into Portland Rd, into Babbacombe Downs Rd

Positioned on Babbacombe Downs, this elegant Victorian house boasts superb views of the coast of Lyme Bay, a World Heritage Site. Bedrooms are individually styled with most having French doors leading onto balconies overlooking the spectacular bay. Many period features have been retained which add to the character and appeal of the building. A spacious guest lounge is also available, whilst the excellent breakfasts are served in the pretty dining room.

Rooms 6 rms (4 en suite) (2 pri facs) S £45-£57; D £60-£72* **Facilities** FTV DVD iPod docking station Lounge TVL tea/coffee Cen ht Wi-fi ♨ **Extras** Speciality toiletries **Parking** 4 **Notes** LB ✕ No Children 5yrs

Iona

★★★★ GUEST ACCOMMODATION

5 Cleveland Rd TQ2 5BD
☎ 01803 294918 📠 01803 294918
e-mail: stay@hoteliona.co.uk
dir: A380 to Riviera rdbt, 1st exit onto A3022 towards seafront. Take left into Vine Rd, right into Cleveland Rd

Dating back to the 1860s, this grand Victorian villa is situated in a quiet location just a short stroll from the town centre, harbour and many attractions. A variety of bedroom sizes is offered; all provide good levels of comfort and the expected necessities. Public areas are elegant with a number of period features retained. Dinner

and breakfast are served in the light and airy conservatory, and a bar is also provided.

Rooms 9 en suite (2 fmly) **Facilities** FTV TVL tea/coffee Dinner available Cen ht Licensed Wi-fi **Parking** 8

Kelvin House

★★★★ GUEST ACCOMMODATION

46 Bampfylde Rd TQ2 5AY
☎ 01803 209093 📠 01803 209093
e-mail: kelvinhousehotel@hotmail.com
dir: M5 junct 31, A380, A3032 (Newton Rd) into Torquay. At lights at Torre Station right into Avenue Rd. Bampfylde Rd on left

This attractive Victorian house was built in the 1880s and sits on a lovely tree-lined road. All bedrooms are en suite and have been appointed to a high standard with many extras. A large elegant sitting room is available for guests and hearty breakfasts are served in the dining room or on the patio in good weather. This is a family-run property with a relaxed, friendly home-from-home atmosphere. Close to transport links, it makes an ideal base for touring the Torquay Riviera.

Rooms 8 en suite (1 fmly) (2 GF) S £45-£50; D £50-£70* **Facilities** FTV TVL tea/coffee Cen ht Licensed Wi-fi **Parking** 6 **Notes** LB ✕

Kingsholm

★★★★ GUEST ACCOMMODATION

539 Babbacombe Rd TQ1 1HQ
☎ 01803 297794 📠 01803 897121
e-mail: thekingsholm@sky.com
dir: From A3022 left onto Torquay seafront, left at clock tower rdbt, Kingsholm 400mtrs on left

An elegant, personally-run establishment situated in a conservation area, only 350 metres from the bustling harbour, this fine Edwardian house offers excellent accommodation appointed to a high standard, and many rooms overlook Torwood Gardens. All bedrooms have Freeview TV, free Wi-fi, hairdryers and hospitality trays. There is also a guest lounge, a spacious dining room with separate tables and a licensed bar. Parking is free. The owners, June and Carl offer a friendly welcome.

Rooms 9 en suite S £30-£35; D £49-£65* **Facilities** FTV TVL tea/coffee Cen ht Licensed Wi-fi **Parking** 9 **Notes** ✕ No Children 10yrs

TORQUAY *continued*

Newton House

★★★★ GUEST ACCOMMODATION

31 Newton Rd TQ2 5DB
☎ 01803 297520 🖷 01803 297520
e-mail: newtonhouse_torquay@yahoo.com
web: www.newtonhouse-tq.co.uk
dir: *From Torre station bear left at lights, Newton House 40yds on left*

You are assured of a warm welcome at Newton House, which is close to the town centre and attractions. The comfortable bedrooms, some at ground level, have thoughtful extras, and a lounge is available. Breakfast is enjoyed in the pleasant dining room.

Rooms 9 en suite (3 fmly) (5 GF) **Facilities** FTV tea/coffee Cen ht Wi-fi Drying room for hikers **Parking** 15 **Notes** ⊗

Peppers

★★★★ GUEST ACCOMMODATION

551 Babbacombe Rd TQ1 1HQ
☎ 01803 293856 🖷 07006 037547
e-mail: enquiries@hotel-peppers.co.uk
web: www.hotel-peppers.co.uk
dir: *A3022 to seafront, left on to B3199 towards harbour. At clock tower rdbt, turn left, 250mtrs on left*

Peppers is a very well-placed bed and breakfast near to the harbour and town centre with free off-road parking. The bedrooms are bright and comfortable, and there is a well-appointed guest lounge. Hearty breakfasts are served in the light and airy breakfast room.

Rooms 10 rms (9 en suite) (1 pri facs) S £28-£38; D £50-£72 **Facilities** FTV TVL tea/coffee Cen ht Licensed Wi-fi **Extras** Bottled water - complimentary **Parking** 9 **Notes** LB ⊗ No Children 10yrs Closed 18 Dec-9 Jan

Robin Hill

★★★★ GUEST ACCOMMODATION

74 Braddons Hill Road East TQ1 1HF
☎ 01803 214518 🖷 01803 291410
e-mail: stay@robinhillhotel.co.uk
web: www.robinhillhotel.co.uk
dir: *From A38 to seafront then left to Babbacombe. Pass theatre to Clock Tower rdbt, take 1st exit & through 2 sets of lights, Braddons Hill Road East on left*

Dating back to 1896, this fascinating building has character in abundance and is located a short stroll from the harbour and shops. Every effort is made to ensure a stay is enjoyable; assistance is readily available at all times. Bedrooms, in varying styles, provide all the expected necessities. Public areas include the inviting lounge and light and airy dining room where breakfast can be enjoyed.

Robin Hill

Rooms 10 en suite (2 fmly) (1 GF) **Facilities** FTV TVL tea/coffee Cen ht Licensed Wi-fi ♨ ♨ 18 **Parking** 10 **Notes** Closed Nov-Mar

Stover Lodge

★★★★ GUEST ACCOMMODATION

29 Newton Rd TQ2 5DB
☎ 01803 297287 🖷 01803 297287
e-mail: enquiries@stoverlodge.co.uk
web: www.stoverlodge.co.uk
dir: *Follow signs to Torquay town centre, at station/ Halfords left lane. Lodge on left after lights*

Located close to the town centre, the family-run Stover Lodge is relaxed and friendly. Children and babies are welcome, and a cot and high chair can be provided on request. Hearty breakfasts, with a vegetarian option, are served in the dining room. There is a garden to enjoy in summer.

Rooms 9 rms (8 en suite) (1 pri facs) (3 fmly) (2 GF) S £30-£45; D £52-£66* **Facilities** FTV tea/coffee Cen ht Wi-fi **Parking** 10 **Notes** LB ⊗

Summerlands

★★★★ GUEST ACCOMMODATION

19 Belgrave Rd TQ2 5HU
☎ 01803 299844
e-mail: summerlands@fsmail.net
web: www.summerlandsguesthousetorquay.com
dir: *A3022 into Newton Rd, towards seafront & town centre, into Belgrave Rd. Summerlands on left just past lights*

Located just five minutes walk from the seafront, Summerlands offers a friendly and relaxed environment. There are six well equipped, modern and comfortable bedrooms, all of which are en suite. Breakfasts are served on the lower-ground floor and provide a satisfying start to the day.

Rooms 6 en suite (2 fmly) (1 GF) **Facilities** FTV tea/coffee Cen ht Wi-fi **Parking** 4 **Notes** ⊗ No Children 5yrs

The Norwood

★★★★ 🅰 GUEST ACCOMMODATION

60 Belgrave Rd TQ2 5HY
☎ 01803 294236 & 07792 186806 🖷 01803 294224
e-mail: enquiries@norwoodhoteltorquay.co.uk
dir: *From Princess Theatre towards Paignton, 1st lights right into Belgrave Rd, over x-rds, 3rd building on left*
Rooms 10 en suite (5 fmly) (1 GF) S £30-£45; D £50-£64 **Facilities** FTV tea/coffee Dinner available Cen ht Licensed Wi-fi **Extras** Speciality toiletries - complimentary **Parking** 3 **Notes** LB

The Sandpiper Guest House

★★★★ 🅰 GUEST HOUSE

Rowdens Rd TQ2 5AZ
☎ 01803 292779 🖷 01803 292806
e-mail: enquiries@sandpiperguesthouse.co.uk
dir: *From A380 onto A3022 (Riviera Way) follow signs for seafront along Avenue Rd. Left into Bampfylde Rd, right into Rowdens Rd*
Rooms 11 rms (9 en suite) (2 pri facs) (1 fmly) (2 GF) **Facilities** FTV TVL tea/coffee Dinner available Cen ht Licensed Wi-fi **Parking** 8

Walnut Lodge

★★★★ 🅰 GUEST ACCOMMODATION

48 Bampfylde Rd TQ2 5AY
☎ 01803 200471 🖷 01803 200571
e-mail: stay@walnutlodgetorquay.co.uk
dir: *M5 onto A3032 into Torquay, through lights at Torre Station, right signed seafront. After 1st lights next left into Bampfylde Rd*
Rooms 6 en suite (1 fmly) (2 GF) S £45; D £64-£84*

Save on B&Bs and Hotels. Book at **theAA.com/hotel**

DEVON 129 ENGLAND

Atlantis

★★★ GUEST ACCOMMODATION

68 Belgrave Rd TQ2 5HY
☎ 01803 292917 📠 01803 292917
e-mail: info@atlantis-torquay.co.uk
dir: *Follow signs to Torquay seafront, left, left at lights into Belgrave Rd, over next lights, premises on left*

Convenient for the beach, theatre and conference centre, the Atlantis is a thoughtfully equipped home-from-home. There is a genuine welcome here with each bedroom offering good levels of comfort. There is a guest lounge leading through to the dining room, where tasty breakfasts provide a satisfying start to the day.

Rooms 10 rms (9 en suite) (1 pri facs) (7 fmly)
S £30-£45; D £40-£60* **Facilities** FTV TVL tea/coffee
Cen ht Wi-fi **Parking** 3 **Notes** LB ⊗

Tyndale Guest House

★★★ GUEST ACCOMMODATION

68 Avenue Rd TQ2 5LF
☎ 01803 380888
e-mail: info@tyndaletorquay.co.uk
dir: *A380 onto A3022, follow sea front signs onto Avenue Rd, on right hand side of 1st lights*

Tyndale is a traditional bed and breakfast operation within walking distance of the town and beach, with good off-road parking. Rooms are comfortable and well presented, breakfast is cooked to order, and the hosts are friendly and helpful.

Rooms 4 en suite (1 fmly) (1 GF) S £30-£40; D £45-£60*
Facilities FTV DVD tea/coffee Cen ht Wi-fi **Parking** 7
Notes LB ⊗

TOTNES Map 3 SX86

The Durant Arms

★★★★ INN

Ashprington TQ9 7UP
☎ 01803 732240
e-mail: info@durantarms.co.uk
web: www.durantarms.co.uk
dir: *A381 from Totnes for Kingsbridge, 1m left for Ashprington*

A traditional inn serving good home-made food and offering high standards of accommodation, service and hospitality from the owners and their team. Rooms are comfortable and well maintained, and The Durant Arms enjoys a peaceful location not far from town.

Rooms 2 en suite 5 annexe en suite (1 fmly) (2 GF)
Facilities FTV TVL tea/coffee Dinner available Cen ht Wi-fi
Parking 10 **Notes** Closed 6-22 Jan

Steam Packet Inn

★★★★ 🍽 INN

St Peter's Quay TQ9 5EW
☎ 01803 863880 📠 01803 862754
e-mail: steampacket@buccaneer.co.uk
web: www.steampacketinn.co.uk
dir: *Off A38 at Totnes to Dartington & Totnes. Over 1st lights, pass railway station, signs for town centre at next rdbt. Over mini-rdbt, River Dart on left, inn 100yds on left*

This friendly and popular riverside inn offers a warm welcome to visitors and locals alike. Complete with its own quay, the property has a long history. Bedrooms are well equipped and comfortable, and some have river views. Public areas have open fires and a choice of dining options including the heated waterside patio area, ideal for relaxing on warmer days. Interesting and well-cooked dishes are offered at lunch and dinner, while breakfast provides a satisfying start to the day.

Rooms 4 en suite (1 fmly) S £50-£80; D £79.50-£99.50*
Facilities FTV tea/coffee Dinner available Cen ht Wi-fi 🍴 4 private moorings **Extras** Speciality toiletries, water
Parking 15 **Notes** LB

WIDECOMBE IN THE MOOR Map 3 SX77

Manor Cottage

★★★ BED AND BREAKFAST

TQ13 7TB
☎ 01364 621218
e-mail: di.richard@btinternet.com
dir: *A382 to Bovey Tracey, left onto B3387 to Widecombe, cottage on right after old inn*

Located in the centre of the historic village, this attractive cottage, standing in a large and pleasant garden, has a lot of character. It offers friendly hospitality and spacious, comfortable bedrooms. Breakfast is served in the cosy dining room and features good home cooking that uses fresh, local produce.

Rooms 3 rms (1 en suite) S £40; D £50-£60 **Facilities** FTV
TV2B tea/coffee Cen ht Wi-fi 🐴 Riding **Parking** 3
Notes ⊗ No Children 15yrs Closed Xmas 🍴

YELVERTON Map 3 SX56

Harrabeer Country House

★★★★ GUEST ACCOMMODATION

Harrowbeer Ln PL20 6EA
☎ 01822 853302
e-mail: reception@harrabeer.co.uk
web: www.harrabeer.co.uk
dir: *In village. Exit A386 (Tavistock Rd) into Grange Rd, right into Harrowbeer Ln*

A warm welcome awaits at this historic Devon longhouse situated on the edge of Dartmoor. It provides an excellent base for exploring this beautiful area; the accommodation has all the expected modern comforts with a lounge, bar and dining room overlooking the garden. Dinners are available by arrangement with special diets catered for. There are also two self-catering units.

Rooms 6 rms (5 en suite) (1 pri facs) (2 fmly) (1 GF)
S £61-£85; D £71-£95* **Facilities** Lounge tea/coffee
Dinner available Direct Dial Cen ht Licensed Wi-fi 🎣 18 🍴
Conf Max 20 Board 20 **Parking** 10 **Notes** Closed 3rd wk
Dec, 1st wk Feb

Overcombe House

★★★★ 🅰 GUEST HOUSE

Old Station Rd, Horrabridge PL20 7RA
☎ 01822 853501
e-mail: enquiries@overcombehotel.co.uk
web: www.overcombehotel.co.uk
dir: *Signed 100yds off A386 at Horrabridge*
Rooms 8 en suite (2 GF) S £50-£60; D £75-£90*
Facilities FTV tea/coffee Cen ht Licensed Wi-fi 🍴
Parking 7 **Notes** ⊗ No Children 12yrs Closed 25 Dec

DORSET

ABBOTSBURY   Map 4 SY58

East Farm House (SY578853)

★★★ FARMHOUSE

2 Rosemary Ln DT3 4JN
☎ 01305 871363 📠 01305 871363 Mrs W M Wood
e-mail: eastfarmhouse@uwclub.net
web: www.eastfarmhouse.co.uk
dir: From B3157 W into Abbotsbury, Swan Inn on left, 1st right into Rosemary Ln

This unspoiled and charming farmhouse is in the centre of the pretty village and has been in the owner's family since 1729. The house has a homely atmosphere, traditionally furnished with much character, and filled with memorabilia. Hearty breakfasts are served in the lounge-dining room, where a log fire burns in winter.

Rooms 3 en suite **Facilities** tea/coffee Dinner available Cen ht **Parking** 3 **Notes** No Children 14yrs 20 acres horse stud/rare breed pigs

ASKERSWELL   Map 4 SY59

The Spyway Inn

★★★★ INN

DT2 9EP
☎ 01308 485250 📠 01308 485250
e-mail: spywayinn@sky.com
dir: From A35 follow Askerswell sign, then follow Spyway Inn sign

Peacefully located in the rolling Dorset countryside, this family-run inn offers a warm and genuine welcome. Bedrooms are spacious and well appointed with a number of extras provided, including bath robes. Real ales are on tap in the bar, where locals congregate to put the world to rights. Menus feature home-cooked food with many dishes utilising local produce both at dinner and breakfast. The extensive beer garden, with wonderful views, is popular in summer.

Rooms 3 en suite (1 fmly) S £45; D £80 **Facilities** FTV tea/coffee Dinner available Cen ht Wi-fi **Parking** 40 **Notes** LB ⊗

BEAMINSTER   Map 4 ST40

Watermeadow House (ST535001)

★★★★★ ⏃ FARMHOUSE

Bridge Farm, Hooke DT8 3PD
☎ 01308 862619 Mrs P M Wallbridge
e-mail: enquiries@watermeadowhouse.co.uk
web: www.watermeadowhouse.co.uk
dir: 3m E of Beaminster, in Hooke

Rooms 2 rms (1 en suite) (1 pri facs) (1 fmly) S £40-£45; D £65-£70* **Facilities** DVD tea/coffee Cen ht Wi-fi 🛁 **Parking** 6 **Notes** LB ⊗ Closed Nov-Mar 280 acres dairy/beef

BLANDFORD FORUM   Map 4 ST80

Portman Lodge

★★★★ BED AND BREAKFAST

Whitecliff Mill St DT11 7BP
☎ 01258 453727 📠 01258 453727
e-mail: enquiries@portmanlodge.co.uk
web: www.portmanlodge.co.uk
dir: On NW end of Blandford's one-way system, to access follow signs from town centre to Shaftesbury & hospital

Built in the Victorian period and once used as a music school, this substantial detached house now provides elegant accommodation and a warm welcome. All bedrooms and bathrooms are well decorated and comfortably furnished. Breakfast utilises good quality ingredients and is served at a communal table.

Rooms 3 en suite S £60-£75; D £90-£100* **Facilities** STV TVL tea/coffee Cen ht Wi-fi **Parking** 8 **Notes** ⊗ No Children Closed 24-31 Dec 🚭

See advert on opposite page

The Anvil Inn

★★★★ INN

Salisbury Rd, Pimperne DT11 8UQ
☎ 01258 453431 📠 01258 480182
e-mail: theanvil.inn@btconnect.com
web: www.anvilinn.co.uk
dir: 2m NE of Blandford on A354 in Pimperne

Dating back to the 16th century, this picturesque thatched inn is located in the village of Pimperne, just a couple of miles from Blandford. There's a warm and welcoming atmosphere here with a convivial bar and choice of dining areas in which to enjoy a meal from the extensive menu. Bedrooms and bathrooms offer impressive standards of comfort for both business and leisure guests. This is a great location for exploring the many historic towns, countryside and coastline which the region has to offer.

Rooms 12 en suite S £65-£80; D £85-£130* **Facilities** STV FTV tea/coffee Dinner available Direct Dial Cen ht Wi-fi **Parking** 18 **Notes** LB No coaches

St Martin's House

★★★★ BED AND BREAKFAST

White Cliff Mill St DT11 7BP
☎ 01258 451245 & 07818 814381
e-mail: info@stmartinshouse.co.uk
dir: Market Place into Salisbury St, left into White Cliff Mill St, on right before traffic island

Dating from 1866, this restored property was once part of the choristers' house for a local church. The bedrooms are comfortable, homely and well equipped. The hosts offer warm hospitality and attentive service. Breakfast, which features local and home-made items, is enjoyed around a communal table.

Rooms 2 rms (2 pri facs) (1 fmly) S £45-£70; D £65-£70* **Facilities** FTV DVD tea/coffee Cen ht Wi-fi 🛁 **Parking** 3 **Notes** LB ⊗ 🚭

Save on B&Bs and Hotels. Book at **theAA.com/hotel**

DORSET 131 **ENGLAND**

The Old Bakery Bed & Breakfast

★★★ BED AND BREAKFAST

Church Rd, Pimperne DT11 8UB
☎ 01258 455173 & 07799 853784
e-mail: jjtanners@hotmail.com
web: www.theoldbakerydorset.co.uk
dir: *2m NE of Blandford. Off A354 into Pimperne*

Dating from 1890 and once, as the name suggests, the village bakery, this family home offers comfortable accommodation in a convenient location. Popular with business travellers, families can also be accommodated, with cots available. Substantial breakfasts featuring home-made bread and marmalade are served in the dining room.

Rooms 3 en suite (1 GF) **Facilities** TVL tea/coffee Dinner available Cen ht Wi-fi **Parking** 2 **Notes** ⊗ ⊜

BOURNEMOUTH   Map 5 SZ09

Fenn Lodge

★★★★ GUEST ACCOMMODATION

11 Rosemount Rd, Alum Chine BH4 8HB
☎ 01202 761273 📠 01202 761273
e-mail: fennlodge@btconnect.com
web: www.fennlodge.co.uk
dir: *A338 into Poole, at rdbt onto B3065 signed Alum Chime & Sandbanks. Left at lights, right at rdbt into Alumhurst Rd, 3rd left into Rosemount Rd*

Located within walking distance of Alum Chine and the beach, this stylish accommodation is friendly and relaxed. The hosts ensure their guests are well cared for and provide many thoughtful extras. Bournemouth and Poole are just a short drive away. Guests have use of an elegant comfortable lounge.

Rooms 11 rms (10 en suite) (1 pri facs) (1 fmly) (1 GF)
Facilities TVL tea/coffee Cen ht Wi-fi **Parking** 6 **Notes** ⊗
Closed Nov-Apr

The Living Room

★★★★ GUEST ACCOMMODATION

2 Drury Rd, Alum Chine BH4 8HA
☎ 01202 761135
e-mail: stay@livingroombournemouth.co.uk
dir: *Signs for Alum Chine Beach. On corner of Alumhurst Rd & Drury Rd*

A delightful and friendly Edwardian house, ideally located for the Jurassic Coast, the New Forest and within walking distance of Westbourne and Alum Chine beaches. The bedrooms are filled with many homely extras and the whole house can be hired for a party or special event.

Rooms 7 rms (6 en suite) (1 pri facs) (1 fmly)
S £30-£37.50; D £60-£80* **Facilities** FTV TVL tea/coffee Cen ht Licensed Wi-fi **Parking** 5 **Notes** LB ⊗

Portman Lodge

Built in 1873, *Portman Lodge* is the main wing and entrance into a large Victorian property, originally part of Lord Portmans estate. It is thought to have been a residence for choristers for St Martins Church. Many of the original fixtures and fittings remain, in particular the attractive Victorian tiled floor in the entrance hall and corridor.

The individually decorated bedrooms, with twin, double or kingsize beds, are supremely comfortable, with ensuite rooms, plentiful hot water, powerful showers and white fluffy towels.

Substantial cooked tasty breakfasts, including a varied range of locally sourced produce, are served around a large table in our lovely dining room.

There is a good choice of pubs and restaurants for lunch and dinner in the beautiful Georgian market town of Blandford, just five minutes walk away, so no need to get into your car.

Recommended in the area: Kingston Lacey, Lulworth Cove, Jurassic Coast, Corfe Castle, Abbotsbury Swannery and Gardens

Whitecliff Mill Street, Blandford Forum, Dorset DT11 7BP
Tel: 01258 453727
Mobile: 07860 424235 (Gerry) • 07785 971743 (Pat)
Website: www.portmanlodge.co.uk
Email: enquiries@portmanlodge.co.uk

BOURNEMOUTH *continued*

The Maples

★★★★ BED AND BREAKFAST

1 Library Rd, Winton BH9 2QH
☎ 01202 529820
e-mail: jeffreyhurrell@yahoo.co.uk
dir: *1.5m N of town centre. Exit A3060 (Castle Ln West) into Wimborne Rd. The Maples 1m on right after police station*

A warm welcome awaits you at The Maples, which is just off Winton High Street. The atmosphere is friendly and bedrooms are quiet, comfortable and equipped with considerate extras. Breakfast is enjoyed in the pleasant dining room around a communal table.

Rooms 2 en suite (1 fmly) S £25-£30; D £50-£60
Facilities FTV Lounge tea/coffee Cen ht Wi-fi 🔒 **Parking** 2 **Notes** ⊗ No Children 7yrs 🖴

Newlands

★★★★ GUEST ACCOMMODATION

14 Rosemount Rd, Alum Chine BH4 8HB
☎ 01202 761922 📄 01202 769872
e-mail: newlandshotel@totalise.co.uk
web: www.newlandsguesthouse.com
dir: *A338, A35 to Liverpool Victoria rdbt, exit for Alum Chine, left at lights, right at small rdbt into Alumhurst Rd, 3rd left*

A warm welcome is guaranteed at this attractive Edwardian house which is in a quiet area near Alum Chine beach and within easy driving distance of Bournemouth and Poole centres. Offering comfortable accommodation with Wi-fi and a guest lounge.

Rooms 8 en suite (3 fmly) **Facilities** TVL tea/coffee Cen ht Wi-fi **Parking** 8 **Notes** ⊗ Closed Dec, Jan & Feb

Rosscourt Guest House

★★★★ GUEST ACCOMMODATION

6 St Johns Rd, Boscombe Spa BH5 1EL
☎ 01202 397537
e-mail: enquiries@rosscourthotel.co.uk
dir: *M27/A338 for Bournemouth, follow until 'Kings Park Football' turnoff, right at rdbt, follow signs for Boscombe*

Located just a moment's walk from Boscombe town centre, this accommodation is suitable for both business and leisure travellers looking to relax in child-free surroundings. Bedrooms are designed with comfort in mind; en suite shower rooms are well furnished. Guests have access to complimentary Wi-fi and use of the guest lounge. A genuine warm and friendly welcome is assured here, whilst a hearty breakfast sets you up for the day ahead. Off-road parking is an additional plus.

Rooms 8 en suite (1 GF) S £40-£65; D £60-£110 (room only) **Facilities** FTV TVL tea/coffee Cen ht Wi-fi 🔒 **Parking** 9 **Notes** LB ⊗ No Children 18yrs Closed 21-30 Dec RS Jan/Mar

Wood Lodge

★★★★ GUEST ACCOMMODATION

10 Manor Rd, East Cliff BH1 3EY
☎ 01202 290891 📄 01202 290892
e-mail: enquiries@woodlodgehotel.co.uk
web: www.woodlodgehotel.co.uk
dir: *A338 to St Pauls rdbt, 1st exit left. Straight over next 2 rdbts, immediate left*

Expect a warm welcome from this family-run establishment. Set in beautiful gardens just minutes from the seafront and a 10-minute walk from the town centre. Bedrooms, which vary in size, are well presented. Home-cooked evening meals and hearty breakfasts are served in the smart dining room.

Rooms 15 rms (14 en suite) (1 pri facs) (1 fmly) (4 GF) **Facilities** TVL tea/coffee Dinner available Cen ht Licensed Wi-fi 🏊 Pool table **Conf** Max 30 Thtr 30 Class 30 Board 30 **Parking** 12

The Woodside

★★★★ GUEST HOUSE

29 Southern Rd, Southbourne BH6 3SR
☎ 01202 427213 & 07772 450403
e-mail: enquiries@the-woodside.co.uk
dir: *Follow A35 from Bournemouth. Take B3059 at Pokesdown Station. Right at Boots. Straight on to Southern Rd*

Expect a warm welcome at The Woodside, located within walking distance of the beach at Southbourne. Bedrooms are all individually designed and very comfortable. There is a dedicated guest lounge, and breakfast is served in the light and airy dining room. Off-street parking is a bonus.

Rooms 7 rms (6 en suite) (1 pri facs) S £40-£45; D £60-£70* **Facilities** FTV Lounge tea/coffee Dinner

available Cen ht Wi-fi **Parking** 4 **Notes** LB ⊗ No Children 16yrs

Blue Palms

★★★★ 🅰 BED AND BREAKFAST

26 Tregonwell Rd, West Cliff BH2 5NS
☎ 01202 554968 📄 01202 294197
e-mail: bluepalmshotel@btopenworld.com
web: www.bluepalmshotel.com
dir: *Exit A338 at Bournemouth West rdbt signed town centre, Triangle, at next rdbt into Durley Chine Rd, at rdbt into West Hill Rd. Tregonwell Rd 3rd left*

Rooms 7 en suite D £65-£95 **Facilities** FTV DVD TVL tea/coffee Cen ht Licensed Wi-fi **Parking** 8 **Notes** LB ⊗ No Children 5yrs Closed Dec-5 Jan

Carlton Lodge

★★★ GUEST ACCOMMODATION

12 Westby Rd, Boscombe BH5 1HD
☎ 01202 303650 📄 01202 303650
e-mail: enquiries@thecarltonlodge.com
dir: *A338 (Wessex Way) turn left signed football ground, right at rdbt, left into Ashley Rd then into Christchurch Rd. 1st right into Crabton Close Rd, 2nd right into Westby Rd*

This relaxing home-from-home, family-run guest accommodation is only a five minute stroll from the beach and shopping centre at Boscombe. The en suite bedrooms are spacious and individually decorated. Hearty breakfasts feature home-made preserves and excellent locally sourced bacon and sausages. Bournemouth is a short drive away with Poole, Swanage and Christchurch on the doorstep.

Rooms 5 en suite (2 fmly) (2 GF) S £50-£70; D £70-£90 **Facilities** FTV tea/coffee Cen ht **Parking** 6 **Notes** LB ⊗

Commodore

★★★ INN

Overcliff Dr, Southbourne BH6 3TD
☎ 01202 423150 📄 01202 423519
e-mail: 7688@greeneking.co.uk
web: www.thecommodore.co.uk
dir: *1m E of town centre on seafront*

Situated on the cliff top at Southbourne, the Commodore is adjacent to Fisherman's Walk. Popular with locals, the bar boasts spectacular views across Poole Bay and serves an extensive range of dishes.

Rooms 12 en suite (1 fmly) **Facilities** tea/coffee Dinner available Cen ht Lift ♿ 18 **Conf** Max 30 Thtr 30 Class 18 Board 20 **Parking** 12 **Notes** ⊗

Save on B&Bs and Hotels. Book at **theAA.com/hotel**

DORSET 133 ENGLAND

Denewood

★★★ GUEST ACCOMMODATION

1 Percy Rd, Boscombe BH5 1JE
☎ 01202 394493 & 309913 📠 01202 391155
e-mail: info@denewood.co.uk
dir: *500yds NE of Boscombe Pier, signed*

Located within walking distance of the beach and Boscombe shopping centre, and close to Bournemouth centre, the Denewood offers individually decorated bedrooms. A full English breakfast is served at individual tables in the delightful dining room, and the beauty salon is perfect for a little indulgence.

Rooms 10 en suite (2 fmly) **Facilities** FTV DVD TVL tea/coffee Cen ht Wi-fi ⚑ 18 health & beauty salon **Conf** Thtr 35 Class 30 Board 20 **Parking** 14 **Notes** LB

Pinedale

★★★ GUEST ACCOMMODATION

40 Tregonwell Rd, West Cliff BH2 5NT
☎ 01202 553733 & 292702 📠 01202 553733
e-mail: thepinedalehotel@btconnect.com
dir: *A338 at Bournemouth West rdbt, signs to West Cliff, Tregonwell Rd 3rd left after passing Wessex Hotel*

This friendly guest accommodation is enthusiastically run by two generations of the same family, and offers comfortable accommodation within a short walk of the seafront and local attractions. The fresh-looking bedrooms are equipped with useful extras. There is also an attractive licensed bar and an airy dining room where you can enjoy wholesome home-cooked meals.

Rooms 15 rms (10 en suite) (1 fmly) S £20-£35; D £40-£70* **Facilities** FTV TVL tea/coffee Dinner available Direct Dial Licensed Wi-fi 🐾 **Parking** 15 **Notes** ⊗

Trouville Lodge

★★★ GUEST ACCOMMODATION

9 Priory Rd BH2 5DF
☎ 01202 552262 📠 01202 293324
e-mail: reception@trouvillehotel.com

Professionally run, this well managed establishment offers an impressive standard of accommodation and facilities. Bedrooms are situated in an annexe to the Trouville Hotel next door. All rooms are stylishly appointed and comfortably furnished. Facilities are in the hotel. The Deauville restaurant offers a very good menu choice, and the well-stocked Le Café Bar provides an informal and pleasant environment. There is also a large pool and sauna as well as a resident beautician.

Rooms 19 en suite (4 fmly) (4 GF) S £40.95-£50.95; D £81.90-£101.90 (room only)* **Facilities** FTV tea/coffee Cen ht Wi-fi Leisure facilities available at Trouville Hotel **Parking** 14 **Notes** LB

BRIDPORT   Map 4 SY49

See also Chideock

PREMIER COLLECTION

The Shave Cross Inn

★★★★★ 🍴 INN

Marshwood Vale DT6 6HW
☎ 01308 868358 📠 01308 867064
e-mail: roy.warburton@virgin.net
web: www.theshavecrossinn.co.uk
dir: *From B3165 turn at Birdsmoorgate & follow brown signs*

This historic inn has been providing refreshment to weary travellers for centuries and continues to offer a warm and genuine welcome. The snug bar is dominated by a wonderful fireplace with crackling logs creating just the right atmosphere. Bedrooms are located in a separate Dorset flint and stone building. Quality is impressive throughout with wonderful stone floors and oak beams, combined with feature beds and luxurious bathrooms. Food, using excellent local produce, has a distinct Caribbean and international slant, including a number of authentic dishes.

Rooms 7 en suite (1 fmly) (3 GF) **Facilities** STV FTV tea/coffee Dinner available Direct Dial Cen ht Wi-fi Pool table **Parking** 29 **Notes** LB No Children RS Mon (ex BH) closed for lunch & dinner No coaches

PREMIER COLLECTION

The Roundham House

★★★★★ GUEST ACCOMMODATION

Roundham Gardens, West Bay Rd DT6 4BD
☎ 01308 422753 📠 01308 421500
e-mail: cyprencom@compuserve.com
dir: *A35 into Bridport, at Crown Inn rdbt take exit signed West Bay. House 400yds on left*

The hosts here are always on hand to welcome guests to their lovely home, which has well-tended gardens and views to the coast. Bedrooms come in a variety of sizes and are filled with useful extras. Public areas include a comfortable lounge and well-appointed dining room.

Rooms 8 rms (7 en suite) (1 fmly) S £50-£58; D £85-£98* **Facilities** FTV Lounge tea/coffee Cen ht Licensed Wi-fi **Parking** 10 **Notes** No Children 5yrs Closed Nov-Apr

---

Willowhayne Farm

★★★★ BED AND BREAKFAST

DT6 6HY
☎ 01297 489042
e-mail: wickes@willowhayne.co.uk
dir: *A35 E of Chideock, turn S towards sea (by speed camera), last house on left (with flag pole)*

This lovely farmhouse has now been updated to provide an engaging blend of traditional and contemporary. Situated just a 15-minute walk from the Jurassic Coast, its setting means stunning views across the rolling countryside. Bedrooms have a wonderful outlook and provide equal measures of comfort and quality, allied with excellent modern bathrooms. The atmosphere here is relaxed and homely, typified by the convivial breakfasts, which use local produce, and are served around the dining room table.

Rooms 2 en suite S £75-£85; D £75-£85 **Facilities** FTV Lounge TVL tea/coffee Cen ht Wi-fi ⚑ 18 Fishing **Parking** 6 **Notes** LB ⊗ No Children 16yrs ♿

Bredy House

★★★★ BED AND BREAKFAST

122 West Bay Rd DT6 4AZ
☎ 01308 422195
e-mail: bredyhouse@btinternet.com
dir: *A35 Bridport bypass, take 2nd exit off Crown Public House rdbt towards West Bay. Bredy House on right*

Located on the main road into West Bay, guests have the option of a few minutes' drive or a short stroll to the harbour. Bedrooms and bathrooms have been refurbished to a very high standard and provide plenty of quality and comfort including welcome extras such as massage showers. Freshly cooked breakfasts offer a good range of options, served in the stylish dining room overlooking the garden.

Rooms 3 en suite (1 fmly) (1 GF) S £45; D £65-£75* **Facilities** FTV DVD tea/coffee Cen ht Wi-fi 🐾 **Extras** Speciality toiletries, local biscuits - complimentary **Parking** 3 **Notes** ⊗

Britmead House

★★★★ GUEST ACCOMMODATION

West Bay Rd DT6 4EG
☎ 01308 422941 & 07973 725243
e-mail: britmead@talk21.com
web: www.britmeadhouse.co.uk
dir: *1m S of town centre, exit A35 into West Bay Rd*

Britmead House is located south of Bridport, within easy reach of the town centre and West Bay harbour. Family-run, the atmosphere is friendly and the accommodation well appointed and comfortable. As it is suitable for business and leisure, many guests return regularly. A choice of breakfast is served in the light and airy dining room.

Rooms 8 en suite (2 fmly) (2 GF) S £40-£60; D £64-£80* **Facilities** FTV Lounge tea/coffee Cen ht Wi-fi 🐾 **Parking** 12 **Notes** LB Closed 24-27 Dec

BRIDPORT *continued*

Oxbridge Farm (SY475977)

★★★★ FARMHOUSE

DT6 3UA
☎ 01308 488368 & 07766 086543 Mrs C Marshall
e-mail: jojokillin@hotmail.com
web: www.oxbridgefarm.co.uk
dir: *From A3066 Bridport to Beaminster. Take 1st right
signed Oxbridge 1m*

Oxbridge Farm sits in the rolling hills of west Dorset in an
Area of Outstanding Natural Beauty. The bedrooms are
well equipped and offer a very good level of comfort. A
hearty breakfast is served in the attractive dining room
which benefits from the wonderful views.

Rooms 3 rms (2 en suite) (1 pri facs) (2 fmly)
Facilities FTV TVL tea/coffee Dinner available Cen ht Wi-fi
⚓ 18 **Parking** 6 **Notes** ⊗ ⊜ 40 acres sheep

CERNE ABBAS   Map 4 ST60

Abbots

★★★ BED AND BREAKFAST

7 Long St DT2 7JF
☎ 01300 341349
dir: *From A352 follow signs to village centre, next to
village stores opp New Inn public house*

Located in the pleasant village of Cerne Abbas, guests
here can enjoy a cream tea in the downstairs tea room
before retiring to the relaxing bedrooms; all are located
upstairs. A choice of pubs offering a selection of evening
meals is just a few minutes' stroll away. Home-cooked
breakfasts are also served in the comfortable tea room.

Rooms 5 rms (4 en suite) (1 pri facs) (1 fmly) S £45-£50;
D £75-£85* **Facilities** FTV tea/coffee Cen ht Licensed
Wi-fi

CHIDEOCK   Map 4 SY49

Rose Cottage

★★★★ BED AND BREAKFAST

Main St DT6 6JQ
☎ 01297 489994 & 07980 400904
e-mail: enquire@rosecottage-chideock.co.uk
web: www.rosecottage-chideock.co.uk
dir: *On A35 in village centre, on left in W direction*

Located in the centre of a charming village, this
300-year-old cottage provides very well-appointed,
attractive accommodation and a friendly welcome is
assured. A delicious breakfast can be enjoyed in the
renovated dining room which has many interesting
features, and in finer weather guests can relax in the
pretty garden.

Rooms 2 en suite S £55; D £78* **Facilities** FTV tea/coffee
Cen ht Wi-fi **Parking** 2 **Notes** LB ⊗ No Children 12yrs
Closed 31 Dec

CHRISTCHURCH   Map 5 SZ19

PREMIER COLLECTION

Druid House

★★★★★ ⌂ GUEST ACCOMMODATION

26 Sopers Ln BH23 1JE
☎ 01202 485615 📠 01202 473484
e-mail: reservations@druid-house.co.uk
web: www.druid-house.co.uk
dir: *From A35 exit at Christchurch main rdbt into
Sopers Ln, establishment on left*

Overlooking the park, this delightful family-run
establishment is just a stroll from the high street, the
priory and the quay. Bedrooms, some with balconies,
are very comfortably furnished, and have many
welcome extras including CD players. There is a
pleasant rear garden, patio and relaxing lounge and
bar areas.

Rooms 8 en suite (3 fmly) (4 GF) **Facilities** STV tea/
coffee Direct Dial Cen ht Licensed **Parking** 8 **Notes** ⊗

PREMIER COLLECTION

The Lord Bute & Restaurant

★★★★★ ⊛ GUEST ACCOMMODATION

179-181 Lymington Rd, Highcliffe on Sea BH23 4JS
☎ 01425 278884 📠 01425 279258
e-mail: mail@lordbute.co.uk
web: www.lordbute.co.uk
dir: *A337 towards Highcliffe*

The elegant Lord Bute stands directly behind the
original entrance lodges of Highcliffe Castle close to
the beach and historic town of Christchurch. Bedrooms
have been finished to a very high standard with many
thoughtful extras including spa baths. Excellent food is
available in the smart restaurant, and conferences and
weddings are catered for.

Rooms 9 en suite 4 annexe en suite (1 fmly) (6 GF)
Facilities FTV tea/coffee Dinner available Direct Dial
Cen ht Licensed **Conf** Max 25 Thtr 25 Class 15 Board
18 **Parking** 40 **Notes** RS Mon Restaurant closed (open
bkfst)

The Manor

★★★★★ ⌂ GUEST ACCOMMODATION

15-17 Salisbury Rd, Burton BH23 7JG
☎ 01202 477189 📠 0872 110 8939
e-mail: info@themanorchristchurch.co.uk
dir: *Exit A35 (Christchurch bypass) into Salisbury Rd*

Rooms 10 en suite (1 fmly) S £55-£85; D £95-£125*
Facilities FTV TVL tea/coffee Dinner available Cen ht
Licensed Wi-fi **Parking** 100 **Notes** LB

Beautiful South

★★★★ BED AND BREAKFAST

87 Barrack Rd BH23 2AJ
☎ 01202 568183 & 07958 597686
e-mail: kevin.lovett1@ntlworld.com
web: www.christchurchbandb.co.uk
dir: *0.25m from Christchurch town centre on A35,
opposite Pizza Hut at Bailey Bridge*

A convenient location near to the main road on the
outskirts of Christchurch makes this friendly bed and
breakfast a good choice for leisure and business. The
public areas and bedrooms are bright and inviting, and
hearty dinners, by arrangement, can be enjoyed in the
pleasantly appointed dining room.

Rooms 3 en suite (1 fmly) **Facilities** FTV tea/coffee Dinner
available Cen ht Wi-fi **Parking** 4 **Notes** ⊗ ⊜

Bure Farmhouse

★★★★ BED AND BREAKFAST

107 Bure Ln, Friars Cliff BH23 4DN
☎ **01425 275498**
e-mail: info@burefarmhouse.co.uk
dir: A35 & A337 E from Christchurch towards Highcliffe,
1st rdbt right onto The Runway. Bure Ln 3rd turn sharp
right onto service road, farmhouse on left

A friendly welcome is assured at this family home.
Individually decorated bedrooms offer comfort and
provide useful extras. Hearty breakfasts are served
farmhouse style in the dining room overlooking the
attractive gardens.

Rooms 3 rms (2 en suite) (1 pri facs) (1 fmly) S £40-£45;
D £60-£70 **Facilities** DVD tea/coffee Cen ht Wi-fi
Parking 3 **Notes** LB ⊗ No Children 4yrs ⊛

Grosvenor Lodge

★★★★ GUEST HOUSE

53 Stour Rd BH23 1LN
☎ **01202 499008** 🖷 **01202 486041**
e-mail: bookings@grosvenorlodge.co.uk
web: www.grosvenorlodge.co.uk
dir: A35 from Christchurch to Bournemouth, at 1st lights
left into Stour Rd. Lodge on right

A friendly and popular guest house near the centre of this
historic town. The bedrooms are brightly and individually
decorated and have lots of useful extras. Hearty
breakfasts are served in the cheerful dining room and
there is an extensive selection of local restaurants for
lunch and dinner.

Rooms 7 en suite (4 fmly) (1 GF) **Facilities** FTV tea/coffee
Cen ht Wi-fi **Parking** 10 **Notes** ⊗

Riversmead

★★★★ GUEST ACCOMMODATION

61 Stour Rd BH23 1LN
☎ **01202 487195**
e-mail: riversmead.dorset@googlemail.com
dir: A338 to Christchurch. Left turn to town centre, turn
right over railway bridge

Ideally located close to the town centre, beaches and the
New Forest with excellent access to all local transport,
Riversmead is the perfect base for a short break or longer
stay. This comfortable house offers a range of facilities
including enclosed off-road parking, fridges in rooms and
an excellent breakfast.

Rooms 3 en suite (1 fmly) S £45-£50; D £50-£70*
Facilities FTV tea/coffee Cen ht Wi-fi **Parking** 9 **Notes** LB
⊗ ⊛

The Rothesay

★★★★ GUEST ACCOMMODATION

175, Lymington Rd, Highcliffe BH23 4JS
☎ **01425 274172**
e-mail: reservations@therothesayhotel.com
web: www.therothesayhotel.com
dir: A337 to Highcliffe towards The Castle, 1m on left

Set on the edge of Highcliffe, The Rothesay is a great
base for exploring the Dorset and Hampshire coast.
Highcliffe Castle is just a five-minute walk away, and
there are cliff top walks and views to the Isle of Wight.
The indoor pool is a real benefit, as are the pretty gardens
and large car park.

Rooms 12 en suite 3 annexe en suite (1 fmly) (7 GF)
Facilities FTV TVL tea/coffee Cen ht Licensed Wi-fi ⊗
Sauna Pool table **Conf** Max 30 Thtr 30 Class 30 Board 30
Parking 21 **Notes** ⊗ No Children 8yrs

The White House

★★★★ GUEST ACCOMMODATION

428 Lymington Rd, Highcliffe on Sea BH23 5HF
☎ **01425 271279** 🖷 **01425 276900**
e-mail: enquiries@thewhitehouse-christchurch.co.uk
dir: Off A35, signs to Highcliffe. After rdbt The White
House 200yds on right

This charming Victorian house is just a short drive from
Highcliffe beach, the New Forest and the historic town of
Christchurch. Comfortable, well-appointed
accommodation is provided, and a generous, freshly-
cooked breakfast is served in the cosy dining room.

Rooms 6 en suite **Facilities** tea/coffee Cen ht Wi-fi
Parking 6 **Notes** LB ⊗

Brantwood Guest House

★★★ GUEST ACCOMMODATION

55 Stour Rd BH23 1LN
☎ **01202 473446** 🖷 **01202 473446**
e-mail: brantwoodbookings@gmail.com
dir: A338 Bournemouth, 1st exit to Christchurch, right
after railway bridge, cross lights, 200yds on right

Brantwood offers relaxed and friendly guest
accommodation where the proprietors create a home-
from-home atmosphere. Bedrooms and bathrooms are all
well decorated and comfortably furnished. The town
centre is just a stroll away and off-road parking is
available.

Rooms 5 rms (4 en suite) (1 pri facs) (2 fmly) (1 GF)
Facilities tea/coffee Cen ht Wi-fi **Parking** 5 **Notes** ⊗ ⊛

Southern Comfort Guest House

★★★ GUEST ACCOMMODATION

51 Stour Rd BH23 1LN
☎ **01202 471373**
e-mail: scomfortgh@aol.com
dir: A338 onto B3073 towards Christchurch, 2m onto
B3059 (Stour Rd)

Convenient for Bournemouth, Christchurch and
Southbourne, this practical and friendly guest
accommodation offers spacious bedrooms. Breakfast,
served in the bright lounge-dining room, is a relaxed
affair with a good choice of hot items.

Rooms 3 en suite (3 fmly) S £25-£30; D £55-£70
Facilities FTV TVL tea/coffee Cen ht Wi-fi **Parking** 4
Notes LB ⊗

Three Gables

★★★ BED AND BREAKFAST

11 Wickfield Av BH23 1JB
☎ **01202 481166**
e-mail: enquiries@three-gables.co.uk
web: www.three-gables.co.uk
dir: A35 to Christchurch, at Fountain rdbt exit onto Sopers
Ln. 1st left onto Wickfield Av

Located in a residential area and only five minutes' walk
for the town centre, this family-run establishment offers
comfortable bedrooms and bathrooms which have now
been redecorated. Wi-fi is available throughout the house.
Breakfast is served at the communal table in the dining
room and there is off-road parking.

Rooms 3 en suite (1 fmly) S £40-£50; D £50-£70
Facilities FTV tea/coffee Cen ht Wi-fi **Parking** 5 **Notes** LB
⊗ ⊛

CORFE MULLEN
Map 4 SY99

Kenways
★★★ BED AND BREAKFAST

90a Wareham Rd BH21 3LQ
☎ 01202 280620
e-mail: eileen@kenways.com
web: www.kenways.com
dir: *2m SW of Wimborne. Off A31 to Corfe Mullen. Over B3074 rdbt, B&B 0.3m on right*

Expect to be welcomed as one of the family at this homely bed and breakfast between Wimborne Minster and Poole. The spacious bedrooms are well provisioned with thoughtful extras, and breakfast is served in the pleasant conservatory overlooking the attractive gardens.

Rooms 3 rms (3 pri facs) (2 GF) S £30; D £60*
Facilities FTV DVD TVL tea/coffee Cen ht Wi-fi Table tennis Snooker table **Parking** 4

DORCHESTER
Map 4 SY69

PREMIER COLLECTION

Little Court
★★★★★ 🏠 GUEST ACCOMMODATION

5 Westleaze, Charminster DT2 9PZ
☎ 01305 261576 📄 01305 261359
e-mail: info@littlecourt.net
web: www.littlecourt.net
dir: *A37 from Dorchester, 0.25m right at Loders Garage, Little Court 0.5m on right*

Built in 1909 in the style of Lutyens, Little Court sits in over four acres of attractive grounds and gardens. The property has been appointed to a very high standard and the friendly proprietors are on hand to ensure a pleasant stay. A delicious breakfast, including home-grown produce, can be enjoyed in the stylish dining room.

Little Court

Rooms 8 en suite (1 fmly) **Facilities** FTV Lounge tea/coffee Cen ht Licensed Wi-fi 🎾 🏊 ♨ 18 **Parking** 10 **Notes** LB ⊗ Closed Xmas & New Year

Baytree House Dorchester
★★★★ BED AND BREAKFAST

4 Athelstan Rd DT1 1NR
☎ 01305 263696
e-mail: info@baytreedorchester.com
dir: *0.5m SE of town centre*

A friendly, family-run bed and breakfast situated in the heart of Dorchester, not far from the village of Higher Bockham - the birthplace of Thomas Hardy. The bedrooms are furnished in an appealing contemporary style and provide high levels of comfort. Breakfast is served farmhouse style in the open-plan kitchen/dining area. Parking is available.

Rooms 3 en suite **Facilities** FTV TVL tea/coffee Cen ht **Parking** 3 **Notes** ⊗ 📧

Westwood House
★★★★ GUEST ACCOMMODATION

29 High West St DT1 1UP
☎ 01305 268018
e-mail: reservations@westwoodhouse.co.uk
web: www.westwoodhouse.co.uk
dir: *On B2150 in town centre*

Built in 1815, Westwood House is centrally located in the historic town of Dorchester and is ideal for leisure visitors as well as business travellers. This attractive property, run by a husband and wife team, offers well-appointed rooms with modern facilities presented in an informal, stylish environment.

Rooms 7 rms (5 en suite) (2 pri facs) (2 fmly) S £60-£75; D £75-£95* **Facilities** FTV DVD tea/coffee Cen ht Wi-fi 🔋 **Notes** ⊗

EVERSHOT
Map 4 ST50

The Acorn Inn
★★★★ 🏵 INN

DT2 0JW
☎ 01935 83228 📄 01935 83707
e-mail: stay@acorn-inn.co.uk
web: www.acorn-inn.co.uk
dir: *From A37 between Yeovil & Dorchester, follow Evershot & Holywell signs, 0.5m to inn*

This delightful 16th-century coaching inn is located in the heart of the village. Many of the bedrooms feature interesting four-poster beds, and all the rooms have been individually decorated and furnished. The public areas retain many original features including oak panelling, open fires and stone-flagged floors. Fresh local produce is included on the varied menu.

Rooms 10 en suite (2 fmly) S £79-£194; D £99-£194*
Facilities STV FTV TVL tea/coffee Dinner available Direct Dial Cen ht Wi-fi ch fac 🔋 Use of spa opposite - charged **Conf** Max 30 Thtr 30 Board 30 **Parking** 40 **Notes** LB

Save on B&Bs and Hotels. Book at **theAA.com/hotel**

DORSET 137 **ENGLAND**

FARNHAM — Map 4 ST91

PREMIER COLLECTION

Farnham Farm House

★★★★★ GUEST ACCOMMODATION

DT11 8DG
☎ 01725 516254 📠 01725 516306
e-mail: info@farnhamfarmhouse.co.uk
web: www.farnhamfarmhouse.co.uk
dir: *Exit A354 Thickthorn x-rds into Farnham, continue NW from village centre T-junct, 1m bear right at sign*

Farnham Farm House sits in 350 acres of arable farmland, offering a high level of quality, comfort and service. The atmosphere is friendly and the accommodation charming and spacious. In winter, a log fire burns in the attractive dining room, where a delicious breakfast, featuring local produce, is served; from here views across the rolling countryside can be enjoyed. Added features include an outdoor pool and the Sarpenela Natural Therapies Centre in the converted stable.

Rooms 3 en suite (1 fmly) **Facilities** FTV tea/coffee 🍵 🍴 Holistic Therapies Centre **Parking** 7 **Notes** ⊗ Closed 25-26 Dec

FERNDOWN — Map 5 SU00

City Lodge

★★★★ GUEST ACCOMMODATION

Ringwood Rd BH22 9AN
☎ 01202 578828 📠 01202 572620
e-mail: bournemouth@citylodge.co.uk

Close to Bournemouth and the airport, City Lodge provides an ideal base for exploring the Dorset coastline. Situated on the edge of the River Stour, many of the rooms have the benefit of beautiful riverside views. The bedrooms offer modern facilities such as en suite bathrooms, LCD TVs and free Wi-fi. The large bar and restaurant serve meals and snacks. Parking is gated and secure.

Rooms 45 en suite (4 fmly) (11 GF) S £29.95-£89.95; D £29.95-£89.95 (room only)* **Facilities** FTV Lounge tea/coffee Dinner available Cen ht Licensed Wi-fi Fishing **Conf** Max 120 Thtr 80 Class 60 Board 40 **Parking** 300 **Notes** LB ⊗ Civ Wed 120

HIGHCLIFFE

For accommodation details see Christchurch

LOWER ANSTY — Map 4 ST70

The Fox Inn

★★★★ INN

DT2 7PN
☎ 01258 880328 📠 01258 881440
e-mail: fox@anstyfoxinn.co.uk
web: www.anstyfoxinn.co.uk
dir: *Off A354 at Millbourne St Andrew, follow brown signs to Ansty*

This popular inn has a long and interesting history including strong links to the Hall & Woodhouse Brewery. Surrounded by beautiful Dorset countryside, this is a great base for exploring the area. Bedrooms are smartly appointed and offer high levels of comfort. The interesting menu focuses on excellent local produce, with a choice of dining options including the oak-panelled dining room. An extensive garden and patio area are also available.

The Fox Inn

Rooms 11 en suite (7 fmly) S £45-£85; D £50-£110* **Facilities** FTV TVL tea/coffee Dinner available Direct Dial Cen ht Wi-fi **Conf** Max 60 Thtr 60 Class 40 Board 45 **Parking** 30 **Notes** LB

LYME REGIS — Map 4 SY39

See also Axminster (Devon)

Old Lyme Guest House

★★★★ GUEST ACCOMMODATION

29 Coombe St DT7 3PP
☎ 01297 442929
e-mail: oldlyme.guesthouse@virgin.net
web: www.oldlymeguesthouse.co.uk
dir: *In town centre into Coombe St at lights*

Comfort is a high priority at this delightful 18th-century former post office, which is just a short walk from the seafront. Bedrooms, which vary in size, are all well equipped and include many thoughtful extras. A wide choice is offered at breakfast, served in the cheerful dining room.

Rooms 5 rms (4 en suite) (1 pri facs) (1 fmly) D £78-£90* **Facilities** FTV TVL tea/coffee Cen ht Wi-fi **Notes** LB ⊗ No Children 5yrs Closed Xmas & New Year 📶

St Cuthberts

★★★★ BED AND BREAKFAST

Charmouth Rd DT7 3HG
☎ 01297 445901
e-mail: info@stcuthbertsoflyme.co.uk
web: www.stcuthbertsoflyme.co.uk
dir: *A35 from Dorchester, at Charmouth rdbt onto B3052 for 2m. Establishment on opposite side of road to "Welcome to Lyme Regis" sign*

Located just a ten minute walk above the main town and harbour, this detached home is set within mature gardens and has its own parking. Bedrooms and bathrooms offer plenty of quality and comfort, as well as many extras that add to guest enjoyment. A lounge with log burner is available in addition to a decked terrace. Breakfast, served around one large table, offers a varied choice including delicious pancakes, with bacon and maple syrup.

Rooms 3 en suite (1 GF) S fr £65; D fr £85* **Facilities** FTV TVL tea/coffee Cen ht 🍴 18 **Parking** 3 **Notes** ⊗ No Children 7yrs 📶

LYME REGIS *continued*

Albany Guest House

★★★★ GUEST ACCOMMODATION

Charmouth Rd DT7 3DP
☎ 01297 443066
e-mail: albany@lymeregis.com
dir: *300yds NE of town centre on A3052*

Situated on the outskirts of this popular town and within easy walking distance of the seafront, this attractive house provides comfortable accommodation and a home-from-home atmosphere. Bedrooms are comfortably furnished, the public rooms are inviting and guests are welcome to use the garden. Breakfast, featuring local ingredients, is served in the homely dining room.

Rooms 5 en suite S £39-£45; D £68-£160* **Facilities** FTV TVL tea/coffee Cen ht Wi-fi **Parking** 5 **Notes** LB ⊗ No Children 10yrs Closed Jan ⊕

Cleveland

★★★★ BED AND BREAKFAST

Pound St DT7 3JA
☎ 01297 442012 & 07879 823674
e-mail: clevelandlyme@aol.com
dir: *A3052 Lyme Regis/Sidmouth road, 250yds up hill from Lyme Regis High St*

Delightfully positioned just a short stroll from the main high street and a five-minute walk from the sea, this relaxing bed and breakfast offers a range of welcome extras including the benefit of off-street parking. The stylish bedrooms and bathrooms are very comfortable, as is the breakfast room where a range of carefully chosen produce is available.

Rooms 3 en suite (3 GF) S £75-£90; D £80-£95 **Facilities** FTV tea/coffee Cen ht Wi-fi ⚓ **Parking** 3 **Notes** ⊗ No Children 18yrs

The Mariners

★★★★ ⊚ INN

Silver St DT7 3HS
☎ 01297 442753 🖷 01297 442431
e-mail: enquiry@hotellymeregis.co.uk
dir: *A35 onto B3165 (Lyme Rd). Mariners is pink building opposite road to The Cobb (Pound Rd)*

This delightful building combines traditional character and ambience with a modern and stylish upgrade. Bedrooms and bathrooms vary in size, but include a range of welcome extras; many have views over the bay. Public areas include a relaxing lounge, comfortable bar and modern restaurant. Guests can choose a full dinner, utilising local fish and seafood, or a varied range of lighter options from the bar menu. Outdoor seating is available.

Rooms 14 en suite (2 fmly) S £34.50-£125; D £59.50-£155* **Facilities** FTV Lounge tea/coffee Dinner available Direct Dial Cen ht Wi-fi **Conf** Max 30 Thtr 24 Class 16 Board 30 **Parking** 20 **Notes** LB ⊗

MILTON ABBAS   Map 4 ST80

Fishmore Hill Farm *(ST799013)*

★★★ FARMHOUSE

DT11 0DL
☎ 01258 881122 & 07708 003561
🖷 01258 881122 Mr & Mrs N Clarke
e-mail: sarah@fishmorehillfarm.com
dir: *Off A354 signed Milton Abbas, 3m left on sharp bend, up steep hill, 1st left*

This working sheep farm and family home is surrounded by beautiful Dorset countryside, close to historic Milton Abbas and only a short drive from the coast. Bedrooms, which vary in size, are comfortable and have useful extras. The atmosphere is friendly and relaxed. Breakfast is served in the smart dining room around a communal table.

Rooms 3 en suite S £35; D £70* **Facilities** FTV TVL tea/coffee Cen ht **Parking** 4 **Notes** Closed Xmas & New Year ⊕ 50 acres sheep/horses

---

MOTCOMBE   Map 4 ST82

The Coppleridge Inn

★★★ INN

SP7 9HW
☎ 01747 851980 🖷 01747 851858
e-mail: thecoppleridgeinn@btinternet.com
web: www.coppleridge.com
dir: *Exit A350 to Motcombe, under railway bridge, 400yds, right to Mere, inn 300yds on left*

This village inn set within its own 15 acres of land offers ten en suite bedrooms located in a pretty courtyard. All bedrooms have been appointed to a very high standard to provide a very comfortable stay. Staff offer a warm welcome, and the inn serves good food with many daily specials. There are tennis courts and boules, plus a children's play area. Clay pigeon shooting can also be arranged.

The Coppleridge Inn

Rooms 10 en suite (2 fmly) (10 GF) S £55; D £95* **Facilities** FTV DVD TVL tea/coffee Dinner available Direct Dial Cen ht Wi-fi ch fac ⚲ Pool table boules pitch **Conf** Max 60 Thtr 60 Class 60 Board 30 **Parking** 100 **Notes** LB Civ Wed 80

PIDDLEHINTON   Map 4 SY79

Longpuddle

★★★★ BED AND BREAKFAST

4 High St DT2 7TD
☎ 01300 348532
e-mail: ann@longpuddle.co.uk
web: www.longpuddle.co.uk
dir: *From Dorchester (A35) take B3143, after entering village 1st thatched house on left after village cross*

This purpose-built annexed accommodation is perfectly located for exploring the delightful Dorset countryside and coast. Bedrooms are spacious, very well furnished and equipped with thoughtful extras such as mini-fridges. Breakfast is served in the dining room of the main house, where a guest lounge is also located overlooking the lovely gardens.

Rooms 2 annexe en suite (2 fmly) S £40-£50; D £80-£100 **Facilities** FTV DVD TVL tea/coffee Cen ht Wi-fi ⚓ **Parking** 3 **Notes** RS Dec-Jan Prior bookings only ⊕

PLUSH   Map 4 ST70

The Brace of Pheasants

★★★★ ⇐ INN

DT2 7RQ
☎ 01300 348357
e-mail: info@braceofpheasants.co.uk
dir: *A35 onto B3142, right to Plush 1.5m*

Situated in the heart of Dorset, this picturesque thatched pub offers a warm and genuine welcome to both visitors and locals alike. Very much a traditional pub, the atmosphere is convivial, with plenty of good-natured conversation. Bedrooms are split between the main building and the former skittle alley - all offer exceptional standards of comfort and individual style, with wonderful bathrooms. The food here should not be missed, with excellent local produce used to create an appealing menu.

Rooms 4 en suite 4 annexe en suite (4 GF) **Facilities** FTV tea/coffee Dinner available Direct Dial Cen ht Wi-fi **Parking** 15 **Notes** Closed 25 Dec

Save on B&Bs and Hotels. Book at **theAA.com/hotel**

DORSET 139 **ENGLAND**

POOLE
Map 4 SZ09

Bees Knees Guest House
★★★★ 🏠 GUEST HOUSE

28 Davis Rd, Branksome BH12 2BB
☎ 01202 734509 & 07729 244297
e-mail: bees.knees1@ntlworld.com
web: www.beesknees-guesthouse.co.uk
dir: A35 from Bournemouth towards Poole. At rdbt take 2nd exit onto A3040 signed Upper Parkstone. At next rdbt straight on onto B3061 (Ashley Rd). 1st right onto Davis Rd

Located in a quiet residential area, yet close to all nearby attractions, this family-run guest house provides especially welcoming and attentive service from the resident proprietors. Bedrooms are very well decorated and furnished and include welcome extras such as home-made cookies. Carefully prepared breakfasts utilise the highest quality ingredients, and are a highlight of any stay.

Rooms 3 en suite S £45-£55; D £60-£80* **Facilities** FTV TVL tea/coffee Cen ht Wi-fi 🎣 18 🔒 **Extras** Fridge, home-made cookies, county magazines **Conf** Max 8 Thtr 8 Class 6 Board 8 **Parking** 3 **Notes** LB ⊗ No Children 16yrs Closed last 2wks Dec-3 Jan 🍽

Acorns Guest House
★★★★ GUEST ACCOMMODATION

264 Wimborne Rd, Oakdale BH15 3EF
☎ 01202 672901 📄 01202 672901
e-mail: enquiries@acornsguesthouse.co.uk
web: www.acornsguesthouse.co.uk
dir: On A35, approx 1m from town centre, opposite Esso station

A warm welcome is assured at Acorns, located with easy access to the town, ferry terminal, business parks and attractions. The bedrooms are furnished to a high standard, and an English breakfast is served in the charming dining room. There is also a quiet cosy lounge.

Rooms 4 en suite (1 GF) D £62-£72 **Facilities** FTV DVD TVL tea/coffee Cen ht Wi-fi 🔒 **Parking** 6 **Notes** LB ⊗ No Children 14yrs Closed 23 Dec-1 Jan 🍽

Milsoms Poole
★★★★ 🍴 RESTAURANT WITH ROOMS

47 Haven Rd, Canford Cliffs BH13 7LH
☎ 01202 609000
e-mail: poole@milsomshotel.co.uk

Milsoms Poole is located in the Canford Cliffs area, moments from some of the country's best beaches and the picturesque Purbeck Hills. Comfortable and stylish en suite accommodation is situated above the popular seafood Loch Fyne Restaurant. The friendly and helpful team provide a warm welcome. Limited on-site parking is available.

Rooms 8 en suite (1 GF) D £70-£85* **Facilities** FTV tea/coffee Dinner available Cen ht Wi-fi **Parking** 12 **Notes** ⊗ No coaches

Towngate Guest House
★★★ GUEST HOUSE

58 Wimborne Rd BH15 2BY
☎ 01202 668552
e-mail: ayoun19@ntlworld.com
dir: B3093 from town centre, guest house on right

Guests are assured of a warm welcome at this centrally located guest house, within walking distance of the town centre and harbour, and just a short drive from the ferry terminal. The well-equipped bedrooms are comfortable and nicely furnished.

Rooms 3 en suite **Facilities** tea/coffee Cen ht **Parking** 4 **Notes** ⊗ No Children 10yrs Closed mid Dec-mid Jan 🍽

Antelope Inn
★★★ INN

8 High St BH15 1BP
☎ 01202 672029 📄 01202 678286
e-mail: 6603@greeneking.co.uk

Close to Poole Quay, which is one of the town's main attractions, this famous old coaching inn is the oldest licensed premises in Poole, and has long been a popular meeting point. All rooms are furnished to a good standard with modern facilities, and include some feature rooms. Public areas include a busy bar and a restaurant.

Rooms 23 en suite

Centraltown Guest House
★★★ GUEST HOUSE

101 Wimborne Rd BH15 2BP
☎ 01202 674080 📄 01202 674080
dir: From town centre onto A3093, Barclays International building on left, guest house 500yds

This friendly and well-maintained guest house is within easy access of the town centre, ferry terminals, speedway and many other attractions. Bedrooms are attractive and equipped with many useful extra facilities. A full English breakfast is served in the bright, cosy dining room.

Rooms 3 en suite **Facilities** tea/coffee Cen ht Wi-fi **Parking** 6 **Notes** ⊗ No Children

Seacourt
★★★ GUEST ACCOMMODATION

249 Blandford Rd, Hamworthy BH15 4AZ
☎ 01202 674995
dir: Off A3049/A35 signed to Hamworthy

Within a short distance of the ferry port and town centre, this friendly establishment is well maintained and efficiently run. The comfortable bedrooms, some located on the ground floor, are all nicely decorated and equipped with useful extra facilities. Breakfast is served in the pleasant dining room at separate tables.

Rooms 5 en suite (1 fmly) (3 GF) (5 smoking) S £40-£59; D £59* **Facilities** FTV tea/coffee Cen ht Wi-fi **Parking** 5 **Notes** ⊗ No Children 5yrs 🍽

PORTESHAM
Map 4 SY68

Kings Arms
[U]

2 Front St DT3 4ET
☎ 01305 871342

Currently the rating for this establishment is not confirmed. This may be due to a change of ownership or because it has only recently joined the AA rating scheme.

Rooms 3 en suite (1 fmly) (3 GF) **Facilities** tea/coffee Dinner available **Parking** 20

PORTLAND
Map 4 SY67

Queen Anne House
★★★★ GUEST ACCOMMODATION

2/4 Fortuneswell DT5 1LP
☎ 01305 820028
e-mail: margaretdunlop@tiscali.co.uk
dir: A354 to Portland then Fortuneswell. House on left 200mtrs past Royal Portland Arms

This delightful Grade II listed building is a charming and comfortable place to stay; particularly delightful are the Italianate gardens to the rear. Ideal for business and for leisure, Queen Anne House is close to Portland Bill, Weymouth and Chesil Beach. The bedrooms are particularly attractive and pleasantly furnished. At breakfast, where guests are seated at one large table, there is a wide choice of options.

Rooms 3 en suite S £48-£60; D £75-£90 **Facilities** FTV TVL tea/coffee Cen ht Wi-fi **Parking** 4 **Notes** ⊗ 🍽

Beach House
★★★ GUEST HOUSE

51 Chiswell DT5 1AW
☎ 01305 821155
e-mail: pete@beach-house-bandb.co.uk
dir: A354, after causeway take right lane to Victoria Square & into Chiswell. 150mtrs on right

Dating back to the early 19th century, this grand building was formerly a public house, which now provides relaxed and welcoming accommodation. Situated at the edge of the stunning sweep of Chesil Beach, this establishment is also handy for the sailing academy. Bedrooms have good levels of comfort and quality; many have stripped wooden floors and simple, stylish decor. A lounge and bar are available, together with a light and airy breakfast room.

Rooms 7 rms (5 en suite) (2 pri facs) (2 fmly) S £35-£48; D £65-£90* **Facilities** FTV TVL tea/coffee Cen ht Licensed Wi-fi 🔒 **Conf** Max 25 Thtr 25 Class 25 Board 25 **Parking** 8 **Notes** LB ⊗

PORTLAND *continued*

Portland Lodge

★★★ GUEST ACCOMMODATION

Easton Ln DT5 1BW
☎ 01305 820265 📠 01305 860359
e-mail: info@portlandlodge.com
dir: *Signs to Easton/Portland Bill, rdbt at Portland Heights Hotel 1st right. Portland Lodge 200yds*

Situated on the fascinating island of Portland, this modern, lodge-style establishment provides comfortable accommodation including a number of ground-floor bedrooms. Breakfast is served in the spacious dining room with a friendly team of staff on hand. This is an ideal location for those wishing to explore the World Heritage coastline.

Rooms 30 annexe en suite (15 fmly) (7 GF) S £30–£55; D £45–£65 (room only)* **Facilities** FTV tea/coffee Cen ht Wi-fi **Parking** 50 **Notes** LB ⊗

POWERSTOCK   Map 4 SY59

Three Horseshoes Inn

★★★★ 🍴 INN

DT6 3TF
☎ 01308 485328 📠 01308 485760
e-mail: threehorseshoespowerstock@live.co.uk
dir: *3m from Bridport. Powerstock signed off A3066 Bridport to Beaminster*

The Three Horseshoes overlooks rolling hills from its elevated position in the village. The unpretentious bar and cosy dining room appeal to locals and visitors alike. Dinner offers a selection of traditional pub classics with a stylish twist, to suit a wide variety of tastes. Two of the spacious bedrooms have been recently refurbished to provide high levels of quality and comfort.

Rooms 1 en suite 2 annexe en suite (3 fmly) (2 GF) S £75–£95; D £75–£95* **Facilities** FTV tea/coffee Dinner available Cen ht Wi-fi **Parking** 20 **Notes** No coaches

---

PUNCKNOWLE   Map 4 SY58

Offley Bed & Breakfast

★★★★ GUEST ACCOMMODATION

Looke Ln DT2 9BD
☎ 01308 897044 & 07792 624977
dir: *Off B3157 into village centre, left after Crown Inn into Looke Ln, 2nd house on right*

With magnificent views over the Bride Valley, this village house provides comfortable, quality accommodation. Guests are assured of a warm, friendly welcome; an ideal venue to enjoy the numerous local attractions. There are several local inns, one in the village which is just a gentle stroll away.

Rooms 3 rms (2 en suite) (1 pri facs) S fr £45; D fr £70* **Facilities** FTV TVL tea/coffee Cen ht **Parking** 4 **Notes** LB 🅿

ST LEONARDS   Map 5 SU10

St Leonards

★★★ INN

Ringwood Rd BH24 2NP
☎ 01425 471220 📠 01425 480274
e-mail: 9230@greeneking.co.uk
web: www.oldenglish.co.uk
dir: *At end of M27 continue to 1st rdbt. Take slip road on left*

Close to Ringwood and Bournemouth, this inn has an attractive bar and restaurant offering an extensive menu of popular dishes and a children's menu. The spacious bedrooms are furnished to a high standard with modern facilities.

Rooms 35 en suite (5 fmly) (15 GF) **Facilities** tea/coffee Direct Dial Lift **Parking** 500 **Notes** Civ Wed 60

SHAFTESBURY   Map 4 ST82

PREMIER COLLECTION

The Old Chapel

★★★★★ 🛏 BED AND BREAKFAST

9 Breach Ln SP7 8LE
☎ 01747 852404
e-mail: info@theoldchapelbb.co.uk
web: www.theoldchapelbb.co.uk

The Old Chapel is exactly that, a lovingly, and dramatically converted chapel, which has spacious and comfortable accommodation. Bedrooms are particularly comfortable, excellent beds are attractively dressed and the rooms have a host of thoughtful extras. Bathrooms too are very well fitted, with power showers and delightful towels and toiletries. There is a pleasant garden and a lounge area. Breakfasts are also a highlight, featuring fresh and local produce feature. Hospitality is also a notable aspect as the proprietors are particularly welcoming.

Rooms 2 en suite S £60; D £90* **Facilities** FTV tea/coffee Cen ht Wi-fi **Parking** 2 **Notes** ⊗ No Children 15yrs

---

La Fleur de Lys Restaurant with Rooms

★★★★ 🍴🍴 RESTAURANT WITH ROOMS

Bleke St SP7 8AW
☎ 01747 853717 📠 01747 853130
e-mail: info@lafleurdelys.co.uk
web: www.lafleurdelys.co.uk
dir: *From junct of A30 & A350, 0.25m towards town centre*

Located just a few minutes' walk from the famous Gold Hill, this light and airy restaurant with rooms combines efficient service in a relaxed and friendly atmosphere. Bedrooms, which are suitable for both business and leisure guests, vary in size but all are well equipped, comfortable and tastefully furnished. A relaxing guest

---

lounge and courtyard are available for afternoon tea or pre-dinner drinks.

Rooms 7 en suite (2 fmly) (1 GF) S £75–£110; D £100–£175* **Facilities** FTV TVL tea/coffee Dinner available Direct Dial Cen ht Wi-fi **Conf** Max 12 Board 10 **Parking** 10 **Notes** LB ⊗ Closed 3rd wk Jan No coaches

---

SHERBORNE   Map 4 ST61

PREMIER COLLECTION

The Kings Arms

★★★★★ 🍴 INN

Charlton Horethorne DT9 4NL
☎ 01963 220281 📠 01963 220496
e-mail: admin@thekingsarms.co.uk
web: www.thekingsarms.co.uk
dir: *From A303 follow signs for Templecombe & Sherborne onto B3145 to Charlton Horethorne*

Situated in the heart of this engaging village, The Kings Arms offers impressive standards throughout. The experienced owners have created something for everyone with a convivial bar, snug and choice of dining environments, including the garden terrace with lovely countryside views. Bedrooms have individuality, quality and style with marble bathrooms, robes and wonderful showers. Food is taken seriously here with assured cooking from a menu showcasing the best of local produce.

Rooms 10 en suite (1 fmly) S £110; D £110* **Facilities** FTV DVD tea/coffee Dinner available Direct Dial Cen ht Lift Wi-fi 🍴 ♿ 18 **Conf** Thtr 70 Class 45 Board 50 **Parking** 30 **Notes** Closed 25 Dec RS 26 Dec no dinner served No coaches

Save on B&Bs and Hotels. Book at **theAA.com/hotel**

DORSET 141 ENGLAND

PREMIER COLLECTION

Munden House

★★★★★ 😊 GUEST ACCOMMODATION

Munden Ln, Alweston DT9 5HU
☎ 01963 23150
e-mail: stay@mundenhouse.co.uk
dir: *A352 from Sherborne, left onto A3030 to Alweston, pass village shop on right, 250yds on left at Oxfords Bakery sign, turn left into Mundens Ln. Munden House 100yds on right*

Delightful property set in a quiet lane away from the main road, with pleasant views over the surrounding countryside. Bedrooms and bathrooms come in a variety of shapes and styles but all are very well decorated and furnished; the beds are especially comfortable. Guests are welcome to use the lounge and garden, and delicious home-cooked dinners (accompanied by an Italian wine list) are available by prior arrangement. Breakfast includes a selection of high quality hot and cold dishes, all carefully prepared to order.

Rooms 4 en suite 3 annexe en suite (3 fmly) (4 GF) S £70-£100; D £90-£130* **Facilities** FTV Lounge tea/coffee Dinner available Cen ht Licensed Wi-fi 🍴 **Extras** Speciality toiletries, mineral water - complimentary **Parking** 14 **Notes** LB

Avalon Townhouse

★★★★ BED AND BREAKFAST

South St DT9 3LZ
☎ 01935 814748
e-mail: enquiries@avalontownhouse.co.uk
web: www.avalontownhouse.co.uk
dir: *A30 from Shaftesbury, towards Sherborne town centre, left into South St*

Avalon is a spacious and comfortable Edwardian townhouse in the heart of historic Sherborne. The building is appointed to a high standard, and each stylish bedroom has Freeview, flat screen TV, free Wi-fi, tea and coffee-making facilities and luxury toiletries. The husband and wife team extend a warm welcome and offer fine, freshly prepared food that utilises local produce.

Rooms 3 en suite S £70-£80; D £80-£90* **Facilities** FTV TVL tea/coffee Cen ht Wi-fi 🔒 **Notes** ⊗ No Children 18yrs

See advert on this page

Thorn Bank

★★★★ BED AND BREAKFAST

Long St DT9 3BS
☎ 01935 813795
e-mail: savileplatt@hotmail.com
dir: *A30 onto North Rd, then St Swithin's Rd. Right onto Long St, 75yds on right*

Located just a short walk from the centre of town and the abbey, this elegantly appointed, Grade II listed, Georgian townhouse is a perfect base from which to explore the area. The attentive service is noteworthy and every effort is made to ensure guests have an enjoyable and relaxing stay. The spacious bedrooms, with lovely views over the garden, are appointed to an impressive standard. Breakfast makes use of local Dorset produce, and in summer months guests are welcome to eat alfresco on the lovely patio.

Rooms 1 en suite 1 annexe en suite (2 fmly) D £90-£105* **Facilities** FTV DVD tea/coffee Cen ht Wi-fi 🔒 **Parking** 2 **Notes** LB ⊗ No Children 18yrs

SHERBORNE *continued*

The Alders

★★★ BED AND BREAKFAST

Sandford Orcas DT9 4SB
☎ 01963 220666 ▤ 01963 220666
e-mail: info@thealdersbb.com
web: www.thealdersbb.com
dir: *3m N of Sherborne. Off B3148 signed Sandford Orcas, near Manor House in village*

Located in the charming conservation area of Sandford Orcas and set in a lovely walled garden, this delightful property offers attractive, well-equipped bedrooms. Guests have their own entrance leading from the garden. A large inglenook fireplace with a wood-burning stove can be found in the comfortable sitting room, which also features the owner's watercolours. Massage therapies are available.

Rooms 3 en suite (1 fmly) S £50-£65; D £60-£75 **Facilities** FTV TVL tea/coffee Cen ht Wi-fi 🛁 **Extras** Fruit **Parking** 4 **Notes** ⊗ 🐾

Venn Farm *(ST684183)*

★★★ FARMHOUSE

Milborne Port DT9 5RA
☎ 01963 250598 ▤ 01963 250598 Mrs P Tizzard
e-mail: info@colintizzard.co.uk
dir: *3m E of Sherborne on A30 on edge of Milborne Port*

Set in a good location for exploring west Dorset, the owners of this farmhouse specialise in training National Hunt race horses, and extend a friendly welcome. The individually furnished bedrooms are comfortable, and bathrooms are fitted with power showers. Downstairs, a farmhouse breakfast is served in the lounge-dining room.

Rooms 2 en suite S fr £30; D fr £56* **Facilities** FTV TVL tea/coffee Cen ht Fishing **Parking** 6 **Notes** No Children 5yrs Closed Xmas 🐾 375 acres dairy/mixed/race horses

The Old Post Office

★★★ BED AND BREAKFAST

Marnhull Rd, Hinton St Mary DT10 1NG
☎ 01258 475590 ▤ 01258 475590
e-mail: info@northdorsetbandb.co.uk
web: www.northdorsetbandb.co.uk
dir: *A30 onto B3092 signed Sturminster Newton, on right after 5m*

Originally built in the 1830s, The Old Post Office provides pleasant and relaxing accommodation with charming features such as low doorways and unusual angles in the floors and walls. Comfortable beds are provided in the two rooms; one is en suite and the other has private facilities. Guests are welcome to use the pleasant rear garden and relaxing guest lounge where a TV is provided (rather than in the bedrooms). Off-street parking is available.

Rooms 2 rms (1 en suite) (1 pri facs) D £65* **Facilities** TVL tea/coffee Cen ht Wi-fi 🛁 **Parking** 2 **Notes** ⊗ No Children 14yrs 🐾

A Great Escape Guest House

★★★★ GUEST ACCOMMODATION

6 Argyle Rd BH19 1HZ
☎ 01929 475853 & 07867 508724
e-mail: stay@agreatescapeguesthouse.co.uk

A Great Escape is located in a quiet part of Swanage within easy reach of the town centre and the beach. The top floor rooms offer beautiful views of the surrounding areas and beyond. Bedrooms are tastefully decorated and equipped with an ample choice of amenities.

Rooms 5 rms (4 en suite) (1 pri facs) (1 fmly) (1 GF) **Facilities** FTV tea/coffee Cen ht Wi-fi **Notes** ⊗ No Children 3yrs

Rivendell

★★★★ 🏠 GUEST HOUSE

58 Kings Rd BH19 1HR
☎ 01929 421383
e-mail: kevin@rivendellguesthouse.co.uk

This beautiful period house, located within easy reach of the beach and town centre, has been lovingly restored to retain many of the original features. The bedrooms have been upgraded to a very good standard and can accommodate a diverse clientele. An award-winning breakfast is served in the cosy dining room.

Rooms 9 en suite (1 fmly) S £45; D £83-£93* **Facilities** FTV DVD TVL tea/coffee Cen ht Wi-fi **Notes** LB ⊗

Swanage Haven

★★★★ 🏠 GUEST HOUSE

3 Victoria Rd BH19 1LY
☎ 01929 423088 ▤ 01929 421912
e-mail: info@swanagehaven.com
web: www.swanagehaven.com

A boutique-style guest house close to Swanage Beach and the coastal path. Exclusively for adults, the accommodation is modern and contemporary with many extras such as fluffy robes, slippers, Wi-fi and a hot tub. Hands-on owners provide excellent hospitality with relaxed and friendly service. Breakfasts are superb; top quality organic and local produce from an extensive menu.

Rooms 7 en suite **Facilities** FTV TVL tea/coffee Cen ht Licensed Wi-fi 🌿 ♨ Hot tub Holistic treatment room **Parking** 7 **Notes** ⊗ No Children

The Limes

★★★★ GUEST HOUSE

48 Park Rd BH19 2AE
☎ 01929 422664
e-mail: info@limeshotel.net
dir: *Follow one-way system, signed to Durlston Country Park. Pass restaurant on left, right into Park Rd, 200mtrs on right*

Ideally located for both the town centre and the seafront, this comfortable establishment offers a variety of different bedroom shapes and sizes. In addition to the pleasant dining room, guests are free to use a small bar area and a popular games room.

Rooms 12 rms (10 en suite) (7 fmly) **Facilities** FTV tea/coffee Cen ht Licensed Wi-fi Pool table **Parking** 8

Ocean Lodge

★★★ GUEST ACCOMMODATION

3 Park Rd BH19 2AA
☎ 01929 422805 ▤ 01929 425225
e-mail: oceanlodgeswanage@gmail.com

This Victorian townhouse is centrally located in the picturesque coastal town of Swanage, within walking distance of the Blue Flag beach, restaurants, pubs and the shops. Bedrooms are comfortable with modern decor and furnishings. A continental or hearty cooked breakfast can be enjoyed in the dining room.

Rooms 5 en suite (2 fmly) **Facilities** FTV tea/coffee Cen ht Wi-fi **Notes** ⊗ No Children 3yrs

Amber Lodge

★★★ GUEST HOUSE

34 Victoria Av BH19 1AP
☎ 01929 426446
e-mail: stay@amberlodge-swanage.co.uk

Situated just five minutes walk from the sea front, the atmosphere here is friendly. Bedrooms are quiet, comfortable and equipped with considerate extras. There is a small guest lounge and breakfast is enjoyed in the spacious rear dining room at individual tables. On-site parking is available. Half board rates are available.

Rooms 7 en suite 1 annexe en suite (3 fmly) (3 GF) S £30-£37; D £60-£74 **Facilities** FTV TVL tea/coffee Dinner available Cen ht Wi-fi **Parking** 9 **Notes** ⊗

Railway Cottage

★★★ BED AND BREAKFAST

----

26 Victoria Av BH19 1AP
☎ 01929 425542
e-mail: foxysh@btinternet.com

Ideally located and only a short stroll from both the town centre and the seafront, this is a relaxed and welcoming family-run establishment with bedrooms of varying sizes. Breakfast is served in the pleasant dining room; parking is available either to the rear of the property or in the main car park opposite.

Rooms 6 en suite (1 fmly) (1 GF) S £35-£65; D £60-£80*
Facilities FTV tea/coffee Cen ht Wi-fi **Parking** 4 **Notes** LB ⊛

SYDLING ST NICHOLAS   Map 4 SY69

The Greyhound Inn

★★★★ ⊛ INN

----

26 High St DT2 9PD
☎ 01300 341303
e-mail: info@dorsetgreyhound.co.uk
dir: Off A37 into village centre

Located in the peaceful and quintessential English village of Sydling St Nicholas, this comfortable inn is certainly the place to escape to for relaxation. Bedrooms and bathrooms, in an adjacent building, are decorated and furnished to high standards. A choice of tempting dishes is available at both lunch and dinner, including choices based on the daily fish deliveries. Pleasant outdoor seating is available.

Rooms 6 en suite **Facilities** Dinner available

TARRANT MONKTON   Map 4 ST90

The Langton Arms

★★★★ INN

DT11 8RX
☎ 01258 830225 ▤ 01258 830053
e-mail: info@thelangtonarms.co.uk
dir: Exit A354 in Tarrant Hinton to Tarrant Monkton, through ford, Langton Arms opposite

Tucked away in this sleepy Dorset village, The Langton Arms offers stylish, light and airy accommodation and is a good base for touring this attractive area. Bedrooms, all on the ground-floor level in the modern annexe, are very well equipped and comfortable. There is a choice of dining options - the relaxed bar-restaurant or the more formal Stables Restaurant, offering innovative and appetising dishes. Breakfast is served in the conservatory dining room just a few steps through the pretty courtyard.

Rooms 6 annexe en suite (6 fmly) (6 GF) S £70; D £90*
Facilities FTV tea/coffee Dinner available Direct Dial Cen ht Wi-fi **Conf** Max 70 Thtr 70 Class 70 Board 70 **Parking** 100 **Notes** Civ Wed 60

WAREHAM   Map 4 SY98

PREMIER COLLECTION

Kemps Country House

★★★★★ ⊛ GUEST ACCOMMODATION

East Stoke BH20 6AL
☎ 0845 8620315 ▤ 0845 8620316
e-mail: info@kempscountryhouse.co.uk
web: www.kempshotel.com
dir: Follow A352 W from Wareham, 3m on right in village of East Stoke

Located within easy reach of the Dorset coastline, this former rectory provides a calming, friendly atmosphere and is a perfect base for touring the area. The refurbished bedrooms are spacious and well appointed, and benefit from plenty of modern extras; super king-size beds, flat screen TV and power showers. Breakfast and dinner are served in the elegant dining room and offer an imaginative choice of modern British cuisine.

Rooms 4 en suite 12 annexe en suite (2 fmly) (6 GF)
Facilities FTV tea/coffee Dinner available Direct Dial Cen ht Licensed Wi-fi **Parking** 24 **Notes** ⊗

Hyde Cottage Bed & Breakfast

★★★★ BED AND BREAKFAST

Furzebrook Rd, Stoborough BH20 5AX
☎ 01929 553344
e-mail: hydecottagebb@gmail.com
dir: 2m S of Wareham. Exit at A351 rdbt for Furzebrook/ Blue Pool, premises on right

Easy to find, on the Corfe Castle side of Wareham, this friendly bed and breakfast has a great location. Bedrooms are all large with lounge seating and some are suitable for families. All are well equipped with extras such as fridges. Meals are served en famille in the dining area downstairs.

Rooms 3 en suite (2 fmly) (1 GF) S £35-£45; D £60-£70*
Facilities FTV tea/coffee Dinner available Cen ht Wi-fi ▩ **Parking** 4 **Notes** LB ⊗ Closed 24-27 Dec ⊛

Luckford Wood House (SY872864)

★★★★ FARMHOUSE

East Stoke BH20 6AW
☎ 01929 463098 & 07888 719002   Mr & Mrs Barnes
e-mail: luckfordleisure@hotmail.co.uk
web: www.luckfordleisure.co.uk
dir: 3m W of Wareham. A352 onto B3070 to Lulworth, right into Holme Ln, signed East Stoke. 1m right into Church Ln, property 2nd on left

Rurally situated about three miles west of Wareham, this family home offers comfortable accommodation. Situated on the edge of woodland, there is abundant wildlife to see. Guests can be assured of a friendly welcome and an extensive choice at breakfast.

Rooms 6 rms (5 en suite) (1 pri facs) (3 fmly) (1 GF)
Facilities FTV DVD TVL tea/coffee Cen ht Wi-fi ⅃ 27 ▩ **Parking** 6 **Notes** LB

The Old Granary (SY886858)

★★★★ FARMHOUSE

West Holme Farm BH20 6AQ
☎ 01929 552972 Mrs V Goldsack
e-mail: theoldgranarybandb@googlemail.com
web: www.theoldgranarybandb.co.uk
dir: A352 from Wareham onto B3070, turn into Holme for Gardens, house on right

A friendly farmhouse with an experienced host, this is a former granary to the working farm, architect-designed with high ceilings and lots of light. Rooms are comfortable and well maintained and the hearty breakfast is a great start to the day.

Rooms 2 en suite (1 GF) **Facilities** STV FTV tea/coffee Cen ht Wi-fi **Parking** 2 **Notes** ⊗ No Children 16yrs Closed 19 Dec-3 Jan 50 acres horticultural

The Red Lion

★★★★ ▤ INN

----

1 North St BH20 4AB
☎ 01929 550099
e-mail: redlionbookings@btconnect.com

Located in the heart of Wareham town centre (Gateway to the Purbecks and Jurassic coast), this former coaching inn has been tastefully restored to its former glory with modern amenities and comfort in mind. Bedrooms are well appointed and benefit from deeply comfortable beds and newly decorated en suite bathrooms. The popular brasserie style restaurant and bar uses local ingredients where possible and is the ideal place to meet for a drink. Limited car parking is available and can be discussed at time of booking.

Rooms 8 en suite (4 fmly) (2 GF) S £70-£90; D £90-£110* **Facilities** FTV tea/coffee Dinner available Cen ht Wi-fi ▩ **Parking** 8

Worgret Manor

★★★★ GUEST ACCOMMODATION

Worgret Rd BH20 6AB
☎ 01929 552957 ▤ 01929 554804
e-mail: admin@worgretmanorhotel.co.uk
dir: 0.5m from town centre towards Dorchester on A352

On the edge of Wareham, with easy access to major routes, this privately owned Georgian manor house has a friendly, cheerful atmosphere. The bedrooms come in a variety of sizes. Public rooms are well presented and comprise a popular bar and a quiet lounge.

Rooms 13 en suite (1 fmly) (4 GF) S £65; D £95*
Facilities FTV TVL tea/coffee Direct Dial Cen ht Licensed Wi-fi ⅃ 18 ▩ **Conf** Max 65 Thtr 65 Class 65 Board 65 **Parking** 25 **Notes** ⊗ Closed 23 Dec-3 Jan

WAREHAM *continued*

The Bankes Arms

★★★ INN

23 East St, Corfe Castle BH20 5ED
☎ 01929 480206
e-mail: bankescorfe@aol.com
dir: *A35 left onto A351*

An ideal base for exploring the Jurassic Coast, this former coaching inn provides newly refurbished accommodation in a historic setting. It's just moments away from Corfe Castle, and a steam railway passes at the end of the garden. Rooms are tastefully appointed and offer good amenities. A hearty breakfast is served in the popular restaurant, while the dinner menu offers daily-changing specials with a Mediterranean twist. Car parking is available at the rear of the property.

Rooms 10 rms (5 en suite) (5 pri facs) (2 fmly) S fr £35; D £60–£98 **Facilities** FTV TVL tea/coffee Dinner available Direct Dial Cen ht Wi-fi ♨ 18 ♠ **Extras** Mineral water **Conf** Max 20 Board 20 **Parking** 12 **Notes** LB

WEYMOUTH
Map 4 SY67

See also Portland

The Esplanade

★★★★ GUEST ACCOMMODATION

141 The Esplanade DT4 7NJ
☎ 01305 783129 & 07515 657116 📠 01305 783129
e-mail: stay@theesplanadehotel.co.uk
web: www.theesplanadehotel.co.uk
dir: *On seafront, between Jubilee Clock & pier bandstand*

Dating from 1835, this attractive property is located on the seafront and offers wonderful views from the elegant dining room and stylish first-floor lounge. There's a genuine enthusiasm here, with a warm welcome assured. The comfortable bedrooms are thoughtfully equipped including Egyptian cotton sheets and towels, and many rooms have sea views. Breakfast is a showcase of local produce with an extensive menu.

Rooms 11 en suite (3 fmly) (2 GF) **Facilities** FTV TVL tea/coffee Cen ht Licensed Wi-fi **Parking** 9 **Notes** ⊗ Closed Nov-Feb

Kingswood

★★★★ GUEST ACCOMMODATION

55 Rodwell Rd DT4 8QY
☎ 01305 784926
e-mail: robbie.f@btinternet.com
dir: *On A354 up hill towards Portland from inner harbour, on left after lights*

Handily located for both Weymouth and Portland, this welcoming establishment provides spacious guest accommodation, including larger suites with jacuzzi baths. The building has a long and interesting history and was even commandeered during World War II for American officers. The bedrooms are well appointed and

comfortable, as are the public areas with breakfast being served in the attractive dining room. Just a stroll away is Brewers Quay, a lovely area in which to while away an hour or two.

Rooms 10 rms (9 en suite) (1 pri facs) (2 GF) D £64–£120 **Facilities** FTV tea/coffee Cen ht Wi-fi **Parking** 20 **Notes** LB ⊗

St John's Guest House

★★★★ GUEST ACCOMMODATION

7 Dorchester Rd DT4 7JR
☎ 01305 775523
e-mail: stjohnsguesthouse@googlemail.com
dir: *Opposite St John's Church*

Located just 70 yards from the beach, this elegant Victorian property was built around 1880. Hospitality here is warm and genuine, the property has an appealing, uncluttered style, and standards are high throughout. Bedrooms are all well equipped with such extras as DVD players, Wi-fi access and comfy beds. Breakfast is served in the light and airy dining room with a lounge area also available for guests.

Rooms 7 en suite (2 fmly) (2 GF) S £32–£60; D £64–£80* **Facilities** FTV DVD tea/coffee Cen ht Wi-fi **Parking** 10 **Notes** LB ⊗ No Children 4yrs

Wenlock House

★★★★ GUEST ACCOMMODATION

107 The Esplanade DT4 7EE
☎ 01305 786674 & 0800 781 3949
e-mail: stay@wenlockweymouth.co.uk
dir: *On A353 (The Esplanade) King St junct*

Wenlock House offers a good standard of accommodation and a friendly atmosphere. The attractive bedrooms are well equipped and many have excellent views. The hosts are very attentive and always happy to help, and the house is situated on the seafront, just a short walk from the station and town centre.

Rooms 10 rms (8 en suite) (3 fmly) **Facilities** FTV tea/coffee Cen ht Wi-fi **Parking** 10 **Notes** ⊗ No Children 5yrs Closed 30 Nov-Dec

Kimberley Guest House

★★★ GUEST HOUSE

16 Kirtleton Av DT4 7PT
☎ 01305 783333 📠 01305 839603
e-mail: kenneth.jones@btconnect.com
dir: *Exit A384 (Weymouth road) into Carlton Rd North, opposite Rembrandt Hotel, Kirtleton Av on left*

This friendly guest house is in a quiet residential area near the seafront. Bedrooms are well presented, and a hearty breakfast is served.

Rooms 11 rms (10 en suite) (1 pri facs) (1 fmly) (1 GF) S £25–£27; D £52–£56* **Facilities** FTV tea/coffee Cen ht **Parking** 8 **Notes** LB ⊗ Closed 1-29 Dec ⊞

Beaufort Guesthouse

★★★ GUEST HOUSE

24 The Esplanade DT4 8DN
☎ 01305 782088

Just a few steps from the sandy beach, this friendly, family-run establishment is ideally located for a seaside break. Bedrooms are soundly appointed with all the necessary essentials, likewise the modern showers. Some of the rooms have the added bonus of sea views. Breakfast is served in the lounge diner, which also has a bar to refresh and revive after a hard day enjoying the many and varied local attractions.

Rooms 6 rms (5 en suite) (1 pri facs) S £30–£35; D £60–£70 **Notes** Closed Dec-1 Jan

The Bedford Guest House

★★★ BED AND BREAKFAST

17 The Esplanade DT4 8DT
☎ 01305 786995
e-mail: info@thebedfordweymouth.co.uk
dir: *Along The Esplanade W towards harbour, turn right around amusement gardens (one-way), Bedford House on left*

Ideally located right on the sea front and with the added bonus of voucher parking for guests, this welcoming accommodation offers bedrooms in a range of shapes and sizes, with some enjoying sea views. Breakfast is taken in the comfortably furnished downstairs dining area.

Rooms 8 en suite (2 fmly) S £32–£45; D £64–£90* **Facilities** FTV TVL tea/coffee Cen ht Wi-fi **Notes** ⊗ No Children 5yrs Closed Dec-Jan

The Cavendale

★★★ BED AND BREAKFAST

10 The Esplanade DT4 8EB
☎ 01305 786960
e-mail: thecavendale@gmail.com

Conveniently located right on the seafront with splendid views from some of the bedrooms, this cosy bed and breakfast offers a range of bedroom sizes, some with private bathrooms. Guests are welcome to use the lounge, where in addition to a large range of videos, they can join in with the current on-the-go jigsaw. Helpfully, parking permits for nearby car parks are available.

Rooms 9 rms (6 en suite) (3 pri facs) (5 fmly) S £27–£32; D £60–£80* **Facilities** FTV TVL tea/coffee Wi-fi **Notes** LB ⊗ Closed 24 Dec-2 Jan

Save on B&Bs and Hotels. Book at **theAA.com/hotel**

DORSET 145 ENGLAND

The Edenhurst

★★★ GUEST HOUSE

122 The Esplanade DT4 7ER
☎ 01305 771255
e-mail: enquiries@edenhurstweymouth.com

Just a step across the road from the beach and within walking distance of the railway and bus stations, this smartly presented establishment is a perfect base from which to explore the local area. A number of bedroom types are offered, some having wonderful sea views and balconies, and all have modern bathrooms. Breakfast is served in the elegant, sea facing, dining room with a guest lounge also provided.

Rooms 12 rms (11 en suite) (1 pri facs) (4 fmly)
S £34-£40; D £68-£88* **Facilities** FTV TVL tea/coffee
Cen ht Wi-fi **Extras** Bottled water - complimentary
Notes LB ⊗

Molyneux Guest House

★★★ GUEST HOUSE

9 Waterloo Place, The Esplanade DT4 7PD
☎ 01305 774623 & 07947 883235
e-mail: stay@molyneuxguesthouse.co.uk
web: www.molyneuxguesthouse.co.uk
dir: *A354 to Weymouth seafront, onto The Esplanade, Molyneux on right*

Located close to the seafront and beautiful beaches of Weymouth, this guest house offers a genuine warm welcome. Bedrooms are brightly decorated and comfortable and there is also a lounge. Breakfast is enjoyed in the smart dining room. Off-road parking to the rear is a bonus.

Rooms 6 rms (5 en suite) (1 pri facs) (2 fmly) (1 GF)
S £30-£70; D £54-£95* **Facilities** FTV TVL tea/coffee
Cen ht Licensed Wi-fi **Parking** 6 **Notes** LB ⊗

Philbeach Guest House

★★★ GUEST ACCOMMODATION

11 Waterloo Place DT4 7PD
☎ 01305 785344
e-mail: stay@philbeachguesthouse.co.uk

Just across the road from the wonderful beach at Weymouth, this is an ideal property from which to explore the town and attractions. A warm welcome is always on offer together with helpful advice about the area. Bedrooms are thoughtfully equipped and include a family room and ground-floor options. Breakfast is served in the attractive dining room with a generous offering of hot and cold items to enjoy.

Rooms 5 en suite (1 fmly) (1 GF) **Facilities** FTV DVD tea/
coffee Wi-fi **Notes** ⊗

Tara Guest House

★★★ GUEST HOUSE

10 Market St DT4 8DD
☎ 01305 766235
dir: *From Alexandra Gardens on The Esplanade right onto Belle Vue, right & left onto Market St*

Neatly presented, this welcoming establishment is set just back from the seafront at the harbour end of town. Strictly non-smoking, the guest house provides a relaxed and friendly atmosphere. Bedrooms offer good levels of comfort.

Rooms 6 en suite (1 fmly) S £30-£32; D £60-£64
Facilities tea/coffee Dinner available Cen ht **Notes** LB ⊗
No Children 14yrs ⊛

The Trelawney

★★★ GUEST ACCOMMODATION

1 Old Castle Rd DT4 8QB
☎ 01305 783188 ☒ 01305 783181
e-mail: info@trelawneyhotel.com
dir: *From Harbourside follow Portland signs, Trelawney 700yds on left*

This charming Victorian house stands amid attractive gardens in a quiet residential area a short walk from the town centre and beach. The friendly proprietors provide a comfortable environment, and many guests return regularly. Generous English breakfasts are offered in the light and airy dining room, and a comfortable lounge is available.

Rooms 8 en suite (3 fmly) D £80-£90* **Facilities** FTV TVL
tea/coffee Cen ht Licensed Wi-fi **Parking** 12 **Notes** LB ⊗
No Children 5yrs Closed Nov-1 Apr

Wadham Guesthouse

★★★ GUEST HOUSE

22 East St DT4 8BN
☎ 01305 779640
e-mail: p.middleton22@aol.com
dir: *Off S end of A353 The Esplanade*

This pleasant, town centre property offers a range of rooms, and is a good base for touring or for a short stay. The comfortable bedrooms are attractively decorated, and home-cooked breakfasts are served in the ground-floor dining room. Parking permits are available.

Rooms 9 en suite (3 fmly) (1 GF) S £30-£35; D £60-£70*
Facilities FTV TVL tea/coffee Cen ht **Notes** LB ⊗ No
Children 4yrs Closed Xmas ⊛

Fieldbarn House

★★ GUEST ACCOMMODATION

44 Fieldbarn Dr, Southill DT4 0EE
☎ 01305 779140
dir: *1m NW of town centre. Exit A354 Weymouth Way rdbt into Fieldbarn Dr (Southill), 300yds on right*

Located on a residential estate on the outskirts of the town, yet only a short drive from sandy beaches and the town centre, this modern home is family run and provides guests with comfortable accommodation. A full English breakfast is served at a communal table overlooking the well-tended rear garden.

Rooms 3 rms (1 fmly) S £22-£26; D £44-£52*
Facilities FTV DVD tea/coffee Cen ht 🔥 **Parking** 4 **Notes** LB
⊗ No Children 3yrs Closed 15-31 Dec ⊛

Royal Oak

Ⓤ

52 Dorchester Rd DT4 7JZ
☎ 01305 785948

Currently the rating for this establishment is not confirmed. This may be due to a change of ownership or because it has only recently joined the AA rating scheme.

Rooms 7 en suite (3 fmly) (3 GF) **Facilities** FTV tea/coffee
Wi-fi **Parking** 4

WIMBORNE MINSTER Map 5 SZ09

PREMIER COLLECTION

Les Bouviers Restaurant with Rooms

★★★★★ ⊛⊛ 🏠 RESTAURANT WITH ROOMS

Arrowsmith Rd, Canford Magna BH21 3BD
☎ 01202 889555 ☒ 01202 639428
e-mail: info@lesbouviers.co.uk
web: www.lesbouviers.co.uk
dir: *A31 onto A349. Left in 0.6m. In approx 1m right into Arrowsmith Rd. Establishment approx 100yds on right*

An excellent restaurant with rooms in a great location, set in five and a half acres of grounds. Food is a highlight of any stay here as is the friendly, attentive service. Chef patron James Coward's team turn out impressive cooking, which has been recognised with 2 AA Rosettes. Bedrooms are extremely well equipped and beds are supremely comfortable. Cream tea can be taken on the terrace.

Rooms 6 en suite (4 fmly) S £88-£200; D £88-£235*
Facilities FTV tea/coffee Dinner available Direct Dial
Cen ht Wi-fi All bathrooms have steam showers or air baths **Conf** Max 120 Thtr 100 Class 100 Board 100
Parking 50 **Notes** LB RS Sun eve restricted opening &
restaurant closed Civ Wed 120

WIMBORNE MINSTER *continued*

Ashton Lodge

★★★★ GUEST ACCOMMODATION

10 Oakley Hill BH21 1QH
☎ 01202 883423
e-mail: ashtonlodge@tiscali.co.uk
web: www.ashton-lodge.co.uk
dir: *Exit A31 S of Wimborne onto A349 for Poole, left next rdbt signed Wimborne/Canford Magna, house 200yds on right*

A warm welcome is assured at this delightful modern home, which provides comfortable bedrooms, stylishly furnished with attractively co-ordinated decor and fabrics. All rooms are well equipped, with many extra facilities provided. Hearty breakfasts are served in the spacious dining room, which overlooks the well-maintained garden.

Rooms 5 rms (2 en suite) (1 pri facs) (2 fmly) S £39; D £72-£76* **Facilities** FTV DVD TVL tea/coffee Cen ht Wi-fi **Parking** 4 **Notes** LB ⊗ ⊜

The Kings Head

★★★ INN

The Square BH21 1JG
☎ 01202 880101 ≣ 01202 881667
e-mail: 6474@greeneking.co.uk
dir: *From A31 Dorchester take B3073 into Wimborne. Follow signs to town centre, in square on left*

Situated in the town square this establishment offers accommodation that includes one room with a four poster and also a family room. The restaurant specialises in seafood and there is also Laing's Bar that serves bar food and real ales. There are facilities for small meetings and wedding receptions.

Rooms 27 en suite (1 fmly) **Facilities** tea/coffee Direct Dial Lift

CO DURHAM

AYCLIFFE Map 19 NZ22

The County Restaurant with Rooms

★★★★ ⊜ RESTAURANT WITH ROOMS

12 The Green DL5 6LX
☎ 01325 312273 ≣ 01325 317131
e-mail: info@thecountyaycliffevillage.com
dir: *A1(M) junct 59, A167 towards Newton Aycliffe. In Aycliffe turn onto village green*

Located overlooking the pretty village green yet convenient for the A1, the focus here is on fresh, home-cooked meals, real ales and friendly service. There is a relaxed atmosphere in the bar area, and the restaurant where attractive artwork is displayed. The bedrooms in the smart townhouse next door are all furnished to a high standard.

Rooms 7 en suite (3 GF) S £49; D £70-£110* **Facilities** FTV TVL tea/coffee Dinner available Cen ht Wi-fi **Parking** 25 **Notes** LB ⊗ Closed 25 Dec & 1 Jan No coaches

BARNARD CASTLE Map 19 NZ01

Homelands Guest House

★★★★ ⊜ GUEST HOUSE

85 Galgate DL12 8ES
☎ 01833 638757
e-mail: carol@homelandsguesthouse.co.uk
dir: *From A1(M) onto A67 to Barnard Castle. Guest house on left on A67(Galgate)*

This beautiful Victorian town house is conveniently located for the Yorkshire Dales and is only 20 minutes from the A1(M). The friendly proprietors provide a warm welcome; there is a comfortable lounge and delicious home-cooked suppers are available by prior arrangement. The attractively presented bedrooms are thoughtfully equipped and include a garden room.

Rooms 4 rms (3 en suite) (1 pri facs) 1 annexe en suite (1 GF) S £45; D £75* **Facilities** STV FTV Lounge tea/coffee Dinner available Cen ht Licensed Wi-fi ⌖

COWSHILL Map 18 NY84

Low Cornriggs Farm *(NY845413)*

★★★★ ⌂ ⊜ FARMHOUSE

Cowshill-in-Weardale DL13 1AQ
☎ 01388 537600 & 07760 766794 Mrs J Elliott
e-mail: cornriggsfarm@btconnect.com
web: www.cornriggsfarm.co.uk
dir: *0.6m NW of Cowshill on A689*

Situated in the heart of Weardale yet also close to Cumbria, this delightful farmhouse has stunning views. Original stone and stripped pine are combined to provide a house with real character. Excellent home-cooked dinners are offered along with charming hospitality. Bedrooms are attractive and thoughtfully equipped with many homely extras.

Rooms 3 en suite 4 annexe en suite (1 fmly) (3 GF) S £44-£45; D £60-£66* **Facilities** STV FTV TVL tea/coffee Dinner available Cen ht Wi-fi ⌖ 9 ⌂ **Parking** 6 **Notes** LB ⊗ 42 acres beef

DARLINGTON Map 19 NZ21

Raby Hunt Inn and Restaurant with Rooms

★★★★ RESTAURANT WITH ROOMS

Summerhouse DL2 3UD
☎ 01325 374237
e-mail: enquiries@rabyhuntrestaurant.co.uk
web: www.rabyhuntrestaurant.co.uk
dir: *A1(M) junct 58 onto A68 N, B6275 & B6279*

This Grade II listed building, situated in the quiet village of Summerhouse, is a family-owned restaurant with rooms providing well-equipped, stylish and comfortable accommodation. Both bedrooms are en suite and have many thoughtful extras. The comfortable and contemporary restaurant serves modern British and European dishes prepared with flair and creativity.

Rooms 2 en suite S £70–£120; D £120 **Facilities** STV FTV tea/coffee Dinner available Cen ht Wi-fi **Parking** 8 **Notes** ⊗ No Children 13yrs No coaches

DURHAM
Map 19 NZ24

The Old Mill

★★★★ ⇔ INN

Thinford Rd, Metal Bridge DH6 5NX
☎ 01740 652928 📠 01740 657230
e-mail: office@oldmilldurham.co.uk
web: www.oldmilldurham.co.uk
dir: 5m S of Durham. A1(M) junct 61, A688 S for 1.5m, left at rdbt, sharp right

This traditional, family-owned inn is in a countryside setting yet is only a mile from the A1. There is a friendly atmosphere and the bar and dining areas are full of character. Food is served throughout the day and evening, with the vast menu displayed on chalkboards. Bedrooms are spacious and well equipped. Complimentary Wi-fi is provided.

Rooms 8 en suite S £60* **Facilities** STV FTV DVD tea/coffee Dinner available Direct Dial Cen ht Wi-fi 🛁 Jacuzzi/Spa **Conf** Max 40 Thtr 40 Class 40 Board 25 **Parking** 40 **Notes** ⊗ Closed 2 Jan RS 25 Dec

SEAHAM
Map 19 NZ44

The Seaton Lane Inn

★★★★ INN

Seaton Ln, Seaton Village SR7 0LP
☎ 0191 581 2036
e-mail: info@seatonlaneinn.com
dir: A19 S of Sunderland on B1404 between Seaham & Houghton

Set on the edge of the quiet village of Seaton, yet close to Seaham and the A19, the inn is popular with visitors and locals alike and is a blend of the modern and traditional. The emphasis is on food here with interesting home-made dishes offered in the restaurant and bar areas. The bedrooms, located in the adjoining building, are modern, spacious and smartly furnished.

Rooms 18 en suite (1 GF) **Facilities** FTV TVL tea/coffee Dinner available Direct Dial Cen ht Wi-fi ⚓ 18 Fishing **Parking** 36 **Notes** ⊗

STOCKTON-ON-TEES
Map 19 NZ41

The Parkwood Inn

★★★ INN

64-66 Darlington Rd, Hartburn TS18 5ER
☎ 01642 587933
e-mail: theparkwoodhotel@aol.com
web: www.theparkwoodhotel.com
dir: 1.5m SW of town centre. A66 onto A137 signed Yarm & Stockton West, left at lights onto A1027, left into Darlington Rd

Expect a very friendly welcome at this family-run establishment. The well-equipped en suite bedrooms come with many homely extras, and a range of professionally prepared meals are served in the cosy bar lounge, conservatory, or the attractive dining room.

Rooms 6 en suite **Facilities** tea/coffee Dinner available Cen ht **Parking** 36 **Notes** No coaches

ESSEX

CHELMSFORD
Map 6 TL70

The Lion Inn

★★★★ ⇔ INN

Main Rd, Boreham CM3 3JA
☎ 01245 394900 📠 01245 394999
e-mail: info@lioninnhotel.co.uk

The Lion Inn offers stylish and comfortably appointed accommodation, well equipped with flat screen TVs, free Wi-fi, all fully air-conditioned and appealing to leisure and business guests alike. Many rooms benefit from balconies or direct access to the private garden. The spacious bar and restaurant have been completely revamped in an open-plan style with additional space in the Victorian conservatory. Guests can enjoy a wide selection of good classic pub dishes with a continental flair. A cooked and continental breakfast is served daily.

The Lion Inn

Rooms 15 en suite **Facilities** tea/coffee Dinner available Wi-fi **Notes** Closed 24-26 Dec

CHIPPING ONGAR
Map 6 TL50

PREMIER COLLECTION

Diggins Farm *(TL582082)*

★★★★★ FARMHOUSE

Fyfield CM5 0PP
☎ 01277 899303 Mrs M Frost
dir: B184 N from Fyfield, right after Black Bull pub, farm 0.75m on left

This delightful Grade II listed 16th-century farmhouse is set amid open farmland in the Roding Valley, and is only a short drive from Stansted Airport. The spacious bedrooms are attractively decorated, carefully furnished and well equipped.

Rooms 2 rms (1 en suite) (1 pri facs) S fr £40; D fr £80 **Facilities** tea/coffee Cen ht 🛁 **Parking** 20 **Notes** ⊗ No Children 12yrs Closed 15 Dec-3 Jan ⊛ 440 acres arable

CLACTON-ON-SEA
Map 7 TM11

The Chudleigh

★★★★ GUEST ACCOMMODATION

13 Agate Rd, Marine Parade West CO15 1RA
☎ 01255 425407 📠 01255 470280
e-mail: chudleighhotel@btconnect.com
dir: With sea on left, cross lights at pier, turn into Agate Rd

Conveniently situated for the seafront and shops, this immaculate property has been run by the friendly owners Peter and Carol Oleggini for more than 30 years. Bedrooms are most attractive with co-ordinating decor and well chosen fabrics. Breakfast is served in the smart dining room and there is a cosy lounge with plush sofas.

Rooms 10 en suite (2 fmly) (2 GF) S £50-£55; D £70-£85* **Facilities** FTV TVL tea/coffee Direct Dial Cen ht Licensed Wi-fi 🛁 **Extras** Speciality toiletries **Parking** 7 **Notes** No Children 1yr Closed Oct RS 1wk Mar/Apr

COLCHESTER   Map 13 TL92

Fridaywood Farm *(TL985213)*

★★★★ FARMHOUSE

Bounstead Rd CO2 0DF
☎ 01206 573595 📠 01206 547011 **Mrs J Lochore**
e-mail: lochorem8@aol.com
dir: *3m S of Colchester, from A12 follow signs for zoo to Mersea, cross B1026. At Maypole pub, right for Bounstead Rd*

Fridaywood Farm is a traditional farmhouse surrounded by wooded countryside. Bedrooms are generally quite spacious, and each one is carefully decorated, furnished with well-chosen pieces, and equipped with many thoughtful touches. Public rooms include an elegant dining room where breakfast is served at a large communal table, and a cosy sitting room.

Rooms 2 en suite S £55-£65; D £70-£80* **Facilities** FTV DVD Lounge tea/coffee Cen ht Wi-fi 🌐 🔓 **Extras** Bottled water **Parking** 6 **Notes** ⊗ No Children 12yrs ⊕ 500 acres sheep/arable

The Old Manse

★★★★ BED AND BREAKFAST

15 Roman Rd CO1 1UR
☎ 01206 545154 & 07773 948082 📠 01206 545153
e-mail: wendyanderson15@hotmail.com
web: www.theoldmanse.uk.com
dir: *In town centre, 250yds E of castle. Exit High St/East Hill into Roman Rd*

Expect a warm welcome from the caring host at this Victorian house, situated just a short walk from the castle and High Street. Bedrooms are carefully decorated with co-ordinated soft furnishings and equipped with many thoughtful touches. Breakfast is served seated at a large communal table in the attractive dining room and there is a comfortable lounge.

Rooms 3 rms (2 en suite) (1 pri facs) S £50-£65; D £70-£78* **Facilities** tea/coffee Cen ht Wi-fi **Parking** 1 **Notes** ⊗ No Children 8yrs Closed 23-31 Dec ⊕

Black Bond Hall Bed and Breakfast

★★★★ BED AND BREAKFAST

Lodge Ln, Langenhoe CO5 7LX
☎ 01206 735776
e-mail: gill@blackbondhall.co.uk
dir: *A12 junct 26 signed to Mersea (B1025). Through Abberton, in Langenhoe pass Langenhoe Lion public house, 1st left signed Fingringhoe Range. 1st right onto Lodge Ln, on right*

This charming country house is packed with original features and surrounded on all sides by beautifully landscaped gardens. Situated approximately five miles from Colchester (Britain's oldest recorded town), and close to Mersea Island, famous for its sailing and seafood restaurants. Guests have use of the tennis court and the area is popular with walkers and cyclists. Bedrooms are very comfortable and freshly cooked breakfasts are not to be missed.

Rooms 2 en suite **Facilities** FTV tea/coffee Cen ht Wi-fi 🌐 **Extras** Snacks **Parking** 8 **Notes** LB ⊗ No Children 12yrs ⊕

DEDHAM   Map 13 TM03

The Sun Inn

★★★★★ ⊚ 🍴 INN

High St CO7 6DF
☎ 01206 323351
e-mail: office@thesuninndedham.com
dir: *In village centre opposite church*

A charming 15th-century coaching inn situated in the centre of Dedham opposite the church. The carefully decorated bedrooms include four-poster and half tester beds, along with many thoughtful touches. The open-plan public rooms have a wealth of character with inglenook fires, oak beams and fine oak panelling.

Rooms 7 en suite S £65-£120; D £85-£160* **Facilities** DVD iPod docking station tea/coffee Dinner available Cen ht 🔓 **Parking** 15 **Notes** LB Closed 25-28 Dec

Marlborough Head Inn

★★★ INN

Mill Ln CO7 6DH
☎ 01206 323250
e-mail: jen.pearmain@tiscali.co.uk

A period building with many original features, the Marlborough Head is ideally located to explore "Constable Country". The three en suite bedrooms are traditionally appointed and offer modern amenities. There are two bars, two restaurants and a comfortable lounge. In addition parking is provided as well as a well maintained garden.

Rooms 3 en suite S £55-£90; D £55-£100 (room only)* **Facilities** FTV Lounge tea/coffee Dinner available Cen ht Wi-fi Pool table **Parking** 20 **Notes** ⊗ No Children 16yrs Closed 24-28 Dec

FRINTON-ON-SEA   Map 7 TM22

Uplands Guest House

★★★ GUEST ACCOMMODATION

41 Hadleigh Rd CO13 9HQ
☎ 01255 674889 & 07921 640772 📠 01255 674889
e-mail: info@uplandsguesthouse.co.uk
web: www.uplandsguesthouse.com
dir: *B1033 into Frinton, over level crossing, Hadleigh Rd 3rd left, Uplands 250yds on left*

This large Edwardian house stands in a peaceful side road just a short walk from the shops and seafront. Bedrooms are pleasantly decorated and thoughtfully equipped with a good range of useful extras. Public rooms include a large lounge-dining room where breakfast is served at individual tables.

Rooms 5 rms (4 en suite) (1 fmly) S £34-£45; D £62-£67* **Facilities** FTV TVL tea/coffee Dinner available Cen ht Wi-fi 🔓 **Parking** 4 **Notes** LB ⊗

Save on B&Bs and Hotels. Book at **theAA.com/hotel**

ESSEX 149 **ENGLAND**

GREAT DUNMOW — Map 6 TL62

Homelye Farm

★★★★ GUEST ACCOMMODATION

Homelye Chase, Braintree Rd CM6 3AW
☎ 01371 872127 & 07572 466981 📠 01371 876428
e-mail: info@homelye.co.uk
web: www.homelye.co.uk
dir: *1.5m E of Great Dunmow. Exit B1256 at water tower*

Expect a warm welcome at this working farm situated in a peaceful rural location just a short drive from the town centre. The spacious bedrooms are in converted outbuildings; each one features exposed beams, co-ordinated fabrics and attractive pine furnishings. Breakfast is taken at individual tables in the original farmhouse.

Rooms 13 annexe en suite (1 fmly) (13 GF) S £49-£65; D £59-£100 **Facilities** FTV TVL tea/coffee Cen ht Licensed Wi-fi 🔒 **Parking** 16 **Notes** ✖ Closed 24-27 Dec

GREAT TOTHAM — Map 7 TL81

The Bull at Great Totham

★ ★ ★ ★ 🏵🏵 RESTAURANT WITH ROOMS

2 Maldon Rd CM9 8NH
☎ 01621 893385 & 894020 📠 01621 894029
e-mail: reservations@thebullatgreattotham.co.uk
dir: *Exit A12 at Witham junct to Great Totham*

A 16th-century coaching inn located in the village of Great Totham, The Bull is now a very stylish restaurant with rooms that offers en suite bedrooms with satellite TVs with Freeview; Wi-fi is available throughout. Guests can enjoy dinner in the gastro-pub or in the award-winning, fine dining restaurant, The Willow Room.

Rooms 4 en suite (2 GF) S £75; D £85* **Facilities** STV FTV tea/coffee Dinner available Cen ht Wi-fi ⚲ 18 **Conf** Max 60 Thtr 40 Class 40 Board 16 **Parking** 80 **Notes** LB

GREAT YELDHAM — Map 13 TL73

The White Hart

★ ★ ★ ★ 🏵🏵 RESTAURANT WITH ROOMS

Poole St CO9 4HJ
☎ 01787 237250 📠 01787 238044
e-mail: mjwmason@yahoo.co.uk
dir: *On A1017 in village*

A large timber-framed character building houses the main restaurant and bar areas whilst the bedrooms are located in the converted coach house; all are smartly appointed and well equipped with many thoughtful extras. A comfortable lounge-bar area and beautifully landscaped gardens provide areas for relaxation. Locally sourced produce is used in the main house restaurant, popular with local residents and guests alike.

Rooms 11 en suite (2 fmly) (6 GF) **Facilities** FTV TVL tea/coffee Dinner available Direct Dial Cen ht Wi-fi **Conf** Max 200 Thtr 200 Class 200 Board 50 **Parking** 80 **Notes** Civ Wed 130

HALSTEAD — Map 13 TL83

The Bull

★★★ INN

Bridge St CO9 1HU
☎ 01787 472144 📠 01787 472496
e-mail: bull.halstead@oldenglishinns.co.uk
dir: *Off A131 at bottom of hill on High St*

A charming inn situated in the heart of this bustling town that is between Sudbury and Braintree. Public areas include a large lounge bar, cosy restaurant and meeting rooms. Bedrooms are full of original character; each one is pleasantly decorated and equipped with modern facilities.

Rooms 10 en suite 6 annexe en suite **Facilities** tea/coffee Direct Dial **Parking** 25 **Notes** Civ Wed 50

HATFIELD HEATH — Map 6 TL51

Lancasters Farm *(TL544149)*

★ ★ ★ ★ FARMHOUSE

Chelmsford Rd CM22 7BB
☎ 01279 730220 📠 01279 730220 **Mrs M Hunt**
dir: *A1060 from Hatfield Heath for Chelmsford, 1m left on sharp right bend, through white gates*

Guests are made to feel at home at this delightfully spacious house, which is the heart of this large working arable farm close to Stansted Airport. Bedrooms vary in size and style but all are smartly decorated and thoughtfully equipped. Garaging can be arranged, as can transport to and from the airport.

Rooms 4 rms (2 en suite) (2 pri facs) S fr £40; D fr £80* **Facilities** FTV Lounge tea/coffee Cen ht Wi-fi **Parking** 6 **Notes** ✖ No Children 12yrs Closed 14 Dec-4 Jan ☕ 260 acres arable

MANNINGTREE — Map 13 TM13

PREMIER COLLECTION

Dairy House Farm *(TM148293)*

★ ★ ★ ★ ★ FARMHOUSE

Bradfield Rd CO11 2SR
☎ 01255 870322 **Mrs B Whitworth**
e-mail: bridgetwhitworth@btinternet.com
web: www.dairyhousefarm.info

(For full entry see Wix)

SOUTHEND-ON-SEA — Map 7 TQ88

The Ilfracombe House

★★★★ GUEST ACCOMMODATION

9-13 Wilson Rd SS1 1HG
☎ 01702 351000 📠 01702 393989
e-mail: info@ilfracombe-hotel.co.uk
web: www.ilfracombe-hotel.co.uk
dir: *500yds W of town centre. Exit A13 at Cricketers pub into Milton Rd, 3rd left into Cambridge Rd, 4th right, car park in Alexandra Rd*

Ilfracombe House lies in Southend's conservation area, just a short walk from the cliffs, gardens and the beach. The public rooms include a dining room, lounge and a cosy bar, and the well-equipped bedrooms include deluxe options and two four-poster rooms.

Rooms 20 en suite (4 fmly) (2 GF) S £54-£59; D £69-£79 **Facilities** STV FTV DVD TVL tea/coffee Dinner available Direct Dial Cen ht Licensed Wi-fi **Extras** Mini-fridge **Conf** Max 15 **Parking** 9 **Notes** LB ✖

Terrace Guest House

★★★ GUEST ACCOMMODATION

8 Royal Ter SS1 1DY
☎ 01702 348143 📠 01702 348143
e-mail: info@terraceguesthouse.co.uk
dir: *From pier up Pier Hill into Royal Terrace*

Set on a terrace above the Western Esplanade, this comfortable guest house has an informal atmosphere. There is an elegant sitting room and breakfast room. The spacious, well-planned bedrooms include four en suite front and rear-facing rooms, and several front-facing rooms that share two bathrooms.

Rooms 9 rms (6 en suite) (2 fmly) **Facilities** FTV TVL tea/coffee Cen ht Wi-fi **Notes** LB Closed 21 Dec-4 Jan

STANSTED AIRPORT   Map 6 TL52

See also Bishop's Stortford (Hertfordshire)

The White House

★★★★ GUEST ACCOMMODATION

Smiths Green CM22 6NR
☎ 01279 870257 📠 01279 870423
e-mail: enquiries@whitehousestansted.co.uk
web: www.whitehousestansted.co.uk
dir: M11 junct 8, B1256 towards Takeley. Through lights
at Four Ashes x-rds. 400yds, corner of B1256 & Smiths
Green

The White House is a delightful 16th-century property
situated close to Stansted Airport (but not on the flight
path). The stylish bedrooms feature superb beds,
luxurious bathrooms and many thoughtful touches.
Traditional breakfasts are served in the farmhouse-style
kitchen, using local ingredients. Evening meals are
available at the Lion and Lamb, a nearby pub/restaurant
owned by the proprietors, who can usually provide
transport.

Rooms 3 rms (2 en suite) (1 pri facs) (3 fmly) S £65-£75;
D £75-£85 **Facilities** FTV DVD tea/coffee Dinner available
Cen ht Wi-fi **Conf** Max 25 **Parking** 6 **Notes** ⊗ Closed
24-25, 31 Dec & 1 Jan

THAXTED   Map 12 TL63

The Farmhouse Inn

★★★ INN

Monk St CM6 2NR
☎ 01371 830864 📠 01371 831196
e-mail: info@farmhouseinn.org
dir: M11 to A120 to B184, 1m from Thaxted, between
Thaxted & Great Dunmow

This 16th-century inn overlooks the Chelmer Valley, and
is surrounded by open countryside. The property is ideally
situated in the quiet hamlet of Monk Street about two
miles from the historic town of Thaxted. Bedrooms are
pleasantly decorated and equipped with modern
facilities. Public rooms include a cosy lounge bar and a
large smartly appointed restaurant.

Rooms 11 annexe en suite **Facilities** FTV tea/coffee
Dinner available Cen ht Wi-fi **Conf** Max 80 Thtr 80 Class
60 Board 50 **Parking** 35

The Swan

★★★ INN

Bullring, Watling St CM6 2PL
☎ 01371 830321 📠 01371 831186
e-mail: swan.thaxted@greeneking.co.uk
web: www.oldenglish.co.uk
dir: M11 junct 8, A120 to Great Dunmow, then B164 to
Thaxted. At N end of high street, opposite church

This popular village inn is situated in the town centre
opposite the parish church. Public areas feature a large
open-plan beamed bar/restaurant serving real ales and
appealing dishes. Bedrooms are located in the main
building or the more peaceful rear annexe; each one is
pleasantly decorated and well equipped.

Rooms 13 en suite 6 annexe en suite (2 fmly) (3 GF)
Facilities FTV tea/coffee Dinner available Cen ht Wi-fi
Conf Max 20 Thtr 20 Class 20 Board 20 **Parking** 15

THORPE BAY

See Southend-on-Sea

TOPPESFIELD   Map 12 TL73

Ollivers Farm

★★★ BED AND BREAKFAST

CO9 4LS
☎ 01787 237642 📠 01787 237602
e-mail: bandbolliversfarm@tesco.net
web: www.essex-bed-breakfast.co.uk
dir: 500yds SE of village centre. Off A1017 in Great
Yeldham to Toppesfield, farm 1m on left before T-junct
to village

This impressive 16th-century farmhouse, full of charm
and character, set amid pretty landscaped gardens in a
peaceful rural location. Bedrooms are pleasantly
decorated and thoughtfully equipped. Public rooms have
a wealth of original features including exposed beams
and a huge open fireplace in the reception hall.

Rooms 3 rms (1 en suite) (1 pri facs) S £50; D £75-£80*
Facilities FTV Lounge tea/coffee Wi-fi 🔧 Shed for bikes
Parking 4 **Notes** ⊗ No Children 10yrs Closed 23 Dec-1
Jan 🍽

WESTCLIFF-ON-SEA   Map 7 TQ88

See also Southend-on-Sea

The Trinity

★★★ GUEST ACCOMMODATION

3 Trinity Av SS0 7PU
☎ 01702 342282
e-mail: enquiries@thetrinityhotel.co.uk
dir: A13 to Milton Rd, at lights turn right towards Cliffs
Pavilion, left into Cambridge Rd, right into Trinity Av

The Trinity is a contemporary establishment with en suite
accommodation within a short distance of the Westcliff
sea front. All rooms are beautifully appointed and
comfortably equipped. A freshly prepared breakfast is
taken at the communal table in the attractive breakfast
room.

Rooms 7 en suite (1 fmly) **Facilities** FTV tea/coffee Cen ht
Notes ⊗

WIX   Map 13 TM12

PREMIER COLLECTION

Dairy House Farm *(TM148293)*

★★★★★ FARMHOUSE

Bradfield Rd CO11 2SR
☎ 01255 870322 Mrs B Whitworth
e-mail: bridgetwhitworth@btinternet.com
web: www.dairyhousefarm.info
dir: *Exit A120 into Wix, turn at x-rds to Bradfield, farm 1m on left*

This Georgian house stands amid 700 acres of arable land, with stunning views of the surrounding countryside. Extensively renovated in the Victorian style, it still retains original decorative tiled floors, moulded cornices and marble fireplaces. The spacious bedrooms are carefully furnished and equipped with many thoughtful touches. Breakfast is served in the elegant antique-furnished dining room and there is a cosy lounge.

Rooms 3 en suite S £44-£50; D £64-£75*
Facilities FTV DVD TVL tea/coffee Cen ht Wi-fi 🛜 🔒
Farm reservoir fishing **Extras** Home-made cake
Parking 8 **Notes** ⊗ No Children 12yrs 🐾 700 acres arable

GLOUCESTERSHIRE

ALDERTON   Map 10 SP03

Tally Ho Bed & Breakfast

★★★★ BED AND BREAKFAST

20 Beckford Rd GL20 8NL
☎ 01242 621482 & 07966 593169
e-mail: tallyhobb@aol.com
web: www.cotswolds-bedandbreakfast.co.uk
dir: *M5 junct 9, A46 signed Evesham, through Ashchurch. Take B4077 signed Stow-on-the-Wold & Alderton. Left in 1.5m opp garage signed Alderton*

Convenient for the M5, this friendly establishment stands in a delightful quiet village. Bedrooms, including two on the ground floor, offer modern comforts and attractive co-ordinated furnishings. Breakfast is served in the stylish dining room, and for dinner, the village pub is just a stroll away.

Tally Ho Bed & Breakfast

Rooms 3 en suite (1 fmly) (2 GF) S £45-£50; D £65-£70*
Facilities FTV DVD tea/coffee Cen ht Wi-fi **Parking** 3
Notes LB

See advert on this page

ARLINGHAM   Map 4 SO71

The Old Passage Inn

★★★★ ◉◉ 🍴 RESTAURANT WITH ROOMS

Passage Rd GL2 7JR
☎ 01452 740547 📠 01452 741871
e-mail: oldpassage@btconnect.com
dir: *A38 onto B4071 through Frampton on Severn. 4m to Arlingham, through village to river*

Delightfully located on the very edge of the River Severn, this relaxing restaurant with rooms combines high quality food with an air of tranquillity. Bedrooms and bathrooms are decorated in a modern style and include a range of welcome extras such as air conditioning and a well-stocked mini-bar. The menu offers a wide range of seafood and shellfish dishes including crab, oysters and lobsters from Cornwall (kept alive in seawater tanks). An outdoor terrace is available in warmer months.

Rooms 3 en suite S £60-£130; D £80-£130*
Facilities FTV DVD Lounge tea/coffee Dinner available Cen ht Wi-fi ◉ **Extras** Mini-bar - chargeable **Parking** 30
Notes Closed 25 & 26 Dec RS Jan-Feb closed for dinner Tue & Wed No coaches

BERKELEY   Map 4 ST69

The Malt House

★★★ INN

22 Marybrook St GL13 9BA
☎ 01453 511177 📠 01453 810257
e-mail: the-malthouse@btconnect.com
web: www.themalthouse.uk.com
dir: *A38 into Berkeley, at town hall follow road to right, premises on right past hospital & opposite school*

Well located for business and leisure, this family-run inn has a convivial atmosphere. Bedrooms are soundly appointed while public areas include a choice of bars, a skittle alley and an attractive restaurant area. Local attractions include Berkeley Castle, and the Wildfowl & Wetlands Trust at Slimbridge.

The Malt House

Rooms 10 rms (9 en suite) (2 fmly) **Facilities** FTV tea/coffee Dinner available Cen ht Wi-fi Pool table Skittle Alley **Parking** 30 **Notes** ⊗

BIBURY   Map 5 SP10

The Catherine Wheel

★★★★ 🍴 INN

Arlington GL7 5ND
☎ 01285 740250
e-mail: rooms@catherinewheel-bibury.co.uk
dir: *On B4425 between Burford & Cirencester*

Located in the middle of a pleasant village, this family-run inn provides a pleasant welcome and traditional country inn ambience. A range of seating is available from the cosy bar or more formal dining room where a selection of carefully prepared dishes is offered throughout the day and evening. Bedrooms are in an adjacent building and include smaller standard rooms or larger superior rooms - all comfortably furnished and with some welcome extras.

Rooms 4 annexe en suite (4 GF) **Facilities** FTV TVL tea/coffee Dinner available Cen ht Wi-fi **Parking** 23

BLOCKLEY   Map 10 SP13

PREMIER COLLECTION

Lower Brook House

★★★★★ 🍴 GUEST ACCOMMODATION

Lower St GL56 9DS
☎ 01386 700286 📠 01386 701400
e-mail: info@lowerbrookhouse.com
web: www.lowerbrookhouse.com
dir: *In village centre*

Dating from the 17th century, this enchanting house is the perfect place to relax. Genuine hospitality and attentive service are hallmarks here, and bedrooms come in all shapes and sizes. There's a lot of character in the public areas, with beams, flagstone floors, huge fireplace and deep stone walls. Enjoy a delicious breakfast and an aperitif in the garden, but leave room for the skilfully prepared dinner.

Rooms 6 en suite S £80-£190; D £80-£190
Facilities FTV Lounge tea/coffee Dinner available Cen ht Licensed Wi-fi ⅃ 18 ◉ **Extras** Mineral water, fruit **Parking** 6 **Notes** ⊗ No Children 10yrs Closed Xmas

BOURTON-ON-THE-WATER   Map 10 SP12

Larks Rise

★★★★ BED AND BREAKFAST

Old Gloucester Rd GL54 3BH
☎ 01451 822613 & 07884 438498
e-mail: larks.rise@virgin.net
web: www.larksrisehouse.co.uk
dir: *0.5m W of village. A249 onto A436, 1st driveway on left*

A relaxed and welcoming establishment that sits in an acre of gardens on the edge of the village. Comfort and style are of paramount importance at this delightful property where the proprietors offer a very warm welcome. The bedrooms are really comfortable with cotton sheets on pocket sprung mattresses and high quality en suite facilities. Breakfasts feature locally sourced produce, and there is ample parking. Larks Rise was a Finalist in the AA Friendliest B&B of the Year Award 2012-13.

Rooms 3 rms (2 en suite) (1 pri facs) (1 GF)
Facilities FTV tea/coffee Cen ht Wi-fi **Parking** 6 **Notes** ⊗ No Children 12yrs

Old Manse

★★★★ INN

Victoria St GL54 2BX
☎ 01451 820082 📠 01451 810381
e-mail: 6488@greeneking.co.uk
web: www.oldenglish.co.uk
dir: *A429 Bourton turn off, property at far end of village high street next to Cotswold Motor Museum*

Formerly a residence for Baptist ministers back in 1748, this establishment has lots of traditional Cotswold charm, and is located just a few feet from the River Windrush. There is an extensive bar menu and a very good restaurant menu. Bedrooms are modern and well equipped with comfortable beds. In the winter guests can relax by a roaring log fire and in the summer enjoy the beer garden overlooking the river.

Rooms 12 en suite 3 annexe en suite **Facilities** FTV tea/coffee Dinner available Direct Dial Cen ht Wi-fi **Conf** Max 40 Thtr 40 Class 20 Board 16 **Parking** 12

The Cotswold House

★★★ BED AND BREAKFAST

Lansdowne GL54 2AR
☎ 01451 822373
e-mail: meadowscotswoldhouse@btinternet.com
dir: *Exit A429 into Landsowne, 0.5m to Cotswold House on right opposite Mousetrap Inn*

A warm welcome is assured at this well maintained, mellow-stone house. Just a short walk from the church and the many attractions of this popular village, this is a great base for touring the Cotswolds. Bedrooms are comfortably furnished, and one is a self-contained conversion of the former village telephone exchange, set within immaculate gardens.

Rooms 3 en suite 1 annexe en suite (2 fmly) (1 GF) S £35-£60; D £55-£70* **Facilities** Lounge tea/coffee Cen ht Wi-fi 🔒 **Parking** 5 **Notes** LB ⊗ Closed Xmas ⊛

The Mousetrap Inn

★★★ INN

Lansdowne GL54 2AR
☎ 01451 820579
e-mail: thebatesies@gmail.com

A traditional and informal Cotswold inn located on the edge of this idyllic village just a few minutes' stroll from the centre. A selection of real ales and also home-cooked dinners (except Sundays and Mondays) are offered in the relaxed bar. Bedrooms and bathrooms vary in size and include three at ground floor level that have easy access. Breakfast includes home-made sausages and free-range eggs.

Rooms 10 en suite (3 GF) **Facilities** tea/coffee Dinner available Cen ht Wi-fi **Parking** 10 **Notes** ⊗ No Children 10yrs

Halford House

Ⓤ

Station Rd GL54 2AA
☎ 01451 822244 📠 01451 657345
e-mail: info@halfordhouse.com

Currently the rating for this establishment is not confirmed. This may be due to a change of ownership or because it has only recently joined the AA rating scheme.

Rooms 8 en suite **Notes** Closed 1-14 Jan

CHELTENHAM Map 10 SO92

PREMIER COLLECTION

Beaumont House

GUEST ACCOMMODATION

56 Shurdington Rd GL53 0JE
☎ 01242 223311 📠 01242 520044
e-mail: reservations@bhhotel.co.uk
web: www.bhhotel.co.uk
dir: *S side of town on A46 to Stroud*

Built as a private residence, this popular establishment exudes genteel charm. Public areas include a large lounge and an elegant dining room which overlooks the garden. There are studio bedrooms on the top floor, as well as bedrooms themed around Asia and Africa, which are luxuriously furnished and very well equipped. Bedrooms situated to the rear of the building have views over Leckhampton Hill and there are also bedrooms on the lower ground floor.

Rooms 16 en suite (3 fmly) S £69-£79; D £89-£190* **Facilities** STV FTV Lounge tea/coffee Dinner available Direct Dial Cen ht Licensed Wi-fi **Extras** Fruit, mineral water - complimentary **Parking** 16 **Notes** LB ⊗ RS 25-26 Dec No bkfst or housekeeping services

PREMIER COLLECTION

Cleeve Hill House

★★★★★ GUEST ACCOMMODATION

Cleeve Hill GL52 3PR
☎ 01242 672052 📠 01242 679969
e-mail: info@cleevehill-hotel.co.uk
dir: *3m N of Cheltenham on B4632*

Many of the bedrooms and the lounge at this Edwardian property have spectacular views across to the Malvern Hills. Room shapes and sizes vary but all are comfortably furnished with many welcome extras; some have four-poster beds. In addition to the relaxing guest lounge, an honesty bar is in place. Breakfast, served in the pleasant conservatory, offers a good selection of carefully presented hot and cold items.

Rooms 10 en suite (1 GF) S £50-£60; D £85-£95* **Facilities** STV FTV DVD Lounge tea/coffee Direct Dial Cen ht Licensed Wi-fi **Parking** 11 **Notes** ⊗ No Children 8yrs

PREMIER COLLECTION

Georgian House

★★★★★ BED AND BREAKFAST

77 Montpellier Ter GL50 1XA
☎ 01242 515577 📠 01242 545929
e-mail: penny@georgianhouse.net
web: www.georgianhouse.net
dir: *M5 junct 11, A40 into town centre, into Montpellier Terrace. Georgian House on right after park*

Dating from 1807, this elegant Georgian house is located in the fashionable area of Montpellier. Renovation has resulted in delightful accommodation with quality and comfort throughout. Bedrooms are individually styled, with contemporary comforts cleverly interwoven with period furnishings to great effect. Warm hospitality and attentive service ensure a memorable stay.

Rooms 3 en suite S £70-£90; D £90-£115* **Facilities** FTV Lounge tea/coffee Cen ht Wi-fi **Extras** Fridge in all rooms, milk & complimentary drinks **Parking** 2 **Notes** ⊗ No Children 16yrs Closed Xmas & New Year

PREMIER COLLECTION

Lypiatt House

★★★★★ GUEST ACCOMMODATION

Lypiatt Rd GL50 2QW
☎ 01242 224994 📠 01242 224996
e-mail: stay@lypiatt.co.uk
web: www.lypiatt.co.uk
dir: *M5 junct 11 to town centre. At Texaco petrol station mini-rdbt take exit signed Stroud. Fork right, pass shops, sharp left into Lypiatt Rd*

Close to the fashionable area of Montpellier, set in its own grounds with ample parking, Lypiatt House is built in a typical Victorian style. Contemporary decor enhances the traditional features of the building. Bedrooms and bathrooms come in a range of shapes and sizes but all rooms are decorated and maintained to high standards, and include a range of welcome extras. Guests may use the elegant drawing room and the conservatory, which has an honesty bar.

Rooms 10 en suite (2 GF) S £78-£95; D £95-£130* **Facilities** FTV Lounge tea/coffee Direct Dial Cen ht Licensed Wi-fi **Parking** 10 **Notes** LB ⊗ No Children 10yrs

CHELTENHAM *continued*

Clarence Court

★★★★ 🛏 GUEST ACCOMMODATION

Clarence Square GL50 4JR
☎ 01242 580411 ▤ 01242 224609
e-mail: enquiries@clarencecourthotel.com
web: www.clarencecourthotel.com

Situated in an attractive, tree-lined Georgian square, this property was once owned by the Duke of Wellington. Recent refurbishment has returned the building to its former glory with elegant public rooms reflecting the grace of a bygone age. Spacious bedrooms offer ample comfort and quality, with many original features retained. The convenience of the peaceful location is a great asset, only a 5-minute stroll from the town centre. A varied range of carefully prepared dishes is offered in the relaxing café-restaurant from noon to 9pm.

Rooms 20 en suite (3 fmly) (7 GF) S £60-£75;
D £70-£120* **Facilities** FTV TVL tea/coffee Dinner available Direct Dial Cen ht Licensed Wi-fi **Parking** 21

Badger Towers

★★★★ GUEST ACCOMMODATION

133 Hales Rd GL52 6ST
☎ 01242 522583
e-mail: mrbadger@badgertowers.co.uk
web: www.badgertowers.co.uk
dir: *Exit A40 (London Rd) into Hales Rd, 0.5m on right towards Prestbury & racecourse*

Located in the residential area of Battledown, close to the racecourse, town centre and GCHQ, this elegant Victorian house offers thoughtfully furnished bedrooms, a light and airy breakfast room, and a spacious lounge complete with piano. The well-cooked breakfasts, with an emphasis on local produce, are a satisfying start to the day.

Rooms 6 en suite (2 GF) **Facilities** FTV DVD Lounge tea/coffee Cen ht Wi-fi **Parking** 6 **Notes** LB Closed Xmas & New Year

The Battledown Bed and Breakfast

★★★★ GUEST HOUSE

125 Hales Rd GL52 6ST
☎ 01242 233881 & 07807 142069
e-mail: battledown125@hotmail.com
dir: *0.5m E of town centre. A40 onto B4075, 0.5m on right*

This family-run guest house is just outside the main town, yet within easy walking distance of it. Bedrooms and bathrooms are generally spacious and all are well equipped with thoughtful extras. The bright and comfortable breakfast room provides an ideal setting for the carefully prepared breakfasts.

Rooms 7 en suite (2 fmly) S £55-£125; D £75-£250* **Facilities** FTV DVD Lounge tea/coffee Cen ht Wi-fi **Parking** 7 **Notes** LB ⊗

Cotswold Grange

★★★★ 🛏 GUEST ACCOMMODATION

Pittville Circus Rd GL52 2QH
☎ 01242 515119 ▤ 01242 241537
e-mail: info@cotswoldgrange.co.uk
dir: *From town centre, follow Prestbury signs. Right at 1st rdbt, next rdbt straight over, 100yds on left*

A delightful building located in a quieter, mainly residential area of Cheltenham, The Grange is near Pitville Park and just a short walk from the town centre. There's a relaxed and welcoming atmosphere, and there are many useful extras such as Wi-fi in the bedrooms. A range of carefully cooked and presented dishes is served in the comfortable restaurant.

Rooms 24 en suite (3 fmly) S £65-£80; D £75-£100* **Facilities** FTV TVL tea/coffee Dinner available Direct Dial Cen ht Licensed Wi-fi ⓘ 18 ⚲ Complimentary access to nearby gym **Conf** Max 60 Board 30 **Parking** 21 **Notes** LB Closed 25-31 Dec

Hope Orchard

★★★★ GUEST ACCOMMODATION

Gloucester Rd, Staverton GL51 0TF
☎ 01452 855556 ▤ 01452 530037
e-mail: info@hopeorchard.com
web: www.hopeorchard.com
dir: *A40 onto B4063 at Arlecourt rdbt. Hope Orchard 1.25m on right*

Situated midway between Gloucester and Cheltenham, Hope Orchard is a good base for exploring the area. The comfortable bedrooms are next to the main house, and all are on the ground floor with their own separate entrances. There is a large garden, and ample off-road parking is available.

Rooms 8 en suite (8 GF) **Facilities** FTV DVD tea/coffee Direct Dial Cen ht Wi-fi ⚲ **Extras** Fridge, microwave - complimentary **Parking** 10 **Notes** Closed 23 Dec-2 Jan

Malvern View

★★★★ GUEST ACCOMMODATION

Cleeve Hill GL52 3PR
☎ 01242 672017
dir: *B4632 from Cheltenham towards Winchcombe & Stratford-upon-Avon. Through Southam & Cleeve Hill, Malvern View on right*

This family-run guest accommodation is located just four miles north of Cheltenham. The property backs onto the Cotswold Way and Cleeve Common which has amazing views that reach as far as the Black Mountains of Wales. The six bedrooms, mostly en suite, are all individually styled and offer an impressive level of quality and comfort.

Rooms 6 rms (5 en suite) (1 pri facs) S £60-£75; D £90-£125* **Facilities** FTV Lounge tea/coffee Cen ht Licensed Wi-fi ⓘ 18 ⚲ **Extras** Speciality toiletries **Parking** 15 **Notes** ⊗ Closed 2-15 Jan

Wishmoor House

★★★★ GUEST ACCOMMODATION

147 Hales Rd GL52 6TD
☎ 01242 238504 ▤ 01242 226090
e-mail: wishmoor@hotmail.co.uk
dir: *A40 onto B4075 (Hales Rd) signed Prestbury, Racecourse & Crematorium. House 0.5m on right*

Wishmoor House is an elegantly modernised, spacious Victorian residence situated between the town centre and the racecourse, with easy access to all major roads. Guests can expect a warm welcome, wonderful views and a charming period interior. Free Wi-fi and ample parking are available.

Rooms 10 rms (9 en suite) (1 pri facs) (2 fmly) S £39-£55; D £69-£75* **Facilities** FTV tea/coffee Cen ht Wi-fi ⚲ **Conf** Max 10 Thtr 10 Class 10 Board 10 **Parking** 9 **Notes** ⊗

| CHIPPING CAMPDEN | Map 10 SP13 |

See also Blockley

PREMIER COLLECTION

The Malt House

★★★★★ 🛏 GUEST HOUSE

Broad Campden GL55 6UU
☎ 01386 840295 ▤ 01386 841334
e-mail: info@malt-house.co.uk
web: www.malt-house.co.uk
dir: *0.8m SE of Chipping Campden in Broad Campden, by church*

Formed from the village malt house and adjacent cottages, this beguiling house dates from the 16th century. Original features are mixed with contemporary comforts, and bedrooms have quality soft fabrics and period furniture. There is a choice of lounges, an elegant breakfast room, and a wonderful garden with croquet lawn and relaxing seating.

Rooms 4 en suite 3 annexe en suite (3 fmly) (1 GF) S fr £85; D £135-£165* **Facilities** FTV TVL tea/coffee Cen ht Licensed Wi-fi 🔌 **Conf** Max 8 Board 8 **Parking** 10 **Notes** ⊗ Closed 22-28 Dec

Save on B&Bs and Hotels. Book at **theAA.com/hotel**

GLOUCESTERSHIRE 155 ENGLAND

PREMIER COLLECTION

Staddlestones

★★★★★ 🏠 BED AND BREAKFAST

7 Aston Rd GL55 6HR
☎ 01386 849288
e-mail: info@staddle-stones.com
web: www.staddle-stones.com
dir: *From Chipping Campden take B4081 signed Mickleton, 200mtrs. House on right opposite gravel lane*

A warm welcome can be expected from host Pauline Kirton at this delightful property, situated just a short walk from the Cotswold village of Chipping Campden, this makes an ideal base for walking, cycling, golf or just relaxing. There are three bedrooms offering quality and comfort plus some thoughtful extras. A hearty breakfast is served in the dining room around the communal table, and there's a good choice of mostly organic produce sourced from local farms.

Rooms 2 en suite 1 annexe en suite (1 fmly) S £75; D £75-£105* **Facilities** FTV DVD iPod docking station tea/coffee Cen ht Wi-fi 🛁 **Extras** Fridge in Garden Room **Parking** 6 **Notes** No Children 12yrs ⊗

Bramley House Bed & Breakfast

★★★★ BED AND BREAKFAST

6 Aston Rd GL55 6HR
☎ 01386 840066 & 07855 760113
e-mail: povey@bramleyhouse.co.uk
dir: *From High St onto B4081 towards Mickleton, house 0.5m opposite cul-de-sac Grevel Ln & post box*

A warm welcome and refreshments on arrival await at Bramley House. With ample off-road parking and situated just a stroll from the centre of the popular market town, this friendly, family home offers attractively co-ordinated accommodation, with many thoughtful extras. The tranquil rear room offers superb field views. A delicious breakfast, featuring organic produce whenever possible, is served in the smart dining room around a large communal table.

Rooms 2 en suite S fr £60; D £80-£90* **Facilities** tea/coffee Cen ht Wi-fi **Parking** 3 **Notes** ⊗ No Children 12yrs Closed 6-14 Feb ⊗

The Chance

★★★★ 🏠 BED AND BREAKFAST

1 Aston Rd GL55 6HR
☎ 01386 849079
e-mail: enquiries@the-chance.co.uk
web: www.the-chance.co.uk
dir: *B4081 towards Mickleton from Chipping Campden, signed on right hand side*

Located just a short stroll from the pleasant town of Chipping Campden, The Chance offers three well decorated and well maintained bedrooms where a range of extras are helpfully provided for guests. A friendly welcome from the resident proprietor may well include the offer of tea and home-made cakes. Breakfast is a real treat with a varied menu utilising fresh local produce with something to suit all tastes.

Rooms 3 en suite S £70-£75; D £75-£95* **Facilities** FTV DVD Lounge tea/coffee Cen ht Wi-fi **Parking** 6 **Notes** ⊗ No Children 12yrs Closed Xmas & New Year RS mid Dec-mid Jan ⊗

The Kings

★★★★ ⊚⊚ 🏠 RESTAURANT WITH ROOMS

The Square GL55 6AW
☎ 01386 840256 & 841056 📠 01386 841598
e-mail: info@kingscampden.co.uk
dir: *In centre of town square*

Located in the centre of this delightful Cotswold town, The Kings effortlessly blends a relaxed and friendly welcome with efficient service. Bedrooms and bathrooms come in a range of shapes and sizes but all are appointed to high levels of quality and comfort. Dining options, whether in the main restaurant or the comfortable bar area, include a tempting menu to suit all tastes, from light salads and pasta to meat and fish dishes.

Rooms 14 en suite 5 annexe en suite (3 fmly) (3 GF) **Facilities** FTV TV14B tea/coffee Dinner available Direct Dial Cen ht Wi-fi **Conf** Thtr 30 Class 20 Board 20 **Parking** 8 **Notes** Civ Wed 60

Seagrave Arms

★★★★ ⊚ INN

Friday St, Weston-sub-Edge GL55 6QH
☎ 01386 840192
e-mail: info@seagravearms.co.uk
web: www.seagravearms.co.uk
dir: *From Moreton-in-Marsh take A44 towards Evesham. Approx 7m right onto B4081 signed Chipping Campden. Becomes Sheep St. At junct with High Street, left into Dyers Ln. 0.5m over Dovers Hill, into Weston-sub-Edge, becomes Church St. Pub on left*

Ideally located for exploring many of the popular Cotswold villages, the Seagrave Arms is a Grade II listed building with parts dating back to the 16th century. The inn now offers a delightful combination of contemporary bedrooms and bathrooms together with plenty of character retained in the bar and restaurant areas. The food at breakfast and dinner is a highlight, and carefully sourced, high quality produce is used.

Rooms 5 en suite 1 annexe en suite (1 GF) D £95-£115* **Facilities** STV Lounge tea/coffee Dinner available Cen ht Wi-fi **Parking** 15 **Notes** No coaches

CHIPPING CAMPDEN *continued*

Catbrook House

★★★★ BED AND BREAKFAST

Catbrook GL55 6DE
☎ 01386 841499
e-mail: m.klein@virgin.net
dir: *B4081 into Chipping Campden, signs for Broad Campden until Catbrook House on right*

Along with stunning rural views and close proximity to the town centre, this mellow-stone house provides comfortable, homely bedrooms. The attentive hosts extend a friendly welcome. A traditional English breakfast is served in the comfortably furnished dining room.

Rooms 2 rms (1 en suite) (1 pri facs) S fr £48; D fr £58* **Facilities** tea/coffee Cen ht 🛁 **Parking** 3 **Notes** ⊗ No Children 9yrs Closed Xmas ⊛

Holly House

★★★★ BED AND BREAKFAST

Ebrington GL55 6NL
☎ 01386 593213
e-mail: jeffreyhutsby@yahoo.co.uk
web: www.hollyhousebandb.co.uk
dir: *B4035 from Chipping Campden towards Shipston on Stour, 0.5m left to Ebrington & signed*

Set in the heart of the pretty Cotswold village of Ebrington, this late Victorian house offers thoughtfully equipped accommodation. Bedrooms are housed in buildings that were formerly used by the local wheelwright, and offer level access, seclusion and privacy. Quality English breakfasts are served in the light and airy dining room. For other meals, the village pub is just a short walk away.

Rooms 2 en suite 1 annexe en suite (2 fmly) (3 GF) S £50-£60; D £70-£75* **Facilities** FTV Lounge tea/coffee Cen ht Wi-fi **Parking** 5 **Notes** ⊗ Closed Xmas ⊛

Lygon Arms

★★★★ 🖥 🚭 INN

High St GL55 6HB
☎ 01386 840318 & 840089 🖨 01386 841088
e-mail: sandra@lygonarms.co.uk
dir: *In town centre near church*

This charming and welcoming inn sits on the High Street of this delightful village - a tranquil location with lots of tempting antique shops and restaurants. Well managed by a friendly team, the inn has a cosy bar with open log fires and oak beams. Spacious and very well appointed accommodation is provided in the main building and in mews houses. Dinner and breakfast are not to be missed.

Rooms 10 en suite (3 fmly) (1 GF) **Facilities** FTV tea/coffee Dinner available Direct Dial Wi-fi **Parking** 12 **Notes** No coaches

Manor Farm (SP124412)

★★★★ FARMHOUSE

Weston-sub-Edge GL55 6QH
☎ 01386 840390 & 07889 108812   Mrs L King
e-mail: lucy@manorfarmbnb.demon.co.uk
web: www.manorfarmbnb.demon.co.uk
dir: *2m NW of Chipping Campden. On B4632 in Weston-sub-Edge*

A genuine welcome is extended at this 17th-century mellow Cotswold-stone farmhouse. Bedrooms are comfortable and homely with thoughtful extras. Facilities include a lounge with a wood-burning stove, and an elegant dining room where mouth-watering breakfasts are served.

Rooms 3 en suite S £60-£75; D £70-£75 **Facilities** STV FTV iPod docking station TVL tea/coffee Cen ht Wi-fi ⚓ 18 **Parking** 8 **Notes** LB ⊗ 800 acres arable/cattle/horses/sheep

Stonecroft Bed & Breakfast

★★★★ BED AND BREAKFAST

Stonecroft, George Ln GL55 6DA
☎ 01386 840486
e-mail: info@stonecroft-chippingcampden.co.uk

Quietly located in a residential area just a stroll from the High Street, this well-maintained property offers relaxing accommodation. Guests have the key to their own entrance and can come and go as they please. Breakfast is served around one large table in the compact but well-furnished dining room.

Rooms 2 en suite (1 fmly) **Facilities** FTV DVD tea/coffee Cen ht Wi-fi **Parking** 2 **Notes** ⊗ No Children 12yrs ⊛

CHIPPING SODBURY   Map 4 ST78

The Moda House

★★★★ GUEST ACCOMMODATION

1 High St BS37 6BA
☎ 01454 312135 🖨 01454 850090
e-mail: enquiries@modahouse.co.uk
web: www.modahouse.co.uk
dir: *In town centre*

This popular Grade II listed Georgian house has an imposing position at the top of the High Street. It has been appointed to provide modern bedrooms of varying shapes and sizes and comfortable public areas, while retaining many original features. Room facilities include satellite TV and phones.

Rooms 8 en suite 3 annexe en suite (3 GF) **Facilities** STV TVL tea/coffee Direct Dial Cen ht Licensed Wi-fi **Conf** Max 20 Thtr 10 Board 10

CIRENCESTER   Map 5 SP00

PREMIER COLLECTION

The Fleece at Cirencester

★★★★★ 🚭 INN

Market Place GL7 2NZ
☎ 01285 658507 🖨 01285 651017
e-mail: relax@fleecehotel.co.uk

Located in the heart of the market town of Cirencester, this newly refurbished inn has been sympathetically brought up-to-date with guest quality and comfort in mind. Bedrooms are deeply comfortable, and many thoughtful touches add to the stay. Public areas include a traditional bar featuring Thwaites cask ales and a comfortable cosy lounge and popular restaurant. The Fleece is nestled in the centre of town, moments walk from eclectic shops and attractions.

Rooms 28 en suite (1 fmly) S £75-£160; D £81-£200* **Facilities** FTV Lounge tea/coffee Dinner available Direct Dial Cen ht Wi-fi **Extras** Home-made biscuits **Parking** 8

Hare & Hounds

★★★★ ◎ INN

Fosse-Cross, Chedworth GL54 4NN
☎ 01285 720288
e-mail: stay@hareandhoundsinn.com
dir: *4.5m NE of Cirencester. On A429 by speed camera*

This traditional country inn built of Cotswold stone, near the Fosse Way, offers delicious home-cooked food in one of the elegant dining rooms and in the garden in fine weather. The smart and comfortable en suite bedrooms are set round a peaceful courtyard. Ample parking is available to the rear of the inn.

Rooms 10 en suite (2 fmly) (8 GF) **Facilities** tea/coffee Dinner available Direct Dial Cen ht Wi-fi **Parking** 40 **Notes** ⊗

CLEEVE HILL	Map 10 SO92

Rising Sun

★ ★ ★   INN

GL52 3PX
☎ 01242 676281 ▤ 01242 673069
e-mail: 9210@greeneking.co.uk
dir: On B4632, 4m N of Cheltenham

This popular establishment is situated on Cleeve Hill and offers commanding views across the Severn Vale to the Malvern Hills and beyond. There is a pleasant range of public rooms which include a large bar-bistro and a reception lounge. Bedrooms are well equipped and smartly presented, and many have glorious views. A large garden is also available for summer drinking and dining.

Rooms 24 en suite (3 fmly) (6 GF) S £40–£70; D £50–£100* Facilities STV Lounge tea/coffee Dinner available Direct Dial Cen ht Wi-fi ⚓ 18 Parking 70 Notes LB

COLEFORD	Map 4 SO51

Dryslade Farm (SO581147)

★ ★ ★ ★   FARMHOUSE

English Bicknor GL16 7PA
☎ 01594 860259 ▤ 01594 860259 Mrs D Gwilliam
e-mail: daphne@drysladefarm.co.uk
web: www.drysladefarm.co.uk
dir: 3m N of Coleford. A4136 onto B4432, right towards English Bicknor, farm 1m

Visitors are warmly welcomed at this 184-acre working farm, which dates from 1780 and has been in the same family for almost 100 years. The en suite bedrooms are attractively furnished in natural pine and are well equipped. The lounge leads onto a conservatory where hearty breakfasts are served.

Rooms 3 en suite (1 GF) S £50; D £66–£72* Facilities FTV DVD Lounge TVL tea/coffee Cen ht Wi-fi ⚓ Parking 6 Notes LB ⊕ 184 acres beef

The Rock B&B

★ ★ ★ ★   GUEST ACCOMMODATION

GL16 7NY
☎ 01594 837893
e-mail: chris@stayattherock.com
web: www.stayattherock.com
dir: A40 at Monmouth onto A4136. 5m, left at Five Acres into Park Rd. At Christchurch right, immediately left towards Symonds Yat Rock, 0.75m S of Symonds Yat Rock

The Rock offers stylish modern accommodation and is located on the outskirts of Coleford, near the famous Symonds Yat Rock. Bedrooms are attractively presented and very comfortable, with the new garden rooms making the most of the spectacular views over the Wye Valley. Very popular with walkers, The Rock also caters well for business guests. Breakfasts are served in the spacious dining room overlooking the garden.

Rooms 7 annexe en suite (5 GF) Facilities FTV Lounge tea/coffee Cen ht Wi-fi ⚓ Hot tub Parking 20 Notes LB No Children 12yrs

COLN ST ALDWYNS	Map 5 SP10

PREMIER COLLECTION

The New Inn at Coln

★ ★ ★ ★ ★   ⑳⑳ INN

GL7 5AN
☎ 01285 750651 ▤ 01285 750657
e-mail: info@new-inn.co.uk
dir: 8m E of Cirencester, between Bilbury & Fairford

This delightful village inn has origins dating back to the 16th century. The stylish, individually designed bedrooms retain original features yet include all the modern amenities such as flat screen TVs and power showers. The rooms come in a variety of shapes and sizes and display bold, impressive colour schemes. Relaxed and welcoming hospitality mixes easily with efficient service from a dedicated team of staff. Dinner, utilising the best of local produce, is a real treat whether served in the relaxing dining room or outside on the terrace.

Rooms 8 rms (7 en suite) 6 annexe rms 4 annexe en suite S £60–£170; D £80–£190 Facilities TVL tea/coffee Dinner available Direct Dial Cen ht Wi-fi Fishing Riding Notes LB

COWLEY	Map 10 SO91

The Green Dragon

★ ★ ★ ★   ⊜ INN

Cockleford GL53 9NW
☎ 01242 870271
e-mail: green-dragon@buccaneer.co.uk

This establishment offers all the charm and character of an English country pub including a relaxed atmosphere and carefully prepared food made from local produce. Bedrooms, some at ground floor level, are individually furnished and vary in size. There is a terrace to the front where guests may enjoy a drink on warm sunny days.

Rooms 9 en suite (4 GF) S fr £70; D £95–£150* Facilities iPod docking station tea/coffee Dinner available Direct Dial Cen ht Wi-fi Conf Max 100 Thtr 100 Class 65 Board 65 Parking 11 Notes LB

EBRINGTON	Map 10 SP14

The Ebrington Arms

★ ★ ★ ★   ⑳⑳ INN

GL55 6NH
☎ 01386 593223
e-mail: info@theebringtonarms.co.uk
web: www.theebringtonarms.co.uk
dir: From Chipping Campden take B4035 towards Shipston-on-Stour, left to Ebrington

Located in the quiet, unspoilt village of Ebrington, just a couple of miles from Chipping Campden, this 17th-century inn provides an excellent selection of real ales, fine wines and really enjoyable award-winning dishes utilising the finest of produce. Food is served in the traditional ambience of the bar or the cosy dining room with roaring open fire. Bedrooms are full of character and include some welcome extras. A large beer garden and car park are also available.

Rooms 3 en suite Facilities FTV tea/coffee Dinner available Cen ht Conf Max 32 Thtr 32 Class 32 Board 25 Parking 10

EWEN	Map 4 SU09

The Wild Duck

★ ★ ★ ★   INN

Drakes Island GL7 6BY
☎ 01285 770310 ▤ 01285 770492
e-mail: duckreservations@aol.com
dir: From Cirencester take A429 towards Malmesbury, at Kemble left to village centre

This lovely 16th-century, family run inn sits in a delightful Cotswold location and offers a wealth of character and interest. Log fires crackle and there are heaps of nooks and crannies in the bar and restaurant where guests can enjoy the hearty cuisine and an extensive choice of beers and wines. There is a lovely courtyard for alfresco dining in the warmer weather. The individually designed bedrooms have a contemporary look, and each has a black lacquered four-poster; the Chinese Suite is in the oldest part of the building.

Rooms 4 en suite 8 annexe en suite (8 GF) S £39–£70; D £59–£165 Facilities FTV Lounge tea/coffee Dinner available Direct Dial Cen ht Wi-fi ⚓ 18 Parking 50 Notes Closed 25 Dec evening

FORD | Map 10 SP02

The Plough Inn

★★★★ 🍽 INN

GL54 5RU
☎ 01386 584215 📄 01386 584042
e-mail: info@theploughinnatford.co.uk
web: www.theploughinnatford.co.uk
dir: On B4077 in village

Popular with locals and the racing fraternity, this charming 16th-century inn retains many original features such as Cotswold stone walls, open fires and beamed ceilings. Cheltenham, Tewkesbury and many popular Cotswold towns and villages are in close proximity. Home-cooked food featuring local produce is a highlight. Bedrooms are situated in a restored stable block across a courtyard, adjacent to the delightful beer garden.

Rooms 3 annexe en suite (2 fmly) S £60; D £80*
Facilities FTV tea/coffee Dinner available Cen ht
Parking 50 Notes LB ⊗

FOSSEBRIDGE | Map 5 SP01

The Inn at Fossebridge

★★★★ 🍽 INN

GL54 3JS
☎ 01285 720721
e-mail: info@fossebridgeinn.co.uk
dir: On A429, 3m S of A40 & 6m N of Cirencester

Located not too far from Stratford-upon-Avon, Cheltenham and Cirencester this inn is around 300 years old, and was once a coaching inn on the old Fosse Way. Today it is a beautiful Cotswold retreat with wonderful accommodation and grounds. Fine food is served in the character bar and dining areas, and a warm welcome awaits all visitors.

Rooms 9 en suite (1 fmly) D £85-£165* Facilities FTV TVL tea/coffee Dinner available Cen ht Wi-fi ch fac

Fishing Extras Bottled mineral water, speciality toiletries
Conf Max 70 Thtr 50 Class 40 Board 16 Parking 50
Notes LB Civ Wed 70

FRAMPTON MANSELL | Map 4 SO90

The Crown Inn

★★★★ INN

GL6 8JG
☎ 01285 760601
e-mail: enquiries@thecrowninn-cotswolds.co.uk
dir: Off A419 signed Frampton Mansell, 0.75m at village centre

This establishment was a cider house in the 17th century, and guests today will find that roaring log fires, locally brewed ales and traditional, home-cooked food are all on offer. The comfortable, well-equipped bedrooms are in an annexe, and ample parking is available.

Rooms 12 annexe en suite (1 fmly) (4 GF) Facilities tea/coffee Dinner available Cen ht Wi-fi Conf Max 40 Parking 35

GLOUCESTER | Map 10 SO81

The Wharf House Restaurant with Rooms

★★★★ 🏆 RESTAURANT WITH ROOMS

Over GL2 8DB
☎ 01452 332900 📄 01452 332901
e-mail: thewharfhouse@yahoo.co.uk
dir: From A40 between Gloucester & Highnam exit at lights for Over. Establishment signed

The Wharf House was built to replace the old lock cottage and, as the name suggests, it is located at the very edge of the river; it has pleasant views and an outdoor terrace. The bedrooms and bathrooms have been decorated and appointed to high levels of quality and comfort, and there are plenty of guest extras. Seasonal, local produce can be enjoyed both at breakfast and dinner in the delightfully relaxing restaurant.

Rooms 7 en suite (1 fmly) (1 GF) S £79-£99; D £85-£125* Facilities STV FTV DVD Lounge tea/coffee Dinner available Cen ht Wi-fi Fishing ♨ Parking 37 Notes Closed 24 Dec-4 Jan No coaches

GUITING POWER | Map 10 SP02

Guiting Guest House

★ ★ ★ ★ GUEST HOUSE

Post Office Ln GL54 5TZ
☎ 01451 850470
e-mail: info@guitingguesthouse.com
web: www.guitingguesthouse.com
dir: In village centre

In keeping with all the surrounding houses, this engaging family home is built of mellow Cotswold stone. Charming and comfortable bedrooms offer both individuality and character, as do the public rooms, which include the stylish dining room and snug lounge. Breakfast (and dinner by arrangement) uses excellent local produce whenever possible.

Rooms 3 rms (2 en suite) (1 pri facs) 2 annexe en suite (2 GF) D £78-£88* Facilities TVL tea/coffee Dinner available Cen ht Wi-fi ♨ Extras Fresh fruit Parking 2 Notes LB

LECHLADE ON THAMES | Map 5 SU29

Cambrai Lodge

★★★★ GUEST ACCOMMODATION

Oak St GL7 3AY
☎ 01367 253173 & 07860 150467
e-mail: cambrailodge@btconnect.com
web: www.cambrailodgeguesthouse.co.uk
dir: In town centre, from High St onto A361 (Oak St)

This delightful house is just a stroll from the centre of the historic market town with its many pubs that serve meals. The individually styled bedrooms offer plenty of quality and comfort, and include a four-poster room and two ground-floor rooms. Breakfast is served in the pleasant conservatory overlooking the gardens.

Rooms 3 en suite (2 GF) S £50-£60; D £65-£90 Facilities FTV tea/coffee Direct Dial Cen ht Wi-fi Parking 12 Notes ⊗

LONGHOPE | Map 10 SO61

New House Farm B&B (SO685229)

★★★★ FARMHOUSE

Barrel Ln, Aston Ingham GL17 0LS
☎ 01452 830484 & 07768 354922
📄 01452 830484 Ms R Smith
e-mail: scaldbrain@btinternet.com
dir: A40 onto B4222, Barrel Ln on right before Aston Ingham; or M50 junct 3 towards Newent, right at Kilcot to Aston Ingham

Located in tranquil wooded countryside, this working farm is a good touring base on the Gloucestershire-Herefordshire border. Set in 80 acres, the welcoming farmhouse will certainly appeal to nature lovers, and there is a comfortable lounge. Breakfast consists of a good selection of carefully prepared local produce.

Rooms 3 en suite (1 fmly) S £40-£60; D £65-£80* Facilities FTV DVD Lounge TVL tea/coffee Dinner available Cen ht Wi-fi 🐾 ♨ Conf Max 15 Parking 10 Notes LB ⊗ No Children 10yrs Closed Xmas & New Year 80 acres sheep/cattle/woodland

Save on B&Bs and Hotels. Book at **theAA.com/hotel**

GLOUCESTERSHIRE 159 ENGLAND

MORETON-IN-MARSH — Map 10 SP23

Red Lion Inn

★★★ ⇔ INN

Little Compton GL56 0RT
☎ 01608 674397
e-mail: info@theredlionlittlecompton.co.uk
dir: On A44 between Chipping Norton & Moreton-in-Marsh

Built in 1748 as a coaching inn the Red Lion retains much of the charm and character of a friendly country pub. It has been sympathetically restored and the inglenook fireplaces, stone walls and oak beams remain a real feature. The comfortable bedrooms are stylishly presented and overlook the neat gardens with the beautiful Cotswold countryside beyond. Comprehensive breakfast choices are available, and evening meals should not be missed.

Rooms 2 en suite S £80; D £80* **Facilities** FTV tea/coffee Dinner available Cen ht Wi-fi Riding Pool table **Parking** 15 **Notes** LB No Children 13yrs

NAILSWORTH — Map 4 ST89

Wild Garlic Restaurant and Rooms

★★★★ ⑳⑳ RESTAURANT WITH ROOMS

3 Cossack Square GL6 0DB
☎ 01453 832615
e-mail: info@wild-garlic.co.uk
dir: M4 junct 18, A46 towards Stroud. Enter Nailsworth, left at rdbt, immediately left. Establishment opposite Britannia pub

Situated in a quiet corner of this charming Cotswold town, this restaurant with rooms offers a delightful combination of welcoming, relaxed hospitality and high quality cuisine. The spacious and well-equipped bedrooms are situated above the restaurant. The small and friendly team of staff ensure guests are very well looked after throughout their stay.

Rooms 3 rms (2 en suite) (1 pri facs) (2 fmly) S £65-£85; D £75-£90* **Facilities** STV FTV DVD Lounge tea/coffee Dinner available Cen ht Wi-fi ⚓ 18 Fishing Riding Shooting **Extras** Spring water - complimentary **Notes** ⊗ No coaches

NAUNTON — Map 10 SP12

Mill View Guest House

★★★★ GUEST HOUSE

2 Mill View GL54 3AF
☎ 01451 850586 & 07887 553571
e-mail: patricia@millview.myzen.co.uk
web: www.millviewguesthousecotswolds.com
dir: Exit B4068 to E end of village

Lying opposite a historic watermill, this former family home has been extended and modernised to provide every comfort. A warm welcome and attentive care is assured in this non-smoking house, which has one bedroom equipped for easier access. The accommodation provides a good base for walkers or for touring Gloucestershire.

Rooms 3 en suite (1 GF) S £50-£60; D £65-£80* **Facilities** FTV DVD iPod docking station TVL tea/coffee Dinner available Cen ht Wi-fi **Extras** Snacks, sherry decanter - complimentary **Parking** 4 **Notes** LB ⊗ ⇔

NETHER WESTCOTE — Map 10 SP22

PREMIER COLLECTION

The Feathered Nest Inn

★★★★★ ⑳⑳ ⌂ INN

OX7 6SD
☎ 01993 833030 📠 01993 833031
e-mail: info@thefeatherednestinn.co.uk
web: www.thefeatherednestinn.co.uk
dir: A424 between Burford & Stow-on-the-Wold, follow signs

Located in the picturesque Cotswold village of Nether Westcote with rolling views over the Evenlode Valley, this charming village inn has been restored with care, offering a cosy base from which to explore the idyllic Cotswolds. There are four luxurious en suite bedrooms, all individually designed combining quality antiques and modern extras. Service is attentive and helpful while the food is a delight, offering a selection of carefully crafted dishes using the best of quality, seasonal produce.

Rooms 4 en suite (1 fmly) **Facilities** STV FTV TVL tea/coffee Dinner available Direct Dial Cen ht Wi-fi **Parking** 45 **Notes** ⊗ Closed 25 Dec No coaches Civ Wed 200

NEWENT — Map 10 SO72

Three Choirs Vineyards

★★★★ ⑳⑳ RESTAURANT WITH ROOMS

GL18 1LS
☎ 01531 890223 📠 01531 890877
e-mail: info@threechoirs.com
web: www.threechoirs.com
dir: On B4215 N of Newent, follow brown tourist signs

This thriving vineyard continues to go from strength to strength and provides a wonderfully different place to stay. The restaurant, which overlooks the 100-acre estate, enjoys a popular following thanks to well-executed dishes that make good use of local produce. Spacious, high quality bedrooms are equipped with many extras, and each opens onto a private patio area which has wonderful views.

Rooms 11 annexe en suite (1 fmly) (11 GF) D £135-£195* **Facilities** FTV DVD Lounge tea/coffee Dinner available Direct Dial Cen ht Wi-fi Wine tasting Vineyard Tours **Conf** Max 20 Thtr 20 Class 15 Board 20 **Parking** 11 **Notes** LB Closed 24-27 Dec No coaches

OLD SODBURY — Map 4 ST78

The Sodbury House

★★★★ GUEST HOUSE

Badminton Rd BS37 6LU
☎ 01454 312847 📠 01454 273105
e-mail: info@sodburyhouse.co.uk
web: www.sodburyhouse.co.uk
dir: M4 junct 18, A46 N, 2m left onto A432 to Chipping Sodbury, house 1m on left

This comfortably furnished 19th-century farmhouse stands in six acres of grounds. The bedrooms, many located on the ground floor and in buildings adjacent to the main house, have many extra facilities. Breakfast offers a varied choice and is served in the spacious breakfast room.

Rooms 6 en suite 9 annexe en suite (2 fmly) (7 GF) **Facilities** FTV TVL tea/coffee Direct Dial Cen ht Wi-fi ⚓ **Conf** Thtr 40 Class 25 Board 20 **Parking** 30 **Notes** ⊗ Closed 24 Dec-3 Jan

OLD SODBURY *continued*

The Cross Hands

★★★ INN

BS37 6RJ
☎ 01454 313000 📠 01454 324409
e-mail: 6435@greeneking.co.uk
dir: *M4 junct 18 signed to Cirencester/Stroud on A46. After 1.5m, on right at 1st lights*

The Cross Hands is a former posting house dating back to the 14th century that is just off the main road, and within easy reach of both Bath and Bristol. The bedrooms are well equipped and some are at ground-floor level. The public areas include a bar, comfortable seating area and a spacious split-level restaurant which offers a selection of home-cooked dishes. Alternatively, guests may choose to eat from the extensive menu in the bar area.

Rooms 21 en suite (1 fmly) (9 GF) **Facilities** tea/coffee Dinner available Direct Dial Cen ht Wi-fi **Conf** Max 80 Thtr 80 Class 24 Board 16 **Parking** 120 **Notes** Civ Wed 80

PAINSWICK	Map 4 SO80

St Michaels

★★★★ 🍴 RESTAURANT WITH ROOMS

Victoria St GL6 6QA
☎ 01452 814555 📠 01452 814606
e-mail: info@stmickshouse.co.uk

This 17th-century Grade II listed building has a wealth of character and overlooks the famous Church of St Michaels with its 99 yew trees. Each stylish bedroom has its own theme and is equipped with a host of thoughtful extras. The award-winning restaurant has an imaginative menu based on the best local produce, and the delicious breakfasts should not be missed. Situated in the heart of the very pretty Cotswold village of Painswick this establishment makes an ideal base for exploring the beautiful Cotswolds. A warm welcome is guaranteed.

Rooms 3 en suite **Facilities** Dinner available Cen ht Wi-fi ⚓ 18 **Notes** Closed 21 Dec-1 Feb & 6-15 Jun No coaches

Hambutts Mynd Guest House

★★★ GUEST ACCOMMODATION

Edge Rd GL6 6UP
☎ 01452 812352
e-mail: ewarland@supanet.com

Built in the 1700s as a corn mill, this property has an interesting history. In 1801 it was converted into a school, and much later it commenced its role of offering guest accommodation. Homely and welcoming hospitality is delivered and the bedrooms benefit from delightful views over the valley and the hills. A number of pleasant Cotswold walks start directly from the house, and Painswick itself is a just a five-minute stroll away.

Rooms 3 en suite **Facilities** STV FTV TVL tea/coffee Cen ht **Parking** 3 **Notes** No Children 10yrs Closed Jan RS Mar 🐾

PAXFORD	Map 10 SP13

Churchill Arms

★★★★ 🍷🍷 🏠 INN

GL55 6XH
☎ 01386 594000
e-mail: info@thechurchillarms.com
dir: *A429 onto A44 to Bourton-on-the-Hill, through village, turn right. Through Blockley to Paxford, pub on right*

Set in the peaceful village of Paxford, this delightful Cotswold inn combines the atmosphere of a traditional village hostelry (real ale, log fires, wooden beams etc) with modern comforts in the well-appointed bedrooms and bathrooms. All food here, from the bar menu's light options to the carefully-prepared dishes at dinner and at breakfast, is of the highest quality.

Rooms 4 en suite (2 fmly) S £60-£100; D £90-£120* **Facilities** FTV tea/coffee Dinner available Direct Dial Cen ht Wi-fi **Notes** No coaches

ST BRIAVELS	Map 4 SO50

The Florence

★★★★ GUEST ACCOMMODATION

Bigsweir GL15 6QQ
☎ 01594 530830 📠 01594 530830
e-mail: enquiries@florencehotel.co.uk
dir: *On A466 between Monmouth & Chepstow*

Located on the Wye Valley road, The Florence has delightful views across the river and stands in over five acres of gardens with woodland walks. Bedrooms, some in the main house and the others in an adjacent cottage, come in a range of sizes and styles. Guests can enjoy cream teas in the garden, a drink in the snug, and choose from a wide selection of carefully prepared dishes at both lunch and dinner.

Rooms 4 en suite 4 annexe en suite (1 fmly) (2 GF) S £52.50; D £105* (incl.dinner) **Facilities** FTV DVD Lounge tea/coffee Dinner available Cen ht Licensed Wi-fi Fishing **Parking** 30 **Notes** LB ⊗ No Children 10yrs Closed Nov-Mar

Green Gables B&B

★★★ BED AND BREAKFAST

Mork GL15 6QH
☎ 01594 531039 & 07786 880498
e-mail: greengablesmork@gmail.com
dir: *A466 cross river at Bigsweir Bridge, 1st right up hill. Green Gables past farm on left*

This welcoming bed and breakfast is ideally located for enjoying delightful walks in all directions over the surrounding countryside. Bedrooms are comfortably furnished and include especially relaxing beds. Breakfast utilises a selection of well-prepared local produce, and home-cooked dinners are also available by prior arrangement. Guests are welcome to use the small guest lounge, and off-street car parking is also provided.

Rooms 2 en suite (2 fmly) (1 GF) S £37.50-£50; D £75 **Facilities** FTV DVD Lounge tea/coffee Dinner available Cen ht Wi-fi ch fac 🐾 🔒 **Parking** 8 **Notes** LB 🐾

STOW-ON-THE-WOLD	Map 10 SP12

Woodlands Guest House

★★★★ GUEST ACCOMMODATION

Upper Swell GL54 1EW
☎ 01451 832346
e-mail: amandak247@talktalk.net
web: www.woodlands-guest-house.co.uk
dir: *Upper Swell 1m from Stow-on-the-Wold, take B4077 (Tewkesbury Road)*

Situated in the small hamlet of Upper Swell, Woodlands provides an ideal base for exploring many charming nearby villages. This establishment enjoys delightful rural views and has comfortably appointed bedrooms with a good range of extra accessories. Breakfast is served in the welcoming dining room around the communal dining table. Off-road parking is available.

Rooms 5 en suite (2 GF) **Facilities** FTV tea/coffee Cen ht Wi-fi **Parking** 8 **Notes** ⊗ 🐾

The Kings Head Inn

★★★★ ❀ INN

The Green, Bledington OX7 6XQ
☎ 01608 658365 ▤ 01608 658902
e-mail: info@kingsheadinn.net
web: www.kingsheadinn.net
dir: *4m SE off B4450*

Located on the delightful village green near the river, this 16th-century inn has spacious public areas with open fires, wobbly floors, beams and wood furnishings. The comfortable restaurant offers excellent dining and the bedrooms have been creatively decorated and well furnished; some rooms are in a converted annexe.

Rooms 6 en suite 6 annexe en suite (3 GF) **Facilities** FTV TVL tea/coffee Dinner available Direct Dial Cen ht Wi-fi **Parking** 24 **Notes** ⊗ Closed 25-26 Dec RS wkdays Closed every afternoon 3-6 low season No coaches

Corsham Field Farmhouse *(SP217249)*

★★★ FARMHOUSE

Bledington Rd GL54 1JH
☎ 01451 831750 ▤ 01451 832247 **Mr R Smith**
e-mail: farmhouse@corshamfield.co.uk
dir: *2m SE of Stow on B4450*

This establishment, which has views of the surrounding countryside from its elevated position, is a popular choice with walking groups and families. The modern bedrooms are practically equipped and located in two separate houses. Enjoyable breakfasts are taken in the spacious dining room, which also provides a lounge. The local pub is just a short walk away and has a reputation for good food.

Rooms 7 rms (5 en suite) (2 pri facs) (3 fmly) (2 GF) S £40-£60; D £50-£70 **Facilities** FTV Lounge tea/coffee Cen ht Wi-fi **Parking** 10 **Notes** LB ⊗ ❀ 100 acres arable

STROUD   Map 4 SO80

1 Woodchester Lodge

★★★★ 🛏 BED AND BREAKFAST

Southfield Rd, North Woodchester GL5 5PA
☎ 01453 872586
e-mail: anne@woodchesterlodge.co.uk
web: www.woodchesterlodge.co.uk
dir: *A46 into Selsley Rd, 2nd left, house 200yds on left*

Close to the newly re-routed Cotswold Way, this late Victorian former timber merchant's house is set in the peaceful village of North Woodchester and is just a short drive from Stroud. In its own landscaped gardens, this large house has spacious, sympathetically restored bedrooms and a comfortable lounge. Evening meals and freshly prepared breakfasts are not to be missed.

1 Woodchester Lodge

Rooms 3 rms (1 en suite) (2 pri facs) (1 fmly) S £50-£55; D £75-£80* **Facilities** FTV DVD Lounge TVL tea/coffee Dinner available Cen ht Wi-fi ▤ **Extras** Speciality toiletries **Parking** 4 **Notes** ⊗ Closed Xmas & Etr

The Withyholt Guest House

★★★★ GUEST HOUSE

Paul Mead, Edge GL6 6PG
☎ 01452 813618 ▤ 01452 813618
e-mail: info@thewithyholtbedandbreakfast.com

A peacefully located property in a quiet residential area very close to Painswick; delightful walks in the Cotswolds are available right from the doorstep. The bedrooms and bathrooms are comfortably appointed, and the spacious public areas include a lounge and snooker room. Breakfast offers a good selection of well cooked and well presented hot and cold dishes.

Rooms 4 rms (2 en suite) (1 pri facs) 1 annexe en suite (1 GF) **Facilities** STV FTV DVD TVL tea/coffee Dinner available Cen ht Wi-fi Snooker ▤ **Parking** 4 **Notes** ⊗

TETBURY   Map 4 ST89

The Great Tythe Barn Accommodation

★★★ GUEST ACCOMMODATION

Folly Farm, Long Newton GL8 8XA
☎ 01666 502475 ▤ 01666 502358
e-mail: info@gtb.co.uk
web: www.gtb.co.uk
dir: *M4 junct 17, B4014 signed Tetbury, on right after Welcome to Tetbury sign*

Folly Farm is located amidst rolling countryside just a 10-minute walk from Tetbury. The well-equipped bedrooms are adjacent to a huge tithe barn, that together with the pleasant grounds surrounding it, makes this a popular wedding venue. Breakfast is taken in the comfortable and relaxing Orangery that offers a well presented continental selection.

Rooms 12 en suite (2 fmly) (6 GF) S £55-£100; D £65-£100* **Facilities** FTV tea/coffee Cen ht Licensed Wi-fi ⛳ **Conf** Max 180 Thtr 100 Class 64 Board 65 **Parking** 100 **Notes** LB ⊗ Civ Wed 180

Hunters Hall

★★★ INN

Kingscote GL8 8XZ
☎ 01453 860393 ▤ 01453 860707
e-mail: huntershall.kingscote@greeneking.co.uk
dir: *M4 junct 18, take A46 towards Stroud. Turn left signed Kingscote, to T-junct left, 0.5m on left*

Situated close to Tetbury, this 16th-century inn has a wealth of charm and character, enhanced by beamed ceilings and open fires. There are three bars and a restaurant offering freshly prepared home-cooked, traditional food from an extensive menu. The bedrooms, situated in the converted stable block, are comfortable with a good range of extras. One ground-floor room has facilities for disabled guests. There is a large garden and play area.

Rooms 12 annexe en suite (1 fmly) (8 GF) **Facilities** tea/coffee Direct Dial Pool table **Parking** 100

TEWKESBURY   Map 10 SO83

The Bell

★★★★ INN

52 Church St GL20 5SA
☎ 01684 293293 ▤ 01684 295938
e-mail: 6408@greeneking.co.uk
dir: *M5 junct 9, follow brown tourist signs for Tewkesbury Abbey, directly opposite Abbey*

This 14th-century former coaching house is situated on the edge of the town, opposite the Norman abbey. The bar and lounge are the focal point of this atmospheric and friendly establishment, with a large open fire providing warmth. Bedrooms offer good levels of comfort and quality with some welcome extra facilities provided.

Rooms 24 en suite (1 fmly) (4 GF) **Facilities** tea/coffee Direct Dial Wi-fi **Parking** 20

Willow Cottages

★★★ GUEST ACCOMMODATION

Shuthonger Common GL20 6ED
☎ 01684 298599 ▤ 01684 298599
e-mail: RobBrd1@aol.com
dir: *1m N of Tewkesbury, on A38, house on right; or 1m S of M50 junct 1, on A38 house on left*

Located to the north of Tewkesbury in pretty rural surroundings, this welcoming house offers comfortable homely bedrooms with efficient modern bathrooms and a cosy, pine furnished breakfast room. This establishment makes an excellent base for those visiting this picturesque area whether for work or pleasure.

Rooms 3 en suite (1 fmly) S £32; D £54* **Facilities** DVD tea/coffee Dinner available Cen ht ▤ **Parking** 6 **Notes** LB ❀

Thornbury Golf Lodge

★★★★ GUEST ACCOMMODATION

Bristol Rd BS35 3XL
☎ 01454 281144 📠 01454 281177
e-mail: info@thornburygc.co.uk
web: www.thornburygc.co.uk
dir: *M5 junct 16, A38 towards Thornbury. At lights (Berkeley Vale Motors) turn left, 1m on left*

With good access to both the M4 and M5 this golfing lodge offers a popular retreat for both business and leisure guests. Surrounded by pleasant scenery including the golf course, dinner and breakfast can be enjoyed in the clubhouse-style dining area where a good choice is offered. Spacious and comfortable bedrooms are located in a lodge adjacent to the main clubhouse. An excellent golf driving range is also available.

Rooms 11 en suite (11 fmly) (7 GF) S £64; D £74*
Facilities STV FTV tea/coffee Dinner available Direct Dial Cen ht Licensed ♨ 36 **Conf** Max 165 Thtr 165 Class 60 Board 40 **Parking** 200 **Notes** LB ⊗ Closed 25 Dec Civ Wed 120

Southwood House B&B

★★★ BED AND BREAKFAST

2 Bath Rd BS30 5RL
☎ 0117 937 2649 & 07792 980087 📠 0117 937 3361
e-mail: mail@southwoodhouse.com

Conveniently located with easy access to both Bristol and Bath, this welcoming, family-run B&B offers a peaceful ambience and comfortable rooms. Two rooms are located in the main house, and one larger room in an adjacent building. Breakfasts utilise fresh, local produce including eggs from the hens in the back garden, and also home-made jams. There's a good choice of pubs nearby including a couple within easy walking distance.

Rooms 2 en suite 1 annexe en suite (1 GF) S £45-£50; D £65-£70* **Facilities** FTV tea/coffee Cen ht Wi-fi ♨ **Parking** 3 **Notes** LB ⊗ No Children

Manor Farm *(SP025300)*

★★★★ FARMHOUSE

Greet GL54 5BJ
☎ 01242 602423 & 07748 077717
📠 01242 602423   Mr & Mrs R Day
e-mail: janet@dickandjanet.fsnet.co.uk
dir: *M5 junct 9, A46, B4077 towards Stow-on-the-Wold, right onto B4078. In 2m left to Greet*

Peacefully located in the quiet village of Greet, this impressive building is full of character and charm. Bedrooms and bathrooms come in a range of shapes and sizes but all are comfortable and well equipped. Breakfast is taken in traditional farmhouse style at one large table in the well furnished dining room. The views from this working farm over the surrounding hills are delightful whatever the time of year.

Rooms 3 en suite **Facilities** FTV TVL tea/coffee Cen ht ♨ **Parking** 50 **Notes** ⊗ Closed 22-28 Dec 🐄 500 acres arable/beef

Sudeley Hill Farm *(SP038276)*

★★★★ FARMHOUSE

GL54 5JB
☎ 01242 602344 📠 01242 602344   Mrs B Scudamore
e-mail: scudamore4@aol.com
dir: *Exit B4632 in Winchcombe into Castle St. White Hart Inn on corner, farm 0.75m on left*

Located on an 800-acre mixed arable and sheep farm, this 15th-century mellow stone farmhouse is full of original features including fires and exposed beams. Genuine hospitality is always on offer here with a relaxed and welcoming atmosphere. The comfortable bedrooms are filled with thoughtful extras, and memorable breakfasts are served in the elegant dining room overlooking immaculate gardens.

Sudeley Hill Farm

Rooms 3 en suite (1 fmly) S £45-£50; D £75-£80
Facilities FTV DVD TVL tea/coffee Cen ht ♨ **Parking** 10 **Notes** ⊗ Closed Xmas 🐄 800 acres sheep/arable

Wesley House

★★★★ ⊛⊛ 🍴 RESTAURANT WITH ROOMS

High St GL54 5LJ
☎ 01242 602366 📠 01242 609046
e-mail: enquiries@wesleyhouse.co.uk
web: www.wesleyhouse.co.uk
dir: *In town centre*

This 15th-century, half-timbered property is named after John Wesley, founder of the Methodist Church, who stayed here while preaching in the town. Bedrooms are small but full of character. In the rear dining room, a unique lighting system changes colour to suit the mood required, and also highlights the various floral creations by a world-renowned flower arranger. A glass atrium covers the outside terrace.

Rooms 5 en suite S £65-£75; D £90-£100* **Facilities** FTV Lounge tea/coffee Dinner available Cen ht Wi-fi **Conf** Thtr 30 Class 40 **Notes** LB ⊗ RS Sun eve Restaurant closed Civ Wed 60

See advert on opposite page

GREATER MANCHESTER

ALTRINCHAM   Map 15 SJ78

Ash Farm Country House

★★★★ GUEST ACCOMMODATION

Park Ln, Little Bollington WA14 4TJ
☎ 0161 929 9290
e-mail: ashfarm@googlemail.com
dir: *Exit A56 at Home pub into Park Ln, house at bottom
of lane on right, just before The Swan with Two Nicks pub*

A warm welcome is guaranteed at this charming 18th-
century National Trust farmhouse, which enjoys a
peaceful rural location along a quiet country lane. The
bedrooms are attractively presented and public areas
include a book-filled lounge with its crackling log fire and
cosy sofas. Free Wi-fi is available and the house is
equally popular with business and leisure guests. The
Dunham Massey Hall and Deerpark is a short stroll from
the house while Manchester Airport is just a 15-minute
drive.

Rooms 3 en suite 1 annexe en suite (1 GF) S £49-£63;
D £79-£89* **Facilities** FTV Lounge tea/coffee Cen ht
Licensed Wi-fi ⏰ **Extras** Robes **Conf** Max 10 Class 10
Parking 12 **Notes** LB ⊗ No Children 12yrs Closed 22
Dec-9 Jan

BOLTON   Map 15 SD70

Broomfield House

★★★ GUEST HOUSE

33-35 Wigan Rd, Deane BL3 5PX
☎ 01204 61570 🗎 01204 650932
e-mail: contact@broomfieldhotel.co.uk
dir: *M61 junct 5, A58 to 1st lights, straight onto A676,
premises on right*

Close to the motorway and west of the town centre,
Broomfield House has a friendly and relaxed
atmosphere. There is a comfy lounge and separate bar
area. Hearty breakfasts are served in the dining room.

Rooms 20 en suite (2 fmly) (2 GF) (6 smoking)
Facilities FTV TVL tea/coffee Cen ht Licensed Wi-fi
Parking 12

CHEADLE   Map 16 SJ88

The Governors House

★★★ INN

43 Ravenoak Rd, Cheadle Hulme SK8 7EQ
☎ 0161 488 4222
e-mail: 4718@greeneking.co.uk
web: www.gkpubs.co.uk/cheadle-hulme/governors-house

Located close to Manchester and Stockport, this
establishment is an ideal base for exploring the Cheshire
countryside. Bedrooms are tastefully decorated and
furnished, with a good range of accessories. The bar and
restaurant are popular with residents and locals, and
alfresco dining can be enjoyed in the summer months.
Children are welcome. Park and Fly Manchester is
available.

Rooms 9 en suite (1 fmly) **Facilities** FTV tea/coffee Dinner
available Direct Dial Cen ht Wi-fi **Conf** Thtr 20 Class 14
Board 14 **Parking** 87 **Notes** ⊗ No coaches

DELPH   Map 16 SD90

Wellcroft House

★★★★ 🍽 GUEST ACCOMMODATION

Bleak Hey Nook OL3 5LY
☎ 01457 875017
e-mail: wellcrofthouse@hotmail.co.uk
web: www.wellcrofthouse.co.uk
dir: *Off A62 on Standedge Foot Rd near A670 junct*

Commanding superb views down the valley below, this
former weaver's cottage offers warm traditional
hospitality to walkers on the Pennine Way and those
touring the Pennine towns and villages. Modern comforts
in all bedrooms and transport from local railway or walks
is routinely provided by the friendly proprietors.

Rooms 3 rms (2 en suite) (1 pri facs) (1 GF) S £35-£65;
D £55-£65* **Facilities** FTV TVL tea/coffee Dinner available
Cen ht Wi-fi Pool table ⏰ **Parking** 1 **Notes** LB ⊗

MANCHESTER   Map 15 SJ89

The Ascott

★★★★ GUEST ACCOMMODATION

6 Half Edge Ln, Ellesmere Park, Eccles M30 9GJ
☎ 0161 950 2453 🗎 0161 661 7063
e-mail: ascotthotelmanchester@yahoo.co.uk
web: www.ascotthotelmanchester.co.uk
dir: *M602 junct 2, left into Wellington Rd, 0.25m, right
into Abbey Grove & left into Half Edge Ln*

Set in a mainly residential area close to major routes, this
early Victorian house, once the home of the mayor of
Eccles, has been renovated to provide thoughtfully
furnished bedrooms with smart modern bathrooms. A
choice of breakfast rooms is available and there is an
elegant lounge.

Rooms 14 en suite (1 fmly) (4 GF) S £45-£75;
D £65-£105* **Facilities** FTV TVL tea/coffee Direct Dial
Cen ht Wi-fi **Parking** 12 **Notes** ⊗ Closed 22 Dec-2 Jan RS
Sun & Fri Closed 1-5pm

MANCHESTER *continued*

Thistlewood

★★★ GUEST HOUSE

203 Urmston Ln, Stretford M32 9EF
☎ **0161 865 3611** 📠 **0161 866 8133**
e-mail: iain.campbell30@ntlworld.com
dir: *M60 junct 7, A56 towards Stretford, left onto A5181 & Sandy Ln, left onto A5213*

This grand Victorian house is set in attractive grounds in a residential area close to the M60, and within easy reach are Old Trafford football and cricket grounds, and the airport. The bedrooms are well equipped, and the public rooms, including a lounge, are spacious and comfortable. Complimentary Wi-fi is also provided.

Rooms 9 en suite **Facilities** FTV TVL tea/coffee Cen ht Licensed Wi-fi **Parking** 12 **Notes** ⊗

MELLOR   Map 16 SJ98

The Moorfield Arms

★★★★ INN

Shiloh Rd SK6 5NE
☎ **0161 427 1580** 📠 **0161 427 1582**
e-mail: info@moorfieldarms.co.uk
dir: *1m NE of Mellor. Exit A6015 towards Mellor, right into Shiloh Rd, 0.3m on left*

Located in an elevated position with stunning views of the surrounding countryside including Kinder Scout, this 400-year-old property has been renovated and extended to provide spacious, comfortable public areas and tastefully furnished modern bedrooms in a sympathetic barn conversion.

Rooms 4 annexe en suite (1 fmly) (3 GF) S £65; D £80-£100* **Facilities** FTV tea/coffee Dinner available Cen ht **Conf** Max 90 Class 40 Board 25 **Parking** 100 **Notes** LB ⊗ Closed Mon (ex BHs)

STOCKPORT   Map 16 SJ89

Innkeeper's Lodge Stockport

★★★ INN

271 Wellington Rd, North Heaton Chapel SK4 5BP
☎ **0845 112 6027**
e-mail: info@innkeeperslodge.com
web: www.innkeeperslodge.com

At Innkeeper's Lodge you'll find accommodation with comfort and character in equal measure, and everything needed for a relaxing stay, from easy check-in and free parking to complimentary breakfast and a cosy pub serving great value food and drink on the doorstep. Each Lodge has quality rooms, and there are Lodges in a variety of locations from towns and cities to countryside settings across the UK.

Rooms 22 en suite (1 fmly) (1 GF) **Facilities** FTV tea/coffee Dinner available Direct Dial Wi-fi **Parking**

WIGAN   Map 15 SD50

The Beeches

★★★ RESTAURANT WITH ROOMS

School Ln, Standish WN6 0TD
☎ **01257 426432 & 421316** 📠 **01257 427503**
e-mail: mail@beecheshotel.co.uk
dir: *M6 junct 27, A5209 into Standish & into School Ln*

Located a short drive from the M6, this elegant Victorian house has been appointed to provide high standards of comfort. Bedrooms are equipped with practical and homely extras, and public areas include spacious lounges, a popular brasserie, and a self-contained function suite.

Rooms 10 en suite (4 fmly) S £35-£45; D £35-£50* **Facilities** FTV Lounge tea/coffee Dinner available Cen ht Wi-fi **Conf** Max 120 Thtr 100 Board 40 **Parking** 120 **Notes** LB ⊗ Civ Wed 60

HAMPSHIRE

ALRESFORD

See New Alresford

ALTON   Map 5 SU73

PREMIER COLLECTION

The Anchor Inn

★★★★★ ◉◉ RESTAURANT WITH ROOMS

Lower Froyle GU34 4NA
☎ **01420 23261**
e-mail: info@anchorinnatlowerfroyle.co.uk
dir: *From A3 follow Bentley signs & inn signs*

The Anchor Inn is located in the tranquil village of Lower Froyle. Luxury rooms are designed to reflect the traditional English inn style with charming decor, pictures and a selection of books. The restaurant welcomes both residents and the public with classic pub cooking, in impressive surroundings, with wooden floors and period furnishings.

Rooms 5 en suite S £120-£150; D £120-£150* **Facilities** STV FTV DVD tea/coffee Dinner available Direct Dial Cen ht Wi-fi ♨ **Parking** 30 **Notes** Closed 25 Dec Civ Wed 60

The Angel

★★★★ GUEST ACCOMMODATION

City Lodge, Gosport Rd GU34 3NN
☎ **01730 828111** 📠 **01730 828057**
e-mail: alton@citylodge.co.uk
dir: *On A32 between Alton & Petersfield*

This refurbished establishment is conveniently located on the A32 and has easy access to Alton, Winchester and Petersfield. The en suite bedrooms are very comfortable and have Hypnos beds, flat screen TVs and free Wi-fi. Breakfast, lunch and dinner are served in the pub-style restaurant, and a popular carvery is offered each day.

Rooms 21 en suite 19 annexe en suite (2 fmly) (27 GF) S £49.95-£99.95; D £49.95-£99.95 (room only)* **Facilities** FTV Lounge tea/coffee Dinner available Cen ht Licensed Wi-fi **Conf** Thtr 120 Class 60 Board 40 **Parking** 100 **Notes** LB ⊗

The Swan

★★★ INN

High St GU34 1AT
☎ **01420 83777** 📠 **01420 87975**
e-mail: 6518@greeneking.co.uk
dir: *B3004 into Alton, follow signs for town centre*

Located in the centre of the town, The Swan is a traditional coaching inn where guests have been welcomed for centuries. Bedrooms and bathrooms vary in size but are generally comfortably furnished and include some welcome extras. A varied choice of enjoyable meals is available from the all-day menu, and a good selection of well-prepared dishes is offered at breakfast.

Rooms 37 en suite (1 fmly) **Facilities** STV FTV TVL tea/coffee Dinner available Direct Dial Cen ht Wi-fi ♨ 9 **Conf** Max 120 Thtr 120 Class 80 Board 80 **Parking** 50 **Notes** Civ Wed 120

ANDOVER   Map 5 SU34

The Barn House B&B

★★★★★ 🅰 BED AND BREAKFAST

Forton SP11 6NU
☎ **01264 720544**
e-mail: hello@thebarnhousebandb.co.uk
web: www.thebarnhousebandb.co.uk
dir: *M3 junct 8, A303, B3048 to Longparish. Right to Forton, 2nd drive on left*

Rooms 2 en suite **Facilities** FTV tea/coffee Cen ht Wi-fi **Parking** 4 **Notes** ⊗

Save on B&Bs and Hotels. Book at theAA.com/hotel

HAMPSHIRE 165 ENGLAND

May Cottage

★★★★ 🅰 BED AND BREAKFAST

SP11 8LZ
☎ 01264 771241 & 07768 242166 📠 01264 771770
e-mail: info@maycottage-thruxton.co.uk
web: www.maycottage-thruxton.co.uk
dir: 3.5m W of Andover. Off A303 signed Thruxton (Village Only), opposite George Inn

Rooms 3 en suite (1 GF) S £45-£65; D £75-£90
Facilities STV FTV TVL tea/coffee Cen ht Wi-fi ⬩ 18 ⬩
Parking 5 Notes LB ⊗ ✉

ASHURST   Map 5 SU31

Kingswood Cottage

★★★★ 🏠 BED AND BREAKFAST

10 Woodlands Rd SO40 7AD
☎ 023 8029 2582 & 07866 455322
e-mail: kingswoodcottage@yahoo.co.uk
dir: Off A35 Lyndhurst to Ashurst, in village turn right over bridge signed Woodlands. Gates on right after 1st turning

Kingswood Cottage is located in Ashurst Village, a quiet area just three miles from Lyndhurst with easy access to Southampton, just six miles away. Bedrooms are comfortably appointed with traditional style decor and furnishings, guests can enjoy home-made refreshments on arrival, and bedrooms are well equipped with beverage trays and Freeview TVs making this a true home-from-home experience. Bedrooms benefit from views of the spacious well tended gardens which guests can enjoy year round. A hearty cooked or continental breakfast is served in the dining room and conservatory area.

Rooms 3 en suite S £30-£55; D £66-£75* Facilities FTV TVL tea/coffee Cen ht Wi-fi ⬩ Extras Robes, bottled water - complimentary Parking 3 Notes LB ⊗ No Children 5yrs Closed 12 Dec-2 Jan ✉

The Willows

★★★ BED AND BREAKFAST

72 Lyndhurst Rd SO40 7BE
☎ 023 8029 2745 & 07980 937862
e-mail: thewillowsashurst@hotmail.co.uk
dir: M27 junct 3 onto M271. 1.5m, at rdbt take A35 signed Lyndhurst. In Ashurst ,The Willows on right before bus stop

This property is on the edge of the New Forest, and is close to Ashurst railway station and the M27. The bedrooms are traditional in style but with modern fixtures and furnishings including free Wi-fi; the bathrooms have high quality fixtures following a complete refurbishment. Guests can enjoy a cooked or continental breakfast in the dining room.

Rooms 3 en suite (1 fmly) S £40-£45; D £70-£75*
Facilities FTV tea/coffee Cen ht Wi-fi ⬩ Parking 4
Notes No Children 5yrs Closed 2wks Xmas & New Year

Forest Gate Lodge

★★★ 🏠 GUEST HOUSE

161 Lyndhurst Rd SO40 7AW
☎ 023 8029 3026 📠 023 8029 3026
e-mail: forestgatelodge@hotmail.co.uk
dir: On A35 in village

Rooms 4 en suite (1 fmly) D £64-£74* Facilities FTV DVD tea/coffee Cen ht Wi-fi ⬩ Parking 6 Notes LB ⊗ No Children 5yrs ✉

BARTON-ON-SEA   Map 5 SZ29

PREMIER COLLECTION

Pebble Beach

★★★★★ ⬩ RESTAURANT WITH ROOMS

Marine Dr BH25 7DZ
☎ 01425 627777 📠 01425 610689
e-mail: mail@pebblebeach-uk.com
dir: A35 from Southampton onto A337 to New Milton, left into Barton Court Av to clifftop

Situated on the clifftop the restaurant at this establishment boasts stunning views towards The Needles. Bedrooms and bathrooms, situated above the restaurant, are well equipped and provide a range of accessories to enhance guest comfort. A freshly cooked breakfast is served in the main restaurant.

Rooms 4 rms (3 en suite) (1 pri facs) S £55.96; D £71.95-£99.95* Facilities FTV tea/coffee Dinner available Cen ht Wi-fi Conf Max 8 Thtr 8 Class 8 Board 8 Parking 20 Notes ⊗ RS 25 Dec & 1 Jan dinner not available No coaches

Watersedge Guest House

★★★★ GUEST ACCOMMODATION

10 Marine Drive West BH25 7QH
☎ 01425 615485 & 07922 263986
e-mail: info@watersedgeguesthouse.co.uk

Located close to New Milton and just a few miles from the New Forest, this cliff-top guest house offers modern and comfortably appointed bedrooms, and all front-facing rooms benefit from fantastic uninterrupted sea views. There are lots of extras provided, making this a true home-from-home experience. There is a spacious lounge area and a garden for guests to use, while a hearty cooked or continental breakfast can be enjoyed daily in the dining room.

Rooms 7 rms (6 en suite) (1 pri facs) (1 fmly) (2 GF) S £60; D £80-£90* Facilities FTV DVD TVL tea/coffee Cen ht Licensed Wi-fi ⬩ Hot tub - chargeable Extras Mini-fridges in all rooms Parking 8 Notes ✉

BASINGSTOKE   Map 5 SU65

Innkeeper's Lodge Basingstoke

★★★ INN

Andover Rd, Clerken Green, Oakley RG23 7EP
☎ 0845 112 6113
e-mail: info@innkeeperslodge.com
web: www.innkeeperslodge.com

At Innkeeper's Lodge you'll find accommodation with comfort and character in equal measure, and everything needed for a relaxing stay, from easy check-in and free parking to complimentary breakfast and a cosy pub serving great value food and drink on the doorstep. Each Lodge has quality rooms, and there are Lodges in a variety of locations from towns and cities to countryside settings across the UK.

Rooms 22 en suite (4 fmly) (22 GF) Facilities FTV tea/coffee Dinner available Direct Dial Wi-fi Parking 45

BRANSGORE   Map 5 SZ19

Tothill House

★★★★ BED AND BREAKFAST

Black Ln, off Forest Rd BH23 8EA
☎ 01425 674414
e-mail: enquiries@tothillhouse.com
dir: M27 onto A31 or A35, house is 0.75m NE of Bransgore centre

Built for an admiral in 1908, Tothill House is located in the southern part of the New Forest. The garden backs on to the forest, where deer, ponies and other wildlife are frequent visitors. The spacious bedrooms are furnished to a high standard, reflecting the character of the house. There is an elegant library, and a generous breakfast is served in the dining room.

Rooms 3 rms (2 en suite) (1 pri facs) S £45-£50; D £80
Facilities FTV tea/coffee Cen ht Wi-fi ⬩ Parking 6
Notes ⊗ No Children 16yrs Closed Nov-Feb ✉

BROCKENHURST   Map 5 SU30

PREMIER COLLECTION

The Cottage Lodge

★★★★★ ≜ GUEST ACCOMMODATION

Sway Rd SO42 7SH
☎ 01590 622296 📠 01590 623014
e-mail: enquiries@cottagelodge.co.uk
web: www.cottagelodge.co.uk
dir: *Exit A337 opposite Careys Manor Hotel into Grigg Ln, 0.25km over x-rds, cottage next to war memorial*

This 17th-century forester's cottage in the town centre is a good base for exploring the New Forest. The comfortable bedrooms are individually furnished and thoughtfully equipped. There is a cosy bar lounge with a fire, where tea can be served and a small selection of drinks is available.

Rooms 11 en suite 4 annexe en suite (7 GF) **Facilities** tea/coffee Cen ht Licensed Wi-fi **Parking** 15 **Notes** LB No Children 10yrs Closed Xmas

The Filly Inn

[U]

Lymington Rd SO42 7UF
☎ 01590 623449

Currently the rating for this establishment is not confirmed. This may be due to a change of ownership or because it has only recently joined the AA rating scheme.

Rooms 5 en suite **Facilities** FTV tea/coffee Dinner available Wi-fi **Parking** 40

COLDEN COMMON   Map 5 SU42

The Dell

★★★★ BED AND BREAKFAST

27 Main Rd SO21 1RP
☎ 01962 714710 & 07554 882131
e-mail: thedellguesthouse@googlemail.co.uk
dir: *M3 junct 11, B3335 to Twyford/Fair Oak through Twyford to Colden Common. On left on entering village opposite restaurant*

This beautiful 15th-century house oozes charm and boasts colourful gardens which lead to a stunning small wooded clearing; hence the name 'The Dell'. Winchester is only a few miles away and this establishment is located within walking distance of a number of dining options; the bus stop is just a stroll away. Original features have been retained in the smart, comfortable bedrooms and bathrooms, and guests can enjoy a delicious home-cooked breakfast in the charming dining room.

Rooms 2 en suite (1 fmly) (1 GF) S £60; D £80-£90 **Facilities** STV Lounge tea/coffee Cen ht Wi-fi ♨ **Extras** Fruit, water, chocolates - complimentary **Parking** 6 **Notes** ✖

DUMMER   Map 5 SU54

Tower Hill House

★★★ BED AND BREAKFAST

Tower Hill, Winchester Rd RG25 2AL
☎ 01256 398340 📠 01256 398340
e-mail: martin.hyndman@virgin.net
web: www.accommodationinbasingstoke.co.uk
dir: *In village. M3 junct 7, A30 towards Winchester, 2nd left, opposite sign for North Waltham*

Ideally situated for access to the M3 and A30, while overlooking fields and countryside, this family-run bed and breakfast is in the pretty village of Dummer, just 10 minutes away from the centre of Basingstoke. Bedrooms are simply, but comfortably furnished and a well-prepared breakfast is served in the cheerful dining room.

Rooms 4 rms (2 en suite) (1 pri facs) **Facilities** tea/coffee Cen ht Wi-fi **Parking** 6

EMSWORTH   Map 5 SU70

36 on the Quay

★★★★ ◉◉◉ RESTAURANT WITH ROOMS

47 South St PO10 7EG
☎ 01243 375592 & 372257

Occupying a prime position with far-reaching views over the estuary, this 16th-century house is the scene for some accomplished and exciting cuisine. The elegant restaurant occupies centre stage with peaceful pastel shades, local art and crisp napery together with glimpses of the bustling harbour outside. The contemporary bedrooms offer style, comfort and thoughtful extras.

Rooms 5 en suite **Facilities** tea/coffee Dinner available Cen ht **Parking** 6 **Notes** Closed 3wks Jan, 1wk late May & 1wk late Oct

Hollybank House

★★★★ BED AND BREAKFAST

Hollybank Ln PO10 7UN
☎ 01243 375502 📠 01243 378118
e-mail: anna@hollybankhouse.com
web: www.hollybankhouse.com
dir: *1m N of town centre. A259 onto B2148, 1m right into Southleigh Rd, 3rd left into Hollybank Ln, house at top*

The Georgian country house stands in a 10-acre woodland garden with a tennis court on the outskirts of Emsworth, and looks out to Chichester Harbour. Emsworth has a variety of restaurants, pubs and harbour walks.

Rooms 4 rms (3 en suite) (1 pri facs) (1 fmly) S £50-£60; D £75-£95 **Facilities** FTV DVD Lounge tea/coffee Cen ht Wi-fi ♨ ♨ ♨ **Parking** 85

Jingles

★★★★ GUEST ACCOMMODATION

77 Horndean Rd PO10 7PU
☎ 01243 373755 📠 01243 431377
e-mail: info@thejingles.co.uk
dir: *A3 (M) junct 2, follow signs for Emsworth, 4m, 1st building in Emsworth*

Jingles is a family-run business, located in the charming maritime village of Emsworth. Situated adjacent to open farmland, it's a great location for discovering both Portsmouth and Chichester. All bedrooms are en suite and decorated to a high standard. The dining room is the setting for a cooked English breakfast, and a drawing room is available for relaxing in. Wi-fi is available if required.

Rooms 28 en suite (2 fmly) (7 GF) **Facilities** FTV tea/coffee Cen ht Wi-fi **Parking** 35 **Notes** ✖

Save on B&Bs and Hotels. Book at theAA.com/hotel

HAMPSHIRE 167 ENGLAND

The Crown

★★★ INN

High St PO10 7AW
☎ 01243 307461 📠 01243 370082
e-mail: thecrownemsworth@aol.co.uk

An historic property conveniently located in the centre of town with ample parking at the back. Long winding stairs and uneven corridors lead to well-appointed bedrooms which offer a range of amenities such as flat screen TVs and Wi-fi. Freshly prepared food is served in the well-stocked bar and the restaurant.

Rooms 9 rms (7 en suite) (2 pri facs) (2 fmly) **Facilities** FTV tea/coffee Dinner available Cen ht Wi-fi **Conf** Max 24 Board 24 **Parking** 16

FAREHAM   Map 5 SU50

Wisteria House

★ ★ ★ ★   BED AND BREAKFAST

14 Mays Ln, Stubbington PO14 2EP
☎ 01329 511940 & 07742 400242
e-mail: info@wisteria-house.co.uk
dir: M27 junct 9, A27 to Fareham. Right onto B3334, at rdbt left into Mays Ln

Wisteria House is located on the edge of the village of Stubbington, just a short walk from local amenities, and only one mile from the beach at Lee-on-the-Solent. The charming and comfortable bedrooms have en suite bathrooms, are located on the ground floor, and also have Wi-fi. Off-road parking is available.

Rooms 2 en suite (2 GF) S £50; D £65* **Facilities** FTV tea/coffee Cen ht Wi-fi **Parking** 2 **Notes** ⊗ No Children 8yrs

Catisfield Cottage

★★ 🅰 BED AND BREAKFAST

1 Catisfield Ln PO15 5NW
☎ 01329 843301
dir: Exit A27 at Highlands Rd lights. Catisfield Ln 2nd left
Rooms 6 rms (3 en suite) (1 fmly) S £30-£40; D £58-£71* **Facilities** FTV TVL tea/coffee Cen ht **Parking** 6 **Notes** Closed 24 Dec-5 Jan

FARNBOROUGH   Map 5 SU85

Tudorwood Guest House

★★★★ GUEST HOUSE

164 Farnborough Rd GU14 7JJ
☎ 01252 541123
e-mail: info@tudorwood.net
dir: From A325 (Farnborough Rd) left into Sycamore Rd, left into Salisbury Rd, left into Cedar Rd, right into Farnborough Rd

A delightful Tudor-style house located just a few minutes from the town centre. Individually decorated bedrooms are well appointed with a range of useful facilities. Public areas include a pleasant conservatory lounge and intimate dining room where home-cooked dinners are available. Ample parking is provided to the front of the property.

Rooms 2 en suite 4 annexe en suite (1 fmly) (4 GF) S £45-£60; D £60-£75* **Facilities** FTV DVD TVL tea/coffee Dinner available Cen ht Wi-fi 🔒 DVD & CD library **Conf** Max 20 Thtr 20 Class 16 Board 16 **Parking** 7 **Notes** ⊗ Closed 24-29 Dec

GRAYSHOTT   Map 5 SU83

Aspects of Lynton

★★★★ BED AND BREAKFAST

Headley Rd GU26 6DL
☎ 01428 604892 & 07896 172280
dir: Approaching from N on A3, 1st left after tunnel. Follow signs for Grayshott, through village, pass church. 0.25m on left past elderly people sign

Located just a minute from Grayshott and in an elevated position with views of Ludshot Common, this property has undergone a complete renovation. There is a stylish and open-plan lounge area with a log-burning stove and a comfortable seating area. Bedrooms and bathrooms offer spacious accommodation complete with en suite facilities; Wi-fi is available throughout. A cooked and continental breakfast can be enjoyed in the conservatory.

Rooms 3 en suite D £50-£60* **Facilities** TVL tea/coffee Cen ht Wi-fi 🔒 **Extras** Snacks - complimentary **Parking** 3 **Notes** LB ⊗ No Children 10yrs 🐾

HAVANT   Map 5 SU70

The Bear

★★★ INN

15-17 East St PO9 1AA
☎ 023 9248 6501 📠 023 9247 0551
e-mail: 9110@greeneking.co.uk

This listed, former coaching inn is located in the heart of the town and has informal public rooms, which include a small cocktail bar and the Elizabethan public bar. The fully equipped bedrooms are well laid out and equally suited to both the business and leisure guest.

Rooms 42 en suite (3 fmly) **Facilities** TVL tea/coffee Dinner available Direct Dial Cen ht Wi-fi ch fac Pool table **Conf** Max 100 Thtr 100 Class 40 Board 40 **Parking** 80

HAWKLEY   Map 5 SU72

The Hawkley Inn

★★★ INN

Pococks Ln GU33 6NE
☎ 01730 827205 📠 01730 827954
e-mail: info@hawkleyinn.co.uk
web: www.hawkleyinn.co.uk
dir: A3 Liss rdbt towards Liss B3006. Right at Spread Eagle 2.5m turn left at Pococks Ln

This inn is conveniently situated just off the A3 and is a perfect base for ramblers. The rustic bar areas are in contrast to the style of contemporary, thoughtfully-equipped bedrooms; the bathrooms have powerful showers. Delicious home-made 'comfort food' is on offer at lunchtime and in the evenings, and breakfast provides a great start to the day.

Rooms 5 en suite (1 fmly) (1 GF) **Facilities** FTV tea/coffee Dinner available Cen ht Wi-fi **Parking** 2 **Notes** ⊗ No coaches

---

HAYLING ISLAND — Map 5 SU70

Ravensdale

★★★★ BED AND BREAKFAST

19 St Catherines Rd PO11 0HF
☎ 023 9246 3203 & 07802 188259
e-mail: phil.taylor@tayloredprint.co.uk
web: www.ravensdale-hayling.co.uk
dir: A27 onto A3023 at Langstone, cross Hayling Bridge, 3m to mini-rdbt, right into Manor Rd, 1m. Right by Barley Mow into Station Rd, 3rd left into St Catherines Rd

A warm welcome awaits you to this comfortable home, quietly situated near the beach and golf course. Bedrooms are attractive, very comfortable and enhanced with numerous thoughtful extras. Home cooking can be enjoyed at breakfast (and dinner by arrangement) in the dining room, and there is also a lounge area.

Rooms 3 rms (2 en suite) (1 pri facs) S £44; D £68
Facilities FTV DVD TVL tea/coffee Dinner available Cen ht Wi-fi **Extras** Flowers, chocolates **Parking** 4 **Notes** ⊗ No Children 8yrs Closed last 2wks Dec ⊜

Redwalls

★★ BED AND BREAKFAST

66 Staunton Av PO11 0EW
☎ 023 9246 6109
e-mail: daphne@redwalls.co.uk
dir: A3023 to South Hayling seafront, right along seafront & 4th right

Built around the turn of the 20th century, the characterful home of Daphne and Noel Grover offers a peaceful retreat close to the seafront and local attractions. The bedrooms and public areas enjoy a homely ambience and there is a garden and conservatory lounge for guests to use.

Rooms 3 en suite **Facilities** TVL tea/coffee Cen ht **Parking** 4 **Notes** ⊗ No Children Closed Xmas & New Year ⊜

HOOK — Map 5 SU75

Oaklea Guest House

★★★★ GUEST HOUSE

London Rd RG27 9LA
☎ 01256 762673
e-mail: reception@oakleaguesthouse.co.uk
dir: From village centre, 500yds on right on A30 towards Basingstoke

You can be sure of a warm welcome at this Victorian house located just a short drive from the M3. Bedrooms are well appointed with modern facilities. There is a comfortable lounge, and the large dining room has a bar.

Rooms 15 en suite (2 fmly) (1 GF) S £50-£60; D £65-£70* **Facilities** FTV DVD TVL tea/coffee Cen ht Licensed Wi-fi **Extras** Bottled water - complimentary **Parking** 15

Cherry Lodge Guest Accommodation

★★★ GUEST ACCOMMODATION

Reading Rd RG27 9DB
☎ 01256 762532
e-mail: cherrylodge@btinternet.com
dir: On B3349 (Reading Rd), next to Hook garden centre

This pleasant bungalow is peacefully set back from the Reading Road, and is convenient for the M3. Cherry Lodge provides extremely friendly hospitality and is popular with business guests. Breakfast is served from 6.30am. A spacious lounge is provided and bedrooms are well equipped.

Rooms 7 en suite (1 fmly) (7 GF) S £37-£47; D £52-£62 (room only)* **Facilities** STV FTV Lounge tea/coffee Direct Dial Cen ht Wi-fi **Extras** Fridge **Parking** 20 **Notes** ⊗ Closed Xmas-New Year

Poachers

Ⓤ

Alton Rd, South Warnborough RG29 1RP
☎ 01256 862218

Currently the rating for this establishment is not confirmed. This may be due to a change of ownership or because it has only recently joined the AA rating scheme.

Rooms 6 en suite **Facilities** FTV tea/coffee Dinner available Direct Dial Wi-fi **Parking** 20

HYTHE — Map 5 SU40

Four Seasons B&B

★★★★ GUEST ACCOMMODATION

Hamilton Rd SO45 3PD
☎ 023 8084 5151 & 07973 194660 ☒ 023 8084 6285
e-mail: the-four-seasons@btconnect.com
dir: M27 junct 2 onto A326. Continue towards Fawley/Hythe, at 4th rdbt take exit signed Hythe & Marine Park, on left after 500mtrs

The Four Seasons B&B is located in Hythe with easy access to both Southampton and the New Forest. Bedrooms are tastefully decorated with modern decor and furnishings, and all rooms are equipped with Freeview TV and free Wi-fi throughout. The dining room and guest lounge is open plan with a small preparation kitchen area, there is a TV and DVD library and a computer with broadband. A cooked and continental breakfast is available, and for the early riser is served from 6:30am on weekdays.

Rooms 12 rms (7 en suite) (2 fmly) (2 GF) S £32-£35; D £72* **Facilities** FTV TVL tea/coffee Cen ht Wi-fi ⌚ **Parking** 11 **Notes** LB ⊗

ISLE OF WIGHT

See Wight, Isle of

LEE-ON-THE-SOLENT — Map 5 SU50

West Wind Guest House

★★★★ GUEST ACCOMMODATION

197 Portsmouth Rd PO13 9AA
☎ 023 9255 2550
e-mail: info@west-wind.co.uk
dir: M27 junct 11 follow Gosport & Fareham signs, B3385 for Lee-on-the-Solent. At seafront left along Marine Pde, 600mtrs left into Portsmouth Rd. West Wind on right

This family-run guest accommodation is found in a quiet, residential location and within walking distance of the beach and town centre. The bedrooms are comfortable and nicely appointed, some with flat screen TV and all with free Wi-fi. There is an attractive breakfast room and off-street parking.

Rooms 6 en suite (1 GF) S fr £50; D fr £65* **Facilities** FTV DVD iPod docking station tea/coffee Cen ht Wi-fi **Parking** 6 **Notes** ⊗ No Children 8yrs

Apple Tree Cottage B&B

★★★ BED AND BREAKFAST

159 Portsmouth Rd PO13 9AD
☎ 023 9255 1176 ☒ 023 9235 2492
e-mail: appletreecottage@ntlworld.com
web: www.leeonthesolentbedandbreakfast.com
dir: From Marine Pde pass Old Ship public house into Portsmouth Rd. Pass Inn by the Sea on right, 4th house

Situated just 50 yards from the seafront and Sailing Club, Apple Tree Cottage is a small, family-run establishment offering a warm welcome, individual attention, and high standards of comfort. Rooms have a maritime theme and enjoy a wide range of useful facilities including DVD players and Wi-fi, along with high quality linen and towels. The Lighthouse Room has a four-poster with drapes, and the Solent can be seen from the bedrooms. Breakfast is served in the pretty dining room.

Rooms 3 en suite (1 fmly) **Facilities** FTV tea/coffee Cen ht Wi-fi **Parking** 3 **Notes** ⊗ No Children 6yrs ⊜

LYMINGTON　　　　　　　　　Map 5 SZ39

See also Milford-on-Sea

The Olde Barn

★★★★ BED AND BREAKFAST

Christchurch Rd, Downton SO41 0LA
☎ 01590 644939 & 07813 679757 ▤ 01590 644939
e-mail: julie@theoldebarn.co.uk
dir: On A337 3m W of Lymington, in Downton

A 17th-century barn and associated buildings have been restored to provide stylish accommodation. Bedrooms are smartly decorated and furnished, and the spacious bathrooms have power showers. There is a comfortable lounge, and a traditional English breakfast is served around a farmhouse table in the attractive dining room.

Rooms 3 annexe en suite (3 GF) S £50–£75; D £50–£80* **Facilities** FTV DVD TVL tea/coffee Cen ht Wi-fi ♨ 27 ♨ **Parking** 6 **Notes** ⊗ No Children 10yrs

---

LYNDHURST　　　　　　　　　Map 5 SU30

Temple Lodge

★★★★ ⬠ GUEST ACCOMMODATION

2 Queens Rd SO43 7BR
☎ 023 8028 2392 ▤ 023 8000 0091
e-mail: templelodge@btinternet.com
web: www.templelodge-guesthouse.com
dir: M27 junct 2/3 onto A35 to Ashurst & Lyndhurst. Temple Lodge on 2nd corner on right, opposite forest

Temple Lodge is a well appointed Victorian house with very friendly hosts. Guests will enjoy easy access to the New Forest and Lyndhurst town centre, with good off-road parking. The bedrooms feature lots of thoughtful extras including mini-bars. The breakfasts should not be missed.

Rooms 6 en suite (1 fmly) D £60–£100* **Facilities** FTV DVD TVL tea/coffee Cen ht Wi-fi ♨ **Extras** Mini-fridge with snacks/soft drinks - chargeable **Parking** 6 **Notes** LB ⊗ No Children 12yrs

---

Whitemoor House

★★★★ ⬠ GUEST ACCOMMODATION

Southampton Rd SO43 7BU
☎ 023 8028 3043
e-mail: enquiries@whitemoorhouse.co.uk
dir: 0.5m NE of town centre on A35

A warm welcome is assured at this well-run establishment in the New Forest. The comfortable bedrooms are brightly decorated and well equipped. A full English breakfast is served with home-made preserves in the tastefully appointed breakfast room.

Rooms 6 en suite (1 fmly) S £45–£60; D £70–£90 **Facilities** FTV TVL tea/coffee Cen ht Licensed Wi-fi ♨ 9 ♨ **Parking** 6 **Notes** ⊗ No Children 10yrs Closed Dec-25 Jan ⊜

Clayhill House

★★★★ BED AND BREAKFAST

SO43 7DE
☎ 023 8028 2304
e-mail: clayhillhouse@tinyworld.co.uk
web: www.clayhillhouse.co.uk
dir: Exit M27 junct 2. A35 to Lyndhurst then A337 signed Brockenhurst, 0.75m from village

Set at the edge of this attractive town, and convenient for visiting the New Forest and coastal attractions nearby, Clayhill House is a well-appointed property, which offers friendly service and comfortable accommodation. The bedrooms are particularly well equipped with thoughtful extras. Freshly-cooked breakfasts are served in the dining room.

Rooms 3 en suite (1 fmly) S £50–£80; D £70–£80* **Facilities** FTV tea/coffee Cen ht Wi-fi **Parking** 6 **Notes** LB ⊗ No Children 7yrs Closed 22 Dec-4 Jan

---

Little Hayes

★★★★ GUEST ACCOMMODATION

43 Romsey Rd SO43 7AR
☎ 023 8028 3816
e-mail: wendy@littlehayes.co.uk
dir: M27 junct 1, A337. On entering Lyndhurst, 200yds on right

A friendly, well-run guest accommodation located a few moments walk from the town centre, pubs and restaurants. Breakfast featuring local produce is served in the cosy dining room. Little Hayes provides an ideal base for touring the New Forest National Park, and benefits from off-road parking.

Rooms 5 rms (4 en suite) (1 pri facs) D £70–£84* **Facilities** FTV DVD tea/coffee Cen ht Wi-fi ♨ **Parking** 6 **Notes** ⊗ No Children 14yrs Closed Dec-Jan

---

The Rufus House

★★★★ ⬠ GUEST ACCOMMODATION

Southampton Rd SO43 7BQ
☎ 023 8028 2930
e-mail: stay@rufushouse.co.uk
dir: From Lyndhurst centre onto A35 (Southampton Rd), 300yds on left

Located on the edge of town, this delightful family-run Victorian property is well situated for exploring the New Forest. The brightly decorated bedrooms are appointed to a high standard, while the turret lounge and the garden terrace are great spots for relaxing.

Rooms 10 en suite (1 fmly) (2 GF) **Facilities** tea/coffee Cen ht Wi-fi ♨ 18 **Parking** 12 **Notes** ⊗ No Children 5yrs

---

Burwood Lodge

★★★★ ⬛ GUEST ACCOMMODATION

27 Romsey Rd SO43 7AA
☎ 023 8028 2445 & 07717 767997 ▤ 023 8028 2057
e-mail: burwoodlodge@yahoo.co.uk
Rooms 7 en suite (2 fmly) (1 GF) **Facilities** FTV TVL tea/coffee Cen ht Wi-fi **Parking** 10 **Notes** ⊗ No Children 6yrs ⊜

LYNDHURST *continued*

Heather House

★ ★ ★ GUEST ACCOMMODATION

Southampton Rd SO43 7BQ
☎ 023 8028 4409 📠 023 8028 4431
e-mail: enquiries@heatherhouse.co.uk
web: www.heatherhouse.co.uk
dir: *M27 junct 1, A337 to Lyndhurst. At lights in centre turn left, establishment 800yds on left*

This impressive double-fronted Edwardian house stands in attractive gardens on the edge of town with views of the New Forest. Bedrooms are comfortably appointed with one suitable for families. Breakfast is served in the pleasant dining room.

Rooms 10 en suite (1 fmly) S £25-£45; D £60-£90*
Facilities FTV TVL tea/coffee Cen ht Licensed Wi-fi 🔒
Parking 12 **Notes** LB ⊗ No Children 7yrs Closed 23 Dec-2 Jan

---

MICHELDEVER   Map 5 SU53

The Dove Inn

★ ★ ★ ★ 🍴 INN

Andover Rd SO21 3AU
☎ 01962 774288 📠 01962 774952
e-mail: info@the-dove-inn.co.uk
web: www.the-dove-inn.co.uk
dir: *M3 junct 8 merge onto A303, take exit signed Micheldever Station, follow station signs into Andover Rd, on left*

Set in the Hampshire countryside close to Micheldever station, this traditional inn serves guest ales and has a popular dining room with both blackboard specials and carte options. Bedrooms feature a range of comfortable accessories to enhance guest comfort, and the en suite bathrooms are well appointed with good quality toiletries. There's complimentary Wi-fi throughout the building. Ample parking is available.

Rooms 5 en suite (1 fmly) S £65; D £85* **Facilities** STV FTV tea/coffee Dinner available Cen ht Wi-fi Pool table **Conf** Max 50 Thtr 50 Class 20 Board 30 **Parking** 20

MILFORD ON SEA   Map 5 SZ29

PREMIER COLLECTION

Ha'penny House

★ ★ ★ ★ ★ 🏠 GUEST ACCOMMODATION

16 Whitby Rd SO41 0ND
☎ 01590 641210
e-mail: info@hapennyhouse.co.uk
web: www.hapennyhouse.co.uk
dir: *A337 at Everton onto B3058, through village into Cliff Rd, right into Cornwallis Rd, right at T-junct into Whitby Rd, house 50yds on left*

This delightful house is in a peaceful residential area, close to the cliff top from which there are stunning views towards the Isle of Wight. Individually styled bedrooms are beautifully appointed and equipped with a host of thoughtful extras. There is a stylish lounge and an elegant dining room where superb breakfasts are served.

Rooms 4 en suite S £48-£55; D £75-£89*
Facilities FTV TVL tea/coffee Cen ht Wi-fi **Parking** 7
Notes LB ⊗ No Children 12yrs

Pilgrims Rest

★ ★ ★ ★ GUEST ACCOMMODATION

Westover Rd SO41 0PW
☎ 01590 641167
e-mail: pilgrimsrestbandb@yahoo.co.uk
dir: *From Lymington follow New Milton signs, in 2m left onto B3058 through village, 2nd left*

A traditional establishment with friendly hosts, very well appointed rooms and a breakfast that is a great start to the day. Pilgrims Rest lies within walking distance of the beach and the town of Milford on Sea. All rooms are en suite.

Rooms 4 en suite **Facilities** FTV tea/coffee Cen ht Wi-fi **Parking** 6 **Notes** LB ⊗ 🚭

NEW ALRESFORD   Map 5 SU53

Haygarth

★ ★ ★ 🅰 BED AND BREAKFAST

82 Jack Lyns Ln SO24 9LJ
☎ 01962 732715 & 07986 372895
dir: *B3046 from New Alresford centre for Cheriton, Haygarth 0.5m on right*

Rooms 3 rms (2 en suite) (1 pri facs) (3 GF) S fr £35; D fr £65 **Facilities** TVL tea/coffee Cen ht **Parking** 7 **Notes** LB ⊗ 🚭

PETERSFIELD   Map 5 SU72

Border Cottage

★ ★ ★ ★ 🅰 BED AND BREAKFAST

4 Heath Rd GU31 4DU
☎ 01730 263179
e-mail: lawrence@bordercottage.co.uk
web: www.bordercottage.co.uk
dir: *From A3 take A272 Midhurst exit. Right at rdbt, stay on left in one-way system. Turn left after Red Lion into Heath Rd*

Rooms 1 en suite S £35-£45; D £65-£70 **Facilities** FTV tea/coffee Cen ht Wi-fi **Notes** ⊗ No Children

Save on B&Bs and Hotels. Book at theAA.com/hotel

HAMPSHIRE 171 ENGLAND

PORTSMOUTH & SOUTHSEA
Map 5 SU60

St Margaret's Lodge
★★★★ GUEST HOUSE

3 Craneswater Gate PO4 0NZ
☎ 023 9282 0097 ▤ 023 9282 0097
e-mail: enquiries@stmargarets-southsea.co.uk
web: www.stmargarets-southsea.co.uk
dir: *From South Parade Pier E along A288 St Helens Parade, 2nd left*

This establishment is in a quiet residential area close to the seafront and town centre. The attractive bedrooms have co-ordinated soft furnishings and many thoughtful extras. Breakfast is served in the smart dining room and there are two lounges and a cosy bar.

Rooms 14 en suite (1 fmly) S £38–£50; D £60–£95*
Facilities FTV Lounge TVL tea/coffee Cen ht Wi-fi
Parking 5 Notes ⊗ Closed 21 Dec–2 Jan

Upper Mount House
★★★★ GUEST ACCOMMODATION

The Vale, Southsea PO5 2EQ
☎ 023 9282 0456 ▤ 023 9282 0456
e-mail: uppermountportsmouth@btconnect.com
dir: *Exit M275 for D-Day Museum into road opposite museum, over x-rds, right at T-junct, right again*

This impressive Victorian villa retains many original features and is peacefully located in a residential cul-de-sac. Public areas include a comfortable lounge and an attractive dining room where a fine collection of Venetian glassware is displayed. The bedrooms are spacious and well equipped, and come in a variety of styles.

Rooms 15 en suite (3 fmly) (7 GF) Facilities FTV TVL tea/coffee Direct Dial Cen ht Wi-fi Parking 17 Notes ⊗ Closed 2wks Xmas

Amberley Court
★★★ GUEST ACCOMMODATION

97 Waverley Rd, Southsea PO5 2PL
☎ 023 9273 7473 ▤ 023 9275 2343
e-mail: mail@amberleycourt.co.uk
dir: *Exit A288 (South Parade) near pier onto B2155 (Clarendon Rd) then Waverley Rd*

Amberley Court has a convenient location less than half a mile from the seafront and attractions. The comfortable bedrooms have bright modern co-ordinated fabrics, and come with good facilities. Some rooms and a smart conservatory-dining room are in a second house nearby.

Rooms 9 en suite (4 fmly) Facilities TVL tea/coffee Cen ht Wi-fi Parking 4 Notes ⊗

RINGWOOD
Map 5 SU10

Moortown Lodge
★★★★ GUEST ACCOMMODATION

244 Christchurch Rd BH24 3AS
☎ 01425 471404 ▤ 01425 476527
e-mail: enquiries@moortownlodge.co.uk
dir: *1m S of Ringwood. Exit A31 at Ringwood onto B3347, follow signs to Sopley. Lodge adjacent to David Lloyds Leisure Club*

Just five minutes south of Ringwood, Moortown Lodge offers free Wi-fi, well-equipped rooms with DVD players, and full English breakfasts. Rooms are individually decorated and have comfortable bedding, telephone, tea and coffee making facilities, and digital TV. Breakfasts are cooked to order daily. Moortown Lodge was originally a Georgian hunting lodge. It is ten miles from Dorset's coastline and 20 minutes from Christchurch.

Rooms 7 en suite (3 fmly) (2 GF) S £76–£86; D £86–£96*
Facilities FTV DVD tea/coffee Direct Dial Cen ht Wi-fi Access to facilities of adjoining leisure club Parking 9 Notes LB

Amberwood
★★★★ GUEST ACCOMMODATION

3/5 Top Ln BH24 1LF
☎ 01425 476615 ▤ 01425 476615
e-mail: maynsing1@sky.com
dir: *A31 onto B3347, over rdbt, left into School Ln, left into Top Ln*

This delightful Victorian home is situated in a quiet residential area within easy walking distance of the town centre. Bedrooms are attractively furnished and decorated, with many thoughtful extras. A substantial breakfast is served around one large table in the conservatory, which overlooks the well-tended garden. A lounge is also available.

Rooms 2 en suite (1 fmly) Facilities FTV TVL tea/coffee Direct Dial Cen ht Wi-fi Parking 2 Notes ⊗ No Children 12yrs Closed Xmas & New Year ⊗

Little Forest Lodge
★★★★ GUEST HOUSE

Poulner Hill BH24 3HS
☎ 01425 478848 ▤ 01425 473564
dir: *1.5m E of Ringwood on A31*

A warm welcome is given to guests, and their pets, at this charming Edwardian house set in two acres of woodland. Bedrooms are pleasantly decorated and equipped with thoughtful extras. Both the attractive wood-panelled dining room and the delightful lounge, with bar and wood-burning fire, overlook the gardens.

Rooms 6 en suite (3 fmly) (1 GF) S £45–£50; D £70
Facilities FTV Lounge tea/coffee Cen ht Licensed ⊌
Parking 10

Candlesticks Inn
★★★ GUEST HOUSE

136 Christchurch Rd BH24 3AP
☎ 01425 472587 ▤ 01425 471600
e-mail: info@hotelnewforest.co.uk
web: www.hotelnewforest.co.uk
dir: *0.5m SE of town centre on B3347*

This 15th-century thatched property offers accommodation with a restaurant on the edge of town, and is convenient for Bournemouth and the New Forest National Park. Ample parking.

Rooms 8 annexe en suite (1 fmly) (4 GF) S £49–£70; D £60–£75* Facilities FTV Lounge tea/coffee Dinner available Direct Dial Cen ht Licensed Wi-fi Sauna ⑧ Sauna also available for wheelchair users Parking 30 Notes LB ⊗ Closed 23 Dec–10 Jan

SOUTHAMPTON
Map 5 SU41

PREMIER COLLECTION

White Star Tavern, Dining and Rooms
★★★★★ ◉◉ INN

28 Oxford St SO14 3DJ
☎ 023 8082 1990 ▤ 023 8090 4982
e-mail: reservations@whitestartavern.co.uk
web: www.whitestartavern.co.uk
dir: *M3 junct 14, A33 towards Ocean Village*

This stylish tavern is conveniently located in the popular Oxford Street area, a moment's walk to the city centre. Bedrooms take their name from the ships of the White Star Line, and are smartly appointed and well equipped with many thoughtful extras. The main bar and restaurant areas provide comfortable seating in well styled surroundings. Award-winning cuisine is served in the White Star restaurant whilst in the morning an à la carte breakfast is served in the bar area. Private meeting space is also available.

Rooms 13 en suite S £65–£105; D £95–£145 (room only)* Facilities FTV DVD iPod docking station TVL tea/coffee Dinner available Direct Dial Cen ht Wi-fi Extras Mini-bar, fresh milk & water, robes in some rooms Conf Max 12 Thtr 12 Board 12 Notes LB ⊗ Closed 25–26 Dec

SOUTHAMPTON *continued*

Heather Gables

★★★★ 🏠 GUEST ACCOMMODATION

Dodwell Ln, Bursledon SO31 1DJ
☎ 023 8040 4925
e-mail: heather.gables@talktalk.net
web: www.heathergables.co.uk
dir: *M27 junct 8, 600yds N on Dodwell Ln, towards Hedge End*

Suitable for both business and leisure travellers, Heather Gables offers comfortable en suite accommodation. Both bedrooms feature balconies overlooking the well manicured garden and countryside. Friendly proprietors are on hand to assist with local dining recommendations. Award-winning breakfasts are served at the communal dining table or on the terrace in the warmer months. Off-road parking is an additional plus.

Rooms 2 en suite S £49; D £69 **Facilities** FTV DVD tea/coffee Cen ht Wi-fi **Parking** 2 **Notes** ⊗ 🐾

Alcantara Guest House

★★★★ 🏠 GUEST ACCOMMODATION

20 Howard Rd, Shirley SO15 5BN
☎ 023 8033 2966 📠 023 8049 6163
e-mail: alcantaraguesthouse@sky.com
dir: *0.5m NW of city centre. Exit A3057 into Howard Rd*

A warm welcome is assured at this Victorian property, named after the ocean liner to reflect the establishment's shipping connections and location close to the city centre. Bedrooms are comfortable and well decorated and have many thoughtful extras. An appetising breakfast can be served in the bright and airy dining room. Secure off-road parking is available.

Rooms 9 rms (6 en suite) (1 fmly) (2 GF) S fr £34; D fr £68* **Facilities** FTV tea/coffee Cen ht Wi-fi 🐾 **Parking** 7 **Notes** ⊗ No Children 12yrs RS 2wks Xmas

Hunters Lodge

★★★★ GUEST ACCOMMODATION

25 Landguard Rd, Shirley SO15 5DL
☎ 023 8022 7919
e-mail: hunterslodge.hotel@virgin.net
web: www.hunterslodgehotel.net
dir: *500yds NW of Southampton Central station. Exit A3057 (Shirley Rd) into Languard Rd*

Located in a leafy residential area close to the city centre and convenient for the docks, ferry terminal, university and hospital, this double-fronted Victorian house provides business and leisure guests with comfortable, well-equipped bedrooms. Full English breakfast is served at shared tables in the elegant dining room. There is also a television lounge and a well-stocked bar.

Rooms 14 en suite (1 fmly) (1 GF) S £46-£50; D £77-£80* **Facilities** FTV DVD TVL tea/coffee Direct Dial Cen ht Licensed Wi-fi **Parking** 16 **Notes** ⊗

Landguard Lodge

★★★ GUEST HOUSE

21 Landguard Rd SO15 5DL
☎ 023 8063 6904 📠 023 8063 2258
e-mail: info@landguardlodge.co.uk
web: www.landguardlodge.co.uk
dir: *500yds NW of Southampton Central station. Off A3057 Shirley Rd into Landguard Rd*

This Victorian house is in a quiet residential area a short walk from the railway station. The bedrooms are bright, comfortable and well equipped with many thoughtful extras.

Rooms 11 en suite (1 fmly) (2 GF) S fr £42; D fr £68* **Facilities** FTV tea/coffee Cen ht Wi-fi **Parking** 3 **Notes** ⊗ No Children 5yrs

The Brimar Guest House

★★ GUEST ACCOMMODATION

10-14 High St, Totton SO40 9HN
☎ 023 8086 2950 📠 023 8086 1301
e-mail: info@brimar-guesthouse.co.uk
dir: *3m W of city centre, exit A35 (Totton bypass) into Totton High St*

This property offers practical, comfortable accommodation at reasonable prices. Not all rooms are en suite but bathrooms are well situated. Breakfast is served in the dining room or as a take-away option. The Brimar is well placed for the M27 and Southampton docks, and off-road parking is available.

Rooms 21 rms (8 en suite) (13 pri facs) (2 fmly) (8 GF) **Facilities** FTV Cen ht Wi-fi **Parking** 20 **Notes** ⊗

Mayview Guest House

★★ 🅰 GUEST HOUSE

30 The Polygon SO15 2BN
☎ 023 8022 0907 & 07973 874194 📠 07977 017921
e-mail: info@mayview.co.uk
Rooms 9 rms (1 en suite) (1 fmly) (1 GF) **Facilities** FTV tea/coffee Cen ht Wi-fi **Notes** ⊗ Closed 25 Dec

SOUTHSEA

See Portsmouth & Southsea

STOCKBRIDGE   Map 5 SU33

York Lodge

★★★★ BED AND BREAKFAST

Five Bells Ln, Nether Wallop SO20 8HE
☎ 01264 781313 & 07765 412254
e-mail: bradley@york-lodge.co.uk
web: www.york-lodge.co.uk
dir: *Exit A30 or A343 onto B3084, into Hosketts Ln, fork left into Five Bells Ln, 1st house on right. Automatic gates (drive car close to open)*

Located in the picturesque village used as one of the sets for Agatha Christie's *Miss Marple* TV series, this charming house has comfortable accommodation in a self-contained wing. Bedrooms are stylishly presented with many thoughtful extra facilities. The dining room overlooks peaceful gardens.

Rooms 2 en suite (2 GF) S £40-£50; D £75-£80* **Facilities** STV FTV Lounge tea/coffee Cen ht Wi-fi 🐾 **Parking** 4 **Notes** No Children 8yrs 🐾

The Three Cups Inn

★★★ INN

High St SO20 6HB
☎ 01264 810527
e-mail: manager@the3cups.co.uk

A former coaching inn on the high street in a popular town, with its own parking. The bedrooms are comfortable and well equipped, and food is available every evening.

Rooms 8 en suite (3 fmly) **Facilities** tea/coffee Dinner available Cen ht Wi-fi Fishing **Parking** 15

Save on B&Bs and Hotels. Book at theAA.com/hotel

HAMPSHIRE 173 ENGLAND

The Grosvenor

★★★ INN

23 High St SO20 6EU
☎ 01264 810606 ≣ 01264 810747
e-mail: 9180@greeneking.co.uk

Located between the historic cathedral cities of Winchester and Salisbury and a stone's throw from the River Test, The Grosvenor provides en suite accommodation within the traditional setting of this Georgian building. Bedrooms have been designed with guest comfort in mind. The Tom Cannon Restaurant is popular with both residents and locals alike, and provides a good range of locally sourced produce including game when in season.

Rooms 14 en suite 12 annexe en suite (6 GF) S £49-£59; D £79-£89* Facilities FTV tea/coffee Dinner available Direct Dial Cen ht Wi-fi Fishing 🔒 Conf Max 105 Thtr 105 Class 85 Board 40 Parking 16 Notes Civ Wed 85

The Peat Spade Inn

Ⓤ

Village St, Longstock SO20 6DR
☎ 01264 810612
e-mail: info@peatspadeinn.co.uk

Currently the rating for this establishment is not confirmed. This may be due to a change of ownership or because it has only recently joined the AA rating scheme.

Rooms 8 en suite S £90-£145; D £90-£145*

WARNFORD — Map 5 SU62

George & Falcon

★★★★ INN

Warnford Rd SO32 3LB
☎ 01730 829623 ≣ 01730 352222
e-mail: reservations@georgeandfalcon.com
web: www.georgeandfalcon.com
dir: Adjacent to A32 in village

Set within the picturesque village of Warnford located close to major transport links to Winchester, Portsmouth and Southampton. Following a refurbishment, the bedrooms are tastefully appointed to retain the charm and character of this coaching inn yet provide modern facilities. Traditional fayre is served in the popular restaurant and bar, and there is a large decking area which proves a welcome addition in summer months.

Rooms 6 en suite (1 fmly) S £55-£85; D £71-£109* Facilities FTV Lounge tea/coffee Dinner available Cen ht Wi-fi ♨ 18 Fishing Riding 🔒 Extras Speciality toiletries Conf Max 30 Thtr 30 Class 15 Board 15 Parking 47 Notes LB Closed Xmas & 1 Jan Civ Wed 135

WHERWELL — Map 5 SU34

The White Lion

Ⓤ

Winchester Rd SP11 7JF
☎ 01264 860317

Currently the rating for this establishment is not confirmed. This may be due to a change of ownership or because it has only recently joined the AA rating scheme.

Rooms 6 en suite Facilities tea/coffee Dinner available Wi-fi Parking 22

WINCHESTER — Map 5 SU42

PREMIER COLLECTION

Giffard House

★★★★★ GUEST HOUSE

50 Christchurch Rd SO23 9SU
☎ 01962 852628 ≣ 01962 856722
e-mail: giffardhotel@aol.com
dir: M3 junct 11, at rdbt 3rd exit onto A333 (St Cross road) for 1m. Pass BP garage on right, next left, 2nd right. 150mtrs on left

A warm welcome awaits at this stunning 19th-century Victorian house. The accommodation is luxurious, comfortable and well equipped for both the business and leisure traveller. There is also a fully licensed bar set in the elegant conservatory.

Rooms 13 en suite (1 fmly) (4 GF) Facilities STV FTV Lounge tea/coffee Direct Dial Cen ht Licensed Wi-fi Conf Max 15 Thtr 15 Class 15 Board 13 Parking 13 Notes ⊗ Closed 24 Dec-2 Jan

PREMIER COLLECTION

Orchard House

★★★★★ 🏠 BED AND BREAKFAST

3 Christchurch Gardens, St Cross SO23 9TH
☎ 01962 861544 ≣ 01962 861988
e-mail: h.hope@hotmail.co.uk
dir: B3335 to Winchester & St Cross, after 2nd lights left into Barnes Close, right into Christchurch Rd, right again into Christchurch Gdns, last house on right

This friendly, family-run B&B is in a peaceful cul-de-sac, close to Winchester and the famous college, yet within easy reach of the M3. It offers a relaxed atmosphere, professional service and warm hospitality. The bedroom is spacious, comfortable and very well equipped. Gardens are well tended, and the balcony overlooking the rear garden can be used for breakfast on warmer summer mornings. There is also ample parking.

Rooms 1 en suite S £55-£65; D £85-£90* Facilities STV FTV DVD TVL tea/coffee Cen ht Wi-fi 🔒 Extras Speciality toiletries, fruit/snacks - complimentary Parking 2 Notes ⊗ No Children 6yrs 🐾

PREMIER COLLECTION

29 Christchurch Road

★★★★★ BED AND BREAKFAST

29 Christchurch Rd SO23 9SU
☎ 01962 868661 ≣ 01962 868661
e-mail: dilke@waitrose.com
dir: M3 junct 11 follow signs for Winchester & St Cross (B3335), through 2 sets of lights, pass BP garage, left into Ranelagh Rd. 2nd right into Christchurch Rd, house at junct with Grafton Rd

Located a short distance from the historic city of Winchester, this quality accommodation is tastefully appointed and offers comfortable bedrooms and bathrooms. The guest terrace is the ideal place to relax on a summer's afternoon within the well kept garden. A wide selection of breakfast items are served in the dining room around the communal table. Ample on-street parking is available.

Rooms 3 rms (2 en suite) (1 pri facs) Facilities FTV Lounge tea/coffee Cen ht Wi-fi 🔒 Notes ⊗ No Children 5yrs 🐾

The Old Vine

★★★★ INN

8 Great Minster St SO23 9HA
☎ 01962 854616
e-mail: reservations@oldvinewinchester.com
web: www.oldvinewinchester.com
dir: M3 junct 11 towards St Cross, right at Green Man Pub, left into Symonds St, left into Little Minster St

Overlooking the cathedral, this historic inn has been extensively and sympathetically restored and updated. Rooms are named and themed after various designers, there is permit parking, and food is served in the restaurant and bar downstairs.

Rooms 5 en suite (1 fmly) S £90-£155; D £100-£195* Facilities FTV tea/coffee Dinner available Cen ht Wi-fi 🔒 Extras Speciality toiletries, water, fruit juices - complimentary Notes No coaches

WINCHESTER *continued*

Running Horse Inn

★★★★ @ @ INN

88 Main Rd, Littleton SO22 6QS
☎ 01962 880218 ▤ 01962 886596
e-mail: runninghorseinn@btconnect.com
web: www.runninghorseinn.co.uk
dir: *B3049 out of Winchester 1.5m, turn right into Littleton after 1m, Running Horse on right*

Situated in a pretty rural location, yet with easy access to the M3, this is a great location for business and leisure travellers visiting Hampshire. Offering quality accommodation, the Running Horse is minimalist in its design, and provides comfortable beds and a small workstation area. Highlights of a stay here are a meal in the smart restaurant or a drink in the bar.

Rooms 9 annexe en suite (1 fmly) (9 GF) S £67.50; D £90* **Facilities** FTV tea/coffee Dinner available Cen ht Wi-fi **Parking** 40 **Notes** No coaches
See advert on this page

24 Clifton Road

★★★ BED AND BREAKFAST

SO22 5BU
☎ 01962 851620
e-mail: a.williams1997@btinternet.com
dir: *500yds NW of city centre. B3090 Romsey Rd W from city centre, Clifton Rd 2nd right*

This delightful house is in a quiet residential area close to the railway station and High Street. It combines town-house elegance with a homely cottage charm, and is handy for local walks. The bedroom is comfortably furnished and the bathroom has a deep claw-foot bath. There is a lounge and a dining room.

Rooms 1 rm (1 pri facs) S £35; D £60 **Facilities** TVL tea/coffee Cen ht Wi-fi **Parking** 2 **Notes** ⊗ No Children 6yrs ⊠

The Westgate Inn

★★★ INN

2 Romsey Rd SO23 8TP
☎ 01962 820222 ▤ 01962 820222
e-mail: wghguy@yahoo.co.uk
dir: *M3 junct 9 follow signs to city centre, on corner of Romsey Rd & Upper High St*

The Westgate Inn is well placed at the west end of the city near the castle. A popular restaurant serves good, home-prepared Indian meals and snacks. The traditional bar is always busy. The attractive and good-sized bedrooms on two floors are well equipped.

Rooms 8 rms (6 en suite) D £75-£90* **Facilities** FTV DVD iPod docking station tea/coffee Dinner available Cen ht Wi-fi **Conf** Max 12 Board 12 **Notes** No Children 10yrs No coaches

My Home

★★ BED AND BREAKFAST

29 Wordsworth Close SO22 5BY
☎ 01962 890337 & 07503 738759
dir: *From N: M3 junct 9 follow signs to railway station. Right, under bridge, 2nd left at rdbt, keep left. Straight over at T-junct, right then left*

Located in a residential area approximately twenty minutes walk from the centre of Winchester. You are guaranteed a warm welcome at this bed and breakfast which offers two bedrooms with shared bathroom facilities. A hearty breakfast will set you up for the day which is served around the family table in the dining room.

Rooms 2 rms (1 pri facs) S fr £37.50; D fr £65* **Facilities** FTV tea/coffee Cen ht Wi-fi **Extras** Snacks & fresh fruit **Notes** LB ⊗ No Children 5yrs ⊠

HEREFORDSHIRE

ADFORTON Map 9 SO47

Brick House Farm

★★★★ ⌂ BED AND BREAKFAST

SY7 0NF
☎ 01568 770870
e-mail: info@adforton.com
dir: *On A4110 in Adforton opposite St Andrew's Church*

Very much at the heart of the village community, this 16th-century longhouse provides high standards of comfort and good facilities. Superb beds and smart, modern private bathrooms can be found in the thoughtfully furnished accommodation. Comprehensive breakfasts featuring locally-sourced produce, are served in the cosy combined sitting and dining room. A warm welcome is assured.

Rooms 2 rms (2 pri facs) S £75; D £75* **Facilities** STV FTV Lounge tea/coffee Cen ht Wi-fi **Parking** 2 **Notes** LB No Children 12yrs

---

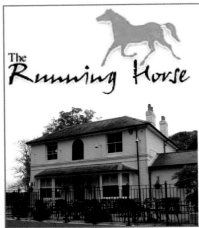

Save on B&Bs and Hotels. Book at **theAA.com/hotel**

HEREFORDSHIRE 175 ENGLAND

BODENHAM
Map 10 SO55

The Coach House at England Gate's Inn

★★★★ ⊜ INN

HR1 3HU

☎ 01568 797286

e-mail: englandsgate@btconnect.com

This fine black and white 16th-century inn is run by the McNeil family, who pride themselves on quality service. The inn is set in attractive gardens which are ideal for alfresco dining on warmer days. The detached coach house has comfortable bedrooms with modern en suite facilities; the views are spectacular from the upstairs rooms. Continental breakfast is served in the coach house dining area on weekdays, and a full cooked breakfast is available at weekends.

Rooms 7 en suite (2 fmly) (4 GF) **Facilities** FTV DVD tea/coffee Dinner available Direct Dial Cen ht Wi-fi ৪ **Extras** Bottled water **Conf** Max 12 Board 12 **Parking** 30

BROCKHAMPTON
Map 10 SO53

Ladyridge Farm

★★★★ ⊜ GUEST HOUSE

HR1 4SE

☎ 01989 740220 📠 01989 740220

e-mail: carolgrant@ladyridgefarm.fsworld.co.uk

dir: Exit B4224 signed Brockhampton Church between How Caple & Fownhope. 400yds on right after thatched church

This working farm, set in delightful countryside, provides a peaceful haven and is also home to rare breed ducks, poultry and sheep. The traditional styled bedrooms are spacious and thoughtfully equipped. Meals, served family-style in the attractive dining room, use local, fresh ingredients and home-produced free-range eggs.

Rooms 3 rms (2 pri facs) (1 fmly) S £32; D £60* **Facilities** DVD tea/coffee Dinner available Cen ht Wi-fi ৪ **Extras** Robes **Parking** 6 **Notes** LB ⊗

BROMYARD
Map 10 SO65

Linton Brook Farm (SO676538)

★★★★ FARMHOUSE

Malvern Rd, Bringsty WR6 5TR

☎ 01885 488875 Mrs S Steeds

e-mail: stay@lintonbrookfarm.com

dir: Exit A44 1.5m E of Bromyard onto B4220 signed Malvern. Farm 0.5m on left

Dating back some 400 years, this large house has a wealth of character and has been renovated to provide modern comforts. Accommodation is spacious and there is a comfortable sitting room with a welcoming wood-burning stove. The breakfast room has exposed beams, antique furniture and an inglenook fireplace.

Rooms 3 rms (2 en suite) (1 pri facs) **Facilities** STV FTV TVL tea/coffee Dinner available Cen ht Wi-fi **Parking** 12 **Notes** ⊗ Closed Xmas & New Year RS Nov-Feb No single person single night bookings ⊜ 68 acres grassland

GARWAY HILL
Map 9 SO42

Garway Moon Inn

Ⓤ

HR2 8RQ

☎ 01600 750270

e-mail: info@garwaymooninn.co.uk

dir: From Hereford, S on A49. Right onto A466, right again onto B4521. At Broad Oak turn right to Garway

Currently the rating for this establishment is not confirmed. This may be due to a change of ownership or because it has only recently joined the AA rating scheme.

Rooms 3 en suite (2 fmly) S £62.50-£82.50; D £70-£90* **Facilities** STV FTV DVD tea/coffee Dinner available Cen ht Licensed Wi-fi ৪ **Extras** Snacks - complimentary **Parking** 20

HEREFORD
Map 10 SO53

See also Little Dewchurch

PREMIER COLLECTION

Somerville House

★★★★★ GUEST ACCOMMODATION

12 Bodenham Rd HR1 2TS

☎ 01432 273991 📠 01432 268719

e-mail: enquiries@somervillehouse.net

web: www.somervillehouse.net

dir: A465, at Aylestone Hill rdbt towards city centre, left at Southbank Rd, leading to Bodenham Rd

Situated in a quiet tree-lined residential road, Somerville House is a detached late-Victorian villa that provides a boutique-style experience. Expect a warm and friendly welcome from Rosie and Bill who offer quality accommodation with high standards of luxury and comfort. All bedrooms are spacious, with a good range of quality extras. Breakfast is served in the light and contemporary dining room at individual tables. There is a terraced garden to the rear where guests can sit and relax, or indoors, they can make use of the comfortable lounge. There is ample parking.

Rooms 12 en suite (2 fmly) (1 GF) **Facilities** FTV tea/coffee Cen ht Licensed Wi-fi Arrangement with health spa **Conf** Max 10 Thtr 10 Class 10 Board 10 **Parking** 10 **Notes** ⊗

The Bay Horse Inn

★★★★ INN

236 Kings Acre Rd HR4 0SD

☎ 01432 273351

e-mail: info@bayhorseinnhereford.co.uk

dir: On A438, pass Wyevale, 1000yds on left

Located just outside the city centre The Bay Horse combines comfortable bedrooms and bathrooms with an excellent range of food available during the day and evening. With a relaxed ambience and welcoming service throughout the inn, guests also benefit from the use of a car park and a range of outdoor seating for warmer weather. A good selection of real ales, wine and bottled ciders are also available.

Rooms 8 annexe en suite (1 fmly) (4 GF) S £59; D £69* **Facilities** FTV TVL tea/coffee Dinner available Cen ht Wi-fi ৬ **Conf** Max 20 Thtr 20 Class 20 Board 20 **Parking** 30 **Notes** LB ⊗

HEREFORD *continued*

Norfolk House

★★★★ GUEST ACCOMMODATION

23 Saint Martin St HR2 7RD
☎ 01432 340900
e-mail: info@norfolkhousehereford.co.uk
web: www.norfolkhousehereford.co.uk

Norfolk House is a large mid-terraced Georgian property situated south of the River Wye in Hereford, only 100 metres from the city's old bridge and the Left Bank Village. An ideal location for exploring the nearby towns of Leominster, Ludlow, Ledbury, Kington, Ross-on-Wye and Worcester. There are five comfortable en suite bedrooms including doubles (with king-sized beds) and twin rooms. In the welcoming dining room a hearty breakfast, made from fresh local produce, is provided. Wi-fi is available.

Rooms 5 en suite (1 fmly) **Facilities** FTV tea/coffee Cen ht Wi-fi **Parking** 3 **Notes** ⊗ No Children 5yrs

No 21

★★★★ GUEST ACCOMMODATION

21 Aylestone Hill HR1 1HR
☎ 01432 279897 & 07967 525403
e-mail: jane@21aylestonehill.co.uk
dir: On A4103 from Worcester to rdbt at approach to Hereford. Take 1st exit to town centre (A465)

A warm welcome from Ken and Jane awaits at this fine detached property, not far from the train station, that offers peace and quiet. The property has recently undergone a total renovation, and all bedrooms and smart modern bathrooms are appointed to a high standard. The bedrooms are spacious with many extras; one ground-floor room, with a wet room, is ideal for guests that have difficulty with stairs. Breakfast is served in the spacious dining room at the front of the property. There is ample secure parking.

No 21

Rooms 4 en suite (1 GF) S £45-£65; D £70-£80* **Facilities** FTV TVL tea/coffee Cen ht Wi-fi **Parking** 8 **Notes** ⊛

Sink Green Farm (SO542377)

★★★★ FARMHOUSE

Rotherwas HR2 6LE
☎ 01432 870223 📠 01432 870223 **Mr D E Jones**
e-mail: enquiries@sinkgreenfarm.co.uk
web: www.sinkgreenfarm.co.uk
dir: 3m SE of city centre. Exit A49 onto B4399 for 2m

This charming 16th-century farmhouse stands in attractive countryside and has many original features, including flagstone floors, exposed beams and open fireplaces. Bedrooms are traditionally furnished and one has a four-poster bed. The pleasant garden has a comfortable summer house, hot tub and barbecue.

Rooms 3 en suite S £40-£45; D £75-£85 **Facilities** FTV iPod docking station Lounge TVL tea/coffee Cen ht Wi-fi Hot tub **Parking** 10 **Notes** LB ⊛ 180 acres beef

Heron House

★★★ 🅰 BED AND BREAKFAST

Canon Pyon Rd, Portway HR4 8NG
☎ 01432 761111 📠 01432 760603
e-mail: info@theheronhouse.com
web: www.theheronhouse.com
dir: A4103 onto A4110to Portway x-rds, Heron House 200yds on left

Rooms 2 rms (1 en suite) **Facilities** tea/coffee Cen ht **Parking** 5 **Notes** ⊗ No Children 10yrs ⊛

HOLME LACY Map 10 SO53

Prickett's Place

⊔

Bolstone HR2 6LZ
☎ 01432 870221

Currently the rating for this establishment is not confirmed. This may be due to a change of ownership or because it has only recently joined the AA rating scheme.

Rooms 2 en suite D £34-£40* **Notes** Closed 25-31 Dec

LEDBURY Map 10 SO73

Moor Court Farm (SO639447)

★★★★ FARMHOUSE

Stretton, Grandison HR8 2TP
☎ 01531 670408 📠 01531 670408 **Mrs E Godsall**
dir: 1.5m E of A417 at Upper Eggleton

This 15th-century house is situated on a mixed farm with working oast houses where hops are dried. Bedrooms are thoughtfully equipped and furnished, and one has a four-poster. Public areas include a comfortable lounge with an impressive stone fireplace and a dining room, where breakfast includes local produce and eggs from the farm.

Rooms 3 en suite **Facilities** tea/coffee Dinner available Cen ht Licensed Fishing **Parking** 5 **Notes** ⊗ No Children 8yrs ⊛ 200 acres mixed/livestock/hops

The Seven Stars

★★★★ 🍺 INN

11 The Homend HR8 1BN
☎ 01531 635800
e-mail: paulford@sevenstars.co.uk
web: www.sevenstarsledbury.co.uk
dir: 4m from M50

This 16th-century high street inn is reputedly the oldest in this picturesque market town. Owners Paul and Sharon are welcoming and friendly. The interior of the inn is modern and contemporary with a stylish dining area to the rear. The bedrooms have very comfortable beds and good space with some thoughtful extras. Breakfast is freshly prepared and hearty. Parking is available at the nearby public car park.

Rooms 3 en suite (2 fmly) **Facilities** STV tea/coffee Dinner available Cen ht Wi-fi **Notes** ⊗ No coaches

Save on B&Bs and Hotels. Book at **theAA.com/hotel**

HEREFORDSHIRE 177 ENGLAND

LEINTWARDINE Map 9 SO47

PREMIER COLLECTION

The Lion

★★★★★ ⓖ 🍴 RESTAURANT WITH ROOMS

High St SY7 0JZ
☎ 01547 540203 & 540747 📠 01547 540747
e-mail: enquiries@thelionleintwardine.co.uk
web: www.thelionleintwardine.co.uk
dir: *Beside bridge on A4113 (Ludlow to Knighton road) in Leintwardine*

This quiet country inn in the picturesque village of Leintwardine, and set beside the River Teme, is just a short distance from Ludlow and Craven Arms. The interior has been totally renovated and all the contemporary bedrooms are en suite. Dining is taken seriously here and the modern, imaginative food uses the freshest local ingredients. The well-stocked bar offers a selection of real ales and lagers and there is a separate drinkers' bar too. The inn is particularly popular with families as the garden has a secure children's play area, and in warmer months guests can eat alfresco. The friendly staff help to make any visit memorable.

Rooms 8 en suite (1 fmly) S £75–£90; D £100–£120*
Facilities FTV Lounge tea/coffee Dinner available Direct Dial Cen ht Wi-fi Fishing 🅿 **Conf** Max 25 Class 25 Board 25 **Parking** 25 **Notes** ⊗ Closed 25 Dec

LEOMINSTER Map 10 SO45

PREMIER COLLECTION

The Old Rectory Pembridge

★★★★★ BED AND BREAKFAST

Bridge St, Pembridge HR6 9EU
☎ 01544 387968
e-mail: lynnpickard@hotmail.co.uk
web: www.theoldrectorypembridge.co.uk
dir: *A44 to Pembridge into Bridge St towards river, house on right before bridge*

Set in a peaceful location close to the River Arrow on the Black & White Village Trail, this 1852 Gothic building provides luxurious accommodation and the owners extend a warm welcome to all their guests. The bedrooms have antique furniture and quality soft furnishings along with a range of thoughtful extras; the spacious en suite bathrooms add to the luxury experience. Public areas include a large lounge with a log fire, and an elegant dining room where excellent breakfasts are served around a communal table.

Rooms 3 en suite **Facilities** FTV DVD TVL tea/coffee Cen ht Wi-fi 🅿 **Parking** 6 **Notes** ⊗ No Children

PREMIER COLLECTION

Hills Farm (SO564638)

★★★★★ 🏠 FARMHOUSE

Leysters HR6 0HP
☎ 01568 750205 Mrs J Conolly
e-mail: info@thehillsfarm.co.uk
web: www.thehillsfarm.co.uk
dir: *Off A4112 (Leominster to Tenbury Wells), on outskirts of Leysters*

Set in a peaceful location with views over the countryside, this property dates in part from the 16th century. The friendly, attentive proprietors provide a relaxing and homely atmosphere. The attractive bedrooms, in the converted barns, are spacious and comfortable. Breakfasts, served in the dining room and conservatory, feature fresh local produce.

Rooms 3 annexe en suite (1 GF) S £50–£52; D £82–£84
Facilities FTV iPod docking station Lounge tea/coffee Cen ht Wi-fi 🅿 **Parking** 8 **Notes** ⊗ No Children 12yrs Closed Dec-Feb 120 acres arable

LITTLE DEWCHURCH Map 10 SO53

Cwm Craig Farm (SO535322)

★★★★ FARMHOUSE

HR2 6PS
☎ 01432 840250 Mrs G Lee
e-mail: cwmcraigfarm@gmail.com
dir: *Exit A49 into Little Dewchurch, right in village, Cwm Craig 1st farm on left*

This Georgian farmhouse is situated on the outskirts of the village in glorious countryside and offers spacious accommodation. Bedrooms are carefully furnished and public areas consist of a comfortable lounge, games room and dining rooms; one of which is offered for the use of families. Hearty breakfasts include eggs from the farm's hens.

Rooms 3 en suite (1 fmly) S £35–£40; D £64–£74
Facilities FTV TVL tea/coffee Cen ht Wi-fi Pool table **Parking** 6 **Notes** ⊗ Closed Xmas & New Year 190 acres organic/arable

ROSS-ON-WYE Map 10 SO52

PREMIER COLLECTION

Wilton Court Restaurant with Rooms

★★★★★ ⓖⓖ 🍴 RESTAURANT WITH ROOMS

Wilton Ln HR9 6AQ
☎ 01989 562569 📠 01989 768460
e-mail: info@wiltoncourthotel.com
dir: *M50 junct 4, A40 towards Monmouth at 3rd rdbt left signed Ross-on-Wye, 1st right, on right*

Dating back to the 16th century, this establishment has great charm and a wealth of character. Standing on the banks of the River Wye and just a short walk from the town centre, there is a genuinely relaxed, friendly and unhurried atmosphere created by hosts Roger and Helen Wynn and their reliable team. Bedrooms are tastefully furnished and well equipped, while public areas include a comfortable lounge, traditional bar and pleasant restaurant with a conservatory extension overlooking the garden. High standards of food, using fresh, locally sourced ingredients, are offered.

Rooms 10 en suite (1 fmly) S £90–£155; D £125–£175*
Facilities FTV TVL tea/coffee Dinner available Direct Dial Cen ht Wi-fi 🛶 ♿ 18 Fishing 🅿 **Conf** Thtr 50 Class 20 Board 20 **Parking** 20 **Notes** LB Closed 3-15 Jan Civ Wed 50

PREMIER COLLECTION

Orles Barn

★★★★★ ⓖⓖ 🍴 RESTAURANT WITH ROOMS

Wilton HR9 6AE
☎ 01989 562155 📠 01989 768470
e-mail: reservations@orles-barn.co.uk
web: www.orles-barn.co.uk
dir: *A49/A40 rdbt outside Ross-on-Wye, take slip road between petrol station & A40 to Monmouth. 100yds on left*

The proprietors of this character property offer a warm welcome to all their guests. Older sections of the property date back to the 14th and 17th centuries when it was a farmhouse with a barn. The property offers comfortable bedrooms, a smart cosy lounge with a bar and a spacious restaurant. Dinner and Sunday lunch are offered on a balanced menu of fresh local and seasonal ingredients. Breakfast also utilises quality local produce and makes a good start to the day.

Rooms 6 en suite (1 fmly) (1 GF) S £80–£130; D £130–£180* **Facilities** FTV DVD iPod docking station tea/coffee Dinner available Cen ht Wi-fi **Conf** Max 100 Thtr 100 Class 50 Board 40 **Parking** 20 **Notes** LB Civ Wed 100

ROSS-ON-WYE *continued*

Caradoc Court

★★★★★ 🅰 BED AND BREAKFAST

Sellack HR9 6LS
☎ 01989 730257 & 07836 296607
e-mail: kathy@caradoccourt.co.uk
web: www.caradoccourt.co.uk
dir: *M50 junct 4 onto A40. At 2nd rdbt onto A49 for Hereford, then 2nd right for Sellack. 2m to Lough Pool Inn, driveaway opposite*

Rooms 4 en suite D £90-£120 Facilities FTV DVD TVL Cen ht Licensed Wi-fi 🏊 Snooker Extras Fruit, flowers - complimentary Parking 20 Notes ⊗ No Children 12yrs Closed Nov-Feb Civ Wed 100

Brookfield House

★★★★ GUEST ACCOMMODATION

Over Ross St HR9 7AT
☎ 01989 562188 & 07595 041613
e-mail: info@brookfield-house.co.uk
dir: *500yds N of town centre. Exit B4234 (Over Ross St) into Brookmead & into driveway*

Dating from the 18th century, this large detached house lies just north of the town centre with easy access to the M50 then the M5. The new owners Robin and Kaye extend a warm welcome to all their guests. Bedrooms are very spacious, comfortably appointed and well equipped with many thoughtful extras. Breakfast is served in the light and airy dining room at separate tables. A relaxing lounge is available for guest use, as are the attractive gardens. Parking is available to the rear of the property.

Rooms 3 en suite (1 fmly) S fr £58; D fr £76*
Facilities Lounge tea/coffee Cen ht Wi-fi Parking 12 Notes ⊗

Benhall Farm

★★★★ 🏠 BED AND BREAKFAST

Wilton HR9 6AG
☎ 01989 563900 & 07900 264612 📠 01989 563900
e-mail: info@benhallfarm.co.uk
web: www.benhallfarm.co.uk
dir: *From Wilton rdbt (A40 & A49 junct), take exit towards M50. On dual-carriageway immediately left at No Through Road sign. Benhall Farm at end of lane*

A warm welcome can be expected at Benhall Farm, a working dairy and arable farm of 335 acres which has been part of the Duchy of Cornwall Estate since 2000. The location is on the outskirts of Ross-on-Wye on the banks of the River Wye and has easy access to the M50, Hereford, Abergavenny, Monmouth, and the Forest of Dean. The bedrooms are comfortable, spacious and many guest extras are provided, including Wi-fi. A lounge is available for guests' use and the dining room is where hearty breakfasts are served at the communal table. Parking is available to the front of the property.

Rooms 3 en suite S £50-£80; D £72-£80* Facilities FTV TVL tea/coffee Cen ht Wi-fi Fishing 🎣 Extras Fridges in all rooms, home-made biscuits Parking 6 Notes LB ⊗ Closed 20 Dec-10 Jan

Lea House

★★★★ 🍴 🚃 GUEST ACCOMMODATION

Lea HR9 7JZ
☎ 01989 750652 📠 01989 750652
e-mail: enquiries@leahouse.co.uk
web: www.leahouse.co.uk
dir: *4m SE of Ross on A40 towards Gloucester in Lea*

This former coaching inn, near Ross-on-Wye, makes a good base for exploring the Forest of Dean and the Wye Valley, and the atmosphere is relaxed and comfortable. The individually furnished bedrooms are thoughtfully equipped and very homely. Breakfast in the oak-beamed dining room offers home-made breads, freshly squeezed juice, fresh fruit platters, local sausages and fish choices. Home-cooked dinners are available by prior arrangement.

Rooms 3 rms (2 en suite) (1 pri facs) (1 fmly) S £45-£55; D £68-£88* Facilities FTV TVL tea/coffee Dinner available Cen ht Wi-fi 🛜 Parking 4 Notes LB

Thatch Close

★★★★ GUEST ACCOMMODATION

Llangrove HR9 6EL
☎ 01989 770300
e-mail: info@thatchclose.co.uk
web: www.thatchclose.co.uk
dir: *Off A40 at Symonds Yat West/Whitchurch junct to Llangrove, right at x-rds after Post Office & before school. Thatch Close 0.6m on left*

Standing in 13 acres, this sturdy 18th-century farmhouse is full of character. Expect a wonderfully warm atmosphere with a genuine welcome from your hosts. The homely bedrooms are equipped for comfort with many thoughtful extras. Breakfast is served in the elegant dining room, and a lounge is available. The extensive patios and gardens are popular in summer, providing plenty of space to find a quiet corner and relax with a good book.

Rooms 3 en suite S £45-£50; D £65-£75* Facilities TVL tea/coffee Cen ht Wi-fi Parking 8 Notes LB 🐾

The Whitehouse Guest House

★★★ GUEST HOUSE

Wye St HR9 7BX
☎ 01989 763572
e-mail: whitehouseross@aol.com
dir: *Exit A40 dual-carriageway at Wilton, pass over bridge, take 1st left White House on right*

A warm welcome awaits at this 18th-century guest house which is located adjacent to the River Wye and just a short walk from the town centre. The bedrooms are tastefully appointed and provide a thoughtful range of extras including Wi-fi access. There are four-poster rooms and single rooms available. A hearty breakfast is provided at individual tables in the dining room, and evening meals are available with prior notice. Parking is on the road to the front.

Rooms 7 en suite (2 fmly) (2 smoking) S £45; D £65* Facilities FTV tea/coffee Dinner available Cen ht Licensed Wi-fi 🛜 Extras Sweets Notes LB Closed 24-25 Dec

---

SHOBDON   Map 9 SO46

The Bateman Arms

★★★★ INN

HR6 9LX
☎ 01568 708374 📠 08701 236418
e-mail: diana@batemanarms.co.uk
web: www.batemanarms.co.uk
dir: *On B4362 in Shobdon*

Located in the village, parts of this inn date back over 400 years; Bill and Diana Mahood offer a warm welcome to all their guests. The accommodation comprises six modern bedrooms located in a separate building, all are comfortable and well appointed. There are plenty of oak beams and a large log fire adds to the warm ambience of the public areas. In addition to the friendly welcome, the food, using carefully prepared local produce, is a key feature.

Rooms 6 annexe en suite (2 fmly) (3 GF) S £55-£60; D £85-£95* Facilities FTV DVD tea/coffee Dinner available Cen ht Wi-fi Pool table 🎱 Games room Parking 40 Notes LB

STAPLOW   Map 10 SO64

The Oak Inn

★★★★ INN

HR8 1NP
☎ 01531 640954
e-mail: oakinn@wyenet.co.uk
dir: *2m N of Ledbury on B4214*

The Oak Inn is a privately owned, delightful country inn surrounded by a cider apple orchard. Situated north of the market town of Ledbury, yet within easy access of the Malvern Hills, this 17th-century building has been totally renovated. The bedrooms are modern, spacious and well appointed with under-floor heating, and beds that have quality pocket-sprung mattresses. The public areas feature log-burning fires, flagstone floors and wooden beams. Dining is available seven days a week, and the open-plan kitchen allows diners to see their meals being prepared. Wi-fi is accessible throughout.

Rooms 4 en suite (1 fmly) S £55-£60; D £80-£90* Facilities FTV DVD tea/coffee Dinner available Cen ht Wi-fi 🛜 Parking 40 Notes No coaches

Save on B&Bs and Hotels. Book at **theAA.com/hotel**

HEREFORDSHIRE 179 **ENGLAND**

SYMONDS YAT (EAST) Map 10 SO51

See also Coleford (Gloucestershire)

The Royal Lodge

★★★★ 🏠 🍴 GUEST ACCOMMODATION

HR9 6JL
☎ 01600 890238 📠 01600 891425
e-mail: info@royalhotel-symondsyat.com
web: www.royallodgesymondsyat.co.uk
dir: *Midway between Ross and Monmouth exit A40 at signs for Goodrich & B4229 to Symonds Yat East*

The Royal Lodge stands at the top end of the village overlooking the River Wye. Bedrooms are spacious and comfortable, and come complete with flat screen TVs and many guest extras; the bathrooms offer modern facilities. There is a cosy lounge with an open fireplace and two bars are available. Meals are offered in the welcoming restaurant which provides carefully prepared meals, using fresh and local ingredients. Staff are pleasant and friendly.

Rooms 20 en suite (5 fmly) **Facilities** FTV DVD TVL tea/coffee Dinner available Direct Dial Cen ht Licensed Wi-fi Fishing ⚓ **Extras** Mineral water **Conf** Max 70 Thtr 70 Class 20 Board 30 **Parking** 150 **Notes** LB Civ Wed 80

Saracens Head Inn

★★★★ 🍴 INN

HR9 6JL
☎ 01600 890435
e-mail: contact@saracensheadinn.co.uk
web: www.saracensheadinn.co.uk
dir: *Exit A40 at South Herefordshire Motorcaravan Centre, signed Symonds Yat East, 2m*

Dating from the 16th century, the friendly, family-run Saracens Head faces the River Wye and has wonderful views. The well-equipped bedrooms are decorated in a cottage style, and there is a cosy lounge, an attractive dining room, and a popular public bar with a riverside patio. All meals are offered from a regularly-changing and comprehensive menu, and include locally-sourced produce.

Saracens Head Inn

Rooms 8 en suite 2 annexe en suite (1 GF) S £59-£75; D £89-£138* **Facilities** FTV TVL tea/coffee Dinner available Direct Dial Cen ht Wi-fi Fishing Pool table **Conf** Max 25 Thtr 25 Class 25 Board 25 **Parking** 35 **Notes** LB No Children 7yrs No coaches

See advert on this page

VOWCHURCH Map 9 SO33

Yew Tree House

★★★★ 🅰 BED AND BREAKFAST

Bacho Hill HR2 9PF
☎ 01981 251195 📠 01981 251195
e-mail: enquiries@yewtreehouse-hereford.co.uk
web: www.yewtreehouse-hereford.co.uk
dir: *On B4348 between Kingstone & Vowchurch*

Rooms 3 en suite (2 fmly) D £80-£95* **Facilities** FTV DVD Lounge TVL tea/coffee Dinner available Cen ht Wi-fi ⚓ **Extras** Chocolates, mineral water - complimentary **Parking** 4 **Notes** LB 🐾

WHITCHURCH   Map 10 SO51

Norton House Bed & Breakfast & Cottages

★★★★ 🛏 BED AND BREAKFAST

Old Monmouth Rd HR9 6DJ
☎ **01600 890046 & 07805 260890** 📠 **08723 526284**
e-mail: enquiries@norton-house.com

Built as a farmhouse, the original property dates back 300 years and retains much character such as flagstone floors and beamed ceilings. A warm and friendly welcome awaits all guests from hosts Jayne and Bill. The bedrooms, including a four-poster room, are individually styled and furnished for maximum comfort. Excellent local produce is used to create an imaginative range of breakfast dishes. The charming public areas include a snug lounge, with a wood-burning stove, and a breakfast room with a communal table. Parking is off-road, and self-catering cottages are also available. Norton House was a Finalist in the AA Friendliest B&B of the Year Award 2012-13.

Rooms 3 en suite S £55-£60; D £75-£80* **Facilities** FTV iPod docking station Lounge TVL tea/coffee Cen ht Wi-fi ♿ **Extras** Fruit - complimentary **Parking** 5 **Notes** LB

Portland House Guest House

★★★★ 🛏 GUEST ACCOMMODATION

HR9 6DB
☎ **01600 890757**
e-mail: info@portlandguesthouse.co.uk
web: www.portlandguesthouse.co.uk
dir: Exit A40 between Monmouth & Ross-on-Wye. Follow signs for Whitchurch & Symonds Yat West

Portland House is an impressive property, dating in part to the 17th century, and situated in the picturesque Wye Valley. Comfortable bedrooms include a large family room, an accessible bedroom on the ground floor, and a four-poster suite. All have a thoughtful range of extras. Walkers can use the Boot Room and guests have use of the laundry, the terrace garden area, and the attractive lounge. Breakfast, with home-made bread and up to eight kinds of home-made preserve, is served around the shared dining table, or at a separate table in the cosy elegant dining room. With prior arrangement, evening meals can be provided.

Rooms 6 en suite (2 fmly) (1 GF) S £55-£70; D £70-£95* **Facilities** FTV DVD Lounge tea/coffee Dinner available Cen ht Licensed Wi-fi ♿ **Extras** Speciality toiletries, mini-bar, fruit - chargeable **Parking** 6 **Notes** LB Closed 23 Dec-Jan

YARKHILL   Map 10 SO64

Garford Farm (SO600435)

★★★★ FARMHOUSE

HR1 3ST
☎ **01432 890226** 📠 **01432 890707 Mrs H Parker**
e-mail: garfordfarm@btconnect.com
dir: Exit A417 at Newtown x-rds onto A4103 for Hereford, farm 1.5m on left

This black and white timber-framed farmhouse, set on a large arable holding, dates from the 17th century. Its character is enhanced by period furnishings, and fires burn in the comfortable lounge during colder weather. The traditionally furnished bedrooms, including a family room, have modern facilities.

Rooms 2 en suite (1 fmly) S fr £40; D fr £60* **Facilities** Lounge tea/coffee Cen ht ♿ **Parking** 6 **Notes** No Children 2yrs Closed 25-26 Dec 🚫 700 acres arable

HERTFORDSHIRE

ASHWELL   Map 12 TL23

The Three Tuns

★★★ 🅰 INN

6 High St SG7 5NL
☎ **01462 742101** 📠 **01462 743662**
e-mail: info@threetunshotel.co.uk
dir: A1M junct 10, after 1m signs for Ashwell

Rooms 6 en suite (2 fmly) **Facilities** FTV tea/coffee Dinner available Cen ht Wi-fi **Conf** Max 36 Thtr 24 Class 36 Board 18 **Parking** 24 **Notes** Civ Wed 150

BALDOCK   Map 12 TL23

The White House

★★★★ BED AND BREAKFAST

Newnham SG7 5JU
☎ **01462 742745 & 07836 260865**
e-mail: info@thenewnhamwhitehouse.com
web: www.thenewnhamwhitehouse.com
dir: A1(M) junct 10 onto A507 towards Baldock. After 500yds turn left signed Newnham & Ashwell. At T-junct turn right, last house on left before narrow bridge

A warm welcome is assured at this delightful home. Refreshment on arrival can be served either in the drawing room or weather permitting on the terrace. All bedrooms are well appointed and offer guests a good range of amenities with comfort in mind. Quality breakfast featuring local sourced ingredients is served around a communal table in the dining room.

Rooms 2 rms (1 en suite) (1 pri facs) (2 fmly) S £40-£60; D £50-£70* **Facilities** FTV Lounge tea/coffee Cen ht Wi-fi **Extras** Fruit & snacks - complimentary **Parking** 3 **Notes** 🚫 Closed 20 Dec-5 Jan 🚫

BISHOP'S STORTFORD   Map 6 TL42

Broadleaf Guest House

★★★ BED AND BREAKFAST

38 Broadleaf Av CM23 4JY
☎ **01279 835467**
e-mail: b-pcannon@sky.com
dir: 1m SW of town centre. Exit B1383 into Whittinton Way & Friedburge Av; Broadleaf Av 6th left

A delightful detached house situated in a peaceful residential area close to the town centre, and within easy striking distance of the M11 and Stansted Airport. The pleasantly decorated bedrooms are carefully furnished and equipped with many thoughtful touches. Breakfast is served in the smart dining room, which overlooks the pretty garden.

Rooms 2 rms (1 fmly) **Facilities** FTV tea/coffee Cen ht **Parking** 2 **Notes** 🚫

BUNTINGFORD   Map 12 TL32

Sword Inn Hand

★★★★ INN

Westmill SG9 9LQ
☎ **01763 271356**
e-mail: welcome@theswordinnhand.co.uk
web: www.theswordinnhand.co.uk
dir: In Westmill, off A10 S of Buntingford

Set within the peaceful village of Westmill amid rolling countryside, this charming 14th-century inn offers excellent accommodation and a friendly and relaxed atmosphere. The purpose-built, ground-floor bedrooms are located just off the rear gardens; they are very well-equipped and carefully appointed rooms that have their own access. Character public rooms offer a choice of restaurant and bar dining options, along with a choice of draught ales.

Rooms 4 en suite (4 GF) **Facilities** STV FTV TVL tea/coffee Dinner available Cen ht Wi-fi **Parking** 25 **Notes** 🚫

HARPENDEN   Map 6 TL11

The Silver Cup

★★★★ INN

5 St Albans Rd AL5 2JF
☎ **01582 713095** 📠 **01582 469713**
e-mail: info@silvercup.co.uk
web: www.silvercup.co.uk
dir: 200yds SW of Harpenden station on A1081 St Albans Rd

Located south of Harpenden High Street opposite the common, this small family-owned inn offers comfortable, well equipped rooms with many additional extras such as an honesty bar and home-made biscuits. Public areas are stylish and well presented and the attractive restaurant

Save on B&Bs and Hotels. Book at **theAA.com/hotel**

HERTFORDSHIRE 181 **ENGLAND**

serves a superior quality menu, complemented by real ales and a good wine list. Service is friendly and helpful.

Rooms 6 en suite (1 fmly) **Facilities** TVL tea/coffee Dinner available Cen ht Wi-fi **Parking** 7 **Notes** ⊗ No coaches

HERTFORD — Map 6 TL31

PREMIER COLLECTION

Rigsbys Guest House

★★★★★ GUEST HOUSE

25 Saint Andrew St SG14 1HZ
☎ 01992 535999
e-mail: matt@rigsbysguesthouse.com
dir: In town centre

This charming townhouse enjoys a prominent position in the busy market town of Hertford. Built in the 18th century it is very well appointed with luxurious spacious bedrooms and stylish modern bathrooms. There is a small courtyard at the rear and Rigsbys Restaurant is a popular venue for lunch or afternoon tea. There is ample parking at the rear of the house and free Wi-fi is available in all bedrooms.

Rooms 4 en suite (1 fmly) **Facilities** FTV Cen ht Licensed Wi-fi **Notes** ⊗

HERTFORD HEATH — Map 6 TL31

PREMIER COLLECTION

Brides Farm

★★★★★ BED AND BREAKFAST

The Roundings SG13 7PY
☎ 01992 463315 📠 01992 478776
e-mail: rjbartington@btinternet.com
dir: Take B1197 to Hertford Heath. Right at College Arms into The Roundings. Left to Brides Farm

This is an elegant country house in a parkland setting with quiet gardens for guests to enjoy. The accommodation is very comfortable and well equipped. There is a large sitting room overlooking the gardens and a formal dining room where continental and English breakfasts are served. Ample parking is available.

Rooms 3 en suite 1 annexe en suite S £40; D £70* **Facilities** STV FTV tea/coffee Cen ht Wi-fi 🔋 **Parking** 10

PREMIER COLLECTION

Rushen

★★★★★ BED AND BREAKFAST

Mount Pleasant SG13 7QY
☎ 01992 581254 📠 01992 534737
e-mail: wilsonamwell@btinternet.com
dir: From A10 exit at Hertford slip road, 1st left onto B1502. 1st right at top of lane, bear left at village green. Rushen on left at end of green

Guests will receive a warm welcome at Rushen, which is situated at the end of the village green in Hertford Heath. Bedrooms are comfortable and well appointed. Breakfast offers a good choice and local and organic produce is used whenever possible.

Rooms 3 rms (2 en suite) (1 pri facs) S £40; D £80* **Facilities** FTV DVD tea/coffee Cen ht Wi-fi **Extras** Robes, slippers, chocolates, water **Parking** 3 **Notes** ⊗ Closed 22 Dec-3 Jan

HITCHIN — Map 12 TL12

The Sun

★★★ INN

Sun St SG5 1AF
☎ 01462 432092 & 438411 📠 01462 431488
e-mail: sun.hitchin@greeneking.co.uk
web: www.sunhotel-hitchin.com
dir: A1(M) junct 8, A602 to Hitchin. At 1st rdbt 4th exit. Straight over at mini-rdbt. 2nd left into Biggin Ln, to car park

This attractive 16th-century coaching inn is situated in the centre of town. Bedrooms are equipped with modern facilities and some retain their original character with exposed beams. Public areas offer an informal restaurant and a comfortably appointed bar.

Rooms 26 en suite 6 annexe en suite (6 GF) (6 smoking) **Facilities** tea/coffee Dinner available Direct Dial Cen ht **Conf** Max 100 Thtr 100 Class 60 Board 30 **Parking** 20 **Notes** Civ Wed 100

MUCH HADHAM — Map 6 TL41

High Hedges Bed & Breakfast

★★★★ BED AND BREAKFAST

High Hedges, Green Tye SG10 6JP
☎ 01279 842505
e-mail: info@high-hedges.co.uk
web: www.high-hedges.co.uk
dir: From B1004 turn off to Green Tye at Prince of Wales pub, turn into private road, 1st on right

Expect a warm welcome at High Hedges. Bedrooms are well presented and comfortable, and come with many thoughtful extra touches. A substantial breakfast is served in the comfortable dining room. Half Moon Holistic Therapies is part of the B&B, and offers a range of massages and other treatments.

Rooms 3 rms (2 en suite) (1 pri facs) (1 GF) **Facilities** FTV tea/coffee Cen ht Wi-fi Holistic therapies **Parking** 3 **Notes** ⊗ Closed 25-26 Dec & 31 Dec-1 Jan 🚭

NUTHAMPSTEAD — Map 12 TL43

The Woodman Inn

★★★ INN

SG8 8NB
☎ 01763 848328 📠 01763 848328
e-mail: woodman.inn@virgin.net
dir: M11 junct 20, A505 towards Royston, left onto B1368 to Barkway, 1st left past Tally Ho, right in 2m. Inn on left. Or from Royston take A505 signed motorway (M11) & Newmarket. Right onto B1368 & then as above

This 17th-century inn has many fine features, and is close to the Duxford Imperial War Museum. The practical bedrooms are decorated in a traditional style. The kitchen offers a good range of British meals, plus a generous breakfast.

Rooms 4 rms (3 en suite) (1 pri facs) (2 GF)
Facilities TVL TV2B tea/coffee Dinner available Cen ht Wi-fi ⅃ 18 Pool table Shooting range by arrangement
Parking 30 **Notes** ⊗ RS Sun eve & Mon lunch, bar & restaurant closed

ST ALBANS — Map 6 TL10

Innkeeper's Lodge St Albans, London Colney

★★★★ INN

Barnet Rd, London Colney AL2 1BL
☎ 0845 112 6058
e-mail: info@innkeeperslodge.com
web: www.innkeeperslodge.com

At Innkeeper's Lodge you'll find accommodation with comfort and character in equal measure, and everything needed for a relaxing stay, from easy check-in and free parking to complimentary breakfast and a cosy pub serving great value food and drink on the doorstep. Each Lodge has quality rooms, and there are Lodges in a variety of locations from towns and cities to countryside settings across the UK.

Rooms 13 en suite **Facilities** FTV tea/coffee Dinner available Direct Dial Wi-fi **Parking**

Fern Cottage

★★★★ 🅰 BED AND BREAKFAST

116 Old London Rd AL1 1PU
☎ 01727 834200
e-mail: bookinginfo@ferncottage.uk.net
dir: M25 junct 22, A1081 to St Albans, 3rd exit at London Colney rdbt, 1m, under railway bridge, over mini-rdbt, 2nd left into Old London Rd. Fern Cottage 400yds on left
Rooms 3 en suite (1 GF) S £35-£55; D £68-£75*
Facilities tea/coffee Cen ht Wi-fi 🔴 **Parking** 3 **Notes** ⊛

STAPLEFORD — Map 6 TL31

Papillon Woodhall Arms

★★★ INN

17 High Rd SG14 3NW
☎ 01992 535123 📠 01992 587030
e-mail: papillonwoodhall@aol.com
web: www.papillonrestaurant.co.uk
dir: 2.5m from Hertford town on A119 (Hertford to Stevenage road)

Located in the village centre, this Victorian house has been sympathetically renovated and extended to provide good standards of comfort and facilities. Bedrooms are equipped with both practical and thoughtful extras and public areas include a spacious restaurant offering a wide range of international dishes.

Rooms 10 en suite (1 fmly) S £29.50-£35; D £46-£55 (room only)* **Facilities** Lounge TVL tea/coffee Dinner available Cen ht Wi-fi **Conf** Max 50 Thtr 50 Class 30 Board 20 **Parking** 33 **Notes** ⊗

WARE — Map 6 TL31

Feathers Inn

★★★ INN

Wadesmill SG12 0TN
☎ 01920 462606 📠 01920 469994
e-mail: feathers.wadesmill@newbridgeinns.co.uk

This coaching inn is situated beside the A10 on the Cambridge side of Ware. An adjacent modern annexe provides cottage-style rooms and a good array of modern facilities. Meals are taken in the inn where there is a choice of a carvery and informal restaurant operations; the bar remains open all day.

Rooms 31 en suite

WATFORD — Map 6 TQ19

Travel Stop Inn

★★★ GUEST ACCOMMODATION

26-28 Upton Rd WD18 0JF
☎ 01923 224298 📠 01923 253553
e-mail: info@travelstopinn.com
web: www.travelstopinn.com
dir: M1 junct 5, A4008 to Watford centre. On ring road stay in centre lane, past lights at Market St, bus stop on left. Take next left Upton Rd

Located within easy walking distance of the town centre, this renovation of two Edwardian houses provides a range of bedrooms equipped with lots of homely extras. There is a cocktail bar and restaurant in the White House Hotel opposite, which is under the same ownership; it is here that guests check in and take breakfast.

Rooms 26 annexe en suite (1 fmly) (7 GF) **Facilities** STV TVL tea/coffee Dinner available Direct Dial Cen ht Licensed Complimentay use of local gym **Conf** Max 200 Thtr 200 Class 80 Board 60 **Parking** 35 **Notes** ⊗ RS Xmas/New Year Reduced restaurant service Civ Wed 120

WELWYN GARDEN CITY — Map 6 TL21

The Fairway Tavern

★★★ INN

Old Herns Ln AL7 2ED
☎ 01707 336007 & 339349 📠 01707 376154
e-mail: info@fairwaytavern.co.uk
web: www.fairwaytavern.co.uk
dir: Exit A1 junct 6 to B1000 through Digswell for 2m, follow signs for golf complex

Enjoying a picturesque location, this property is located on Panshanger Golf Complex, with lodge style bedrooms opening out onto views of the golf course and rolling countryside. Bedrooms are smartly presented and are well equipped for business and leisure guests. Breakfast and evening meals are served by the friendly staff in the adjacent pub. Evening meals are available Monday to Thursday, between 6.30pm and 9.30pm. A large peaceful garden and a function room for private hire are available.

Rooms 7 en suite (2 fmly) (7 GF) **Facilities** tea/coffee Dinner available Direct Dial Cen ht Lift Wi-fi ⅃ 18 **Conf** Thtr 120 Class 80 Board 25 **Parking** 200 **Notes** ⊗ Civ Wed 100

KENT

ASHFORD — Map 7 TR04

The Wife of Bath

★★★★★ ⊛⊛ 🍴 RESTAURANT WITH ROOMS

4 Upper Bridge St, Wye TN25 5AF
☎ 01233 812232 📠 01233 813630
e-mail: relax@thewifeofbath.com
dir: 4m NE of Ashford. M20 junct 9, A28 for Canterbury, 3m right to Wye

The Wife of Bath is set in the medieval village of Wye which is close to Dover, Canterbury and Ashford. Bedrooms are tastefully decorated and provide guests with comfortable accommodation; each is equipped with LCD TVs and DVD players (a range of DVDs is available). The stylish restaurant, with a small separate bar area, is open for lunch and dinner daily; a cooked or continental breakfast is served here in the morning. Free Wi-fi is available throughout.

Rooms 3 en suite 2 annexe en suite (2 GF) S £75; D £95*
Facilities FTV DVD Lounge tea/coffee Dinner available Cen ht Wi-fi **Extras** Speciality toiletries **Parking** 12 **Notes** Closed 25-26 Dec No coaches

Save on B&Bs and Hotels. Book at **theAA.com/hotel**

KENT 183 ENGLAND

The Croft

★★★ GUEST ACCOMMODATION

Canterbury Rd, Kennington TN25 4DU
☎ 01233 622140 📠 01233 635271
e-mail: info@thecroft.biz
dir: M20 junct 10, 2m on A28 signed Canterbury

An attractive red-brick house situated in two acres of landscaped grounds just a short drive from Ashford railway station. The generously proportioned bedrooms are in the main house and in pretty cottages; all are pleasantly decorated and thoughtfully equipped. Public rooms include a smart Italian restaurant, a bar, and a cosy lounge.

Rooms 14 en suite (4 GF) **Facilities** tea/coffee Dinner available Direct Dial Cen ht Licensed Wi-fi **Conf** Max 40 Thtr 40 Class 20 Board 22 **Parking** 30 **Notes** Civ Wed 40

BENENDEN Map 7 TQ83

Apple Trees B&B

★★★★ BED AND BREAKFAST

Goddards Green TN17 4AR
☎ 01580 240622
e-mail: garryblanch@aol.com
web: www.appletreesbandb.co.uk
dir: 3m E of Cranbrook. Exit A262 at Sissinghurst S into Chaple Ln, over x-rds, 2m left to Goddards Green, 1m on right

This spacious rural cottage is situated in the heart of the Kentish countryside, and is convenient for those visiting Sissinghurst Castle and Great Dixter. Bedrooms are attractively presented and include plenty of thoughtful extras such as flat screen TVs and internet connection. Breakfast is served in the rustic dining room with picturesque views of the garden.

Rooms 3 rms (1 en suite) (2 pri facs) (3 GF) **Facilities** TVL TV1B tea/coffee Cen ht Wi-fi ch fac ⚓ 18 **Parking** 6 **Notes** ⊗ ⌨

BIDDENDEN Map 7 TQ83

Heron Cottage

★★★★ GUEST ACCOMMODATION

TN27 8HH
☎ 01580 291358 📠 01580 291358
e-mail: susantwort@hotmail.com
web: www.heroncottage.info
dir: 1m NW of Biddenden. A262 W from Biddenden, 1st right, 0.25m across sharp left bend through stone pillars, left onto unmade road

Expect a warm welcome at this picturesque extended cottage, set in immaculate, mature gardens in peaceful Kent countryside. The bedrooms are thoughtfully equipped and have co-ordinated soft furnishings. Breakfast is served in the smart dining room, and the cosy sitting room has an open fireplace.

Rooms 7 rms (6 en suite) (2 fmly) (1 GF) S £60-£70; D £70-£80* **Facilities** FTV Lounge TVL tea/coffee Dinner available Cen ht Wi-fi 🎣 Fishing **Parking** 8 **Notes** Closed Dec-Feb ⌨

BROADSTAIRS Map 7 TR36

Bay Tree Broadstairs

★★★★ GUEST ACCOMMODATION

12 Eastern Esplanade CT10 1DR
☎ 01843 862502 📠 01843 860589
dir: A255 into Rectory Rd & Eastern Esplanade

Expect a warm welcome at this family-run establishment, situated on an elevated position overlooking East Cliff. The attractive bedrooms are well equipped and some have a balcony with a sea view. There is a comfortable lounge bar, and a good breakfast menu is offered in the dining room.

Rooms 10 en suite (1 GF) S £47-£72; D £94-£104 **Facilities** FTV TVL tea/coffee Cen ht Licensed **Parking** 11 **Notes** LB ⊗ No Children 10yrs Closed Xmas & New Year

BROOKLAND Map 7 TQ92

Dean Court

★★★★ BED AND BREAKFAST

TN29 9TD
☎ 01797 344244 📠 01797 344102
e-mail: anne_furnival@hotmail.com
dir: M20 junct 10, A2070 towards Hastings (follow Brenzett signs). At Brenzett take A259 signed Hastings & Rye. Through Brookland, sharp left. In 0.5m to house

A very warm welcome is assured at this Victorian farmhouse located on a working farm in the middle of Romney Marsh. The bedrooms are well appointed and suitable for both the leisure and business guest. There is a spacious seating room and a well-kept garden for the warmer months.

Rooms 2 rms (1 en suite) (1 pri facs) (1 fmly) S £45-£55; D £75-£85* **Facilities** FTV iPod docking station Lounge tea/coffee Cen ht Wi-fi 🔌 **Parking** 5 **Notes** No Children 12yrs Closed 20 Dec-4 Jan ⌨

CANTERBURY — Map 7 TR15

PREMIER COLLECTION

Magnolia House
★★★★★ GUEST ACCOMMODATION

36 St Dunstans Ter CT2 8AX
☎ 01227 765121 & 07776 236459 📠 01227 765121
e-mail: info@magnoliahousecanterbury.co.uk
web: www.magnoliahousecanterbury.co.uk
dir: *A2 E onto A2050 for city centre, left at 1st rdbt signed University of Kent. St Dunstans Terrace 3rd right*

This charming property combines a warm welcome with superbly appointed bedrooms, equipped with lots of extra amenities including internet access. Evening meals (by arrangement from November to February) are delightful, served in the dining room overlooking the attractive walled garden. A wide range of items are offered at breakfast.

Rooms 6 en suite (1 GF) S £55; D £95-£125 **Facilities** FTV DVD tea/coffee Dinner available Cen ht Wi-fi **Extras** Hand-made toiletries, fridges, complimentary drinks **Parking** 5 **Notes** ⊗ No Children 12yrs

BijouAbode
★★★★ GUEST ACCOMMODATION

Chaucer House, 15 The Friars CT1 2AS
☎ 01227 472861 & 07891 343998
e-mail: contact@bijouabode.co.uk
dir: *A2050 into Canterbury, left at rdbt into London Rd. Right at next rdbt into Saint Dunstans St. Before Westgate, left into North Ln then right into The Causeway. Turn right into Pound Ln & car park*

Located right in the heart of Canterbury, directly opposite the new Marlow Theatre, BijouAbode offers comfortable bedrooms that are spacious and of very high quality, both with large wet rooms and free standing baths. There are a number of extras including free Wi-fi and satellite TV in addition to a sun lounge and large living room which guests can use during their stay. Both cooked and continental breakfasts are served daily either in your room or in the dining area. Guests will either be greeted on arrival or provided with a code to access the property.

Rooms 2 en suite (2 fmly) S £129-£149; D £129-£149 **Facilities** STV FTV iPod docking station Lounge TVL tea/coffee Cen ht Wi-fi **Extras** Speciality toiletries, chocolates - complimentary **Notes** ⊗

Castle House
★★★★ GUEST ACCOMMODATION

28 Castle St CT1 2PT
☎ 01227 761897
e-mail: enquiries@castlehousehotel.co.uk
web: www.castlehousehotel.co.uk
dir: *Opposite Canterbury Castle ruins, off A28 (ring road)*

Conveniently located in the city centre opposite the imposing ruins of the ancient Norman castle; part of the building dates back to 1730s. Bedrooms are spacious, all with en suite facilities and many little extras such as Wi-fi. There is a walled garden in which to relax during the warm months.

Rooms 7 en suite 5 annexe en suite (4 fmly) (2 GF) **Facilities** TVL tea/coffee Dinner available Cen ht Wi-fi **Conf** Max 35 **Parking** 12 **Notes** ⊗

Chislet Court Farm (TR224644)
★★★★ FARMHOUSE

Chislet CT3 4DU
☎ 01227 860309 & 07980 841890
📠 01227 860444 Mrs K Wilkinson
e-mail: kathy@chisletcourtfarm.com
web: www.chisletcourtfarm.com
dir: *Exit A28 in Upstreet, farm on right 100yds past church*

This delightful 18th-century house is situated in a pretty village close to Canterbury. The house is smartly

maintained and set in delightful grounds. The en suite bedrooms are extremely spacious, well appointed, and have smart modern bathrooms. A hearty Aga-cooked breakfast is served in the charming conservatory overlooking the garden.

Chislet Court Farm

Rooms 2 en suite S £50; D £80* **Facilities** FTV Lounge tea/coffee Cen ht Wi-fi **Parking** 4 **Notes** ⊗ No Children 12yrs Closed Xmas 🐾 800 acres arable

House of Agnes
★★★★ GUEST ACCOMMODATION

71 Saint Dunstans St CT2 8BN
☎ 01227 472185 📠 01227 470478
e-mail: info@houseofagnes.co.uk
dir: *On A290 between London Rd & Orchard St, 300mtrs from West Gate*

This historic 14th-century property has been appointed to provide luxury guest accommodation and offers individually themed rooms, ranging from the traditional to the more exotic. All bedrooms have a good range of amenities such as flat screen TVs and Wi-fi. This establishment is also licensed for weddings.

Rooms 8 en suite 8 annexe en suite (2 fmly) (8 GF) **Facilities** FTV tea/coffee Cen ht Licensed Wi-fi 🐾 Boules **Conf** Thtr 30 Class 12 Board 20 **Parking** 13 **Notes** ⊗ No Children 5yrs Closed 24-26 Dec Civ Wed 46

The White House
★★★★ GUEST ACCOMMODATION

6 St Peters Ln CT1 2BP
☎ 01227 761836
e-mail: info@whitehousecanterbury.co.uk
dir: *A2 into Canterbury. At London Rd rdbt take 2nd exit (A2050), at next rdbt 1st exit into St Peters Pl. Right at Westgate Tower rdbt, right before next rdbt. Left at end, St Peters Ln on right*

This listed Regency establishment is ideally located in the heart of Canterbury, within a two-minute walk of the famous cathedral. All bedrooms are modern with a bright, airy decor and have LCD TVs and Wi-fi. Breakfast can be enjoyed in the ground-floor dining room and there's additional space for guests to relax during their stay.

Rooms 7 en suite S £65-£75; D £80-£140* **Facilities** FTV tea/coffee Cen ht Wi-fi **Notes** ⊗ No Children 16yrs Closed Jan

Yorke Lodge

★★★★ GUEST ACCOMMODATION

50 London Rd CT2 8LF
☎ 01227 451243 🖷 01227 462006
e-mail: info@yorkelodge.com
web: www.yorkelodge.com
dir: *M2 junct 7, A2, exit left signed Canterbury. At 1st rdbt turn left into London Rd*

The charming Victorian property stands in a tree-lined road just a ten-minute walk from the town centre and railway station. The spacious bedrooms are thoughtfully equipped and carefully decorated; some rooms have four-poster beds. The stylish dining room leads to a conservatory-lounge, which opens onto a superb terrace.

Rooms 8 en suite (1 fmly) S £58-£70; D £80-£120*
Facilities FTV tea/coffee Cen ht Wi-fi **Parking** 5 **Notes** LB No Children 5yrs

Beech Bank

★★★★ GUEST ACCOMMODATION

Duckpit Ln, Waltham CT4 5QA
☎ 01227 700302 🖷 01227 700302
e-mail: grandbeech@hotmail.com
dir: *5.5m S of Canterbury. Off B2068 through Petham, left by telephone onto Duckpit Ln, 2m on left*

A 15th-century coach house set in landscaped grounds with magnificent views of the surrounding countryside. Original features include a minstrels' gallery, oak beams and exposed brickwork. Bedrooms are carefully decorated and thoughtfully equipped, and one room has a four-poster bed. Breakfast is served in the elegant Victorian conservatory.

Rooms 3 rms (2 en suite) (1 pri facs) (1 fmly) (2 GF)
Facilities tea/coffee Cen ht 🏃 🥾 **Parking** 10 **Notes** ⊗ No Children 4yrs Closed 20 Dec-5 Jan 🐾

Peregrine House

★★★★ GUEST ACCOMMODATION

18 Hawks Ln CT1 2NU
☎ 01227 761897
e-mail: enquiries@castlehousehotel.co.uk

Peregrine House is centrally located right in the heart of historic Canterbury. This is a sister property to Castle House, guests register at Castle House and then take a short walk to Peregrine House, alternatively a courtesy car is available to help transport guests and their luggage. Bedrooms and bathrooms offer clean, modern comfortable accommodation. Within seconds, guests are on the main high street close to Canterbury Cathedral, shops and restaurants.

Rooms 13 rms (11 en suite) (2 pri facs) (5 fmly) (3 GF)
Facilities TVL tea/coffee Dinner available Cen ht Licensed Wi-fi **Parking** 14 **Notes** ⊗

Canterbury Cathedral Lodge

★★★★ 🄰 GUEST ACCOMMODATION

The Precincts CT1 2EH
☎ 01227 865350 🖷 01227 865388
e-mail: stay@canterbury-cathedral.org

Rooms 29 en suite 6 annexe en suite (1 fmly) (13 GF)
S £65-£81; D £165-£129* **Facilities** FTV Lounge TVL tea/coffee Direct Dial Cen ht Lift Licensed Wi-fi **Conf** Max 250 Thtr 250 **Parking** 15 **Notes** LB ⊗

Duke William

★★★ 🍺 INN

Ickham CT3 1QP
☎ 01227 721308 & 721244
e-mail: goodfood@dukewilliam.biz
dir: *A257 (Canterbury to Sandwich) into Littlebourne, left opposite The Anchor into Nargate St. 0.5m, right into Drill Ln, right into The Street*

Located in the quiet village of Ickham and just five miles from Canterbury, this family-run pub has a spacious bar and restaurant boasting original features and a large open fireplace. There is also a rear garden with seating for guests to enjoy lunch with great views of the East Kent countryside. Bedrooms are well appointed with modern, comfortable decor and free Wi-fi throughout. Lunch and dinner are available daily and a cooked or continental breakfast is served in the restaurant.

Rooms 4 en suite D £70* **Facilities** STV tea/coffee Dinner available Cen ht Wi-fi ⚓ 18 **Conf** Class 30 Board 30

Cathedral Gate

★★★ GUEST ACCOMMODATION

36 Burgate CT1 2HA
☎ 01227 464381 🖷 01227 462800
e-mail: cgate@cgate.demon.co.uk
dir: *In city centre. Next to main gateway into cathedral precincts*

Dating from 1438, this house has an enviable central location next to the cathedral. Old beams and winding corridors are part of the character of the property. Bedrooms are traditionally furnished, equipped to modern standards and many have cathedral views. Luggage can be unloaded at reception before parking in a nearby car park.

Rooms 13 rms (2 en suite) 12 annexe rms 10 annexe en suite (5 fmly) **Facilities** FTV tea/coffee Dinner available Direct Dial Cen ht Licensed Wi-fi

Ersham Lodge

★★★ GUEST ACCOMMODATION

12 New Dover Rd CT1 3AP
☎ 01227 463174
e-mail: info@ersham-lodge.co.uk
dir: *From Canterbury ring road take A2050 (signs for Dover, A2) premises on right 40mtrs after lights opposite road entrance to Canterbury College*

This attractive twin-gabled Victorian house is just a short walk from the college, cathedral and the city's attractions. Bedrooms are smartly decorated and comfortable, and there is a cosy lounge and a spacious breakfast room which looks out onto the well-kept patio and garden. Free guest parking is available.

Rooms 10 en suite (1 fmly) (5 GF) S £55; D £85*
Facilities Lounge tea/coffee Cen ht Wi-fi 🛁 **Conf** Max 30 Class 30 Board 20 **Parking** 10 **Notes** LB ⊗

Innkeeper's Lodge Canterbury

★★★ INN

162 New Dover Rd CT1 3EL
☎ 0845 112 6099
e-mail: info@innkeeperslodge.com
web: www.innkeeperslodge.com

At Innkeeper's Lodge you'll find accommodation with comfort and character in equal measure, and everything needed for a relaxing stay, from easy check-in and free parking to complimentary breakfast and a cosy pub serving great value food and drink on the doorstep. Each Lodge has quality rooms, and there are Lodges in a variety of locations from towns and cities to countryside settings across the UK.

Rooms 9 en suite (1 fmly) **Facilities** FTV tea/coffee Dinner available Direct Dial Wi-fi **Parking**

St Stephens Guest House

★★★ GUEST ACCOMMODATION

100 St Stephens Rd CT2 7JL
☎ 01227 767644
e-mail: info@ststephensguesthouse.co.uk
dir: *A290 from city, Westgate & sharp right into North Ln, 2nd rdbt left into St Stephens Rd, right into Market Way, car park on right*

St Stephens Guest House offers well-appointed accommodation. All rooms are well equipped with beverage making facilities and free Wi-fi throughout. It is located just ten minutes' walk from Canterbury town centre and conveniently located near the University of Kent and Christchurch College. The dining room is traditionally decorated and has views of the garden; guests can enjoy a cooked and continental breakfast.

Rooms 1 en suite 8 annexe en suite (1 fmly) (3 GF)
S £50-£55; D £70-£80* **Facilities** FTV tea/coffee Cen ht Wi-fi **Parking** 8 **Notes** ⊗ Closed mid Dec-mid Jan

CRANBROOK — Map 7 TQ73

PREMIER COLLECTION

Waters End

★★★★★ 🍴 BED AND BREAKFAST

**Waters End Farm, Standen Street,
Iden Green TN17 4LA**
☎ 01580 850731 & 07768 131317
e-mail: jill@watersendfarm.co.uk
web: www.watersendfarm.co.uk
dir: M25 junct 5, A51, A268. Through Hawkhurst &
Sandhurst, 1st left on Crouch Ln. 1.5m, 1st left to
Standen Street, pass house on right, entrance on left

Located in a very quiet and tranquil part of the Kent
countryside, this 46-acre site offers barn converted
styled bedrooms with high quality decor and soft
furnishings. All come equipped with flat screen TVs,
Wi-fi and Vi-spring beds. Bedrooms are spacious and
benefit from views of the garden and a ten-acre lake. A
hearty cooked and continental breakfast can be enjoyed
in the dining room or on the outdoor terrace.

Rooms 3 annexe en suite (3 GF) **Facilities** FTV TVL tea/
coffee Cen ht Wi-fi **Parking** 10 **Notes** No Children 10yrs
Closed Nov-Mar

DARTFORD — Map 6 TQ57

The Rising Sun Inn

★★★ INN

Fawkham Green DA3 8NL
☎ 01474 872291 📠 01474 872779
web: www.risingsun-fawkham.co.uk
dir: M25 junct 3, A20 Brands Hatch. Turn onto Scratchers
Ln until sign for Fawkham. Left onto Brandshatch Rd,
inn on left

This popular inn overlooks the village green just a short
drive from Brands Hatch. All the en suite bedrooms are
spacious, pleasantly decorated and comfortable. There is
a busy character bar, restaurant, and a patio for alfresco
dining in warmer weather.

The Rising Sun Inn

Rooms 5 en suite (1 fmly) (2 GF) **Facilities** FTV tea/coffee
Dinner available Cen ht Wi-fi **Parking** 20 **Notes** ⊗ No
coaches

DEAL — Map 7 TR35

PREMIER COLLECTION

Sutherland House

★★★★★ GUEST ACCOMMODATION

186 London Rd CT14 9PT
☎ 01304 362853 📠 01304 381146
e-mail: info@sutherlandhouse.fsnet.co.uk
dir: 0.5m W of town centre/seafront on A258

This stylish accommodation demonstrates impeccable
taste with its charming, well-equipped bedrooms and a
comfortable lounge. A fully stocked bar, books, free Wi-
fi, Freeview TV and radio are some of the many
amenities offered. The elegant dining room is the venue
for a hearty breakfast and dinner is available by prior
arrangement.

Rooms 4 en suite (1 GF) S £67-£75; D £75-£90
Facilities FTV tea/coffee Dinner available Direct Dial
Cen ht Licensed Wi-fi ⚹ **Conf** Max 12 Thtr 12 Class 12
Board 12 **Parking** 7 **Notes** LB No Children 5yrs

Sondes Lodge

★★★ GUEST ACCOMMODATION

14 Sondes Rd CT14 7BW
☎ 01304 368741 & 07817 178186
e-mail: info@sondeslodge.co.uk
web: www.sondeslodge.co.uk
dir: From Dover take A258 to Deal, pass Deal Castle,
towards town centre. 4th right into Sondes Rd. Lodge
on right

Expect a warm welcome at this smart guest
accommodation situated in a side road just off the
seafront and a short walk from the town centre. The
pleasant bedrooms have co-ordinated fabrics and many
thoughtful touches. Breakfast is served at individual
tables in the lower ground-floor dining room.

Rooms 3 en suite (1 fmly) (1 GF) S fr £40; D £60-£70*
Facilities FTV TVL tea/coffee Cen ht Wi-fi **Extras** Bath
robes **Notes** ⊗

DODDINGTON — Map 7 TQ95

PREMIER COLLECTION

The Old Vicarage

★★★★★ GUEST ACCOMMODATION

Church Hill ME9 0BD
☎ 01795 886136 📠 01795 886136
e-mail: claire@oldvicaragedoddington.co.uk
web: www.oldvicaragedoddington.co.uk
dir: From A2 take Faversham Rd signed Doddington for
4.4m. Turn right towards church

The Old Vicarage is a stunning Grade II listed property
situated at the edge of the village beside the old
church. Spacious rooms come with flat screen TVs, and
special touches such as binoculars and bird reference
books. Guests can relax in the elegant lounge, and a
bountiful breakfast is served in the stylish dining room
overlooking endless trees and green fields.

Rooms 3 en suite (2 fmly) S £55-£69; D £79-£89
Facilities FTV Lounge tea/coffee Cen ht Wi-fi ⚹ **Parking** 6
Notes ⊗ No Children 3yrs Closed 25 Dec-2 Jan

DOVER — Map 7 TR34

PREMIER COLLECTION

The Marquis at Alkham

★★★★★ ◉◉ 🍴 RESTAURANT WITH ROOMS

Alkham Valley Rd, Alkham CT15 7DF
☎ 01304 873410 & 822945 📠 01304 873418
e-mail: info@themarquisatalkham.co.uk
web: www.themarquisatalkham.co.uk
dir: A256 from Dover, at rdbt 1st exit into London Rd,
left into Alkham Rd, Alkham Valley Rd. Establishment
1.5m after sharp bend

Located between Dover and Folkestone, this modern,
contemporary restaurant with rooms offers luxury
accommodation with modern features - flat screen TVs,
Wi-fi, power showers and bathrobes to name but a few.
All the stylish bedrooms are individually designed and
have fantastic views of the Kent Downs. The award-
winning restaurant, open for lunch and dinner, serves
modern British cuisine. Both continental and a choice
of cooked breakfasts are offered.

Rooms 10 en suite (3 fmly) (1 GF) S £79-£119;
D £89-£249* **Facilities** FTV DVD Lounge TVL Dinner
available Direct Dial Cen ht Wi-fi **Conf** Max 20 Thtr 20
Class 20 Board 16 **Parking** 22 **Notes** LB ⊗ Civ Wed 55

Hubert House Guesthouse & Bistro

★★★★ GUEST HOUSE

9 Castle Hill Rd CT16 1QW
☎ 01304 202253 ◫ 01304 210142
e-mail: stay@huberthouse.co.uk
web: www.huberthouse.co.uk
dir: On A258 by Dover Castle, down hill, 1st left. Next to White Horse pub

This charming Georgian house is within walking distance of the ferry port and the town centre. Bedrooms are sumptuously decorated and furnished with an abundance of practical extras. Breakfast, including full English and healthy options, is served in the smart coffee house, which is open all day. Families are especially welcome.

Rooms 6 en suite (4 fmly) S £40-£55; D £55-£100*
Facilities FTV tea/coffee Cen ht Licensed Wi-fi **Parking** 6
Notes LB Closed 24-27 Dec & 31 Dec-2 Jan

Beulah House

★★★★ GUEST ACCOMMODATION

94 Crabble Hill, London Rd CT17 0SA
☎ 01304 824615 ◫ 01304 828850
e-mail: owen@beulahhouse94.freeserve.co.uk
web: www.beulahguesthouse.co.uk
dir: On A256

An impressive Victorian house located just a stroll from the town centre and close to the ferry port. The spacious bedrooms are pleasantly decorated and thoughtfully equipped. Public rooms include two conservatories and a comfortable lounge. The impressive garden has an interesting display of topiary and a small menagerie.

Rooms 8 en suite **Facilities** TVL tea/coffee Cen ht Wi-fi
Parking 8 **Notes** ⊗ No Children 12yrs

Bleriot's

★★★ GUEST ACCOMMODATION

Belper House, 47 Park Av CT16 1HE
☎ 01304 211394
e-mail: info@bleriots.net
dir: A20 to Dover, left onto York St, right at lights into Ladywell. Left at next lights onto Park Av

This large, family-run Victorian property is convenient for the ferry port and town centre. Guests receive a warm welcome and can enjoy a range of comfortable, spacious en suite bedrooms. The attractive dining room is the venue for a wholesome breakfast to start the day.

Rooms 8 en suite (2 fmly) S £34-£35; D £50-£62 (room only) **Facilities** FTV Lounge tea/coffee Cen ht Wi-fi
Parking 8 **Notes** LB ⊗

Ardmore Guest House

★★★ GUEST ACCOMMODATION

18 Castle Hill Rd CT16 1QW
☎ 01304 205895 ◫ 01304 208229
e-mail: res@ardmoreph.co.uk
web: www.ardmoreph.co.uk
dir: On A258 by Dover Castle

Dating from 1796, this delightful house is adjacent to Dover Castle. Convenient for the town centre and ferry port, the Ardmore offers comfortable accommodation and friendly hospitality. The non-smoking bedrooms are spacious and airy. Public rooms include a comfortable lounge and a well-appointed breakfast room.

Rooms 4 en suite (1 fmly) D £60-£70* **Facilities** FTV
Lounge tea/coffee Cen ht Wi-fi **Notes** ⊗ Closed Xmas

St Martins Guest House

★★★ GUEST ACCOMMODATION

17 Castle Hill Rd CT16 1QW
☎ 01304 205938 ◫ 01304 208229
e-mail: res@stmartinsgh.co.uk
web: www.stmartinsgh.co.uk
dir: On A258 by Dover Castle

Located close to the castle, ferry port and town centre, this smart guest accommodation offers a friendly welcome. The thoughtfully equipped en suite bedrooms are attractively decorated, and most rooms enjoy a sunny aspect. Breakfast is served in the pine-furnished dining room, and there is also a comfortable lounge.

Rooms 6 en suite (3 fmly) D £50-£56* **Facilities** FTV
Lounge tea/coffee Cen ht Wi-fi **Notes** ⊗ Closed Xmas

EDENBRIDGE   Map 6 TQ44

Ye Old Crown

★★★ INN

74-76 The High St TN8 5AR
☎ 01732 867896 & 866107
e-mail: yeoldcrown@gmail.com
dir: In town centre

Located off the high street in Edenbridge, this family-run inn offers six tastefully appointed bedrooms with modern decor and furnishings, and includes free Wi-fi throughout. A range of bar snacks and traditional pub meals is offered for both lunch and dinner. There is also a courtyard area, and breakfast is served daily in the pub. Parking is available on site and the inn is conveniently located near Chartwell, Hever Castle and Penshurst Place.

Rooms 6 annexe en suite (1 fmly) (2 GF) S £69; D £79*
Facilities FTV tea/coffee Dinner available Cen ht Wi-fi
Parking 15

FAVERSHAM   Map 7 TR06

Judd's Folly

★★★ GUEST ACCOMMODATION

Syndale Park, London Rd ME13 0RH
☎ 01795 591818 & 532595 ◫ 01795 532595
e-mail: jason@juddsfollyhotel.co.uk
web: www.juddsfollyhotel.co.uk
dir: M2 junct 6 follow signs for Faversham. Onto A2 towards Sittingbourne, through Ospringe, over mini-rdbt, 50yds on left

Located on an elevated position with far-reaching views, Judd's Folly is just a five minute drive from the market town of Faversham and just a couple of minutes drive from the M2. Bedrooms are all tastefully decorated with modern decor and soft furnishings, and are split between courtyard buildings and the main building which hosts the bar and restaurant area. Dinner is served here daily and is also the venue where guests can enjoy a cooked and continental breakfast. Functions and weddings can also be accommodated.

Rooms 13 en suite 13 annexe en suite (4 fmly) (16 GF)
Facilities FTV TVL tea/coffee Dinner available Licensed
Wi-fi Arrangement with gym, charges payable **Conf** Max
100 Thtr 80 Class 30 Board 30 **Parking** 100 **Notes** LB Civ
Wed 80

FOLKESTONE   Map 7 TR23

PREMIER COLLECTION

The Relish

★★★★★ GUEST ACCOMMODATION

4 Augusta Gardens CT20 2RR
☎ 01303 850952 ◫ 01303 850958
e-mail: reservations@hotelrelish.co.uk
web: www.hotelrelish.co.uk
dir: Off A2033 (Sandgate Rd)

Expect a warm welcome at this impressive Victorian terrace property, which overlooks Augusta Gardens in the fashionable West End of town. The bedrooms feature beautiful contemporary natural-wood furniture, lovely co-ordinated fabrics and many thoughtful extras like DVD players and free broadband access. Public rooms include a modern lounge-dining room, and a sun terrace where breakfast is served in the summer.

Rooms 10 en suite (2 fmly) S £69-£135; D £95-£145*
Facilities FTV DVD Lounge tea/coffee Direct Dial Cen ht
Wi-fi **Conf** Max 20 Thtr 20 Class 10 Board 20 **Notes** ⊗
Closed 23 Dec-2 Jan

FOLKESTONE continued

Rocksalt Rooms

★★★★ ◉◉ RESTAURANT WITH ROOMS

2 Back St CT19 6NN
☎ 01303 212070
e-mail: info@rocksaltfolkestone.co.uk
dir: M20 junct 13 follow signs to harbour (A259). At
harbour left onto Fish Market

Overlooking the busy harbour, crowded with small leisure
boats, and having wonderful sea views, Rocksalt enjoys a
great location in Folkestone. Bedrooms are stylish, well
appointed with original antique beds and equipped with
a host of thoughtful little extras. Continental breakfasts
are delivered promptly to the guests' rooms each
morning, and dinner is served in the award-winning
restaurant that has panoramic views.

Rooms 4 en suite (1 fmly) D £75–£85* **Facilities** FTV iPod
docking station tea/coffee Dinner available Cen ht Wi-fi
Notes ⊗ No coaches

Chandos Guest House

★★★ GUEST ACCOMMODATION

77 Cheriton Rd CT20 1DG
☎ 01303 851202 & 07799 886297
e-mail: don@chandosguesthouse.com
web: www.chandosguesthouse.co.uk
dir: M20 junct 13. Right towards Folkestone. At 2nd set of
lights, take middle lane. Continue for 1m, straight over
rdbt, premises 0.25m on right

Close to the town centre and only a five minute drive from
the Eurotunnel, this pleasant guest accommodation is
ideal for continental travellers. Bedrooms and bathrooms
are well equipped, bright and comfortable. Free Wi-fi is
available. A hearty breakfast is served in the spacious
ground-floor dining room. Early morning departures are
catered for.

Rooms 10 rms (6 en suite) (4 pri facs) (4 fmly)
Facilities FTV tea/coffee Cen ht Wi-fi **Parking** 6 **Notes** ⊗

Langhorne Garden

★★★ GUEST ACCOMMODATION

10-12 Langhorne Gardens CT20 2EA
☎ 01303 257233 ▤ 01303 242760
e-mail: info@langhorne.co.uk
web: www.langhorne.co.uk
dir: Exit M20 junct 13, follow signs for The Leas, 2m

Once a Victorian villa, Langhorne Garden is close to the
seafront, shops and restaurants. Bright spacious
bedrooms are traditionally decorated with plenty of
original charm. Public rooms include a choice of
comfortable lounges and a bar, a spacious dining room
and a popular basement bar with billiards, darts and
table football.

Rooms 29 en suite (8 fmly) **Facilities** STV FTV tea/coffee
Dinner available Direct Dial Cen ht Lift Licensed Wi-fi
Pool table **Notes** Closed Xmas RS Jan-Etr no evening
meal

Save on B&Bs and Hotels. Book at **theAA.com/hotel**

KENT 189 ENGLAND

GOUDHURST
Map 6 TQ73

The Star & Eagle
★★★★ 🍺 INN

High St TN17 1AL
☎ 01580 211512 📠 01580 212444
e-mail: starandeagle@btconnect.com
web: www.starandeagle.co.uk
dir: *Off A21 to Hastings rd, take A262, inn at top of village next to church*

A warm welcome is assured at this 15th-century inn located in the heart of a delightful village. Within easy reach of Royal Tunbridge Wells and the Weald this is a great base for walkers. Both bedrooms and public areas boast original features and much character. A wide range of delicious home-made dishes is available in the restaurant and bar.

Rooms 10 rms (8 en suite) (2 pri facs) D £85-£150 **Facilities** FTV tea/coffee Dinner available Direct Dial Cen ht Wi-fi ♠ **Conf** Max 30 Thtr 30 Class 15 Board 12 **Parking** 20 **Notes** ⊗ RS 25-26 Dec eve closed Civ Wed 50

HALSTEAD
Map 6 TQ46

7 Motel Diner
★★★★ GUEST ACCOMMODATION

London Rd, Polhill TN14 7AA
☎ 01959 535890
e-mail: reservations@7hoteldiner.co.uk
dir: *M25 junct 4, 2m towards Sevenoaks*

This motel is conveniently located off the M25 and is just a short drive from Sevenoaks. The well-equipped bedrooms have been stylishly decorated to offer modern, comfortable accommodation; all have custom-made furniture, flat screen TVs and free Wi-fi. There is an American-themed diner complete with authentic jukebox and leather booths, and all-day dining is available from 7am in the 7 Lounge. Secure parking is available.

Rooms 25 en suite (2 fmly) (6 GF) **Facilities** STV tea/coffee Dinner available Wi-fi **Notes** ⊗

HAWKHURST
Map 7 TQ73

PREMIER COLLECTION

Southgate-Little Fowlers
★★★★★ 🏠 GUEST ACCOMMODATION

Rye Rd TN18 5DA
☎ 01580 752526 📠 01580 752526
e-mail: susan.woodard@southgate.uk.net
dir: *0.25m E of Hawkhurst on A268*

A warm welcome is assured at this wonderful 300-year-old former dower house. Set in immaculate mature gardens, the renovated property provides attractive accommodation throughout. Spacious bedrooms are carefully decorated and equipped with many thoughtful extras. A hearty breakfast is served at individual tables in the delightful Victorian conservatory.

Rooms 2 en suite (1 fmly) **Facilities** TVL tea/coffee Cen ht Wi-fi **Parking** 5 **Notes** ⊗ No Children 8yrs Closed Nov-Feb 🚭

HYTHE
Map 7 TR13

Seabrook House
★★★★ GUEST ACCOMMODATION

81 Seabrook Rd CT21 5QW
☎ 01303 269282 📠 01303 237822
e-mail: seabrookhouse@hotmail.co.uk
web: www.seabrook-house.co.uk
dir: *0.9m E of Hythe on A259*

Seabrook House is a stunning Victorian house situated just a few miles from the M20 and Eurotunnel. The property is set in pretty gardens and within easy walking distance of the beach. The attractive bedrooms are carefully furnished and thoughtfully equipped. Public rooms include an elegant lounge, where tea and coffee are served in the evening, a sunny conservatory and large dining room.

Seabrook House

Rooms 13 en suite (4 fmly) (4 GF) **Facilities** TVL tea/coffee Cen ht **Parking** 13 **Notes** ⊗

IVYCHURCH
Map 7 TR02

PREMIER COLLECTION

Olde Moat House
★★★★★ 🏠 GUEST ACCOMMODATION

TN29 0AZ
☎ 01797 344700 📠 01797 343919
e-mail: oldemoathouse@hotmail.com
web: www.oldemoathouse.co.uk
dir: *Exit A2070 & A259 junct into Ivychurch, left, 0.75m on left*

Situated eight miles north-east of Rye this charming character property sits peacefully amongst carefully tended gardens. Spacious bedrooms are elegantly furnished and an abundance of accessories are provided for guest comfort. The elegant dining room overlooks the gardens, and a cosy lounge with oak beams and open fireplace is furnished with comfortable sofas.

Rooms 3 en suite D £70-£110 **Facilities** FTV TVL tea/coffee Dinner available Cen ht Wi-fi **Parking** 10 **Notes** LB ⊗ No Children 16yrs

MAIDSTONE
Map 7 TQ75

See also Marden

The Black Horse Inn
★★★★ 🍺 INN

Pilgrims Way, Thurnham ME14 3LD
☎ 01622 737185 & 630830 📠 01622 739170
e-mail: info@wellieboot.net
web: www.wellieboot.net
dir: *M20 junct 7, N A249. Right into Detling, opposite pub into Pilgrims Way for 1m*

This charming inn dates from the 17th century, and the public areas have a wealth of oak beams, exposed brickwork and open fireplaces. The stylish bedrooms are in a series of cosy cabins behind the premises; each one is attractively furnished and thoughtfully equipped.

Rooms 27 annexe en suite (8 fmly) (27 GF) S £65-£75; D £85-£95 **Facilities** FTV tea/coffee Dinner available Cen ht Wi-fi ♠ **Parking** 40 **Notes** LB No coaches Civ Wed 40

MAIDSTONE *continued*

Aylesbury House

★★★★ GUEST ACCOMMODATION

56-58 London Rd ME16 8QL
☎ 01622 762100 ▤ 01622 664673
e-mail: mail@aylesburyhouse.co.uk
dir: *M20 junct 5, A20 to Maidstone. Aylesbury House on left before town centre*

Located just a short walk from the town centre, this smartly maintained establishment offers a genuine welcome. The carefully decorated bedrooms have co-ordinated soft fabrics and many thoughtful touches. Breakfast is served in the smart dining room overlooking a walled garden.

Rooms 8 en suite S £58-£65; D £69-£80 Facilities FTV DVD tea/coffee Cen ht Wi-fi Parking 8 Notes ⊗

Innkeeper's Lodge Maidstone

★★★ INN

Sandling Rd ME14 2RF
☎ 0845 112 6103
e-mail: info@innkeeperslodge.com
web: www.innkeeperslodge.com

At Innkeeper's Lodge you'll find accommodation with comfort and character in equal measure, and everything needed for a relaxing stay, from easy check-in and free parking to complimentary breakfast and a cosy pub serving great value food and drink on the doorstep. Each Lodge has quality rooms, and there are Lodges in a variety of locations from towns and cities to countryside settings across the UK.

Rooms 12 en suite (1 fmly) Facilities FTV tea/coffee Dinner available Direct Dial Wi-fi Parking

Rock House Bed & Breakfast

★★★ GUEST ACCOMMODATION

102 Tonbridge Rd ME16 8SL
☎ 01622 751616 ▤ 01622 756119
e-mail: rock.house@btconnect.com
web: www.rockhousebandb.co.uk
dir: *On A26, 0.5m from town centre*

This friendly, family-run property is just a short walk from the town centre. Breakfast is served in the conservatory dining room that overlooks the attractive walled garden.

Bedrooms are brightly decorated and equipped with modern facilities.

Rooms 14 rms (8 en suite) (4 fmly) (3 GF) Facilities FTV TVL tea/coffee Cen ht Wi-fi Parking 7 Notes ⊗

Maidstone Lodge

★★★ ⚠ GUEST ACCOMMODATION

22/24 London Rd ME16 8QL
☎ 01622 758778 ▤ 01622 609984
e-mail: maidstonelodge@btinternet.com
dir: *400yds W of town centre on A20*
Rooms 6 rms (1 GF) (3 smoking) S £40-£45; D £80 Facilities FTV TVL tea/coffee Cen ht Licensed Parking 10 Notes ⊗ Closed 24 Dec-1 Jan

---

MARDEN Map 6 TQ74

PREMIER COLLECTION

Merzie Meadows

★★★★★ BED AND BREAKFAST

Hunton Rd TN12 9SL
☎ 01622 820500 & 07762 713077 ▤ 01622 820500
e-mail: pamela@merziemeadows.co.uk
dir: *A229 onto B2079 for Marden, 1st right into Underlyn Ln, 2.5m at large Chainhurst sign, right onto drive*

Merzie Meadows is a detached property set in 20 acres of mature gardens in the Kent countryside. The generously proportioned bedrooms are housed in two wings, which overlook a terrace; each room is carefully decorated, thoughtfully equipped and furnished with well-chosen pieces. The attractive breakfast room has an Italian tiled floor and superb views of the garden.

Rooms 2 en suite (1 fmly) (2 GF) S £90; D £98-£110* Facilities STV FTV TVL tea/coffee Cen ht Wi-fi Extras Speciality toiletries, chocolates Parking 4 Notes ⊗ No Children 15yrs Closed mid Dec-mid Feb ⊛

Tanner House

★★★★ BED AND BREAKFAST

Tanner Farm, Goudhurst Rd TN12 9ND
☎ 01622 831214 ▤ 01622 832472
e-mail: lesley@tannerhouse.wanadoo.co.uk
dir: *From A21 or A229 onto B2709, between Marden & Goudhurst*

This traditional style Tudor farmhouse is located just outside the village of Marden. Part of a 150-acre family-run farm with caravan and camping park on site, this bed and breakfast is completely separate and boasts views of the spacious gardens and period outbuildings. Bedrooms are traditional in style and combine comfort with modern amenities including free Wi-fi and Freeview TVs. There is a guest lounge which provides additional space for guests to relax, and breakfast can be enjoyed in the dining room which boasts a large inglenook fireplace.

Rooms 3 en suite S £50-£75; D £65-£75* Facilities FTV TVL tea/coffee Cen ht Wi-fi Fishing ⚓ Extras Speciality toiletries, snacks, chocolates Conf Max 24 Thtr 24 Class 24 Board 12 Parking 3 Notes ⊗ No Children 12yrs Closed 25-26 Dec

---

NEW ROMNEY Map 7 TR02

Honeychild Manor Farmhouse *(TR062276)*

★★★★ 🏠 FARMHOUSE

St Mary In The Marsh TN29 0DB
☎ 01797 366180 & 07951 237821
▤ 01797 366925 Mrs V Furnival
e-mail: honeychild@farming.co.uk
web: www.honeychild-farm-bnb.co.uk
dir: *2m N of New Romney off A259. S of village centre*

This imposing Georgian farmhouse is part of a working dairy farm on Romney Marsh. Walkers and dreamers alike will enjoy the stunning views and can relax in the beautifully landscaped gardens or play tennis on the full-sized court. A hearty breakfast is served in the elegant dining room and features quality local produce. Bedrooms are pleasantly decorated, well furnished and thoughtfully equipped. This establishment is pet friendly.

Rooms 3 rms (1 en suite) (2 pri facs) (1 fmly) Facilities tea/coffee Dinner available Cen ht Wi-fi ⛳ Parking 10 Notes LB ⊛ 1500 acres arable/dairy

Save on B&Bs and Hotels. Book at **theAA.com/hotel**

KENT 191 ENGLAND

PEMBURY | Map 6 TQ64

Camden Arms

★★★★ INN

1 High St TN2 4PH
☎ **01892 822012**
e-mail: food@camdenarms.co.uk
dir: *Off A21, opposite village green*

Located in a central position and just a couple of minutes drive from Tunbridge Wells, this inn offers guests comfortable, well equipped accommodation with LCD TVs, free Wi-fi throughout and spacious en suite bathrooms. The inn is spacious with a large garden with outdoor seating, restaurant and bar area. The latter has a large variety of local beers which change on a regular basis and pub meals are served seven days a week. Guests can enjoy a continental breakfast in the morning or for an additional supplement, can have a hearty traditional English breakfast.

Rooms 15 annexe en suite (1 fmly) (8 GF) D £98
Facilities FTV tea/coffee Dinner available Wi-fi
Extras Trouser press **Conf** Max 50 Thtr 50 Class 24 Board 16 **Parking** 68

SANDGATE | Map 7 TR23

The Suite at Tsunami

★★★★ GUEST ACCOMMODATION

Helena Corniche CT20 3TD
☎ **01303 268535**
e-mail: thesuite@btinternet.com
dir: *M20 junct 12, A20 signed Cheriton. 1st right (across dual carriageway). Left at lights into Horn St, over bridge, left into Church Rd. 3rd right into North Rd, at T-junct. Becomes Hospital Hill, left into Helena Corniche*

Located in the quiet area of Sandgate, this establishment benefits from views of the English Channel and is in close proximity to both Folkestone and Dover. There is one main suite, which includes a private patio, a spacious bedroom with modern decor and furnishings, and an en suite bathroom. There is a comfortable lounge where breakfast is also served.

Rooms 1 rm (1 pri facs) **Facilities** FTV DVD iPod docking station TVL tea/coffee Cen ht Wi-fi **Extras** Mini-fridge, robes - complimentary **Parking** 2 **Notes** LB No Children 1yr

SANDWICH | Map 7 TR35

The New Inn

★★★ INN

2 Harnet St CT13 9ES
☎ **01304 612335** 🖨 **01304 619133**
e-mail: new.inn@thorleytaverns.com
dir: *Off A256, one-way system into town centre, inn on right*

The New Inn is situated in the heart of this busy historic town. The large open-plan lounge bar offers an extensive range of beers and an interesting choice of home-made dishes. Bedrooms are furnished in pine and have many useful extras.

Rooms 5 en suite (3 fmly) (2 smoking) **Facilities** STV tea/coffee Dinner available Direct Dial Cen ht **Parking** 17 **Notes** No coaches

SEVENOAKS | Map 6 TQ55

Yew Tree Barn

★★★★ GUEST ACCOMMODATION

Long Mill Ln, Crouch, Borough Green TN15 8QB
☎ **01732 780461 & 07811 505798**
e-mail: tricia@yewtreebarn.com
web: www.yewtreebarn.com
dir: *A25 (Maidstone Road) turn left after Esso garage. Crouch Lane 1m, right to Crouch. Yew Tree Barn on left*

Situated in the picturesque village of Crouch this attractively converted barn is in an ideal position from which to explore the beautiful Kent countryside. Brands Hatch racing circuit and The London Golf Club are just a short drive away as well as Leeds and Lullingstone Castles. Welcoming hosts Tricia and James offer spaciously comfortable bedrooms with free Wi-fi. The charming dining room and guest lounge overlook the well-tended gardens.

Rooms 2 en suite (2 fmly) (1 GF) S £50-£90; D £75-£90*
Facilities FTV Lounge TVL tea/coffee Cen ht Wi-fi **Parking** 5 **Notes** LB

SITTINGBOURNE | Map 7 TQ96

The Beaumont

★★★★ GUEST ACCOMMODATION

74 London Rd ME10 1NS
☎ **01795 472536** 🖨 **01795 425921**
e-mail: info@thebeaumont.co.uk
web: www.thebeaumont.co.uk
dir: *From M2 or M20 take A249 N. Exit at A2, 1m on left towards Sittingbourne*

This Georgian farmhouse is a charming family-run property that offers the best hospitality and service. Comfortable bedrooms and bathrooms are well equipped for business and leisure guests. Breakfast in the bright, spacious conservatory makes good use of local produce and home-made preserves. Off-road parking is available.

Rooms 9 rms (6 en suite) (3 pri facs) (3 GF)
Facilities STV TVL tea/coffee Cen ht Wi-fi **Conf** Max 12 Thtr 12 Class 12 Board 12 **Parking** 9 **Notes** Closed 24 Dec-1 Jan

Sandhurst Farm Forge

★★★ BED AND BREAKFAST

Seed Rd, Newnham ME9 0NE
☎ **01795 886854**
e-mail: rooms.forge@btinternet.com
dir: *Exit A2 into Newnham, into Seed Rd by church, establishment 1m on right*

A warm welcome is assured at this peaceful location, which also features a working forge. The spacious bedrooms are in a converted stable block and provide smartly furnished accommodation. Breakfast is served in the dining room adjoining the bedrooms. The owner has won an award for green tourism by reducing the impact of the business on the environment.

Rooms 2 annexe en suite (2 GF) S £45; D £75
Facilities STV FTV DVD tea/coffee Cen ht Wi-fi Riding **Parking** 6 **Notes** LB No Children 12yrs Closed 23 Dec-2 Jan

STELLING MINNIS | Map 7 TR14

Heathwood Lodge B&B

★★★★ BED AND BREAKFAST

Wheelbarrow Town CT4 6AH
☎ **01227 709315 & 07831 347395** 🖨 **01227 709475**
e-mail: enquiries@heathwoodlodge.co.uk
dir: *B2068 from Canterbury, left into Stelling Minnis. Right at T-junct, pass village hall, after 0.5m round right-hand corner, last yellow house on left*

Heathwood Lodge is located in a quiet village area of Stelling Minnis, boasting scenic views, spacious gardens for guests to enjoy during summer months, and easily access from both Canterbury and Dover. Bedrooms are tastefully appointed, comfortable and all have en suite facilities. The guest lounge provides additional space for guests to relax and features an open fireplace. The traditionally styled dining room serves both a cooked and continental breakfast with high quality ingredients sourced from the surrounding area.

Rooms 3 en suite **Facilities** FTV TVL tea/coffee Cen ht Wi-fi **Parking** 8 **Notes**

TUNBRIDGE WELLS (ROYAL) — Map 6 TQ53

PREMIER COLLECTION

Danehurst House

★★★★★ BED AND BREAKFAST

41 Lower Green Rd, Rusthall TN4 8TW
☎ 01892 527739 📠 01892 514804
e-mail: info@danehurst.net
web: www.danehurst.net
dir: 1.5m W of Tunbridge Wells in Rusthall. Exit A264 into Coach Rd & Lower Green Rd

Situated in pretty gardens in a quiet residential area, this Victorian gabled house is located to the west of the historic spa town. The house retains many original features and is attractively decorated throughout. Public areas include a comfortable lounge with a small bar. The homely bedrooms come with a wealth of thoughtful extras, and excellent breakfasts are served in the conservatory.

Rooms 4 en suite (1 fmly) **Facilities** TVL tea/coffee Cen ht Licensed **Parking** 6 **Notes** ⊗ No Children 8yrs Closed Xmas

The Beacon

★★★★ INN

Tea Garden Ln, Rusthall TN3 9JH
☎ 01892 524252 📠 01892 534288
e-mail: beaconhotel@btopenworld.com
web: www.the-beacon.co.uk
dir: 1.5m W of Tunbridge Wells. Signed from A264 into Tea Garden Ln

This charming 18th-century inn is situated on an elevated position amid 16 acres of land and surrounded by open countryside. The open-plan public areas are full of character and include ornate fireplaces and stained glass windows. The spacious bedrooms are attractively

decorated, comfortably furnished and have many thoughtful touches.

Rooms 3 en suite **Facilities** TV2B tea/coffee Dinner available Direct Dial Cen ht Wi-fi Fishing **Conf** Thtr 50 Class 40 Board 30 **Parking** 42 **Notes** No coaches Civ Wed 100

Innkeeper's Lodge Tunbridge Wells

★★★ INN

London Rd, Southborough TN4 0QB
☎ 0845 112 6109
e-mail: info@innkeeperslodge.com
web: www.innkeeperslodge.com

At Innkeeper's Lodge you'll find accommodation with comfort and character in equal measure, and everything needed for a relaxing stay, from easy check-in and free parking to complimentary breakfast and a cosy pub serving great value food and drink on the doorstep. Each Lodge has quality rooms, and there are Lodges in a variety of locations from towns and cities to countryside settings across the UK.

Rooms 14 en suite (2 fmly) **Facilities** FTV tea/coffee Dinner available Direct Dial Wi-fi **Parking**

WESTERHAM — Map 6 TQ45

Corner Cottage

★★★★ GUEST ACCOMMODATION

Toys Hill TN16 1PY
☎ 01732 750362 📠 01732 750754
e-mail: cornercottagebandb@jshmanco.com
dir: A25 to Brasted, into Chart Ln signed Fox & Hounds. Right into Puddledock Ln, 1st house on left

Set in a charming village this property offers a spacious, well-equipped annexe bedroom that is comfortably furnished and includes many thoughtful touches. In the main cottage a hearty Aga-cooked breakfast is served in the rustic dining room with stunning views of the countryside.

Rooms 1 annexe en suite (1 fmly) S £60-£70; D £80-£85* **Facilities** FTV tea/coffee Dinner available Cen ht Wi-fi 🐾 **Parking** 2 **Notes** ⊗

Kings Arms

★★★ INN

Market Square TN16 1AN
☎ 01959 562990 📠 01959 561240
e-mail: 6471@greeneking.co.uk
dir: Exit M25 junct 6 & follow A25 to Westerham

The Kings Arms is located in the centre of Westerham and is in close proximity to Sevenoaks, Tunbridge Wells and Maidstone. The bedrooms are spacious and feature original oak beams; some have four-poster beds. The bar and restaurant are modern, and breakfast can be enjoyed in the conservatory. Free Wi-fi is available throughout.

Rooms 18 en suite (4 fmly) S £59-£99; D £79-£119* **Facilities** tea/coffee Dinner available Direct Dial Cen ht Wi-fi **Extras** Pamper packs - chargeable **Conf** Max 50 Thtr 50 Class 40 Board 24 **Parking** 33 **Notes** LB Civ Wed 50

WORTH — Map 7 TR35

Chilton Villa B&B

★★★★ BED AND BREAKFAST

The Street CT14 0DD
☎ 01304 614415
e-mail: info@chiltonvilla.co.uk
dir: A2 or A20 onto A256 towards Sandwich, then A258 towards Deal. Turn left to Worth

Located in the heart of the village and just a mile from Sandwich and close to Canterbury, this former post office has been converted to create two spacious en suite bedrooms offering very good quality and comfortable accommodation; each is equipped with modern fixtures including digital TV and free Wi-fi. There is a cosy dining room, with separate access, where a cooked and continental breakfast is served daily.

Rooms 2 annexe en suite (2 fmly) (2 GF) S £60; D £80* **Facilities** FTV tea/coffee Cen ht Wi-fi ♿ 🐾 **Parking** 2

WROTHAM — Map 6 TQ65

The Bull

★★★★ ⑱ INN

Bull Ln TN15 7RF
☎ 01732 789800 📠 01732 886288
e-mail: info@thebullhotel.com
web: www.thebullhotel.com
dir: In centre of village

Dating back to 1385 and first licensed in 1495, this property offers modern facilities yet retains many traditional features including original exposed beams. High quality meals can be enjoyed at breakfast, lunch and dinner; the inn sources local produce from nearby farms, south coast landed fish and real ales from Dark Star micro-brewery. The bedrooms, including one four-poster room, are decorated with modern furnishings. The Buttery function room was originally the village bakery.

Save on B&Bs and Hotels. Book at **theAA.com/hotel**

KENT – LANCASHIRE 193 ENGLAND

The Bull

Rooms 11 en suite **Facilities** FTV tea/coffee Dinner available Cen ht Wi-fi **Conf** Max 40 Thtr 40 Class 40 Board 30 **Parking** 30 **Notes** ⊗

LANCASHIRE

ACCRINGTON
Map 18 SD72

The Maple Lodge

★★★★ GUEST ACCOMMODATION

70 Blackburn Rd, Clayton-le-Moors BB5 5JH
☎ **01254 301284** 📠 **0560 112 5380**
e-mail: info@stayatmaplelodge.co.uk
dir: *M65 junct 7, follow signs for Clitheroe, right at T-junct into Blackburn Rd*

This welcoming house is convenient for the M65, and provides comfortable, well-equipped bedrooms, as well as an inviting lounge with well-stocked bar. Freshly cooked dinners (by arrangement) and hearty breakfasts are served in the attractive dining room.

Rooms 4 en suite 4 annexe en suite (1 fmly) (4 GF) **Facilities** FTV TVL tea/coffee Dinner available Direct Dial Cen ht Licensed Wi-fi 🎱 **Parking** 6 **Notes** LB

Pilkington's Guest House

★★★ GUEST HOUSE

135 Blackburn Rd BB5 0AA
☎ **01254 237032** 📠 **01254 237032**
e-mail: pilkybuses@hotmail.com
dir: *M65 junct 7 follow signs to Accrington town centre, establishment opposite railway station. M66 onto A56 to Accrington town centre*

Located close to the railway station, this family-run property has two comfortable bedrooms in the main house and four further bedrooms in the terrace which is just a short way along the street. Home-cooked breakfasts are served in the main house.

Rooms 2 rms (2 pri facs) 4 annexe rms (2 fmly) (2 GF) S £30; D £60 **Facilities** FTV TVL tea/coffee Cen ht Wi-fi Snooker Pool table 🎱 **Conf** Max 60 Thtr 60 Class 60 Board 60 **Parking** 6 **Notes** ⊗

BLACKPOOL
Map 18 SD33

Bona Vista

★★★★ GUEST ACCOMMODATION

104-106 Queens Promenade FY2 9NX
☎ **01253 351396** 📠 **01253 594985**
e-mail: enquires@bonavistahotel.com
web: www.bonavistahotel.com
dir: *0.25m N of Uncle Toms Cabin & Casino*

The Bona Vista has a peaceful seafront location on North Shore within reach of the town's amenities. Its attractive bedrooms are well equipped and some have sea views. There is a spacious dining room and a comfortable bar and lounges. Sixteen parking spaces are available, a boon in busy Blackpool.

Rooms 19 rms (17 en suite) (4 fmly) S £27-£35; D £54-£70* **Facilities** FTV Lounge TVL tea/coffee Dinner available Cen ht Licensed Wi-fi Pool table **Conf** Max 50 Thtr 50 Class 50 Board 50 **Parking** 16 **Notes** LB

The Craigmore

★★★★ GUEST HOUSE

8 Willshaw Rd, Gynn Square FY2 9SH
☎ **01253 355098**
e-mail: enquiries@thecraigmore.com
dir: *1m N of Tower. A584 N over Gynn rdbt, 1st right into Willshaw Rd. The Craigmore 3rd on left*

This well-maintained property is in an attractive location overlooking Gynn Square gardens, with the Promenade and tram stops just yards away. Several of the smart modern bedrooms are suitable for families. There is a comfortable lounge, a sun lounge and patio, and the pretty dining room has a small bar.

Rooms 7 en suite (3 fmly) S £30-£40; D £50-£70* **Facilities** FTV Lounge TVL tea/coffee Dinner available Cen ht Licensed Wi-fi **Notes** LB ⊗ Closed Nov-Feb RS Mar open wknds & BHs

The Ramsay

★★★★ GUEST ACCOMMODATION

90-92 Queen Promenade FY2 9NS
☎ **01253 352777** 📠 **01253 351207**
e-mail: enquiries@theramsayhotel.co.uk
dir: *M55 exit towards Blackpool, left into Central Drive, 1st left towards promenade. Right at lights. At Gynn rdbt straight over, establishment just past Uncle Toms Cabin*

This family-run guest accommodation occupies a prime location on the North Shore promenade. The bedrooms are restful and those at the front enjoy panoramic sea views. The public rooms are spacious, and include a cosy lounge with comfortable seating providing an ideal area to relax and have a drink from the bar. Dinner is available on request.

Rooms 22 en suite (2 fmly) **Facilities** FTV TVL tea/coffee Dinner available Cen ht Lift Licensed Wi-fi ♿ **Parking** 8 **Notes** LB ⊗

The Baron

★★★★ 🅰 GUEST ACCOMMODATION

296 North Promenade FY1 2EY
☎ **01253 622729** 📠 **0161 297 0464**
e-mail: baronhotel@f2s.com
web: www.baronhotel.co.uk
Rooms 21 en suite (1 fmly) (3 GF) (2 smoking) **Facilities** FTV tea/coffee Dinner available Cen ht Lift Licensed Wi-fi **Conf** Max 20 Thtr 20 Class 20 Board 20 **Parking** 16 **Notes** ⊗ No Children 12yrs

Homecliffe

★★★★ 🅰 GUEST ACCOMMODATION

5-6 Wilton Pde FY1 2HE
☎ **01253 625147** 📠 **01253 292667**
e-mail: enquiry@homecliffehotel.com
dir: *From promenade at North Pier, turn right into Wilton Parade after Imperial Hotel, establishment half way along on left*

Rooms 22 en suite (1 fmly) S £40-£60; D £50-£90* **Facilities** FTV Lounge TVL tea/coffee Direct Dial Cen ht Licensed Wi-fi ♿ 18 Pool table **Conf** Max 100 Thtr 100 Class 80 Board 60 **Parking** 10 **Notes** LB ⊗

The Valentine

★★★★ 🅰 GUEST ACCOMMODATION

35 Dickson Rd FY1 2AT
☎ **01253 622775**
e-mail: anthony@anthonypalmer.orangehome.co.uk
Rooms 12 en suite (1 fmly) **Facilities** FTV TVL tea/coffee Dinner available Cen ht Licensed Wi-fi **Notes** ⊗ Closed Nov-Mar

BLACKPOOL *continued*

Hartshead

★★★ GUEST ACCOMMODATION

17 King Edward Av, North Shore FY2 9TA
☎ 01253 353133 & 357111
e-mail: info@hartshead-hotel.co.uk
dir: *M55 junct 4, A583, A584 to North Shore, exit Queens Promenade into King Edward Av*

Popular for its location near the seafront, this enthusiastically run establishment has modern bedrooms of various sizes, equipped with a good range of practical extras. A verandah-sitting room is available, in addition to a comfortable lounge bar, and breakfast and pre-theatre dinners are served in the attractive dining room.

Rooms 9 en suite (3 fmly) S £24–£40; D £48–£62*
Facilities FTV DVD Lounge TVL tea/coffee Dinner available Cen ht Licensed Wi-fi **Parking** 6 **Notes** LB ⊗

Sunny Cliff Guest House

★★★ GUEST ACCOMMODATION

98 Queens Promenade, North Shore FY2 9NS
☎ 01253 351155
dir: *On A584, 1.5m N of Blackpool Tower, just past Sheraton Hotel*

Under the same ownership for four decades, this friendly guest accommodation overlooking the seafront offers a genuine home-from-home atmosphere. The pretty bedrooms, some with sea views, are neatly furnished. There is a cosy bar, a sun lounge, a comfortable lounge, and a smart dining room where good home cooking features.

Rooms 9 en suite (3 fmly) (2 smoking) S £26–£28; D £52–£56* **Facilities** FTV TVL tea/coffee Dinner available Cen ht Licensed **Parking** 6 **Notes** LB ⊗ Closed 9 Nov-Etr 🍽

Denely

★★★ GUEST HOUSE

15 King Edward Av, North Shore FY2 9TA
☎ 01253 352757
e-mail: denely-hotel@btconnect.com
dir: *1m N of Blackpool Tower*

Just a stroll from the Promenade and Gynn Square Gardens, this welcoming guest house offers a spacious lounge and a bright dining room along with simply furnished bedrooms. The friendly resident owners provide attentive service, and evening meals are available by arrangement.

Rooms 9 en suite (3 fmly) S £25–£30; D £40–£45*
Facilities FTV DVD TVL tea/coffee Dinner available Cen ht Wi-fi **Parking** 6 **Notes** LB ⊗ Closed Dec-Jan

Funky Towers

★★★ GUEST ACCOMMODATION

297 The Promenade FY1 6AL
☎ 01253 400123
e-mail: stay@funkytowers.com
web: www.funkytowers.com
dir: *On seafront promenade halfway between The Tower & Pleasure Beach*

The friendly, family-run property has a prime location facing the sea, between the Pleasure Beach and Central Pier. There is a spacious bar and a modern café with direct access to the seafront. The bedrooms are equipped with lots of extras; some feature four-posters and others have great sea views.

Rooms 14 en suite (5 fmly) S £38–£45; D £70–£99
Facilities FTV DVD Lounge TVL tea/coffee Cen ht Licensed Wi-fi Pool table ⊛ **Parking** 3 **Notes** ⊗

The Fairway

★★★ Ⓐ GUEST ACCOMMODATION

34-36 Hull Rd FY1 4QB
☎ 01253 623777 📠 01253 297970
e-mail: impulsedh@aol.com
Rooms 19 en suite

The Edenfield Guest House

Ⓤ

17 Cocker St FY1 2BY
☎ 01253 624009 📠 01253 624009
e-mail: info@edenfieldguesthouse.com

Currently the rating for this establishment is not confirmed. This may be due to a change of ownership or because it has only recently joined the AA rating scheme.

Rooms 6 en suite D £55–£75* **Notes** Closed 3 Jan-12 Feb

BOLTON-BY-BOWLAND Map 18 SD74

Middle Flass Lodge

★★★★ GUEST HOUSE

Settle Rd BB7 4NY
☎ 01200 447259 📠 01200 447300
e-mail: middleflasslodge@btconnect.com
web: www.middleflasslodge.co.uk
dir: *2m N of Bolton by Bowland. Off A59 for Sawley, N to Forest Becks, over bridge, 1m on right*

Set in peaceful countryside in the Forest of Bowland, this smart house provides a warm welcome. Stylishly converted from farm outbuildings, exposed timbers feature throughout, including the attractive restaurant and cosy lounge. The modern bedrooms include a family room, with stairlift access to the first floor. Thanks to the accomplished chef the restaurant is popular with residents.

Rooms 5 en suite 2 annexe en suite (1 fmly) S £48–£54; D £68–£75 **Facilities** FTV TVL tea/coffee Dinner available Cen ht Licensed Wi-fi ⊛ **Parking** 14 **Notes** LB ⊗

CHORLEY

See Eccleston

COLNE Map 18 SD83

The Alma Inn

★★★★ 🍽 INN

Emmott Ln, Laneshaw Bridge BB8 7EG
☎ 01282 857830 📠 01282 857831
e-mail: reception@thealmainn.com
web: www.thealmainn.com
dir: *At end of M65 onto A6068 (Vivary Way) towards Skipton. At 3rd rdbt, 1st exit onto Skipton Old Rd, after 0.5m right onto Hill Ln. 0.5m on right*

Nestling in the magnificent Pendle countryside, dating back to 1725 this rural coaching inn features open fires, stone floor and original beams. Guest can dine well in the lounge style bars or the restaurant. The stylish rooms come in a variety of sizes, and all are thoughtfully equipped. Function facilities available along with ample car parking and a helicopter landing pad.

Rooms 10 en suite (8 fmly) (1 GF) S £65.95–£109.95; D £69.95–£109.95* **Facilities** FTV DVD iPod docking station tea/coffee Dinner available Direct Dial Cen ht Wi-fi ⅃ 9 ⊛ **Extras** Speciality toiletries - complimentary **Conf** Max 150 Thtr 100 Class 50 Board 40 **Parking** 45 **Notes** LB Civ Wed 170

ECCLESTON Map 15 SD51

Parr Hall Farm

★★★★ GUEST ACCOMMODATION

8 Parr Ln PR7 5SL
☎ 01257 451917
e-mail: enquiries@parrhallfarm.com
dir: *M6 junct 27, B5250 N for 5m to Parr Ln on right. 1st property on left*

This attractive, well-maintained farmhouse, located in a quiet corner of the village, yet close to the M6, dates back to the 18th century. The majority of bedrooms are located in a sympathetic barn conversion and include luxury en suite bathrooms and lots of thoughtful extras. A comprehensive continental breakfast is included in the room price.

Rooms 10 annexe en suite (1 fmly) (5 GF) S £45–£50; D £70–£80 **Facilities** FTV tea/coffee Cen ht Wi-fi ⅃ 9 ⊛ Guided Walks **Parking** 20 **Notes** ⊗

Save on B&Bs and Hotels. Book at **theAA.com/hotel**

LANCASHIRE 195 **ENGLAND**

LYTHAM ST ANNES Map 18 SD32

Strathmore

★★★ GUEST ACCOMMODATION

305 Clifton Drive South FY8 1HN
☎ 01253 725478
dir: *In centre of St Annes opposite Post Office*

This friendly, family-run property has a central location close to the promenade. The long-established Strathmore offers smartly furnished and well-equipped bedrooms. There is an elegant lounge where you can enjoy a relaxing drink, and a smart dining room.

Rooms 8 rms (5 en suite) S £24-£31; D £48-£62
Facilities Lounge tea/coffee Cen ht Wi-fi 🔋 **Parking** 8
Notes LB ⊗ No Children 9yrs 🚭

MORECAMBE Map 18 SD46

Yacht Bay View

★★★★ GUEST HOUSE

359 Marine Road East LA4 5AQ
☎ 01524 414481
e-mail: yachtbayview@hotmail.com
dir: *0.5m NE of town centre on seafront promenade*

Overlooking Morecambe Bay, this family-run property offers comfortable bedrooms, some with impressive views, and all with en suite shower rooms. Guests are given a warm welcome and breakfast is served in the dining room, which also has a lounge area. Yacht Bay View was a Finalist in the AA Friendliest B&B of the Year Award 2012-13.

Rooms 7 en suite (1 fmly) S £32-£35; D £64-£70*
Facilities FTV TVL tea/coffee Wi-fi **Extras** Speciality toiletries - complimentary **Parking** 1 **Notes** LB ⊗

Broadwater Guest House

★★★ GUEST HOUSE

356 Marine Road East LA4 5AQ
☎ 01524 41333
e-mail: enquiries@thebroadwaterhotel.co.uk
web: www.thebroadwaterhotel.co.uk
dir: *M6 junct 34 follow signs for Morecambe, then signs for E Promenade*

Located on Morecambe's sea front this guest house offers a refreshingly friendly welcome. Bedrooms vary in size, but all are en suite, and well equipped with thoughtful extras including free Wi-fi. Substantial breakfasts are served in the pleasant dining room with sea views.

Rooms 8 en suite S £28-£30; D £56-£66* **Facilities** FTV DVD Lounge tea/coffee Wi-fi **Notes** ⊗

Beach Mount

★★★ GUEST ACCOMMODATION

395 Marine Road East LA4 5AN
☎ 01524 420753
e-mail: beachmounthotel@aol.com
dir: *M6 junct 34/35, follow signs to Morecambe. Beach Mount 0.5m from town centre on E Promenade*

This spacious property overlooks the bay and features a range of room styles that includes a junior suite. Guests have use of a comfortable lounge with fully licensed bar, and breakfasts are served in a pleasant separate dining room.

Rooms 10 en suite (1 GF) (10 smoking) S £25.50-£28.75; D £53-£59.50* **Facilities** FTV tea/coffee Cen ht Licensed **Notes** LB Closed Nov-Mar

Belle Vue

★★★ GUEST ACCOMMODATION

330 Marine Rd LA4 5AA
☎ 01524 411375 & 411214 📄 01524 411375
dir: *On seafront between lifeboat house & bingo hall*

With fine views over the promenade and Morecambe Bay, the Belle Vue provides a range of bedrooms styles on three floors; most are accessible by lift. There are comfortable lounges, and a spacious lounge bar where entertainment is provided at peak times. A choice of dishes is available in the large dining room.

Rooms 41 rms (34 en suite) (3 fmly) S £25-£35; D £50-£60* **Facilities** FTV Lounge TVL tea/coffee Dinner available Cen ht Lift Licensed **Parking** 3 **Notes** LB ⊗ No Children 14yrs Closed Jan-Mar

The Wimslow

★★★ GUEST ACCOMMODATION

374 Marine Road East LA4 5AH
☎ 01524 417804 & 07942 861948
e-mail: thewimslow@yahoo.co.uk
web: www.thewimslow.co.uk
dir: *From S: M6 junct 33 follow signs for Lancaster/Morecambe. In Morecambe take A589, turn left at Broadway Hotel, 0.25m on left. From N: M6 junct 35 via Carnforth/Bolton-le-Sands, after 0.25m right at lights. After 3m, 200mtrs past Emmanuel Church*

A very warm welcome is assured at The Wimslow, where the owner's first concern is your comfort and enjoyment. Bedrooms are comfortable, with modern decor and furnishings, and offer a range of guest amenities. Hearty breakfasts are served overlooking Morecambe Bay towards the Lake District on a fine day. Binoculars and guides are provided for breakfast birdwatching.

Rooms 10 en suite (2 GF) S £27-£30; D £54-£60*
Facilities FTV Lounge tea/coffee Cen ht Wi-fi 🔋 **Parking** 2
Notes ⊗ No Children 18yrs Closed 24 Dec-2 Jan

PRESTON Map 18 SD52

Birch Croft Bed & Breakfast

★★★ BED AND BREAKFAST

Gill Ln, Longton PR4 4SS
☎ 01772 613174 & 07761 817187
e-mail: johnsuts@btinternet.com
web: www.birchcroftbandb.co.uk
dir: *From A59 right at rdbt to Midge Hall. Premises 4th on left*

Located only ten minutes away from major motorway links (M6, M65, M61) this establishment is on the doorstep of many attractions and close to Southport, Preston and Blackpool. This is a friendly, family-run business which offers comfortable accommodation in a very peaceful location.

Rooms 3 en suite (1 fmly) S £32-£36; D £50-£56*
Facilities FTV TVL tea/coffee Cen ht Wi-fi **Parking** 11
Notes LB ⊗ 🚭

Ashton Lodge Guest House

★★ GUEST ACCOMMODATION

37 Victoria Pde, Ashton PR2 1DT
☎ 01772 728414 📄 01772 720580
e-mail: greathospitality@btconnect.com
dir: *M6 junct 31, A59 onto A5085, 3.3m onto A5072 (Tulketh Rd), 0.3m, into Victoria Pde*

This detached Victorian guest house offers good value accommodation. Bedrooms vary in size, and some are located on the ground floor. The dining room is the setting for hearty traditional breakfasts served at individual tables.

Rooms 8 rms (3 en suite) (5 fmly) (3 GF) S £28-£35; D £40-£48* **Facilities** FTV TVL tea/coffee Cen ht Wi-fi 🔋 **Parking** 7 **Notes** ⊗

WHITEWELL — Map 18 SD64

PREMIER COLLECTION

The Inn at Whitewell

★★★★★ @ INN

Forest of Bowland, Clitheroe BB7 3AT
☎ 01200 448222 ▣ 01200 448298
e-mail: reception@innatwhitewell.com
dir: M6 junct 31a, B6243 to Longridge. Left at mini-
rdbt. After 3 rdbts (approx 3m) sharp left (with white
railings), then right. Approx 1m, left, right at T-junct.
Next left, 3m to Whitewell

This long-established culinary destination is hidden
away in quintessential Lancashire countryside just 20
minutes from the M6. The fine dining restaurant is
complemented by two historic and cosy bars with
roaring fires, real ales and polished service. Bedrooms
are richly furnished with antiques and eye-catching
bijouterie, while many of the bathrooms have Victorian
brass showers.

Rooms 19 en suite 4 annexe en suite (1 fmly) (2 GF)
S £88-£194; D £120-£240* Facilities STV FTV DVD
iPod docking station tea/coffee Dinner available Direct
Dial Cen ht Wi-fi ↕ 18 Fishing Riding ⚓ Horse stabling
can be arranged Conf Max 45 Thtr 45 Board 35
Parking 60 Notes No coaches Civ Wed 80

WHITWORTH — Map 16 SD81

The Sportsman

★★★ GUEST HOUSE

464 Market St OL12 8AN
☎ 01706 854402 & 07973 693853
e-mail: steve@sportsman.biz
dir: M62 junct 21, follow signs for Burnley (A671)

This family-run sports bar is situated in Whitworth,
recently re-opened by the Butterworth's. The Sportsman
has strong ties with the community and is home to the
local rugby team. Guests can enjoy live sporting events
on large screen TVs and live bands are popular most
weekends. Bedrooms are situated above the pub, they are
comfortable and include a number of family rooms.

Rooms 4 en suite (3 fmly) S fr £30; D fr £50*
Facilities STV FTV DVD TVL tea/coffee Dinner available
Cen ht Licensed Wi-fi ⚓ Parking 40 Notes LB

LEICESTERSHIRE

BELTON — Map 11 SK42

The Queen's Head

★★★★ @ RESTAURANT WITH ROOMS

2 Long St LE12 9TP
☎ 01530 222359 ▣ 01530 224680
e-mail: enquiries@thequeenshead.org
dir: From Loughborough take A6 N, left onto B5324, 3m
to Belton

Situated in the pretty village of Belton, close to East
Midlands Airport, this popular restaurant with rooms
offers good quality food and comfortable accommodation.
All the bedrooms are en suite, individually decorated and
well equipped - Wi-fi is available. Food is the focus with
good quality locally sourced ingredients, blackboard
specials and a range of ales from the local area.

Rooms 6 en suite (2 fmly) S £70-£100; D £80-£150*
(incl.dinner) Facilities Dinner available Wi-fi Conf Max
40 Thtr 40 Class 18 Board 30

CROFT — Map 11 SP59

Fossebrook B&B

★★★★ GUEST ACCOMMODATION

Coventry Rd LE9 3GP
☎ 01455 283517 ▣ 01455 283517
dir: 0.6m SE of village centre on B4114

This friendly guest accommodation stands in a quiet
rural location with good access to major roads. Bedrooms
are spacious, very comfortable and offer an excellent
range of facilities including a range of videos in all
rooms. Breakfast is served in the bright dining room,
which overlooks pleasant gardens and grounds.

Rooms 4 en suite (4 GF) Facilities tea/coffee Cen ht
Wi-fi ⚓ Extras Fruit, snacks Parking 16 Notes ⊗ Closed
24 Dec-2 Jan

EAST LANGTON — Map 11 SP79

The Bell Inn

★★★ INN

Main St LE16 7TW
☎ 01858 545278
e-mail: nickatthebell@btconnect.com
web: www.thebellinn-eastlangton.co.uk
dir: Between A47 & A6, East Langton off B6047

Set in the pretty village of East Langton, The Bell Inn is a
traditional English pub with two comfortable en suite
bedrooms, both of which come with TV and Wi-fi. Staff
are on hand to offer a warm and friendly welcome. A wide
range of food and ales is available, and is served seven
days a week in the spacious restaurant. In the summer
months, guests can enjoy alfresco dining in the attractive
garden.

Rooms 2 en suite (1 fmly) S £55-£65; D £65-£95*
Facilities FTV TVL tea/coffee Dinner available Cen ht Wi-fi
Parking 20 Notes No coaches

EAST MIDLANDS AIRPORT — Map 11 SK42

PREMIER COLLECTION

Kegworth House

★★★★★ ⌂ GUEST HOUSE

42 High St DE74 2DA
☎ 01509 672575 ▣ 01509 670645
e-mail: info@kegworthhouse.co.uk
web: www.kegworthhouse.co.uk
dir: M1 junct 24, A6 to Loughborough. 0.5m 1st right
onto Packington Hill. Left at junct, Kegworth House
50yds on left

Convenient for major roads and East Midlands Airport,
this impressive Georgian house with an immaculate
walled garden has been lovingly restored. The
individually styled bedrooms are luxuriously appointed
and equipped with a wealth of thoughtful extras. The
elegant dining room is the setting for memorable
dinners by arrangement for six or more, and wholesome
breakfasts featuring local produce are served in the
kitchen.

Rooms 11 en suite (1 fmly) (2 GF) S £84-£144;
D £104-£200* Facilities FTV DVD Lounge TVL tea/
coffee Direct Dial Cen ht Licensed Wi-fi Free access to
health club & swimming pool Conf Max 12 Board 12
Parking 25 Notes LB ⊗ No Children 8yrs

HUSBANDS BOSWORTH — Map 11 SP68

Croft Farm B&B (SP634860)

★★★★ FARMHOUSE

Leicester Rd LE17 6NW
☎ 01858 880679 Mrs Smith
e-mail: janesmith06@aol.com
web: www.croftfarm.org.uk
dir: A5199 from Husbands Bosworth towards Leicester.
Croft Farm 0.25m on left

This very spacious and delightfully furnished house
stands on the edge of the village in very well cared for
grounds. Bedrooms are thoughtfully equipped and there
is a very comfortable guests' lounge. Expect a substantial
breakfast together with friendly and attentive service.

Rooms 4 en suite S fr £40; D £70* Facilities DVD TVL
tea/coffee Cen ht Wi-fi Parking 15 Notes ⊗ No Children
10yrs ◉ 350 acres sheep/arable/beef/mixed

KEGWORTH

See East Midlands Airport

KNIPTON   Map 11 SK83

The Manners Arms

★★★★ ⊜ RESTAURANT WITH ROOMS

Croxton Rd NG32 1RH
☎ 01476 879222 📄 01476 879228
e-mail: info@mannersarms.com
web: www.mannersarms.com
dir: *From A607 follow signs to Knipton*

Part of the Rutland Estate and built as a hunting lodge
for the 6th Duke, The Manners Arms offers thoughtfully
furnished bedrooms designed by the present Duchess.
Public areas include the intimate Beater's Bar and
attractive Red Coats Restaurant, popular for its
imaginative menus.

Rooms 10 en suite (1 fmly) **Facilities** TVL tea/coffee
Dinner available Direct Dial Cen ht Wi-fi **Conf** Max 50 Thtr
50 Class 25 Board 20 **Parking** 60 **Notes** No coaches Civ
Wed 50

LEICESTER   Map 11 SK50

Stoney Croft

★★★ GUEST ACCOMMODATION

5-7 Elmfield Av, Off London Rd LE2 1RB
☎ 0116 270 7605 📄 0116 270 6067
e-mail: reception@stoneycrofthotel.co.uk
web: www.stoneycrofthotel.co.uk
dir: *Near city centre on A6 to Market Harborough*

Stoney Croft provides comfortable accommodation and
helpful service. Public rooms include a foyer-lounge area,
breakfast room and conference facilities. The modern
bedrooms come with desks. There is also a large
restaurant-bar where a good selection of freshly cooked
dishes is available.

Rooms 41 en suite (4 fmly) (6 GF) **Facilities** FTV TVL tea/
coffee Dinner available Direct Dial Cen ht Licensed Wi-fi
Pool table **Conf** Max 150 Thtr 150 Class 20 Board 30
Parking 30 **Notes** LB Civ Wed 120

LONG WHATTON   Map 11 SK42

The Royal Oak

★ ★ ★ ★ ★ ⊕ ⌂ INN

26 The Green LE12 5DB
☎ 01509 843694
e-mail: enquiries@theroyaloaklongwhatton.co.uk

The Royal Oak is a popular gastro pub with rooms located
in a small village just four miles from East Midlands
airport. The young team offer a warm welcome and
service is attentive. The seven spacious en suite
bedrooms are set externally to the rear of the property and
have been designed with comfort and style in mind. There
is plenty of parking available and a small garden for the
warmer months.

Rooms 7 en suite (1 fmly) (7 GF) D £85-£99*
Facilities FTV tea/coffee Dinner available Cen ht Wi-fi
Extras Speciality toiletries, mineral water **Parking** 28
Notes ⊗

The Falcon Inn

★★★ INN

64 Main St LE12 5DG
☎ 01509 842416 📄 01509 646802
e-mail: enquiries@thefalconinnlongwhatton.com
dir: *M1 junct 23 N or junct 24 S, follow signs to Airport.
After lights 1st left to Diseworth, left at T-junct, left
towards Long Whatton, on right*

This late 18th-century traditional country pub sits in the
quiet village of Long Whatton. Inside, the relaxed and
friendly atmosphere is complemented by a good choice of
freshly made meals, real ales and efficient service.
Smartly appointed bedrooms are housed in a converted
former school house and stable block at the rear of the
main inn. Ample private parking is provided. Helicopter
landing pad available.

Rooms 11 annexe en suite (5 GF) **Facilities** FTV tea/
coffee Dinner available Cen ht Wi-fi petanque pitch
Conf Max 30 Thtr 20 Class 20 Board 20 **Parking** 46
Notes ⊗

MARKET BOSWORTH   Map 11 SK40

Softleys

★★★ GUEST ACCOMMODATION

2 Market Place CV13 0LE
☎ 01455 290464
e-mail: softleysrestaurant@tiscali.co.uk
dir: *On B585 in Market Place*

Softleys is a Grade II listed building dating back to 1794.
The bedrooms are en suite and set on the third floor

offering picturesque views over Market Bosworth. Quality
food is served using locally sourced ingredients.

Rooms 3 en suite (1 fmly) S fr £69; D fr £85*
Facilities FTV tea/coffee Dinner available Direct Dial
Cen ht Licensed Wi-fi **Conf** Max 26 Thtr 26 Class 26 Board
26 **Notes** RS Sun eve & Mon no food available

MEDBOURNE   Map 11 SP89

Medbourne Grange *(SP815945)*

★★★★ FARMHOUSE

LE16 8EF
☎ 01858 565249 & 07730 956116
📄 01858 565257 Mrs S Beaty
e-mail: sally.beaty@googlemail.com
dir: *2m NE of Medbourne. Between Market Harborough &
Uppingham off B664*

This 150-year-old working farm has unrivalled views of
the Welland Valley and is well situated for Rutland Water,
Uppingham or Market Harborough. Mrs Beaty is a natural
host, ensuring that guests receive a warm welcome and
friendly service. Individually furnished bedrooms are
complemented by comfortable day rooms, and freshly
prepared breakfasts are served in the smart dining room.

Rooms 3 en suite S £36-£46; D £60-£70* **Facilities** FTV
DVD TVL tea/coffee Cen ht Wi-fi ⚲ **Parking** 6 **Notes** ⊗
⊜ 500 acres arable

MELTON MOWBRAY   Map 11 SK71

Bryn Barn

★★★★ GUEST ACCOMMODATION

38 High St, Waltham-on-the-Wolds LE14 4AH
☎ 01664 464783 & 07914 222407
e-mail: glenarowlands@onetel.com
web: www.brynbarn.co.uk
dir: *4.5m NE of Melton. Off A607, in Waltham-on-the-
Wolds centre*

A warm welcome awaits at this attractive, peacefully
located cottage within easy reach of Melton Mowbray,
Grantham, Rutland Water and Belvoir Castle. Bedrooms
are smartly appointed and comfortably furnished, while
public rooms include an inviting lounge overlooking a
wonderful courtyard garden. Meals are available at one of
the nearby village pubs.

Rooms 4 rms (3 en suite) (1 pri facs) (2 fmly) (1 GF)
S £45-£50; D £65-£70* **Facilities** FTV TVL tea/coffee
Cen ht Wi-fi 🕯 **Parking** 4 **Notes** LB Closed 21 Dec-4 Jan

MOUNTSORREL — Map 11 SK51

The Swan Inn

★★★★ INN

10 Loughborough Rd LE12 7AT
☎ 0116 230 2340 ▤ 0116 237 6115
e-mail: office@swaninn.eu
web: www.the-swan-inn.eu
dir: *In village centre*

This traditional 17th-century inn is in the centre of the village and offers well produced meals in the bar, together with a wide range of real ales. The accommodation consists of a luxury suite which includes a double bedroom, a lounge, a large bathroom and an office. Continental breakfast is available in the suite.

Rooms 1 en suite £98; D £108* **Facilities** FTV DVD Lounge TVL tea/coffee Dinner available Direct Dial Cen ht Wi-fi **Parking** 12 **Notes** No coaches

RAVENSTONE — Map 11 SK41

Ravenstone Guesthouse

★★★★ 🅖 GUEST HOUSE

Church Lane Farm House LE67 2AE
☎ 01530 810536
e-mail: annthorne@ravenstone-guesthouse.co.uk
web: www.ravenstone-guesthouse.co.uk
dir: *1.5m W of Coalville. Exit A447 into Church Ln, 2nd house on left*

Situated in the heart of Ravenstone village, this early 18th-century house is full of character. The bedrooms are individually decorated and feature period furniture. Local produce is used for dinner and in the extensive breakfast menu. The beamed dining room has an honesty bar and there is also a cosy lounge.

Rooms 4 en suite **Facilities** FTV TVL tea/coffee Dinner available Cen ht Licensed Wi-fi Painting tuition **Parking** 6 **Notes** Closed 23-30 Dec & 1 Jan RS 31 Dec-1 Jan No breakfast on 1 Jan

SIBSON — Map 11 SK30

The Millers

★★★ INN

Twycross Rd CV13 6LB
☎ 01827 880223 ▤ 01827 880990
e-mail: millerssibsonreservations@greeneking.co.uk
dir: *A5 onto A444 towards Burton. Property 3m on right*

This inn was once a bakery and water mill and several original features have been retained - the water wheel is a feature of the public bar along with the log-burning fireplace. The well-equipped bedrooms have modern facilities. The bar and restaurant are popular with the locals, and there is a conference suite in a separate building which is ideal for small groups.

Rooms 39 en suite (2 fmly) (15 GF) **Facilities** tea/coffee Dinner available Direct Dial Cen ht Wi-fi **Conf** Max 60 Thtr 60 Class 30 Board 40 **Parking** 60 **Notes** ⊗ Civ Wed 60

SUTTON IN THE ELMS — Map 11 SP59

The Mill on the Soar

★★★ INN

Coventry Rd LE9 6QA
☎ 01455 282419 ▤ 01455 285937
e-mail: 1968@greeneking.co.uk
web: www.oldenglish.co.uk
dir: *M1 junct 21, follow signs for Narborough, 3m, inn on left*

This is a popular inn, set in grounds with two rivers and a lake, that caters especially well for family dining. The open-plan bar offers meals and snacks throughout the day, and is divided into family and adults-only areas; for the summer months, there is also an attractive patio. Practical bedrooms are housed in a lodge-style annexe in the grounds.

Rooms 20 en suite 5 annexe en suite (19 fmly) (13 GF) **Facilities** FTV tea/coffee Direct Dial Children's outdoor play area Pool room **Parking** 80 **Notes** ⊗

WOODHOUSE EAVES — Map 11 SK51

The Wheatsheaf Inn

★★★★ 🍴 INN

90 Brand Hill LE12 8SS
☎ 01509 890320
e-mail: richard@wheatsheafinn.net
web: www.wheatsheafinn.net

Originally built around 1800 by the local miners of Swithland slate mines, this charming inn offers a friendly service, good food and modern accommodation in the adjacent self-contained cottage. The first-floor restaurant proves very popular with locals, offering specials and bistro menus that include traditional English dishes, and fresh fish appears on the blackboard specials.

The Wheatsheaf Inn

Rooms 2 annexe en suite S £60-£70; D £80* **Facilities** FTV TVL tea/coffee Dinner available Cen ht Wi-fi **Conf** Thtr 18 Class 12 Board 14 **Parking** 70 **Notes** No coaches

LINCOLNSHIRE

ALFORD — Map 17 TF47

Field Cottage Farm House

🅤

Field Cottage, Church Ln, South Thoresby LN13 0AS
☎ 01507 481830 & 07771 962619
e-mail: gary.attwater@googlemail.com
dir: *A16 follow signs to Alford. At staggered x-rds take exit signed South Thoresby, continue, opposite The Vine pub*

Currently the rating for this establishment is not confirmed. This may be due to a change of ownership or because it has only recently joined the AA rating scheme.

Rooms 2 rms (1 pri facs) D £55-£60* **Facilities** Lounge TVL tea/coffee Cen ht Wi-fi 🛁 **Extras** Fruit, snacks, flowers **Parking** 4 **Notes** ⊗

CLEETHORPES — Map 17 TA30

Adelaide

★★★★ GUEST ACCOMMODATION

41 Isaac's Hill DN35 8JT
☎ 01472 693594 ▤ 01472 329717
e-mail: adelaide.hotel@ntlworld.com
dir: *500yds W of seafront. At A180 & A46 junct onto A1098 (Isaac's Hill), house on right at bottom of hill*

This beautifully presented house offers well-equipped bedrooms and comfortable public rooms. Hospitality is a major strength. Good home cooking is provided and there is a small lounge with a bar. Secure parking is available.

Rooms 5 rms (3 en suite) (1 fmly) **Facilities** STV TVL tea/coffee Dinner available Cen ht Licensed **Notes** ⊗ No Children 4yrs

Save on B&Bs and Hotels. Book at theAA.com/hotel

LINCOLNSHIRE 199 ENGLAND

Aristocrat Guest House

★★★★ GUEST HOUSE

15 Clee Rd DN35 8AD
☎ 01472 234027 & 07957 388475 🖷 01472 318086
e-mail: aristocrat@ntlworld.com
web: www.aristocrat-guesthouse.co.uk
dir: *From A180 follow signs for Cleethorpes, over flyover, through 3 sets of lights. At rdbt right into Clee Rd, 30yds on left*

Located just a few minutes' walk from the seafront, restaurants, bars and main attractions, this lovely house is family run. The attractively decorated bedrooms are well equipped with thoughtful accessories such as fridges and DVD players, and Wi-fi is available.

Rooms 4 rms (2 en suite) (2 pri facs) (1 fmly) S fr £30; D fr £55 **Facilities** FTV tea/coffee Cen ht Wi-fi **Parking** 2 **Notes** LB ⊗

The Comat

★★★★ GUEST ACCOMMODATION

26 Yarra Rd DN35 8LS
☎ 01472 694791 🖷 01472 238113
e-mail: comat-hotel@ntlworld.com
web: www.comat-hotel.co.uk
dir: *Exit A1098 (Alexandra Rd), left of library*

A short walk from the shops and seafront, the welcoming Comat offers cosy, well-equipped bedrooms. The Superior double has a leather settee, four-poster bed and sitting area. Tasty English breakfasts are served in the bright dining room, and a quiet sitting room and bar overlook the colourful flower terrace.

Rooms 6 en suite (2 fmly) (2 GF) D £65-£70* **Facilities** FTV DVD TVL tea/coffee Cen ht Wi-fi **Notes** LB ⊗ No Children 3yrs

Alpine House

★★★ GUEST ACCOMMODATION

55 Clee Rd DN35 8AD
☎ 01472 690804
e-mail: nw.sanderson@ntlworld.com
dir: *On A46 before junct A180 & A1098 Isaac's Hill rdbt*

Carefully run by the resident owners, and convenient for the town centre and attractions, this friendly guest accommodation offers compact, well-equipped bedrooms and a comfortable lounge.

Rooms 5 rms (2 fmly) **Facilities** FTV TVL tea/coffee Cen ht Wi-fi **Parking** 3 **Notes** ⊗ No Children 2yrs ⊛

Brier Park Guest House

★★★ GUEST ACCOMMODATION

27 Clee Rd DN35 8AD
☎ 01472 605591 & 07849 639923
e-mail: graham.sherwood2@ntlworld.com
web: www.brierparks-guesthouse.co.uk
dir: *Left at bottom of Isaac's Hill, 150yds on left*

A private house personally managed by the owner offering a friendly atmosphere and comfortable compact bedrooms that are brightly decorated. Breakfast is freshly cooked to order, and convenient parking in front is a bonus.

Rooms 6 rms (3 en suite) (3 pri facs) (1 fmly) (2 GF) **Facilities** FTV TVL tea/coffee Cen ht Wi-fi **Parking** 2 **Notes** LB ⊗ No Children 5yrs ⊛

Holmhirst

★★★ GUEST ACCOMMODATION

3 Alexandra Rd DN35 8LQ
☎ 01472 692656 🖷 01472 692656
e-mail: holmhirst@aol.com

Overlooking the sea and the pier, this Victorian terraced house offers simply furnished bedrooms, many with en suite shower rooms. The public areas have recently been refurbished and relaunched as Apples Wine & Cider Bar Bistro with a stylish New York theme, well-stocked bar and wide range of meals available.

Rooms 8 rms (5 en suite) **Facilities** TVL TV7B tea/coffee Dinner available Cen ht Licensed **Notes** ⊗

Ginnie's Guest House

★★★ 🄰 GUEST HOUSE

27 Queens Pde DN35 0DF
☎ 01472 694997 🖷 01472 593153
e-mail: enquiries@ginnies.co.uk
dir: *From Kingsway (seafront) into Queens Parade (A1098)*

Rooms 7 rms (5 en suite) (2 pri facs) (3 fmly) (1 GF) D £50-£65* **Facilities** FTV DVD iPod docking station TVL tea/coffee Cen ht Wi-fi **Extras** Speciality toiletries **Parking** 4 **Notes** LB ⊗ RS 24 Dec-2 Jan 24-25 & 31 Dec room only

GAINSBOROUGH   Map 17 SK88

See also Marton (Village)

Eastbourne House

★★★★ GUEST HOUSE

81 Trinity St DN21 1JF
☎ 01427 679511
e-mail: info@eastbournehouse.co.uk
dir: *In town centre. A631 onto A159 (Trinity St)*

Located in a residential area west of the town centre, this impressive Victorian house has been restored to provide high standards of comfort and facilities. Bedrooms are thoughtfully furnished and the comprehensive breakfast uses quality local produce.

Rooms 5 rms (3 en suite) (2 pri facs) (1 fmly) **Facilities** FTV DVD tea/coffee Cen ht Wi-fi 🖧 **Parking** 1 **Notes** ⊗

GRANTHAM   Map 11 SK93

The Welby Arms

★★★★ INN

The Green, Allington NG32 2EA
☎ 01400 281361 🖷 01400 281361
dir: *4m NW of Grantham. Exit A52 into Allington*

Set in the pleasant village of Allington, The Welby Arms is just off the busy A1, handy for Grantham but deep in the countryside. There are three purpose built en suites in a former byre behind a popular village inn that serves a wide range of real ales and an extensive menu that is very popular with locals.

Rooms 3 annexe en suite **Facilities** FTV Dinner available Cen ht **Parking** 30 **Notes** ⊗

Beaver House

★★★ BED AND BREAKFAST

School Ln, Old Somerby NG33 4AH
☎ 01476 565011 & 07779 002206
e-mail: cuttlers@btinternet.com
web: www.beaverhouse.co.uk
dir: *From Grantham A52 E for 2m. At rdbt take exit signed Old Somerby, then 1st left, 1st house on right*

Located on a mainly residential avenue in the quiet village of Old Somerby, just five minutes' drive from Grantham, a warm welcome awaits you at Beaver House. The accommodation has been thoughtfully designed, and is well equipped and very comfortable. Breakfasts are served in the dining room overlooking the manicured garden, and there is a restaurant within walking distance. For those with children a highchair and travel cot can be provided.

Rooms 3 rms (1 en suite) (1 pri facs) S £35-£40; D £45-£50 **Facilities** FTV TVL tea/coffee Cen ht Wi-fi **Parking** 3 **Notes** ⊗ ⊛

HEMSWELL　　　　　Map 17 SK99

PREMIER COLLECTION

Hemswell Court

★★★★★ 　GUEST ACCOMMODATION

Lancaster Green, Hemswell Cliff DN21 5TQ
☎ 01427 668508 ⬚ 01427 667335
e-mail: function@hemswellcourt.com
dir: 1.5m SE of Hemswell on A631 in Hemswell Cliff

Originally an officers' mess, Hemswell Court is now a venue for conferences, weddings or private gatherings. The modern bedrooms and many suites are ideal for families or groups of friends, and all rooms are well equipped. The lounges and dining rooms are enhanced by many antique pieces.

Rooms 23 en suite (2 fmly) (4 GF) S £75-£95; D £85-£145* **Facilities** TVL tea/coffee Dinner available Cen ht Licensed Wi-fi 🐾 🛥 **Conf** Max 200 Thtr 200 Class 150 Board 150 **Parking** 150 **Notes** ⊗ Closed Xmas & New Year Civ Wed 200

HORNCASTLE　　　　Map 17 TF26

Greenfield Farm *(TF175745)*

★ ★ ★ ★ 　FARMHOUSE

Mill Ln/Cow Ln, Minting LN9 5PJ
☎ 01507 578457 & 07768 368829
⬚ 01507 578457 　Mrs J Bankes Price
e-mail: info@greenfieldfarm.net
web: www.greenfieldfarm.net
dir: A158 NW from Horncastle. 5m left at The New Midge pub, farm 1m on right

A beautifully appointed, spacious farmhouse located just one mile from the A158 and within easy reach of many attractions. The stunning grounds, wildlife pond and surrounding countryside ensure a peaceful stay. A warm welcome is certain along with comfortable, fully equipped bedrooms (two doubles and a twin room available) and a hearty Lincolnshire breakfast. There is also a lovely sitting room and complimentary Wi-fi access.

Rooms 3 en suite S £45; D £64-£70* **Facilities** FTV TVL tea/coffee Cen ht Wi-fi Farm trail **Parking** 12 **Notes** LB ⊗ No Children 10yrs Closed Xmas & New Year 🐾 387 acres arable

HOUGH-ON-THE-HILL　　　Map 11 SK94

PREMIER COLLECTION

The Brownlow Arms

★★★★★ ◉ INN

High Rd NG32 2AZ
☎ 01400 250234 ⬚ 01400 271193
e-mail: armsinn@yahoo.co.uk
web: www.thebrownlowarms.com

This beautiful 16th-century property enjoys a peaceful location in the picturesque village, located between Newark and Grantham. Tastefully appointed and spacious public areas have many original features, and include a choice of luxurious lounges and an elegant restaurant offering imaginative cuisine. The bedrooms are stylish, comfortable and particularly well equipped.

Rooms 4 en suite 1 annexe en suite (1 GF) S £65; D £98 **Facilities** FTV DVD tea/coffee Dinner available Wi-fi 🔒 **Parking** 20 **Notes** ⊗ No Children 10yrs Closed 25-27 Dec & 31 Dec-1 Jan No coaches

LINCOLN　　　　　Map 17 SK97

See also Horncastle & Marton

PREMIER COLLECTION

Minster Lodge

★★★★★ GUEST ACCOMMODATION

3 Church Ln LN2 1QJ
☎ 01522 513220 ⬚ 01522 513220
e-mail: info@minsterlodge.co.uk
dir: 400yds N of cathedral

A charming house in a convenient location close to the cathedral and castle. Spacious bedrooms are enhanced by good bathrooms and are full of thoughtful extras. A large comfortable sitting room with deep sofas, and an attractive dining room, where Aga-cooked breakfasts can be enjoyed, ensure guests have a memorable stay.

Rooms 6 en suite (3 fmly) **Facilities** FTV TVL tea/coffee Direct Dial Cen ht Wi-fi **Parking** 11

Carholme Guest House

★★★★ GUEST HOUSE

175 Carholme Rd LN1 1RU
☎ 01522 531059 & 07795 964706
e-mail: root@carholmeguesthouse.com
dir: From A1 take A57. From A46 take A57, 0.5m on left after racecourse

Situated a short walk from Lincoln Marina and the University, this small family-run guest house provides well appointed accommodation that is attractively decorated and well maintained, equipped with many useful extras; a ground floor bedroom is available. A freshly cooked breakfast is served in a pleasant dining area and guests have use of a comfortable ground floor lounge.

Rooms 5 rms (4 en suite) (1 pri facs) (1 fmly) (1 GF) S £30-£40; D £50-£80* **Facilities** FTV Lounge tea/coffee Cen ht Wi-fi 🔒 **Parking** 3 **Notes** ⊗ Closed 23 Dec-2 Jan

Carline Guest House

★★★★ GUEST HOUSE

1-3 Carline Rd LN1 1HL
☎ 01522 530422
e-mail: sales@carlineguesthouse.co.uk
dir: Left off A1102, A15 N. Premises 1m from A46 bypass & A57 into city

This smart double-fronted Edwardian house is within easy walking distance of the castle and the cathedral. Bedrooms are particularly smartly appointed and have a host of useful extras. Breakfast is served at individual tables in the spacious dining room.

Rooms 9 en suite (1 fmly) (3 GF) **Facilities** tea/coffee Cen ht Wi-fi **Parking** 6 **Notes** LB ⊗ No Children 3yrs Closed Xmas & New Year 🐾

Eagles Guest House

★★★★ GUEST ACCOMMODATION

552A Newark Rd, North Hykeham LN6 9NG
☎ 01522 686346
e-mail: eaglesguesthouse@yahoo.co.uk
dir: A46 onto A1434, signed Lincoln South, North Hykeham & South Hykeham. 0.5m on right opposite Cornflower Way

This large, modern detached house is situated within easy access of the A46 and the historic city of Lincoln. The smartly appointed, thoughtfully equipped bedrooms are bright and fresh in appearance. A substantial breakfast is served in the pleasant dining room and free Wi-fi is available throughout the property.

Rooms 5 en suite (1 fmly) (1 GF) S £38-£42; D £50-£70* **Facilities** FTV tea/coffee Cen ht Wi-fi **Parking** 6 **Notes** ⊗ No Children 9yrs

The Loudor

★★★★ GUEST ACCOMMODATION

37 Newark Rd, North Hykeham LN6 8RB
☎ 01522 680333 ⬚ 01522 802770
e-mail: info@loudorhotel.co.uk
dir: 3m from city centre. A46 onto A1434 for 2m, on left opposite shopping centre

Opposite the Forum shopping centre and a short walk from the sports centre, this friendly house offers well-equipped bedrooms. Breakfast is served at individual tables in the spacious dining room. There is ample parking.

Rooms 9 en suite 2 annexe rms (1 fmly) (2 GF) S £40; D £58* **Facilities** FTV Lounge tea/coffee Cen ht Wi-fi **Extras** Home-made biscuits **Conf** Max 30 **Parking** 8 **Notes** ⊗

The Old Bakery

★★★★ ◉◉ RESTAURANT WITH ROOMS

26/28 Burton Rd LN1 3LB
☎ 01522 576057 & 07949 035554
e-mail: enquiries@theold-bakery.co.uk
dir: *Exit A46 at Lincoln North follow signs for cathedral. 3rd exit at 1st rdbt, 1st exit at next rdbt*

Situated close to the castle at the top of the town, this converted bakery offers well-equipped bedrooms and a delightful dining operation. The cooking is international and uses much local produce. Expect good friendly service from the dedicated staff.

Rooms 4 rms (2 en suite) (2 pri facs) (1 fmly) S £50; D £55-£65 (room only)* **Facilities** FTV tea/coffee Dinner available Cen ht Wi-fi 🔒 **Notes** ✖

St Clements Lodge

★★★★ GUEST ACCOMMODATION

21 Langworth Gate LN2 4AD
☎ 01522 521532 & 07906 184266 📠 01522 521532
e-mail: enquiries@stclementslodge.co.uk
dir: *350yds E of cathedral, down Eastgate into Langworth Gate*

A warm welcome awaits at St Clements Lodge, which is just a short walk from Lincoln Cathedral and Castle. This constantly improving accommodation offers three very comfortable bedrooms, two of which are en suite. Off-road parking is available.

Rooms 3 rms (2 en suite) (1 pri facs) (1 fmly) S £55; D £70-£75 **Facilities** FTV tea/coffee Cen ht Wi-fi **Parking** 3 **Notes** ✖ ☺

South Park Guest House

★★★★ GUEST HOUSE

11 South Park LN5 8EN
☎ 01522 887136 📠 01522 887136
e-mail: enquiry@southparkguesthouse.co.uk
dir: *1m S of city centre on A15*

A Victorian house situated on the inner ring road facing South Park. The staff are friendly and attentive, and bedrooms, though compact, are well equipped. Breakfast is served in a modern dining room overlooking the park.

Rooms 6 en suite 1 annexe en suite (2 fmly) (1 GF) **Facilities** FTV tea/coffee Dinner available Cen ht Wi-fi **Parking** 7 **Notes** ✖

The Manse B&B

★★★ BED AND BREAKFAST

Middlesykes Ln, Grimoldby LN11 8TE
☎ 01507 327495
e-mail: knowles578@btinternet.com
dir: *Grimoldby 4m from Louth on B1200. Into Tinkle St, right into Middlesykes Ln*

Located in a quiet country lane, this pleasantly appointed house offers comfortable accommodation and a warm welcome. Bedrooms offer a range of homely extras along with flat screen TV. Proprietors are enthusiastic and helpful, making every effort to make guests feel welcomed to their home, and freshly cooked evening meals are available by prior arrangement. The Manse is an ideal location for exploring the delights of the Wolds.

Rooms 4 rms (3 en suite) (1 pri facs) (1 fmly) (1 GF) S £45; D £55-£65* **Facilities** FTV TVL tea/coffee Dinner available Cen ht Wi-fi **Parking** 5 **Notes** LB ✖ No Children 5yrs Closed 25 Dec ☺

Park View Guest House

★★★ GUEST HOUSE

48 Gibraltar Rd LN12 2AT
☎ 01507 477267 & 07906 847841 📠 01507 477267
e-mail: malcolm@pvgh.freeserve.co.uk
dir: *Take A1104 to Mablethorpe. At beach turn right into Gibraltar Rd*

This well-established guest house is ideally situated just beside Mablethorpe's golden beach and the Queens Park, and also within easy walking distance of the main town centre amenities. Service is both helpful and friendly, provided by the resident proprietors, Debbie and Malcolm. The accommodation is soundly presented and of varying sizes, the ground-floor bedrooms proving particularly popular.

Rooms 5 rms (2 en suite) (1 fmly) (3 GF) S £25-£27.50; D £50-£55* **Facilities** FTV TVL tea/coffee Dinner available Cen ht Licensed Wi-fi **Parking** 6 **Notes** LB ☺

PREMIER COLLECTION

The Advocate Arms

★★★★★ ◉ RESTAURANT WITH ROOMS

2 Queen St LN8 3EH
☎ 01673 842364
e-mail: info@advocatearms.co.uk
dir: *In town centre*

Appointed to a high standard this 18th-century property is located in the heart of Market Rasen and combines historic character and contemporary design. The operation centres around the stylish restaurant where service is friendly yet professional and the food is a highlight. The attractive bedrooms are very well equipped and feature luxury bathrooms.

Rooms 10 en suite (2 fmly) S £50-£70; D £55-£100 (room only)* **Facilities** FTV tea/coffee Dinner available Cen ht Wi-fi 🛗 18 **Conf** Max 22 Thtr 18 Class 22 Board 18 **Parking** 6 **Notes** ✖

Wold View House B&B

★★★ 🏠 BED AND BREAKFAST

Bully Hill Top, Tealby LN8 6JA
☎ 01673 838226 & 07976 563473
e-mail: enquiries@woldviewhouse.co.uk
dir: *A46 onto B1225 towards Horncastle, after 7m Wold View House at x-rds*

Situated at the top of Bully Hill with expansive views across The Wold, this smart bed and breakfast offers modern bedrooms and warm hospitality. Ideal for walking, riding, or touring the charming nearby villages and coastline, the house is also only a short drive from Lincoln.

Rooms 3 rms (2 en suite) (1 pri facs) (1 fmly) S £35-£40; D £60-£65* **Facilities** TVL tea/coffee Cen ht Licensed Wi-fi **Parking** 15 **Notes** LB ☺

MARTON (VILLAGE) Map 17 SK88

Black Swan Guest House

★★★★ GUEST ACCOMMODATION

21 High St DN21 5AH
☎ 01427 718878
e-mail: info@blackswanguesthouse.co.uk
web: www.blackswanguesthouse.co.uk
dir: On A156 in village centre at junct A1500

Centrally located in the village, this 18th-century former coaching inn retains many original features, and offers good hospitality and homely bedrooms with modern facilities. Tasty breakfasts are served in the cosy dining room and a comfortable lounge with Wi-fi access is available. Transport to nearby pubs and restaurants can be provided.

Rooms 6 en suite 4 annexe en suite (3 fmly) (4 GF) S £48-£55; D £68-£78 **Facilities** FTV TVL tea/coffee Cen ht Licensed Wi-fi 🛁 **Parking** 10 **Notes** LB

SKEGNESS Map 17 TF56

Sunnyside B&B

★★★ GUEST ACCOMMODATION

34 Scarborough Av PE25 2TA
☎ 01754 765119 & 07435 764160
e-mail: form@skegness-accommodation.co.uk
dir: From A52 or A158 follow signs for seafront. Scarborough Av opposite pier, Sunnyside on left before church

Sunnyside B&B is ideally situated in a quiet avenue, close to Skegness Pier and the northern promenade. The bedrooms are pleasantly decorated and have a good range of useful facilities such as fridges, Freeview TV and DVD players. Breakfast is served at individual tables in the breakfast room and guests also have the use of a conservatory.

Rooms 8 en suite (2 fmly) (1 GF) D £50-£55*
Facilities FTV DVD TVL tea/coffee Cen ht Wi-fi
Extras Fridges in all bedrooms **Parking** 4 **Notes** LB ⊗
Closed 20-28 Dec

SKILLINGTON Map 11 SK82

The Cross Swords Inn

★★★ INN

The Square NG33 5HB
☎ 01476 861132
e-mail: harold@thecross-swordsinn.co.uk
dir: Exit A1 at Colsterworth junct between Grantham & Stamford

Located at the crossroads at the centre of the award-winning village of Skillington, and very popular with the local community, this traditional inn offers three modern, well-equipped bedrooms that are housed in an attractive cottage at the top of the courtyard, and named in keeping with the history of the village. All are very comfortable and coupled with smart modern bathrooms. The inn provides imaginative food and a range of real ales in a rustic period atmosphere.

Rooms 3 annexe en suite (3 GF) S fr £55; D fr £68*
Facilities FTV tea/coffee Dinner available Cen ht Gliding club **Parking** 12 **Notes** ⊗ No Children 10yrs RS Sun eve & Mon lunch bar & restaurant closed No coaches

STAMFORD Map 11 TF00

PREMIER COLLECTION

Meadow View

★★★★★ BED AND BREAKFAST

Wothorpe Rd PE9 2JR
☎ 01780 762133 & 07833 972577
dir: Off A1 signed Stamford, follow road past entrance to Burley House, bottom of hill, left at lights. Follow road round, 1st house on left

A stylish property situated just a short walk from the town centre and Burghley House. The tastefully appointed bedrooms are contemporary in style with lovely co-ordinated soft furnishings and many thoughtful touches. Breakfast is served at a large communal table in the open-plan kitchen/dining room, and guests have the use of a smartly appointed lounge with plush sofas.

Rooms 3 en suite S £55-£65; D £75-£85*
Facilities FTV iPod docking station TVL tea/coffee Cen ht **Extras** Chocolates **Parking** 2 **Notes** LB ⊗ ⊛

The Bull & Swan at Burghley

★★★★ ⊛ INN

St Martins PE9 2LJ
☎ 01780 766412 📠 01780 767061
e-mail: enquiries@thebullandswan.co.uk
dir: A1 onto Old Great North Rd, left onto B1081, follow Stamford signs

This delightful inn dates back to the 16th century when it is said to have been a gentleman's drinking club. The public rooms include a large bar with a range of ales. There is also a separate restaurant. The stylish bedrooms are extremely well appointed with lovely co-ordinated soft furnishings and a range of thoughtful touches.

Rooms 7 en suite (2 fmly) **Facilities** FTV tea/coffee Dinner available Direct Dial Cen ht Wi-fi **Parking** 7 **Notes** No coaches

Candlesticks

★★★ RESTAURANT WITH ROOMS

1 Church Ln PE9 2JU
☎ 01780 764033 📠 01780 756071
e-mail: info@candlestickshotel.co.uk
dir: B1081 into Stamford. Left onto A43. Right into Worthorpe Rd, right into Church Ln

Candlesticks is a 17th-century property situated in a quiet lane in the oldest part of Stamford just a short walk from the centre of town. The bedrooms are pleasantly decorated and equipped with a good range of useful extras. Public rooms feature Candlesticks restaurant, a small lounge and a cosy bar.

Rooms 8 en suite **Facilities** STV FTV tea/coffee Dinner available Direct Dial Cen ht **Parking** 8 **Notes** LB ⊗ RS Mon No restaurant or bar service No coaches

SUTTON ON SEA Map 17 TF58

Athelstone Lodge

★★★ GUEST ACCOMMODATION

25 Trusthorpe Rd LN12 2LR
☎ 01507 441521
e-mail: athelstone@googlemail.com
dir: On A52, N of village

Situated between Mablethorpe and Skegness and close to the promenade, Athelstone Lodge has pleasant, soundly maintained bedrooms equipped with many useful extras. Breakfast is served in the dining room and a bar and a lounge are also available. A variety of enjoyable home-cooked dinners is served.

Rooms 6 rms (5 en suite) (1 fmly) S £32-£34; D £64-£68* **Facilities** FTV TVL tea/coffee Dinner available Cen ht Licensed **Parking** 6 **Notes** LB Closed Nov-Feb

Save on B&Bs and Hotels. Book at theAA.com/hotel

LINCOLNSHIRE – LONDON 203 ENGLAND

WHAPLODE
Map 12 TF32

Westgate House & Barn
★★★★ BED AND BREAKFAST

Little Ln PE12 6RU
☎ 01406 370546
e-mail: enquiries@westgatehousebandb.co.uk
web: www.westgatehousebandb.co.uk
dir: *Follow brown signs in Whaplode (on A151)*

Set in a peaceful rural location, in well-established cottage gardens and grounds, Westgate House offers comfortably appointed accommodation in a delightful barn conversion. Breakfast is taken in the main house, in a charming room with wood-burning stove and garden views. The freshly cooked breakfast includes good locally sourced ingredients and home-made preserves.

Rooms 2 annexe en suite **Facilities** FTV tea/coffee Cen ht Wi-fi **Parking** 2 **Notes** LB ⊗ No Children 6yrs ⊜

WINTERINGHAM
Map 17 SE92

PREMIER COLLECTION

Winteringham Fields
★★★★★ ⚫⚫ RESTAURANT WITH ROOMS

DN15 9ND
☎ 01724 733096 🖨 01724 733898
e-mail: reception@winteringhamfields.co.uk
dir: *In village centre at x-rds*

This highly regarded restaurant with rooms, located deep in the countryside in the village of Winteringham, is just six miles west of the Humber Bridge. Public rooms and bedrooms, some of which are housed in renovated barns and cottages, are delightfully cosseting. Award-winning food is served in the restaurant.

Rooms 4 en suite 7 annexe en suite (2 fmly) (3 GF) S £145-£220; D £145-£220 **Facilities** iPod docking station tea/coffee Dinner available Direct Dial Cen ht Wi-fi **Conf** Max 50 Thtr 50 Class 50 Board 50 **Parking** 14 **Notes** LB Closed 25 Dec for 2wks, last wk Oct, 2wks Aug No coaches Civ Wed 60

WOODHALL SPA
Map 17 TF16

The Claremont Guest House
★★★ GUEST HOUSE

9/11 Witham Rd LN10 6RW
☎ 01526 352000
e-mail: claremontgh@live.co.uk
web: www.theclaremontguesthouse.co.uk
dir: *In town centre on B1191 near mini-rdbt*

A Victorian townhouse with a lovely dining room, guest lounge and Wi-fi access. The owners are very friendly and offer bedrooms that are well equipped and vary in size from cosy singles to a family room. The house is pet friendly, with lock up facilities for cyclists and golfers also available.

Rooms 10 en suite (1 fmly) (2 GF) S £40; D £70*
Facilities FTV TVL tea/coffee Dinner available Cen ht Wi-fi
🔒 **Conf** Max 20 Thtr 20 Class 20 Board 10 **Parking** 4 **Notes** LB

LONDON

N4

Best Western London Highbury
PLAN 2 F5
★★★ GUEST ACCOMMODATION

372-374 Seven Sisters Rd N4 2PG
☎ 020 8802 6551 🖨 020 8802 9461
e-mail: reservations@highbury.com
dir: *0.5m from Finsbury Park Station*

Located opposite Finsbury Park and only a short tube ride from the centre of London, this newly refurbished establishment offers well-appointed and well-equipped accommodation. There is ample and secure parking; a well stocked bar and a buffet style continental breakfast is available daily.

Rooms 45 en suite (6 fmly) (7 GF) **Facilities** STV FTV tea/coffee Direct Dial Lift Wi-fi **Parking** 20 **Notes** ⊗

N12
Map 6 TQ29

Glenlyn Guest House
★★★ GUEST ACCOMMODATION

6 Woodside Park Rd N12 8RP
☎ 020 8445 0440 🖨 020 8446 2902
e-mail: contactus@glenlynhotel.com
web: www.glenlynhotel.com
dir: *M25 junct 23 towards High Barnet, A1000 into North Finchley on right after Sainsburys*

Located in the heart of Finchley and set in four large Victorian terraced houses, the Glenlyn offers a choice of rooms spanning from cosy loft rooms to interconnecting family rooms. Guests can relax in the private bar or unwind in the garden. Breakfast is served in the airy conservatory.

Rooms 27 en suite (4 fmly) (3 GF) S £70; D £80*
Facilities FTV Lounge TVL tea/coffee Direct Dial Cen ht Licensed Wi-fi **Parking** 14 **Notes** ⊗

NW1

MIC
PLAN 1 C5

★★★★ 🍴 GUEST ACCOMMODATION

81-103 Euston St NW1 2EZ
☎ 020 7380 0001 ▤ 020 7387 5300
e-mail: reception@micentre.com
web: www.micentre.com
dir: *Euston Rd left at lights onto Melton St, 1st left onto Euston St, 100yds on left*

Located within walking distance of Euston station, this smart property is convenient for central London. Stylish air-conditioned bedrooms are thoughtfully equipped for business and leisure. The airy Atrium Bar and Restaurant offers drinks, light snacks and an evening menu. Extensive conference and meeting facilities are available.

Rooms 28 en suite (2 fmly) **Facilities** STV iPod docking station TVL tea/coffee Dinner available Direct Dial Cen ht Lift Licensed Wi-fi **Extras** Speciality toiletries, safe **Conf** Max 150 Thtr 150 Class 50 Board 45 **Notes** LB ⊗ Civ Wed

Euston Square
PLAN 1 C5

★★★ GUEST ACCOMMODATION

152-156 North Gower St NW1 2LU
☎ 020 7388 0099 ▤ 020 7788 9699
e-mail: reservations@euston-square-hotel.com
web: www.euston-square-hotel.com
dir: *On junct Euston Rd, next to Euston Square tube station*

Over the tube station, this property is ideal for both the business and leisure markets. The smart compact bedrooms and en suite bathrooms are well designed. Conference facilities and a modern reception area are available. Zone One Restaurant & Bar serves a well-balanced and good value menu.

Rooms 75 en suite (4 GF) **Facilities** STV TVL tea/coffee Dinner available Direct Dial Cen ht Lift Licensed Wi-fi **Conf** Thtr 120 Class 50 Board 50 **Notes** ⊗

NW3

The Langorf
PLAN 2 E4

★★★★ GUEST ACCOMMODATION

20 Frognal, Hampstead NW3 6AG
☎ 020 7794 4483 ▤ 020 7435 9055
e-mail: info@langorfhotel.com
web: www.langorfhotel.com
dir: *Off A41 (Finchley Rd), near Finchley Road tube station*

Located on a leafy and mainly residential avenue within easy walking distance of shops and restaurants, this elegant Edwardian property has been appointed to provide high standards of comfort and facilities. Bedrooms are furnished with flair and a warm welcome is assured.

Rooms 31 en suite (4 fmly) (3 GF) **Facilities** STV TVL tea/coffee Direct Dial Cen ht Lift Licensed Wi-fi **Conf** Max 30 Thtr 30 Class 20 Board 15 **Parking Notes** ⊗

La Gaffe
PLAN 2 E4

★★★ 🍴 GUEST ACCOMMODATION

107-111 Heath St NW3 6SS
☎ 020 7435 8965 & 7435 4941 ▤ 020 7794 7592
e-mail: info@lagaffe.co.uk
dir: *On A502, 250yds N of Hampstead tube station*

This family-owned and run guest accommodation, just north of Hampstead High Street, offers charm and warm hospitality. The Italian restaurant, which is open most lunchtimes and for dinner, is popular with locals. Bedrooms are compact, but all are en suite.

La Gaffe

Rooms 11 en suite 7 annexe en suite (2 fmly) (2 GF) **Facilities** FTV tea/coffee Dinner available Direct Dial Cen ht Licensed Wi-fi **Conf** Max 10 Board 10 **Notes** ⊗ RS 26 Dec Restaurant closed

NW9

Kingsland
PLAN 2 C5

★★★ GUEST ACCOMMODATION

Kingsbury Circle, Kingsbury NW9 9RR
☎ 020 8206 0666 ▤ 020 8206 0555
e-mail: stay@kingslandhotel.co.uk
web: www.kingslandhotel.co.uk
dir: *Kingsbury Circle junct A4006 & A4140*

Located at the roundabout near Kingsbury Station, shops, restaurants and Wembley complex, the Kingsland provides modern bedrooms with smart bathrooms en suite. A continental breakfast is supplied, and a passenger lift and car park are available.

Rooms 28 en suite (5 fmly) (6 GF) S £45-£65; D £65-£95* **Facilities** STV FTV tea/coffee Direct Dial Cen ht Lift Wi-fi **Parking** 30 **Notes** ⊗

SW1

Sidney London-Victoria
PLAN 1 C1

★★★★ GUEST ACCOMMODATION

68-76 Belgrave Rd SW1V 2BP
☎ 020 7834 2738 ▤ 020 7630 0973
e-mail: reservations@sidneyhotel.com
web: www.sidneyhotel.com
dir: *A202 (Vauxhall Bridge Rd) into Charlwood St & junct with Belgrave Rd*

This smart property near Pimlico offers brightly decorated bedrooms that are well equipped for business use, while several rooms are suitable for families. Public areas include a bar lounge and an airy breakfast room.

Rooms 82 en suite (13 fmly) (9 GF) **Facilities** STV Lounge TVL tea/coffee Direct Dial Cen ht Lift Licensed Wi-fi **Conf** Max 30 Thtr 30 Class 15 Board 14 **Notes** ⊗

Save on B&Bs and Hotels. Book at theAA.com/hotel

LONDON 205 ENGLAND

The Windermere PLAN 1 C1

★★★★ GUEST ACCOMMODATION

142/144 Warwick Way, Victoria SW1V 4JE
☎ 020 7834 5163 📠 020 7630 8831
e-mail: reservations@windermere-hotel.co.uk
web: www.windermere-hotel.co.uk
dir: On B324 off Buckingham Palace Rd, at junct with
Alderney St

The Windermere is a relaxed, informal and family-run
establishment within easy reach of Victoria Station and
many of the capital's attractions. Bedrooms, although
varying in size, are stylish, comfortable and well
equipped. The Pimlico restaurant serves delicious evening
meals and hearty cooked breakfasts.

Rooms 19 en suite (3 fmly) (3 GF) **Facilities** FTV TVL tea/
coffee Dinner available Direct Dial Cen ht Lift Licensed
Wi-fi **Notes** ✕

Best Western Victoria Palace PLAN 1 C1

★★★ GUEST ACCOMMODATION

60-64 Warwick Way SW1V 1SA
☎ 020 7821 7113 📠 020 7630 0806
e-mail: info@bestwesternvictoriapalace.co.uk
web: www.bestwesternvictoriapalace.co.uk

An elegant, 19th-century building located in the heart of
London, near to Belgravia and a five minute walk from
Victoria rail, underground and coach stations. The
bedrooms have en suite shower rooms. A buffet-style
breakfast is served in the basement dining room.

Rooms 50 en suite (4 fmly) (4 GF) **Facilities** STV TVL tea/
coffee Direct Dial Cen ht Lift **Notes** ✕

Central House PLAN 1 C1

★★★ GUEST ACCOMMODATION

39 Belgrave Rd SW1V 2BB
☎ 020 7834 8036 📠 020 7834 1854
e-mail: info@centralhousehotel.co.uk
dir: Near Victoria station

Located a short walk from Victoria station, the Central
House offers sound accommodation. Bedroom sizes vary,
and each room is suitably appointed, with en suite
compact modular shower rooms. A self-service
continental breakfast is offered in the lower ground-floor
dining room.

Rooms 54 en suite (4 fmly) **Facilities** TVL tea/coffee
Direct Dial Cen ht Lift

Comfort Inn PLAN 1 C1

★★★ GUEST ACCOMMODATION

8-12 St George's Dr SW1V 4BJ
☎ 020 7834 2988 📠 020 7821 5814
e-mail: info@comfortinnbuckinghampalacerd.co.uk
dir: From Buckingham Palace Rd into St George's Dr.
Inn on left

Located just a short walk south from Victoria station, this
establishment is a good base for visiting the capital's
attractions. All bedrooms and public areas are smartly
appointed and offer very good levels of comfort. An
extensive continental breakfast is served.

Rooms 81 en suite (13 fmly) (15 GF) **Facilities** STV TVL
tea/coffee Direct Dial Cen ht Lift **Conf** Max 20 Thtr 20
Class 20 Board 20 **Notes** ✕

Comfort Inn Victoria PLAN 1 C1

★★★ GUEST ACCOMMODATION

18-24 Belgrave Rd, Victoria SW1V 1QF
☎ 020 7233 6636 📠 020 7932 0538
e-mail: stay@comfortinnvictoria.co.uk

Having a prime location close to Victoria station, this
property offers brightly appointed en suite
accommodation that is thoughtfully equipped for
business and leisure guests. A continental breakfast is
offered in the basement dining room.

Rooms 50 rms (48 en suite) (16 fmly) (9 GF)
Facilities STV FTV TVL tea/coffee Direct Dial Cen ht Lift
Wi-fi **Notes** ✕

The Victoria Inn PLAN 1 C1

★★★ GUEST HOUSE

65-67 Belgrave Rd, Victoria SW1V 2BG
☎ 020 7834 6721 & 7834 0182 📠 020 7931 0201
e-mail: welcome@victoriainn.co.uk
web: www.victoriainn.co.uk
dir: On A3213, 0.4m SE of Victoria station, near Pimlico
tube station

A short walk from Victoria station, this Victorian property
offers modern, well-equipped accommodation for
business and leisure guests. There is a comfortable
reception lounge, and a limited self-service buffet
breakfast is available in the basement breakfast room.

Rooms 43 en suite (7 fmly) **Facilities** STV tea/coffee
Direct Dial Cen ht Lift Wi-fi **Notes** ✕

Stanley House PLAN 1 C1

★★ ◬ BED AND BREAKFAST

19-21 Belgrave Rd, Victoria SW1V 1RB
☎ 020 7834 5042 & 7834 7292 📠 020 7834 8439
e-mail: cmahotel@aol.com
web: www.londonbudgethotels.co.uk
dir: Near Victoria station

Rooms 44 rms (41 en suite) (7 fmly) (8 GF) S £45-£55;
D £60-£75* **Facilities** FTV TVL Direct Dial Cen ht Wi-fi
Notes LB ✕ No Children 5yrs

SW3

PREMIER COLLECTION

San Domenico House PLAN 1 B1

★★★★★ GUEST ACCOMMODATION

29-31 Draycott Place SW3 2SH
☎ 020 7581 5757 📠 020 7584 1348
e-mail: info@sandomenicohouse.com

This stunning property in the heart of Chelsea offers
beautiful, individually styled bedrooms, all with
antique and period pieces, and well appointed en
suites complete with Italian Spa toiletries. A
sumptuous drawing room with wonderful works of art is
available for guests to relax in or maybe to enjoy
afternoon tea. Breakfast is served either in guests'
bedrooms or in the lower ground floor elegant dining
room. Staff are friendly and attentive.

Rooms 13 en suite (9 smoking) **Facilities** STV Direct
Dial Cen ht Lift Licensed **Notes** ✕

SW5

Best Western The Boltons PLAN 2 E3

★★★★ GUEST ACCOMMODATION

19-21 Penywern Rd, Earls Court SW5 9TT
☎ 020 7373 8900 📠 020 7244 6835
e-mail: reservations@theboltonshotel.co.uk
dir: A3220 from Cromwell Rd, follow road past Earls Court
station, 1st right into Penywern Rd. Located on left

This smart property boasts an excellent location, just
seconds walk from Earls Court tube station and exhibition
centre, and within easy reach of museums and major
shopping areas. Both public areas and bedrooms have an
airy contemporary feel with stylish furnishings and
fittings. En suite bedrooms have comfy beds, flat screen
satellite TV and Wi-fi. 24-hour room service and buffet
breakfast are available.

Rooms 57 en suite (4 fmly) (4 GF) S £75-£165;
D £105-£215* **Facilities** STV FTV iPod docking station
TVL tea/coffee Direct Dial Cen ht Lift Wi-fi **Notes** ✕

SW5 *continued*

Best Western Shaftesbury Kensington
PLAN 2 E3

★★★★ GUEST ACCOMMODATION

33-37 Hogarth Rd, Kensington SW5 0QQ
☎ 020 7370 6831 📠 020 7373 6179

Well appointed to a high standard, this property has a smart modern feel and is conveniently located for the exhibition centre, the West End and local transport links. Bedrooms are furnished and decorated to a very high standard, offering guests a comprehensive range of modern facilities and amenities.

Rooms 133 en suite (7 GF) S £89-£349; D £99-£399*
Facilities STV tea/coffee Dinner available Direct Dial
Cen ht Lift Licensed Wi-fi Gym Fitness centre **Conf** Max 15
Board 15 **Notes** ⊗

The Mayflower
PLAN 2 E3

★★★★ GUEST ACCOMMODATION

26-28 Trebovir Rd SW5 9NJ
☎ 020 7370 0991 📠 020 7370 0994
e-mail: info@mayflower-group.co.uk
web: www.mayflowerhotel.co.uk
dir: *Left from Earls Court tube station & 1st left into Trebovir Rd, premises on left in 50yds*

This smart guest accommodation is a short walk from Earls Court, and close to Olympia and West London's museums and attractions. Stylish, individually designed bedrooms vary in size but all are extremely well equipped and have smart, modern en suites. There is a comfortable, stylish lounge and an airy dining room where breakfast is served.

The Mayflower

Rooms 47 en suite (4 fmly) (5 GF) **Facilities** FTV tea/coffee Direct Dial Cen ht Lift Wi-fi **Conf** Max 25 Thtr 25 Class 25 Board 25 **Notes** ⊗

See advert on this page

The Mayflower

Stylish & boutique. Featuring 48 individually decorated rooms, complimented with modern marbled bathrooms

'The difference is in the detail....' Time Out

Recommended by Johansens...

'West London's best kept secret......' Conde Nast

www.themayflowerhotel.co.uk
www.mayflowercollection.com

Save on B&Bs and Hotels. Book at theAA.com/hotel

LONDON 207 **ENGLAND**

Quality Crown Kensington
PLAN 2 E3

★★★★ GUEST ACCOMMODATION

162 Cromwell Rd, Kensington SW5 0TT
☎ 020 7244 2400 ▤ 020 7244 2500
e-mail: stay@qualitycrown.com

This delightful property enjoys a prime location adjacent to the famous Cromwell Road Hospital, within easy reach of the V&A Museum and the chic shops of Knightsbridge and South Kensington. Bedrooms are extremely well equipped and along with the comfortable public areas have a stylish, contemporary feel. The popular smart bar is a feature.

Rooms 82 en suite **Facilities** STV TVL tea/coffee Dinner available Direct Dial Cen ht Lift Licensed **Parking** 8 **Notes** ⊗

SW7

Best Western The Cromwell
PLAN 1 A2

★★★★ GUEST ACCOMMODATION

110-112 Cromwell Rd, Kensington SW7 4ES
☎ 020 7244 1720 ▤ 020 7373 3706
e-mail: reception@thecromwell.co.uk
dir: M4/A4 towards London, pass Cromwell Hospital, 0.5m

Just minutes away from the tube station and within easy access of all main tourist attractions, this property offers comfortable, modern accommodation. Fully air conditioned and with free Wi-fi, this is an ideal location for both leisure and business guests. Amenities include an on-site meeting room, and secure parking is available nearby.

Rooms 85 en suite (11 GF) **Facilities** STV TVL tea/coffee Direct Dial Cen ht Lift Licensed Wi-fi Fitness room **Conf** Max 8 Board 8 **Notes** ⊗

The Gainsborough
PLAN 1 A2

★★★★ GUEST ACCOMMODATION

7-11 Queensberry Place, South Kensington SW7 2DL
☎ 020 7957 0000 ▤ 020 7970 1805
e-mail: reservations@eeh.co.uk
web: www.eeh.co.uk
dir: Off A4 (Cromwell Rd) opposite Natural History Museum, near South Kensington tube station

This smart Georgian house is in a quiet street near South Kensington's museums. Bedrooms are individually designed with fine fabrics, quality furnishings and co-ordinated colours. A choice of breakfasts is offered in the attractive dining room. There is also a delightful lobby lounge, and 24-hour room service is available.

Rooms 48 en suite (5 fmly) **Facilities** STV tea/coffee Dinner available Direct Dial Cen ht Lift Licensed Wi-fi **Conf** Max 40 Class 40 Board 30 **Notes** ⊗

The Gallery
PLAN 1 A2

★★★★ GUEST ACCOMMODATION

8-10 Queensberry Place, South Kensington SW7 2EA
☎ 020 7915 0000 ▤ 020 7970 1805
e-mail: reservations@eeh.co.uk
web: www.eeh.co.uk
dir: Exit A4 (Cromwell Rd) opposite Natural History Museum, near South Kensington tube station

This stylish property, close to Kensington and Knightsbridge, offers friendly hospitality, attentive service and sumptuously furnished bedrooms, some with a private terrace. Public areas include a choice of lounges (one with internet access) and an elegant bar. There is an option of English or continental breakfast, and 24-hour room service is available.

Rooms 36 en suite **Facilities** STV tea/coffee Dinner available Direct Dial Cen ht Lift Licensed Wi-fi **Conf** Max 40 Thtr 40 Board 30 **Notes** ⊗

W1

AA GUEST ACCOMMODATION OF THE YEAR FOR LONDON

PREMIER COLLECTION

The Marble Arch by Montcalm
PLAN 1 B4

GUEST ACCOMMODATION

31 Great Cumberland Place W1H 7TA
☎ 020 7258 0777 ▤ 020 7258 0999

Located just a short walk from Marble Arch and Oxford Street, this boutique property offers elegant, stylish and lavish accommodation. Bedrooms are well equipped for the modern traveller with all rooms offering executive work desks, telephone with voicemail, flat screen TVs, and well stocked mini-bar. Bathrooms have opulent marble baths with special rain showers. Free Wi-fi is also available. Guests can also enjoy complimentary access to the Club Lounge located in sister property The Montcalm London Marble Arch. The Club lounge serves a light continental breakfast along with snacks and beverages all day. The Marble Arch by Montcalm is the AA Guest Accommodation of the Year for London 2012-13.

Rooms 43 en suite (1 fmly) **Facilities** STV FTV TVL tea/coffee Cen ht Lift Licensed Wi-fi **Notes** ⊗

The Sumner
PLAN 1 B4

★★★★ GUEST ACCOMMODATION

54 Upper Berkeley St, Marble Arch W1H 7QR
☎ 020 7723 2244 ▤ 020 7705 8767
e-mail: hotel@thesumner.com

Centrally located just five minutes' walk from Marble Arch, The Sumner is part of a Georgian terrace. Appointed throughout to a very high standard, this delightful property combines much of the original character of the building with modern comfort. The air-conditioned bedrooms have all been designer decorated and feature widescreen LCD TVs, free broadband, as well as a range of traditional amenities. The breakfast buffet is included in the rate and there is also an elegant lounge for guests to relax in.

Rooms 20 en suite **Facilities** FTV Direct Dial Cen ht Lift Licensed Wi-fi **Notes** ⊗ No Children 5yrs

Best Western Premier Shaftesbury
PLAN 1 D3

★★★★ GUEST ACCOMMODATION

65-73 Shaftesbury Av W1D 6EX
☎ 020 7871 6000
e-mail: reservations@shaftesburyhotel.co.uk
dir: From Piccadilly Circus 300yds up Shaftesbury Av, at junct with Dean St

In the centre of the West End, this boutique property offers plenty of warm, traditional hospitality. The Shaftesbury is next to two major underground stations, with comfortably sized public areas, a refreshment lounge, the Premier Bar, restaurants, conference facilities, and a fitness room.

Rooms 67 en suite (2 fmly) **Facilities** STV tea/coffee Direct Dial Lift Licensed Gym **Conf** Max 12 Board 12 **Notes** ⊗

W1 *continued*

Hart House
PLAN 1 B4

★★★★ GUEST ACCOMMODATION

51 Gloucester Place, Portman Sq W1U 8JF
☎ 020 7935 2288 📠 020 7935 8516
e-mail: reservations@harthouse.co.uk
web: www.harthouse.co.uk
dir: *Off Oxford St behind Selfridges, near Baker Street & Marble Arch tube stations*

This elegant Georgian house is only a short walk from Oxford Street, Selfridges and Madame Tussaud's. Bedrooms and public areas are smartly furnished, stylishly decorated and have been carefully restored to retain much of the house's original character. English breakfast is served in the stylish dining room.

Rooms 15 en suite (4 fmly) (4 GF) S £75-£125; D £110-£175 **Facilities** FTV tea/coffee Direct Dial Cen ht Wi-fi **Notes** ✗

See advert on this page

The St George
PLAN 1 B4

★★★★ GUEST ACCOMMODATION

49 Gloucester Place W1U 8JE
☎ 020 7486 8586 📠 020 7486 6567
e-mail: reservations@stgeorge-hotel.net
dir: *Off Marylebone Rd, between Marble Arch & Baker Street tube stations*

This attractive, Grade II listed house is in the heart of the West End near Oxford Street. Bedrooms are furnished to a high standard and offer many facilities such as modem points, safes, hairdryers and mini-fridges. There is a smart breakfast room and the friendly staff offer a very warm welcome.

Rooms 19 en suite (3 fmly) (3 GF) **Facilities** STV FTV TVL tea/coffee Direct Dial Cen ht Wi-fi **Extras** Soft drinks & water **Conf** Max 20 Thtr 15 Class 20 Board 20 **Notes** LB ✗

The Regency
PLAN 1 B4

★★★ GUEST ACCOMMODATION

19 Nottingham Place W1U 5LQ
☎ 020 7486 5347 📠 020 7224 6057
e-mail: enquiries@regencyhotelwestend.co.uk
web: www.regencyhotelwestend.co.uk
dir: *A501 (Marylebone Rd) S into Baker St, left into Paddington St, left into Nottingham Place*

The Regency, a converted mansion, is close to Baker Street tube station, Madame Tussaud's, the West End shops and Harley Street. Bedrooms are well equipped and some rooms are suitable for families. Breakfast is served in the brightly appointed basement breakfast room. Free Wi-fi is available.

Rooms 20 en suite (2 fmly) (5 smoking) **Facilities** STV TVL tea/coffee Dinner available Direct Dial Cen ht Lift Wi-fi **Notes** ✗

W2

Park Grand Paddington
PLAN 1 A4

★★★★ GUEST ACCOMMODATION

1-2 Queens Gardens, Paddington W2 3BA
☎ 020 7298 9800 📠 020 7262 5414
e-mail: info@parkgrandlondon.co.uk
dir: *Exit Paddington station via Praed St, turn right. After 3 sets of lights right into Devonshire Terrace. 100mtrs to Park Grand Paddington*

Park Grand Paddington enjoys a central location moments walk from Paddington Station and Hyde Park not to mention the main shopping districts and attractions. Rooms vary in size and are completed to a very high standard. A number of stylish suites are also available. The Atlantic bar serves a range of light snacks throughout the day and evening. Additional facilities include state of the art technology with free internet access, satellite TV and fridges. Park Grand Paddington was last year's AA Guest Accommodation of the Year for London (2011-2012).

Rooms 157 en suite (11 fmly) (23 GF) **Facilities** FTV TVL tea/coffee Dinner available Direct Dial Cen ht Lift Licensed Wi-fi Fitness room **Notes** ✗

Best Western Mornington
PLAN 1 A3

★★★★ GUEST ACCOMMODATION

12 Lancaster Gate W2 3LG
☎ 020 7262 7361 📠 020 7706 1028
e-mail: london@mornington.co.uk
dir: *N of Hyde Park, off A402 Bayswater Rd*

This fine Victorian building is located in a quiet road, close to Lancaster Gate station for easy access to the West End. The bedrooms have been appointed to provide comfortable, stylish accommodation. There is a lounge/

Save on B&Bs and Hotels. Book at theAA.com/hotel

LONDON 209 ENGLAND

bar and an attractive dining room where an extensive Scandinavian-style breakfast is served.

Rooms 70 en suite (10 fmly) (4 GF) **Facilities** STV FTV tea/coffee Direct Dial Cen ht Lift Licensed Wi-fi **Extras** Mini-bar **Conf** Max 14 Thtr 14 Class 14 Board 14 **Notes** ⊗

Best Western Shaftesbury Paddington Court London
PLAN 1 A4

★★★★ GUEST ACCOMMODATION

27 Devonshire Ter W2 3DP
☎ 020 7745 1200 ▤ 020 7745 1221
e-mail: info@paddingtoncourt.com
web: www.paddingtoncourt.com
dir: *From A40 take exit before Paddington flyover, follow Paddington Station signs. Devonshire Ter is off Craven Rd*

This establishment benefits from its convenient location close to Paddington mainline train station including links to the underground and the Heathrow Express terminal. Situated next to Hyde Park and Kensington Palace Gardens, this establishment offers smart and comfortable guest accommodation and a guaranteed substantial breakfast. Club Rooms are also available with additional extras including the exclusive use of the Club Lounge. A room is available for small meetings by prior arrangement.

Rooms 165 en suite 35 annexe en suite (43 fmly) **Facilities** STV TVL tea/coffee Direct Dial Lift Licensed

Commodore
PLAN 1 A3

★★★★ GUEST ACCOMMODATION

50 Lancaster Gate, Hyde Park W2 3NA
☎ 020 7402 5291 ▤ 020 7262 1088
e-mail: reservations@commodore-hotel.com

Located in a quiet area of Bayswater, close to Hyde Park and the buzzy shopping area of Oxford Street, is the Commodore. This attractive establishment was originally three townhouses, and facilities include a stylish dining area where evening meals and substantial breakfasts are served daily. 24-hour room service and day-time refreshments are available in the ornate, high ceilinged lounge area.

Rooms 83 en suite (1 fmly) (8 GF) (8 smoking)
S £140-£175; D £180-£240* **Facilities** STV tea/coffee Dinner available Direct Dial Cen ht Lift Licensed Wi-fi Gym **Notes** ⊗

Grand Royale London Hyde Park
PLAN 2 E3

★★★★ GUEST ACCOMMODATION

1 Inverness Ter W2 3JP
☎ 020 7313 7900 ▤ 020 7221 1169
e-mail: info@shaftesburyhotels.com
dir: *On A40 Bayswater Rd*

Located adjacent to Hyde Park, fashionable Notting Hill and within easy reach of the West End, the Grand Royale

combines its rich heritage with the needs of the modern traveller. The accommodation is contemporary in style and very well equipped. Breakfast is served in the staterooms.

Rooms 188 en suite (2 GF) **Facilities** tea/coffee Direct Dial Cen ht Lift Licensed Wi-fi **Conf** Max 20 Thtr 20 Class 20 Board 20 **Notes** ⊗

Hyde Park Radnor
PLAN 1 A4

★★★★ GUEST ACCOMMODATION

7-9 Sussex Place, Hyde Park W2 2SX
☎ 020 7723 5969 ▤ 020 7262 8955
e-mail: hydeparkradnor@btconnect.com
web: www.hydeparkradnor.com
dir: *A402 (Bayswater Rd) into Lancaster Ter & Sussex Gardens, right into Sussex Place*

This smart property is within walking distance of Paddington station and close to all London's central attractions. The smart bedrooms are brightly appointed, well equipped and have modern en suites. English breakfast is served in the lower ground-floor dining room.

Rooms 36 en suite (10 fmly) (5 GF) **Facilities** STV TVL tea/coffee Direct Dial Cen ht Lift **Parking** 2 **Notes** ⊗

Mercure London Paddington
PLAN 1 A4

★★★★ GUEST ACCOMMODATION

144 Praed St, Paddington W2 1HU
☎ 020 7835 2000 ▤ 020 7706 8800
e-mail: stay@mercurepaddington.com
web: www.mercurepaddington.com

This contemporary, stylish property enjoys a central location, adjacent to Paddington Station. Bedrooms and en suites vary in size but all are extremely smartly appointed and boast a host of extra facilities including CD players, flat screen TVs, room safes and internet access. A small gym, stylish lounge and meeting rooms are also available.

Rooms 83 en suite **Facilities** STV TVL tea/coffee Dinner available Direct Dial Cen ht Lift Licensed **Conf** Max 22 Board 22 **Notes** ⊗

The New Linden
PLAN 2 E3

★★★★ GUEST ACCOMMODATION

59 Leinster Square, Notting Hill W2 4PS
☎ 020 7221 4321 ▤ 020 7727 3156
e-mail: newlindenhotel@mayflower-group.co.uk
web: www.newlinden.co.uk
dir: *Off A402, Bayswater Rd*

The friendly New Linden has a good location north of Kensington Gardens. Its stylish en suite bedrooms are richly furnished and thoughtfully equipped with CD players and safes. A good continental breakfast is served in the basement dining room.

Rooms 50 en suite **Facilities** STV FTV TVL tea/coffee Direct Dial Cen ht Lift Wi-fi **Notes** ⊗

See advert on page 210

Park Grand London Hyde Park
PLAN 1 A4

★★★★ GUEST ACCOMMODATION

78-82 Westbourne Ter, Paddington W2 6QA
☎ 020 7262 4521 ▤ 020 7262 7610
e-mail: reservations@londonpremierhotels.co.uk
dir: *A40 into Lancaster Terrace, at crossing left onto slip road*

This attractive property enjoys a central location within easy reach of central London shops and attractions. The en suite bedrooms and public areas have a smart contemporary feel. Although rooms vary in size, all boast many useful facilities such as free internet access, mini-fridges and irons.

Rooms 119 en suite (10 fmly) (19 GF) **Facilities** FTV Lounge tea/coffee Direct Dial Cen ht Lift Licensed Wi-fi **Parking** 11 **Notes** ⊗

W2 *continued*

Quality Crown Hyde Park

PLAN 1 A4

★★★★ GUEST ACCOMMODATION

8-14 Talbot Square W2 1TS
☎ 020 7262 6699 ▤ 020 7723 3233
e-mail: res.hydepark@lth-hotels.com
dir: *SE of Paddington station off Sussex Gardens*

This well-presented property is convenient for Hyde Park, Paddington and Marble Arch. The modern bedrooms are furnished to a good standard and the executive rooms are particularly impressive. Public areas include a compact but stylish bar and lounge, and a basement restaurant where hearty breakfasts are served.

Rooms 75 en suite (8 fmly) (8 GF) **Facilities** FTV TVL tea/coffee Direct Dial Cen ht Lift Licensed Wi-fi **Notes** ⊗

Shaftesbury Hyde Park International

PLAN 2 E3

★★★★ GUEST ACCOMMODATION

52-55 Inverness Ter W2 3LB
☎ 020 7985 8300 ▤ 020 7792 0157
e-mail: info@shaftesburyhotels.com
dir: *On A40 Bayswater road*

This smart, modern establishment is located near to Bayswater, Queensway and Paddington underground stations and it is within walking distance of a myriad of dining options. Bedrooms and bathrooms are decorated to a very high standard with a good range of in-room facilities including flat screen TV, iron and ironing board and complimentary internet or Wi-fi access. Continental and cooked buffet breakfasts are served daily. There is a limited number of off-road parking spaces.

Rooms 70 en suite (2 GF) **Facilities** STV TVL tea/coffee Direct Dial Cen ht Lift Licensed Wi-fi Gym **Parking** 3 **Notes** ⊗

Shaftesbury Metropolis London Hyde Park

PLAN 1 A4

★★★★ GUEST ACCOMMODATION

78-84 Sussex Gardens, Hyde Park W2 1UH
☎ 020 7723 7723 ▤ 020 7402 6318
e-mail: gurpreet@shaftesburymetropolitan.com

This establishment is in an ideal location close to Paddington station with express links to Heathrow Airport. Smartly decorated bedrooms with highly comfortable beds are available in a range of bedroom sizes, all with stylish en suite provision. On-site facilities include complimentary internet or Wi-fi, and continental and full English breakfasts are served every day. Reception is staffed 24 hours a day.

Rooms 90 en suite (14 GF) **Facilities** STV FTV TVL tea/coffee Direct Dial Cen ht Lift Licensed Wi-fi small fitness centre **Extras** Mini-bar **Notes** ⊗

Shaftesbury Premier London Notting Hill

PLAN 2 E3

★★★★ GUEST ACCOMMODATION

5-7 Princes Square, Bayswater W2 4NP
☎ 020 7792 1414 ▤ 020 7792 0099

This smart establishment offers friendly, professional service and comfortable rooms. Situated conveniently for many attractions yet peacefully located in a quiet, leafy square, the property has stylish public rooms and offers free Wi-fi as well as hard-wire connectivity in the extremely well equipped bedrooms. Breakfast is served in the dining room and offers a good choice of fresh cooked traditional breakfast and continental items.

Rooms 68 en suite (2 GF) **Facilities** STV TVL tea/coffee Direct Dial Cen ht Lift Wi-fi Gym

Save on B&Bs and Hotels. Book at **theAA.com/hotel**

LONDON 211 ENGLAND

Shaftesbury Premier Paddington
PLAN 1 A4

★★★ GUEST ACCOMMODATION

55-61 Westbourne Ter W2 6QA
☎ **020 7723 3434** 🖷 **020 7402 0433**
dir: *Exit A40 into Lancaster Terrace*

This smart property enjoys a convenient location within walking distance of Hyde Park and of many of London's major shops and attractions. Bedrooms are smartly appointed and boast modern technology. A hearty breakfast is served in the airy dining room. Limited off-street parking (chargeable) is a bonus. The staff are friendly and attentive.

Rooms 118 en suite (2 GF) **Facilities** STV tea/coffee Dinner available Direct Dial Cen ht Lift Licensed Wi-fi **Notes** ⊗

Soroptimist Residential Club
PLAN 1 A3

★★★ GUEST ACCOMMODATION

63 Baywater Rd W2 3PH
☎ **020 7723 8575** 🖷 **020 7723 1061**
e-mail: info@soropclub63.org.uk

This friendly establishment offers a surprisingly tranquil environment located less than one minute's walk from Lancaster Gate Underground and situated directly opposite Hyde Park. All bedrooms are comfortable with en suite facilities and consist of a range of singles and twins; there is also a room which can accommodate three guests. Hot snacks are available throughout the afternoon and evening by prior arrangement and a good continental or cooked breakfast is served in the mornings. A room is available for meetings and private functions. Parking arrangements can be made.

Rooms 16 en suite (1 fmly) **Facilities** TVL tea/coffee Dinner available Cen ht Lift Licensed Wi-fi **Conf** Max 40 Class 40 Board 20 **Notes** ⊗ Closed 21-31 Dec

Admiral
PLAN 1 A4

★★★ GUEST ACCOMMODATION

143 Sussex Gardens, Hyde Park W2 2RY
☎ **020 7723 7309** 🖷 **020 7723 8731**
e-mail: enquiries@admiral-hotel.com

The Admiral is a short walk from Paddington station and is convenient for Hyde Park and the West End. The smart bedrooms are enhanced with attractive artworks, and a full English breakfast is provided.

Rooms 21 en suite (12 fmly) (1 GF) **Facilities** STV FTV TVL tea/coffee Dinner available Direct Dial Cen ht Licensed Wi-fi **Conf** Max 30 Class 25 Board 25 **Parking** 3 Notes ⊗

Comfort Inn
PLAN 1 A3

★★★ GUEST ACCOMMODATION

73 Queensborough Ter, Bayswater W2 3SU
☎ **020 7229 6424** 🖷 **020 7221 4772**
e-mail: info@comforthydepark.com
dir: *Off Bayswater Rd near Queensway tube station*

A short walk from Kensington Gardens and fashionable Queensway, this property has been converted to provide practically equipped bedrooms, with bright and well appointed bathrooms. Breakfast is served in the basement dining room.

Rooms 29 en suite (1 fmly) (3 GF) **Facilities** STV FTV tea/coffee Direct Dial Cen ht Lift **Notes** ⊗

Kingsway Park Guest Accommodation
PLAN 1 A4

★★★ GUEST ACCOMMODATION

139 Sussex Gardens W2 2RX
☎ **020 7723 5677 & 7724 9346** 🖷 **020 7402 4352**
e-mail: info@kingswaypark-hotel.com
web: www.kingswaypark-hotel.com
dir: *A40 Ebound junct for Paddington, through to Sussex Gdns*

This Victorian property has a central location within walking distance of Marble Arch, Hyde Park and Paddington. Bedrooms offer well-equipped value accommodation. Public areas include a reception lounge and a basement breakfast room adorned with interesting artwork. A limited number of parking spaces is available.

Rooms 22 en suite (5 fmly) (2 GF) **Facilities** STV FTV TVL tea/coffee Direct Dial Cen ht Licensed **Conf** Max 30 **Parking** 3 **Notes** LB ⊗

Parkwood at Marble Arch
PLAN 1 B4

★★★ GUEST ACCOMMODATION

4 Stanhope Place, Marble Arch W2 2HB
☎ **020 7402 2241** 🖷 **020 7402 1574**
e-mail: reception@parkwoodhotel.com
web: www.parkwoodhotel.com
dir: *Near Marble Arch tube station*

Located in a quiet residential street next to Marble Arch and Oxford Street, the friendly Parkwood provides a central base for budget-conscious shoppers and tourists. A family room is available, and a freshly cooked breakfast is served in the attractive basement dining room.

Rooms 16 rms (12 en suite) (1 fmly) (2 GF) **Facilities** STV FTV TVL tea/coffee Direct Dial Cen ht Wi-fi **Notes** ⊗

Princes Square
PLAN 2 E3

★★★ GUEST ACCOMMODATION

23-25 Princes Square, off Ilchester Gardens, Bayswater W2 4NJ
☎ **020 7229 9876** 🖷 **020 7229 4664**
e-mail: info@princessquarehotel.co.uk
dir: *From Bayswater 1st left into Moscow Rd, 3rd right into Ilchester Gardens*

This fine building is in a quiet road close to tube stations for easy access to the West End. The comfortable bedrooms provide stylish accommodation, and there is a small bar and an attractive dining room where a continental breakfast is served.

Rooms 50 en suite (3 fmly) (6 GF) **Facilities** STV tea/coffee Direct Dial Cen ht Lift Wi-fi **Notes** ⊗

W2 *continued*

Barry House
PLAN 1 A4

★★★ 🅰 BED AND BREAKFAST

12 Sussex Place, Hyde Park W2 2TP
☎ 020 7723 7340 📠 020 7723 9775
e-mail: hotel@barryhouse.co.uk
web: www.barryhouse.co.uk
dir: *300yds SE of Paddington station*

Rooms 18 rms (16 en suite) (5 fmly) (2 GF) D £70–£130
Facilities FTV tea/coffee Direct Dial Cen ht Wi-fi **Notes** ⊗

W8

Seraphine, Kensington Gardens
PLAN 2 E3

★★★★ GUEST ACCOMMODATION

7-11 Kensington High St W8 5NP
☎ 020 7368 2222 & 7938 5911 📠 020 7368 2221
e-mail: info@seraphinehotel.co.uk
dir: *B325 Gloucester Road, continue for 0.5m, left at A315 Kensington Road*

This smart property enjoys a prime location opposite Kensington Palace and is ideally positioned for Hyde Park, The Royal Albert Hall, shops and museums. Bedrooms vary in size but all are well equipped with interactive flat screen TV, iPod docking, laptop safes and free Wi-fi. En suites are modern with powerful showers. An extensive continental breakfast is included.

Rooms 22 en suite **Facilities** STV FTV TVL tea/coffee Direct Dial Cen ht Lift Licensed Wi-fi **Notes** ⊗

Seraphine Kensington Olympia
PLAN 2 E3

★★★★ GUEST ACCOMMODATION

225 Kensington High St W8 6SA
☎ 020 7938 5911 📠 020 7938 5912
e-mail: olympia@seraphinehotel.co.uk
dir: *A4 left onto A330, then right onto A315. On corner of Kensington High St & Abingdon Rd*

This chic and intimate property enjoys a prime location in the heart of High Street Kensington, and is ideally positioned for Holland Park, local attractions, shops and museums. Bedrooms vary in size but all are well equipped with interactive flat screen TV, iPod docking, laptop safes and free Wi-fi. En suites are modern with powerful showers. An extensive continental breakfast is included and full cooked breakfasts upon request.

Rooms 17 en suite **Facilities** FTV iPod docking station TVL tea/coffee Direct Dial Cen ht Lift Licensed Wi-fi **Notes** ⊗

WC1

The George
PLAN 1 D5

★★★ GUEST ACCOMMODATION

58-60 Cartwright Gardens WC1H 9EL
☎ 020 7387 8777 📠 020 7387 8666
e-mail: ghotel@aol.com
web: www.georgehotel.com
dir: *From St Pancras 2nd left onto Marchmont St & 1st left onto Cartwright Gardens*

The George is within walking distance of Russell Square and the tube, and convenient for London's central attractions. The brightly appointed bedrooms vary in size, many have en suites, and some rooms are suitable for families. A substantial breakfast is served in the attractive ground-floor dining room.

Rooms 40 rms (14 en suite) (14 fmly) (4 GF)
Facilities STV TVL tea/coffee Direct Dial Cen ht Wi-fi 🌐 Free Internet access **Notes** ⊗

GREATER LONDON

BARNET
Map 6 TQ29

Savoro Restaurant with Rooms

★★★★ ⊛ RESTAURANT WITH ROOMS

206 High St EN5 5SZ
☎ 020 8449 9888 📠 020 8449 7444
e-mail: savoro@savoro.co.uk
web: www.savoro.co.uk
dir: *M25 junct 23, A1000. Establishment in crescent behind Hadley Green Jaguar Garage*

Set back from the main high street, the traditional frontage of this establishment belies the stylishly modern bedrooms and well designed bathrooms within. The award-winning restaurant is an additional bonus.

Rooms 11 rms (9 en suite) (2 pri facs) (2 fmly) (3 GF)
Facilities FTV tea/coffee Dinner available Cen ht Wi-fi
Parking 9 **Notes** LB ⊗ No coaches

BECKENHAM

See London Plan 2 G1

Innkeeper's Lodge Beckenham

★★★ INN

422 Upper Elmers End Rd BR3 3HQ
☎ 0845 112 6126
e-mail: info@innkeeperslodge.com
web: www.innkeeperslodge.com

At Innkeeper's Lodge you'll find accommodation with comfort and character in equal measure, and everything needed for a relaxing stay, from easy check-in and free parking to complimentary breakfast and a cosy pub serving great value food and drink on the doorstep. Each Lodge has quality rooms, and there are Lodges in a variety of locations from towns and cities to countryside settings across the UK.

Save on B&Bs and Hotels. Book at theAA.com/hotel

GREATER LONDON 213 **ENGLAND**

Rooms 24 en suite (1 fmly) (8 GF) **Facilities** FTV tea/coffee Dinner available Direct Dial Wi-fi **Parking** 40

CRANFORD

See London Plan 2 A3 For accommodation details see Heathrow Airport

CROYDON   Map 6 TQ36

Kirkdale

★★★ GUEST ACCOMMODATION

22 St Peters Rd CRO 1HD
☎ 020 8688 5898 📠 020 8680 6001
e-mail: reservations@kirkdalehotel.co.uk
web: www.kirkdalehotel.co.uk
dir: A23 onto A232 W & A212 (Lower Coombe St), 500yds right

Close to the town centre, this Victorian property retains many original features. Public areas include a small lounge bar and an attractive breakfast room, and the bedrooms have good facilities. There is a sheltered patio for the summer.

Rooms 16 en suite (5 GF) S £50-£109; D £60-£159
Facilities FTV TVL tea/coffee Direct Dial Cen ht Licensed Wi-fi **Parking** 12 **Notes** ⊗

HARROW ON THE HILL

See London Plan 2 B5

Old Etonian

★★★ 🖱 GUEST ACCOMMODATION

36-38 High St HA1 3LL
☎ 020 8423 3854 & 8422 8482 📠 020 8423 1225
e-mail: info@oldetonian.com
web: www.oldetonian.com
dir: In town centre. On B458 opposite Harrow School

In the heart of this historic part of London and opposite the prestigious school, this friendly guest accommodation

is a delight. Bedrooms are attractive, well appointed and comfortable. A continental breakfast is served in the dining room, which in the evening is home to a lively restaurant. On-road parking is available.

Rooms 9 en suite (1 GF) S £67.50-£75; D £75-£85*
Facilities FTV TVL tea/coffee Dinner available Direct Dial Cen ht Licensed 🔒 **Conf** Max 30 Thtr 20 Class 20 Board 20 **Parking** 3 **Notes** ⊗

HEATHROW AIRPORT

See London plan 2 A2

The Cottage

★★★★ GUEST ACCOMMODATION

150-152 High St TW5 9WB
☎ 020 8897 1815
e-mail: info@the-cottage.eu
web: www.the-cottage.eu
dir: M4 junct 3, A312 towards Feltham, left at lights, left after 1st pub on left

This beautiful property is a peacefully situated, family-run oasis, within five minutes of Heathrow Airport. It offers comfortable and spacious accommodation, decorated tastefully in the main house and six bedrooms located at the rear of the garden, connected to the main building by a covered walkway overlooking the stunning courtyard.

Rooms 14 en suite 6 annexe en suite (4 fmly) (12 GF)
Facilities tea/coffee Cen ht Wi-fi **Parking** 20 **Notes** ⊗ Closed 24-26 Dec & 31 Dec-1 Jan

Crompton Guest House

★★★★ GUEST HOUSE

49 Lampton Rd TW3 1JG
☎ 020 8570 7090 📠 020 8577 1975
e-mail: cromptonguesthouse@btinternet.com
web: www.cromptonguesthouse.co.uk
dir: M4 junct 3, follow signs for Hounslow. Into Bath Rd (A3005), left at Yates pub. 200yds on right just before bridge

Located just a moment's walk away from Hounslow underground station this accommodation is popular with both business and leisure travellers. Bedrooms and bathrooms are comfortable and well equipped with good facilities. Breakfast is served in the intimate dining room where a freshly prepared breakfast is served. Ample off-street parking is a plus.

Rooms 11 en suite (5 fmly) (2 GF) **Facilities** STV FTV tea/coffee Dinner available Direct Dial Cen ht Wi-fi **Parking** 12 **Notes** ⊗

HORNCHURCH   Map 6 TQ58

Innkeeper's Lodge Hornchurch

★★★ INN

Station Ln RM12 6SB
☎ 0845 112 6010
e-mail: info@innkeeperslodge.com
web: www.innkeeperslodge.com

At Innkeeper's Lodge you'll find accommodation with comfort and character in equal measure, and everything needed for a relaxing stay, from easy check-in and free parking to complimentary breakfast and a cosy pub serving great value food and drink on the doorstep. Each Lodge has quality rooms, and there are Lodges in a variety of locations from towns and cities to countryside settings across the UK.

Rooms 12 en suite (1 fmly) **Facilities** FTV tea/coffee Dinner available Direct Dial Wi-fi **Parking**

HOUNSLOW

See London Plan 2 B2 For accommodation details see under Heathrow Airport

ILFORD

See London Plan 2 H5

Best Western Ilford

★★★★ GUEST ACCOMMODATION

3-5 Argyle Rd IG1 3BH
☎ 020 8911 6083 ▤ 020 8554 4726
e-mail: manager@expresslodging.co.uk
dir: *From A406 E towards Ilford, then A118 & 1st left after Ilford Station*

This refurbished establishment is conveniently located for easy access to the Olympic Village and central London. The accommodation is very comfortable and offers a range of amenities such as free internet and a new, state-of-the-art Media Hub. 24-hour room service and parking is also provided.

Rooms 34 en suite (4 fmly) (15 GF) S £35-£65; D £45-£109 **Facilities** FTV Lounge TVL tea/coffee Dinner available Direct Dial Wi-fi **Conf** Max 30 Thtr 30 Class 30 Board 30 **Parking** 12 **Notes** LB ⊗

RICHMOND (UPON THAMES)

See London Plan 2 C2

Hobart Hall

★★★ GUEST ACCOMMODATION

43-47 Petersham Rd TW10 6UL
☎ 020 8940 0435 ▤ 020 8332 2996
e-mail: hobarthall@aol.com
dir: *200yds S of Richmond Bridge on A307*

Built around 1690, this impressive yet friendly establishment stands beside the River Thames close to Richmond Bridge. Many of the spacious bedrooms have river views and a good range of modern facilities. There is a comfortable lounge, an attractive breakfast room, and a meeting room that overlooks the river.

Rooms 33 rms (18 en suite) (5 fmly) (3 GF) **Facilities** TVL tea/coffee Direct Dial Cen ht Wi-fi **Parking** 14 **Notes** ⊗ RS 25-26 Dec & 1 Jan

MERSEYSIDE

BROMBOROUGH
Map 15 SJ38

The Dibbinsdale

★★★★ INN

Dibbinsdale Rd CH63 0HQ
☎ 0151 334 9818
e-mail: info@thedibbinsdale.co.uk
dir: *M53 junct 4 towards Bebbington. Right at 1st lights, after 1.8m on this road*

Located in a peaceful residential area, a few minutes' walk from shops and transport links, this popular inn has been sympathetically renovated to offer high standards of comfort and facilities. Bedrooms are equipped for both business and leisure guests, and spacious public areas are a perfect setting for freshly prepared food, a wide selection of real ales and regular live entertainment.

Rooms 11 en suite (1 fmly) **Facilities** FTV tea/coffee Dinner available Cen ht Wi-fi **Parking** 20

LIVERPOOL
Map 15 SJ39

Blenheim Lakeside

Ⓤ

37 Aigburth Dr, Aigburth L17 4JE
☎ 0151 727 7380 ▤ 0151 211 1980
e-mail: enquiries@blenheimlakesidehotel.co.uk
web: www.blenheimlakesidehotel.co.uk

Currently the rating for this establishment is not confirmed. This may be due to a change of ownership or because it has only recently joined the AA rating scheme.

Rooms 16 rms (15 en suite) (1 pri facs) (7 fmly) (2 GF) S £40-£95; D £55-£135 (room only) **Facilities** FTV TVL Dinner available Cen ht Licensed Wi-fi **Conf** Max 60 Thtr 60 Class 40 Board 40 **Parking** 12 **Notes** LB

SOUTHPORT
Map 15 SD31

Bay Tree House B&B

★★★★ GUEST ACCOMMODATION

No1 Irving St, Marine Gate PR9 0HD
☎ 01704 510555 ▤ 0870 753 6318
e-mail: info@baytreehousesouthport.co.uk
web: www.baytreehousesouthport.co.uk
dir: *3rd road right off Leicester St, approaching from rdbt off Lord St*

A warm welcome is assured at this immaculately maintained house, located a short walk from the promenade and central attractions. Bedrooms are equipped with a wealth of thoughtful extras, and delicious imaginative breakfasts are served in an attractive dining room overlooking the pretty front patio garden.

Rooms 6 en suite S £45-£60; D £69-£85* **Facilities** FTV DVD iPod docking station Lounge Direct Dial Cen ht Licensed Wi-fi Discounts available for local swimming

baths & gym **Extras** Speciality toiletries, mini-bar, snacks, robes **Parking** 2 **Notes** Closed 17 Dec-4 Jan

The Baytrees

★★★★ GUEST ACCOMMODATION

4 Queens Rd PR9 9HN
☎ 01704 536513 ▤ 01704 536513
e-mail: baytreeshotel@hotmail.com
web: www.baytreeshotel.co.uk
dir: *From B565 (Lord St) towards fire station, right at rdbt into Manchester Rd, left at lights, 200yds on right*

Located a short walk from Lord Street, this elegant late Victorian house has been well appointed to provide thoughtfully furnished bedrooms with smart modern en suite bathrooms. Breakfast is served in the attractive dining room overlooking the pretty rear garden, and a lounge is also available.

Rooms 12 en suite (5 fmly) (2 GF) S £29.50-£40; D £39.50-£67.50* **Facilities** FTV DVD TVL tea/coffee Cen ht Wi-fi ♨ **Parking** 11 **Notes** ⊗ Closed Xmas

Bowden Lodge

★★★★ GUEST ACCOMMODATION

18 Albert Rd PR9 0LE
☎ 01704 543531 ▤ 01704 539112
e-mail: stay@bowdenlodge.co.uk
web: www.bowdenlodge.co.uk
dir: *A565 N from town centre, over rdbt, 150yds on right*

This stylish house is in a quiet residential area just a stroll from Lord Street and the town's attractions. Bedrooms, some suitable for families, are smartly furnished and well equipped. Day rooms include a lounge with deep sofas, and a bright dining room where hearty cooked breakfasts are served. Value for money and a friendly welcome are assured. Ideal venue for walkers and cyclists.

Rooms 10 en suite (3 fmly) S £35-£60; D £65-£100* **Facilities** FTV TVL tea/coffee Dinner available Cen ht Licensed Wi-fi ♨ **Parking** 10 **Notes** LB ⊗

NORFOLK

ALBURGH
Map 13 TM28

The Dove Restaurant with Rooms

★★★★ ◉◉ ≌ RESTAURANT WITH ROOMS

Holbrook Hill IP20 0EP
☎ 01986 788315 ▤ 01986 788315
e-mail: info@thedoverestaurant.co.uk
dir: *Between Harleston & Bungay at junct A143 & B1062*

A warm welcome awaits at this restaurant with rooms. Bedrooms are pleasantly decorated, furnished with pine pieces and have modern facilities. Public rooms include a lounge area with a small bar, and a smart restaurant with well-spaced tables.

Rooms 2 rms (1 en suite) (1 pri facs) (1 fmly) **Facilities** tea/coffee Dinner available Cen ht Wi-fi **Parking** 20 **Notes** ⊗ No coaches

Save on B&Bs and Hotels. Book at theAA.com/hotel

NORFOLK 215 ENGLAND

ATTLEBOROUGH — Map 13 TM09

Rylstone B&B

★★★★ BED AND BREAKFAST

Bell Rd, Rockland St Peter NR17 1UL
☎ 01953 488199 📠 0844 7744562
e-mail: margaret@hneale.f9.co.uk
dir: *4m W of Attleborough. B1077 to Rockland St Peter, at x-rds into Chapel St & Bell Rd*

A delightful detached property situated in a peaceful rural location on the edge of the village. The pleasantly decorated bedrooms have co-ordinated fabrics and many thoughtful touches. Public rooms include a large lounge with a log burner, and a conservatory with views of the surrounding countryside.

Rooms 3 rms (2 en suite) (1 pri facs) S £40; D £70* **Facilities** FTV tea/coffee Cen ht Wi-fi 🔒 **Parking** 3 **Notes** LB ⊗ 🐾

BLAKENEY — Map 13 TG04

PREMIER COLLECTION

Blakeney House

★★★★★ GUEST HOUSE

High St NR25 7NX
☎ 01263 740561 📠 01263 741750
e-mail: admin@blakeneyhouse.com
web: www.blakeneyhouse.com
dir: *In village centre*

Blakeney House is a stunning Victorian manor house set amid two acres of attractive landscaped grounds just a short walk from the quay and town centre. The stylish, individually decorated bedrooms have co-ordinated fabrics and many thoughtful touches. Breakfast is served at individual tables in the smart dining room, which overlooks the well-stocked front garden.

Rooms 8 rms (7 en suite) (1 pri facs) (1 fmly) S £60-£95; D £70-£150 **Facilities** tea/coffee Cen ht Wi-fi ⅃ 18 **Parking** 8 **Notes** ⊗ No Children 12yrs

BRISLEY — Map 13 TF92

The Brisley Bell Inn & Restaurant

★★★ INN

The Green NR20 5DW
☎ 01362 668686
e-mail: info@brisleybell-inn.co.uk
web: www.brisleybell-inn.co.uk
dir: *Between Fakenham & East Dereham on B1145*

This delightful village inn is situated in a peaceful location just a short drive from the town centre. The bedrooms are generally quite spacious, and each one is smartly appointed with modern furniture and co-ordinated soft furnishings. Public rooms include a beamed bar and a cosy restaurant serving an interesting choice of dishes.

Rooms 3 rms (1 en suite) (1 fmly) **Facilities** FTV DVD tea/coffee Dinner available Cen ht Wi-fi **Conf** Max 40 Thtr 40 Class 36 Board 20 **Parking** 30

BROOKE — Map 13 TM29

The Old Vicarage

★★★★ BED AND BREAKFAST

48 The Street NR15 1JU
☎ 01508 558329
dir: *Exit B1332, in village centre near church*

Set in mature gardens in a peaceful village, this charming house is within easy driving distance of Norwich. The individually decorated bedrooms are thoughtfully furnished and equipped, and one room has a lovely four-poster bed. There is an elegant dining room and a cosy lounge, and dinner is available by arrangement. Service is genuinely helpful, provided in a relaxed and friendly manner.

Rooms 2 en suite S £40; D £66* **Facilities** TVL tea/coffee Dinner available Cen ht **Parking** 4 **Notes** LB ⊗ No Children 15yrs 🐾

CASTLE ACRE — Map 13 TF81

Lodge Farm

★★★★ BED AND BREAKFAST

PE32 2BS
☎ 01760 755506
e-mail: stay@lodgefarmcastleacre.co.uk
web: www.lodgefarmcastleacre.co.uk
dir: *From Swaffham on A1065, after 4m turn left to Castle Acre. Follow signs for Rougham, farm road on right*

This charming 18th-century farmhouse was built as a hunting lodge for the Earl of Leicester, and is situated in a peaceful rural location amidst rolling countryside. The bedrooms are spacious, equipped with modern facilities and have lovely views. Breakfast is served at a large communal table in the dining room and features locally sourced produce, including their own free-range eggs.

Rooms 3 rms (2 en suite) (1 pri facs) **Facilities** FTV tea/coffee Cen ht Wi-fi **Parking** 10 **Notes** Closed Xmas 🐾

Ostrich Inn

★★★★ 🍽 INN

Stocks Green PE32 2AE
☎ 01760 755398
e-mail: info@ostrichcastleacre.com
web: www.ostrichcastleacre.com
dir: *0.3m on right of Castle Acre Priory*

This 15th-century inn is situated adjacent to the village green in the centre of Castle Acre. The warm and inviting public areas have a wealth of original features such as exposed brickwork, oak beams and open fires. The spacious bedrooms are in an adjacent building; each

room has been sympathetically renovated and has modern facilities.

Rooms 6 en suite (1 fmly) (1 GF) **Facilities** FTV tea/coffee Dinner available Direct Dial Cen ht Wi-fi **Conf** Max 25 Thtr 25 Class 25 Board 25 **Parking** 30

CLEY NEXT THE SEA — Map 13 TG04

PREMIER COLLECTION

Old Town Hall House

★★★★★ 🏠 BED AND BREAKFAST

Coast Rd NR25 7RB
☎ 01263 740284
e-mail: louise@oldtownhallhouse.co.uk
web: www.oldtownhallhouse.co.uk
dir: *On A149 in centre of Cley. Opposite old red phone box*

Expect a warm welcome from the caring hosts at this delightful detached property situated in the heart of a bustling North Norfolk village, which has been designated as an Area of Outstanding Natural Beauty, and has a superb bird-watching reserve on its outskirts. The tastefully appointed bedrooms have lovely co-ordinated soft fabrics and many thoughtful touches. Breakfast, using locally sourced produce, is served at individual tables in the stylish dining room.

Rooms 3 en suite **Facilities** tea/coffee Cen ht Wi-fi **Notes** ⊗ No Children Closed Xmas & Jan

COLTON — Map 13 TG10

The Ugly Bug Inn

★★★★ INN

High House Farm Ln NR9 5DG
☎ 01603 880794
e-mail: info@uglybuginn.co.uk

This popular inn is located in a peaceful rural location on the edge of the village, close to the A47 that has links to Norwich and the Norfolk coast. Public rooms include a large lounge bar and a smart restaurant. The bedrooms are smartly appointed with modern facilities, and most rooms have views of the countryside.

Rooms 4 en suite (1 GF) **Facilities** FTV tea/coffee Dinner available Cen ht Wi-fi ⅃ 18 **Parking** 40 **Notes** No Children 16yrs

CROMER
Map 13 TG24

See also Sheringham

Shrublands Farm (TG246393)

★★★★ ⌂ FARMHOUSE

Church St, Northrepps NR27 0AA
☎ 01263 579297 📠 01263 579297 Mrs A Youngman
e-mail: youngman@farming.co.uk
web: www.shrublandsfarm.com
dir: Exit A149 to Northrepps, through village, past
Foundry Arms, cream house 50yds on left

Expect a warm welcome from the caring host at this
delightful 18th-century farmhouse, set in landscaped
grounds and surrounded by 300 acres of arable farmland.
Public areas include a cosy lounge with a wood-burning
stove, and breakfast is served at a communal table in the
elegant dining room.

Rooms 2 rms (1 en suite) (1 pri facs) S £45-£47.50;
D £70-£75* Facilities FTV TVL tea/coffee Cen ht 🔒
Parking 5 Notes LB ⊗ No Children 12yrs 300 acres
arable

The White Horse Overstrand

★★★★ ⊛⊛ INN

34 High St, Overstrand NR27 0AB
☎ 01263 579237
e-mail: reservations@whitehorseoverstrand.co.uk
dir: From A140, before Cromer, turn right into Mill Rd. At
bottom right into Station Rd. After 2m, bear left into High
St, White Horse on left

A smartly appointed inn ideally situated in the heart of
this popular village on the north Norfolk coastline. The
modern bedrooms are tastefully appointed and equipped
with a good range of useful extras. Public rooms include
a large open-plan lounge bar with comfortable seating
and a relaxed dining area.

Rooms 8 en suite (2 fmly) Facilities TVL tea/coffee Dinner
available Cen ht Wi-fi Pool table Parking 6 Notes LB

Beachcomber Guest House

★★★★ GUEST HOUSE

17 Macdonald Rd NR27 9AP
☎ 01263 513398
e-mail: info@beachcomber-guesthouse.co.uk
dir: Off A149 Runton Rd, 500yds W of pier

A smartly maintained Edwardian house situated in a
peaceful side road close to the seafront and town centre.
The pleasant bedrooms are carefully furnished and
equipped with many thoughtful touches. Breakfast is
served in the smart dining room and there is a
comfortable lounge with sofas.

Rooms 5 en suite (1 fmly) S £40-£55; D £60-£68*
Facilities FTV TVL tea/coffee Cen ht Wi-fi Notes LB ⊗ No
Children 8yrs ⊜

Bon Vista

★★★★ GUEST ACCOMMODATION

12 Alfred Rd NR27 9AN
☎ 01263 511818
e-mail: jim@bonvista-cromer.co.uk
web: www.bonvista-cromer.co.uk
dir: From pier onto A148 (coast road), in 400yds left onto
Alfred Rd

The owners of this delightful Victorian terraced house,
situated in a peaceful side road adjacent to the seafront,
just a short walk from the town centre, extend a warm
welcome. The individually decorated bedrooms have co-
ordinated soft fabrics, and the public rooms include an
attractive dining room and a spacious first-floor lounge.

Rooms 5 en suite (2 fmly) Facilities TVL tea/coffee Cen ht
Wi-fi Parking 2 Notes ⊗ ⊜

Homefield Guest House

★★★★ GUEST HOUSE

48 Cromer Rd, West Runton NR27 9AD
☎ 01263 837337
e-mail: homefield@hotmail.co.uk
web: www.homefieldguesthouse.co.uk
dir: On A149 (coast road) between Sheringham & Cromer

This large Victorian house was previously owned by the
Canon of Cromer and is situated in the peaceful village of
West Runton between Cromer and Sheringham. The
pleasantly co-ordinated bedrooms have many useful
extras. Breakfast, which includes locally sourced produce,
is served at individual tables in the smart dining room.

Rooms 6 en suite Facilities STV TVL tea/coffee Cen ht
Wi-fi Parking 8 Notes ⊗ No Children 14yrs

The Red Lion Food and Rooms

★★★★ ⇌ INN

Brook St NR27 9HD
☎ 01263 514964 📠 01263 512834
e-mail: info@redlion-cromer.co.uk

The Red Lion is a charming Victorian inn situated in an
elevated position in the heart of the town centre
overlooking the beach and the sea. The open-plan public
areas include a lounge bar, a popular restaurant and
sunny conservatory. The spacious bedrooms are tastefully
decorated with co-ordinated soft furnishings and include
many thoughtful touches.

Rooms 15 en suite S £62.50-£97.50; D £105-£125*
Facilities FTV tea/coffee Dinner available Cen ht Wi-fi ⅃
Parking 20 Notes LB

Glendale Guest House

★★★ GUEST HOUSE

33 Macdonald Rd NR27 9AP
☎ 01263 513278
e-mail: glendalecromer@btconnect.com
dir: A149 (coast road) from Cromer centre, 4th left

Victorian property situated in a peaceful side road
adjacent to the seafront, just a short walk from the town
centre. Bedrooms are pleasantly decorated, well
maintained and equipped with a good range of useful
extras. Breakfast is served at individual tables in the
smart dining room.

Rooms 5 rms (1 en suite) S £28-£40; D £56-£80
Facilities FTV tea/coffee Parking 2 Notes LB Closed 11
Oct-28 Mar

The Sandcliff

★★★ GUEST HOUSE

Runton Rd NR27 9AS
☎ 01263 512888 📠 01263 512785
e-mail: admin@sandcliffhotel.com
dir: 500yds W of town centre on A149

Ideally situated on the seafront just a short walk from the
town centre, this guest house offers a large lounge bar
with comfortable seating and a spacious dining room
where breakfast and dinner are served. The bedrooms are
pleasantly decorated, thoughtfully equipped and some
have superb sea views.

Rooms 23 rms (17 en suite) (10 fmly) (3 GF) S £47-£65;
D £65-£95 Facilities FTV TVL tea/coffee Dinner available
Licensed Wi-fi ⅃ 18 🔒 Parking 10 Notes LB

Westgate Lodge B&B

★★★ BED AND BREAKFAST

10 MacDonald Rd NR27 9AP
☎ 01263 512840
e-mail: info@westgatelodge.co.uk
dir: *Along seafront & left after the Cliftonville Hotel, Westgate Lodge 50yds on right*

Situated in a peaceful side road next to the seafront and just a short walk from the centre of town. Bedrooms vary in size and style; each one is pleasantly decorated and has a few thoughtful touches. Breakfast is served in the smart dining room and there is a cosy lounge.

Rooms 3 en suite S £31-£38; D £52-£66* **Facilities** FTV tea/coffee Cen ht **Parking** 5 **Notes** LB ⊗ No Children 3yrs Closed Xmas & New Year ⊛

DEREHAM   Map 13 TF91

Orchard Cottage

★★★★ BED AND BREAKFAST

The Drift, Gressenhall NR20 4EH
☎ 01362 860265
e-mail: ann@walkers-norfolk.co.uk
dir: *2m NE of Dereham. Exit B1146 in Beetley to Gressenhall, right at x-rds into Bittering St, right at x-rds, 2nd right*

Orchard Cottage is an attractive newly-built Norfolk flint building situated in the historic rural village of Gressenhall near Dereham. The comfortable country style bedrooms are smartly decorated and situated on the ground floor; one of the rooms has a superb wet room. Public rooms include a lounge, a dining room and a study. Dinner is available by arrangement.

Rooms 2 en suite (2 GF) S £48-£54; D £68-£74 **Facilities** FTV Lounge TVL tea/coffee Dinner available Cen ht Wi-fi 🛆 **Parking** 2 **Notes** LB ⊗ ⊛

DOCKING   Map 13 TF73

Jubilee Lodge

★★★★ GUEST ACCOMMODATION

Station Rd PE31 8LS
☎ 01485 518473 📠 01485 518473
e-mail: eghoward62@hotmail.com
web: www.jubilee-lodge.com
dir: *400yds N of village centre on B1153*

Ideally placed for touring the North Norfolk coast, with Sandringham, Hunstanton, Burnham Market and Fakenham within easy striking distance. Bedrooms are pleasantly decorated, thoughtfully equipped and come with en suite facilities. Public rooms include a cosy guest lounge, and breakfast is served at individual tables in the smart dining room.

Rooms 3 en suite **Facilities** FTV TVL tea/coffee Cen ht 🛆 Fishing **Parking** 3 **Notes** ⊗ No Children 16yrs ⊛

DOWNHAM MARKET   Map 12 TF60

Crosskeys Riverside House

★★★★ BED AND BREAKFAST

Bridge St, Hilgay PE38 0LD
☎ 01366 387777 📠 01366 387777
e-mail: crosskeyshouse@aol.com
web: www.crosskeys.info
dir: *2m S of Downham Market. Off A10 into Hilgay, Crosskeys on bridge*

Situated in the small village of Hilgay on the banks of the River Wissey, this former coaching inn offers comfortable accommodation that includes a number of four-poster bedrooms; many rooms have river views. Public rooms include a dining room with oak beams and inglenook fireplace, plus a small, rustic residents' bar.

Rooms 4 en suite (1 fmly) (2 GF) S £35-£65; D £60-£80* **Facilities** FTV DVD Lounge tea/coffee Cen ht Wi-fi Fishing 🛆 Rowing boat for guests use **Parking** 10

FAKENHAM   Map 13 TF92

Abbott Farm *(TF975390)*

★★★ FARMHOUSE

Walsingham Rd, Binham NR21 0AW
☎ 01328 830519 📠 01328 830519 Mrs E Brown
e-mail: abbot.farm@btinternet.com
web: www.abbottfarm.co.uk
dir: *NE of Fakenham. From Binham SW onto Walsingham Rd, farm 0.6m on left*

A detached red-brick farmhouse set amidst 190 acres of arable farmland and surrounded by open countryside. The spacious bedrooms are pleasantly decorated and thoughtfully equipped; they include a ground-floor room with a large en suite shower. Breakfast is served in the attractive conservatory, which has superb views of the countryside.

Rooms 3 en suite (1 GF) S £30-£40; D £60* **Facilities** DVD TVL tea/coffee Cen ht **Parking** 20 **Notes** Closed 24-26 Dec ⊛ 190 acres arable

Fieldview Guest House

★★★ GUEST HOUSE

West Barsham Rd, East Barsham NR21 0AR
☎ 01328 820083
e-mail: info@fieldview.net

Ideally situated in a peaceful location just off the beaten track and well placed for touring the area, RSPB reserves, North Norfolk coast and Thursford. The spacious bedrooms have pine furniture, matching soft furnishings and thoughtful touches; breakfast is served at individual tables in the smart dining room.

Rooms 4 en suite

GORLESTON ON SEA   Map 13 TG50

Avalon

★★★★ GUEST ACCOMMODATION

54 Clarence Rd NR31 6DR
☎ 01493 662114 📠 01493 668528
e-mail: info@avalon-gorleston.co.uk
web: www.avalon-gorleston.co.uk
dir: *A12 past James Paget Hospital. Take 2nd exit at rdbt towards Gorleston. Next rdbt 2nd exit, 1st right*

This Edwardian terraced house is just a short walk from the promenade and beach. Breakfast and evening meals are served in the smart dining room and there is a cosy lounge bar; service is both helpful and friendly. Bedrooms are pleasantly appointed, each thoughtfully equipped and well furnished.

Rooms 10 en suite (6 fmly) (1 GF) **Facilities** TVL tea/coffee Dinner available Cen ht Licensed Wi-fi **Notes** ⊗

Jennis Lodge

★★★★ GUEST HOUSE

63 Avondale Rd NR31 6DJ
☎ 01493 662840
e-mail: bookings@jennis-lodge.co.uk
dir: *A12, past James Paget Hospital, rdbt 2nd exit, next rdbt 2nd exit, left & 2nd right*

Jennis Lodge is a friendly, family-run guest house situated close to the seafront, marine gardens and town centre. The smartly decorated bedrooms have pine furniture and many thoughtful touches that include TV, DVD or video plus broadband connection. Breakfast and dinner are served in the smart dining room and guests have the use of a cosy lounge with comfy sofas.

Rooms 8 en suite (2 fmly) S £30-£35; D £52-£55* **Facilities** FTV TVL tea/coffee Dinner available Cen ht 🛆 **Notes** LB

GREAT ELLINGHAM   Map 13 TM09

Aldercarr Hall

★★★★ GUEST ACCOMMODATION

Attleborough Rd NR17 1LQ
☎ 01953 455766 & 07710 752213 📠 01953 457993
e-mail: bedandbreakfast@aldercarr-limited.com
dir: *On B1077 500yds SE of village*

Aldercarr Hall is set in extensive grounds and surrounded by open countryside on the edge of Great Ellingham. Public rooms include a comfortably appointed conservatory and a delightful dining room where breakfast is served around a large table. The excellent facilities include a health, beauty and hairdressing studio, an indoor swimming pool, a jacuzzi and a large function suite.

Rooms 3 annexe en suite (1 fmly) (3 GF) S £51.50-£67.50; D £57.50-£67.50* **Facilities** FTV TVL tea/coffee Cen ht Licensed Wi-fi 🎱 ♪ Fishing Riding Snooker Sauna Pool table 🛆 **Parking** 200 **Notes** LB

GREAT HOCKHAM — Map 13 TL99

PREMIER COLLECTION

Home Hall Organic B&B

★★★★★ BED AND BREAKFAST

Vicarage Rd IP24 1PE
☎ 01953 498985
e-mail: homehall@hotmail.co.uk
dir: A11 Thetford left onto A1075 towards Watton. After Wretham turn right into Great Hockham, at village green left then 2nd left onto Vicarage Rd. Home Hall 1st on left

Enjoy a cream tea on arrival at this delightful detached property, which is set in landscaped gardens. There are three tastefully furnished bedrooms - the Edwardian Suite, the Victorian Suite and the Georgian Suite; each one has beautiful co-ordinated soft fabrics and Freeview TV, DVD, Wi-fi and many thoughtful touches. Organic free-range produce is served at breakfast, with guests seated around a large communal table in the oak-panelled dining room; dinner is also available.

Rooms 3 en suite (2 fmly) S fr £58; D £98-£145*
Facilities FTV DVD iPod docking station Lounge tea/coffee Dinner available Cen ht Wi-fi ♨ Extras Organic toiletries & chocolates - complimentary Parking 3 Notes LB No Children 12yrs

GREAT YARMOUTH — Map 13 TG50

PREMIER COLLECTION

Andover House

★★★★★ ◎◎ RESTAURANT WITH ROOMS

28-30 Camperdown NR30 3JB
☎ 01493 843490 📠 01493 852546
e-mail: info@andoverhouse.co.uk
web: www.andoverhouse.co.uk
dir: Opposite Wellington Pier turn into Shadingfield Close, right into Kimberley Terrace, follow into Camperdown. Property on left

A lovely three-storey Victorian town house which was totally transformed by the current owners a few years ago. The property features a series of contemporary spaces that include a large open-plan lounge bar, a brasserie-style restaurant serving modern British cuisine, a cosy lounge and a smart sun terrace. Bedrooms are tastefully appointed with co-ordinated soft furnishings and have many thoughtful touches.

Rooms 20 en suite S £67-£69; D £77-£109*
Facilities STV FTV Lounge TVL tea/coffee Dinner available Direct Dial Cen ht Wi-fi Conf Max 30 Thtr 30 Class 30 Board 15 Notes ⊗ No Children 16yrs No coaches

PREMIER COLLECTION

3 Norfolk Square

★★★★★ GUEST HOUSE

3 Norfolk Square NR30 1EE
☎ 01493 843042 & 07734 735001 📠 01493 857276
e-mail: info@3norfolksquare.co.uk
web: www.3norfolksquare.co.uk
dir: From Britannia Pier, 200yds N along seafront, left into Albemarle Rd

A delightful property situated in a peaceful side road just a short walk from the seafront and town centre. The bedrooms are smartly decorated, with co-ordinated soft furnishings and many thoughtful touches. Breakfast is served in the lower-ground floor dining room/bar, and guests also have the use of a large lounge.

Rooms 8 en suite (2 GF) Facilities FTV TVL tea/coffee Cen ht Licensed Wi-fi Conf Max 20 Class 20 Board 20 Parking 3 Notes ⊗ No Children 18yrs

Barnard House

★★★★ BED AND BREAKFAST

2 Barnard Crescent NR30 4DR
☎ 01493 855139
e-mail: enquiries@barnardhouse.com
dir: 0.5m N of town centre. Exit A149 into Barnard Crescent

A friendly, family-run bed and breakfast, set in mature landscaped gardens in a residential area. The smartly decorated bedrooms are thoughtfully equipped. Breakfast is served in the stylish dining room and there is an elegant lounge with comfy sofas. A warm welcome is assured.

Rooms 3 rms (2 en suite) (1 pri facs) S £45-£50; D £65-£75 Facilities FTV DVD TVL tea/coffee Cen ht Wi-fi ♨ Parking 3 Notes LB Closed Xmas & New Year

The Classic Lodge

★★★★ BED AND BREAKFAST

13 Euston Rd NR30 1DY
☎ 01493 852851 📠 01493 852851
web: www.classiclodge.com
dir: A12 to A47, follow signs for seafront. Turn left at Sainsbury's, ahead at lights 200mtrs on right, 100mtrs from seafront

The Classic Lodge is an impressive Victorian villa situated just a short stroll from the seafront and town centre. Breakfast is served at individual tables in the large lounge-dining room, and the spacious bedrooms are carefully furnished and equipped with a very good range of facilities. Secure parking is provided at the rear of the property.

Rooms 3 en suite Facilities FTV TVL tea/coffee Cen ht Wi-fi Parking 7 Notes LB ⊗ No Children 18yrs Closed Nov-Apr ☺

All Seasons Guest House

★★★★ GUEST HOUSE

10 Nelson Road South NR30 3JL
☎ 01493 852713 & 07543 036475
e-mail: mpilgrimmcd@hotmail.co.uk
dir: Enter Great Yarmouth on A47, at rdbt 2nd exit onto A149 for 0.3m. Next rdbt 3rd exit onto B1141 for 0.4m. Left into Queens Rd, after 0.2m left into Nelson Rd

All Seasons is a smartly presented family-run guest house that enjoys an ideal location close to the sea front and the historic South Quay area. A warm welcome is guaranteed and the freshly cooked hot breakfasts are not to be missed. There is a good range of comfortable well-appointed bedrooms available including some more spacious family rooms. Free Wi-fi is available and there is ample on-street parking.

Rooms 8 en suite (3 fmly) (1 GF) S £28-£35; D £50-£70*
Facilities FTV TVL tea/coffee Cen ht Wi-fi Extras Snacks - complimentary Conf Max 16 Thtr 16 Class 16 Board 16 Notes LB ⊗

Arden Court

★★★★ 🍽 GUEST ACCOMMODATION

93-94 North Denes Rd NR30 4LW
☎ 01493 855310 📠 01493 843413
e-mail: info@ardencourthotel.co.uk
web: www.ardencourthotel.co.uk
dir: At seafront left along North Drive. At boating lake left along Beaconsfield Rd. At mini-rdbt right into North Denes Rd

A friendly, family-run property situated in a residential area just a short walk from the seafront. The individually decorated bedrooms are smartly furnished and equipped with a good range of useful extras. Public rooms are attractively presented, and include a smart lounge bar and a restaurant serving an interesting choice of home-cooked dishes.

Rooms 14 en suite (5 fmly) (2 GF) Facilities tea/coffee Dinner available Wi-fi Parking 10 Notes ⊗

The Chequers

★★★★ GUEST HOUSE

27 Nelson Road South NR30 3JA
☎ 01493 853091
e-mail: mitchellsatchequers@hotmail.co.uk
dir: Exit A47 signed sea front, right into Marine Parade & Kings Rd, 1st right

Guests will receive a warm welcome from the caring hosts at this privately-run establishment situated just a short walk from Wellington pier and the beach. Public rooms include a cosy bar, residents' lounge and a smart dining room. Bedrooms are cheerfully decorated and have many thoughtful touches.

Rooms 8 rms (7 en suite) (1 pri facs) (2 fmly) Facilities FTV TVL tea/coffee Dinner available Cen ht Licensed Wi-fi Notes ⊗

The Hamilton

★★★★ GUEST HOUSE

23-24 North Dr NR30 4EW
☎ 01493 844662 ▤ 01493 745772
e-mail: enquiries@hamilton-hotel.co.uk

Overlooking the beach with fantastic views of the sea, this property is ideally situated for the theatre, tourist attractions, town centre and Yarmouth Racecourse. Public rooms include a smart lounge bar with plush leather seating, a breakfast room and a residents' lounge with comfy sofas. Bedrooms are bright and airy with many thoughtful touches; most rooms have lovely sea views.

Rooms 21 en suite (1 fmly) (1 GF) **Facilities** TVL tea/coffee Dinner available Cen ht Licensed Wi-fi **Conf** Max 40 Thtr 40 Class 26 Board 26 **Parking** 20 **Notes** LB ⊗

Marine Lodge

★★★★ GUEST ACCOMMODATION

19-20 Euston Rd NR30 1DY
☎ 01493 331120
e-mail: res@marinelodge.co.uk
dir: *Follow signs for sea front, 300mtrs N of Britannia Pier*

This establishment's enviable seafront position has panoramic views of the bowling greens and beach, and is within easy walking distance of Britannia Pier. Bright modern bedrooms are complemented by smart public areas that include a bar area where light snacks are available during the evening. Guests also have complimentary use of the indoor swimming pool at the sister Palm Court Hotel.

Rooms 40 en suite (5 fmly) (5 GF) **Facilities** FTV TVL tea/coffee Cen ht Lift Licensed Wi-fi **Conf** Thtr 50 Class 35 Board 25 **Parking** 38 **Notes** ⊗

Swiss Cottage B&B Exclusively for Non Smokers

★★★★ GUEST ACCOMMODATION

31 North Dr NR30 4EW
☎ 01493 855742 & 07986 399857 ▤ 01493 843547
e-mail: info@swiss-cottage.info
dir: *0.5m N of town centre. Exit A47 or A12 to seafront, 750yds N of pier. Left at Britannia Pier. Swiss Cottage on left opposite Water Gardens*

A charming detached property situated in the peaceful part of town overlooking the Venetian waterways and the sea beyond. The comfortable bedrooms are pleasantly decorated with co-ordinated fabrics and have many useful extras. Breakfast is served in the smart dining room and guests have use of an open-plan lounge area.

Rooms 8 en suite 1 annexe en suite (2 GF) S £35-£44; D £58-£88* **Facilities** FTV Lounge tea/coffee Cen ht Wi-fi ⚿ **Parking** 9 **Notes** LB No Children 11yrs Closed Nov-Feb

The Winchester

★★★★ GUEST ACCOMMODATION

12 Euston Rd NR30 1DY
☎ 01493 843950
e-mail: enquiries@winchesterprivatehotel.com
dir: *A12 onto A47, signs for seafront, left at Sainsbury's over lights, premises 400yds on right*

Just off the sea front, the friendly hosts at The Winchester give a warm welcome. The pleasant bedrooms vary in size and style and are thoughtfully equipped. Public rooms include a large lower ground-floor dining room, a small conservatory and a foyer with plush sofas.

Rooms 14 en suite (2 fmly) (5 GF) S £27.50-£35; D £55-£70* **Facilities** TVL tea/coffee Dinner available Cen ht Wi-fi ⚿ **Parking** 10 **Notes** LB ⊗ No Children 12yrs Closed Dec-Jan RS Oct-Etr No evening meals ⊠

The Harbour

★★★ GUEST HOUSE

20 Pavilion Rd, Gorleston on Sea NR31 6BY
☎ 01493 661031 & 07816 891900
e-mail: sales@theharbourhotel.co.uk
web: www.theharbourhotel.co.uk
dir: *A47 signs for Gorleston on Sea, pier & Quay Rd, premises near lighthouse*

A friendly, family-run guest house situated on the seafront just a short walk from the town centre. The pleasant, well-equipped bedrooms vary in size and style, and some rooms have lovely sea views. Breakfast is served at individual tables in the dining room, and evening meals are available by prior arrangement.

Rooms 10 rms (4 en suite) (5 fmly) S £28-£46; D £44-£60* **Facilities** STV TVL TV7B tea/coffee Dinner available Cen ht Licensed Wi-fi **Parking** 1 **Notes** LB ⊗

Haydee

★★★ GUEST HOUSE

27 Princes Rd NR30 2DG
☎ 01493 844580 ▤ 01493 844580
e-mail: info@haydee.co.uk
web: www.haydee.co.uk
dir: *Exit A47 to seafront, Princes Rd opposite Britannia Pier*

The Haydee is in a side road just a stroll from the seafront, pier and town centre. The pleasant bedrooms vary in size and style, but all are well equipped. Breakfast is served in the smart dining room and there is a cosy lounge bar.

Rooms 8 en suite (2 fmly) (2 smoking) S £24-£27; D £48-£54 **Facilities** FTV DVD TVL tea/coffee Cen ht Licensed **Notes** LB ⊗

Senglea Lodge

★★★ GUEST ACCOMMODATION

7 Euston Rd NR30 1DX
☎ 01493 859632 & 07775 698819
e-mail: senglealodge@fsmail.net
dir: *From A4 straight over 1st 2 rdbts. At lights left towards seafront. Through next lights, Lodge on right*

Delightful terrace property situated just off the seafront and very close to the town centre. Bedrooms are pleasantly decorated, have co-ordinated soft furnishings and a good range of useful extras. Breakfast is served at individual tables in the smart open-plan lounge/dining room.

Rooms 6 rms (4 en suite) (2 fmly) (2 smoking) S £23; D £46* **Facilities** FTV DVD TVL tea/coffee Cen ht Wi-fi **Notes** LB ⊗ Closed 23 Dec-2 Jan

Shemara Guest House

★★★ GUEST HOUSE

11 Wellesley Rd NR30 2AR
☎ 01493 844054 & 07771 882054
e-mail: info@shemaraguesthouse.co.uk
dir: *A47 to Great Yarmouth, follow signs for seafront, take 4th right, Shemara on right*

Shemara is ideally situated in the heart of this busy resort, as it is just a short walk from the town centre and seafront. Bedrooms come in a variety of sizes and styles, each one is pleasantly decorated and well equipped. Breakfast is served at individual tables in the open-plan lounge/dining room.

Rooms 7 en suite (2 fmly) S £22-£28; D £44-£56 **Facilities** FTV tea/coffee Dinner available Cen ht Wi-fi **Parking** 4 **Notes** LB ⊗

GREAT YARMOUTH *continued*

Victoria

★★★ GUEST ACCOMMODATION

2 Kings Rd NR30 3JW
☎ 01493 843872 & 842132 📠 01493 718921
e-mail: booking@hotelvictoria.org.uk
web: www.hotelvictoria.org.uk
dir: *Off seafront, opposite model village*

Large detached property situated just off the seafront close to Wellington Pier and the town centre. Bedrooms come in a variety of sizes and styles; each one is pleasantly decorated and thoughtfully equipped. Dinner and breakfast are served in the open plan lounge/dining room. The Victoria also has a smart outdoor swimming pool.

Rooms 35 en suite 10 annexe en suite (13 fmly) (2 GF) S £25-£40; D £49-£70* **Facilities** FTV DVD TVL tea/coffee Dinner available Cen ht Lift Licensed Wi-fi ⚡ Pool table 🏆 **Conf** Max 50 Thtr 50 Class 50 Board 30 **Parking** 20 **Notes** LB ⊗

Rhonadean

★★ GUEST HOUSE

110-111 Wellesley Rd NR30 2AR
☎ 01493 842004
e-mail: barbara@6wheeler0.wanadoo.co.uk
dir: *500yds N of town centre. A47 onto B1141 (Fuller's Hill) towards seafront, into St Nicholas Rd, 3rd right*

Rhonadean is situated in a side road adjacent to the seafront and just a short walk from the town centre. Public rooms include a small lounge bar and a dining room where breakfast and dinner are served at individual tables. Bedrooms vary in size and style; each one is pleasantly decorated and well equipped.

Rooms 18 rms (17 en suite) (1 pri facs) (7 fmly) (8 GF) **Facilities** TVL tea/coffee Dinner available Cen ht Licensed Pool table **Notes** ⊗ Closed 24-26 Dec

Villa Rose

★★ GUEST ACCOMMODATION

30-31 Princes Rd NR30 2DG
☎ 01493 843507 📠 01493 843507
e-mail: thevillarosehotel@gmail.com

Situated on a side road adjacent to the seafront within easy walking distance of the town centre and local amenities. Public rooms include a spacious lounge with plush seating and large screen TV. Breakfast is served at individual tables in the smart dining room.

Rooms 23 rms (22 en suite) (1 pri facs)

White Horse Farm

★★★★ BED AND BREAKFAST

Sharrington Rd NR24 2PB
☎ 01263 860693 & 07831 336210
e-mail: enquiries@white-horse-farm.co.uk
dir: *1m off A148 to Gunthorpe, left at village green, last property on right*

White Horse Farm has a range of converted outbuildings set amid lovely landscaped grounds in a peaceful rural location close to the north Norfolk coast. Sweetpea is a self-contained bed and breakfast unit situated in a courtyard next to the self-catering units which are themselves adjacent to the main building. Sweetpea is tastefully furnished and has a separate lounge with exposed beams and a wood-burner.

Rooms 1 en suite (1 GF) S £95-£115; D £95-£115* **Facilities** STV FTV tea/coffee Dinner available Cen ht Wi-fi 🏇 18 Riding 🏆 **Parking** 8 **Notes** LB ⊗

Heath Farmhouse

★★★★ BED AND BREAKFAST

Homersfield IP20 0EX
☎ 01986 788417
e-mail: julia.john.hunt@googlemail.com
dir: *A143 onto B1062 towards Flixton, over bridge past Suffolk sign, 2nd farm entrance on left at AA sign*

A charming 16th-century farmhouse set amid attractive landscaped grounds that include a croquet lawn. The property retains much of its original character with exposed beams, open fireplaces and wood-burning stoves. The pleasant bedrooms are carefully furnished and have many thoughtful touches. Breakfast and dinner are served in the smart dining room overlooking the garden.

Rooms 2 rms (1 fmly) S £35; D £60* **Facilities** Lounge TVL tea/coffee Dinner available Cen ht Wi-fi 🏇 🏆 Table tennis **Extras** Mineral water **Parking** 8 **Notes** ⊗ 🐾

The Old Bakery B&B

★★★★ BED AND BREAKFAST

34 The Street NR20 5DF
☎ 01263 862802 & 07771 391967
e-mail: mike@theoldbakerynorfolk.co.uk
web: www.theoldbakerynorfolk.co.uk
dir: *From A148 exit at Little Snoring signed Fulmodeston, follow signs to Hindolveston. At next junct continue for 1.3m, house on corner of turn to Foulsham*

A delightful detached property which was originally the village bakery and dates back to the 17th century. The spacious, well-equipped bedroom has pine furniture and many thoughtful touches. Breakfast, which includes locally-sourced ingredients is served at a large communal

---

table in the smart dining room, guests have the use of a comfortable lounge with leather sofas and a log fire.

Rooms 1 en suite S £68-£75; D £68-£75* **Facilities** FTV DVD iPod docking station TVL tea/coffee Dinner available Cen ht Wi-fi 🏇 🏆 **Extras** Fridges in room, cakes on arrival - complimentary **Parking** 4 **Notes** LB ⊗ No Children ⊗

PREMIER COLLECTION

Field House

★★★★★ 🍴 BED AND BREAKFAST

Moorgate Rd NR21 0PT
☎ 01328 878726
e-mail: stay@fieldhousehindringham.co.uk
web: www.fieldhousehindringham.co.uk
dir: *Exit A148 to Hindringham, into Moorgate Rd at Lower Green. Field House on left*

A warm friendly welcome and genuine hospitality are offered by the caring hosts at this delightful property. Field House is situated in a peaceful rural location amid pretty landscaped gardens. The individually decorated bedrooms are tastefully furnished and have co-ordinated soft fabrics as well as many thoughtful touches. Breakfast is served in the lounge-dining room and features quality, locally sourced produce. Field House was a Finalist in the AA Friendliest B&B of the Year Award 2012-13.

Rooms 2 en suite 1 annexe en suite **Facilities** FTV tea/coffee Cen ht Wi-fi 🏇 **Parking** 3 **Notes** ⊗ No Children 10yrs Closed 25-26 Dec ⊗

Save on B&Bs and Hotels. Book at theAA.com/hotel

NORFOLK 221 ENGLAND

HOLT — Map 13 TG03

Kadina

★★★★ BED AND BREAKFAST

Warren Close, High Kelling NR25 6QX
☎ 01263 710116 & 07900 928729 ▤ 01263 710116
e-mail: enquiries@kadinanorfolk.co.uk
dir: Exit A148 into Bridge Rd, right into Warren Rd. Right into Warren Close. Kadina 4th left

Modern detached chalet bungalow situated close to the Georgian town of Holt, in the peaceful village of High Kelling. The smartly appointed bedrooms have pine furniture, co-ordinated soft furnishings and many thoughtful touches. Breakfast is served at a large pine table in the kitchen/dining room, and dinner is available by prior arrangement.

Rooms 2 en suite (1 GF) S £50-£55; D £70-£75*
Facilities tea/coffee Dinner available Cen ht Wi-fi
Parking 5 Notes LB ⊗ No Children ⊛

The Lawns Wine Bar

★★★★ ⊛ RESTAURANT WITH ROOMS

26 Station Rd NR25 6BS
☎ 01263 713390
e-mail: mail@lawnsatholt.co.uk
dir: A148 (Cromer road). 0.25m from Holt rdbt, turn left, 400yds along Station Rd

A superb Georgian house situated in the centre of this delightful north Norfolk market town. The open-plan public areas include a large wine bar, a conservatory and a smart restaurant. The spacious bedrooms are tastefully appointed with co-ordinated soft furnishings and have many thoughtful touches.

Rooms 8 en suite 2 annexe en suite (2 GF) S £95;
D £95-£125* Facilities FTV DVD TVL TV8B tea/coffee
Dinner available Cen ht Wi-fi Extras Speciality toiletries
Conf Max 20 Thtr 20 Class 12 Parking 14

The Old Telephone Exchange Bed & Breakfast

★★★★ BED AND BREAKFAST

37 New St NR25 6JH
☎ 01263 712992
e-mail: christopher.manders@btinternet.com
dir: From High St into New St, establishment 200yds on left

Expect a warm welcome at this small, family-run bed and breakfast situated in a quiet side road close to the town centre. The immaculate bedrooms are tastefully appointed and equipped with many thoughtful touches. Public rooms feature a comfortable lounge-dining area with a wide-screen TV, sofas, books and games. The Old Telephone Exchange was a Finalist in the AA Friendliest B&B of the Year Award 2012-13.

Rooms 3 rms (2 en suite) (1 pri facs) (3 GF) D £60-£75
Facilities FTV DVD TVL tea/coffee Cen ht 🔒 Parking 3
Notes LB ⊗ No Children 10yrs ⊛

White Cottage B&B

★★★★ GUEST ACCOMMODATION

Norwich Rd NR25 6SW
☎ 01263 713353
e-mail: enquiries@whitecottageholt.co.uk
dir: From A148 from Holt take B1149, 0.5m on left after police station

A delightful detached cottage situated just a short walk from this busy town centre. Breakfast is served at individual tables in the smart dining room and guests have the use of a cosy lounge. The bedrooms are pleasantly decorated and equipped with a good range of useful extras.

Rooms 2 en suite D £60-£75* Facilities tea/coffee
Cen ht Notes ⊗ No Children 10yrs Closed 21 Dec-7 Jan
RS Jan-Feb Telephone to confirm ⊛

HORNING — Map 13 TG31

Innkeeper's Lodge Norfolk Broads, Horning

★★★ INN

10 Lower St NR12 8AA
☎ 0845 112 6060
e-mail: info@innkeeperslodge.com
web: www.innkeeperslodge.com

At Innkeeper's Lodge you'll find accommodation with comfort and character in equal measure, and everything needed for a relaxing stay, from easy check-in and free parking to complimentary breakfast and a cosy pub serving great value food and drink on the doorstep. Each Lodge has quality rooms, and there are Lodges in a variety of locations from towns and cities to countryside settings across the UK.

Rooms 8 en suite (3 fmly) Facilities FTV tea/coffee Dinner available Direct Dial Wi-fi Parking

HUNSTANTON — Map 12 TF64

Claremont Guest House

★★★★ GUEST HOUSE

35 Greevegate PE36 6AF
☎ 01485 533171
e-mail: claremontgh@tiscali.co.uk
dir: Exit A149 into Greevegate, house before St Edmund's Church

This Victorian guest house, close to the shops, beach and gardens, has individually decorated bedrooms with a good range of useful extras. There are also a ground-floor room, two feature rooms, one with a four-poster, and another with a canopied bed.

Rooms 7 en suite (1 fmly) (1 GF) S £28-£37; D £56-£74*
Facilities TVL tea/coffee Cen ht Parking 4 Notes LB No
Children 5yrs Closed 15 Nov-15 Mar ⊛

The Neptune Restaurant with Rooms

★★★★ ⊛⊛⊛ RESTAURANT WITH ROOMS

85 Old Hunstanton Rd, Old Hunstanton PE36 6HZ
☎ 01485 532122
e-mail: reservations@theneptune.co.uk
web: www.theneptune.co.uk
dir: On A149, past Hunstanton, 200mtrs on left after post office

This charming 18th-century coaching inn, now a restaurant with rooms, is ideally situated for touring the Norfolk coastline. The smartly appointed bedrooms are brightly finished with co-ordinated fabrics and hand-made New England furniture. Public rooms feature white clapboard walls, polished dark wood floors, fresh flowers and Lloyd Loom furniture. The food is very much a draw here with the carefully prepared, award-winning cuisine utilising excellent local produce, from oysters and mussels from Thornham to quinces grown on a neighbouring farm.

Rooms 6 en suite Facilities FTV tea/coffee Dinner available Direct Dial Cen ht Wi-fi Parking 6 Notes ⊗ No Children 10yrs Closed 2wks Nov & 3wks Jan RS Oct-Apr Closed Mon No coaches

Gemini Lodge Guest House

★★★★ GUEST HOUSE

5 Alexandra Rd PE36 5BT
☎ 01485 533902

This guest house is situated in an elevated position close to the centre of town and seafront. The bedrooms are smartly decorated in neutral colours with lovely co-ordinated soft furnishings and fabrics; some rooms have lovely views of the sea. Public rooms include a smart lounge with plush sofas, and breakfast is served at a large communal table in the contemporary dining room.

Rooms 3 en suite Facilities FTV TVL tea/coffee Cen ht
Parking 3 Notes No Children ⊛

The King William IV Country Inn & Restaurant

★★★★ Ⓐ INN

Heacham Rd, Sedgeford PE36 5LU
☎ 01485 571765 ▤ 01485 571743
e-mail: info@thekingwilliamsedgeford.co.uk
web: www.thekingwilliamsedgeford.co.uk
dir: A149 to Hunstanton, right at Norfolk Lavender in Heacham onto B1454, signed Docking. 2m to Sedgeford

Rooms 9 en suite (4 fmly) S £60-£70; D £90-£115*
Facilities tea/coffee Dinner available Cen ht Wi-fi ⚓ 18 🔒
Leisure/Tennis centre 0.5m by arrangement Parking 60
Notes LB No coaches

HUNSTANTON *continued*

Rosamaly Guest House

★★★★ Ⓐ GUEST ACCOMMODATION

14 Glebe Av PE36 6BS
☎ 01485 534187 & 07775 724484
e-mail: vacancies@rosamaly.co.uk
dir: *A149 to Hunstanton. At rdbt take 3rd exit staying on A149 towards Cromer. In 1m church on left, Glebe Av 2nd left, Rosamaly 50yds on left*
Rooms 6 en suite (1 fmly) (1 GF) D £64-£70*
Facilities FTV TVL tea/coffee Dinner available Cen ht
Notes LB Closed 24 Dec-1 Jan ⊜

The White Cottage

★★★ GUEST ACCOMMODATION

19 Wodehouse Rd PE36 6JW
☎ 01485 532380

A charming cottage situated in a quiet side road in Old Hunstanton, The White Cottage has been owned and run by Mrs Burton for 30 years. The spacious bedrooms are attractively decorated, and some have lovely sea views. Dinner is served in the smart dining room and there is a cosy sitting room with a television.

Rooms 3 rms (1 en suite) **Facilities** TVL TV1B tea/coffee Dinner available Cen ht **Parking** 4 **Notes** LB No Children 10yrs ⊜

Richmond House Bed & Breakfast

★★★ GUEST HOUSE

6-8 Westgate PE36 5AL
☎ 01485 532601
e-mail: richmondhousehotel@xln.co.uk
dir: *Exit A149 into Westgate*

This well-maintained guest house is well situated for the seafront and town centre. Its pleasant bedrooms vary in size and style, but all are well equipped and some rooms have superb sea views. Public rooms feature a smart restaurant and a cosy lounge bar.

Rooms 14 rms (10 en suite) (5 GF) S £35-£45; D £65-£70* **Facilities** tea/coffee Dinner available Cen ht Lift Licensed **Notes** ⊗ No Children 18yrs Closed Nov-Etr ⊜

LITCHAM   Map 13 TF81

Bramley

★★★★ BED AND BREAKFAST

Weasenham Rd PE32 2QT
☎ 01328 701592 📠 01328 701592
e-mail: bramleybandb@hotmail.co.uk
web: www.bramley-litcham.co.uk
dir: *A1065 onto B1145. Left at x-rds, left at school, 4th house on left*

A warm welcome awaits at this delightful detached house, set in a peaceful location on the village fringe, with ample safe parking in generous grounds. The mostly spacious bedrooms are thoughtfully furnished to ensure guest comfort and have smartly appointed en suite shower rooms. A hearty, freshly-cooked breakfast is served at individual tables in the separate elegant dining room.

Rooms 4 en suite (1 fmly) **Facilities** FTV TV3B tea/coffee Cen ht Wi-fi ⓟ **Parking** 4 **Notes** LB ⊗ ⊜

LITTLE WALSINGHAM   Map 13 TF93

The Old Bakehouse Tea Room & Guest House

★★★★ GUEST HOUSE

33 High St NR22 6BZ
☎ 01328 820454 📠 01328 820454
e-mail: theoldbakehouseguesthouse@yahoo.co.uk
dir: *Exit A148 (Fakenham bypass) to Wells & Walsingham (B1105). NB Do not turn left at x-rds, continue straight ahead into Walsingham. Next to post office*

Ideally situated in the heart of the historical shrine village of Little Walsingham, The Old Bakehouse offers spacious bedrooms with pine furniture, co-ordinated soft furnishings and many thoughtful touches. Breakfast is served in the large dining room, which is now a traditional tea room during the day.

Rooms 3 en suite S £50-£55; D £80-£85* **Facilities** FTV DVD Lounge tea/coffee Cen ht Wi-fi ⓟ **Extras** Speciality toiletries, mineral water - complimentary **Notes** ⊗ Closed Jan

---

NORTH WALSHAM   Map 13 TG23

Chimneys

★★★★ ⊜ BED AND BREAKFAST

51 Cromer Rd NR28 0HB
☎ 01692 406172 & 07952 117701
e-mail: jenny.harmer6172@gmail.com
dir: *0.5m NW of town centre on A149*

A delightful Edwardian-style town house set amidst mature secluded grounds close to the town centre. Bedrooms are tastefully furnished and thoughtfully equipped, the superior room has a jacuzzi bath. Breakfast is served in the smart dining room and guests are welcome to sit on the balcony, which overlooks the garden. Dinner is available by prior arrangement. Chimneys was a Finalist in the AA Friendliest B&B of the Year Award 2012-13.

Rooms 3 en suite (1 fmly) S £45-£55; D £65-£75*
Facilities STV FTV DVD iPod docking station tea/coffee Dinner available Cen ht Wi-fi ⓟ **Parking** 6

The Scarborough Hill Country Inn

★★★★ INN

Old Yarmouth Rd NR28 9NA
☎ 01692 402151 📠 01692 406686
e-mail: scarboroughhill@nascr.net
web: www.arlingtonhotel.co.uk
dir: *From Norwich B1150, straight through lights, across mini-rdbt, right at next rdbt, 1m on right*

This is a delightful inn with a country house feel situated on the outskirts of town, in a peaceful location amidst landscaped grounds. Public rooms include a smart lounge bar with plush sofas, an intimate dining room and a large conservatory. Bedrooms are generally quite spacious; each one is pleasantly furnished and thoughtfully equipped.

Save on B&Bs and Hotels. Book at **theAA.com/hotel**

NORFOLK 223 ENGLAND

Rooms 8 en suite 1 annexe en suite (1 fmly) (1 GF)
Facilities FTV TVL tea/coffee Dinner available Direct Dial
Cen ht Wi-fi **Parking** 80 **Notes** ⊗ Civ Wed

NORWICH   Map 13 TG20

PREMIER COLLECTION

Brasteds

★★★★★ ◉◉ 🏠 RESTAURANT WITH ROOMS

Manor Farm Barns, Framingham Pigot NR14 7PZ
☎ 01508 491112 📠 01508 491113
e-mail: enquiries@brasteds.co.uk
web: www.brasteds.co.uk
dir: *A11 onto A47 towards Great Yarmouth, then A146.*
0.5m, right into Fox Rd, 0.5m on left

Brasteds is a lovely detached property set in 20 acres
of mature, landscaped parkland on the outskirts of
Norwich. The tastefully appointed bedrooms have
beautiful soft furnishings and fabrics along with
comfortable seating and many thoughtful touches.
Public rooms include a cosy snug with plush sofas, and
a smart dining room where breakfast is served. Dinner
is available in Brasteds Restaurant, which can be
found in an adjacent building.

Rooms 6 en suite (1 fmly) (3 GF) **Facilities** FTV DVD
iPod docking station TVL tea/coffee Dinner available
Direct Dial Cen ht Wi-fi ch fac 🏋 **Extras** Mini-bar
Conf Max 120 Thtr 120 Class 100 Board 40 **Parking** 50
Notes LB No coaches Civ Wed 160

Gothic House Bed & Breakfast

★★★★ GUEST ACCOMMODATION

King's Head Yard, Magdalen St NR3 1JE
☎ 01603 631879
e-mail: charvey649@aol.com
dir: *Follow signs for A147, exit at rdbt past flyover into*
Whitefriars. Right into Fishergate, at end, right into
Magdalen St

Gothic House is an elegant Grade II listed Regency
townhouse set in a quiet courtyard in the heart of
Norwich. The property has been lovingly restored and
retains much of its original character. The spacious
bedrooms are individually decorated and have many
thoughtful touches. Breakfast, which includes locally
sourced produce, is served in the elegant dining room.

Rooms 2 rms (2 pri facs) S £65; D £95 **Facilities** STV FTV
tea/coffee Cen ht Wi-fi **Parking** 2 **Notes** ⊗ No Children
18yrs Closed Feb 🖃

Old Thorn Barn

★★★★ GUEST ACCOMMODATION

Corporation Farm, Wymondham Rd, Hethel NR14 8EU
☎ 01953 607785 & 07894 203208
e-mail: enquiries@oldthornbarn.co.uk
web: www.oldthornbarn.co.uk
dir: *6m SW of Norwich. Follow signs for Lotus Cars from*
A11 or B1113, on Wymondham Rd

A delightful Grade II listed barn situated in a peaceful
rural location just a short drive from the city centre. The
property has stylish, thoughtfully equipped bedrooms
with polished wood floors and antique pine furniture.
Breakfast is served in the open-plan barn, which also has
a wood-burning stove and a cosy lounge area.

Rooms 5 en suite 2 annexe en suite (7 GF) S £38-£42;
D £68-£72 **Facilities** FTV TVL tea/coffee Cen ht Wi-fi
Parking 14 **Notes** ⊗

Church Farm

★★★★ GUEST ACCOMMODATION

Church St, Horsford NR10 3DB
☎ 01603 898020 & 898582 📠 01603 755010
e-mail: churchfarmgh@aol.com
dir: *5m NW of city centre. A140 onto B1149, right at x-rds*

Church Farm is set in a peaceful rural location just a
short drive from Norwich airport and the city centre. The
spacious bedrooms are smartly decorated, pleasantly
furnished and have many thoughtful touches. Breakfast
is served at individual tables in the conservatory-style
lounge-dining room, which overlooks the garden and sun
terrace.

Rooms 10 en suite (1 fmly) (3 GF) S £40-£50;
D £55-£75* **Facilities** FTV TVL tea/coffee Cen ht Wi-fi
Parking 20 **Notes** ⊗

Cringleford Guest House

★★★★ GUEST HOUSE

1 Gurney Ln, Cringleford NR4 7SB
☎ 01603 451349 & 07775 725933
e-mail: robandkate@cringlefordguesthouse.co.uk
web: www.cringlefordguesthouse.co.uk
dir: *From A11 & A47 Thickthorn rdbt follow signs to*
Norwich, 0.25m slip road to Cringleford, left at junct into
Colney Ln. Gurney Ln 5th on right

A delightful property, situated just a short drive from the
hospital, University of East Anglia and major roads. The
pleasant, well-equipped bedrooms have co-ordinated
fabrics and pine furniture. Breakfast is served at
individual tables in the smart dining room.

Rooms 6 en suite 1 annexe en suite (4 fmly) (2 GF)
S £45-£55; D £65-£75* **Facilities** FTV DVD TVL tea/coffee
Cen ht Wi-fi **Conf** Max 10 Thtr 10 Class 10 Board 10
Parking 7 **Notes** LB ⊗

The Larches Guest House

★★★★ GUEST ACCOMMODATION

345 Aylsham Rd NR3 2RU
☎ 01603 415420 📠 01603 465340
e-mail: info@thelarches.com
dir: *50yds from Norwich ring road*

A large detached property set in mature gardens and
situated just off the Norwich outer ring road. The public
rooms include a large open-plan lounge and breakfast
room with a TV and sofas. The well-equipped bedrooms
are smartly decorated and have matching soft
furnishings.

Rooms 7 en suite (1 fmly) (1 GF) (7 smoking) S £32;
D £55* **Facilities** STV FTV TVL tea/coffee Cen ht Wi-fi 🏋
Parking 10

Wensum Guest House

★★★★ GUEST HOUSE

225 Dereham Rd NR2 3TF
☎ 01603 621069 📠 01603 618445
e-mail: info@wensumguesthouse.co.uk
dir: *From A47 1st exit into Norwich A1074 Dereham Rd*

Expect a warm welcome at this modern guest house
situated just a short walk from the city centre. Public
rooms include a smart open-plan dining room and a cosy
lounge with flat screen TV and plush leather sofas. The
contemporary bedrooms are pleasantly decorated and
thoughtfully equipped.

Rooms 9 rms (5 en suite) (4 pri facs) 9 annexe rms 7
annexe en suite (2 pri facs) (4 fmly) (8 GF) **Facilities** FTV
tea/coffee Cen ht Wi-fi **Parking** 16 **Notes** LB ⊗ Closed 24
Dec-3 Jan

NORWICH *continued*

Edmar Lodge

★ ★ ★ GUEST ACCOMMODATION

64 Earlham Rd NR2 3DF
☎ 01603 615599 ▤ 01603 495599
e-mail: mail@edmarlodge.co.uk
web: www.edmarlodge.co.uk
dir: *Exit A47 (S bypass) onto B1108 (Earlham Rd), follow university & hospital signs*

Located just a ten-minute walk from the city centre, this friendly family-run establishment offers a convenient location and ample private parking. Individually decorated bedrooms are smartly appointed and well equipped. Freshly prepared breakfasts are served in the cosy dining room; a microwave and a fridge are also available.

Rooms 5 en suite (1 fmly) S £40-£50; D £45-£60
Facilities FTV tea/coffee Cen ht Wi-fi ⚓ **Parking** 6

Innkeeper's Lodge Norwich

★ ★ ★ INN

18-22 Yarmouth Rd NR7 0EF
☎ 0845 112 6063
e-mail: info@innkeeperslodge.com
web: www.innkeeperslodge.com

At Innkeeper's Lodge you'll find accommodation with comfort and character in equal measure, and everything needed for a relaxing stay, from easy check-in and free parking to complimentary breakfast and a cosy pub serving great value food and drink on the doorstep. Each Lodge has quality rooms, and there are Lodges in a variety of locations from towns and cities to countryside settings across the UK.

Rooms 14 en suite (5 fmly) **Facilities** FTV tea/coffee Dinner available Direct Dial Wi-fi **Parking**

RINGSTEAD — Map 12 TF74

The Gin Trap Inn

★ ★ ★ ★ ⊛ INN

6 High St PE36 5JU
☎ 01485 525264
e-mail: thegintrap@hotmail.co.uk
dir: *A149 from King's Lynn towards Hunstanton. In 15m right at Heacham for Ringstead, into village centre*

This delightful 17th-century inn is in a quiet village just a short drive from the coast. The public rooms include a large open-plan bar and a cosy restaurant. The accommodation is luxurious. Each individually appointed bedroom has been carefully decorated and thoughtfully equipped.

Rooms 3 en suite S £39-£60; D £78-£120* **Facilities** FTV tea/coffee Dinner available Cen ht Wi-fi ⚓ **Parking** 20
Notes No Children No coaches

SHERINGHAM — Map 13 TG14

See also Cromer

The Eight Acres

★ ★ ★ ★ ★ ▤ BED AND BREAKFAST

Glebe Farm, Holt Rd, Aylmerton NR11 8QA
☎ 01263 838094 & 07891 717713 ▤ 01263 838094
dir: *On A148 3m from Cromer, 6m from Holt*

A warm welcome is assured at this modern detached farmhouse, which is set amid open countryside just off the A148. Bedrooms are smartly decorated with co-ordinated soft furnishings, lovely pine furniture and many extras such as flat screen digital TVs with built-in DVD. Public rooms feature a large open-plan lounge/dining room.

Rooms 2 en suite S £55; D £70* **Facilities** FTV Lounge tea/coffee Cen ht Wi-fi DVD players available in rooms **Parking** 2 **Notes** ⊗ No Children 16yrs Closed Nov-Feb ⊛

Ashbourne House

★ ★ ★ ★ ★ ▤ BED AND BREAKFAST

1 Nelson Rd NR26 8BT
☎ 01263 821555 & 07807 629868
e-mail: nailligill@yahoo.co.uk
dir: *Take A149 Cromer road towards Cromer, turn left over Beeston Common. Under bridge, at top of Curtis Ln turn left, situated on right*

This superb detached property has been tastefully appointed to a very high standard. The smart bedrooms have lovely soft furnishings and are full of thoughtful touches. Public rooms include a large entrance hall and a guest lounge. Breakfast is served in the stylish panelled dining room, which overlooks the landscaped gardens that slope upwards to the cliff top.

Rooms 3 en suite S £50-£60; D £70-£75 **Facilities** STV FTV DVD TVL tea/coffee Cen ht Wi-fi **Parking** 3 **Notes** ⊗ No Children 12yrs ⊛

The Eiders Bed & Breakfast

★ ★ ★ ★ ★ BED AND BREAKFAST

Holt Rd, Aylmerton NR11 8QA
☎ 01263 837280
e-mail: enquiries@eiders.co.uk
web: www.eiders.co.uk
dir: *From Cromer on A148, enter Aylmerton, pass garage on left. After x-rds, 2nd entrance on right*

The Eiders is situated just a short drive from the centre of town and is ideally placed for touring the north Norfolk coast. The tastefully appointed bedrooms have lovely co-ordinated fabrics and many thoughtful touches. Breakfast is served at individual tables in the conservatory which overlooks the gardens and duck pond. Guests have the use of a heated swimming pool which is open from May to September.

Rooms 6 en suite (2 fmly) (6 GF) S £75-£85; D £95-£130* **Facilities** FTV DVD iPod docking station TVL tea/coffee Cen ht Wi-fi ↘ **Extras** Bottled water - complimentary **Parking** 7 **Notes** LB ⊗

At Knollside

★ ★ ★ ★ BED AND BREAKFAST

43 Cliff Rd NR26 8BJ
☎ 01263 823320 & 07771 631980
e-mail: avril@at-knollside.co.uk
web: www.at-knollside.co.uk
dir: *250yds E of town centre. A1082 to High St, into Wyndham St & Cliff Rd*

Expect a warm welcome from the caring hosts at this delightful Victorian house overlooking the beach and sea. Bedrooms are tastefully furnished, have co-ordinated fabrics and enjoy many thoughtful touches. Breakfast is served in the elegant dining room and features local produce. Guests also have the use of a comfortable lounge.

Rooms 3 en suite D £60-£80* **Facilities** DVD Lounge tea/coffee Cen ht ⅃ 36 **Parking** 3 **Notes** LB ⊗ No Children 3yrs ⊛

Bay Leaf Guest House

★ ★ ★ ★ BED AND BREAKFAST

10 St Peters Rd NR26 8QY
☎ 01263 823779
e-mail: bayleafgh@aol.com
dir: *A149 (Weybourne Rd) into Church St, 2nd right*

This lovely Victorian property is situated just a short walk from the golf course, steam railway and town centre. There is a smart lounge bar, and breakfast is served in the conservatory-dining room which overlooks the patio.

Rooms 7 en suite (2 fmly) (2 GF) S £40-£50; D £64-£76 **Facilities** FTV tea/coffee Cen ht Licensed **Parking** 5 **Notes** LB ⊗ No Children 8yrs ⊛

Save on B&Bs and Hotels. Book at **theAA.com/hotel**

NORFOLK 225 ENGLAND

Brambles Bed & Breakfast

★★★★ GUEST ACCOMMODATION

5 Nelson Rd NR26 8BT
☎ 01263 825567 & 07791 429093 📠 01263 825567
e-mail: enquiries@stayatbrambles.co.uk
dir: Exit A148 into Sheringham, across rdbt, right at
Lobster pub. Left into Cliff Rd, right into Nelson Rd

A warm welcome is offered by the caring hosts at this
delightful detached property situated just a short walk
from the seafront and town centre. The well-equipped
bedrooms are pleasantly decorated. Breakfast is served
in the smart dining room.

Rooms 3 en suite (2 fmly) (1 GF) S £47-£57;
D £62.70-£77* **Facilities** FTV DVD tea/coffee Cen ht Wi-fi
Extras Mini-fridges **Parking** 6 **Notes** LB ⊗

Highfield Guest House

★★★★ GUEST HOUSE

5 Montague Rd NR26 8LN
☎ 01263 825524 & 07769 628817
e-mail: gmcaldwell@aol.com
dir: Exit A148, left at mini-rdbt, 1st right. Left at church,
left into South St & Montague Rd

This delightful guest house is situated in a peaceful side
road within easy walking distance of the shops and
beach. It offers smart, thoughtfully equipped bedrooms,
and breakfast is served at individual tables in the
attractive dining room.

Rooms 6 rms (5 en suite) (1 pri facs) (2 fmly)
Facilities TVL tea/coffee Cen ht **Conf** Max 20 Board 20
Parking 2 **Notes** ⊗ No Children 8yrs Closed 22 Dec-1
Feb 🏦

Roman Camp Inn

★★★★ INN

Holt Rd, Aylmerton NR11 8QD
☎ 01263 838291 📠 01263 837071
e-mail: enquiries@romancampinn.co.uk
dir: On A148 between Sheringham & Cromer, approx 1.5m
from Cromer

A smartly presented inn ideally situated for touring the
north Norfolk coastline. The property provides spacious,
tastefully appointed bedrooms with a good range of
useful facilities including hair dryers. Five rooms are
presented as Deluxe, and two are suitable for disabled
guests. Public rooms include a smart conservatory-style
restaurant, a comfortable open-plan lounge/bar and a
dining area. Room service is available, guests have
complimentary use of local leisure facilities, and there is
ample free parking.

Rooms 15 en suite (1 fmly) (10 GF) **Facilities** tea/coffee
Direct Dial Wi-fi Free use of nearby leisure complex & pool
Parking 50 **Notes** ⊗ Closed 25-26 Dec

The Old Barn

★★★★ Ⓐ BED AND BREAKFAST

Cromer Rd, West Runton NR27 9QT
☎ 01263 838285
e-mail: mkelliott2@aol.com
dir: A149 from Cromer to West Runton, 2m opposite
church

Rooms 3 rms (2 en suite) (1 pri facs) (1 GF) D £70-£80*
Facilities TVL tea/coffee Cen ht Wi-fi **Parking** 6 **Notes** ⊗
No Children 18yrs 🏦

STALHAM
Map 13 TG32

Wayford Bridge Inn

Ⓤ

Wayford NR12 9LL
☎ 01692 582414
e-mail: wayfordbridge@norfolkbroadsinns.co.uk

Currently the rating for this establishment is not
confirmed. This may be due to a change of ownership or
because it has only recently joined the AA rating scheme.

Rooms 15 en suite D £60-£125*

SWAFFHAM

See Castle Acre

THETFORD
Map 13 TL88

The Bell

★★★ INN

King St IP24 2AZ
☎ 01842 754455 📠 01842 755552
e-mail: bell.thetford@oldenglishinns.co.uk
dir: From S exit A11, 2m to 1st lights, right onto A134.
100yds, left into Bridge St, 150yds over bridge

A 15th-century coaching inn situated in the heart of the
old part of town. The historic charm and character
permeates through much of the building. The
accommodation is split between the main building and
the more modern bedroom wings. Public areas include a
bar, a lounge, and restaurant as well as conference
facilities.

Rooms 46 en suite (1 fmly) **Facilities** tea/coffee Direct
Dial **Parking** 55

THOMPSON
Map 13 TL99

The Chequers Inn

★★★★ Ⓐ INN

Griston Rd IP24 1PX
☎ 01953 483360
e-mail: richard@thompsonchequers.co.uk
dir: NE of Thetford. Off A1075 to Thompson village x-rds
Rooms 3 annexe en suite (1 fmly) (3 GF) S £45; D £65
Facilities FTV DVD tea/coffee Dinner available Direct Dial
Cen ht Wi-fi Fishing 🛇 **Extras** Fruit **Parking** 35

THORNHAM
Map 12 TF74

The Old Coach House

Ⓤ

High St PE36 6LY
☎ 01485 512229 📠 01485 512091
e-mail: info@oldcoachousethornham.com

Currently the rating for this establishment is not
confirmed. This may be due to a change of ownership or
because it has only recently joined the AA rating scheme.

Rooms 12 en suite S £50-£90; D £69-£130*

THURSFORD
Map 13 TF93

PREMIER COLLECTION

Holly Lodge

★★★★★ 🛏 BED AND BREAKFAST

The Street NR21 0AS
☎ 01328 878465 📠 01328 878465
e-mail: info@hollylodgeguesthouse.co.uk
dir: Exit A148 into Thursford (village green on left) 2nd
driveway on left past green

Holly Lodge is an award-winning 18th-century property
situated in a picturesque location surrounded by open
farmland. The stylish cottage bedrooms are in a
converted stable block, each room individually
decorated, beautifully furnished and equipped with
many useful extras. The attractive public rooms have a
wealth of character, with flagstone floors, oak beams
and open fireplaces. There are also superb landscaped
grounds to enjoy.

Rooms 3 en suite (3 GF) S £70-£100; D £90-£120*
Facilities TVL tea/coffee Dinner available Cen ht Wi-fi
Parking 6 **Notes** LB ⊗ No Children 14yrs

The Old Forge Seafood Restaurant

★★★★ ⊛ RESTAURANT WITH ROOMS

Fakenham Rd NR21 0BD
☎ 01328 878345
e-mail: sarah.goldspink@btconnect.com
dir: On A148 (Fakenham to Holt road)

Expect a warm welcome at this delightful relaxed
restaurant with rooms. The open-plan public areas
include a lounge bar area with comfy sofas, and an
intimate restaurant with pine tables. Bedrooms are
pleasantly decorated and equipped with a good range of
useful facilities.

Rooms 3 en suite S £32.50; D £65* **Facilities** STV FTV
Lounge tea/coffee Dinner available Cen ht Wi-fi Riding
Parking 14 **Notes** No Children 5yrs No coaches

TIVETSHALL ST MARGARET — Map 13 TM18

Red House Farm Bed & Breakfast

★★★★ BED AND BREAKFAST

Station Rd NR15 2DJ
☎ 01379 676566 & 07719 437007
e-mail: office@redhousefarm.info
dir: 500mtrs from Pulham rdbt A140

A warm welcome is assured at this delightful 17th-century barn conversion, situated on a small working farm in a peaceful rural location. The tastefully appointed bedrooms have modern furniture and lovely countryside views. Breakfast, which includes home-grown produce, is served at a large communal table in the smart kitchen.

Rooms 2 en suite (2 GF) S £40-£50; D £70-£75*
Facilities FTV TVL tea/coffee Cen ht Wi-fi **Parking** 4
Notes ⊛

WELLS-NEXT-THE-SEA — Map 13 TF94

Kilcoroon

★★★ BED AND BREAKFAST

Chancery Ln NR23 1ER
☎ 01328 710270 & 07733 112108
e-mail: terry@kilcoroon.co.uk
dir: Exit B1105 into Mill Rd. 3rd right into Buttlands. Property on left of Crown Hotel

Delightful detached period property situated by the green, just off the Buttlands and a short walk from the town centre. The spacious bedrooms are pleasantly decorated with co-ordinated fabrics and equipped with modern facilities. Breakfast is served at a large communal table in the elegant dining room.

Rooms 2 en suite **Facilities** tea/coffee Cen ht Wi-fi
Notes ⊛ No Children 10yrs Closed 23-31 Dec ⊛

WESTON LONGVILLE — Map 13 TG11

The Parson Woodforde

★★★★ @ INN

Church St NR9 5JU
☎ 01603 881675
e-mail: info@theparsonwoodforde.com
dir: W past Norwich on A47. At Easton rdbt A47 to Dereham, right onto Wood Ln. After 3m, establishment on left opposite church

This 18th-century inn has recently reopened after undergoing a total refurbishment. The spacious open plan public rooms include a range of seating areas, a large bar area and a restaurant which opens out onto a smart terrace; there are many original features such as exposed brickwork, beams and open fireplaces. Bedrooms are tastefully appointed and well equipped.

Rooms 4 en suite (2 fmly) S £75-£85; D £85-£95*
Facilities FTV iPod docking station tea/coffee Dinner available Cen ht Wi-fi **Parking** 50 **Notes** Closed 1 Jan RS 25 Dec open for drinks only No coaches

---

NORTHAMPTONSHIRE

CASTLE ASHBY — Map 11 SP85

The Falcon

★★★ INN

NN7 1LF
☎ 01604 696200 📠 01604 696673
e-mail: 6446@greeneking.co.uk
dir: Follow signs for Castle Ashby from A428

Set in the heart of a peaceful village, the inn consists of a main house and a neighbouring cottage. Bedrooms are all individually decorated and provide a wealth of thoughtful extras. Character public rooms, in the main house, include a cellar bar, a choice of lounges and a pretty restaurant serving good quality cuisine.

Rooms 5 en suite 10 annexe en suite (1 fmly)
Facilities TVL tea/coffee Dinner available Cen ht Wi-fi
Conf Max 100 Thtr 100 Class 60 Board 30 **Parking** 75
Notes Civ Wed 60

COLLYWESTON — Map 11 SK90

Collyweston Slater

★★★★ INN

87-89 Main Rd PE9 3PQ
☎ 01780 444288
e-mail: enquiries@collywestonslaterpub.co.uk

A delightful village inn with a modern contemporary feel; the public rooms include a choice of dining areas and a comfortable lounge with plush sofas. A range of cask beers are available along with good pub food at affordable prices. The stylish bedrooms are individually decorated and equipped with modern facilities.

Rooms 3 en suite (1 fmly) S £55-£70; D £70-£120*
Facilities FTV tea/coffee Dinner available Cen ht Wi-fi
Conf Max 12 Board 12 **Parking** 50 **Notes** LB ⊛ Closed 25-26 Dec RS 1 Jan

---

EASTON-ON-THE-HILL — Map 11 TF00

The Exeter Arms

★★★★ @ INN

21 Stamford Rd PE9 3NS
☎ 01780 756321 📠 01780 753171
e-mail: reservations@theexeterarms.net
dir: A1 Nbound take exit signed Easton-on-the-Hill; A1 Sbound take exit signed A47/A43 Corby/Kettering, on left entering village

This lovely village inn is situated in north-eastern Northamptonshire just a short drive from Stamford. The public rooms have many original features such as stone walls and open fireplaces; they include a lounge bar and the Orangery Restaurant which opens out onto the terrace for alfresco dining. The modern, well-equipped bedrooms are very stylish.

Rooms 5 en suite 1 annexe en suite (2 fmly) S £65-£165; D £70-£170* **Facilities** FTV tea/coffee Dinner available Direct Dial Cen ht Wi-fi ⅃ 18 **Parking** 40

ECTON — Map 11 SP86

The World's End

★★★★ INN

Main St NN6 0QN
☎ 01604 414521 📠 01604 400334
e-mail: info@theworldsend.org
dir: On A4500 on outskirts of Ecton. A45 for Cogenhoe/Great Billing, follow Ecton signs

The World's End is a modern inn with striking interior, wooden floors, leather sofas, mirrors and downlighters. Smart, well appointed, bedrooms have flat screen TVs, broadband and power showers along with all the expected amenities. The restaurant offers plenty of choice to suit all appetites. There is an outdoor decking area for alfresco dining.

Rooms 20 en suite (9 GF) **Facilities** tea/coffee Dinner available Direct Dial Cen ht Lift Wi-fi **Conf** Max 35 Thtr 35 Class 16 Board 16 **Parking** 50 **Notes** ⊗

NASSINGTON
Map 12 TL09

The Queens Head Inn

★★★★ ⊛ INN

54 Station Rd PE8 6QB
☎ **01780 784006** 📠 **01780 781539**
e-mail: info@queensheadnassington.co.uk
web: www.queensheadnassington.co.uk
dir: *A1 Nbound exit junct 17, follow signs for Yarwell, then Nassington. Queens Head on left on entering the village*

A friendly atmosphere and a warm welcome are to be expected at this delightful inn situated on the banks of the River Nene in the picturesque village of Nassington. The adjacent bedrooms are constructed from local stone; each one is smartly appointed and well equipped. Public rooms include a smart lounge bar, a restaurant and a smart conservatory dining room.

Rooms 9 en suite (2 fmly) (9 GF) S £50–£120; D £50–£130 **Facilities** FTV tea/coffee Dinner available Direct Dial Cen ht Wi-fi Fishing 🛁 **Extras** Bottled water **Conf** Max 50 Thtr 50 Class 20 Board 20 **Parking** 45 **Notes** LB ⊗

TOWCESTER
Map 11 SP64

The Saracens Head

★★★ INN

219 Watling St NN12 7BX
☎ **01327 350414 & 0800 917 3085** 📠 **01327 359879**
e-mail: saracenshead.towcester@greeneking.co.uk
dir: *M1 junct 15a, A43, at rdbt 1st exit onto A5 signed Towcester, premises on right*

This historic coaching inn is rumoured to be an inspiration for Dickens' *Pickwick Papers*, and provides smart bedrooms and a convivial bar and restaurant. Staff are young and friendly and The Saracens Head provides an excellent base for horse-racing enthusiasts visiting the Towcester course and for motor-racing fans heading for Silverstone.

Rooms 21 en suite (5 fmly) **Facilities** FTV tea/coffee Direct Dial Cen ht Wi-fi **Conf** Max 100 Thtr 100 Class 60 Board 50 **Parking** 32 **Notes** ⊗ No coaches Civ Wed 90

NORTHUMBERLAND

ALNWICK
Map 21 NU11

Bondgate House

★★★★ 🏠 GUEST HOUSE

20 Bondgate Without NE66 1PN
☎ **01665 602025**
e-mail: enquiries@bondgatehouse.co.uk
web: www.bondgatehouse.co.uk
dir: *A1 onto B6346 into town centre, 200yds past war memorial on right*

Originally a doctor's house, this Georgian building stands close to the historic gateway into the town centre. Friendly service complements an attractive breakfast room, memorable breakfasts and the cosy lounge. Bedrooms are all well equipped and thoughtfully furnished and include three rooms in converted stables set in a secluded garden behind the house.

Rooms 3 en suite 3 annexe en suite (1 fmly) (1 GF) D £75–£100* **Facilities** FTV DVD iPod docking station TVL tea/coffee Cen ht Wi-fi 🛁 **Parking** 8 **Notes** ⊗ No Children 5yrs Closed Xmas ⊚

BERWICK-UPON-TWEED
Map 21 NT95

Lindisfarne Inn

★★★ INN

Beal TD15 2PD
☎ **01289 381223** 📠 **01289 381223**
e-mail: enquiries@lindisfarneinn.co.uk
dir: *Exit A1 for Holy Island*

The Lindisfarne Inn stands on the site of the old Plough Hotel at Beal, on the road leading to Holy Island. The inn has a traditional bar, rustic-style restaurant and comfortably equipped courtyard bedrooms in the adjacent wing. Food is available all day.

Rooms 21 annexe en suite (20 fmly) (10 GF) **Facilities** FTV TVL tea/coffee Dinner available Cen ht Wi-fi **Parking** 25

CRAMLINGTON
Map 21 NZ27

Innkeeper's Lodge Cramlington

★★★ INN

Blagdon Ln NE23 8AU
☎ **0845 112 6013**
e-mail: info@innkeeperslodge.com
web: www.innkeeperslodge.com

At Innkeeper's Lodge you'll find accommodation with comfort and character in equal measure, and everything needed for a relaxing stay, from easy check-in and free parking to complimentary breakfast and a cosy pub serving great value food and drink on the doorstep. Each Lodge has quality rooms, and there are Lodges in a variety of locations from towns and cities to countryside settings across the UK.

Rooms 18 en suite (4 fmly) (10 GF) **Facilities** FTV tea/coffee Dinner available Direct Dial Wi-fi **Parking** 50

FALSTONE
Map 21 NY78

Pheasant Inn

★★★★ ⇔ INN

Stannersburn NE48 1DD
☎ **01434 240382** 📠 **01434 240382**
e-mail: stay@thepheasantinn.com
web: www.thepheasantinn.com
dir: *From A69 (N of Hexham) take A6079 signed Otterburn & Bellingham. Left onto B6320 signed Bellingham. Before Bellingham follow Hesleyside sign, then signs for Kielder & Stannersburn*

This charming establishment epitomises the traditional country inn; it has character, good food and warm hospitality. Bright modern bedrooms, some with their own entrances, are all contained in stone buildings adjoining the inn. Delicious home-cooked meals are served in the bar with its low-beamed ceilings and exposed stone walls, or in the attractive dining room.

Rooms 8 annexe en suite (1 fmly) (5 GF) S £50–£60; D £90–£95 **Facilities** tea/coffee Dinner available Cen ht ch fac ⚖ 18 🛁 **Parking** 40 **Notes** LB ⊗ Closed 4 days Xmas RS Nov–Mar closed Mon & Tue No coaches

---

FELTON
Map 21 NU10

Birchwood House

★★★★ 🏠 GUEST ACCOMMODATION

Kitswell Dene NE65 9NZ
☎ **01670 787828** 📠 **01670 787828**
e-mail: gbblewitt@btinternet.com
web: www.birchwood-house.co.uk
dir: *Just off A1. Take Swarland exit, bear left, left again*

Ideally located for the A1, this spacious house combines very high standards of accommodation with warmth and great hospitality. Modern bedrooms and en suites cater well for the needs of the guest, and a fantastic large lounge is also made available. A well-cooked breakfast will set you up for your day regardless of your planned activities.

Rooms 3 en suite (3 GF) S fr £50; D £70–£80* **Facilities** FTV TVL tea/coffee Cen ht Wi-fi **Parking** 20 **Notes** ⊗ No Children 14yrs Closed Nov-1 Mar

HALTWHISTLE   Map 21 NY76

See also Brampton (Cumbria)

Vallum Lodge

★★★★ GUEST HOUSE

Twice Brewed, Bardon Mill NE47 7AN
☎ 01434 344248
e-mail: stay@vallum-lodge.co.uk
web: www.vallum-lodge.co.uk
dir: *On B6318, 200yds W of Once Brewed National Park visitors' centre*

Vallum Lodge is located in the wonderfully named village of Twice Brewed on the Military Road just a few hundred meters from Hadrian's Wall. Expect a warm welcome with comfortable bedrooms and public areas. A hearty breakfast will set you up for the day regardless of your planned activities. The property is licensed and all bedrooms are on the ground floor.

Rooms 6 en suite (1 fmly) (6 GF) **Facilities** FTV TVL tea/coffee Licensed Wi-fi ⬛ **Parking** 10 **Notes** ⊗

HEXHAM   Map 21 NY96

Peth Head Cottage

★★★★ ⬛ BED AND BREAKFAST

Juniper NE47 0LA
☎ 01434 673286 ⬛ 01434 673038
e-mail: peth_head@btopenworld.com
web: www.peth-head-cottage.co.uk
dir: *B6306 S from Hexham, 200yds fork right, next left. Continue 3.5m, house 400yds on right after Juniper sign*

Warm and caring hospitality is assured at this lovely sandstone cottage located in the peaceful hamlet of Juniper. Guests can enjoy home-made biscuits on arrival and home-baked bread and preserves at breakfast. The attractive bedrooms are equipped with lots of thoughtful extras and day rooms feature a cosy lounge-breakfast room. Self-catering is also available.

Peth Head Cottage

Rooms 2 en suite **Facilities** FTV TVL tea/coffee Cen ht **Parking** 2 **Notes** LB ⊗

MORPETH   Map 21 NZ18

PREMIER COLLECTION

Eshott Hall

★★★★★ ◉ ⬛ GUEST ACCOMMODATION

Eshott NE65 9EN
☎ 01670 787454 ⬛ 01670 786011
e-mail: info@eshotthall.co.uk
dir: *Eshott signed from A1. N of Morpeth*

Eshott Hall dates back to the 16th century and is set behind walled gardens in the heart of Northumberland just a few miles from the A1. Bedrooms are extremely comfortable and very well appointed, in keeping with the style and character of the house. Award-winning food uses the best from the local larder with public areas offering a real wow factor.

Rooms 11 en suite 5 annexe en suite (3 fmly) (2 GF) S £80-£120; D £100-£180* (incl.dinner) **Facilities** FTV iPod docking station Lounge tea/coffee Dinner available Cen ht Licensed Wi-fi ⬛ ⬛ ⬛ 18 Fishing ⬛ **Extras** Speciality toiletries - complimentary **Conf** Max 100 Thtr 100 Class 50 Board 20 **Parking** 50 **Notes** LB Civ Wed 100

NEWTON-ON-THE-MOOR   Map 21 NU10

The Cook and Barker Inn

★★★★ ⬛ INN

NE65 9JY
☎ 01665 575234 ⬛ 01665 575234
e-mail: info@cookandbarkerinn.co.uk
dir: *North on A1, pass Morpeth. A1 becomes single carriageway for 8m, then dual carriageway. Up slight incline 3m, follow signs on left to Newton-on-the-Moor*

Set in the heart of a quiet village this inn is popular with visitors and locals. The emphasis is on food here with interesting home-made dishes offered in the restaurant and bar areas. Bedrooms are smartly furnished and well equipped and are split between the main house and the adjacent annexe.

Rooms 4 en suite 14 annexe en suite (2 fmly) (7 GF) S fr £65; D fr £85* **Facilities** tea/coffee Dinner available Direct Dial Cen ht Wi-fi **Conf** Max 50 Thtr 50 Class 50 Board 25 **Parking** 64 **Notes** LB ⊗

OTTERBURN   Map 21 NY89

Dunns Houses Farmhouse *(NY868930)*

★★★★ FARMHOUSE

NE19 1LB
☎ 01830 520677 & 07808 592701
⬛ 01830 520677 Ms J Walton
e-mail: dunnshouses@hotmail.com
dir: *Situated on the A68, 7m E of Bellingham & 3m W of Otterburn*

Dunns Houses Farmhouse is a peaceful period residence that dates back to the 15th century and is part of a 960-hectare working farm in the beautiful Northumberland National Park. The wonderful secluded garden offers breath-taking views over the countryside, and this is an ideal place for walkers or anyone who just wants to relax. There is a lock-up garage available for bicycles or motorbikes.

Rooms 3 en suite (1 fmly) S £45; D £60-£80* **Facilities** FTV TVL tea/coffee Dinner available Cen ht Wi-fi ch fac ⬛ ⬛ 18 Fishing Pool table **Parking** 6 **Notes** LB 2372 acres beef/sheep/horses

RIDING MILL   Map 21 NZ06

Low Fotherley Farm *(NZ030581)*

★★★★ FARMHOUSE

NE44 6BB
☎ 01434 682277 & 07707 821202
⬛ 01434 682277 Mrs L Adamson
e-mail: hugh@lowfotherley.fsnet.co.uk
web: www.lowfotherleyfarmhouse.co.uk
dir: *1.5m N of Kilnpit Hill, on left*

Low Fotherley Farm is a traditional Victorian farmhouse on a working farm just off the A68 in the heart of the Northumbrian countryside. Bedrooms are spacious and comfortable, while customer care and hospitality are very warm. A hearty breakfast is served family-style in the dining room.

Rooms 3 rms (2 en suite) (1 pri facs) S £45-£50; D £65-£75* **Facilities** FTV tea/coffee Cen ht Wi-fi **Parking** 6 **Notes** ⊗ No Children 8yrs Closed Xmas & New Year ⬛ 225 acres sheep

SEAHOUSES   Map 21 NU23

The Olde Ship Inn
★★★★ INN

NE68 7RD
☎ 01665 720200 ▤ 01665 721383
e-mail: theoldeship@seahouses.co.uk
dir: *Lower end of main street above harbour*

Under the same ownership since 1910, this friendly inn overlooks the harbour and is full of character. Lovingly maintained, its sense of history is evident by the amount of nautical memorabilia on display. Public areas include a character bar, cosy snug, restaurant and guests' lounge. The individual bedrooms are smartly presented. Two separate buildings contain executive apartments, all with sea views.

Rooms 12 en suite 6 annexe en suite (4 GF) S £51-£59; D £115-£130* **Facilities** FTV Lounge TVL tea/coffee Dinner available Direct Dial Cen ht Wi-fi Pool table **Parking** 18 **Notes** LB ⊗ No Children 10yrs Closed Dec-Jan No coaches

Bamburgh Castle Inn
★★★ INN

NE68 7SQ
☎ 01665 720283 ▤ 01665 720284
e-mail: enquiries@bamburghcastleinn.co.uk
web: www.bamburghcastleinn.co.uk
dir: *A1 onto B1341 to Bamburgh, B1340 to Seahouses, follow signs to harbour*

Situated in a prime location on the quayside in the popular coastal resort of Seahouses, this establishment has arguably the best viewpoint along the coast. Dating back to the 18th century, the inn has been transformed in recent years and has superb dining and bar areas, with outside seating available in warmer weather. There are smart, comfortable bedrooms, many with views of the Farne Islands and the inn's famous namesake Bamburgh Castle.

Rooms 27 en suite 2 annexe en suite (6 fmly) (8 GF) **Facilities** FTV TVL tea/coffee Dinner available Cen ht Sauna Gym Access to Ocean Club Spa **Conf** Max 50 **Parking** 35 **Notes** LB

WOOLER   Map 21 NT92

PREMIER COLLECTION

The Old Manse
★★★★★ 🏠 GUEST ACCOMMODATION

New Rd, Chatton NE66 5PU
☎ 01668 215343 & 07811 411808
e-mail: chattonbb@aol.com
web: www.oldmansechatton.co.uk
dir: *4m E of Wooler. On B6348 in Chatton*

Built in 1875, this elegant former manse is located on the edge of the village convenient for St Cuthbert's Way. There is a four-poster and double room upstairs, and a ground-floor room with its own entrance, sitting room and patio; all are thoughtfully equipped with a wealth of thoughtful extras including fridge with fruit, CD player, juices and biscuits. Sumptuous day rooms include wood-burning stoves. Impressive breakfasts are served in a conservatory overlooking the pretty gardens and a warm welcome is assured.

Rooms 3 en suite (1 GF) S £50-£85; D £85-£100* **Facilities** FTV DVD iPod docking station TVL tea/coffee Cen ht Wi-fi 🔒 **Extras** Speciality toiletries, fruit, bottled water - complimentary **Parking** 4 **Notes** ⊗ No Children 14yrs Closed Nov-Feb ☺

NOTTINGHAMSHIRE

COTGRAVE   Map 11 SK63

Jerico Farm *(SK654307)*
★★★★ 🏠 FARMHOUSE

Fosse Way NG12 3HG
☎ 01949 81733 Mrs S Herrick
e-mail: info@jericofarm.co.uk
web: www.jericofarm.co.uk
dir: *Off A46, signposted Kinoulton. N of intersection with A606*

A friendly relaxed atmosphere is offered at this attractive farmhouse, which stands in the beautiful Nottinghamshire countryside just off the A46, close to Nottingham, Trent Bridge Cricket and the National Water Sports Centre. Day rooms include a comfortable lounge and a separate dining room, in which substantial tasty breakfasts are served overlooking the gardens. Spacious bedrooms are individually appointed and thoughtfully equipped.

Rooms 3 en suite (1 fmly) **Facilities** FTV TVL tea/coffee Cen ht Wi-fi Fishing **Parking** 4 **Notes** ⊗ No Children 10yrs Closed 24 Dec-2 Jan 150 acres mixed

EASTWOOD   Map 11 SK44

The Sun Inn
★★★ INN

6 Derby Rd NG16 3NT
☎ 01773 712940 ▤ 01773 531563

Built in 1705, this Grade II listed building is located right in the centre of Eastwood with easy access to the Derbyshire Dales for walkers, and Nottingham for shoppers. The well-equipped bedrooms are all en suite and offer modern facilities.

Rooms 15 en suite (1 fmly) **Facilities** FTV tea/coffee Dinner available Cen ht Wi-fi Pool table **Conf** Max 15 Thtr 15 Class 8 Board 15 **Parking** 8 **Notes** ⊗

EDWINSTOWE   Map 16 SK66

The Forest Lodge
★★★★ INN

Church St NG21 9QA
☎ 01623 824443 ▤ 01623 824686
e-mail: reception@forestlodgehotel.co.uk
dir: *A614 into Edwinstowe. On B6034, opposite St Mary's church*

Situated in the heart of Sherwood Forest, The Forest Lodge is a 17th-century coaching inn that provides the visitor with a warm and homely base from which to explore the unique attractions of this fascinating and historic area. The bedrooms have been tastefully modernised and the bar provides home comforts and good company. Food is served in the bar and in the restaurant.

Rooms 8 en suite 5 annexe en suite (2 fmly) (5 GF) **Facilities** FTV tea/coffee Dinner available Cen ht Wi-fi 🔒 **Conf** Max 75 Thtr 75 Class 45 Board 50 **Parking** 35

The Dukeries Lodge
★★★ INN

Main St NG21 9HS
☎ 01623 822553
e-mail: mark.gallagher@pubpeople.com
dir: *In town centre*

Set in the pleasant village of Edwinstowe, this 18th-century inn offers live music, a games area with a pool table and free Wi-fi throughout. Bedrooms are comfortable with en suite facilities. A varied menu is available in the traditional restaurant or light snacks are offered in the bar. On-site car parking available.

Rooms 17 en suite **Facilities** FTV tea/coffee Dinner available

ELTON	Map 11 SK73

PREMIER COLLECTION

The Grange

★★★★★ BED AND BREAKFAST

Sutton Ln NG13 9LA
☎ 07887 952181
web: www.thegrangebedandbreakfastnotts.co.uk
dir: From Grantham A1 onto A52 to Elton x-rds, left 200yds, B&B on right

Parts of this lovely house date back to the early 17th century and the rooms command fine views across the gardens and rolling open countryside. Bedrooms contain many thoughtful extras and fine hospitality is assured from the proprietors.

Rooms 3 en suite S £45-£55; D £70-£75*
Facilities FTV DVD Lounge TVL tea/coffee Cen ht Wi-fi 🔒
Parking 8 **Notes** ⊗ 🐾

HOLBECK	Map 16 SK57

PREMIER COLLECTION

Browns

★★★★★ 🏡 BED AND BREAKFAST

The Old Orchard Cottage, Holbeck Ln S80 3NF
☎ 01909 720659 📠 01909 720659
e-mail: browns.holbeck@btconnect.com
dir: 0.5m off A616 Sheffield-Newark road, turn for Holbeck at x-rds

Set amid beautifully tended gardens with lily-ponds and extensive lawns, this mid 18th-century cottage is a tranquil rural hideaway. Breakfasts are served in the Regency-style dining room, and the elegant bedrooms have four-poster beds and many extras. The friendly owners provide attentive service, including courtesy transport to nearby restaurants if required.

Rooms 3 annexe en suite (3 GF) S £59-£69;
D £79-£89* **Facilities** FTV DVD tea/coffee Cen ht 🔒
Parking 3 **Notes** ⊗ No Children 15yrs Closed Xmas wk 🐾

HOLME PIERREPONT	Map 11 SK63

Holme Grange Cottage

★★★ GUEST ACCOMMODATION

Adbolton Ln NG12 2LU
☎ 0115 981 0413
e-mail: jean.colinwightman@talk21.com
dir: Exit A52 SE of Nottingham onto A6011. After 500yds turn right into Regatta Way, 1.25m on right

A stone's throw from the National Water Sports Centre, this establishment with its own all-weather tennis court is ideal for the active guest. Indeed, when not providing warm hospitality and freshly cooked breakfasts, the proprietor is usually on the golf course.

Rooms 3 rms (1 en suite) (1 fmly) S £31-£36;
D £52-£56* **Facilities** FTV TVL tea/coffee Cen ht Wi-fi 🌙 🔒
Parking 6 **Notes** Closed Xmas 🐾

MANSFIELD	Map 16 SK56

Bridleways Holiday Homes & Guest House

★★★★ GUEST HOUSE

Newlands Rd, Forest Town NG19 0HU
☎ 01623 635725 📠 01623 635725
e-mail: bridleways@webnet2000.net
dir: From Mansfield take B6030 towards New Clipstone. Right at rdbt, follow Crown Farm Industrial Park sign. 1st left into Newlands Rd. Guest house on left

Beside a quiet bridleway that leads to Vicar Water Country Park and Sherwood Pines Forest Park this friendly guest house is a good touring base for walking, cycling or sightseeing. The double, twin and family bedrooms are particularly spacious and all are en suite. Lovely breakfasts are served in a cottage style dining room.

Rooms 9 en suite (1 fmly) (2 GF) S £37; D £70*
Facilities FTV tea/coffee Wi-fi 🔒 **Parking** 14 **Notes** ⊗

NEWARK-ON-TRENT	Map 17 SK75

Compton House

★★★★ 🏡 🍽 GUEST HOUSE

117 Baldertongate NG24 1RY
☎ 01636 708670
e-mail: info@comptonhousenewark.com
web: www.comptonhousenewark.com
dir: 500yds SE of town centre. B6326 into Sherwood Av, 1st right into Baldertongate

Located a short walk from the central attractions, this elegant period house has been renovated to provide high standards of comfort. Individually themed bedrooms come with a wealth of thoughtful extras and smart modern bathrooms. Comprehensive breakfasts, and wholesome dinners by arrangement, are served in the attractive dining room and a lounge is available. Lisa Holloway was last year's AA Friendliest Landlady of the Year (2011-12).

Rooms 7 rms (6 en suite) (1 pri facs) (1 fmly) (1 GF)
S £45-£65; D £90-£120* **Facilities** FTV Lounge tea/coffee Dinner available Cen ht Wi-fi **Extras** Magazines - complimentary **Conf** Max 10 Thtr 10 Class 10 Board 10
Parking 2 **Notes** ⊗ Closed Xmas

NOTTINGHAM	Map 11 SK53

See also Cotgrave

PREMIER COLLECTION

Restaurant Sat Bains with Rooms

★★★★★ 🟥🟥🟥🟥🟥 🏡
RESTAURANT WITH ROOMS

Trentside, Lenton Ln NG7 2SA
☎ 0115 986 6566 📠 0115 986 0343
e-mail: info@restaurantsatbains.net
dir: M1 junct 24, A453 Nottingham S. Over River Trent into central lane to rdbt. Left, left again towards river. Establishment on left after bend

This charming restaurant with rooms, a stylish conversion of Victorian farm buildings, is situated on the river and close to the industrial area of Nottingham. The bedrooms create a warm atmosphere by using quality soft furnishings together with antique and period furniture; suites and four-poster rooms are available. Public areas are chic and cosy, and the delightful restaurant complements the truly outstanding, much acclaimed cuisine.

Rooms 4 en suite 4 annexe en suite (6 GF)
Facilities STV Dinner available Direct Dial Cen ht
Parking 22 **Notes** ⊗ Closed 1st wk Jan & 2wks mid Aug RS Sun & Mon rooms & restaurant closed

Save on B&Bs and Hotels. Book at **theAA.com/hotel**

NOTTINGHAMSHIRE 231 ENGLAND

Cockliffe Country House

★ ★ ★ ★ ⊛ RESTAURANT WITH ROOMS

Burntstump Country Park, Burntstump Hill, Arnold NG5 8PQ
☎ 0115 968 0179 📄 0115 968 0623
e-mail: enquiries@cockliffehouse.co.uk

Expect a warm welcome at this delightful property situated in a peaceful rural location amidst neat landscaped grounds, close to Sherwood Forest. Public areas include a smart breakfast room, a tastefully appointed restaurant and a cosy lounge bar. The individually decorated bedrooms have co-ordinated soft furnishings and many thoughtful touches.

Rooms 7 en suite 4 annexe en suite (5 GF) S £79-£119; D £99-£189* **Facilities** FTV tea/coffee Dinner available Direct Dial Cen ht Wi-fi ⤳ **Conf** Max 30 Thtr 30 Class 25 Board 30 **Parking** 60 **Notes** No coaches Civ Wed 60

Beech Lodge

★ ★ ★ ★ GUEST ACCOMMODATION

222 Porchester Rd NG3 6HG
☎ 0115 952 3314 & 07961 075939
e-mail: paulinegoodwin222@hotmail.co.uk
web: www.beechlodgeguesthouse.com
dir: From A684 into Porchester Rd, 8th left, (Punchbowl pub on right corner), Beech Lodge on left corner

A friendly welcome is assured at Beech Lodge and the modern accommodation is well presented and suitably equipped. The ground-floor lounge is particularly comfortable, and there is a small conservatory. Breakfast is a good choice of freshly cooked and carefully presented fare served in the dining area next to the lounge.

Rooms 4 en suite (1 fmly) S £30-£35; D £60-£65* **Facilities** FTV TVL tea/coffee Cen ht Wi-fi **Parking** 4 **Notes** LB ⊗

The Yellow House

★ ★ ★ ★ BED AND BREAKFAST

7 Littlegreen Rd, Woodthorpe NG5 4LE
☎ 0115 926 2280
e-mail: suzanne.prewsmith1@btinternet.com
web: www.bandb-nottingham.co.uk
dir: Exit A60 (Mansfield Rd) N from city centre into Thackeray's Ln, over rdbt, right into Whernside Rd to x-rds, left into Littlegreen Rd, house on left

This semi-detached private house is in a quiet residential suburb to the north-east of the city, with easy access. A warm welcome is assured; the one purpose-built bedroom contains many thoughtful extras, and the family's pet dog is also very friendly.

Rooms 1 en suite S fr £45; D fr £65* **Facilities** FTV tea/coffee Cen ht **Parking** 1 **Notes** ⊗ No Children Closed Xmas & New Year ⊛

Old Rectory Farm B&B

★ ★ ★ 🏠 BED AND BREAKFAST

Main St, Strelley Village NG8 6PE
☎ 0115 929 8838
e-mail: enq@oldrectoryfarm.com
dir: M1 junct 26, A6002, after 1m turn right to Strelley Village, 0.5m opposite church

Located in the pretty village of Strelley opposite the notable All Saints parish church, this period property has been sympathetically restored to provide modern comfort in a home-from-home atmosphere. Bedrooms are equipped with lots of thoughtful extras, and memorable breakfasts feature eggs from the farm's own chickens, along with home-made preserves.

Rooms 4 rms (2 en suite) (1 fmly) (1 GF) D £65-£70* **Facilities** Lounge TVL tea/coffee Cen ht Wi-fi Riding Access to gym & pool **Extras** Fruit, snacks - complimentary **Parking** 6 **Notes** LB ⊛

Fairhaven

★ ★ GUEST ACCOMMODATION

19 Meadow Rd, Beeston NG9 1JP
☎ 0115 922 7509 📄 0115 922 5344
e-mail: info@fairhavennottingham.com
web: www.fairhavennottingham.com
dir: A52 onto B6005 for Beeston station, 200yds after bridge

This well-established guest accommodation is in the quiet residential suburb of Beeston on the outskirts of Nottingham. The public rooms offer a stylish reception lounge, and breakfast is served in the cosy dining room. The bedrooms vary in style and size.

Rooms 14 rms (10 en suite) (1 fmly) (1 GF) S £29-£42; D £57* **Facilities** tea/coffee Cen ht Licensed Wi-fi **Parking** 13

The Old Forge

★ ★ ★ GUEST HOUSE

Burgage Ln NG25 0ER
☎ 01636 812809
e-mail: theoldforgesouthwell@yahoo.co.uk
dir: Exit A612 past Minster, Church St, left into Newark Rd, 2nd left into Burgage Ln

An interesting house packed with pictures and antique furniture, The Old Forge is central and handy for the Minster, while its own parking also makes this a good touring base. Bedrooms are comfortable, and a secluded conservatory-lounge and spacious breakfast room are available.

Rooms 3 en suite 1 annexe en suite (1 GF) S £50-£60; D £80* **Facilities** tea/coffee Cen ht Wi-fi **Parking** 4

Scotts Farm B&B

★ ★ ★ BED AND BREAKFAST

Wellow Park Stables, Rufford Ln NG22 0EQ
☎ 01623 861040 & 07860 869378 📄 01623 835292
e-mail: wellowpark@btconnect.com
web: www.wellowpark.co.uk
dir: A616 SE from New Ollerton, 1m right into Rufford Ln

Scotts Farm is a part of Wellow Park Stables, a family equestrian centre located on the quiet outskirts of Wellow in Sherwood Forest. Breakfast is served in the kitchen. Stabling, dressage instruction, showjumping and cross-country rides are available by arrangement.

Rooms 3 rms (1 en suite) (3 fmly) **Facilities** tea/coffee Cen ht Riding **Parking** 6 **Notes** ⊗

Acorn Lodge

★ ★ ★ ★ GUEST ACCOMMODATION

85 Potter St S80 2HL
☎ 01909 478383 📄 01909 478383
e-mail: info@acornlodgeworksop.co.uk
dir: A1 onto A57. Take B6040 (town centre) through Manton. Lodge on right, 100mtrs past Priory

Originally part of the community house of the Priory Church, this property has been modernised to offer comfortable, well-appointed accommodation. Good breakfasts are served in the pleasant breakfast room and ample private parking is available at the rear.

Rooms 7 en suite (2 fmly) **Facilities** FTV tea/coffee Cen ht Wi-fi **Parking** 15 **Notes** ⊗

OXFORDSHIRE

ABINGDON-ON-THAMES — Map 5 SU49

PREMIER COLLECTION

B&B Rafters

★★★★★ ⬛ BED AND BREAKFAST

Abingdon Rd, Marcham OX13 6NU
☎ 01865 391298 & 07824 378720 📠 01865 391173
e-mail: enquiries@bnb-rafters.co.uk
web: www.bnb-rafters.co.uk
dir: A34 onto A415 towards Witney. Rafters on A415 in Marcham adjacent to pedestrian crossing, on right

Set amid immaculate gardens, this modern house is built in a half-timbered style and offers spacious accommodation together with a warm welcome. Bedrooms are stylishly furnished and equipped with a range of homely extras. Comprehensive breakfasts feature local and organic produce when possible.

Rooms 4 en suite S £52-£85; D £95-£120*
Facilities FTV DVD iPod docking station Lounge tea/coffee Cen ht Wi-fi Extras Speciality toiletries, fruit, water Parking 4 Notes ⊛

The Dog House

★★★ INN

Faringdon Rd, Frilford Heath OX13 6QJ
☎ 01865 390830 📠 01865 390860
e-mail: doghouse.frilfordheath@oldenglishinns.co.uk

As its name suggests, The Dog House was once the kennels (and the stables) for a local manor house. Situated in the heart of the Oxfordshire countryside, this is a popular inn with a spacious bar and restaurant that offer a wide variety of meals and lighter options, with carvery available on Sundays. Conference facilities and weddings are also catered for.

Rooms 20 en suite (2 fmly) (4 GF) Facilities tea/coffee Dinner available Direct Dial Cen ht Wi-fi Conf Thtr 30 Class 10 Board 18 Parking 40

ADDERBURY — Map 11 SP43

Red Lion

★★★ INN

The Green, Oxford Rd OX17 3LU
☎ 01295 810269 📠 01295 811906
e-mail: 6496@greeneking.co.uk
web: www.oldenglish.co.uk
dir: M40 junct 11 into Banbury, take A4260 towards Bodicote into Adderbury, on left

This charming former coaching inn was once an important stop-over on the old Banbury to Oxford road. The atmosphere typifies an English inn, and dedicated staff provide a warm welcome. The comfortable and spacious bedrooms are attractively decorated - some are

split-level and one has a four-poster. Honest, fresh food is served in the restaurant and the bar.

Rooms 12 en suite (1 GF) Facilities FTV tea/coffee Direct Dial Wi-fi Notes ⊛

ARDINGTON — Map 5 SU48

The Boar's Head

★★★★ ⬟⬟ INN

Church St OX12 8QA
☎ 01235 833254 📠 01235 833254
e-mail: info@boarsheadardington.co.uk
dir: In village next to church

This characterful inn has been serving the local community for over 150 years and is set in a beautiful and seemingly timeless village. Great care has gone into creating a stylish ambience in the comfortable bedrooms, and the welcoming bar and restaurant where Bruce Buchan's accomplished cuisine can be enjoyed.

Rooms 3 en suite (1 fmly) Facilities tea/coffee Dinner available Direct Dial Cen ht Wi-fi Parking 20 Notes No coaches

ASTON ROWANT — Map 5 SU79

Lambert Arms

★★★★★ ⬟ ⬛ INN

London Rd OX49 5SB
☎ 0845 4593736 📠 01844 351893
e-mail: info@lambertarms.com
web: www.lambertarms.com
dir: M40 junct 6, follow signs to Chinnor (B4009) then left to Thame (A40)

Completely transformed inside, yet retaining original, historical features, this lovely coaching inn has been caringly restored to its former glory, with a modern twist. You'll find a comfortable and friendly bar with open log fires, real ales and a mouth-watering array of food, including favourite pub classics using fresh, seasonal locally sourced produce.

Rooms 9 rms (8 en suite) (1 pri facs) 35 annexe en suite (13 fmly) (16 GF) Facilities STV FTV tea/coffee Dinner available Direct Dial Cen ht Lift Wi-fi ♪ Gym Ella Bache Treatment rooms Conf Max 140 Thtr 120 Class 62 Board 38 Parking 75 Notes Civ Wed 120

BAMPTON — Map 5 SP30

Upham House Bed & Breakfast

★★★★ BED AND BREAKFAST

The Lanes OX18 2JG
☎ 01993 852703 & 07946 625563 📠 01993 852703
e-mail: pat@uphamhouse.co.uk
web: www.uphamhouse.co.uk
dir: A4095 between Faringdon & Brize Norton

A delightful stone-built house in a traditional country style, Upham House provides well-appointed and

tastefully decorated accommodation, with a welcoming atmosphere; quality linens and towels, comfortable beds, fresh flowers and local produce used wherever possible. Situated in part of the Conservation Area of Bampton, with no passing traffic, yet only five minutes' walk from the village centre, it is just a short drive from the River Thames and Kelmscott Manor - home of William Morris. Bampton is just eight miles from Burford, 'the gateway to the Cotswolds.'

Rooms 2 rms (1 en suite) (1 pri facs) S £45-£50; D £70-£80* Facilities FTV TVL tea/coffee Cen ht Wi-fi Extras Snacks - complimentary Parking 3 Notes ⊛ No Children 2yrs Closed 10 Dec-5 Jan ⬟

BANBURY — Map 11 SP44

PREMIER COLLECTION

Tree Tops Guest House

★★★★★ GUEST ACCOMMODATION

28 Dashwood Rd OX16 5HD
☎ 01295 254444 & 07951 095479
e-mail: enquiries@treetopsbanbury.co.uk
dir: M40 junct 11 onto A422. At Concord rdbt 1st exit onto A4260, next rdbt 1st exit. Over 1st set of lights, right at next lights into George St, 2nd left into Broad St. At junct of Newlands Rd & Dashwood Rd

Located just a short walk from the town centre, a warm welcome is certainly assured here. Stylishly decorated bedrooms are well equipped, spacious and are a perfect respite for the business traveller or holiday-makers alike. Hearty breakfasts and daily specials are served at individual tables in the modern dining room.

Rooms 4 en suite S £45-£50; D £65-£70*
Facilities FTV DVD tea/coffee Cen ht Wi-fi ⬟
Extras Water Parking 2 Notes ⊛ No Children 12yrs Closed 24 Dec-2 Jan

The Cromwell Lodge

★★★★ INN

9-11 North Bar OX16 0TB
☎ 01295 259781 📠 01295 276619
e-mail: 6434@greeneking.co.uk
dir: M40 junct 11 towards Banbury, through 3 sets of lights, property on left just before Banbury Cross

Enjoying a central location, this 17th-century property is full of character. Diners can choose between the lounge, the smart restaurant or the delightful walled garden and patio. The comfortable bedrooms are furnished and equipped to a good standard. Parking is available at the rear of the building.

Rooms 23 en suite (1 fmly) (3 GF) Facilities Direct Dial Parking 20

The Blinking Owl

★★★ INN

Main St, North Newington OX15 6AE
☎ 01295 730650
e-mail: theblinkingowl@btinternet.com
dir: B4035 from Banbury, 2m, sharp bend, right to North Newington, inn opposite green

An important part of the community in the pretty village of North Newington, this former 17th-century inn retains many original features including impressive open fires. Straightforward food and a range of real ales are served in the beamed bar-lounges. The converted barn houses the three bedrooms and the restaurant, which is open at weekends.

Rooms 3 en suite S £60; D £70* **Facilities** tea/coffee Dinner available Cen ht **Parking** 14 **Notes** ✪ 🐕

Fairlawns Guest House

★★★ GUEST ACCOMMODATION

60 Oxford Rd OX16 9AN
☎ 01295 262461 & 07831 330220 🖷 01295 261296
e-mail: fairlawnsgh@gmail.com
dir: 0.5m S of Banbury Cross on A4260 opposite Horton Hospital

This extended Edwardian house retains many original features and has a convenient location. Bedrooms are mixed in size, and all are neatly furnished, some with direct access to the car park. A comprehensive breakfast is served in the traditional dining room and a selection of soft drinks and snacks is also available.

Rooms 11 rms (10 en suite) 6 annexe en suite (5 fmly) (9 GF) S £45-£58; D £68* **Facilities** FTV tea/coffee Cen ht Wi-fi ⚓ 18 **Parking** 17

Manor Farm B&B

★★★★ BED AND BREAKFAST

Hethe OX27 8ES
☎ 01869 277602
e-mail: chrmanor@aol.com
web: www.freewebs.com/manorfarm
dir: Off B4100 signed Hardwick, 2m to Hethe. In village 1st house after church (entrance through thatched arch)

Guests are warmly welcomed at this delightful stone farmhouse in the peaceful village of Hethe, close to the M40 and Bicester, and a short drive from Oxford. The property retains many original features such as Georgian beams and open fireplaces, and offers comfortable spacious accommodation with beautiful stylish bathrooms. A hearty breakfast with home-made preserves is included.

Rooms 2 rms (1 en suite) (1 pri facs) S fr £45; D fr £80 **Facilities** FTV Lounge tea/coffee Cen ht Wi-fi 🔒 **Parking** 2 **Notes** LB ✪ 🐕

PREMIER COLLECTION

Burford House

🏠 GUEST ACCOMMODATION

99 High St OX18 4QA
☎ 01993 823151 🖷 01993 823240
e-mail: stay@burfordhouse.co.uk
web: www.burfordhouse.co.uk
dir: A40 onto A361, on right half way down hill

This charming house provides superb quality with a professional and friendly welcome. The bedrooms offer very good quality, space and comfort. Wonderful lunches and afternoon teas are served daily, while dinners are available by prior arrangement.

Rooms 8 en suite (1 fmly) (1 GF) **Facilities** STV tea/coffee Dinner available Direct Dial Cen ht Licensed Wi-fi **Notes** ✪

The Bull at Burford

★★★★ 🏵🏵 🏠 RESTAURANT WITH ROOMS

105 High St OX18 4RG
☎ 01993 822220 🖷 01993 824055
e-mail: info@bullatburford.co.uk
dir: In town centre

Situated in the heart of a pretty Cotswold town, The Bull was originally built in 1475 as a rest house for the local priory. It now has stylish, attractively presented bedrooms that still reflect charm and character. Dinner is a must and the award-winning restaurant has an imaginative menu along with an excellent choice of wines. Lunch is served daily and afternoon tea is popular. There is a residents' lounge, and free Wi-fi is available.

Rooms 12 en suite (1 fmly) S £70-£110; D £75-£160* **Facilities** FTV Lounge tea/coffee Dinner available Cen ht Wi-fi **Conf** Thtr 24 Class 12 Board 12 **Parking** 6 **Notes** LB

Potters Hill Farm (SP300148)

★★★★ FARMHOUSE

Leafield OX29 9QB
☎ 01993 878018 🖷 01993 878018 Mrs K Stanley
e-mail: potterabout@freenet.co.uk
dir: 4.5m NE of Burford. A361 onto B4437, 1st right, 1st left, 1.5m on left

Located on a working farm in peaceful parkland with diverse wildlife, this converted coach house stands next to the farmhouse. It has been appointed to offer comfortable bedrooms with many original features. Breakfast served in the main farmhouse features local produce.

Rooms 3 annexe en suite (1 fmly) (2 GF) **Facilities** tea/coffee Dinner available Cen ht Wi-fi **Parking** 5 **Notes** ✪ 🏞 770 acres mixed/sheep

The Inn For All Seasons

★★★ RESTAURANT WITH ROOMS

The Barringtons OX18 4TN
☎ 01451 844324 🖷 01451 844375
e-mail: sharp@innforallseasons.com
web: www.innforallseasons.com
dir: 3m W of Burford on A40 towards Cheltenham

This charming 16th-century coaching inn is close to the pretty village of Burford. The individually styled bedrooms are comfortable, and include a four-poster room, as well as a family room that sleeps four. The public areas include a cosy bar with oak beams and real fires. There is a good choice on the bar menu, and evening meals feature the best of local Cotswold produce. The inn is a dog-friendly establishment and there are ground-floor bedrooms with direct access to the garden and an exercise area.

Rooms 10 en suite (1 fmly) **Facilities** Dinner available

PREMIER COLLECTION

The Feathered Nest Inn

★★★★★ 🏵🏵 🏠 INN

OX7 6SD
☎ 01993 833030 🖷 01993 833031
e-mail: info@thefeatherednestinn.co.uk
web: www.thefeatherednestinn.co.uk

(For full entry see Nether Westcote (Gloucestershire))

CHIPPING NORTON *continued*

Wild Thyme Restaurant with Rooms

★★★★ ◎◎ RESTAURANT WITH ROOMS

10 New St OX7 5LJ
☎ 01608 645060
e-mail: enquiries@wildthymerestaurant.co.uk
dir: *On A44 in town centre off market square*

Located in the bustling Cotswold market town of Chipping Norton, this restaurant with rooms offers three en suite bedrooms that are individually designed, well equipped and have many thoughtful extras. The restaurant serves exciting modern British food along with relaxed and friendly service.

Rooms 3 en suite **Facilities** FTV DVD tea/coffee Dinner available Cen ht Wi-fi **Extras** Mineral water, home-made biscuits **Notes** ⊗ Closed 2wks Jan & 1wk spring No coaches

---

CHISELHAMPTON	Map 5 SU59

Coach & Horses Inn

★★★ INN

Watlington Rd OX44 7UX
☎ 01865 890255 📠 01865 891995
e-mail: enquiries@coachhorsesinn.co.uk
dir: *On B480*

Located six miles south-east of Oxford, this 16th-century inn retains original exposed beams and open fires, while furniture styles enhance the character of the building. A wide range of imaginative food is served, and the practically equipped chalet-style bedrooms have lovely rural views.

Rooms 9 annexe en suite **Facilities** tea/coffee Dinner available Direct Dial Cen ht **Conf** Max 12 **Parking** 30

FARINGDON	Map 5 SU29

PREMIER COLLECTION

Buscot Manor B&B

★★★★★ BED AND BREAKFAST

SN7 8DA
☎ 01367 252225 & 07973 831690
e-mail: romneypargeter@hotmail.co.uk

Delightfully located in a peaceful village, Buscot Manor, a Queen Anne manor house built in 1692, is full of character and quality. Guests are welcome to use the two comfortable lounges in addition to the pleasant gardens where tea may be enjoyed in the summer months. The two upper-floor bedrooms have private bathrooms and traditional four-poster beds. A more contemporary room is located on the ground floor. Breakfast is taken around one large table in the elegant dining room.

Rooms 2 en suite 1 annexe en suite (3 fmly) (1 GF) **Facilities** FTV DVD Lounge TVL tea/coffee Cen ht Wi-fi ch fac Fishing Riding Sauna Gym ⬦ **Extras** Speciality toiletries, fruit, snacks **Conf** Max 12 Board 12 **Parking** 30

Chowle Farmhouse Bed & Breakfast *(SU272925)*

★ ★ ★ ★ FARMHOUSE

SN7 7SR
☎ 01367 241688 Mr & Mrs Muir
e-mail: info@chowlefarmhouse.co.uk
web: www.chowlefarmhouse.co.uk
dir: *From Faringdon rdbt on A420, 2m W on right. From Watchfield rdbt 1.5m E on left*

Chowle is a delightful modern farmhouse in a quiet setting, just off the A420 and ideally placed for visiting Oxford and Swindon. Bedrooms are very well equipped, and there is a charming and airy downstairs breakfast room. An outdoor pool and hot tub are available to guests. There is ample parking space.

Rooms 4 en suite (1 GF) S £65; D £90* **Facilities** FTV tea/coffee Cen ht Wi-fi ⬦ ⬦ 9 Fishing Riding Sauna Gym ⬦ Clay pigeon shooting Indoor spa **Parking** 10 **Notes** LB 10 acres pedigree beef cattle

---

The Eagle

★★★★ ◎◎ INN

Little Coxwell SN7 7LW
☎ 01367 241879
e-mail: eaglelittlecoxwell@gmail.com
dir: *M4 junct 15, A419, A420 signed Oxford, right into village*

Located in the peaceful village of Little Coxwell, The Eagle is a traditional inn with a welcoming atmosphere and a selection of real ales. The upstairs bedrooms, in a range of shapes and sizes, offer good comfort and ease of use. At both breakfast and dinner there's a very good selection of carefully prepared, quality dishes.

Rooms 6 en suite **Facilities** FTV Dinner available Cen ht Wi-fi **Notes** No coaches

---

The Trout at Tadpole Bridge

★★★★ ◎ INN

Buckland Marsh SN7 8RF
☎ 01367 870382 📠 01367 870912
e-mail: info@troutinn.co.uk
web: www.troutinn.co.uk
dir: *A420 Swindon to Oxford road, turn signed Bampton. Inn 2m on right*

The Trout is located 'where the River Thames meets the Cotswolds'. The peaceful location offers riverside walks from the door and berthing for up to six boats. Bedrooms and bathrooms are located adjacent to the inn and all rooms are very comfortable and well equipped with welcome extras. The main bar and restaurant offer an excellent selection of carefully prepared local produce at both lunch and dinner, together with cask ales and a varied choice of wines by the glass.

Rooms 3 en suite 3 annexe en suite (1 fmly) (4 GF) **Facilities** FTV tea/coffee Dinner available Cen ht Wi-fi Fishing **Conf** Max 20 Thtr 20 Class 20 Board 20 **Parking** 40 **Notes** Closed 25-26 Dec No coaches

---

HENLEY-ON-THAMES   Map 5 SU78

The Baskerville

★★★★ INN

Station Rd, Lower Shiplake RG9 3NY
☎ 0118 940 3332
e-mail: enquiries@thebaskerville.com
web: www.thebaskerville.com
dir: 2m S of Henley in Lower Shiplake. Exit A4155 into Station Rd, inn signed

Located close to Shiplake station and just a short drive from Henley, this smart accommodation is perfect for a business or leisure break. It is a good base for exploring the Oxfordshire countryside, and the enjoyable hearty meals served in the cosy restaurant use good local produce.

Rooms 4 en suite (1 fmly) S £82; D £92* **Facilities** STV DVD tea/coffee Dinner available Cen ht Wi-fi 🔒 **Conf** Max 15 Thtr 15 Class 15 Board 15 **Parking** 15 **Notes** Closed 25 Dec & 1 Jan No coaches

---

Leander Club

★★★★ 🏠 GUEST ACCOMMODATION

Leander Way RG9 2LP
☎ 01491 575782 📠 01491 410291
e-mail: events@leander.co.uk
web: www.leander.co.uk
dir: M4 junct 8/9 follow signs for Henley (A404M & A4130). Turn right immediately before Henley Bridge to Club & car park

This historic rowing club has opened its doors and made its delightful facilities available to guests. The location is breathtaking, particularly in the morning, when the rowers can be seen setting out on the river. The rooms are each named after various colleges and universities, and each is packed with interesting photos and memorabilia linking them with the Leander Club. Public areas also feature lots of trophies, pictures and artefacts, and it all makes for a most interesting place to stay.

Rooms 11 en suite (1 fmly) S fr £120; D fr £145* **Facilities** STV FTV TVL tea/coffee Dinner available Direct Dial Cen ht Lift Licensed Wi-fi **Conf** Max 120 Thtr 120 Class 40 Board 20 **Parking** 60 **Notes** ⊗ No Children 10yrs Closed Xmas-New Year RS 1st wk Jul Henley Royal Regatta Civ Wed 120

Milsoms Henley-on-Thames

★★★★ RESTAURANT WITH ROOMS

20 Market Place RG9 2AH
☎ 01491 845780 & 845789
e-mail: henley@milsomshotel.co.uk
dir: In centre of town, close to town hall

The seven en suite bedrooms are located in a listed building above the Loch Fyne Restaurant in Henley's Market Place. Each bedroom is individually appointed and equipped to meet the needs of the modern traveller; particular care has been taken to incorporate original features into the contemporary design. The restaurant has a commitment to offer ethically sourced seafood.

Rooms 7 en suite (2 fmly) (1 GF) **Facilities** FTV tea/coffee Dinner available Cen ht Wi-fi **Extras** Still & sparkling water - complimentary **Parking** 7 **Notes** ⊗ No coaches

---

Phyllis Court Club

★★★★ GUEST ACCOMMODATION

Marlow Rd RG9 2HT
☎ 01491 570500 📠 01491 570528
e-mail: enquiries@phylliscourt.co.uk
dir: A404 onto A4130 into town centre. Follow A4155, 150mtrs on right

Phyllis Court was founded in 1906 as a private members' club and has welcomed many distinguished visitors over the years. Set in 18 acres, with lawns sweeping down to the River Thames, it offers a unique blend of traditional elegance and modern comforts. The club takes centre stage during Henley Royal Regatta week, being positioned opposite the race finishing line. The individually styled bedrooms are well appointed and very comfortable. There is restricted meal service two days before and after the regattas in June and July. An excellent range of function venues is available, and the Grade II listed Grandstand Pavilion is perfect for weddings.

Rooms 17 en suite **Facilities** FTV Lounge TVL tea/coffee Dinner available Direct Dial Cen ht Lift Licensed Wi-fi 🛎 **Extras** Speciality toiletries, trouser press, magazines **Conf** Max 250 Thtr 250 Class 100 Board 30 **Parking** 200 **Notes** RS 26-28 Dec, 2-3 Jan, regattas Jun-Jul Civ Wed 250

Slater's Farm

★★★ 🅰 BED AND BREAKFAST

Peppard Common RG9 5JL
☎ 01491 628675
e-mail: stay@slatersfarm.co.uk
dir: 3m W of Henley. A4130 onto B481 to Rotherfield Peppard, pass Ruchetta Restaurant, left to primary school, house 200yds on right

Rooms 3 rms (1 pri facs) S fr £45; D fr £65* **Facilities** FTV tea/coffee Dinner available Cen ht Wi-fi 🛎 🎣 18 🔒 **Parking** 7 **Notes** ⊗ Closed Xmas 🐕

IDBURY   Map 10 SP21

Bould Farm (SP244209)

★★★★ FARMHOUSE

OX7 6RT
☎ 01608 658850 📠 01608 658850 Mrs L Meyrick
e-mail: meyrick@bouldfarm.co.uk
web: www.bouldfarm.co.uk
dir: Off A424 signed Idbury, through village, down hill, round two bends, on right

This delightful 17th-century farmhouse stands amid pretty gardens between Stow-on-the-Wold and Burford. The spacious bedrooms are carefully furnished and thoughtfully equipped, and some have stunning views of the surrounding countryside. Breakfast is served in the cosy dining room which features a cast-iron stove and stone-flagged floors.

Rooms 3 rms (2 en suite) (1 pri facs) (1 fmly) **Facilities** FTV TVL tea/coffee Cen ht Wi-fi **Parking** 6 **Notes** ⊗ Closed Dec-Jan 🐕 400 acres arable/sheep/beef cows

---

KINGHAM   Map 10 SP22

The Kingham Plough

★★★★★ ◉◉ ☗ INN

The Green OX7 6YD
☎ 01608 658327
e-mail: book@thekinghamplough.co.uk
dir: *From Chipping Norton, take B4450 to Churchill. Take 2nd right to Kingham, left at T-junct in Kingham. Pub on right.*

The Kingham Plough is a quintessential Cotswold inn set in the pretty village of Kingham, just minutes away from the well-known Daylesford Organic Estate. The en suite bedrooms have Cotswold character and offer impressive quality and comfort. Eating here is memorable both whether at breakfast or in the evening; the team deliver excellent results using locally sourced produce.

Rooms 7 en suite (2 fmly) S £75-£130; D £90-£130* **Facilities** FTV DVD tea/coffee Dinner available Cen ht Wi-fi **Extras** Speciality toiletries **Parking** 25 **Notes** Closed 25 Dec No coaches

Moat End

★★★★ ☗ BED AND BREAKFAST

The Moat OX7 6XZ
☎ 01608 658090 & 07765 278399
e-mail: moatend@gmail.com
web: www.moatend.co.uk
dir: *Exit B4450 or A436 into village centre*

This converted barn lies in a peaceful Cotswold village and has splendid country views. Its well-appointed bedrooms either have a jacuzzi or large shower cubicles, one with hydro-massage jets. The attractive dining room leads to a comfortable beamed sitting room with a stone fireplace. Quality local ingredients are used in the wholesome breakfasts. The owner has won an award for green tourism by reducing the impact of the business on the environment.

Rooms 3 en suite (1 fmly) S £58-£65; D £73-£80* **Facilities** FTV TVL tea/coffee Cen ht Wi-fi ☗ **Parking** 4 **Notes** LB Closed Xmas & New Year

The Tollgate Inn & Restaurant

★★★★ ☗ INN

Church St OX7 6YA
☎ 01608 658389
e-mail: info@thetollgate.com

Situated in the idyllic Cotswold village of Kingham, this Grade II listed Georgian building has been lovingly restored to provide a complete home-from-home among some of the most beautiful countryside in Britain. The Tollgate provides comfortable, well-equipped accommodation in pleasant surroundings. A good choice of menu for lunch and dinner is available with fine use made of fresh and local produce. Guests can also be sure of a hearty breakfast which is served in the modern, well-equipped dining room.

Rooms 5 en suite 4 annexe en suite (1 fmly) (4 GF) **Facilities** tea/coffee Dinner available Cen ht Wi-fi **Conf** Max 15 **Parking** 12

MILTON COMMON   Map 5 SP60

Byways

★★★★ ☗ BED AND BREAKFAST

Old London Rd OX9 2JR
☎ 01844 279386 📠 01844 279386
e-mail: byways.mott@tiscali.co.uk
web: www.bywaysbedandbreakfast.co.uk
dir: *Between M40 juncts 7 & 8A*

A friendly welcome awaits you at Byways, situated a few minutes from the M40. Bedrooms are comfortable and tastefully decorated, and the emphasis is on a peaceful and relaxing stay away from it all. Breakfast is home produced, organic and obtained locally where possible. There is a large garden for guests to enjoy. Please note that Byways is a TV-free establishment.

Rooms 3 rms (2 en suite) (1 pri facs) (3 GF) S £40; D £70-£80 **Facilities** DVD tea/coffee Cen ht Wi-fi ☗ **Parking** 3 **Notes** ⊗ No Children 7yrs ☺

OXFORD   Map 5 SP50

PREMIER COLLECTION

Burlington House

★★★★★ ☗ GUEST ACCOMMODATION

374 Banbury Rd, Summertown OX2 7PP
☎ 01865 513513 📠 01865 311785
e-mail: stay@burlington-house.co.uk
dir: *Opposite Oxford Conference Centre on A4165 on corner of Hernes Rd & Banbury Rd*

Guests are assured of a warm welcome and attentive service at this smart, beautifully maintained Victorian house, within walking distance of Summertown's fashionable restaurants. Elegant, contemporary bedrooms are filled with a wealth of thoughtful extras, and some open onto a pretty patio garden. Memorable breakfasts, served in the delightful dining room, include home-made preserves, fruit breads, granola and excellent coffee.

Rooms 10 en suite 2 annexe en suite **Facilities** FTV tea/coffee Direct Dial Cen ht Wi-fi **Parking** 5 **Notes** ⊗ No Children 12yrs Closed 24 Dec-2 Jan

PREMIER COLLECTION

The Bocardo

★★★★★ GUEST ACCOMMODATION

24-26 George St OX1 2AE
☎ 01865 591234
e-mail: reservations@thebocardo.co.uk

Located right in the heart of Oxford City Centre on George Street directly above Jamie's Italian Restaurant, The Bocardo offers bedrooms that are all tastefully decorated, following a complete refurbishment, with stylish decor and comfortably appointed soft furnishings. All rooms are equipped with flat screen TVs, free Wi-fi and high quality bathrooms including power showers. This is a Room Only establishment with breakfast not available, but there are endless bars, restaurants and cafés right on the doorstep for guests to enjoy.

Rooms 10 en suite S £69-£110; D £99-£130 (room only)* **Facilities** Wi-fi

---

Save on B&Bs and Hotels. Book at theAA.com/hotel

OXFORDSHIRE 237 ENGLAND

Claddagh Guest House

★★★★ GUEST HOUSE

112 The Slade, Headington OX3 7DX
☎ 01865 751641
e-mail: info@claddaghguesthouse.co.uk
dir: *At Headington rdbt 1st exit onto A420 signed city centre. At lights left into Windmill Rd (B4495) signed Nuffield Orthopaedic Centre. 0.6m, on left into The Slade*

A family-run guest house, where guests can relax and unwind. Three rooms are en suite whilst the single room has a private bathroom. All have TVs and courtesy trays as well as thoughtful extras including Wi-fi. Breakfast is served at the communal table in the attractive breakfast room overlooking the garden.

Rooms 4 rms (3 en suite) (1 pri facs) **Facilities** STV FTV tea/coffee Cen ht Wi-fi ♨ **Parking** 8 **Notes** ⊗ 🐾

Conifers Guest House

★★★★ GUEST ACCOMMODATION

116 The Slade, Headington OX3 7DX
☎ 01865 763055 📠 01865 742232
e-mail: stay@conifersguesthouse.co.uk
web: www.conifersguesthouse.co.uk
dir: *Exit ring road onto A420 towards city centre. Left onto B4495 (Windmill Rd), straight over at lights, house on left past Nuffield Orthopaedic Centre*

Located in a residential area close to the hospitals, this impressive Edwardian house has been renovated to provide attractive, pine-furnished bedrooms. Breakfast is served in a smart, front-facing dining room. Private car park.

Rooms 11 en suite (4 fmly) **Facilities** FTV TV9B tea/coffee Cen ht Wi-fi **Parking** 8 **Notes** ⊗

Cotswold House

★★★★ GUEST ACCOMMODATION

363 Banbury Rd OX2 7PL
☎ 01865 310558 📠 08721 107068
e-mail: d.r.walker@talk21.com
web: www.cotswoldhouse.co.uk
dir: *A40 onto A423 into city centre, follow signs to Summertown, house 0.5m on right*

Situated in a leafy avenue close to the northern ring road and Summertown, this well-maintained house offers comfortable, well-equipped bedrooms and a relaxed atmosphere. Enjoy a traditional, hearty breakfast with vegetarian choice, including home-made muesli and fresh fruit, served in the bright attractive dining room.

Rooms 8 en suite (2 fmly) (2 GF) S £65-£75; D £99-£120 **Facilities** FTV Lounge tea/coffee Cen ht Wi-fi ♨ **Parking** 6 **Notes** ⊗

Galaxie

★★★★ GUEST ACCOMMODATION

180 Banbury Rd OX2 7BT
☎ 01865 515688 📠 01865 556824
e-mail: info@galaxie.co.uk
web: www.galaxie.co.uk
dir: *1m N of Oxford centre, on right before shops in Summertown*

Situated in the popular Summertown area of the city, the Galaxie has a welcoming atmosphere and very good quality accommodation. The well-equipped bedrooms are all very comfortable and have a good range of extra facilities. The attractive conservatory-dining room looks over the Oriental garden.

Rooms 32 rms (28 en suite) (3 fmly) **Facilities** TVL TV31B tea/coffee Direct Dial Cen ht Lift **Parking** 30 **Notes** ⊗

Marlborough House

★★★★ GUEST ACCOMMODATION

321 Woodstock Rd OX2 7NY
☎ 01865 311321 📠 01865 515329
e-mail: enquiries@marlbhouse.co.uk
web: www.marlbhouse.co.uk
dir: *1.5m N of city centre. Exit at A34 & A44 junct for city centre, onto A4144 (Woodstock Rd), premises on right by lights*

Marlborough House is just 1.5 miles north of Oxford's historic city centre, and is within easy reach of the M40 and the A34 ring road. Custom built in 1990 to a traditional design, the house sits comfortably alongside its Victorian neighbours in a predominantly residential area. All 17 bedrooms have en suite facilities, kitchenettes and mini-bars so guests aren't tied to any routine. Wi-fi covers the lounge and many of the rooms.

Rooms 13 en suite 4 annexe en suite (3 fmly) (4 GF) **Facilities** FTV Lounge tea/coffee Direct Dial Cen ht Licensed Wi-fi **Extras** Mini-bar - chargeable **Parking** 6 **Notes** ⊗

Red Mullions Guest House

★★★★ GUEST HOUSE

23 London Rd, Headington OX3 7RE
☎ 01865 742741 📠 01865 769944
e-mail: stay@redmullions.co.uk
dir: *M40 junct 8, A40. At Headington rdbt, 2nd exit signed Headington into London Rd*

Red Mullions takes its name from the brick columns between the windows of the building. Modern bedrooms provide comfortable accommodation set within easy reach of motorway networks and Oxford city centre. Hearty breakfasts provide a good start to any day.

Rooms 13 rms (12 en suite) (1 pri facs) (3 fmly) (4 GF) S £80-£85; D £90-£110* **Facilities** FTV DVD tea/coffee Cen ht Wi-fi **Extras** Water - complimentary **Parking** 9 **Notes** ⊗

Remont

★★★★ GUEST ACCOMMODATION

367 Banbury Rd OX2 7PL
☎ 01865 311020 📠 01865 552080
e-mail: info@remont-oxford.co.uk

Location in Summertown, just two miles from Oxford city centre. The well-equipped bedrooms, and bathrooms, are modern and stylish and come with flat screen TVs, complimentary Wi-fi and well stocked beverage trays; all offer high quality and comfort. Parking is available and there is a delightful garden for guests to enjoy. Cooked and continental buffet breakfasts are served in the light and airy dining room.

Rooms 25 en suite (2 fmly) (8 GF) **Facilities** FTV tea/coffee Cen ht Lift Wi-fi **Parking** 18 **Notes** ⊗

OXFORD *continued*

Green Gables

★ ★ ★ GUEST ACCOMMODATION

326 Abingdon Rd OX1 4TE
☎ 01865 725870 ▤ 01865 723115
e-mail: green.gables@virgin.net
web: www.greengables.uk.com
dir: *Exit ring road onto B4144 towards city centre, Green Gables 0.5m on left*

A warm welcome is assured at this Edwardian house, located within easy walking distance of the city centre. Bedrooms are equipped with a range of practical and homely extras, and a comprehensive breakfast is served in the cosy dining room. Guests have free access to the internet in the smart conservatory-lounge, and private parking is available.

Rooms 11 en suite (2 fmly) (4 GF) **Facilities** FTV TVL tea/coffee Direct Dial Cen ht Wi-fi **Parking** 9 **Notes** ⊗ Closed 23-31 Dec

Acorn Guest House

★ ★ ★ GUEST ACCOMMODATION

260-262 Iffley Rd OX4 1SE
☎ 01865 247998
e-mail: kate@oxford-acorn.co.uk
dir: *Exit ring road onto A4158 towards city centre, house 1m on left after VW garage*

This double-fronted Victorian house is located between the ring road and the city centre, and offers good value accommodation. The lounge leads out to a quiet enclosed rear garden.

Rooms 15 rms (7 en suite) (1 pri facs) (1 fmly) **Facilities** tea/coffee Cen ht Lift Wi-fi **Parking** 6

All Seasons Guest House

★ ★ ★ GUEST ACCOMMODATION

63 Windmill Rd, Headington OX3 7BP
☎ 01865 742215 ▤ 01865 429667
e-mail: info@allseasonshouse.com
web: www.allseasonshouse.com
dir: *Exit ring road onto A420 towards city centre. 1m, left at lights into Windmill Rd, house 300yds on left*

Within easy walking distance of the suburb of Headington, this double-fronted Victorian house provides comfortable homely bedrooms equipped with practical and thoughtful extras. The elegant dining room features an original fireplace, and secure parking is available behind the property.

Rooms 7 rms (5 en suite) (2 pri facs) (1 fmly) (1 GF) S £45-£70; D £68-£85* **Facilities** FTV TVL tea/coffee Cen ht Wi-fi **Parking** 6 **Notes** ⊗

Athena Guest House

★ ★ ★ GUEST ACCOMMODATION

255 Cowley Rd, Cowley OX4 1XQ
☎ 01865 425700 & 07748 837144 ▤ 01865 240566
e-mail: info@athenaguesthouse.com
web: www.athenaguesthouse.com
dir: *1.5m SE of city centre on B480*

Located close to the shops and amenities in Cowley, this Victorian brick house offers smart modern bedrooms on three floors with many useful extras. Breakfast is served in the bright and relaxing dining room, and limited parking is available.

Rooms 6 en suite (2 fmly) (2 GF) **Facilities** STV TVL tea/coffee Cen ht Wi-fi **Conf** Max 15 **Parking** 4 **Notes** ⊗

Heather House

★ ★ ★ GUEST ACCOMMODATION

192 Iffley Rd OX4 1SD
☎ 01865 249757 ▤ 01865 249757
e-mail: stay@heatherhouseoxford.com
web: www.heatherhouseoxford.com
dir: *Exit A40 at Headington rdbt, S onto A4142 to Littlemore rdbt onto A4158 (Iffley Rd) then house 1.25m. On left after pedestrian crossing near Chester St*

A short walk from the colleges, city centre and Oxford Brookes campus, this detached Edwardian house stands in a residential area and has its own parking. The en suite bedrooms are bright and comfortable, and come complete with useful facilities including TV and CD/DVD players. There is Wi-fi, a computer station (with Skype) and a relaxing lounge with lots of tourist information. A choice of breakfasts is available.

Rooms 6 rms (5 en suite) (1 pri facs) (2 fmly) (1 GF) S £42-£48; D £74-£80* **Facilities** FTV DVD TVL tea/coffee Direct Dial Cen ht Wi-fi **Extras** Speciality toiletries **Parking** 6 **Notes** ⊗

Highfield Guest House

★ ★ ★ GUEST ACCOMMODATION

91 Rose Hill OX4 4HT
☎ 01865 774083
e-mail: highfield.house@tesco.net
dir: *Exit A4142 (Eastern Bypass Rd) onto A4158, house 250yds*

This attractive detached house stands in immaculate gardens close to Cowley and provides homely bedrooms equipped with quality pine furniture. The attractive front dining room is the setting for comprehensive breakfasts and there is also a spacious lounge.

Rooms 7 rms (5 en suite) (2 pri facs) (1 fmly) **Facilities** FTV TVL tea/coffee Cen ht Wi-fi **Parking** 6 **Notes** ⊗ Closed Xmas

Lina Guest House

★ ★ ★ GUEST HOUSE

308 Banbury Rd OX2 7ED
☎ 01865 511070 ▤ 01865 510060
e-mail: info@linaguesthouse.com

This beautiful Victorian townhouse offers well-appointed accommodation with all the modern facilities to provide a base for leisure and business guests alike. Breakfast is served in the front room whilst the rear garden can be enjoyed in the warmer months. Parking is available on a first-come, first-served basis.

Rooms 7 en suite (1 fmly) (1 GF) S £55-£75; D £80-£95* **Facilities** FTV DVD TVL Cen ht Wi-fi **Parking** 5 **Notes** ⊗

Sports View Guest House

★ ★ ★ GUEST ACCOMMODATION

106-110 Abingdon Rd OX1 4PX
☎ 01865 244268 ▤ 01865 249270
e-mail: stay@sportsviewguesthouse.co.uk
web: www.sportsviewguesthouse.co.uk
dir: *Exit Oxford S at Kennington rdbt towards city centre, 1.25m on left*

This family-run Victorian property, overlooks the Queens College sports ground. Situated south of the city it is within walking distance of the centre. Rooms are comfortable, and the property benefits from off-road parking.

Rooms 20 rms (19 en suite) (1 pri facs) (4 fmly) (5 GF) S £42-£57; D £70-£84* **Facilities** FTV Lounge tea/coffee Direct Dial Cen ht Wi-fi **Parking** 10 **Notes** ⊗ No Children 3yrs Closed 25-26 Dec & 1 Jan

Save on B&Bs and Hotels. Book at **theAA.com/hotel**

OXFORDSHIRE 239 **ENGLAND**

Tower House

★★★ GUEST ACCOMMODATION

15 Ship St OX1 3DA
☎ 01865 246828 📄 01865 247508
e-mail: generalmanager.towerhousehotel@ohiml.com
dir: *Follow signs to city centre, turn left into Turl St, then right into Ship St*

Tower House is a charming 17th-century house set on a quiet street in the heart of Oxford city centre. Bedrooms are all individually decorated in keeping with the age of the property. A light continental breakfast is served in the quaint breakfast room on the ground floor.

Rooms 7 rms (4 en suite) (1 fmly) **Facilities** FTV tea/coffee Cen ht Wi-fi **Notes** ⊗

Newton House

★★★ 🅰 BED AND BREAKFAST

82-84 Abingdon Rd OX1 4PL
☎ 01865 240561 📄 01865 244647
e-mail: newton.house@btinternet.com
dir: *On A4144 (Abingdon Rd)*

Rooms 14 rms (2 en suite) (12 pri facs) (3 fmly) (4 GF)
S £60-£80; D £60-£89* **Facilities** FTV tea/coffee Direct Dial Cen ht Wi-fi **Parking** 8 **Notes** LB ⊗

SOUTH STOKE — Map 5 SU58

Perch & Pike

★★★ INN

The Street RG8 0JS
☎ 01491 872415 📄 01491 871001
e-mail: info@perchandpike.co.uk
dir: *From A4074 take B4009 S to South Stoke*

Set in the quiet village of South Stoke, minutes from the River Thames, this cosy inn offers a very warm welcome. The four en suite bedrooms are comfortable and well equipped. Public areas are spacious and include a separate dining room. Enjoy local asparagus, when in season, or trout caught that day by the proprietor.

Rooms 4 en suite (1 fmly) **Facilities** FTV tea/coffee Dinner available Cen ht **Parking** 25 **Notes** ⊗ No coaches

STADHAMPTON — Map 5 SU69

PREMIER COLLECTION

The Crazy Bear

★★★★★ ⚘⚘ 🛒 GUEST ACCOMMODATION

Bear Ln OX44 7UR
☎ 01865 890714 📄 01865 400481
e-mail: enquiries@crazybear-stadhampton.co.uk
web: www.crazybeargroup.co.uk
dir: *M40 junct 7, A329. In 4m left after petrol station, left into Bear Ln*

This popular and attractive guest accommodation successfully combines modern chic with old world character. Cuisine is extensive and varied, with award-winning Thai and English restaurants under the same roof (both with AA Rosettes). Those choosing to make a night of it can enjoy the concept bedrooms, all presented to a very high standard and styled with exciting themes; the 'infinity suites' have state-of-the-art facilities.

Rooms 5 en suite 12 annexe en suite (3 fmly) (4 GF)
Facilities STV FTV Dinner available Direct Dial Cen ht Licensed Wi-fi 🏌 **Conf** Max 40 Thtr 30 Class 30 Board 30 **Parking** 100 **Notes** ⊗ Civ Wed 200

SWINBROOK — Map 5 SP21

The Swan Inn

★★★★★ ⚘⚘ INN

OX18 4DY
☎ 01993 823339
e-mail: swaninnswinbrook@btconnect.com
web: www.theswanswinbrook.co.uk
dir: *1m from A40, 2m E of Burford*

The idyllic location and award-winning food are only two of the reasons why this is the perfect place for a comfortable business visit or a relaxed weekend. The bar offers real ales, local lagers and an appealing wine list. The accommodation is sumptuous and combines modern facilities with traditional comfort.

Rooms 6 en suite (1 fmly) (4 GF) **Facilities** FTV tea/coffee Dinner available Cen ht Wi-fi ⚲ 18 Riding **Parking** 20 **Notes** Closed 25 Dec No coaches

WANTAGE — Map 5 SU38

PREMIER COLLECTION

Brook Barn Country House

★★★★★ 🚲 🛒 GUEST ACCOMMODATION

Brook Barn, Letcombe Regis OX12 9JD
☎ 01235 766502 📄 01235 766873
e-mail: info@brookbarn.com
web: www.brookbarn.com
dir: *M4 junct 14, A338 to Wantage. Left onto B4507 signed Ashbury, 1m, left signed Letcombe Regis. House 0.75m on left*

A bijou country house hideaway with luxurious bedrooms, Brook Barn is set in over an acre of gardens which include an orchard, and a beautiful chalk stream allowing guests to enjoy the tranquillity of the Oxfordshire countryside. This house is equipped to the highest standards, and is a perfect respite for business travellers or holiday-makers alike.

Rooms 5 rms (4 en suite) (1 pri facs) (4 GF)
Facilities STV FTV tea/coffee Dinner available Direct Dial Cen ht Licensed Wi-fi 🏌 Outdoor hot tub **Parking** 6 **Notes** ⊗ No Children 16yrs

La Fontana Restaurant with Accommodation

★★★★ 🍽 RESTAURANT WITH ROOMS

Oxford Rd, East Hanney OX12 0HP
☎ 01235 868287 📄 01235 868019
e-mail: anna@la-fontana.co.uk
dir: *A338 from Wantage towards Oxford. Restaurant on right in East Hanney*

Guests are guaranteed a warm welcome at this family-run Italian restaurant which is located on the outskirts of the busy town of Wantage. The stylish bedrooms are individually designed, well equipped and very comfortable. Dinner should not to be missed - the menu features a wide range of regional Italian specialities.

Rooms 8 en suite 7 annexe en suite (2 fmly) (4 GF)
S £65-£75; D £85-£100* **Facilities** FTV TVL tea/coffee Dinner available Direct Dial Cen ht Wi-fi **Parking** 30 **Notes** LB ⊗

WANTAGE *continued*

Hill Barn *(SU337852)*

★★★ FARMHOUSE

Sparsholt Firs OX12 9XB
☎ 01235 751236 & 07885 368918 Mrs J Whittington
e-mail: jmw@hillbarn.plus.com
dir: W of B4001 on The Ridgeway, 4m N of Wantage

This working farm offers en suite bedrooms with beautiful
distant views over the countryside. The atmosphere is
friendly, and guests are able to relax either in the sitting
room or in the garden. Breakfast is a highlight with
home-made jams and produce from the farm, when
available.

Rooms 2 en suite D fr £80* **Facilities** Lounge TVL tea/
coffee Dinner available Cen ht Wi-fi **Parking** 3 **Notes** LB
⊛ 100 acres horses

WATLINGTON   Map 5 SU69

The Fat Fox Inn

★★★ ⊛ INN

13 Shirburn St OX49 5BU
☎ 01491 613040
e-mail: info@thefatfoxinn.co.uk

This inn is conveniently located for both the leisure guest,
especially walkers of the nearby Ridgeway and the
business traveller looking for a quiet location just 20
minutes out of Oxford city. Guests can enjoy lunch and
dinner in the relaxed bar or in the restaurant where the
kitchen team offers well-sourced, quality seasonal food.

Rooms 9 en suite **Facilities** Dinner available

WHEATLEY   Map 5 SP50

Gidleigh House

★★★★ BED AND BREAKFAST

27 Old London Rd OX33 1YW
☎ 01865 875150 & 07733 026882
dir: M40 junct 8 follow signs to Wheatley. Pass Asda on
left & right turn to Hotton/Waterperry. Next right, marked
private road

You are assured of a warm, personal welcome at this
modern home which is located on a private road in a
quiet village just ten minutes from Oxford city centre with
easy access to the M40. The two en suite rooms are
spacious, very comfortable and equipped with thoughtful
extras. Relax over a newspaper in the conservatory at the
family style table while your breakfast is freshly prepared.

Rooms 2 en suite (2 fmly) S £55-£65; D £75-£85*
Facilities tea/coffee Cen ht **Extras** Fruit, chocolates
Parking 4 **Notes** ⊗ No Children 10yrs Closed 18 Dec-5
Jan ⊜

WITNEY   Map 5 SP31

PREMIER COLLECTION

Old Swan & Minster Mill

★★★★★ ⊛ 🍴 INN

Old Minster OX29 0RN
☎ 01993 774441 📠 01993 702002
e-mail: enquiries@oldswanandminstermill.com
web: www.oldswanandminstermill.com

Located within its own stunning grounds and gardens
including a private stretch of the River Windrush, the
Old Swan and Minster Mill are two distinct
accommodation areas, both with quality and
individuality. Check-in is at the Minster Mill, where
guests are welcomed and escorted to their room or
suite. Old Swan rooms are traditional, with old oak
beams and fireplaces in some rooms, whilst Mill rooms
are more contemporary in style many of which feature
great views of the river and grounds. Award-winning
cuisine is served in the dining room.

Rooms 60 en suite (4 fmly) (7 GF) S £145-£305;
D £165-£325* **Facilities** FTV tea/coffee Dinner
available Direct Dial Cen ht Wi-fi 🛉 🏊 Fishing Gym
Conf Thtr 55 Class 22 Board 24 **Parking** 40 **Notes** LB
Civ Wed 50

Corn Croft Guest House

★★★★ GUEST ACCOMMODATION

69-71 Corn St OX28 6AS
☎ 01993 773298 📠 01993 773298
e-mail: enquiries@corncroft.co.uk
web: www.corncroft.co.uk
dir: A40 to town centre, from Market Square into Corn
Street, 400mtrs on left

Located in the quieter end of town, yet close to the centre,
Corn Croft offers comfortable well equipped
accommodation in a friendly atmosphere. Substantial
breakfasts featuring local produce are served in the
attractive dining room.

Rooms 11 en suite (1 fmly) (2 GF) **Facilities** FTV DVD tea/
coffee Cen ht Wi-fi **Notes** Closed 24-26 Dec

The Fleece

★★★ 🍴 INN

11 Church Green OX28 4AZ
☎ 01993 892270 📠 0871 8130458
e-mail: fleece@peachpubs.com
dir: A40 to Witney town centre, on Church Green

Set in the centre of Witney overlooking the church green,
The Fleece offers ten well-equipped, en suite modern
bedrooms. This popular destination pub offers food all
day including breakfast, and a great selection of wines
and real ales.

Rooms 7 en suite 3 annexe en suite (1 fmly) (1 GF)
S £55-£85; D £55-£95* **Facilities** FTV tea/coffee Dinner
available Direct Dial Cen ht Wi-fi **Conf** Max 30 Thtr 25
Class 16 Board 22 **Parking** 12 **Notes** LB Closed 25 Dec

Crofters Guest House

[U]

29 Oxford Hill OX28 3JU
☎ 01993 778165 & 07930 539021
e-mail: countycolours@hotmail.co.uk
web: www.bedandbreakfastwitney.co.uk
dir: Off A40 onto B4022 (Witney East). On right just after
1st set of lights

Currently the rating for this establishment is not
confirmed. This may be due to a change of ownership or
because it has only recently joined the AA rating scheme.

Rooms 4 rms (2 en suite) (1 fmly) (2 GF) S £40-£50;
D £65-£90* **Facilities** FTV TVL tea/coffee Cen ht Wi-fi
Parking 5 **Notes** ⊗

WOODSTOCK Map 11 SP41

Duke of Marlborough Country Inn

★★★★ INN

Woodleys OX20 1HT
☎ 01993 811460 📠 01993 810165
e-mail: sales@dukeofmarlborough.co.uk
dir: *1m N of Woodstock on A44 x-rds*

The Duke of Marlborough is just outside the popular town of Woodstock, convenient for local attractions including Blenheim Palace. Bedrooms and bathrooms are in an adjacent lodge-style building and offer high standards of quality and comfort. Dinner includes many tempting home-cooked dishes, complemented by a good selection of ales and wines.

Rooms 13 annexe en suite (2 fmly) (7 GF) S £66-£90; D £75-£120* **Facilities** FTV tea/coffee Dinner available Direct Dial Cen ht Wi-fi 🛁 **Conf** Max 20 Thtr 20 Class 16 Board 12 **Parking** 42 **Notes** LB ⊗

The Blenheim Guest House & Tea Rooms

★★★★ 🅰 GUEST ACCOMMODATION

17 Park St OX20 1SJ
☎ 01993 813814 📠 01993 813810
e-mail: theblenheim@aol.com
web: www.theblenheim.com
dir: *Off A44 in Woodstock to County Museum, after museum on left*

Rooms 6 rms (5 en suite) (1 pri facs) (2 fmly) **Facilities** tea/coffee Cen ht Licensed Wi-fi

The Townhouse

★★★ GUEST ACCOMMODATION

15 High St OX20 1TE
☎ 01993 810843
e-mail: townhousewoodstock@hotmail.co.uk
dir: *Off A44 onto High St*

This early 18th-century character, stone townhouse offers five individually styled, cosy en suite bedrooms. Situated in the heart of the town just a short walk from Blenheim Palace, it is an ideal base for exploring many famous Cotswold locations. Breakfasts are cooked to order and served in the small conservatory room overlooking the walled garden.

Rooms 5 en suite (1 fmly) S £60-£65; D £80-£120 **Facilities** FTV TVL tea/coffee Cen ht Wi-fi **Notes** ⊗

RUTLAND

CLIPSHAM Map 11 SK91

Beech House

★★★★★ ◉◉ 🛏 INN

Main St LE15 7SH
☎ 01780 410355 📠 01780 410000
e-mail: rooms@theolivebranchpub.com
dir: *From A1 take B668 signed Stretton & Clipsham*

Beech House stands over the road from the Olive Branch restaurant. It offers very well furnished bedrooms which include DVD players. Breakfasts are served in the Olive Branch. Excellent lunches and dinners are also available.

Rooms 5 en suite 1 annexe en suite (2 fmly) (3 GF) S £97.50-£112.50; D £115-£195* **Facilities** FTV DVD tea/coffee Dinner available Direct Dial Cen ht Wi-fi 🛁 **Extras** Speciality toiletries - complimentary; fruit - chargeable **Conf** Max 20 Thtr 20 Class 16 Board 16 **Parking** 10 **Notes** LB No coaches

EMPINGHAM Map 11 SK90

The White Horse Inn

★★★ INN

Main St LE15 8PS
☎ 01780 460221 📠 01780 460521
e-mail: info@whitehorserutland.co.uk
web: www.whitehorserutland.co.uk
dir: *On A606 (Oakham to Stamford road)*

This attractive stone-built inn, offering bright, comfortable accommodation, is conveniently located just minutes from the A1. Bedrooms in the main building are spacious and include a number of family rooms. Public areas include a well-stocked bar, a bistro and restaurant where a wide range of meals is served.

Rooms 4 en suite 9 annexe en suite (4 fmly) (5 GF) S £53; D £70* **Facilities** FTV TVL tea/coffee Dinner available Direct Dial 🛁 **Conf** Max 25 Thtr 25 Class 20 Board 20 **Parking** 60 **Notes** Closed 25 Dec

LYDDINGTON Map 11 SP89

The Marquess of Exeter

★★★★ 🛏 INN

52 Main St LE15 9LT
☎ 01572 822477 📠 08082 801159
e-mail: info@marquessexeter.co.uk
dir: *M1 junct 19, A14 to Kettering, then A6003 to Caldecott. Right into Lyddington Rd, 2m to village*

Situated in the picturesque Rutland countryside, the inn is appointed with contemporary touches whilst retaining many original features such as timber beam ceilings, open log fires and flagstone floors. The stylish bedrooms, situated across a courtyard, are individually decorated and comfortable. The food is imaginative with the chef's 'sharing dishes' being particularly noteworthy.

Rooms 17 en suite (3 fmly) (10 GF) S £69.50-£99.50; D £89.50-£124.50* **Facilities** FTV tea/coffee Dinner available Direct Dial Cen ht Wi-fi **Conf** Max 50 Thtr 50 Class 40 Board 40 **Parking** 60

LYDDINGTON *continued*

Old White Hart

★★★★ INN

51 Main St LE15 9LR
☎ 01572 821703 📠 01572 821978
e-mail: mail@oldwhitehart.co.uk
dir: *1m S of Uppingham on main street, opposite village green*

Set opposite the village green in the heart of Lyddington, the Old White Hart offers a personal, attentive welcome. The accommodation is set in converted cottages situated alongside the public house. All bedrooms have been thoughtfully renovated, and each is individually designed to offer quality and comfort. Enjoy home-prepared food either in one of the cosy restaurants, the bar, or alfresco dining in the garden during the summer months.

Rooms 2 en suite 9 annexe en suite (1 fmly) (2 GF) S £65–£75; D £90–£100* **Facilities** FTV Lounge tea/coffee Dinner available Direct Dial Cen ht Wi-fi ⚲ Petanque **Conf** Max 20 Thtr 15 Class 15 Board 18 **Parking** 50 **Notes** LB ⊗ Closed 25 Dec

OAKHAM	Map 11 SK80

Kirkee House

★★★★ BED AND BREAKFAST

35 Welland Way LE15 6SL
☎ 01572 757401
e-mail: carolbeech@kirkeehouse.demon.co.uk
dir: *S of town centre. Exit A606 (High St) into Mill St, over level crossing, 400yds on left*

Located on a leafy avenue a short walk from the town centre, this immaculately maintained modern house provides comfortable bedrooms filled with homely extras. Comprehensive breakfasts, including local sausages and home-made jams, are served in the elegant conservatory-dining room, which overlooks the pretty garden.

Rooms 2 en suite **Facilities** FTV tea/coffee Cen ht Wi-fi **Parking** 2 **Notes** ⊗ No Children 7yrs ⊠

UPPINGHAM	Map 11 SP89

The Lake Isle

★★★★ ⊛⊛ ⊞ RESTAURANT WITH ROOMS

16 High Street East LE15 9PZ
☎ 01572 822951 📠 01572 824400
e-mail: info@lakeisle.co.uk
web: www.lakeisle.co.uk
dir: *From A47, turn left at 2nd lights, 100yds on right*

This attractive townhouse centres round a delightful restaurant and small elegant bar. There is also an inviting first-floor guest lounge, and the bedrooms are extremely well appointed and thoughtfully equipped; spacious split-level cottage suites situated in a quiet courtyard are also available. The imaginative cooking and an extremely impressive wine list are highlights.

Rooms 9 en suite 3 annexe rms (3 pri facs) (1 fmly) (1 GF) **Facilities** FTV tea/coffee Dinner available Direct Dial Cen ht Wi-fi **Conf** Max 16 Board 16 **Parking** 7 **Notes** ⊗ RS Sun eve & Mon lunch closed No coaches

WING	Map 11 SK80

Kings Arms Inn & Restaurant

★★★★ ⊛⊛ ⊞ INN

13 Top St LE15 8SE
☎ 01572 737634 📠 01572 737255
e-mail: info@thekingsarms-wing.co.uk
web: www.thekingsarms-wing.co.uk
dir: *1.5m off A6003 in village centre*

This traditional village inn, with its open fires, flagstone floors and low beams, dates from the 17th century. The restaurant is more contemporary and offers a wide range of interesting, freshly produced dishes. Service is attentive and friendly. The spacious, well-equipped bedrooms are in The Old Bake House and Granny's Cottage, in the nearby courtyard.

Rooms 8 en suite (2 fmly) (4 GF) **Facilities** FTV tea/coffee Dinner available Cen ht Wi-fi **Conf** Max 20 Thtr 16 Class 16 Board 16 **Parking** 30 **Notes** RS Nov-Apr closed Mon, Tue lunch & Sun eve (ex BHs)

SHROPSHIRE	

BISHOP'S CASTLE	Map 15 SO38

The Coach House

★★★★ ⊞ ⊜ INN

Norbury SY9 5DX
☎ 01588 650680
e-mail: coachhouse.norbury@virginmedia.com
web: www.thecoachhousenorbury.co.uk
dir: *3m NE of Bishop's Castle. Exit A488/A489 into Norbury*

This delightful stone-built inn stands in the quiet village of Norbury. The interior with its exposed beams and log-burning stoves is enhanced by period furnishings, and the attractive, traditionally appointed bedrooms have modern facilities. Wholesome, home-cooked food is available in the elegant dining room or in the popular bar.

Rooms 3 rms (2 en suite) (1 pri facs) 3 annexe en suite (1 GF) D £90–£120* **Facilities** FTV Lounge tea/coffee Dinner available Cen ht ⚲ **Parking** 20 **Notes** LB ⊗ No Children 12yrs No coaches

Boars Head

★★★★ INN

Church St SY9 5AE
☎ 01588 638521
e-mail: info@boarsheadhotel.co.uk
web: www.boarsheadhotel.co.uk

The Boars Head is situated in the centre of Bishop's Castle, with easy access, and is a traditional inn with separate annexe-style bedrooms which are comfortable and spacious. The inn incorporates a post office with a cash machine and phone top-up facilities, and a hair salon. Food is on offer all day and good quality ingredients are used to create a well balanced menu. Parking is to the rear of the inn.

Rooms 3 annexe en suite (1 fmly) (3 GF) S £45–£80; D £60–£80 (room only)* **Facilities** FTV DVD iPod docking station Lounge tea/coffee Dinner available Cen ht Wi-fi **Extras** Fridge, digital safe, mineral water **Parking** 60 **Notes** ⊗

Shuttocks Wood

★★★★ BED AND BREAKFAST

Norbury SY9 5EA
☎ 01588 650433 & 07712 443283 📠 01588 650433
e-mail: info@shuttocks.co.uk
dir: *From A489, turn left signed Norbury 3m, on the left past Norbury school*

Peacefully located in rural Norbury, this modern detached house stands on pretty mature gardens and provides good standards of comfort and facilities. Bedrooms are equipped with thoughtful extras; there is a separate annexe, and breakfasts feature local fresh produce. Kennels are available for dogs.

Rooms 3 en suite 1 annexe en suite (1 fmly) (2 GF) S £45–£55; D £60–£70* **Facilities** FTV DVD Lounge tea/coffee Dinner available Cen ht Wi-fi ⚲ **Parking** 10 **Notes** LB No Children 10yrs

BRIDGNORTH	Map 10 SO79

PREMIER COLLECTION

The Albynes

★★★★★ BED AND BREAKFAST

Nordley WV16 4SX
☎ 01746 762261
e-mail: thealbynes@hotmail.com
dir: *In Nordley on B4373, 500yds past Nordley sign*

This imposing farmhouse features grand staircases, high ceilings and idyllic views. Melissa Woolley is a charming hostess, while husband Hayden looks after the crops and sheep. Bedrooms are comfortable, spacious and offer many thoughtful extras. Day rooms retain many original features and guests can enjoy traditional breakfasts, home-cooked on the Aga.

Rooms 3 en suite S £45–£55; D £65–£80 **Facilities** FTV TVL tea/coffee Cen ht **Parking** 6 **Notes** ⊗ No Children 12yrs Closed Xmas-New Year ⊠

Save on B&Bs and Hotels. Book at theAA.com/hotel

SHROPSHIRE 243 **ENGLAND**

The Laurels

★★★★ GUEST HOUSE

Broadoak, Six Ashes WV15 6EQ
☎ 01384 221546 & 07813 925319
e-mail: george.broadoak75@btinternet.com
web: www.thelaurelsbandb.co.uk
dir: On right 5m from Bridgnorth towards Stourbridge
on A458

Located on pretty gardens in a hamlet between
Bridgnorth and Stourbridge, this immaculately
maintained property provides a range of homely
bedrooms, some of which are in converted stables.
Breakfast is served in an attractive conservatory-dining
room, and a lounge and indoor swimming pool are
additional attractions.

Rooms 2 en suite 5 annexe en suite (1 fmly) (5 GF)
Facilities FTV TVL tea/coffee Dinner available Cen ht Wi-fi
🕑 **Parking** 9 **Notes** ✖ 🐾

Bearwood Lodge Guest House

★★★★ GUEST ACCOMMODATION

10 Kidderminster Rd WV15 6BW
☎ 01746 762159
e-mail: dawnjones604@yahoo.co.uk
dir: On A442, 50yds S of Bridgnorth bypass island

This friendly guest house is situated on the outskirts of
Bridgnorth. It provides soundly maintained, modern
accommodation, including one bedroom on the ground
floor. The bright and pleasant breakfast room has an
adjacent conservatory, which opens onto the attractive
and colourful garden. There is also a comfortable lounge.

Rooms 4 en suite (1 GF) S £45; D £65* **Facilities** FTV
Lounge TVL tea/coffee Cen ht Wi-fi 🕑 **Parking** 8 **Notes** LB
🐾

The Halfway House Inn

★★★ INN

Cleobury Mortimer Rd WV16 5LS
☎ 01746 762670 📠 01746 802020
e-mail: info@halfwayhouseinn.co.uk
web: www.halfwayhouseinn.co.uk
dir: 1.5m from town centre on B4363 to Cleobury
Mortimer

Located in a rural area, this 16th-century inn has been
renovated to provide good standards of comfort, while
retaining its original character. The bedrooms, some in
converted stables and cottages, are especially suitable
for families and groups.

Rooms 10 en suite (10 fmly) (6 GF) S £50-£65;
D £65-£95* **Facilities** FTV TVL tea/coffee Dinner available
Cen ht Wi-fi ⚓ 18 Fishing Pool table 🕑 **Conf** Max 30 Thtr 30
Class 24 Board 20 **Parking** 30 **Notes** LB Closed 25-26
Dec RS Sun eve (ex BHs)

BURLTON   Map 15 SJ42

Burlton Inn

★★★★ 🍽 INN

SY4 5TB
☎ 01939 270284
e-mail: enquiries@burltoninn.com
dir: A528 Ellesmere to Shrewsbury road

This 18th-century building, in its own grounds, is
situated between Shrewsbury and Ellesmere. Hosts,
Lindsay and Paul, and their staff offer a warm welcome
to all guests. The en suite bedrooms are furnished in a
modern style and located in a separate building at the
rear. Classic cuisine, using fresh, locally sourced
ingredients, is offered. There is a terrace area for guests
to enjoy on warmer days.

Rooms 6 en suite (3 GF) S £68-£95; D £68-£95*
Facilities FTV tea/coffee Dinner available Cen ht Wi-fi 🕑
Parking 30 **Notes** ✖ Closed 24-26 Dec RS Sun eve
closed No coaches

CHURCH STRETTON   Map 15 SO49

PREMIER COLLECTION

Field House

★★★★★ GUEST HOUSE

Cardington Moor, Cardington SY6 7LL
☎ 01694 771485
e-mail: pjsecrett@talktalk.net
dir: A49 onto B4371 at lights in Church Stretton. Left
after 3.5m signed Cardington, left in 1m, house 0.5m
on right

This delightful old cottage is set by nine acres of
grounds and gardens quietly located in a picturesque
valley. It has been considerably renovated and
extended to provide tastefully appointed, modern
accommodation including a bedroom on the ground-
floor. Separate tables are provided in the pleasant
dining room where a hearty breakfast is served. There
is also a conservatory lounge with views out to the well
maintained gardens.

Rooms 3 en suite (1 GF) S £45; D £67-£71*
Facilities FTV Lounge tea/coffee Direct Dial Cen ht
Licensed Wi-fi Pool table 🕑 Table tennis
Extras Speciality toiletries, kitchen for guests' use
Parking 3 **Notes** ✖ Closed Nov-Feb 🐾

PREMIER COLLECTION

Willowfield Guest House

★★★★★ GUEST HOUSE

Lower Wood SY6 6LF
☎ 01694 751471
e-mail: willowfieldlowerwood@tiscali.co.uk
dir: A5 onto A49 to Leebotwood, follow sign for Lower
Wood, 0.5m on left

Set in spacious and immaculate gardens, this
Edwardian house, parts of which are much older,
provides high standards of comfort. The bedrooms are
well equipped and have many thoughtful extras as well
as stunning views, while stylish decor and period
furnishings add to the charm. A comfortable lounge is
available, plus two elegant dining rooms where hearty
breakfasts are served.

Rooms 4 en suite (1 GF) S £40-£45; D £60-£70*
Facilities FTV tea/coffee Cen ht **Parking** 6 **Notes** LB ✖

Belvedere Guest House

★★★★ GUEST HOUSE

Burway Rd SY6 6DP
☎ 01694 722232
e-mail: info@belvedereguesthouse.co.uk
dir: Exit A49 into town centre, over x-rds into Burway Rd

Popular with walkers and cyclists and located on the
lower slopes of the Long Mynd, this impressive, well-
proportioned Edwardian house has a range of homely
bedrooms, equipped with practical extras and
complemented by modern bathrooms. Ground-floor areas
include a cottage-style dining room overlooking the pretty
garden and a choice of lounges.

Rooms 7 rms (6 en suite) (2 fmly) S £34-£40; D £58-£68
Facilities TVL tea/coffee Cen ht Wi-fi 🕑 **Extras** Mini-fridge,
snacks, water - chargeable **Parking** 9 **Notes** LB

Brereton's Farm (SO424871)

★★★★ FARMHOUSE

Woolston SY6 6QD
☎ 01694 781201 📠 01694 781201 Mrs J Brereton
e-mail: info@breretonsfarm.co.uk
web: www.breretonsfarm.co.uk
dir: A49 N from Craven Arms, at Jewsons turn left A489.
Under bridge turn right Wistonstow, top of village signed
left 1.75m to Woolston. Farm on right

Located among undulating hills in the pretty hamlet of
Woolston, this impressive early-Victorian red-brick house
provides thoughtfully equipped bedrooms with stunning
country views. Comprehensive breakfasts are served in
an elegant dining room, and the lounge has a wood-
burning fire.

Rooms 2 en suite **Facilities** TVL tea/coffee Cen ht
Parking 6 **Notes** ✖ Closed 30 Nov-Mar 🐾 350 acres
mixed

CHURH STRETTON *continued*

The Bucks Head

★★★★ INN

42 High St SY6 6BX
☎ 01694 722898 & 07811 364416
e-mail: lloyd.nutting@btconnect.com
web: www.the-bucks-head.co.uk
dir: *A49 N or S, turn into Church Stretton. At top of town turn left, Bucks Head on right*

Located in the heart of an historic market town, this period hostelry has become a vibrant modern inn after a total renovation. There are high levels of comfort and up-to-date facilities together with original charm and character. The comfortable bedrooms are complemented by smart en suite bathrooms, and the attractive open-plan public areas are the perfect setting for enjoying food and drinks. The hospitality is warm and genuine.

Rooms 4 en suite **Facilities** FTV tea/coffee Dinner available Cen ht Wi-fi **Notes** ⊗ No Children 5yrs No coaches

Court Farm *(SO514951)*

★★★★ FARMHOUSE

Gretton SY6 7HU
☎ 01694 771219 ≣ 01694 771219 General Manager
e-mail: alison@courtfarm.eu
dir: *Turn off B4371 at Longville, left at x-rds, 1st on left*

Located in the pretty village of Gretton, this 17th-century impressive stone-built Tudor house has been sympathetically renovated to provide high standards of comfort and facilities. The bedrooms overlook the pretty gardens and are equipped with a wealth of thoughtful extras. Comprehensive breakfasts are taken in an elegant dining room and a comfortable guest lounge is also available.

Rooms 2 en suite S £40; D £65-£70* **Facilities** FTV TVL tea/coffee Cen ht **Parking** 4 **Notes** ⊗ No Children 12yrs 🐾 330 acres mixed

North Hill Farm

★★★★ BED AND BREAKFAST

Cardington SY6 7LL
☎ 01694 771532
e-mail: cbrandon@btinternet.com
dir: *From Cardington S onto Church Stretton road, right signed Cardington Moor, farm at top of hill on left*

This delightful house has been modernised to provide comfortable accommodation. It is located on a fairly remote 20-acre sheep-rearing holding amid the Shropshire hills and wonderful views can be seen from the property. There is a small but cosy sitting area in the main house for guests to relax in. Guests sit at one large table in the breakfast room. There are two bedrooms in the main house and a further two in different buildings; one provides high quality, spacious family accommodation.

Rooms 2 rms (2 pri facs) 2 annexe en suite (2 GF) S £35-£45; D £56-£80* **Facilities** FTV Lounge tea/coffee Cen ht Wi-fi 🐾 **Parking** 6 **Notes** LB Closed Xmas 🐾

Castle View

★★★★ BED AND BREAKFAST

Stokesay SY7 9AL
☎ 01588 673712
e-mail: castleviewb_b@btinternet.com
dir: *On A49 S of Craven Arms opposite turn to Stokesay Castle*

The Victorian cottage, extended about 20 years ago, stands in delightful gardens on the southern outskirts of Craven Arms, close to Stokesay Castle. Bedrooms are thoughtfully furnished, and breakfasts, featuring local produce, are served in the cosy, traditionally furnished dining room.

Rooms 3 rms (1 en suite) (2 pri facs) S £35-£40; D £60-£70* **Facilities** FTV tea/coffee Cen ht 🐾 **Parking** 4 **Notes** LB No Children 3yrs 🐾

Strefford Hall Farm *(SO444856)*

★★★★ FARMHOUSE

Strefford SY7 8DE
☎ 01588 672383 ≣ 0870 132 3818 Mrs C Morgan
e-mail: strefford@btconnect.com
dir: *A49 from Church Stretton, S for 5.5m to Strefford, 0.25m past Travellers Rest Inn signed left. Strefford Hall 0.25m on right*

This well-proportioned Victorian house stands at the foot of Wenlock Edge. The spacious bedrooms, filled with homely extras, have stunning views of the surrounding countryside. Breakfast is served in the elegant dining room and a comfortable lounge is also available.

Rooms 3 en suite (1 fmly) (3 smoking) **Facilities** TVL tea/coffee Cen ht **Parking** 3 **Notes** ⊗ RS end Feb-end Oct 🐾 350 acres arable/beef/sheep/pigs

Caro's Bed & Breakfast

★★★ BED AND BREAKFAST

1 Higher Netley SY5 7JY
☎ 01743 718790 & 07739 285263
e-mail: info@carosbandb.co.uk
dir: *1m SW of Dorrington. Exit A49 in Dorrington signed Picklescott, 1m left onto driveway by stone bridge, signed Higher Netley*

Self-contained accommodation is provided in this converted barn, south-west of Dorrington. Bedrooms, with smart modern bathrooms, are equipped with thoughtful extras and the open-plan ground floor contains a dining area and a comfortable lounge with a wood-burning stove.

Rooms 2 en suite (1 fmly) S £40-£60; D £60
Facilities FTV DVD Lounge tea/coffee Cen ht Wi-fi 🐾 **Parking** 4 **Notes** LB Closed 21-28 Dec 🐾

The Inn at Grinshill

★ ★ ★ ★ ★ ⚜⚜ INN

The High St SY4 3BL
☎ 01939 220410 ≣ 01939 220397
e-mail: info@theinnatgrinshill.co.uk
dir: *N of Shrewsbury on A49, after 7m turn left, inn 500yds on left*

This inn is part Grade II listed and many areas have been restored to highlight the original features. It is located under the lee of Grinshill in a delightful village with beautiful countryside close by; the Welsh border is within easy driving distance as are Shrewsbury, Telford and Welshpool. The accommodation is comfortable and real ales and award-winning food is available in spacious restaurant. Guests are very welcome to make use of the grounds.

Rooms 6 en suite **Facilities** FTV Dinner available Cen ht Wi-fi 🦽 ♿ 36 **Parking** 30 **Notes** No coaches

Saracens at Hadnall

★★★★ ⚜⚜ RESTAURANT WITH ROOMS

Shrewsbury Rd SY4 4AG
☎ 01939 210877 ≣ 01939 210877
e-mail: reception@saracensathadnall.co.uk
web: www.saracensathadnall.co.uk
dir: *M54 onto A5 towards Shrewsbury, take A49 towards Whitchurch. In Hadnall, property diagonally opposite church*

This Georgian Grade II listed former farmhouse and village pub has been tastefully converted into a very smart restaurant with rooms, without any loss of original charm and character. The bedrooms are thoughtfully equipped. Skilfully prepared meals are served in either the elegant dining room or the adjacent conservatory where there is a glass-topped well.

Rooms 5 en suite S £35-£45; D £60-£85* **Facilities** tea/coffee Dinner available Cen ht **Parking** 20 **Notes** LB ⊗ Closed 26-31 Dec RS Sun eve-Mon closed No coaches

Save on B&Bs and Hotels. Book at **theAA.com/hotel**

SHROPSHIRE 245 ENGLAND

IRONBRIDGE
Map 10 SJ60

PREMIER COLLECTION

The Library House
★★★★ GUEST ACCOMMODATION

11 Severn Bank TF8 7AN
☎ 01952 432299
e-mail: info@libraryhouse.com
web: www.libraryhouse.com
dir: *50yds from Iron Bridge*

A warm welcome is assured at this renovated Georgian house, once the local library. In keeping with its history the bedrooms are named after notable writers. They are beautifully appointed and provide a wealth of thoughtful extras. Gardens are immaculate and stunning when in flower. The Garden Room, very popular in summer, has a small private outdoor seating area. Memorable breakfasts are served in the elegant dining room, and a comfortable guest lounge is also available.

Rooms 4 en suite **Facilities** FTV TVL tea/coffee Cen ht Licensed Wi-fi **Notes** ⊗ No Children

Broseley House
★ ★ ★ ★ GUEST HOUSE

1 The Square, Broseley TF12 5EW
☎ 01952 882043 & 07790 732723
e-mail: info@broseleyhouse.co.uk
web: www.broseleyhouse.co.uk
dir: *1m S of Ironbridge in Broseley town centre*

A warm welcome is assured at this impressive Georgian house in the centre of Broseley. Quality, individual decor and soft furnishings highlight the many original features, and the thoughtfully furnished bedrooms are equipped with a wealth of homely extras. Comprehensive breakfasts are taken in an elegant dining room; a stylish apartment is also available.

Rooms 7 en suite (2 fmly) (2 GF) S £50-£60; D £70-£90* **Facilities** FTV DVD iPod docking station tea/coffee Cen ht Wi-fi ⌁ **Extras** Fridges **Notes** LB No Children 5yrs

LUDLOW
Map 10 SO57

PREMIER COLLECTION

The Clive Bar & Restaurant with Rooms
★ ★ ★ ★ ★ @@ RESTAURANT WITH ROOMS

Bromfield SY8 2JR
☎ 01584 856565 & 856665 📄 01584 856661
e-mail: info@theclive.co.uk
web: www.theclive.co.uk
dir: *2m N of Ludlow on A49 in Bromfield*

The Clive is just two miles from the busy town of Ludlow and is a convenient base for visiting the local attractions or for business. The bedrooms, located outside the main restaurant area, are spacious and very well equipped; some are suitable for families and many are on the ground-floor level. Meals are available in the well-known Clive Restaurant or in the bar areas. The property also has a small meeting room.

Rooms 15 annexe en suite (9 fmly) (11 GF) S £68-£95; D £95-£120* **Facilities** FTV tea/coffee Dinner available Direct Dial Cen ht Wi-fi **Extras** Mini-bar with local produce **Conf** Max 40 Thtr 40 Class 40 Board 24 **Parking** 100 **Notes** LB ⊗ Closed 25-26 Dec

PREMIER COLLECTION

De Greys of Ludlow
★ ★ ★ ★ ★ GUEST HOUSE

5-6 Broad St SY8 1NG
☎ 01584 872764 📄 01584 879764
e-mail: degreys@btopenworld.com
web: www.degreys.co.uk
dir: *Off A49, in town centre, 50yds beyond clock tower*

This 16th-century timber-framed property is situated in the town centre. It provides high quality accommodation with modern facilities, including two suites and one bedroom on the ground floor level; all rooms have an electronic security system. Careful renovation of the original beams combined with lush fabrics and beautiful wooden furniture has created a successful fusion of the past and present. Breakfast is taken in the adjacent tearoom/restaurant and bakery shop.

Rooms 9 en suite (1 GF) **Facilities** tea/coffee Cen ht Licensed **Notes** ⊗ Closed 26 Dec & 1 Jan

LUDLOW *continued*

Number Twenty Eight

★ ★ ★ ★ 🏠 BED AND BREAKFAST

28 Lower Broad St SY8 1PQ
☎ 01584 875466
e-mail: enquiries@no28ludlow.co.uk
dir: *In town centre. Over Ludford Bridge into Lower Broad St, 3rd house on right*

A warm welcome is assured at this 200-year-old property just a stroll from the centre. There are two double bedrooms, each well-equipped and containing thoughtful extras and welcoming touches. Day rooms include an antique furnished combined lounge and sitting room, and a small roof terrace that overlooks the pretty rear garden.

Rooms 2 en suite S £65-£75; D £85-£90 **Facilities** FTV Lounge tea/coffee Cen ht Wi-fi **Notes** ⊗ No Children 16yrs Closed Nov-May

37 Gravel Hill

★ ★ ★ ★ BED AND BREAKFAST

SY8 1QR
☎ 01584 877524
e-mail: angelastraker@btinternet.com
dir: *Close to town centre*

This charming old house is within walking distance of the town centre. It provides good quality, thoughtfully equipped accommodation, and there is also a comfortable sitting room. Guests share one large table in the elegant breakfast room.

Rooms 2 rms (1 en suite) (1 pri facs) **Facilities** TVL tea/coffee Cen ht Wi-fi **Notes** ◉

Angel House

★ ★ ★ ★ BED AND BREAKFAST

Angel Bank, Bitterley SY8 3HT
☎ 01584 891377 🖳 08723 520921
e-mail: angelhousebandb@googlemail.com
dir: *On A4117, 4m E of Ludlow on Clee Hill*

Located in an elevated position four miles from Ludlow, this sympathetically renovated 17th-century former pub provides high standards of comfort and facilities. Thoughtfully furnished bedrooms have stunning rural views, and comprehensive breakfasts are served in the attractive dining room. A guest lounge is also available and a warm welcome is assured.

Rooms 2 en suite (1 fmly) S £65; D £80* **Facilities** FTV DVD Lounge tea/coffee Dinner available Cen ht Wi-fi ❀ **Extras** Snacks **Parking** 7 **Notes** No Children 7yrs

The Charlton Arms

★ ★ ★ ★ 🍴 INN

Ludford Bridge SY8 1PJ
☎ 01584 872813
dir: *From town centre into Broad St, over Ludford Bridge. Charlton Arms on right*

The accommodation at this riverside inn reflects the character of the historic building whilst offering all the comforts of modern living. The restaurant provides fresh locally-sourced ingredients, and as a free house also offers a fine selection of local beers. There is one bedroom which has a private terrace and a hot tub, and there are decking areas to enjoy drinks or a meal on warmer days.

Rooms 10 en suite (2 fmly) **Facilities** tea/coffee Dinner available Cen ht Wi-fi Fishing **Conf** Max 100 Thtr 100 Class 80 Board 70 **Parking** 25 **Notes** Civ Wed 80

The Church Inn

★ ★ ★ ★ INN

The Buttercross SY8 1AW
☎ 01584 872174 🖳 01584 877146
web: www.thechurchinn.com
dir: *In town centre at top of Broad St, behind Buttercross*

Set right in the heart of the historic town, this Grade II listed inn has been renovated to provide quality accommodation with smart modern bathrooms, some with spa baths. Other areas include a small lounge, a well-equipped meeting room, and cosy bar areas where imaginative food and real ales are served.

Rooms 10 en suite (3 fmly) **Facilities** TVL tea/coffee Dinner available Direct Dial Cen ht **Conf** Max 38 **Notes** No coaches

Haynall Villa *(SO543674)*

★ ★ ★ ★ FARMHOUSE

Little Hereford SY8 4BG
☎ 01584 711589 🖳 01584 711589 Mrs R Edwards
e-mail: rachelmedwards@hotmail.com
web: www.haynallvilla.co.uk
dir: *A49 onto A456, at Little Hereford right signed Leysters & Middleton on the Hill. Villa 1m on right*

Located in immaculate gardens in the pretty hamlet of Little Hereford, this Victorian house retains many original features, which are enhanced by the furnishings and decor. Bedrooms are filled with lots of homely extras and the lounge has an open fire.

Rooms 3 rms (2 en suite) (1 pri facs) (1 fmly) **Facilities** FTV TVL tea/coffee Dinner available Cen ht Wi-fi Fishing **Parking** 3 **Notes** No Children 6yrs Closed mid Dec-mid Jan ◉ 72 acres arable

Moor Hall

★ ★ ★ ★ GUEST HOUSE

Cleedownton SY8 3EG
☎ 01584 823209
e-mail: enquiries@moorhall.co.uk
dir: *From A4117 (Ludlow to Kidderminster) left to Bridgnorth. B4364, 3.2m, Moor Hall on right*

This impressive Georgian house, once the home of Lord Boyne, is surrounded by extensive gardens and farmland. Bedrooms are richly decorated, well equipped, and one room has a sitting area. Public areas are spacious and comfortably furnished. There is a choice of sitting rooms and a library bar. Guests dine family-style in an elegant dining room.

Rooms 3 en suite S £40-£45; D £70-£80* **Facilities** FTV Lounge tea/coffee Dinner available Cen ht Licensed Wi-fi ❀ **Parking** 7 **Notes** LB Closed 25-26 Dec ◉

130 Corve Street

★ ★ ★ ★ BED AND BREAKFAST

130 Corve St SY8 2PG
☎ 01584 875548 🖳 08723 523397
e-mail: info@130corvestreet.co.uk
dir: *N side of town on B4361, adjacent to Tesco supermarket*

Expect a warm welcome at this Grade II listed building, situated within easy access of the town's many interesting attractions and restaurants. The attractive bedrooms, situated on the ground floor at the rear, are comfortable and have their own independent entrances. Hearty breakfasts are served in the first-floor dining room. There is off-road parking close by.

Rooms 3 en suite (3 GF) **Facilities** FTV tea/coffee Cen ht Wi-fi **Parking** 3 **Notes** ⊗ No Children 12yrs

Tean House

★ ★ ★ ★ BED AND BREAKFAST

8 Ledwyche Close, Middleton SY8 3EP
☎ 01584 875891
e-mail: tean.bandb@btinternet.com
dir: *A4117 onto B4364, 0.7m on right*

Located in a small rural hamlet a few minutes' drive from the town centre, this impressive modern detached house offers comfortable bedrooms equipped with a range of homely extras. Comprehensive breakfasts provide a good start to the day and a warm welcome is assured.

Rooms 3 rms (1 en suite) (1 pri facs) (2 fmly) S £42; D £65* **Facilities** FTV DVD TVL tea/coffee Cen ht Wi-fi ❀ **Extras** Snacks, bottled water - complimentary **Parking** 3 **Notes** ⊗ No Children 5yrs

Save on B&Bs and Hotels. Book at theAA.com/hotel

SHROPSHIRE 247 ENGLAND

MARKET DRAYTON Map 15 SJ63

PREMIER COLLECTION

Ternhill Farm House & The Cottage Restaurant

★★★★★ ◉◉ 🍴 RESTAURANT WITH ROOMS

Ternhill TF9 3PX
☎ 01630 638984
e-mail: info@ternhillfarm.co.uk
web: www.ternhillfarm.co.uk
dir: On junct A53 & A41, archway off A53 to back of property

This elegant Grade II listed Georgian farmhouse stands in a large pleasant garden and has been modernised to provide quality accommodation. There is a choice of comfortable lounges, and The Cottage Restaurant features imaginative dishes using local produce. Secure parking is an additional benefit.

Rooms 7 rms (6 en suite) (1 pri facs) (2 fmly) S £45-£65; D £70-£90* Facilities FTV DVD Lounge tea/coffee Dinner available Cen ht Wi-fi Extras Speciality toiletries Parking 18 Notes LB ⊗

The Four Alls Inn

★★★ INN

Woodseaves TF9 2AG
☎ 01630 652995 ▤ 01630 653930
e-mail: inn@thefouralls.com
web: www.thefouralls.com
dir: On A529 1m S of Market Drayton

This country inn provides spacious open-plan public areas and has a strong local following for its food and real ales. Bedrooms, which are in a purpose-built chalet block, offer a good balance between practicality and homeliness. The superb beer gardens are adorned with attractive floral displays in summer.

Rooms 9 annexe en suite (4 fmly) (9 GF) S £47; D £67-£70* Facilities FTV tea/coffee Dinner available Direct Dial Cen ht Wi-fi ⚓ Conf Max 100 Thtr 100 Class 100 Board 30 Parking 60 Notes LB ⊗ Closed 24-26 Dec

The Tudor House

★★★ INN

1 Cheshire St TF9 1PD
☎ 01630 657523 & 01257 248012 ▤ 01630 657806
e-mail: tudor@alfatravel.co.uk
web: www.thetudorhousehotel.com
dir: A53 onto A529 (Adderley Rd), at next rdbt 2nd exit into Cheshire St

This beautiful property and former coaching inn is located in the heart of the town and has a public bar full of character. The fully equipped bedrooms are well laid out and are equally suited to both business and leisure guests. Parking is shared with a hotel just a short distance away.

Rooms 10 en suite (3 fmly) S £45-£55; D £70-£90 Facilities FTV TVL tea/coffee Dinner available Cen ht Wi-fi ⚓ Extras Speciality toiletries - complimentary Conf Thtr 40 Class 6 Board 12 Notes ⊗ No coaches

MARTON Map 15 SJ20

The Lowfied Inn

★★★★ ⚑ INN

SY21 9JX
☎ 01743 891313
e-mail: lowfieldinn@tiscali.co.uk
dir: From A5 (Shrewsbury ring road) onto B4386 signed Montgomery

Rooms 4 en suite (1 fmly) S £50; D £70 Facilities FTV DVD tea/coffee Dinner available Cen ht Wi-fi Pool table ⚓ Parking 30

MUCH WENLOCK Map 10 SO69

Yew Tree Farm (SO543958)

★★★★ ⚑ FARMHOUSE

Longville in the Dale TF13 6EB
☎ 01694 771866 Mr & Mrs Hilbery
e-mail: enquiries@yewtreefarmshropshire.co.uk
dir: 5m SW of Much Wenlock. N off B4371 at Longville, left at pub, right at x-rds, farm 1.2m on right

Yew Tree Farm is peacefully located between Much Wenlock and Church Stretton, in ten acres of unspoiled countryside, where pigs, sheep and chickens are reared. Own produce is a feature on the comprehensive breakfast menu, bedrooms are equipped with thoughtful extras, and a warm welcome is assured.

Rooms 2 rms (1 en suite) (1 pri facs) S £35-£45; D £60-£70* Facilities FTV TVL tea/coffee Cen ht Wi-fi ⚓ Extras Snacks, bottled water Parking 4 Notes LB Closed 24-30 Dec ⊜ 10 acres small holding/sheep/pigs

Talbot Inn

★★★ ⚑ INN

High St TF13 6AA
☎ 01952 727077 ▤ 01952 728436
e-mail: the_talbot_inn@hotmail.com
web: www.the-talbot-inn.com
dir: In village centre on A458

Rooms 6 annexe en suite (1 GF) Facilities TVL tea/coffee Dinner available Cen ht Parking 6 Notes ⊗ Closed 25 Dec

MUNSLOW Map 10 SO58

Crown Country Inn

★★★★ ◉◉ 🍴 INN

SY7 9ET
☎ 01584 841205
e-mail: info@crowncountryinn.co.uk
dir: Off B4368 into village

Located between Much Wenlock and Craven Arms, this impressive pastel-coloured and half-timbered Tudor inn is full of character and charm with stone floors, exposed beams and blazing log fires during winter. The smart pine-furnished bedrooms are in a converted stable block, and the spacious public areas include two dining rooms.

Rooms 3 en suite (1 fmly) (1 GF) S £65-£110; D £95-£110* Facilities DVD tea/coffee Dinner available Cen ht Wi-fi Extras Fruit Conf Max 30 Thtr 30 Class 30 Board 20 Parking 20 Notes LB ⊗ Closed 25 Dec RS Closed Sun eve & Mon for food & drink

NEWPORT Map 15 SJ71

Moreton Hall Farm B&B

★★★★ GUEST HOUSE

Moreton TF10 9DY
☎ 01952 691544 & 07816 755045
e-mail: sarabloor@moretonhallfarm.com
web: www.moretonhallfarm.com
dir: Exit M54 junct 3, A41 Chester. Turn right Stockton, Moreton, Church Eaton 1.5m, turn left to farm

Peacefully located close to major road links, a warm welcome is assured at this 18th-century farmhouse, which stands in pretty mature gardens and benefits from a swimming pool. Bedrooms are equipped with lots of homely extras, and locally-sourced produce is featured in the breakfast selection.

Rooms 3 rms (2 en suite) (1 pri facs) (1 fmly) S £35-£100; D £55-£150* Facilities FTV DVD tea/coffee Cen ht Wi-fi ⚓ ⚓ Extras Fresh milk, bottled water Parking 6 Notes ⊗ ⊜

NORTON Map 10 SJ70

The Hundred House

★★★★ @@ INN

Bridgnorth Rd TF11 9EE
☎ 01952 580240 & 0845 644 6100 ⓘ 01952 580260
e-mail: reservations@hundredhouse.co.uk
dir: *M54 junct 5, follow signs for Bridgnorth (A442),
midway between Bridgnorth & Telford*

This unique property holds a genuine rural charm, setting
it apart from the modern style of country 'food
destination' pubs. A rabbit warren of public bars and
restaurants, it provides respite for weary travellers and
locals alike, many of whom come for the excellent meals.
Bedrooms are individually designed, with quirky
furnishings and decor, and are well equipped. A large
beer garden provides for good weather, with well stocked
herb and flower gardens to encourage a wander.

Rooms 9 en suite (4 fmly) S £65-£99; D £69-£140*
Facilities FTV tea/coffee Dinner available Direct Dial
Cen ht Wi-fi ♨ 18 ♦ **Extras** Water, sweets **Conf** Max 100
Thtr 80 Class 30 Board 35 **Parking** 50 **Notes** LB Civ Wed
120

OSWESTRY Map 15 SJ22

PREMIER COLLECTION

Greystones

★ ☕ GUEST HOUSE

Crickheath SY10 8BW
☎ 07976 740141
e-mail: enquiry@stayatgreystones.co.uk
web: www.stayatgreystones.co.uk
dir: *From A483 follow B4396, turn right through village
take No Through Road, Greystones on right*

A warm welcome is assured at this impressive
detached house, located on pretty, mature gardens in
the hamlet of Crickheath. The bedrooms are equipped
with a wealth of thoughtful extras and smart modern
bathrooms. Comprehensive breakfasts and imaginative
dinners, featuring the best seasonal produce, are
available in the elegant dining room. A comfortable
guest lounge is also available.

Rooms 3 en suite (2 fmly) **Facilities** FTV TVL tea/coffee
Dinner available Cen ht Licensed Wi-fi ⤸ Fishing
Conf Board 10 **Parking** 20 **Notes** ⊗ No Children 14yrs

The Pentre

★★★★ ☕ GUEST HOUSE

Trefonen SY10 9EE
☎ 01691 653952
e-mail: helen@thepentre.com
web: www.thepentre.com
dir: *4m SW of Oswestry. Exit Oswestry-Treflach road into
New Well Ln, The Pentre signed*

This 500-year-old stone farmhouse retains many original
features, including a wealth of exposed beams and a
superb inglenook fireplace with blazing wood burner
during colder months. Bedrooms are equipped with a
range of thoughtful extras, and breakfast and dinner are
memorable, with quality produce cooked with flair on an
Aga.

Rooms 3 en suite (1 fmly) (1 GF) **Facilities** FTV TVL tea/
coffee Dinner available Cen ht ♦ **Parking** 10 **Notes** LB ⊗
⊜

The Bradford Arms

★★★★ INN

Llanymynech SY22 6EJ
☎ 01691 830582 ⓘ 01691 839009
e-mail: catelou@tesco.net
web: www.bradfordarmshotel.com
dir: *5.5m S of Oswestry on A483 in Llanymynech*

Once a coaching inn on the Earl of Bradford's estate, The
Bradford Arms provides a range of carefully furnished
bedrooms with a wealth of thoughtful extras. The elegant
ground-floor areas include lounges, bars, and a choice of
formal or conservatory restaurants, the settings for
imaginative food and fine wines.

Rooms 5 en suite (2 fmly) (2 GF) S £40; D £60*
Facilities FTV tea/coffee Dinner available Direct Dial
Cen ht Wi-fi ♨ 18 Fishing Riding Pool table ♦ **Parking** 20

Riseholme

★★★★ BED AND BREAKFAST

4 Hampton Rd SY11 1SJ
☎ 01691 656508
e-mail: ssparnell1234@googlemail.com

Located in a residential area within easy walking
distance of the town centre, via the attractive memorial
gardens, this attractive house offers comfortable
bedrooms complemented by smart modern bathrooms.
Comprehensive breakfasts are taken in a cosy dining
room and a spacious guest lounge is also available.

Rooms 3 en suite (1 fmly) **Facilities** TVL tea/coffee Cen ht
Wi-fi **Parking** 5 **Notes** No Children 12yrs ⊜

Carreg-Y-big Farm

★★★ BED AND BREAKFAST

Carreg-y-big, Selattyn SY10 7HX
☎ 01691 654754
e-mail: info@carreg-y-bigfarm.co.uk
dir: *Off B4580 at Old Racecourse, signed Selattyn. 1m on
right on Offa's Dyke*

Incorporated within The Oswestry Equestrian Centre on
the edge of Selattyn, this former farmhouse provides a
range of simply appointed bedrooms, ideal for walkers on
nearby Offas's Dyke. Comprehensive breakfasts, and
dinners by arrangement, are served at one table in an
attractive beamed dining room; a small guest lounge is
also available.

Rooms 4 rms (1 pri facs) (1 GF) **Facilities** TVL Dinner
available Cen ht Riding **Parking** 10 **Notes** ⊜

RUYTON-XI-TOWNS Map 15 SJ32

Brownhill House

★★★ BED AND BREAKFAST

SY4 1LR
☎ 01939 261121 ⓘ 01939 260626
e-mail: brownhill@eleventowns.co.uk
web: www.eleventowns.co.uk
dir: *A5 onto B4397, 2m to Ruyton-XI-Towns. Through
village. Brownhill House on left at right bend*

A warm welcome is assured at this charming house,
parts of which date from the 18th century. The large
terraced garden has been painstakingly created on the
side of a steep hill above the River Perry, and guests are
welcome to explore. All bedrooms have modern facilities
and guests share one large table in a cosy kitchen-dining
room.

Rooms 3 en suite (1 GF) S £31.50-£35; D £55-£66*
Facilities DVD TVL tea/coffee Cen ht Wi-fi ⤸ Fishing ♦
Parking 5 **Notes** LB ⊗ RS Xmas

Save on B&Bs and Hotels. Book at theAA.com/hotel

SHROPSHIRE 249 **ENGLAND**

SHIFNAL
Map 10 SJ70

The Anvil Lodge
★★★★ GUEST ACCOMMODATION

22 Aston Rd TF11 8DU
☎ 01952 460125 📠 01952 460125
e-mail: michaeldavies234@btinternet.com

A friendly welcome is assured at Anvil Lodge, just a short stroll from the market town of Shifnal. Delicious, freshly cooked breakfasts are served around the dining room table. The bedrooms are spacious, fresh in appearance and very comfortable with modern bathrooms complete with bath and separate shower. Off-road secure parking is available.

Rooms 4 annexe en suite (2 fmly) (2 GF) **Facilities** FTV Cen ht **Parking** 8 **Notes** ⊗

SHREWSBURY
Map 15 SJ41

See also Criggion (Powys), Ruyton-XI-Towns, Wem & Westbury

PREMIER COLLECTION

Drapers Hall
★★★★★ ◉◉ RESTAURANT WITH ROOMS

10 Saint Mary's Place SY1 1DZ
☎ 01743 344679
e-mail: goodfood@drapershallrestaurant.co.uk
dir: From A5191 (Saint Mary's St) on one-way system into St Mary's Place

This 16th-century timber-framed property is situated in the heart of the market town of Shrewsbury. It provides high quality accommodation, including two suites, with modern facilities. Careful renovation of the original beams and wood panels together with beautiful wooden furniture has created a harmony of the past and present. Accomplished dining, headed up by Nigel Huxley, can be enjoyed in the main restaurant, Huxleys at Drapers Hall.

Rooms 4 en suite (2 fmly) **Facilities** FTV TVL tea/coffee Dinner available Cen ht Wi-fi **Conf** Max 20 Thtr 20 Class 20 Board 20 **Notes** ⊗

PREMIER COLLECTION

Mad Jack's Restaurant & Bar
★★★★★ ◉ RESTAURANT WITH ROOMS

15 Saint Mary's St SY1 1EQ
☎ 01743 358870 & 761220 📠 01743 344422
e-mail: info@madjacks.uk.com
dir: Follow one-way system around town, opposite St Mary's church

This fine property is located in the heart of the town. Its name comes from a eccentric squire in the 18th century who squandered a fortune and then landed in jail for his drunken and riotous behaviour. The four individually designed bedrooms, including a suite, are very comfortable and have spacious and contemporary bathrooms. Downstairs the award-winning, vibrant bar and restaurant specialises in British food with a classic twist. Breakfast offers a quality range of dishes. Secure parking is available in a nearby public car park.

Rooms 4 en suite (1 fmly) S £70-£100; D £80-£145* **Facilities** tea/coffee Dinner available Cen ht Wi-fi **Notes** LB ⊗ Closed 25 Dec No coaches

Tudor House
★★★★ 🏠 GUEST HOUSE

2 Fish St SY1 1UR
☎ 01743 351735 & 07870 653040
e-mail: enquiry@tudorhouseshrewsbury.co.uk
web: www.tudorhouseshrewsbury.co.uk
dir: Enter town over English Bridge, ascend Wyle Cop, in 50yds take 1st right

Located in the beautiful medieval town centre, this fine 15th-century house has original beams and fireplaces, enhanced by the stylish decor and furnishings. The bedrooms are filled with thoughtful extras, and breakfast features local organic produce.

Rooms 3 rms (2 en suite) (1 pri facs) **Facilities** tea/coffee Cen ht **Notes** ⊗ No Children 11yrs 🍽

TELFORD
Map 10 SJ60

Church Farm Guest House & Basils Restaurant
★★★★★ ◉ 🏠 GUEST ACCOMMODATION

Wrockwardine Village, Wellington TF6 5DG
☎ 01952 251927 & 07976 897528 📠 01952 427511
e-mail: info@churchfarm-shropshire.co.uk
dir: M54 junct 7 towards Wellington, 1st left, 1st right, right at end of road. 0.5m on left opposite St Peters Church

Located in the pretty rural village of Wrockwardine, this impressive period former farmhouse provides high standards of comfort and good facilities. Attractive bedrooms, furnished in minimalist style, offer a wealth of thoughtful extras including complimentary Wi-fi. The spacious day rooms include a comfortable lounge and an elegant dining room, the setting for imaginative cooking.

Rooms 4 rms (3 en suite) (1 pri facs) S £55-£65; D £70-£85* **Facilities** FTV DVD tea/coffee Dinner available Cen ht Wi-fi ⊥ 18 🔒 **Conf** Max 20 Class 20 Board 14 **Parking** 12 **Notes** LB

WELLINGTON
Map 10 SJ61

The Old Orleton Inn
★★★★★ 🅰 INN

Holyhead Rd TF1 2HA
☎ 01952 255011 & 07515 352538
e-mail: info@theoldorleton.com
dir: M54 junct 7, towards Wellington then 400yds on left on corner of Haygate Rd & Holyhead Rd

Rooms 10 en suite S £79-£89; D £79-£118* **Facilities** FTV iPod docking station tea/coffee Dinner available Direct Dial Cen ht Wi-fi ⊥ 18 Discounted access to local gym/spa **Conf** Max 15 Thtr 15 Class 15 Board 15 **Parking** 25 **Notes** LB ⊗ No Children 5yrs Closed 1st 2wks Jan

Clairmont Guest House
★★★★ 🅰 GUEST HOUSE

54 Haygate Rd TF1 1QN
☎ 01952 414214 & 07590 335000 📠 01952 897997
e-mail: info@clairmontguesthouse.co.uk

Rooms 5 en suite (1 fmly) (2 GF) S £40-£45; D £65-£70* **Facilities** FTV DVD iPod docking station tea/coffee Cen ht Wi-fi 🔒 **Extras** Mini-bar, bottled water **Parking** 5 **Notes** ⊗

WEM
Map 15 SJ52

Soulton Hall

★★★★ 🍽 GUEST ACCOMMODATION

Soulton SY4 5RS
☎ 01939 232786 📠 01939 234097
e-mail: enquiries@soultonhall.co.uk
web: www.soultonhall.co.uk
dir: From A49 between Shrewsbury & Whitchurch take B5065 towards Wem. Soulton Hall 2m E of Wem

Located two miles from historic Wem, this 16th-century manor house incorporates part of an even older building. The house stands in 560 acres and provides high levels of comfort. Bedrooms are equipped with homely extras and the ground-floor areas include a spacious hall-sitting room, lounge-bar and an attractive dining room, the setting for imaginative dinners.

Rooms 4 en suite 3 annexe en suite (2 fmly) (3 GF) **Facilities** FTV tea/coffee Dinner available Direct Dial Cen ht Licensed Wi-fi ch fac 🐾 ♿ 18 Fishing Birdwatching in 50 acre private woodland **Conf** Max 100 Thtr 100 Class 60 Board 50 **Parking** 52 **Notes** Civ Wed 450

WESTBURY
Map 15 SJ30

Barley Mow House

★★★★ BED AND BREAKFAST

Aston Rogers SY5 9HQ
☎ 01743 891234 📠 01743 891234
e-mail: colinrigby@astonrogers.fsnet.co.uk
web: www.barleymowhouse.co.uk
dir: 2m S of Westbury. Exit B4386 into Aston Rogers, house 400yds opposite Aston Hall

Dating in part from the 17th century and extended in the 18th, this charming property has been restored to provide comfortable accommodation with modern facilities. The house stands in a peaceful village and is surrounded by beautifully maintained gardens.

Rooms 3 en suite (1 fmly) (1 GF) **Facilities** FTV TVL tea/coffee Cen ht Wi-fi 🔒 **Parking** 4 **Notes** LB 🐾

SOMERSET

BALTONSBOROUGH
Map 4 ST53

Lower Farm (ST572346)

★★★★ FARMHOUSE

Lottisham BA6 8PF
☎ 01458 850206 & 07773 497188   Ms D Board
e-mail: dboard51@btinternet.com
dir: From Shepton Mallet take A37 over Wraxall Hill past Queens Arms. Follow road 3rd turning on right to Marsh Lottisham, 1st on right

Peacefully located and surrounded by pleasant countryside, this working farm offers a genuine welcome and traditional farmhouse hospitality. The one en suite bedroom is spacious and well equipped, and is located on the ground floor at one end of the main building. Breakfast is taken in the comfortable dining room where a wood-burning fire adds to the ambience during the winter.

Rooms 1 en suite (1 GF) **Facilities** FTV TVL tea/coffee Cen ht ♿ **Parking Notes** 🚭 🐾

BATCOMBE
Map 4 ST63

The Three Horseshoes Inn

★★★★ INN

BA4 6HE
☎ 01749 850359
e-mail: info@thethreehorseshoesinn.co.uk
dir: 3m from Bruton signed on A359

This traditional village inn has a delightful rural setting and provides a peaceful and relaxing stay. Welcoming hospitality combines with a fine selection of good food and real ales. Bedrooms, while not large, are comfortably furnished and well equipped. Guests have the option of sitting beside a log fire in the bar or relaxing in the garden depending on the season.

Rooms 3 en suite **Facilities** FTV tea/coffee Dinner available Cen ht Wi-fi **Parking** 30 **Notes** 🚭

BATH
Map 4 ST76

For other locations surrounding Bath see also Box (Wiltshire), Bradford on Avon (Wiltshire), Farmborough, Frome & Trowbridge (Wiltshire).

PREMIER COLLECTION

The Ayrlington

★★★★★ GUEST ACCOMMODATION

24/25 Pulteney Rd BA2 4EZ
☎ 01225 425495 📠 01225 469029
e-mail: mail@ayrlington.com
web: www.ayrlington.com
dir: A4 onto A36, pass Holburne Museum, premises 200yds on right

The charm of this impressive Victorian house is evident in the attractive exterior and throughout the rooms, many of which feature Oriental artefacts and pictures. The bedrooms, some with spa baths, four-poster beds and views over Bath cricket ground, are very comfortable. Breakfast is served in the elegant dining room, which shares the enjoyable view.

Rooms 16 en suite (3 fmly) (3 GF) **Facilities** tea/coffee Cen ht Licensed Wi-fi Unlimited free golf at local golf club **Conf** Max 20 **Parking** 16 **Notes** 🚭 No Children 14yrs Closed 22 Dec-5 Jan

PREMIER COLLECTION

One Three Nine

★★★★★ GUEST ACCOMMODATION

139 Wells Rd BA2 3AL
☎ 01225 314769 📠 01225 443079
e-mail: info@139bath.co.uk
dir: M4 junct 19, A46. A4 towards Bath, A367 towards Wells & Shepton Mallet. Establishment on left 500mtrs up hill

Overlooking the historic city of Bath, this quality establishment provides spacious accommodation paired with thoughtful design. The bedrooms are comfortably equipped with a very good range of accessories. A number of feature bathrooms add a dash of luxury. Breakfast is served in the bright and airy dining room, where an excellent choice of continental and hot items is available. Off-street parking is an advantage.

Rooms 10 en suite (1 fmly) (2 GF) S £69-£170; D £79-£190 **Facilities** FTV DVD tea/coffee Direct Dial Cen ht Wi-fi **Parking** 10 **Notes** 🚭 Closed 24-25 Dec

Save on B&Bs and Hotels. Book at **theAA.com/hotel**

SOMERSET 251 ENGLAND

PREMIER COLLECTION

Paradise House

★★★★★ GUEST ACCOMMODATION

Holloway BA2 4PX
☎ 01225 317723 📄 01225 482005
e-mail: info@paradise-house.co.uk
web: www.paradise-house.co.uk
dir: *A36 onto A367 (Wells Rd), 3rd left, down hill Into cul-de-sac, house 200yds on left*

Set in half an acre of lovely walled gardens, this Georgian house, built of mellow Bath stone, is within walking distance of the city centre. Many bedrooms have fine views over the city, and all are decorated in opulent style. Furnishings are elegant and facilities modern. The lounge is comfortable and relaxing, and breakfast is served in the smart dining room. Hospitality and service are friendly and professional.

Rooms 11 en suite (2 fmly) (4 GF) S £59–£180; D £69–£200* **Facilities** FTV DVD tea/coffee Direct Dial Cen ht Licensed Wi-fi **Parking** 11 **Notes** LB ✖ Closed 24–25 Dec

PREMIER COLLECTION

Apsley House

★★★★★ 🏠 BED AND BREAKFAST

Newbridge Hill BA1 3PT
☎ 01225 336966 📄 01225 425462
e-mail: info@apsley-house.co.uk
dir: *1.3m W of city centre on A431*

Built in 1830 for the Duke of Wellington, Apsley House is within walking distance (allow around half an hour) of the city centre. The house is extremely elegant, and the spacious bedrooms have pleasant views. There are family rooms and rooms with four-poster beds. A smart breakfast room and a delightful lounge are also available.

Rooms 11 en suite (2 fmly) (1 GF) S £65–£150; D £75–£200* **Facilities** STV FTV DVD Lounge tea/coffee Direct Dial Cen ht Licensed Wi-fi **Extras** Speciality toiletries, bottled water **Parking** 12 **Notes** LB ✖ Closed 3 days Xmas

PREMIER COLLECTION

Cheriton House

★★★★★ GUEST ACCOMMODATION

9 Upper Oldfield Park BA2 3JX
☎ 01225 429862 📄 01225 428403
e-mail: info@cheritonhouse.co.uk
web: www.cheritonhouse.co.uk
dir: *A36 onto A367 (Wells Rd), 1st right*

Expect a friendly welcome and a relaxed atmosphere at this well-presented Victorian house with panoramic views over Bath. The carefully decorated bedrooms are well equipped and include a two-bedroom suite in a converted coach house. A substantial breakfast is served in the conservatory-breakfast room overlooking the rear garden. There is also a comfortable lounge.

Rooms 11 en suite (2 fmly) (2 GF) **Facilities** tea/coffee Direct Dial Cen ht Wi-fi **Parking** 11 **Notes** LB ✖ No Children 12yrs

PREMIER COLLECTION

Chestnuts House

★★★★★ 🏠 GUEST ACCOMMODATION

16 Henrietta Rd BA2 6LY
☎ 01225 334279 📄 01225 312236
e-mail: reservations@chestnutshouse.co.uk
web: www.chestnutshouse.co.uk
dir: *Enter Bath on A46, under flyover, right at rdbt. Follow signs for A36 Warminster, over Cleveland Bridge & turn right. 50mtrs on left*

Located just a few minutes' walk from the city centre and totally renovated using light shades and oak, the accommodation is fresh and airy. Bedrooms are attractively co-ordinated, well equipped and comfortable. Added enhancements, such as Wi-fi make the rooms suitable for both business and leisure guests. Breakfast, which features quite an extensive buffet and daily specials, is served in the dining room that opens onto the pretty rear garden. There is a cosy lounge, and the small car park is a bonus.

Rooms 5 en suite (1 fmly) (2 GF) S £70–£95; D £80–£120* **Facilities** STV FTV DVD TVL tea/coffee Cen ht Wi-fi Riding **Extras** Speciality toiletries **Parking** 5 **Notes** ✖

PREMIER COLLECTION

Dorian House

★★★★★ GUEST ACCOMMODATION

1 Upper Oldfield Park BA2 3JX
☎ 01225 426336 📄 01225 444699
e-mail: info@dorianhouse.co.uk
web: www.dorianhouse.co.uk
dir: *A36 onto A367 (Wells Rd), right into Upper Oldfield Park, 3rd building on left*

This elegant Victorian property has stunning views over the city. The atmosphere is welcoming and the accommodation of high quality. Several of the rooms have fine period four-poster beds and all offer a range of extra facilities. The attractive lounge has an honesty bar and views of the terraced gardens.

Rooms 13 en suite (4 fmly) (2 GF) **Facilities** FTV tea/coffee Direct Dial Cen ht Licensed Wi-fi **Parking** 9 **Notes** ✖ Closed 25–26 Dec

BATH *continued*

Tasburgh House

★★★★★ 🏠 GUEST ACCOMMODATION

Warminster Rd BA2 6SH
☎ 01225 425096 🖷 01225 463842
e-mail: stay@tasburghhouse.co.uk
dir: *On N side of A36, next to Bathampton Ln junct*

Located on the main road just outside Bath, this elegant, detached property has undergone a complete refurbishment and provides high levels of quality and comfort throughout. Relaxing public areas include a guest lounge and the delightful conservatory-style breakfast room. Bedrooms vary in size but each includes a host of extras and very comfortable beds. Guests also have use of outdoor seating on the terrace, the large garden and off-street parking.

Rooms 12 en suite (3 fmly) (2 GF) S £85–£105; D £120–£180 **Facilities** FTV DVD Lounge tea/coffee Dinner available Direct Dial Cen ht Licensed Wi-fi 🏊 ♨ 18 Fishing 🔒 **Extras** Speciality toiletries, home-made brownies - complimentary **Conf** Max 15 Thtr 10 Class 10 Board 15 **Parking** 16 **Notes** ⊗ No Children 8yrs Closed 21 Dec-14 Jan

---

The Bailbrook Lodge

★★★★ GUEST HOUSE

35-37 London Road West BA1 7HZ
☎ 01225 859090 🖷 01225 852299
e-mail: hotel@bailbrooklodge.co.uk
web: www.bailbrooklodge.co.uk
dir: *M4 junct 18, A46 S to A4 junct, left signed Batheaston. Lodge 1st on left*

Set in extensive gardens on the east edge of the city, this imposing Georgian building provides smart accommodation. The well-equipped bedrooms include some with four-poster beds and period furniture, and service is professional and efficient. The inviting lounge has a small bar, and light snacks are available from noon until evening. Breakfast is served in the elegant dining room.

Rooms 15 rms (14 en suite) (1 pri facs) (5 fmly) (1 GF) S £69–£79; D £89–£145 **Facilities** FTV DVD iPod docking station Lounge tea/coffee Cen ht Licensed Wi-fi 🔒 **Extras** Mineral water, bath robes in some rooms **Conf** Max 20 Thtr 20 Class 10 Board 12 **Parking** 15 **Notes** LB ⊗

Corston Fields Farm *(ST674648)*

★★★★ FARMHOUSE

Corston BA2 9EZ
☎ 01225 873305 & 07900 056568 Mr & Mrs Addicott
e-mail: corston.fields@btinternet.com
web: www.corstonfields.com
dir: *300mtrs off A39 between Corston & Marksbury on lane running adjacent to Wheatsheaf pub*

Located in peaceful countryside and surrounded by a variety of crops, this traditional farmhouse offers a relaxing stay. Spacious and well-furnished bedrooms are located in the main property with an additional room in a separate building with its own entrance and patio. Guests are welcome to use the comfortable lounge, and walk the family dog in the fields if you wish. The delicious breakfasts use high quality ingredients including free-range eggs from the farm.

Rooms 3 rms (2 en suite) (1 pri facs) 1 annexe en suite (1 GF) S £60–£65; D £94–£98* **Facilities** STV FTV Lounge tea/coffee Cen ht Wi-fi Walk around farm **Parking** 4 **Notes** ⊗ No Children 13yrs Closed 23 Dec-2 Jan 312 acres arable

---

Cranleigh

★★★★ 🏠 BED AND BREAKFAST

159 Newbridge Hill BA1 3PX
☎ 01225 310197 🖷 01225 423143
e-mail: cranleigh@btinternet.com
dir: *1.2m W of city centre on A431*

This pleasant Victorian house is in a quiet location near the city centre. The well-equipped bedrooms, some of which are on the ground floor, are decorated in the style of the period, and two rooms have four-poster beds. Breakfast is served in the elegant dining room, and there is also an attractive garden which includes a popular hot tub.

Rooms 9 en suite (3 fmly) (2 GF) S £65–£75; D £65–£140* **Facilities** FTV DVD iPod docking station tea/coffee Cen ht Licensed Wi-fi Garden hot tub **Parking** 5 **Notes** ⊗ No Children 5yrs Closed 25-26 Dec

---

The Hollies

★★★★ GUEST ACCOMMODATION

Hatfield Rd BA2 2BD
☎ 01225 313366
e-mail: davcartwright@lineone.net
dir: *A36 onto A367 Wells Rd & Wellsway, 0.7m right opposite Devonshire Arms*

This delightful house stands in impressive gardens overlooking a magnificent church, and is within easy reach of the city centre. The individually decorated, themed bedrooms are appointed to provide excellent levels of comfort and good facilities. Breakfast in the elegant dining room is an enjoyable start to the day.

Rooms 3 rms (2 en suite) (1 pri facs) S £70; D £90* **Facilities** FTV Lounge tea/coffee Cen ht Wi-fi 🔒

Extras Sweets **Parking** 3 **Notes** ⊗ No Children 16yrs Closed 15 Dec-15 Jan

---

The Kennard

★★★★ 🏠 GUEST ACCOMMODATION

11 Henrietta St BA2 6LL
☎ 01225 310472 🖷 01225 460054
e-mail: reception@kennard.co.uk
web: www.kennard.co.uk
dir: *A4 onto A36 (Bathwick St), 2nd right into Henrietta Rd & Henrietta St*

This attractive Georgian house dates from 1794 and is situated just off famous Great Pulteney Street, making it convenient for the city centre. The house is decorated and furnished in keeping with the elegance of the architecture. Bedrooms, some located at ground floor level, vary in style and size. Breakfast is served in the lower garden dining room and includes an excellent cold buffet, as well as a selection of hot items.

Rooms 12 rms (10 en suite) (2 GF) **Facilities** FTV tea/coffee Direct Dial Cen ht Licensed Wi-fi **Notes** ⊗ No Children 8yrs Closed 1wk Xmas

---

Marlborough House

★★★★ GUEST ACCOMMODATION

1 Marlborough Ln BA1 2NQ
☎ 01225 318175 🖷 01225 466127
e-mail: mars@manque.dircon.co.uk
web: www.marlborough-house.net
dir: *450yds W of city centre, at A4 junct with Marlborough Ln*

Marlborough House is situated opposite Royal Victoria Park and close to the Royal Crescent. Some original features remain and the rooms are decorated with period furniture and pictures. The atmosphere is relaxed, and service is attentive and friendly. The breakfast, served from an open-plan kitchen, is vegetarian and organic.

Rooms 6 en suite (3 fmly) (1 GF) **Facilities** FTV tea/coffee Direct Dial Cen ht Licensed Wi-fi 🛇 **Extras** Organic toiletries; mini-bar - chargeable **Parking** 3 **Notes** LB Closed 24-26 Dec

Oldfields

★★★★ GUEST ACCOMMODATION

102 Wells Rd BA2 3AL
☎ 01225 317984 📠 01225 444471
e-mail: info@oldfields.co.uk
dir: A4 to city centre, left at lights (A36/A367). At large rdbt, under railway viaduct, 1st exit A367 signed Radstock. After 0.5m 1st right, then left

Located in an elevated position with excellent views over Bath from many of the bedrooms, Oldfields provides a range of various-sized rooms decorated and furnished to provide very good levels of quality and comfort. Guests are welcome to use the relaxing lounge and a DVD library is available. At breakfast, taken in the relaxing dining room, there is a choice of high-quality cooked dishes. The property has a small car park.

Rooms 16 en suite (2 GF) S £55-£79; D £74-£174*
Facilities FTV DVD TVL tea/coffee Direct Dial Cen ht Wi-fi **Parking** 14 **Notes** LB ⊗

School Cottages Bed & Breakfast

★★★★ BED AND BREAKFAST

The Street, Near Bath BA2 0AR
☎ 01761 471167 & 07989 349428
e-mail: tim@schoolcottages.co.uk
web: www.schoolcottages.co.uk

(For full entry see Farmborough)

Villa Claudia

★★★★ BED AND BREAKFAST

19 Forester Rd, Bathwick BA2 6QE
☎ 01225 329670 📠 01225 329670
e-mail: claudiaamato77@aol.com
dir: From A4 into Cleveland Place East (A36), at next rdbt 1st exit into Beckford Rd, left into Forester Rd

Villa Claudia is a beautiful Victorian property located on a quiet tree-lined residential street within easy walking distance of the city's attractions and restaurants. The Italian owners of this family-run bed and breakfast provide attentive and personal service. The bedrooms and bathrooms are beautifully decorated and very comfortable; a four-poster room is available. Delicious breakfasts are served in the charming dining room at a communal table.

Rooms 3 rms (1 en suite) (2 pri facs) (1 fmly) S £65-£70; D £120-£140* **Facilities** FTV DVD tea/coffee Cen ht Wi-fi **Parking** 4 **Notes** ⊗

Waterhouse

★★★★ GUEST ACCOMMODATION

Waterhouse Ln, Monkton Combe BA2 7JB
☎ 01225 721999 📠 01225 721998
e-mail: jane.curtis@wilsher-group.com
dir: From Bath on A36 to Monkton Combe

This newly restored 18th-century manor house is in a peaceful location just a couple of miles outside of Bath. It offers modern bedrooms and bathrooms with plenty of welcome guest extras, and a range of relaxing lounges. Guests can enjoy the garden and country walks straight from the front door. Breakfast is served in the contemporary dining room, and meeting rooms are also available.

Rooms 8 en suite **Facilities** STV FTV Lounge TVL tea/coffee Cen ht Lift Wi-fi Fishing 🛇 Arrangement with leisure centre **Conf** Max 40 Thtr 40 Class 20 Board 16 **Parking** 40 **Notes** LB ⊗

The Bath House

★★★★ GUEST ACCOMMODATION

40 Crescent Gardens BA1 2NB
☎ 0117 937 4495 & 07711 119847 📠 0117 337 6791
e-mail: info@thebathhouse.org
dir: 100yds from Queen Sq on A431

Appointed to high specifications, this accommodation is stylish and just a few minutes' level walk from the city. Bedrooms are attractive, spacious, light and airy, and equipped with modern accessories, including flat screen TVs. Wi-fi is available. Breakfast is room service only and a full height dining table provided in the bedroom ensures guests enjoy their meal experience. Limited parking space is available.

Rooms 5 en suite (1 GF) S £69-£110; D £79-£125*
Facilities FTV iPod docking station tea/coffee Cen ht Wi-fi 🛇 **Extras** Mini-fridge **Parking** 5 **Notes** LB ⊗ No Children 8yrs

Bathwick Gardens

★★★★ BED AND BREAKFAST

95 Sydney Place BA2 6NE
☎ 01225 469435 & 07737 793772
e-mail: visitus@bathwickgardens.co.uk
web: www.bathwickgardens.co.uk
dir: A46 onto A4 for 2m. At lights left, over bridge, at next lights right, pass Holburne Museum, then immediately left

Situated close to the city centre, this substantial Regency town house featured in the 1995 film version of Jane Austen's *Persuasion*. Architecturally restored with many original features, the house provides an insight into the 18th century. The en suite bedrooms are very spacious and decorated with period wallpapers. Breakfast is a choice of traditional English or the house special, an Austrian continental breakfast. Parking is by arrangement.

Rooms 3 rms (2 en suite) **Facilities** TVL TV1B tea/coffee Cen ht Wi-fi **Parking** 2 **Notes** ⊗ 🍽

Beckford House B&B

★★★★ BED AND BREAKFAST

59 Upper Oldfield Park BA2 3LB
☎ 01225 310005
e-mail: info@beckford-house.com
web: www.beckford-house.com
dir: Off A36 Lower Bristol Rd onto Lower Oldfield Park at Green Park Tavern opp Skoda, 3rd left

Close to the city's attractions, this Victorian house provides a relaxed and friendly welcome in a quiet location. The spacious bedrooms are carefully furnished and decorated. A varied choice is offered at breakfast including local and organic produce.

Rooms 2 en suite (1 fmly) S £68-£75; D £75-£110 **Facilities** FTV DVD iPod docking station Cen ht Wi-fi 🛇 **Parking** 2 **Notes** LB ⊗ No Children 11yrs Closed 25-31 Dec 🍽

Brocks Guest House

★★★★ GUEST ACCOMMODATION

32 Brock St BA1 2LN
☎ 01225 338374 📠 01225 338425
e-mail: brocks@brocksguesthouse.co.uk
web: www.brocksguesthouse.co.uk
dir: Just off A4 between Circus & Royal Crescent

A warm welcome is extended at this delightful Georgian property, located in the heart of the city just a few hundred yards from Royal Crescent. All rooms reflect the comfortable elegance of the Georgian era. A traditional breakfast is served in the charming dining room, which also offers a lounge area with comfortable seating.

Rooms 6 en suite (2 fmly) **Facilities** FTV tea/coffee Cen ht Wi-fi **Parking** **Notes** ⊗ Closed 24 Dec-1 Jan

Devonshire House

★★★★ GUEST ACCOMMODATION

143 Wellsway BA2 4RZ
☎ 01225 312495
e-mail: enquiries@devonshire-house.uk.com
web: www.devonshire-house.uk.com
dir: 1m S of city centre. A36 onto A367 (Wells Rd becomes Wellsway)

Located within walking distance of the city centre, this charming house has maintained its Victorian style, and the friendly proprietors make every effort to ensure a stay here is pleasant and memorable. The attractive bedrooms, some appointed to a very high quality standard, have many thoughtful extras. There is a small lounge area, and freshly cooked breakfasts are served in the pleasant dining room. Secure parking is available.

Rooms 4 en suite (1 fmly) (2 GF) S £50-£88; D £68-£88*
Facilities FTV DVD iPod docking station tea/coffee Cen ht Wi-fi 🛇 **Parking** 6 **Notes** LB ⊗

BATH *continued*

Grove Lodge

★★★★ GUEST ACCOMMODATION

11 Lambridge BA1 6BJ
☎ 01225 310860 📠 01225 429630
e-mail: stay@grovelodgebath.co.uk
web: www.grovelodgebath.co.uk
dir: *0.6m NE of city centre. Exit A4, 400yds W from junct A46*

This fine Georgian house lies within easy reach of the city centre and is accessed via a stone path through a neat garden surrounded by trees. The spacious bedrooms have period character and all are well equipped. There is an attractive breakfast room, and parking is available in nearby side streets. Guests may venture into the city for evening meals or alternatively, a short stroll along the canal leads to an inn which serves food.

Rooms 4 rms (3 en suite) (1 pri facs) S £60-£75;
D £78-£95* **Facilities** FTV tea/coffee Cen ht Wi-fi ⓐ
Notes LB ⊗ No Children 7yrs Closed Xmas & New Year

Highways House

★★★★ GUEST ACCOMMODATION

143 Wells Rd BA2 3AL
☎ 01225 421238 📠 01225 481169
e-mail: stay@highwayshouse.co.uk
dir: *A36 onto A367 (Wells Rd), 300yds on left*

This elegant Victorian house is just a ten-minute walk from the city centre; alternatively, there is a frequent bus service. The bedrooms are individually styled, well equipped and homely. A spacious, attractive lounge is available, and breakfast is served in the dining room at separate tables. Parking is a bonus.

Rooms 5 en suite 2 annexe en suite (2 fmly) (3 GF)
Facilities FTV tea/coffee Cen ht Wi-fi **Parking** 7 **Notes** ⊗
No Children 8yrs

Milsoms Bath

★★★★ 🍴 RESTAURANT WITH ROOMS

24 Milsom St BA1 1DG
☎ 01225 750128 📠 01225 750121
e-mail: bath@milsomshotel.co.uk
dir: *M4 junct 18, A46 (Bath), 3m, through Pennsylvania. 3rd exit on rdbt onto A420 (Bristol). 1st left signed Hamswell/Park & Ride, left at junct towards Lansdown. Right at next T-junct. 5th right into George St. 1st left into Milsom St*

Located at the end of the main street in busy, central Bath, this stylish restaurant with rooms offers a range of comfortable, well-equipped accommodation. The ground-floor Loch Fyne Restaurant serves an excellent selection of dishes at both lunch and dinner with an emphasis on freshest quality fish and shellfish. A good selection of hot and cold items is also available in the same restaurant at breakfast.

Rooms 9 en suite D £85-£125* **Facilities** FTV tea/coffee
Dinner available Direct Dial Cen ht **Notes** LB ⊗ No
coaches

Pulteney House

★★★★ GUEST ACCOMMODATION

14 Pulteney Rd BA2 4HA
☎ 01225 460991 📠 01225 460991
e-mail: pulteney@tinyworld.co.uk
web: www.pulteneyhotel.co.uk
dir: *On A36*

This large detached property, situated in a colourful garden is within walking distance of the city centre. Bedrooms vary in size including some annexe rooms, and are well equipped with useful facilities. Full English breakfasts are served in the dining room at individual tables. A guest lounge and car park are both welcome features.

Rooms 12 rms (11 en suite) (1 pri facs) 5 annexe en suite
(3 fmly) (2 GF) S £50-£70; D £75-£130* **Facilities** STV

FTV TVL tea/coffee Cen ht Wi-fi ⓐ **Parking** 18 **Notes** LB ⊗
Closed 24-26 Dec

Rivers Street Rooms

★★★★ BED AND BREAKFAST

39 Rivers St BA1 2QA
☎ 07787 500345
e-mail: sharonabrahams3@yahoo.co.uk
dir: *M4 junct 18, A46, through Pennsylvania to mini-rdbt, right onto A420 signed Bristol. 0.5m, left at staggered x-rds into lane. Left at end, pass racecourse, 2m. At church right into Lansdown Rd towards city. Right into Julian Rd. 1st left into Rivers St. Establishment 50mtrs on left*

This centrally located, five-storey, 1770s townhouse offers modern contemporary styling that blends seamlessly with the wealth of original features. There's a family suite that comprises two rooms, and a double room with king-size bed and the exclusive use of a small courtyard garden; both rooms have flat screen Freeview TVs and refreshment trays. Breakfast is continental style but very generous, offering a wide variety of delicious home-baked goodies such as mini-quiches, pastries, scones and fresh fruits.

Rooms 2 rms (1 en suite) (1 pri facs) (1 fmly)
Facilities FTV tea/coffee Cen ht Wi-fi **Notes** 🐾

Elgin Villa

★★★ BED AND BREAKFAST

6 Marlborough Ln BA1 2NQ
☎ 01225 424557
e-mail: elginvilla@hotmail.co.uk
web: www.elginvilla.co.uk
dir: *From one way system at Queen Sq, exit NW & follow signs for A4, Bristol. By pedestrian crossing, right into car park, parking in far left corner behind wooden gate*

Located near the park and just a ten-minute walk from the centre of Bath, Elgin Villa offers a range of variously sized bedrooms. Most rooms have en suite facilities, although two just have a shower and washbasin in the room, and share a toilet. Continental breakfast, including scrambled eggs and croissants, is served in the comfortable dining room. Private parking is available to the rear of the property.

Rooms 6 rms (4 en suite) (2 fmly) D £85-£110*
Facilities FTV tea/coffee Wi-fi **Parking** 6 **Notes** ⊗

The Parade Park and Lambrettas Bar

★★★ GUEST ACCOMMODATION

8-10 North Pde BA2 4AL
☎ 01225 463384 📠 01225 442322
e-mail: info@paradepark.co.uk
web: www.paradepark.co.uk
dir: *In city centre. Exit A36 (Pulteney Rd) into North Parade Rd & North Parade*

This attractive Georgian property was formerly the home of William Wordsworth. The restored rooms are brightly

Save on B&Bs and Hotels. Book at theAA.com/hotel

SOMERSET 255 ENGLAND

decorated, and well equipped with modern facilities. A varied continental style breakfast is served in the impressive, panelled first-floor dining room. The mod scooter-themed Lambretta bar is open to the public.

Rooms 38 rms (32 en suite) (6 pri facs) (8 fmly) (2 GF) S £55-£75; D £75-£105* **Facilities** FTV tea/coffee Cen ht Licensed Wi-fi **Notes** LB ⊗ Closed Xmas

Roman City Guest House

★★★ GUEST HOUSE

18 Raby Place, Bathwick Hill BA2 4EH
☎ 01225 463668 & 07899 777953
e-mail: enquire@romancityguesthouse.co.uk
dir: A4 onto A36 Bathwick St, turn right at lights, straight on at rdbt. Turn left at St Mary's church onto Bathwick Hill, on left

A warm welcome is assured at this 18th-century end-of-terrace house, located just a stroll from the heart of the historic city. The spacious bedrooms, some with four-poster beds, are comfortable and well equipped with many extra facilities. A pleasant lounge is also available.

Rooms 4 rms (3 en suite) (1 pri facs) (2 fmly)
Facilities FTV tea/coffee Cen ht Wi-fi **Conf** Board 12
Notes ⊗

Waltons Guest House

★★★ GUEST HOUSE

17-19 Crescent Gardens, Upper Bristol Rd BA1 2NA
☎ 01225 426528
e-mail: rose@waltonsguesthouse.co.uk
web: www.bathguesthouse.com
dir: On A4 350yds W of city centre

There is a warm welcome at Waltons, situated within strolling distance of the centre of Bath. The cosy bedrooms come with useful extra facilities, and a traditional English breakfast is served at individual tables in the dining room.

Rooms 7 en suite **Facilities** FTV tea/coffee Direct Dial Cen ht **Notes** ⊗

The Hermitage

★★ GUEST ACCOMMODATION

Bath Rd SN13 8DT
☎ 01225 744187
e-mail: hermitagebb@btconnect.com
web: www.thehermitage-box.co.uk

(For full entry see Box (Wiltshire))

BECKINGTON   Map 4 ST85

Woolpack Inn

★★★★ INN

BA11 6SP
☎ 01373 831244 📠 01373 831223
e-mail: 6534@greeneking.co.uk
web: www.oldenglish.co.uk

This charming coaching inn dates back to the 16th century and retains many original features including flagstone floors, open fireplaces and exposed beams. The bar is popular with visitors and locals alike. There is a garden room lounge and a choice of places to eat: the bar for light snacks, the Oak Room for more substantial meals, or the Garden Room which leads onto a pleasant courtyard.

Rooms 11 en suite (3 fmly) S £69-£100; D £79-£100*
Facilities tea/coffee Dinner available Direct Dial Cen ht
Wi-fi ⅃ 18 **Conf** Max 40 Thtr 40 Class 20 Board 20
Parking 16 **Notes** LB

BRIDGWATER   Map 4 ST23

Ash-Wembdon Farm (ST281382)

★★★★ FARMHOUSE

Hollow Ln, Wembdon TA5 2BD
☎ 01278 453097 📠 01278 445856 Mr & Mrs Rowe
e-mail: mary.rowe@btinternet.com
web: www.farmaccommodation.co.uk
dir: M5, A38, A39 to Minehead, at rdbt 3rd exit into Homeburg Way, at lights take B3339, right into Hollow Ln

Near the Quantock Hills, this is a 17th-century farmhouse on a working beef and arable farm offering homely and comfortable accommodation. All rooms have en suite showers or private bathrooms, and English or continental breakfasts are served in the guest dining room. Guests also have use of a lounge and landscaped garden.

Rooms 3 rms (2 en suite) (1 pri facs) S £35-£40;
D £54-£60 **Facilities** FTV Lounge tea/coffee Cen ht Wi-fi 🐾
Parking 3 **Notes** LB ⊗ No Children 10yrs Closed 22
Dec-3 Jan 340 acres arable/beef

Blackmore Farm (ST247385)

★★★★ FARMHOUSE

Blackmore Ln, Cannington TA5 2NE
☎ 01278 653442 Mrs A Dyer
e-mail: dyerfarm@aol.com
dir: 3m W of Bridgwater. Follow brown tourist signs on A39, before Carrington

Dating back to the 15th century, this Grade I listed manor house is truly unique; there is a wealth of original features such as oak beams, huge open fireplaces, stone archways and even a chapel. Bedrooms located in the main house are individual in style and one has a wonderful four-poster and a lofty oak-beamed ceiling. Additional, more conventional bedrooms are located in a separate courtyard area. Breakfast is taken in the grandeur of the dining room around one, incredibly long table - a truly memorable experience. Blackmore Farm was last year's AA Guest Accommodation of the Year for England (2011-2012).

Rooms 3 en suite 2 annexe en suite (1 fmly) (2 GF)
S £50-£55; D £90-£100* **Facilities** FTV TVL tea/coffee
Cen ht Licensed Wi-fi 🐾 ⅃ 18 Fishing 🔒 Farm shop café
Extras Fruit, bath robes in some rooms **Conf** Max 30
Board 30 **Parking** 10 **Notes** LB ⊗ 900 acres dairy/arable

The Malt Shovel

★★★ INN

Blackmore Ln, Cannington TA5 2NE
☎ 01278 653432
e-mail: maltshovel@butcombe.com
dir: A39 from Bridgwater, left into Blackmore Ln, just before Bridgwater Mowers

Located in a quiet rural area and just a couple of miles from Bridgwater, this popular hostelry has a broad appeal. There's plenty of character here with log fires, low beams and a warm and genuine welcome. The well-stocked bar has a range of Butcombe Ales as well as guest beers, while the menu offers plenty of choice in addition to the impressive carvery. The bedrooms are located in the converted skittle alley, and provide good levels of space and comfort. Spacious gardens and patios make the perfect venues for a refreshing drink in the summer.

Rooms 8 annexe en suite (1 fmly) (8 GF) S £45; D £70
Facilities FTV TVL tea/coffee Dinner available Cen ht Wi-fi
Parking 50 **Notes** LB

BROMPTON REGIS   Map 3 SS93

Holworthy Farm *(SS978308)*

★★★★ FARMHOUSE

TA22 9NY
☎ 01398 371244 📠 01398 371244 **Mrs G Payne**
e-mail: holworthyfarm@aol.com
web: www.holworthyfarm.co.uk
dir: *2m E of Brompton Regis. Exit A396 on E side of Wimbleball Lake*

Set in the south-east corner of Exmoor, this working livestock farm has spectacular views over Wimbleball Lake. Bedrooms are traditionally furnished and well equipped. The dining room overlooking the garden is the attractive setting for breakfast. Dinner is available by arrangement.

Rooms 5 rms (3 en suite) (2 pri facs) (2 fmly) (1 GF)
Facilities Lounge TVL tea/coffee Dinner available Cen ht
Conf Max 20 **Parking** 8 **Notes** LB ⊗ 200 acres beef/sheep

BURNHAM-ON-SEA   Map 4 ST34

Magnolia House

★★★★ GUEST HOUSE

26 Manor Rd TA8 2AS
☎ 01278 792460
e-mail: enquiries@magnoliahouse.gb.com
web: www.magnoliahouse.gb.com
dir: *M5 junct 22, follow signs to Burnham-on-Sea, at 2nd rdbt, Magnolia House on right*

Within walking distance of the town centre and beach, this elegant Edwardian house has been appointed to an impressive standard. Contemporary bedrooms offer comfort and quality with many extras such as Wi-fi and a large DVD film library. Bathrooms are also modern and stylish with invigorating showers. A family suite is offered with separate, interconnecting bedrooms. Traditional full English breakfasts are served in the attractive, air-conditioned breakfast room, with vegetarian and continental options also available.

Rooms 4 en suite (2 fmly) **Facilities** FTV tea/coffee Cen ht Wi-fi ♿ 18 **Parking** 7 **Notes** ⊗ No Children 5yrs

The Victoria

Ⓤ

25 Victoria St TA8 1EQ
☎ 01278 783085

Currently the rating for this establishment is not confirmed. This may be due to a change of ownership or because it has only recently joined the AA rating scheme.

Rooms 5 en suite **Facilities** FTV tea/coffee Dinner available Wi-fi **Parking** 6

CASTLE CARY   Map 4 ST63

Clanville Manor *(ST618330)*

★★★★ FARMHOUSE

BA7 7PJ
☎ 01963 350124 & 07966 512732 **Mrs S Snook**
e-mail: info@clanvillemanor.co.uk
web: www.clanvillemanor.co.uk
dir: *A371 onto B3153, 0.75m, entrance to Clanville Manor via white gate & cattle grid under bridge*

Built in 1743, Clanville Manor is situated on a beef farm, and has been owned by the Snook family since 1898. A polished oak staircase leads up to the individually decorated bedrooms, which retain a great deal of their original character. Hearty breakfasts are served in the elegant dining room, which looks over open meadows. There is also a spacious and comfortable sitting room.

Rooms 4 en suite S £40-£60; D £80-£110* **Facilities** FTV iPod docking station TVL tea/coffee Cen ht Wi-fi 🐾 🐶 **Parking** 6 **Notes** LB ⊗ No Children 12yrs Closed 21 Dec-2 Jan 140 acres beef

The Pilgrims

★★★★ ⊛ INN

Lovington BA7 7PT
☎ 01963 240600
e-mail: jools@thepilgrimsatlovington.co.uk
web: www.thepilgrimsatlovington.co.uk
dir: *On B3153, 1.5m E of lights on A37 at Lydford*

This popular establishment describes itself as 'the pub that thinks it's a restaurant', which is pretty accurate. With a real emphasis on fresh, local and carefully prepared produce, both dinner and breakfast are the focus of any stay here. In addition, the resident family proprietors provide a friendly and relaxed atmosphere. Comfortable and well-equipped bedrooms are available in the adjacent, converted cider barn.

Rooms 5 annexe en suite (5 GF) S £80; D £95-£120* **Facilities** FTV DVD Lounge tea/coffee Dinner available Cen ht Wi-fi **Parking** 5 **Notes** LB No Children 14yrs Closed 1st 2wks Oct RS Sun eve-Tue lunch Restaurant & bar closed to non-residents No coaches

CATCOTT   Map 4 ST33

Honeysuckle

★★★★ GUEST ACCOMMODATION

King William Rd TA7 9HU
☎ 01278 722890
dir: *Exit A39 to Catcott, pass King William pub, house 200yds on right*

Situated in the village centre, this delightful modern house is a good base for visiting the many attractions in the area, including the bird-watching haven of the Somerset Levels. Bedrooms are comfortable, and there is a spacious lounge and a charming garden. Breakfast is served around a communal table in the pleasant dining room.

Rooms 3 rms (1 en suite) (1 pri facs) (1 GF) S £27; D £56-£64* **Facilities** DVD tea/coffee Cen ht Wi-fi **Parking** 3 **Notes** ⊗ No Children 7yrs Closed 20 Dec-3 Jan 🐾

CHARD   Map 4 ST30

Hornsbury Mill

★★★★ 🅰 GUEST ACCOMMODATION

Eleighwater TA20 3AQ
☎ 01460 63317 📠 01460 67758
e-mail: info@hornsburymill.co.uk

Rooms 10 en suite (2 fmly) (1 GF) S £75; D £99* **Facilities** STV FTV DVD tea/coffee Dinner available Direct Dial Cen ht Licensed Wi-fi **Conf** Max 150 Thtr 150 Class 50 Board 50 **Parking** 80 **Notes** ⊗ Closed 30 Dec-10 Jan RS Sun eve closed Civ Wed 120

Save on B&Bs and Hotels. Book at **theAA.com/hotel**

SOMERSET 257 ENGLAND

Watermead Guest House

★★★ GUEST HOUSE

83 High St TA20 1QT
☎ 01460 62834 📠 01460 67448
e-mail: trudy@watermeadguesthouse.co.uk
dir: On A30 in town centre

Guests will feel at home at this family-run house, a smart establishment in a convenient location. Hearty breakfasts are served in the dining room overlooking the garden. Bedrooms are neat, and the spacious, self-contained suite is popular with families. Free Wi-fi access is available.

Rooms 9 rms (6 en suite) 1 annexe en suite (1 fmly)
S £38-£45; D £65-£75* Facilities FTV TVL tea/coffee
Cen ht Wi-fi 🛁 Parking 10 Notes LB

CHEDDAR

See Draycott

CLUTTON   Map 4 ST65

The Hunters Rest

★★★★ INN

King Ln, Clutton Hill BS39 5QL
☎ 01761 452303 📠 01761 453308
e-mail: paul@huntersrest.co.uk
web: www.huntersrest.co.uk
dir: Off A37 onto A368 towards Bath, 100yds right onto lane, left at T-junct, inn 0.25m on left

This establishment was originally built around 1750 as a hunting lodge for the Earl of Warwick. Set in delightful countryside, it is ideally located for Bath, Bristol and Wells. Bedrooms and bathrooms are furnished and equipped to excellent standards, and the ground floor combines the character of a real country inn with an excellent range of home-cooked meals.

Rooms 5 en suite (2 fmly) S £67.50-£77.50; D £95-£130*
Facilities FTV iPod docking station tea/coffee Dinner available Direct Dial Cen ht Wi-fi ⅃ 18 🛁 Conf Max 40 Thtr 40 Class 25 Board 25 Parking 90 Notes LB

CORTON DENHAM   Map 4 ST62

The Queens Arms

★★★★ ⌘ INN

DT9 4LR
☎ 01963 220317 📠 01963 220797
e-mail: relax@thequeensarms.com
web: www.thequeensarms.com
dir: A303 exit Chapel Cross signed South Cadbury & Corton Denham. Follow signs to South Cadbury. Through village, after 0.25m turn left up hill signed Sherborne & Corton Denham. Left at top of hill, pub at end of village on right

This is a proper inn located in peaceful countryside and complete with roaring log fire, a friendly welcome from the staff and a labrador in the bar. Bedrooms and bathrooms come in a range of shapes and sizes, and all are well decorated and comfortably furnished. In addition to a very good selection of real ales, this is a paradise for bottled beer lovers with a great choice from around the world. Excellent, quality local produce is utilised to provide a choice of delicious dinners which may be enjoyed in the traditional bar or character restaurant.

Rooms 5 en suite 3 annexe en suite (1 GF) S £80-£85;
D £95-£120* Facilities FTV DVD iPod docking station Lounge tea/coffee Dinner available Direct Dial Cen ht Wi-fi ⅃ 18 Riding 🛁 Extras Speciality toiletries, robes/slippers some rooms Conf Max 35 Thtr 35 Class 25 Board 35 Parking 20 Notes LB

See advert on page 258

CREWKERNE   Map 4 ST40

Manor Farm

★★★★ GUEST ACCOMMODATION

Wayford TA18 8QL
☎ 01460 78865 & 0776 7620031 📠 01460 78865
e-mail: theresaemery@hotmail.com
web: www.manorfarm.biz
dir: B3165 from Crewkerne to Lyme Regis. 3m, in Clapton right into Dunsham Ln, Manor Farm 0.5m up hill on right

Located off the beaten track, this fine Victorian country house has extensive views over Clapton towards the Axe Valley. The comfortably furnished bedrooms are well equipped, and front-facing rooms enjoy splendid views. Breakfast is served at separate tables in the dining room, and a spacious lounge is also provided.

Rooms 4 en suite 1 annexe en suite (2 fmly) S £35-£40;
D £70-£75* Facilities STV FTV TVL TV4B tea/coffee
Cen ht Wi-fi Fishing Riding 🛁 Parking 14 Notes ⊗ ⊛

The George

★★★ INN

Market Square TA18 7LP
☎ 01460 73650 📠 01460 72974
e-mail: georgecrewkerne@btconnect.com
web: www.thegeorgehotelcrewkerne.co.uk
dir: In town centre on A30

Situated in the heart of town, this welcoming inn has been providing rest and sustenance for over 400 years. The atmosphere is warm and inviting, and the bar is the ideal place for a natter and a refreshing pint. Comfortable bedrooms are traditionally styled and include four-poster rooms. A choice of menus is available, served either in the bar or attractive restaurant.

Rooms 13 rms (8 en suite) (2 pri facs) (2 fmly)
S £40-£100; D £70-£150 Facilities FTV DVD TVL tea/coffee Dinner available Direct Dial Cen ht Wi-fi George Suite has a hydro-therapy spa bath Conf Max 100 Thtr 100 Class 100 Board 50 Notes LB ⊗

CROSCOMBE — Map 4 ST54

The Bull Terrier

★★★ INN

BA5 3QJ

☎ 01749 343658

e-mail: barry.vidler@bullterrierpub.co.uk

dir: *On A371 by village cross*

Located in the centre of the village, this attractive country inn has a relaxed and friendly atmosphere. The character of the inn has been retained with the flagstone floors and inglenook fireplace, and the public areas are particularly welcoming. Bedrooms are brightly decorated and well equipped. Freshly prepared lunches and dinners are available.

Rooms 2 en suite S £30-£35; D £65-£70* **Facilities** FTV tea/coffee Dinner available Cen ht ⓐ **Parking** 3 **Notes** No Children 10yrs RS Oct-Mar closed Mon

DRAYCOTT — Map 4 ST45

Oakland House

★★★★ ⬤ GUEST ACCOMMODATION

Wells Rd BS27 3SU

☎ 01934 744195 🖷 01934 744195

e-mail: enquiries@oakland-house.co.uk

web: www.oakland-house.co.uk

dir: *Off A371 at S end of village*

Situated a short distance from Cheddar, this friendly home provides comfortable and spacious accommodation. There are splendid views of the Somerset Moors and Glastonbury Tor from the sun lounge and the well-appointed and attractive bedrooms. Dinner features fresh fruit and vegetables from the garden.

Oakland House

Rooms 3 en suite (1 fmly) S fr £45; D fr £70* **Facilities** TVL tea/coffee Dinner available Cen ht Pool table ⓐ **Parking** 6 **Notes** LB ⊗

See advert on opposite page

Save on B&Bs and Hotels. Book at **theAA.com/hotel**

SOMERSET 259 ENGLAND

DULVERTON
Map 3 SS92

PREMIER COLLECTION

Tarr Farm Inn
★★★★★ ⦿ INN

Tarr Steps, Exmoor National Park TA22 9PY
☎ 01643 851507 📠 01643 851111
e-mail: enquiries@tarrfarm.co.uk
web: www.tarrfarm.co.uk
dir: *4m NW of Dulverton. Off B3223 signed Tarr Steps, signs to Tarr Farm Inn*

Tarr Farm, dating from the 16th century, nestles on the lower slopes of Exmoor overlooking the famous old clapper bridge, Tarr Steps. The majority of rooms are in the bedroom block that provides very stylish and comfortable accommodation with an impressive selection of thoughtful touches. Tarr Farm Inn, with much character and traditional charm, draws the crowds for cream teas and delicious dinners which are prepared from good local produce.

Rooms 9 en suite (4 GF) **Facilities** STV tea/coffee Dinner available Direct Dial Cen ht Wi-fi Fishing Riding **Conf** Max 18 **Parking** 10 **Notes** No Children 14yrs No coaches

FARMBOROUGH
Map 4 ST66

School Cottages Bed & Breakfast
★★★★ BED AND BREAKFAST

The Street, Near Bath BA2 0AR
☎ 01761 471167 & 07989 349428
e-mail: tim@schoolcottages.co.uk
web: www.schoolcottages.co.uk
dir: *Exit A39 in Farmborough into The Street, 1st left opposite village school*

This lovingly restored country house is conveniently located to the south-west of Bath in the pretty Somerset village of Farmborough. The contemporary, stylish bedrooms are equipped with Wi-fi, while the excellent bathrooms may include a power shower or a spa bath. Home-made jams and freshly-laid eggs contribute to the delicious breakfasts served in a charming conservatory overlooking the garden.

School Cottages Bed & Breakfast

Rooms 3 en suite **Facilities** FTV TVL tea/coffee Cen ht Wi-fi ⅃ 18 🔒 **Parking** 3 **Notes** LB ⊗ No Children 10yrs

FROME
Map 4 ST74

PREMIER COLLECTION

Lullington House
★★★★★ BED AND BREAKFAST

Lullington BA11 2PG
☎ 01373 831406 & 07979 290146 📠 01373 831406
e-mail: info@lullingtonhouse.co.uk
web: www.lullingtonhouse.co.uk
dir: *2.5m N of Frome. Off A36 into Lullington*

Built in 1866 as a rectory, this quintessentially English stone country house stands in extensive grounds and gardens which convey an air of peace, quiet and tranquillity. The luxurious large bedrooms, some with four-poster beds, are decorated to high standards using beautiful fabrics, fine antique furniture and many extras such as Wi-fi, decanters of sherry, fresh flowers and well-stocked beverage trays. Breakfast is served in the impressive dining room with an excellent selection of dishes available.

Rooms 3 en suite **Facilities** FTV tea/coffee Cen ht Wi-fi ⅃ 18 **Parking** 4 **Notes** ⊗ Closed Xmas & New Year 🚭

GLASTONBURY — Map 4 ST53

See also Catcott & Somerton

Belle-Vue Bed & Breakfast

★★★ GUEST ACCOMMODATION

2 Bere Ln BA6 8BA
☎ 01458 830385
e-mail: info@bellevueglastonbury.co.uk
web: www.bellevueglastonbury.co.uk
dir: M5 junct 23, A39, A361 signed Glastonbury. B&B on right, after Fisher Hill junct

This 1920s property, close to the town centre, provides a relaxed and cosy atmosphere. All bedrooms are en suite, and some have fabulous and far-reaching views; they are all decorated in a contemporary style with many extras provided. A hearty breakfast, using quality produce, is served in the charming dining room.

Rooms 6 en suite (1 fmly) (2 GF) S £30-£35; D £60-£70 Facilities FTV tea/coffee Cen ht Licensed Wi-fi ⅃ 18 Fishing Riding 🔒 Parking 6 Notes LB ⊗

No 1 Park Terrace

★★★ GUEST HOUSE

Street Rd BA6 9EA
☎ 01458 835845 📠 01458 833296
e-mail: info@no1parkterrace.co.uk
dir: From High St into Magdalene St. Right at mini-rdbt, house 100mtrs on right

A spacious and charming Victorian guest house located within walking distance of the High Street and the Abbey ruins. The proprietors are friendly and welcoming; bedrooms are bright and airy with single rooms available. The fully licensed restaurant offers a Spanish influenced menu. Limited parking is available at the rear of the property.

Rooms 5 rms (2 en suite) (1 pri facs) S £40; D £70-£80* Facilities FTV tea/coffee Dinner available Cen ht Licensed Wi-fi Conf Max 20 Parking 5 Notes LB ⊗

HIGHBRIDGE — Map 4 ST34

The Greenwood

★★★★ GUEST ACCOMMODATION

76 Main Rd, West Huntspill TA9 3QU
☎ 01278 795886 📠 01278 795886
e-mail: info@the-greenwood.co.uk
web: www.the-greenwood.co.uk
dir: On A38 in West Huntspill, between Orchard Inn & Sundowner Hotel

Set in two acres of land, this 18th-century former farmhouse and family home offers comfortable accommodation in a friendly environment. Breakfast, featuring home-made preserves, is served in the dining room and home-cooked dinners are available by arrangement. There is a lounge for relaxation.

Rooms 7 rms (6 en suite) (1 pri facs) (3 fmly) (1 GF) S £49.50-£55; D £75-£80* Facilities FTV TVL tea/coffee Dinner available Cen ht Licensed Wi-fi ch fac Holistic treatments Conf Max 30 Thtr 30 Class 20 Board 12 Parking 8 Notes LB

HOLCOMBE — Map 4 ST64

PREMIER COLLECTION

Holcombe Inn

★★★★★ ⚛⚛ INN

Stratton Rd BA3 5EB
☎ 01761 232478
e-mail: bookings@holcombeinn.co.uk
dir: From Bath or Shepton Mallet take A367 (Fosse Way) to Stratton. Follow inn signs

Dating back to the 16th century this inn has views towards Downside Abbey in the distance. The attentive owners and pleasant staff create a friendly and relaxed atmosphere. Bedrooms are individually furnished and very comfortable. Real ales are served in the open-plan bar which has an attractive split-level restaurant.

Rooms 7 en suite (4 fmly) S £65-£75; D £80-£100* Facilities FTV tea/coffee Dinner available Direct Dial Cen ht Wi-fi Extras Speciality toiletries - complimentary Conf Thtr 40 Class 40 Parking 40

ILCHESTER — Map 4 ST52

Liongate House B&B

★★★★ BED AND BREAKFAST

Northover BA22 8NG
☎ 01935 841741
e-mail: info@liongatehouse.com
dir: A303 onto A37 towards Yeovil, after 800mtrs left at rdbt signed Ilchester. Through village, over river, opposite petrol station, through gates, House on left

Located in the central area of the pleasant town of Ilchester, this purpose-built bed and breakfast provides guests with comfortable, well-furnished bedrooms and modern bathrooms; one bedroom is on the ground floor. The welcoming resident proprietors greet guests with tea on arrival which may be taken in the pleasant rear garden if the weather allows. A choice of pubs and restaurants is available just a short stroll away.

Rooms 3 en suite (1 fmly) (1 GF) S £60-£65; D £75* Facilities FTV DVD tea/coffee Cen ht Wi-fi 🔒 Parking 3 Notes LB ⊗ Closed 23 Dec-2 Jan

ILMINSTER Map 4 ST31

Herne Lea Guest House
★★★★ GUEST ACCOMMODATION

15 Station Rd TA19 9BE
☎ 01460 53067
e-mail: enquiries@hernelea-ilminster.co.uk
web: www.hernelea-ilminster.co.uk
dir: M5 junct 25, A358 follow Ilminster signs, 50mtrs after Best Western Hotel

This welcoming Edwardian house provides impressive levels of quality and character. The bedrooms are comfortable, with well appointed and stylish bathrooms. Breakfast utilises local produce and is served in the elegant dining room which opens into the conservatory lounge with lovely views towards Herne Hill.

Rooms 3 en suite (1 fmly) S £45-£50; D £60-£65* Facilities FTV tea/coffee Cen ht Wi-fi Extras Fruit Notes LB ⊗

The New Inn
★★★★ ⬛ INN

Dowlish Wake TA19 0NZ
☎ 01460 52413
e-mail: newinn-ilminster@btconnect.com
dir: A358 or A303, follow signs for Perry's Cider, well-signed in village

Situated in the tranquil and unspoilt village of Dowlish Wake, The New Inn is a proper local pub with a warm welcome at the convivial bar. All the bedrooms are on the ground floor; they are contemporary in style and located to the rear overlooking the garden. The menu offers a range of enduring favourites and daily specials with good local produce used whenever possible. Breakfast is a substantial offering, just right for healthy appetites.

Rooms 4 annexe en suite (4 GF) Facilities FTV tea/coffee Dinner available Cen ht Parking 20

Square & Compass
★★★★ INN

Windmill Hill, Ashill TA19 9NX
☎ 01823 480467 ▤ 01823 480467
e-mail: squareandcompass@tiscali.co.uk
dir: M5 junct 25 onto A358. After 5m, turn right into Wood Rd, signed Windmill Hill; From Ilminster, 2m N on A358

This peacefully located inn provides a genuinely warm welcome and traditional hospitality. The bedrooms and modern bathrooms provide high standards of quality and comfort, and are situated in converted stables adjacent to the main building. In addition to a range of excellent home-cooked meals, a selection of real ales is also available. Outdoor seating is provided in the warmer months.

Rooms 8 en suite (8 fmly) (8 GF) S £65; D £85* Facilities FTV Lounge tea/coffee Dinner available Cen ht Wi-fi Conf Max 100 Class 100 Board 50 Parking 50 Notes Closed 24-26 Dec No coaches Civ Wed 120

KEYNSHAM Map 4 ST66

Grasmere Court
★★★★ GUEST HOUSE

22-24 Bath Rd BS31 1SN
☎ 0117 986 2662 ▤ 0117 986 2762
e-mail: grasmerecourt@aol.com
web: www.grasmerecourthotel.co.uk
dir: On B3116 just off A4 between Bath & Bristol

This very friendly, family-run establishment is located between Bath and Bristol, and once served as accommodation for senior management at the local chocolate manufacturers, J.S.Fry & Sons. Bedrooms vary in size and one has a four-poster bed. A comfortable lounge and a well-stocked bar are available, and good-value, freshly prepared food is served in the attractive dining room.

Rooms 16 en suite (2 fmly) (4 GF) S fr £63.50; D fr £79.95 Facilities STV FTV TVL tea/coffee Dinner available Direct Dial Cen ht Licensed Wi-fi ♨ 18 Extras Bottled water Conf Max 30 Thtr 30 Class 20 Board 20 Parking 11 Notes LB ⊗

KILVE Map 3 ST14

Hood Arms Inn
★★★★ INN

TA5 1EA
☎ 01278 741210 & 741969 ▤ 01278 741210
e-mail: info@thehoodarms.com
web: www.thehoodarms.com
dir: W of Bridgwater on A39, halfway between Bridgwater & Minehead

The Hood Arms is a traditional inn providing good food, comfortable bedrooms and a range of local beers in the bar. Bedrooms are well equipped, and both the bar and restaurant have a cosy feel enhanced by the open fire. Food is available daily and fresh local produce features on the extensive menu.

Rooms 8 en suite 4 annexe en suite (2 GF) Facilities FTV TVL tea/coffee Dinner available Direct Dial Wi-fi Riding Boules Bar billiards Parking 11

LOWER LANGFORD Map 4 ST46

The Langford Inn
★★★★ INN

BS40 5BL
☎ 01934 863059 ▤ 01934 863539
e-mail: langfordinn@aol.com
web: www.langfordinn.com
dir: M5 junct 21, A370 towards Bristol. At lights right onto B3133 to Langford, at mini-rdbt left signed Lower Langford

Located in a peaceful village on the edge of The Mendips, this traditional country pub offers a varied selection of real ales, well chosen wines and carefully prepared, home-made dishes at dinner. Bedrooms and bathrooms,

appointed to a high standard, are housed in two converted 17th-century barns that are adjacent to the inn. They feature exposed beams, original brickwork and oak floors combined with modern luxuries.

Rooms 7 annexe en suite (3 fmly) (6 GF) S £79; D £79-£110 (room only)* Facilities FTV TVL Dinner available Cen ht Wi-fi ♨ Conf Max 30 Thtr 30 Class 20 Board 20 Parking 20

LOWER VOBSTER Map 4 ST74

The Vobster Inn
★★★★ ⚫⚫ INN

BA3 5RJ
☎ 01373 812920 ▤ 01373 812920
e-mail: rdavila@btinternet.com
dir: From A361 follow signs for Whatley & Mells, then Vobster

Peacefully located in four acres, this is a village inn where the resident proprietors offer a genuine welcome and personal attention. Bedrooms and bathrooms provide high levels of quality and comfort. Dinner menus place an emphasis on high quality, simply prepared dishes with regular seasonal changes; several dishes demonstrate the Spanish heritage of the chef proprietor.

Rooms 3 annexe en suite (2 fmly) (3 GF) Facilities FTV tea/coffee Dinner available Cen ht Wi-fi Petanque Conf Max 40 Thtr 25 Class 32 Board 32 Parking 60 Notes ⊗ RS Sun eve & Mon (ex BH lunch) No food or drinks available

LYMPSHAM Map 4 ST35

Batch Country House
★★★★ GUEST ACCOMMODATION

Batch Ln BS24 0EX
☎ 01934 750371 ▤ 01934 750501
web: www.batchcountryhouse.co.uk
dir: M5 junct 22, take last exit on rdbt signed A370 to Weston-Super-Mare. After 3.5m, left into Lympsham, 1m, sign at end of road

In a rural location between Weston-Super-Mare and Burnham-on-Sea, this former farmhouse offers a relaxed, friendly and peaceful environment. The comfortable bedrooms have views to the Mendip and Quantock hills. Spacious lounges overlook the extensive, well-tended gardens and the comfortably furnished function room, together with the restaurant, make this a popular venue for wedding ceremonies.

Rooms 19 en suite (3 fmly) (9 GF) D £85-£95* Facilities Lounge TVL tea/coffee Dinner available Direct Dial Cen ht Licensed Wi-fi ♨ Conf Max 250 Thtr 250 Class 200 Board 200 Parking 140 Notes LB ⊗ RS 25-26 Dec bookings only Civ Wed 260

MIDSOMER NORTON — Map 4 ST65

The Moody Goose at The Old Priory

★★★★ ◉◉ RESTAURANT WITH ROOMS

Church Square BA3 2HX
☎ 01761 416784 📠 01761 417851
e-mail: info@theoldpriory.co.uk
dir: *From E: on A362 at mini-rdbt left into High St signed town centre. Right at lights. Right by church. Old Priory signed*

Dating back to the 12th century, this relaxing establishment, with plenty of historic charm and character has been sensitively restored to maintain original features. The bedrooms, including one with a four-poster, are individually styled with plenty of welcome extras. The intimate, open-plan restaurant serves innovative, carefully prepared dishes utilising local produce whenever possible. There are two cosy lounges with log fires blazing in the colder months.

Rooms 6 en suite (1 fmly) S £65-£125; D £75-£150 **Facilities** FTV Lounge tea/coffee Dinner available Cen ht Wi-fi ⚓ 9 Fishing ⚓ **Conf** Max 14 Thtr 12 Class 14 Board 14 **Parking** 15 **Notes** ✕ Closed 25 Dec & 2 Jan No coaches

MILVERTON — Map 3 ST12

The Globe

★★★ ◉ INN

Fore St TA4 1JX
☎ 01823 400534
e-mail: adele@theglobemilverton.co.uk
web: www.theglobemilverton.co.uk
dir: *M5 junct 27 follow B3277 to Milverton. In village centre*

This popular village local was once a coaching inn, and even though it has been given contemporary styling it still retains much traditional charm. The welcome is warm and genuine with a convivial atmosphere always guaranteed. Bedrooms are appointed in a similar modern style and have comfy beds. The hard-working kitchen is committed to quality, with excellent locally-sourced produce used in impressive dishes. Continental breakfast is served.

Rooms 3 en suite (1 fmly) **Facilities** tea/coffee Dinner available Cen ht Wi-fi **Parking** 4 **Notes** ✕ Closed 20 Dec-2 Jan No coaches

MINEHEAD — Map 3 SS94

Alcombe House

★★★★ GUEST ACCOMMODATION

Bircham Rd, Alcombe TA24 6BG
☎ 01643 705130
e-mail: alcombehouse@talktalkbusiness.net
web: www.alcombehouse.co.uk
dir: *A39 E towards Minehead, pass junct for Dunster, straight over at floral rdbt. Alcombe House on left*

Located midway between Minehead and Dunster on the coastal fringe of Exmoor National Park, this Grade II listed, Georgian house offers a delightful combination of efficient service and genuine hospitality delivered by the very welcoming resident proprietors. Public areas include a comfortable lounge and a candlelit dining room where a range of carefully prepared dishes is offered by prior arrangement.

Rooms 7 en suite S £46.50; D £73* **Facilities** FTV Lounge tea/coffee Dinner available Cen ht Licensed Wi-fi ⚓ **Extras** Speciality toiletries **Parking** 9 **Notes** LB No Children 15yrs Closed Nov-16 Mar

Kenella House

★★★★ GUEST ACCOMMODATION

7 Tregonwell Rd TA24 5DT
☎ 01643 703126 & 07710 889079 📠 01643 703128
e-mail: kenellahouse@fsmail.net
dir: *Off A39 onto Townsend Rd & right onto Ponsford Rd & Tregonwell Rd*

A warm welcome and relaxed atmosphere is found at Kenella House. Located close to the town centre, this guest house is also convenient for visitors to the steam railway, and walkers (a heated boot cupboard is available). The well-furnished bedrooms are very comfortable and have many extras. Home-cooked dinners (available by prior arrangement) and hearty breakfasts are served in the smart dining room.

Rooms 6 en suite (1 GF) D £60-£70* **Facilities** FTV tea/coffee Dinner available Cen ht Wi-fi ⚓ **Parking** 8 **Notes** LB ✕ No Children 14yrs Closed 23-26 Dec ◉

NORTH WOOTTON — Map 4 ST54

Crossways

★★★★ INN

Stocks Ln BA4 4EU
☎ 01749 899000 📠 01749 890476
e-mail: enquiries@thecrossways.co.uk
dir: *Exit M5 junct 22 towards Shepton Mallet, 0.2m from Pilton*

This family-run establishment is tucked away down a quiet lane, yet is with easy reach of Wells, Glastonbury and other interesting areas of Wiltshire and Somerset. The bedrooms and bathrooms are spacious and have undergone a major refurbishment to provide high levels of quality and comfort. There is a large bar-restaurant and a smaller dining room where breakfast is served. The extensive menu (served Wednesday to Sunday) features many home-cooked dishes.

Rooms 21 en suite (4 fmly) **Facilities** tea/coffee Dinner available Cen ht Pool table **Conf** Max 40 Thtr 40 Class 40 Board 25 **Notes** ✕ Closed 25 Dec RS 26 Dec-2 Jan Civ Wed 100

NORTON ST PHILIP — Map 4 ST75

PREMIER COLLECTION

Bath Lodge Castle

★★★★★ GUEST ACCOMMODATION

Warminster Rd BA2 7NH
☎ 01225 723043
e-mail: bathlodge@amazingretreats.com
dir: *On A36 between Woolverton & Farleigh Hungerford turning*

This delightful property has all the character and charm expected of a genuine castle right down to the turrets and towers. Bedrooms offer a range of shapes and sizes and all are very comfortably furnished and equipped. Some of the larger rooms have balconies with outdoor seating. Guests are welcome to use the comfortable lounge with roaring fire in the winter or relax on the rear patio in warmer months. Breakfast is served around one large table.

Rooms 7 en suite 1 annexe en suite (1 fmly) (1 GF) **Facilities** FTV iPod docking station Lounge TVL tea/coffee Dinner available Cen ht Licensed Wi-fi ⚓ Sauna ⚓ Outdoor hot tub **Extras** Speciality toiletries **Conf** Max 18 Thtr 18 Class 18 Board 16 **Parking** 30 **Notes** LB ✕

OAKHILL — Map 4 ST64

The Oakhill Inn

★★★★ ◉ INN

Fosse Rd BA3 5HU
☎ 01749 840442 📠 01749 840289
e-mail: info@theoakhillinn.com
dir: *On A367 between Stratton-on-the-Fosse & Shepton Mallet*

A welcoming country inn, offering warm hospitality, locally sourced food and a wide selection of fine ales from local micro-breweries. The comfortable bedrooms include luxuries such as Egyptian cotton sheets and DVD players. Dinner here should not be missed. In addition to lighter bar snacks, a full range of high quality dishes utilising fresh local produce is also available.

Rooms 5 en suite (1 fmly) **Facilities** FTV tea/coffee Dinner available Cen ht Wi-fi ⚓ **Parking** 12

Save on B&Bs and Hotels. Book at theAA.com/hotel

SOMERSET 263 ENGLAND

PORLOCK
Map 3 SS84

Tudor Cottage

★★★★ GUEST ACCOMMODATION

TA24 8HQ
☎ 01643 862255 & 07855 531593
e-mail: tudorcottagebossington@btconnect.com
dir: *M5 junct 25, A358, A39 through Minehead. 5m, follow signs for Allerford & Bossington. 1m, 1st house on left*

Parts of this engaging cottage date back to the 15th century, and many period features have been retained. The welcome couldn't be warmer with tea and cakes in the lovely garden to get the stay off to a relaxing start. The setting is a haven of peace and tranquillity with a wonderful wooded hillside as a backdrop. Bedrooms are reassuringly cosseting with all the expected modern comforts. Breakfast features a host of locally sourced produce, and light snacks are also offered in the evenings.

Rooms 3 rms (1 en suite) (2 pri facs) S £50-£75; D £70-£75* **Facilities** FTV DVD TVL tea/coffee Dinner available Licensed Wi-fi ⓑ **Extras** Books; mini-bar - chargeable **Parking** 3 **Notes** LB ⊗ No Children 10yrs

RUDGE
Map 4 ST85

The Full Moon Inn

★★★ INN

BA11 2QF
☎ 01373 830936
e-mail: info@thefullmoon.co.uk
dir: *From A36 S from Bath, 10m, left at Standerwick by The Bell pub. 4m from Warminster*

Peacefully located in the quiet village of Rudge, this traditional inn offers a warm welcome and a proper country pub atmosphere. In the bar area, guests mix happily with the locals to enjoy a selection of real ales and a log fire in the colder months. In addition to bar meals, a comfortable restaurant serving excellent home-cooked dishes is also available. Bedrooms include some at the main inn and more in an adjacent annexe - all are comfortable and well equipped.

Rooms 5 en suite 12 annexe en suite (2 fmly) (3 GF) **Facilities** tea/coffee Dinner available Cen ht ⓒ **Conf** Max 65 Thtr 30 Class 12 Board 18 **Parking** 25

SHEPTON MALLET
Map 4 ST64

Cannards Grave Farmhouse

★★★★ GUEST ACCOMMODATION

Cannards Grave BA4 4LY
☎ 01749 347091 📠 01749 347091
e-mail: sue@cannardsgravefarmhouse.co.uk
web: www.cannardsgravefarmhouse.co.uk
dir: *On A37 between Shepton Mallet & The Bath and West Showground, 100yds from Highwayman pub towards showground on left*

Conveniently located for the Royal Bath & West Showground, Longleat, Glastonbury and Wells, this 17th-century house provides thoughtfully equipped en suite bedrooms. There is also a well-furnished lounge, and breakfast is served in the conservatory dining room. The proprietors provide warm hospitality.

Rooms 4 en suite 1 annexe en suite (2 fmly) (1 GF) **Facilities** FTV TVL tea/coffee Cen ht Wi-fi **Parking** 6 **Notes** ⊗

The Thatched Cottage

★★★★ ⚙ INN

63-67 Charlton Rd BA4 5QF
☎ 01749 342058 📠 01749 901100
e-mail: enquiries@thatchedcottageinn.com
dir: *0.6m E of town centre on A361*

With a change of owners, this popular inn offers a warm welcome and traditional hospitality. Bedrooms and bathrooms come in a range of shapes and sizes but all are comfortably furnished. There is a choice of seating areas for either drinking or dining, in addition to outdoor seating in the pleasant garden. Guests have a choice of carefully prepared quality food at dinner from menus of pub classics to a more fine-dining option - all meals are served in a welcoming atmosphere.

Rooms 8 en suite (1 fmly) D £75-£89* **Facilities** FTV Lounge Dinner available Direct Dial Cen ht Wi-fi ⓑ **Conf** Max 45 Thtr 45 Class 25 Board 35 **Parking** 48 **Notes** LB ⊗

The Abbey Barn

★★★ BED AND BREAKFAST

Doulting BA4 4QD
☎ 01749 880321
e-mail: abbeybarn@btconnect.com
dir: *2m E of Shepton Mallet on A361 in Doulting centre*

Situated on the edge of the Mendips in the pretty village of Doulting, this Grade II listed property is renowned for its friendly welcome and top quality breakfasts. A licensed cosy residents' lounge bar provides a relaxing area to enjoy a drink or two. Log fires burn in the winter, and guests can enjoy the attractive garden in the summer. Private parking is available.

Rooms 3 en suite (1 fmly) S £49-£69; D £69-£74* **Facilities** FTV Lounge tea/coffee Licensed Wi-fi ⓑ **Extras** Fruit, snacks **Parking** 10 **Notes** LB ⊗ No Children

SOMERTON
Map 4 ST42

The Devonshire Arms

★★★★ ⚙ INN

Long Sutton TA10 9LP
☎ 01458 241271 📠 01458 241037
e-mail: mail@thedevonshirearms.com
web: www.thedevonshirearms.com
dir: *A303 onto A372 at Podimore rdbt. After 4m left onto B3165, signed Martock & Long Sutton*

This popular village inn offers an appealing blend of traditional and contemporary styling throughout the spacious public areas and accommodation. Bedrooms are individually designed and provide impressive levels of comfort and quality. Public areas include the convivial bar and elegant restaurant where excellent local produce is utilised in skilfully executed dishes.

Rooms 7 rms (6 en suite) (1 pri facs) 2 annexe en suite (1 fmly) (2 GF) **Facilities** FTV tea/coffee Dinner available Cen ht Wi-fi ⓑ ⚐ 18 **Parking** 6 **Notes** Closed 25-26 Dec & 1 Jan

Somerton Court Country House

★★★★ GUEST ACCOMMODATION

TA11 7AH
☎ 01458 274694 📠 01458 274694
e-mail: enquiries@somertoncourt.com
web: www.somertoncourt.com
dir: *From A303 onto A372 at Podimore rdbt. In 3m right onto B3151 to Somerton & follow signs*

Dating back to the 17th century and set in extensive gardens and grounds, this house provides a tranquil haven away from the pressures of modern life. The comfortable bedrooms have lovely views, and breakfast is served in a delightful dining room that overlooks the gardens.

Rooms 4 en suite 2 annexe en suite (2 fmly) S fr £50; D fr £80* **Facilities** tea/coffee Cen ht Licensed Riding **Conf** Max 200 Thtr 200 Class 150 **Parking** 30 **Notes** ⊗ Closed Xmas & New Year

STANTON DREW · Map 4 ST56

Greenlands (ST597636)

★★★★ FARMHOUSE

BS39 4ES
☎ 01275 333487 🖹 01275 331211 Mrs J Cleverley
dir: A37 onto B3130, on right before Stanton Drew Garage

Situated near the ancient village of Stanton Drew in the heart of the Chew Valley, Greenlands is convenient for Bristol Airport and Bath, Bristol and Wells. There are comfortable, well-equipped bedrooms and a downstairs lounge, and breakfast is the highlight of any stay here.

Rooms 4 en suite **Facilities** STV FTV TVL tea/coffee Cen ht Wi-fi **Parking** 8 **Notes** No Children 12yrs ⊗ 3 acres hobby farm/poultry

Valley Farm

★★★★ BED AND BREAKFAST

Sandy Ln BS39 4EL
☎ 01275 332723 & 07799 768161
e-mail: valleyfarm2010@btinternet.com
dir: Exit B3130 into Stanton Drew, right onto Sandy Ln

Located on a quiet country lane, Valley Farm offers relaxing and friendly accommodation. All bedrooms are comfortable and well equipped, and each has pleasant views over the countryside. Breakfast is served around a communal table in the dining room, and although dinner is not available, a number of village pubs are just a stroll away. Also conveniently located for Bath and Bristol.

Rooms 3 en suite (1 fmly) (1 GF) S £38-£42; D £70-£75* **Facilities** FTV TVL tea/coffee Cen ht Wi-fi **Parking** 6 **Notes** ⊗ No Children 12yrs Closed Xmas ⊗

STAPLE FITZPAINE · Map 4 ST21

Greyhound Inn

★★★★ ➡ INN

TA3 5SP
☎ 01823 480227 🖹 01823 481117
e-mail: thegreyhound-inn@btconnect.com
web: www.thegreyhoundinn.biz
dir: M5 junct 25, A358 signed Yeovil. In 3m turn right, signed Staple Fitzpaine

Set in the heart of Somerset in the Blackdown Hills, this picturesque village inn has great atmosphere and character, complete with flagstone floors and open fires. An imaginative choice of freshly-prepared seasonal dishes using locally sourced ingredients is featured on the ever-changing blackboard menu. The delightful bedrooms are spacious, comfortable, and well equipped with many extra facilities.

Rooms 4 en suite **Facilities** FTV tea/coffee Dinner available Direct Dial Cen ht Wi-fi Pool table **Conf** Max 60 Thtr 60 Class 30 Board 20 **Parking** 40 **Notes** No Children 10yrs

STOGUMBER · Map 3 ST03

Wick House

★★★★ ⚄ GUEST HOUSE

Brook St TA4 3SZ
☎ 01984 656422
e-mail: sheila@wickhouse.co.uk
web: www.wickhouse.co.uk
dir: Off A358 into village, left at the x-rds, Wick House 3rd on left

Rooms 9 en suite (1 GF) S £35-£50; D £70-£80* **Facilities** FTV Lounge tea/coffee Dinner available Licensed Wi-fi ★ **Extras** Sweets - complimentary **Parking** 6 **Notes** LB ⊗

STREET · Map 4 ST43

The Two Brewers

★★★★ INN

38 Leigh Rd BA16 0HB
☎ 01458 442421
e-mail: richard@thetwobrewers.co.uk
web: www.thetwobrewers.co.uk

This traditional inn is very popular with locals and tourists alike and offers a genuine welcome, excellent home-cooked food and a selection of fine, real ales. The bedrooms are located in an annexe to the rear of the inn, and are well equipped and comfortable. The absence of music and machines in the bar adds to the relaxing atmosphere, and the menu choices include regularly-changing blackboard specials and guest real ales.

Rooms 3 annexe en suite (1 GF) D £49 **Facilities** FTV tea/coffee Dinner available Cen ht Wi-fi ★ Skittle alley **Parking** 3 **Notes** LB ⊗ Closed 25-26 Dec No coaches

Kasuli Bed & Breakfast

★★★ BED AND BREAKFAST

71 Somerton Rd BA16 0DN
☎ 01458 442063
dir: B3151 from Street rdbt for Somerton, house 400yds past Street Inn on left

This family home is located close to Clarks Village Outlet Centre and with easy access to local places of historical interest. Friendliness and a homely atmosphere are offered, and bedrooms are neatly presented. An enjoyable traditional breakfast is served in the dining room around the family dining table.

Rooms 2 rms S £28; D £52 **Facilities** FTV tea/coffee Cen ht Wi-fi ★ **Parking** 2 **Notes** ⊗ No Children 10yrs Closed 1-27 Jan ⊗

TAUNTON · Map 4 ST22

See also Staple Fitzpaine

PREMIER COLLECTION

Elm Villa

★★★★★ BED AND BREAKFAST

1 Private Rd, Staplegrove Rd TA2 6AJ
☎ 01823 336165 & 07704 469820
e-mail: ferguson@elmvilla10.freeserve.co.uk
dir: M5 junct 25, A358 (Minehead road) to Staplegrove Inn, left, left again into Private Rd

This spacious and comfortable Victorian villa enjoys distant views of the Blackdown Hills, yet is within walking distance of the town centre, theatre, station and county cricket ground. Both bedrooms are en suite and have plenty of facilities. Ample parking is available.

Rooms 2 en suite **Facilities** FTV Lounge tea/coffee Cen ht Wi-fi ★ **Parking** 2 **Notes** ⊗ No Children 10yrs ⊗

Meryan House

★★★★ ⚄ GUEST ACCOMMODATION

Bishop's Hull TA1 5EG
☎ 01823 337445 🖹 01823 322355
e-mail: meryanhousehotel@yahoo.co.uk
web: www.meryanhouse.co.uk
dir: 1.5m W of town centre. Off Silk Mills Rd (A358)

Located in its own grounds just over a mile from the town centre, this 17th-century property has delightful individually furnished rooms, featuring antiques along with modern facilities. Interesting dishes are available at dinner, and there is also a cosy bar and a spacious lounge.

Rooms 12 en suite (2 fmly) (2 GF) S £65-£80; D £70-£90* **Facilities** STV FTV DVD iPod docking station TVL tea/coffee Dinner available Cen ht Licensed Wi-fi ★ **Conf** Max 25 Thtr 25 Class 25 Board 18 **Parking** 17 **Notes** LB RS Sun No evening meal

Save on B&Bs and Hotels. Book at theAA.com/hotel

SOMERSET 265 ENGLAND

Wick House B&B

★ ★ ★ ★ ★ BED AND BREAKFAST

Norton Fitzwarren TA4 1BT
☎ 01823 289614 & 07772 052063
e-mail: info@wick-house.co.uk
dir: *From Taunton take B3227 through Norton Fitzwarren, after old railway bridge, 1st house on right*

This family-run establishment is handily placed just a few minutes from Taunton and within 15 minutes of the M5. Bedrooms are located away from the main house, allowing guests the flexibility to come and go as they please. All bedrooms provide impressive levels of comfort and quality, including spacious wet rooms and a kitchenette area for preparation of beverages. Breakfast is taken in the well-appointed dining room which has lovely views across the orchard.

Rooms 3 annexe en suite (3 GF) S £45-£55; D £65-£80
Facilities FTV DVD tea/coffee Cen ht Wi-fi ⬤ **Extras** Bottled water **Parking** 3 **Notes** ⊗ No Children

Blorenge House

★ ★ ★ ★ GUEST ACCOMMODATION

57 Staple Grove Rd TA1 1DG
☎ 01823 283005 🖷 01823 283005
e-mail: enquiries@blorengehouse.co.uk
dir: *M5 junct 25, towards cricket ground & Morrisons on left, left at lights, right at 2nd lights, house 150yds on left*

This fine Victorian property offers spacious accommodation and is within walking distance of the town centre. The bedrooms, some at ground-floor level and some with four-poster beds, are individually furnished and vary in size. A lounge is available, and the garden, with an outdoor swimming pool, is open to guests during daytime hours most days of the week. There is also ample parking.

Rooms 23 rms (19 en suite) (4 pri facs) (2 fmly) (2 GF)
Facilities FTV TVL tea/coffee Cen ht Wi-fi ⬌ **Conf** Max 20 **Parking** 23

Brookfield House

★ ★ ★ ★ GUEST HOUSE

16 Wellington Rd TA1 4EQ
☎ 01823 272786 🖷 01823 240003
e-mail: info@brookfieldguesthouse.uk.com
web: www.brookfieldguesthouse.uk.com
dir: *From town centre follow signs to Musgrove Hospital, onto A38 (Wellington Rd), on right opposite turn to hospital*

This charming Grade II listed Georgian house is just a five-minute, level walk from the town centre. The family take great pride in caring for guests, and the brightly decorated bedrooms are well equipped. Breakfast, featuring local produce, is served in the attractive dining room. The property is entirely non-smoking.

Rooms 7 en suite (1 fmly) S £62-£68; D £75-£98*
Facilities FTV Lounge tea/coffee Dinner available Cen ht Wi-fi **Parking** 8 **Notes** ⊗ No Children 7yrs

Creechbarn Bed & Breakfast

★ ★ ★ ★ BED AND BREAKFAST

Vicarage Ln, Creech St Michael TA3 5PP
☎ 01823 443955
e-mail: mick@somersite.co.uk
dir: *M5 junct 25, A358 to Creech St Michael, follow canal boat signs to end Vicarage Ln. Through brick gateposts, turn right*

Located next to the canal and on a Sustrans cycle route, this traditional Somerset barn was lovingly converted by the current owners. Bedrooms are comfortable and there is a spacious sitting room with books and TV. Breakfast is carefully prepared with free-range eggs and home-made bread.

Rooms 2 rms (1 en suite) (1 pri facs) S £46; D £56-£60*
Facilities TVL TV1B tea/coffee Direct Dial Cen ht Wi-fi ⬤ **Parking** 6 **Notes** LB Closed 20 Dec-6 Jan ⊛

Lower Farm (ST281241)

★ ★ ★ ★ FARMHOUSE

Thornfalcon TA3 5NR
☎ 01823 443549 Mrs D Titman
e-mail: doreen@titman.eclipse.co.uk
web: www.thornfalcon.co.uk
dir: *M5 junct 25, 2m SE on A358, left opposite Nags Head pub, farm signed 1m on left*

This charming, thatched, 15th-century farmhouse is set in lovely gardens and is surrounded by open countryside. Hearty breakfasts, served in the farmhouse kitchen, feature home-produced eggs. Some bedrooms are located in the converted granary, some on the ground floor. There is a comfortable sitting room with a log fire.

Rooms 2 rms (1 en suite) (1 pri facs) 9 annexe rms 7 annexe en suite (2 pri facs) (2 fmly) (7 GF) S £45-£50; D £70-£75* **Facilities** FTV TVL TV9B tea/coffee Cen ht Wi-fi ⬤ **Parking** 10 **Notes** LB ⊗ No Children 5yrs 10 acres beef/cows/poultry

Lower Marsh Farm (ST224279)

★ ★ ★ ★ FARMHOUSE

Kingston St Mary TA2 8AB
☎ 01823 451331 🖷 01823 451331 Mr & Mrs J Gothard
e-mail: b&b@lowermarshfarm.co.uk
web: www.lowermarshfarm.co.uk
dir: *M5 junct 25. Farm between Taunton & Kingston St Mary just past King's Hall School on right*

Located at the foot of the Quantock Hills, this delightful family-run farm provides a warm welcome with a pot of tea and cake ready and waiting. Bedrooms are individually styled and reflect the traditional charm of the house; they provide impressive levels of quality and are complemented by numerous thoughtful extras. The Aga-cooked breakfast is a real treat, served in the dining room around one grand table; evening meals are available by prior arrangement. There is also a spacious lounge warmed by a crackling log fire in winter.

Rooms 3 en suite (1 fmly) S fr £40; D fr £75*
Facilities TVL tea/coffee Dinner available Cen ht Wi-fi ⬤ **Parking** 6 **Notes** ⊗ 300 acres arable

TAUNTON *continued*

Higher Dipford Farm *(ST216205)*

★★★ FARMHOUSE

Trull TA3 7NU
☎ 01823 275770 ▤ 01823 275770 Mrs M Fewings
e-mail: mafewings@tesco.net
web: www.higherdipfordfarm.com
dir: *From Taunton town centre on A38 towards Wellington left into Trull Rd signed Trull & Blagdon. Becomes Honiton Rd. In Trull, right into Dipford Rd, farm on left*

This Grade II listed, 17th-century longhouse is part of a working farm. Steeped in character with elm beams and inglenook fireplaces, the house provides well-equipped and homely accommodation. Bedrooms are comfortable and individually decorated, and there is an honesty bar and lounge. Breakfasts and home-cooked dinners, featuring local produce, are served in the spacious dining room.

Rooms 3 en suite (1 fmly) Facilities STV FTV TVL tea/coffee Dinner available Cen ht Licensed ⛴ Parking 6 Notes ⊗ ⊜ 120 acres beef

---

TINTINHULL   Map 4 ST41

Crown & Victoria

★★★★ ⊕ INN

Farm St BA22 8PZ
☎ 01935 823341 ▤ 01935 825786
e-mail: info@thecrownandvictoria.co.uk
web: www.thecrownandvictoria.co.uk
dir: *Off A303, signs for Tintinhull Gardens*

Appointed to a high standard, the light and airy property has very well-equipped bedrooms. The staff ensure guests are well cared for, and the contemporary bar and restaurant provide a good selection of carefully prepared dishes.

Rooms 5 en suite Facilities tea/coffee Dinner available Cen ht Wi-fi Parking 60 Notes No coaches

---

WATCHET   Map 3 ST04

The Georgian House

★★★★ GUEST HOUSE

28 Swain St TA23 0AD
☎ 01984 639279
e-mail: georgianhouse_watchet@virgin.net
dir: *From A39 over railway bridge into main street*

This elegant Georgian property is situated in the heart of the increasingly popular coastal resort and is within a short walk of the impressive marina. The comfortable bedrooms combine quality and individuality. Breakfast (and dinner by arrangement) is served in the well-appointed dining room. Additional facilities for guests include a lounge and the use of the garden.

Rooms 3 en suite Facilities Dinner available Cen ht Parking 2 Notes ⊗ ⊜

WATERROW   Map 3 ST02

The Rock Inn

★★★★ ⊜ INN

TA4 2AX
☎ 01984 623293 ▤ 01984 623293
e-mail: enquiries@rockinn.co.uk
dir: *On B3227*

Set in the lush greenery of the Tone Valley, this 16th-century inn, as its name suggests, is built against a rock face. There is an abundance of character, and the friendly atmosphere draws both locals and visitors alike. A range of freshly prepared, imaginative meals is available in the bar and restaurant, including Aberdeen Angus steaks from the owner's farm. The bedrooms are comfortable, light and airy.

Rooms 8 en suite (1 fmly) Facilities FTV TVL tea/coffee Dinner available Direct Dial Cen ht Wi-fi Parking 25

WEDMORE   Map 4 ST44

The Swan

★★★★ ⊜ INN

Cheddar Rd BS28 4EQ
☎ 01934 710337
e-mail: info@theswanwedmore.com
dir: *M5 junct 22 onto A38 towards Highbridge/Burnham-on-Sea. At rdbt take 3rd exit onto A370. Right into Harp Rd, then left onto B3139. At junct of Church Rd & Cheddar Rd*

Having recently undergone a complete refurbishment, The Swan offers high quality and comfortable accommodation in the centre of this delightful village. Bedrooms and bathrooms offer a range of shapes and sizes and are all well equipped with plenty of useful extras including Wi-fi. The restaurant offers a stylish, contemporary feel and additional seating is available in the comfortable bar and pleasant rear garden. High quality produce is utilised at both dinner and breakfast.

Rooms 6 en suite S £85-£110; D £85-£110*
Facilities FTV DVD iPod docking station tea/coffee Dinner available Cen ht Wi-fi 🔲 Conf Max 60 Thtr 60 Class 40 Board 40 Parking 12

WELLINGTON   Map 3 ST12

The Cleve Spa

★★★★ GUEST ACCOMMODATION

Mantle St TA21 8SN
☎ 01823 662033 ▤ 01823 660874
e-mail: reception@clevehotel.com
web: www.clevehotel.com
dir: *M5 junct 26 follow signs to Wellington town centre. Continue for 600mtrs, entrance on left*

This elegant Victorian country house is situated in an elevated position with commanding views. Bedrooms provide high levels of comfort and quality with well appointed and stylish bathrooms. Dinner and breakfast are served in the attractive restaurant, after which a stroll around the extensive grounds may be appropriate. An impressive array of leisure facilities is also offered, including indoor pool, spa bath, steam room and fully-equipped fitness studio.

Rooms 20 en suite (5 fmly) (3 GF) S £65-£85; D £80-£110* Facilities FTV tea/coffee Dinner available Direct Dial Cen ht Licensed Wi-fi 🔲 Sauna Gym Spa beauty treatments Conf Max 250 Thtr 250 Class 100 Board 60 Parking 100 Notes LB Civ Wed 200

WELLS   Map 4 ST54

See also Croscombe

PREMIER COLLECTION

Beaconsfield Farm

★★★★★ ▤ BED AND BREAKFAST

Easton BA5 1DU
☎ 01749 870308
e-mail: carol@beaconsfieldfarm.co.uk
web: www.beaconsfieldfarm.co.uk
dir: *2.5m from Wells on A371, on right just before Easton*

Set in pleasant, well-tended gardens on the west side of the Mendip Hills, Beaconsfield Farm is a convenient base for exploring this attractive area. The welcoming hosts are really friendly and attentive, and many guests return on a regular basis. The comfortable bedrooms are delightfully decorated with co-ordinated fabrics and have many guest extras. A choice of well-cooked dishes featuring fresh local produce is offered at breakfast.

Rooms 3 en suite Facilities FTV TVL tea/coffee Cen ht Wi-fi Parking 10 Notes ⊗ No Children 8yrs Closed 22 Dec-3 Jan ⊜

Beryl

★★★★★ 🅰 BED AND BREAKFAST

Hawkers Ln BA5 3JP
☎ **01749 678738** 📠 **01749 670508**
e-mail: stay@beryl-wells.co.uk
dir: *Exit B3139 (Radstock Rd), signed The Horringtons, onto Hawkers Ln opposite BP garage, to end*

Rooms 11 rms (10 en suite) (1 pri facs) (3 fmly) S £75-£95; D £90-£150* **Facilities** FTV TVL tea/coffee Direct Dial Cen ht Lift Licensed Wi-fi ch fac ↘ 🐾 childrens play area **Parking** 20 **Notes** LB Closed 25-26 Dec

Double-Gate Farm *(ST484424)*

★★★★ FARMHOUSE

Godney BA5 1RZ
☎ **01458 832217** 📠 **01458 835612** Mr Millard
e-mail: doublegatefarm@aol.com
web: www.doublegatefarm.com
dir: *A39 from Wells towards Glastonbury, at Polsham right signed Godney/Polsham. 2m to x-rds, continue to farmhouse on left after inn*

Expect a warm welcome not only from the owners, but also their friendly Labradors. Set on the banks of the River Sheppey on the Somerset Levels, this comfortable farmhouse is well known for its attractive summer flower garden, as well as delicious breakfasts. Guests have use of a games room and free internet access in the lounge.

Double-Gate Farm

Rooms 3 en suite 4 annexe en suite (4 fmly) (4 GF) S £60-£85; D £70-£120* **Facilities** FTV DVD TVL tea/coffee Direct Dial Cen ht Wi-fi Fishing Snooker 🎱 Table tennis **Extras** Mini-fridges in 4 rooms **Parking** 9 **Notes** ⊗ Closed 20 Dec-5 Jan 100 acres mixed

See advert on this page

The Crown at Wells

★★★★ INN

Market Place BA5 2RP
☎ **01749 673457** 📠 **01749 679792**
e-mail: stay@crownatwells.co.uk
web: www.crownatwells.co.uk
dir: *On entering Wells follow signs for Hotels & Deliveries, in Market Place, car park at rear*

Retaining its original features and period charm, this historic inn is situated in the heart of the city, just a short stroll from the cathedral. The building's frontage has been used in many film productions. Bedrooms, all with modern facilities, vary in size and style. Public areas focus around Anton's, the popular bistro, which has a light, airy environment and relaxed atmosphere. The Penn Bar offers an alternative eating option and real ales.

Rooms 15 en suite (2 fmly) S £65-£95; D £95-£115* **Facilities** FTV Lounge tea/coffee Dinner available Cen ht Wi-fi ♨ 18 🏃 **Parking** 10 **Notes** LB

Highfield

★★★★ BED AND BREAKFAST

93 Portway BA5 2BR
☎ **01749 675330**
dir: *Enter Wells & signs for A371 Cheddar, Highfield on Portway after last lights at top of hill*

Within walking distance of the city and cathedral, this delightful home maintains Edwardian style and provides comfortable accommodation. Pleasant views can be enjoyed over the countryside - some from the comfort of your own bedroom balcony. A carefully prepared breakfast is served around one large table in the well furnished breakfast room. Welcome extra features include the well tended garden and off-street parking.

Rooms 3 en suite (1 fmly) S £45-£55; D £65-£70* **Facilities** FTV tea/coffee Cen ht Wi-fi **Parking** 7 **Notes** LB ⊗ No Children 2yrs Closed 23 Dec-1 Jan 🐾

WELLS *continued*

Hollow Tree Farm

★★★★ GUEST ACCOMMODATION

Launcherley BA5 1QJ
☎ 01749 673715 & 07704 506513 ▤ 01749 673715
e-mail: jennifercoombes1@hotmail.co.uk
dir: *A39 from Wells for Glastonbury, 1st left at Brownes Garden Centre, farm 0.5m on right*

Delightfully appointed rooms with bright, cheery colour schemes and comfortable furnishings are provided at this non-working farm. Spectacular views of Wells Cathedral and Glastonbury Tor and delightful flower-filled gardens add to the charm. The friendly hosts are most welcoming and attentive, and home-baked bread, jams and marmalade are only a part of the delicious breakfast.

Rooms 2 en suite (2 GF) S £35-£40; D £55-£60*
Facilities TVL tea/coffee Cen ht Wi-fi **Parking** 4 **Notes** LB
⊗ No Children 12yrs Closed mid Dec-mid Jan ⊜

Amber House

★★★ BED AND BREAKFAST

Coxley BA5 1QZ
☎ 01749 679612
e-mail: amberhouse.wells@gmail.com
dir: *On A39 in village, 0.25m S past Pound Inn on right*

Located less than two miles south of the centre of Wells, and ideally placed for touring the area's historic sites and countryside, this friendly family home offers a relaxed atmosphere. Bedrooms are well equipped; some look out over open countryside and farmland to the rear. A traditional English breakfast is served at separate tables, in the cosy dining room, which guests are welcome to use at other times.

Rooms 3 en suite S £35; D £50-£60* **Facilities** FTV DVD tea/coffee Cen ht Wi-fi 🔒 **Parking** 3 **Notes** ⊗ ⊜

Birdwood House

★★★ GUEST ACCOMMODATION

Birdwood, Bath Rd BA5 3EW
☎ 01749 679250
e-mail: info@birdwood-bandb.co.uk
web: www.birdwood-bandb.co.uk
dir: *1.5m NE of city centre. On B3139 between South & West Horrington*

Set in extensive grounds and gardens just a short drive from the town centre, this imposing detached house dates from the 1850s. The bedrooms are comfortable and equipped with a number of extra facilities. Breakfast is served around a communal table in the pleasant dining room or conservatory, which is also available for guest use throughout the day.

Rooms 3 rms (2 en suite) (1 pri facs) (1 fmly)
Facilities TVL tea/coffee Cen ht 🐾 **Parking** 12 **Notes** ⊜

19 St Cuthbert Street

★★ BED AND BREAKFAST

BA5 2AW
☎ 01749 673166
dir: *At bottom of High St opposite St Cuthbert's Church*

Guests are assured of a friendly welcome at this charming terrace house, which is within walking distance of the cathedral and bus station. The accommodation is fresh, light and comfortable and the atmosphere homely. Bedrooms are well appointed and there is a comfortable lounge. Breakfast, featuring home-made marmalade, is served in the dining room around a family table.

Rooms 2 rms S £35-£45; D £58-£64* **Facilities** FTV TVL tea/coffee Cen ht **Notes** ⊗ No Children 5yrs ⊜

WEST HUNTSPILL	Map 4 ST34

Crossways Inn

★★★★ INN

Withy Rd TA9 3RA
☎ 01278 783756
e-mail: info@crosswaysinn.com
dir: *On main A38*

Crossways is a traditional inn serving good food and offering a very high standard of accommodation. Service is warm and friendly; bedrooms are very comfortable, and offer a host of extras such as iPod docks and Wi-fi.

Rooms 7 en suite (2 GF) D £54.95-£89.95* **Facilities** FTV iPod docking station tea/coffee Dinner available Cen ht Wi-fi Pool table **Parking** 72

WESTON-SUPER-MARE	Map 4 ST36

Church House

★★★★★ BED AND BREAKFAST

27 Kewstoke Rd, Kewstoke BS22 9YD
☎ 01934 633185
e-mail: churchhouse@kewstoke.net
web: www.churchhousekewstoke.co.uk
dir: *From M5 junct 21 follow signs for Kewstoke 2.5m, next to Kewstoke Church*

In a peaceful location at the foot of Monk's Hill, this delightful property enjoys wonderful views of the Bristol Channel and as far as Wales on clear days. The bedrooms are stylish and spacious, with lots of thoughtful extras and well-appointed en suites. Public areas include a pleasant conservatory and an elegant dining room where impressive breakfasts are served.

Rooms 5 en suite **Facilities** tea/coffee Cen ht Wi-fi **Parking** 10

PREMIER COLLECTION

9 The Park

★★★★★ GUEST ACCOMMODATION

9 Ellenborough Park Rd BS23 1XJ
☎ 01934 415244 & 07792 184230
e-mail: info@9theparkbandb.co.uk
dir: A370 towards town centre, through 5 rdbts, 1st exit
at next rdbt into Station Approach. Pass station, into
Neva Rd, left into Ellenborough Park Rd, 40mtrs on left

This elegant property is peacefully located in a
residential area, just a short walk from the beach and
town centre. Bedrooms and bathrooms are all
decorated and furnished to high standards, and the
beds are especially comfortable. The attentive
proprietors ensure guests are very well looked after at
all times. Breakfast is a highlight, with plenty of fresh
local produce, including a varied choice of hot dishes,
a wide range of fruits, cheeses and other items.

Rooms 3 en suite (2 fmly) S £60; D £85* **Facilities** FTV
tea/coffee Cen ht Wi-fi 🛆 **Parking** 4 **Notes** ⊗

Oakover Guest House

★★★★ GUEST HOUSE

25 Clevedon Rd BS23 1DA
☎ 01934 620125 📠 01934 620173
e-mail: info@oakover.co.uk
web: www.oakover.co.uk
dir: Exit A370 (Beach Rd) near Sea Life Aquarium into
Clevedon Rd

Oakover is a substantial Victorian property situated a
short level walk from the town centre and seafront.
Bedrooms and bathrooms offer very good levels of quality
and comfort. A varied breakfast menu is offered in the
bright dining room. The friendly resident proprietor
maintains an easy-going and welcoming establishment.

Rooms 6 en suite (2 GF) S £45-£75; D £60-£100
Facilities FTV DVD tea/coffee Cen ht Wi-fi **Parking** 7
Notes ⊗ No Children 12yrs

Beverley Guest House

★★★★ GUEST HOUSE

11 Whitecross Rd BS23 1EP
☎ 01934 622956 & 07824 512085 📠 01934 622956
e-mail: beverley11@hushmail.com
dir: Exit A370 (Beach Rd) into Ellenborough Park Rd
South, 2nd right

This charming guest house is located in a quieter
residential area, yet is only a short stroll from both the
beach and the town centre. The bedrooms and bathrooms
come in a range of shapes and sizes but all are equipped
with a number of welcome extras. A good selection of hot
and cold items is offered at breakfast and served in the
comfortable dining room.

Rooms 5 en suite (1 fmly) (1 GF) S £30-£38; D £60-£76*
Facilities FTV DVD tea/coffee Cen ht Wi-fi **Notes** LB ⊗
Closed 20 Dec-2 Jan

Camellia Lodge

★★★★ BED AND BREAKFAST

76 Walliscote Rd BS23 1ED
☎ 01934 613534 📠 01934 613534
e-mail: dachefs@aol.com
dir: 200yds from seafront

Guests return regularly for the warm welcome at this
immaculate Victorian family home, which is just off the
seafront and within walking distance of the town centre.
Bedrooms have a range of thoughtful touches, and
carefully prepared breakfasts are served in the relaxing
dining room. Home-cooked dinners are also available by
prior arrangement.

Rooms 5 en suite (2 fmly) S £30-£35; D £60-£70*
Facilities FTV tea/coffee Dinner available Cen ht Wi-fi

Jamesfield Guest House

★★★★ GUEST HOUSE

1A Ellenborough Park North BS23 1XH
☎ 01934 642898
e-mail: jamesfield1@aol.com

A well-maintained property in an ideal location, a short
walk from the seafront and only a few minutes stroll from
town. The bedrooms are comfortably furnished and well
decorated, and include rooms on the ground floor. Guests
are welcome to use the relaxing lounge, and the property
also benefits from its own car park.

Rooms 7 rms (6 en suite) (1 pri facs) (2 GF) S £35;
D £60* **Facilities** FTV TVL tea/coffee Cen ht Wi-fi
Parking 9 **Notes** ⊗

Linden Lodge Guest House

★★★★ GUEST ACCOMMODATION

27 Clevedon Rd BS23 1DA
☎ 01934 645797
e-mail: info@lindenlodge.com
dir: Follow signs to seafront. 0.5m S of grand pier turn
into Clevedon Rd

Just a short walk from the town centre and the seafront,
Linden Lodge offers a traditional style of welcoming
hospitality and guest care. Bedrooms come in a range of
shapes and sizes, and all are well decorated and
equipped. A good selection is offered at breakfast which
is served in the pleasant conservatory.

Rooms 5 en suite (1 fmly) **Facilities** tea/coffee Cen ht
Parking 3 **Notes** ⊗

The Owls Crest House

★★★★ BED AND BREAKFAST

39 Kewstoke Rd, Kewstoke BS22 9YE
☎ 01934 417672 & 07929 350017
e-mail: theowlscrest1@btinternet.com
dir: M5 junct 21, A370 towards Weston, 1st left towards
Kewstoke. Through 4 rdbts, to T-junct in Kewstoke. Turn
left. Owls Crest House after New Inn pub

Guests will find an especially friendly welcome from the
resident Irish hosts at this relaxed establishment, located
in the pleasant village of Kewstoke. The comfortable
bedrooms provide plenty of useful extras, and the
traditional home-cooked breakfasts are served in the
dining room. Guests are welcome to use the lounge.

Rooms 4 en suite (1 fmly) S £45-£50; D £60-£65*
Facilities STV FTV TVL tea/coffee Cen ht Licensed Wi-fi
Parking 5 **Notes** LB No Children 7yrs Closed 28 Dec-5 Jan
& annual holidays

Goodrington Guest House

★★★ GUEST HOUSE

23 Charlton Rd BS23 4HB
☎ 01934 623229
e-mail: vera.bishop@talk21.com
web: www.goodrington.info
dir: A370 Beach Rd S onto Uphill Rd, left onto Charlton
Rd

The owners make every effort to ensure guests enjoy their
stay at this charming Victorian house tucked away in a
quiet residential area. The bedrooms are comfortably
furnished, and there is an attractive lounge. Families are
especially welcome and this makes a good holiday base.

Rooms 3 rms (2 en suite) (1 pri facs) (1 fmly) (1 GF)
S £35-£40; D £56-£60* **Facilities** FTV TVL tea/coffee
Dinner available Cen ht Wi-fi **Notes** LB ⊗ Closed Oct-Etr
🚭

Parasol Guest House

★★★ GUEST HOUSE

49 Walliscote Rd BS23 1EE
☎ 01934 636409 & 07592 357619
e-mail: parasol49@hotmail.com

Located in a residential area with the seafront and town
centre just a short stroll away, Parasol Guest House offers
a range of well decorated bedrooms in various sizes.
Breakfast is served at individual tables in the
comfortable dining room. Wi-fi is among the welcome
extras available in the bedrooms.

Rooms 8 en suite (2 fmly) (1 GF) S £25-£35; D £45-£66
Facilities FTV DVD iPod docking station TVL tea/coffee
Dinner available Cen ht Wi-fi 🛆 Pass available to fitness
club **Parking** 2 **Notes** LB ⊗

WESTON-SUPER-MARE *continued*

Corbiere Guest House

★★★ GUEST HOUSE

24 Upper Church Rd BS23 2DX
☎ 01934 629607 & 07932 029732 ▤ 01934 629607
e-mail: corbierehotel@btinternet.com
dir: *M5 junct 21, A370, follow town & seafront signs.
Right towards pier along Knightstone Rd. Right in approx
300yds into Upper Church Rd, right at x-rds*

Located within walking distance of the city centre, this
charming house maintains Victorian style. The friendly
proprietors make every effort to ensure a stay is pleasant
and memorable, and the attractive bedrooms have many
considerate extras. There is a lounge, and freshly cooked
breakfasts are served in the pleasant dining room.

Rooms 10 en suite (4 fmly) (2 GF) S £25–£30;
D £50–£60* **Facilities** FTV DVD TVL tea/coffee Dinner
available Cen ht **Notes** LB ⌖

Edelweiss Guest House

★★★ GUEST HOUSE

24 Clevedon Rd BS23 1DG
☎ 01934 624705 ▤ 01934 624705
e-mail: edelweissguesthouse@tiscali.co.uk
dir: *Into Clevedon Rd off Beach Rd (Seafront) opposite
Tropicana. Edelweiss 75yds on right*

Located in a residential area approximately 100 yards
from the seafront and beach, Edelweiss is a traditional
and comfortable guest house run in a welcoming manner.
Bedrooms vary in size but all are nicely decorated.
Although dinner is not available, guests are welcome to
select from a light snack and beverage menu up until
10pm.

Rooms 5 rms (4 en suite) (1 pri facs) (3 fmly) (2 GF)
Facilities FTV tea/coffee Cen ht **Notes** LB ⌖ Closed Xmas
wk

Weston Bay Guest House

★★★ GUEST HOUSE

2-4 Clevedon Rd BS23 1DG
☎ 01934 628903 ▤ 01934 417661
e-mail: westonbayhotel@btinternet.com
web: www.westonbayhotel.co.uk
dir: *Opposite Sea Quarium on seafront*

Located on the seafront, this family-run property has
generally spacious, well-equipped bedrooms with modern
en suites. The comfortable lounge and attractive
breakfast room have sea views, and packed lunches are
available on request. There is a small private car park.

Rooms 9 en suite (5 fmly) (1 GF) **Facilities** FTV TVL tea/
coffee Cen ht Wi-fi **Parking** 11 **Notes** ⌖ Closed mid Nov–
mid Mar

WEST PENNARD — Map 4 ST53

The Lion

🛈

Glastonbury Rd BA6 8NH
☎ 01458 832941

Currently the rating for this establishment is not
confirmed. This may be due to a change of ownership or
because it has only recently joined the AA rating scheme.

Rooms 6 en suite **Facilities** FTV tea/coffee Dinner
available Wi-fi **Parking** 20

WHEDDON CROSS — Map 3 SS93

North Wheddon Farm (SS923385)

★★★★ ⌂ ⌸ FARMHOUSE

TA24 7EX
☎ 01643 841791 **Mrs R Abraham**
e-mail: rachael@go-exmoor.co.uk
dir: *500yds S of village x-rds on A396. Pass Moorland
Hall on left, driveway next right*

North Wheddon Farm is a delightfully friendly and
comfortable environment with great views, a perfect base
for exploring the delights of Exmoor. The tranquil grounds
include a pleasant garden and guests are welcome to
roam the fields and say hello to the pigs, sheep, goats
and any other new arrivals. Memorable dinners and
breakfasts feature excellent produce, much of it straight
from the farm. The bedrooms are thoughtfully equipped
and individual in style with lovely comfy beds.

Rooms 3 rms (2 en suite) (1 pri facs) **Facilities** FTV tea/
coffee Dinner available Cen ht Licensed Wi-fi Riding
Parking 5 **Notes** 20 acres mixed

The Rest and Be Thankful Inn

★★★★ INN

TA24 7DR
☎ 01643 841222 ▤ 01643 841813
e-mail: stay@restandbethankful.co.uk
web: www.restandbethankful.co.uk
dir: *M5 junct 25, A358 to Minehead, left onto B3224 at
Wheddon Cross sign*

The Rest and Be Thankful Inn is situated in the highest
village on Exmoor overlooking Dunkery Beacon. The

comfortable bedrooms are extremely well equipped with
extras such as mini-bars and trouser presses. The
convivial bar, complete with crackling log fires, is a
popular meeting point for locals and visitors alike. A
range of wholesome dishes is offered either in the bar,
restaurant or outside on the patio, from where lovely
countryside views can be enjoyed.

The Rest and Be Thankful Inn

Rooms 8 en suite (1 fmly) **Facilities** FTV tea/coffee Dinner
available Direct Dial Cen ht Wi-fi Pool table Skittle alley
Table Tennis **Extras** Mini-bar - chargeable **Conf** Max 50
Class 50 Board 50 **Parking** 10 **Notes** Closed 25 Dec

WILLITON — Map 3 ST04

The White House

★★★★ GUEST ACCOMMODATION

11 Long St TA4 4QW
☎ 01984 632306
e-mail: whitehouse@btconnect.com
dir: *A39 Bridgwater to Minehead, in Williton on right prior
to Watchet turning*

This Grade II listed Georgian house is in the perfect
location for guests wishing to explore the beautiful
countryside and coast. Many original features have been
retained which add to the character of the house. Rooms
are well equipped and guests have a choice of rooms in
the main house or in the courtyard, and the use of a
guest lounge.

Rooms 8 rms (7 en suite) (1 pri facs) 6 annexe en suite
(2 fmly) (6 GF) S £39–£44; D £78–£98* **Facilities** TVL
Cen ht **Parking** 12

Save on B&Bs and Hotels. Book at theAA.com/hotel

SOMERSET 271 ENGLAND

| WITHYPOOL | Map 3 SS83 |

PREMIER COLLECTION

Kings Farm

★★★★★ 🏠 BED AND BREAKFAST

TA24 7RE
☎ 01643 831381
e-mail: info@kingsfarmexmoor.co.uk
dir: Off B3223 to Withypool, over bridge & sharp left to farm

This delightful farmhouse is set in over two acres of landscaped gardens in an idyllic valley beside the River Barle. It combines the character and charm of its 19th-century origins with modern comforts. From the carefully planned bedrooms to the sumptuously furnished sitting room, delicious home-cooked breakfasts and the warmest of welcomes, top quality is most definitely the hallmark of Kings Farm. Both stabling and fishing are available.

Rooms 2 rms (1 en suite) (1 pri facs) S £60; D £95-£105* **Facilities** STV FTV Lounge tea/coffee Cen ht Wi-fi Fishing 🎣 **Extras** Speciality toiletries, fruit, chocolates - complimentary **Parking** 3 **Notes** No Children 14yrs

The Royal Oak Inn

★★★★ 🍽 INN

TA24 7QP
☎ 01643 831506 📠 01643 831659
e-mail: enquiries@royaloakwithypool.co.uk
dir: 7m N of Dulverton, off B3223

Set at the heart of Exmoor, this long established and popular inn continues to provide rest and sustenance for weary travellers. The atmosphere is warm and engaging with the bar always frequented by cheery locals. Bedrooms and bathrooms are stylish and very well appointed with added touches of luxury such as Egyptian cotton linen, bath robes and cosseting towels. Menus feature local produce and can be enjoyed either in the bars or in the elegant restaurant.

Rooms 8 rms (7 en suite) (1 pri facs) **Facilities** tea/coffee Dinner available Direct Dial Cen ht **Parking** 10 **Notes** LB No Children 10yrs No coaches

| WIVELISCOMBE | Map 3 ST02 |

North Down Farm B&B (ST066261)

★★★★ FARMHOUSE

Pyncombe Ln TA4 2BL
☎ 01984 623730 Ms J Blackshaw
e-mail: jennycope@btinternet.com
dir: From Taunton on B3227 towards Wiveliscombe, at lights turn left down hill. After 150mtrs at end of 30mph limit, turn right, 1st farm on left

A well established farmhouse bed and breakfast with superb views across the countryside. The bedrooms are comfortable and well maintained, well appointed and decorated. Breakfasts, using quality local produce, are hearty and a great start to the day.

Rooms 4 rms (3 en suite) (1 pri facs) (1 fmly) S £38; D £76 **Facilities** FTV Lounge TVL tea/coffee Dinner available Cen ht Wi-fi Fishing 🎣 **Parking** 10 **Notes** LB Closed Xmas 🐾 102 acres mixed

White Hart

★★★★ INN

West St TA4 2JP
☎ 01984 623344 📠 01984 624748
e-mail: reservations@whitehartwiveliscombe.co.uk
dir: M5 junct 25 then A38 to Taunton. Follow signs for A358 to Minehead then B3227 to Wiveliscombe

The White Hart is the focal point of this delightful town situated near the foot of the Quantock Hills. Exmoor is on the doorstep and the coast is just a few miles away. Bedrooms offer contemporary, comfortable accommodation with a good range of facilities. Innovative dishes are offered in the restaurant, and the bar has a good range of locally brewed beers.

Rooms 16 en suite (2 fmly) **Facilities** FTV tea/coffee Dinner available Direct Dial Cen ht Wi-fi Skittle alley **Conf** Max 30 Thtr 30 Class 15 Board 15 **Parking** 12

| WRINGTON | Map 4 ST46 |

Stablegrove Bed & Breakfast

★★★★ BED AND BREAKFAST

West Hay Rd BS40 5NR
☎ 01934 862032
e-mail: info@stablegrovebedandbreakfast.co.uk
web: www.stablegrovebedandbreakfast.co.uk
dir: M5 junct 20 follow signs for Yatton (B3133), through Yatton, at x-rds left onto A370. 0.25m, right into Wrington Rd, B&B on left in 1.7m

Peacefully located with delightful views towards the Mendip Hills, Stablegrove is only a short drive from the M5 and also Bristol Airport. Guests are welcome to use the very comfortable, stylish lounge/dining room where a welcoming fire and glass of port await. Bedrooms and bathrooms come in a range of shapes and sizes but all are well appointed and include some useful extras. Breakfast utilises fresh produce including eggs from the hens that live at the back of the property. Keep an eye out for the pet llamas too.

Rooms 5 rms (1 en suite) (2 pri facs) (1 fmly) D £60-£85* **Facilities** FTV tea/coffee Cen ht Licensed Wi-fi Pool table Table tennis **Parking** 8 **Notes** LB 🚫 No Children 5yrs Closed Xmas & New Year 🐾

YEOVIL
Map 4 ST51

See also Crewkerne

PREMIER COLLECTION

Little Barwick House

⭐⭐⭐⭐⭐ ☻☻☻ 🏱 RESTAURANT WITH ROOMS

Barwick Village BA22 9TD
☎ 01935 423902 📠 01935 420908
e-mail: littlebarwick@hotmail.com
dir: From Yeovil A37 towards Dorchester, left at 1st
rdbt, 1st left, 0.25m on left

Situated in a quiet hamlet in three and half acres of
gardens and grounds, this listed Georgian dower house
is an ideal retreat for those seeking peaceful
surroundings and good food. Just one of the highlights
of a stay here is a meal in the restaurant, where good
use is made of local ingredients. Each of the bedrooms
has its own character, and a range of thoughtful extras
such as fresh flowers, bottled water and magazines is
provided.

Rooms 6 en suite **Facilities** FTV iPod docking station
tea/coffee Dinner available Direct Dial Cen ht
Parking 30 **Notes** LB No Children 5yrs RS Sun eve &
Mon closed No coaches

The Masons Arms

⭐⭐⭐⭐ 🏱 ☻ INN

41 Lower Odcombe BA22 8TX
☎ 01935 862591 📠 01935 862591
e-mail: paula@masonsarmsodcombe.co.uk
web: www.masonsarmsodcombe.co.uk
dir: From A303 take A3088 to Yeovil, follow signs to
Montacute after village, 3rd turning on right

Dating back to the 16th century, this charming inn claims
to be the oldest building in this small country village on
the outskirts of Yeovil. The spacious bedrooms are
contemporary in style, with clean lines, a high level of
comfort and a wide range of considerate extras. The
friendly hosts run their own micro-brewery, and their ales
are available at the bar along with others. Public areas
include the bar/restaurant, which offers a full menu of
freshly prepared dishes, along with a choice of lighter
snacks.

Rooms 6 en suite (1 fmly) (6 GF) S £55-£70; D £75-£85*
Facilities FTV tea/coffee Dinner available Direct Dial
Cen ht Wi-fi ☻ **Extras** Mineral water/beer in room fridge
Conf Max 15 Class 15 Board 15 **Parking** 35 **Notes** No
coaches

The Manor

⭐⭐⭐⭐ INN

Hendford BA20 1TG
☎ 01935 423116 📠 01935 706607
e-mail: manor.yeovil@oldenglishinns.co.uk
dir: A303 onto A3088 to Yeovil. Over River Yeo, 2nd exit at
rdbt immediately left into Hendford

This manor house, dating from 1735, stands in the centre
of Yeovil and has the benefit of its own spacious car park.
There is a bar and an open-plan lounge area where
afternoon tea may be enjoyed. Breakfast and dinner are
served in the light and airy conservatory dining area.

Rooms 21 rms (20 en suite) (1 pri facs) 21 annexe en
suite (10 GF) **Facilities** tea/coffee Dinner available Direct
Dial Cen ht Wi-fi **Conf** Max 150 Thtr 120 Class 80 Board
60 **Parking** 60 **Notes** ⊗ Civ Wed 60

The Halfway House Inn Country Lodge

⭐⭐⭐ INN

Ilchester Rd BA22 8RE
☎ 01935 840350 & 849005 📠 01935 849006
e-mail: paul@halfwayhouseinn.com
web: www.halfwayhouseinn.com
dir: A303 onto A37 (Yeovil road) at Ilchester, inn 2m
on left

This roadside inn offers comfortable accommodation,
which consists of bedrooms in the main house, in
addition to contemporary annexe rooms, each with a front
door; all bedrooms are bright and well equipped. Meals
are available in the cosy restaurant and bar where
friendly staff ensure a warm welcome.

Rooms 11 en suite 9 annexe en suite (7 fmly) (9 GF)
Facilities STV tea/coffee Dinner available Cen ht Wi-fi
Fishing Pool table **Conf** Max 120 Thtr 120 Class 50 Board
40 **Parking** 49

At Your Service B&B

⭐⭐⭐ BED AND BREAKFAST

102 West Coker Rd BA20 2JG
☎ 01935 706932 & 07590 960339
e-mail: randall9ee@btinternet.com

Conveniently located on the main through road, this
relaxed bed and breakfast makes an ideal base from
which to explore the various nearby attractions. Bedrooms
come in a range of shapes and sizes including some on
the ground floor. Guests have use of the lounge and there
is a car park to the rear of the property.

Rooms 4 en suite (4 GF) S £40; D £60* **Facilities** FTV tea/
coffee Cen ht **Parking** 4 **Notes** LB

The Half Moon Inn

⭐⭐⭐ INN

Main St, Mudford BA21 5TF
☎ 01935 850289 📠 01935 850842
e-mail: enquiries@thehalfmooninn.co.uk
dir: A303 at Sparkford onto A359 to Yeovil, 3.5m on left

Situated north of Yeovil, this delightful village inn dates
from the 17th century. It has a wealth of character
including exposed beams and flagstone floors. The inn
proves very popular for its extensive range of wholesome
food, and there is a choice of bar and dining areas. Most
of the spacious, well-equipped bedrooms are on the
ground floor and situated in an adjacent building.

Rooms 14 en suite (4 fmly) (9 GF) **Facilities** STV FTV tea/
coffee Dinner available Cen ht Wi-fi ☻ **Parking** 36
Notes ⊗ Closed 25-26 Dec

The Helyar Arms

⭐⭐⭐ INN

Moor Ln, East Coker BA22 9JR
☎ 01935 862332 📠 01935 864129
e-mail: info@helyar-arms.co.uk
dir: 3m S of Yeovil. Off A30 or A37 into East Coker

A charming 15th-century inn, serving seasonal British
food in the heart of a pretty Somerset village. The
traditional friendly bar with hand-drawn ales retains
many original features while the bedrooms offer well
equipped, attractive accommodation and modern
facilities.

Rooms 6 en suite (3 fmly) **Facilities** tea/coffee Dinner
available Direct Dial Cen ht Wi-fi Skittle alley **Conf** Max
40 Thtr 40 Class 20 Board 30 **Parking** 40

STAFFORDSHIRE

ABBOTS BROMLEY
Map 10 SK02

Marsh Farm (SK069261)

⭐⭐⭐⭐ FARMHOUSE

WS15 3EJ
☎ 01283 840323 Mrs M K Hollins
e-mail: marshfarm@meads1967.co.uk
dir: 1m N of Abbots Bromley on B5013

Guests are welcome to walk around the fields at this
working farm and watch the activities. The farmhouse
has been modernised, and bedrooms are carefully
furnished and equipped; three rooms are located in a
sympathetic barn conversion. Comprehensive breakfasts
are served in the spacious cottage-style dining room,
which operates as a popular tea room during the summer.

Rooms 5 rms (3 en suite) (1 fmly) (1 GF) S £30-£35;
D £55-£60* **Facilities** TVL tea/coffee Cen ht ☻ **Parking** 6
Notes ⊗ Closed 25-27 Dec 20 acres mixed

BURTON UPON TRENT — Map 10 SK22

The Delter

★★★★ GUEST ACCOMMODATION

5 Derby Rd DE14 1RU
☎ 01283 535115 📠 01283 845261
e-mail: info@delterhotel.co.uk
web: www.thedelter.co.uk
dir: *A511 rdbt onto A5121 (Derby Rd), 50yds on left*

This relaxing guest accommodation is on the outskirts of Burton upon Trent, close to the famous Bass Museum. Bedrooms are thoughtfully equipped and carefully decorated, and there is a pleasant breakfast room. Expect friendly and attentive service.

Rooms 7 en suite (2 fmly) (2 GF) S £42–£45; D £55–£60*
Facilities FTV tea/coffee Cen ht Wi-fi 🔒 **Parking** 8
Notes ✖ Closed Xmas

The Riverside

★★★ INN

Riverside Dr, Branston DE14 3EP
☎ 01283 511234 📠 01283 511441
e-mail: 6498@greeneking.co.uk
web: www.oldenglishinns.co.uk
dir: *From A38 onto A5121 to Burton upon Trent, property on right entering Branston*

With its quiet residential location and well-kept terraced garden stretching down to the River Trent, this inn has all the ingredients for a relaxing stay. Many of the tables in the Garden Room restaurant have views over the garden. Bedrooms are tastefully furnished and provide a good range of extras.

Rooms 23 en suite (15 GF) **Facilities** TVL tea/coffee Dinner available Direct Dial Cen ht Wi-fi ⚡ 18 Fishing **Conf** Max 150 Thtr 150 Class 30 Board 40 **Parking** 60
Notes LB Civ Wed 170

CHEDDLETON — Map 16 SJ95

Prospect House

★★★★ GUEST HOUSE

334 Cheadle Rd ST13 7BW
☎ 01782 550639
e-mail: prospect@talk21.com
web: www.prospecthouse.tv
dir: *4m S of Leek on A520*

Prospect House was built from local stone in 1838, and is situated between Cheddleton and Wetley Rocks. Bedrooms are in a converted coach house behind the house, and facilities include a traditionally-furnished dining room together with a cosy lounge, and a pleasant garden with a conservatory.

Rooms 4 en suite (1 GF) **Facilities** FTV TVL tea/coffee Dinner available Cen ht Wi-fi **Parking** 4 **Notes** ✖

ECCLESHALL — Map 15 SJ82

Slindon House Farm *(SJ826324)*

★★★★ FARMHOUSE

Slindon ST21 6LX
☎ 01782 791237 Mrs H Bonsall
e-mail: bonsall@btconnect.com
dir: *2m N of Eccleshall on A519*

This large, charming, Victorian farmhouse is fronted by a lovely garden and situated on a dairy, arable and sheep farm in the village of Slindon some two miles from Eccleshall. It has one twin and one double-bedded room, both of which are thoughtfully equipped. Breakfast is served at individual tables in the traditionally-furnished combined breakfast room and lounge.

Rooms 2 rms (1 en suite) (1 pri facs) S £40; D £65–£70*
Facilities FTV TVL tea/coffee Cen ht Wi-fi **Parking** 4
Notes ✖ Closed 23 Dec-3 Jan 🐄 175 acres arable/dairy/sheep/beef

FOXT — Map 16 SK04

Shawgate Farm Guest House

★★★★ GUEST ACCOMMODATION

Shay Ln ST10 2HN
☎ 01538 266590
e-mail: ken@shawgatefarm.co.uk
dir: *1m off A52 (Stoke to Ashbourne road)*

Situated in five acres of grounds, this property is quietly located overlooking the picturesque Churnet Valley. Original farm buildings have been converted to guest bedrooms, ideal for families. Two bedrooms are able to accommodate five people each and one room has a four-poster bed. Shawgate Farm is a family-run establishment, and offers an evening meal in the bar lounge and a patio is available in warmer months. The property is licensed for civil wedding ceremonies and is handy for visiting Alton Towers.

Rooms 5 en suite (4 fmly) D £60–£80* **Facilities** FTV DVD TVL tea/coffee Dinner available Cen ht Licensed Wi-fi ⚡ 18 Fishing Pool table **Parking** 8 **Notes** LB ✖ Closed 10 Nov-15 Mar Civ Wed 50

FROGHALL — Map 10 SK04

Hermitage Working Farm *(SK037497)*

★★★ FARMHOUSE

ST10 2HQ
☎ 01538 266515 📠 01538 266155 Mrs W Barlow
e-mail: wilma@hermitagefarm.co.uk
web: www.hermitagefarm.co.uk
dir: *A52 onto B5053 in Froghall, farm 0.5m on left at top of hill*

Parts of this charming sandstone house date from the 16th century. It is quietly located on an elevated position with panoramic views. There is traditionally-furnished accommodation in the main house as well as a converted barn that offers rooms suitable for families. Handy for visiting Alton Towers.

Rooms 3 en suite 6 annexe en suite (3 fmly) (3 GF)
Facilities tea/coffee Cen ht Wi-fi Shooting **Parking** 13
Notes ✖ 100 acres beef/sheep/poultry

HALMER END — Map 15 SJ74

The Lodge

★★★★ BED AND BREAKFAST

Red Hall Ln ST7 8AX
☎ 01782 729047 & 07973 776797 📠 01782 729047
e-mail: freelancedobies@aol.com
dir: *M6 junct 16, A500 signed Stoke, follow Audley Head sign. At mini-rdbt right into Nantwich Rd (B5500). 0.75m, left into Shraleybrook Rd (B5367), right into Red Hall Ln*

Beside a quiet bridleway, situated next to Bateswood nature reserve bird sanctuary this friendly bed and breakfast is a good touring base for walkers, cyclists or sightseers. The new double bedrooms are particularly spacious and both bedrooms are en suite. Lovely breakfasts, using free range hen and duck eggs are served in a dining room which overlooks the guest patio.

Rooms 2 en suite **Facilities** FTV TVL tea/coffee Cen ht Wi-fi Fishing **Parking** 5 **Notes** ✖ 🐄

KINGSLEY — Map 10 SK04

The Church Farm *(SK013466)*

★★★★ FARMHOUSE

Holt Ln ST10 2BA
☎ 01538 754759 Mrs J Clowes
e-mail: thechurchfarm@yahoo.co.uk
dir: *From A52 in Kingsley into Holt Ln, 150mtrs on right opposite school drive*

A warm welcome is assured at this charming farmhouse situated in the village of Kingsley. Thoughtfully equipped bedrooms with stylish furnishings are available in the main house. A hearty breakfast is served on individual tables overlooking the cottage gardens.

Rooms 3 en suite S £35–£40; D £55–£60* **Facilities** FTV DVD TVL TV2B tea/coffee Cen ht Wi-fi garden
Extras Speciality toiletries **Parking** 6 **Notes** ✖ 🐄 100 acres dairy/beef

LICHFIELD — Map 10 SK10

PREMIER COLLECTION

Pipe Hill House

BED AND BREAKFAST

Walsall Rd, Pipehill WS13 8JU
☎ 01543 255751 & 07779 291219
🖷 0871 978 9286
e-mail: nick@pipehillhouse.co.uk
dir: From A5 rdbt at junct with A461towards Lichfield. 1m on right

Located two miles from the centre of the cathedral city of Lichfield, this beautiful 300-year-old Georgian house is personally run by owners Nick and Annmarie. Individually designed bedrooms offering high levels of comfort and warm hospitality, ensure an enjoyable stay. The comprehensive breakfast features free-range eggs and locally sourced produce, while gluten free, dairy free, low sodium and diabetic diets are catered for. Full office services available in an adjoining barn conversion.

Rooms 2 en suite D £85–£125* **Facilities** FTV iPod docking station Lounge tea/coffee Cen ht Licensed Wi-fi **Extras** Speciality toiletries **Conf** Max 12 Thtr 12 Class 8 Board 8 **Parking** 4 **Notes** ⊗ No Children 16yrs

PREMIER COLLECTION

St Johns House

★★★★★ GUEST ACCOMMODATION

Saint Johns St WS13 6PB
☎ 01543 252080 🖷 01543 254623
e-mail: luxury@stjohnshouse.co.uk
dir: In Lichfield City, Saint John St opposite Frog Ln, entrance through gateway on left hand side of building

St Johns House is a Grade II listed Regency house which was once a preparatory school. The present owner Johann Popp has lovingly restored the property and retained authentic features in the main building. The modern bedrooms are situated across the courtyard in a separate stable building; stylishly designed with comfort in mind, they each have a bathroom of the highest quality. The breakfasts use freshly cooked, home-made and locally sourced ingredients that make for a good start to the day.

Rooms 4 annexe en suite (2 GF) **Facilities** FTV tea/coffee Direct Dial Cen ht Wi-fi **Parking** 4 **Notes** ⊗ No Children 12yrs

Netherstowe House

★★★★ ⬥ GUEST HOUSE

Netherstowe Ln WS13 6AY
☎ 01543 254270 🖷 01543 419998
e-mail: reception@netherstowehouse.com
web: www.netherstowehouse.com
dir: A38 onto A5192, 0.3m on right into Netherstowe Ln. 1st left, 1st right down private drive

Located in a residential area a few minutes drive from city centre, this elegant Georgian house provides a range of bedrooms, some of which are quite spacious. Comprehensive breakfasts are taken in a cosy dining room and a comfortable guest lounge is also available, along with a well-equipped gym.

Rooms 9 en suite 8 annexe en suite (8 fmly) (4 GF) D £85–£125* **Facilities** STV FTV DVD Lounge tea/coffee Dinner available Licensed Wi-fi ⬥ 18 Gym ⬥ **Extras** Robes, fruit, flowers - chargeable **Conf** Max 14 Thtr 14 Class 14 Board 14 **Parking** 35 **Notes** LB ⊗ No Children 12yrs

The Hawthorns

★★★ BED AND BREAKFAST

30 Norwich Close WS13 7SJ
☎ 01543 250151 & 07794 709240
e-mail: bambrushton@hotmail.com
dir: 1m N of city centre. Exit A5192 (Eastern Av) near Bristol Street Motors left into Norwich Close

Located in a residential area on the outskirts of the city, this modern house provides two homely bedrooms with separate side entrance. Breakfast is taken in an attractive kitchen/dining room overlooking a pretty rear garden.

Rooms 2 en suite (2 GF) S £38; D £50 **Facilities** FTV tea/coffee Cen ht **Parking** 2 **Notes** ⊗ No Children ⬥

Innkeeper's Lodge Lichfield

★★★ INN

Stafford Rd WS13 8JB
☎ 0845 112 6071
e-mail: info@innkeeperslodge.com
web: www.innkeeperslodge.com

At Innkeeper's Lodge you'll find accommodation with comfort and character in equal measure, and everything needed for a relaxing stay, from easy check-in and free parking to complimentary breakfast and a cosy pub serving great value food and drink on the doorstep. Each Lodge has quality rooms, and there are Lodges in a variety of locations from towns and cities to countryside settings across the UK.

Rooms 9 en suite (2 fmly) **Facilities** FTV tea/coffee Dinner available Direct Dial Wi-fi **Parking**

OAKAMOOR — Map 10 SK04

The Beehive Guest House

★★★★ GUEST HOUSE

Churnet View Rd ST10 3AE
☎ 01538 702420 🖷 01538 703735
e-mail: thebeehiveoakamoor@btinternet.com
web: www.thebeehiveguesthouse.co.uk
dir: Off B5417 in village N onto Eaves Ln, sharp left onto Churnet View Rd

Standing in the centre of the village and overlooking the river, this spacious detached house offers thoughtfully equipped and comfortable bedrooms. There is also a comfortable lounge-dining room, where substantial breakfasts are served. This guest house is renowned for its hospitality.

Rooms 5 en suite (1 fmly) (1 GF) S £39–£58; D £58–£65* **Facilities** FTV DVD TVL tea/coffee Cen ht Wi-fi **Parking** 6 **Notes** LB ⊗ No Children 5yrs

Crowtrees Farm (SK049459)

★★★★ FARMHOUSE

Eaves Ln ST10 3DY
☎ 01538 702260 Mrs D Bickle
e-mail: dianne@crowtreesfarm.co.uk
web: www.crowtreesfarm.co.uk
dir: Exit B5417 in village N into Eaves Ln, farm 1m on left

This impeccably maintained 200-year-old farmhouse is convenient for the Potteries, the Peak District and Alton Towers. Bedrooms are comfortable and well equipped. It is still a working farm with splendid views, and has a variety of pets. The friendly owners create a relaxing atmosphere.

Rooms 2 en suite 5 annexe en suite (3 fmly) (4 GF) **Facilities** FTV tea/coffee Cen ht **Parking** 8 **Notes** ⊗ Closed 25-26 Dec 70 acres sheep

The Laurels Guest House

★★★★ GUEST HOUSE

Star Bank ST10 3BN
☎ 01538 702629 🖷 01538 702796
e-mail: bbthelaurels@aol.com
web: www.thelaurels.co.uk
dir: On B5147 from Cheadle, 250yds on right past Cricketers Arms public house in Oakamoor

Situated on the edge of Oakamoor, offering comfortable bedrooms, a bar lounge and a spacious dining room, this friendly guest house is ideally located for families wishing to visit Alton Towers or tour rural Staffordshire and the Potteries.

Rooms 9 en suite (5 fmly) (1 GF) **Facilities** FTV TVL tea/coffee Dinner available Cen ht Licensed Wi-fi Pool table **Parking** 9 **Notes** ⊗

Save on B&Bs and Hotels. Book at **theAA.com/hotel**

STAFFORDSHIRE 275 **ENGLAND**

The Admiral Jervis Inn

★★★ INN

Mill Rd ST10 3AG
☎ **01538 702187**
e-mail: admiralshouse@btinternet.com
dir: *A52 onto B5417. In Oakamoor opposite picnic site*

At the heart of the village a few minutes drive from Alton Towers, this half-timbered house is a popular community meeting point, and offers a range of tasty bar meals and real ales. Homely bedrooms are equipped with thoughtful extras and family rooms are also available.

Rooms 6 en suite (4 fmly) (1 GF) **Facilities** tea/coffee Dinner available Cen ht **Parking** 10 **Notes** ⊗ Closed 23 Dec-3 Jan RS Nov-Mar Restaurant closed Sun & Mon eve No coaches

---

ONNELEY Map 15 SJ74

The Wheatsheaf Inn

★★★★ 🍴 INN

Barhill Rd CW3 9QF
☎ **01782 751581** 📠 **01782 751499**
e-mail: pub@wheatsheafpub.co.uk
web: www.wheatsheafpub.co.uk
dir: *On A525 between Madeley & Woore*

The Wheatsheaf is a beautifully appointed 18th-century inn that retains many original features. A wide choice of home-cooked meals is served in the spacious dining areas where there are also cosy alcoves, comfortable lounge seating and real fires. The bedrooms are spacious and well equipped. A function room is also available.

Rooms 6 en suite 4 annexe en suite (4 GF) **Facilities** FTV tea/coffee Dinner available Cen ht Wi-fi ⅃ 18 Pool table **Conf** Thtr 60 Class 30 Board 30 **Notes** ⊗ Civ Wed 60

RUGELEY Map 10 SK01

PREMIER COLLECTION

Colton House

★★★★★ 🏠 GUEST HOUSE

Colton WS15 3LL
☎ **01889 578580** 📠 **01889 578580**
e-mail: mail@coltonhouse.com
web: www.coltonhouse.com
dir: *1.5m N of Rugeley. Exit B5013 into Colton, 0.25m on right*

Set in the pretty village of Colton, this elegant early 18th-century house has been restored to retain original character and provide high standards of comfort and facilities. Bedrooms have a wealth of thoughtful extras; there is a spacious and comfortable lounge and a one and half acre garden.

Rooms 10 en suite S £61-£93; D £80-£190 **Facilities** FTV TVL tea/coffee Dinner available Cen ht Licensed Wi-fi **Conf** Max 15 Thtr 15 Class 15 Board 15 **Parking** 15 **Notes** ⊗ No Children 12yrs

---

STAFFORD Map 10 SJ92

Leonards Croft

★★★ GUEST HOUSE

80 Lichfield Rd ST17 4LP
☎ **01785 223676** 📠 **01785 223676**
e-mail: leonardscroft@hotmail.com
dir: *A34 from town centre signed Cannock, 0.5m on left*

Located south of the town centre, this well-proportioned late Victorian house has been carefully renovated and is convenient for both business and leisure guests. Bedrooms are practically furnished, with two situated on the ground floor. A spacious lounge and complimentary Wi-fi are also provided. The gardens are extensive.

Rooms 9 en suite (3 fmly) (2 GF) S £33-£45; D £53-£65* **Facilities** FTV TVL tea/coffee Dinner available Cen ht Licensed Wi-fi **Parking** 12

The Old School

★★★ BED AND BREAKFAST

Newport Rd, Haughton ST18 9JH
☎ **01785 780358** 📠 **01785 780358**
e-mail: info@theoldsc.co.uk
dir: *A518 W from Stafford, 3m to Haughton, Old School next to church*

Located in the heart of Haughton, this Grade II listed former Victorian school has been renovated to provide a range of bedrooms; a single, a double and a twin. All are appropriately equipped and complimentary Wi-fi is also provided. Breakfast is served at a family table in the homely dining room.

Rooms 3 rms (3 GF) S £25; D £50* **Facilities** FTV tea/coffee Cen ht Wi-fi **Parking** 3 **Notes** No Children 14yrs 🐾

STONE Map 10 SJ93

Field House

★★★ BED AND BREAKFAST

59 Stafford Rd ST15 0HE
☎ **01785 605712** 📠 **01785 605712**
e-mail: fieldhouse@ntlworld.com
dir: *From A34, NW into town centre, right into Stafford Rd, opposite Walton Grange*

This family home stands in secluded, pretty gardens close to the town centre. The Georgian house has traditionally furnished bedrooms, some with family pieces. Guests breakfast together in the lounge-dining room, and hospitality is very welcoming.

Rooms 2 rms (1 en suite) (1 pri facs) **Facilities** STV FTV TVL tea/coffee Cen ht Art tuition on request **Parking** 4 **Notes** ⊗ 🐾

TAMWORTH
Map 10 SK20

PREMIER COLLECTION

Oak Tree Farm

★★★★★ GUEST ACCOMMODATION

Hints Rd, Hopwas B78 3AA
☎ 01827 56807 📠 01827 67271
e-mail: oaktreefarm1@aol.com
web: www.oaktreefarmhotel.co.uk
dir: 2m NW of Tamworth. Off A51 in Hopwas

A warm welcome is assured at this sympathetically restored farmhouse, located in peaceful rural surroundings yet only a short drive from the NEC. Spacious bedrooms are filled with homely extras. The elegant dining room, adorned with Oriental artefacts, is the setting for memorable breakfasts. A small conference room is available.

Rooms 4 en suite 10 annexe en suite (4 fmly) (7 GF) Facilities FTV TVL tea/coffee Cen ht Wi-fi 🎣 Fishing Conf Max 15 Thtr 15 Class 9 Board 15 Parking 20

Globe Inn

★★★ INN

Lower Gungate B79 7AW
☎ 01827 60455 📠 01827 63575
e-mail: info@theglobetamworth.com

Located in the centre of Tamworth, this popular inn provides well-equipped and pleasantly decorated accommodation. The public areas include a spacious lounge bar and a relaxed dining area where a varied selection of dishes is available. There is also a function room and adjacent parking.

Rooms 18 en suite (2 fmly) (18 smoking) S £40; D £60* Facilities STV FTV tea/coffee Dinner available Cen ht Wi-fi Conf Thtr 90 Class 90 Board 90 Parking 30 Notes ⊗ Closed 25 Dec, 1 Jan

UTTOXETER
Map 10 SK03

High View Cottage

★★★★ GUEST ACCOMMODATION

Toothill Rd ST14 8JU
☎ 01889 568183 & 07980 041670
e-mail: info@highviewcottage.co.uk
dir: 1m S of town centre. Exit B5017 (Highwood Rd) into Toothill Rd

Located on the edge of Uttoxeter and close to the racecourse, High View Cottage offers comfortable, well-equipped accommodation and a friendly atmosphere. Bedrooms are equipped with lots of thoughtful extras, and hearty breakfasts are served in the attractive Garden Room which overlooks the courtyard.

Rooms 5 en suite (2 fmly) (5 GF) S £35-£70; D £60-£75* Facilities FTV DVD tea/coffee Cen ht Wi-fi Conf Max 8 Board 8 Parking 10 Notes ⊗

WOODSEAVES
Map 15 SJ72

Tunstall Hall Farm (SJ771273)

★★★★ FARMHOUSE

ST20 0NH
☎ 01785 280232 📠 01785 280232 Mrs Cooke
e-mail: isabel.cooke@btinternet.com
dir: 2m NW of Woodseaves. A41 onto A519, 1st left to Shebdon, in 3m right towards Woodseaves. Bishops Offley 1m on right

Located in a quiet hamlet, this impressive renovated farmhouse dates from the early 18th century and retains original exposed beams and open fires. The thoughtfully furnished bedrooms have smart modern shower rooms en suite, and breakfast is served in the attractive conservatory.

Rooms 2 en suite (1 fmly) Facilities TVL tea/coffee Cen ht Wi-fi Parking 6 Notes ⊗ 🐾 280 acres mixed/dairy

SUFFOLK

ALDEBURGH
Map 13 TM45

The Toll House

★★★★ GUEST HOUSE

50 Victoria Rd IP15 5EJ
☎ 01728 453239
e-mail: mail@tollhousealdeburgh.com
web: www.tollhousealdeburgh.com
dir: B1094 into town until rdbt, on right

Expect a warm welcome at this delightful red brick property situated just a short walk from the seafront and town centre. Bedrooms are tastefully furnished, have co-ordinated fabrics and many thoughtful touches. Breakfast is served at individual tables in the smart dining room, which overlooks the garden.

The Toll House

Rooms 7 en suite (3 GF) S £60-£65; D £70-£80* Facilities DVD tea/coffee Cen ht Parking 6 Notes ⊗

BURY ST EDMUNDS
Map 13 TL86

PREMIER COLLECTION

Clarice House

★★★★★ ⑧ GUEST ACCOMMODATION

Horringer Court, Horringer Rd IP29 5PH
☎ 01284 705550 📠 01284 716120
e-mail: bury@claricehouse.co.uk
web: www.claricehouse.co.uk
dir: 1m SW from town centre on A143 towards Horringer

A large country property set amidst pretty landscaped grounds a short drive from the historic town centre. The spacious, well-equipped bedrooms have co-ordinated fabrics and many thoughtful touches. Public rooms have a wealth of charm and include a smart lounge bar, an intimate restaurant, a further lounge and a conservatory. The property also has superb leisure facilities.

Rooms 13 en suite S £80-£100; D £120-£160* Facilities FTV tea/coffee Dinner available Direct Dial Cen ht Lift Licensed 🎣 Sauna Gym Spa & Beauty facilities Conf Max 50 Thtr 50 Class 50 Board 50 Parking 85 Notes LB ⊗ No Children 5yrs Closed 24-26 Dec & 31 Dec-1 Jan Civ Wed 70

The Abbey

★★★★ GUEST ACCOMMODATION

35 Southgate St IP33 2AZ
☎ 01284 762020 📠 01284 330279
e-mail: reception@abbeyhotel.co.uk
dir: A14 junct 44, A1302 to town centre, into Southgate St, premises 400yds

The Abbey is well placed for visiting the historic town centre. The property is split between several historic buildings, the main core dating from the 15th century. The public rooms in the Tudor inn section feature a comfortable lounge and an informal dining area.

Save on B&Bs and Hotels. Book at **theAA.com/hotel**

SUFFOLK 277 ENGLAND

Bedrooms vary in size and style, but all are comfortably furnished and well equipped.

Rooms 12 en suite (1 fmly) (2 GF) **Facilities** FTV tea/coffee Cen ht Wi-fi **Parking** 12 **Notes** ⊗ No Children 3yrs

The Black Boy
★★★★ INN

69 Guildhall St IP33 1QD
☎ 01284 752723
dir: *Exit A14 to town centre*

The Black Boy is a popular inn situated in the centre of this historic town. The spacious bedrooms have co-ordinated fabrics, pine furniture and many thoughtful touches. Public areas feature a large open-plan bar with a good selection of ales and a range of bar snacks are also available.

Rooms 5 en suite **Facilities** tea/coffee Dinner available Cen ht Wi-fi Pool table **Parking** 6 **Notes** ⊗ No coaches

The Chantry
★★★★ GUEST ACCOMMODATION

8 Sparhawk St IP33 1RY
☎ 01284 767427 📠 01284 760946
e-mail: chantryhotel1@aol.com
dir: *From cathedral S into Crown St, left into Honey Hill then right into Sparhawk St*

Expect a warm welcome at this attractive Georgian property, just a short walk from the town centre. The individually decorated bedrooms are furnished with well-chosen pieces and have many thoughtful touches. Dinner and breakfast are served in the smart restaurant, and there is a cosy lounge-bar.

Rooms 11 en suite 3 annexe en suite (1 fmly) (1 GF) S £60-£77; D £87-£117* **Facilities** FTV Lounge tea/coffee Dinner available Direct Dial Cen ht Licensed Wi-fi **Parking** 16 **Notes** LB

83 Whiting Street
★★★★ BED AND BREAKFAST

83 Whiting St IP33 1NX
☎ 01284 704153 & 07703 601072
e-mail: gordon.wagstaff@btinternet.com
dir: *In town centre*

An attractive three-storey terrace property convenient for exploring this historic town. The spacious, individually decorated bedrooms are furnished with pine and equipped with modern facilities. Breakfast is served in the beamed dining room that features an open fireplace and a wall painting dating from 1530.

Rooms 4 en suite (1 fmly) S £50; D £75 **Facilities** FTV iPod docking station tea/coffee Cen ht Wi-fi ⛱ **Notes** LB ⊗ ⌂

St Andrews Lodge
★★★★ BED AND BREAKFAST

30 Saint Andrews Street North IP33 1SZ
☎ 01284 756733
e-mail: standrewslodge@hotmail.com
web: www.thestandrewslodge.co.uk
dir: *A14 junct 43, A134 towards town centre, left into Saint Andrews St North. Lodge on right*

This delightful property is situated close to the A14 and the town centre. The well-equipped modern bedrooms are on the ground floor of a separate purpose-built building to the rear of the house. Breakfast is served at individual tables in the smart dining room, which overlooks the neat courtyard.

Rooms 3 annexe en suite (3 GF) S £50; D £68* **Facilities** FTV DVD tea/coffee Cen ht Wi-fi **Parking** 3

The Six Bells at Bardwell
★★★★ INN

The Green, Bardwell IP31 1AW
☎ 01359 250820 📠 01359 250820
e-mail: sixbellsbardwell@aol.com
web: www.sixbellsbardwell.co.uk
dir: *8m NE, off A143 on edge of village. Follow brown signs from A143*

This 16th-century inn lies in the peaceful village of Bardwell. The bedrooms are in a converted stable block next to the main building, and are furnished in a country style and thoughtfully equipped. Public rooms have original character and provide a choice of areas in which to relax.

Rooms 10 annexe en suite (1 fmly) (10 GF) S £50-£85; D £62.50-£120* **Facilities** FTV tea/coffee Dinner available Cen ht **Parking** 50 **Notes** LB Closed 25 Dec-3 Jan

The Three Kings
★★★★ INN

Hengrave Rd, Fornham All Saints IP28 6LA
☎ 01284 766979
e-mail: thethreekings@keme.co.uk
web: www.the-three-kings.com
dir: *A14 junct 42, B1106 to Fornham, left onto B1101, establishment on left*

Attractive inn situated in the pleasant village of Fornham All Saints. The bedrooms are in a building adjacent to the main property; each one is smartly furnished and thoughtfully equipped. Public rooms feature a smart lounge bar, a conservatory and a comfortable restaurant.

Rooms 9 annexe en suite (2 fmly) (6 GF) **Facilities** FTV tea/coffee Dinner available Direct Dial Cen ht Wi-fi ⛱ **Conf** Max 45 Thtr 12 Class 24 Board 24 **Parking** 28 **Notes** ⊗

Dog & Partridge, The Old Brewers House
★★★ 🍴 INN

29 Crown St IP33 1QU
☎ 01284 764792
e-mail: 1065@greeneking.co.uk
web: www.oldenglish.co.uk
dir: *In town centre. Exit A134 (Parkway) into Westgate St & left into Crown St*

This charming inn is situated just a short walk from the town centre. Public rooms include a smart conservatory, a lounge bar, a small dining area and a smartly decked terrace to the rear of the property for alfresco dining. Bedrooms are pleasantly decorated, have co-ordinated fabrics, natural wood furniture and many thoughtful touches.

Rooms 9 en suite (2 fmly) (3 GF) **Facilities** STV tea/coffee Dinner available Direct Dial **Parking** 11 **Notes** ⊗

The Old Cannon Brewery
★★★ INN

86 Cannon St IP33 1JR
☎ 01284 768769
e-mail: stay@oldcannonbrewery.co.uk
dir: *A14 junct 43, A134 towards town centre. At rdbt after Tesco left then sharp right onto Cadney Ln, left onto Cannon St, on left*

A delightful Victorian property which was originally a beer house and brewery, the property has been renovated in recent years and the brewery has now re-opened - the finished products can be sampled in the bar. The open-plan bar and dining area features the polished stainless steel mash tun and kettle. The well-equipped bedrooms are located in an adjacent building.

Rooms 7 annexe en suite (3 GF) S £85; D £110* **Facilities** FTV tea/coffee Dinner available Cen ht Wi-fi ⛱ **Parking** 7 **Notes** ⊗ No coaches

BURY ST EDMUNDS *continued*

Hamilton House

★★★ BED AND BREAKFAST

4 Nelson Rd IP33 3AG
☎ 01284 703022 & 07787 146553
e-mail: hamiltonhouse@hotmail.co.uk
dir: *A14 junct 42, follow A1302 across rdbt, then 1st right*

A warm welcome awaits at this relaxing Edwardian villa, which is situated in a quiet side road just a short walk from the town centre. The bedrooms are brightly decorated with co-ordinated fabrics and have a good range of facilities. Breakfast is served at a large communal table in the dining room.

Rooms 4 rms (2 en suite) (1 fmly) S £25-£35; D £55-£65* **Facilities** FTV tea/coffee Cen ht Wi-fi 🛝 **Notes** ⊗ 🚭

6 Orchard Street

★★★ BED AND BREAKFAST

IP33 1EH
☎ 01284 705146 & 07946 590265
e-mail: mariellascarlett@me.com
dir: *In town centre near St John's Church on one-way system; Northgate St turn right into Looms Ln, 2nd right into Well St, straight on into Orchard St*

Expect a warm welcome from the caring hosts at this terrace property situated just a short walk from the town centre. The pleasant bedrooms are comfortably appointed and have a good range of useful extras. Breakfast is served at a large communal table in the cosy dining room.

Rooms 2 rms (1 en suite) (1 pri facs) S £30-£35; D £45-£60* **Facilities** FTV tea/coffee Cen ht Wi-fi 🛝 **Notes** No Children 6yrs 🚭

CAVENDISH Map 13 TL84

The George

★★★★ ⚘ RESTAURANT WITH ROOMS

The Green CO10 8BA
☎ 01787 280248
e-mail: thegeorgecavendish@gmail.com
web: www.thecavendishgeorge.co.uk
dir: *A1092 into Cavendish, The George next to village green*

The George is situated in the heart of the pretty village of Cavendish and has five very stylish bedrooms. The front-facing rooms overlook the village; the comfortable, spacious bedrooms retain many of their original features. The award-winning restaurant is very well appointed and dinner should not be missed. Guests are guaranteed to receive a warm welcome, attentive friendly service and great food.

Rooms 5 en suite (1 fmly) S £50; D £75-£85* **Facilities** FTV tea/coffee Dinner available Cen ht Wi-fi **Extras** Speciality toiletries, mineral water **Notes** ⊗ Closed 25 Dec & 1 Jan

---

CLARE Map 13 TL74

Ship Stores

★★★★ GUEST ACCOMMODATION

22 Callis St CO10 8PX
☎ 01787 277834 🖷 01787 277183
e-mail: shipclare@aol.com
dir: *A1092 to Clare, onto B1063, pass church, 100yds on right*

A charming property situated in the heart of an historic market town. Bedrooms are split between the main house and a converted stable block; each room is furnished in a country style with bright, co-ordinated soft furnishings and many thoughtful touches. Public areas include a lounge with comfy sofas, and a contemporary breakfast room with a stripped pine floor.

Rooms 4 en suite 2 annexe en suite (1 fmly) (3 GF) S £45-£60; D £65-£75* **Facilities** tea/coffee Cen ht Wi-fi **Parking** 3 **Notes** LB ⊗

ELMSWELL Map 13 TL96

Kiln Farm Guest House

★★★★ GUEST HOUSE

Kiln Ln IP30 9QR
☎ 01359 240442
e-mail: davejankilnfarm@btinternet.com
dir: *A14 junct 47 onto A1088. Entrance to Kiln Ln off E'bound slip road*

A delightful Victorian farmhouse situated in a peaceful rural location amid three acres of landscaped grounds. The bedrooms are housed in converted farm buildings, and each one is smartly decorated and furnished in country style. Breakfast is served in the smart conservatory and there is also a cosy lounge and bar area.

Kiln Farm Guest House

Rooms 2 en suite 6 annexe en suite (2 fmly) (6 GF) S £35-£40; D £70-£80* **Facilities** FTV DVD Lounge TVL tea/coffee Dinner available Cen ht Licensed Wi-fi **Parking** 20

ELVEDEN Map 13 TL88

The Elveden Inn

Ⓤ

Brandon Rd IP24 3TP
☎ 01842 890876 🖷 01842 221822
e-mail: info@elvedeninn.com
dir: *On Brandon Road (B1106), off A11 at lights*

Currently the rating for this establishment is not confirmed. This may be due to a change of ownership or because it has only recently joined the AA rating scheme.

Rooms 4 en suite (2 fmly) S £105; D £125* **Facilities** FTV tea/coffee Dinner available Direct Dial Cen ht Licensed Wi-fi **Extras** Speciality toiletries, fruit, bottled water - complimentary **Parking** 50

EYE Map 13 TM17

The White Horse Inn

★★★★ INN

Stoke Ash IP23 7ET
☎ 01379 678222 🖷 01379 678800
e-mail: mail@whitehorse-suffolk.co.uk
web: www.whitehorse-suffolk.co.uk
dir: *On A140 halfway between Ipswich & Norwich*

A 17th-century coaching inn situated in the village of Stoke Ash. Bedrooms are located in an annexe adjacent to the main building; each one is smartly decorated in pastel shades, tastefully furnished with co-ordinated fabrics, and thoughtfully equipped. An interesting choice of dishes is served in the restaurant, which features exposed beams and inglenook fireplaces.

Rooms 11 annexe en suite (1 fmly) (9 GF) **Facilities** FTV tea/coffee Dinner available Direct Dial Cen ht Wi-fi **Conf** Max 50 Thtr 50 Class 50 **Parking** 60 **Notes** LB ⊗

Save on B&Bs and Hotels. Book at **theAA.com/hotel**

SUFFOLK 279 **ENGLAND**

FRAMLINGHAM   Map 13 TM26

Church Farm *(TM605267)*

★★★★ FARMHOUSE

Church Rd, Kettleburgh IP13 7LF
☎ 01728 723532 Mrs A Bater
e-mail: jbater@suffolkonline.net
web: www.churchfarmkettleburgh.co.uk
dir: *Off A12 to Wickham Market, signs to Easton Farm Park & Kettleburgh 1.25m, house behind church*

A charming 300-year-old farmhouse situated close to the village church amid superb grounds with a duck pond, mature shrubs and sweeping lawns. The converted property retains exposed beams and open fireplaces. Bedrooms are pleasantly decorated and equipped with useful extras, and ground-floor rooms are available.

Rooms 2 rms (1 en suite) (1 pri facs) 2 annexe rms 1 annexe en suite (1 pri facs) (3 GF) S £35-£40; D £70-£80 **Facilities** TVL tea/coffee Dinner available Cen ht Wi-fi Fishing 🎣 **Extras** Home-made biscuits - complimentary **Parking** 10 **Notes** 🐾 70 acres mixed

---

HOLTON   Map 13 TM47

PREMIER COLLECTION

Valley Farm

★★★★★ BED AND BREAKFAST

Bungay Rd IP19 8LY
☎ 01986 874521 & 07971 669270
e-mail: mail@valleyfarmholton.co.uk
web: www.valleyfarmholton.co.uk
dir: *A144 onto B1123 to Holton, left at fork in village, left at school, 500yds on left*

Expect a warm welcome from the caring hosts at this charming red-brick farmhouse situated in a peaceful rural location a short drive from Halesworth. The individually decorated bedrooms are tastefully appointed with co-ordinated soft furnishings and many thoughtful touches. Breakfast, which features locally sourced and home-grown produce, is served at a large communal table in the smartly appointed dining room. The property has lovely landscaped grounds, a summer house, and an indoor heated swimming pool.

Rooms 2 en suite (1 fmly) S £75-£95; D £75-£95* **Facilities** FTV DVD Lounge tea/coffee Cen ht Wi-fi 🐾 ⛳ 🎱 Boules piste **Extras** Speciality toiletries, sweets **Parking** 15 **Notes** LB 🐾

INGHAM   Map 13 TL87

The Cadogan Arms

★★★★ 🍴 INN

The Street IP31 1NG
☎ 01284 728443
e-mail: info@thecadogan.co.uk
dir: *4m from Bury St Edmunds, follow A134 towards Thetford*

The Cadogan Arms is a popular inn situated four miles from the centre of town. The smartly appointed bedrooms

---

have been thoughtfully designed and have many useful touches such as, flat screen TVs, Freeview and CD/radios. The open-plan public rooms are contemporary in style; they include a range of seating areas with plush leather sofas and a smart restaurant.

Rooms 7 en suite S £80; D £100* **Facilities** FTV tea/coffee Dinner available Cen ht Wi-fi **Parking** 30 **Notes** LB

IPSWICH   Map 13 TM14

Evelyn B&B

★★★ BED AND BREAKFAST

London Rd IP2 0SS
☎ 01473 604769 & 07850 415544
e-mail: cliffb@btinternet.com
dir: *A1214 into Ipswich, 0.5m pass Tesco, 500yds into bus lane, Evelyn on left*

This comfortable establishment is located just outside Ipswich town centre and within easy reach of the main arterial roads. The husband and wife team extends a warm welcome. Bedrooms are well-appointed and offer a good range of amenities. A home-cooked breakfast is served in the cosy breakfast room.

Rooms 2 en suite (2 GF) S fr £40; D fr £60* **Facilities** FTV DVD tea/coffee Cen ht **Extras** Trouser press **Parking** 6 **Notes** 🚫 No Children 12yrs 🐾

LAVENHAM   Map 13 TL94

PREMIER COLLECTION

Lavenham Great House 'Restaurant With Rooms'

★★★★★ 🍴🍴 RESTAURANT WITH ROOMS

Market Place CO10 9QZ
☎ 01787 247431 📠 01787 248007
e-mail: info@greathouse.co.uk
web: www.greathouse.co.uk
dir: *Exit A1141 into Market Ln, behind cross on Market Place*

The 18th-century frontage on Market Place conceals a 15th-century timber-framed building that is now a restaurant with rooms. The Great House remains a pocket of France offering high-quality rural cuisine served by French staff. The spacious bedrooms are individually decorated and thoughtfully equipped with many useful extras; some rooms have a separate lounge area.

Rooms 5 en suite (1 fmly) S £95-£195; D £95-£225 (room only)* **Facilities** FTV DVD tea/coffee Dinner available Direct Dial Cen ht Wi-fi 🎱 Free bicycle use for guests **Extras** Mini-bar, fruit, sherry - complimentary **Notes** LB 🚫 Closed Jan RS Sun eve & Mon Restaurant closed No coaches

LAVENHAM *continued*

PREMIER COLLECTION

Lavenham Old Rectory

★★★★★ 🛏 BED AND BREAKFAST

Church St CO10 9SA
☎ 01787 247572
e-mail: susie_dwright@hotmail.co.uk

After years of restoration work, the Old Rectory has recently been reborn and offers sumptuous en suite accommodation where classic style meets modern technology to suit a discerning clientele. The two suites are decorated in understated contemporary style, while the other room has a more traditional, elegant feel. Three acres of garden include a classical formal pond, herbaceous borders, a rose garden with an arched walk, and a thatched summer house.

Rooms 3 en suite **Facilities** FTV Cen ht Wi-fi **Parking** 10 **Notes** ⊗ No Children Closed 24-26 Dec

PREMIER COLLECTION

Lavenham Priory

★★★★★ 🛏 BED AND BREAKFAST

Water St CO10 9RW
☎ 01787 247404 📠 01787 248472
e-mail: mail@lavenhampriory.co.uk
web: www.lavenhampriory.co.uk
dir: A1141 to Lavenham, turn by side of The Swan onto Water St & right after 50yds onto private drive

This superb Grade I listed building, dating from the 15th century, once belonged to Benedictine monks and has been lovingly restored to maintain its original character. Individually decorated bedrooms are very spacious; each is beautifully furnished and thoughtfully equipped. Breakfast is served in the spectacular dining room or in the sheltered courtyard herb garden. Guests also have use of the Great Hall, with inglenook fireplace, and an adjoining lounge.

Rooms 6 en suite (1 fmly) S £87-£97; D £120-£183* **Facilities** FTV Lounge TVL tea/coffee Cen ht Licensed Wi-fi 🔒 **Extras** Speciality toiletries **Parking** 11 **Notes** No Children 10yrs Closed 21 Dec-2 Jan

LEISTON   Map 13 TM46

Field End

★★★★ GUEST HOUSE

1 Kings Rd IP16 4DA
☎ 01728 833527 & 07946 287451
e-mail: herbert@herbertwood.wanadoo.co.uk
web: www.fieldendbedandbreakfast.co.uk
dir: In town centre off B1122

This Edwardian house has been appointed to a high standard and is impeccably maintained by the present owners. Bedrooms have co-ordinated soft furnishings and

many thoughtful touches. Breakfast is served in an attractive dining room, which has a large sofa and a range of puzzles and games.

Rooms 5 rms (2 en suite) (1 pri facs) (1 fmly) (1 GF) **Facilities** TVL tea/coffee Cen ht **Parking** 5 **Notes** ⊗ No Children 6mths ⊛

LOWESTOFT   Map 13 TM59

Somerton House

★★★★ GUEST ACCOMMODATION

7 Kirkley Cliff NR33 0BY
☎ 01502 565665 & 07742 127706
e-mail: somerton7@hotmail.co.uk
dir: Opposite Claremont Pier, on seafront

Somerton House is a Victorian Grade II listed building situated on the seafront with great views of the beach and sea. The bedrooms are sympathetically decorated and furnished to enhance the original Victorian features. Breakfast is served at individual tables in the lower ground floor dining room, and features locally sourced produce.

Rooms 7 rms (4 en suite) (3 pri facs) (1 fmly) (1 GF) S £36; D £57* **Facilities** FTV tea/coffee Cen ht Wi-fi **Notes** LB

Wavecrest Guest House

★★★★ GUEST HOUSE

31 Marine Pde NR33 0QN
☎ 01502 561268
e-mail: wavecrestguesthouse@googlemail.com
dir: On seafront just S of Lowestoft Bridge

This Victorian terrace house is situated on the seafront, overlooking the award-winning beach and within easy walking distance of the town centre. The bedrooms are smartly decorated with co-ordinated soft furnishings and equipped with modern facilities. Public areas include an elegant dining room where breakfast is served at individual tables.

Rooms 5 rms (4 en suite) (1 pri facs) (1 fmly) S £29-£45; D £50-£60* **Facilities** FTV DVD tea/coffee Cen ht Wi-fi 🔒 **Notes** ⊗ Closed 24-31 Dec

Coventry House

★★★ GUEST HOUSE

8 Kirkley Cliff NR33 0BY
☎ 01502 573865
dir: On seafront

A well presented Victorian property situated on the seafront overlooking the beach with superb views of the sea. Breakfast is served at individual tables in the spacious dining room, which is situated on the lower ground floor. The bedrooms have co-ordinated soft furnishings and modern facilities such as Wi-fi and flat screen TVs.

Rooms 7 rms (5 en suite) (2 pri facs) (3 fmly) (1 GF) **Facilities** FTV tea/coffee Cen ht Wi-fi **Parking** 4 **Notes** Closed 22-28 Dec ⊛

Seavilla

★★★ GUEST ACCOMMODATION

43 Kirkley Cliff Rd NR33 0DF
☎ 01502 574657
dir: A12 into town, right at South Beach, 300yds past Claremont Pier

Expect a warm welcome at the Seavilla which is situated on the southern side of town overlooking the beach. The pleasant bedrooms are thoughtfully equipped and many have superb sea views. Breakfast is served at individual tables in the attractive dining room and guests have the use of a cosy lounge.

Rooms 9 rms (5 en suite) S £25-£35; D £50-£60* **Facilities** FTV tea/coffee Cen ht 🔒 **Parking** **Notes** LB ⊗

MENDHAM   Map 13 TM28

Weston House Farm *(TM292828)*

★★★★ FARMHOUSE

IP20 0PB
☎ 01986 782206   Mrs J E Holden
e-mail: holden@farmline.com
web: www.westonhousefarm.co.uk
dir: Off A143 or B1123 signed Mendham, signs from village centre

Weston House is a well maintained, Grade II listed, 17th-century farmhouse set in an acre of pleasant gardens in the heart of the Waveney Valley. The individually decorated bedrooms are thoughtfully furnished, well-equipped and generally quite spacious. Breakfast is served in the smart dining room which overlooks the garden.

Rooms 3 en suite (1 GF) S £40-£50; D £60-£72* **Facilities** FTV TVL tea/coffee Cen ht Wi-fi **Extras** Snacks - complimentary **Parking** 6 **Notes** No Children 10yrs Closed Dec-Feb 600 acres mixed

NEWMARKET   Map 12 TL66

The Garden Lodge

★★★★ BED AND BREAKFAST

11 Vicarage Ln, Woodditton CB8 9SG
☎ 01638 731116
e-mail: swedishgardenlodge@hotmail.com
web: www.gardenlodge.net
dir: 3m S of Newmarket in Woodditton

A warm welcome is assured in this home-from-home, not far from the famous racecourse. The accommodation, in quality chalets, is very well equipped and features a wealth of thoughtful extras. Freshly prepared home-cooked breakfasts are served in an elegant dining room in the main house.

Save on B&Bs and Hotels. Book at **theAA.com/hotel**

SUFFOLK 281 ENGLAND

Rooms 3 en suite (3 GF) S £45* **Facilities** FTV tea/coffee Dinner available Cen ht Wi-fi **Parking** 6 **Notes** ⊛

SAXMUNDHAM   Map 13 TM36

Sandpit Farm

★★★★ BED AND BREAKFAST

Bruisyard IP17 2EB
☎ 01728 663445
e-mail: smarshall@aldevalleybreaks.co.uk
web: www.aldevalleybreaks.co.uk
dir: *4m W of Saxmundham. A1120 onto B1120, 1st left for Bruisyard, house 1.5m on left*

Sandpit Farm is a delightful Grade II listed farmhouse set in 20 acres of grounds. Bedrooms have many thoughtful touches and lovely country views, and there are two cosy lounges to enjoy. Breakfast features quality local produce and freshly laid free-range eggs.

Rooms 2 en suite S £50-£65; D £60-£100 **Facilities** FTV TVL TV1B tea/coffee Cen ht Wi-fi ⬡ 🔒 **Parking** 5 **Notes** LB Closed 24-26 Dec ⊛

SIBTON   Map 13 TM36

Sibton White Horse Inn

★★★★ ⊛ INN

Halesworth Rd IP17 2JJ
☎ 01728 660337
e-mail: info@sibtonwhitehorseinn.co.uk
dir: *From A12 in Yoxford take A1120 signed Sibton & Peasenhall. 3m, in Peasenhall right opposite butcher's shop. White Horse 600mtrs*

The Sibton White Horse Inn is a delightful Grade II listed 16th-century Tudor inn set in a rural location surrounded by open countryside, a few miles from the Suffolk coast. Public rooms include a traditional beamed bar with exposed brick fireplaces and a choice of dining areas. The attractive bedrooms are situated in a converted building adjacent.

Rooms 6 annexe en suite (3 GF) S £65-£75; D £80-£90* **Facilities** FTV DVD tea/coffee Dinner available Cen ht Wi-fi ⬡ 18 🔒 **Extras** Bottled water **Parking** 50 **Notes** LB No Children 12yrs Closed 26-27 Dec No coaches

SOUTHWOLD   Map 13 TM57

PREMIER COLLECTION

Sutherland House

★★★★★ ⊛⊛ RESTAURANT WITH ROOMS

56 High St IP18 6DN
☎ 01502 724544
e-mail: enquiries@sutherlandhouse.co.uk
web: www.sutherlandhouse.co.uk
dir: *A1095 into Southwold, on High St on left after Victoria St*

A delightful 16th-century house situated in the heart of the bustling town centre with a wealth of character, Sutherland House has oak beams, exposed brickwork, open fireplaces and two superb ornate plasterwork ceilings. The stylish bedrooms are tastefully decorated, have co-ordinated fabrics and many thoughtful touches. Public rooms feature a large open-plan contemporary restaurant with plush furniture.

Rooms 4 en suite (1 fmly) **Facilities** FTV tea/coffee Dinner available Direct Dial Cen ht Wi-fi **Conf** Max 80 Thtr 80 Class 30 Board 30 **Parking** 1 **Notes** ⊗ RS Mon Restaurant closed in winter No coaches

Home @ 21 Bed and Breakfast

★★★★ BED AND BREAKFAST

21 North Pde IP18 6LT
☎ 01502 722573
e-mail: pauline.archer@btconnect.com
web: www.homeat21.co.uk
dir: *A12 onto B1095. At mini-rdbt, left into Pier Av, right into North Parade. Premises 100yds on right*

This delightful Victorian property is situated on the promenade overlooking the sea. The stylish bedrooms have co-ordinated soft furnishings and many thoughtful touches, also some rooms have superb sea views.

Breakfast, which includes fresh local produce, is served in the smart lounge/dining room at a large polished table.

Rooms 3 rms (2 en suite) (1 pri facs) S £75-£100; D £80-£110 **Facilities** FTV tea/coffee Cen ht Wi-fi ⬡ **Notes** LB ⊗ No Children 10yrs Closed Xmas & New Year ⊛

STOWMARKET   Map 13 TM05

PREMIER COLLECTION

Bays Farm

★★★★★ GUEST ACCOMMODATION

Forward Green IP14 5HU
☎ 01449 711286
e-mail: info@baysfarmsuffolk.co.uk
web: www.baysfarmsuffolk.co.uk
dir: *A14 junct 50, A1120. 1m after Stowupland, right at sharp left bend signed Broad Green. Bays Farm 1st house on right*

Tea and home-made cake are offered on arrival at this delightful 17th-century former farmhouse, situated amid four acres of mature grounds. The property has a wealth of character. Bedrooms are carefully decorated and have co-ordinated soft furnishings as well as many thoughtful touches. Breakfast, which includes locally sourced produce, is served around a large polished table in the stylish dining room.

Rooms 3 en suite 1 annexe en suite S £65-£85; D £80-£95* **Facilities** FTV DVD iPod docking station Lounge tea/coffee Cen ht Licensed Wi-fi 🔒 **Extras** Speciality toiletries **Parking** 6 **Notes** No Children 12yrs

SUDBURY   Map 13 TL84

The Case Restaurant with Rooms

★★★★ ⊛ RESTAURANT WITH ROOMS

Further St, Assington CO10 5LD
☎ 01787 210483 ▤ 01787 211725
e-mail: restaurant@thecaserestaurantwithrooms.co.uk
dir: *Exit A12 at Colchester onto A134 to Sudbury. 7m, establishment on left*

The Case Restaurant with Rooms offers dining in comfortable surroundings, along with luxurious accommodation in bedrooms that all enjoy independent access. Some bathrooms come complete with corner jacuzzi, while internet access comes as standard. In the restaurant, local produce is used in all dishes, and fresh bread and desserts are made every day.

Rooms 7 en suite (2 fmly) (7 GF) S £69-£89; D £89-£125 **Facilities** FTV Lounge tea/coffee Dinner available Cen ht Wi-fi **Extras** Speciality toiletries - complimentary; snacks -chargeable **Parking** 25 **Notes** LB ⊗

WOODBRIDGE
Map 13 TM24

Grove House
★★★ GUEST HOUSE

39 Grove Rd IP12 4LG
☎ 01394 382202
e-mail: reception@grovehousehotel.ltd.uk
dir: W of town centre on A12

A warm welcome is assured at this owner-managed establishment on the west side of town. The bedrooms are pleasantly decorated and thoughtfully equipped with a good range of useful facilities. The smart public rooms include a cosy bar, a comfortable lounge and a large dining room with individual tables.

Rooms 10 en suite (1 fmly) (6 GF) **Facilities** tea/coffee Dinner available Cen ht Licensed Wi-fi **Conf** Max 20 Thtr 20 Class 20 Board 20 **Parking** 12 **Notes** ⊗

YAXLEY
Map 13 TM17

PREMIER COLLECTION

The Auberge
★★★★★ ◉◉ RESTAURANT WITH ROOMS

Ipswich Rd IP23 8BZ
☎ 01379 783604 📠 01379 788486
e-mail: aubmail@the-auberge.co.uk
web: www.the-auberge.co.uk
dir: On A140 between Norwich & Ipswich at x-rds with B1117

A warm welcome awaits at this charming 15th-century property, which has been lovingly converted by the present owners from a rural pub into a smart restaurant with rooms. The restaurant has gained AA Rosettes for the good use of fresh, quality produce. The public areas have a wealth of character, such as exposed brickwork and beams, and the grounds are particularly well-kept and attractive. The spacious bedrooms are tastefully appointed and have many thoughtful touches; one bedroom has a four-poster.

Rooms 11 annexe en suite (2 fmly) (6 GF) **Facilities** FTV tea/coffee Dinner available Direct Dial Cen ht Wi-fi **Conf** Max 46 Thtr 30 Class 30 Board 20 **Parking** 40 **Notes** ⊗ No coaches

SURREY

ALBURY
Map 6 TQ04

The Drummond at Albury
★★★ ◡ INN

High St GU5 9AG
☎ 01483 202039 📠 01483 205361

The Drummond is centrally located in this picturesque village, with attractive gardens running down to a small river at the rear of the property. The bedrooms are individually appointed and offer all the modern comforts. Breakfast is served in the light and airy conservatory whilst the restaurant offers mouth-watering dishes.

Rooms 9 en suite **Facilities** Dinner available **Conf** Max 40 Thtr 40 Class 40

CAMBERLEY
Map 6 SU86

Hatsue Guest House
★★★★ GUEST ACCOMMODATION

17 Southwell Park Rd GU15 3PU
☎ 01276 22160 & 07791 267620 📠 01276 671415
e-mail: welcome@hatsueguesthouse.com
dir: M3 junct 4, A331 N, A30 E, at Arena sports centre turn right. At T-junct, turn right, 2nd house on left before church

Hatsue Guest House offers comfortable, well-appointed accommodation within a period house, which has been sympathetically modernised to meet the needs of the modern guest. Flat screen TV and free Wi-fi are examples of the amenities provided. The breakfast room overlooks the quiet rear garden. Ample parking is available.

Rooms 5 en suite **Facilities** FTV DVD tea/coffee Direct Dial Cen ht Wi-fi **Parking** 5 **Notes** ⊗

Burwood House
★★★★ ◡ GUEST ACCOMMODATION

15 London Rd GU15 3UQ
☎ 01276 685686 📠 01276 62220
e-mail: enquiries@burwoodhouse.co.uk
dir: On A30 between Camberley & Bagshot

Burwood House is a very stylish establishment with individually designed bedrooms that offer all modern conveniences including Wi-fi. Every Monday to Thursday evening the kitchen offers a varied menu full of traditional favourites, as well as seasonal house specialties. Breakfast can be taken either buffet-style or as a fresh-cooked meal prepared upon request. Public areas include a lounge, bar and garden.

Rooms 22 en suite (3 fmly) (7 GF) S £75-£95; D £95-£145* **Facilities** FTV tea/coffee Dinner available Direct Dial Cen ht Licensed Wi-fi ↻ ♨ 18 ♣ **Extras** Speciality toiletries, mini-bar **Conf** Max 60 Thtr 50 Class 16 Board 20 **Parking** 22 **Notes** Closed 22 Dec-4 Jan

CHARLWOOD

For accommodation details see under Gatwick Airport (London), (Sussex, West)

CHIDDINGFOLD
Map 6 SU93

PREMIER COLLECTION

The Crown Inn
★★★★★ INN

The Green, Petworth Rd GU8 4TX
☎ 01428 682255 📠 01428 683313
e-mail: enquiries@thecrownchiddingfold.com

Set in a tranquil location in a picturesque village, the inn dates back to as early as 1216. This charming property has been completely renovated and offers stylish, modern accommodation which has been tastefully renovated without losing any period features. Breakfast and dinner can be enjoyed in the oak-panelled dining room, and there is a spacious bar, outside seating and small courtyard.

Rooms 8 en suite (4 fmly) S £100-£125; D £135-£200 **Facilities** FTV DVD iPod docking station Lounge tea/coffee Dinner available Direct Dial Cen ht Wi-fi **Conf** Max 40 Thtr 40 Class 25 Board 28 **Parking** 15 **Notes** ⊗

Save on B&Bs and Hotels. Book at **theAA.com/hotel**

SURREY 283 **ENGLAND**

The Swan Inn
★★★★ ⓐ INN

Petworth Rd GU8 4TY
☎ 01428 684688 ▤ 01428 685991
e-mail: info@theswaninnchiddingfold.com
web: www.theswaninnchiddingfold.com
dir: M25 junct 10, A3 to Milford junct. At rdbt 1st exit onto A283, left at lights. At next rdbt 2nd exit, 5m to Swan Inn

The Swan Inn offers well-sourced, seasonal food within an elegant environment. The well-appointed bedrooms are air-conditioned and equipped to meet the needs of both the leisure and business traveller. The rear garden is a peaceful option during the warm months.

Rooms 10 en suite (1 fmly) D £100-£180* **Facilities** STV DVD tea/coffee Dinner available Direct Dial Wi-fi **Conf** Max 20 Thtr 20 Class 20 Board 20 **Parking** 30 **Notes** No coaches

---

CHOBHAM
Map 6 SU96

Pembroke House
★★★★ GUEST ACCOMMODATION

Valley End Rd GU24 8TB
☎ 01276 857654
e-mail: pembroke_house@btinternet.com
dir: A30 onto B383 signed Chobham, 3m right into Valley End Rd, 1m on left

Proprietor Julia Holland takes obvious pleasure in welcoming guests to her beautifully appointed and spacious home. The elegantly proportioned public areas include an imposing entrance hall and dining room with views over the surrounding countryside. Bedrooms are restful and filled with thoughtful extras.

Rooms 4 rms (2 en suite) (2 pri facs) (1 fmly) S £40-£60; D £100-£200* **Facilities** STV FTV DVD tea/coffee Cen ht Wi-fi ⌂ ☖ **Parking** 10 **Notes** ⊛

CRANLEIGH
Map 6 TQ03

The Cranley
★★★ INN

The Common GU6 8SQ
☎ 01483 272827 ▤ 01483 548576
e-mail: thecranleyhotel@gmail.com
dir: From Guildford on A281 left to Cranleigh

This traditional pub, located in the picturesque village of Cranleigh, offers freshly prepared food, using local produce, at lunch and dinner. Regular entertainment is provided, and the rear garden is popular with families. The comfortable bedrooms have TVs and tea- and coffee-making facilities.

Rooms 7 en suite **Facilities** TVL tea/coffee Dinner available Cen ht Wi-fi Pool table **Parking** 50 **Notes** ⊛

EAST HORSLEY
Map 6 TQ05

The Duke of Wellington
★★★ INN

Guildford Rd KT24 6AA
☎ 01483 282164
e-mail: info@dukeofwellington.uk.com

Built in the 16th century, and once a coaching inn, this establishment is close to Guildford, Leatherhead and the M25. The courtyard, previously a stable block, houses all the en suite bedrooms; each is spacious and modern yet retains original features. A hearty breakfast is served, and a selection of home-cooked meals is available for both lunch and dinner.

Rooms 9 en suite (2 fmly) (9 GF) **Facilities** FTV tea/coffee Dinner available Wi-fi Pool table **Parking** 30

EFFINGHAM
Map 6 TQ15

Sir Douglas Haig
★★★ INN

The Street KT24 5LU
☎ 01372 456886 ▤ 01372 450987
e-mail: sirdouglashaig@hotmail.com
dir: M25 junct 9, A243 then A24, at rdbt take 2nd exit onto A246. Through Bookham, at lights with golf club on left, turn right. Pub on right

A traditional public house located in the village centre, the Sir Douglas Haig has retained a country atmosphere and offers comfortable accommodation for the modern traveller. The bar is well stocked and provides regular entertainment whilst the restaurant serves a choice of traditional dishes. Ample parking is available.

Rooms 7 en suite (1 fmly) **Facilities** FTV tea/coffee Dinner available Cen ht Wi-fi **Parking** 15 **Notes** LB

FARNHAM
Map 5 SU84

Sandiway
★★★ BED AND BREAKFAST

24 Shortheath Rd GU9 8SR
☎ 01252 710721
e-mail: john@shortheath.freeserve.co.uk
dir: Onto A287 Hindhead, at lights at top of hill right onto Ridgway Rd, past green on left, Sandiway 300yds on right

Guests are warmly welcomed at this delightful house, set in attractive gardens in a quiet residential area. Smart bedrooms have a thoughtful range of facilities and share a spacious, well-appointed bathroom. Guests have use of a comfortable lounge during the day and evening, which doubles as the dining room at breakfast.

Rooms 3 rms S £35-£40; D £50-£55 **Facilities** FTV TVL tea/coffee Cen ht Wi-fi **Extras** Bottled water **Parking** 3 **Notes** ⊛ No Children 10yrs Closed 21-31 Dec ⊛

GODALMING
Map 6 SU94

Innkeeper's Lodge Godalming
★★★★ ⌟ INN

Ockford Rd GU7 1RH
☎ 0845 112 6102
e-mail: info@innkeeperslodge.com
web: www.innkeeperslodge.com

At Innkeeper's Lodge you'll find accommodation with comfort and character in equal measure, and everything needed for a relaxing stay, from easy check-in and free parking to complimentary breakfast and a cosy pub serving great value food and drink on the doorstep. Each Lodge has quality rooms, and there are Lodges in a variety of locations from towns and cities to countryside settings across the UK.

Rooms 14 en suite (4 fmly) **Facilities** FTV tea/coffee Dinner available Direct Dial Wi-fi **Parking**

GUILDFORD
Map 6 SU94

Asperion Hillside
★★★★ ⌟ GUEST ACCOMMODATION

Perry Hill, Worplesdon GU3 3RF
☎ 01483 232051 ▤ 01483 237015
e-mail: info@thehillsidehotel.com

Located just a short drive away from central Guildford this accommodation is popular with both business and leisure travellers. Bedrooms are comfortable and well equipped with good facilities. Public areas include a spacious lounge bar where dinner is served, and a bright well-styled breakfast room. Gardens are well maintained and are enhanced by a guest terrace. Intimate meetings and events can also be catered for here.

Rooms 15 en suite (6 GF) **Facilities** FTV tea/coffee Dinner available Cen ht Licensed Wi-fi **Conf** Max 20 Thtr 20 Class 10 Board 12 **Parking** 15 **Notes** ⊛ Closed 21 Dec-7 Jan

GUILDFORD *continued*

Asperion

★★★★ GUEST ACCOMMODATION

73 Farnham Rd GU2 7PF
☎ 01483 579299 ▤ 01483 457977
e-mail: enquiries@asperion.co.uk
dir: *Exit A3 at Surrey University only, 2nd exit from rdbt into Chase Rd. Right into Agraria Rd to Farnham Rd junct. Turn right into Farnham Rd (A31), 3rd on right*

The stylish Asperion provides comfortable, modern, and contemporary styled bedrooms in a convenient location close to the city centre of Guildford. The owners are committed to a "more than for profit" business ethos, part of which involves a healthy organic breakfast.

Rooms 15 rms (14 en suite) (1 pri facs) (1 fmly) (9 GF) S £50-£65; D £85-£120 Facilities STV FTV TVL tea/coffee Direct Dial Cen ht Licensed Notes ⊗ No Children 12yrs Closed 21 Dec-5 Jan

HASLEMERE   Map 6 SU93

The Wheatsheaf Inn

★★★ ⇥ INN

Grayswood Rd, Grayswood GU27 2DE
☎ 01428 644440 ▤ 01428 641285
e-mail: ken@thewheatsheafgrayswood.co.uk
web: www.thewheatsheafgrayswood.co.uk
dir: *1m N of Haslemere on A286 in Grayswood*

Situated in a small village just outside Haslemere, this well-presented inn has a friendly atmosphere. The smart conservatory restaurant is a new addition, which complements the attractive dining area and popular bar. Bedrooms are furnished to a good standard, all but one on the ground floor.

Rooms 7 en suite (6 GF) S £59; D £79* Facilities tea/coffee Dinner available Direct Dial Cen ht Wi-fi Parking 21 Notes No coaches

HORLEY

For accommodation details see under Gatwick Airport (London), (Sussex, West)

RIPLEY   Map 6 TQ05

The Talbot Inn

★★★★★ ◉ ⇥ INN

High St GU23 6BB
☎ 01483 225188 ▤ 01483 211332
e-mail: info@thetalbotinn.com
web: www.thetalbotinn.com
dir: *Exit A3 signed Ripley, on left on High St*

The Talbot Inn simply oozes charm and character and has retained many of its historical features despite having undergone a major transformation. Public areas are very comfortable, with real ales and delicious home-cooked food on offer; alfresco dining is available in summer

months. The Classic Rooms in the Ripley Wing are contemporary in design, and there are nine bedrooms in the main building, all of which have traditional character and original features; four newly refurbished deluxe rooms, with hi-spec furnishing, are available.

Rooms 9 en suite 34 annexe en suite (17 GF) Facilities STV FTV tea/coffee Dinner available Cen ht Wi-fi Conf Max 120 Thtr 120 Class 58 Board 36 Parking 60 Notes Civ Wed 120

WEYBRIDGE   Map 6 TQ06

Innkeeper's Lodge Weybridge

★★★ INN

25 Oatlands Chase KT13 9RW
☎ 0845 112 6111
e-mail: info@innkeeperslodge.com
web: www.innkeeperslodge.com

At Innkeeper's Lodge you'll find accommodation with comfort and character in equal measure, and everything needed for a relaxing stay, from easy check-in and free parking to complimentary breakfast and a cosy pub serving great value food and drink on the doorstep. Each Lodge has quality rooms, and there are Lodges in a variety of locations from towns and cities to countryside settings across the UK.

Rooms 19 en suite (5 fmly) (2 GF) Facilities FTV tea/coffee Dinner available Direct Dial Wi-fi Parking

WOKING   Map 6 TQ05

Innkeeper's Lodge Woking

★★★ INN

Chobham Rd, Horsell GU21 4AL
☎ 0845 112 6112
e-mail: info@innkeeperslodge.com
web: www.innkeeperslodge.com

At Innkeeper's Lodge you'll find accommodation with comfort and character in equal measure, and everything needed for a relaxing stay, from easy check-in and free parking to complimentary breakfast and a cosy pub serving great value food and drink on the doorstep. Each Lodge has quality rooms, and there are Lodges in a variety of locations from towns and cities to countryside settings across the UK.

Rooms 34 en suite (3 fmly) (13 GF) Facilities FTV tea/coffee Dinner available Direct Dial Wi-fi Parking 28

SUSSEX, EAST

BECKLEY   Map 7 TQ82

Woodgate Farm

★★★★ BED AND BREAKFAST

Church Ln TN31 6UH
☎ 01797 260763
e-mail: info@woodgate-farm.co.uk
dir: *Off B2088 into Church Ln or off A268 into Stoddards Ln*

Set in 22 acres of tranquil countryside, yet convenient for both Rye and Hastings, this B&B offers two comfortably appointed bedrooms with modern decor and furnishings. The owners also offer a friendly welcome and home-made refreshments. Guests are more than welcome to explore the property's garden and meadows. Enjoy a hearty cooked and continental breakfast in the open-plan kitchen.

Rooms 2 rms (1 en suite) (1 pri facs) (2 GF) S £60; D £72-£78* Facilities STV tea/coffee Cen ht Wi-fi jacuzzi Extras Speciality toiletries, filtered water Parking 4 Notes ⊗ No Children Closed Xmas wk

BODIAM   Map 7 TQ72

Spring Farm

★★★★★ BED AND BREAKFAST

Northlands TN32 5UX
☎ 01580 831222
e-mail: springfarmbandb@tiscali.co.uk
web: www.springfarmbodiam.co.uk
dir: *A21, 1m S of Hurst Green, turn left, follow signs for Bodiam Castle. After 2m across x-rds, 400mtrs on left*

Spring Farm is located just one mile from Bodiam Castle and is convenient for Hastings, Rye and Tenterden. Bedrooms and bathrooms are stylishly decorated, providing guests with comfortable accommodation that includes flat screen LCD TVs; free Wi-fi is available throughout. The guest lounge on the ground floor provides additional space for relaxing during the day, and is the venue for a cooked or continental breakfast. There is an outdoor swimming pool in the beautiful gardens.

Rooms 3 en suite S £60-£75; D £70-£95* Facilities FTV TVL tea/coffee Dinner available Cen ht Wi-fi ⤬ ⬤ Parking 3 Notes LB ⊗ No Children 12yrs ✉

Save on B&Bs and Hotels. Book at theAA.com/hotel

SUSSEX, EAST 285 ENGLAND

BRIGHTON & HOVE — Map 6 TQ30

Brighton Pavilions
★★★★ GUEST ACCOMMODATION

7 Charlotte St BN2 1AG
☎ 01273 621750 📠 01273 622477
e-mail: sanchez-crespo@lineone.net
web: www.brightonpavilions.com
dir: *A23 to Brighton Pier, left onto A259 (Marine Parade), take 15th left into Charlotte St*

This well-run operation is in one of Brighton's Regency streets, a short walk from the seafront and town centre. Bedrooms have themes such as Mikado or Pompeii, and are very smartly presented with many thoughtful extras, including room service breakfast in superior rooms, and free Wi-fi. The bright breakfast room has doors opening out onto a patio.

Rooms 10 rms (7 en suite) (1 fmly) (1 GF) S £46-£50; D £86-£150* **Facilities** FTV DVD tea/coffee Direct Dial Cen ht Wi-fi **Extras** Chocolate, soft drinks, bottled water **Notes** LB

Five
★★★★ GUEST ACCOMMODATION

5 New Steine BN2 1PB
☎ 01273 686547 📠 0871 522 7472
e-mail: info@fivehotel.com
dir: *On A259 towards E, 8th turn on left into square*

An attractive townhouse in a traditional Georgian square just a stone's throw from the famous Brighton beaches, cafés and shops. Comfortable bedrooms and bathrooms are well equipped. A copious organic breakfast is served by cheerful hosts in the spacious, contemporary dining room.

Rooms 10 en suite **Facilities** FTV TVL tea/coffee Cen ht Wi-fi **Conf** Max 20 Board 20 **Notes** ⊗ No Children 5yrs

New Steine
★★★★ 🛏 🍽 GUEST ACCOMMODATION

10-11 New Steine BN2 1PB
☎ 01273 695415 & 681546 📠 01273 622663
e-mail: reservation@newsteinehotel.com
web: www.newsteinehotel.com
dir: *A23 to Brighton Pier, left into Marine Parade, New Steine on left after Wentworth St*

Close to the seafront, off the Esplanade, the New Steine provides spacious and well-appointed accommodation. The Bistro offers simple yet appealing dishes with a French and British influence; produce from farms in Sussex is used for the breakfasts. There are two meeting rooms suitable for a range of occasions. Street parking can be arranged.

Rooms 20 rms (16 en suite) (4 pri facs) (4 fmly) (2 GF) S £34.50-£59; D £62.50-£119* **Facilities** FTV Lounge tea/coffee Dinner available Direct Dial Cen ht Licensed Wi-fi 🛏 **Extras** Speciality toiletries **Conf** Max 50 Thtr 50 Class 20 Board 26 **Notes** LB No Children 4yrs

The Twenty One
★★★★ GUEST ACCOMMODATION

21 Charlotte St, Marine Pde BN2 1AG
☎ 01273 686450
e-mail: enquiries@thetwentyone.co.uk
web: www.thetwentyone.co.uk
dir: *From Brighton Pier turn left into Marine Parade, 16th left turn*

This stylishly appointed townhouse property is situated in Kemp Town within easy reach of clubs, bars and restaurants, and just a short walk from the beach. Bedrooms are elegantly furnished and comfortable, with an abundance of thoughtful extras provided. The smart dining room is the setting for a delicious, freshly-cooked breakfast.

Rooms 8 en suite (1 fmly) S £55-£65; D £90-£149* **Facilities** FTV DVD iPod docking station Lounge tea/coffee Cen ht Wi-fi ⊗ No Children 10yrs

See advert on this page

BRIGHTON & HOVE *continued*

The White House

★★★★ ☖ GUEST ACCOMMODATION

6 Bedford St BN2 1AN
☎ 01273 626266
e-mail: info@whitehousebrighton.com
web: www.whitehousebrighton.com
dir: *A23 to Brighton, follow signs to town centre. At rdbt opposite pier 1st exit, through 2 sets of lights, left into Bedford St*

The White House is a small Regency residence only 100 metres from the seafront, and a short walk from Brighton's centre. There are sea views from the south-facing rooms and a courtyard garden where guests may sit and relax. All rooms are smartly and stylishly decorated and there is a relaxed atmosphere. Breakfast is served in the dining room, or alfresco. The extensive breakfast menu uses only best quality ingredients.

Rooms 10 rms (8 en suite) (2 GF) **Facilities** tea/coffee Cen ht Wi-fi **Notes** ✖ Closed Jan

Brighton House

★★★★ ☖ GUEST ACCOMMODATION

52 Regency Square BN1 2FF
☎ 01273 323282
e-mail: info@brighton-house.co.uk
web: www.brighton-house.co.uk
dir: *Opposite West Pier*

Situated close to the seafront is the elegant, environmentally-friendly, Brighton House. Comfortably appointed bedrooms and bathrooms come in a variety of sizes and are located on four floors. An impressively abundant, organic continental breakfast is served in the spacious elegant dining room. Parking is in the nearby underground car park.

Rooms 16 en suite (2 fmly) **Facilities** tea/coffee Cen ht Licensed **Notes** ✖ No Children 12yrs

Four Seasons Guest House

★★★★ GUEST ACCOMMODATION

3 Upper Rock Gardens BN2 1QE
☎ 01273 673574
e-mail: info@fourseasonsbrighton.com
web: www.fourseasonsbrighton.com
dir: *A23 signed town centre & seafront to Brighton Pier. At rdbt 1st exit, left into Marine Parade. At next lights left into Lower Rock Gardens*

Caring hosts William and Thommy provide smart accommodation with a variety of stylish contemporary bedrooms, each with ample facilities including Wi-fi and hairdryers. A healthy breakfast is served in the sunny dining room. Beaches, restaurants and shops are within close walking distance.

Rooms 7 rms (6 pri facs) (1 GF) S £50-£65; D £60-£130* **Facilities** FTV tea/coffee Cen ht Wi-fi **Notes** LB ✖ No Children 10yrs

Gullivers

★★★★ GUEST ACCOMMODATION

12a New Steine BN2 1PB
☎ 01273 681546 & 695415 ▤ 01273 622663
e-mail: reservation@gullivershotel.com
web: www.gullivershotel.com
dir: *A23 to Brighton Pier, left into Marine Parade, premises 300yds on left*

Situated in an impressive Regency square close to the town and seafront, Gullivers has much to offer. Compact rooms use clever design and contemporary colours to ensure comfort, and some have quality shower rooms en suite. The lounge and brasserie, decorated with fine art, are super areas in which to relax and dine.

Rooms 12 rms (9 en suite) (3 pri facs) (2 GF) (4 smoking) S £32.50-£55; D £60-£115* **Facilities** FTV Lounge tea/coffee Dinner available Direct Dial Cen ht Licensed Wi-fi ⚓ **Extras** Speciality toiletries - complimentary **Conf** Max 30 Thtr 30 Class 10 Board 20 **Notes** LB ✖ No Children 4yrs

Marine View

★★★★ GUEST ACCOMMODATION

24 New Steine BN2 1PD
☎ 01273 603870 ▤ 01273 357257
e-mail: info@mvbrighton.co.uk
web: www.mvbrighton.co.uk
dir: *From A23, left into Marine Pde, left into New Steine, 300mtrs*

Overlooking the elegant Steine Square with the sea just a glance away, this 18th-century property offers comfortable, well-designed accommodation. Plenty of accessories are provided, including free Wi-fi. A hearty breakfast is available in the bright lounge/dining room.

Rooms 11 rms (8 en suite) (1 pri facs) (2 fmly) (2 GF) **Facilities** tea/coffee Cen ht Wi-fi **Notes** ✖

Nineteen

★★★★ GUEST ACCOMMODATION

19 Broad St BN2 1TJ
☎ 01273 675529 ▤ 01273 675531
e-mail: info@hotelnineteen.co.uk
web: www.hotelnineteen.co.uk
dir: *A23 to Brighton Pier, left into Marine Parade, 1st left into Manchester St, right into Saint James St. 2nd right into Broad St*

This contemporary establishment lies close to the town centre, only minutes from Brighton Pier. Bedrooms are decorated with white walls, wooden floors and stylish artworks. The continental breakfast (served with champagne at the weekend) is superb, providing a fine start to the day.

Rooms 7 en suite (2 GF) S £50-£90; D £72-£250* **Facilities** FTV DVD iPod docking station Cen ht Wi-fi Outdoor hot tub in 1 bedroom **Extras** Speciality toiletries, mineral water, fruit **Notes** ✖ No Children 10yrs Closed 24-26 Dec

The Oriental

★★★★ GUEST ACCOMMODATION

9 Oriental Place BN1 2LJ
☎ 01273 205050 ▤ 01273 205050
e-mail: info@orientalbrighton.co.uk
dir: *A23 right onto A259 at seafront, right into Oriental Place, on right*

The Oriental is situated close to the seafront and enjoys easy access to all areas. The accommodation is comfortable and modern, and there is a licensed bar. A tasty Sussex breakfast using locally sourced produce is offered in a friendly, relaxed atmosphere.

Rooms 9 en suite (4 fmly) (1 GF) S £45-£85; D £65-£150* **Facilities** FTV Lounge tea/coffee Cen ht Licensed Wi-fi ⚓ Massage Aromatherapy Beauty treatments **Conf** Max 10 Thtr 10 Class 10 Board 10

Paskins Town House

★★★★ ☖ GUEST ACCOMMODATION

18/19 Charlotte St BN2 1AG
☎ 01273 601203 ▤ 01273 621973
e-mail: welcome@paskins.co.uk
web: www.paskins.co.uk
dir: *A23 to pier, turn left, Charlotte St 11th left*

This environmentally-friendly, family-run Victorian house is in a quiet street within walking distance of the seafront and town centre. Bedrooms are a comfortable mix of Victorian and art nouveau styles. The Art Deco breakfast room offers a variety of vegetarian and vegan dishes and traditional English breakfasts, featuring home-made vegetarian sausages and much organic produce.

Rooms 19 rms (16 en suite) (2 fmly) (3 GF) S £40-£60; D £60-£145 **Facilities** FTV tea/coffee Cen ht Wi-fi **Notes** LB

Snooze

★★★★ GUEST ACCOMMODATION

25 St George Ter BN2 1JJ
☎ 01273 605797
e-mail: info@snoozebrighton.com

This splendid Victorian terraced property is close to the beach and the popular Kemptown bars and restaurants. Bedrooms have a distinctly 'retro' feel and all are comfortably presented. A choice of hearty breakfasts is served in the spacious dining room enhanced with large bay windows.

Rooms 8 en suite (2 GF) **Facilities** FTV tea/coffee Cen ht Wi-fi **Notes** ✖

Save on B&Bs and Hotels. Book at theAA.com/hotel

SUSSEX, EAST 287 ENGLAND

Motel Schmotel

★★★ 🏠 GUEST ACCOMMODATION

37 Russell Square BN1 2EF
☎ 01273 326129
e-mail: info@motelschmotel.co.uk

A charming family-run establishment situated in a quiet square just minutes away from the beach and the shops. The bright en suite bedrooms include thoughtful amenities such as free Wi-fi and Freeview TV. The substantial breakfast menu uses fresh, local produce and is served in the comfort of the guest's own room or the newly renovated breakfast room.

Rooms 8 en suite (1 fmly) (2 GF) Facilities FTV tea/coffee Cen ht Wi-fi Parking 2 Notes ⊗

Regency Landsdowne Guest House

★★★ GUEST ACCOMMODATION

45 Landsdowne Place BN3 1HF
☎ 01273 321830 📠 01273 777067
e-mail: regencylandsdowne@aol.com
web: www.regencylandsdowne.co.uk
dir: A23 to Brighton Pier, right onto A259, 1m right into Lansdowne Place, house on left before Western Rd

A warm welcome is guaranteed at this Regency house, located only minutes from the seafront. Comfortable bedrooms are functionally equipped with a good range of facilities. An extensive continental breakfast is served at a communal table overlooking attractive gardens. On-road parking is a short walk away.

Rooms 7 rms (5 en suite) (2 pri facs) Facilities FTV tea/coffee Cen ht Lift Wi-fi Notes ⊗ Closed 20-27 Dec

Ainsley House

★★★ GUEST ACCOMMODATION

28 New Steine BN2 1PD
☎ 01273 605310 📠 01273 688604
e-mail: rooms@ainsleyhotel.com

Situated on the stylish Steine Square and with good views of the Pier, this popular property has a range of well equipped rooms; most are en suite and all are comfortably presented. Breakfast, served by the cheerful proprietor, is in the well positioned dining room with views over the square.

Rooms 12 rms (10 en suite) (3 fmly) S £25-£65; D £40-£120* Facilities TVL TV11B tea/coffee Cen ht Notes LB

Avalon

★★★ GUEST ACCOMMODATION

7 Upper Rock Gardens BN2 1QE
☎ 01273 692344
e-mail: info@avalonbrighton.co.uk
dir: A23 to Brighton Pier, left into Marine Parade, 300yds at lights left into Lower Rock Gdns, over lights, Avalon on left

A warm welcome is assured at this guest accommodation just a short walk from the seafront and The Lanes. The en suite bedrooms vary in size and style but all are attractively presented with plenty of useful accessories including free Wi-fi. Parking vouchers are available for purchase from the proprietor.

Rooms 7 en suite (3 fmly) (1 GF) D £75-£105* Facilities FTV DVD tea/coffee Cen ht Wi-fi

Innkeeper's Lodge Brighton, Patcham

★★★ INN

Black Lion Harvester, London Rd, Patcham BN1 8YQ
☎ 0845 112 6097
e-mail: info@innkeeperslodge.com
web: www.innkeeperslodge.com

At Innkeeper's Lodge you'll find accommodation with comfort and character in equal measure, and everything needed for a relaxing stay, from easy check-in and free parking to complimentary breakfast and a cosy pub serving great value food and drink on the doorstep. Each Lodge has quality rooms, and there are Lodges in a variety of locations from towns and cities to countryside settings across the UK.

Rooms 17 en suite (6 fmly) (1 GF) Facilities FTV tea/coffee Dinner available Direct Dial Wi-fi Parking

The Market Inn

★★★ INN

1 Market St BN1 1HH
☎ 01273 329483
e-mail: marketinn@reallondonpubs.com
web: www.reallondonpubs.com/market.html
dir: In city centre, on pedestrian road 50yds from junct North St & East St

This lively period inn is within walking distance of many local attractions. Bedrooms are attractively decorated and feature a range of extra facilities. Breakfast is served in the bedrooms, and popular bar food is served at lunchtimes in the bar, which retains its original character.

Rooms 2 en suite S £50-£60; D £75-£85 Facilities FTV tea/coffee Dinner available Cen ht Wi-fi Notes LB No Children 18yrs No coaches

Westbourne Guest House

★★★ GUEST ACCOMMODATION

46 Upper Rock Gardens BN2 1QF
☎ 01273 686920 📠 01273 686920
e-mail: welcome@westbournehotel.net
dir: A23 to Brighton Pier, left into Marine Parade, 100yds left at lights, premises on right

Just a short walk from the seafront, this Victorian house is run by friendly owners. The attractive bedrooms are bright and well furnished, and some have flat screen TVs. Spacious dining area is complemented by a large bay window.

Rooms 11 rms (7 en suite) (1 fmly) (2 GF) (2 smoking) S £25-£59; D £40-£100* Facilities FTV tea/coffee Licensed Wi-fi Parking 1 Notes ⊗ Closed 23-30 Dec

Sandpiper Guest House

★★★ 🅰 GUEST HOUSE

11 Russell Square BN1 2EE
☎ 01273 328202 📠 01273 329974
e-mail: sandpiper@brighton.co.uk
dir: After conference centre on King's Rd, right into Cannon Place. Russell Sq at end

Rooms 6 rms (1 fmly) Facilities tea/coffee Cen ht Notes ⊗

DITCHLING   Map 6 TQ31

PREMIER COLLECTION

Tovey Lodge

GUEST ACCOMMODATION

Underhill Ln BN6 8XE
☎ 01273 256156 & 07515 753802 📠 01273 256156
e-mail: info@toveylodge.co.uk
dir: From Ditchling N on Beacon Rd. 0.5m, left into Underhill Ln, 100yds, 1st drive on left

Tovey Lodge is set within three acres of gardens and great views of the South Downs. There is an indoor swimming pool, sauna and hot tub. Bedrooms and bathrooms are spacious and stylishly decorated. Bedrooms also include Wi-fi and DVD plasma TVs. There is a guest lounge which backs on to a patio offering additional space to relax. The lounge is spacious and features a 50-inch plasma TV. A cooked or continental breakfast can be enjoyed in the dining room.

Rooms 5 en suite (4 fmly) (2 GF) S £55-£150; D £60-£170 Facilities FTV DVD TVL tea/coffee Dinner available Cen ht Licensed Wi-fi Ⓢ☐ ♨ 18 Riding Sauna Gym ♨ Hot tub spa Extras Speciality toiletries, sweets Conf Max 12 Thtr 12 Board 12 Parking 28 Notes LB

DITCHLING *continued*

The Bull

★★★★ ⬭ INN

2 High St BN6 8TA
☎ 01273 843147 🖷 01273 843147
e-mail: info@thebullditchling.com
dir: *Exit A23 signed Pyecombe, left onto A273 signed Hassocks. Up hill, pass Pyecombe Golf Club on right, 2nd right into New Rd (B2112) to Ditchling. Right at mini-rdbt, next left into car park*

Dating back to 1563, The Bull is one of the oldest buildings in this famously pretty Sussex village. First used as an overnight resting place for travelling monks, the inn has also served as a courthouse and staging post for the London-Brighton coach. Home-cooked meals and local ales are available in the restaurant. A huge garden commands stunning views over the South Downs, and the modern en suite bedrooms are stylishly decorated and comfortably furnished.

Rooms 4 en suite D £80-£120* **Facilities** FTV DVD iPod docking station Dinner available Cen ht Wi-fi ⚐ 18 🛁 **Extras** Speciality toiletries, mineral water, chocolates - complimentary **Parking** 30 **Notes** LB No coaches

---

EASTBOURNE — Map 6 TV69

PREMIER COLLECTION

The Manse B&B

☆☆☆☆☆ BED AND BREAKFAST

7 Dittons Rd BN21 1DW
☎ 01323 737851
e-mail: anne@themansebb.com
web: www.themansebb.com
dir: *A22 to town centre railway station, into Old Orchard Rd, right into Arlington Rd*

This delightful home is in a quiet residential area only a five minute walk from the town centre. Built as a Presbyterian manse at the turn of the 19th century, much of the original character has been retained. The beautifully decorated bedrooms are very comfortable and have a wide range of accessories such as flat screen TV and DVD. Breakfast is served in the elegant dining room, with its stripped wooden floors and pretty courtyard view.

The Manse B&B

Rooms 3 en suite S £55-£60; D £84-£96 **Facilities** FTV DVD iPod docking station Lounge tea/coffee Cen ht Wi-fi 🛁 **Extras** Fruit - complimentary **Parking** 2

PREMIER COLLECTION

Ocklynge Manor

☆☆☆☆☆ BED AND BREAKFAST

Mill Rd BN21 2PG
☎ 01323 734121 & 07979 627172
e-mail: ocklyngemanor@hotmail.com
web: www.ocklyngemanor.co.uk
dir: *From Eastbourne Hospital follow town centre/ seafront sign, 1st right into Kings Av, Ocklynge Manor at top of road*

This charming home has seen a variety of uses through the years, including serving as a commanderie for the Knights of St John in the 12th century. An air of peace and relaxation is evident in the delightful public rooms, well-tended gardens and the spacious, comfortable bedrooms filled with thoughtful extras, including free Wi-fi. Hospitality is a plus and home-baked bread is just one of the delights on offer.

Rooms 3 rms (2 en suite) (1 pri facs) D £90-£110* **Facilities** FTV DVD Lounge tea/coffee Cen ht Wi-fi 🛁 Walks **Extras** Snacks - complimentary **Parking** 3 **Notes** ⊗ No Children 16yrs ⊗

PREMIER COLLECTION

The Berkeley

★★★★★ GUEST ACCOMMODATION

3 Lascelles Ter BN21 4BJ
☎ 01323 645055 🖷 01323 400128
e-mail: info@theberkeley.net
dir: *Follow seafront from pier, take 7th turn on right*

The Berkeley's central location is convenient for the seafront, theatres and town centre. Spacious bedrooms are smartly furnished and decorated, and some offer sea views and views over the South Downs and Devonshire Park. A stylish lounge is provided for guests' relaxation. Here they can enjoy a drink and a snack while choosing a book from the library or playing one of the many board games available. Continental and full English breakfasts are served in the attractive dining room.

Rooms 13 en suite (4 fmly) (1 GF) **Facilities** STV tea/ coffee Cen ht Wi-fi

---

The Camelot Lodge

★★★★ GUEST ACCOMMODATION

35 Lewes Rd BN21 2BU
☎ 01323 725207 🖷 01323 722799
e-mail: info@camelotlodgehotel.com
web: www.camelotlodgehotel.com
dir: *A22 onto A2021, premises 0.5m after hospital on left*

This delightful Edwardian property is within walking distance of the seafront and local amenities. The beautifully styled bedrooms feature a range of facilities including free Wi-fi access, and there is a spacious lounge-bar area. Meals are served in the conservatory dining room, and dinner is available by arrangement.

Rooms 8 en suite (3 fmly) (1 GF) S £30-£50; D £60-£90 **Facilities** FTV Lounge TVL tea/coffee Dinner available Cen ht Licensed Wi-fi **Extras** Mini-bar - chargeable **Parking** 8 **Notes** LB ⊗

Save on B&Bs and Hotels. Book at theAA.com/hotel

SUSSEX, EAST 289 ENGLAND

The Mowbray

★★★★ 🏠 GUEST ACCOMMODATION

2 Lascelles Ter BN21 4BJ
☎ 01323 720012 📠 01323 733579
e-mail: info@themowbray.com
web: www.themowbray.com
dir: *Opposite Devonshire Park Theatre*

This elegant townhouse is located opposite The Devonshire Park Theatre and a few minutes' walk from the seafront. Bedrooms are accessible by a lift to all floors, and vary in size, but all are attractively furnished and comfortable. Public areas include a spacious well presented lounge, small modern bar and a stylish dining room. Breakfast is home-cooked, as are evening meals, available by prior arrangement

Rooms 13 en suite (1 fmly) (1 GF) S £39-£45;
D £79-£110* **Facilities** FTV DVD TVL tea/coffee Dinner available Cen ht Lift Licensed Wi-fi 🔒 **Extras** Superior rooms - robes, fruit, water, slippers **Conf** Max 20 Thtr 20 Class 10 Board 10 **Notes** LB

Arden House

★★★★ GUEST ACCOMMODATION

17 Burlington Place BN21 4AR
☎ 01323 639639 📠 01323 417840
e-mail: info@theardenhotel.co.uk
dir: *On seafront, towards W, 5th turn after pier*

This attractive Regency property sits just minutes away from the seafront and town centre. Bedrooms are comfortable and bright, many with new en suite bathrooms. Guests can enjoy a hearty breakfast at the beginning of the day then relax in the cosy lounge in the evening.

Rooms 11 rms (10 en suite) (1 pri facs) (1 fmly)
Facilities STV FTV TVL tea/coffee Cen ht Wi-fi **Parking** 3

The Bay Lodge

★★★★ GUEST ACCOMMODATION

61-62 Royal Pde BN22 7AQ
☎ 01323 732515 📠 01323 735009
e-mail: baylodgehotel@fsmail.net
web: www.baylodge.org.uk
dir: *From A22 follow signs to seafront. Bay Lodge on right opposite Pavilion Tea Gardens*

This family-run guest accommodation offers a warm welcome in comfortable surrounds opposite the Redoubt and Pavilion gardens. Bedrooms are bright and spacious, some with balconies. There is a sun lounge and a cosy bar that enjoy superb sea views.

Rooms 10 en suite (2 fmly) (2 GF) S £32.50-£40;
D £60-£80* **Facilities** TVL tea/coffee Cen ht Licensed Wi-fi 🔒 **Extras** Bottled water - complimentary **Parking** 6 **Notes** LB ⊗ Closed 23 Dec-3 Jan

Bella Vista

★★★★ GUEST ACCOMMODATION

30 Redoubt Rd BN22 7DH
☎ 01323 724222
e-mail: enquiries@hotelbellavista.co.uk
dir: *500yds NE of town centre. Off A259 (Seaside Rd)*

Situated on the east side of town, just off the seafront, this is an attractive flint house with the bonus of a car park. Bedrooms are generally spacious, comfortable and neatly appointed with modern facilities including free Wi-fi. There is a large lounge and a dining room where dinner and breakfast is served.

Rooms 9 en suite (1 fmly) (3 GF) **Facilities** TVL tea/coffee Dinner available Cen ht Licensed **Parking** 10 **Notes** ⊗

Ivydene

★★★★ GUEST ACCOMMODATION

5-6 Hampden Ter, Latimer Rd BN22 7BL
☎ 01323 720547 📠 01323 411247
e-mail: ivydenehotel@hotmail.co.uk
web: www.ivydenehotel-eastbourne.co.uk
dir: *From town centre/pier NE along seafront, towards Redoubt Fortress, onto St Aubyns Rd, 1st right onto Hampden Terrace*

This friendly family-run property is situated a short walk from the pier and seafront. Bedrooms are bright and cheerful with comfortable, stylish furnishings. Public areas include a spacious lounge/bar, sunny conservatory and attractive dining room.

Rooms 14 en suite (2 fmly) (1 GF) S £33-£38;
D £64-£75* **Facilities** FTV TVL tea/coffee Dinner available Cen ht Licensed Wi-fi **Notes** LB ⊗ RS Oct-Etr No evening meal

The Royal

★★★★ GUEST ACCOMMODATION

8-9 Marine Pde BN21 3DX
☎ 01323 649222 📠 0560 1500 065
e-mail: info@royaleastbourne.org.uk
dir: *On seafront 100mtrs E of pier*

This property enjoys a central seafront location close to the pier and within easy walking distance of the town centre. Spectacular uninterrupted sea views are guaranteed. Now fully renovated and eco-friendly, the comfortable bedrooms are modern with flat screen TVs and free Wi-fi. One of the ten rooms has private facilities, while the others are fully en suite. A substantial continental breakfast is served. The Royal offers a full pet-sitting service and dogs stay free of charge.

Rooms 10 rms (9 en suite) (1 pri facs) (1 fmly) (1 GF)
S £40-£59; D £70-£98* **Facilities** STV FTV DVD tea/coffee Cen ht Wi-fi ⅃ 18 Free Wi-fi **Notes** LB No Children 12yrs

The Sheldon

★★★★ GUEST ACCOMMODATION

9-11 Burlington Place BN21 4AS
☎ 01323 724120 & 07803 147082 📠 01323 644327
e-mail: info@thesheldonhotel.co.uk
dir: *Just off The Grand Parade near bandstand*

New life has been injected into The Sheldon since the arrival of its new owner. The accommodation has been updated and improved, including the addition of flat screen TVs with 110 satellite channels, whilst the public areas have been refurbished to a very high standard. These factors, together with an excellent location, make for a very enjoyable stay. Ample, secure parking is available.

Rooms 21 en suite (6 fmly) (4 GF) **Facilities** STV FTV Lounge tea/coffee Cen ht Lift Wi-fi **Extras** Speciality toiletries **Parking** 21 **Notes** ⊗ Closed 31 Oct-Mar

EASTBOURNE *continued*

The Sherwood

★★★★ GUEST ACCOMMODATION

7 Lascelles Ter BN21 4BJ
☎ 01323 724002 📠 01323 400133
e-mail: info@thesherwood.net
dir: *Follow signs to seafront (Grand Parade). Next to Eastbourne Centre*

Attractive Victorian property just a minute's walk from the seafront, offering well-appointed bedrooms with comfortable, co-ordinated furnishings. The cosy lounge is a nice environment for relaxation, and the attractive dining room serves a robust breakfast.

Rooms 13 en suite (5 fmly) (1 GF) S £39-£46; D £78-£92 **Facilities** STV FTV DVD TVL tea/coffee Cen ht Licensed Wi-fi

Beach Haven

★★★ GUEST ACCOMMODATION

61 Pevensey Rd BN21 3HS
☎ 01323 726195
e-mail: enquiries@beach-haven.co.uk
web: www.beach-haven.co.uk
dir: *250yds E of town centre off A259*

This attractive terrace property is just a short walk from the seafront and attractions. Bedrooms are located on three floors, some offer en suite facilities and all have a thoughtful range of guest extras. There is also a comfortable dining room, a cosy lounge and a small private chapel.

Rooms 7 rms (3 en suite) (1 GF) S £30-£45; D £60-£90* **Facilities** Lounge tea/coffee Cen ht **Extras** Bottled water **Notes** ⊗ No Children 1yr Closed Nov-Mar (ex Xmas)

Beachy Rise Guest House

★★★ GUEST HOUSE

5 Beachy Head Rd BN20 7QN
☎ 01323 639171 📠 01323 645006
e-mail: susanne234@hotmail.co.uk
dir: *1m SW of town centre. Off B2103 Upper Dukes Rd*

This friendly family-run guest house has a quiet residential location close to Meads Village. Bedrooms are individually styled with co-ordinated soft furnishings and feature some useful extras. Breakfast is served in the light and airy dining room overlooking the garden, which guests are welcome to use.

Rooms 4 en suite (2 fmly) S £30-£50; D £55-£70* **Facilities** tea/coffee Cen ht Wi-fi

---

FOREST ROW	Map 6 TQ43

The Roebuck

★★★ INN

Wych Cross RH18 5JL
☎ 01342 823811 📠 01342 824790
e-mail: 6499@greeneking.co.uk

This 17th-century country house is located just minutes from Forest Row just off the A22. Public areas have many original features and log fires are lit during the winter months. Free Wi-fi is available throughout. Bedrooms are well equipped and offer comfortable facilities. Dinner and breakfast are served in Antlers Restaurant.

Rooms 28 en suite (8 GF) **Facilities** TVL tea/coffee Dinner available Direct Dial Cen ht Wi-fi Pool table **Conf** Max 100 Thtr 10 Class 20 **Parking** 100 **Notes** Civ Wed 100

HALLAND	Map 6 TQ41

Beechwood B&B

★★★★★ Ⓐ GUEST ACCOMMODATION

Eastbourne Rd BN8 6PS
☎ 01825 840936 📠 01825 840936
e-mail: chyland1956@aol.com
web: www.beechwoodbandb.co.uk
dir: *On A22 directly before speed camera in Halland*

Rooms 3 rms (2 en suite) (1 pri facs) (1 fmly) **Facilities** TVL tea/coffee Cen ht Wi-fi ⌇ Hot tub **Parking** 5

HASTINGS & ST LEONARDS	Map 7 TQ80

PREMIER COLLECTION

Stream House

★★★★★ BED AND BREAKFAST

Pett Level Rd, Fairlight TN35 4ED
☎ 01424 814916 & 0794 191 1379
e-mail: info@stream-house.co.uk
web: www.stream-house.co.uk
dir: *4m NE of Hastings. Exit A259 onto unclassified road between Fairlight & Cliff End*

Lovingly converted from three cottages, the Stream House stands in three acres of tranquil grounds, just one mile from Winchelsea beach. The well-appointed bedrooms are beautifully decorated. Delicious breakfasts are served in the lounge-dining room with an original inglenook fireplace, and during warmer

---

months you can enjoy the extensive garden with its rippling stream and Koi pond.

Stream House

Rooms 3 rms (2 en suite) (1 pri facs) D £75-£100 **Facilities** FTV TVL tea/coffee Cen ht Wi-fi **Extras** Speciality toiletries, chocolates - complimentary **Parking** 4 **Notes** LB ⊗ No Children 10yrs Closed Dec-Feb ⊜

PREMIER COLLECTION

Barn House Seaview B&B

★★★★★ BED AND BREAKFAST

Warren Rd, Fairlight TN35 4AN
☎ 01424 813821
e-mail: enquiries@seaviewbnb.co.uk
web: www.seaviewbnb.co.uk
dir: *From Hastings on A259, right into Fairlight Rd to Battery Hill. Right at Warren Rd*

Barn House Seaview B&B is located in Fairlight, just a couple of miles from Hastings. In a quiet location down a country lane, this 16th-century converted barn has an elevated position with far reaching sea views, and is set in 14 acres of garden and woodland. During summer months guests can enjoy the tennis court or play petang. Rooms are stylishly decorated and equipped with a number of thoughtful extras including well stocked beverage trays and free Wi-fi. There are also two large guest lounges. Dinner is available on request and guests can enjoy authentic Chinese cooking. A cooked and continental breakfast can be enjoyed in the conservatory.

Rooms 3 en suite (1 fmly) **Facilities** STV FTV TVL tea/coffee Dinner available Direct Dial Cen ht Wi-fi ⌣ Boules **Conf** Max 12 Thtr 12 Class 12 Board 12 **Parking** 6 **Notes** ⊜

Save on B&Bs and Hotels. Book at **theAA.com/hotel**

SUSSEX, EAST 291 ENGLAND

PREMIER COLLECTION

The Cloudesley

★★★★★ GUEST ACCOMMODATION

7 Cloudesley Rd TN37 6JN
☎ 01424 442524 & 07507 000148
e-mail: info@thecloudesley.co.uk
dir: *A21 (London Rd) onto A2102, left into Tower Rd. Right into Cloudesley Rd, house at top on left*

The Cloudesley is located just minutes from Hastings in the quiet residential area of St Leonard's, and offers high standards of quality and comfort. The bedrooms have been environmentally designed - the walls have been eco-limewashed, the beds are hand-made and have Siberian goosedown pillows, and the shampoos are free of parabens and sodiam lauryl sulphate. There is a treatment room for holistic therapies. The two guest lounges are stylish and decorated with photographs taken by the proprietor. An extensive selection of cooked and continental dishes is available for breakfast, which includes locally sourced, organic ingredients.

Rooms 4 en suite **Facilities** tea/coffee Dinner available Cen ht Licensed Wi-fi Holistic therapies & massage **Notes** ⊗ No Children

PREMIER COLLECTION

The Laindons

★★★★★ BED AND BREAKFAST

23 High St, Old Town TN34 3EY
☎ 01424 437710
e-mail: jacksonchris2007@yahoo.co.uk
dir: *A21 onto seafront, left towards old town. Left at lights into High St. Lodge adjacent to pharmacy*

The Laindons is a Georgian townhouse, formerly a coaching house, set on this attractive High Street in Hastings. Bedrooms have been stylishly decorated offering guests comfortable accommodation; rooms include satellite TV and Wi-fi. Whilst bedrooms are spacious, there is a guest lounge providing additional space for guests to relax. A cooked or continental breakfast can be enjoyed in the upper-floor conservatory with views of the Downs and Hastings church.

Rooms 3 en suite S £80-£90; D £110-£125
Facilities STV DVD TVL tea/coffee Cen ht Wi-fi ⚽
Extras Speciality toiletries **Notes** ⊗ No Children 5yrs Closed Dec-Jan

Parkside House

★★★★ GUEST ACCOMMODATION

59 Lower Park Rd TN34 2LD
☎ 01424 433096
e-mail: bkentparksidehse@aol.com
dir: *A2101 to town centre, right at rdbt, 1st right*

You can expect a friendly welcome at this attractive Victorian house overlooking Alexandra Park, just a 10-minute walk from the town centre and seafront. The bedrooms are carefully furnished and have an abundance of thoughtful touches including free Wi-fi and a 'tuck shop' for midnight snackers. Breakfast is served at individual tables in the elegant dining room.

Rooms 5 rms (4 en suite) (1 pri facs) (1 fmly)
Facilities TVL tea/coffee Cen ht Wi-fi **Notes** ⊗

Seaspray Bed & Breakfast

★★★★ 🅰 GUEST HOUSE

54 Eversfield Place TN37 6DB
☎ 01424 436583
e-mail: jo@seaspraybb.co.uk
web: www.seaspraybb.co.uk
dir: *A21 to town centre & seafront, Seaspray 100yds W of pier*

Rooms 10 rms (8 en suite) (2 pri facs) (1 fmly) (1 GF)
Facilities FTV tea/coffee Cen ht Wi-fi **Notes** LB ⊗ Closed 10 Jan-10 Feb

Eagle House

★★★ GUEST ACCOMMODATION

Pevensey Rd TN38 0JZ
☎ 01424 430535 & 437771 📠 01424 400035
e-mail: info@eaglehousehotel.co.uk
web: www.eaglehousehotel.co.uk
dir: *Exit seafront into London Rd, 5th turn on left into Pevensey Rd. 150mtrs on right*

Eagle House is a Victorian property situated in a peaceful residential area within easy walking distance of the shops, college and seafront. Public areas are sumptuously decorated in a traditional style and the spacious 'retro' bedrooms are simply furnished. A hearty breakfast can be enjoyed in the dining room, which overlooks the gardens.

Rooms 19 en suite (4 fmly) (3 GF) S £45-£50;
D £70-£80* **Facilities** FTV TVL tea/coffee Direct Dial Cen ht Licensed Wi-fi **Parking** 13 **Notes** ⊗

HEATHFIELD Map 6 TQ52

Holly Grove

★★★★ BED AND BREAKFAST

Little London TN21 0NU
☎ 01435 863375 & 07814 398854
e-mail: andy-christie@btconnect.com
dir: *A267 to Horam, turn right at Little London garage into Spinney Ln, proceed to bottom of lane*

Holly Grove is set in a quiet rural location with heated outdoor swimming pool, satellite TV, Wi-fi and parking facilities. Bedrooms are appointed to a very high standard. There is a separate lounge available for guests, and breakfast is served in the dining room or on the terrace, weather permitting.

Rooms 3 rms (2 en suite) (1 pri facs) (1 fmly) (2 GF)
S £55-£80; D £65-£90* **Facilities** STV TVL tea/coffee Dinner available Cen ht Wi-fi ⚽ 🔒 **Parking** 7

HERSTMONCEUX Map 6 TQ61

PREMIER COLLECTION

Wartling Place

★★★★★ GUEST ACCOMMODATION

Wartling Place, Wartling BN27 1RY
☎ 01323 832590 📠 01323 831558
e-mail: accom@wartlingplace.prestel.co.uk
dir: *2.5m SE of Herstmonceux. Exit A271 to Wartling. Wartling Place opposite village church*

Located in a sleepy village, this beautiful Grade II listed country home is set in two acres of well-tended gardens. The individually decorated bedrooms, two featuring four-poster beds, are luxurious and have a host of thoughtful extras. Delicious breakfasts are served in the elegant dining room. Guests can also enjoy free broadband access.

Rooms 4 en suite (1 fmly) **Facilities** tea/coffee Dinner available Cen ht **Conf** Max 12 **Parking** 10 **Notes** ⊗

HERSTMONCEUX *continued*

Cleavers Lyng Country House

★ ★ ★ ★ GUEST ACCOMMODATION

Church Rd BN27 1QJ
☎ 01323 833644
e-mail: cleaverslyng@btinternet.com
web: www.cleaverslyng.co.uk
dir: *Exit A271 at Herstmonceux, into Chapel Row leading into Church Rd, 1.5m on right*

Expect a warm welcome at this Grade II listed country house, parts of which date back to 1577. A spacious downstairs lounge and breakfast room offers the perfect place to relax with its log burning fireplace. Alternatively guests can enjoy the peaceful, landscaped gardens with fantastic views of beautiful Sussex countryside. Rooms are well appointed with LCD TVs, free Wi-fi and many enjoy amazing scenic views.

Rooms 4 en suite (1 fmly) **Facilities** tea/coffee Cen ht Wi-fi **Parking** 10

HOVE

See Brighton & Hove

LEWES
Map 6 TQ41

The Blacksmiths Arms

★ ★ ★ ★ ⊖ INN

London Rd, Offham BN7 3QD
☎ 01273 472971
e-mail: blacksmithsarms@shineadsl.co.uk
web: www.theblacksmithsarms-offham.co.uk
dir: *1m N of Lewes. On A275 in Offham*

Situated just outside Lewes, this is a great location for touring the South coast, offering high quality accommodation in comfortable bedrooms. Enjoyable meals are available in the cosy bar downstairs, and this is where the hearty cooked breakfast is also served.

Rooms 4 en suite **Facilities** FTV tea/coffee Dinner available Cen ht Wi-fi **Extras** Water, fruit, sweets **Parking** 22 **Notes** ⊗ No coaches

---

Orchard B&B

[U]

22 St Annes Crescent BN7 1SB
☎ 01273 487719 ▤ 08703 305802
e-mail: bookings@orchardbedandbreakfast.co.uk
dir: *A27 onto A277 proceed to x-rds/lights. Turn right, then sharp left into St Annes Crescent*

Currently the rating for this establishment is not confirmed. This may be due to a change of ownership or because it has only recently joined the AA rating scheme.

Rooms 1 en suite (1 fmly) D £90–£110* **Facilities** FTV DVD tea/coffee Cen ht Wi-fi ch fac ⚬ **Extras** Home-baked produce **Notes** ⊗

ROTTINGDEAN
Map 6 TQ30

White Horse

★ ★ ★ INN

Marine Dr BN2 7HR
☎ 01273 300301 ▤ 01273 308716
e-mail: 5308@greeneking.co.uk
dir: *A27 Lewes towards Rottingdean on B1223*

The White Horse is conveniently located just a couple of miles from Brighton, and is right on the seafront with uninterrupted views. Bedrooms are comfortable with modern fixtures and fittings, and there is free Wi-fi throughout. Dinner is served daily and a cooked or continental breakfast can be enjoyed in the restaurant. There is plenty of outside seating available.

Rooms 18 en suite (1 fmly) S £64; D £79–£99* **Facilities** FTV tea/coffee Dinner available Direct Dial Cen ht Wi-fi ⚬ **Conf** Max 60 Thtr 60 Class 30 Board 30 **Parking** 40 **Notes** No coaches

Save on B&Bs and Hotels. Book at **theAA.com/hotel**

SUSSEX, EAST 293 ENGLAND

RYE
Map 7 TQ92

See also Hastings & St Leonards

PREMIER COLLECTION

Jeake's House

★★★★★ 🏛 GUEST ACCOMMODATION

Mermaid St TN31 7ET
☎ 01797 222828
e-mail: stay@jeakeshouse.com
web: www.jeakeshouse.com
dir: *Approach from High St or The Strand*

Previously a 17th-century wool store and then a 19th-century Baptist school, this delightful house stands on a cobbled street in one of the most beautiful parts of this small, bustling town. The individually decorated bedrooms combine elegance and comfort with modern facilities. Breakfast is served at separate tables in the galleried dining room, and there is an oak-beamed lounge as well as a stylish book-lined bar with old pews.

Rooms 11 rms (10 en suite) (1 pri facs) (2 fmly) S £75-£100; D £90-£140 **Facilities** FTV Lounge tea/coffee Direct Dial Cen ht Licensed Wi-fi 🐾 **Parking** 20 **Notes** LB No Children 5yrs

PREMIER COLLECTION

Manor Farm Oast

★★★★★ 🏛 ➾ BED AND BREAKFAST

Windmill Ln TN36 4WL
☎ 01424 813787 & 07866 818952 📠 01424 813787
e-mail: manor.farm.oast@lineone.net
web: www.manorfarmoast.co.uk
dir: *4m SW of Rye. A259 W past Icklesham church, left at x-rds into Windmill Ln, after sharp left bend, left (follow sign) into farmland*

A charming 19th-century, environmentally-friendly oast house peacefully located amid orchards in open countryside. Spacious bedrooms are individually styled and include numerous thoughtful extras including free Wi-fi. A choice of lounges is available, one heated by a roaring log fire during the winter, and locally sourced, home-produced dinners are a feature of any stay.

Rooms 3 rms (2 en suite) (1 pri facs) (1 fmly) S £85-£105; D £105 **Facilities** FTV Lounge tea/coffee Dinner available Cen ht Licensed Wi-fi 🐾 **Extras** Speciality toiletries, fruit, chocolates **Conf** Max 20 Thtr 20 Board 12 **Parking** 8 **Notes** LB ⊗ No Children 11yrs Closed 31 Dec Civ Wed 50

PREMIER COLLECTION

Olde Moat House

★★★★★ 🏛 GUEST ACCOMMODATION

TN29 0AZ
☎ 01797 344700 📠 01797 343919
e-mail: oldemoathouse@hotmail.com
web: www.oldemoathouse.co.uk

(For full entry see Ivychurch (Kent))

PREMIER COLLECTION

White Vine House

★★★★★ ➾ RESTAURANT WITH ROOMS

24 High St TN31 7JF
☎ 01797 224748
e-mail: info@whitevinehouse.co.uk
dir: *In town centre*

Situated in the heart of the ancient Cinque Port town of Rye, this property's origins go back to the 13th century. The cellar is the oldest part, but the current building dates from 1560 and boasts an impressive Georgian frontage. The original timber framework is visible in many areas, and certainly adds to the house's sense of history. The bedrooms have period furniture along with luxury bath or shower rooms; one bedroom has an antique four-poster.

Rooms 7 en suite (1 fmly) **Facilities** tea/coffee Dinner available Cen ht Wi-fi **Conf** Max 30 Thtr 30 Class 30 Board 30 **Notes** ⊗ No coaches Civ Wed 30

The Rise

★★★★★ 🅰 BED AND BREAKFAST

82 Udimore Rd TN31 7DY
☎ 01797 222285
e-mail: theriserye@aol.com
dir: *A21 Johns Cross take B2089 towards Rye. On entering Rye on right on bottom of hill*

Rooms 3 en suite S £70-£95; D £90-£120* **Facilities** FTV DVD tea/coffee Cen ht Wi-fi 🐾 **Parking** 3 **Notes** ⊗ No Children 12yrs Closed 23 Dec-3 Jan

RYE *continued*

Strand House

★★★★ 🏠 🍽 GUEST ACCOMMODATION

Tanyards Ln, Winchelsea TN36 4JT
☎ 01797 226276 📠 01797 224806
e-mail: info@thestrandhouse.co.uk
web: www.thestrandhouse.co.uk
dir: *M20 junct 10, A2070 to Lydd. A259 through Rye to
Winchelsea, house in 2m*

This charming 15th-century house is just a few miles
drive from Rye. Traditional character is maintained in
comfortably appointed rooms and the public areas whilst
the annexe rooms offer a more contemporary style. Local
produce is a feature of the home-cooked evening meals
and breakfasts.

Rooms 10 rms (9 en suite) (1 pri facs) 3 annexe en suite
(4 fmly) (3 GF) S £50-£155; D £65-£180* **Facilities** FTV
DVD iPod docking station Lounge tea/coffee Dinner
available Cen ht Licensed Wi-fi 🔒 **Extras** Mini-fridge in
annexe rooms **Parking** 15 **Notes** LB No Children 5yrs RS
wknds (high season) 2 night bookings only Civ Wed 30

Little Saltcote

★★★★ GUEST ACCOMMODATION

22 Military Rd TN31 7NY
☎ 01797 223210 & 07940 742646 📠 01797 224474
e-mail: info@littlesaltcote.co.uk
web: www.littlesaltcote.co.uk
dir: *0.5m N of town centre. Exit A268 into Military Rd
signed Appledore, house 300yds on left*

This delightful family-run establishment stands in quiet
surroundings within walking distance of Rye town centre.
The bright and airy en suite bedrooms are equipped with
modern facilities including Wi-fi, and guests can enjoy
afternoon tea in the garden conservatory. A hearty
breakfast is served at individual tables in the dining
room.

Rooms 4 en suite (2 fmly) (1 GF) S £40-£75; D £70-£80*
Facilities FTV tea/coffee Cen ht Wi-fi **Parking** 5 **Notes** LB

The Windmill Guest House

★★★★ GUEST ACCOMMODATION

Ferry Rd TN31 7DW
☎ 01797 224027
e-mail: info@ryewindmill.co.uk
web: www.ryewindmill.co.uk

This white smock windmill has been a Rye landmark
since 1820 and was more recently a bakery. Bedrooms
located in the purpose-built extension have good beds
and en suite facilities are generously proportioned.
Breakfast taken in the old granary is a freshly-cooked
affair from well-sourced local ingredients including
butchers' sausages and some good fruit juices.

Rooms 10 en suite (1 fmly) (4 GF) S £45-£65;
D £75-£155* **Facilities** FTV Lounge TVL tea/coffee Cen ht
Licensed Wi-fi 🔒 **Conf** Thtr 25 Class 30 Board 12
Parking 12 **Notes** No Children 12yrs Closed 24-26 Dec

Cliff Farm *(TQ933237)*

★★★ FARMHOUSE

Military Rd, Iden Lock TN31 7QD
☎ 01797 280331 📠 01797 280331 Mrs P Sullivin
e-mail: info@cliff-farm.com
dir: *2m along Military Rd to Appledore, turn left at
hanging milk churn*

Beautiful views and wonderful hospitality are what you'll
find at this farmhouse situated in a peaceful rural
location just a short drive from Rye and Hastings.
Bedrooms are pleasantly decorated and comfortably
furnished. Breakfast is served at individual tables in the
dining room, and there is also a cosy sitting room with a
wood-burning stove and TV.

Rooms 3 rms (1 fmly) **Facilities** TVL tea/coffee Cen ht
Parking 6 **Notes** LB Closed Nov-Feb 🐾 6 acres small
holding

Save on B&Bs and Hotels. Book at **theAA.com/hotel**

SUSSEX, EAST 295 **ENGLAND**

Tower House

★★★ BED AND BREAKFAST

Hilders Cliff TN31 7LD
☎ **01797 226865 & 07940 817438** 📠 **01797 226865**
dir: *Follow one-way system, signs to town centre. Through medieval archway, 30mtrs on right*

This expansive Georgian property is conveniently located in the heart of historic Rye. Benefiting from off-road car parking, the house is set back off the road within its own well tended gated gardens. Bedrooms are traditionally decorated, and there is a TV lounge, as well as a spacious dining room where guests can enjoy a cooked or continental breakfast. There is a large snooker room with full size table, large inglenook fireplace and seating for guests to relax.

Rooms 3 rms (2 en suite) (1 pri facs) (1 GF) S £55-£58; D £85-£95* **Facilities** TVL tea/coffee Cen ht Licensed Snooker **Parking** 3 **Notes** ⊗ No Children 12yrs Closed Dec-Wed before Etr ⊛

ST LEONARDS

See Hastings & St Leonards

SEAFORD   Map 6 TV49

Ab Fab Rooms

★★★★ 🛏 BED AND BREAKFAST

11 Station Rd, Bishopstone BN25 2RB
☎ **01323 895001 & 07713 197915** 📠 **0705 360 3204**
e-mail: stay@abfabrooms.co.uk
web: www.abfabrooms.co.uk

Just a short walk from Bishopstone station and sandy beaches, this is a perfect base for visiting local sights and attractions. Contemporary-styled bedrooms offer superior comfort and amenities. Breakfast, served in the garden conservatory, includes home-made jams and local Sussex produce.

Ab Fab Rooms

Rooms 3 en suite **Facilities** STV tea/coffee Cen ht Wi-fi **Parking** 2 **Notes** ⊗ ⊛

The Avondale

★★★ GUEST ACCOMMODATION

Avondale Rd BN25 1RJ
☎ **01323 890008** 📠 **01323 490598**
e-mail: info@theavondale.co.uk
web: www.theavondale.co.uk
dir: *In town centre, off A259 behind war memorial*

A warm welcome is offered by the caring owners at this friendly, family-run guest accommodation which is ideally placed for the Newhaven to Dieppe ferry service. The bedrooms are pleasantly furnished and thoughtfully equipped. Breakfast is served in the attractive dining room and guests also have the use of a cosy lounge.

Rooms 14 rms (8 en suite) (4 fmly) S £35-£65; D £60-£85* **Facilities** FTV TVL tea/coffee Cen ht Lift Licensed Wi-fi **Conf** Max 15 Class 15 Board 15 **Notes** LB ⊗

SEDLESCOMBE   Map 7 TQ71

Kester House B&B

★★★★ 🛏 BED AND BREAKFAST

The Street TN33 0QB
☎ **01424 870035**
e-mail: derek@kesterhouse.co.uk
dir: *A21 onto B2244 signed Sedlescombe, left after 0.75m. On entering village, Kester House on right*

This 16th-century, Grade II listed house is located in the tranquil village of Sedlescombe, close to Hastings, Battle and Rye. The bedrooms have been tastefully appointed to offer stylish, comfortable accommodation while still retaining many of the building's original features. There is a guest lounge next to the dining room area where guests can enjoy home-made refreshments on arrival, and a hearty cooked or continental breakfast which features top quality, locally sourced produce.

Rooms 3 rms (1 en suite) (2 pri facs) (1 fmly) **Facilities** DVD iPod docking station Lounge tea/coffee Cen ht Wi-fi 🛁 Arrangement with local riding stables **Notes** ⊗ No Children 7yrs Closed 24 Dec-2 Jan

---

WADHURST   Map 6 TQ63

Little Tidebrook Farm (TQ621304)

★★★★ FARMHOUSE

Riseden TN5 6NY
☎ 01892 782688 & 07970 159988   Mrs S Marley-Ward
e-mail: info@littletidebrook.co.uk
web: www.littletidebrook.co.uk
dir: A267 from Tunbridge Wells to Mark Cross, left onto
B2100, 2m, right at Best Beech Inn, left after 1m into
Riseden Rd, farm on left

This traditional farmhouse has cosy log fires in winter
and wonderful garden dining in warm months. The
imaginative decor combines with modern amenities such
as Wi-fi to provide leisure and business travellers with
the ideal setting. Close to Bewl Water and Royal
Tunbridge Wells.

Rooms 3 rms (2 en suite) (1 pri facs) Facilities FTV TVL
tea/coffee Cen ht Wi-fi Parking 8 Notes No Children 12yrs
50 acres horses

The Greyhound Inn

★★★ INN

High St TN5 6AP
☎ 01892 783224
e-mail: info@thegreyhoundwadhurst.co.uk
web: www.thegreyhoundwadhurst.co.uk
dir: In village centre

This 16th-century inn is located in the centre of
Wadhurst. The pub and restaurant area are traditional in
style and feature a large open fireplace. Breakfast, lunch
and dinner are served daily. Bedrooms are all annexed
and have been converted from the original stable blocks.
They are spacious and comfortable and combine
traditional features such as exposed oak beams with
modern decor and furnishings.

Rooms 5 en suite (1 fmly) (3 GF) Facilities FTV tea/coffee
Dinner available Cen ht Wi-fi Parking 8

WILMINGTON   Map 6 TQ50

Crossways

★★★★★ @@ RESTAURANT WITH ROOMS

Lewes Rd BN26 5SG
☎ 01323 482455 ☐ 01323 487811
e-mail: stay@crosswayshotel.co.uk
web: www.crosswayshotel.co.uk
dir: On A27 between Lewes & Polegate, 2m E of Alfriston
rdbt

Amidst stunning gardens and attractively tended grounds
sits this well-established, popular restaurant. The well-
presented bedrooms are tastefully decorated and provide
an abundance of thoughtful amenities including free Wi-
fi. Guest comfort is paramount and the naturally warm
hospitality ensures guests often return.

Rooms 7 en suite S £79-£85; D £135-£170*
Facilities FTV tea/coffee Dinner available Direct Dial
Cen ht Wi-fi ☖ Extras Speciality toiletries, mini-bar, fresh
milk Parking 30 Notes LB ⊗ No Children 12yrs Closed
24 Dec-23 Jan No coaches

SUSSEX, WEST

AMBERLEY   Map 6 TQ01

Woody Banks Cottage

★★★★ BED AND BREAKFAST

Crossgates BN18 9NR
☎ 01798 831295 & 07719 916703
e-mail: woodybanks@btinternet.com
web: www.woodybanks.co.uk
dir: Off B2139 into village, right at Black Horse pub,
Woody Banks 0.5m on left past Sportsman pub

Located close to Arundel on an elevated position with
stunning views over the Wildbrooks, this immaculately
maintained house and gardens is very popular with
walkers. It provides two comfortable, homely bedrooms
filled with thoughtful extras. Imaginative breakfasts are
served in the panoramic lounge-dining room.

Rooms 2 rms (1 pri facs) (1 fmly) S £40; D £70-£75
Facilities TVL tea/coffee Cen ht ☖ Parking 3 Notes LB ⊗
No Children 6yrs Closed 24-27 Dec

ANGMERING   Map 6 TQ00

Angmering Manor

★★★★ ➾ GUEST ACCOMMODATION

High St BN16 4AG
☎ 01903 859849 ☐ 01903 783268
e-mail: angmeringmanor@thechapmansgroup.co.uk
web: www.relaxinnz.co.uk
dir: Follow A27 towards Portsmouth, exit A280, follow
signs for Angmering

This former manor house in the heart of the village has
been stylishly appointed. It offers good food, a bar, an
indoor pool, and good parking. Staff are friendly and
helpful and rooms are very comfortable.

Rooms 17 en suite (3 fmly) (4 GF) Facilities FTV TVL tea/
coffee Dinner available Direct Dial Cen ht Licensed Wi-fi
⊗ Sauna Gym Beauty salon Parking 25 Notes LB ⊗ Civ
Wed 50

ARUNDEL   Map 6 TQ00

See also Amberley

Hanger Down House B&B

★★★★ BED AND BREAKFAST

Priory Ln, Tortington BN18 0BG
☎ 01903 882904 & 07753 595191
e-mail: aayling@btinternet.com
web: www.hangerdownhouse.co.uk
dir: A27 to Arundel, take road signed Ford/Climping at
Arundel rdbt. Priory Ln 0.5m on right

Set in picturesque Sussex countryside, Hanger Down
House is conveniently and quietly located one mile from
the historic town of Arundel. All three bedrooms are
stylishly decorated and provide comfortable
accommodation for guests. Bedrooms include king-sized
beds, a leather sofa, refrigerators, digital LCD TVs and
free Wi-fi. There are great views of the local countryside
and a walled garden which guests are free to use. A
cooked or continental breakfast can be enjoyed
downstairs in the dining room.

Rooms 3 en suite (2 fmly) (1 GF) S £60-£90; D £90-£120
Facilities FTV Lounge tea/coffee Cen ht Wi-fi ❧ Pool
table ☖ Trampoline Football pitch Outdoor table tennis
Extras Speciality toiletries - complimentary, fridges
Parking 5 Notes LB ⊗

The Town House

★★★★ @@ RESTAURANT WITH ROOMS

65 High St BN18 9AJ
☎ 01903 883847
e-mail: enquiries@thetownhouse.co.uk
web: www.thetownhouse.co.uk
dir: A27 to Arundel, into High Street, establishment on
left at top of hill

This is an elegant, Grade II-listed Regency building
overlooking Arundel Castle, just a short walk from the
shops and centre of the town. Bedrooms and public areas
retain the building's unspoilt character. The ceiling in the
dining room is particularly spectacular and originated in
Florence in the 16th century.

Rooms 4 en suite S fr £75; D £95-£130* Facilities FTV
tea/coffee Dinner available Cen ht Wi-fi ☖ Notes ⊗ Closed
2wks Etr & 2wks Oct RS Sun-Mon Restaurant closed No
coaches

Save on B&Bs and Hotels. Book at **theAA.com/hotel**

SUSSEX, WEST 297 ENGLAND

White Swan

★★★★ INN

16 Chichester Rd BN18 0AD
☎ 01903 882677 📠 01903 684154
e-mail: thewhiteswan.arundel@pebblehotels.com

The White Swan offers very comfortable and stylish accommodation. There are a character bar, lounge and restaurant, and an informal service is provided by the friendly team. Substantial snacks and meals can be ordered throughout the day and evening. Complimentary Wi-fi is available in the public areas.

Rooms 20 en suite **Facilities** Dinner available Wi-fi

Arden Guest House

★★★ GUEST ACCOMMODATION

4 Queens Ln BN18 9JN
☎ 01903 882544
e-mail: info@ardenguesthouse.net
dir: From station, at rdbt take turn for town centre. Next left into Queens Ln

This is a comfortable guest accommodation situated a few minutes from the town centre and station. The property has a selection of single, double and twin bedrooms, some of which are en suite. Traditional cooked breakfasts are served in the well-lit dining room. Off-street parking is available.

Rooms 8 rms (5 en suite) (2 GF) S £40-£55; D £60-£75*
Facilities FTV tea/coffee Cen ht 🔒 **Parking** 5 **Notes** ⊗ No Children 14yrs Closed 31 Dec

BOGNOR REGIS Map 6 SZ99

Arbor D'Oak

★★★★ BED AND BREAKFAST

221 Hawthorn Rd PO21 2UW
☎ 01243 861280
e-mail: arbordoak@uwclub.net
dir: A29 to Bognor Regis, pass hospital, take last exit from rdbt onto A259 (Chichester Rd). Over lights, next left into Hawthorn Rd, past sports field, 50yds on left

Arbor D'Oak is a modern property offering guests stylish, comfortable accommodation. Bedrooms and bathrooms are spacious with excellent quality fixtures and fittings. Useful features include hairdryers and irons in the rooms. The guest lounge on the ground floor creates additional space in which to relax. Breakfast can be enjoyed around the family-style breakfast table in the conservatory that looks out over the garden.

Rooms 2 rms (1 en suite) (1 pri facs) S £55-£85; D £90-£130* **Facilities** FTV DVD Lounge tea/coffee Cen ht 🔒 cycle storage available **Extras** Speciality toiletries, chocolates - complimentary **Parking** 4 **Notes** LB ⊗ No Children Closed Oct-Mar

The Old Priory

★★★★ GUEST HOUSE

80 North Bersted St PO22 9AQ
☎ 01243 863580 📠 01243 826597
e-mail: old.priory@btinternet.com
web: www.old-priory.com
dir: 1.6m NW of Bognor. Off A259 (Chichester road) to North Bersted. Old Priory sign on left

Located in the mainly residential area of North Bersted, this 400-year-old property retains many original features. Bedrooms which are all individual in style are homely, and one has a four-poster waterbed and a double air bath. There is an outdoor pool and attractive grounds, perfect for the summer.

Rooms 3 rms (2 en suite) (1 pri facs) 3 annexe en suite (3 GF) S £50; D £70-£100 **Facilities** STV tea/coffee Cen ht Wi-fi ↘ Hot tub **Parking** 6

Jubilee Guest House

★★★ GUEST ACCOMMODATION

5 Gloucester Rd PO21 1NU
☎ 01243 863016
dir: A259 to seafront, house opposite Day Entrance to Butlins

This property is conveniently located opposite Butlins and in close proximity to the sea front and town centre. Comfortably appointed bedrooms come well equipped with free Wi-fi, flat screen digital TVs and heating/cooling

systems. A cooked breakfast can be enjoyed in the attractive dining room.

Jubilee Guest House

Rooms 6 rms (2 en suite) (4 pri facs) (3 fmly) **Facilities** tea/coffee Cen ht Wi-fi **Parking** 4 **Notes** ⊗ Closed Xmas, Jan & Feb

BOLNEY Map 6 TQ22

8 Bells Bed & Breakfast

★★★★ 🍴 INN

The Long House, The Street RH17 5QP
☎ 01444 881396
e-mail: stay@8bellsbandb.com
dir: A23/A272 junct. Village situated between Ansty & Cowfold on A272

Situated in a peaceful village and in close proximity to both Heathfield and Crawley, this Tudor property has been restored following a complete refurbishment. Many original features, including exposed beams, remain, along with high quality, modern and comfortable accommodation. Guests check in at the establishment's pub located directly opposite and it is here that breakfast, lunch and dinner can be enjoyed.

Rooms 3 en suite (1 fmly) (1 GF) **Facilities** FTV DVD Lounge tea/coffee Dinner available Cen ht Wi-fi ↧ 18 Pool table Billiards **Extras** Bottled water - complimentary **Parking** 15 **Notes** LB ⊗

BOSHAM — Map 5 SU80

White Barn Guest House

★★★★ ⋒ BED AND BREAKFAST

Crede Ln PO18 8NX
☎ 01243 573113 📠 01243 573113
e-mail: chrissie@whitebarn.biz
web: www.whitebarn.biz
dir: *A259 Bosham rdbt, turn S signed Bosham Quay, 0.5m to T-junct, left signed White Barn, 0.25m turn left signed White Barn, 50yds turn right*

This delightful single storey property is close to Bosham Harbour, Goodwood Race Circuit, Chichester and Portsmouth, and has cosy bedrooms with colour co-ordinated soft furnishings and many thoughtful extras. The open-plan dining room overlooks an attractive garden, where breakfast is served if the weather permits.

Rooms 2 en suite 1 annexe en suite (3 GF) S £70-£80; D £80-£110* Facilities FTV DVD tea/coffee Cen ht Wi-fi Parking 3 Notes LB ⊗ No Children 12yrs Closed Xmas & New Year

BURGESS HILL — Map 6 TQ31

Abbey House

★★★★ BED AND BREAKFAST

2 The Holt RH15 0RF
☎ 01444 233299
e-mail: info@abbey-house.biz
dir: *0.5m E of town centre. A2113 (Folders Ln) into Kings Way, 3rd left into The Holt*

This excellent accommodation is set in a comfortable family home, in a pleasant residential area, just a short walk from the town centre and railway station. The modern bedrooms are well equipped and include hairdryers, TVs, fridges and CD players. Welcoming touches include wine and fruit. A good breakfast is served around a large communal dining table.

Rooms 4 rms (3 en suite) (1 pri facs) (1 GF) Facilities FTV tea/coffee Direct Dial Cen ht Wi-fi Parking 5 Notes ⊗ No Children 11yrs Closed 24 Dec-2 Jan

CHARLTON — Map 6 SU81

The Fox Goes Free

★★★★ INN

PO18 0HU
☎ 01243 811461 📠 01243 811712
e-mail: enquiries@thefoxgoesfree.com
dir: *In village centre*

This former hunting lodge has retained much original character and is located in lovely countryside at the foot of the South Downs National Park. The bedrooms are well appointed and the pub boasts low ceilings, brick floors and three inglenook fireplaces. The inn serves its own ale and has an inviting daily-changing menu. During the summer months, guests can take advantage of the rear garden.

Rooms 5 en suite Facilities FTV tea/coffee Dinner available Cen ht Wi-fi Parking 50

CHICHESTER — Map 5 SU80

See also Bosham & West Marden

PREMIER COLLECTION

Rooks Hill

★★★★★ ⋒ BED AND BREAKFAST

Lavant Rd, Lavant PO18 0BQ
☎ 01243 528400
e-mail: enquiries@rookshill.co.uk

Rooks Hill occupies a convenient and picturesque location near Goodwood and the city of Chichester. The warm and friendly proprietors create a wonderful home-from-home atmosphere. Rooms offer powerful thermostatic showers and additional thoughtful extras. A delicious breakfast served in the stylish dining room or on the patio overlooking the pretty gardens in warmer weather provides a substantial start to the day.

Rooms 3 en suite (1 GF) Facilities FTV TVL tea/coffee Cen ht Wi-fi ⅃ 19 Parking 6 Notes ⊗ No Children 12yrs

PREMIER COLLECTION

The Royal Oak Inn

★★★★★ ⊚ ⋒ INN

Pook Ln, East Lavant PO18 0AX
☎ 01243 527434
e-mail: info@royaloakeastlavant.co.uk
dir: *2m N of Chichester. Exit A286 to East Lavant centre*

Located close to the Goodwood estate and Rolls Royce HQ this delightful inn is full of character with beamed ceilings, timber floors and open fires in the public areas. Bedrooms are finished to a very high standard with comfortable beds and state-of-the-art electronic equipment. AA Rosette award-winning meals are served in the popular restaurant.

The Royal Oak Inn

Rooms 3 en suite 5 annexe en suite (1 fmly) (2 GF) S £95-£145; D £130-£195 Facilities FTV DVD iPod docking station tea/coffee Dinner available Direct Dial Cen ht Wi-fi ch fac ⅃ 27 Riding Extras Speciality toiletries, chocolate - complimentary Parking 25 Notes ⊗ No coaches

Old Chapel Forge

★★★★ ⋒ BED AND BREAKFAST

Lower Bognor Rd, Lagness PO20 1LR
☎ 01243 264380
e-mail: info@oldchapelforge.co.uk
dir: *4m SE of Chichester. Exit A27 (Chichester bypass) at Bognor rdbt signed Pagham & Runcton, onto B2166 (Pagham Rd & Lower Bognor Rd). Old Chapel Forge on right*

Great local produce features in the hearty breakfasts at this comfortable, eco-friendly property, an idyllic 17th-century house and chapel set in mature gardens with panoramic views of the South Downs. Old Chapel Forge is a short drive from Chichester, Goodwood, Pagham Harbour Nature Reserve and the beach. Bedrooms, including suites in the chapel, are luxurious, and all have internet access.

Rooms 4 annexe en suite (2 fmly) (4 GF) Facilities tea/coffee Dinner available Cen ht Wi-fi ⅃ 18 Parking 6

Richmond House Boutique B&B

★★★★ ⋒ BED AND BREAKFAST

230 Oving Rd PO19 7EJ
☎ 01243 771464 & 07909 971736
e-mail: richmondhousechichester@hotmail.co.uk
web: www.richmondhousechichester.co.uk
dir: *From A27 bypass enter Chichester from lights E of city on Oving Rd. 1m on left*

Richmond House is conveniently located within a short walking distance of the town centre. Bedrooms and bathrooms are stylishly decorated and offer guests high quality comfort. All bedrooms come equipped with digital TVs, free Wi-fi and beverage making facilities. An extensive cooked or continental breakfast can be enjoyed in the private dining area

Rooms 3 en suite D £85-£125* Facilities FTV iPod docking station tea/coffee Cen ht Wi-fi 🛁 Extras Speciality toiletries, home-made snacks - complimentary Parking 1 Notes LB ⊗

Save on B&Bs and Hotels. Book at **theAA.com/hotel**

SUSSEX, WEST 299 **ENGLAND**

Abelands Barn B&B

★★★★ BED AND BREAKFAST

Bognor Rd, Merston PO20 1DY
☎ 01243 533826 📠 01243 783576
e-mail: snooze@abelandsbarn.co.uk
dir: 2.5m E of city centre on A259

Abelands Barn is located just two miles south of Chichester on the A259 with close proximity to Goodwood, Bognor Regis and Arundel. Bedrooms in the main house are traditionally decorated and comfortable, with far reaching countryside views and large open-plan lounge area. The annexed flint stone barn conversion offers stylish, modern and spacious rooms. Breakfast is served in the main house where guests can enjoy a cooked or continental breakfast.

Rooms 1 en suite 1 annexe en suite **Facilities** FTV TVL tea/coffee Cen ht Wi-fi ch fac **Parking** 5 **Notes** LB ⊗ ⌂

The Bull's Head

★★★★ INN

99 Fishbourne Road West PO19 3JP
☎ 01243 839895
e-mail: julie@bullsheadfishbourne.net
dir: A27 onto A259, 0.5m on left

The Bull's Head is a charming traditionally-styled inn which has a roaring open fire during winter months. By contrast, the accommodation is modern and contemporary and offers very good levels of comfort, spacious showers and generously sized fluffy towels. Evening meals and enjoyable breakfasts are provided daily. The establishment is perfectly located for Fishbourne Roman Palace, Goodwood, Portsmouth, Chichester Theatre and Bosham Harbour.

Rooms 4 en suite (1 fmly) (4 GF) **Facilities** FTV tea/coffee Dinner available Cen ht Wi-fi **Parking** 35

82 Fishbourne

★★★★ BED AND BREAKFAST

82 Fishbourne Road West PO19 3JL
☎ 07854 051013
e-mail: nik@nikwestacott.plus.com
dir: A27 at Chichester rdbt, towards Fishbourne & Bosham on A259. 0.5m on right diagonally opposite Woolpack pub

Warm and friendly hospitality abounds at 82 Fishbourne which is located only a short drive from the historic city of Chichester. Accommodation is spacious and well equipped. Breakfast provides a substantial start to the day and includes delicious fresh eggs from the free range hens which live in the back garden. Scheduled activities include 'Mushroom Hunts' and wine tastings held throughout the year.

Rooms 3 en suite (1 fmly) (1 GF) S £54.50-£85; D £59.50-£95* **Facilities** FTV tea/coffee Dinner available Cen ht Licensed Wi-fi 🍴 Cookery lessons **Parking** 3

Englewood B&B

★★★★ 🏠 BED AND BREAKFAST

East Ashling PO18 9AS
☎ 01243 575407
e-mail: sjenglewood@hotmail.co.uk
dir: Bosham rdbt A259, N exit. At T-junct turn right, next left to B2178, left again, Englewood on left

Set well back from the main road and in the South Downs National Park, Englewood has a very pretty garden, and is surrounded by pleasant lanes and footpaths. The two bedrooms have lots of thoughtful facilities and extras including bottled water, boiled sweets and fruit squash.

Rooms 2 rms (1 en suite) (1 pri facs) (2 GF) S £35-£45; D £50-£75 **Facilities** FTV DVD tea/coffee Cen ht Wi-fi 🍴 **Extras** Sweets, bottled water - complimentary **Parking** 2 **Notes** LB ⊗ No Children ⌂

Gable End

★★★★ BED AND BREAKFAST

Main Rd, Nutbourne PO18 8RT
☎ 01243 573356
e-mail: jill@po188rt.freeserve.co.uk
dir: A259 W past Barleycorn pub on left, 0.3m, left, immediately right, 150yds, 4th house on left, set back from road

You are guaranteed a genuinely warm welcome at Gable End which occupies a peaceful location close to Bosham and Emsworth Marina. Enjoy a delicious home-cooked breakfast in attractive surroundings, with views from the rear of the property overlooking the sea and pretty garden.

Rooms 1 rm (1 pri facs) D £76-£80* **Facilities** tea/coffee Cen ht Wi-fi 🍴 **Parking** 8 **Notes** ⊗ No Children 11yrs Closed 23 Dec-2 Jan ⌂

Horse and Groom

★★★★ INN

East Ashling PO18 9AX
☎ 01243 575339
e-mail: info@thehorseandgroomchichester.co.uk
web: www.thehorseandgroomchichester.co.uk
dir: 3m N of Chichester, on B2178 towards Rowland's Castle

The Horse and Groom is a unique 17th-century country pub and restaurant offering spacious and comfortable accommodation and warm, friendly hospitality. The substantial, freshly prepared breakfasts, lunches and

dinners make good use of freshly caught fish and locally sourced ingredients.

Horse and Groom

Rooms 11 en suite (11 GF) S £45-£55; D £70-£80* **Facilities** tea/coffee Dinner available Cen ht Wi-fi 🍴 **Parking** 40 **Notes** RS Sun eve Bar & Restaurant close 6pm

Musgrove House

★★★★ 🏠 BED AND BREAKFAST

63 Oving Rd PO19 7EN
☎ 01243 790179 & 07885 586344
e-mail: enquiries@musgrovehouse.co.uk
dir: From A27 onto B2144 towards city centre, at corner of Oving Rd & St James Rd

Located just outside Chichester city centre, this establishment has undergone a complete refurbishment and offers guests three stylish bedrooms with light airy decor and modern fixtures and fittings, including free Wi-fi and digital TVs. Expect a friendly welcome on arrival and a choice of both cooked and continental dishes at breakfast which make good use of high quality and locally sourced produce.

Rooms 3 en suite **Facilities** FTV tea/coffee Cen ht Wi-fi **Extras** Speciality toiletries **Parking** 3 **Notes** ⊗ No Children 12yrs

The Vestry

★★★ INN

23 Southgate PO19 1ES
☎ 01243 773358 📠 08720 220801
e-mail: info@the-vestry.com

The Vestry is conveniently located in the town centre. Bedrooms are spacious and well equipped including beverage making facilities and Wi-fi. The bar and restaurant are spacious with comfortable seating areas; during the winter months guests can keep cosy in front of the log fires. Lunch and dinner are served daily; both continental and a range of wholesome cooked breakfasts are available.

Rooms 11 en suite (2 fmly) **Facilities** FTV tea/coffee Dinner available Wi-fi **Notes** Closed 24-26 Dec & 31 Dec-1 Jan

Derwent House

★★★★ BED AND BREAKFAST

Climping St BN17 5RQ
☎ 01903 726204
e-mail: jonshorrock@yahoo.co.uk
dir: *Turn S from A259 at Yapton into Climping St*

Derwent House is situated in the Conservation Area of the Climping Gap, the last undeveloped stretch of coastline between Brighton and Bognor Regis. Guests will find a warm and friendly welcome at this attractive country house, which offers well-appointed rooms, a dining room and a cosy lounge overlooking the garden.

Rooms 2 en suite **Facilities** FTV TVL tea/coffee Cen ht Wi-fi ⚓ 18 Fishing Riding Snooker **Parking** 8 **Notes** No Children

CRAWLEY

For accommodation details see Gatwick Airport (London)

GATWICK AIRPORT (LONDON) — Map 6 TQ24

Acorn Lodge Gatwick

★★★★ GUEST ACCOMMODATION

79 Massetts Rd RH6 7EB
☎ 01293 774550
e-mail: info@acornlodgegatwick.co.uk
web: www.acornlodgegatwick.co.uk
dir: *M23 junct 9, A23 into Horley, off A23 Brighton Rd*

This property provides a 24-hour transfer service to the airport and has on-site parking. Bedrooms are comfortably furnished, come with a practical desk area and useful touches. The breakfasts served in the comfortable dining room make a good start to the day; dinner is also available.

Rooms 15 en suite (4 fmly) (7 GF) **Facilities** FTV TVL tea/coffee Dinner available Cen ht Licensed Wi-fi **Parking** 20 **Notes** ⊗

The Lawn Guest House

★★★★ GUEST HOUSE

30 Massetts Rd RH6 7DF
☎ 01293 775751 ▤ 01293 821803
e-mail: info@lawnguesthouse.co.uk
web: www.lawnguesthouse.com
dir: *M25 junct 7, M23 S towards Brighton/Gatwick Airport. Exit at junct 9. At either South or North Terminal rdbts take A23 towards Redhill. At 3rd rdbt (Esso garage on left) take 3rd exit (Texaco garage on right). In 200yds right at lights onto Massetts Rd. Guest house 400yds on left*

Once a Victorian school, this friendly guest house is well-positioned on a quiet leafy street close to Gatwick. Bedrooms are spacious with thoughtful amenities such as free Wi-fi, and fans for use in warm weather. Airport parking is available.

Rooms 12 en suite (4 fmly) **Facilities** STV tea/coffee Direct Dial Cen ht Wi-fi **Parking** 4

Trumbles

★★★★ GUEST ACCOMMODATION

Stan Hill RH6 0EP
☎ 01293 863418 ▤ 01293 862925
e-mail: stay@trumbles.co.uk
web: www.trumbles.co.uk
dir: *0.5m N of Charlwood. From village centre onto Norwoodhill Rd, 1st left onto Stan Hill*

This attractive house, within easy reach of Gatwick, enjoys a quiet and secluded setting in this charming village. Bedrooms are spacious with a good range of facilities. The conservatory offers an ideal environment for guests to relax and enjoy either continental or full English breakfast. Parking is available, along with airport transfers.

Rooms 6 en suite (2 fmly) (1 GF) S fr £60; D £74-£79* **Facilities** FTV TVL tea/coffee Cen ht Wi-fi 🔒 **Parking** 20 **Notes** ⊗ Closed 24-25 Dec

Vulcan Lodge Guest House

★★★★ BED AND BREAKFAST

27 Massetts Rd RH6 7DQ
☎ 01293 771522 & 07980 576012 ▤ 01737 720153
e-mail: reservations@vulcan-lodge.com
web: www.vulcan-lodge.com
dir: *M23 junct 9, A23 into Horley, off A23 Brighton Rd*

A particularly warm and friendly welcome is offered by the hosts of this charming period house, which sits back from the main road and is convenient for Gatwick Airport. Bedrooms are well equipped and feature many thoughtful extras. A choice of breakfast is offered, including vegetarian, and is served in a delightful dining room.

Vulcan Lodge Guest House

Rooms 4 rms (3 en suite) (1 pri facs) (1 fmly) S £47-£54; D £68 **Facilities** FTV TVL tea/coffee Cen ht Wi-fi **Parking** 13

Gainsborough Lodge

★★★ GUEST ACCOMMODATION

39 Massetts Rd RH6 7DT
☎ 01293 783982 ▤ 01293 785365
e-mail: enquiries@gainsborough-lodge.co.uk
dir: *2m NE of airport off A23 Brighton Rd*

Close to Gatwick, this fine Edwardian house offers a courtesy service to and from the airport. The bright bedrooms are comfortably appointed, and a varied breakfast, including a vegetarian option, is served in the cheerful conservatory-dining room. There is also an attractive lounge and bar.

Rooms 16 rms (14 en suite) 14 annexe en suite (5 fmly) (12 GF) **Facilities** TVL tea/coffee Direct Dial Cen ht Free membership of local Gym **Parking** 30 **Notes** ⊗

Gatwick White House

★★ GUEST ACCOMMODATION

50-52 Church Rd RH6 7EX
☎ 01293 402777 & 784322 ▤ 01293 424135
e-mail: hotel@gwhh.com
web: www.gwhh.com
dir: *In Horley centre off A23 (Brighton Rd)*

Convenient for the airport and major routes, this establishment offers efficient and functional accommodation. There is a bar, restaurant with good curries as well as traditional dishes, parking, and a 24-hour transfer service to Gatwick that is available on request.

Rooms 27 en suite (2 fmly) (10 GF) **Facilities** TVL tea/coffee Dinner available Direct Dial Cen ht Licensed Wi-fi **Parking** 30 **Notes** ⊗

HORSHAM	Map 6 TQ13

Random Hall

★★★★ GUEST ACCOMMODATION

Stane St, Slinfold RH13 0QX
☎ 01403 790558 ▤ 01403 330475
e-mail: nigelrandomhall@btconnect.com
web: www.randomhall.co.uk
dir: *4m W of Horsham. On A29 W of Slinfold*

This 16th-century farmhouse combines character with good quality accommodation and service from the resident proprietors. The comfortable bedrooms are equipped with useful extras. Beams, flagstone floors and quality fabrics add style to the bar and public areas, and an enjoyable dinner is served Monday to Saturday.

Rooms 13 en suite (5 GF) **Facilities** STV tea/coffee Dinner available Direct Dial Cen ht Licensed Wi-fi ♨ 18 **Conf** Max 20 Thtr 20 Class 10 Board 10 **Parking** 40 **Notes** ⊗

LITTLEHAMPTON	Map 6 TQ00

Leeside

★★★★ GUEST ACCOMMODATION

Rope Walk BN17 5DE
☎ 01903 723666 & 07791 797131
e-mail: leeside1@tiscali.co.uk
dir: *From A259 into Ferry Rd signed Rope Walk & West Beach. 1m, turn right into Rope Walk, Leeside on right*

This bright bungalow is close to local sailing clubs, the River Arun and the beach. Visitors will enjoy a warm welcome and comfortable modern bedrooms have flat screen TVs and free Wi-fi. The hearty breakfasts make a good start to the day.

Rooms 4 en suite (3 GF) S fr £40; D fr £70* **Facilities** TVL tea/coffee Cen ht Wi-fi **Parking** 4 **Notes** ⊗ No Children 14yrs

East Beach Guest House

★★★★ GUEST HOUSE

71 South Ter BN17 5LQ
☎ 01903 714270 ▤ 01903 714270
e-mail: info@eastbeachguesthouse.co.uk
web: www.eastbeachguesthouse.co.uk
dir: *On South Terrace, opposite beach, 200mtrs from junct with Pier Rd*

This guest house offers individually styled and comfortable accommodation; all rooms are equipped with a good range of amenities including flat screen TVs and Wi-fi; some bedrooms have sea views. A freshly cooked breakfast, using local produce, is served on the first-floor breakfast room that overlooks the sea.

Rooms 9 en suite (2 fmly) (2 GF) **Facilities** FTV TVL tea/coffee Cen ht Wi-fi **Extras** Speciality toiletries **Notes** LB ⊗ No Children 3yrs

MIDHURST	Map 6 SU82

See also Rogate

Loves Farm *(SU912235)*

★★★★ FARMHOUSE

Easebourne St GU29 0BG
☎ 01730 813212 & 07789 228400   Mr J Renwick
e-mail: renwick@lovesl.fsnet.co.uk
dir: *2m NE of town centre. Exit A272 at Easebourne church into Easebourne St, follow signs for Loves Farm*

This 17th-century farmhouse is set on a 300-acre farm with wonderful views of the South Downs from the windows. The comfortable rooms have their own entrance and benefit from king-size beds and en suite or private shower rooms. This is a great location for access to Midhurst, Cowdray Park and Goodwood.

Rooms 3 rms (2 en suite) (1 pri facs) (2 fmly) (1 GF) S £50-£55; D £75-£100* **Facilities** FTV tea/coffee Cen ht Wi-fi **Parking** 3 **Notes** ⊗ ⊜ 300 acres arable/horses

PETWORTH	Map 6 SU92

The Angel Inn

★★★★ INN

Angel St GU28 0BG
☎ 01798 344445 & 342153
e-mail: reception@angelinnpetworth.co.uk
dir: *Leave one-way system onto A283 E, 100yds on left*

Located in the heart of the historic town of Petworth, this inn has recently been refurbished to offer guests stylish yet traditionally decorated bedrooms and bathrooms. Guests can enjoy breakfast, lunch or dinner in the bar and restaurant area, and there is a large walled garden for alfresco dining during the warmer months. There is parking on site and the inn is just a two minute walk from the town centre.

Rooms 6 en suite S £75-£110; D £95-£130* **Facilities** FTV tea/coffee Dinner available Cen ht Wi-fi **Parking** 15 **Notes** No coaches

ROGATE	Map 5 SU82

PREMIER COLLECTION

Mizzards Farm

★★★★★ BED AND BREAKFAST

GU31 5HS
☎ 01730 821656 ▤ 01730 821655
e-mail: francis@mizzards.co.uk
dir: *0.6m S from Rogate x-rds, over river & signed 300yds on right*

This charming 16th-century house stands near the River Rother in two acres of beautiful landscaped gardens with a lake and the proprietor's own sculptures. Guests can relax in either the conservatory or the split-level drawing room, and the airy, well-appointed bedrooms look over the grounds. There is an entrance hall, dining room, and a swimming pool is available in summer.

Rooms 3 en suite S £60-£65; D £82-£92 **Facilities** FTV tea/coffee Cen ht Wi-fi ♫ ✦ **Parking** 12 **Notes** ⊗ No Children 9yrs Closed Xmas ⊜

RUSTINGTON	Map 6 TQ00

Kenmore Guest House

★★★★ GUEST ACCOMMODATION

Claigmar Rd BN16 2NL
☎ 01903 784634
e-mail: enquiries@kenmoreguesthouse.co.uk
dir: *A259 follow signs for Rustington, turn for Claigmar Rd by war memorial. Kenmore on right as Claigmar Rd bends*

A warm welcome is assured at this Edwardian house, located close to the sea and convenient for touring West Sussex. Spacious bedrooms, all individually decorated, are provided with many useful extras. There is a comfortable lounge in which to relax and a bright dining room where a good choice of breakfast is served.

Rooms 8 rms (7 en suite) (1 pri facs) (1 fmly) (2 GF) S £35-£45; D £69-£74* **Facilities** FTV Lounge tea/coffee Cen ht Wi-fi ♨ **Parking** 7 **Notes** No Children 6yrs

Rustington Manor

★★★★ ⊜ GUEST ACCOMMODATION

12 Broadmark Ln BN16 2HH
☎ 01903 788782
e-mail: enquiries@rustingtonmanor.com

A warm welcome is assured at this family-run establishment where guests are made to feel at home. Attentive service and excellent food make for a wonderful dining experience. Six comfortable en suite rooms offer all the amenities that the modern guest requires. The establishment is located a short walk from the beach.

Rooms 6 en suite **Facilities** TVL tea/coffee Dinner available Direct Dial Cen ht Licensed Wi-fi ♨ **Conf** Max 40 Thtr 40 Class 40 Board 40 **Parking** 14 **Notes** ⊗

SELSEY
Map 5 SZ89

Greenacre Bed & Breakfast

★★★★ A BED AND BREAKFAST

5 Manor Farm Court PO20 0LY
☎ 01243 602912
e-mail: greenacre@zoom.co.uk
dir: B2145 to Selsey, over a small rdbt, next left (Manor Farm Court), bear left & Greenacre on left

Rooms 4 rms (3 en suite) (1 fmly) (1 GF) Facilities STV TVL tea/coffee Cen ht Wi-fi Parking 7

St Andrews Lodge

★★★★ A GUEST ACCOMMODATION

Chichester Rd PO20 0LX
☎ 01243 606899 📠 01243 607826
e-mail: info@standrewslodge.co.uk
web: www.standrewslodge.co.uk
dir: B2145 into Selsey, on right just before church

Rooms 5 en suite 5 annexe en suite (3 fmly) (5 GF) S £45-£65; D £65-£90* Facilities FTV Lounge tea/coffee Direct Dial Cen ht Licensed Wi-fi Extras Sweets - complimentary Conf Max 15 Parking 14 Notes LB

SIDLESHAM
Map 5 SZ89

PREMIER COLLECTION

The Crab & Lobster

★★★★★ ⑩ RESTAURANT WITH ROOMS

Mill Ln PO20 7NB
☎ 01243 641233
e-mail: enquiries@crab-lobster.co.uk
dir: A27 onto B2145 signed Selsey. 1st left after garage at Sidlesham into Rookery Ln to Crab & Lobster

Hidden away on the south coast near Pagham Harbour and only a short drive from Chichester is the stylish Crab & Lobster. Bedrooms are superbly appointed, and bathrooms are a feature with luxury toiletries and powerful 'raindrop' showers. Guests can enjoy lunch or dinner in the smart restaurant where the menu offers a range of locally caught fresh fish amongst other regionally-sourced, seasonal produce.

Rooms 4 en suite S £80-£90; D £140-£180* Facilities FTV DVD iPod docking station tea/coffee Dinner available Cen ht Wi-fi Extras Speciality toiletries Parking 12 Notes ⊗ No coaches

PREMIER COLLECTION

Lockgate Dairy

★★★★★ BED AND BREAKFAST

Sidlesham Common PO20 7QH
☎ 01243 641452
e-mail: buchanan.j@virgin.net
dir: 4.5m S of Chichester, access from A286 or B2145

Set in a quiet, rural location just a couple of miles from Chichester, this recently renovated property offers guests large, spacious bedrooms that have fresh, modern decor and high quality fixtures and fittings. Expect a friendly welcome with home-made refreshments. Bedrooms come complete with Freeview TVs, free Wi-fi and well stocked beverage trays. There is a conservatory area as well as a walled garden with exotic plants and seating areas for guests. A cooked or continental breakfast is served in the dining room.

Rooms 2 annexe en suite (2 GF) S £60-£80; D £90-£110* Facilities FTV DVD iPod docking station tea/coffee Cen ht Wi-fi 🔒 Parking 4 Notes LB ⊗ No Children 12yrs

The Jolly Fisherman B&B

★★★★ BED AND BREAKFAST

Selsey Rd PO20 7LS
☎ 01243 641544
e-mail: pamela.brett@btinternet.com
dir: From Chichester take B2145 (Selsey Rd)

The Jolly Fisherman B&B benefits from its location halfway between the historic city of Chichester and Selsey. It is perfect for exploring the South coast harbours and ideal for Goodwood. Accommodation is comfortable and a traditional substantial breakfast is available in the dining room or on the rear patio overlooking fields, weather permitting.

Rooms 3 en suite Facilities FTV Cen ht Wi-fi ⚓ Parking 3 Notes ⊗ ♨

TILLINGTON
Map 6 SU92

The Horse Guards Inn

★★★★ ⑩ INN

GU28 9AF
☎ 01798 342332 📠 01798 345126
e-mail: info@thehorseguardsinn.co.uk
dir: Off A272 to Tillington, up hill opposite All Hallows church

This inn is conveniently located close to Petworth and Midhurst in a quiet village setting opposite the quaint church, and is perfect for exploring the beautiful surrounding countryside. The comfortable bedrooms are simply decorated, and delicious breakfasts are prepared to order using the finest local ingredients. The same principles apply to the substantial and flavoursome meals served in the cosy restaurant/bar dining areas.

Rooms 2 en suite 1 annexe en suite (1 fmly) S £85-£115; D £85-£115* Facilities FTV tea/coffee Dinner available Cen ht Wi-fi

WEST CHILTINGTON
Map 6 TQ01

The Roundabout

U

Monkmead Ln RH20 2PF
☎ 01798 817336
e-mail: roundabout@relax.co.uk

Currently the rating for this establishment is not confirmed. This may be due to a change of ownership or because it has only recently joined the AA rating scheme.

Rooms 26 en suite

WEST MARDEN
Map 5 SU71

PREMIER COLLECTION

West Marden Farmhouse (SU770135)

★★★★★ 🏠 FARMHOUSE

PO18 9ES
☎ 023 9263 1761 Mrs C M Edney
e-mail: carole.edney@btinternet.com

Located in the small rural village of West Marden is the delightful West Marden Farmhouse, (a working arable farm) which provides extremely comfortable and stylish accommodation as well as a fabulous private lounge with sofas, where the log fire is lit in cooler weather. The farmhouse provides a sumptuous home-cooked, freshly prepared breakfast for all of its welcome visitors. Free Wi-fi is available throughout.

Rooms 2 en suite 2 annexe en suite (1 GF) D £115-£150* Facilities FTV Lounge tea/coffee Cen ht Wi-fi 🔒 Parking 5 Notes ⊗ No Children Closed 20 Dec-7 Jan 1000 acres arable

Grandwood House

★★★★ GUEST ACCOMMODATION

Watergate PO18 9EG
☎ 07971 845153 & 023 9263 1436
e-mail: info@grandwoodhouse.co.uk
web: www.grandwoodhouse.co.uk

Set in the South Downs and built in 1907, Grandwood House was originally a lodge belonging to Watergate House, which was accidentally burnt down by troops during WWII. Only a short walk away is the local pub in nearby Walderton which serves lunches and evening meals. All rooms are en suite and enjoy views of the garden, open farmland or both. Large security gates leading onto the driveway ensure secure parking at all times.

Rooms 4 annexe en suite (4 GF) S £45-£55; D £60-£95* Facilities FTV DVD tea/coffee Cen ht Wi-fi Riding 🔒 Parking 8 Notes LB

WORTHING
Map 6 TQ10

The Beacons

★★★★ GUEST ACCOMMODATION

18 Shelley Rd BN11 1TU
☎ 01903 230948
e-mail: thebeacons@btconnect.com
dir: 0.5m W of town centre. Exit A259 Richmond Rd into
Crescent Rd, 3rd left

This splendid Edwardian property is ideally situated close
to the shopping centre, marine garden and pier.
Bedrooms are bright, spacious and attractively furnished
with many thoughtful amenities, including free Wi-fi.
Guests can enjoy the comfortable lounge with honesty bar
and breakfast is served in the sunny dining room.

Rooms 8 en suite (1 fmly) (3 GF) S £45-£50; D £72-£80*
Facilities FTV Lounge tea/coffee Cen ht Licensed Wi-fi
Parking 8

The Burlington

★★★★ GUEST ACCOMMODATION

Marine Pde BN11 3QL
☎ 01903 211222 📠 01903 209561
e-mail: info@theburlingtonworthing.co.uk
web: www.theburlingtonworthing.co.uk
dir: On seafront 0.5m W of Worthing Pier, Wordsworth
Rd junct

This imposing seafront building offers a modern
contemporary look that appeals to a mainly youthful
clientele. The light bar and terrace extends to a night
club open at the weekends. Bedrooms are spacious and
thoughtfully furnished with some modern touches.
Friendly staff.

Rooms 26 en suite (6 fmly) S £60-£75; D £75-£95*
Facilities FTV Lounge tea/coffee Dinner available Direct
Dial Cen ht Licensed Wi-fi **Conf** Max 100 Thtr 50 Class 35
Board 40 **Notes** ⊗

The Conifers

★★★★ 🏠 GUEST ACCOMMODATION

43 Parkfield Rd BN13 1EP
☎ 01903 265066 & 07947 321096
e-mail: conifers@hews.org.uk
dir: A24 or A27 onto A2031 at Offington rdbt, over lights,
Parkfield Rd 5th right

This charming home is located in a quiet residential area
of West Worthing close to the town centre and seafront.
Bedrooms are traditionally decorated and offer guests
comfortable accommodation. There are a number of
thoughtful extras which make this a true home-from-
home experience. Guests can enjoy a selection of both
cooked and continental dishes for breakfast which has
achieved an AA Breakfast Award. There is a well kept
garden for guests to enjoy during the summer months.

Rooms 2 rms (1 pri facs) (2 fmly) S £50; D £80-£100
Facilities FTV tea/coffee Cen ht Wi-fi **Extras** Chocolates,
robes, water - complimentary **Notes** LB ⊗ No Children
12yrs Closed Xmas & New Year

Moorings

★★★★ GUEST ACCOMMODATION

4 Selden Rd BN11 2LL
☎ 01903 208882
e-mail: themooringsworthing@hotmail.co.uk
dir: 0.5m E of pier off A259 towards Brighton

This well-presented Victorian house is located in a quiet
residential street just a short walk from the seafront and
town centre. Bedrooms are attractively co-ordinated with
plenty of extras such as Wi-fi and Freeview TV. Breakfast
is served in a smart dining room and there is a small
lounge with books and games.

Rooms 7 en suite (1 fmly) (1 GF) S £40-£50; D £70-£80*
Facilities FTV DVD Lounge tea/coffee Direct Dial Cen ht
Wi-fi **Notes** LB ⊗ No Children 3yrs

Olinda Guest House

★★★★ GUEST ACCOMMODATION

199 Brighton Rd BN11 2EX
☎ 01903 206114
e-mail: info@olindaguesthouse.co.uk
web: www.olindaguesthouse.co.uk
dir: 1m E of pier on Brighton Rd along Worthing seafront

Guests are assured a warm welcome at this
establishment which is located on the seafront just a
walk away from the town centre. The bedrooms are cosy
and comfortable, and breakfast is taken in the
attractively appointed dining room overlooking the
seafront.

Rooms 6 rms (3 en suite) S £27-£35; D £56-£75
Facilities FTV DVD tea/coffee Cen ht Wi-fi **Notes** ⊗ No
Children 12yrs

Merton House

★★★★ 🅰 GUEST HOUSE

96 Broadwater Rd BN14 8AW
☎ 01903 238222
e-mail: stay@mertonhouse.co.uk
dir: 0.5m from A27, S onto A24 towards pier. 0.25m after
St Marys Church

Rooms 7 en suite (2 GF) S £50-£75; D £82-£86*
Facilities FTV Lounge tea/coffee Dinner available Cen ht
Wi-fi 🛁 **Parking** 7 **Notes** LB ⊗ No Children 10yrs

High Beach Guest House

★★★ GUEST ACCOMMODATION

201 Brighton Rd BN11 2EX
☎ 01903 236389
e-mail: info@highbeachworthing.com
web: www.highbeachworthing.com
dir: On A259, 200yds past Aquarena swimming pool

This property is situated within a short walking distance
of Worthing town centre, and its seafront location offers
uninterrupted sea views from front facing rooms and the
breakfast room. Bedrooms are traditionally decorated and
come well-equipped. A conservatory with comfortable
seating leads onto the front garden which guests can
enjoy during summer months.

Rooms 7 rms (3 en suite) (1 GF) **Facilities** FTV Lounge
TVL tea/coffee Cen ht Wi-fi 🛁 **Parking** 3 **Notes** ⊗

Marina Guest House

★★★ GUEST ACCOMMODATION

191 Brighton Rd BN11 2EX
☎ 01903 207844
e-mail: marinaworthing@ntlworld.com
dir: M27 onto A259 to Worthing; or M23 onto A24 to
Worthing

This Victorian establishment is in a great location with
uninterrupted sea views, and just a short distance from
the town centre. The property is well maintained with
comfortable accommodation. A cooked breakfast can be
enjoyed in the family-style breakfast room that looks out
over the sea.

Rooms 5 rms (2 en suite) (2 fmly) **Facilities** tea/coffee
Direct Dial Cen ht Wi-fi **Notes** ⊗

TYNE & WEAR

NEWCASTLE UPON TYNE
Map 21 NZ26

Kenilworth

★★★★ GUEST ACCOMMODATION

44 Osborne Rd, Jesmond NE2 2AL
☎ 0191 281 8111 📠 0191 281 9476
e-mail: info@kenilworthhotel.co.uk
dir: A1058 signed Tynemouth for 1m. Left at lights onto
Osborne Rd, 0.5m on right

Kenilworth is located in the heart of Jesmond amongst
the other hotels and bars which have created a very
cosmopolitan feel to the whole area. On-going
refurbishment of bedrooms and en suites is creating
comfortable modern accommodation. Public areas are
limited but the bar, restaurant and staff are very relaxed
and informal, reflecting the feel of the area.

Rooms 11 en suite (5 fmly) **Facilities** FTV tea/coffee Wi-fi
Access to leisure centre nearby **Parking** 11

SOUTH SHIELDS — Map 21 NZ36

Forest Guest House

★★★★ GUEST HOUSE

117 Ocean Rd NE33 2JL
☎ 0191 454 8160 & 07834 690989 ▤ 0191 454 8160
e-mail: enquiries@forestguesthouse.com

Forest Guest House is centrally located, close to both beach and town centre. It offers comfortable and modern bedrooms with en suites and many thoughtful extras provided as standard. The hospitable owners are always on hand to offer help and recommendations. A well-cooked breakfast is served on individual tables giving a great start to the day.

Rooms 6 rms (5 en suite) (1 pri facs) (3 fmly) S £30-£33; D £60-£65* Facilities STV FTV Cen ht Wi-fi Notes ⊗

Ocean Breeze

★★★★ GUEST HOUSE

11 Urfa Ter NE33 2ES
☎ 0191 456 7442
e-mail: info@oceanbreezeguesthouse.co.uk
dir: A183 towards town centre, into Lawe Rd, 3rd left

Situated just a short walk from the seafront and town centre, this smartly appointed terrace house offers modern, fully-equipped bedrooms, most with en suite shower rooms. Guests are given a genuine warm welcome, and hearty breakfasts made using fresh local ingredients are served in the pleasant dining room.

Rooms 6 rms (3 en suite) (1 fmly) Facilities FTV tea/coffee Cen ht Wi-fi Notes ⊗ No Children 5yrs Closed 16 Dec-6 Jan

SUNNISIDE — Map 19 NZ25

PREMIER COLLECTION

Hedley Hall Country House

★★★★★ GUEST ACCOMMODATION

Hedley Ln NE16 5EH
☎ 01207 231835
e-mail: hedleyhall@aol.com
web: www.hedleyhall.com
dir: From A1 follow signs for Lamsely, at mini-rdbt turn right 2m, left at Birkheads Garden/Nursery sign. Straight over x-rds, turn left to Hedley Hall Country House

Located within easy reach of Beamish, Hedley Hall Country House was once a working farm that was part of the Queen Mother's estate. A warm welcome and quality accommodation is guaranteed. The stylish modern bedrooms, one with a super-king-sized bed, are very thoughtfully equipped. Delightful day rooms include a spacious lounge with deep sofas. Breakfasts are served in the conservatory or the elegant dining room.

Rooms 4 en suite (1 fmly) S £57-£68; D £88* Facilities Lounge TVL tea/coffee Dinner available Cen ht Wi-fi ♨ Extras Fruit, snacks Parking 6 Notes LB ⊗ Closed 22 Dec-2 Jan

WHITLEY BAY — Map 21 NZ37

Park Lodge

★★★★ GUEST HOUSE

158-160 Park Av NE26 1AU
☎ 0191 253 0288 ▤ 0191 252 6879
e-mail: parklodgehotel@hotmail.com
dir: From S A19 through Tyne Tunnel, right onto A1058 to seafront. Left, after 2m left at lights onto A191. On left

Located on a leafy avenue, overlooking the park and just minutes from the town centre and coastline, you can expect a friendly atmosphere at this Victorian house. Bedrooms are very comfortable, stylishly furnished and feature homely extras. A hearty breakfast is served and free Wi-fi is available.

Rooms 5 en suite (1 fmly) (2 GF) S £55-£70; D £75-£95* Facilities FTV DVD TVL tea/coffee Cen ht Wi-fi Parking 2 Notes ⊗ Closed 24-30 Dec

Sandsides Guest House

★★★ GUEST ACCOMMODATION

122 Park Av NE26 1AY
☎ 0191 253 0399 & 07947 447695
e-mail: sandsides@btinternet.com
dir: A19 Tyne Tunnel exit A1058. At rdbt follow A192 Whitley Bay, next rdbt turn left. Located in one-way system

Situated opposite the park and close to the beach and town centre, Sandsides offers a variety of room sizes, two with en suite shower rooms and the others with shared facilities. Freshly-cooked breakfasts are served in the dining room.

Rooms 5 rms (2 en suite) (2 fmly) S £20-£25; D £45-£55* Facilities FTV DVD tea/coffee Cen ht Wi-fi ♨ Parking 1 Notes LB ⊗ ⊛

Save on B&Bs and Hotels. Book at **theAA.com/hotel**

WARWICKSHIRE 305 **ENGLAND**

WARWICKSHIRE

ATHERSTONE
Map 10 SP39

PREMIER COLLECTION

Chapel House Restaurant With Rooms

★★★★★ ⑳ RESTAURANT WITH ROOMS

Friar's Gate CV9 1EY
☎ 01827 718949 🖻 01827 717702
e-mail: info@chapelhouse.eu
web: www.chapelhouse.eu
dir: *A5 to town centre, right into Church St. Right into Sheepy Rd, left into Friar's Gate*

Sitting next to the church, this 18th-century town house offers excellent hospitality and service while the cooking, using much local produce, is very notable. Bedrooms are well equipped and lounges are extensive; there is also a delightful walled garden for guests to use.

Rooms 11 en suite **Facilities** Lounge tea/coffee Dinner available Direct Dial Cen ht Wi-fi **Notes** LB ⊗ Closed Etr wk, Aug BH wk & Xmas wk No coaches

BAGINTON
Map 11 SP37

The Oak

★★★ INN

Coventry Rd CV8 3AU
☎ 024 7651 8855 🖻 024 7651 8866
e-mail: thebagintonoak@aol.com
web: www.thebagintonoak.co.uk

Located close to major road links and Coventry Airport, this popular inn provides a wide range of food throughout the themed, open-plan public areas. Families are especially welcome. Modern, well-equipped bedrooms are situated in a separate accommodation building.

Rooms 13 annexe en suite (1 fmly) (6 GF) S £45-£75; D £45-£75* **Facilities** FTV tea/coffee Dinner available Cen ht Wi-fi **Conf** Max 40 Thtr 40 Class 40 Board 25 **Parking** 110

COLESHILL
Map 10 SP28

Coleshill

★★★ INN

152 High St B46 3BG
☎ 01675 465527 🖻 01675 464013
e-mail: 9130@greeneking.co.uk
dir: *M6 junct 4, A446 signed Coleshill & Lichfield. Turn right (across dual carriageway) into Coventry Rd to Coleshill. Straight on at mini-rdbt, establishment on left*

The Coleshill is in a convenient location for both the NEC and Birmingham International Airport. Bedrooms, some of which are in a separate house opposite, provide comfortable and well-equipped facilities. The bar and bistro are attractively appointed, and there are additional features including a car park and self-contained function suite.

Rooms 15 en suite 8 annexe en suite (3 fmly) (3 GF) **Facilities** tea/coffee Direct Dial **Parking** 30

Innkeeper's Lodge Birmingham (NEC) Coleshill

★★★ INN

High St B46 3BL
☎ 0845 112 6061
e-mail: info@innkeeperslodge.com
web: www.innkeeperslodge.com

At Innkeeper's Lodge you'll find accommodation with comfort and character in equal measure, and everything needed for a relaxing stay, from easy check-in and free parking to complimentary breakfast and a cosy pub serving great value food and drink on the doorstep. Each Lodge has quality rooms, and there are Lodges in a variety of locations from towns and cities to countryside settings across the UK.

Rooms 33 en suite (7 fmly) (1 GF) **Facilities** FTV tea/coffee Dinner available Direct Dial Wi-fi **Parking** 44

ETTINGTON
Map 10 SP24

PREMIER COLLECTION

Fulready Manor

★★★★★ 🖘 BED AND BREAKFAST

Fulready CV37 7PE
☎ 01789 740152
e-mail: stay@fulreadymanor.co.uk
web: www.fulreadymanor.co.uk
dir: *2.5m SE of Ettington. 0.5m S off A422 at Pillerton Priors*

Located in 120 acres of arable farmland, this impressive, new Cotswold-stone house provides very high levels of comfort. The spacious ground-floor areas are furnished with quality and flair, and feature fine furniture and art. The individually themed bedrooms have a wealth of thoughtful extras, and memorable breakfasts are served in the elegant dining room overlooking immaculate gardens.

Rooms 3 en suite D £95-£120 **Facilities** iPod docking station Cen ht Wi-fi 🔒 **Parking** 6 **Notes** ⊗ No Children 15yrs ⊛

FILLONGLEY
Map 10 SP28

Heart of England Conference & Events Centre

★★★★ GUEST ACCOMMODATION

Meriden Rd CV7 8DX
☎ 01676 540333 🖻 01676 540365
e-mail: pa@heartofengland.co.uk
web: www.heartofengland.co.uk

This charming stone-built house offers attractively presented, well-equipped bedrooms and sleek modern bathrooms. This fine old house has bags of character and the spacious, comfortable lounge has a wood burning stove, which is a real feature on cooler evenings. Delicious hot breakfasts are served at individual tables in the well-appointed breakfast room. The nearby Quicken Tree restaurant serves an extensive choice of imaginative dishes and is an ideal dinner venue. First-rate conference and business facilities are available on site.

Rooms 7 en suite (1 GF) S £70-£120; D £75-£120* **Facilities** FTV TVL tea/coffee Dinner available Direct Dial Cen ht Licensed Wi-fi Fishing **Conf** Max 450 Thtr 450 Class 200 Board 50 **Parking** 36 **Notes** LB ⊗ Civ Wed 200

KENILWORTH | Map 10 SP27

Milsoms Kenilworth

★★★★ 🍴 INN

Clarendon House Hotel, High St CV8 1LZ
☎ 01926 515450 🖨 01926 515451
e-mail: kenilworth@milsomshotel.co.uk
web: www.milsomshotel.co.uk
dir: A452 signs to town centre, at small rdbt with clock tower, 2nd exit Abbey Hill. At lights, Milsoms immediately on left

Milsoms enjoys a prominent position in the heart of Kenilworth and benefits from secure car parking for guests. The bedrooms are beautifully appointed and very well equipped; complimentary Wi-fi is available. Dinner in the Loch Fyne Restaurant should not be missed as guests are assured of great food along with attentive and friendly service. There is also a charming bar and a comfortable lounge. The NEC and Birmingham Airport are a short drive away.

Rooms 28 en suite 3 annexe en suite (1 fmly) (5 GF) Facilities FTV tea/coffee Dinner available Wi-fi Conf Max 25 Thtr 16 Class 18 Parking 19 Notes ⊗

Stoneleigh Park Lodge

★★★★ GUEST HOUSE

Stoneleigh Park CV8 2LZ
☎ 024 7669 0123 🖨 024 7669 0789
e-mail: info@stoneleighparklodge.com
web: www.stoneleighparklodge.com
dir: 2m E of Kenilworth in Stoneleigh Park

This house lies within the grounds of the National Agricultural Centre and provides modern, well-equipped accommodation. Meals, using local produce, are served in the Park View Restaurant overlooking the showground. Various conference and meeting facilities are available.

Rooms 58 en suite (4 fmly) (26 GF) S £55-£100; D £65-£130* Facilities FTV TVL tea/coffee Dinner available Direct Dial Cen ht Licensed Wi-fi Fishing Conf Max 10 Parking 60 Notes Closed Xmas

Victoria Lodge

★★★★ GUEST ACCOMMODATION

180 Warwick Rd CV8 1HU
☎ 01926 512020 🖨 01926 858703
e-mail: info@victorialodgekenilworth.co.uk
dir: 250yds SE of town centre on A452 opposite St John's Church

Situated within walking distance of Kenilworth Castle and the historic town's many acclaimed restaurants, Victoria Lodge is a family-run establishment. All of the well-appointed rooms are en suite and thoughtfully furnished with homely extras. There is a Victorian walled garden for guests' use, plus a car park.

Rooms 10 en suite (1 fmly) (2 GF) S £52-£65; D £75-£83* Facilities FTV tea/coffee Direct Dial Cen ht Licensed Wi-fi Parking 9 Notes ⊗ Closed 24 Dec-1 Jan

Hollyhurst Guest House

★★★ GUEST HOUSE

47 Priory Rd CV8 1LL
☎ 01926 853882 🖨 01926 853882
e-mail: admin@hollyhurstguesthouse.co.uk
dir: On A452 in town centre

Located on a mainly residential avenue within easy walking distance of the castle and town centre, this constantly improving establishment offers a range of bedrooms, some of which have the benefit of modern shower rooms. Ground-floor areas include a comfortable lounge in addition to an attractive dining room.

Rooms 4 rms (3 en suite) (1 pri facs) (1 fmly) S £36-£39; D £58* Facilities FTV DVD Lounge tea/coffee Cen ht Wi-fi Parking 7 Notes ⊗ Closed Xmas & New Year

Howden House

★★★ BED AND BREAKFAST

170 Warwick Rd CV8 1HS
☎ 01926 850310
e-mail: howdenhouse@hotmail.co.uk
dir: From A46 take Leamington exit onto A452 towards Kenilworth, follow town centre signs. Becomes Warwick Rd. House on left at junct with Saint John St

Guests will find a warm welcome awaits them at Howden House which is situated at the end of the main street, convenient for the town centre, the National Exhibition Centre and motorway networks. The bedrooms are homely and comfortable.

Rooms 3 rms (1 en suite) (1 fmly) (1 GF) Facilities TVL tea/coffee Cen ht 🐾 🎣 36 Parking 1 Notes ⊗ Closed Xmas & New Year 🍴

LEAMINGTON SPA (ROYAL) | Map 10 SP36

The Adams

★★★★ GUEST ACCOMMODATION

22 Avenue Rd CV31 3PQ
☎ 01926 450742 🖨 01926 313110
e-mail: bookings@adams-hotel.co.uk
dir: 500yds W of town centre. Exit A452 (Adelaide Rd) into Avenue Rd

Just a short walk from the town centre, this elegant 1827 Regency house offers a relaxing setting and quality accommodation. Public areas include a lounge bar with leather armchairs, and a pretty garden. The attractive bedrooms are very well appointed, and have modem points and bathrobes.

Rooms 10 en suite (2 GF) Facilities tea/coffee Direct Dial Cen ht Licensed Wi-fi Parking 14 Notes ⊗ No Children 12yrs Closed 23 Dec-2 Jan

LIGHTHORNE | Map 10 SP35

Redlands Farm

★★★★ BED AND BREAKFAST

Banbury Rd CV35 0AH
☎ 01926 651241
e-mail: redlandsfarm@btinternet.com
dir: Off B4100, 5m S of Warwick

Redlands Farm offers a tranquil location, just six miles from Warwick, Leamington Spa and Stratford-upon-Avon. Bedrooms promise a comfortable stay and breakfast features fresh eggs laid by the chickens in the garden.

Rooms 3 en suite (1 fmly) S £35-£45; D £60-£70* Facilities FTV TVL tea/coffee Cen ht Wi-fi 🐾 Parking 7 Notes ⊗ Closed Xmas & New Year

LONG COMPTON | Map 10 SP23

The Red Lion

★★★★ 🍴 INN

Main St CV36 5JS
☎ 01608 684221 🖨 01608 684968
e-mail: info@redlion-longcompton.co.uk
dir: 5m S of Shipston on Stour on A3400

Located in the pretty rural village of Long Compton, this mid 18th-century posting house retains many original features which are complemented by rustic furniture in the public areas. A good range of ales is offered, and interesting menus make good use of quality local produce. The bedrooms are well appointed, and have a good range of facilities.

Rooms 5 en suite (1 fmly) Facilities tea/coffee Dinner available Cen ht Wi-fi Parking 60 Notes No coaches

Save on B&Bs and Hotels. Book at **theAA.com/hotel**

WARWICKSHIRE 307 ENGLAND

Tallet Barn B&B

★★★★ BED AND BREAKFAST

Yerdley Farm CV36 5LH
☎ 01608 684248 📠 01608 684248
e-mail: talletbarn@googlemail.com
dir: *From A3400 in village into Vicarage Ln opposite village store, 3rd entrance on right at sharp bend*

This converted barn and grain store in the heart of an unspoiled Cotswold village provides comfortable bedrooms with thoughtful extras. Comprehensive breakfasts are served in the elegant beamed dining room in the main house.

Rooms 2 annexe en suite (1 GF) S £45-£50; D £65-£70 **Facilities** tea/coffee Cen ht **Parking** 2 **Notes** ⊗ No Children ⊛

RUGBY   Map 11 SP57

Innkeeper's Lodge Rugby, Dunchurch

★★★ INN

The Green, Dunchurch CV22 6NJ
☎ 0845 112 6073
e-mail: info@innkeeperslodge.com
web: www.innkeeperslodge.com

At Innkeeper's Lodge you'll find accommodation with comfort and character in equal measure, and everything needed for a relaxing stay, from easy check-in and free parking to complimentary breakfast and a cosy pub serving great value food and drink on the doorstep. Each Lodge has quality rooms, and there are Lodges in a variety of locations from towns and cities to countryside settings across the UK.

Rooms 16 en suite (2 fmly) (6 GF) **Facilities** FTV tea/coffee Dinner available Direct Dial Wi-fi **Parking**

Number Seven Guest House

★★★ GUEST HOUSE

7 Eastfield Place CV21 3AT
☎ 01788 541010 📠 01788 544996
dir: *Follow signs to town centre & Rugby school, onto Hillmorton Rd then Littlechurch St. 1st right onto Eastfield Pl, before black & white pub*

Located in a quiet side road, just minutes from Rugby town centre, this guest house, originally a private residence, offers good quality accommodation, some with en suite facilities. Ground-floor areas include a comfortable lounge in addition to an open plan kitchen/dining room where hearty breakfasts are served.

Rooms 7 rms (1 en suite) (6 pri facs) 3 annexe en suite (1 fmly) (4 GF) **Facilities** FTV TVL tea/coffee Cen ht Wi-fi **Notes** ⊛

SHIPSTON ON STOUR   Map 10 SP24

Holly End Bed & Breakfast

★★★★ 🏠 BED AND BREAKFAST

London Rd CV36 4EP
☎ 01608 664064
e-mail: hollyend.hunt@btinternet.com
web: www.holly-end.co.uk
dir: *0.5m S of Shipston on Stour on A3400, just beyond Methodist church*

Located between Oxford and Stratford-upon-Avon and a short walk from the town centre, this immaculate detached house offers bedrooms with lots of thoughtful extras. Comprehensive breakfasts use the best of local produce.

Rooms 2 rms (1 en suite) (1 pri facs) S £60-£65; D £75-£85* **Facilities** FTV tea/coffee Cen ht Wi-fi **Parking** 6 **Notes** LB ⊗ No Children 9yrs ⊛

STRATFORD-UPON-AVON   Map 10 SP25

PREMIER COLLECTION

Cherry Trees

★★★★★ 🏠 GUEST HOUSE

Swans Nest Ln CV37 7LS
☎ 01789 292989
e-mail: cherrytreesstratforduponavon@gmail.com
web: www.cherrytrees-stratford.co.uk
dir: *M40 junct 15 to A439, one-way system (A3400) over bridge, pass Cherry Trees, continue on to rdbt & double back. Then take 1st left onto Swan's Nest Ln*

Comfortably located close to the theatre and the centre of town, Cherry Trees offers three spacious, luxurious and well-equipped rooms. The Garden Room has a king-size four-poster, while the Terrace Room and the Tiffany Suite both include king-size beds. The Tiffany Suite is so named thanks to its round Tiffany stained-glass window. Guests have a separate entrance and hearty breakfasts are served in the attractive upstairs dining room. As well as continental and full English choices, guests can enjoy Belgian waffles or eggs Benedict.

Rooms 3 en suite (3 GF) D £105-£125 **Facilities** FTV tea/coffee Cen ht Wi-fi **Parking** 4 **Notes** LB ⊗ No Children 12yrs Closed Jan-1 Mar

Adelphi Guest House

★★★★ 🏠 GUEST ACCOMMODATION

39 Grove Rd CV37 6PB
☎ 01789 204469
e-mail: info@adelphi-guesthouse.com

The Adelphi is a Victorian town house just minutes from the centre of Stratford-upon-Avon and within walking distance of all the town's theatres and historic attractions. The property is decorated in period style and a warm welcome awaits from the proprietors. The comfortable bedrooms are suitably decorated and provide a good range of extras. Breakfast offers an excellent choice and is served in the elegant dining room which has views out over the park. Parking is provided to the rear of the property.

Rooms 6 en suite S £38-£40; D £70-£85* **Facilities** FTV DVD iPod docking station tea/coffee Cen ht Wi-fi **Parking** 5 **Notes** ⊗ No Children 10yrs

Ambleside Guest House

★★★★ GUEST HOUSE

41 Grove Rd CV37 6PB
☎ 01789 297239
e-mail: peter@amblesideguesthouse.com
dir: *250mtrs from town centre on A4390 opposite Firs Gdns*

Ambleside is a very comfortable house in the heart of Stratford. Breakfast is served in the bright and airy dining room, which overlooks the park at the front. Free on-site parking and Wi-fi are provided.

Rooms 7 rms (5 en suite) (2 pri facs) (2 fmly) (2 GF) S £30-£45; D £55-£85 **Facilities** FTV tea/coffee Cen ht Wi-fi **Parking** 9 **Notes** ⊗ No Children 7yrs

Arden Way Guest House

★★★★ GUEST HOUSE

22 Shipston Rd CV37 7LP
☎ 01789 205646 📠 01789 205646
e-mail: info@ardenwayguesthouse.co.uk
web: www.ardenwayguesthouse.co.uk
dir: *On A3400, S of River Avon, 100mtrs on left*

A warm welcome is assured at this constantly improving non-smoking house, located within easy walking distance of the Butterfly Farm and cricket ground. The homely bedrooms are filled with lots of thoughtful extras and an attractive dining room, overlooking the pretty rear garden, is the setting for comprehensive breakfasts.

Rooms 6 en suite (1 fmly) (2 GF) **Facilities** FTV DVD Lounge tea/coffee Cen ht Wi-fi **Parking** 6 **Notes** LB ⊗

STRATFORD-UPON-AVON *continued*

Clopton Orchard Farm *(SP165455)*

★★★★ FARMHOUSE

Lower Clopton, Upper Quinton CV37 8LH
☎ 01386 438669 & 07765 414636
🖷 01386 438669 Mrs A Coldicott
e-mail: mail@clopton-orchard.fsnet.co.uk
dir: *6m S of Stratford on B4632. S through Lower Clopton, on right opposite farm shop*

A warm welcome is assured at this attractive modern farmhouse located between Broadway and Stratford-upon-Avon. The spacious bedrooms come with practical and thoughtful extras, and comprehensive breakfasts are served around a family table in the cosy pine-furnished first-floor dining room.

Rooms 2 en suite (1 fmly) S £50-£70; D £70-£75 **Facilities** FTV iPod docking station tea/coffee Cen ht Wi-fi 🛇 **Extras** Flowers, fridge **Parking** 5 **Notes** LB ⊛ 300 acres arable/sheep/mixed

Monk's Barn Farm *(SP206516)*

★★★★ FARMHOUSE

Shipston Rd CV37 8NA
☎ 01789 293714 & 205886 Mrs R M Meadows
e-mail: ritameadows@btconnect.com
dir: *2m S of Stratford on A3400, on right after bungalows on left*

With stunning views of the surrounding countryside, a warm welcome is assured at this impressive renovated house. Bedrooms, some of which are located in former outbuildings, are filled with a wealth of thoughtful extras. Memorable breakfasts are served in the spacious and cosy lounge-dining room.

Rooms 2 en suite 3 annexe en suite (1 fmly) (3 GF) S £30-£33; D £60-£65 **Facilities** FTV DVD Lounge TVL tea/coffee Cen ht Wi-fi 🛇 **Parking** 7 **Notes** ⊛ Closed 25-27 Dec 75 acres mixed

Moonraker House

★★★★ GUEST ACCOMMODATION

40 Alcester Rd CV37 9DB
☎ 01789 268774 🖷 01789 268774
e-mail: info@moonrakerhouse.com
web: www.moonrakerhouse.com
dir: *200yds from rail station on A422 (Alcester Rd)*

Just a short walk from the railway station and the central attractions, this establishment provides a range of stylish bedrooms. The sitting area during the day is the setting for the freshly cooked breakfasts. The attractive exterior is enhanced by a magnificent floral display during the warmer months.

Rooms 7 en suite (1 fmly) (2 GF) S £40-£50; D £65-£87* **Facilities** FTV tea/coffee Cen ht Wi-fi **Parking** 7 **Notes** LB ⊛ No Children 6yrs

Twelfth Night

★★★★ GUEST ACCOMMODATION

13 Evesham Place CV37 6HT
☎ 01789 414595
e-mail: twelfthnight@fsmail.net
web: www.twelfthnight.co.uk
dir: *In town centre off A4390 Grove Rd*

This delightful Victorian villa is within easy walking distance of the town centre. Quality decor and furnishings enhance the charming original features, and the elegant dining room is the setting for imaginative English breakfasts.

Rooms 7 rms (6 en suite) (1 pri facs) **Facilities** tea/coffee Cen ht **Parking** 6 **Notes** ⊛ Closed 11-25 Feb

Victoria Spa Lodge

★★★★ GUEST HOUSE

Bishopton Ln, Bishopton CV37 9QY
☎ 01789 267985 🖷 01789 204728
e-mail: ptozer@victoriaspalodge.demon.co.uk
web: www.victoriaspa.co.uk
dir: *A3400 1.5m N to junct A46, 1st left into Bishopton Ln, 1st house on right*

Located within immaculate mature gardens beside the canal on the outskirts of town, this impressive Victorian house retains many original features enhanced by the lovely furnishings and decor. Bedrooms are filled with thoughtful extras and the spacious dining room, furnished with quality antiques and ornaments, also contains a cosy lounge area.

Rooms 7 en suite (3 fmly) S £50-£55; D £65-£70* **Facilities** FTV Lounge tea/coffee Cen ht Wi-fi **Parking** 12 **Notes** ⊛

Travellers Rest

★★★ GUEST ACCOMMODATION

146 Alcester Rd CV37 9DR
☎ 01789 266589
e-mail: enquiries@travellersrest.biz
web: www.travellersrest.biz
dir: *0.5m W of town centre on A422, past railway station*

Located with easy access to the town centre, this attractive semi-detached house provides cosy bedrooms, each with a modern shower room and filled with thoughtful extras. Breakfast is taken in an attractive front-facing dining room, and a warm welcome is assured.

Rooms 4 en suite (1 fmly) S £30-£50; D £55-£80 **Facilities** FTV tea/coffee Cen ht Wi-fi 🛇 **Parking** 5 **Notes** LB Closed 24-26 Dec

Barbette Guest House

★★★ BED AND BREAKFAST

165 Evesham Rd CV37 9BP
☎ 01789 297822
e-mail: barbette@sitgetan.demon.co.uk
dir: *B439 S, 0.5m from town centre*

Expect a friendly welcome at this guest house, a compact but comfortable establishment close to the main road with ample parking and a landscaped rear garden.

Bedrooms are comfortable and well-equipped, and guests have use of a TV lounge.

Barbette Guest House

Rooms 4 rms (2 en suite) **Facilities** FTV TVL tea/coffee Cen ht Wi-fi **Parking** 5 **Notes** ⊗ 🐾

Clomendy Guest House

★★★ BED AND BREAKFAST

10 Broad Walk CV37 6HS
☎ 01789 266957
e-mail: clomendy@amserve.com
dir: *In town centre, left from B439 at Evesham Place into Broad Walk*

Located on a peaceful avenue within easy walking distance of central attractions, this wonderfully maintained house offers homely, thoughtfully-equipped bedrooms with modern bathrooms. All bedrooms are rear-facing, overlooking the garden and a peaceful night's sleep is assured. Breakfast is served at a family table in the elegant dining room, which opens onto the pretty patio garden.

Rooms 2 rms (1 en suite) (1 pri facs) S £45; D £50–£60 **Facilities** FTV Lounge tea/coffee Cen ht 🐾 **Parking** 1 **Notes** LB ⊗ No Children 5yrs 🐾

Stretton House

★★★ GUEST ACCOMMODATION

38 Grove Rd CV37 6PB
☎ 01789 268647
e-mail: shortpbshort@aol.com
web: www.strettonhouse.co.uk
dir: *On A439 in town centre road behind police station*

This attractive Edwardian terrace house is within easy walking distance of the railway station and Shakespeare's birthplace. Bedrooms are carefully decorated, well equipped, and many have modern shower rooms en suite. The pretty front garden is a very welcoming feature.

Rooms 6 rms (5 en suite) (1 pri facs) (3 fmly) (1 GF) S £35–£40; D £60–£70* **Facilities** FTV tea/coffee Cen ht Wi-fi 🐾 **Parking** 7

Salamander Guest House

★★★ 🅰 GUEST HOUSE

40 Grove Rd CV37 6PB
☎ 01789 205728 📠 01789 205728
e-mail: p.delin@btinternet.com
web: www.salamanderguesthouse.co.uk
dir: *250yds W of town centre on A439 ring road, opposite Firs Garden*

Rooms 7 rms (6 en suite) (1 pri facs) (5 fmly) (1 GF) **Facilities** FTV tea/coffee Dinner available Cen ht Wi-fi **Parking** 12 **Notes** ⊗

TEMPLE GRAFTON   Map 10 SP15

The Blue Boar

★★★ INN

B49 6NR
☎ 01789 750010 📠 01789 750635
e-mail: info@theblueboar.co.uk

A warm welcome is guaranteed at this country inn. The bedrooms are comfortable and homely, and the dining room and bar menus offer extensive choice, plus additional specials. There is also a beer garden to sit in when the weather allows.

Rooms 14 en suite (5 fmly) (1 GF) S £55–£65; D £75–£95 **Facilities** FTV Dinner available Cen ht Wi-fi **Conf** Max 30 Thtr 30 Class 40 Board 30 **Parking** 35

WELLESBOURNE   Map 10 SP25

Innkeeper's Lodge Stratford-upon-Avon

★★★ INN

Wartwick Rd CV35 9LX
☎ 0845 112 6075
e-mail: info@innkeeperslodge.com
web: www.innkeeperslodge.com

At Innkeeper's Lodge you'll find accommodation with comfort and character in equal measure, and everything needed for a relaxing stay, from easy check-in and free parking to complimentary breakfast and a cosy pub serving great value food and drink on the doorstep. Each Lodge has quality rooms, and there are Lodges in a variety of locations from towns and cities to countryside settings across the UK.

Rooms 9 en suite (2 fmly) **Facilities** FTV tea/coffee Dinner available Direct Dial Wi-fi **Parking** 35

WEST MIDLANDS

BIRMINGHAM   Map 10 SP08

PREMIER COLLECTION

Westbourne Lodge

★★★★★ 🍴 GUEST ACCOMMODATION

25-31 Fountain Rd, Edgbaston B17 8NJ
☎ 0121 429 1003 📠 0121 429 7436
e-mail: info@westbournelodge.co.uk
web: www.westbournelodge.co.uk
dir: *100yds from A456*

Located on a quiet residential avenue close to Hagley Road, this well-maintained property provides a range of no-smoking, thoughtfully furnished bedrooms, two of which are on the ground floor. Breakfasts (and dinner by arrangement) are served in the attractive dining room overlooking a pretty patio garden. A comfortable sitting room and lounge bar are also available.

Rooms 18 en suite (4 fmly) (2 GF) S £49.50–£69.50; D £69.50–£89.50* **Facilities** FTV TVL tea/coffee Dinner available Cen ht Licensed Wi-fi **Parking** 12 **Notes** Closed 24 Dec-1 Jan

Black Firs

★★★★ GUEST HOUSE

113 Coleshill Rd, Marston Green B37 7HT
☎ 0121 779 2727 📠 0121 778 1149
e-mail: julie@b-firs.co.uk
web: www.b-firs.co.uk
dir: *M42 junct 6, A45 W, onto B4438, follow signs for Marston Green*

This elegant house is set in immaculate gardens in a mainly residential area close to the NEC. Thoughtfully equipped bedrooms with Wi-fi access are complemented by smart shower rooms. Memorable breakfasts are served in an attractive dining room and a lounge is also available.

Rooms 6 en suite **Facilities** TVL tea/coffee Cen ht Wi-fi **Conf** Max 14 **Parking** 6 **Notes** ⊗ 🐾

Olton Cottage Guest House

★★★★ GUEST HOUSE

School Ln, Old Yardley Village, Yardley B33 8PD
☎ 0121 783 9249 📠 0121 789 6545
e-mail: olton.cottage@virgin.net
dir: *3.5m E of city centre. A45 onto A4040 to Yardley. Into Stoney Ln via Yew Tree rdbt. In 1m right into Vicarage Rd, right into Church Rd, left into School Ln*

A warm welcome is assured at this carefully renovated Victorian house, located in a peaceful residential area close to the city centre. The cosy bedrooms contain a wealth of thoughtful extras, and ground-floor areas include a cottage-style dining room and comfortable lounge overlooking the pretty enclosed garden.

Rooms 5 rms (2 en suite) **Facilities** FTV TVL tea/coffee Cen ht Wi-fi **Parking** 2 **Notes** Closed Xmas & New Year 🐾

BIRMINGHAM *continued*

Tri-Star

★★★ GUEST ACCOMMODATION

Coventry Rd, Elmdon B26 3QR
☎ 0121 782 1010 & 782 6131 🖷 0121 782 6131
e-mail: info@tristarhotel.co.uk
dir: On A45

Located a short drive from the airport, the international station and the NEC, this owner-managed property provides a range of thoughtfully furnished bedrooms with modern bathrooms. The open-plan ground-floor area includes a bright, attractive dining room and a comfortable lounge and bar. A separate room is available for conferences or functions.

Rooms 15 en suite (3 fmly) (6 GF) Facilities FTV TVL tea/coffee Dinner available Cen ht Licensed Wi-fi Pool table Games room Conf Max 20 Thtr 20 Class 10 Board 20 Parking 25 Notes ⊗

Innkeeper's Lodge Birmingham West (Quinton)

★★★ INN

563 Hagley Road West, Quinton B32 1HP
☎ 0845 112 6066
e-mail: info@innkeeperslodge.com
web: www.innkeeperslodge.com

At Innkeeper's Lodge you'll find accommodation with comfort and character in equal measure, and everything needed for a relaxing stay, from easy check-in and free parking to complimentary breakfast and a cosy pub serving great value food and drink on the doorstep. Each Lodge has quality rooms, and there are Lodges in a variety of locations from towns and cities to countryside settings across the UK.

Rooms 24 en suite (8 fmly) (8 GF) Facilities FTV tea/coffee Dinner available Direct Dial Wi-fi Parking

Rollason Wood

★★ GUEST ACCOMMODATION

130 Wood End Rd, Erdington B24 8BJ
☎ 0121 373 1230 🖷 0121 382 2578
e-mail: rollwood@globalnet.co.uk
web: www.rollasonwoodhotel.co.uk
dir: M6 junct 6, A5127 to Erdington, right onto A4040, house 0.25m on left

Well situated for many road networks and the city centre, this owner-managed establishment is popular with contractors. The choice of three different bedroom styles suits most budgets, and rates include full English breakfasts. Ground-floor areas include a popular bar, cosy TV lounge and a dining room.

Rooms 35 rms (11 en suite) (5 fmly) (9 smoking) Facilities TVL tea/coffee Dinner available Cen ht Licensed Wi-fi Pool table Parking 35

BIRMINGHAM (NATIONAL EXHIBITION CENTRE)

See Solihull

COVENTRY   Map 10 SP37

Innkeeper's Lodge Birmingham (NEC) Meriden

★★★★ 🍽 INN

Main Rd, Meriden CV7 7NN
☎ 0845 112 6072
e-mail: info@innkeeperslodge.com
web: www.innkeeperslodge.com

At Innkeeper's Lodge you'll find accommodation with comfort and character in equal measure, and everything needed for a relaxing stay, from easy check-in and free parking to complimentary breakfast and a cosy pub serving great value food and drink on the doorstep. Each Lodge has quality rooms, and there are Lodges in a variety of locations from towns and cities to countryside settings across the UK.

Rooms 13 en suite (3 fmly) (4 GF) Facilities FTV tea/coffee Dinner available Direct Dial Wi-fi Parking

DORRIDGE   Map 10 SP17

The Forest

★★★★ ◉◉ RESTAURANT WITH ROOMS

25 Station Rd B93 8JA
☎ 01564 772120 🖷 01564 732680
e-mail: info@forest-hotel.com
web: www.forest-hotel.com
dir: In town centre near station

This very individual and stylish restaurant with rooms is well placed for routes to Birmingham, Stratford-upon-Avon and Warwick. The individually designed bedrooms are very well equipped with modern facilities, and imaginative food is served in the bars and intimate restaurant. A warm welcome is assured.

Rooms 12 en suite S £80-£100; D £100-£130 Facilities FTV tea/coffee Dinner available Direct Dial Cen ht Wi-fi Conf Max 100 Thtr 100 Class 60 Board 40 Parking 50 Notes ⊗ RS Sun eve Restaurant closed No coaches Civ Wed 120

MERIDEN   Map 10 SP28

Grove House Bed & Breakfast

★★★★ BED AND BREAKFAST

8 Whichcote Av CV7 7LR
☎ 01676 523295
e-mail: enquiries@grovehousebandb.co.uk
web: www.grovehousebandb.co.uk
dir: M42 junct 6, A45, A452, at rdbt onto B4102 signed Meriden. At next rdbt 3rd exit. Pass Bulls Head on left, 3rd left into Leys Ln, Whichcote Av on left

Located in the quiet village of Meriden just ten minutes from Birmingham International Airport and the NEC, a

---

warm welcome is guaranteed at Grove House. Bedrooms are spacious and well equipped providing impressive quality and comfort. Ground-floor areas include a comfortable lounge in addition to the cosy breakfast room that overlooks the garden.

Rooms 2 rms (1 en suite) (1 pri facs) Facilities FTV TVL tea/coffee Dinner available Cen ht Wi-fi Parking 6 Notes LB ⊗ ⊜

Swallowfield Country House

★★★★ GUEST ACCOMMODATION

Hampton Ln CV7 7JR
☎ 01676 521262

Swallowfield Country House is a beautifully presented house located on a quiet side road in the busy town of Meriden. The house is a five-minute drive from the NEC and is ideally situated for Birmingham Airport and The Bullring shopping complex. Bedrooms are all very attractively presented; free Wi-fi is available along with ample secure car parking. Breakfast is not to be missed and is served in the light filled conservatory. Guests are assured of a warm welcome from the very friendly proprietors.

Rooms 8 en suite (5 GF) Facilities TVL Cen ht Wi-fi Parking 15 Notes ⊗ No Children Closed 22 Dec-6 Jan

SOLIHULL   Map 10 SP17

The Gate House

★★★ BED AND BREAKFAST

Barston Ln, Barston B92 0JN
☎ 01675 443274
e-mail: enquiries@gatehousesolihull.co.uk
web: www.gatehousesolihull.co.uk
dir: 4m E of Solihull. Off B4101 or B4102 to Barston, on W side of village

This elegant Victorian building stands in landscaped grounds with secure parking, and is within easy driving distance of the NEC and Birmingham. A warm welcome and a comfortable night's rest are guaranteed. Enjoy breakfast in the elegant dining room, overlooking the gardens, which are stunning in spring and summer.

Rooms 4 rms (2 en suite) Facilities tea/coffee Cen ht Wi-fi Parking 20 Notes ⊗ No Children 5yrs ⊜

Innkeeper's Lodge Solihull, Knowle

★★★ INN

Warwick Rd, Knowle B93 0EE
☎ 0845 112 6070
e-mail: info@innkeeperslodge.com
web: www.innkeeperslodge.com

At Innkeeper's Lodge you'll find accommodation with comfort and character in equal measure, and everything needed for a relaxing stay, from easy check-in and free parking to complimentary breakfast and a cosy pub serving great value food and drink on the doorstep. Each Lodge has quality rooms, and there are Lodges in a variety of locations from towns and cities to countryside settings across the UK.

Rooms 11 en suite (1 fmly) **Facilities** FTV tea/coffee Dinner available Direct Dial Wi-fi **Parking**

SUTTON COLDFIELD Map 10 SP19

Windrush

★★★★ 🏠 BED AND BREAKFAST

337 Birmingham Rd, Wylde Green B72 1DL
☎ **0121 384 7534 & 07884 226552**
e-mail: windrush59@hotmail.com
dir: M6 junct 6, on A5127 to Sutton Coldfield, pass shopping centre on left. 75yds then house just before Hawthorn's Surgery on right immediately before traffic bollards

A very warm welcome is extended at this Victorian family house, which offers a relaxed home-from-home atmosphere within easy reach of city centre facilities and shops, as well as the NEC, NIA, ICC and the airport. Bedrooms provide welcoming spaces to relax in, with comfortable beds and a wide range of guest amenities. Award-winning breakfasts are served in the elegant dining room.

Rooms 2 rms (1 en suite) (1 pri facs) S £40-£45; D £60-£65 **Facilities** FTV DVD tea/coffee Cen ht Wi-fi **Parking** 5 **Notes** ⊗ No Children 16yrs Closed 19 Dec-3 Jan 🐾

WIGHT, ISLE OF

ARRETON Map 5 SZ58

Blandings

★★★★ BED AND BREAKFAST

Horringford PO30 3AP
☎ **01983 865720 & 865331** 📠 **01983 862099**
e-mail: robin.oulton@horringford.com
web: www.horringford.com/bedandbreakfast.htm
dir: S through Arreton (B3056), pass Stickworth Hall on right, 300yds on left farm entrance signed Horringford Gdns. U-turn to left, at end of poplar trees turn right. Blandings on left

This detached home stands in the grounds of Horringford Gardens. One bedroom has private access and a decking area for warm summer evenings. Breakfast is a highlight with local island produce gracing the table.

Blandings

Rooms 2 en suite (1 GF) **Facilities** FTV TV1B tea/coffee Cen ht **Parking** 3 **Notes** LB 🐾

BEMBRIDGE Map 5 SZ68

The Crab & Lobster Inn

★★★★ INN

32 Forelands Field Rd PO35 5TR
☎ **01983 872244** 📠 **01983 873495**
e-mail: info@crabandlobsterinn.co.uk
web: www.crabandlobsterinn.co.uk
dir: From Bembridge village, 1st left after Boots into Forelands Rd to Windmill Hotel. Left into Lane End Rd, 2nd right into Egerton Rd, left into Howgate Rd & immediately right into Forelands Field Rd

A traditional beamed inn enjoying a coastal location overlooking Bembridge Ledge with panoramic sea views. Bedrooms and bathrooms are traditionally fitted, comfortable and spacious, offering a good range of accessories. Locally-caught crab and lobster is the specialty during lunch and dinner at this popular dining destination.

Rooms 5 en suite (1 fmly) S £25-£70; D £60-£100* **Facilities** FTV DVD tea/coffee Dinner available Cen ht Wi-fi **Parking** 20 **Notes** Closed 24-26 Dec No coaches

---

Windmill Inn

★★★★ INN

1 Steyne Rd PO35 5UH
☎ **01983 872875** 📠 **01983 874760**
e-mail: enquiries@windmill-inn.com

This popular inn is in the quiet village of Bembridge. Bedrooms are modern throughout with good quality decor and comfortable furnishings. Food is served throughout the day in the popular bar and restaurant. Guests can choose from snacks, meals including locally sourced Bembridge lobster and a carvery on Sunday.

Rooms 14 en suite (2 fmly) S £45-£55; D £90-£110* **Facilities** FTV TVL tea/coffee Dinner available Cen ht Wi-fi 🅿 **Parking** 50 **Notes** No coaches

---

BONCHURCH Map 5 SZ57

The Lake

★★★★ GUEST ACCOMMODATION

Shore Rd PO38 1RF
☎ **01983 852613**
e-mail: enquiries@lakehotel.co.uk
dir: 0.5m E of Ventnor. Exit A3055 to Bonchurch, opposite village pond

A warm welcome is assured at this friendly, family-run property set in two acres of well-tended gardens close to the sea. Bedrooms are equipped with modern facilities and the elegant public rooms offer a high standard of comfort. The breakfast menu offers a good choice of hot and cold options.

Rooms 11 en suite 9 annexe en suite (7 fmly) (4 GF) S £36-£49; D £78-£98* **Facilities** FTV Lounge TVL tea/coffee Cen ht Licensed Wi-fi ⚡ 9 **Parking** 20 **Notes** LB No Children 3yrs Closed 20 Dec-2 Jan

---

CHALE Map 5 SZ47

The Old House

★★★★ 🏠 BED AND BREAKFAST

Gotten Manor, Gotten Ln PO38 2HQ
☎ **01983 551368 & 07746 453398**
e-mail: aa@gottenmanor.co.uk
web: www.gottenmanor.co.uk
dir: 1m N of Chale. Turn right from B3399 into Gotten Ln (opposite chapel), house at end

Located in countryside close to the coast, this 17th-century house has 18th- and 19th-century additions. Restoration has created comfortable, rustic bedrooms with antique bathtubs. Comprehensive breakfasts using the finest ingredients are served in the cosy dining room, and there is a spacious lounge with an open fire.

Rooms 2 en suite **Facilities** STV FTV tea/coffee Cen ht Wi-fi 🛁 **Parking** 3 **Notes** ⊗ No Children 12yrs 🐾

COWES — Map 5 SZ49

Duke of York Inn

★★★ INN

Mill Hill Rd PO31 7BT
☎ 01983 295171 ◻ 01983 295047
e-mail: bookings@dukeofyorkcowes.co.uk

This family-run inn is situated very close to the town centre of Cowes. Comfortable bedrooms are divided between the main building and a separate building only seconds away. Home-cooked meals, with a number of fish and seafood dishes, feature on the menu every evening and are served in the bar and dining area. Parking is a bonus at this location, and outdoor, covered dining is also an option.

Rooms 8 en suite 5 annexe en suite (1 fmly) (1 GF)
S £49-£70; D £79-£100* **Facilities** FTV tea/coffee Dinner available Wi-fi **Parking** 10

The Fountain Inn

★★★ INN

High St PO31 7AW
☎ 01983 292397 ◻ 01983 299554
e-mail: fountain.cowes@oldenglishinns.co.uk
dir: Adjacent to Red Jet passenger ferry in town centre

The Fountain Inn, located in the heart of this harbourside town, offers a number of bedrooms that have beautiful views across the water. Bedrooms and bathrooms are modern in design and provide comfortable accommodation. Substantial bar meals are served in the public areas, and breakfast offers a wide range of options. There is a regular transport service with a convenient drop-off point at the rear of the inn; a pay-and-display car park is a short walk away.

Rooms 20 en suite **Facilities** FTV tea/coffee Dinner available Direct Dial Cen ht Wi-fi **Notes** LB No coaches

---

FISHBOURNE — Map 5 SZ59

The Fishbourne

★★★★ ⇔ INN

111 Fishbourne Ln PO33 4EU
☎ 01983 882823 & 811784 ◻ 01983 884779
e-mail: info@thefishbourne.co.uk
web: www.thefishbourne.co.uk
dir: Off A3054 Newport to Ryde road, next to Wightlink Ferry Terminal

The Fishbourne is conveniently located just along from the Wightlink Fishbourne terminal. Following a complete refurbishment the inn offers five stylishly decorated bedrooms with light and airy decor and modern fixtures including LCD TV and free Wi-fi. Guests can enjoy breakfast, lunch or dinner served in the open-plan bar and restaurant area. On offer are a wide range of traditional pub dishes, with all produce locally sourced.

Rooms 5 en suite (2 fmly) S £45-£65; D £80-£100* **Facilities** FTV DVD iPod docking station tea/coffee Dinner available Cen ht Wi-fi ⚟ 9 **Parking** 40 **Notes** LB No coaches

---

GODSHILL — Map 5 SZ58

PREMIER COLLECTION

Godshill Park Farm House

★★★★★ 🏠 BED AND BREAKFAST

Shanklin Rd PO38 3JF
☎ 01983 840781
e-mail: info@godshillparkfarm.uk.com
web: www.godshillparkfarm.uk.com
dir: From ferry teminal towards Newport, onto A3020 follow signs to Sandown, at Blackwater Corner right to Godshill, farm on right after Griffin pub

This delightful 200-year-old stone farmhouse is set in 270 acres of organic farmland with lakes and woodlands. Bedrooms, one with a four-poster bed and the other overlooking the millpond, are comfortably furnished with many extra facilities. Delicious full English breakfasts are served at one large table in the oak panelled Great Hall.

Rooms 2 en suite S £40-£60; D £80-£110
Facilities FTV Lounge tea/coffee Cen ht Fishing ⚓
Extras Speciality toiletries - complimentary **Parking** 4
Notes ⊗ No Children 8yrs

PREMIER COLLECTION

Koala Cottage

★★★★★ 🏠 BED AND BREAKFAST

Church Hollow PO38 3DR
☎ 07921 183621 & 01983 842031
e-mail: info@koalacottage.co.uk
web: www.koalacottage.co.uk
dir: From Ryde on A3055, after 7m onto A3056 then A3020, left onto Church Hollow

Located in the heart of the picturesque village of Godshill, Koala Cottage offers three spacious and comfortably appointed bedrooms, all with external access and on-site parking. Bedrooms and bathrooms are of a high quality and guests can expect a number of thoughtful extras on arrival including locally-made chocolates plus wine and flowers. There is patio area and indoor hot tub for guests to enjoy. Both cooked and continental breakfasts are served in the conservatory. There are a number of good pubs within a couple of minutes walking distance for evening meals.

Rooms 3 en suite (3 GF) **Facilities** FTV DVD tea/coffee Cen ht Licensed Wi-fi Sauna ⚓ jacuzzi
Extras Chocolates, snacks - complimentary; mini-bar - chargeable **Parking** 3 **Notes** ⊗ No Children 18yrs

---

Arndale

★★★★ BED AND BREAKFAST

High St PO38 3HH
☎ 01983 842003
e-mail: arndalebandb@aol.com
dir: On A3020 High St

Arndale is situated in the pretty village of Godshill. Expect a warm welcome from the resident dogs, Bayley and Arrow. Breakfast is served in the private lounge-dining room. Guests have access to the patio and garden during the warmer months of the year

Rooms 2 rms (2 pri facs) (1 GF) **Facilities** TVL Cen ht Riding **Parking** 4 **Notes** ⊗ No Children 14yrs 🐾

NEWPORT — Map 5 SZ58

Castle Lodge

★★★ GUEST ACCOMMODATION

54 Castle Rd PO30 1DP
☎ 01983 527862 & 07789 228203
e-mail: castlelodge@hotmail.co.uk
web: www.castlelodgeiow.co.uk
dir: 0.5m SW of town centre. On B3323 towards Carisbrooke Castle

This well-presented establishment is located in a quiet residential area within close walking distance of the famous Carisbrooke Castle. A comfortable stay is assured in attractive and restful bedrooms, together with a bright and airy dining room where a substantial breakfast can be enjoyed.

Rooms 2 en suite 5 annexe en suite (1 fmly) (5 GF)
Facilities FTV DVD tea/coffee Cen ht Wi-fi ⚓ **Parking** 5
Notes ⊗

NITON — Map 5 SZ57

PREMIER COLLECTION

Enchanted Manor

★★★★★ GUEST ACCOMMODATION

Sandrock Rd PO38 2NG
☎ 01983 730215
e-mail: info@enchantedmanor.co.uk
web: www.enchantedmanor.co.uk

This delightful property, set in charming grounds, enjoys an enviable location within walking distance of the sea. The unusual theme of magic and enchantment prevails throughout the beautifully appointed suites and spacious public areas, all of which are furnished and decorated to a very high standard. A host of extra touches are provided such as DVD players, well-stocked mini-fridges and welcome baskets. Guests are ensured of friendly, attentive personalised service and an excellent breakfast.

Rooms 7 en suite (2 GF) **Facilities** STV FTV tea/coffee Cen ht Licensed Wi-fi Snooker Pool table Spa/hot tub Massage beauty treatment room **Conf** Max 30 Board 30 **Parking** 15 **Notes** No Children Civ Wed 50

Save on B&Bs and Hotels. Book at **theAA.com/hotel**

WIGHT, ISLE OF 313 ENGLAND

RYDE
Map 5 SZ59

Lisle Court
★★★★ BED AND BREAKFAST

Woodside, Wootton PO33 4JR
☎ **01983 882860 & 07773 870376**
e-mail: welcome@lislecourt.org.uk
dir: *A3054 to Wootton Bridge. In High St onto New Rd, 1m to Lisle Court*

In a prime location with views of Wooton Creek, this Victorian property offers comfortably appointed bedrooms and bathrooms. The house stands in approximately two acres of garden, mainly mature trees, shrubs and lawns with a small pond and swimming pool. For anyone with a boat the property has its own jetty and pontoons which dry out at low tide. A small boat/summer house on the foreshore provides a tranquil spot to sit and watch boats and wildlife on the creek.

Rooms 3 en suite S £55-£65; D £90-£100 **Facilities** FTV TVL tea/coffee Wi-fi ⚡ Fishing Private jetty & pontoons **Parking** 12 **Notes** LB No Children 16yrs Closed 24 Dec-4 Jan ⊛

Ryde Castle
★★★ INN

The Esplanade PO33 1JA
☎ **01983 563755** 🖷 **01983 566906**
e-mail: 6505@greeneking.co.uk

Located overlooking Ryde Esplanade with sea views out to the Solent and beyond, this historic building provides comfortable bedroom accommodation with en suite facilities. This majestic setting houses a popular brasserie and lounge/bar whilst the external decking areas are a welcome place to relax for a summer-time drink. Ample off-road parking is an additional bonus.

Rooms 18 en suite (1 fmly) **Facilities** FTV tea/coffee Dinner available Cen ht Wi-fi **Conf** Max 100 Thtr 100 Class 75 Board 30 **Parking** 70 **Notes** ⊗ No coaches Civ Wed 120

SANDOWN
Map 5 SZ58

The Lawns
★★★★ GUEST ACCOMMODATION

72 Broadway PO36 9AA
☎ **01983 402549**
e-mail: lawnshotel@aol.com
web: www.lawnshotelisleofwight.co.uk
dir: *On A3055 N of town centre*

The Lawns stands in grounds just a short walk from the beach, public transport and town centre. There is a comfortable lounge and bar, while evening meals (by arrangement) and breakfast are served in the bright dining room. Service is friendly and attentive, and the bedrooms are comfortably equipped.

Rooms 13 en suite (2 fmly) (2 GF) S £50-£55; D £72-£84 **Facilities** FTV TVL tea/coffee Dinner available Cen ht Licensed Wi-fi 🛁 **Parking** 13 **Notes** LB ⊗ Closed Nov-Jan

Montague House
★★★★ GUEST HOUSE

109 Station Av PO36 8HD
☎ **01983 404295**
e-mail: enquiries@montaguehousehotel.fsnet.co.uk
dir: *A3055 from Ryde to Sandown, into Station Av, follow signs for beach*

This large, detached, late Victorian house is just a short walk from the town centre and seafront. The friendly hosts provide good quality, well-equipped modern accommodation. Separate tables are provided in the very attractive dining room and you can relax in the pleasant conservatory.

Rooms 10 rms (9 en suite) (1 pri facs) (2 fmly) (2 GF) S £35; D £70 **Facilities** TVL tea/coffee Cen ht **Notes** LB ⊗ No Children 5yrs ⊛

Carisbrooke House
★★★★ GUEST HOUSE

11 Beachfield Rd PO36 8NA
☎ **01983 402257** 🖷 **01983 402257**
e-mail: wmch583@aol.com
dir: *Opposite Ferncliff Gardens*

Expect a friendly welcome at this family-run guest house situated opposite Ferncliff Gardens and within walking distance of the town centre and seafront. A full English breakfast is served in the dining room overlooking the sun terrace. Enjoy a drink in the bar/lounge. Dinner by arrangement.

Rooms 11 rms (9 en suite) (2 pri facs) (3 fmly) (3 GF) **Facilities** TVL tea/coffee Dinner available Cen ht Licensed Wi-fi **Parking** 3

The Sandhill
★★★ ⚑ GUEST ACCOMMODATION

6 Hill St PO36 9DB
☎ **01983 403635** 🖷 **01983 403695**
e-mail: sandhillsandown@aol.com
dir: *In Sandown on main broadway, into Leed St. The Sandhill at top of road*

Rooms 16 en suite (6 fmly) (4 GF) S £30-£40; D £60-£80 **Facilities** FTV Lounge TVL tea/coffee Dinner available Direct Dial Cen ht Licensed Wi-fi ch fac **Parking** 10 **Notes** LB

SEAVIEW
Map 5 SZ69

The Boathouse
★★★★ ⇔ INN

Springvale Rd PO34 5AW
☎ **01983 810616 & 811784** 🖷 **01983 811784**
e-mail: info@theboathouseiow.co.uk

This very pleasant inn has a shore side location and is a relaxing, friendly and comfortable place to stay. Food is a focus here with fresh, local produce and speciality lobster and crab dishes. The inn provides a contemporary style throughout; bedrooms are pleasantly spacious and most have beach views. There is ample parking and a garden where in warmer times food and drink are served.

Rooms 4 en suite (1 fmly) S £55-£75; D £100-£120* **Facilities** FTV DVD iPod docking station tea/coffee Dinner available Cen ht Wi-fi **Parking** 20 **Notes** LB No coaches

SHANKLIN Map 5 SZ58

Fernbank

★★★★ GUEST ACCOMMODATION

6 Highfield Rd PO37 6PP
☎ 01983 862790
e-mail: fernbank2010@btconnect.com
dir: *Approaching Shanklin on A3020, right into Highfield Rd. 300yds on left*

Located in the Shanklin Old Village, this newly renovated establishment offers modern, comfortable and spacious accommodation. Home-made refreshments are available throughout the afternoon and guests can enjoy a wide range of both cooked and continental breakfasts in the airy dining room. There is an indoor swimming pool and plenty of outside space within the sup-tropical landscaped gardens in which to relax. Free Wi-fi is available throughout.

Rooms 17 en suite (2 fmly) (2 GF) **Facilities** FTV tea/coffee Cen ht Licensed Wi-fi 🐾 Petanque **Parking** 13 **Notes** ⊗ No Children 5yrs Closed Nov-Feb

The Avenue

★★★★ GUEST ACCOMMODATION

6 Avenue Rd PO37 7BG
☎ 01983 862746
e-mail: info@avenuehotelshanklin.co.uk
dir: *A3055 from Sandown, through Lake, right into Avenue Rd before x-rds lights*

This friendly, family-run guest accommodation is in a quiet location just a five minute walk from the town centre and beaches. The well-equipped bedrooms are generally spacious, and there is a bar-lounge, a conservatory and a comfortable breakfast room. An attractive terraced courtyard lies to the rear.

Rooms 10 en suite (2 GF) S £35-£45; D £78-£82*
Facilities FTV Lounge tea/coffee Cen ht Licensed Wi-fi **Parking** 6 **Notes** LB ⊗ Closed Nov-Feb

The Bedford Lodge

★★★★ GUEST ACCOMMODATION

4 Chine Av PO37 6AA
☎ 01983 862416 📠 01983 868704
e-mail: mail@bedfordlodge.co.uk
web: www.bedfordlodge.co.uk
dir: *A3055 into Chine Av opposite Tower Cottage Gardens*

A particularly warm welcome is guaranteed at this delightful property. The Bedford Lodge benefits from an unspoilt and quiet location with pretty gardens and is extremely close to Shanklin Old Village and Shanklin beach. Bedrooms are well equipped and comfortable. A delicious breakfast is served at individual dining tables in the attractive dining room; in addition a bar and lounge is available for guests' use.

Rooms 14 en suite (1 fmly) (2 GF) **Facilities** TVL tea/coffee Cen ht Wi-fi **Parking** 8 **Notes** No Children 5yrs

The Belmont

★★★★ GUEST ACCOMMODATION

8 Queens Rd PO37 6AN
☎ 01983 862864 & 867875
e-mail: enquiries@belmont-iow.co.uk
dir: *From Sandown (on A3055), half turn left at Fiveways lights signed Ventnor. Belmont 400mtrs on right, opposite St Saviour's Church*

Situated less than ten minutes' walk from Shanklin beach and only five minutes from Shanklin Old Village is The Belmont. This establishment offers comfortable accommodation and several rooms have stunning sea views. The Belmont is licensed, and beverages and sandwiches are available during the day time and evening. Off-road parking is a benefit, and during summer months guests can enjoy the outdoor swimming pool.

Rooms 13 en suite (2 fmly) (2 GF) **Facilities** FTV tea/coffee Direct Dial Licensed Wi-fi 🐾 **Parking** 9 **Notes** ⊗ No Children 5yrs

The Grange

★★★★ GUEST ACCOMMODATION

9 Eastcliff Rd PO37 6AA
☎ 01983 867644 📠 01983 865537
e-mail: jenni@thegrangebythesea.com
web: www.thegrangebythesea.com
dir: *Off A3055, High St*

This delightful house specialises in holistic breaks and enjoys a tranquil yet convenient setting in manicured grounds close to the seafront and village centre. Extensive refurbishment has resulted in beautifully presented bedrooms and spacious public areas. Breakfast is taken en famille (outside in fine weather).

Rooms 16 en suite (2 fmly) (6 GF) S £69-£83; D £88-£116* **Facilities** TVL tea/coffee Cen ht Licensed Wi-fi Sauna Beauty treatments & massage **Parking** 8 **Notes** LB ⊗ Civ Wed 100

Hayes Barton

★★★★ GUEST ACCOMMODATION

7 Highfield Rd PO37 6PP
☎ 01983 867747
e-mail: williams.2000@virgin.net
web: www.hayesbarton.co.uk
dir: *A3055 onto A3020 Victoria Ave, 3rd left*

Hayes Barton has the relaxed atmosphere of a family home and provides well-equipped bedrooms and a range of comfortable public areas. Dinner is available from a short selection of home-cooked dishes, and there is a cosy bar lounge. The old village, beach and promenade are all within walking distance.

Rooms 9 en suite (4 fmly) (2 GF) S £31-£35; D £62-£70* **Facilities** FTV TVL tea/coffee Dinner available Cen ht Licensed Wi-fi **Parking** 9 **Notes** LB Closed Nov-Mar

Save on B&Bs and Hotels. Book at theAA.com/hotel

WIGHT, ISLE OF 315 ENGLAND

Hopecliff Guest House

★★★★ GUEST ACCOMMODATION

12 Northcliff Gardens PO37 6ES
☎ 01983 866235 📠 01983 866235
e-mail: hopecliff@hotmail.co.uk
dir: On A3055, pass Wiltons garage on right, turn left onto St Martins Av, at end on right

This is a family-run guest accommodation located on a quiet road just a couple of minutes walk along the coastal path into Shanklin. Bedrooms are comfortable throughout and come well equipped with Wi-fi and TV/DVD available. Well stocked beverage trays and lots of little extras make this a true home-from-home experience. There is additional space for guests to relax in the lounge area and a selection of cooked and continental dishes at breakfast is served in the conservatory.

Rooms 4 rms (3 en suite) (1 pri facs) (1 fmly) (1 GF) D £50-£60* **Facilities** STV FTV DVD TVL tea/coffee Cen ht Wi-fi 🅿 **Parking** 4 **Notes** 🚭

The Rowborough

★★★★ GUEST ACCOMMODATION

32 Arthurs Hill PO37 6EX
☎ 01983 866072 & 863070
e-mail: susanpatricia@btconnect.com
web: www.rowboroughhotel.com
dir: Between Sandown & Shanklin

Located on the main road into town, this charming, family-run establishment provides comfortable bedrooms with many extra facilities. The non-smoking conservatory overlooks the garden, along with a lounge and a bar. Dinner is available by arrangement.

Rooms 9 en suite (5 fmly) (1 GF) S £34-£40; D £68-£80* **Facilities** FTV Lounge TVL tea/coffee Dinner available Cen ht Licensed Wi-fi DVD players in all rooms **Parking** 5 **Notes** LB

St Georges House

★★★★ GUEST ACCOMMODATION

2 St Georges Rd PO37 6BA
☎ 01983 863691 📠 01983 861597
e-mail: info@stgeorgesiow.com
web: www.stgeorgesiow.com
dir: S from Fiveways turn 2nd right off A3055, next right

A warm welcome is assured at this family-run property located in a quiet area between the town centre and cliff top. Bedrooms vary in size but all are comfortable and well appointed. Guests have use of the lounge and bar.

Rooms 9 en suite (1 fmly) (1 GF) S £32-£44; D £64-£88* **Facilities** FTV TVL tea/coffee Cen ht Licensed Wi-fi 🅿 **Parking** 7 **Notes** LB Closed mid Dec-mid Jan

The Braemar

★★★ GUEST HOUSE

1 Grange Rd PO37 6NN
☎ 01983 863172 📠 01983 863172
e-mail: djsherfield@aol.com

Tucked away in Shanklin Old Village, expect a warm welcome at this family-run, licensed guest house. Bedrooms are comfortable and vary in size. Breakfast is served in the bright dining room overlooking the gardens.

Rooms 11 en suite (2 fmly) (3 GF) **Facilities** TVL tea/coffee Cen ht Licensed Wi-fi Pool table **Parking** 10

TOTLAND BAY	Map 5 SZ38

PREMIER COLLECTION

Sentry Mead

★★★★★ GUEST ACCOMMODATION

Madeira Rd PO39 0BJ
☎ 01983 753212 📠 01983 754710
e-mail: info@sentrymead.co.uk
dir: From Yarmouth onto A3054 to Freshwater, 2m, straight over at rdbt, right at next rdbt into Madeira Rd, 300yds on right

This country house is located in Totland Bay, the West Wight part of the Isle of Wight. Bedrooms have been tastefully decorated to offer guests traditional yet stylish accommodation, all well equipped with Wi-fi and digital TV. Public areas are spacious; guests can relax in the main lounge or conservatory area, both with views of the large well tended garden. Guests can enjoy a selection of cooked breakfasts and continental dishes in the dining room.

Rooms 11 en suite (1 fmly) S £55-£60; D £70-£135* **Facilities** FTV iPod docking station tea/coffee Direct Dial Cen ht Licensed Wi-fi ⚓ 18 🅿 Day membership to West Bay Country Club **Parking** 9 **Notes** LB

Whitefield

★★★★ BED AND BREAKFAST

Madeira Rd PO39 0BJ
☎ 01983 752041
e-mail: whitefieldiow@btinternet.com

Whitefield is located in the West Wight area in Totland Bay and just a few miles away from Yarmouth. The two bedrooms are well presented and offer guests comfortable accommodation. There's a spacious art studio on the top floor which guests can use during their stay, as well as a comfortable guest lounge where beverages on arrival can be enjoyed, and a family style dining room where guests can enjoy both a cooked and continental breakfast.

Rooms 2 en suite **Facilities** FTV tea/coffee Cen ht Wi-fi ⚓ 18 **Parking** **Notes** ⊗ No Children 12yrs 🚭

The Golf House

★★★★ 🍴 BED AND BREAKFAST

Alum Bay New Rd PO39 0JA
☎ 01983 753293
e-mail: sue@thegolfhouse.info
web: www.thegolfhouse.info
dir: A3054 (or A3055) into Totland, onto A3322 (The Broadway). At Totland War Memorial rdbt 2nd exit into Church Hill towards Alum Bay. Approx 1m, house on left

The Golf House is a detached house in its own grounds situated at the western tip of the Isle of Wight with all rooms enjoying amazing views. Two bedrooms, each with TVs, create a two-bedroom suite with one bathroom which can accommodate up to four guests, and the second bedroom has en suite facilities. Local produce is used where possible and evening snacks are available by prior arrangement. Transport to and from Yarmouth can be arranged.

Rooms 3 rms (1 en suite) (2 pri facs) S £50-£60; D £75-£100* **Facilities** STV FTV DVD TVL tea/coffee Cen ht Wi-fi Snooker 🅿 **Parking** 3 **Notes** LB

The Hoo

★★★★ BED AND BREAKFAST

Colwell Rd PO39 0AB
☎ 01983 753592 📠 01983 753592
e-mail: the.hoo@btinternet.com
dir: From Yarmouth ferry right onto A3054, 2.25m enter Colwell Common. The Hoo on corner of Colwell Rd & Warden Rd

Located close to the port and beaches, this friendly family home provides a peaceful setting. The house has many Japanese features and guests are asked to wear slippers. The spacious bedrooms are well equipped and comfortably furnished. English breakfast is most enjoyable and is served overlooking the attractive gardens.

Rooms 3 rms (1 en suite) (2 fmly) **Facilities** FTV tea/coffee Cen ht Wi-fi **Parking** 1 **Notes** No Children 5yrs

TOTLAND BAY *continued*

The Hermitage

★★★ GUEST ACCOMMODATION

Cliff Rd PO39 0EW
☎ **01983 752518**
e-mail: blake_david@btconnect.com
web: www.thehermitagebnb.co.uk
dir: *From Church Hill (B3322), right into Eden Rd, left into Cliff Rd, 0.5m on right*

The Hermitage is an extremely pet and people friendly establishment which occupies a stunning and unspoilt location near to the cliff top in Totland Bay. Extensive gardens are well maintained and off-road parking is a bonus. Accommodation is comfortable and guests are assured of a genuinely warm welcome at this traditionally styled establishment. A range of delicious items at breakfast provide a substantial start to the day.

Rooms 6 rms (5 en suite) (1 pri facs) (1 fmly)
Facilities FTV Lounge TVL tea/coffee Dinner available ⓑ
Parking 6 **Notes** LB

VENTNOR	Map 5 SZ57

PREMIER COLLECTION

The Hambrough

★★★★★ ⊛⊛⊛ RESTAURANT WITH ROOMS

Hambrough Rd PO38 1SQ
☎ **01983 856333** 🖷 **01983 857260**
e-mail: reservations@robert-thompson.com
dir: *Telephone for directions*

A former Victorian villa set on the hillside above Ventnor and with memorable views out to sea, The Hambrough has a modern, stylish interior with well equipped and boutique-style accommodation. The kitchen team's passion for food is clearly evident in the superb cuisine served in the minimalistic styled restaurant.

Rooms 7 en suite (3 fmly) S £119-£210; D £170-£300*
Facilities STV DVD Lounge tea/coffee Dinner available Direct Dial Cen ht Wi-fi ⓑ **Extras** Fruit - complimentary; mini-bar, snacks - chargeable **Notes** LB ⊗ RS Restaurant closed 1.5wks Apr, 2wks Nov & 2wks Jan No coaches Civ Wed 40

PREMIER COLLECTION

The Leconfield

★★★★★ ⊛ ⓑ GUEST ACCOMMODATION

85 Leeson Rd, Upper Bonchurch PO38 1PU
☎ **01983 852196**
e-mail: enquiries@leconfieldhotel.com
web: www.leconfieldhotel.com
dir: *On A3055, 3m from Shanklin Old Village*

This country house is situated on an elevated position with panoramic sea views above the historic village of Bonchurch. Luxury bedrooms and suites are spacious and individually styled. Public rooms include two lounges and a conservatory, in addition to the Sea Scape restaurant, named after the views, where freshly prepared breakfast and imaginative dinner menus are served. Additional facilities include the outdoor pool, terrace area and ample off-road parking.

Rooms 6 en suite 5 annexe en suite (3 GF) S £48-£185; D £80-£200* **Facilities** DVD iPod docking station Lounge tea/coffee Dinner available Cen ht Licensed Wi-fi ⓑ **Extras** Bath robes **Parking** 14 **Notes** LB ⊗ No Children 16yrs Closed 24-26 Dec & 3-27 Jan

St. Augustine Villa

★★★★ GUEST ACCOMMODATION

Esplanade PO38 1TA
☎ **01983 852285**
e-mail: info@harbourviewhotel.co.uk
web: www.harbourviewhotel.co.uk
dir: *Opposite harbour*

Located on an elevated position with spectacular sea views, this delightful Victorian property next to the Winter Gardens provides well-equipped and comfortable bedrooms. Public areas include a conservatory dining room, lounge, small garden and patio area, all with sea views.

Rooms 9 en suite **Facilities** STV FTV TVL tea/coffee Direct Dial Cen ht Wi-fi **Parking** 8 **Notes** ⊗ No Children 21yrs Closed 5 Jan-1 Feb

St Maur

★★★★ GUEST ACCOMMODATION

Castle Rd PO38 1LG
☎ **01983 852570 & 853645** 🖷 **01983 852306**
e-mail: sales@stmaur.co.uk
dir: *Exit A3055 at end of Park Av into Castle Rd, premises 150yds on left*

A warm welcome awaits guests at this Victorian villa, which is pleasantly and quietly located in an elevated position overlooking the bay. The well-equipped bedrooms are traditionally decorated, while public areas include a spacious lounge and cosy residents' bar. The gardens here are a delight.

Rooms 9 en suite (2 fmly) **Facilities** STV tea/coffee Dinner available Cen ht Licensed **Parking** 9 **Notes** ⊗ No Children 5yrs Closed Dec

Gothic View B&B

★★★ ⓑ ⓦ BED AND BREAKFAST

Town Ln, Chale Green PO38 2JS
☎ **01983 551120 & 07818 864967**
e-mail: info@gothicview.co.uk
dir: *From Cowes A3021, A3054 to Newport (or from Fishbourne B3339 to Newport). Then B3323 to Shorwell, B3399 to Chale. From Yarmouth A3054 to Totland, A3055 to Chale*

This establishment provides comfortable accommodation in a converted Gothic chapel located in the picturesque village of Chale Green. Delicious meals are prepared with the personal tastes of the guest fully catered for, and breakfast is also a treat with a number of home-made, freshly created and healthy items available.

Rooms 3 rms (2 en suite) (1 pri facs) (2 fmly) (3 GF) S £30-£35; D £60-£70* **Facilities** DVD tea/coffee Dinner available Cen ht Wi-fi ⓑ **Extras** Mineral water **Parking** 2 **Notes** LB ⊗ ⓦ

WILTSHIRE

AMESBURY	Map 5 SU14

Mandalay

★★★★ GUEST ACCOMMODATION

15 Stonehenge Rd SP4 7BA
☎ **01980 623733**
e-mail: nick.ramplin@btinternet.com
web: www.mandalayguesthouse.com
dir: *500yds W of town centre, exit High St into Church St & Stonehenge Rd*

Quietly located on the edge of the town, yet within easy reach of Stonehenge and Salisbury Cathedral, this delightful property provides individually decorated rooms. Freshly cooked breakfasts are served in the pleasant breakfast room, which overlooks the landscaped gardens. Please note that a 48-hour cancellation policy is in operation.

Rooms 5 en suite (1 fmly) (1 GF) S £50-£60; D £60-£70 **Facilities** FTV iPod docking station TVL tea/coffee Cen ht Wi-fi ⓑ **Parking** 5 **Notes** ⊗

Save on B&Bs and Hotels. Book at theAA.com/hotel

WILTSHIRE 317 **ENGLAND**

Park House Motel

★★★★ GUEST ACCOMMODATION

SP4 0EG
☎ 01980 629256 ⬚ 01980 629256
e-mail: info@parkhousemotel.com
dir: 5m E of Amesbury. Junct A303 & A338

This family-run establishment offers a warm welcome and is extremely convenient for the A303. Bedrooms are practically equipped with modern facilities and come in a variety of sizes. There is a large dining room where dinner is served during the week, and a cosy bar in which to relax.

Rooms 30 rms (27 en suite) (1 pri facs) (9 fmly) (25 GF)
Facilities STV FTV TVL tea/coffee Dinner available Cen ht Licensed Wi-fi **Parking** 40

Catkin Lodge

★★★ BED AND BREAKFAST

93 Countess Rd SP4 7AT
☎ 01980 624810 & 622139 ⬚ 01980 622139
e-mail: info@catkinlodge.fsnet.co.uk
web: www.catkinlodge.fsnet.co.uk
dir: From A303 at Amesbury onto A345 (Marlborough road), 400yds on left

Popular for business and leisure, Catkin Lodge is close to Stonehenge and offers off-road parking. The two bedrooms offer good levels of comfort and can accommodate children if required. The artwork of the talented proprietor is displayed around the property, adding further interest.

Rooms 2 en suite (2 GF) **Facilities** FTV tea/coffee Cen ht **Parking** 7 **Notes** ⊗ No Children 7yrs ⊛

BOX	Map 4 ST86

PREMIER COLLECTION

The Northey Arms

★★★★★ ⬭ INN

Bath Rd SN13 8AE
☎ 01225 891166
web: www.ohhcompany.co.uk

Refurbished throughout, this stylish inn combines modern comfort and quality with relaxed and welcoming hospitality. The bedrooms and bathrooms are especially comfortable and well equipped, with large walk-in showers, luxurious towels and toiletries. Food is served throughout the day and utilises high quality produce on a menu which has something for everyone.

Rooms 3 en suite **Facilities** Dinner available

The Hermitage

★★ GUEST ACCOMMODATION

Bath Rd SN13 8DT
☎ 01225 744187
e-mail: hermitagebb@btconnect.com
web: www.thehermitage-box.co.uk
dir: On A4 at W end of village

This 16th-century house is located in a pleasant village five miles from Bath. The spacious bedrooms are comfortably furnished, with two rooms in a small adjacent cottage. Breakfast is served in the dining room. There is also a lounge area, and delightful gardens with a heated swimming pool.

Rooms 3 en suite 2 annexe en suite (1 fmly) (1 GF)
Facilities FTV tea/coffee Cen ht ⚓ **Parking** 6 **Notes** ⊗ Closed 22 Dec-6 Jan ⊛

BRADFORD-ON-AVON	Map 4 ST86

Midway Place

★★★★ BED AND BREAKFAST

10 Farleigh Wick BA15 2PU
☎ 01225 863932
e-mail: info@midwayplace.co.uk
web: www.midwayplace.co.uk
dir: On A363 between Bath & Bradford-on-Avon, next to Fox & Hounds pub

This property has been extensively renovated throughout and now offers contemporary bedrooms and bathrooms, and a breakfast area. The resident host offers a naturally relaxed, welcoming style of hospitality. Bedrooms vary in size but are well laid out for guests' comfort and include useful extras. Dinner and lunch are available at the pub next door where guests can usually park their cars while they stay at Midway Place.

Rooms 6 en suite **Facilities** FTV TVL tea/coffee Cen ht Wi-fi **Parking** 6 **Notes** ⊗ Closed 14 Dec-14 Jan

Serendipity

★★★★ BED AND BREAKFAST

19f Bradford Rd, Winsley BA15 2HW
☎ 01225 722380 & 07941 778397
e-mail: vanda.shepherd@tesco.net
dir: A36 onto B3108, 1.5m right into Winsley, establishment on right on main road

Set in a quiet residential area, Serendipity is convenient for visiting nearby Bath. The proprietors are friendly and welcoming, and bedrooms are brightly decorated and equipped with a range of extras. Two bedrooms are on the ground floor. Guests can watch badgers and other wildlife in the gardens during the evening. Breakfast is served in the conservatory overlooking the garden.

Rooms 3 en suite (1 fmly) (2 GF) S £55-£73; D £62-£73
Facilities FTV DVD tea/coffee Cen ht Wi-fi ⬇ ⚲ 36
Parking 5 **Notes** LB ⊗ ⊛

The Tollgate Inn

★★★★ ⚘⚘ INN

Ham Green, Holt BA14 6PX
☎ 01225 782326 ⬚ 01225 782805
e-mail: alison@tollgateholt.co.uk
web: www.tollgateholt.co.uk
dir: A363 Bradford-on-Avon turn left onto B3105, left onto B3107, 100yds on right at W end of Holt

The Tollgate combines the comforts of a traditional inn with excellent food served in delightful surroundings. It stands near the village green in Holt, and is only a short drive from Bath. The bedrooms, varying in size, are well decorated and thoughtfully equipped with welcome extras.

Rooms 4 en suite S £70-£110; D £90-£110 **Facilities** FTV tea/coffee Dinner available Direct Dial Cen ht Wi-fi ⬚ Farm shop & animals **Conf** Max 36 Thtr 36 Board 30 **Parking** 40 **Notes** ⊗ Closed 25-26 Dec & 1 Jan No coaches

BRADFORD-ON-AVON *continued*

Stillmeadow

★★★★ 🅰 BED AND BREAKFAST

18 Bradford Rd, Winsley BA15 2HW
☎ 01225 722119
e-mail: sue.gilby@btinternet.com
dir: *From Bradford-on-Avon on B3108 to rdbt, take 1st exit, 0.25m on left*

Rooms 3 en suite (2 fmly) **Facilities** tea/coffee Cen ht Wi-fi ⚓ 18 Storage for bicycles **Parking** 6 **Notes** ⊗ Closed 24-26 Dec

The Kings Arms

Ⓤ

Monkton Farleigh BA15 2QH
☎ 01225 858705

Currently the rating for this establishment is not confirmed. This may be due to a change of ownership or because it has only recently joined the AA rating scheme.

Rooms 4 en suite **Facilities** FTV tea/coffee Dinner available Direct Dial Wi-fi **Parking** 20

Wayside

★★★ BED AND BREAKFAST

Chittoe Heath SN15 2EH
☎ 01380 850695 & 07770 774460 📠 01380 850696
e-mail: mail@waysideofwiltshire.co.uk
web: www.waysideofwiltshire.co.uk
dir: *From A342 take road signed Spye Park & Chittoe, Wayside 1st on right*

Peacefully located yet only just off the main road, Wayside offers relaxed and comfortable accommodation and bedrooms in a range of shapes and sizes. Guests are welcome to use the lounge and there is even a wood to the rear of the property where guests can enjoy a quiet walk. Good quality ingredients are offered at breakfast, and a wide choice of local inns and restaurants is available for dinner.

Rooms 2 en suite (1 fmly) (1 GF) (2 smoking) S £40; D £70* **Facilities** STV FTV DVD TVL tea/coffee Cen ht Wi-fi ⚓ 18 Riding ♨ 12 acres of private woodland **Parking** 3 **Notes** LB ⊜

PREMIER COLLECTION

The Old House at Home

★★★★★ 🍴 INN

SN14 7LT
☎ 01454 218227
e-mail: office@ohhcompany.co.uk
web: www.ohhcompany.co.uk
dir: *M4 junct 18, A46, B4040 to Acton Turvill, right onto B4039. 1.5m to Burton*

In a pleasant setting, just a couple of miles from the delightful village of Castle Combe, this well-established country inn is run personally by the resident proprietors and their family. Six purpose-built, high quality bedrooms and bathrooms provide plenty of welcome extras, and are located in a stylish block adjacent to the main building. Dinner here should not be missed, with a varied selection of high quality, carefully prepared ingredients used in the dishes, including daily specials.

Rooms 6 annexe en suite (6 GF) S £89-£150; D £89-£150* **Facilities** FTV tea/coffee Dinner available Direct Dial Cen ht Wi-fi **Parking** 20 **Notes** LB ⊗ Closed 25 Dec

Fosse Farmhouse Chambre d'Hote

★★★★ 🍴 BED AND BREAKFAST

Nettleton Shrub SN14 7NJ
☎ 01249 782286 📠 01249 783066
e-mail: caroncooper@fossefarmhouse.com
web: www.fossefarmhouse.com
dir: *1.5m N from Castle Combe on B4039, left at Gib, 1m on right*

Set in quiet countryside not far from Castle Combe, this bed and breakfast has well-equipped bedrooms decorated in keeping with its 18th-century origins. Excellent dinners are served in the farmhouse, and cream teas can be enjoyed in the old stables or the delightful garden.

Rooms 2 en suite (1 fmly) S £70-£80; D £95-£125 **Facilities** FTV DVD Lounge tea/coffee Dinner available Cen ht Licensed Wi-fi ch fac ⚓ 18 ♨ badminton & ping pong in garden **Extras** Speciality toiletries, bottled water, flowers **Conf** Max 15 Thtr 10 Class 10 Board 10 **Parking** 12 **Notes** LB

The Old Rectory

★★★★ BED AND BREAKFAST

SP3 5SU
☎ 01747 820000 📠 01747 820000
e-mail: lynda@theoldrectory-bandb.co.uk
dir: *On A303 in village behind lay-by*

Located on the A303 close to Stonehenge and Longleat, this beautifully restored rectory is an ideal location for those wishing to explore the North Dorset countryside, or as an overnight stop for those travelling onto the West Country. You are guaranteed a warm welcome and a traditional breakfast to set you up for the day. The three en suite bedrooms are individually designed. One of them is a family suite and all offer impressive quality and comfort.

Rooms 3 en suite (1 fmly) S £60-£75; D £75-£90 **Facilities** FTV Lounge tea/coffee Cen ht Wi-fi ♨ **Parking** 6 **Notes** LB Closed Xmas ⊜

Diana Lodge Bed & Breakfast

★★★ BED AND BREAKFAST

Grathie Cottage, 72 Marshfield Rd SN15 1JR
☎ 01249 650306
e-mail: diana.lodge@talktalk.net
dir: *500yds NW of town centre on A420, into West End Club car park*

A cheerful welcome awaits guests at this late 19th-century cottage that is within walking distance of the town centre and the railway station. The comfortable bedrooms are well appointed, and adjacent parking is available.

Rooms 5 rms (3 en suite) (2 pri facs) (1 fmly) (2 GF) **Facilities** FTV tea/coffee Cen ht Wi-fi **Parking** 1 **Notes** ⊗

Save on B&Bs and Hotels. Book at **theAA.com/hotel**

WILTSHIRE 319 ENGLAND

CORSHAM — Map 4 ST87

PREMIER COLLECTION

The Methuen Arms

★★★★★ ⑥⑥ RESTAURANT WITH ROOMS

2 High St SN13 0HB
☎ **01249 717060**
e-mail: info@themethuenarms.com
web: www.themethuenarms.com
dir: M4 junct 17, A350 towards Chippenham, at rdbt take A4 towards Bath. 1m after lights, at next rdbt sharp left into Pickwick Rd, establishment 0.5m on left

This well-established restaurant with rooms in the centre of the thriving town of Corsham provides very high levels of quality and comfort. The bedrooms are modern and stylish with large comfortable beds and spacious, well-equipped bathrooms. Guests can enjoy a drink in the relaxing bar, a light snack in the day or evening, and should not miss the award-winning, high quality, carefully prepared dishes at dinner.

Rooms 12 en suite (3 fmly) **Facilities** FTV tea/coffee Dinner available Direct Dial Cen ht Wi-fi **Conf** Thtr 50 Board 14 **Parking** 50

Thurlestone Lodge

★★★★ BED AND BREAKFAST

13 Prospect SN13 9AD
☎ **01249 713397 & 07815 731131**
e-mail: thurlestonelodge@gmail.com
web: www.thurlestone.webeden.co.uk
dir: 0.25m from Corsham Centre on B3353. 150yds on right after Great Western pub halfway between turnings to Lypiatt Rd & Dicketts Rd

This charming Victorian house is delightfully located in the attractive town of Corsham, convenient for the attractions of the Cotswolds and of Bath. Bedrooms are comfortable, spacious and well appointed. Breakfast is served in the spacious dining room and provides a hearty start to the day.

Rooms 2 en suite (1 fmly) S £52-£65; D £70-£82* **Facilities** FTV DVD iPod docking station tea/coffee Cen ht Wi-fi ⚓ **Parking** 5 **Notes** ⊗ No Children 7yrs Closed Xmas & New Year RS 22 Dec-2 Jan

Pickwick Lodge Farm B&B (ST857708)

★★★★ ⌂ FARMHOUSE

Guyers Ln SN13 0PS
☎ **01249 712207 Mrs G Stafford**
e-mail: bandb@pickwickfarm.co.uk
web: www.pickwickfarm.co.uk
dir: Exit A4, Bath side of Corsham, into Guyers Ln, farmhouse at end on right

This Grade II listed, 17th-century farmhouse is peacefully located on a 300-acre beef and arable farm, within easy reach of Bath. The spacious bedrooms are well equipped with modern facilities and many thoughtful extras. A hearty breakfast using the best local produce is served at a communal table in the dining room.

Rooms 3 rms (2 en suite) (1 pri facs) S £45-£55; D £75-£85* **Facilities** FTV TVL tea/coffee Cen ht Wi-fi Fishing ⚓ **Extras** Speciality toiletries, fruit, home-made cake **Parking** 6 **Notes** LB ⊗ No Children 12yrs ⊜ 300 acres arable/beef

CRICKLADE — Map 5 SU09

Upper Chelworth Farm

★★★ BED AND BREAKFAST

Upper Chelworth SN6 6HD
☎ **01793 750440**
dir: 1.5m W of Cricklade. Off B4040 x-rds for Chelworth Upper Green

Close to the M4 and Swindon, Upper Chelworth Farm offers a genuinely friendly welcome in addition to comfortable bedrooms of varying sizes. There is a spacious lounge with a wood-burning stove, a games room with a pool table and a lovely garden. Breakfast is served in the dining room.

Rooms 7 rms (6 en suite) (1 fmly) **Facilities** TVL TV6B tea/coffee Cen ht Pool table **Parking** 10 **Notes** No Children 5yrs Closed mid Dec-mid Jan ⊜

DEVIZES — Map 4 SU06

PREMIER COLLECTION

Blounts Court Farm

★★★★★ ⌂ BED AND BREAKFAST

Coxhill Ln, Potterne SN10 5PH
☎ **01380 727180**
e-mail: carys@blountscourtfarm.co.uk
dir: A360 to Potterne, into Coxhill Ln opposite George & Dragon, at fork turn left, follow drive uphill to farmhouse

A warm welcome is assured at this peacefully located, delightful arable farm, overlooking the village cricket field. The character barn has been converted to provide three attractive bedrooms on the ground floor - one has a four-poster bed. The elegant decor is in keeping with the character of the house. Breakfast, which features home-made and local produce, is served in the farmhouse dining room.

Rooms 3 en suite (3 GF) S £40-£55; D £70-£78* **Facilities** FTV DVD iPod docking station TVL tea/coffee Cen ht Wi-fi ⚓ **Parking** 5 **Notes** ⊗ No Children 8yrs

Summerhayes B&B

★★★★★ ⌂ BED AND BREAKFAST

143 High St, Littleton Panell SN10 4EU
☎ **01380 813521**
e-mail: summerhayesbandb@btinternet.com
web: www.summerhayesbandb.co.uk
dir: 5m S of Devizes on A360, near x-rds with B3098
Rooms 2 rms (1 en suite) (1 pri facs) (1 fmly) S £55-£60; D £75-£80* **Facilities** STV FTV DVD Lounge TVL tea/coffee Cen ht Wi-fi Sauna ⚓ Hot tub **Extras** Speciality toiletries, bottled water, fruit **Parking** 6 **Notes** LB ⊗

EDINGTON — Map 4 ST95

PREMIER COLLECTION

The Three Daggers

★★★★★ INN

Westbury Rd BA13 4PG
☎ 01380 830940
e-mail: hello@threedaggers.co.uk
dir: A36 towards Warminster then A350 to Westbury then A303 to Edington

Stylishly refurbished to offer luxurious standards of quality and comfort throughout, The Three Daggers combines traditional inn hospitality with contemporary furnishings and decor. Bedrooms and bathrooms are in a range of shapes and sizes but all are appointed with high quality Egyptian cotton bedding, large shower heads and a generous range of welcome extras. The bar and dining area menus offer high quality, carefully prepared ingredients at both dinner and breakfast. A large lounge with a real fire and comfortable seating is also available to guests.

Rooms 3 en suite (1 fmly) Facilities FTV Dinner available Wi-fi Parking 20

FIRSDOWN — Map 5 SU23

Junipers

★★★★ BED AND BREAKFAST

3 Juniper Rd SP5 1SS
☎ 01980 862330
e-mail: junipersbedandbreakfast@btinternet.com
web: www.junipersbedandbreakfast.co.uk
dir: 5m from Salisbury on A30, A343 to London follow Junipers brown signs into Firsdown

Located in a quiet residential area, just five miles from the city, Junipers offers ground floor bedrooms that are well equipped with thoughtful extras. The hosts, who have craft skills, are happy to show guests their interesting items constructed in medieval style. Breakfast, featuring local produce, is served in the cosy dining room/lounge. Junipers was a Runner up in the AA Friendliest B&B of the Year Award 2012-13.

Rooms 3 en suite (3 GF) S £55; D £75 Facilities FTV Lounge tea/coffee Cen ht Wi-fi Parking 6 Notes LB ⊗ No Children

FONTHILL BISHOP — Map 4 ST93

The River Barn

★★★ ⇔ GUEST HOUSE

SP3 5SF
☎ 01747 820232
dir: From Wincanton towards Amesbury on A303 take B3089, through Hindon to Fonthill Bishop. Property on right. Or from Amesbury on A303 left onto unclassified road after Wylye signed Fonthill Bishop. Property on left

Surrounded by lawns stretching down to the river, The River Barn is the central hub of the village of Fonthill Bishop. Parts of the barn are 600 years old and it has operated as a business for the last 100 years. The annexe bedrooms are spacious and well appointed. The café-bar offers sumptuous cakes and cream teas, light lunches and evening meals.

Rooms 4 annexe en suite (1 fmly) (3 GF) Facilities tea/coffee Dinner available Cen ht Licensed Parking 20 Notes ⊗

GRITTLETON — Map 4 ST88

Staddlestones

★★ BED AND BREAKFAST

SN14 6AW
☎ 01249 782458 🖷 01249 782458
e-mail: staddlestonesbb@btinternet.com
dir: 500yds E of village x-rds

The large modern bungalow lies at the east end of the small village, and is convenient for the M4. The local pub is just a stroll away and ample parking is available.

Rooms 3 rms (3 GF) S £40-£60; D £60-£80 Facilities FTV DVD TVL tea/coffee Cen ht Parking 5 Notes ⊗

HINDON — Map 4 ST93

The Lamb Inn

★★★★ ⊛ INN

SP3 6DP
☎ 01747 820573 🖷 01747 820605
e-mail: info@thelambathindon.co.uk
web: www.lambathindon.co.uk
dir: Off B3089 in village centre

This 17th-century coaching inn is in a pretty village within easy reach of Salisbury and Bath. It has been appointed in an eclectic style, and some of the well-equipped bedrooms have four-poster beds. Enjoyable, freshly prepared dishes are available at lunch and dinner in the restaurant or bar, where log fires provide a welcoming atmosphere on colder days.

The Lamb Inn

Rooms 19 rms (13 en suite) 6 annexe en suite (1 fmly) (3 GF) Facilities FTV tea/coffee Dinner available Direct Dial Cen ht Wi-fi Boules court Conf Max 40 Thtr 40 Class 16 Board 24 Parking 16

HORNINGSHAM — Map 4 ST84

The Bath Arms at Longleat

★★★★ ⊛⊛ INN

Longleat Estate BA12 7LY
☎ 01985 844308 🖷 01985 845187
e-mail: enquiries@batharms.co.uk
dir: In village, on Longleat Estate

Peacefully located at the edges of The Longleat Estate, this delightful inn has perhaps best been described as 'quirky luxury'. Bedrooms come in a variety of shapes and sizes; each individually decorated in a range of styles and designs. High quality produce is used to prepare delicious dishes at dinner which is served in the relaxed main restaurant.

Rooms 9 en suite 6 annexe en suite (9 fmly) (1 GF) Facilities FTV tea/coffee Dinner available Direct Dial Cen ht Wi-fi ৬ 18 Parking 6

LOWER CHICKSGROVE — Map 4 ST92

Compasses Inn

★★★★ ⊛ INN

SP3 6NB
☎ 01722 714318 🖷 01722 714318
e-mail: thecompasses@aol.com
web: www.thecompassesinn.com
dir: Exit A30 signed Lower Chicksgrove, 1st left into Lagpond Ln, single-track lane to village

This charming 17th-century inn, within easy reach of Bath, Salisbury, Glastonbury and the Dorset coast, offers comfortable accommodation in a peaceful setting. Carefully prepared dinners are enjoyed in the warm atmosphere of the bar-restaurant, while breakfast is served in a separate dining room.

Rooms 5 en suite (2 fmly) S £50-£65; D £90 **Facilities** FTV iPod docking station tea/coffee Dinner available Cen ht Wi-fi ch fac ♿ **Conf** Max 16 Thtr 16 Class 16 Board 14 **Parking** 40 **Notes** LB Closed 25-26 Dec

---

LUDWELL　Map 4 ST92

The Grove Arms

★★★★ INN

SP7 9ND
☎ 01747 828811 📠 01747 828844
e-mail: info@grovearms-ludwell.co.uk
web: www.grovearms-ludwell.co.uk
dir: 2m E of Shaftesbury on A30

This 16th-century, Grade II listed building is located between Salisbury and Shaftesbury, and provides a great base for exploring the Wiltshire and Dorset countryside. The six en suite bedrooms are comfortable and well equipped. Lunch and dinner menus offer a great choice, enhanced with daily specials; traditional ales are also available.

Rooms 6 en suite (2 fmly) S £48-£75; D £64-£100* **Facilities** Lounge tea/coffee Dinner available Cen ht Wi-fi ♿ 18 ♿ **Parking** 32 **Notes** No coaches

---

MARLBOROUGH　Map 5 SU16

The Lamb Inn

★★★ 🛏 INN

The Parade SN8 1NE
☎ 01672 512668 & 07885 275568 📠 01672 512668
e-mail: thelambinnmarlboro@fsmail.net
web: www.thelambinnmarlborough.com
dir: From High St, right into The Parade, establishment 50yds on left

Located in a quieter area of Marlborough, yet just a couple of minutes from the bustle of the main street, this traditional inn provides a friendly welcome and relaxed ambience. Bedrooms vary in size and are located above the main inn, and in modernised stables adjacent to the pleasant rear garden. Dinner here is a highlight with a good selection of very well cooked and presented dishes using fresh ingredients.

The Lamb Inn

Rooms 3 en suite 3 annexe en suite (1 fmly) S £55-£60; D £80-£90* **Facilities** tea/coffee Dinner available Cen ht Wi-fi ♿ 18 ♿ **Conf** Max 24 **Notes** No coaches

---

MERE　Map 4 ST83

The Walnut Tree Inn

★★★★ 🛏 INN

Shaftesbury Rd BA12 6BH
☎ 01747 861220 & 07763 001119
e-mail: markcassidy661@btinternet.com
dir: A303 take exit signed Mere towards town centre. At clock tower onto Boar St, post office on right. 1m on left

This comfortable inn is located just outside the village and provides quality accommodation. The bedrooms and bathrooms have undergone a refurbishment and are appointed to a high standard including a number of welcome guest extras. The excellent menu, wine and real ale choices offer something for everyone, and meals are served throughout the day and evening. Outdoor seating is provided at both the rear and front of the inn.

Rooms 3 en suite (2 fmly) **Facilities** FTV Dinner available Cen ht Wi-fi **Parking** 16 **Notes** ⊗

REDLYNCH　Map 5 SU22

Rookseat B&B

★ ★ ★ BED AND BREAKFAST

Grove Ln SP5 2NR
☎ 01725 512522 & 07748 550481
e-mail: deanransome@btinternet.com

Expect a friendly welcome at this family-run bed and breakfast situated in the quiet New Forest village of Redlynch, perfect for visiting Salisbury and Bournemouth. Comfortable bedrooms all have en suite shower rooms. A delicious breakfast with plenty of choice is served in the dining room.

Rooms 3 en suite S £45; D £65* **Facilities** FTV tea/coffee Cen ht Wi-fi ♿ **Parking** 3 **Notes** ⊗ No Children 12yrs 🐾

ROWDE　Map 4 ST96

The George & Dragon

★★★★ ◉◉ RESTAURANT WITH ROOMS

High St SN10 2PN
☎ 01380 723053
e-mail: thegandd@tiscali.co.uk
dir: 1.5m from Devizes on A350 towards Chippenham

The George & Dragon dates back to the 14th century when it was a meeting house. Exposed beams, wooden floors, antique rugs and open fires create a warm atmosphere in the bar and restaurant. Bedrooms and bathrooms are very well decorated and equipped with some welcome extras. Dining in the bar or restaurant should not be missed, as local produce and fresh fish deliveries from Cornwall are offered on the daily-changing blackboard menu.

Rooms 3 rms (2 en suite) (1 pri facs) (1 fmly) D fr £65* **Facilities** FTV DVD iPod docking station Lounge TVL tea/coffee Dinner available Cen ht Wi-fi ♿ **Extras** Mini-bar, snacks - complimentary **Parking** 15 **Notes** No coaches

---

SALISBURY　Map 5 SU12

See also Amesbury

PREMIER COLLECTION

Quidhampton Mill

★★★★★ 🛏 BED AND BREAKFAST

Lower Rd, Quidhampton SP2 9BB
☎ 01722 741171
e-mail: quidhamptonmill@waitrose.com
dir: From Salisbury on A36 towards Wilton, at lights left onto B3094 signed Blandford. On left just after turn for Quidhampton

A warm welcome is assured here at Quidhampton Mill. Situated just two miles out of Salisbury, this makes for an ideal base from which to explore the many attractions that Wiltshire has to offer. There are three en suite bedrooms each with its own external access. Rooms are tastefully designed and offer excellent quality and comfort. Award-winning breakfasts are served in the main house and feature a range of excellent coffees and daily specials. Secure off-road parking is available. Quidhampton Mill was a Finalist in the AA Friendliest B&B of the Year Award 2012-13.

Rooms 3 en suite (1 fmly) (2 GF) **Facilities** STV FTV tea/coffee Dinner available Cen ht Wi-fi ♿ 18 **Parking** 7 **Notes** ⊗

SALISBURY *continued*

St Anns House

★★★★ GUEST ACCOMMODATION

32-34 Saint Ann St SP1 2DP
☎ 01722 335657
e-mail: info@stannshouse.co.uk
web: www.stannshouse.co.uk
dir: *From Brown St left into Saint Ann St*

St Anns House is a former public house situated close to the cathedral and city centre. Lovingly restored with many original features and modern creature comforts such as flat screen TVs, this is a high quality operation with a friendly host.

Rooms 8 en suite S £54-£60; D £74-£89* **Facilities** FTV Lounge tea/coffee Cen ht Wi-fi **Extras** Water - complimentary **Conf** Max 16 Thtr 14 Class 14 Board 16 **Notes** ⊗ Closed 23 Dec-2 Jan

Salisbury Old Mill House

★★★★ BED AND BREAKFAST

Warminster Rd, South Newton SP2 0QD
☎ 01722 742458
e-mail: salisburymill@yahoo.com
dir: *4m NW of Salisbury on A36 in South Newton*

This restored watermill exudes character, and the mill machinery is still on view. Friendly and welcoming, the property offers comfortable, well-appointed bedrooms, a lounge with wood-burning stove, and a dining area where dinner is available by arrangement. The garden features the original millpond.

Rooms 3 rms (2 en suite) (1 pri facs) 1 annexe en suite (2 fmly) (2 GF) S £40-£50* **Facilities** FTV Lounge tea/coffee Dinner available Cen ht Licensed Wi-fi ⌣ ⅃ 9 Riding 🏓 Outdoor table tennis **Parking** 6 **Notes** ⊗ Closed 25 Dec & 1 Jan 🖼

Websters

★★★★ GUEST HOUSE

11 Hartington Rd SP2 7LG
☎ 01722 339779
e-mail: enquiries@websters-bed-breakfast.com
dir: *From city centre onto A360 (Devizes Rd), 1st turn on left*

A warm welcome is assured at this delightful property, located in a quiet cul-de-sac close to the city centre. The charming, well-presented bedrooms are equipped with numerous extras including broadband. There is one ground-floor room with easier access.

Rooms 5 en suite (1 GF) **Facilities** FTV TVL tea/coffee Cen ht Wi-fi **Parking** 5 **Notes** ⊗ No Children 12yrs Closed 31 Dec & 1 Jan RS Xmas & New Year continental breakfast only at Xmas

Avonlea House

★★★★ BED AND BREAKFAST

231 Castle Rd SP1 3RY
☎ 01722 338351
e-mail: guests@avonleahouse.co.uk
web: www.avonleahouse.co.uk
dir: *1.5m N of city centre. On A345 near Old Sarum*

Avonlea House has very comfortable and well equipped bedrooms. Breakfast is offered with a choice of fresh local items. The property is located close to Old Sarum and within walking distance of Salisbury city centre, the Cathedral and riverside walks. There are leisure facilities close by in the shape of a swimming pool and gym, and there is easy access to Stonehenge, the New Forest and the South coast.

Rooms 3 en suite S £45-£55; D £65-£75* **Facilities** FTV DVD Lounge tea/coffee Cen ht Wi-fi **Parking** 3 **Notes** ⊗ No Children 12yrs

Cricket Field House

★★★★ GUEST ACCOMMODATION

Skew Bridge, Wilton Rd SP2 9NS
☎ 01722 322595 📠 01722 444970
e-mail: cricketfieldcottage@btinternet.com
dir: *A36, 1m W of Salisbury, towards Wilton & Warminster*

The 19th-century gamekeeper's cottage stands in award-winning gardens overlooking the South Wiltshire Cricket Ground. Within walking distance of the city centre and railway station, Cricket Field House provides a high level of accommodation, hospitality and customer care.

Rooms 7 en suite 10 annexe en suite (10 GF) S £50-£75; D £75-£135* **Facilities** FTV tea/coffee Cen ht Licensed Wi-fi **Conf** Thtr 20 Class 14 Board 16 **Parking** 25 **Notes** ⊗ No Children 14yrs RS 24-26 Dec room only

Newton Farmhouse *(SU230223)*

★★★★ FARMHOUSE

Southampton Rd SP5 2QL
☎ 01794 884416 Mr & Mrs Guild
e-mail: lizzie@newtonfarmhouse.com
web: www.newtonfarmhouse.com

(For full entry see Whiteparish)

The Old House

★★★★ GUEST ACCOMMODATION

161 Wilton Rd SP2 7JQ
☎ 01722 333433 📠 01722 335551
dir: *1m W of city centre on A36*

Located close to the city centre, this non-smoking property dates from the 17th century. Bedrooms have modern facilities and one room has a four-poster bed. There is a spacious lounge and large gardens to enjoy - weather permitting.

Rooms 7 en suite (1 fmly) S £50-£80; D £70-£80* **Facilities** FTV Lounge TVL tea/coffee Cen ht Wi-fi ⅃ 9 **Parking** 10 **Notes** LB ⊗ No Children 7yrs

2 Park Lane

★★★★ GUEST ACCOMMODATION

2 Park Ln SP1 3NP
☎ 01722 321001
web: www.2parklane.co.uk

A stylish period property that has been completely renovated, within walking distance of the city centre and its attractions. Light, airy rooms, comfortable beds and good off-road parking are available.

Rooms 4 en suite **Facilities** FTV tea/coffee Cen ht Wi-fi **Parking** 6 **Notes** ⊗ No Children 6yrs

Melbury House

★★★ BED AND BREAKFAST

46 Stonehenge Rd, Durrington SP4 8BP
☎ 01980 653151
e-mail: jonandcarol@daytons.co.uk
dir: *From A303 (Countess Rd rdbt) take A345. At rdbt right signed Durrington, 5yds, left into Stonehenge Rd*

Melbury House is a traditional small bed and breakfast with warm, friendly hosts. Rooms are fresh and comfortable and it has a great location, handy for Stonehenge and Salisbury. Breakfast is at a family table and is freshly cooked to order - a good start to the day.

Rooms 2 rms (1 en suite) (1 pri facs) (2 fmly) (2 GF) **Facilities** FTV tea/coffee Cen ht Wi-fi **Parking** 4 **Notes** ⊗ No Children 10yrs 🖼

Sarum Heights

★★★ BED AND BREAKFAST

289 Castle Rd SP1 3SB
☎ 01722 421596 & 07931 582357
e-mail: reservations@sarumheights.co.uk

Sarum Heights is a large family home on the outskirts of the city with good off-road parking. Rooms are smart, clean and well appointed with quality beds and linen. Freshly-cooked breakfasts are served at a family table in the kitchen.

Rooms 3 rms (2 en suite) (1 pri facs) S £50-£65; D £60-£70* **Facilities** FTV DVD tea/coffee Cen ht Wi-fi **Parking** 3 **Notes** ⊗ 🖼

Save on B&Bs and Hotels. Book at **theAA.com/hotel**

WILTSHIRE 323 **ENGLAND**

Byways Guest House

★★★ GUEST ACCOMMODATION

31 Fowlers Rd SP1 2QP
☎ **01722 328364** 🖷 **01722 322146**
e-mail: info@bywayshouse.co.uk
web: www.bywayshouse.co.uk
dir: *500yds E of city centre. A30 onto A36 signed Southampton, follow Youth Hostel signs to hostel. Fowlers Rd opposite*

Located in a quiet street with off-road parking, Byways is within walking distance of the town centre. Several bedrooms have been decorated in a Victorian style and another two have four-poster beds. All rooms offer good levels of comfort, with one adapted for easier access.

Rooms 20 rms (19 en suite) (6 fmly) (13 GF) **Facilities** tea/coffee Cen ht Licensed Wi-fi **Conf** Max 8 **Parking** 15 **Notes** Closed Xmas & New Year

Old Mill

★★★ 🍽 INN

Town Path SP2 8EU
☎ **01722 327517** 🖷 **01722 333367**
e-mail: theoldmill@simonandsteve.com
web: www.simonandsteve.com
dir: *A338 onto A3094, turn 3rd right*

Full of character, The Old Mill has an interesting history going back well over five hundred years. Located in tranquil water meadows, the medieval city of Salisbury is just a ten-minute walk along the footpath. Bedrooms come in a range of shapes and sizes and include two above the lively bar. Dinner here is a highlight; the carefully prepared dishes, utilising local produce, should suit all tastes.

Old Mill

Rooms 11 en suite S £50-£70; D £65-£115* **Facilities** FTV DVD tea/coffee Dinner available Direct Dial Cen ht Wi-fi Fishing 🔒 **Extras** Bottled water - complimentary **Conf** Max 43 Class 43 Board 28 **Parking** 17

SEMINGTON Map 4 ST86

The Somerset Arms

★★★★ INN

High St BA14 6JR
☎ **01380 870067**
e-mail: contact@somersetarmssemington.co.uk
dir: *From Melksham take 3rd exit at Semington rdbt signed High St, 1st exit from Trowbridge Way*

Located in a quiet village, this former coaching inn has been providing a warm welcome to visitors for centuries. Its tradition of hospitality is endorsed by the crackling log fires, comfy sofas and an engaging blend of old and new. The bedrooms offer high standards of comfort and quality that include those little extras which make all the difference. The exciting menu utilises local produce whenever possible, and can be enjoyed in the elegant informality of the restaurant.

Rooms 3 en suite S fr £70; D fr £80* **Facilities** FTV DVD Lounge TVL tea/coffee Dinner available Wi-fi 🔒 **Parking** 20 **Notes** LB No coaches

STAPLEFORD Map 5 SU03

Oak Bluffs

★★★ BED AND BREAKFAST

4 Church Furlong SP3 4QE
☎ **01722 790663 & 07796 893502** 🖷 **01722 790663**
dir: *In village centre off B3083*

A warm and friendly welcome awaits at this immaculately presented bungalow situated in a delightful village, complete with an ancient church and many thatched properties. Convenient for visiting Stonehenge, the well appointed bedroom has its own separate entrance, with lots of thoughtful extras provided. A couple of pubs are within walking distance.

Rooms 1 en suite (1 GF) S £35-£40; D £45-£55* **Facilities** STV FTV tea/coffee Cen ht 🔒 9 **Parking** 1 **Notes** 🚭

STOURTON Map 4 ST73

Spread Eagle Inn

★★★★ 🍽 INN

Church Lawn BA12 6QE
☎ **01747 840587**
e-mail: enquiries@spreadeagleinn.com
web: www.spreadeagleinn.com
dir: *0.5m W off B3092 at entrance to Stourhead Gardens*

Set in the beautiful grounds of Stourhead House with its Palladian temples, lakes and inspiring vistas, the Spread Eagle is an impressive red-brick building with a good reputation for simple, honest and locally-sourced food. In the bedrooms, National Trust antiques sit side by side with modern comforts. The large Georgian windows, low ceilings and uneven floors add to the authentic atmosphere of this delightful country house.

Rooms 5 en suite **Facilities** tea/coffee Dinner available Direct Dial Cen ht Wi-fi **Conf** Max 30 Thtr 30 Board 20 **Notes** 🚫

SWINDON Map 5 SU18

Ardecca

★★★★ GUEST ACCOMMODATION

Fieldrise Farm, Kingsdown Ln, Blunsdon SN25 5DL
☎ **01793 721238 & 07791 120826**
e-mail: chris-graham.ardecca@fsmail.net
web: www.ardecca-bedandbreakfast.co.uk
dir: *A419 onto B4019 to Blunsdon/Highworth, then into Turnpike Rd at Cold Harbour pub, left into Kingsdown Ln*

Ardecca is quietly located in 16 acres of pastureland with easy access to Swindon and the Cotswolds. All bedrooms are on the ground floor and are well furnished and equipped. An especially friendly welcome is provided and Arts & Crafts workshops are available on site.

Rooms 4 rms (4 pri facs) (1 fmly) (4 GF) (4 smoking) **Facilities** FTV tea/coffee Cen ht Wi-fi Art & Crafts workshops **Conf** Class 16 **Parking** 5 **Notes** 🚫 No Children 6yrs 🚭

SWINDON *continued*

The Old Post Office Guest House

★★★★ GUEST HOUSE

Thornhill Rd, South Marston SN3 4RY
☎ 01793 823114 📠 01793 823441
e-mail: theoldpostofficeguesthouse@yahoo.co.uk
web: www.theoldpostofficeguesthouse.co.uk
dir: *M4 junct 15, A419 signed Cirencester/Swindon
(East), approx 3m, left onto A420 towards Oxford, at
next rdbt 2nd exit into Merlin Way, 0.3m, at White Hart
rdbt 3rd exit onto A420. At Gablecross rdbt follow South
Marston signs*

Sympathetically extended, this attractive property is
about two miles from Swindon. Guests are welcomed by
the enthusiastic owner, a professional opera singer with
a wonderful sense of humour. The comfortable bedrooms
vary in size, and all are equipped with numerous
facilities. An extensive choice is offered at breakfast,
which is freshly cooked and uses the best local produce.

Rooms 5 en suite (1 fmly) **Facilities** STV tea/coffee
Cen ht Wi-fi **Parking** 6 **Notes** ⊗

Tawny Owl

★★★★ INN

Queen Elizabeth Dr, Taw Hill SN25 1WP
☎ 01793 706770 📠 01793 706785
e-mail: tawnyowl@arkells.com
web: www.arkells.com
dir: *2.5m NW of town centre, signed from A419*

Expect a genuinely friendly welcome from the staff at this
modern inn on the north-west outskirts of Swindon. It has
comfortable, well-equipped bedrooms and bathrooms. A
varied selection of enjoyable home-cooked meals is on
offer at both lunch and dinner together with a range of
Arkells ales and wines. A private function room is
available.

Rooms 5 en suite (1 fmly) **Facilities** TVL tea/coffee Dinner
available Direct Dial Cen ht Stairlift **Conf** Max 55 Thtr 55
Class 55 Board 55 **Parking** 75 **Notes** ⊗ RS Xmas/New
Year Civ Wed 50

Fairview Guest House

★★★ GUEST HOUSE

52 Swindon Rd, Royal Wootton Bassett SN4 8EU
☎ 01793 852283
e-mail: fairviewguesthouse@mail.com
web: www.fairviewguesthouse.com
dir: *On A3102 to Royal Wootton Bassett. 1.25m from M4
junct 16. 5m from Swindon centre*

A welcoming, family-run property with easy access to the
M4 and the town of Swindon. Bedrooms are split between
the main house and the bungalow annexe, and breakfast
is served in an open-plan dining/sitting room with an
open fire on cooler mornings.

Rooms 8 rms (3 en suite) 4 annexe rms 3 annexe en suite
(1 pri facs) (2 fmly) (4 GF) S £32-£39.50; D £50-£60*
Facilities FTV Lounge TVL tea/coffee Cen ht Wi-fi
Parking 14 **Notes** LB ⊗ 🐾

Heart in Hand

★★★ INN

43 High St, Blunsdon SN26 7AG
☎ 01793 721314 📠 01793 727026
e-mail: leppardsteve@aol.com
dir: *Exit A419 into High St, 200yds on right*

Located in the village centre, this family-run inn offers a
friendly welcome together with a wide selection of home-
cooked food. Bedrooms are spacious, well equipped and
offer a number of useful extras. A pleasant patio and rear
garden with seating is also available.

Rooms 4 en suite (1 fmly) **Facilities** tea/coffee Dinner
available Cen ht **Parking** 17 **Notes** ⊗

Internos B&B

★★★ BED AND BREAKFAST

3 Turnpike Rd, Blunsdon SN26 7EA
☎ 01793 721496 📠 01793 721496
web: www.internos-bedandbreakfast.co.uk
dir: *4m N of Swindon. Alongside A419 access from Cold
Harbour End*

Situated just off the A419, this establishment offers
comfortable accommodation and a relaxed and informal
atmosphere. The gardens open onto a field, which is a
haven for wildlife. Guests can enjoy the freshly-cooked
breakfasts, served in the dining room, and a cosy lounge
is also available.

Rooms 3 rms (1 fmly) S £25-£27; D £42-£54*
Facilities FTV TVL tea/coffee Cen ht Wi-fi **Parking** 6
Notes ⊗ 🐾

Saracens Head

★★ INN

High St, Highworth SN6 7AG
☎ 01793 762284 📠 01793 767869
e-mail: arkells@arkells.com
dir: *5m NE of Swindon*

This establishment stands on the main street of a
pleasant market town, close to Swindon. It offers plenty
of character, including a popular bar dating from 1828. A
fine selection of real ales and home-cooked food are
highlights. Bedrooms, which vary in size, are generally
compact. A rear car park and a patio area are available.

Rooms 13 en suite (2 fmly) S £35-£90; D £50-£110*
Facilities tea/coffee Dinner available Direct Dial Cen ht
Wi-fi **Conf** Max 10 Thtr 10 Class 10 Board 10 **Parking** 30
Notes LB

TROWBRIDGE   Map 4 ST85

Eastbrook Cottage

★★★★ BED AND BREAKFAST

Hoopers Pool, Southwick BA14 9NG
☎ 01225 764403
e-mail: enquiries@eastbrookcottage.co.uk
web: www.eastbrookcottage.co.uk
dir: *2m SW of Trowbridge. Off A361 between Rode &
Southwick*

This cottage, situated just off the main Frome road, offers
fresh, smart accommodation. Although the bedrooms are
not the most spacious, they are finished to a high
standard and are equipped with many thoughtful extras.
Guests may not want to move from the wood-burning
stove in the snug lounge. Breakfast, featuring local
produce whenever possible, is enjoyed around a large oak
table. The host offers genuine hospitality and
friendliness.

Rooms 3 rms (2 en suite) (1 pri facs) **Facilities** tea/
coffee Cen ht Wi-fi **Parking** 5 **Notes** ⊗ No Children 10yrs
🐾

The Mill House (ST810576)

★★★★ FARMHOUSE

Stowford Manor Farm, Wingfield BA14 9LH
☎ 07916 138072 & 01225 781318   Mr & Mrs Bryant
e-mail: stowford1@supanet.com
web: www.stowfordmanorfarm.co.uk
dir: *On A366 3m W of Trowbridge, on left*

Peacefully located and surrounded by delightful
countryside, this traditional farmhouse accommodation
proves to be a relaxing retreat. Guests can watch the
various animals and birdlife from the breakfast room. The
bedrooms come in a variety of shapes and sizes, and are
on the first floor accessed by fairly steep steps; one room
looks directly over the river. Breakfast is a real treat and
utilises fresh fruit and much produce from the farm
including milk, sausages and bacon.

Rooms 3 en suite (1 fmly) S £45-£60; D £80-£90*
Facilities FTV tea/coffee Dinner available Cen ht Wi-fi
Fishing 🐾 **Parking** 4 **Notes** LB ⊗ Closed Dec 100 acres
mixed

WARMINSTER   Map 4 ST84

The George Inn

★★★★ INN

Longbridge Deverill BA12 7DG
☎ 01985 840396 📠 01985 841333
e-mail: info@the-georgeinn.co.uk
web: www.the-georgeinn.co.uk
dir: 3m S on A350

The George Inn combines a friendly village pub
atmosphere with modern well-equipped bedrooms; one
with a four-poster bed. In addition to the pleasant bar/
restaurant, there is a cosy first-floor lounge and a
charming river garden in which to enjoy a cool summer
drink. There is an extensive menu available featuring a
selection of home-cooked dishes.

Rooms 12 en suite (5 fmly) S £65-£70; D £80-£90*
Facilities FTV tea/coffee Dinner available Direct Dial
Cen ht Wi-fi **Extras** Bottled water - complimentary
Conf Max 120 Thtr 50 Class 50 Board 30 **Parking** 100
Notes LB ⊗ RS Xmas closed pm

The Dove Inn

★★★ ⊛ INN

Corton BA12 0SZ
☎ 01985 850109 📠 01985 851041
e-mail: info@thedove.co.uk
dir: 5m SE of Warminster. Exit A36 to Corton

Quietly located in the village of Corton, this traditional
inn has undergone many changes and now provides,
along with a friendly welcome, plenty of quality and
comfort. In addition to lighter options, a range of well-
sourced, quality produce is used in the enjoyable dinners
served in the main restaurant. There is a choice of
standard bedrooms adjacent to the inn, and two more
luxurious rooms in a cottage appointed to high standards.

Rooms 7 annexe en suite (1 fmly) (5 GF) **Facilities** FTV
tea/coffee Dinner available Cen ht Wi-fi **Parking** 24

WHITEPARISH   Map 5 SU22

Brayford

★★★★ BED AND BREAKFAST

Newton Ln SP5 2QQ
☎ 01794 884216
e-mail: reservations@brayford.org.uk
dir: Exit A36 at Newton x-rds into Newton Ln towards
Whiteparish. Brayford 150yds on right

A genuine welcome awaits guests at this comfortable
family home. Peacefully located with views over
neighbouring farmland, the house is just a short drive
from the A36. Suitable for business and leisure travellers,
bedrooms are well equipped with many thoughtful extras.
Guests are invited to relax in the lounge dining room,
where a tasty breakfast is served.

Rooms 3 rms (2 pri facs) (1 fmly) (2 GF) S £40-£50;
D £70-£80* **Facilities** FTV DVD TVL tea/coffee Cen ht
Wi-fi 🐾 **Parking** 2 **Notes** ⊗ Closed Xmas & New Year 🐾

Newton Farmhouse (SU230223)

★★★★ FARMHOUSE

Southampton Rd SP5 2QL
☎ 01794 884416 Mr & Mrs Guild
e-mail: lizzie@newtonfarmhouse.com
web: www.newtonfarmhouse.com
dir: 7m SE of Salisbury on A36, 1m S of A27 junct

Dating back to the 16th century, this delightful
farmhouse was gifted to Lord Nelson's family as part of
the Trafalgar estate. The house has been thoughtfully
restored and bedrooms, most with four-poster beds, have
been adorned with personal touches. Delicious breakfasts
are available in the relaxing conservatory. The pleasant
gardens include an outdoor swimming pool.

Rooms 6 en suite 2 annexe en suite (3 fmly) (4 GF)
S £55-£90; D £90-£150* **Facilities** FTV DVD TVL tea/
coffee Cen ht Wi-fi ⤴ 🐾 🐾 **Extras** Speciality toiletries,
sweets **Parking** 8 **Notes** LB ⊗ 2.5 acres non-working

WHITLEY   Map 4 ST86

Marco Pierre White The Pear Tree Inn

Ⓤ

Top Ln SN12 8QX
☎ 01225 709131

Currently the rating for this establishment is not
confirmed. This may be due to a change of ownership or
because it has only recently joined the AA rating scheme.

Rooms 6 en suite **Facilities** FTV tea/coffee Dinner
available Direct Dial Wi-fi **Parking** 30

ZEALS   Map 4 ST73

Cornerways Cottage

★★★★ BED AND BREAKFAST

Longcross BA12 6LL
☎ 01747 840477
e-mail: cornerways.cottage@btinternet.com
dir: A303 onto B3092 signed Stourhead. At bottom of slip
road, right under bridge, follow signs for Zeals. On left
by 40mph sign

A warm friendly welcome, comfortable rooms and hearty
breakfasts await in this charming 250-year-old stone
cottage. Situated right on the borders of Somerset, Dorset
and Wiltshire it is ideal for visiting Longleat, Stourhead
House and Gardens or for simply touring the local area.
Horseriding, fishing, the Wiltshire Cycleway and plenty of
great walks are all on the doorstep.

Rooms 3 rms (2 en suite) (1 pri facs) S fr £50; D £65*
Facilities FTV Lounge TVL tea/coffee Cen ht Wi-fi ⤴ 9 🐾
Extras Bottled water **Parking** 10 **Notes** ⊗ No Children
8yrs Closed Xmas & New Year

WORCESTERSHIRE

ALVECHURCH   Map 10 SP07

Alcott Farm (SP056739)

★★★ 🅰 FARMHOUSE

Icknield St, Weatheroak B48 7EH
☎ 01564 824051 📠 01564 829799 Mrs J Poole
e-mail: alcottfarm@btinternet.com
web: www.alcottfarm.co.uk
dir: 2m NE of Alvechurch. M42 junct 3, A435 for
Birmingham, left signed Weatheroak, left at x-rds down
steep hill, left opposite pub, farm 0.5m on right up long
driveway

Rooms 4 en suite (1 GF) **Facilities** TVL tea/coffee Cen ht
Wi-fi Fishing **Parking** 20 **Notes** ⊗ No Children 10yrs 66
acres horses

ASTWOOD BANK   Map 10 SP06

Corner Cottage

★★★ BED AND BREAKFAST

1194 Evesham Rd B96 6AA
☎ 01527 459122 & 07917 582884 📠 01527 459122
e-mail: marilyn_alan1194@hotmail.co.uk
dir: A441 through Astwood Bank, Corner Cottage at lights

A warm welcome awaits you at Corner Cottage, a
beautiful Victorian cottage set in a pristine village
location within walking distance of pubs, shops and
restaurants. Convenient for Statford-upon-Avon,
Evesham, Warwick, Birmingham and Worcester.

Rooms 3 rms (2 en suite) (1 pri facs) (3 fmly)
D £50-£55* **Facilities** FTV TVL tea/coffee Cen ht Wi-fi
Notes LB ⊗ 🐾

BECKFORD
Map 10 SO93

The Beckford Inn
★★★★ INN

Cheltenham Rd GL20 7AN
☎ 01386 881532
e-mail: enquiries@thebeckford.com
dir: M5 junct 9, A46 towards Evesham, inn on left

Looking more like a country mansion than a typical inn, this is a superb Cotswold-stone building with 18th-century origins. Comfortable accommodation is provided and there's a good range of choices at dinner and breakfast; a snug is available with a widescreen TV. The Beckford is a good venue for parties, weddings or conferences. There is ample parking and disabled access.

Rooms 11 rms (8 en suite) (3 pri facs) 2 annexe en suite (2 fmly) **Facilities** FTV tea/coffee Dinner available Cen ht Wi-fi **Conf** Max 100 Thtr 100 Class 60 Board 100 **Parking** 70 **Notes** Civ Wed 60

BEWDLEY
Map 10 SO77

PREMIER COLLECTION

Kateshill House
★★★★★ 👤 GUEST ACCOMMODATION

Red Hill DY12 2DR
☎ 01299 401563
e-mail: info@kateshillhouse.co.uk
web: www.kateshillhouse.co.uk
dir: A456 onto B4195 signed Bewdley. Bear left over bridge, 1st left into Severnside South. Right into Lax Ln, at T-junct turn left, up hill on right

A very warm welcome awaits at this Georgian manor house overlooking Bewdley. Two acres of landscaped gardens provide a dramatic backdrop to the house, as well as fruit for breakfasts and home-made jams. The elegant bedrooms are individually styled, sumptuously decorated with rich fabrics and period furniture, and equipped with a wealth of amenities for guests' use. Small private functions are also catered for.

Rooms 7 en suite S £65-£75; D £85-£100 **Facilities** FTV TVL tea/coffee Cen ht Wi-fi ch fac **Parking** 10 **Notes** LB ⊗

PREMIER COLLECTION

Number Thirty
★★★★★ BED AND BREAKFAST

30 Gardners Meadow DY12 2DG
☎ 01299 402404
e-mail: info@numberthirty.net
dir: From A456 take B4195 (Stourport Rd) signed Bewdley. Bear left, over Bewdley Bridge (Load St). 1st left into Severnside South, 2nd right into Gardners Meadow

A warm welcome is assured at this smart modern house, a short stroll from the River Severn and the Georgian town centre. Bedrooms are luxuriously furnished and have lots of thoughtful extras. Comprehensive breakfasts are taken in an attractive dining room that overlooks the immaculate gardens and cricket ground; guests can enjoy watching a game from a raised sun deck. A sumptuous guest lounge is also available.

Rooms 3 en suite S fr £60; D fr £75 **Facilities** STV TVL tea/coffee Cen ht Wi-fi ⚡ 18 **Extras** Robes, sherry, sweets - complimentary **Parking** 6 **Notes** ⊗ No Children 10yrs ⊗

The Mug House Inn
★★★★★ 🍴 INN

12 Severnside North DY12 2EE
☎ 01299 402543
e-mail: drew@mughousebewdley.co.uk
web: www.mughousebewdley.co.uk
dir: In town centre on riverfront

Located on the opposite side of the River Severn to Bewdley Rowing Club, this 18th-century inn has been renovated to combine high standards of comfort and facilities with many original features. Bedrooms are thoughtfully furnished, there is a separate breakfast room, and imaginative dinners are served in the restaurant.

Rooms 4 en suite 3 annexe en suite (2 fmly) (1 GF) S £67-£97; D £77-£97* **Facilities** tea/coffee Dinner available Cen ht Wi-fi **Notes** No Children 10yrs No coaches

Royal Forester Country Inn
★★★★ 🍴 INN

Callow Hill DY14 9XW
☎ 01299 266286
e-mail: contact@royalforesterinn.co.uk

Located opposite The Wyre Forest on the town's outskirts, this inn dates back to 1411 and has been sympathetically restored to provide high standards of comfort. Stylish modern bedrooms are complemented by smart bathrooms, and equipped with many thoughtful extras. Decor styles throughout the public areas highlight the many period features, and the restaurant serves imaginative food featuring locally sourced produce.

Rooms 7 en suite (2 fmly) **Facilities** STV FTV tea/coffee Dinner available Cen ht Wi-fi **Parking** 40 **Notes** No coaches

Welchgate Guest House
★★★★ GUEST HOUSE

1 Welch Gate DY12 2AT
☎ 01299 402655
e-mail: info@welchgate-guesthouse.co.uk
web: www.welchgate-guesthouse.co.uk

A warm welcome is assured at this 400-year-old former inn, which has been sympathetically restored to provide modern comforts and good facilities. Bedrooms are equipped with fine furnishings and thoughtful extras, and have smart modern en suite shower rooms. Hearty breakfasts are taken in a rustically furnished café which is also open to the public during the day.

Rooms 4 en suite **Facilities** tea/coffee Cen ht Licensed Wi-fi **Parking** 4 **Notes** LB ⊗ No Children

Bank House
★★★ BED AND BREAKFAST

14 Lower Park DY12 2DP
☎ 01299 402652
e-mail: fleur.nightingale@virgin.net
web: www.bewdley-accommodation.co.uk
dir: In town centre. From junct High St & Lax Ln, Bank House after junct on left

Once a private bank, this Victorian house retains many original features and offers comfortable accommodation. The cosy dining room is the setting for tasty English breakfasts served at one family table. Owner Mrs Nightingale has a comprehensive knowledge of the town and its history.

Rooms 4 rms (1 fmly) S £34-£37; D £58-£62 **Facilities** FTV tea/coffee Cen ht Wi-fi 🐾 **Parking** 2 **Notes** ⊗ Closed 24-26 Dec ⊗

Woodcolliers Arms
★★★ INN

76 Welch Gate DY12 2AU
☎ 01299 400589
e-mail: roger@woodcolliers.co.uk
web: www.woodcolliers.co.uk
dir: Exit A456, follow road behind church, left into Welch Gate (B4190)

Dating from before 1780, the Woodcolliers Arms is a family-run establishment located in the renowned Georgian town of Bewdley. This is a traditional inn offering an interesting menu with both traditional British pub food and a speciality Russian menu. Accommodation is comfortable and rooms are well equipped.

Rooms 5 rms (4 en suite) (1 pri facs) S £20-£35; D £50-£70 (room only)* **Facilities** FTV DVD tea/coffee Dinner available Cen ht Wi-fi 🐾 **Parking** 2 **Notes** LB No Children 12yrs

BROADWAY
Map 10 SP03

PREMIER COLLECTION

Abbots Grange
★★★★★ 🏠 GUEST HOUSE

Church St WR12 7AE
☎ 020 8133 8698
e-mail: rooms@abbotsgrange.com
web: www.abbotsgrange.com
dir: *M5 junct 9 follow signs to Evesham & Broadway*

A warm welcome waits at this 14th-century monastic manor house believed to be the oldest dwelling in Broadway; a Grade II listed building it stands proudly in eight acres of grounds. The bedrooms are luxurious and comprise twin and four-poster suites. The stunning medieval Great Hall is the guests' lounge and makes a romantic setting with its log fire and candles. The quality breakfasts are served at the large communal table in the wood-panelled dining room. The Grange has a tennis court and croquet lawn along with a helicopter landing pad. Abbots Grange was a Finalist in the AA Friendliest B&B of the Year Award 2012-13.

Rooms 4 rms (3 en suite) (1 pri facs) S £100-£135; D £150* **Facilities** STV FTV DVD Lounge TVL tea/coffee Cen ht Wi-fi 🌐 🍴 🚲 **Extras** Port, whiskey, sherry, soft drinks, mineral water **Conf** Board 10 **Parking** 8 **Notes** ⊗ No Children 6yrs

---

AA GUEST ACCOMMODATION OF THE YEAR FOR ENGLAND

PREMIER COLLECTION

East House
★★★★★ 🏠 GUEST ACCOMMODATION

162 High St WR12 7AJ
☎ 01386 853789 & 07738 290855
e-mail: enquiries@vacationcotswolds.co.uk
dir: *M40 junct 8 then A44 to Broadway, left at mini-rdbt to Upper High Street. 600mtrs on left*

A very warm welcome is assured at this fine house, located in a quiet residential area of Broadway. Day rooms include an elegant reception room with open fire, a drawing room with grand piano and a cosy breakfast room where memorable breakfasts are served. Individually furnished bedrooms, equipped with many thoughtful extras are decorated and furnished in keeping with the rest of the house. Off-road parking is a bonus. East House is the AA's Guest Accommodation of the Year for England 2012-13.

Rooms 4 en suite D £165-£195 **Facilities** FTV DVD iPod docking station Lounge tea/coffee Cen ht Wi-fi 🔒 Table tennis Treadmill **Extras** Speciality toiletries **Parking** 7 **Notes** ⊗ No Children 18yrs

---

PREMIER COLLECTION

Mill Hay House
★★★★★ 🏠 GUEST ACCOMMODATION

Snowshill Rd WR12 7JS
☎ 01386 852498 📠 01386 858038
e-mail: info@millhay.co.uk
web: www.millhay.co.uk
dir: *0.7m S of Broadway towards Snowshill, house on right*

Set in three acres of immaculate grounds beside a medieval watermill, this impressive early 18th-century stone house has many original features complemented by quality decor, period furniture and works of art. The spacious bedrooms are filled with thoughtful extras and one has a balcony. Imaginative breakfasts are served in the elegant dining room, and there is a spacious drawing room.

Rooms 3 en suite S £125-£195; D £160-£210* **Facilities** FTV TVL tea/coffee Direct Dial Cen ht Wi-fi **Parking** 15 **Notes** LB ⊗ No Children 12yrs

---

PREMIER COLLECTION

Russell's
★★★★★ ⚏⚏ 🍴 RESTAURANT WITH ROOMS

20 High St WR12 7DT
☎ 01386 853555 📠 01386 853555
e-mail: info@russellsofbroadway.co.uk
dir: *Opposite village green*

Situated in the centre of a picturesque Cotswold village this restaurant with rooms makes a great base for exploring local attractions. The superbly appointed bedrooms, each with its own character, have air conditioning and a wide range of extras for guests. The cuisine is a real draw here with freshly-prepared, local produce skilfully utilised.

Rooms 4 en suite 3 annexe en suite (4 fmly) (2 GF) D £105-£300* **Facilities** FTV DVD iPod docking station tea/coffee Dinner available Direct Dial Cen ht Wi-fi **Conf** Max 12 Board 12 **Parking** 16 **Notes** No coaches

---

Bowers Hill Farm *(SP086420)*
★★★★ FARMHOUSE

Bowers Hill, Willersey WR11 7HG
☎ 01386 834585 & 07966 171861
📠 01386 830234 Mr & Mrs M Bent
e-mail: sarah@bowershillfarm.com
web: www.bowershillfarm.com
dir: *3m NW of Broadway. A44 onto B4632 to Willersey, at mini-rdbt signs to Badsey & Willersey Industrial Estate, farm 2m on right by post box*

An impressive Victorian house set in immaculate gardens on a diverse farm, where point-to-point horses are bred. The house has been renovated to provide very comfortable bedrooms with modern bathrooms. Breakfast is served in the elegant dining room or the magnificent conservatory, and a lounge, with an open fire, is available to guests.

Rooms 3 en suite (1 fmly) **Facilities** FTV TVL tea/coffee Cen ht Wi-fi **Conf** Max 8 Class 8 Board 8 **Parking** 5 **Notes** ⊗ 98 acres horse breeding/grassland

---

Mount Pleasant Farm *(SP056392)*
★★★★ FARMHOUSE

Childswickham WR12 7HZ
☎ 01386 853424 & 07515 651560
📠 01386 853424 Mrs H Perry
e-mail: helen@mountpleasantfarm.biz
dir: *From A44, S of Evesham, onto B4632 for Cheltenham & Winchcombe, 50yds right to Childswickham (3m). Farm 1.5m W on left*

Located in immaculate, mature grounds in a pretty hamlet, this impressive Victorian house provides spacious, traditionally furnished bedrooms with smart modern bathrooms. Comprehensive breakfasts are served in an elegant dining room, and a comfortable lounge is available.

Rooms 3 en suite (1 fmly) **Facilities** tea/coffee Cen ht ♿ **Parking** 10 **Notes** ⊗ No Children 5yrs 950 acres arable

BROADWAY *continued*

Cowley House

★★★★ GUEST ACCOMMODATION

Church St WR12 7AE
☎ 01386 858148
e-mail: joan.peter@cowleyhouse-broadway.co.uk
dir: *Follow signs for Broadway. Church St adjacent to village green, 3rd on left*

A warm welcome is assured at this 18th-century Cotswold-stone house, just a stroll from the village green. Fine period furniture enhances the interior, and the elegant hall has a polished flagstone floor. Tastefully equipped bedrooms include thoughtful extras and smart modern shower rooms. Comprehensive breakfasts feature local produce.

Rooms 7 rms (6 en suite) (1 pri facs) (2 fmly) (2 GF)
S £60-£88; D £72-£104* **Facilities** FTV TVL tea/coffee Cen ht Wi-fi **Parking** 7 **Notes** LB

Horse & Hound

★★★★ INN

54 High St WR12 7DT
☎ 01386 852287 📠 01386 853784
e-mail: djttruesdale@msn.com
dir: *Off A46 to Evesham*

The Horse & Hound is at the heart of the beautiful Cotswold village of Broadway. There are many areas of interest to visit within easy distance of this well established inn. A warm welcome is guaranteed from hosts David and Diane whether dining in the inviting pub or staying overnight in attractive and well-appointed bedrooms. Breakfast and dinner provide quality ingredients which are freshly prepared.

Rooms 5 en suite (1 fmly) S £60-£80; D £70-£90*
Facilities FTV tea/coffee Dinner available Cen ht Wi-fi 🦮 **Parking** 15 **Notes** LB RS Winter

Windrush House

★★★★ 🅰 GUEST ACCOMMODATION

Station Rd WR12 7DE
☎ 01386 853577
e-mail: info@windrushhouse.com
dir: *From A44 take turn for Broadway, Windrush House is opposite junct with B4632*

Rooms 5 en suite S £75; D £90* **Facilities** FTV TVL tea/coffee Cen ht Wi-fi **Extras** Speciality toiletries, home-made biscuits, robes **Parking** 5 **Notes** ⊗ No Children 7yrs

---

Boot Inn

★★★★ 🍽 INN

Radford Rd WR7 4BS
☎ 01386 462658 📠 01386 462547
e-mail: enquiries@thebootinn.com
web: www.thebootinn.com
dir: *In village centre, signed from A422*

An inn has occupied this site since the 13th century, though the Boot itself dates from the Georgian period. Modernisation has retained historic charm, while the bedrooms, furnished in antique pine, are equipped with practical extras and have modern bathrooms. A range of ales, wines and imaginative food is offered in the cosy public areas, which include an attractive conservatory and patio.

Rooms 5 annexe en suite (2 GF) S £50-£60; D £65-£90
Facilities FTV DVD iPod docking station Lounge tea/coffee Dinner available Cen ht Wi-fi ⚓ 27 Pool table **Parking** 30 **Notes** LB

The Swan Inn

★★★★ INN

Worcester Rd WR8 0EA
☎ 01684 311870
e-mail: info@theswanhanleyswan.co.uk
web: www.theswanhanleyswan.co.uk
dir: *M5 junct 7, follow signs for Three Counties Showground, inn 1m before showground*

This 17th-century property, often described as a quintessential country inn, is located right on the village green, and has a warm, cosy, home-from-home atmosphere. Ideally situated at the foot of the beautiful Malvern Hills, it has five en suite bedrooms that are pleasantly furnished, modern and comfortable. Dining, particularly on warmer days in the garden and the patio,

---

is a delight. There is ample parking to the rear of the property.

Rooms 5 en suite (2 fmly) **Facilities** tea/coffee Dinner available Cen ht Wi-fi **Parking** 30

Walter de Cantelupe Inn

★★★ INN

Main Rd WR5 3NA
☎ 01905 820572
e-mail: walter.depub@fsbdial.co.uk
web: www.walterdecantelupeinn.com
dir: *On A38 in village centre*

This inn provides cosy bedrooms with smart bathrooms, and is convenient for the M5 and Worcester. The intimate, open-plan public areas are the setting for a range of real ales, and imaginative food featuring local produce and a fine selection of British cheeses.

Rooms 3 rms (2 en suite) (1 pri facs) **Facilities** tea/coffee Dinner available Cen ht Wi-fi **Parking** 24 **Notes** No coaches

---

The Dell House

★★★★ BED AND BREAKFAST

Green Ln, Malvern Wells WR14 4HU
☎ 01684 564448 📠 01684 893974
e-mail: burrage@dellhouse.co.uk
web: www.dellhouse.co.uk
dir: *2m S of Great Malvern on A449. Left into Green Ln. House at top of road on right, just below old church*

This impressive, well-proportioned Victorian house retains many unique features, several of which were introduced by the resident vicar, during the time it was a rectory. The spacious bedrooms are filled with thoughtful extras, and a comprehensive breakfast is served in an elegant dining room that has superb views over the mature gardens to the countryside beyond. Babies under one year are catered for.

Rooms 3 en suite **Facilities** TVL tea/coffee Cen ht Wi-fi **Parking** 3 **Notes** ⊗ No Children 10yrs

---

Appleby

★★★★ BED AND BREAKFAST

213 Worcester Rd WR14 1SP
☎ 01684 562106
e-mail: davidwatkins_07@hotmail.co.uk
dir: *On A449, opposite United Reform church*

This fine Victorian building, on the main road leading into Great Malvern, is where a warm and friendly welcome can be expected from the friendly host, David Watkins. The bedrooms are spacious, comfortable and offer modern facilities including Wi-fi. Breakfast in the dining room is freshly prepared and served with impeccable style. There

---

Save on B&Bs and Hotels. Book at **theAA.com/hotel**

WORCESTERSHIRE 329 ENGLAND

is a small lounge for guests, and some parking is available at the rear of the property.

Rooms 2 rms (1 en suite) (1 pri facs) S £40-£60; D £60-£70* **Facilities** TVL tea/coffee Cen ht Wi-fi **Extras** Bottled water - complimentary **Parking** 6 **Notes** ⊗ No Children Closed Xmas & New Year ⊜

Gilberts End Farm B&B

★★★★ BED AND BREAKFAST

Gilberts End, Harley Castle WR8 0AR
☎ 01684 311392 📠 01684 311392
e-mail: chrissy.bacon@btinternet.com
dir: *From Hanley Castle (B4211) onto B4209 signed Malvern Wells. Immediately left to Gilberts End, follow brick wall on right round sharp right bend (approx 1m), entrance on right on exit of bend*

A warm welcome awaits guests from hosts Chrissy and Roy Bacon at this Grade II listed farm building, parts of which date back some 600 years. Peacefully located in its own grounds, the house is close to Upton-upon-Severn and Hanley Swan, and just a short drive to the Malvern Hills and Worcester for sightseeing or walking. Therapeutic massage treatments and other complementary therapies are available. The bedrooms are comfortable with a good range of extras. The farmhouse breakfasts are served at individual tables in the welcoming dining room.

Rooms 3 en suite S £55-£75; D £70-£75 **Facilities** FTV DVD tea/coffee Cen ht Wi-fi Complementary therapies available **Extras** Fruit, snacks, mini-fridges **Parking** 6 **Notes** LB ⊗ No Children 5yrs

Wyche Inn

★★★★ INN

74 Wyche Rd WR14 4EQ
☎ 01684 575396
e-mail: thewycheinn@googlemail.com
web: www.thewycheinn.co.uk
dir: *1.5m S of Malvern. On B4218 towards Malvern & Colwall. Off A449 (Worcester to Ross/Ledbury road)*

Located in an elevated position on the outskirts of Malvern, this inn is popular with locals and visiting walkers. The thoughtfully furnished bedrooms provide good levels of comfort with suitable guest extras; all bathrooms have a bath and shower. Each bedroom benefits from stunning countryside views. The menus feature home-cooked dishes, including good-value options, and a comprehensive range of real ales is available from the bar.

Rooms 4 en suite 2 annexe rms (2 pri facs) (1 GF) **Facilities** FTV tea/coffee Dinner available Cen ht Wi-fi Pool table **Parking** 6 **Notes** LB No coaches

The Pembridge

★★★ GUEST ACCOMMODATION

114 Graham Rd WR14 2HX
☎ 01684 574813 📠 01684 566885
e-mail: info@thepembridge.co.uk
dir: *From A449 into Church St, 1st left*

Located on a leafy residential road close to the town centre, this large Victorian house retains many original features, including a superb staircase. Bedrooms, which include a ground-floor room, are well equipped. Other areas include a comfortable sitting room with a small bar and an elegant dining room.

Rooms 8 en suite (1 fmly) (1 GF) S £48-£60; D £59-£69* **Facilities** FTV TVL tea/coffee Direct Dial Cen ht Wi-fi **Conf** Max 8 **Parking** 10 **Notes** LB ⊗ No Children 7yrs RS 25-26 Dec No cooked English breakfast

Portocks End House

★★★ BED AND BREAKFAST

Little Clevelode WR13 6PE
☎ 01684 310276
e-mail: email@portocksendbandb.co.uk
dir: *On B4424, 4m N of Upton upon Severn, opposite Riverside Caravan Park*

Peacefully located, yet convenient for the showground and major road links, this period house retains many original features; the traditional furnishings and decor highlight its intrinsic charm. The bedrooms are equipped with lots of thoughtful extras, and breakfasts are taken in a cosy dining room overlooking the pretty garden.

Rooms 2 rms (1 en suite) (1 pri facs) (1 fmly) S £30; D £56 **Facilities** Lounge tea/coffee 🔒 **Extras** Speciality toiletries - complimentary **Parking** 4 **Notes** Closed Dec-Feb ⊜

Sidney House

★★★ GUEST ACCOMMODATION

40 Worcester Rd WR14 4AA
☎ 01684 574994 📠 01684 574994
e-mail: info@sidneyhouse.co.uk
web: www.sidneyhouse.co.uk
dir: *On A449, 200yds N from town centre*

This impressive Grade II listed Georgian house is close to the central attractions and has stunning views. Bedrooms are filled with thoughtful extras, and some have small, en suite shower rooms. The spacious dining room overlooks the Cotswold escarpment and a comfortable lounge is also available.

Rooms 8 rms (6 en suite) (2 pri facs) (1 fmly) S £25-£55; D £59-£75* **Facilities** FTV TVL tea/coffee Cen ht Licensed Wi-fi 🔒 **Parking** 9 **Notes** Closed 24 Dec-3 Jan

Four Hedges

★★ GUEST ACCOMMODATION

The Rhydd, Hanley Castle WR8 0AD
☎ 01684 310405
e-mail: fredgies@aol.com
dir: *4m E of Malvern at junct of B4211 & B4424*

Situated in a rural location, this detached house stands in mature grounds with wild birds in abundance. The bedrooms are equipped with thoughtful extras. Tasty English breakfasts, using free-range eggs, are served in a cosy dining room at a table made from a 300-year-old elm tree.

Rooms 4 rms (2 en suite) S £25; D £50 **Facilities** FTV iPod docking station Lounge TVL TV2B tea/coffee Cen ht 🎣 Fishing 🔒 **Extras** Snacks - complimentary **Parking** 5 **Notes** No Children 1yr Closed Xmas ⊜

MARTLEY   Map 10 SO76

Admiral Rodney Inn

★★★★ INN

Berrow Green WR6 6PL
☎ 01886 821375
e-mail: rodney@admiral.fslife.co.uk
dir: *A44 onto B4197 at Knightwick, 2m on left*

Located in the pretty village of Berrow Green, this 16th-century inn has been renovated to provide high standards of comfort and facilities. Karen and Desmond offer a warm welcome to all their customers, and provide spacious, carefully furnished bedrooms, complemented by luxurious modern bathrooms. Ground-floor areas include quality bars with log fires, and a unique tiered and beamed restaurant, where imaginative dishes are served. There are also outside seating areas to front and rear, and excellent parking facilities.

Rooms 3 en suite **Facilities** tea/coffee Cen ht Wi-fi Pool table **Parking** 40

WORCESTER   Map 10 SO85

Bants

★★★★ INN

Worcester Rd WR7 4NN
☎ 01905 381282 📠 01905 381173
e-mail: info@bants.co.uk
web: www.bants.co.uk
dir: *5m E of Worcester. On A422 at Upton Snodsbury*

Bants is a family-run, 16th-century pub with a modern atmosphere. Bedrooms are carefully decorated and well equipped, with some rooms separate from the inn. A wide range of freshly-cooked meals is available in the free-house bar or served in the large conservatory.

Rooms 4 en suite 5 annexe en suite (3 GF) **Facilities** FTV tea/coffee Dinner available Cen ht Wi-fi **Conf** Max 50 **Parking** 40

WORCESTER *continued*

Oaklands B&B

★★★★ GUEST ACCOMMODATION

Claines WR3 7RS
☎ 01905 458871 🖷 01905 759362
e-mail: barbara.gadd@btinternet.com
dir: M5 junct 6, A449. At rdbt take 1st exit signed
Claines. 1st left into School Bank. Oaklands 1st house
on right

A warm welcome is guaranteed at this converted stable,
which is well located in a peaceful setting just a short
drive from major routes. The property stands in abundant
mature gardens, and the well-appointed bedrooms are
mostly spacious. There is also a snooker room. Parking is
available.

Rooms 4 en suite (2 fmly) S £40-£45; D £70-£80*
Facilities FTV DVD Lounge tea/coffee Cen ht Wi-fi Snooker
🔒 **Parking** 7 **Notes** LB Closed Xmas & New Year ⊛

Wyatt Guest House

★★★★ GUEST HOUSE

40 Barbourne Rd WR1 1HU
☎ 01905 26311
e-mail: wyatt.guest@virgin.net
dir: On A38 0.5m N from city centre

Located within easy walking distance of shops,
restaurants and central attractions, this constantly
improving Victorian house provides a range of
thoughtfully furnished bedrooms. Breakfast is served in
an attractive dining room, a warm welcome is assured,
and the lovely frontage is a regular winner in the
Worcester Britain in Bloom competition.

Rooms 8 rms (7 en suite) (1 fmly) (1 GF) S £35-£45;
D £58-£60* **Facilities** FTV DVD Lounge tea/coffee Cen ht
Wi-fi

Ye Olde Talbot

★★★ INN

Friar St WR1 2NA
☎ 01905 23573 🖷 01905 612760
e-mail: 9250@greeneking.co.uk
web: www.oldenglish.co.uk

Located in the heart of the city, close to the Cathedral,
this period inn has been sympathetically renovated to
provide attractive and cosy public areas where guests
can enjoy a wide range of imaginative food, wine and real
ales. Bedrooms are thoughtfully furnished. Parking is
available at the adjacent NCP Cathedral car park.

Rooms 29 en suite (6 fmly) (6 GF) **Facilities** FTV tea/
coffee Direct Dial Wi-fi **Notes** ⊛

Croft Guest House

★★ GUEST HOUSE

Bransford WR6 5JD
☎ 01886 832227
e-mail: accom@brianporter.orangehome.co.uk
web: www.croftguesthouse.com
dir: 4m SW of Worcester. On A4103 Leigh exit at
Bransford rdbt, driveway on left after 30yds

This cottage-style property, dating in parts from the 16th
century, is convenient for the city centre and the Malvern
Hills, and offers homely bedrooms. Freshly-cooked
breakfasts feature home-made sausages. Dogs are
welcome provided they have a current vaccination
certificate.

Rooms 3 en suite (1 fmly) **Facilities** TVL tea/coffee Cen ht
Licensed **Parking** 5

YORKSHIRE, EAST RIDING OF

BEVERLEY   Map 17 TA03

PREMIER COLLECTION

Burton Mount Country House

☆☆☆☆☆ 🗎 GUEST ACCOMMODATION

Malton Rd, Cherry Burton HU17 7RA
☎ 01964 550541
e-mail: pg@burtonmount.co.uk
web: www.burtonmount.co.uk
dir: 2m NW of Beverley. B1248 for Malton, 2m right at
x-rds, house on left

Burton Mount is a charming country house three miles
from Beverley, set in delightful gardens and offering
luxurious accommodation. Bedrooms are well equipped
and have thoughtful extra touches. The spacious
drawing room has a blazing fire in the cooler months,
and an excellent, Aga-cooked Yorkshire breakfast is
served in the morning room. Pauline Greenwood is
renowned locally for her customer care, culinary skills
and warm hospitality.

Rooms 3 en suite **Facilities** STV TVL tea/coffee Dinner
available Cen ht Licensed Wi-fi 🥂 **Conf** Max 30 Thtr 30
Class 20 Board 20 **Parking** 20 **Notes** LB ⊛ No Children
12yrs

The Ferguson Fawsitt Arms & Country Lodge

★★★★ 🅰 INN

East End, Walkington HU17 8RX
☎ 01482 882665 🖷 01482 882665
e-mail: admin@fergusonfawsitt.com
web: www.fergusonfawsitt.co.uk
dir: M62 junct 38, B1230, left onto A1034, right onto
B1230, on left in centre of Walkington

Rooms 10 en suite (2 fmly) (10 GF) **Facilities** FTV tea/
coffee Dinner available Cen ht Wi-fi **Conf** Max 80 Thtr 60
Class 40 Board 20 **Parking** 120 **Notes** ⊛ RS 25-26 & 31
Dec No breakfast available

BRIDLINGTON   Map 17 TA16

PREMIER COLLECTION

Marton Grange

★★★★★ GUEST ACCOMMODATION

Flamborough Rd, Marton cum Sewerby YO15 1DU
☎ 01262 602034 & 07891 682687 🖷 01262 602034
e-mail: info@marton-grange.co.uk
web: www.marton-grange.co.uk
dir: 2m NE of Bridlington. On B1255, 600yds W of Links
golf club

This Grade II listed former farmhouse is set in well
maintained gardens offering high levels of comfort,
service and hospitality. Bedrooms are well appointed
with quality fixtures and fittings. Public areas offer
wonderful views of the gardens. Thoughtful extras,
provided as standard, help create a delightful guest
experience.

Rooms 11 en suite (3 GF) D £67-£120* **Facilities** FTV
DVD Lounge tea/coffee Cen ht Lift Licensed Wi-fi ⅃ 18 🔒
Extras Home-made shortbread, bottled water -
complimentary **Parking** 11 **Notes** LB RS Nov-Jan
Restricted opening for refurbishments

The Brockton

★★★★ GUEST ACCOMMODATION

4 Shaftesbury Rd YO15 3NP
☎ 01262 673967 & 401771 🖷 01262 673967
e-mail: brocktonhotel@yahoo.co.uk
dir: Off A167 coast road, right at golf course, through
lights, 2nd on left

Located close to the seafront, this family-run property
offers comfortable bedrooms, some with sea views, and
all with en suite shower rooms. A lounge and bar area is
available and dinner and breakfast is served in the
dining room.

Rooms 10 en suite (1 fmly) (2 GF) S £32-£35;
D £64-£70* **Facilities** FTV DVD TVL tea/coffee Dinner
available Cen ht Licensed Wi-fi ⅃ 18 🔒 **Conf** Max 20
Parking 10 **Notes** LB ⊛

Burlington Quays

★★★★ GUEST ACCOMMODATION

20 Meadowfield Rd YO15 3LD
☎ 01262 676052
e-mail: burlingtonquays@axis-connect.com
dir: A165 into Bridlington, 1st right past golf course into
Kingston Rd. Bear left to seafront, take 3rd left

In a peaceful street close to the seafront, this spacious
house features modern, well appointed bedrooms, all with
en suite bath or shower rooms. Guests also have use of a
comfortable lounge and a cosy, fully licensed bar. Tasty
breakfasts are served in the pleasant dining room at
individual tables.

Rooms 5 en suite (4 fmly) **Facilities** TVL tea/coffee Cen ht
Licensed Wi-fi **Parking** 2 **Notes** ⊛

Longleigh

★★★★ BED AND BREAKFAST

12 Swanland Av YO15 2HH
☎ 01262 676234 & 07980 310777
e-mail: geraldineross@hotmail.co.uk
dir: *Flamborough Rd, N past Holy Trinity Church*

In a quiet location ten minutes walk from the town centre or beach, Longleigh offers comfortable, tastefully appointed accommodation in a friendly atmosphere. Rooms are well equipped and breakfast is served in the attractive dining room. Free parking permits are available for on-street parking.

Rooms 2 en suite S £30–£35; D £56–£60* **Facilities** STV FTV TVL tea/coffee Cen ht Wi-fi **Notes** ⊗ No Children

The Royal Bridlington

★★★★ GUEST ACCOMMODATION

1 Shaftesbury Rd YO15 3NP
☎ 01262 672433 ▤ 01262 672118
e-mail: info@royalhotelbrid.co.uk
dir: *A615 N to Bridlington (Kingsgate), right into Shaftesbury Rd*

Located just off the promenade, this immaculate property has a range of thoughtfully furnished bedrooms with smart modern bathrooms. Spacious public areas include a large dining room, conservatory-sitting room, and a cosy television lounge. Freshly-cooked dinners are a feature and a warm welcome is assured.

Rooms 14 rms (13 en suite) (1 pri facs) 4 annexe en suite (7 fmly) (4 GF) S £40–£45; D £70–£80* **Facilities** FTV DVD Lounge TVL tea/coffee Dinner available Cen ht Licensed Wi-fi ⌿ 18 ⚓ **Conf** Max 85 Thtr 85 Class 20 Board 40 **Parking** 7 **Notes** LB ⊗

The Marina

★★★★ 🅰 GUEST HOUSE

8 Summerfield Rd YO15 3LF
☎ 01262 677138 & 0800 970 0591
e-mail: themarina8@hotmail.com
web: www.themarina-bridlington.com
dir: *From A165 take 1st right after Broadacres pub on left. Onto promenade, take 5th left*

Rooms 7 en suite (1 fmly) (1 GF) S £23–£30; D £50–£60* **Facilities** FTV tea/coffee Dinner available Cen ht Licensed Wi-fi **Notes** LB No Children 4yrs

The Tennyson

★★★ GUEST ACCOMMODATION

19 Tennyson Av YO15 2EU
☎ 01262 604382 & 07729 149729
e-mail: dianew2@live.co.uk
web: www.thetennyson-brid.co.uk
dir: *500yds NE of town centre. Take B1254 (Promenade) from town centre towards Flamborough. Tennyson Av on left*

Situated in a quiet side road close to the town centre and attractions, this friendly establishment offers attentive service and comfortable bedrooms. Dinner is also available by prior arrangement.

Rooms 8 rms (7 en suite) (1 pri facs) (2 fmly) (1 GF) S £25–£28; D £50–£72* **Facilities** FTV tea/coffee Dinner available Cen ht Wi-fi ⚓ **Notes** LB

The Ransdale

★★★ GUEST ACCOMMODATION

30 Flamborough Rd YO15 2JQ
☎ 01262 674334
e-mail: info@ransdalehotel.com

Close to all main attractions this establishment offers comfortable bedrooms and friendly service. Guests have use of a small, modern lounge. Evening meals and tasty breakfasts are served in the spacious dining room which also has a bar area. Limited off-street parking is also available.

Rooms 16 en suite (4 fmly) (4 GF) **Facilities** FTV TVL tea/coffee Dinner available Cen ht Licensed Wi-fi ⌿ 18 **Parking** 10 **Notes** ⊗

The Wolds Inn

★★★ 🍴 INN

Driffield Rd YO42 1YH
☎ 01377 288217
e-mail: huggate@woldsinn.freeserve.co.uk
dir: *Huggate signed off A166 & brown signs to Wolds Inn*

At the end of the highest village in the Yorkshire Wolds, midway between York and the coast, this ancient inn is a rural haven beside the Wolds Way walk. Substantial meals are served in the dining room and a good range of well-kept beers is available in the bar. Bedrooms, varying in size, are well equipped and comfortable.

Rooms 3 en suite S £50; D £76 **Facilities** FTV tea/coffee Dinner available Cen ht Pool table ⚓ **Parking** 30 **Notes** ⊗

Robeanne House

★★★ GUEST ACCOMMODATION

Towthorpe Ln, Shiptonthorpe YO43 3PW
☎ 01430 873312 & 07720 468811 ▤ 01430 879142
e-mail: enquiries@robeannehouse.co.uk
web: www.robeannehouse.co.uk
dir: *1.5m NW on A614*

Set back off the A614 in a quiet location, this delightful modern family home was built as a farmhouse. York, the coast, and the Yorkshire Moors and Dales are within easy driving distance. All bedrooms have country views and include a large family room. A charming wooden chalet is available in the garden.

Rooms 2 en suite 6 annexe en suite (2 fmly) (3 GF) S £40–£45; D £65–£75 **Facilities** FTV TVL tea/coffee Dinner available Cen ht Wi-fi ⚓ **Extras** Robes, guest kitchen **Conf** Max 8 Board 8 **Parking** 10 **Notes** LB

Innkeeper's Lodge Hull, Willerby

★★★ INN

Beverley Rd HU10 6NT
☎ 0845 112 6036
e-mail: info@innkeeperslodge.com
web: www.innkeeperslodge.com

At Innkeeper's Lodge you'll find accommodation with comfort and character in equal measure, and everything needed for a relaxing stay, from easy check-in and free parking to complimentary breakfast and a cosy pub serving great value food and drink on the doorstep. Each Lodge has quality rooms, and there are Lodges in a variety of locations from towns and cities to countryside settings across the UK.

Rooms 32 en suite (12 fmly) (8 GF) **Facilities** FTV tea/coffee Dinner available Direct Dial Wi-fi **Parking** 70

YORKSHIRE, NORTH

AA FRIENDLIEST B&B
OF THE YEAR

ALLERSTON — Map 19 SE88

Rains Farm (SE888808)

★★★★ 🏠 FARMHOUSE

YO18 7PQ
☎ 01723 859333 Miss N Allanson
e-mail: rainsholidays@btconnect.com
web: www.rains-farm-holidays.co.uk
dir: 1.5m S of A170 Pickering to Scarborough road, through village, 1m on right

This 17th-century farmhouse located on the edge of the North Yorkshire Moors and central for Pickering Moors, the coast, and steam train, is a quiet and peaceful destination. The accommodation is comfortable and the lounge and attractive garden provide a relaxing place to sit and view the wildlife. Exclusively for adults. Rains Farm is the Winner of the AA Friendliest B&B of the Year Award 2012-13.

Rooms 3 en suite (1 GF) S £40-£70; D £70-£100 **Facilities** FTV TVL tea/coffee Cen ht Wi-fi **Parking** 7 **Notes** LB ⊗ No Children Closed mid Sep-Etr 7 acres non-working

AMPLEFORTH — Map 19 SE57

PREMIER COLLECTION

Shallowdale House

🏠 GUEST ACCOMMODATION

West End YO62 4DY
☎ 01439 788325 📠 01439 788885
e-mail: stay@shallowdalehouse.co.uk
web: www.shallowdalehouse.co.uk
dir: Off A170 at W end of village, on turn to Hambleton

An outstanding example of an architect-designed 1960s house, Shallowdale lies in two acres of hillside gardens. There are stunning views from every room, and the elegant public rooms include a choice of lounges. Spacious bedrooms blend traditional and 1960s style with many home comforts. Expect excellent service and genuine hospitality from Anton and Phillip. The very imaginative, freshly cooked dinners are not to be missed.

Shallowdale House

Rooms 3 rms (2 en suite) (1 pri facs) S £80-£105; D £99-£135* **Facilities** FTV Lounge tea/coffee Dinner available Cen ht Licensed Wi-fi 🔒 **Parking** 3 **Notes** ⊗ No Children 12yrs Closed Xmas & New Year

APPLETREEWICK — Map 19 SE06

PREMIER COLLECTION

Knowles Lodge

★★★★★ 🏠 BED AND BREAKFAST

BD23 6DQ
☎ 01756 720228 📠 01756 720381
e-mail: pam@knowleslodge.com
web: www.knowleslodge.com
dir: From Bolton Abbey on B6160, 3.5m, right after Barden Tower, 1.5m, entrance on left

Located in the heart of Wharfedale and surrounded by 17 acres of meadow and woodland, this delightful Canadian-style ranch has been lovingly restored. The house is attractively furnished, with well appointed bedrooms, and whether guests are there to walk, cycle, fish, or simply relax and enjoy the scenery, they are sure to be given a warm welcome. Delicious breakfasts featuring home-made dishes are served around a large table.

Rooms 4 en suite (1 fmly) (3 GF) **Facilities** TVL tea/coffee Cen ht Wi-fi 🎣 Fishing **Parking** 6 **Notes** No Children 8yrs Civ Wed 100

ASENBY — Map 19 SE37

PREMIER COLLECTION

Crab Manor

★★★★★ ⚜⚜ 🍴 RESTAURANT WITH ROOMS

YO7 3QL
☎ 01845 577286 📠 01845 577496
dir: A1(M) junct 49, on outskirts of village

This stunning 18th-century Grade II listed Georgian manor is located in the heart of the North Yorkshire Dales. Each bedroom is themed around the world's most famous hotels and each is uniquely designed with high quality furnishings, beautiful wallpaper, and thoughtful extras. Scandinavian log cabins are also available within the grounds, which have their own terrace with hot tubs. There is a comfortable lounge bar where guests can relax in the Manor before enjoying dinner next door in the Crab & Lobster Restaurant, which specialises in fresh local seafood. The attractive gardens offer a lovely backdrop, and provide a pleasant place in which to relax.

Rooms 8 en suite 6 annexe en suite (3 fmly) D £160-£240 **Facilities** FTV tea/coffee Dinner available Cen ht Wi-fi Sauna **Conf** Max 16 Board 16 **Parking** 90 **Notes** ⊗ No coaches Civ Wed 105

ASKRIGG — Map 18 SD99

The White Rose Inn

★★★★ INN

Main St DL8 3HG
☎ 01969 650515 📠 01969 650176
e-mail: stay@thewhiterosehotelaskrigg.co.uk
dir: M6 or A1 onto A685, follow signs to Askrigg, White Rose Inn in village centre

This family-run inn set in the small village of Askrigg has been carefully refurbished to provide a perfect place to stay and dine in the North Yorkshire Dales. The accommodation offers standard rooms as well as king-sized rooms, some with original fireplaces. The large bar/lounge is welcoming with its open fire and real ales. The new dining room provides ample space for residents and

Save on B&Bs and Hotels. Book at **theAA.com/hotel**

YORKSHIRE, NORTH 333 ENGLAND

guests to dine in comfort. Ample private off-road parking is also available.

The White Rose Inn

Rooms 12 en suite D £75-£85* **Facilities** tea/coffee Dinner available Cen ht **Parking** 20 **Notes** Closed 24-25 Dec

---

AUSTWICK
Map 18 SD76

The Traddock

★★★★ ◉◉ 🍴 RESTAURANT WITH ROOMS

LA2 8BY
☎ 015242 51224 📠 015242 51796
e-mail: info@austwicktraddock.co.uk
dir: *From Skipton take A65 towards Kendal, 3m after Settle turn right signed Austwick, cross hump back bridge, 100yds on left*

Situated within the Yorkshire Dales National Park and a peaceful village environment, this fine Georgian country house with well-tended gardens offers a haven of calm and good hospitality. There are two comfortable lounges with real fires and fine furnishings, as well as a cosy bar and an elegant dining room serving fine cuisine. Bedrooms are individually styled with many homely touches.

Rooms 12 en suite (2 fmly) (1 GF) S £85-£95; D £89-£195* **Facilities** FTV DVD Lounge tea/coffee Dinner available Direct Dial Cen ht Wi-fi 🐾 ♨ 18 🔒 **Conf** Max 24 Thtr 24 Class 16 Board 16 **Parking** 20 **Notes** LB No coaches

---

AYSGARTH
Map 19 SE08

Stow House

★★★★ 🅰 GUEST ACCOMMODATION

DL8 3SR
☎ 01969 663635
e-mail: info@stowhouse.co.uk
web: www.stowhouse.co.uk
dir: *0.6m E of Aysgarth on A684*

Rooms 9 en suite (1 GF) S £42-£57; D £84-£104* **Facilities** FTV Lounge tea/coffee Dinner available Cen ht Licensed Wi-fi 🐾 ☺ 🔒 **Extras** Speciality toiletries **Parking** 10 **Notes** LB Closed 24-26 Dec

---

BAINBRIDGE
Map 18 SD99

PREMIER COLLECTION

Yorebridge House

★★★★★ ◉◉ 🍴 RESTAURANT WITH ROOMS

DL8 3EE
☎ 01969 652060 📠 01969 650258
e-mail: enquiries@yorebridgehouse.co.uk
dir: *A648 to Bainbridge. Yorebridge House N of centre on right before river*

Yorebridge House is situated by the river on the edge of Bainbridge, in the heart of the North Yorkshire Dales. In the Victorian era this was a schoolmaster's house and school, but this building now offers luxury boutique-style accommodation. Each bedroom is individually designed with high quality furnishings and thoughtful extras. All rooms have stunning views of the Dales and some have their own terrace with hot tubs. There is a comfortable lounge bar where guests can relax before enjoying dinner in the attractive and elegant dining room.

Rooms 7 en suite 4 annexe en suite (11 fmly) (5 GF) **Facilities** STV FTV DVD iPod docking station tea/coffee Dinner available Direct Dial Cen ht Wi-fi **Extras** Speciality toiletries **Conf** Max 70 Thtr 70 Class 60 Board 30 **Parking** 30 **Notes** LB No coaches Civ Wed 100

BEDALE
Map 19 SE28

The Castle Arms Inn

★★★★ 🍺 INN

Snape DL8 2TB
☎ 01677 470270 📠 01677 470837
e-mail: castlearms@aol.com
web: www.castlearmsinn.com
dir: *2m S of Bedale. Off B6268 into Snape*

Nestled in the quiet village of Snape, this former coaching inn is full of character. Bedrooms are in a converted barn, and each room is very comfortable and carefully furnished. The restaurant and public bar offer a good selection of fine ales, along with an interesting selection of freshly-prepared dishes.

The Castle Arms Inn

Rooms 9 annexe en suite (8 GF) S £60-£65; D £70-£80* **Facilities** FTV tea/coffee Dinner available Cen ht Wi-fi **Parking** 15 **Notes** LB No coaches

---

Elmfield House

★★★★ 🅰 GUEST HOUSE

Arrathorne DL8 1NE
☎ 01677 450558
e-mail: stay@elmfieldhouse.co.uk
dir: *4m NW of Bedale. A684 from Bedale for Leyburn, right after Patrick Brompton towards Richmond, 1.5m on right*

Rooms 4 en suite (1 fmly) **Facilities** FTV Lounge tea/coffee Cen ht Wi-fi Fishing **Parking** 4 **Notes** LB ⊗

BISHOP MONKTON
Map 19 SE36

Lamb & Flag Inn

★★★★ INN

Boroughbridge Rd HG3 3QN
☎ 01765 677322
e-mail: carol@lambandflagbarn.co.uk
dir: *From A61 turn E into Moor Rd (cross Knaresbrough Rd)*

The Lamb & Flag is a delightful country inn set in the countryside close to Harrogate, York and Leeds. The inn provides a warm welcome and freshly-prepared local food. The three comfortably furnished and equipped bedrooms are a conversion from a barn and are annexed next to the pub. A continental-style breakfast is provided in your bedroom.

Rooms 3 annexe en suite (1 fmly) (3 GF) **Facilities** FTV tea/coffee Dinner available Cen ht Wi-fi Pool table **Parking** 20 **Notes** ⊗ No coaches

BOLTON ABBEY · Map 19 SE05

Howgill Lodge

★★★★ GUEST ACCOMMODATION

Barden BD23 6DJ
☎ 01756 720655
e-mail: info@howgill-lodge.co.uk
dir: B6160 from Bolton Abbey signed Burnsall, 3m right at Barden Tower signed Appletreewick, Howgill Lodge 1.25m on right at phone box

Having an idyllic position high above the valley, this converted stone granary provides a quality get-away-from-it-all experience. The uniquely styled bedrooms provide a host of thoughtful touches and are designed to feature original stonewalls, flagstone floors and timber beams. All of the rooms boast spectacular, memorable views. Breakfasts make excellent use of fresh local ingredients.

Rooms 4 en suite (1 fmly) (4 GF) S £49; D £78*
Facilities FTV tea/coffee Cen ht Parking 6 Notes LB ⊗ Closed 24-26 Dec

BOROUGHBRIDGE · Map 19 SE36

PREMIER COLLECTION

The Crown Inn

★★★★★ ◉ RESTAURANT WITH ROOMS

Roecliffe YO51 9LY
☎ 01423 322300 ▤ 01423 322033
e-mail: info@crowninnroecliffe.com
web: www.crowninnroecliffe.com
dir: A1(M) junct 48, follow signs for Boroughbridge. At rdbt exit towards Roecliffe & brown tourist signs

The Crown is a 16th-century coaching inn providing an excellent combination of traditional charm and modern comforts. Service is friendly and professional and food is a highlight of any stay. The kitchen team use the finest of Yorkshire produce from the best local suppliers to create a weekly-changing seasonal menu. Bedrooms are attractively furnished with stylish en suite bathrooms.

Rooms 4 en suite (1 fmly) S £90-£100; D £100-£120*
Facilities FTV DVD tea/coffee Dinner available Cen ht Wi-fi ⓑ Extras Sherry - complimentary Conf Max 100 Thtr 100 Class 60 Board 30 Parking 40 Notes Civ Wed 120

BURNSALL · Map 19 SE06

The Devonshire Fell

★★★★ ◉◉ RESTAURANT WITH ROOMS

BD23 6BT
☎ 01756 729000 & 718111 ▤ 01756 729009
e-mail: manager@devonshirefell.co.uk
web: www.devonshirefell.co.uk
dir: On B6160, 6m from Bolton Abbey rdbt, A59 junct

Located on the edge of the attractive village of Burnsall, this establishment offers comfortable, well-equipped accommodation in a relaxing atmosphere. There is an extensive menu featuring local produce, and meals can be taken either in the bar area or the more formal restaurant. A function room with views over the valley is also available.

Rooms 12 en suite (2 fmly) S £89-£219; D £129-£259*
Facilities STV FTV DVD tea/coffee Dinner available Direct Dial Cen ht Wi-fi Fishing Free use of Spa facilities at sister hotel Conf Max 50 Thtr 50 Class 30 Board 24 Parking 40 Notes LB Civ Wed 120

CARPERBY · Map 19 SE08

The Wheatsheaf

★★★ 🅰 INN

DL8 4DF
☎ 01969 663216 ▤ 01969 663019
e-mail: wheatsheaf@paulmit.globalnet.co.uk
dir: Off A684 signed Aysgarth Falls to village centre
Rooms 12 en suite 1 annexe en suite (2 fmly) (1 GF) S £36-£57; D £70-£87* Facilities FTV Lounge tea/coffee Dinner available Cen ht Wi-fi 🔒 Conf Max 20 Board 20 Parking 40 Notes LB No coaches

CATTERICK · Map 19 SE29

Rose Cottage Guest House

★★★ GUEST ACCOMMODATION

26 High St DL10 7LJ
☎ 01748 811164
dir: Exit A1 in village centre, opposite village pharmacy

Convenient for exploring the Dales and Moors, this well-maintained guest accommodation lies in the middle of Catterick. Bedrooms are nicely presented and comfortable. The cosy public rooms include a cottage-style dining room adorned with Mrs Archer's paintings, and a lounge. Dinner is available by arrangement during the summer.

Rooms 3 rms (2 en suite) (1 pri facs) (1 fmly) (3 smoking) S £35-£38; D £52-£58 Facilities FTV Lounge tea/coffee Dinner available Cen ht Parking 3 Notes Closed 24-26 Dec

CAWOOD · Map 16 SE53

Maypole Farm B&B

★★★ BED AND BREAKFAST

14 Wistowgate YO8 3SH
☎ 01757 268849
e-mail: bookings@maypole-farm.co.uk
web: www.maypole-farm.co.uk

Located in a quiet village, Maypole Farm B&B offers a peaceful and relaxing stay. Each of the three bedrooms are uniquely designed, with thoughtful accessories. The conservatory overlooking the garden offers a relaxing place to sit, or even a game of pool. Breakfast is served in the very pleasant and well-appointed dining room.

Rooms 3 en suite Facilities FTV tea/coffee Cen ht Wi-fi ⓛ 18 Pool table Parking 3 Notes ⊗

CLAPHAM · Map 18 SD76

Brookhouse Guest House

★★★★ 🍴 GUEST HOUSE

Station Rd LA2 8ER
☎ 015242 51580
e-mail: admin@brookhouseclapham.co.uk
web: www.brookhouse-clapham.co.uk
dir: Off A65 into village

Located in the pretty conservation village of Clapham beside the river, this well-maintained and friendly guest house provides thoughtfully furnished bedrooms and a popular evening bistro, offering an interesting selection of home-made meals.

Rooms 3 rms (2 en suite) (1 pri facs) (1 fmly)
Facilities FTV tea/coffee Dinner available Cen ht Licensed Wi-fi ⓑ ⓛ 18 Notes ⊗ ⓦ ⓔ

CLOUGHTON · Map 19 TA09

Blacksmiths Arms

★★★★ INN

High St YO13 0AE
☎ 01723 870244
e-mail: enquiries@blacksmithsarmsinn.co.uk
dir: On A171 in village centre. 6m N of Scarborough

Located six miles north of Scarborough, this inn features smartly furnished bedrooms. Four are in converted stone

Save on B&Bs and Hotels. Book at **theAA.com/hotel**

YORKSHIRE, NORTH 335 ENGLAND

buildings that have private entrances. A good range of dishes is served in the bar and dining room, which have the ambience of a country inn, including open fires and traditional furniture.

Blacksmiths Arms

Rooms 6 en suite 4 annexe en suite (1 fmly) (4 GF) **Facilities** FTV tea/coffee Dinner available Cen ht Wi-fi **Parking** 35 **Notes** ⊗ RS 25-27 Dec No breakfast or room service No coaches

---

CRAYKE   Map 19 SE57

The Durham Ox

★★★★ ⚠ RESTAURANT WITH ROOMS

Westway YO61 4TE
☎ 01347 821506 📠 01347 823326
e-mail: enquiries@thedurhamox.com
dir: *A19 to Easingwold. Through market place to Crayke, 1st left up hill*

Rooms 1 en suite 4 annexe en suite (2 fmly) (2 GF) S £80; D £100* **Facilities** DVD tea/coffee Dinner available Wi-fi Shooting, fishing, riding by arrangement **Extras** Speciality toiletries **Parking** 35 **Notes** LB Closed 25 Dec No coaches

---

FLIXTON   Map 17 TA07

Orchard Lodge

★★★★ GUEST ACCOMMODATION

North St YO11 3UA
☎ 01723 890202 📠 01723 890202
e-mail: c.pummell@btinternet.com
web: www.orchard-lodge.com
dir: *Off A1039 in village centre*

Located six miles south of Scarborough, just off the main road, this establishment offers spacious and comfortable bedrooms. It is a good base for touring the coast, the North York Moors or the Wolds. Hearty breakfasts feature home-made preserves.

Rooms 6 en suite S £45-£50; D £65-£70* **Facilities** FTV tea/coffee Cen ht **Parking** 8 **Notes** LB ⊗ No Children 3yrs Closed Jan-Feb

---

GIGGLESWICK   Map 18 SD86

Harts Head Inn

★★★★ ⚠ INN

Belle Hill BD24 0BA
☎ 01729 822086 & 07894 939495
e-mail: info@hartsheadinn.co.uk
web: www.hartsheadinn.co.uk
dir: *On B6480, 1m from A65*

Rooms 7 en suite 3 annexe en suite (1 fmly) S fr £45; D fr £70* **Facilities** STV FTV tea/coffee Dinner available Cen ht Wi-fi ⅃ 9 Snooker Pool table 🔒 **Conf** Max 30 Class 30 Board 20 **Parking** 25 **Notes** LB

GOLDSBOROUGH   Map 19 SE35

PREMIER COLLECTION

Goldsborough Hall

★★★★★ ⬅ GUEST ACCOMMODATION

Church St HG5 8NR
☎ 01423 867321 📠 08723 310728
e-mail: accommodation@goldsboroughhall.com
dir: *A1(M) junct 47, A59 to Knaresborough. 2nd left into Station Rd, at T-junct left into Church St*

It's not everyday that you get the chance to stay in the former residence of a Royal Princess, in this case HRH Princess Mary. Hospitality at Goldsborough Hall is second to none. The luxury bedrooms are appointed to the highest standards, and the bathrooms have a real wow factor. Bedrooms feature hand-made mahogany four-poster beds, Chesterfields and 50-inch TVs.

Rooms 6 en suite (3 fmly) **Facilities** FTV DVD iPod docking station Lounge tea/coffee Dinner available Direct Dial Cen ht Lift Licensed Wi-fi ⅃ 18 Outdoor Hot Tub **Extras** Speciality toiletries; mini-bar - chargeable **Conf** Max 150 Thtr 150 Class 50 Board 30 **Parking** 50 **Notes** LB ⊗ Civ Wed 110

GRASSINGTON   Map 19 SE06

PREMIER COLLECTION

Ashfield House

★★★★★ 🏆 ⬅ GUEST ACCOMMODATION

Summers Fold BD23 5AE
☎ 01756 752584 📠 07092 376562
e-mail: sales@ashfieldhouse.co.uk
web: www.ashfieldhouse.co.uk
dir: *B6265 to village centre, from main street left into Summers Fold*

Guests are greeted like old friends at this beautifully maintained 17th-century house, peacefully tucked away a few yards from the village square. The smart lounges offer a high level of comfort and an honesty bar. The freshly prepared three-course dinner (by arrangement) is a highlight of any stay. The attractive bedrooms are well furnished and thoughtfully equipped.

Rooms 7 en suite 1 annexe en suite **Facilities** FTV tea/coffee Dinner available Cen ht Licensed Wi-fi **Conf** Max 8 Board 8 **Parking** 8 **Notes** ⊗ No Children 5yrs RS Nov-Mar No dinner on Sun & Wed eve

GRASSINGTON *continued*

PREMIER COLLECTION

Grassington House

★★★★★ @@ 🍴 RESTAURANT WITH ROOMS

5 The Square BD23 5AQ
☎ 01756 752406 📠 01756 752050
e-mail: bookings@grassingtonhousehotel.co.uk
web: www.grassingtonhousehotel.co.uk
dir: *A59 into Grassington, in town square opposite post office*

Located in the square of the popular village of Grassington this beautifully converted Georgian house is personally run by owners John and Sue. Delicious food, individually designed bedrooms and warm hospitality ensure an enjoyable stay. There is a stylish lounge bar looking out to the square and the restaurant is split between two rooms; here guests will find the emphasis is on fresh, local ingredients and attentive, yet friendly service.

Rooms 9 en suite (2 fmly) S £90-£175; D £100-£210*
Facilities STV FTV tea/coffee Dinner available Direct Dial Cen ht Wi-fi **Conf** Thtr 26 Class 20 Board 20
Parking 25 **Notes** LB ⊗

GREAT AYTON   Map 19 NZ51

Royal Oak

★★★ INN

123 High St TS9 6BW
☎ 01642 722361 & 723270 📠 01642 724047
e-mail: info@royaloak-hotel.co.uk
dir: *Off the A173, on High Street*

This 18th-century former coaching inn is very popular with locals and visitors to the village. Bedrooms are all comfortably equipped. The restaurant and public bar retain many original features and offer a good selection of fine ales; an extensive range of food is available all day and is served in the bar or the dining room.

Rooms 5 rms (4 en suite) **Facilities** tea/coffee Dinner available Direct Dial Cen ht Wi-fi **Conf** Max 30 Thtr 30 Class 30 Board 30 **Notes** Closed 25 Dec

GUISBOROUGH   Map 19 NZ61

The Kings Head at Newton

★★★★ GUEST ACCOMMODATION

The Green TS9 6QR
☎ 01642 722318 📠 01642 724750
e-mail: info@kingsheadhotel.co.uk
web: www.kingsheadhotel.co.uk
dir: *A171 towards Guisborough, at rdbt onto A173 to Newton-under-Roseberry, under Roseberry Topping landmark*

Converted from a row of traditional cottages, the friendly, family-owned Kings Head offers modern accommodation yet retains original features. The stylish bedrooms are thoughtfully equipped, and the adjacent restaurant offers a very good range of dishes.

Rooms 8 en suite (1 fmly) (2 GF) S £62.50-£87.50;
D £77.50-£115* **Facilities** FTV Lounge TVL tea/coffee Direct Dial Cen ht Licensed Wi-fi 🛇 Mountain biking
Parking 100 **Notes** ⊗ Closed 25 Dec & 1 Jan

HACKNESS   Map 19 SE99

Troutsdale Lodge

★★★★ GUEST ACCOMMODATION

Troutsdale YO13 0BS
☎ 01723 882209
e-mail: captroutsdale@yahoo.co.uk
web: www.troutsdalelodge.com
dir: *Off A170 at Snainton signed Troutsdale*

Commanding magnificent views across a peaceful valley and the forest beyond, this Edwardian house showcases many original features combined with modern art. Bedrooms offer good all-round comforts and guests receive fine hospitality from the resident owners.

Rooms 4 en suite (1 fmly) (4 GF) **Facilities** TVL tea/coffee Dinner available Cen ht Licensed 🍴 **Parking** 8 **Notes** ⊗

HARROGATE   Map 19 SE35

Alexa House

★★★★ GUEST HOUSE

26 Ripon Rd HG1 2JJ
☎ 01423 501988
e-mail: enquiries@alexa-house.co.uk
web: www.alexa-house.co.uk
dir: *On A61, 0.25m from junct A59*

This popular establishment has stylish, well-equipped bedrooms split between the main house and cottage rooms. All come with homely extras. The opulent day rooms include an elegant lounge with honesty bar, and a bright dining room. The hands-on proprietors ensure high levels of customer care.

Rooms 9 en suite 4 annexe en suite (2 fmly) (4 GF) S £50-£62; D £75-£94* **Facilities** iPod docking station Lounge tea/coffee Cen ht Licensed Wi-fi **Parking** 10 **Notes** Closed 23-26 Dec

The Grafton Boutique B&B

★★★★ GUEST ACCOMMODATION

1-3 Franklin Mount HG1 5EJ
☎ 01423 508491 📠 01423 523168
e-mail: enquiries@graftonhotel.co.uk
web: www.graftonhotel.co.uk
dir: *Follow signs to International Centre, into Kings Rd (with Centre on left), Franklin Mount 450yds on right*

The delightful family-run Grafton is in a quiet location just a short walk from the conference centre and town. This smartly appointed period property provides stylish accommodation; bedrooms vary between modern and traditional. There is a beautifully appointed lounge looking out to the garden.

Rooms 14 en suite (1 GF) D £90-£140 **Facilities** FTV TVL tea/coffee Direct Dial Cen ht Licensed Wi-fi ⚓ 18
Parking 1 **Notes** LB ⊗ Closed 15 Dec-6 Jan

Shelbourne House

★★★★ 🍴 GUEST ACCOMMODATION

78 Kings Rd HG1 5JX
☎ 01423 504390
e-mail: sue@shelbournehouse.co.uk
web: www.shelbournehouse.co.uk
dir: *Follow signs to International Centre, over lights by Holiday Inn, premises on right*

Situated opposite the conference centre and close to the town centre, this elegant Victorian house features attractive bedrooms that are well equipped. There is a beautifully presented guest lounge and smart dining room. The friendly owners provide attentive service and offer a wide choice at breakfast, with emphasis on local ingredients. Complimentary Wi-fi access is provided.

Rooms 8 en suite (2 fmly) S £45-£60; D £70-£90*
Facilities DVD iPod docking station TVL tea/coffee Cen ht Wi-fi **Conf** Board 16 **Parking** 1 **Notes** LB ⊗

Save on B&Bs and Hotels. Book at theAA.com/hotel

YORKSHIRE, NORTH 337 ENGLAND

Wynnstay House

★★★★ 🏠 GUEST ACCOMMODATION

60 Franklin Rd HG1 5EE
☎ 01423 560476
e-mail: wynnstayhouse@tiscali.co.uk
web: www.wynnstayhouse.com
dir: *Exit A61 in town centre into Kings Rd, right into Strawberry Dale, left at top of road into Franklin Rd*

Located in a residential area a short distance from the conference centre, shops and attractions, this friendly, family-run guest accommodation is ideal for business or leisure. There is a passion for ruined castles at Wynnstay House: the attractive, well-equipped bedrooms are each named after a spectacular fortress.

Rooms 5 en suite S £55-£89; D £75-£89* **Facilities** FTV iPod docking station Lounge tea/coffee Cen ht Wi-fi 🐾 **Notes** LB ⊗ No Children 14yrs

April House

★★★★ GUEST ACCOMMODATION

3 Studley Rd HG1 5JU
☎ 01423 561879
e-mail: info@aprilhouse.com
dir: *Exit A59/A61 into Kings Rd signed Harrogate International Centre. Opposite Holiday Inn turn into Alexandra Rd. Establishment at top of road on right*

Located in a quiet residential area just a short walk from the conference centre, this impeccable Victorian house retains many original features. The comfortable bedrooms come with an array of homely touches, and breakfast is served in an attractive dining room.

Rooms 3 en suite D £70-£90* **Facilities** FTV tea/coffee Wi-fi **Notes** LB ⊗

Ashwood House Guest House

★★★★ GUEST ACCOMMODATION

7 Spring Grove HG1 2HS
☎ 01423 560081 📠 01423 527928
e-mail: ashwoodhouse@aol.com
web: www.ashwoodhouse.co.uk
dir: *A61 (Ripon Rd) into Springfield Av, 3rd left*

This delightfully decorated and furnished Edwardian house is situated in a quiet area of town. The spacious bedrooms are individually styled and thoughtfully equipped, and one has a four-poster bed. There is a cosy lounge and an elegant dining room where full English breakfasts are served.

Rooms 5 en suite (1 fmly) S £35-£45; D £65-£75* **Facilities** FTV TVL tea/coffee Cen ht Wi-fi **Parking** 3 **Notes** LB ⊗ No Children 7yrs Closed Xmas & New Year

Harrogate Brasserie with Rooms

★★★★ GUEST ACCOMMODATION

28-30 Cheltenham Pde HG1 1DB
☎ 01423 505041 📠 01423 722300
e-mail: info@harrogatebrasserie.co.uk
web: www.harrogatebrasserie.co.uk
dir: *On A61 town centre behind theatre*

This town centre establishment is distinctly continental in style. The brasserie covers three cosy dining areas, richly decorated and adorned with artefacts. Live jazz is featured on Wednesday, Friday and Sunday nights. The individual bedrooms feature period collectibles; many rooms have DVD players and all have lots of reading material.

Rooms 15 en suite 1 annexe en suite (3 fmly) **Facilities** tea/coffee Dinner available Direct Dial Cen ht Licensed Wi-fi **Parking** 12 **Notes** LB

Innkeeper's Lodge Harrogate (West)

★★★★ INN

Beckwith Knowle, Otley Rd HG3 1UE
☎ 0845 112 6034
e-mail: info@innkeeperslodge.com
web: www.innkeeperslodge.com

At Innkeeper's Lodge you'll find accommodation with comfort and character in equal measure, and everything needed for a relaxing stay, from easy check-in and free parking to complimentary breakfast and a cosy pub serving great value food and drink on the doorstep. Each Lodge has quality rooms, and there are Lodges in a variety of locations from towns and cities to countryside settings across the UK.

Rooms 12 en suite (4 fmly) **Facilities** FTV tea/coffee Dinner available Direct Dial Wi-fi **Parking** 60

Ruskin

★★★★ GUEST ACCOMMODATION

1 Swan Rd HG1 2SS
☎ 01423 502045 📠 01423 506131
e-mail: ruskin.hotel@virgin.net
dir: *Off A61(Ripon road), left opposite The Majestic Hotel*

The mid 19th-century house stands in secluded tree-studded gardens, only a 5-minute walk from the town centre. It retains many original features and has a relaxing lounge. Breakfasts are served in the elegant dining room, and the thoughtfully equipped bedrooms range from compact to spacious, all furnished in stylish Victorian pine.

Rooms 7 en suite (2 fmly) (1 GF) **Facilities** tea/coffee Direct Dial Cen ht Licensed **Parking** 7

HAWNBY | **Map 19 SE58**

The Inn at Hawnby

★★★★★ 🏵 INN

YO62 5QS
☎ 01439 798202 📠 01439 798344
e-mail: info@innathawnby.co.uk
web: www.innathawnby.co.uk
dir: *Exit B1257 between Stokesley & Helmsley*

This charming 19th-century inn is located in a peaceful village. Service is attentive and friendly, with guests able to relax and browse menus in the cosy bar where there is a good wine list and range of ales. Delicious, home-cooked meals are served in the restaurant, overlooking the gardens and surrounding countryside. Bedrooms are well equipped, with some in the converted stables.

Rooms 6 en suite 3 annexe en suite (1 fmly) (3 GF) S £79; D £90-£99* **Facilities** FTV DVD tea/coffee Dinner available Direct Dial Cen ht Wi-fi Fishing Riding **Extras** Speciality toiletries, sherry - complimentary **Conf** Max 20 Thtr 12 Class 20 **Parking** 9 **Notes** LB ⊗ Closed 25 Dec RS Feb & Mar Restricted lunch service Mon & Tue

Laskill Grange

★★★★ GUEST ACCOMMODATION

YO62 5NB
☎ 01439 798268
e-mail: laskillgrange@tiscali.co.uk
web: www.laskillgrange.co.uk
dir: *From York A19 to Thirsk, A170 to Helmsley then B1257 N, after 6m sign on left to Laskill Grange*

Lovers of the countryside will enjoy this charming 19th-century farmhouse. Guests can take a walk in the surrounds, fish the River Seph, which runs through the grounds, or visit nearby Rievaulx Abbey. The comfortable, well furnished bedrooms are in the main house and are supplied with many thoughtful extras.

Rooms 3 rms (2 en suite) (1 pri facs) (3 GF) S £40-£50; D £80-£90* **Facilities** FTV Lounge TVL tea/coffee Dinner available Cen ht Licensed Wi-fi ch fac Fishing Riding Outdoor activity area Hot tubs **Extras** Speciality toiletries - complimentary **Conf** Max 20 **Parking** 20 **Notes** LB Civ Wed 620

HELMSLEY
Map 19 SE68

See also Hawnby

Shallowdale House

★★★★★ 🍽 GUEST ACCOMMODATION

West End YO62 4DY
☎ 01439 788325 🖷 01439 788885
e-mail: stay@shallowdalehouse.co.uk
web: www.shallowdalehouse.co.uk

(For full entry see Ampleforth)

Plumpton Court

★★★★ GUEST ACCOMMODATION

High St, Nawton YO62 7TT
☎ 01439 771223
e-mail: mail@plumptoncourt.com
web: www.plumptoncourt.com
dir: *2.5m E of Helmsley. Exit A170 in Nawton, signed*

Located in the village of Nawton, in the foothills of the North Yorkshire Moors, this characteristic 17th-century, stone-built house offers a warm welcome. The cosy lounge bar has an open fire. Bedrooms are comfortable, modern and well equipped, one with a four-poster bed.

Rooms 6 en suite (1 GF) S £55; D £70-£76* **Facilities** FTV tea/coffee Cen ht Licensed Wi-fi ♨ 18 🍷 **Parking** 8 **Notes** ⊗ No Children 12yrs Closed 22-29 Dec

HETTON
Map 18 SD95

The Angel Inn

★★★★★ 🍽🍽 RESTAURANT WITH ROOMS

BD23 6LT
☎ 01756 730263 🖷 01756 730363
e-mail: info@angelhetton.co.uk
dir: *B6265 from Skipton towards Grassington. At Rylstone turn left by pond, follow signs to Hetton*

This roadside inn is steeped in history; parts of the building go back over 500 years. The restaurant and bar are in the main building which has ivy and green canopies at the front. The large and stylish bedrooms are across the road in a converted barn which has great views of the Dales, its own wine cave and private parking.

Rooms 9 en suite (3 GF) **Facilities** FTV tea/coffee Dinner available Direct Dial Cen ht Wi-fi Wine tasting cave **Conf** Max 16 Board 14 **Parking** 40 **Notes** LB Closed 25 Dec & 1wk Jan No coaches Civ Wed 40

HUBY
Map 19 SE56

The New Inn Motel

★★★ GUEST ACCOMMODATION

Main St YO61 1HQ
☎ 01347 810219 🖷 01347 810219
e-mail: enquiries@newinnmotel.freeserve.co.uk
web: www.newinnmotel.co.uk
dir: *Exit A19 E into village centre, motel on left*

Just nine miles north of York and situated in a quiet location behind The New Inn, this establishment offers modern motel-style accommodation. Comfortable bedrooms are spacious and neatly furnished, and breakfast is served in the cosy dining room. The reception area has an array of tourist information and the resident owners provide a friendly and helpful service.

Rooms 8 en suite (3 fmly) (8 GF) S £40-£50; D £70-£80* **Facilities** FTV tea/coffee Cen ht **Parking** 8 **Notes** LB Closed mid Nov-mid Dec & part Feb

INGLETON
Map 18 SD67

Gale Green Cottage

★★★★ BED AND BREAKFAST

Westhouse LA6 3NJ
☎ 015242 41245 & 077867 82088
e-mail: jill@galegreen.com
dir: *2m NW of Ingleton. S of A65 at Masongill x-rds*

Peacefully located in a rural hamlet, this 300-year-old house has been lovingly renovated to provide modern facilities without compromising original charm and character. Thoughtfully furnished bedrooms feature smart modern en suite shower rooms, and a guest lounge is also available.

Rooms 3 en suite (1 fmly) S £35-£39; D £58-£64* **Facilities** FTV TVL tea/coffee Cen ht **Parking** 6 **Notes** Closed Xmas & New Year ⊛

KIRKBY FLEETHAM
Map 19 SE29

The Black Horse

★★★★★ 🍽🍽 RESTAURANT WITH ROOMS

Lumley Ln DL7 0SH
☎ 01609 749010 & 749011 🖷 01423 507836
e-mail: gm@blackhorsekirkbyfleetham.com
web: www.blackhorsekirkbyfleetham.com
dir: *A1 onto A648 towards Northallerton. Left into Ham Hall Ln, through Scruton. At T-junct left into Fleetham Ln. Through Great Fencote to Kirkby Fleetham, into Lumley Ln, inn on left past post office*

Set in a small village, The Black Horse provides everything needed for a getaway break including award-winning food. The spacious bedrooms, named after famous racehorses, are beautifully designed in New England/French style with pastel colours, co-ordinating fabrics and excellent beds; many of the superb bathrooms feature slipper or roll-top baths. There is a large dining room and bar that attracts locals as well as visitors from further afield.

Rooms 7 en suite (1 fmly) (2 GF) **Facilities** FTV tea/coffee Dinner available Cen ht Wi-fi ch fac ♨ 18 Fishing quoits pitch **Conf** Max 40 Thtr 40 Class 30 Board 24 **Parking** 90

KNARESBOROUGH
Map 19 SE35

General Tarleton Inn

★★★★★ 🍽🍽 RESTAURANT WITH ROOMS

Boroughbridge Rd, Ferrensby HG5 0PZ
☎ 01423 340284 🖷 01423 340288
e-mail: gti@generaltarleton.co.uk
dir: *A1(M) junct 48 at Boroughbridge, take A6055 to Knaresborough. 4m on right*

This beautiful 18th-century coaching inn has been stylishly renovated. Though the physical aspects are impressive, the emphasis here is on food with high quality, skilfully prepared dishes served in the smart bar/brasserie and in the Orangery. There is also a richly furnished cocktail lounge with a galleried private dining room above it. Bedrooms are very comfortable and business guests are also well catered for.

Rooms 13 en suite (7 GF) S £75-£137; D £129-£150* **Facilities** FTV Lounge tea/coffee Dinner available Direct Dial Cen ht Wi-fi **Conf** Max 40 Thtr 40 Class 35 Board 20 **Parking** 40 **Notes** LB ⊗ Closed 24-26 Dec, 1 Jan No coaches

Newton House

★★★★ 🔒 GUEST ACCOMMODATION

5-7 York Place HG5 0AD
☎ 01423 863539
e-mail: info@newtonhousehotel.com
web: www.newtonhouseyorkshire.com
dir: A1(M) junct 47 onto A59 towards Knaresborough.
Right at 1st rdbt, continue to town centre, on right before
lights

This elegant Georgian guest accommodation is only a
short walk from the river, castle and market square. The
property is entered by an archway into the courtyard. The
attractive, very well equipped bedrooms include some
four-poster beds and also king-sized doubles. There is a
comfortable lounge with honesty bar and memorable
breakfasts are served in the attractive dining rooms.

Rooms 9 rms (8 en suite) (1 pri facs) 3 annexe en suite
(2 fmly) (4 GF) Facilities FTV TVL tea/coffee Direct Dial
Cen ht Licensed Wi-fi ♨ 18 Parking 9

Innkeeper's Lodge Harrogate (East)

★★★ INN

Wetherby Rd, Plompton HG5 8LY
☎ 0845 112 6033
e-mail: info@innkeeperslodge.com
web: www.innkeeperslodge.com

At Innkeeper's Lodge you'll find accommodation with
comfort and character in equal measure, and everything
needed for a relaxing stay, from easy check-in and free
parking to complimentary breakfast and a cosy pub
serving great value food and drink on the doorstep. Each
Lodge has quality rooms, and there are Lodges in a
variety of locations from towns and cities to countryside
settings across the UK.

Rooms 10 en suite (2 fmly) Facilities FTV tea/coffee
Dinner available Direct Dial Wi-fi Parking

LEEMING BAR   Map 19 SE57

Little Holtby

★★★★ 🅰 BED AND BREAKFAST

DL7 9LH
☎ 01609 748762
e-mail: littleholtby@yahoo.co.uk
dir: 2m N of A684 (junct with A1)
Rooms 3 en suite S £42.50-£45; D £80-£85*
Facilities FTV DVD TVL tea/coffee Cen ht Wi-fi ♨ 18
Extras Speciality toiletries, fruit, snacks - complimentary
Parking 6 Notes LB ⊗ No Children 12yrs ⊜

LEVISHAM   Map 19 SE89

The Horseshoe Inn

★★★★ INN

Main St YO18 7NL
☎ 01751 460240 📠 01751 460052
e-mail: info@horseshoelevisham.co.uk
dir: From Pickering on A169, after 4m past Fox & Rabbit
Inn on right. 0.5m left to Lockton, then steep winding
road to village

A charming 19th-century inn with a peaceful location in
Levisham village. The spacious bar and dining area are
traditionally furnished and food is a highlight with a wide
choice and generous portions. The attractive bedrooms
include two garden rooms, and most rooms in the main
house have lovely views of the village.

Rooms 9 en suite (3 fmly) (3 GF) S £40-£45; D £60-£90*
Facilities FTV tea/coffee Dinner available Cen ht Wi-fi
Parking 30 Notes LB No coaches

LEYBURN   Map 19 SE19

PREMIER COLLECTION

Capple Bank Farm

★★★★★ BED AND BREAKFAST

West Witton DL8 4ND
☎ 01969 625825 & 07836 645238
e-mail: julian.smithers@btinternet.com
dir: A1 to Bedale, onto A684 to Leyburn, turn left to
Hawes, through Wensley, 1st left in West Witton. Up
hill, left bend, gates straight ahead

Ideal for walking and touring in the Yorkshire Dales
National Park, this is a spacious house. Guests have
use of a lovely lounge with a real fire lit on cooler days,
and breakfast is served at a beautiful table in the
open-plan kitchen and dining room.

Rooms 2 en suite 2 annexe en suite S £70;
D £100-£110* Facilities STV FTV Lounge TV3B tea/
coffee Cen ht 🔒 Parking 6 Notes ⊗ No Children 10yrs
⊜

The Queens Head

★★★★ ⊜ INN

Westmoor Ln, Finghall DL8 5ND
☎ 01677 450259
e-mail: enquiries@queensfinghall.co.uk
web: www.queensfinghall.co.uk
dir: From Bedale follow A684 W towards Leyburn, just
after pub & caravan park turn left signed to Finghall.
Follow road, on left

Located in the quiet village of Finghall this country inn
dates back to the 18th century, and has original oak
beams. A wide choice of freshly prepared meals are
served in either the bar or more contemporary restaurant,
which has lovely views of the surrounding countryside.
Bedrooms are spacious and located in an adjacent
annexe.

Rooms 3 annexe en suite (1 fmly) (3 GF) D £60-£90*
Facilities FTV TVL tea/coffee Dinner available Cen ht Pool
table Parking 40 Notes LB

LONG PRESTON   Map 18 SD85

The Boars Head

★★★ INN

9 Main St BD23 4ND
☎ 01729 840217 📠 01729 840217
e-mail: boardsheadhotel@hotmail.co.uk

Situated in the pleasant village of Long Preston, the inn
was built in the 18th century and features beamed
ceilings and open fires. It's a lively inn with
entertainment including live bands, discos, bingo and
quizzes. A wide range of food and ales are available in
the pub restaurant. Bedrooms are en suite and
comfortable. The property has ample parking.

Rooms 5 en suite Facilities FTV tea/coffee Dinner
available Cen ht Wi-fi Pool table 🚭 Parking 26

LOW ROW   Map 18 SD99

The Punch Bowl Inn

★★★★ 🔒 ⊜ INN

DL11 6PF
☎ 01748 886233 📠 01748 886945
e-mail: info@pbinn.co.uk
dir: From Scotch Corner take A6108 to Richmond then
B6270 to Low Row

This friendly inn is appointed in a contemporary style.
Real ales and freshly-cooked meals are served in either
the spacious bar or dining room. The modern bedrooms
are stylish yet simply furnished, with well-equipped
bathrooms. Guests also have use of a lounge which has
stunning views of the Dales.

Rooms 9 en suite 2 annexe en suite (1 fmly) (1 GF)
D £92-£123* Facilities FTV Lounge tea/coffee Dinner
available Direct Dial Cen ht Wi-fi Fishing
Extras Speciality toiletries, home-made shortbread
Parking 20 Notes LB ⊗ Closed 25 Dec

| MALHAM | Map 18 SD96 |

The Lister Arms

★★★★ INN

BD23 4DB
☎ 01729 830330
e-mail: relax@listerarms.co.uk
dir: From A59 into Malham, right in centre of village

Located in Malham in the Yorkshire Dales National Park, The Lister Arms is a traditional country inn with wood beams and open fires. It is close to the village green and a babbling stream. The accommodation is comfortable and well equipped, and a wide selection of imaginative dishes together with real ales and fine wines are served in the busy bar and restaurant, where the atmosphere is relaxed and comfortable.

Rooms 9 en suite (1 fmly) **Facilities** FTV tea/coffee Dinner available Cen ht Wi-fi **Parking** 20 **Notes** No coaches

---

River House

★★★★ ⌂ ☕ GUEST HOUSE

BD23 4DA
☎ 01729 830315
e-mail: info@riverhousehotel.co.uk
web: www.riverhousehotel.co.uk
dir: Off A65, N to Malham

A warm welcome awaits guests at this attractive house, which dates from 1664. The bedrooms are bright and comfortable, with one on the ground floor. Public areas include a cosy lounge and a large, well-appointed dining room. Breakfasts and evening meals offer choice and quality above expectation.

Rooms 8 en suite (1 GF) S £65-£80; D £70-£85* **Facilities** FTV Lounge tea/coffee Dinner available Cen ht Licensed Wi-fi Fishing ⌂ **Extras** Wine, flowers, fruit - chargeable **Parking** 5 **Notes** LB No Children 12yrs

---

Beck Hall

★★★ GUEST HOUSE

Cove Rd BD23 4DJ
☎ 01729 830332
e-mail: alice@beckhallmalham.com
web: www.beckhallmalham.com
dir: A65 to Gargrave, turn right to Malham. Beck Hall 100yds on right after mini-rdbt

A small stone bridge over Malham Beck leads to this delightful property. Dating from 1710, the house has true character, and bedrooms come complete with four-poster beds. Delicious afternoon teas are available in the colourful garden in warmer months, while roaring log fires welcome the guests in the winter.

Rooms 11 en suite 7 annexe en suite (4 fmly) (4 GF) S £45-£80; D £60-£75* **Facilities** STV Lounge tea/coffee Cen ht Licensed Wi-fi ⌂ **Parking** 40 **Notes** LB

| MASHAM | Map 19 SE28 |

Bank Villa Guest House

★★★★ ⌂ ☕ GUEST HOUSE

HG4 4DB
☎ 01765 689605
e-mail: stay@bankvilla.com
web: www.bankvilla.com
dir: Enter on A6108 from Ripon, property on right

An elegant Georgian house set in a pretty walled garden. Individually decorated bedrooms feature stripped pine, period furniture and crisp, white linen. Imaginative home-cooked meals are served in the attractive dining room. Character public rooms include a choice of lounges, or you can relax in the garden in summer.

Rooms 5 rms (4 en suite) (1 pri facs) (2 fmly) S £45-£65; D £55-£115* **Facilities** FTV DVD iPod docking station Lounge TVL tea/coffee Dinner available Cen ht Licensed Wi-fi ⌂ **Conf** Max 10 Thtr 10 Class 10 Board 10 **Parking** 6 **Notes** LB ⊗ No Children 5yrs

---

| MIDDLESBROUGH | Map 19 NZ41 |

The Grey House

★★★★ GUEST ACCOMMODATION

79 Cambridge Rd, Linthorpe TS5 5NL
☎ 01642 817485 📠 01642 817485
e-mail: denistaylor-100@btinternet.com
web: www.greyhousehotel.co.uk
dir: A19 N onto A1130 & A1032 (Acklam Rd), right at lights

This Edwardian mansion stands in mature gardens in a quiet residential area, and is lovingly maintained to provide a relaxing retreat. The master bedrooms are well sized, and the upper rooms, though smaller, also offer good comfort. Downstairs there is an attractive lounge and the breakfast room.

Rooms 9 en suite (1 fmly) **Facilities** FTV TVL tea/coffee Direct Dial Cen ht Wi-fi **Parking** 10

| MUKER | Map 18 SD99 |

Oxnop Hall (SD931973)

★★★★ FARMHOUSE

Low Oxnop, Gunnerside DL11 6JJ
☎ 01748 886253 📠 01748 886253 Mrs A Porter
dir: Off B6270 between Muker & Gunnerside

Set in beautiful Swaledale scenery, this smartly presented 17th-century farmhouse has been furnished with thought and care. The attractive bedrooms are well equipped and some boast original exposed beams and mullion windows. Hearty farmhouse breakfasts are served, using local and home-made produce where possible. A cosy lounge is also available.

Rooms 4 en suite 1 annexe en suite (1 GF) S £41-£51; D £76-£84* **Facilities** FTV tea/coffee Cen ht **Parking** 10 **Notes** ⊗ No Children 10yrs Closed Nov-Mar ⊛ 1300 acres beef/sheep/hill farming

---

| OLDSTEAD | Map 19 SE57 |

The Black Swan at Oldstead

★★★★★ ⊛⊛⊛ ⌂ RESTAURANT WITH ROOMS

YO61 4BL
☎ 01347 868387
e-mail: enquiries@blackswanoldstead.co.uk
dir: Exit A19, 3m S Thirsk for Coxwold, left in Coxwold, left at Byland Abbey for Oldstead

The Black Swan is set amidst the stunning scenery of the North Yorkshire National Park, and parts of the building date back to the 16th century. Well appointed, very comfortable bedrooms and bathrooms provide the perfect get-away-from-it-all. Open fires, a traditional bar and a restaurant, serving award-winning food, is the icing on the cake for this little gem of a property.

Rooms 4 en suite (4 GF) **Facilities** FTV DVD tea/coffee Dinner available Cen ht Wi-fi **Extras** Home-made biscuits, speciality toiletries - complimentary **Parking** 24 **Notes** LB ⊗ No Children 10yrs Closed 2wks Jan No coaches

---

PATELEY BRIDGE | Map 19 SE16

Roslyn House

★★★★ GUEST ACCOMMODATION

9 King St HG3 5AT
☎ 01423 711374 ▤ 01423 715995
e-mail: enquiries@roslynhouse.co.uk
web: www.roslynhouse.co.uk
dir: *B6165 into Pateley Bridge, right at end of High St at newsagents into King St, house 200yds on left*

You are assured of a very warm welcome at this well-maintained guest accommodation in the village centre. Bedrooms are sensibly furnished and offer many homely touches. A very comfortable lounge is available, and hearty breakfasts set you up for the day. Roslyn House caters well for cyclists and walkers on the famous Nidderdale Way.

Rooms 6 en suite (1 fmly) S £49-£55; D £70-£74*
Facilities FTV TVL tea/coffee Cen ht Wi-fi
Extras Chocolates, water - complimentary **Conf** Max 8 Board 8 **Parking** 6 **Notes** LB ⊗ No Children 3yrs

PICKERING | Map 19 SE78

PREMIER COLLECTION

17 Burgate

★★★★★ ⌂ GUEST ACCOMMODATION

17 Burgate YO18 7AU
☎ 01751 473463
e-mail: info@17burgate.co.uk
dir: *From A170 follow sign to Castle. 17 Burgate on right*

An elegant market town house close to the centre and the castle, offering comfortable individually designed bedrooms with all modern facilities, including free broadband. Public areas include a comfortable lounge bar, and breakfast includes a wide choice of local, healthy foods.

Rooms 5 en suite S £65-£105; D £78-£115*
Facilities FTV DVD iPod docking station Lounge tea/coffee Cen ht Licensed Wi-fi 🔒 **Extras** Chocolate, snacks **Parking** 7 **Notes** LB No Children 10yrs Closed Xmas

Fox & Hounds Country Inn

★★★★ INN

Main St, Sinnington YO62 6SQ
☎ 01751 431577 ▤ 01751 432791
e-mail: fox.houndsinn@btconnect.com
dir: *3m W of Pickering, off A170, betwen Pickering & Helmsley*

An attractive village inn offering smart, well-equipped bedrooms. The public areas include a bar, a cosy lounge and a restaurant which offers an impressive range of well presented and well cooked dishes.

Rooms 10 en suite (4 GF) **Facilities** tea/coffee Dinner available Direct Dial Wi-fi **Parking** 40 **Notes** Closed 25-26 Dec

PICKHILL | Map 19 SE38

Nags Head Country Inn

★★★★ ⊛⊛ INN

YO7 4JG
☎ 01845 567391 ▤ 01845 567212
e-mail: reservations@nagsheadpickhill.co.uk
dir: *Leave A1 junct 50 (travelling N) onto A6055; junct 51 (travelling S) onto A684, then A6055*

This country inn, situated in the centre of the attractive village, is only a mile from the A1, and nine miles northwest of Thirsk. It is renowned for the excellence of its food and traditional real ales, complemented by the atmosphere and character of its cosy bars. Some bedrooms are in a cottage next door, and they all have en suite bathrooms and are very well equipped with TV, clock radios, telephones and tea and coffee making facilities. The smartly appointed restaurant and cocktail bar is open to both residents and non-residents for dinner.

Rooms 7 en suite 6 annexe en suite (1 fmly) (3 GF) S £50-£77.50; D £67-£97* **Facilities** FTV TVL tea/coffee Dinner available Direct Dial Cen ht Wi-fi 🏊 ⚓ 18 🔒 **Extras** Fruit **Conf** Thtr 30 Class 18 Board 16 **Parking** 40 **Notes** LB ⊗ Closed 25 Dec

RAVENSCAR | Map 19 NZ90

Smugglers Rock Country House

★★★★ ⌂ GUEST HOUSE

YO13 0ER
☎ 01723 870044
e-mail: info@smugglersrock.co.uk
dir: *0.5m S of Ravenscar. Off A171 towards Ravenscar, opposite stone windmill*

Rooms 8 en suite (3 fmly) S £39-£47; D £68-£84
Facilities FTV TVL tea/coffee Cen ht Wi-fi 🔒 **Parking** 12 **Notes** LB ⊗ Closed Nov-Mar RS Etr-early Oct

REDCAR | Map 19 NZ62

Springdale House

★★★★ BED AND BREAKFAST

3 Nelson Ter TS10 1RX
☎ 01642 297169 & 07834 615147
e-mail: reservations@springdalehouse.co.uk

This renovated Victorian townhouse situated on a quiet terraced row offers delightful and friendly accommodation with a focus on quality furnishings and comfort. It is situated only five minutes walk from the town's bars and restaurants, and near to the promenade.

Rooms 4 en suite D £75-£80* **Facilities** STV tea/coffee Cen ht Wi-fi 🔒 **Notes** ⊗ No Children 16yrs

REETH | Map 19 SE09

Charles Bathurst Inn

★★★★ ⊜ INN

Arkengarthdale DL11 6EN
☎ 01748 884567 ▤ 01748 884599
e-mail: info@cbinn.co.uk
dir: *B6270 to Reeth, at Buck Hotel turn N to Langthwaite, pass church on right, inn 0.5m on right*

The CB Inn, as it is known, is surrounded by magnificent scenery high in the Dales. Food is the focus of the pub, where a choice of rustic eating areas makes for atmospheric dining. The well-equipped bedrooms blend contemporary and traditional styles, and cosy lounge areas are available. A well-equipped function suite is also available.

Rooms 19 en suite (3 fmly) (5 GF) D £92-£123*
Facilities FTV Lounge tea/coffee Dinner available Direct Dial Cen ht Wi-fi Fishing Riding Pool table
Extras Speciality toiletries, home-made shortbread
Conf Max 70 Thtr 70 Class 30 Board 30 **Parking** 35 **Notes** LB ⊗ Closed 25 Dec

RICCALL | Map 16 SE63

White Rose Villa

★★★★ ⚑ BED AND BREAKFAST

33 York Rd YO19 6QG
☎ 01757 248115
e-mail: whiterosevilla@btinternet.com
web: www.whiterosevilla.info
dir: *S of York, from A19, signed Riccall, 50mtrs on right*
Rooms 3 en suite (2 fmly) S £30-£35; D £60-£70*
Facilities FTV DVD TVL tea/coffee Cen ht Wi-fi **Parking** 4 **Notes** LB ⊗ Closed 24-26 & 31 Dec 🚭

RICHMOND | Map 19 NZ10

See also Reeth

Rosedale Guest House

★★★★ ⌂ GUEST HOUSE

2 Pottergate DL10 4AB
☎ 01748 823926 & 07854 698027
e-mail: gary53uk@hotmail.com
dir: *A1(M), A6108 to Richmond. Pottergate 0.5m before town centre*

A short stroll away from the small town of Richmond, this attractive Grade II listed building has been tastefully decorated throughout. Warm hospitality features alongside stylishly furnished and comfortably equipped bedrooms. The public rooms include a dining area and a private lounge offering free Wi-fi. Rosedale Guest House was a Finalist in the AA Friendliest B&B of the Year Award 2012-13.

Rooms 4 en suite (1 fmly) S £55-£72; D £80-£88*
Facilities FTV Lounge tea/coffee Cen ht Wi-fi 🔒 **Notes** LB ⊗ No Children 5yrs

RICHMOND continued

Whashton Springs Farm (NZ149046)

★★★★ FARMHOUSE

DL11 7JS
☎ 01748 822884 📠 01748 826285 **Mrs J M Turnbull**
e-mail: whashtonsprings@btconnect.com
web: www.whashtonsprings.co.uk
dir: In Richmond N at lights towards Ravensworth, 3m
down steep hill, farm at bottom on left

A friendly welcome awaits at this farmhouse
accommodation, situated in the heart of the countryside
yet convenient for major routes. Bedrooms are split
between the courtyard rooms and the main farmhouse.
Hearty breakfasts are served in the spacious dining room
overlooking the gardens. A stylish lounge is also
available.

Rooms 3 en suite 5 annexe en suite (2 fmly) (5 GF)
Facilities FTV tea/coffee Cen ht Wi-fi **Conf** Max 16 Board
16 **Parking** 10 **Notes** ⊗ No Children 3yrs Closed late
Dec-Jan ⊛ 600 acres arable/beef/mixed/sheep

The Frenchgate Guest House

★★★★ GUEST HOUSE

66 Frenchgate DL10 7AG
☎ 01748 823421 & 07889 768696 📠 01748 823421
e-mail: info@66frenchgate.co.uk
dir: From Scotch Corner, enter Richmond, straight over
rdbt & lights. Right at 2nd rdbt, turn left after 100mtrs

Tucked away on a charming cobbled street in an historic
market town, this attractively presented Victorian
townhouse has an elevated position with stunning views.
Bedrooms are comfortable and well equipped with
complimentary Wi-fi access provided. The spacious
conservatory lounge and breakfast room has panoramic
south-facing views of the Swale Valley and Easby Abbey.

Rooms 8 rms (7 en suite) (1 pri facs) (3 fmly) (2 GF)
S £55-£90; D £75-£94 **Facilities** FTV Lounge tea/coffee

Cen ht Wi-fi ⌦ 18 🏌 **Extras** Fridges, bottled water **Conf** Max
20 Thtr 15 Class 15 Board 15 **Notes** LB ⊗ No Children
5yrs

RIPON   **Map 19 SE37**

PREMIER COLLECTION

Mallard Grange (SE270704)

★★★★★ FARMHOUSE

Aldfield HG4 3BE
☎ 01765 620242 📠 01765 620242 **Mrs M Johnson**
e-mail: maggie@mallardgrange.co.uk
web: www.mallardgrange.co.uk
dir: B6265 W fom Ripon, Mallard Grange 2.5m on right

Located near Fountains Abbey a genuine welcome is
always guaranteed at Mallard Grange. The original
features of this early 16th-century, Grade II listed
farmhouse are highlighted by quality furnishings and
decor. Bedrooms, two of which are in a converted
smithy, are filled with a wealth of thoughtful extras,
and comprehensive breakfasts feature home-reared
and local produce.

Rooms 2 en suite 2 annexe en suite (2 GF) D £75-£100
Facilities FTV Lounge tea/coffee Cen ht Wi-fi
Extras Speciality toiletries, home-made biscuits
Parking 6 **Notes** LB ⊗ No Children 12yrs Closed Xmas
& New Year 500 acres mixed/beef/sheep/arable

The Old Coach House

★★★★★ GUEST ACCOMMODATION

2 Stable Cottages, North Stainley HG4 3HT
☎ 01765 634900 📠 01765 635352
e-mail: enquiries@oldcoachhouse.info
web: www.oldcoachhouse.info
dir: From Ripon take A6108 to Masham. Once in North
Stainley, on left opposite Staveley Arms

Rooms 8 en suite (4 GF) S £45-£55; D £75-£99*
Facilities FTV iPod docking station tea/coffee Direct Dial
Cen ht Wi-fi ⌦ 18 🏌 **Extras** Speciality toiletries -
complimentary **Parking** 8 **Notes** ⊗ No Children 14yrs

Bay Tree Farm (SE263685)

★★★★ FARMHOUSE

Aldfield HG4 3BE
☎ 01765 620394 📠 01765 620394 **Mrs V Leeming**
e-mail: val@btfarm.entadsl.com
web: www.baytreefarm.co.uk
dir: 4m W of Ripon. S off B6265 in village of Aldfield

A warm welcome awaits at this farmhouse set in the
countryside close to Fountains Abbey and Studley Park.
Bedrooms are suitably equipped, there is a cosy lounge
with a log-burning stove, and breakfast is traditional
home-cooked fare. Dinner is available for groups of eight
or more by arrangement.

Rooms 4 en suite 2 annexe en suite (1 fmly) (3 GF)
Facilities FTV tea/coffee Dinner available Cen ht Wi-fi
Parking 10 **Notes** LB 400 acres beef/arable

The George at Wath

★★★★ ⊛ INN

Main St, Wath HG4 5EN
☎ 01765 641324
e-mail: reception@thegeorgeatwath.co.uk
web: www.thegeorgeatwath.co.uk
dir: From A1 (dual carriageway) N'bound, left signed
Melmerby & Wath. From A1 S'bound, exit at slip road
signed A61. Right at T-junct signed Ripon. Approx 0.5m,
right for Melmerby & Wath

Located in the centre of the beautiful North Yorkshire
village of Wath, this popular village inn provides well-
equipped and pleasantly decorated accommodation. The
public areas include a spacious lounge bar complete with
log burning stove, and a relaxed dining area where a
varied selection of dishes is available. Wi-fi is available
throughout.

Rooms 5 en suite (1 fmly) S £50-£65; D £80-£120*
Facilities FTV iPod docking station tea/coffee Dinner
available Cen ht Wi-fi Pool table 🏌 **Extras** Home-made
cookies **Conf** Max 45 Thtr 45 Class 32 Board 20
Parking 25 **Notes** Civ Wed 60

The Royal Oak

★★★★ ⊛ INN

36 Kirkgate HG4 1PB
☎ 01765 602284
e-mail: info@royaloakripon.co.uk
dir: In town centre

Ideally located in the heart of the city centre close to the
Cathedral and museum, The Royal Oak offers modern,
stylish, and comfortable en suite rooms with a genuine
warm welcome on arrival. The inn has a restaurant and
separate bar area which organises food and wine tasting
events on a regular basis. The menu boasts a varied
range of traditional dishes with a European influence in
the attractively designed restaurant. A good selection of
Timothy Taylor ales can be found along with a varied
selection of wines.

Rooms 6 en suite (1 fmly) **Facilities** FTV tea/coffee Dinner
available Cen ht Wi-fi 🏌 **Parking** 4 **Notes** ⊗ No coaches

Save on B&Bs and Hotels. Book at **theAA.com/hotel**

YORKSHIRE, NORTH 343 ENGLAND

St George's Court (SE237697)

★★★★ 🏠 FARMHOUSE

Old Home Farm, Grantley HG4 3PJ
☎ 01765 620618 Mrs Hitchen
e-mail: info@stgeorgescourt.co.uk
web: www.stgeorges-court.co.uk
dir: *B6265 W from Ripon, up hill 1m past Risplith sign & next right, 1m on right*

This renovated farmhouse is a great location to get away from it all, in the delightful countryside close to Fountains Abbey. The attractive, well-equipped, upgraded ground-floor bedrooms are located around a central courtyard. Imaginative breakfasts are served in the breakfast room, and a guest lounge is available, both with views of the surrounding countryside.

Rooms 5 en suite (1 fmly) (5 GF) S £50-£60; D £75-£85*
Facilities Lounge tea/coffee Cen ht Wi-fi Fishing 🎣
Conf Max 12 **Parking** 12 **Notes** LB 20 acres beef /sheep/ pigs

---

SCARBOROUGH   Map 17 TA08

Columbus

★★★★ GUEST ACCOMMODATION

124 Columbus Ravine YO12 7QZ
☎ 01723 374634 & 07930 545964
e-mail: hotel.columbus@lineone.net
dir: *On A165 towards North Bay, near Peasholm Park*

Yorkshire hospitality at its best is offered here, and Bonnie Purchon is a welcoming hostess. The establishment is well located for the beach and attractions. Bedrooms are compact, well equipped and homely. A very comfortable lounge is provided. In the dining room a good breakfast is served, as are evening meals during the main season.

Rooms 10 en suite (2 fmly) S £30-£35; D £60-£70*
Facilities FTV DVD tea/coffee Dinner available Cen ht
Parking 8 **Notes** LB ⊗ No Children 3yrs Closed Dec

Foulsyke Farm House B&B (TA008912)

★★★★ FARMHOUSE

Barmoor Ln, Scalby YO13 0PG
☎ 01723 507423 Mr K Gregory
e-mail: foulsykebandb@btinternet.com
dir: *A171 from Scarborough follow signs to Whitby. Pass through Newby & Scalby. Left onto Barmoor Ln, 50yds past pond*

Foulsyke Farm is situated in the quiet village of Scalby three miles north of Scarborough. The house is on a working farm and is part of the Duchy of Lancaster estate. Gardens offer space to sit and enjoy the surrounding peaceful countryside. Bedrooms all provide a good level of comfort, and the new refurbished loft room offers luxury accommodation with wine, chocolates and flowers ideal for a special occasion.

Rooms 4 en suite S £50-£60; D £65-£85* **Facilities** FTV TVL tea/coffee Dinner available Cen ht Wi-fi 🔒
Extras Speciality toiletries, snacks in some rooms
Parking 8 **Notes** LB ⊗ No Children arable/beef/dairy/ sheep

The Hillcrest

★★★★ GUEST ACCOMMODATION

2 Peasholm Av YO12 7NE
☎ 01723 361981
e-mail: enquiries@hillcresthotel.co.uk
dir: *A165 to North Bay/leisure parks, into Peasholm Drive & Peasholm Crescent*

Hillcrest is in a residential area close to Peasholm Park, within walking distance of the cricket ground and the North Bay attractions, and its individually furnished bedrooms contain many extras. There is a dining room where breakfast and dinner are served.

Rooms 7 en suite (1 fmly) S £29-£37.50; D £56-£70*
Facilities FTV DVD tea/coffee Dinner available Cen ht Licensed Wi-fi **Parking** 2 **Notes** LB ⊗ No Children 4yrs Closed Dec-1 Feb

Olivers

★★★★ GUEST ACCOMMODATION

34 West St YO11 2QP
☎ 01723 368717
e-mail: info@olivershotelscarborough.co.uk
dir: *Take A64 to B1427 (Margarets Rd). Right onto A165 (Filey Rd). 2nd left into Granville Rd*

Well-equipped, spacious bedrooms are a feature of this old Victorian gentleman's residence, and one bedroom was originally the nursery. Close to the cliff lift down to the spa, beaches and gardens, and centrally located on the South Cliff.

Rooms 6 en suite (2 fmly) (1 GF) D £56-£64
Facilities FTV tea/coffee Dinner available Cen ht
Notes LB ⊗ Closed 20-28 Dec

Paragon

★★★★ GUEST ACCOMMODATION

123 Queens Pde YO12 7HU
☎ 01723 372676 📠 01723 372676
web: www.paragonhotel.com
dir: *On A64, follow signs for North Bay. Establishment on clifftop*

This welcoming Victorian terrace house has been carefully renovated to provide stylish, thoughtfully equipped, non-smoking accommodation. Hearty English breakfasts are served in the attractive dining room and there is also a lounge bar with a fabulous sea view.

Rooms 14 en suite (1 fmly) S £35; D £60-£80*
Facilities Lounge tea/coffee Direct Dial Cen ht Licensed Wi-fi **Parking** 6 **Notes** LB Closed 20 Nov-24 Jan

The Whiteley

★★★★ GUEST ACCOMMODATION

99-101 Queens Pde YO12 7HY
☎ 01723 373514 📠 01723 373007
e-mail: whiteleyhotel@bigfoot.com
dir: *A64, A165 to North Bay & Peasholm Park, right into Peasholm Rd, 1st left*

The Whiteley is an immaculately run, sea-facing home-from-home. Bedrooms, though compact, are carefully decorated and have many thoughtful extras. There's a small garden at the rear, a choice of lounges and a bar. The establishment has superb views, and the owners provide personal attention and a substantial breakfast.

Rooms 10 en suite (3 fmly) (1 GF) S £33.50-£35; D £55-£66* **Facilities** TVL tea/coffee Cen ht Licensed Wi-fi **Parking** 8 **Notes** LB ⊗ No Children 3yrs Closed 30 Nov-Jan

The Windmill Bed & Breakfast

★★★★ GUEST ACCOMMODATION

Mill St YO11 1SZ
☎ 01723 372735 📠 01723 377190
e-mail: info@windmill-hotel.co.uk
dir: *A64 into Scarborough, pass Sainsbury's, left into Victoria Rd, 3rd left into Mill St*

Situated in the centre of town but having its own car park, this unique establishment has modern bedrooms situated around a courtyard next to a windmill dating from 1784. The base of the mill includes a spacious breakfast room and a toy museum which is only viewable by guests.

Rooms 7 en suite (2 fmly) (6 GF) **Facilities** FTV tea/coffee Cen ht **Parking** 7 **Notes** ⊗

SCARBOROUGH *continued*

Howdale

★★★★ 🄰 GUEST HOUSE

121 Queens Pde YO12 7HU
☎ 01723 372696
e-mail: mail@howdale.co.uk
web: www.howdale.co.uk
dir: *Left at lights opposite railway station, stay in left lane. Straight over at next lights into Northway then Columbus Ravine. Right into Victoria Park, continue into Queens Parade*

Rooms 15 rms (13 en suite) (1 fmly) S £25-£28; D £50-£70* **Facilities** FTV TVL tea/coffee Cen ht Wi-fi **Parking** 9 **Notes** LB Closed Nov-Feb

See advert on opposite page

The Wharncliffe

★★★★ 🄰 GUEST ACCOMMODATION

26 Blenheim Ter YO12 7HD
☎ 01723 374635
e-mail: info@thewharncliffescarborough.co.uk
dir: *Follow signs to Castle, left into Blenheim St, left into Blenheim Ter*

Rooms 12 en suite D £65-£75* **Facilities** FTV DVD TVL tea/coffee Cen ht Licensed Wi-fi **Notes** LB ⊗ No Children 18yrs

The Chessington

★★★ GUEST ACCOMMODATION

The Crescent YO11 2PP
☎ 01723 365207
e-mail: info@thechessington.co.uk
web: www.thechessington.co.uk
dir: *A64 to town centre lights, right, left at next lights & right at next lights, The Chessington on left*

This Grade II listed building occupies a fine position overlooking The Crescent and is close to the town centre. The bedrooms are well equipped, and the spacious dining room is the setting for comprehensive breakfasts. A sitting room and lounge bar are available.

Rooms 10 en suite (2 fmly) S fr £34; D fr £68* **Facilities** FTV TVL tea/coffee Cen ht Licensed Wi-fi 🛆 **Conf** Max 10 **Notes** LB ⊗ Closed Dec & Jan

The Croft

★★★ 🄰 GUEST ACCOMMODATION

87 Queens Pde YO12 7HT
☎ 01723 373904
e-mail: information@crofthotel.co.uk
web: www.crofthotel.co.uk
dir: *Follow tourist signs for North Bay seafront, along front towards castle headland, right turn up cliff, right at top, premises on left*

A flexible approach to your needs is a key feature of this friendly establishment. It overlooks the bay, so you can enjoy the spectacular view from the comfortable lounge or from the patio in fine weather. Breakfast is served in the very pleasant well-appointed dining room.

Rooms 6 rms (5 en suite) (1 pri facs) (4 fmly) **Facilities** FTV TVL tea/coffee Dinner available Cen ht Licensed **Parking** 4 **Notes** LB ⊗ Closed Nov-Jan

The Danielle

★★★ GUEST ACCOMMODATION

9 Esplanade Rd, South Cliff YO11 2AS
☎ 01723 366206
e-mail: hoteldanielle@yahoo.co.uk
dir: *S of town centre. Exit A165 (Filey Rd) onto Victoria Av, left onto Esplanade, left onto Esplanade Rd*

A warm welcome is assured at this elegant Victorian house situated a short walk from the Spa Cliff Lift. Bedrooms are equipped with thoughtful extras, and day rooms include an attractive dining room and a lounge.

Rooms 9 rms (7 en suite) (2 pri facs) (1 fmly) S £31-£33; D £66-£68 **Facilities** FTV TVL tea/coffee Cen ht Licensed **Notes** LB ⊗ No Children 2yrs Closed Dec-mid Feb

Palace Hill

★★★ GUEST HOUSE

1 Palace Hill, Eastborough YO11 1NL
☎ 01723 374535
e-mail: info@palace-hill.co.uk
web: www.palace-hill.co.uk
dir: *On Foreshore Rd (with sea on right), left at lights into Eastborough, establishment 300yds on right*

With its central location in the Old Town this smartly presented 18th-century building is only a minute's walk from the South Bay beach and seafront. The house is attractively decorated, and the modern bedrooms have good quality en suite shower rooms. Wi-fi access is also available.

Rooms 9 en suite (3 fmly) (1 GF) **Facilities** FTV Cen ht Wi-fi **Notes** LB ⊗

Plane Tree Cottage Farm *(SE999984)*

★★★ FARMHOUSE

Staintondale YO13 0EY
☎ 01723 870796 Mrs M A Edmondson
dir: *A171, N from Scarborough. At Cloughton into Staintondale road, farm 2m N of Cloughton*

The Edmondson family are welcoming hosts, and the animals on the farm include unusual breeds of sheep and hens. This is an interesting and pleasant venue, either for its tranquil, secluded setting, or as a base for walking. Expect good home-cooking, comfortable bedrooms, and a cosy lounge and dining room.

Rooms 3 rms (2 en suite) (1 pri facs) (1 GF) D £60* **Facilities** TVL tea/coffee Dinner available Cen ht **Parking** 3 **Notes** ⊗ No Children Closed Oct-Mar 🐾 60 acres sheep/hens/Highland cattle

Save on B&Bs and Hotels. Book at theAA.com/hotel

YORKSHIRE, NORTH 345 ENGLAND

Argo

★★★ GUEST HOUSE

134 North Marine Rd YO12 7HZ
☎ **01723 375745**
dir: *Close to entrance of Scarborough Cricket Ground*

This friendly house is a haven for cricket fans, with some of the comfortable bedrooms overlooking the championship ground. Day rooms include a well appointed lounge and a dining room where tasty cooked breakfasts are served at individual tables.

Rooms 8 rms (5 en suite) (2 fmly) **Facilities** TVL tea/coffee Cen ht **Notes** ⊗ ⊜

The Barrington Guest House

★★★ GUEST HOUSE

3 Palace Hill, Eastborough YO11 1NL
☎ **01723 379494**
e-mail: valeriehotchin@talktalk.net

This charming house has an elevated position just a short walk from the sandy beaches of South Bay and all the amenities of the town. Bedrooms are ranged over three floors and all are tastefully decorated in a contemporary style; they include family rooms and en suite rooms.

Rooms 6 en suite (2 fmly) **Facilities** FTV tea/coffee Cen ht Wi-fi **Notes** LB Closed 24 Dec-2 Jan

North End Farm Country Guesthouse

★★★ GUEST ACCOMMODATION

88 Main St, Seamer YO12 4RF
☎ **01723 862965**
e-mail: northendfarm@tiscali.co.uk
dir: *A64 N onto B1261 through Seamer, guest house next to rdbt*

Located in Seamer, a village inland from Scarborough, this 18th-century guest house contains comfortable, well-equipped en suite bedrooms. Breakfast is served at individual tables in the smart dining room, and the cosy lounge has a large-screen TV.

Rooms 3 en suite (1 fmly) S £30-£40; D £60-£65*
Facilities FTV TVL tea/coffee Cen ht Wi-fi **Parking** 6
Notes ⊗

Peasholm Park Lodge

★★★ GUEST ACCOMMODATION

21-23 Victoria Park YO12 7TS
☎ **01723 500954**
e-mail: peasholmparkhotel@btconnect.com
web: www.peasholmpark.co.uk
dir: *Opposite entrance to Peasholm Park*

A warm welcome awaits at this family-run guest accommodation, within easy walking distance of the town, beach or open air theatre. Bedrooms are comfortable, and feature homely extras. A full English breakfast uses local produce and is served at individual tables in the dining room, which looks over Peasholm Park.

Rooms 12 en suite (3 fmly) **Facilities** FTV TVL tea/coffee Cen ht Licensed **Parking** 2 **Notes** ⊗ No Children 4yrs RS 22 Dec-2 Jan bed & breakfast only

SCARBOROUGH *continued*

Dolphin Guest House

★★★ **A** GUEST HOUSE

151 Columbus Ravine YO12 7QZ
☎ 01723 341914 📠 08715 284118
e-mail: dolphinguesthouse@btinternet.com
web: www.thedolphin.info
dir: *At train station left into Northway, into Columbus Ravine, guest house on right*

Rooms 6 rms (5 en suite) (1 pri facs) (4 fmly) S £30;
D £52-£56 **Facilities** FTV TVL tea/coffee Cen ht Wi-fi 🛁
Notes LB ⊗ Closed 22-26 Dec

Lyness Guest House

★★★ **A** GUEST HOUSE

145 Columbus Ravine YO12 7QZ
☎ 01723 375952 📠 01723 372550
e-mail: info@thelyness.co.uk
dir: *Follow signs for North Bay, leading onto Northway. Continue onto Columbus Ravine, over 2 rdbts, 200mtrs on right*

Rooms 8 rms (6 en suite) (2 pri facs) (2 fmly) S £26-£28;
D £56-£60* **Facilities** FTV DVD tea/coffee Dinner available Cen ht Wi-fi **Notes** LB ⊗ Closed 20 Dec-3 Jan

The Sheridan

★★★ **A** GUEST ACCOMMODATION

108 Columbus Ravine YO12 7QZ
☎ 01723 372094
e-mail: kim@thesheridan.co.uk
dir: *From railway station left into Northway, over 2 mini-rdbts, establishment 300yds on left*

Rooms 8 en suite (2 fmly) (1 GF) S £35-£40; D £56-£60*
Facilities FTV tea/coffee Dinner available Cen ht
Parking 6 **Notes** LB ⊗ No Children 5yrs Closed Xmas & New Year

Warwick House

★★ GUEST ACCOMMODATION

70 Westborough YO11 1TS
☎ 01723 374343 📠 01723 374343
e-mail: warwick-house@talktalk.net
dir: *On outskirts of town centre, just before railway station on left*

Close to the Stephen Joseph Theatre, station and shops, this friendly guest accommodation has some en suite and some shared facility rooms. Hearty breakfasts are served in the pleasant basement dining room. Private parking is available.

Rooms 6 rms (2 en suite) (4 fmly) S £19-£21; D £38-£46 (room only)* **Facilities** FTV tea/coffee Cen ht Wi-fi
Parking 5 **Notes** LB

SCOTCH CORNER   Map 19 NZ20

The Vintage

★★★ **A** INN

DL10 6NP
☎ 01748 824424 & 822961 📠 01748 826272
e-mail: thevintagescotchcorner@btinternet.com
web: www.thevintagehotel.co.uk
dir: *Exit A1 at Scotch Corner onto A66 towards Penrith, premises 200yds on left*

Rooms 8 rms (5 en suite) S £23.50-£39.50;
D £39.50-£49.50 (room only)* **Facilities** TVL tea/coffee Dinner available Cen ht Wi-fi **Conf** Max 48 Thtr 40 Class 24 Board 20 **Parking** 40 **Notes** LB Closed Xmas & New Year

---

SETTLE   Map 18 SD86

See also Clapham

The Lion at Settle

★★★★ INN

Duke St BD24 9DU
☎ 01729 822203
e-mail: relax@thelionsettle.co.uk
dir: *In town centre opposite Barclays Bank*

Located in the heart of the market town of Settle, this is a traditional coaching inn with an inglenook fireplace. The accommodation is comfortable and well equipped. A wide selection of imaginative dishes together with real ales and fine wines is served in the busy bar, and also the restaurant where the atmosphere is relaxed and comfortable; alfresco dining is possible in the courtyard.

Rooms 14 en suite (3 fmly) **Facilities** FTV tea/coffee Dinner available Cen ht Wi-fi 🛁 **Notes** LB

Whitefriars Country Guesthouse

★★★★ GUEST ACCOMMODATION

Church St BD24 9JD
☎ 01729 823753
e-mail: info@whitefriars-settle.co.uk
dir: *Off A65 through Settle market place, premises signed 50yds on left*

This friendly, family-run house stands in peaceful gardens just a stroll from the town centre and railway station. Bedrooms, some quite spacious, are attractively furnished in a traditional style and thoughtfully equipped. A hearty breakfast is served in the traditional, beamed dining room, and a cosy lounge is available.

Rooms 8 rms (6 en suite) (1 pri facs) (1 fmly) S fr £38;
D £58-£70* **Facilities** FTV Lounge TVL tea/coffee Cen ht Wi-fi **Parking** 10 **Notes** ⊗ Closed 25 Dec 🐾

SKIPTON   Map 18 SD95

Clay Hall

★★★★ GUEST ACCOMMODATION

Broughton Rd BD23 3AA
☎ 01756 794391
dir: *On A6069, 1m from Skipton towards Broughton*

A warm welcome is assured here on the outskirts of the town next to the Leeds and Liverpool canal. The house has been restored to provide carefully furnished bedrooms with smart modern shower rooms en suite, and a wealth of thoughtful extras. Comprehensive breakfasts are served in an attractive dining room.

Rooms 2 en suite **Facilities** tea/coffee Cen ht **Parking** 4 **Notes** ⊗ No Children 12yrs 🐾

Westfield House

★★★★ 🛏 GUEST HOUSE

50 Keighley Rd BD23 2NB
☎ 01756 790849
dir: *500yds S of town centre on A6131, S of canal bridge*

Just a stroll from the town centre, this friendly, non-smoking guest house provides smart accommodation. Bedrooms are well presented and most have large beds and many accessories including bathrobes. A hearty breakfast is served in the cosy dining room. Hospitality here is warm and nothing is too much trouble for the owners.

Rooms 4 en suite D £65 **Facilities** tea/coffee Cen ht **Notes** ⊗ No Children 🐾

The Woolly Sheep

★★★★ INN

38 Sheep St BD23 1HY
☎ 01756 700966
e-mail: woolly.sheep@btconnect.com
dir: *At bottom of High St*

Situated right in the centre of Skipton's vibrant market town, close to the medieval castle and railway station, this popular inn offers good quality and comfortable accommodation. All bedrooms are en suite and well equipped with traditional country pine furniture, colour TV and tea/coffee making facilities. Good home-cooked food is served alongside a range of award-winning Timothy Taylor real ales. Free secure car parking to the rear.

Rooms 9 en suite (3 fmly) **Facilities** FTV tea/coffee Dinner available Cen ht Wi-fi **Parking** 14 **Notes** ⊗ No coaches

Save on B&Bs and Hotels. Book at **theAA.com/hotel**

YORKSHIRE, NORTH 347 ENGLAND

Low Skibeden House *(SD013526)*

★★★ FARMHOUSE

Harrogate Rd BD23 6AB
☎ 01756 793849 Mrs H Simpson
web: www.lowskibeden.co.uk
dir: *1m E of Skipton on right before A59/A65 rdbt, set back from road*

A lovely stone, 16th-century farmhouse located one mile from Skipton and surrounded by open countryside. Bedrooms are traditionally furnished and there is a spacious, comfortable lounge where guests are offered tea or coffee and cake on arrival, and supper time drinks from hosts, Bill and Heather.

Rooms 4 rms (2 en suite) (2 pri facs) (2 fmly) S £40-£56; D £64-£68 **Facilities** TVL tea/coffee Cen ht 🐾 **Parking** 4 **Notes** LB ⊗ No Children 14yrs 40 acres sheep/non-working

Rockwood House

★★★ GUEST ACCOMMODATION

14 Main St, Embsay BD23 6RE
☎ 01756 799755 & 07976 314980 📠 01756 799755
e-mail: rockwood@steadonline.com
web: www.stayinyorkshire.co.uk
dir: *2m NE of Skipton. Off A59 into Embsay village centre*

This Victorian terrace house has a peaceful location in the village of Embsay. Bedrooms are thoughtfully furnished, individually styled and reassuringly comfortable. The traditionally styled dining room sets the venue for hearty breakfasts. Hospitality is a feature here with a genuine and friendly welcome.

Rooms 3 en suite (1 fmly) (1 GF) S £35-£39; D £65-£73* **Facilities** TVL tea/coffee Cen ht Wi-fi 🐾 18 🐾 **Parking** 3 **Notes** LB ⊗

SNAINTON Map 17 SE98

The Coachman Inn

★★★★ ⑳ RESTAURANT WITH ROOMS

Pickering Road West YO13 9PL
☎ 01723 859231 📠 01723 850008
e-mail: info@coachmaninn.co.uk
web: www.coachmaninn.co.uk
dir: *From A170 between Pickering & Scarborough onto B1258 (High St) in Snainton*

This Grade II listed property was built in 1776 as a coaching inn and stands just on the outskirts of Snainton. It now offers comfortable, double, en suite rooms, fine dining in a wonderful large dining room, a locals' bar, a quiet lounge for residents and ample parking.

Rooms 6 en suite (1 fmly) S £60-£80; D £80-£100* **Facilities** FTV tea/coffee Dinner available Cen ht Wi-fi 🐾 9 Riding 🐾 **Conf** Max 60 **Parking** 28 **Notes** No coaches

---

STILLINGTON Map 19 SE56

The Baytree

★★★★ ⑳ RESTAURANT WITH ROOMS

Main St YO61 1JU
☎ 01347 811394
e-mail: info@baytreestillington.com
web: www.baytreestillington.com
dir: *A19 into Tollerton Rd (signed Huby, Public Weighbridge, Sutton Park). In Huby left into Main St, right into Stillington Rd. 0.5m, left into Roseberry Ln. 0.5m, left into Carr Ln (B1363), right into Main St*

Just a 20-minute drive from York, The Baytree enjoys a quiet country village location. It is spacious with comfortable seating, a large conservatory restaurant, and a small, private dining area - perfect for small parties. The bar has open fires, stone-flagged floors and a great ambiance. The accommodation includes rooms suitable for families. The award-winning food is the highlight of any stay; the outside eating areas are delightful, and even if it's chilly, there are patio heaters.

Rooms 4 en suite (2 fmly) (2 GF) **Facilities** FTV tea/coffee Dinner available Direct Dial Cen ht Wi-fi **Parking** 8 **Notes** No coaches

---

SUTTON-ON-THE-FOREST Map 19 SE56

The Blackwell Ox Inn

★★★★★ ⑳ 🍴 INN

Huby Rd YO61 1DT
☎ 01347 810328 📠 01347 812738
e-mail: enquiries@blackwelloxinn.co.uk
web: www.blackwelloxinn.co.uk
dir: *A1237 onto B1363 to Sutton-on-the-Forest. Left at T-junct, 50yds on right*

Standing in the lovely village, this inn and restaurant offers very good bedrooms and pleasing public rooms. Built in 1823 the Blackwell Ox was named after a locally-

---

bred animal that weighed 2278lbs when it was slaughtered in 1779. Chef Steven Holding sources local produce from North Yorkshire, to create simple, honest cooking that has achieved an AA Rosette.

Rooms 7 en suite **Facilities** FTV tea/coffee Dinner available Direct Dial Cen ht Lift Wi-fi **Parking** 18 **Notes** LB ⊗ No coaches

---

TADCASTER Map 16 SE44

The Old Presbytery Guest House

★★★ BED AND BREAKFAST

London Rd, Saxton LS24 9PU
☎ 01937 557708
e-mail: guest@presbytery.plus.com
web: www.presbyteryguesthouse.co.uk
dir: *4m S of Tadcaster on A162. 100yds N of Barkston Ash on E side of road*

Dating from the 18th century, this former dower house has been modernised to provide comfortable accommodation with original features. The hall lounge features a wood-burning stove, and extensive breakfasts are served at an old oak dining table in a cosy breakfast room.

Rooms 4 rms (3 en suite) (1 pri facs) (1 fmly) S £43-£51; D £82 **Facilities** FTV TVL tea/coffee Cen ht Wi-fi 🐾 18 🐾 **Parking** 6 **Notes** ⊗ Closed 21 Dec-6 Jan

---

THIRSK Map 19 SE48

PREMIER COLLECTION

Spital Hill

★★★★★ 🐾 🍴 GUEST ACCOMMODATION

York Rd YO7 3AE
☎ 01845 522273 📠 01845 524970
e-mail: spitalhill@spitalhill.entadsl.com
web: www.spitalhill.co.uk
dir: *1.5m SE of town, set back 200yds from A19, driveway marked by 2 white posts*

Set in gardens, this substantial Victorian country house is delightfully furnished. The spacious bedrooms are thoughtfully equipped with many extras, one even has a piano, but no TVs or kettles; the proprietor prefers to offer tea as a service. Delicious meals feature local and home-grown produce and are served house-party style around one table in the interesting dining room.

Rooms 3 rms (2 en suite) (1 pri facs) 2 annexe en suite (1 GF) **Facilities** TVL Dinner available Direct Dial Cen ht Licensed Wi-fi 🐾 🐾 **Parking** 6 **Notes** ⊗ No Children 12yrs

THORNTON WATLASS — Map 19 SE28

PREMIER COLLECTION

Thornton Watlass Hall

★★★★★ GUEST ACCOMMODATION

HG4 4AS
☎ 01677 422803 📠 01677 424160
e-mail: enquiries@thorntonwatlasshall.co.uk
dir: Exit B6268 to Thornton Watlass. Hall at N end of village

Thornton Watlass Hall dates from the 11th century and has been occupied by the same family for just under 1000 years. The Hall has featured in TV dramas over the years such as *All Creatures Great and Small*, and it has also been the home to Lord Ashfordly, as Ashfordly Hall in *Heartbeat*. The Hall is finely furnished in period style and is unspoilt but still offers all the modern amenities. David and Liz Smith-Dodsworth offer a very friendly welcome and breakfasts are served in the grand dining room offering local produce. Relax in the palatial drawing room with its large open fireplace and honesty bar.

Rooms 6 en suite (1 fmly) **Facilities** FTV TVL tea/coffee Direct Dial Cen ht Licensed Wi-fi 🎱 Snooker **Parking** 50 **Notes** Closed 24 Dec-1 Jan RS Nov-Apr Full house parties only

---

Buck Inn

★★★ INN

HG4 4AH
☎ 01677 422461 📠 01677 422447
e-mail: innwatlass1@btconnect.com
web: www.thebuckinn.net
dir: From A1 at Leeming Bar take A684 towards Bedale, B6268 towards Masham 2m, turn right at x-rds to Thornton Watlass

This traditional country inn is situated on the edge of the village green overlooking the cricket pitch. Cricket prints and old photographs are found throughout, and an open fire in the bar adds to the warm and intimate atmosphere. Wholesome lunches and dinners, from an extensive menu, are served in the bar or dining room. Bedrooms are brightly decorated and well equipped.

Rooms 7 rms (5 en suite) (1 fmly) (1 GF) **Facilities** TVL tea/coffee Dinner available Cen ht Wi-fi Fishing Pool table Quoits **Conf** Max 50 Thtr 50 Class 45 Board 30 **Parking** 10 **Notes** RS 24-25 Dec No accommodation, no food 25 Dec

WESTOW — Map 19 SE76

Woodhouse Farm (SE749637)

★★★★ FARMHOUSE

YO60 7LL
☎ 01653 618378 & 07904 293422
📠 01653 618378 Mrs S Wardle
e-mail: stay@wood-house-farm.co.uk
web: www.wood-house-farm.co.uk
dir: Exit A64 to Kirkham Priory & Westow. Right at T-junct, farm drive 0.5m out of village on right

The owners of this house are a young farming family who open their home and offer caring hospitality. Home-made bread, preserves and farm produce turn breakfast into a feast, and the views from the house across open fields are splendid.

Rooms 2 en suite (1 fmly) S £35-£50; D £65-£80* **Facilities** FTV TVL tea/coffee Cen ht Wi-fi ch fac Fishing 🛁 **Parking** 12 **Notes** LB ⊗ Closed Xmas, New Year & mid Mar-mid Apr 🐄 500 acres arable/sheep

WEST WITTON — Map 19 SE08

The Wensleydale Heifer

★★★★ ◉◉ RESTAURANT WITH ROOMS

Main St DL8 4LS
☎ 01969 622322
e-mail: info@wensleydaleheifer.co.uk
web: www.wensleydaleheifer.co.uk
dir: A1 to Leeming Bar junct, A684 towards Bedale for approx 10m to Leyburn, then towards Hawes 3.5m to West Witton

Describing itself as 'boutique style', this 17th-century former coaching inn is very much in the 21st century. The bedrooms, with Egyptian cotton linen and Molton Brown toiletries as standard, are each designed with a unique and interesting theme - for example, Black Sheep, Night at the Movies, True Romantics and Shooters, and for chocolate lovers there's a bedroom where they can eat as much chocolate as they like! The food is very much the focus here in both the informal fish bar and the contemporary style restaurant. The kitchen prides itself on sourcing the freshest fish and locally reared meats. The Wensleydale Heifer was last year's AA Funkiest B&B of the Year (2011-2012).

Rooms 9 en suite 4 annexe en suite (2 fmly) (2 GF) S £90; D £120-£220* **Facilities** FTV DVD Lounge tea/coffee Dinner available Direct Dial Cen ht Wi-fi **Extras** Speciality toiletries **Parking** 30 **Notes** LB

WHITBY — Map 19 NZ81

Estbek House

★★★★★ ◉◉ 🍴 RESTAURANT WITH ROOMS

East Row, Sandsend YO21 3SU
☎ 01947 893424 📠 01947 893625
e-mail: info@estbekhouse.co.uk
dir: From Whitby take A174. In Sandsend, left into East Row

A speciality seafood restaurant on the first floor is the focus of this listed building in a small coastal village north west of Whitby. The seasonal menu is based on local fresh local ingredients, and is overseen by James the chef, who has guided his team to 2 AA Rosette recognition. There is also a small bar and breakfast room, and four individually appointed bedrooms offering luxury and comfort.

Rooms 4 rms (3 en suite) (1 pri facs) **Facilities** tea/coffee Dinner available Cen ht Wi-fi **Conf** Board 20 **Parking** 6 **Notes** ⊗ No Children 14yrs No coaches

Netherby House

★★★★ 🍴 GUEST ACCOMMODATION

90 Coach Rd, Sleights YO22 5EQ
☎ 01947 810211 📠 01947 810211
e-mail: info@netherby-house.co.uk
web: www.netherby-house.co.uk
dir: In village of Sleights, off A169 (Whitby-Pickering road)

This fine Victorian house offers thoughtfully furnished, individually styled bedrooms together with delightful day rooms. There is a fine conservatory and the grounds are extensive, with exceptional views from the summerhouse at the bottom of the garden. Imaginative dinners feature produce from the extensive kitchen garden.

Rooms 6 en suite 5 annexe en suite (1 fmly) (5 GF) S £40-£49.50; D £80-£99* **Facilities** FTV Lounge TVL tea/

Save on B&Bs and Hotels. Book at theAA.com/hotel

YORKSHIRE, NORTH 349 ENGLAND

coffee Dinner available Cen ht Licensed Wi-fi 🐾 🔒
Parking 17 **Notes** LB ⊗ No Children 2yrs Closed 25-26 Dec

Chiltern Guest House

★★★★ GUEST HOUSE

13 Normanby Ter, West Cliff YO21 3ES
☎ 01947 604981
e-mail: Jjchiltern@aol.com
dir: *Whalebones next to Harbour, sea on right. Royal Hotel on left, 200yds. Royal Gardens turn left, 2nd road on left, 6th house on right*

This Victorian terrace house offers a warm welcome and comfortable accommodation within walking distance of the town centre and seafront. Public areas include a smartly decorated lounge and a bright, attractive dining room. Bedrooms are thoughtfully equipped and many have modern en suites.

Rooms 9 en suite (2 fmly) S £30-£35; D £60-£70*
Facilities FTV tea/coffee Cen ht Wi-fi ⅃ 18 🔒 **Notes** LB

Corra Lynn

★★★★ GUEST ACCOMMODATION

28 Crescent Av YO21 3EW
☎ 01947 602214 📠 01947 602214
dir: *On corner of A174 & Crescent Av*

Occupying a prominent corner position, this property mixes traditional values with a trendy and artistic style. Bedrooms are thoughtfully equipped, individually furnished and have bright colour schemes, but it is the delightful dining room with corner bar, and a wall adorned with clocks that catch the eye.

Rooms 5 en suite (1 fmly) D fr £76* **Facilities** STV FTV tea/coffee Direct Dial Cen ht Licensed **Parking** 5 **Notes** ⊗ Closed 21 Dec-14 Feb 🍽

Kimberley House

★★★★ GUEST ACCOMMODATION

7 Havelock Place YO21 3ER
☎ 01947 604125 📠 01947 604125
e-mail: enquiries@kimberleyhouse.com
web: www.kimberleyhouse.com
dir: *Follow signs for West Cliff, close to Whalebone Arch and Captain Cook Monument, behind Royal Crescent at corner of Hudson St*

With new ownership in place, a warm and genuine hospitality is offered at this attractive house in the centre of Whitby, just a short stroll away from the local attractions. Bedrooms are pleasantly co-ordinated and comfortably furnished. Freshly prepared breakfasts are served in the attractive ground floor dining room.

Rooms 8 rms (7 en suite) (1 pri facs) (2 fmly) (1 GF) S £35; D £65-£75 **Facilities** FTV DVD TVL tea/coffee Cen ht Wi-fi 🔒 **Notes** LB ⊗

Lansbury Guesthouse

★★★★ GUEST ACCOMMODATION

29 Hudson St YO21 3EP
☎ 01947 604821
e-mail: jill@lansbury44.fsnet.co.uk
dir: *In town centre. Exit A174 (Upgang Ln) into Crescent Av, 2nd right*

A short walk from the historic harbour, a warm welcome is assured at this elegant Victorian terrace house which has been renovated to provide good standards of comfort and facilities. Bedrooms are equipped with thoughtful extras, and comprehensive breakfasts using local produce are served in an attractive dining room.

Rooms 7 en suite **Facilities** FTV tea/coffee Cen ht **Parking** 3 **Notes** ⊗

Rosslyn Guest House

★★★★ GUEST HOUSE

11 Abbey Ter YO21 3HQ
☎ 01947 604086
e-mail: rosslynhouse@googlemail.com

Guests are sure of a friendly atmosphere, high standards of cleanliness and comfortable bedrooms at this lovely house, close to the sea front. Breakfast is served in a beautifully appointed dining room. Additional facilities include a small guest kitchen, complimentary Wi-fi, Sky TV and secure outside storage for bikes.

Rooms 6 en suite (2 fmly) (1 GF) **Facilities** STV tea/coffee Cen ht Wi-fi **Parking** 1 **Notes** LB ⊗

Sandpiper Guest House

★★★★ GUEST HOUSE

4 Belle Vue Ter YO21 3EY
☎ 01947 600246
e-mail: enquiries@sandpiperhouse.wanadoo.co.uk
dir: *From A169 2nd left at rdbt signed Whitby, follow signs to West Cliff on N Prom, 4th right, take Esplanade straight into Belle Vue Terrace. Guest house on left*

This well presented Victorian house is just a few minutes' walk from Whitby's golden sands and the quaint streets of its historic harbour area. The contemporary bedrooms vary in size with a choice of singles, twins, a four-poster room and family room available. Hearty breakfasts are served in the cheerful lower ground-floor dining room.

Rooms 7 en suite (1 fmly) (1 GF) **Facilities** tea/coffee Cen ht Wi-fi **Parking** 3 **Notes** ⊗ No Children 4yrs 🍽

Whitehaven Guest House

★★★★ GUEST ACCOMMODATION

29 Crescent Av YO21 3EW
☎ 01947 601569
e-mail: simon@whitehavenguesthouse.co.uk
web: www.whitehavenguesthouse.co.uk
dir: *Follow signs to West Cliff, A174 into Crescent Av*

Occupying a corner position close to the sports complex and indoor swimming pool, this house provides colourful bedrooms in contrasting styles. All rooms have mini-fridges and most have DVD players. Vegetarian options are available at breakfast, which is served in the attractive dining room.

Rooms 4 rms (3 en suite) (1 pri facs) (1 fmly) D £60-£70* **Facilities** FTV DVD tea/coffee Cen ht Wi-fi 🔒 **Notes** LB ⊗ Closed 23-26 Dec 🍽

WOMBLETON — Map 19 SE68

New Buckland

★★★★ BED AND BREAKFAST

Flatts Ln YO62 7RU
☎ 01751 433369 & 07738 430519
e-mail: junedrake138@btinternet.com
dir: *From A170 turn right 3m from Helmsley, left at Plough Inn follow round, last property on right*

New Buckland offers two attractive bedrooms and excellent bathrooms in a well presented countryside property. Whether one or both rooms are booked, guests have exclusive use of the spacious, contemporary lounge and a very well equipped small kitchen. Complimentary Wi-fi access is available. Guests also have use of an area of the attractive garden with summer house and garden furniture.

Rooms 2 rms (2 pri facs) **Facilities** FTV TVL Cen ht Wi-fi **Parking** 2 **Notes** ⊗ No Children

YORK — Map 16 SE65

See also Sutton-on-the-Forest

Burswood Guest House

★★★★ 🍴 GUEST HOUSE

68 Tadcaster Rd, Dringhouses YO24 1LR
☎ 01904 702582 & 708377 📠 01904 708377
e-mail: info@burswoodguesthouse.co.uk
dir: *On A1036 Tadcaster Rd*

Guests are sure of a warm welcome at this modern dormer bungalow. Bedrooms are richly furnished and very well equipped. Freshly cooked breakfasts are served in the conservatory/breakfast room overlooking the attractive garden. Parking is available, and the city centre and racecourse are easily accessible from Burswood.

Rooms 6 en suite (2 fmly) (3 GF) D £65-£130*
Facilities FTV tea/coffee Cen ht Wi-fi **Parking** 6 **Notes** LB ⊗

YORK *continued*

Guy Fawkes Inn

★ ★ ★ ★ ⊛ INN

25 High Petergate YO1 7HP
☎ 01904 623716
e-mail: enquiry@gfyork.com
web: www.gfyork.com
dir: *A64 onto A1036 signed York & inner ring road. Over bridge into Duncombe Place, right into High Petergate*

This inn is only feet away from The Minster and was the birthplace of the notorious plotter, Guy Fawkes. Steeped in history, it is full of character and has been restored to retain many original features including the timber staircase, gas lighting and open fires. The bar is a real gathering place for locals and visitors to the city. The bedrooms are wonderfully appointed with antique furniture, Italian fabrics and luxury beds; some of the modern bathrooms have roll-top baths. An outside courtyard at the back of the inn provides ample space for dining and enjoying a drink.

Rooms 13 en suite (1 fmly) (2 GF) **Facilities** FTV tea/coffee Dinner available Direct Dial Wi-fi

The Lamb & Lion

★ ★ ★ ★ ⊛ INN

2-4 High Petergate YO1 7EH
☎ 01904 612078 & 654112
e-mail: enquiry@lambandlionyork.com
web: www.lambandlionyork.com
dir: *A64 onto A1036. 3.5m, at rdbt 3rd exit, continue on A1036. 2m, right into High Petergate*

This inn, steeped in history and full of character, stands in the shadows of the medieval city gate on Bootham Bar. The stylish bedrooms are well appointed and have wonderfully comfortable beds; some benefit from views of the city wall and The Minster itself. The public areas have winding passages leading to a 'Parlour' dining room complete with church pews and open fire; cosy little rooms off the corridor afford much privacy.

Rooms 12 en suite S £69-£95; D £85-£169*
Facilities FTV tea/coffee Dinner available Cen ht Wi-fi
Extras Bottled mineral water - complimentary **Conf** Max 20 Thtr 20 Class 20 Board 20

Ascot House

★ ★ ★ ★ GUEST ACCOMMODATION

80 East Pde YO31 7YH
☎ 01904 426826 🖷 01904 431077
e-mail: admin@ascothouseyork.com
web: www.ascothouseyork.com
dir: *0.5m NE of city centre. Exit A1036 (Heworth Green) into Mill Ln, 2nd left*

June and Keith Wood provide friendly service at the 1869 Ascot House, a 15-minute walk from the town centre. Bedrooms are thoughtfully equipped, many with four-poster or canopy beds and other period furniture. Reception rooms include a cosy lounge that also retains its original features.

Rooms 12 en suite (3 fmly) (2 GF) S £60-£80; D £72-£95* **Facilities** FTV TVL tea/coffee Cen ht Licensed Wi-fi 🔒 **Parking** 13 **Notes** LB Closed 21-28 Dec

Ashley Guest House

★ ★ ★ ★ GUEST HOUSE

76 Scott St YO23 1NS
☎ 01904 647520 & 07955 250271
e-mail: stay@ashleyguesthouse.co.uk
dir: *From A64 take York West exit onto A1036 (Tadcaster Rd) follow city centre signs. After racecourse (on right) at 2nd lights right into Scarcroft Rd. Scott St 2nd last street before lights*

Ashley Guest House is a Victorian end-terrace that has been given a very modern treatment with stylish interiors and distinctive character. Attractively furnished bedrooms and caring hospitality are hallmarks of this well located city-centre establishment.

Rooms 6 rms (5 en suite) (1 pri facs) (1 fmly) S £40-£53; D £50-£86* **Facilities** FTV Lounge tea/coffee Cen ht Wi-fi 🔒 **Notes** ⊗ No Children 5yrs

City Guest House

★ ★ ★ ★ GUEST ACCOMMODATION

68 Monkgate YO31 7PF
☎ 01904 622483
e-mail: info@cityguesthouse.co.uk
web: www.cityguesthouse.co.uk
dir: *NE of city centre on B1036*

Just a stroll from the historic Monk Bar, this guest accommodation is well located for business, shopping and sightseeing. Carefully furnished bedrooms boast stylish interior design and come equipped with a host of thoughtful touches. The smart dining room is the venue for a good breakfast.

Rooms 7 rms (6 en suite) (1 pri facs) (1 fmly) (1 GF) S £40-£45; D £70-£78* **Facilities** FTV Lounge tea/coffee Cen ht Wi-fi ♪ 9 🔒 **Parking** 6 **Notes** ⊗ No Children 8yrs Closed Xmas & 1st 2wks Jan

The Heathers Guest House

★★★★ GUEST ACCOMMODATION

54 Shipton Rd, Clifton-Without YO30 5RQ
☎ 01904 640989 ▤ 01904 640989
e-mail: aabbg@heathers-guest-house.co.uk
web: www.heathers-guest-house.co.uk
dir: N of York on A19, halfway between A1237 ring road & York city centre

This spacious detached house offers off-street parking and a peaceful setting, only a short drive or walk from the City centre. Each room is individually designed, using quality fabrics. The light, airy breakfast room looks out onto the beautiful large rear garden, which is visited daily by local wildlife. Complimentary Wi-fi access is provided.

Rooms 6 rms (4 en suite) (2 pri facs) (1 fmly)
S £52-£126; D £56-£130 **Facilities** Lounge tea/coffee Cen ht Wi-fi ♿ **Parking** 9 **Notes** ⊗ No Children 10yrs Closed Xmas

Holly Lodge

★★★★ GUEST ACCOMMODATION

204-206 Fulford Rd YO10 4DD
☎ 01904 646005
e-mail: geoff@thehollylodge.co.uk
web: www.thehollylodge.co.uk
dir: On A19 south side, 1.5m on left from A64/A19 junct, or follow A19 Selby signs from city centre to Fulford Rd

Located just a short walk from the historic centre, this pleasant Georgian property has co-ordinated, well-equipped bedrooms. The spacious lounge houses a grand piano, and hearty breakfasts are served in the cosy dining room. You may also enjoy the delightful walled garden. Complimentary Wi-fi is also available.

Rooms 5 en suite (1 fmly) (1 GF) S £58-£88; D £78-£88 **Facilities** FTV Lounge tea/coffee Cen ht Wi-fi **Parking** 6 **Notes** ⊗ No Children 7yrs Closed 24-27 Dec

Midway House

★★★★ ⚠ GUEST ACCOMMODATION

145 Fulford Rd YO10 4HG
☎ 01904 659272 ▤ 01904 638496
e-mail: info@midwayhouseyork.co.uk
dir: A64 to York, 3rd exit A19 to York city centre, over 2nd lights, house 50yds on right
Rooms 12 rms (10 en suite) (3 fmly) (1 GF) S £48-£66; D £60-£84* **Facilities** FTV TVL tea/coffee Cen ht Wi-fi **Parking** 14 **Notes** LB ⊗ No Children 6yrs Closed 18 Dec-20 Jan

Adam's House

★★★ GUEST HOUSE

5 Main St, Fulford YO10 4HJ
☎ 01904 655413 ▤ 01904 643203
e-mail: adams.house2@virgin.net
dir: A64 onto A19, 200yds on right after lights

Adam's House offers comfortable accommodation not far from York centre in the suburb of Fulford, close to the university. It has many fine period features, pleasant, well-proportioned bedrooms, and an attractive dining room. The resident owners are friendly and attentive.

Rooms 8 rms (7 en suite) (4 fmly) (2 GF) **Facilities** FTV tea/coffee Cen ht Wi-fi **Parking** 8 **Notes** ⊗

Dalescroft Guest House

★★★ GUEST HOUSE

10 Southlands Rd YO23 1NP
☎ 01904 626801 ▤ 01904 626801
e-mail: info@dalescroft-york.co.uk
web: www.dalescroft-york.co.uk
dir: A64 onto A1036 towards racecourse, right at lights (Kwik-Fit on left) into Scarcroft Rd (A59). Pass green on left, right into Russell St, at top turn left into Southlands Rd

Originally built in 1908, this smartly appointed Victorian terrace house is located in a quiet residential area just ten minutes walk from the city of York. Bedrooms and bathrooms are comfortably furnished. Freshly cooked breakfasts are served at individual tables in the cosy dining room. Permits are available for the on-street parking.

Rooms 5 en suite **Facilities** FTV tea/coffee Cen ht **Notes** LB ⊗ No Children 12yrs

Greenside

★★★ GUEST HOUSE

124 Clifton YO30 6BQ
☎ 01904 623631 ▤ 01904 623631
e-mail: greenside@onebillnet.co.uk
web: www.greensideguesthouse.co.uk
dir: A19 N towards city centre, over lights for Greenside, on left opposite Clifton Green

Overlooking Clifton Green, this charming detached conservation house is just within walking distance of the city centre. Accommodation consists of comfortably furnished bedrooms and there is a cosy lounge and a dining room, where the traditional full English is served. Secure parking and Wi-fi are additional bonuses.

Rooms 6 rms (3 en suite) (2 fmly) (3 GF) S fr £30; D fr £60 **Facilities** FTV TVL tea/coffee Cen ht Wi-fi **Parking** 6 **Notes** LB Closed Xmas & New Year ⊗

St Georges

★★★ ⚠ GUEST ACCOMMODATION

6 St Georges Place, Tadcaster Rd YO24 1DR
☎ 01904 625056 ▤ 01904 625009
e-mail: breakfastinyork@aol.com
web: www.stgeorgesyork.com
dir: A64 onto A1036 N to city centre, as racecourse ends, St Georges Place on left

Rooms 10 en suite (4 fmly) (1 GF) S £35-£65; D £55-£71* **Facilities** tea/coffee Cen ht Wi-fi ♿ **Parking** 7 **Notes** LB No Children 12yrs Closed mid Dec-mid Jan

YORKSHIRE, SOUTH

DONCASTER
Map 16 SE50

Innkeeper's Lodge Doncaster, Bessacarr

★★★ INN

Bawtry Rd, Bessacarr DN4 7BS
☎ 0845 112 6032
e-mail: info@innkeeperslodge.com
web: www.innkeeperslodge.com

At Innkeeper's Lodge you'll find accommodation with comfort and character in equal measure, and everything needed for a relaxing stay, from easy check-in and free parking to complimentary breakfast and a cosy pub serving great value food and drink on the doorstep. Each Lodge has quality rooms, and there are Lodges in a variety of locations from towns and cities to countryside settings across the UK.

Rooms 25 en suite (3 fmly) (6 GF) **Facilities** FTV tea/coffee Dinner available Direct Dial Wi-fi **Parking**

ROTHERHAM
Map 16 SK49

The Stonecroft

★★★★ GUEST ACCOMMODATION

138 Main St, Bramley S66 2SF
☎ 01709 540922 📠 01709 540922
e-mail: stonecrofthotel@btconnect.com
dir: 3m E of Rotherham. Off A631 into Bramley village centre

These converted stone cottages in the centre of Bramley provide a good base for visiting Rotherham or Sheffield. Some bedrooms are around a landscaped courtyard with private parking, and there is a lounge with a bar. Imaginative home-cooked meals are available.

Rooms 3 en suite 4 annexe en suite (1 fmly) (4 GF) S £45-£60; D £60-£80* **Facilities** FTV TVL tea/coffee Dinner available Cen ht Licensed Wi-fi ⌣ 18 **Parking** 7 **Notes** LB ⊗ Closed 24 Dec-2 Jan

SHEFFIELD
Map 16 SK38

Cross Scythes

★★★★ INN

Baslow Rd, Totley S17 4AE
☎ 0114 236 0204
e-mail: enquiries@cross-scythes.com

Located approximately five miles south of Sheffield city centre and just ten minutes drive from Chatsworth House, this 18th-century building has been sympathetically renovated. There are four tastefully decorated double rooms and all are en suite. Food is served all day throughout the spacious public areas.

Rooms 4 en suite D fr £55 (room only)* **Facilities** FTV tea/coffee Dinner available Cen ht Wi-fi ⌣ 18 **Parking** 51 **Notes** ⊗

Padley Farm B&B

★★★★ GUEST ACCOMMODATION

Dungworth Green S6 6HE
☎ 0114 285 1427 & 07890 937090 📠 0114 285 1427
e-mail: aandlmbestall@btinternet.com
web: www.padleyfarm.co.uk
dir: M1 junct 33 follow ring road (A61 Barnsley), left onto B6077 signed Bradfield

The barn conversion offers high quality en suite rooms with spectacular views of open countryside. An allergy free environment and warm hospitality ensure a pleasant stay.

Rooms 7 en suite (3 fmly) (2 GF) S £37-£60; D £60* **Facilities** FTV DVD tea/coffee Cen ht Fishing Riding Snooker ⌣ **Conf** Max 15 Class 15 **Parking** 8 **Notes** LB ⊗

Westbourne House Guest Accommodation

★★★★ GUEST ACCOMMODATION

25 Westbourne Rd, Broomhill S10 2QQ
☎ 0114 266 0109 📠 0114 266 7778
e-mail: guests@westbournehousehotel.com
dir: A61 onto B6069 Glossop Rd, past university, after Hallamshire Hospital over lights to next T-junct, straight through next lights, left onto Westbourne Rd

Westbourne House is a Victorian residence situated in beautiful gardens close to the university and hospitals. The modern bedrooms are individually furnished and decorated, and extremely well equipped. Wi-fi is available throughout the property. A comfortable lounge overlooks the terrace and garden.

Rooms 8 rms (7 en suite) (1 pri facs) (2 fmly) **Facilities** FTV TVL tea/coffee Cen ht Licensed Wi-fi **Parking** 6 **Notes** ⊗

Innkeeper's Lodge Sheffield, Longshaw

★★★ INN

Hathersage Rd, Longshaw S11 7TY
☎ 0845 112 6041
e-mail: info@innkeeperslodge.com
web: www.innkeeperslodge.com

At Innkeeper's Lodge you'll find accommodation with comfort and character in equal measure, and everything needed for a relaxing stay, from easy check-in and free parking to complimentary breakfast and a cosy pub serving great value food and drink on the doorstep. Each Lodge has quality rooms, and there are Lodges in a variety of locations from towns and cities to countryside settings across the UK.

Rooms 10 en suite (7 fmly) (4 GF) **Facilities** FTV tea/coffee Dinner available Direct Dial Wi-fi **Parking**

THROAPHAM
Map 16 SK58

Throapham House

★★★★★ 🅰 GUEST ACCOMMODATION

Oldcotes Rd S25 2QS
☎ 01909 562208 📠 01909 212005
e-mail: enquiries@throapham-house.co.uk
web: www.throapham-house.co.uk
dir: M1 junct 31, A57 E towards Worksop. 1m, left at lights, at rdbt 2nd exit into Common Rd. In Throapham, 200yds on left after sign

Rooms 3 en suite **Facilities** FTV TVL tea/coffee Cen ht Wi-fi **Parking** 3 **Notes** LB ⊗

TODWICK
Map 16 SK48

The Red Lion

★★★ INN

Worksop Rd S26 1DJ
☎ 01909 771654 📠 01909 773704
e-mail: 7933@greeneking.co.uk
dir: On A57, 1m from M1 junct 31 towards Worksop

Originally a roadside public house, The Red Lion is now a popular bar and restaurant offering a wide range of food and drink. Bedrooms are well equipped, modern and comfortable, and there are three meeting rooms and ample parking facilities.

Rooms 27 en suite (1 fmly) (14 GF) **Facilities** tea/coffee Direct Dial **Parking** 80

Wortley Hall

★★★★ 😊 GUEST ACCOMMODATION

Wortley Village S35 7DB
☎ 0114 288 2100 📠 0114 283 0695
e-mail: info@wortleyhall.org.uk
web: www.wortleyhall.org.uk
dir: *Exit M1 junct 35a, straight over 2nd rdbt signed A616/Manchester. In 3m turn left to Wortley*

Standing in 26 acres of beautiful parkland, this listed country house has been in the custody of the Trades Union Movement for the last 60 years and displays much of their history in the grand day rooms. Function rooms cater well for both conferences and weddings. Bedrooms vary in size but all are comfortable and complimentary Wi-fi is provided.

Rooms 49 en suite (7 fmly) (4 GF) S £48.50-£105; D £97-£137* **Facilities** FTV TVL tea/coffee Dinner available Direct Dial Cen ht Lift Licensed Wi-fi 🔔 **Conf** Max 300 Thtr 150 Class 70 Board 30 **Parking** 60 **Notes** ⊗ Civ Wed 100

Shibden Mill Inn

★★★★ 😊😊 INN

Shibden Mill Fold, Shibden HX3 7UL
☎ 01422 365840 📠 01422 362971
e-mail: enquiries@shibdenmillinn.com
web: www.shibdenmillinn.com
dir: *3m NE of Halifax off A58*

Nestling in a fold of Shibden Dale, this 17th-century inn features exposed beams and open fires. Guests can dine well in the two lounge-style bars, the restaurant, or outside in summer. The stylish bedrooms come in a variety of sizes, and all are thoughtfully equipped and have access to a free video library. Service is friendly and obliging.

Shibden Mill Inn

Rooms 11 en suite (1 GF) **Facilities** FTV DVD tea/coffee Dinner available Direct Dial Cen ht Wi-fi ⅃ 18 Free use of local fitness centre **Conf** Max 50 Thtr 50 Class 21 Board 24 **Parking** 100 **Notes** Closed 25-26 Dec & 1 Jan

PREMIER COLLECTION

Ashmount Country House

★★★★★ 😊 🏠 GUEST HOUSE

Mytholmes Ln BD22 8EZ
☎ 01535 645726 📠 01535 642550
e-mail: info@ashmounthaworth.co.uk
dir: *M65 junct 13A Laneshaw Bridge, turn right over moors to Haworth. Turn left after car park on right, 100yds on right*

This stunning property is located in the heart of the Brontë Country and just a short stroll away from the centre of Haworth. This is an ideal location for those seeking a relaxing retreat with luxurious qualities. Each bedroom is uniquely designed with high quality furnishings, attractive decor, and many thoughtful extras, with some of the rooms having their own terrace with hot tubs or a sauna. There is also a comfortable lounge bar where guests can relax before enjoying dinner in the elegant dining room. The attractive and landscaped gardens offer a lovely backdrop, and provide a pleasant location in which to relax or enjoy afternoon tea on the lawn.

Rooms 8 en suite 4 annexe en suite (5 GF) **Facilities** FTV iPod docking station Lounge tea/coffee Dinner available Cen ht Licensed Wi-fi 🎵 **Extras** Fruit on arrival **Conf** Max 25 Class 25 Board 15 **Parking** 12 **Notes** ⊗ No Children 10yrs Civ Wed 40

Weavers Restaurant with Rooms

★★★★ 😊 RESTAURANT WITH ROOMS

15 West Ln BD22 8DU
☎ 01535 643822 📠 01535 644832
e-mail: weaversltd@btconnect.com
dir: *In village centre. Pass Brontë Weaving Shed on right, 100yds left to Parsonage Museum car park*

Centrally located on the cobbled main street, this family-owned restaurant with rooms provides well-equipped, stylish and comfortable accommodation. Each of the three en suite bedrooms has many thoughtful extras. The kitchen serves both modern and traditional dishes with flair and creativity.

Rooms 3 en suite S £65-£100; D £90-£120 **Facilities** FTV DVD tea/coffee Dinner available Direct Dial Cen ht Wi-fi **Extras** Speciality toiletries, home-made biscuits – complimentary **Notes** ⊗ Closed 24 Dec-10 Jan RS Sun & Mon No arrivals/rest

Moyles

★★★★ 😊 RESTAURANT WITH ROOMS

6-10 New Rd HX7 8AD
☎ 01422 845272 📠 01422 847663
e-mail: enquire@moyles.com
dir: *A646 to Hebden Bridge, opposite marina*

Centrally located in the charming town of Hebden Bridge, this Victorian building as been modernised to offer a high standard of contemporary accommodation. Fresh, local produce features on the imaginative menus served in the bar and in the restaurant. There's a relaxing ambience throughout.

Rooms 12 en suite (6 fmly) **Facilities** FTV tea/coffee Dinner available Cen ht Wi-fi **Conf** Max 12 Thtr 12 Class 12 Board 12 **Notes** ⊗

Uppergate Farm

★★★★ 🅰 GUEST ACCOMMODATION

Hepworth HD9 1TG
☎ 01484 681369 📠 01484 687343
e-mail: info@uppergatefarm.co.uk
dir: *0.5m off A616*

Rooms 2 en suite (1 fmly) S £55; D £85 **Facilities** FTV TVL tea/coffee Cen ht Wi-fi ch fac 🐾 Sauna Pool table 🔔 Table tennis **Parking** 6 **Notes** LB ⊗

HUDDERSFIELD
Map 16 SE11

PREMIER COLLECTION

315 Bar and Restaurant

★★★★★ ⊛ RESTAURANT WITH ROOMS

315 Wakefield Rd, Lepton HD8 0LX
☎ 01484 602613
e-mail: info@315barandrestaurant.co.uk
dir: M1 junct 38, A637 towards Huddersfield. At rdbt take A642 towards Huddersfield. Establishment on right in Lepton

In a wonderful setting 315 Bar and Restaurant is very well presented and benefits from countryside views from the well-appointed dining room and conservatory areas. The interior is modern with open fires that add character and ambiance, while the chef's table gives a real insight into the working of the kitchen. Bedrooms are well-appointed and modern, and most have feature bathrooms. Staff are friendly and attentive, and there are excellent parking facilities.

Rooms 8 en suite (3 fmly) Facilities FTV DVD tea/coffee Dinner available Cen ht Lift Wi-fi Conf Max 150 Thtr 100 Class 75 Board 60 Parking 97 Notes ⊗ Civ Wed 120

The Huddersfield Central Lodge

★★★★ GUEST ACCOMMODATION

11/15 Beast Market HD1 1QF
☎ 01484 515551 ⬛ 01484 432349
e-mail: angela@centrallodge.com
web: www.centrallodge.com
dir: In town centre off Lord St. Follow Beast Market signs from ring road

This friendly, family-run operation offers smart spacious bedrooms with modern en suites. Some bedrooms are in the main building, while newer rooms, many with kitchenettes, are situated across a courtyard. Public rooms include a bar and a conservatory, and there are arrangements for local restaurants to charge meals to guests' accounts. Secure complimentary parking is available.

Rooms 9 en suite 13 annexe en suite (2 fmly) (6 smoking) Facilities FTV Lounge TVL tea/coffee Direct Dial Cen ht Licensed Wi-fi ⬛ Parking 50

The Woodman Inn

★★★★ ⊜ INN

Thunder Bridge Ln HD8 0PX
☎ 01484 605778 ⬛ 01484 604110
e-mail: thewoodman@connectfree.co.uk
web: www.woodman-inn.co.uk

(For full entry see Kirkburton)

Griffin Lodge Guest House

★★★ GUEST HOUSE

273 Manchester Rd HD4 5AG
☎ 01484 431042 ⬛ 01484 431043
e-mail: info@griffinlodge.co.uk
web: www.griffinlodge.co.uk

Located on the outskirts of Huddersfield and close to the villages of Holmfirth and Marsden, Griffin Lodge is family run and offers comfortable well appointed accommodation. Either continental or a full cooked breakfast is served in the small dining room and there is parking to the rear.

Rooms 6 en suite (4 fmly) (6 GF) S £35; D £45* Facilities FTV tea/coffee Cen ht Wi-fi ⬛ Parking 10

Innkeeper's Lodge Huddersfield, Kirkburton

★★★ INN

36a Penistone Rd, Kirkburton HD8 0PQ
☎ 0845 112 6035
e-mail: info@innkeeperslodge.com
web: www.innkeeperslodge.com

At Innkeeper's Lodge you'll find accommodation with comfort and character in equal measure, and everything needed for a relaxing stay, from easy check-in and free parking to complimentary breakfast and a cosy pub serving great value food and drink on the doorstep. Each Lodge has quality rooms, and there are Lodges in a variety of locations from towns and cities to countryside settings across the UK.

Rooms 23 en suite (3 fmly) (13 GF) Facilities FTV tea/coffee Dinner available Direct Dial Wi-fi Parking

ILKLEY
Map 19 SE14

Innkeeper's Lodge Ilkley

★★★ INN

Hangingstone Rd LS29 8BT
☎ 0845 112 6037
e-mail: info@innkeeperslodge.com
web: www.innkeeperslodge.com

At Innkeeper's Lodge you'll find accommodation with comfort and character in equal measure, and everything needed for a relaxing stay, from easy check-in and free parking to complimentary breakfast and a cosy pub serving great value food and drink on the doorstep. Each Lodge has quality rooms, and there are Lodges in a variety of locations from towns and cities to countryside settings across the UK.

Rooms 13 en suite (2 fmly) Facilities FTV tea/coffee Dinner available Direct Dial Wi-fi Parking

KIRKBURTON
Map 16 SE11

The Woodman Inn

★★★★ ⊜ INN

Thunder Bridge Ln HD8 0PX
☎ 01484 605778 ⬛ 01484 604110
e-mail: thewoodman@connectfree.co.uk
web: www.woodman-inn.co.uk
dir: 1m SW of Kirkburton. Off A629 in Thunder Bridge

The Woodman offers traditional innkeeping and is extremely popular with locals. The air-conditioned restaurant holds an extensive range of wines, while the popular bar offers a wide selection of ales and lagers. Bedrooms are comfortable and comprehensively furnished, making this an ideal base for walking, visiting the National Mining Museum, or simply escaping to the country.

Rooms 12 en suite (3 GF) Facilities FTV tea/coffee Dinner available Direct Dial Cen ht Pool table Conf Max 60 Thtr 50 Class 60 Board 30 Parking 50 Notes LB ⊗ Civ Wed

LEEDS
Map 19 SE23

Innkeeper's Lodge Leeds Calverley

★★★ INN

Calverley Ln, Pudsey LS28 5QQ
☎ 0845 112 6043
e-mail: info@innkeeperslodge.com
web: www.innkeeperslodge.com

At Innkeeper's Lodge you'll find accommodation with comfort and character in equal measure, and everything needed for a relaxing stay, from easy check-in and free parking to complimentary breakfast and a cosy pub serving great value food and drink on the doorstep. Each Lodge has quality rooms, and there are Lodges in a variety of locations from towns and cities to countryside settings across the UK.

Rooms 14 en suite (5 fmly) Facilities FTV tea/coffee Dinner available Direct Dial Wi-fi Parking

MARSDEN
Map 16 SE01

The Olive Branch Restaurant with Rooms

★★★★ ⊛ RESTAURANT WITH ROOMS

Manchester Rd HD7 6LU
☎ 01484 844487
e-mail: eat@olivebranch.uk.com
web: www.olivebranch.uk.com
dir: 1m NE of Marsden on A62

The Olive Branch, once a roadside inn, was developed into a popular restaurant with three comfortable bedrooms. The menu features the best of seasonal produce cooked with flair and enthusiasm. The surrounding countryside has many historic attractions and offers pleasant walking opportunities.

Rooms 3 en suite S £65; D £90* **Facilities** FTV DVD tea/coffee Dinner available Cen ht Wi-fi **Parking** 25 **Notes** ⊗ Closed 2-17 Jan No coaches

OSSETT   Map 16 SE22

Heath House

★★★★ GUEST ACCOMMODATION

Chancery Rd WF5 9RZ
☎ 01924 260654 & 07890 385622 📠 01924 263131
e-mail: bookings@heath-house.co.uk
web: www.heath-house.co.uk
dir: *M1 junct 40, A638 towards Dewsbury, at end dual carriageway exit rdbt 2nd left, house 20yds on right*

The spacious Victorian family home stands in four acres of tranquil gardens a short distance from the M1. It has elegant en suite bedrooms, and the courteous and friendly owners provide healthy, freshly-cooked breakfasts.

Rooms 2 en suite (1 fmly) (1 GF) **Facilities** tea/coffee Cen ht Wi-fi **Parking** 16

WAKEFIELD   Map 16 SE32

Midgley Lodge Motel and Golf Course

★★★★ 🅰 GUEST ACCOMMODATION

Barr Ln, Midgley WF4 4JJ
☎ 01924 830069 📠 01924 830087
e-mail: midgleylodgemotel@tiscali.co.uk
dir: *SW of Wakefield. M1 junct 38, A637 Huddersfield road to Midgley*

Rooms 25 en suite (10 fmly) (13 GF) S £48-£54; D £64-£58 (room only) **Facilities** STV FTV TVL tea/coffee Direct Dial Cen ht Licensed Wi-fi ⚓ 9 **Parking** 90 **Notes** ⊗ Closed 25 Dec-2 Jan

Stanley View Guest House

★★★ GUEST HOUSE

226-230 Stanley Rd WF1 4AE
☎ 01924 376803 📠 01924 369123
e-mail: enquiries@stanleyviewguesthouse.co.uk
dir: *M62 junct 30, follow Aberford Rd 3m. Signed on left*

Part of an attractive terrace, this well-established guest house is just half a mile from the city centre and has private parking at the rear. The well equipped bedrooms are brightly decorated, and there is a licensed bar and comfortable lounge. Hearty home-cooked meals are served in the attractive dining room.

Rooms 17 rms (13 en suite) (6 fmly) (7 GF) S £30-£37; D £40-£54* **Facilities** STV DVD TVL tea/coffee Dinner available Direct Dial Cen ht Licensed Wi-fi **Parking** 10

CHANNEL ISLANDS
JERSEY

ST AUBIN   Map 24

PREMIER COLLECTION

The Panorama

★★★★★ 🏠 GUEST ACCOMMODATION

La Rue du Crocquet JE3 8BZ
☎ 01534 742429 📠 01534 745940
e-mail: info@panoramajersey.com
web: www.panoramajersey.com
dir: *In village centre*

Having spectacular views across St Aubin's Bay, The Panorama is a long-established favourite with visitors. The welcome is genuine and many of the well-equipped bedrooms have wonderful views; most bathrooms are newly upgraded. Public areas also look seaward and have attractive antique fireplaces. Breakfast is excellent and served in two dining areas.

Rooms 14 en suite (3 GF) S £42-£78; D £96-£156* **Facilities** STV tea/coffee Cen ht Wi-fi ⚫ **Notes** ⊗ No Children 18yrs Closed mid Oct-mid Apr

Harbour View

★★★★ GUEST HOUSE

Le Boulevard JE3 8AB
☎ 01534 741585 📠 01534 499460
e-mail: harbourview@localdial.com

The Harbour View is situated in a beautiful location overlooking St Aubin Harbour. The guest house has been lovingly restored over recent years and it retains many original features. Bedrooms are all smartly presented and come with a host of facilities. Food can be taken at 'Danny's at the Harbour View' and car parking is an added bonus. A substantial continental breakfast, along with cooked options, is available in the well-appointed breakfast room.

Harbour View

Rooms 16 en suite (4 fmly) (2 GF) **Facilities** STV TVL tea/coffee Cen ht Licensed Wi-fi ⚓ 18 **Parking** 8 **Notes** Closed Dec-Feb

Peterborough House

★★★ GUEST ACCOMMODATION

La Rue du Crocquet JE3 8BZ
☎ 01534 741568 📠 01534 746787
e-mail: fernando@localdial.com
dir: *A13 to St Aubin, left at La Haule Slip, 1st left. Left fork, half way down on left*

Situated on the old St Aubin high street, this well-presented house dates back to 1690. The bedrooms are comfortably appointed and the sea-facing rooms are always in high demand. One of the two lounge areas has a bar, or guests can enjoy the view with a drink on the outdoor terrace. Breakfast has a choice of traditional and continental options.

Rooms 14 rms (12 en suite) (1 fmly) (2 GF) S £32-£43.25; D £54-£76.50* **Facilities** Lounge TVL tea/coffee Cen ht Licensed Wi-fi **Notes** LB ⊗ No Children 12yrs Closed Nov-Feb

ST HELIER   Map 24

Bay View Guest House

★★★★ GUEST ACCOMMODATION

12 Havre des Pas JE2 4UQ
☎ 01534 720950 & 07700 720100 📠 01534 720950
e-mail: bayview.guesthouse@jerseymail.co.uk
dir: *Through tunnel, right at rdbt, down Green St & left, 100yds on left*

The Bay View is located across the road from the Havre des Pas Lido and beach, and just a ten-minute walk from the centre of St Helier. The bedrooms are well equipped, and extra facilities include a bar and a TV lounge with free Wi-fi access. There is a small garden terrace to the front of the establishment and at the rear another secluded terrace and hot tub.

Rooms 13 rms (12 pri facs) (3 fmly) **Facilities** FTV TVL tea/coffee Cen ht Licensed Wi-fi **Notes** ⊗

ISLE OF MAN

DOUGLAS   Map 24 SC37

All Seasons

★★★ ⒶGUEST HOUSE

11 Clifton Ter, Broadway IM2 3HX
☎ **01624 676323** 📠 **08718 553465**
dir: *Off Central Promenade at Villa Marina, premises in 1st row of hotels on left*

Rooms 6 rms (4 en suite) (2 pri facs) (6 fmly) S fr £32; D fr £54* **Facilities** FTV DVD TVL tea/coffee Dinner available Cen ht Licensed Wi-fi **Notes** LB ⊗ No Children 12yrs

PORT ST MARY   Map 24 SC26

PREMIER COLLECTION

Aaron House

★★★★★ 🛏GUEST HOUSE

The Promenade IM9 5DE
☎ **01624 835702** 📠 **01624 837731**
web: www.aaronhouse.co.uk
dir: *Follow signs for South & Port St Mary, left at Post Office. House in centre of Promenade*

Aaron House is truly individual. From the parlour down to the detail of the cast-iron baths, the house, overlooking the harbour, has been restored to its Victorian origins. The family work hard to offer the best quality, whether its providing luxury and comfort in the bedrooms, or offering home-made cakes on arrival.

Rooms 4 rms (3 en suite) (1 pri facs) **Facilities** TVL TV1B tea/coffee Cen ht **Notes** ⊗ No Children 12yrs Closed 21 Dec-3 Jan 🚭

ST JOHN'S   Map 24 SC28

Glen Helen Inn

★★★★ 🍴 INN

Glen Helen IM4 3NP
☎ **01624 801294 & 666186** 📠 **01624 803294**
e-mail: info@glenheleninn.com
web: www.glenheleninn.com

This charming inn is in a glorious location in the heart of the island and close to some lovely country walks. Bedrooms are all very well planned and have a contemporary appearance. The stylish bar is ideal for pre-dinner drinks and there is a popular restaurant, which serves a wide range of dishes.

Rooms 17 en suite (4 fmly) S £40-£55; D £60-£130 **Facilities** FTV Lounge tea/coffee Dinner available Cen ht Wi-fi 🔒 **Conf** Max 80 Thtr 80 Class 24 Board 40 **Parking** 70 **Notes** LB Civ Wed 70

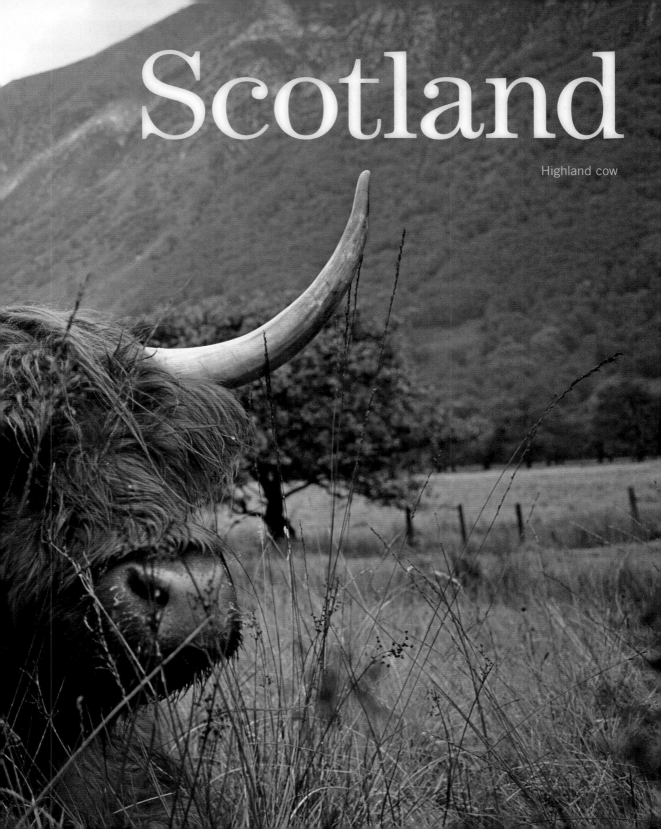

Scotland

Highland cow

CITY OF ABERDEEN

ABERDEEN — Map 23 NJ90

The Jays Guest House

★★★★ GUEST HOUSE

422 King St AB24 3BR
☎ **01224 638295**
e-mail: alice@jaysguesthouse.co.uk
web: www.jaysguesthouse.co.uk
dir: *From S on A90, cross river, at next rdbt right into Holburn St (A9013). At lights right into Union St. Becomes King St. Guest house on right*

Guests are warmly welcomed to this attractive granite house on the north side of the city. Maintained in first-class order throughout, it offers attractive bedrooms, smartly furnished to appeal to business guests and tourists. Freshly prepared breakfasts are enjoyed in the carefully appointed dining room. A private car park is a definite plus.

Rooms 10 rms (8 en suite) (2 pri facs) (1 GF) S £60-£70; D £100-£120* **Facilities** STV FTV tea/coffee Cen ht Wi-fi **Parking** 9 **Notes** ⊗ No Children 12yrs Closed mid Dec-mid Jan

Arkaig Guest House

★★★ GUEST HOUSE

43 Powis Ter AB25 3PP
☎ **01224 638872** 📠 **01224 622189**
e-mail: info@arkaig.co.uk
dir: *On A96 at junct with Bedford Rd*

A friendly welcome and relaxed atmosphere is assured at this well-presented guest house, situated on the north side of the city close to the university and city centre. Bedrooms vary in size, are attractively decorated, and are all thoughtfully equipped to appeal to business and leisure guests. There is a comfortable lounge and an attractive breakfast room where delicious, freshly cooked breakfasts are served. Parking is also available.

Rooms 9 rms (7 en suite) (1 fmly) (5 GF) **Facilities** FTV TVL tea/coffee Direct Dial Cen ht **Parking** 10

PETERCULTER — Map 23 NJ80

Furain Guest House

★★★ Ⓐ GUEST HOUSE

92 North Deeside Rd AB14 0QN
☎ **01224 732189** 📠 **01224 739070**
e-mail: furain@btinternet.com
dir: *7m W of city centre on A93*

Rooms 8 en suite (2 fmly) (3 GF) S £45-£52; D £60-£72* **Facilities** FTV Lounge tea/coffee Cen ht Wi-fi **Parking** 7 **Notes** Closed Xmas & New Year

ABERDEENSHIRE

ABOYNE — Map 23 NO59

The Lodge on the Loch of Aboyne

★★★★ 🚬 GUEST ACCOMMODATION

Aboyne Loch Golf Centre AB34 5BR
☎ **013398 86444**
e-mail: info@thelodgeontheloch.com
dir: *1m E of Aboyne on A93*

The beautiful loch side location of this unique property ensures stunning views and a peaceful stay. The wide range of facilities include a nine-hole golf centre with driving range, osprey viewing deck, fitness centre and a wide range of treatments offered in the Reflect Spa. Dining options include the Loch side Restaurant and Bistro Bar with very good function and wedding facilities also available.

Rooms 6 en suite (2 fmly) (2 GF) S £50-£70; D £75-£130 (room only)* **Facilities** FTV TVL tea/coffee Dinner available Direct Dial Cen ht Licensed Wi-fi ♿ 9 Sauna Gym ♨ Hot tub Spa Therapy treatments **Conf** Max 120 Thtr 120 Class 80 Board 40 **Parking** 30 **Notes** LB ⊗ Closed Jan-Feb Civ Wed 120

BALLATER — Map 23 NO39

The Green Inn

★★★★★ ⊛⊛⊛ 🍴 RESTAURANT WITH ROOMS

9 Victoria Rd AB35 5QQ
☎ **01339 755701**
e-mail: info@green-inn.com
web: www.green-inn.com
dir: *In village centre*

A former temperance hotel, The Green Inn enjoys a central location in the pretty village of Ballater. Bedrooms are of a high standard and attractively presented. The kitchen has a strong reputation for its excellent cuisine, which can be enjoyed in the stylish conservatory restaurant. The head chef is Chris O'Halloran, son of owners Trevor and Evelyn. Breakfast is equally enjoyable and should also not be missed. Genuine hospitality from the enthusiastic proprietors is a real feature of any stay.

Rooms 2 en suite D £79* **Facilities** FTV Lounge TVL tea/coffee Dinner available Cen ht Wi-fi ♨ **Notes** Closed Nov-Jan No coaches

The Auld Kirk

★★★★ ⊛⊛ RESTAURANT WITH ROOMS

Braemar Rd AB35 5RQ
☎ **01339 755762 & 07918 698000** 📠 **0700 6037 559**
e-mail: info@theauldkirk.com
dir: *From Aboyne on A93 into Ballater, establishment on right just before village centre*

A Victorian Scottish Free Church building that is now a contemporary restaurant with rooms, boasting well-appointed bedrooms and bathrooms. Many original features of this kirk have been restored and incorporated in the design. The Spirit Restaurant with its high ceilings and tall windows provides a wonderful setting to enjoy the award-winning, seasonal food. There is a stylish bar with a good selection of malts and a terrace for alfresco eating when the weather permits.

Rooms 7 en suite (1 fmly) S £65-£72.50; D £110-£140* **Facilities** FTV Lounge tea/coffee Dinner available Direct Dial Cen ht Wi-fi ♨ **Conf** Max 25 Thtr 25 Class 18 Board 16 **Parking** 7 **Notes** RS Sun & Mon closed No coaches Civ Wed 34

BRAEMAR — Map 23 NO19

Callater Lodge Guest House

★★★★ GUEST HOUSE

9 Glenshee Rd AB35 5YQ
☎ **01339 741275**
e-mail: info@hotel-braemar.co.uk
web: www.callaterlodge.co.uk
dir: *Next to A93, 300yds S of Braemar centre*

Located in the picturesque village of Braemar, this grand Victorian villa is very well presented with stunning views and lots of period features. Bedrooms are attractively decorated with many thoughtful extras, and the spacious lounge is inviting and homely. Breakfast is served at individual tables and uses quality local ingredients. The gardens are a very pleasant feature.

Rooms 6 en suite (1 fmly) S fr £40; D fr £80*
Facilities FTV Lounge tea/coffee Cen ht Licensed Wi-fi ♿ 18 🅿 **Parking** 6 **Notes** ⊗ Closed Xmas

INVERURIE   Map 23 NJ72

Kintore Arms

★★★★ INN

83 High St AB51 3QJ
☎ 01467 621367 🖨 01467 625620
e-mail: manager.kintore@ohiml.com
web: www.oxfordhotelsandinns.com
dir: *From A96 at rdbt follow Inverurie signs onto B993. At mini-rdbt right, follow town centre signs to High St, establishment on left*

Well situated within easy walking distance of the town centre, and benefiting from off-road parking, this traditional inn is a popular destination. Good-sized bedrooms are thoughtfully equipped for the modern traveller, and regular evening entertainment is provided.

Rooms 28 en suite (1 fmly) **Facilities** FTV TVL tea/coffee Dinner available Cen ht Wi-fi **Conf** Max 150 Thtr 150 Class 75 Board 75 **Parking** 30 **Notes** Civ Wed 150

ANGUS

INVERKEILOR   Map 23 NO64

Gordon's

★★★★ ●●● 🍽 RESTAURANT WITH ROOMS

Main St DD11 5RN
☎ 01241 830364
e-mail: gordonsrest@aol.com
dir: *Exit A92 between Arbroath & Montrose into Inverkeilor*

It's worth a detour off the main road to this family-run restaurant with rooms set in the centre of the village. It has earned AA Rosettes for dinner, and the excellent breakfasts are equally memorable. A huge fire dominates the restaurant on cooler evenings, and there is a small lounge with limited seating. The attractive bedrooms are tastefully decorated and thoughtfully equipped; the larger two are furnished in pine.

Rooms 4 en suite 1 annexe en suite (1 GF) S £55-£85; D £110-£130* **Facilities** FTV Dinner available Cen ht Wi-fi 🅿 **Parking** 6 **Notes** ⊗ No Children 12yrs Closed 2wks Jan No coaches

MONTROSE   Map 23 NO75

Oaklands Guest House

★★★ GUEST HOUSE

10 Rossie Island Rd DD10 9NN
☎ 01674 672018 🖨 01674 672018
e-mail: oaklands1@btopenworld.com
dir: *On A92 at S end of town*

A genuine welcome and attentive service are assured at this smart detached house situated on the south side of the town. Bedrooms come in a variety of sizes and are neatly presented. There is a lounge on the ground floor next to the attractive dining room, where hearty breakfasts are served. Motorcycle guided tours can be arranged for those travelling with their own motorbikes.

Rooms 7 en suite (1 fmly) (1 GF) S £35-£40; D £60-£70* **Facilities** FTV TVL tea/coffee Cen ht Wi-fi 🅿 **Extras** Mints - complimentary **Parking** 8 **Notes** ⊗

ARGYLL & BUTE

APPIN   Map 20 NM94

Pineapple House

★★★★ 🍽 GUEST HOUSE

Duror PA38 4BP
☎ 01631 740557 🖨 01631 740557
e-mail: info@pineapplehouse.co.uk
dir: *In Duror, off A828. 5m S of A82*

Ideally located just south of Glencoe and just north of Appin, this period farmhouse has been lovingly restored and is extremely well presented using a great mix of modern and traditional. Dinners are available on request and use the best local quality produce. Service is friendly and genuine, making it a wonderful base for touring this area of Scotland.

Rooms 6 en suite (1 fmly) **Facilities** FTV tea/coffee Dinner available Cen ht Wi-fi **Parking** 10 **Notes** ⊗ No Children 7yrs Closed Oct-25 Mar

CAIRNDOW   Map 20 NN11

Cairndow Stagecoach Inn

★★★ INN

PA26 8BN
☎ 01499 600286 & 600252 🖨 01499 600220
e-mail: enq@cairndowinn.com
dir: *From N, take either A82 to Tarbet, A83 to Cairndow, or A85 to Palmally, A819 to Inveraray & A83 to Cairndow*

A relaxed, friendly atmosphere prevails at this 18th-century inn, overlooking the beautiful Loch Fyne. Bedrooms offer individual decor and thoughtful extras. Traditional public areas include a comfortable beamed lounge, a well-stocked bar where food is served throughout the day, and a spacious restaurant with conservatory extension. Deluxe bedrooms offer more space and luxury.

Rooms 13 en suite 5 annexe en suite (2 fmly) (5 GF) **Facilities** STV FTV tea/coffee Dinner available Direct Dial Cen ht Wi-fi ♿ 9 Sauna 🅿 **Conf** Max 30 Thtr 30 Class 30 Board 30 **Parking** 30 **Notes** LB

CONNEL   Map 20 NM93

PREMIER COLLECTION

Ards House

★★★★★ 🍽 GUEST HOUSE

PA37 1PT
☎ 01631 710255 & 07703 438341 🖨 01631 710857
e-mail: info@ardshouse.com
web: www.ardshouse.com
dir: *On A85, 4m N of Oban*

This delightful Victorian villa on the approaches to Loch Etive has stunning views over the Firth of Lorne and the Morven Hills beyond. The stylish bedrooms come with added touches such as mineral water and home-made shortbread. There is an inviting drawing room complete with piano, games and books, plus a fire on cooler evenings. The attractive dining room is the setting for delicious breakfasts.

Rooms 4 en suite **Facilities** FTV TVL tea/coffee Cen ht Wi-fi **Parking** 12 **Notes** ⊗ No Children 10yrs Closed mid Dec-mid Jan

LUSS   Map 20 NS39

The Inn at Inverbeg

★★★★ 🍽 INN

Inverbeg G83 8PD
☎ 01436 860678 🖨 01436 860203
e-mail: inverbeg.reception@loch-lomond.co.uk
dir: *A82 N of Balloch*

Dating back to the 18th century this inn offers very stylish, comfortable bedrooms, bathrooms, and equally stylish public areas that boast open fires and cow-hide sofas. Food is as much a feature as the property itself, serving unusual but quality dishes including deep-fried Mars bars and Irn Bru sorbet. The Beach House accommodation is a real treat for that special occasion.

Rooms 12 en suite 8 annexe en suite (1 fmly) (5 GF) **Facilities** STV FTV TVL tea/coffee Dinner available Cen ht Wi-fi **Parking** 60 **Notes** ⊗ Civ Wed 60

OBAN — Map 20 NM82

PREMIER COLLECTION

Blarcreen House

★★★★ GUEST HOUSE

Ardchattan, Connel PA37 1RG
☎ 01631 750272 & 07557 977225
e-mail: info@blarcreenhouse.com
web: www.blarcreenhouse.com
dir: N over Connel Bridge, turn right signed Bonawe, 6.7m to Blarcreen

This elegant Victorian mansion house on the side of Loch Etive is the ideal base for exploring the Highlands. Warm hospitality and log fires await guests arriving at this property, where they can relax and enjoy comfortable bedrooms and fantastic views.

Rooms 3 en suite S £55–£85; D £95–£115*
Facilities FTV DVD iPod docking station TVL tea/coffee Dinner available Cen ht Licensed Wi-fi ⚓ Parking 5 Notes No Children 16yrs

Glenburnie House

★★★★ GUEST HOUSE

The Esplanade PA34 5AQ
☎ 01631 562089 ▤ 01631 562089
e-mail: graeme.strachan@btinternet.com
dir: On Oban seafront. Follow signs for Ganavan

This impressive seafront Victorian house has been lovingly restored to a high standard. Bedrooms (including a four-poster room and a mini-suite) are beautifully decorated and very well equipped. There is a cosy ground-floor lounge and an elegant dining room, where hearty traditional breakfasts are served at individual tables.

Rooms 12 en suite (2 GF) S £50–£60; D £79–£120
Facilities FTV DVD Lounge tea/coffee Cen ht Wi-fi Massage Parking 12 Notes LB ⊗ No Children 12yrs Closed Dec-Feb

High Cliff Guest House

★★★★ ⌂ GUEST HOUSE

Glencruitten Rd PA34 4EW
☎ 01631 564134 & 07766 685819
e-mail: info@highcliffoban.co.uk
web: www.highcliffoban.co.uk

Located just a few minutes walk away from the centre of Oban, this delightful Victorian house has been lovingly restored. The house is attractively furnished, with well-appointed bedrooms and guests are sure to be given a warm welcome. Delicious breakfasts featuring local produce are served around a large communal table. Car parking is available along with a patio area.

Rooms 4 en suite D £80–£85* Facilities STV FTV iPod docking station TVL Cen ht Wi-fi Parking 8 Notes ⊗ No Children 12yrs ⊗

Braeside Guest House

★★★★ GUEST HOUSE

Kilmore PA34 4QR
☎ 01631 770243 ▤ 01631 770343
e-mail: braeside.guesthouse@virgin.net
web: www.braesideguesthouse.net
dir: On A816 5m from Oban

This family-run bungalow stands in gardens overlooking the spectacular Loch Feochan. Bedrooms, all en suite, are bright and airy, well equipped and have easy access. The lounge-dining room has a loch view, a bar with a range of single malts, wines and a wonderful array of local beers, and offers a varied choice of tasty home-cooked evening meals and breakfasts.

Rooms 5 en suite (1 fmly) (5 GF) S £40–£60; D £70–£80*
Facilities FTV DVD iPod docking station Lounge tea/coffee Dinner available Cen ht Licensed Wi-fi Parking 6 Notes LB ⊗ No Children 8yrs

Lancaster

★★ GUEST ACCOMMODATION

Corran Esplanade PA34 5AD
☎ 01631 562587 ▤ 01631 562587
e-mail: lancasteroban@btconnect.com
dir: On seafront next to Columba's Cathedral

Lancaster is a family-run establishment on the esplanade that offers budget accommodation; many bedrooms boast lovely views out over the bay towards the Isle of Mull. Public areas include a choice of lounges and bars that also benefit from the panoramic views. A swimming pool, sauna and jacuzzi are added benefits.

Rooms 27 rms (24 en suite) (3 fmly) (10 smoking)
S £35–£40; D £74–£82* Facilities FTV Lounge TVL tea/coffee Cen ht Licensed ⊗ Sauna Pool table ⚓ Jacuzzi Steam room Conf Max 30 Thtr 30 Class 20 Board 12 Parking 20 Notes LB

DUMFRIES & GALLOWAY

CASTLE DOUGLAS — Map 21 NX76

Craigadam

★★★★ ⌂ ⌂ GUEST HOUSE

Craigadam DG7 3HU
☎ 01556 650233 & 650100 ▤ 01556 650233
e-mail: inquiry@craigadam.com
web: www.craigadam.com
dir: From Castle Douglas E on A75 to Crocketford. In Crocketford turn left on A712 for 2m. House on hill

Set on a farm, this elegant country house offers gracious living in a relaxed environment. The large bedrooms, most set around a courtyard, are strikingly individual in style. Public areas include a billiard room with comprehensive honesty bar, and the panelled dining room which features a magnificent 15-seater table, the setting for Celia Pickup's delightful meals.

Rooms 10 en suite (2 fmly) (7 GF) Facilities FTV TVL tea/coffee Dinner available Cen ht Licensed Wi-fi 🎣 Fishing Snooker Private fishing & shooting Conf Max 22 Parking 12 Notes Closed Xmas & New Year Civ Wed 150

DUMFRIES — Map 21 NX97

Wallamhill House

★★★★ BED AND BREAKFAST

Kirkton DG1 1SL
☎ 01387 248249
e-mail: wallamhill@aol.com
dir: 3m N of Dumfries. Off A701 signed Kirkton, 1.5m on right

Wallamhill House is set in well-tended gardens, in a delightful rural area three miles from Dumfries. Bedrooms are spacious and extremely well equipped. There is a peaceful drawing room, and a mini health club with sauna, steam shower and gym equipment.

Rooms 3 en suite (1 fmly) **Facilities** FTV TVL tea/coffee Cen ht Wi-fi ☼ Sauna Gym Steam room **Parking** 6 **Notes** ⊗

Rivendell
★★★★ GUEST HOUSE
105 Edinburgh Rd DG1 1JX
☎ 01387 252251 📠 01387 263084
e-mail: info@rivendellbnb.co.uk
web: www.rivendellbnb.co.uk
dir: On A701 Edinburgh Rd, 400yds S of A75 junct

Situated just north of the town and close to the bypass, this lovely 1920s house, standing in extensive landscaped gardens, has been restored to reflect the period style of the property. Bedrooms are thoughtfully equipped, many are spacious and all offer modern facilities. Traditional breakfasts are served in the elegant dining room.

Rooms 6 en suite (2 fmly) (1 GF) **Facilities** FTV tea/coffee Cen ht Wi-fi **Parking** 12 **Notes** ⊗

Southpark House
★★★★ GUEST ACCOMMODATION
Quarry Rd, Locharbriggs DG1 1QR
☎ 01387 711188 & 0800 970 1588 📠 01387 711155
e-mail: info@southparkhouse.co.uk
dir: 3.5m NE of Dumfries. Exit A701 in Locharbriggs into Quarry Rd, last house on left

With a peaceful location commanding stunning views, this well-maintained property offers comfortable, attractive and well-equipped bedrooms. The peaceful lounge has a log fire on colder evenings, and fax and e-mail facilities are available. Friendly proprietor Ewan Maxwell personally oversees the hearty Scottish breakfasts served in the conservatory breakfast room.

Rooms 4 en suite (1 fmly) S £29.99-£49.99; D £49.99-£69.99* **Facilities** STV FTV Lounge TVL tea/coffee Cen ht Wi-fi 2 acres of garden **Parking** 13 **Notes** LB ⊗

GRETNA (WITH GRETNA GREEN) Map 21 NY36

Barrasgate
★★★★ GUEST ACCOMMODATION
Millhill DG16 5HU
☎ 01461 337577 & 07711 661938 📠 01461 337577
e-mail: info@barrasgate.co.uk
web: www.barrasgate.co.uk
dir: From N: A74 (M) junct 22 signed Gretna Green/Longtown. At 2nd rdbt right, signed Longtown. Approx 1.5m, establishment on right. From S: M6 junct 45 (A74(M) junct 24) take A6071 signed Gretna/Longtown. Approx 1m turn 2nd left, signed Gretna Green/Springfield. Establishment 1st left

This detached house lies in attractive gardens in a rural setting near Gretna, the Blacksmith Centre and motorway links. Bedrooms are well presented and equipped. Hearty

breakfasts, featuring local produce, are taken in an attractive dining room, overlooking the gardens.

Rooms 5 en suite (2 fmly) (1 GF) **Facilities** FTV tea/coffee Cen ht Wi-fi **Parking** 10 **Notes** Closed Jan-Feb

Surrone House
★★★ GUEST ACCOMMODATION
Annan Rd DG16 5DL
☎ 01461 338341
e-mail: enquiries@surronehouse.co.uk
web: www.surronehouse.co.uk
dir: In town centre on B721

Guests are assured of a warm welcome at this well-maintained guest accommodation set in attractive gardens well back from the road. Bedrooms are sensibly furnished and include a delightful honeymoon suite. Dinner, drinks and light refreshments are available.

Rooms 7 en suite (3 fmly) (2 GF) S £40; D £70-£80* **Facilities** FTV TVL tea/coffee Dinner available Cen ht Licensed Wi-fi 🔒 **Parking** 10 **Notes** ⊗

LANGHOLM Map 21 NY38

Glengarth Guest Rooms
★★★★ GUEST ACCOMMODATION
Maxwell Rd DG13 0DX
☎ 01387 380777 & 07802 771137
e-mail: info@glengarthguestrooms.co.uk
dir: M6 junct 44, A7. In Langholm 500yds past Co-op

Glengarth Guest Rooms is located in a quiet residential area in the Borders town of Langholm. Strong hospitality and customer care is provided. Bedrooms and en suites are well appointed, comfortable and cater well for the needs of the guest. Quality breakfast is served in the lounge/dining room using locally sourced produce.

Rooms 2 en suite (2 GF) S £40; D £60 **Facilities** STV DVD Lounge tea/coffee Cen ht Wi-fi ♨ 9 Fishing **Parking** 1 **Notes** LB ⊗ No Children ⊜

LOCKERBIE Map 21 NY18

Blackyett Mains
★★★★ BED AND BREAKFAST
DG11 3ND
☎ 01461 500750
e-mail: mail@blackyettmains.co.uk
web: www.blackyettmains.co.uk
dir: M74 junct 21 towards Kirkpatrick Fleming, B6357 to Annan. At Hollee turn right to Irvington after 0.5m, left to Blackyett Mains. 1st on left

Set in the rolling Dumfriesshire countryside but just 5 minutes from the M74, Blackyett Mains is a converted farmhouse with many original features along with wonderful wooden floors. Bedrooms and en suites are generous in size and very well appointed. Award-winning breakfasts use locally sourced produce, and a large garden is available for guests to enjoy.

Rooms 3 rms (2 en suite) (1 GF) D £80* **Facilities** FTV iPod docking station TVL tea/coffee Dinner available Cen ht Wi-fi 🔒 **Parking** 3 **Notes** LB ⊗ ⊜

MOFFAT Map 21 NT00

Bridge House
★★★★ ⌒ GUEST HOUSE

Well Rd DG10 9JT
☎ 01683 220558 📠 01683 220558
e-mail: info@bridgehousemoffat.co.uk
dir: Exit A708 (The Holm) into Burnside, bear right into Well Rd, house 0.5m on left

A fine Victorian property, Bridge House lies in attractive gardens in a quiet residential area on the outskirts of the town. The atmosphere is very friendly and relaxed. The chef-proprietor provides interesting dinners (by arrangement) featuring local produce. The cosy guest lounge is the ideal venue for pre-dinner drinks.

Rooms 7 en suite (1 fmly) **Facilities** FTV Lounge tea/coffee Dinner available Cen ht Licensed **Parking** 7 **Notes** LB ⊗ No Children 2yrs Closed Xmas & New Year

MOFFAT *continued*

Hartfell House & The Limetree Restaurant

★★★★ @ GUEST HOUSE

Hartfell Crescent DG10 9AL
☎ 01683 220153
e-mail: enquiries@hartfellhouse.co.uk
web: www.hartfellhouse.co.uk
dir: *From High St at war memorial into Well St & Old Well Rd. Hartfell Crescent on right*

Built in 1850, this impressive Victorian house is in a peaceful terrace high above the town and has lovely countryside views. Beautifully maintained, the bedrooms offer high quality and comfort. The attractive dining room is transformed in the evening into The Limetree Restaurant (previously situated in the town centre) offering chef Matt Seddon's culinary delights.

Rooms 7 en suite (2 fmly) (1 GF) S £35-£45; D £60-£75*
Facilities FTV Lounge tea/coffee Dinner available Cen ht Licensed Wi-fi ♿ 18 Parking 6 Notes LB ⊗ Closed Xmas

Limetree House

★★★★ GUEST ACCOMMODATION

Eastgate DG10 9AE
☎ 01683 220001
e-mail: limetreehousemoffat@yahoo.co.uk
web: www.limetreehouse.co.uk
dir: *From High St into Well St, left into Eastgate, house 100yds on left*

A warm welcome is assured at this well-maintained guest accommodation, quietly situated behind the main high street. Recognisable by its colourful flower baskets in season, it provides an inviting lounge and a bright cheerful breakfast room. Bedrooms are smartly furnished and include a large family room.

Rooms 6 en suite (1 fmly) (1 GF) S £40-£45; D £60-£80*
Facilities FTV TVL tea/coffee Cen ht Wi-fi ♿ 18 ♨
Parking 3 Notes LB No Children 5yrs RS Xmas & New Year

No 29 Well Street

★★★★ BED AND BREAKFAST

29 Well St DG10 9DP
☎ 01683 221905
e-mail: mcleancamm1956@btinternet.com
dir: *M74 junct 15 follow signs to High St, Well St on right*

Located in the heart of Moffat just minutes drive from the rolling countryside of the Scottish Borders, this is a very comfortable and well presented property offering high standards of hospitality and service. Bedrooms are well appointed with many useful extras provided as standard. Breakfast is hearty with local produce used to good effect.

Rooms 3 en suite (2 GF) S £30-£45; D £55-£65
Facilities FTV DVD tea/coffee Cen ht Wi-fi ♨
Extras Speciality toiletries - complimentary Parking 1
Notes No Children 10yrs Closed 24-26 & 31 Dec, 1 Jan

The Balmoral

★★★ INN

High St DG10 9DL
☎ 01683 220288 ▤ 01683 220451
web: www.thebalmoralhotel-moffat.co.uk
dir: *0.5m from A74(M) junct 15, halfway up High St on right*

The Balmoral is situated in the centre of the town with free parking in the town square, and a friendly welcome is guaranteed. Bar meals are available all day until 9.30pm. Bedrooms are very comfortably equipped with thoughtful extras. Moffat is a former spa town and is within easy reach of many major tourist attractions.

Rooms 16 en suite (2 fmly) Facilities tea/coffee Dinner available Cen ht Notes ⊗

Barnhill Springs Country Guest House

★★ GUEST ACCOMMODATION

DG10 9QS
☎ 01683 220580
e-mail: barnhillsprings@yahoo.co.uk
dir: *A74(M) junct 15, A701 towards Moffat. Barnhill Rd 50yds on right*

This former farmhouse is in a quiet, rural location south of the town and within easy reach of the M74. Bedrooms are well proportioned; and have private bathrooms. There is a comfortable lounge and separate dining room. Barnhill Springs continues to welcome pets.

Rooms 5 rms (5 pri facs) (1 fmly) (1 GF) S £34-£36; D £68-£72 Facilities TVL tea/coffee Cen ht ♨
Parking 10 Notes LB ⊛

THORNHILL | Map 21 NX89

Gillbank House

★★★★★ GUEST ACCOMMODATION

8 East Morton St DG3 5LZ
☎ 01848 330597 ▤ 01848 331713
e-mail: hanne@gillbank.co.uk
web: www.gillbank.co.uk
dir: *In town centre off A76*

Gillbank House was originally built for a wealthy Edinburgh merchant. Convenient for the many outdoor pursuits in this area, such as fishing and golfing, this delightful house offers comfortable and spacious bedrooms and smart shower rooms en suite. Breakfast is served at individual tables in the bright, airy dining room, which is next to the comfortable lounge.

Rooms 6 en suite (2 GF) S £50-£60; D £75-£85
Facilities tea/coffee Cen ht Wi-fi ♿ 18 ♨ Parking 8
Notes ⊗ No Children 8yrs

EAST AYRSHIRE

SORN | Map 20 NS52

The Sorn Inn

★★★★ @@ RESTAURANT WITH ROOMS

35 Main St KA5 6HU
☎ 01290 551305 ▤ 01290 553470
e-mail: craig@sorninn.com
dir: *A70 from S or A76 from N onto B743 to Sorn*

Centrally situated in a rural village, which is convenient for many of Ayrshire's attractions, this inn has a fine dining restaurant with a cosy lounge area. There is also a popular chop house with a pub-like environment. The freshly decorated bedrooms have comfortable beds and good facilities.

Rooms 4 en suite (1 fmly) S £40-£50; D £55-£90
Facilities tea/coffee Dinner available Direct Dial Cen ht Wi-fi Fishing Parking 9 Notes Closed 2wks Jan RS Mon closed

EAST LOTHIAN

ABERLADY
Map 21 NT47

Ducks at Kilspindie

★★★★ @@ RESTAURANT WITH ROOMS

Main St EH32 0RE
☎ 01875 870682 📠 01875 870504
e-mail: kilspindie@ducks.co.uk
web: www.ducks.co.uk
dir: *A1 (Bankton junct) take 1st exit to North Berwick. At next rdbt 3rd exit onto A198 signed Longniddry, left towards Aberlady. At T-junct, facing river, right to Aberlady*

The name of this restaurant with rooms is referenced around the building - Ducks Restaurant for award-winning cuisine; Donald's Bistro and the Ducklings informal coffee shop. The warm and welcoming public areas include a great bar offering real ales and various objets d'art. The bedrooms are comfortable and well appointed with well-presented en suites. The team are informal, friendly and take the time to chat to their guests.

Rooms 23 en suite (1 fmly) (6 GF) S £115; D £115*
Facilities FTV TVL tea/coffee Dinner available Direct Dial Cen ht Wi-fi ⚓ **Conf** Max 100 Thtr 100 Class 60 Board 30 **Parking** 15 **Notes** LB

CITY OF EDINBURGH

EDINBURGH
Map 21 NT27

See also East Calder (West Lothian)

PREMIER COLLECTION

Elmview

★★★★★ 🛏 GUEST ACCOMMODATION

15 Glengyle Ter EH3 9LN
☎ 0131 228 1973
e-mail: nici@elmview.co.uk
web: www.elmview.co.uk
dir: *0.5m S of city centre. Exit A702 (Leven St) into Valleyfield St, one-way to Glengyle Terrace*

Elmview offers stylish accommodation on the lower ground level of a fine Victorian terrace house. The bedrooms and smart bathrooms are comfortable and extremely well equipped, with thoughtful extras such as safes, and fridges with fresh milk and water. Breakfasts are excellent and are served at a large, elegantly appointed table in the charming dining room.

Rooms 3 en suite (3 GF) S £65-£110; D £90-£135*
Facilities FTV tea/coffee Direct Dial Cen ht Wi-fi
Notes ⊗ No Children 15yrs Closed Dec-Feb

PREMIER COLLECTION

Kew House

★★★★★ GUEST ACCOMMODATION

1 Kew Ter, Murrayfield EH12 5JE
☎ 0131 313 0700 📠 0131 313 0747
e-mail: info@kewhouse.com
web: www.kewhouse.com
dir: *1m W of city centre A8*

Forming part of a listed Victorian terrace, Kew House lies within walking distance of the city centre, and is convenient for Murrayfield Stadium and tourist attractions. Meticulously maintained throughout, it offers attractive bedrooms in a variety of sizes, all thoughtfully equipped to suit business and leisure guests. There is a comfortable lounge offering a supper and snack menu. Internet access is also available.

Rooms 6 en suite (1 fmly) (2 GF) S £79-£96; D £90-£190* **Facilities** FTV Lounge tea/coffee Direct Dial Cen ht Wi-fi ⚓ **Extras** Speciality toiletries, sherry, chocolates **Parking** 6 **Notes** LB ⊗ Closed approx 5-23 Jan

PREMIER COLLECTION

23 Mayfield

★★★★★ 🛏 GUEST ACCOMMODATION

23 Mayfield Gardens EH9 2BX
☎ 0131 667 5806 📠 0131 667 6833
e-mail: info@23mayfield.co.uk
web: www.23mayfield.co.uk
dir: *A720 bypass S, follow city centre signs. Left at Craigmillar Park, 0.5m on right*

23 Mayfield is well located en route into Edinburgh with the added benefit of off-road parking. The spacious accommodation has retained many of its original period features. Breakfast is a real delight, with the very best local produce used to give guests a great start to their day. 23 Mayfield was last year's AA Guest Accommodation of the Year for Scotland (2011-2012).

Rooms 9 en suite (2 fmly) (2 GF) S £80-£85; D £90-£170* **Facilities** FTV DVD iPod docking station Lounge tea/coffee Cen ht Wi-fi ⚓ Bike hire **Parking** 10 **Notes** LB ⊗

EDINBURGH *continued*

PREMIER COLLECTION

21212

★★★★★ ◉◉◉ RESTAURANT WITH ROOMS

3 Royal Ter EH7 5AB
☎ 0131 523 1030 & 0845 222 1212
e-mail: reservations@21212restaurant.co.uk

A real gem in Edinburgh's crown, this establishment takes its name from the numbers of choices at each course on the five-course dinner menu. Located on the prestigious Royal Terrace this is a light and airy, renovated Georgian townhouse stretching over four floors. The four individually designed bedrooms epitomise luxury living and the bathrooms certainly have the wow factor. At the heart of this restaurant with rooms is the creative, award-winning cooking of Paul Kitching. Service throughout is friendly and very attentive.

Rooms 4 en suite D £175-£325* **Facilities** STV FTV iPod docking station Lounge Dinner available Cen ht Wi-fi **Extras** Speciality toiletries **Notes** ⊗ No Children 5yrs Closed 1wk Jan RS Sun & Mon restaurant closed No coaches

PREMIER COLLECTION

The Witchery by the Castle

★★★★★ ◉ ⏚ RESTAURANT WITH ROOMS

352 Castlehill, The Royal Mile EH1 2NF
☎ 0131 225 5613 ⌨ 0131 220 4392
e-mail: mail@thewitchery.com
web: www.thewitchery.com
dir: *Top of Royal Mile at gates of Edinburgh Castle*

Originally built in 1595, The Witchery by the Castle is situated in a historic building at the gates of Edinburgh Castle. The two luxurious and theatrically decorated suites, known as the Inner Sanctum and the Old Rectory are located above the restaurant and are reached via a winding stone staircase. Filled with antiques, opulently draped beds, large roll-top baths and a plethora of memorabilia, this ancient and exciting establishment is often described as one of the country's most romantic destinations.

Rooms 3 en suite 5 annexe en suite (1 GF) **Facilities** STV FTV tea/coffee Dinner available Direct Dial Cen ht **Notes** ⊗ No Children 12yrs Closed 25-26 Dec No coaches

Bonnington Guest House

★★★★ GUEST HOUSE

202 Ferry Rd EH6 4NW
☎ 0131 554 7610
e-mail: booking@thebonningtonguesthouse.com
web: www.thebonningtonguesthouse.com
dir: *On A902, near corner of Ferry Rd & Newhaven Rd*

This delightful Georgian house offers individually furnished bedrooms on two floors that retain many of their original features. Family rooms are also available. A substantial freshly prepared breakfast is served in the dining room. Off-street parking is an added bonus.

Rooms 7 rms (5 en suite) (2 pri facs) (2 fmly) (1 GF) S £65-£120; D £70-£150* **Facilities** FTV tea/coffee Cen ht Wi-fi **Parking** 9 **Notes** ⊗ Closed Nov-Mar

Fraoch House

★★★★ ⏚ GUEST ACCOMMODATION

66 Pilrig St EH6 5AS
☎ 0131 554 1353
e-mail: info@fraochhouse.com
dir: *1m from Princes St*

Situated within walking distance of the city centre and convenient for many attractions, Fraoch House, which dates from the 1900s, has been appointed to offer well-equipped and thoughtfully furnished bedrooms. Delicious, freshly cooked breakfasts are served in the charming dining room on the ground floor.

Rooms 9 rms (7 en suite) (2 pri facs) (1 fmly) (1 GF) **Facilities** FTV tea/coffee Cen ht Wi-fi Free use of DVDs and CDs & internet access **Notes** ⊗

Southside Guest House

★★★★ ⏚ GUEST HOUSE

8 Newington Rd EH9 1QS
☎ 0131 668 4422 ⌨ 0131 667 7771
e-mail: info@southsideguesthouse.co.uk
web: www.southsideguesthouse.co.uk
dir: *E end of Princes St into North Bridge to Royal Mile, continue S, 0.5m, house on right*

Situated within easy reach of the city centre and convenient for the major attractions, Southside is an elegant sandstone house. Bedrooms are individually styled, comfortable and thoughtfully equipped. Traditional, freshly cooked Scottish breakfasts are served at individual tables in the smart ground-floor dining room.

Rooms 8 en suite (2 fmly) (1 GF) S £65-£80; D £70-£160 **Facilities** FTV tea/coffee Direct Dial Cen ht Licensed Wi-fi **Notes** LB ⊗ No Children 10yrs

Allison House

★★★★ GUEST ACCOMMODATION

17 Mayfield Gardens EH9 2AX
☎ 0131 667 8049 ⌨ 0131 667 5001
e-mail: info@allisonhousehotel.com
web: www.allisonhousehotel.com

Part of a Victorian terrace, Allison House offers modern comforts in a splendid building. It's convenient for the city centre, theatres, tourist attractions, and the main bus route. The attractive bedrooms are generally spacious and very well equipped. Breakfast is served at individual tables in the ground-floor dining room. Off-road parking is available.

Rooms 11 rms (10 en suite) (1 pri facs) (1 fmly) (2 GF) (2 smoking) **Facilities** tea/coffee Direct Dial Cen ht Wi-fi **Parking** 6 **Notes** ⊗

Ashlyn Guest House

★★★★ GUEST HOUSE

42 Inverleith Row EH3 5PY
☎ 0131 552 2954
e-mail: info@ashlynguesthouse.com
web: www.ashlynguesthouse.com
dir: *Adjacent to Edinburgh Botanic Gardens, then follow signs for North Edinburgh & Botanics*

The Ashlyn Guest House is a warm and friendly Georgian home, ideally located to take advantage of Edinburgh's attractions. The city centre is within walking distance and the Royal Botanical Gardens are minutes away. Bedrooms are all individually decorated and furnished to a high standard. A generous and hearty breakfast gives a great start to the day.

Rooms 6 rms (3 en suite) (3 pri facs) (1 fmly) S £35-£40; D £70-£95* **Facilities** FTV TVL tea/coffee Cen ht Wi-fi ⏚ **Extras** Mineral water **Notes** ⊗ No Children 7yrs Closed 23-28 Dec

Save on B&Bs and Hotels. Book at theAA.com/hotel

CITY OF EDINBURGH 367 SCOTLAND

Heriott Park Guest House

★★★★ GUEST HOUSE

256 Ferry Rd, Goldenacre EH5 3AN
☎ 0131 552 3456
e-mail: reservations@heriottpark.co.uk
web: www.heriottpark.co.uk
dir: 1.5m N of city centre on A902

A conversion of two adjoining properties, which retain many original features, Heriott Park is on the north side of the city and has lovely panoramic views of the Edinburgh skyline, including the castle and Arthur's Seat. The attractive bedrooms are well equipped and have excellent en suite bathrooms.

Rooms 15 en suite (7 fmly) (1 GF) S £40-£80;
D £60-£120* **Facilities** FTV tea/coffee Cen ht Wi-fi
Notes ⊗

The International Guest House

★★★★ GUEST HOUSE

37 Mayfield Gardens EH9 2BX
☎ 0131 667 2511 & 0845 241 7551 📠 0131 667 1112
e-mail: intergh1@yahoo.co.uk
web: www.accommodation-edinburgh.com
dir: On A701 1.5m S of Princes St

Guests are assured of a warm and friendly welcome at this attractive Victorian terraced house, situated to the south of the city centre. The smartly presented bedrooms are thoughtfully decorated, comfortably furnished and well equipped. Hearty Scottish breakfasts are served at individual tables in the traditionally styled dining room, which boasts a beautiful ornate ceiling.

The International Guest House

Rooms 9 en suite (3 fmly) (1 GF) **Facilities** FTV tea/coffee
Direct Dial Cen ht Wi-fi **Parking** 3 **Notes** LB ⊗

See advert on this page

Kingsway Guest House

★★★★ GUEST HOUSE

5 East Mayfield EH9 1SD
☎ 0131 667 5029
e-mail: room@edinburgh-guesthouse.com
web: www.edinburgh-guesthouse.com
dir: A701 to city centre, after 4m road name changes to Mayfield Gdns. Right at lights into East Mayfield

Well situated for the city centre and with off-road parking, this well presented Victorian building maintains a number of original features, and genuine and warm hospitality is assured. All the bedrooms are comfortable, and the quality Scottish breakfasts make an excellent start to the day.

Kingsway Guest House

Rooms 7 rms (6 en suite) (1 pri facs) S £40-£60;
D £65-£100* **Facilities** FTV DVD iPod docking station tea/coffee Cen ht Wi-fi ⅃ 18 🔒 **Parking** 4 **Notes** ⊗

Sherwood Guest House

★★★★ GUEST HOUSE

42 Minto St EH9 2BR
☎ 0131 667 1200 📠 0131 667 2344
e-mail: enquiries@sherwood-edinburgh.com
web: www.sherwood-edinburgh.com
dir: On A701, S of city centre

Lying on the south side of the city, this guest house is immaculately maintained and attractively presented throughout. Bedrooms vary in size, the smaller ones being thoughtfully appointed to make the best use of space. All include iron and ironing board, and several come with a fridge and microwave. Continental breakfast is served in the elegant dining room.

Rooms 6 rms (5 en suite) (1 pri facs) (2 fmly) (1 GF)
Facilities FTV tea/coffee Cen ht Wi-fi **Parking** 3 **Notes** ⊗
Closed 20-29 Dec & 5 Jan-2 Mar

EDINBURGH *continued*

Gildun Guest House

★★★★ 🅰 GUEST HOUSE

9 Spence St EH16 5AG
☎ 0131 667 1368 📠 0131 668 4989
e-mail: gildun.edin@btinternet.com
dir: *A720 (city bypass) to Sheriffhall rdbt onto A7. 4m to Cameron Toll rdbt. Under rail bridge follow A7 sign into Dalkeith Rd. Spence St 4th left opposite church*
Rooms 8 rms (7 en suite) (1 pri facs) (5 fmly) (2 GF)
S £30-£68; D £60-£140 Facilities FTV iPod docking station tea/coffee Cen ht Wi-fi 🛁 Parking 4 Notes LB

Arden Guest House

★★★ GUEST HOUSE

126 Old Dalkeith Rd EH16 4SD
☎ 0131 664 3985 📠 0131 621 0866
e-mail: ardenguesthouse@btinternet.com
dir: *2m SE of city centre near Craigmillar Castle. On A7, 200yds W of hospital*

Arden Guest House is well situated on the south-east side of the city, close to the hospital, and benefits from off-road parking. Many thoughtful extras are provided as standard, including Wi-fi. Attentive and friendly service enhances the guest experience.

Rooms 8 en suite (2 fmly) (3 GF) Facilities STV tea/coffee Cen ht Wi-fi Parking 8 Notes Closed 22-27 Dec

Averon City Centre Guest House

★★★ GUEST HOUSE

44 Gilmore Place EH3 9NQ
☎ 0131 229 9932
e-mail: info@averon.co.uk
web: www.averon.co.uk
dir: *From W end of Princes St onto A702, right at Kings Theatre*

Situated within walking distance of the west end of the city and close to the Kings Theatre, Mrs Iliazova's guest house offers comfortable good value accommodation, with a secure car park to the rear.

Rooms 10 rms (6 en suite) (1 pri facs) (3 fmly) (5 GF)
Facilities tea/coffee Cen ht Parking 19 Notes ⊗

See advert on this page

Elder York Guest House

★★★ GUEST HOUSE

38 Elder St EH1 3DX
☎ 0131 556 1926 📠 0131 624 7140
e-mail: reception@elderyork.co.uk
web: www.elderyork.co.uk
dir: *Close to Princes St, next to bus station*

Elder York Guest House is centrally located just minutes from the bus station, Harvey Nichols and the St James Shopping Centre. Accommodation is situated up flights of stairs and all bedrooms are well appointed with many thoughtful extras including Wi-fi. Quality breakfast is served on individual tables overlooking Queen Street.

Rooms 13 rms (10 en suite) (1 fmly) Facilities FTV tea/coffee Cen ht Wi-fi Notes ⊗

Innkeeper's Lodge Edinburgh, Corstorphine

★★★ INN

St Johns Rd, Corstorphine EH12 8AX
☎ 0845 112 6002
e-mail: info@innkeeperslodge.com
web: www.innkeeperslodge.com

At Innkeeper's Lodge you'll find accommodation with comfort and character in equal measure, and everything needed for a relaxing stay, from easy check-in and free parking to complimentary breakfast and a cosy pub serving great value food and drink on the doorstep. Each Lodge has quality rooms, and there are Lodges in a variety of locations from towns and cities to countryside settings across the UK.

Rooms 28 en suite (4 fmly) (6 GF) Facilities FTV tea/coffee Dinner available Direct Dial Wi-fi Parking

Classic House

★★★ 🅰 GUEST HOUSE

50 Mayfield Rd EH9 2NH
☎ 0131 667 5847 📠 0131 662 1016
e-mail: info@classicguesthouse.co.uk
web: www.classichouse.demon.co.uk
dir: *From bypass follow signs for A701 city centre. At Liberton Brae, keep left, 0.5m on left*
Rooms 7 rms (6 en suite) (1 pri facs) (2 fmly)
Facilities TVL Cen ht **Notes** LB ⊗

Ravensdown Guest House

★★★ 🅰 GUEST HOUSE

248 Ferry Rd EH5 3AN
☎ 0131 552 5438
e-mail: david@ravensdownhouse.com
web: www.ravensdownhouse.com
dir: *N of city centre, close to Royal Botanic Gardens, A902 Goldenacre*

Rooms 7 en suite (5 fmly) (1 GF) S £45-£75;
D £80-£120* **Facilities** FTV iPod docking station tea/coffee Cen ht Wi-fi 🅿 **Parking** 2 **Notes** LB ⊗

SOUTH QUEENSFERRY   Map 21 NT17

Innkeeper's Lodge Edinburgh South Queensferry

★★★ INN

7 Newhalls Rd EH30 9TA
☎ 0845 112 6001
e-mail: info@innkeeperslodge.com
web: www.innkeeperslodge.com

At Innkeeper's Lodge you'll find accommodation with comfort and character in equal measure, and everything needed for a relaxing stay, from easy check-in and free parking to complimentary breakfast and a cosy pub serving great value food and drink on the doorstep. Each

Lodge has quality rooms, and there are Lodges in a variety of locations from towns and cities to countryside settings across the UK.

Rooms 14 en suite (5 fmly) (3 GF) **Facilities** FTV tea/coffee Dinner available Direct Dial Wi-fi **Parking** 40

FIFE

ANSTRUTHER   Map 21 NO50

The Spindrift

★★★★ 🛏 ➖ GUEST HOUSE

Pittenweem Rd KY10 3DT
☎ 01333 310573 📠 01333 310573
e-mail: info@thespindrift.co.uk
web: www.thespindrift.co.uk
dir: *Enter town from W on A917, 1st building on left*

This immaculate Victorian villa stands on the western edge of the village. The attractive bedrooms offer a wide range of extra touches; the Captain's Room, a replica of a wood-panelled cabin, is a particular feature. The inviting lounge has an honesty bar, while imaginative breakfasts, and enjoyable home-cooked meals by arrangement, are served in the cheerful dining room. Free Wi-fi is available.

Rooms 8 rms (7 en suite) (1 pri facs) (2 fmly) S £40-£80;
D £68-£90 **Facilities** FTV DVD TVL tea/coffee Dinner available Direct Dial Cen ht Licensed Wi-fi 🅿 18 **Parking** 12 **Notes** LB No Children 10yrs Closed Xmas-late Jan

The Bank

★★★★ INN

23-25 High Street East KY10 3DQ
☎ 01333 310189
e-mail: enquiries@thebank_anstruther.co.uk
web: www.thebank-anstruther.co.uk
dir: *From St Andrews, in Anstruther turn right towards Pittenweem. 50mtrs on left*

Located in the heart of Anstruther where the Dreel Burn meets the Forth, this friendly inn serves real ales and great pub food; there is a separate building next door for the accommodation. Modern, high quality, en suite bedrooms cater well for guests' needs and some offer great views. The beer garden is a real suntrap and has a children's play area.

Rooms 8 en suite (1 fmly) (1 GF) S £35-£50; D £70-£100 **Facilities** STV iPod docking station tea/coffee Dinner available Direct Dial Cen ht Wi-fi 🅿 18 Pool table 🎱 **Extras** Fridge, safe, bottled water - complimentary **Parking** 3 **Notes** LB ⊗

INVERKEITHING   Map 21 NT18

The Roods

★★★★ BED AND BREAKFAST

16 Bannerman Av KY11 1NG
☎ 01383 415049 📠 01383 415049
e-mail: isobelmarley@hotmail.com
web: www.the-roods.co.uk
dir: *N of town centre off B981(Church St/Chapel Place)*

This charming house stands in secluded, well-tended gardens close to the station. Bedrooms are individually styled and have state-of-the-art bathrooms. There is an inviting lounge, and breakfast is served at individual tables in an attractive conservatory.

Rooms 2 en suite (2 GF) **Facilities** FTV TVL tea/coffee Direct Dial Cen ht Wi-fi **Parking** 4 **Notes** ⊗

| LEUCHARS | Map 21 NO42 |

Hillpark House

★★★★ GUEST HOUSE

96 Main St KY16 0HF
☎ 01334 839280 ▤ 01334 839051
e-mail: enquiries@hillparkhouse.co.uk
web: www.hillparkhouse.co.uk
dir: From Leuchars on A919 towards St Michaels, house last on right

Lying peacefully on the edge of the village, Hillpark House is an impressive Edwardian home offering comfortable, well-appointed and equipped bedrooms. There is an inviting lounge, a conservatory and a peaceful dining room.

Rooms 5 rms (3 en suite) (1 pri facs) (1 fmly)
Facilities TVL tea/coffee Cen ht Wi-fi ⌴ **Parking** 6
Notes ⊗

| PEAT INN | Map 21 NO40 |

PREMIER COLLECTION

The Peat Inn

★★★★★ ❀❀❀ ⌂ RESTAURANT WITH ROOMS

KY15 5LH
☎ 01334 840206 ▤ 01334 840530
e-mail: stay@thepeatinn.co.uk
dir: At junct of B940 & B941, 5m SW of St Andrews

This 300-year-old former coaching inn enjoys a rural location, yet is close to St Andrews. The spacious restaurant with rooms is very well appointed and all rooms have lounge areas. The inn is steeped in history and for years has proved a real haven for food lovers. The three dining areas create a romantic setting, and chef/owner Geoffrey Smeddle produces excellent, award-winning dishes. Expect welcoming open fires and a relaxed ambiance.

Rooms 8 annexe en suite (3 fmly) (8 GF) S £125-£150;
D £185-£195 **Facilities** FTV tea/coffee Dinner available
Direct Dial Cen ht Wi-fi ✿ **Extras** Speciality toiletries, fruit, sherry, water - complimentary **Parking** 24
Notes LB ⊗ Closed 25-26 Dec, 2wks Jan, 1wk Nov RS Sun-Mon Closed No coaches

| ST ANDREWS | Map 21 NO51 |

PREMIER COLLECTION

The Paddock

★★★★★ ⌂ GUEST ACCOMMODATION

Sunnyside, Strathkinness KY16 9XP
☎ 01334 850888 ▤ 01334 850870
e-mail: thepaddock@btinternet.com
web: www.thepadd.co.uk
dir: 3m W from St Andrews off B939. The Paddock signed from village centre

Situated in a peaceful village overlooking rolling countryside, this friendly, family-run guest accommodation offers stylish and very well-equipped bedrooms. Superb fish tanks, one freshwater, the other salt, line the entrance hall and contain beautiful and unusual fish. The conservatory is a lovely setting for the delicious breakfasts. Beauty treatments are also available on site.

Rooms 4 en suite (1 fmly) (2 GF) **Facilities** FTV tea/coffee Cen ht Wi-fi **Parking** 8 **Notes** ⊗ No Children 12yrs Closed Nov-Mar

Nethan House

★★★★ ⌂ GUEST HOUSE

17 Murray Park KY16 9AW
☎ 01334 472104 ▤ 01334 850870
e-mail: enquiries@nethan-standrews.com
dir: A91 towards St Andrews, over 2nd rdbt into North St, Murray Park on left before cinema

This large Victorian terrace house is set in the heart of St Andrews; a short walk from the main tourist attractions and the famous golf course. The bright bedrooms are stylish and well appointed. The freshly cooked breakfast is a highlight and is served in the attractive dining room.

Rooms 7 en suite (1 fmly) (1 GF) **Facilities** FTV TVL tea/coffee Cen ht Wi-fi **Notes** ⊗ Closed 24-26 Dec

The Inn at Lathones

★★★★ ❀❀ ⌂ INN

Largoward KY9 1JE
☎ 01334 840494 ▤ 01334 840694
e-mail: lathones@theinn.co.uk
web: www.theinn.co.uk
dir: 5m S of St Andrews on A915, 0.5m before village of Largoward on left just after hidden dip

This lovely country inn, parts of which are 400 years old, is full of character and individuality. The friendly staff help to create a relaxed atmosphere. Smart contemporary bedrooms are in two separate wings. The colourful, cosy restaurant is the main focus, where the menu offers modern interpretations of Scottish and European dishes.

Rooms 21 annexe en suite (1 fmly) (18 GF) **Facilities** STV TVL tea/coffee Dinner available Direct Dial Cen ht Wi-fi

Conf Max 40 Thtr 40 Class 10 Board 20 **Parking** 35
Notes Closed 26 Dec & 3-16 Jan RS 24 Dec Civ Wed 45

Lorimer House

★★★★ 🅰 GUEST HOUSE

19 Murray Park KY16 9AW
☎ 01334 476599 ▤ 01334 476599
e-mail: info@lorimerhouse.com
dir: A91 to St Andrews, left into Golf Place, right into The Scores, right into Murray Park

Rooms 5 en suite (1 GF) D £70-£120 **Facilities** STV FTV TVL tea/coffee Cen ht Wi-fi **Extras** Chilled water, use of fridge **Notes** ⊗ No Children 12yrs

CITY OF GLASGOW

| GLASGOW | Map 20 NS56 |

Clifton Guest House

★★★ GUEST HOUSE

26-27 Buckingham Ter, Great Western Rd G12 8ED
☎ 0141 334 8080 ▤ 0141 337 3468
e-mail: kalam@cliftonhotelglasgow.co.uk
web: www.cliftonhotelglasgow.co.uk
dir: 1.25m NW of city centre off A82 (Inverquhomery Rd)

Located north-west of the city centre, the Clifton forms part of an elegant terrace and is ideal for business and leisure. The attractive bedrooms are spacious, and there is an elegant lounge. Hearty breakfasts are served at individual tables in the dining room.

Rooms 23 rms (17 en suite) (6 fmly) (3 GF) S £39; D £59*
Facilities STV FTV TVL tea/coffee Direct Dial Cen ht Wi-fi
Parking 8 **Notes** ⊗

Georgian House

★★★ GUEST HOUSE

29 Buckingham Ter, Great Western Rd G12 8ED
☎ 0141 339 0008 & 07973 971563
e-mail: thegeorgianhouse@yahoo.com
web: www.thegeorgianhousehotel.com
dir: M8 junct 17 towards Dumbarton, through 4 sets of lights & right onto Queen Margaret Dr, then right onto Buckingham Ter

Georgian House offers good value accommodation at the west end of the city in a peaceful tree-lined Victorian terrace near the Botanic Gardens. Bedrooms vary in size and are furnished in modern style. A continental style breakfast is served in the first-floor lounge-dining room.

Rooms 11 rms (10 en suite) (1 pri facs) (4 fmly) (3 GF)
Facilities FTV tea/coffee Cen ht Wi-fi **Parking** 6

Craigielea House B&B

★★ 🅰 BED AND BREAKFAST

35 Westercraigs G31 2HY
☎ 0141 554 3446 & 07890 991063
e-mail: craigieleahouse@yahoo.co.uk
dir: *1m E of city centre. M8 junct 15, A8, left into Duke St, pass Tennents Brewery, left into road after lights into Craigpark. 3rd left, then right into Westercraigs*
Rooms 3 rms (1 GF) **Facilities** FTV tea/coffee Cen ht Wi-fi **Parking** 3 **Notes** ⊗ No Children 3yrs ⊛

HIGHLAND

ARDELVE   Map 22 NG82

Caberfeidh House

★★★ GUEST HOUSE

IV40 8DY
☎ 01599 555293
e-mail: info@caberfeidh.plus.com
web: www.caberfeidh.plus.com
dir: *A87 over Dornie Bridge 1st left into Ardelve, 100yds on right*

Set in a peaceful location overlooking Lochs Alsh and Duich, Caberfeidh House offers good value, comfortable accommodation in relaxed and friendly surroundings. Bedrooms are traditionally furnished and thoughtfully equipped, and there is a cosy lounge with a wide selection of books, games and magazines. Hearty breakfasts are served at individual tables in the dining room. Discount available for stays of two or more nights.

Rooms 5 rms (4 en suite) (1 pri facs) (3 fmly) S £32; D £64 **Facilities** FTV Lounge tea/coffee Cen ht **Parking** 4 **Notes** ⊗ Closed 25-26 Dec

---

AVIEMORE   Map 23 NH81

PREMIER COLLECTION

The Old Minister's House

★★★★ GUEST HOUSE

Rothiemurchus PH22 1QH
☎ 01479 898079 🖷 01479 898079
e-mail: info@theoldministershouse.co.uk
web: www.theoldministershouse.co.uk
dir: *B970 from Aviemore signed Glenmore & Coylumbridge, 0.75m at Inverdruie*

Built originally as a manse in 1906, The Old Minister's House stands in well-tended grounds close to Aviemore. The house is beautifully furnished and immaculately maintained. Bedrooms are spacious, attractively decorated and thoughtfully equipped. There is an inviting lounge and a dining room where hearty breakfasts are served.

Rooms 4 en suite (1 fmly) S £70; D £110-£150* **Facilities** FTV DVD Lounge tea/coffee Dinner available Cen ht Licensed Wi-fi ♨ **Extras** Sherry in bedrooms **Conf** Max 24 Thtr 24 Class 12 Board 12 **Parking** 8 **Notes** LB ⊗

Ravenscraig Guest House

★★★★ GUEST HOUSE

Grampian Rd PH22 1RP
☎ 01479 810278 🖷 01479 810210
e-mail: info@aviemoreonline.com
web: www.aviemoreonline.com
dir: *N end of main street, 250yds N of police station*

This friendly, family-run guest house is on the north side of the village, a short walk from local amenities. Bedrooms vary between the traditionally styled rooms in the main house and modern spacious rooms in a chalet-style annexe. There is a relaxing lounge and separate dining room, where freshly prepared breakfasts are served at individual tables.

Rooms 6 en suite 6 annexe en suite (6 fmly) (6 GF) S £35-£45; D £66-£84* **Facilities** FTV TVL tea/coffee Cen ht Wi-fi ♨ **Parking** 15 **Notes** ⊗

BALLACHULISH   Map 22 NN05

Lyn-Leven Guest House

★★★★ GUEST HOUSE

West Laroch PH49 4JP
☎ 01855 811392 🖷 01855 811600
e-mail: macleodcilla@aol.com
web: www.lynleven.co.uk
dir: *Off A82 signed on left West Laroch*

Genuine Highland hospitality and high standards are part of the appeal of this comfortable guest house. The attractive bedrooms vary in size, are well equipped, and offer many thoughtful extra touches. There is a spacious lounge, and a smart dining room where delicious home-cooked breakfasts are served at individual tables.

Rooms 8 en suite (3 fmly) (8 GF) S £45-£50; D £60-£70* **Facilities** TVL tea/coffee Cen ht Licensed Wi-fi ♨ **Parking** 12 **Notes** LB Closed Xmas

BOAT OF GARTEN — Map 23 NH91

Moorfield House

★★★★ 🅰 GUEST HOUSE

Deshar Rd PH24 3BN
☎ 01479 831646
e-mail: enquiries@moorfieldhouse.com
dir: Off A9 at Carrbridge junct. Follow signs for Boat of Garten, in centre next to church

Rooms 6 en suite (1 GF) **Facilities** STV Lounge tea/coffee Dinner available Cen ht Licensed Wi-fi ⚓ 18 🔒
Extras Sweets, bottled water - complimentary **Parking** 6
Notes ⊗ No Children 12yrs Closed 31 Oct-26 Dec

BONAR BRIDGE — Map 23 NH69

Kyle House

★★★ GUEST ACCOMMODATION

Dornoch Rd IV24 3EB
☎ 01863 766360
e-mail: kylehouse360@msn.com
dir: On A949 N from village centre

A spacious house with splendid views of the Kyle of Sutherland and the hills beyond. Bedrooms are comfortably furnished in traditional style and equipped with all the expected facilities. There is a lounge, and hearty breakfasts are enjoyed in the dining room.

Rooms 5 rms (3 en suite) (2 fmly) S £33-£45; D £66
Facilities FTV TVL tea/coffee Cen ht **Parking** 5 **Notes** ⊗ No Children 5yrs Closed Dec-Jan RS Oct & Apr occasional closure (phone in advance) 🐾

BRACHLA — Map 23 NH53

PREMIER COLLECTION

Loch Ness Lodge

★★★★★ 😊😊 🍴 RESTAURANT WITH ROOMS

Loch Ness-Side IV3 8LA
☎ 01456 459469 📠 01456 459439
e-mail: escape@loch-ness-lodge.com
dir: A9 from Inverness onto A82 signed Fort William, 9m, at 30mph sign. Lodge on right immediately after Clansman Hotel

This house enjoys a prominent position overlooking Loch Ness, and each of the individually designed bedrooms enjoys views of the loch. The bedrooms are of the highest standard, and are beautifully presented with a mix of traditional luxury and up-to-date technology, including Wi-fi. There is a spa with a hot tub, sauna and a therapy room offering a variety of treatments. Award-winning evening meals are served in the restaurant, and guests have a choice of attractive lounges which feature real fires in the colder months.

Rooms 7 en suite (1 GF) **Facilities** Dinner available Direct Dial Cen ht Wi-fi ⚓ 18 Fishing Sauna Hot tub Therapy room **Conf** Max 14 Thtr 14 Class 10 Board 14 **Parking** 10 **Notes** ⊗ No Children 16yrs Closed 2-31 Jan No coaches Civ Wed 24

CARRBRIDGE — Map 23 NH92

The Pines Country House

★★★ BED AND BREAKFAST

Duthil PH23 3ND
☎ 01479 841520 📠 01479 841520
e-mail: lynn@thepines-duthil.co.uk
dir: 2m E of Carrbridge in Duthil on A938

A warm welcome is assured at this comfortable home in the Cairngorms National Park. The bright bedrooms are traditionally furnished and offer good amenities. Enjoyable home-cooked fare is served around a communal table. Guests can relax in the conservatory-lounge and watch squirrels feed in the nearby wood.

Rooms 3 en suite (1 fmly) S £41.50-£45; D £60-£63.50*
Facilities STV FTV DVD Lounge tea/coffee Dinner available Cen ht Wi-fi ch fac 🔒 **Parking** 4 **Notes** LB

DORNOCH — Map 23 NH78

PREMIER COLLECTION

2 Quail

★★★★★ 🍴 GUEST ACCOMMODATION

Castle St IV25 3SN
☎ 01862 811811
e-mail: theaa@2quail.com
dir: On main street, 200yds from cathedral

The saying 'small is beautiful' aptly applies to this guest accommodation. Set in the main street the careful renovation of its Victorian origins transports guests back in time. Cosy public rooms are ideal for conversation, but there are masses of books for those just wishing to relax. The stylish, individual bedrooms match the character of the house but are thoughtfully equipped to include DVD players. 2 Quail was a Finalist in the AA Friendliest B&B of the Year Award 2012-13.

Rooms 3 en suite (1 fmly) D £80-£120* **Facilities** FTV Lounge tea/coffee Direct Dial Cen ht Licensed Wi-fi
Extras Speciality toiletries **Notes** LB ⊗ No Children 8yrs Closed Xmas & 2wks Feb/Mar RS Nov-Mar winter hours - check when booking

DRUMNADROCHIT — Map 23 NH53

Ferness Cottage

★★★★ BED AND BREAKFAST

Lewiston IV63 6UW
☎ 01456 450564
e-mail: info@lochnessaccommodation.co.uk
web: www.lochnessaccommodation.co.uk
dir: A82, from Inverness turn right after Esso service station; from Fort William left before Esso service station, 100mtrs phone box on left. 100mtrs on right

This rose-covered cottage dating from the 1840s has a peaceful location and is within easy walking distance of the village centre. The two charming bedrooms are well equipped, with many thoughtful extra touches. Traditional breakfasts in the cosy lounge-dining room feature the best of local produce. Guests can use the grass area, with seating, beside the River Coiltie, where fishing is available.

Rooms 2 rms (1 en suite) (1 pri facs) S £65-£75; D £65-£75 **Facilities** STV Lounge tea/coffee Cen ht Wi-fi 🔒 **Parking** 2 **Notes** LB ⊗ No Children 10yrs

FORT WILLIAM — Map 22 NN17

See also Spean Bridge

Distillery Guest House

★★★★ GUEST HOUSE

Nevis Bridge, North Rd PH33 6LR
☎ 01397 700103
e-mail: disthouse@aol.com
dir: A82 from Fort William towards Inverness, on left after Glen Nevis rdbt

Situated in the grounds of the former Glenlochy Distillery, this friendly guest house was once the distillery manager's home. Bedrooms are attractively decorated, comfortably furnished and very well equipped. There is a relaxing lounge, which features a superb range of games, and a bright airy dining room where traditional Scottish breakfasts are served at individual tables.

Rooms 10 en suite (1 fmly) (1 GF) **Facilities** tea/coffee Cen ht Licensed **Parking** 21 **Notes** ⊗

Save on B&Bs and Hotels. Book at **theAA.com/hotel**

HIGHLAND 373 SCOTLAND

Mansefield Guest House

★★★★ GUEST HOUSE

Corpach PH33 7LT
☎ 01397 772262 & 0845 6449432
e-mail: mansefield@btinternet.com
web: www.fortwilliamaccommodation.com
dir: *2m N of Fort William. A82 onto A830, house 2m on A830 in Corpach*

Peacefully set in its own well-tended garden this friendly, family-run guest house provides comfortable, attractively decorated and well-equipped accommodation. There is a cosy lounge, where a roaring coal fire burns on cold evenings, and an attractive dining room where delicious, home-cooked evening meals and breakfasts are served at individual tables.

Rooms 6 en suite (1 GF) **Facilities** FTV TVL tea/coffee Dinner available Cen ht Wi-fi ⌲ 18 ♨ **Parking** 7 **Notes** LB ⊗ No Children 12yrs

Stobhan B&B

★★★ BED AND BREAKFAST

Fassifern Rd PH33 6BD
☎ 01397 702790 📠 01397 702790
e-mail: boggi@supanet.com
dir: *In town centre. A82 into Victoria Rd beside St Mary's Church, right into Fassifern Rd*

Stobhan B&B occupies an elevated location overlooking Loch Linnhe and offers comfortable, good-value accommodation. Bedrooms, one of which is on the ground floor, are traditionally furnished and have en suite facilities. Breakfast is served in the ground-floor dining room, which is adjacent to the lounge.

Rooms 4 en suite (1 GF) **Facilities** FTV tea/coffee Cen ht

FOYERS — Map 23 NH42

Craigdarroch House

★★★★ ◉ RESTAURANT WITH ROOMS

IV2 6XU
☎ 01456 486400 📠 01456 486444
e-mail: info@hotel-loch-ness.co.uk
dir: *Take B862 from either end of loch, then B852 signed Foyers*

Craigdarroch is located in an elevated position high above Loch Ness on the south side. Bedrooms vary in style and size but all are comfortable and well equipped; those that are front-facing have wonderful views. The award-winning food is well worth staying in for, and breakfasts are also memorable.

Rooms 8 en suite (1 fmly) S £60-£120; D £75-£160 **Facilities** FTV Lounge TVL tea/coffee Dinner available Direct Dial Cen ht Wi-fi ♨ **Conf** Max 30 Thtr 30 Class 30 Board 30 **Parking** 24 **Notes** No coaches Civ Wed 30

Foyers Bay Country House

★★★ GUEST HOUSE

Lochness IV2 6YB
☎ 01456 486624
e-mail: info@foyersbay.co.uk
dir: *Off B852 into Lower Foyers*

Situated in sloping grounds with pines and abundant colourful rhododendrons, this delightful Victorian villa has stunning views of Loch Ness. The attractive bedrooms vary in size and are well equipped. There is a comfortable lounge next to the plant-filled conservatory-café, where delicious evening meals and traditional breakfasts are served.

Rooms 6 en suite (1 GF) D £75-£110 **Facilities** FTV TVL tea/coffee Dinner available Cen ht Licensed Wi-fi **Conf** Max 20 Thtr 20 Class 20 Board 20 **Parking** 6 **Notes** LB ⊗ No Children 16yrs

---

GLENCOE — Map 22 NN15

Lyn-Leven Guest House

★★★★ GUEST HOUSE

West Laroch PH49 4JP
☎ 01855 811392 📠 01855 811600
e-mail: macleodcilla@aol.com
web: www.lynleven.co.uk

(For full entry see Ballachulish)

GOLSPIE — Map 23 NC80

Granite Villa Guest House

★★★★ GUEST ACCOMMODATION

Fountain Rd KW10 6TH
☎ 01408 633146
e-mail: info@granite-villa.co.uk
dir: *Left from A9 (N'bound) onto Fountain Rd, immediately before pedestrian crossing lights*

Originally built in 1892 for a wealthy local merchant, this traditional Victorian house has been sympathetically restored in recent years. Bedrooms are comfortable and all come with a range of thoughtful extras. Guests can relax in the large lounge, with its views over the landscaped garden where complimentary tea and coffee is often served. A warm welcome is assured in this charming period house.

Rooms 5 en suite (1 fmly) (1 GF) (2 smoking) S £45; D £70* **Facilities** FTV DVD Lounge tea/coffee Cen ht Wi-fi ⌲ 18 ♨ **Parking** 6 **Notes** ⊛

GRANTOWN-ON-SPEY — Map 23 NJ02

An Cala Guest House

★★★★★ Ⓐ GUEST HOUSE

Woodlands Ter PH26 3JU
☎ 01479 873293 📠 01479 873610
e-mail: ancala@globalnet.co.uk
web: www.ancalaguesthouse.co.uk
dir: *From Aviemore on A95 left onto B9102 at rdbt outside Grantown. After 400yds, 1st left, An Cala opposite*

Rooms 4 en suite (1 fmly) **Facilities** FTV TVL tea/coffee Dinner available Cen ht Wi-fi **Parking** 7 **Notes** ⊗ No Children 3yrs Closed Xmas RS Nov-Mar Phone/e-mail bookings only

---

INVERGARRY — Map 22 NH30

Forest Lodge Guest House

★★★ Ⓐ GUEST HOUSE

South Laggan PH34 4EA
☎ 01809 501219 & 07790 907477
e-mail: info@flgh.co.uk
web: www.flgh.co.uk
dir: *2.5m S of Invergarry. Off A82 in South Laggan*

Rooms 8 rms (7 en suite) (1 pri facs) (3 fmly) (4 GF) S £40; D £64* **Facilities** TVL tea/coffee Cen ht Wi-fi **Parking** 10 **Notes** LB Closed 20 Dec-7 Jan

INVERNESS
Map 23 NH64

PREMIER COLLECTION

Daviot Lodge
🏠 GUEST ACCOMMODATION

Daviot Mains IV2 5ER
☎ 01463 772215 📠 01463 772099
e-mail: margaret.hutcheson@btopenworld.com
dir: *Exit A9 5m S of Inverness onto B851 signed Croy. 1m on left*

Standing in 80 acres of peaceful pasture land, this impressive establishment offers attractive, well-appointed and equipped bedrooms. The master bedroom is furnished with a four-poster bed. There is a tranquil lounge with deep sofas and a real fire, and a peaceful dining room where hearty breakfasts featuring the best of local produce are served. Full disabled access for wheelchairs.

Rooms 4 en suite (1 GF) S £55; D £90–£100*
Facilities FTV DVD Lounge TVL tea/coffee Direct Dial Cen ht Licensed Wi-fi **Extras** Speciality toiletries
Parking 10 **Notes** LB No Children 5yrs Closed 23 Dec–2 Jan

PREMIER COLLECTION

Trafford Bank
🏠 GUEST HOUSE

96 Fairfield Rd IV3 5LL
☎ 01463 241414
e-mail: info@traffordbankguesthouse.co.uk
web: www.traffordbank.co.uk
dir: *Exit A82 at Kenneth St, 2nd left into Fairfield Rd, 600yds on right*

This impressive Victorian house lies in a residential area close to the canal. Lorraine Freel has utilised her interior design skills to blend the best in contemporary styles with the house's period character and the results are simply stunning. Delightful public areas offer a choice of lounges, while breakfast is taken in a beautiful conservatory featuring eye-catching wrought-iron chairs. Each bedroom is unique in design and has TV, DVD and CDs, sherry, silent mini-fridges and much more.

Trafford Bank

Rooms 5 en suite (2 fmly) **Facilities** STV FTV TVL tea/coffee Cen ht Wi-fi **Parking** 10 **Notes** ⊗
See advert on this page

Alexander Guest House
★★★★ 🏠 GUEST HOUSE

16 Ness Bank IV2 4SF
☎ 01463 231151 📠 01463 232220
e-mail: info@thealexander.net
web: www.thealexander.net
dir: *On E bank of river, opposite cathedral*

Built in 1830, this impressive house has been extensively renovated, and many of the original Georgian features have been retained. Bedrooms are simply furnished and beds have luxurious mattresses dressed in fine Egyptian cotton. All rooms have flat screen TVs with DVD players, and ironing facilities are available. Light sleepers will welcome the silent running fridges in each room. Public rooms include a charming lounge with views over the River Ness, and the house is a short walk from the city centre.

Rooms 11 en suite (1 GF) S £55–£65; D £90–£130*
Facilities STV FTV DVD Lounge TVL tea/coffee Cen ht Wi-fi 🔒 **Parking** 10 **Notes** ⊗

Save on B&Bs and Hotels. Book at **theAA.com/hotel**

HIGHLAND 375 SCOTLAND

Avalon Guest House

★★★★ GUEST HOUSE

79 Glenurquhart Rd IV3 5PB
☎ **01463 239075 & 07936 226241** 📠 **01463 709827**
e-mail: avalon@inverness-loch-ness.co.uk
web: www.inverness-loch-ness.co.uk

Avalon Guest House is just a short walk from the city centre, and five minutes drive from Loch Ness. Breakfast can be taken in the well appointed dining room where fresh local produce is the highlight of the menu. Bedrooms are spacious with a host of thoughtful extras including Wi-fi, fridges, fluffy towels and complimentary toiletries. A guest lounge is also provided.

Rooms 6 rms (5 en suite) (1 pri facs) (4 GF) S £55-£70*
Facilities FTV DVD iPod docking station TVL tea/coffee Cen ht Wi-fi **Extras** Fridges, chocolates, flowers **Parking** 10 **Notes** No Children 10yrs

Ballifeary Guest House

★★★★ 🏠 GUEST HOUSE

10 Ballifeary Rd IV3 5PJ
☎ **01463 235572** 📠 **01463 717583**
e-mail: william.gilbert@btconnect.com
web: www.ballifearyguesthouse.co.uk
dir: Exit A82, 0.5m from town centre, left into Bishops Rd, sharp right into Ballifeary Rd

This charming detached house has a peaceful residential location within easy walking distance of the town centre and Eden Court Theatre. The attractive bedrooms are carefully appointed and well equipped. There is an elegant ground-floor drawing room and a comfortable dining room, where delicious breakfasts, featuring the best of local produce, are served at individual tables.

Rooms 7 en suite (1 GF) S £40-£70; D £60-£80
Facilities FTV DVD Lounge tea/coffee Cen ht Wi-fi 🔒
Extras Mineral water **Parking** 6 **Notes** LB ⊗ No Children 15yrs Closed 24-28 Dec

The Ghillies Lodge

★★★★ 🏠 BED AND BREAKFAST

16 Island Bank Rd IV2 4QS
☎ **01463 232137 & 07817 956533**
e-mail: info@ghillieslodge.com
dir: 1m SW from town centre on B862, pink house facing river

Situated on the banks of the River Ness not far from the city centre, Ghillies Lodge offers comfortable accommodation in a relaxed, peaceful environment. The attractive bedrooms, one of which is on the ground floor, are all en suite, and are individually styled and well equipped. There is a comfortable lounge-dining room, and a conservatory that overlooks the river.

Rooms 3 en suite (1 GF) S £45-£55; D £65-£78
Facilities STV FTV tea/coffee Cen ht Wi-fi 🔒 **Parking** 4
Notes ⊗

Moyness House

★★★★ 🏠 GUEST ACCOMMODATION

6 Bruce Gardens IV3 5EN
☎ **01463 233836** 📠 **01463 233836**
e-mail: stay@moyness.co.uk
web: www.moyness.co.uk
dir: Off A82 (Fort William road), almost opposite Highland Regional Council headquarters

Situated in a quiet residential area just a short distance from the city centre, this elegant Victorian villa dates from 1880 and offers beautifully decorated, comfortable bedrooms and well-appointed bathrooms. There is an attractive sitting room and an inviting dining room, where traditional Scottish breakfasts are served. Guests are welcome to use the secluded and well-maintained back garden.

Moyness House

Rooms 6 en suite (1 fmly) (2 GF) S £60-£85;
D £69-£105* **Facilities** FTV DVD Lounge tea/coffee Cen ht Wi-fi **Extras** Speciality toiletries, robes **Parking** 10
Notes LB ⊗ No Children 5yrs

Lyndon Guest House

★★★★ GUEST HOUSE

50 Telford St IV3 5LE
☎ **01463 232551** 📠 **01463 225827**
e-mail: lyndon@invernessbedandbreakfast.com
web: www.invernessbedandbreakfast.com
dir: A9 onto A82, over Friars Bridge, right at rdbt into Telford St. House on right

A warm Highland welcome awaits at this family-run accommodation close to the centre of Inverness. All bedrooms are en suite and are equipped with plenty of useful facilities including full internet access. Gaelic is spoken here.

Rooms 6 en suite (4 fmly) (2 GF) S £25-£40; D £50-£80*
Facilities STV FTV TVL tea/coffee Cen ht Wi-fi 🔒
Parking 6 **Notes** ⊗ Closed 20 Dec-5 Jan

INVERNESS *continued*

Strathness House

★★★★ GUEST HOUSE

4 Ardross Ter IV3 5NQ
☎ 01463 232765 ▤ 01463 232970
e-mail: info@strathnesshouse.com
web: www.strathnesshouse.co.uk
dir: *From A9, A96 to city centre, pass Eastgate shopping centre. At bottom of Academy St turn left, then cross bridge, then left again*

Strathness House offers comfortable accommodation and heartwarming hospitality in the heart of Inverness. Eight of the well equipped bedrooms have river or castle views. Scottish breakfasts are served overlooking the river.

Rooms 12 en suite (4 fmly) **Facilities** FTV Lounge tea/coffee Direct Dial Cen ht Wi-fi **Notes** ⊗ No Children 5yrs Closed Xmas-New Year

Westbourne Guest House

★★★★ ≜ GUEST ACCOMMODATION

50 Huntly St IV3 5HS
☎ 01463 220700 ▤ 01463 220700
e-mail: richard@westbourne.org.uk
dir: *A9 onto A82 at football stadium over 3 rdbts, at 4th rdbt 1st left onto Wells St & Huntly St*

The immaculately maintained Westbourne looks across the River Ness to the city centre. This friendly, family-run house has bright modern bedrooms of varying size, all attractively furnished in pine and very well equipped. A relaxing lounge with internet access, books, games and puzzles is available.

Rooms 9 en suite (2 fmly) **Facilities** FTV tea/coffee Cen ht Wi-fi **Parking** 6 **Notes** Closed Xmas & New Year

Sunnyholm

★★★ GUEST ACCOMMODATION

12 Mayfield Rd IV2 4AE
☎ 01463 231336
e-mail: sunnyholm@aol.com
web: www.invernessguesthouse.com
dir: *500yds SE of town centre. Exit B861 (Culduthel Rd) into Mayfield Rd*

Situated in a peaceful residential area within easy walking distance of the city centre, Sunnyholm offers comfortably proportioned and well-equipped bedrooms. A spacious conservatory-lounge overlooks the rear garden, and there is a another lounge next to the bright, airy dining room.

Rooms 4 en suite (4 GF) S £38-£40; D £64-£68*
Facilities FTV DVD Lounge tea/coffee Cen ht Wi-fi ≜
Parking 6 **Notes** ⊗ No Children 3yrs ⊛

Acorn House

★★★ GUEST HOUSE

2A Bruce Gardens IV3 5EN
☎ 01463 717021 & 240000 ▤ 01463 714236
e-mail: enquiries@acorn-house.freeserve.co.uk
web: www.acorn-house.freeserve.co.uk
dir: *From town centre onto A82, on W side of river, right onto Bruce Gardens*

This attractive detached house is just a five-minute walk from the town centre. Bedrooms are smartly presented and well equipped. Breakfast is served at individual tables in the spacious dining room.

Rooms 6 en suite (2 fmly) **Facilities** STV TVL tea/coffee Cen ht Wi-fi Sauna Hot tub **Parking** 7 **Notes** Closed 25-26 Dec

Fraser House

★★★ GUEST ACCOMMODATION

49 Huntly St IV3 5HS
☎ 01463 716488 & 07900 676799 ▤ 01463 716488
e-mail: fraserlea@btopenworld.com
dir: *A82 W over bridge, left into Wells St leading into Huntly St, house in 100yds*

Situated on the west bank of the River Ness, Fraser House has a commanding position overlooking the city, and is within easy walking distance of the central amenities. Bedrooms, all en suite, vary in size and are comfortably furnished and well equipped. The ground-floor dining room is the setting for freshly cooked Scottish breakfasts.

Rooms 5 en suite (2 fmly) S £35-£40; D £55-£65*
Facilities FTV DVD iPod docking station tea/coffee Cen ht Wi-fi ≜ **Notes** Closed Feb-Mar ⊛

| KINGUSSIE | Map 23 NH70 |

PREMIER COLLECTION

The Cross at Kingussie

★★★★★ ⊛⊛⊛ ≜ RESTAURANT WITH ROOMS

Tweed Mill Brae, Ardbroilach Rd PH21 1LB
☎ 01540 661166 ▤ 01540 661080
e-mail: relax@thecross.co.uk
dir: *From lights in Kingussie centre take Ardbroilach Rd, 300yds left into Tweed Mill Brae*

Situated in the valley near Kingussie, this former tweed mill sits next to a river, with wild flower gardens and a sunny terrace. Hospitality and food are clearly highlights of any stay at this special restaurant with rooms. Locally sourced produce is carefully prepared with passion and skill. Bedrooms are spacious and airy, with little touches such as fluffy towels and hand-made toiletries providing extra luxury.

Rooms 8 en suite (1 fmly) S £140-£190; D £200-£270* (incl.dinner) **Facilities** FTV Lounge tea/coffee Dinner available Direct Dial Cen ht Wi-fi ⚓ 18 ≜ Petanque **Extras** Speciality toiletries, mineral water - complimentary **Conf** Max 20 Thtr 20 Class 20 Board 20 **Parking** 12 **Notes** LB ⊗ No Children 8yrs Closed Xmas & Jan (ex New Year) RS Sun & Mon Accommodation/dinner not available No coaches

Save on B&Bs and Hotels. Book at theAA.com/hotel

HIGHLAND 377 SCOTLAND

Allt Gynack Guest House

★★★ 🅰 GUEST HOUSE

Gynack Villa, 1 High St PH21 1HS
☎ 01540 661081
e-mail: alltgynack@tiscali.co.uk
web: www.alltgynack.com
dir: A9 onto A86 through Newtonmore, 2m to Kingussie,
on left after bridge

Rooms 5 rms (3 en suite) (2 pri facs) S £30-£32;
D £60-£64* Facilities FTV tea/coffee Cen ht Wi-fi ⌁ 18
🚲 Parking 4 Notes LB No Children 15yrs

MUIR OF ORD   Map 23 NH55

Carndaisy House

★★★★ BED AND BREAKFAST

Easter Urray IV6 7UL
☎ 01463 870244 & 07780 923316 📠 0808 280 1771
e-mail: info@carndaisyhouse.co.uk
dir: From A9 at Tore rdbt 1st left onto A832 to Muir of Ord.
At junct with A862 right over bridge, 1st left onto A832.
2m W, right, 0.5m on left

Carndaisy House is a very comfortable bed and breakfast
situated in Easter Urray, a short drive from Muir of Ord
just outside Inverness. The accommodation includes
three en suite rooms including a large family room with
its own entrance and patio. All bedrooms are
contemporarily decorated, and finished to a high
standard. A well-cooked traditional Scottish breakfast
provides a good start to the day.

Rooms 3 en suite (2 fmly) (1 GF) S £35-£70; D £49-£79
Facilities FTV Lounge tea/coffee Cen ht Wi-fi Riding
Extras Home-baking, sweets/snacks - complimentary
Parking 5 Notes LB ⊗

NAIRN   Map 23 NH85

North End

★★★★ BED AND BREAKFAST

18 Waverley Rd IV12 4RQ
☎ 01667 456338
e-mail: reservations@northendnairn.co.uk
dir: On corner of A96 (Academy St) & Waverley Rd

Built in 1895, North End is a delightful Victorian villa
that has been sympathetically restored in recent years.
The spacious bedrooms are comfortable and well
equipped. The cosy lounge has a wood-burning stove and
the original features of the house are complemented by
contemporary furnishings. The house is within easy
walking distance of Nairn and is a 20-minute drive from
Inverness.

Rooms 3 rms (2 en suite) (1 pri facs) S £30; D £60*
Facilities FTV TVL tea/coffee Cen ht Wi-fi Parking 4
Notes LB ⊗ Closed Oct-Apr ✉

POOLEWE   Map 22 NG88

PREMIER COLLECTION

Pool House

★★★★★ GUEST ACCOMMODATION

IV22 2LD
☎ 01445 781272 📠 01445 781403
e-mail: stay@pool-house.co.uk
dir: 6m N of Gairloch on A832 in the centre of village
by bridge

Set on the shores of Loch Ewe where the river meets the
bay, the understated roadside façade gives little hint of
its splendid interior, nor of the views facing the bay.
Memorable features are its delightful public rooms and
stunningly romantic suites, each individually designed
and with feature bathrooms. Pool House is run very
much as a country house - the hospitality and guest
care by the Harrison Family are second to none.

Rooms 5 en suite 1 annexe en suite (2 GF)
S £125-£150; D £195-£295 Facilities FTV DVD iPod
docking station Lounge tea/coffee Dinner available
Direct Dial Cen ht Licensed Wi-fi Fishing Snooker
Parking 12 Notes LB ⊗ No Children 16yrs Closed 2
Jan-1 Mar RS Mon closed

SHIEL BRIDGE   Map 22 NG91

Grants at Craigellachie

★★★★ ⊛ RESTAURANT WITH ROOMS

Craigellachie, Ratagan IV40 8HP
☎ 01599 511331
e-mail: info@housebytheloch.co.uk
dir: From A87 exit for Glenelg, 1st right to Ratagan,
opposite Youth Hostel sign

Sitting on the tranquil shores of Loch Duich and
overlooked by the Five Sisters Mountains, Grants really
does occupy a stunning location. The restaurant has a
well deserved reputation for its cuisine, and the bedrooms
are stylish and have all the creature comforts. Guests are
guaranteed a warm welcome at this charming house.

Rooms 2 en suite 2 annexe en suite (3 GF) D £160-£240*
(incl.dinner) Facilities STV DVD tea/coffee Dinner
available Cen ht Wi-fi Riding Extras Speciality toiletries,
robes, bottled water - complimentary Parking 8 Notes LB
No Children 12yrs Closed Dec-mid Feb RS mid Feb-Nov
reservation only No coaches

SOUTH BALLACHULISH   Map 22 NN05

Craiglinnhe House

★★★★ GUEST HOUSE

Lettermore PH49 4JD
☎ 01855 811270
e-mail: info@craiglinnhe.co.uk
web: www.craiglinnhe.co.uk
dir: From village A82 onto A828, Craiglinnhe 1.5m on left

Built during the reign of Queen Victoria, Craiglinnhe
House enjoys an elevated position with stunning views
across Loch Linnhe to the village of Onich, and up to the
Ballachulish Bridge and the Pap of Glencoe. The
attractive bedrooms vary in size, are stylishly furnished,
and are well equipped. There is a ground-floor lounge and
a charming dining room where delicious breakfasts, and
evening meals by arrangement, are served at individual
tables.

Rooms 5 en suite S £49.50-£55.50; D £66-£85*
Facilities FTV Lounge tea/coffee Dinner available Cen ht
Licensed Wi-fi Parking 5 Notes LB ⊗ No Children 13yrs
Closed 24-26 Dec

SPEAN BRIDGE   Map 22 NN28

Corriechoille Lodge

★★★★ 🚽 GUEST HOUSE

PH34 4EY
☎ 01397 712002
e-mail: mail@corriechoille.co.uk
web: www.corriechoille.com
dir: Off A82 signed Corriechoille, 2.5m, left at fork
(10mph sign). At end of tarmac, turn right up hill & left

This fine country house stands above the River Spean.
There are magnificent views of the Nevis range and
surrounding mountains from the comfortable first-floor
lounge and some of the spacious, well-appointed
bedrooms. Friendly and attentive service is provided, as
are traditional breakfasts and delicious evening meals by
arrangement.

Rooms 4 en suite (2 fmly) (1 GF) S £43-£48; D £66-£76*
Facilities STV FTV DVD iPod docking station Lounge tea/
coffee Dinner available Cen ht Licensed Wi-fi Parking 7
Notes ⊗ No Children 7yrs Closed Nov-Mar RS Sun-Mon
closed

SPEAN BRIDGE *continued*

Smiddy House

★★★★ ◎◎ ▣ RESTAURANT WITH ROOMS

Roy Bridge Rd PH34 4EU
☎ 01397 712335 ▣ 01397 712043
e-mail: enquiry@smiddyhouse.com
web: www.smiddyhouse.com
dir: *In village centre, A82 onto A86*

Set in the Great Glen which stretches from Fort William to Inverness, this was once the village smithy, and is now a very friendly establishment. The attractive bedrooms, named after places in Scotland, are comfortably furnished and well equipped. A relaxing garden room is available for guest use. Delicious evening meals are served in Russell's restaurant. Smiddy House was a Finalist in the AA Friendliest B&B of the Year Award 2012-13.

Rooms 4 en suite (1 fmly) D £90-£120* **Facilities** FTV Lounge tea/coffee Dinner available Wi-fi **Extras** Speciality toiletries, mineral water - complimentary **Parking** 15 **Notes** No coaches

Achnabobane Farmhouse *(NN195811)*

★★★ FARMHOUSE

PH34 4EX
☎ 01397 712919 **Mr and Mrs N Ockenden**
e-mail: enquiries@achnabobane.co.uk
web: www.achnabobane.co.uk
dir: *2m S of Spean Bridge on A82*

With breathtaking views of Ben Nevis, Aonach Mhor and the Grey Corries, the farmhouse offers comfortable, good-value accommodation in a friendly family environment. Bedrooms are traditional in style and well equipped. Breakfast and evening meals are served in the conservatory-dining room. Pets are welcome.

Rooms 4 rms (1 en suite) (1 fmly) (1 GF) S £32-£35; D £64-£66 **Facilities** TVL tea/coffee Dinner available

Cen ht Wi-fi **Parking** 5 **Notes** Closed Xmas red deer/woodland

STRATHPEFFER   Map 23 NH45

Inver Lodge

★★★ GUEST HOUSE

IV14 9DL
☎ 01997 421392
e-mail: derbyshire@inverlg.fsnet.co.uk
dir: *A834 through Strathpeffer centre, turn beside Spa Pavilion signed Bowling Green, Inver Lodge on right*

You are assured of a warm welcome at this Victorian lodge, secluded in its own tree-studded gardens yet within easy walking distance of the town centre. Bedrooms are comfortable and well equipped, and the cosy lounge is ideal for relaxation. Breakfasts, and evening meals (by arrangement), are served at a communal table.

Rooms 2 rms (1 fmly) S £32-£35; D £50* **Facilities** FTV tea/coffee Dinner available Cen ht Wi-fi ▲ **Parking** 2 **Notes** LB ⊗ Closed Xmas & New Year ☻

TOMATIN   Map 23 NH82

Glenan Lodge Guest House

★★★★ GUEST HOUSE

IV13 7YT
☎ 01808 511217 ▣ 08082 801125
e-mail: enquiries@glenanlodge.co.uk
web: www.glenanlodge.co.uk
dir: *Off A9 to Tomatin, turn left to distillery, then right into distillery drive. Proceed to top of hill, take right fork & follow road to Glenan Lodge*

Peacefully located on the edge of the village, this relaxed and homely guest house offers a warm welcome. The comfortable bedrooms are traditionally furnished and suitably equipped. An inviting lounge is available, and delicious home-cooked evening meals and breakfasts are served in the dining room. A two mile stretch of the River Findhorn is available for fly-fishing, and golfers, walkers and bird watchers are also well provided for locally.

Rooms 7 en suite (2 fmly) **Facilities** FTV TVL tea/coffee Dinner available Cen ht Licensed Wi-fi Fishing **Parking** 7 **Notes** ⊗ No Children 5yrs

TORRIDON   Map 22 NG95

The Torridon Inn

★★★★ ⌂ INN

IV22 2EY
☎ 01445 791242 ▣ 01445 712253
e-mail: inn@thetorridon.com

The Torridon Inn enjoys an idyllic location and is set in 58 acres of parkland overlooking Loch Torridon and surrounded by steep mountains on all sides. Bedrooms are lodge style with adjacent parking and are smartly appointed with comfy beds and modern facilities. Freshly prepared food is served in the adjacent inn, where over 80 whiskies, and several real ales including a local Torridon Ale, are firm favourites.

Rooms 12 en suite (3 fmly) (5 GF) S £99; D £99* **Facilities** STV tea/coffee Dinner available Cen ht Wi-fi ⚑ Fishing Pool table ▲ Outdoor adventure activities available **Parking** 12 **Notes** LB Closed Jan

ULLAPOOL   Map 22 NH19

The Arch Inn

★★★ INN

10-11 West Shore St IV26 2UR
☎ 01854 612454
e-mail: info@thearchinn.co.uk

The Arch Inn is situated on Ullapool waterfront on the shores of Loch Broom, only a two-minute walk from the Outer Hebrides ferry terminal. The accommodation provided is comfortable and most rooms have stunning views over the loch to the mountains in the distance. Two dining options are available - the relaxed bar and grill on the ground floor, and a more formal Seafood Restaurant on the first floor.

Rooms 10 en suite (1 fmly) (2 GF) **Facilities** FTV tea/coffee Dinner available Cen ht Wi-fi Pool table **Conf** Max 60 Thtr 40 Class 30 Board 35 **Parking** 5 **Notes** ⊗

WICK   Map 23 ND35

The Clachan

★★★★ BED AND BREAKFAST

13 Randolph Place, South Rd KW1 5NJ
☎ 01955 605384 & 600467
e-mail: enquiry@theclachan.co.uk
dir: *Off A99 0.5m S of town centre*

A warm welcome is assured at this immaculate detached home, by the main road on the south edge of the town. The bright, airy bedrooms (all on the ground floor) though compact, are attractively furnished to make good use of available space. Breakfast offers an extensive choice and is served at individual tables in the cosy dining room.

Rooms 3 en suite (3 GF) S £55-£60; D £70-£80* **Facilities** FTV tea/coffee Cen ht Wi-fi **Parking** 3 **Notes** ⊗ No Children 12yrs Closed Xmas & New Year ☻

MIDLOTHIAN

DALKEITH   Map 21 NT36

The Sun Inn

★★★★ ⊛ INN

Lothian Bridge EH22 4TR
☎ 0131 663 2456
e-mail: thesuninn@live.co.uk
dir: On A7 towards Galashiels, opposite Newbattle
Viaduct

The Sun Inn dates back to 1697 and is situated within
easy striking distance of Edinburgh. It has boutique-style
bedrooms (one featuring a copper bath) and modern
bathrooms. High quality, award-winning food is served in
stylish surroundings; drinks can be enjoyed in the
terraced garden area.

Rooms 5 en suite S £70-£75; D £85-£95* Facilities STV
FTV tea/coffee Dinner available Cen ht Wi-fi ⌁ 18 Fishing
Parking 50 Notes LB ⊗ No coaches

ROSLIN   Map 21 NT26

The Original Rosslyn Inn

★★★★ INN

4 Main St EH25 9LE
☎ 0131 440 2384 ▤ 0131 440 2514
e-mail: enquiries@theoriginalhotel.co.uk
dir: From A701 at rdbt take B7003 signed Roslin &
Rosewell, into Roslin. At T-junct, inn opposite. Or from
mini-rdbt on A701 at Bilston take B7006 to Roslin. Inn
on left

Whether on the Da Vinci Code trail or in the area on
business, this property a very short walk from the famous
Rosslyn Chapel which is well worth visiting. This
delightful village inn offers well-equipped bedrooms with
upgraded en suites. Four of the bedrooms have four-
poster beds. The Grail Restaurant, the lounge and
conservatory offer a comprehensive selection of dining
options.

The Original Rosslyn Inn

Rooms 6 en suite (2 fmly) (1 smoking) Facilities STV tea/
coffee Dinner available Cen ht Wi-fi Conf Max 130 Thtr
130 Class 80 Board 60 Parking 8 Notes LB Civ Wed 180

NORTH AYRSHIRE

LARGS   Map 20 NS25

South Whittlieburn Farm

★★★★ ⌁ BED AND BREAKFAST

Brisbane Glen KA30 8SN
☎ 01475 675881 ▤ 01475 675080
e-mail: largsbandb@southwhittlieburnfarm.freeserve.
co.uk
dir: 2m NE of Largs off A78 signed Brisbane Glen, after
Vikingar centre

This comfortable and welcoming farmhouse is on a
working sheep farm surrounded by gently rolling
countryside. The attractive bedrooms are well equipped
with all having DVD and video players. There is a
spacious ground-floor lounge, and a bright airy dining
room where delicious breakfasts are served.

Rooms 3 en suite (1 fmly) S £38.50-£44; D £62-£68*
Facilities STV FTV DVD TVL tea/coffee Cen ht Wi-fi ⌁ 18
🔒 Parking 10 Notes LB ⊗ RS Xmas ⊛

NORTH LANARKSHIRE

COATBRIDGE   Map 20 NS76

Auchenlea

★★★ GUEST HOUSE

153 Langmuir Rd, Bargeddie G69 7RT
☎ 0141 771 6870 & 07775 791381 ▤ 0141 771 6870
e-mail: helenbarr06@btinternet.com
dir: A8 onto A752 for 0.4m

Backing onto farmland, yet only a short distance from the
motorway, this detached house is well placed for Glasgow
and Edinburgh. Satisfying, well-cooked breakfasts are
served at a communal table in the bright dining room,
and there is an attractive conservatory and adjoining
lounge. The bedrooms, all on the ground floor, are modern
in style with one designed for easier access.

Rooms 6 en suite (1 fmly) (6 GF) S £35; D £65*
Facilities FTV Lounge TVL tea/coffee Cen ht Parking 10
Notes ⊗

PERTH & KINROSS

ALYTH   Map 23 NO24

PREMIER COLLECTION

Tigh Na Leigh Guesthouse

🏠 ⌁ GUEST ACCOMMODATION

22-24 Airlie St PH11 8AJ
☎ 01828 632372 ▤ 01828 632279
e-mail: bandcblack@yahoo.co.uk
web: www.tighnaleigh.co.uk
dir: In town centre on B952

Situated in the heart of this country town, Tigh Na
Leigh is Gaelic for 'The House of the Doctor'. Its
location and somewhat sombre façade are in stunning
contrast to what lies inside. The house has been
completely restored to blend its Victorian architecture
with contemporary interior design. Bedrooms, including
a superb suite, have state-of-the-art bathrooms. There
are three entirely different lounges, while delicious
meals are served in the conservatory/dining room
overlooking a spectacular landscaped garden.

Rooms 5 en suite (1 GF) S £50; D £80-£120*
Facilities FTV DVD iPod docking station Lounge TVL
tea/coffee Dinner available Cen ht Licensed Wi-fi ⌁ 18
🔒 Extras Fruit, snacks Parking 5 Notes No Children
12yrs Closed Dec-Feb

BLAIRGOWRIE
Map 21 NO14

Gilmore House

★★★★ 🏠 BED AND BREAKFAST

Perth Rd PH10 6EJ
☎ 01250 872791 📠 01250 872791
e-mail: jill@gilmorehouse.co.uk
dir: On A93 S

This Victorian villa stands in a well-tended garden on the south side of town. Sympathetically restored to enhance its period features it offers individual bedrooms tastefully furnished in antique pine, and thoughtfully equipped to include modern amenities such as Freeview TV. There are two inviting lounges, one of which has lovely views over the gardens. Hearty traditional breakfasts are served in the attractive dining room.

Rooms 3 en suite D £65-£80* **Facilities** FTV TVL tea/coffee Cen ht Wi-fi **Parking** 3 **Notes** Closed Xmas

CRIEFF
Map 21 NN82

Merlindale

★★★★ BED AND BREAKFAST

Perth Rd PH7 3EQ
☎ 01764 655205 📠 01764 655205
e-mail: merlin.dale@virgin.net
web: www.merlindale.co.uk
dir: On A85, 350yds from E end of High St

Situated in a quiet residential area within walking distance of the town centre, this delightful detached house stands in well-tended grounds and offers a warm welcome. The pretty bedrooms are comfortably furnished and well equipped. There is a spacious lounge, an impressive library, and an elegant dining room where delicious evening meals and traditional breakfasts are served.

Rooms 3 en suite (1 fmly) **Facilities** STV FTV TVL tea/coffee Dinner available Cen ht Wi-fi **Parking** 3 **Notes** LB ⊗ Closed 9 Dec-10 Feb

GLENFARG
Map 21 NO11

The Famous Bein Inn

★★★ ⊛ INN

PH2 9PY
☎ 01577 830216 📠 01577 830211
e-mail: enquiries@beininn.com
web: www.beininn.com
dir: From S: M90 junct 8, A91 towards Cupar. Left onto B996 to Bein Inn. From N: M90 junct 9, A912 towards Gateside

This inn, in a peaceful rural setting, was originally built to accommodate travellers on a journey between

Edinburgh and the Highlands. A friendly welcome is guaranteed and there is a relaxed informal atmosphere with blazing log fires a feature on colder evenings. Short breaks for golf, fishing and shooting are offered. The restaurant has a well deserved reputation for the careful preparation of the finest local produce.

Rooms 7 en suite 4 annexe en suite (4 fmly) (4 GF) **Facilities** tea/coffee Dinner available Direct Dial Cen ht Wi-fi **Conf** Max 32 Thtr 32 Class 25 Board 25 **Parking** 26 **Notes** Closed 25 Dec

MUTHILL
Map 21 NN81

Barley Bree Restaurant with Rooms

★★★★ ⊛⊛ RESTAURANT WITH ROOMS

6 Willoughby St PH5 2AB
☎ 01764 681451 📠 01764 910055
e-mail: info@barleybree.com
dir: A9 onto A822 in centre of Muthill

Situated in the heart of the small village of Muthill, and just a short drive from Crieff, genuine hospitality and quality food are obvious attractions at this charming restaurant with rooms. The property has been transformed by the current owners, and the stylish bedrooms are appointed to a very high standard. The restaurant has a rustic feel with exposed stonework, wooden floors and a log-burning fire in the centre. Choices range from set, carte and tasting menus. Children are welcome too.

Rooms 6 en suite (1 fmly) S £70-£75; D £105-£140* **Facilities** FTV DVD Lounge tea/coffee Dinner available Cen ht 🔒 **Parking** 10 **Notes** LB ⊗ Closed 2wks autumn/Jan RS Mon & Tue Restaurant closed to public No coaches

PERTH
Map 21 NO12

Cherrybank Guesthouse

★★★★ 🏠 GUEST ACCOMMODATION

217-219 Glasgow Rd PH2 0NB
☎ 01738 451982 📠 01738 561336
e-mail: m.r.cherrybank@blueyonder.co.uk
dir: 1m SW of town centre on A93

Convenient for the town and major roads, Cherrybank offers well equipped and beautifully presented bedrooms, one of which is on the ground floor. The delightful lounge is ideal for relaxation, while delicious breakfasts are served at individual tables in the bright airy dining room.

Rooms 5 rms (4 en suite) (1 pri facs) (2 fmly) (1 GF) **Facilities** tea/coffee Cen ht Wi-fi **Parking** 4 **Notes** ⊗

Clunie Guest House

★★★★ GUEST HOUSE

12 Pitcullen Crescent PH2 7HT
☎ 01738 623625 📠 01738 623238
e-mail: ann@clunieguesthouse.co.uk
dir: On A94 on E side of river

Lying on the north east side of town, this family-run guest house offers a friendly welcome. The comfortable bedrooms, which vary in size, are attractively decorated and well equipped. Breakfast is served at individual tables in the elegant ground-floor dining room.

Rooms 7 en suite (1 fmly) **Facilities** tea/coffee Cen ht Wi-fi **Parking** 8 **Notes** ⊗

Ballabeg Guest House

★★★ BED AND BREAKFAST

14 Keir St PH2 7HJ
☎ 01738 620434
e-mail: ballabeg@btopenworld.com
dir: NE of city centre, Keir St accessed from A93 (E of river) or from A94 (Strathmore St)

Well situated for the town centre and benefiting from off-road parking, this property offers modern, comfortable bedrooms of a good overall size with a number of extras provided as standard. Well-cooked breakfasts with warm and genuine hospitality ensure a pleasant stay. All major credit cards are accepted.

Rooms 4 rms (3 en suite) (1 pri facs) D £58-£61* **Facilities** FTV DVD tea/coffee Cen ht Wi-fi **Parking** 4 **Notes** ⊗ No Children 16yrs Closed Dec-Jan

PITLOCHRY
Map 23 NN95

Craigroyston House

★★★★ GUEST HOUSE

2 Lower Oakfield PH16 5HQ
☎ 01796 472053 📠 01796 472053
e-mail: reservations@craigroyston.co.uk
web: www.craigroyston.co.uk
dir: In town centre near information centre car park

The Maxwell family delight in welcoming guests to their home, an impressive detached Victorian villa set in a colourful garden. The bedrooms have pretty colour schemes and are comfortably furnished in period style. There is an inviting sitting room, complete with deep sofas for those wishing to relax and enjoy the peaceful atmosphere. Scottish breakfasts are served at individual tables in the attractive dining room.

Rooms 8 en suite (1 fmly) (1 GF) **Facilities** FTV tea/coffee Cen ht Wi-fi **Parking** 9 **Notes** LB ⊗ ⊛

Wellwood House

★★★★ GUEST HOUSE

13 West Moulin Rd PH16 5EA
☎ 01796 474288 📠 01796 474299
e-mail: wellwoodhouse@aol.com
web: www.wellwoodhouse.com
dir: In town centre opposite town hall

Set in lovely grounds on an elevated position overlooking the town, Wellwood House has stunning views of the Vale of Atholl and the surrounding countryside. The comfortably proportioned bedrooms are attractively decorated and well equipped. The elegant lounge has an honesty bar and a fire on cooler evenings, and the spacious dining room is the setting for hearty breakfasts served at individual tables.

Rooms 10 rms (8 en suite) (2 pri facs) (1 fmly) (1 GF) S £45-£60; D £69-£89* **Facilities** FTV Lounge TVL tea/coffee Cen ht Licensed Wi-fi **Extras** Honesty bar **Parking** 20 **Notes** ✖ Closed 10 Nov-14 Feb Civ Wed 24

SCOTTISH BORDERS

BROUGHTON   Map 21 NT13

The Glenholm Centre

★★★ 🏠 GUEST ACCOMMODATION

ML12 6JF
☎ 01899 830408
e-mail: info@glenholm.co.uk
dir: 1m S of Broughton. Off A701 to Glenholm

Surrounded by peaceful farmland, this former schoolhouse has a distinct African theme. The home-cooked meals and baking have received much praise and are served in the spacious lounge-dining room. The bright airy bedrooms are thoughtfully equipped, and the service is friendly and attentive. Computer courses are available.

Rooms 3 en suite 1 annexe en suite (1 fmly) (2 GF) **Facilities** TVL tea/coffee Dinner available Cen ht Licensed Wi-fi **Conf** Max 24 Thtr 24 Class 24 Board 24 **Parking** 14 **Notes** Closed 20 Dec-1 Feb

EDDLESTON   Map 21 NT24

The Horseshoe Inn

★★★★ 🍴🍴 🏠 RESTAURANT WITH ROOMS

EH45 8QP
☎ 01721 730225 📠 01721 730268
e-mail: reservations@horseshoeinn.co.uk
web: www.horseshoeinn.co.uk
dir: A703, 5m N of Peebles

This inn is five miles north of Peebles and only 18 miles south of Edinburgh. Originally a blacksmith's shop, it has a very good reputation for its delightful atmosphere and excellent cuisine. There are eight luxuriously appointed and individually designed bedrooms.

Rooms 8 en suite (1 fmly) (6 GF) **Facilities** FTV Lounge tea/coffee Dinner available Direct Dial Cen ht Wi-fi Fishing **Extras** Speciality toiletries - complimentary; mini-bar **Parking** 20 **Notes** LB Closed 25 Dec & 2wks Jan RS Sun eve & Mon Restaurant closed, bistro open

GALASHIELS   Map 21 NT43

Over Langshaw (NT524400)

★★★ FARMHOUSE

Langshaw TD1 2PE
☎ 01896 860244 📠 01896 860668 Mrs S Bergius
e-mail: overlangshaw@btconnect.com
dir: 3m N of Galashiels. A7 N from Galashiels, 1m right signed Langshaw, right at T-junct into Langshaw, left signed Earlston. Over Langshaw 1m, signed

There are fine panoramic views from this organic hillside farm which offers two comfortable and spacious bedrooms. Hearty breakfasts are provided at individual tables in the lounge and a friendly welcome is guaranteed.

Rooms 2 en suite (1 fmly) (1 GF) S £35-£37.50; D £65-£75 **Facilities** TVL tea/coffee Cen ht Wi-fi 🐾 **Parking** 4 **Notes** 🐾 500 acres dairy/sheep/organic

JEDBURGH   Map 21 NT62

Ferniehirst Mill Lodge

★★ GUEST HOUSE

TD8 6PQ
☎ 01835 863279
e-mail: ferniehirstmill@aol.com
web: www.ferniehirstmill.co.uk
dir: 2.5m S of Jedburgh on A68, onto private track to end

Reached by a narrow farm track and a rustic wooden bridge, this chalet-style house has a secluded setting by the River Jed. Bedrooms are small and functional, and there is a comfortable lounge in which to relax. Home-cooked and hearty breakfasts are served in the cosy dining room.

Rooms 7 en suite (1 GF) S £30; D £60* **Facilities** TVL tea/coffee Cen ht Fishing Riding 🐾 **Parking** 10

LAUDER   Map 21 NT54

The Black Bull

★★★★ 🍴 INN

Market Place TD2 6SR
☎ 01578 722208 📠 01578 722419
e-mail: enquiries@blackbull-lauder.com
dir: On A68 in village centre

This 18th-century coaching inn has been completely transformed. The lovely bedrooms are furnished in the period character and thoughtfully equipped with modern amenities. The wooden floored cosy bar and four dining areas are charming, the main dining room being a former chapel. A very good range of food makes this a popular gastro-pub.

Rooms 8 en suite (2 fmly) **Facilities** FTV tea/coffee Dinner available Direct Dial Cen ht Wi-fi **Parking** 8

MELROSE — Map 21 NT53

PREMIER COLLECTION

Fauhope House

★★★★★ GUEST HOUSE

Gattonside TD6 9LU
☎ 01896 823184 ▥ 01896 823184
e-mail: info@fauhopehouse.com
dir: 0.7m N of Melrose over River Tweed. N off B6360 at Gattonside 30mph sign (E) up long driveway

It's hard to imagine a more complete experience than a stay at Fauhope, set high on a hillside on the north-east edge of the village. Hospitality is first class, breakfasts are excellent, and the delightful country house has a splendid interior. Bedrooms are luxurious, each individual and superbly equipped. Public areas are elegantly decorated and furnished, and enhanced by beautiful floral arrangements; the dining room is particularly stunning.

Rooms 3 en suite Facilities tea/coffee Dinner available Cen ht ☕ Riding Parking 10 Notes LB ⊗

NEWCASTLETON — Map 21 NY48

Liddesdale

★★★★ INN

Douglas Sq TD9 0QD
☎ 01387 375255 ▥ 01387 752577
e-mail: reception@theliddesdalehotel.co.uk
web: www.theliddesdalehotel.co.uk

Liddesdale is located in the peaceful 17th-century village of Newcastleton overlooking the village square. There are well-appointed bedrooms and bathrooms, and the public areas offer various locations in which to dine. The welcoming public bar is well used by locals and residents alike, and there is also a beer garden. Relaxed and informal menus use the best local produce available.

Rooms 6 en suite (2 fmly) Facilities STV FTV Lounge TVL tea/coffee Dinner available Direct Dial Cen ht Wi-fi ☕ ⚓ ⛳ 9 Fishing ☕ Conf Max 60 Thtr 40 Class 40 Board 40 Notes LB

SOUTH AYRSHIRE

AYR — Map 20 NS32

PREMIER COLLECTION

26 The Crescent

★★★★★ GUEST HOUSE

26 Bellevue Crescent KA7 2DR
☎ 01292 287329 ▥ 01292 201003
e-mail: enquiries@26crescent.co.uk
web: www.26crescent.co.uk
dir: Exit A79 at rdbt, 3rd exit into King St. Left into Bellevue Crescent

Located in a quiet residential area of Ayr, close to the seafront, town centre and race course, this guest house offers a traditional warm welcome with well appointed and comfortable bedrooms. Bathrooms are of a high standard, as is the hearty breakfast served on individual tables in the charming dining room.

Rooms 5 en suite Facilities FTV tea/coffee Cen ht Wi-fi Notes ⊗

Daviot House

★★★★ GUEST HOUSE

12 Queens Ter KA7 1DU
☎ 01292 269678
e-mail: daviothouse@hotmail.com
web: www.daviothouse.com
dir: Exit A719 into Wellington Sq & Bath Place, turn right

This well-maintained Victorian house stands in a peaceful location close to the beach and town centre. Bedrooms are modern in style and well equipped. Hearty breakfasts are served in the dining room. Daviot House is a member of Golf South Ayrshire - a golf booking service for local municipal courses, so let your hosts know if you'd like a round booked.

Rooms 6 rms (5 en suite) (1 pri facs) (1 fmly) (1 GF) Facilities FTV tea/coffee Cen ht Wi-fi Notes ⊗

SOUTH LANARKSHIRE

STRATHAVEN — Map 20 NS74

Rissons at Springvale

★★★ ⊛ RESTAURANT WITH ROOMS

18 Lethame Rd ML10 6AD
☎ 01357 521131 & 520234 ▥ 01357 521131
e-mail: rissons@msn.com
dir: A71 into Strathaven, W of town centre off Townhead St

Guests are assured of a warm welcome at this charming establishment close to the town centre. The bedrooms and bathrooms are stylish and well equipped. The main attraction here is the food - a range of interesting, well-prepared dishes served in Rissons Restaurant.

Rooms 9 en suite (1 fmly) (1 GF) S £42.50-£45;
D £75-£80* **Facilities** Lounge tea/coffee Dinner available
Cen ht Wi-fi ⚿ 18 🅿 **Parking** 10 **Notes** ⊗ Closed 1st wk
Jan No coaches

STIRLING

CALLANDER   Map 20 NN60

Abbotsford Lodge

★★★★ GUEST ACCOMMODATION

Stirling Rd FK17 8DA
☎ 01877 330066 & 07939 538164 📠 01877 339363
e-mail: info@abbotsfordlodge.co.uk
dir: M80 junct 10 to A84 signed Callander. Pass garage
on right, Abbotsford Lodge 0.5m on right

Abbotsford Lodge is situated within easy walking
distance of the centre of town, set in mature and well-
presented gardens that are a definite feature. Bedrooms
are comfortable with very good quality decor and soft
furnishings. Public areas are warm and welcoming with a
licensed residents bar. Breakfast is served on individual
tables in the conservatory and dining room areas.

Rooms 9 rms (5 en suite) 7 annexe rms 6 annexe en suite
(1 pri facs) (3 fmly) (2 GF) S £45-£100; D £50-£120*
Facilities FTV Lounge tea/coffee Cen ht Licensed Wi-fi
⚿ 18 🅿 **Parking** 16 **Notes** LB ⊗ Closed 22 Dec-12 Feb

Callander Meadows

★★★★ ⊛ RESTAURANT WITH ROOMS

24 Main St FK17 8BB
☎ 01877 330181
e-mail: mail@callandermeadows.co.uk
web: www.callandermeadows.co.uk
dir: M9 junct 10, A84 to Callander, house on main street
just past A81 junct

Located on the high street in Callander, this family-run
business offers comfortable accommodation and a
restaurant that has quickly become very popular with the
locals. The bedrooms have been appointed to a high
standard. Private parking is available to the rear.

Rooms 3 en suite **Facilities** STV tea/coffee Dinner
available Cen ht Wi-fi **Parking** 4 **Notes** ⊗ RS Winter
Restaurant open Thu-Sun only No coaches

Lubnaig House

★★★★ 🅰 GUEST HOUSE

Leny Feus FK17 8AS
☎ 01877 330376 📠 01877 330376
e-mail: info@lubnaighouse.co.uk
web: www.lubnaighouse.co.uk
dir: From town centre take A84 W, 1st street on right after
Poppies Hotel

Rooms 6 en suite 2 annexe en suite (4 GF) S £50-£60;
D £70-£80* **Facilities** FTV Lounge tea/coffee Cen ht Wi-fi
🅿 **Parking** 10 **Notes** LB ⊗ No Children 7yrs Closed Nov-
Apr

LOCHEARNHEAD   Map 20 NN52

Tigh Na Crich

★★★★ BED AND BREAKFAST

FK19 8PR
☎ 01567 830235
e-mail: johntippett2@aol.com
web: www.tighnacrich.co.uk
dir: At junct of A84 & A85, adjacent to village shop

Tich Na Crich is located in the heart of the small village
of Lochearnhead, surrounded by mountains on three sides
and Loch Earn on the fourth. Inside is very well presented
accommodation with many thoughtful extras provided.
The generous breakfast is served in the comfortable
dining room on individual tables looking out to the front
of the property.

Rooms 3 en suite (1 fmly) S £42-£45; D £64-£68*
Facilities FTV DVD Lounge tea/coffee Cen ht Wi-fi 🅿
Parking 3 **Notes** Closed Xmas-New Year ⊜

STIRLING   Map 21 NS79

Linden Guest House

★★★★ GUEST HOUSE

22 Linden Av FK7 7PQ
☎ 01786 448850 & 07974 116573 📠 01786 448850
e-mail: fay@lindenguesthouse.co.uk
web: www.lindenguesthouse.co.uk
dir: 0.5m SE of city centre off A9

Situated within walking distance of the town centre, this
friendly guest house offers attractive and very well-
equipped bedrooms, including a large family room that
sleeps five comfortably. There is a bright dining room
where delicious breakfasts are served at individual tables
with quality Wedgwood crockery.

Rooms 4 en suite (2 fmly) (1 GF) D £50-£80
Facilities STV FTV DVD iPod docking station tea/coffee
Cen ht Wi-fi **Parking** 2 **Notes** LB

STRATHYRE   Map 20 NN51

PREMIER COLLECTION

Creagan House

★★★★★ ⊛⊛ 🍴 RESTAURANT WITH ROOMS

FK18 8ND
☎ 01877 384638 📠 01877 384319
e-mail: eatandstay@creaganhouse.co.uk
web: www.creaganhouse.co.uk
dir: 0.25m N of Strathyre on A84

Originally a farmhouse dating from the 17th century,
Creagan House has operated as a restaurant with
rooms for many years. The baronial-style dining room
provides a wonderful setting for the cuisine which is
classic French with some Scottish influences. The warm
hospitality and attentive service are noteworthy.

Rooms 5 en suite (1 fmly) (1 GF) S £75-£95;
D £130-£150 **Facilities** FTV Lounge tea/coffee Dinner
available Cen ht Wi-fi 🅿 **Extras** Speciality toiletries
Conf Max 35 Thtr 35 Class 12 Board 35 **Parking** 16
Notes LB Closed 6-22 Nov, Xmas & 16 Jan-8 Mar RS
Wed & Thu closed

WEST DUNBARTONSHIRE

BALLOCH   Map 20 NS38

The Waterhouse Inn

★★★★ INN

34 Balloch Rd G83 8LE
☎ 01389 752120 📠 01389 752125
e-mail: info@waterhouseinn.co.uk
web: www.waterhouseinn.co.uk
dir: M8 junct 30 onto M898. Over Erskine bridge, take
exit for Crianlarich onto A82 head towards Loch Lomond.
Right at rdbt onto A811

The Waterhouse Inn is located on the high street of
Balloch close to the park and the mouth of Loch Lomond.
Bedrooms are well equipped and spacious, with modern
bright bathrooms. The inn is welcoming and friendly, with
a café that serves home-cooked food throughout the day,
and is a perfect base for touring Loch Lomond and the
Trossachs National Park.

Rooms 7 en suite (2 fmly) **Facilities** STV FTV Lounge TVL
tea/coffee Dinner available Cen ht Wi-fi **Notes** ⊗

BALLOCH *continued*

Innkeeper's Lodge Loch Lomond

★★★ INN

Balloch Rd G83 8LQ
☎ 0845 112 6006
e-mail: info@innkeeperslodge.com
web: www.innkeeperslodge.com

At Innkeeper's Lodge you'll find accommodation with comfort and character in equal measure, and everything needed for a relaxing stay, from easy check-in and free parking to complimentary breakfast and a cosy pub serving great value food and drink on the doorstep. Each Lodge has quality rooms, and there are Lodges in a variety of locations from towns and cities to countryside settings across the UK.

Rooms 11 en suite (4 fmly) **Facilities** FTV tea/coffee Dinner available Direct Dial Wi-fi **Parking** 52

Sunnyside

★★★ BED AND BREAKFAST

35 Main St G83 9JX
☎ 01389 750282 & 07717 397548
e-mail: enquiries@sunnysidebb.co.uk
dir: *From A82 take A811 then A813 for 1m, over mini-rdbt 150mtrs on left*

Set in its own grounds well back from the road by Loch Lomond, Sunnyside is an attractive, traditional detached house, parts of which date back to the 1830s. Bedrooms are attractively decorated and provide comfortable modern accommodation. Free Wi-fi is also available. The dining room is located on the ground floor, and is an appropriate setting for hearty Scottish breakfasts.

Rooms 6 en suite (2 fmly) (1 GF) S £28-£38; D £48-£65* **Facilities** FTV DVD tea/coffee Dinner available Cen ht Wi-fi **Parking** 8

BLACKBURN   Map 21 NS96

Cruachan B&B

★★★★ GUEST ACCOMMODATION

78 East Main St EH47 7QS
☎ 01506 655221 🖷 01506 652395
e-mail: enquiries@cruachan.co.uk
web: www.cruachan.co.uk
dir: *On A705 in Blackburn, 1m from M8 junct 4*

Ideally located for both the leisure and business traveller to central Scotland, with Edinburgh only 30 minutes away by train and Glasgow only 35 minutes away by car. Cruachan is the comfortable, friendly home of the Harkins family. Bedrooms are bright, attractive and very well equipped. Breakfast, featuring the best of local produce is served at individual tables in the ground-floor dining room.

Rooms 4 rms (3 en suite) (1 pri facs) (1 fmly) S £40-£45; D £60-£68* **Facilities** FTV tea/coffee Cen ht Wi-fi 🐾 **Parking** 5 **Notes** ⊗

EAST CALDER   Map 21 NT06

PREMIER COLLECTION

Ashcroft Farmhouse

★★★★★ GUEST HOUSE

EH53 0ET
☎ 01506 881810 & 07788 926239 🖷 01506 884327
e-mail: scottashcroft7@aol.com
web: www.ashcroftfarmhouse.com

(For full entry see Livingston)

Whitecroft Bed & Breakfast

★★★★ BED AND BREAKFAST

7 Raw Holdings EH53 0ET
☎ 01506 882494 🖷 01506 882598
e-mail: lornascot@aol.com
web: www.whitecroftbandb.co.uk

(For full entry see Livingston)

LINLITHGOW   Map 21 NS97

AA GUEST ACCOMMODATION OF THE YEAR FOR SCOTLAND

PREMIER COLLECTION

Arden Country House

★★★★★ 🏠 GUEST ACCOMMODATION

Belsyde EH49 6QE
☎ 01506 670172 🖷 01506 670172
e-mail: info@ardencountryhouse.com
dir: *1.3m SW of Linlithgow. A706 over Union Canal, entrance 200yds on left at Lodge Cottage*

Situated in the picturesque grounds of the Belsyde Country Estate and close to the Royal Burgh of Linlithgow, Arden Country House offers immaculate, stylishly furnished and spacious bedrooms. There is a cosy ground-floor lounge and a charming dining room where delicious breakfasts feature the best of local produce. Arden Country House is the AA Guest Accommodation of the Year for Scotland 2012-13.

Rooms 3 en suite (1 GF) S £58-£90; D £76-£104* **Facilities** FTV DVD tea/coffee Cen ht Wi-fi **Extras** Savoury snacks, chocolates **Parking** 4 **Notes** LB ⊗ No Children 12yrs Closed 25-26 Dec

Belsyde House

★★★★ 🏠 GUEST ACCOMMODATION

Lanark Rd EH49 6QE
☎ 01506 842098 🖷 01506 842098
e-mail: info@belsydehouse.com
web: www.belsyde.com
dir: *1.5m SW on A706, 1st left over Union Canal*

Reached by a tree-lined driveway, this welcoming farmhouse is peacefully situated in attractive grounds close to the Union Canal. There are well-proportioned double, twin and family rooms, and a cosy single. All are nicely furnished and well equipped. Breakfast, including a vegetarian menu, is served at good-sized tables in the dining room, next to the lounge.

Belsyde House

Rooms 3 en suite (1 fmly) **Facilities** FTV TVL tea/coffee Cen ht Wi-fi **Extras** Speciality toiletries, robes **Parking** 10 **Notes** ⊗ No Children 12yrs Closed Xmas

Bomains Farm Guest House

★ ★ ★ ★ GUEST HOUSE

Bo'ness EH49 7RQ
☎ 01506 822188 & 822861 📠 01506 824433
e-mail: bunty.kirk@onetel.net
web: www.bomains.co.uk
dir: *A706, 1.5m N towards Bo'ness, left at golf course x-rds, 1st farm on right*

From its elevated location this friendly farmhouse has stunning views of the Firth of Forth. The bedrooms which vary in size are beautifully decorated, well equipped and enhanced by quality fabrics, with many thoughtful extra touches. Delicious home-cooked fare featuring the best of local produce is served in a stylish lounge-dining room.

Rooms 6 rms (4 en suite) (1 pri facs) (1 fmly) (2 GF) S £35-£45; D £60-£80* **Facilities** STV FTV DVD Lounge TVL tea/coffee Cen ht Wi-fi ⅃ 18 Fishing **Parking** 12

Kirkland House

★ ★ ★ ★ BED AND BREAKFAST

Bomains Farm EH49 7RQ
☎ 01506 822188 & 07974 736480
e-mail: bunty.kirk@onetel.net
dir: *A706, 1.5m N towards Bo'ness, left at golf course x-rds, 1st farm on right*

Kirkland House is a recent purpose-built property adjacent to the family-run Bomains Farm Guest House, where a number of guest services are provided. Large bedrooms come with high quality fixtures and fittings, and patio doors that lead onto the garden which has a children's play area and views onto the River Forth. All in all, a peaceful location within striking distance of Linlithgow, Edinburgh and the Central Belt.

Rooms 3 en suite (1 fmly) (3 GF) **Facilities** FTV TVL tea/coffee Cen ht Wi-fi ⅃ 18 Fishing **Parking** 6 **Notes** ⊗ ⊚

LIVINGSTON	Map 21 NT06

PREMIER COLLECTION

Ashcroft Farmhouse

★ ★ ★ ★ ★ 🏠 GUEST HOUSE

East Calder EH53 0ET
☎ 01506 881810 & 07788 926239 📠 01506 884327
e-mail: scottashcroft7@aol.com
web: www.ashcroftfarmhouse.com
dir: *On B7015, off A71, 0.5m E of East Calder, near Almondell Country Park*

With over 40 years' experience in caring for guests, Derek and Elizabeth Scott ensure a stay at Ashcroft will be memorable. Their modern home sits in lovely award-winning landscaped gardens and provides attractive and well-equipped ground-floor bedrooms. The comfortable lounge includes a video and DVD library. Breakfast, featuring home-made sausages and the best of local produce, is served at individual tables in the stylish dining room. Free Wi-fi is available, and a Park and Ride facility is nearby. Ashcroft Farmhouse was a Finalist in the AA Friendliest B&B of the Year Award 2012-13.

Rooms 6 en suite (2 fmly) (6 GF) S £60-£65; D £80-£90 **Facilities** FTV TVL tea/coffee Cen ht Wi-fi 🔒 **Parking** 8 **Notes** ⊗ No Children 12yrs

Whitecroft Bed & Breakfast

★ ★ ★ ★ BED AND BREAKFAST

7 Raw Holdings, East Calder EH53 0ET
☎ 01506 882494 📠 01506 882598
e-mail: lornascot@aol.com
web: www.whitecroftbandb.co.uk
dir: *A71 onto B7015, establishment on right*

A relaxed and friendly atmosphere prevails at this charming modern bed and breakfast. The bedrooms, all of which are on the ground floor, are attractively colour co-ordinated, well-equipped and contain many thoughtful extra touches. Breakfast is served at individual tables in the smart dining room.

Rooms 3 en suite (3 GF) S £45-£50; D £64-£70* **Facilities** FTV DVD tea/coffee Cen ht Wi-fi **Parking** 5 **Notes** No Children 12yrs

SCOTTISH ISLANDS

ISLE OF ARRAN

BRODICK Map 20 NS03

Allandale Guest House

★★★★ GUEST HOUSE

KA27 8BJ
☎ 01770 302278
e-mail: info@allandalehouse.co.uk
web: www.allandalehouse.co.uk
dir: *500yds S of Brodick Pier, off A841 towards Lamlash, up hill 2nd left at Corriegills sign*

Under enthusiastic ownership, this comfortable guest house is set in delightful gardens in beautiful countryside. Guests can relax in the lounge with its attractive garden views. Bedrooms vary in size and have pleasing colour schemes and mixed modern furnishings, along with thoughtful amenities. In a peaceful location, Allandale is convenient for the CalMac ferry and Brodick centre.

Rooms 4 rms (3 en suite) (1 pri facs) 2 annexe en suite (3 fmly) (2 GF) **Facilities** FTV tea/coffee Cen ht **Parking** 6 **Notes** ⊗ Closed Nov-Feb

Dunvegan House

★★★★ GUEST HOUSE

Dunvegan Shore Rd KA27 8AJ
☎ 01770 302811 🖹 01770 302811
e-mail: dunveganhouse1@hotmail.com
dir: *Turn right from ferry terminal, 500yds along Shore Rd*

Situated close to the shore and enjoying spectacular views of the bay, this establishment is a popular choice for visitors to the island. The property benefits from having a hands-on approach from the friendly owner whilst public areas and bedrooms have great views.

Rooms 9 en suite (3 GF) S fr £50; D fr £80* **Facilities** FTV Lounge tea/coffee Dinner available Cen ht Licensed Wi-fi 🅿 **Parking** 8 **Notes** ⊗ Closed 23 Dec-3 Jan ⊛

ISLE OF HARRIS

SCARISTA (SGARASTA BHEAG) Map 22 NG09

Scarista House

★★★★ ⊛⊛ 🍴 RESTAURANT WITH ROOMS

HS3 3HX
☎ 01859 550238 🖹 01859 550277
e-mail: timandpatricia@scaristahouse.com
dir: *On A859, 15m S of Tarbert*

A former manse, Scarista House is a haven for food lovers who seek to explore this magnificent island. It enjoys breathtaking views of the Atlantic and is just a short stroll from miles of golden sandy beaches. The house is run in a relaxed country-house manner by the friendly hosts. Expect wellies in the hall and masses of books and CDs in one of two lounges. Bedrooms are cosy, and delicious set dinners and memorable breakfasts are provided.

Rooms 3 en suite 3 annexe en suite (1 fmly) (2 GF) S £137-£147; D £210-£235* **Facilities** Lounge tea/coffee Dinner available Cen ht Wi-fi ch fac 🅿 **Extras** Speciality toiletries, fruit **Parking** 12 **Notes** LB Closed Xmas, Jan & Feb No coaches Civ Wed 40

ISLE OF LEWIS

STORNOWAY Map 22 NB43

Stornoway Bed & Breakfast

★ ★ ★ BED AND BREAKFAST

29 Kenneth St HS1 2DR
☎ 0800 234 3271
e-mail: stay@hebgroup.co.uk
web: www.hebrides-selfcatering.co.uk

Situated in an attractive 175 year-old listed building, Stornoway Bed and Breakfast offers comfortable accommodation on a quiet backstreet in Stornoway town centre, a couple of minutes walk from both the ferry and bus terminals, An Lanntair Art Centre, and local shops, pubs and restaurants. Guests can enjoy modern bedrooms and a hearty breakfast in the morning.

Rooms 4 en suite (1 fmly) S £45-£50; D £60-£80* **Facilities** FTV tea/coffee Cen ht Wi-fi 🅿 **Notes** ⊗

ORKNEY

ST MARGARET'S HOPE Map 24 ND49

The Creel Restaurant with Rooms

★★★★ ⊛⊛ RESTAURANT WITH ROOMS

Front Rd KW17 2SL
☎ 01856 831311
e-mail: alan@thecreel.freeserve.co.uk
web: www.thecreel.co.uk
dir: *A961 into village, establishment on seafront*

With wonderful sea views, The Creel enjoys a prominent position in the pretty fishing village of St Margaret's Hope. The award-winning restaurant has a well deserved reputation for the quality of its seafood and a window seat is a must in the charming restaurant. The stylish bedrooms are appointed to a high standard and most enjoy views over the bay. Breakfasts should not be missed, with local Orkney produce and freshly baked breads on the menu.

Rooms 3 en suite **Facilities** Dinner available Cen ht Wi-fi **Parking** 6 **Notes** ⊗ Closed mid Oct-Apr No coaches

SHETLAND

LERWICK
Map 24 HU44

Glen Orchy House

★★★ GUEST HOUSE

20 Knab Rd ZE1 0AX
☎ 01595 692031 📄 01595 692031
e-mail: glenorchy.house@virgin.net
dir: Next to coastguard station

This welcoming and well-presented house lies above the
town with views over the Knab, and is within easy walking
distance of the town centre. Bedrooms are modern in
design and there is a choice of lounges with books and
board games, one with an honesty bar. Substantial
breakfasts are served, and the restaurant offers a
delicious Thai menu.

Rooms 24 en suite (4 fmly) (4 GF) S £75; D £100*
Facilities STV FTV Lounge TVL tea/coffee Dinner available
Cen ht Licensed Wi-fi Parking 10 Notes Closed 25-26 Dec
& 1-2 Jan

ISLE OF SKYE

EDINBANE
Map 22 NG35

Shorefield House

★★★★ 🏠 GUEST HOUSE

IV51 9PW
☎ 01470 582444
e-mail: stay@shorefield-house.com
dir: 12m from Portree & 8m from Dunvegan, off A850 into
Edinbane, 1st on right

Shorefield stands in the village of Edinbane and looks out
to Loch Greshornish. Bedrooms range from single to
family, while one ground-floor room has easier access. All
rooms are thoughtfully equipped and have Wi-fi, fridges,
safes, DVD and CD players. Breakfast is an impressive
choice and there is also a child-friendly garden.

Rooms 3 en suite (2 fmly) (2 GF) S £42-£47; D £82-£110
Facilities STV FTV iPod docking station TVL tea/coffee
Cen ht Wi-fi 🐾 Parking 10 Notes LB ⊗ Closed Xmas

STAFFIN
Map 22 NG46

The Glenview

★★★ @@ RESTAURANT WITH ROOMS

Culnacnoc IV51 9JH
☎ 01470 562248
e-mail: enquiries@glenviewskye.co.uk
dir: 12m N of Portree on A855

The Glenview is located in one of the most beautiful parts
of Skye with stunning sea views; it is close to the famous
rock formation, The Old Man of Storr. The individually
styled bedrooms are very comfortable and front-facing
rooms enjoy the dramatic views. Evening meals should
not to be missed as the restaurant has a well deserved
reputation for its treatment of locally sourced produce.

Rooms 5 en suite (1 GF) Facilities tea/coffee Dinner
available Wi-fi Parking 12 Notes ⊗ RS Sun & Mon closed

STRUAN
Map 22 NG33

PREMIER COLLECTION

Ullinish Country Lodge

★★★★★ @@@ 🍽 RESTAURANT WITH ROOMS

IV56 8FD
☎ 01470 572214 📄 01470 572341
e-mail: ullinish@theisleofskye.co.uk
dir: Take A863 N. Lodge signed on left

Set in some of Scotland's most dramatic landscape,
with views of the Black Cuillin and MacLeod's Tables,
this lodge has lochs on three sides. Samuel Johnson
and James Boswell stayed here in 1773 and were
impressed with the hospitality even then. Hosts Brian
and Pam hope to extend the same welcome to their
guests today. As you would expect, all bedrooms have
amazing views, and come with half-tester beds. The
cuisine in the restaurant is impressive and uses the
best of Skye's produce including locally sourced
seafood and game.

Rooms 6 en suite Facilities FTV Lounge tea/coffee
Dinner available Cen ht Wi-fi Parking 8 Notes LB ⊗ No
Children 16yrs Closed Jan & 1wk Nov No coaches

UIG
Map 22 NG36

Woodbine House

★★★ GUEST ACCOMMODATION

IV51 9XP
☎ 01470 542243 & 07904 267561
e-mail: contact@skyeactivities.co.uk
dir: From Portree into Uig Bay, pass Ferry Inn, right onto
A855 (Staffin road), house 300yds on right

Built in the late 19th century, Woodbine House occupies
an elevated position overlooking Uig Bay and the
surrounding countryside, and is well suited for walking
and bird-watching enthusiasts. The ground-floor dining
room has lovely sea views, as do the front-facing
bedrooms.

Rooms 5 en suite (1 fmly) (1 GF) S £45-£62; D £66-£75*
Facilities FTV TVL tea/coffee Cen ht Wi-fi 🐾 Archery
Mountain Bike/sea kayak hire Boat trips Parking 5
Notes LB ⊗ RS Nov-Feb long stays or group bookings
only

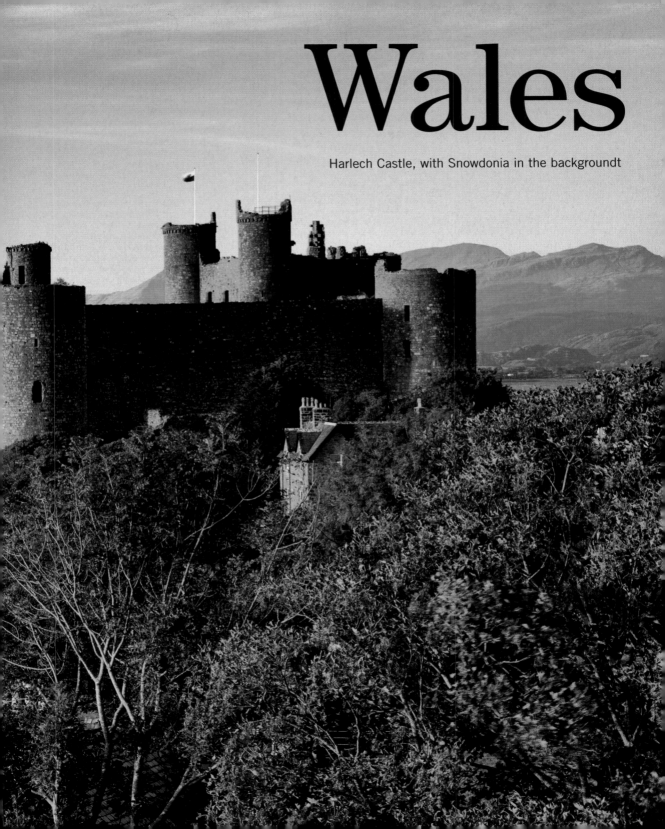

Wales

Harlech Castle, with Snowdonia in the backgroundt

ANGLESEY, ISLE OF

BEAUMARIS   Map 14 SH67

PREMIER COLLECTION

Ye Olde Bulls Head Inn

★★★★★ @ @ INN

Castle St LL58 8AP
☎ 01248 810329 ▤ 01248 811294
e-mail: info@bullsheadinn.co.uk
dir: *Located on Main St in town centre*

Both Charles Dickens and Samuel Johnson were regular visitors to this inn. The interior still features exposed beams and antique weaponry; the inn building has richly decorated, traditional bedrooms, and across a side street is The Townhouse which offers additional boutique bedrooms, each with vibrant decor. The food continues to attract praise in both the Loft Restaurant and the less formal Brasserie, and cask conditioned ales are served in the traditional bar. Meeting and functions can be catered for.

Rooms 25 en suite 1 annexe en suite (2 fmly) (5 GF) S £85-£150; D £105-£175* **Facilities** FTV Lounge tea/coffee Dinner available Direct Dial Cen ht Lift Wi-fi ⌡ 18 **Extras** Speciality toiletries **Parking** 10 **Notes** LB ✖ Closed 25 & 26 Dec No coaches

HOLYHEAD   Map 14 SH28

Blackthorn Farm

★★★★ 🅰 GUEST ACCOMMODATION

Penrhosfeilw, Trearddur Bay LL65 2LT
☎ 01407 765262 ▤ 01407 765336
e-mail: enquiries@blackthornfarm.co.uk
web: www.blackthornleisure.co.uk
dir: *A55 to Holyhead, take 1st exit at rdbt, turn immediately right between two pubs. At end of road, turn right, 0.5m on left*

Rooms 7 rms (5 en suite) (2 fmly) (1 GF) S £55-£73; D £68-£89* **Facilities** FTV DVD tea/coffee Cen ht Wi-fi 🔒 **Conf** Thtr 25 Class 25 Board 20 **Parking** 10 **Notes** LB Closed 22-31 Dec

MENAI BRIDGE   Map 14 SH57

Bryn Aethwy

★★★★ 🅰 GUEST ACCOMMODATION

Pentracth Rd LL59 5HS
☎ 01248 712228
e-mail: info@brynaethwy.com
Rooms 6 en suite S £40-£50; D £65-£85* **Notes** ☺

CARMARTHENSHIRE

CARMARTHEN   Map 8 SN42

Capel Dewi Uchaf Country House

★★★★ 🏠 BED AND BREAKFAST

Capel Dewi SA32 8AY
☎ 01267 290799 ▤ 01267 290003
e-mail: uchaffarm@aol.com
dir: *On B4300 between Capel Dewi & junct B4310*

Located in 35 acres of grounds with stunning views and private fishing in the River Towy, this Grade II listed, 16th-century house retains many magnificent features and has a wealth of character. Generous Welsh breakfasts are a feature here.

Rooms 3 en suite **Facilities** TVL tea/coffee Dinner available Cen ht Fishing Riding **Conf** Max 8 Board 8 **Parking** 10 **Notes** ✖ Closed Xmas

Sarnau Mansion

★★★★ GUEST ACCOMMODATION

Llysonnen Rd SA33 5DZ
☎ 01267 211404 ▤ 01267 211404
e-mail: d.fernihough@btinternet.com
web: www.sarnaumansion.co.uk
dir: *5m W of Carmarthen. Exit A40 onto B4298, becomes Bancyfelin road (signed Bancyfelin), Sarnau Mansion on right*

Located west of Carmarthen in 16 acres of grounds and gardens, including a tennis court, this large Grade II listed, late Georgian house retains much original character and is stylishly decorated. There is a lounge with a log fire, an elegant dining room, and spacious bedrooms with stunning rural views.

Rooms 4 rms (3 en suite) (1 pri facs) S £50-£55; D £80-£90 **Facilities** DVD TVL tea/coffee Dinner available Cen ht Wi-fi 🎾 ⌡ 18 🔒 **Parking** 10 **Notes** ✖ No Children 5yrs

FELINGWM UCHAF   Map 8 SN52

Allt Y Golau Farmhouse *(SN510261)*

★★★★ 🏠 FARMHOUSE

Allt Y Golau Uchaf SA32 7BB
☎ 01267 290455 **Dr C Rouse**
e-mail: alltygolau@btinternet.com
web: www.alltygolau.com
dir: *A40 onto B4310, N for 2m. 1st on left after Felingwm Uchaf*

This delightful Georgian farmhouse has been furnished and decorated to a high standard by the present owners, and enjoys panoramic views over the Tywi Valley to the Black Mountains beyond. Guests are welcome to take a relaxing walk through two acres of mature garden. Many thoughtful extras are provided in the comfortable bedrooms, and there is a separate lounge. Breakfast is provided in the cosy dining room around a communal table.

Rooms 3 rms (2 en suite) (1 pri facs) (2 GF) S £45; D £70 **Facilities** TVL tea/coffee Cen ht 🔒 **Parking** 3 **Notes** ✖ Closed 20 Dec-2 Jan 🐾 2 acres small holding

LLANWRDA   Map 9 SN73

PREMIER COLLECTION

Tyllwyd Hir Bed & Breakfast

★★★★★ BED AND BREAKFAST

Tyllwyd Hir SA19 8AS
☎ 01550 777362 & 07850 330218
e-mail: info@bandbwestwales.co.uk
web: www.bandbwestwales.co.uk
dir: *From Llanwrda on A482 Lampeter Rd for 1.5m, entrance on right with green name sign. 0.5m along lane through neighbouring farmland*

A warm welcome from hosts Philip and Jennifer is promised at this luxury bed and breakfast which has a superb setting in an elevated position with stunning views out across the Brecon Beacons. Recently renovated, this old building has been brought back to life, yet has retained many of its original features. Set in a peaceful location near the village of Llanwrda, it is within easy reach of Lampeter and Landovery. Bedrooms are very comfortable and modern with a host of extras provided. All three bedrooms have en suite facilities of high quality. Breakfast is a highlight of the stay with well prepared fresh ingredients and use of their own hen's eggs.

Rooms 3 en suite S £62.50-£67; D £75-£100 **Facilities** FTV DVD TVL tea/coffee Cen ht Wi-fi 🔒 **Extras** Robes, slippers, fruit, chocolates - complimentary **Parking** 10 **Notes** LB ✖ No Children RS wknds & BHs 2 nights stay min

PREMIER COLLECTION

Coedllys Country House

★★★★★   BED AND BREAKFAST

Coedllys Uchaf, Llangynin SA33 4JY
☎ 01994 231455 📠 01994 231441
e-mail: coedllys@btinternet.com
web: www.coedllyscountryhouse.co.uk
dir: *A40 St Clears rdbt, take 3rd exit, at lights turn left. After 100yds turn right, 3m to Llangynin, pass village sign. 30mph sign on left, turn immediately down track (private drive)*

Set in a peaceful valley, Coedllys is the home of Mr and Mrs Harber, who make visitors feel like honoured guests. Bedrooms are lavishly furnished, and the thoughtful and useful extras make a stay most memorable. There is a cosy, well-furnished lounge, and an extensive breakfast choice is served in the pleasant dining room. A further cottage-style annexe is now available, and is also suitable as a self-catering let. For the energetic there is a fitness suite, but guests can also relax in the sauna or small indoor pool. Coedllys was a Finalist in the AA Friendliest B&B of the Year Award 2012-13.

Rooms 3 en suite 1 annexe en suite (1 fmly) (1 GF)
Facilities FTV tea/coffee Cen ht Wi-fi 🕹 Sauna Gym
Parking 6 **Notes** No Children 12yrs Closed Xmas

PREMIER COLLECTION

Ty Mawr Mansion

★★★★★ ◉◉ 🍴 RESTAURANT WITH ROOMS

Cilcennin SA48 8DB
☎ 01570 470033
e-mail: info@tymawrmansion.co.uk
web: www.tymawrmansion.co.uk
dir: *On A482 (Lampeter to Aberaeron road), 4m from Aberaeron*

Surrounded by rolling countryside in its own naturally beautiful gardens, this fine country mansion house is a haven of peace and tranquillity. Careful renovation has restored it to its former glory and, combined with lush fabrics, top quality beds and sumptuous furnishings, the accommodation is spacious, superbly equipped and very comfortable. Award-winning chefs create mouth-watering dishes from local and seasonal produce. There is also a 27-seat cinema with all the authenticity of the real thing. Martin and Cath McAlpine offer the sort of welcome which makes every visit to Ty Mawr a memorable one.

Rooms 8 en suite 1 annexe en suite (1 fmly) (2 GF)
S £120-£180; D £140-£240* **Facilities** FTV DVD Lounge tea/coffee Dinner available Direct Dial Cen ht Wi-fi

---

Fishing 🎣 Cinema **Extras** Speciality toiletries, home-made biscuits, robes **Conf** Max 25 Thtr 25 Class 25 Board 16 **Parking** 20 **Notes** LB ⊗ No Children 12yrs Closed 28 Dec-10 Jan No coaches Civ Wed 30

PREMIER COLLECTION

Feathers Royal

★★★★★ ⌂ INN

Alban Square SA46 0AQ
☎ 01545 571750 📠 01545 571760
e-mail: enquiries@feathersroyal.co.uk
dir: *A482, Lampeter Road, Feathers Royal opposite recreation grounds*

This is a family-run inn, ideally located in the picturesque Georgian town of Aberaeron. It is a charming, Grade II listed property, built in 1815 as a traditional coaching house, it later underwent a transformation to coincide with the town's bicentenary celebrations. Accommodation is very comfortable with modern fittings and accessories provided, and the public areas are well appointed. There is a large suite available for private or business functions. A friendly welcome can be expected.

Rooms 13 en suite (2 fmly) S £65-£75; D £85-£115*
Facilities FTV tea/coffee Dinner available Direct Dial Cen ht Wi-fi 🎣 **Conf** Max 200 Thtr 200 Class 100 Board 50 **Parking** 20 **Notes** LB ⊗ Civ Wed 200

Arosfa Harbourside Guesthouse

★★★★ 🏠 GUEST HOUSE

SA46 0BU
☎ 01545 570120
e-mail: info@arosfaguesthouse.co.uk
web: www.arosfaguesthouse.co.uk
dir: *A487 in town centre into Market St towards sea, 150yds to Arosfa, harbourside car park*

A warm welcome is assured at this renovated Georgian house, located by the historic harbour. Bedrooms are filled with thoughtful extras and have modern bathrooms. Other areas include a cosy lounge, stairways enhanced by quality art and memorabilia, and a bright, attractive dining room, the setting for imaginative Welsh breakfasts.

Arosfa Harbourside Guesthouse

Rooms 3 en suite 1 annexe en suite (1 fmly) (1 GF)
S £40-£65; D £65-£120 **Facilities** FTV iPod docking station Lounge tea/coffee Dinner available Cen ht Licensed Wi-fi 🎣 **Notes** LB ⊗ 🖼

Gwennaul

★★★★ 🄰 BED AND BREAKFAST

Drefach SA46 0JR
☎ 01545 571756
e-mail: gwennaul@hotmail.co.uk
dir: *From Aberaeron on A487 towards Aberystwyth, after petrol station take 2nd lane on left, 1st bungalow on left*

Rooms 2 en suite (2 GF) D £70-£80 **Facilities** FTV tea/coffee Cen ht **Parking** 2 **Notes** ⊗ No Children 16yrs Closed Dec 🖼

ABERAERON continued

Aromatherapy Reflexology Centre

★★★ BED AND BREAKFAST

The Barn House, Pennant Rd SY23 5LZ
☎ 01974 202581
e-mail: aromareflex@googlemail.com
web: www.aromatherapy-breaks-wales.co.uk
dir: S of Aberystwyth to Llanon, leave village, turn left at 40mph sign. 2nd left to Barn House

Expect a warm welcome from this family-run bed and breakfast where Welsh is spoken. Set in its own grounds in a tranquil position with lovely views of Cardigan Bay. Bedrooms are comfortable and smartly presented, and there is a choice of traditional, vegetarian or vegan breakfasts. Aromatherapy and reflexology are available at the centre.

Rooms 3 rms (2 en suite) (1 pri facs) S £30-£40; D £60-£80 **Facilities** FTV tea/coffee Wi-fi ♨ Massage/Reflexology by appointment **Parking** 7 **Notes** LB ⊛

ABERYSTWYTH	Map 8 SN58

PREMIER COLLECTION

Awel-Deg

★★★★★ BED AND BREAKFAST

Capel Bangor SY23 3LR
☎ 01970 880681
e-mail: awel-deg@tiscali.co.uk
web: www.awel-deg.co.uk
dir: 5m E of Aberystwyth. On A44 in Capel Bangor

Located five miles from the historic university town, this attractive bungalow, set in pretty gardens, provides high standards of hospitality, comfort and facilities. Immaculately maintained throughout, spacious bedrooms are equipped with a wealth of thoughtful extras and smart, modern en suite shower rooms. Comprehensive breakfasts are served at one table in the elegant dining room and a choice of lounges is available.

Rooms 2 en suite (2 GF) D £59* **Facilities** FTV TVL tea/coffee Cen ht **Parking** 8 **Notes** LB ⊛ No Children 11yrs Closed 20-30 Dec ⊛

Bodalwyn Guest House

★★★★ GUEST HOUSE

Queen's Av SY23 2EG
☎ 01970 612578 📠 01970 639261
e-mail: enquiries@bodalwyn.co.uk
web: www.bodalwyn.co.uk
dir: 500yds N of town centre. Exit A487 (Northgate St) into North Rd to end

Located a short walk from the promenade, this imposing Edwardian house, built for a college professor, has been appointed to provide high standards of comfort and good facilities. Smart modern bathrooms complement the spacious bedrooms, which are equipped with a wealth of thoughtful extras; family rooms are available. Comprehensive Welsh breakfasts are served in the elegant conservatory-dining room.

Rooms 8 en suite (2 fmly) **Facilities** FTV tea/coffee Cen ht Wi-fi **Notes** ⊛ Closed 24 Dec-1 Jan ⊛

Glyn-Garth

★★★★ GUEST HOUSE

South Rd SY23 1JS
☎ 01970 615050
e-mail: glyngarth@aol.com
web: www.glyngarth.cjb.net
dir: In town centre. Off A487 into South Rd, off South Promenade

Privately owned and personally run by the same family for over 50 years, this immaculately maintained guest house provides a range of thoughtfully furnished bedrooms with smart modern bathrooms. Breakfast is served in the attractive dining room and a lounge is also available.

Rooms 10 rms (6 en suite) (2 fmly) (1 GF) S £33-£56; D £66-£85 **Facilities** STV FTV TVL tea/coffee Cen ht Wi-fi ⚑ 18 ♨ **Parking** 2 **Notes** ⊛ Closed 2wks Xmas & New Year ⊛

Llety Ceiro Country House

★★★★ GUEST HOUSE

Peggy Ln, Bow St, Llandre SY24 5AB
☎ 01970 821900 📠 01970 820966
e-mail: marinehotel1@btconnect.com
dir: 4m NE of Aberystwyth. Exit A487 onto B4353 for 300yds

Located north of Aberystwyth, this house is well maintained throughout. Bedrooms are equipped with a range of thoughtful extras in addition to smart modern bathrooms. Morning coffees, afternoon teas and dinner are available in an attractive dining room, with a conservatory extension, and bicycle hire is also available.

Rooms 11 en suite (2 fmly) (3 GF) (1 smoking) **Facilities** FTV TVL tea/coffee Dinner available Direct Dial Cen ht Licensed Wi-fi ⚑ 18 Fishing Riding Snooker Sauna Gym Pool table Free use of facilities at sister hotel **Conf** Max 60 Thtr 60 Class 40 Board 40 **Parking** 21 **Notes** LB Civ Wed 65

Yr Hafod

★★★★ GUEST HOUSE

1 South Marine Ter SY23 1JX
☎ 01970 617579
e-mail: johnyrhafod@aol.com
dir: On south promenade between harbour & castle

An immaculately maintained, end of terrace Victorian house in a commanding location overlooking the South Bay. The spacious bedrooms are comfortable and some have smart modern shower rooms. Breakfast is served in the attractive front-facing dining room.

Rooms 6 rms (3 en suite) (1 pri facs) S £32-£33; D £64-£84* **Facilities** STV FTV TVL tea/coffee Cen ht Wi-fi ♨ **Extras** Chocolates, mineral water **Parking** 1 **Notes** ⊛ Closed Xmas & New Year ⊛

Y Gelli

★★★ GUEST HOUSE

Dolau, Lovesgrove SY23 3HP
☎ 01970 617834
e-mail: pat.twigg@virgin.net
web: www.dolau-holidays.co.uk
dir: Off A44 2.75m E of town centre

Located in spacious grounds on the town's outskirts, this modern detached house contains a range of practical furnished bedrooms, with three further rooms available in an adjacent Victorian property. Comprehensive breakfasts are served in the attractive dining room with evening meals available on request. A comfortable lounge is also available for guest use.

Rooms 5 rms (2 en suite) 3 annexe rms 1 annexe en suite (3 fmly) (1 GF) **Facilities** TVL tea/coffee Dinner available Cen ht Snooker Pool table Table tennis Stabling can be provided **Conf** Thtr 30 Class 30 Board 20 **Parking** 20 **Notes** ⊛ ⊛

PONTERWYD   Map 9 SN78

Ffynnon Cadno Guest House

★★★★ 🅰 BED AND BREAKFAST

SY23 3AD
☎ 01970 890224
e-mail: ffynnoncadno@btinternet.com
dir: *Adjacent to A44 (Aberystwyth to Llangurig road), on Aberystwyth side of village*

Rooms 3 rms (2 en suite) (1 pri facs) (1 fmly) S £20-£35; D £40-£70* **Facilities** STV FTV DVD TVL tea/coffee Cen ht Wi-fi Pool table 🔒 **Parking** 6 **Notes** ⊗ No Children 3yrs

CONWY

ABERGELE   Map 14 SH97

PREMIER COLLECTION

The Kinmel Arms

★★★★★ ◎◎ RESTAURANT WITH ROOMS

The Village, St George LL22 9BP
☎ 01745 832207 📠 01745 822044
e-mail: info@thekinmelarms.co.uk
dir: *From A55 junct 24a to St George. E on A55, junct 24. 1st left to Rhuddlan, 1st right into St George. 2nd right*

This converted 17th-century coaching inn stands close to the church in the village of St George, in the beautiful Elwy Valley. The popular restaurant specialises in produce from Wales and north-west England, and friendly and helpful staff ensure you will have an enjoyable stay. The four attractive suites are luxuriously furnished and feature stunning bathrooms. Substantial continental breakfasts are served in the rooms.

Rooms 4 en suite (2 GF) S £115-£175; D £115-£175 **Facilities** STV DVD Lounge tea/coffee Dinner available Cen ht ⌁ 18 🔒 **Extras** Speciality toiletries, fruit/snacks - complimentary **Parking** 50 **Notes** LB No Children 16yrs Closed 25 Dec & 1 Jan RS Sun & Mon closed (ex BHs) No coaches

BETWS-Y-COED   Map 14 SH75

PREMIER COLLECTION

Penmachno Hall

★★★★★ 🍽 GUEST ACCOMMODATION

Penmachno LL24 0PU
☎ 01690 760410 📠 01690 760410
e-mail: stay@penmachnohall.co.uk
web: www.penmachnohall.co.uk
dir: *4m S of Betws-y-Coed. A5 onto B4406 to Penmachno, over bridge, right at Eagles pub signed Ty Mawr. 500yds at stone bridge*

Set in more than two acres of mature grounds including a mountain stream and woodland, this impressive Victorian rectory has been lovingly restored to provide high standards of comfort and facilities. Stylish decor and quality furnishings highlight the many original features throughout the ground-floor areas, and the bedrooms have a wealth of thoughtful extras. Alongside the main building is a superb two-bedroom, self-catering unit created from a sympathetic renovation of a former coach house. Pre-booked set menu, party-style evening meals are served on Saturday nights, while buffet-style meals are served Tuesday through Friday.

Rooms 3 en suite D £85-£100* **Facilities** STV Lounge tea/coffee Dinner available Cen ht Licensed Wi-fi 🔒 **Extras** Fruit, robes - complimentary **Parking** 5 **Notes** LB ⊗ Closed Xmas & New Year RS Sun-Mon no evening meals

PREMIER COLLECTION

Tan-y-Foel Country House

★★★★★ ◎◎◎ 🛏 GUEST HOUSE

Capel Garmon LL26 0RE
☎ 01690 710507 📠 01690 710681
e-mail: enquiries@tyfhotel.co.uk
web: www.tyfhotel.co.uk
dir: *1.5m E of Betws-y-Coed. Off A5 onto A470 N, 2m right for Capel Garmon, establishment signed 1.5m on left*

Situated high above the Conwy valley and set in six acres of woodland with attractive gardens and country walks leading from the grounds, this delightful 17th-century country house has superb views in all directions. The bedrooms are individually decorated and include four-poster king, canopied and king-size beds along with modern facilities. There is a stylish sitting room and restaurant where fires burn in winter, and fresh local produce features on the small but interesting menu.

Rooms 4 en suite 2 annexe en suite (1 GF) S £90-£145; D £125-£245* **Facilities** DVD Lounge tea/coffee Dinner available Direct Dial Cen ht Licensed Wi-fi 🔒 **Extras** Robes **Parking** 14 **Notes** LB ⊗ No Children 12yrs Closed Dec RS Jan limited availability

Afon View Guest House

★★★★ GUEST HOUSE

Holyhead Rd LL24 0AN
☎ 01690 710726 📠 01690 710726
e-mail: welcome@afon-view.co.uk
web: www.afon-view.co.uk
dir: *On A5, 150yds E of HSBC bank*

A warm welcome is assured at this elegant Victorian house, located between Waterloo Bridge and the village centre. Bedrooms are equipped with lots of thoughtful extras, and day rooms include an attractive dining room and comfortable guest lounge.

Rooms 7 en suite (1 fmly) **Facilities** FTV tea/coffee Cen ht Wi-fi **Parking** 7 **Notes** ⊗ No Children 4yrs Closed 23-26 Dec

BETWS-Y-COED *continued*

Bryn Bella Guest House

★★★★ GUEST HOUSE

Lon Muriau, Llanrwst Rd LL24 0HD
☎ 01690 710627
e-mail: welcome@bryn-bella.co.uk
web: www.bryn-bella.co.uk
dir: *A5 onto A470, 0.5m right onto driveway signed Bryn Bella*

Located on an elevated position on the town's outskirts with stunning views of the surrounding countryside, this elegant Victorian house provides a range of thoughtfully equipped bedrooms with smart modern bathrooms. A fine collection of memorabilia adorns the public areas, which include an attractive dining room and a comfortable lounge. A warm welcome is assured and guest services include a daily weather forecast.

Rooms 5 en suite (1 GF) Facilities FTV TVL tea/coffee Cen ht Wi-fi Parking 7 Notes LB ⊗

Cwmanog Isaf Farm *(SH799546)*

★★★★ FARMHOUSE

Fairy Glen LL24 0SL
☎ 01690 710225 & 07808 421634 Mrs H M Hughes
e-mail: h.hughes165@btinternet.com
dir: *1m S of Betws-y-Coed off A470 by Fairy Glen Hotel, 500yds on farm lane*

Peacefully located in 30 acres of undulating land, which also contains the renowned Fairy Glen, this 200-year-old house on a working livestock farm has been restored to provide comfortable, thoughtfully furnished bedrooms. Breakfasts use home-reared or organic produce. The property's elevated position provides stunning views of the surrounding countryside.

Rooms 3 rms (2 en suite) (1 pri facs) (1 GF) S £45-£60; D £62-£75* Facilities STV Lounge tea/coffee Cen ht ⌨ Parking 4 Notes ⊗ No Children 15yrs Closed 15 Nov-1 Mar ⊕ 30 acres sheep

Park Hill

★★★★ GUEST HOUSE

Llanrwst Rd LL24 0HD
☎ 01690 710540 📠 01690 710540
e-mail: welcome@park-hill.co.uk
web: www.park-hill.co.uk
dir: *0.5m N of Betws-y-Coed on A470 (Llanrwst road)*

A warm welcome is assured at this guest house, which benefits from a peaceful location overlooking the village and valley beyond. Well equipped bedrooms, including one with a four-poster, offer comfortable beds and thoughtful extras. There are a choice of lounges, a heated swimming pool, sauna and whirlpool bath for guests' use.

Rooms 8 en suite S £53-£90; D £66-£97.50* Facilities FTV DVD Lounge tea/coffee Cen ht Wi-fi ⌨ ⌁ Sauna ⌨ Parking 11 Notes LB ⊗ No Children 8yrs

Ty Gwyn Inn

★★★ ⊜ INN

LL24 0SG
☎ 01690 710383 📠 01690 710383
e-mail: mratcl1050@aol.com
dir: *Junct of A5 & A470, by Waterloo Bridge*

Situated on the edge of the village, close to the Waterloo Bridge, this historic coaching inn retains many original features. Quality furnishing styles and memorabilia enhance its intrinsic charm. Bedrooms, some with antique beds, are equipped with thoughtful extras. Imaginative food is provided in the cosy bars and the restaurant.

Rooms 13 rms (10 en suite) (3 fmly) (1 GF) Facilities TVL tea/coffee Dinner available Cen ht Wi-fi Parking 14 Notes Closed Mon-Wed in Jan

COLWYN BAY Map 14 SH87

Whitehall

★★★★ GUEST HOUSE

51 Cayley Promenade, Rhos-on-Sea LL28 4EP
☎ 01492 547296
e-mail: mossd.cymru@virgin.net
dir: *A55 onto B5115 (Brompton Av), right at rdbt into Whitehall Rd to seafront*

Overlooking the Rhos-on-Sea promenade, this popular, family-run establishment is convenient for the shops and local amenities. Attractively appointed bedrooms include family rooms and a room on the ground floor; all benefit from an excellent range of facilities such as video and CD players as well as air-conditioning. Facilities include a bar and a foyer lounge. Home-cooked dinners are available.

Rooms 12 en suite (4 fmly) (1 GF) S £28-£32; D £112-£126* Facilities FTV DVD TVL tea/coffee Dinner available Direct Dial Cen ht Licensed Wi-fi ⌨ Parking 5 Notes LB

CONWY Map 14 SH77

The Groes Inn

★★★★★ ⊕ INN

Tyn-y-Groes LL32 8TN
☎ 01492 650545 📠 01492 650855
e-mail: enquiries@thegroes.com
web: www.groesinn.com
dir: *A55, over Old Conwy Bridge, 1st left through Castle Walls on B5106 (Trefriw Road), 2m on right*

Located in the picturesque Conwy Valley, this historic inn dates from 1573 and was the first licensed house in Wales. The exterior and gardens have an abundance of shrubs and seasonal flowers that create an immediate welcome, which is matched by the friendly and professional staff. Public areas are decorated and furnished with flair to highlight the many period features. The spacious bedrooms, in renovated outbuildings, are equipped with a wealth of thoughtful extras; many have balconies overlooking the countryside.

Rooms 14 en suite (1 fmly) (6 GF) Facilities FTV tea/coffee Dinner available Direct Dial Cen ht Wi-fi ⌁ 18 Conf Max 20 Thtr 20 Class 20 Board 20 Parking 100 Notes LB Closed 25 Dec Civ Wed 100

The Old Rectory Country House

★★★★★ ⊜ GUEST ACCOMMODATION

Llanrwst Rd, Llansanffraid Glan Conwy LL28 5LF
☎ 01492 580611
e-mail: info@oldrectorycountryhouse.co.uk
web: www.oldrectorycountryhouse.co.uk
dir: *0.5m S from A470/A55 junct on left, by 30mph sign*

This very welcoming property has fine views over the Conwy estuary towards Snowdonia, and the elegant day rooms are luxurious and comfortable. The thoughtfully furnished bedrooms also benefit from the delightful views. The genuine hospitality creates a real home from home.

Rooms 3 en suite 2 annexe en suite (1 fmly) (2 GF) S £79.90-£99.90; D £99.90-£159.90* Facilities STV FTV tea/coffee Direct Dial Cen ht Wi-fi Extras Speciality toiletries Parking 10 Notes LB No Children 3yrs Closed 14 Dec-15 Jan

Save on B&Bs and Hotels. Book at **theAA.com/hotel**

CONWY 395 WALES

DWYGYFYLCHI | Map 14 SH77

The Gladstone

★★★★ INN

Ygborwen Rd LL34 6PS
☎ 01492 623231
e-mail: thegladstonepub@hotmail.co.uk
dir: *A55 junct 16 turn left, then left again towards Dwygyfylchi, 0.25m on right*

The Gladstone offers modern seaside accommodation; the comfortable, stylish bedrooms are individually designed, equipped with plenty of thoughtful extras and luxurious bathrooms. The bar and front bedrooms have views of Puffin Island and Anglesey. There is seating outside for alfresco dining and for enjoying the sunsets. Off-road parking is available.

Rooms 6 en suite S £60-£90; D £75-£120* **Facilities** FTV TVL tea/coffee Dinner available Cen ht Wi-fi 🔒 **Parking** 25 **Notes** LB ⊗ No coaches Civ Wed 40

LLANDUDNO | Map 14 SH78

PREMIER COLLECTION

Bryn Derwen

★★★★★ GUEST HOUSE

34 Abbey Rd LL30 2EE
☎ 01492 876804 📠 01492 876804
e-mail: brynderwen34@btinternet.com
dir: *A470 into Llandudno, left at The Parade promenade to cenotaph, left, over rdbt, 4th right into York Rd, Bryn Derwen at top*

A warm welcome is assured at this impressive Victorian house, which retains original tiled floors and some fine stained-glass windows. Quality decor and furnishings highlight the historic charm of the property, which is apparent in the sumptuous lounges and attractive dining room, the setting for imaginative breakfasts. Bedrooms are equipped with a wealth of thoughtful extras, and the establishment also has a fully-equipped beauty salon.

Rooms 9 en suite (1 fmly) S £51-£57; D £79-£101 **Facilities** FTV DVD iPod docking station Lounge tea/coffee Cen ht Licensed Wi-fi ⌀ 18 🔒 Beauty Salon **Extras** Speciality toiletries, water, chocolates - complimentary **Parking** 9 **Notes** LB ⊗ No Children 12yrs Closed Dec-Jan

Abbey Lodge

★★★★ GUEST HOUSE

14 Abbey Rd LL30 2EA
☎ 01492 878042
e-mail: enquiries@abbeylodgeuk.com
web: www.abbeylodgeuk.com
dir: *A546 to N end of town, onto Clement Av, right onto Abbey Rd*

This impressive Victorian villa is on a leafy avenue within easy walking distance of the promenade. It has been lovingly restored, and stylish decor and furniture add to its charm. Bedrooms come with a wealth of thoughtful extras, and there is a sumptuous lounge. Breakfasts are served around the elegant dining table.

Rooms 4 en suite S £45; D £80 **Facilities** FTV Lounge tea/coffee Cen ht Wi-fi 🔒 **Parking** 4 **Notes** ⊗ Closed Dec-1 Mar 🚭

Brigstock House

★★★★ GUEST HOUSE

1 St David's Place LL30 2UG
☎ 01492 876416 📠 01492 879292
e-mail: simon.hanson4@virgin.net
dir: *A470 into Llandudno, left into The Parade promenade, left into Lloyd St, left into St David's Rd & left into St David's Place*

This impressive Edwardian property is in a quiet residential cul-de-sac within easy walking distance of the seafront and central shopping area. The attractive bedrooms are well equipped, and a comfortable lounge is available. Substantial breakfasts and dinners, by arrangement, are served in the elegant dining room.

Rooms 8 en suite **Facilities** FTV TVL tea/coffee Dinner available Cen ht Licensed Wi-fi **Parking** 6 **Notes** ⊗ No Children 12yrs Closed Dec-Jan

The Cliffbury

★★★★ GUEST ACCOMMODATION

34 St David's Rd LL30 2UH
☎ 01492 877224
e-mail: info@thecliffbury.co.uk

Located on a leafy avenue within easy walking distance of the town centre, this elegant Edwardian house provides high standards of comfort. Bedrooms, furnished in minimalist style, provide a range of practical and thoughtful extras and smart modern bath/shower rooms are an additional benefit. Breakfast is taken in an attractive dining room and a warm welcome is assured.

Rooms 6 en suite D £62-£82* **Facilities** FTV DVD tea/coffee Cen ht Wi-fi **Parking** 6 **Notes** LB ⊗ No Children 11yrs

St Hilary Guest House

★★★★ GUEST ACCOMMODATION

16 Craig-y-Don Pde, The Promenade LL30 1BG
☎ 01492 875551 📠 01492 877538
e-mail: info@sthilaryguesthouse.co.uk
web: www.sthilaryguesthouse.co.uk
dir: *0.5m E of town centre. On B5115 seafront road near Venue Cymru*

A warm welcome is assured at this constantly improving guest accommodation, located at the Craig-y-Don end of The Promenade, and many of the thoughtfully furnished bedrooms have superb sea views. Day rooms include a spacious attractive front-facing dining room. A cosy guest lounge is also available.

Rooms 9 en suite (1 GF) S £45; D £65-£82* **Facilities** FTV iPod docking station Lounge tea/coffee Cen ht Wi-fi **Notes** LB ⊗ No Children 8yrs Closed end Nov-early Feb

LLANDUDNO *continued*

Stratford House

★★★★ GUEST ACCOMMODATION

8 Craig-y-Don Pde, The Promenade LL30 1BG
☎ **01492 877962**
e-mail: stratfordhtl@aol.com
dir: *A470 at rdbt take 4th exit, on Queens Rd to promenade, on right*

This immaculately presented spacious house is located on the sea front with spectacular views. Bedrooms are attractively decorated, some with four-poster beds and all have an excellent range of accessories, such as flat screen TVs. The traditionally decorated dining room is also beautifully presented. The friendly owners are very welcoming.

Rooms 9 en suite (1 fmly) (1 GF) S £45-£60; D £55-£75*
Facilities FTV tea/coffee Cen ht Wi-fi **Extras** Chocolates - complimentary **Notes** LB ⊗ No Children 8yrs Closed Jan RS Dec & Feb

Britannia Guest House

★★★★ GUEST HOUSE

15 Craig-y-Don Pde, The Promenade LL30 1BG
☎ **01492 877185** 📠 **01492 233300**
e-mail: info@thebritanniaguesthouse.co.uk
web: www.thebritanniaguesthouse.co.uk
dir: *A55 onto A470 to Llandudno, at rdbt take 4th exit signed Craig-y-Don, right at promenade*

This family-run Victorian guest house offers a warm welcome and friendly service. The bedrooms are very comfortable and well equipped, and many have fantastic views of Llandudno's bay. Ground floor rooms are available. Hearty breakfasts are served in the sea view dining room.

Rooms 10 en suite (2 fmly) (2 GF) S £45-£80; D £60-£84* **Facilities** FTV tea/coffee Cen ht Wi-fi **Notes** LB ⊗ No Children 10yrs Closed 28 Nov-13 Feb

Bryn-y-Mor

★★★★ GUEST ACCOMMODATION

25 North Pde LL30 2LP
☎ **01492 876790** 📠 **01492 874990**
e-mail: info@bryn-y-mor.net
web: www.bryn-y-mor.net
dir: *A55 take Llandudno junct, head for Promenade turn left, by pier on left on road beneath the Great Orme*

Located at the foot of the Great Orme and close to the town centre and its main attractions, the family-run Bryn-y-Mor offers comfortable well-equipped rooms, many with sea views. There is an attractive lounge looking over the bay to the Little Orme. There is also a small bar and an outside patio which also overlooks the bay.

Rooms 12 en suite **Facilities** STV FTV Lounge tea/coffee Cen ht Licensed Wi-fi 🔒 **Notes** ⊗ No Children 16yrs Closed Dec-15 Feb

Can-Y-Bae

★★★★ GUEST ACCOMMODATION

10 Mostyn Crescent, Central Promenade LL30 1AR
☎ **01492 874188** 📠 **01492 868376**
e-mail: canybae@btconnect.com
web: www.can-y-baehotel.com
dir: *A55 junct 10, A470, signed Llandudno/Promenade. Can-Y-Bae on seafront promenade between Venue Cymru Theatre & band stand*

A warm welcome is assured at this tastefully renovated house, centrally located on the Promenade. Bedrooms are equipped with both practical and homely extras and upper floors are serviced by a modern lift. Day rooms include a panoramic lounge, cosy bar and attractive basement dining room.

Rooms 16 en suite (2 GF) S £40-£50; D £80-£90*
Facilities FTV Lounge tea/coffee Dinner available Direct Dial Cen ht Lift Licensed Wi-fi **Notes** LB No Children 12yrs

Epperstone

★★★★ GUEST ACCOMMODATION

15 Abbey Rd LL30 2EE
☎ **01492 878746** 📠 **01492 871223**
e-mail: epperstone@btinternet.com
dir: *A550, A470 to Mostyn St. Left at rdbt, 4th right into York Rd. Epperstone at junct of York Rd & Abbey Rd*

This delightful property is located in wonderful gardens in a residential part of town, within easy walking distance of the seafront and shopping area. Bedrooms are attractively decorated and thoughtfully equipped. Two lounges and a Victorian-style conservatory are available. A daily-changing menu is offered in the bright dining room.

Rooms 8 en suite (5 fmly) (1 GF) **Facilities** FTV Lounge tea/coffee Dinner available Direct Dial Cen ht Licensed Wi-fi **Parking** 8 **Notes** LB

Glenavon Guest House

★★★★ GUEST HOUSE

27 St Mary's Rd LL30 2UB
☎ **01492 877687** 📠 **0870 706 2247**
e-mail: postmaster@glenavon.plus.com
dir: *From A470 signed Llandudno, left at lights into Trinity Av. 3rd right into St Mary's Rd. Glenavon on right*

Supporters of Liverpool Football Club are especially welcome here and they can admire the extensive range of memorabilia throughout the comfortable day rooms. Bedrooms are equipped with thoughtful extras and Welsh breakfasts provide a good start to the day.

Rooms 7 en suite (1 fmly) **Facilities** FTV TVL tea/coffee Cen ht Wi-fi **Parking** 4 **Notes** ⊗

The Lilly Restaurant with Rooms

★★★ ◉ RESTAURANT WITH ROOMS

West Pde, West Shore LL30 2BD
☎ **01492 876513**
e-mail: thelilly@live.co.uk
dir: *Telephone for detailed directions*

Located on the seafront on the West Shore with views over the Great Orme, this establishment has bedrooms that offer high standards of comfort and good facilities. Children are very welcome here, and a relaxed atmosphere can be found in Madhatters Brasserie, which takes its name from Lewis Caroll's *Alice in Wonderland* which was written on the West Shore. A fine dining restaurant is also available.

Rooms 12 en suite (2 fmly) (2 GF) **Facilities** FTV tea/coffee Dinner available Direct Dial Cen ht Wi-fi **Conf** Max 35 Thtr 25 Board 20 **Notes** ⊗ No coaches

Minion

★★★ GUEST ACCOMMODATION

21-23 Carmen Sylva Rd, Craig-y-Don LL30 1EQ
☎ **01492 877740**
dir: *A55 junct 19, A470 to Llandudno. At 4th rdbt take Craig-y-Don exit. 2nd right after park*

Situated in a quiet residential area a few minutes' walk from the eastern promenade, the Minion has been owned by the same family for over 60 years and continues to extend a warm welcome. The bedrooms are smart and comfortable, and two are on the ground floor. There is a cosy bar and a colourful garden.

Rooms 10 en suite (1 fmly) (2 GF) **Facilities** FTV TVL tea/coffee Dinner available Licensed **Parking** 8 **Notes** No Children 2yrs Closed Nov-Mar ⊛

LLANFAIRFECHAN　　　Map 14 SH67

Min-Y-Don Guest House

★★★★ Ⓐ GUEST ACCOMMODATION

Promenade LL33 0BY
☎ **01248 680742**
e-mail: minydon1@aol.com
Rooms 4 en suite S £60; D £80*

LLANRWST　　　Map 14 SH86

PREMIER COLLECTION

Plas Maenan Country House

★★★★★ ◎◎ GUEST ACCOMMODATION

Maenan LL26 0YR
☎ **01492 660232** ▤ **01492 660363**
e-mail: james.burt@btconnect.com
dir: *On A470 between Glan Conwy & Llanrwst*

Plas Maenan is a beautiful Edwardian mansion house with stunning views over the Conwy Valley, where friendly owners and their staff provide attentive service. Bedrooms are tastefully furnished and well equipped, and there is an elegant sitting room with open fire, as well as a mountain-view conservatory. An unusual feature is a Steinway piano, located in the Music Room which leads through to the cosy bar. Dinner is a highlight, and features skilfully prepared dishes made with high quality ingredients. Plas Maenan was last year's AA Guest Accommodation of the Year for Wales (2011-2012).

Rooms 10 en suite (2 fmly) **Facilities** FTV DVD Lounge TVL tea/coffee Dinner available Direct Dial Cen ht Licensed Wi-fi **Conf** Max 80 Thtr 80 Class 60 Board 40 **Parking** 60 **Notes** LB No Children 6yrs Closed 1-10 Jan RS Sun eve & Mon closed Civ Wed 85

RHOS-ON-SEA　　　Map 14 SH88

See also Colwyn Bay

PREMIER COLLECTION

Plas Rhos

★★★★★ ▥ GUEST ACCOMMODATION

Cayley Promenade LL28 4EP
☎ **01492 543698**
e-mail: info@plasrhos.co.uk
web: www.plasrhos.co.uk
dir: *A55 junct 20 onto B5115 for Rhos-on-Sea, right at rdbt onto Whitehall Rd to promenade*

Stunning sea views are a feature of this renovated Victorian house, which provides high standards of comfort and hospitality. Cosy bedrooms are filled with a wealth of thoughtful extras, and public areas include a choice of sumptuous lounges featuring smart decor, quality soft furnishings and memorabilia. Breakfast is served in the attractive dining room, overlooking the pretty patio garden.

Rooms 6 en suite S £50-£70; D £70-£100*
Facilities FTV TVL tea/coffee Cen ht Licensed Wi-fi ⊛
Parking 4 **Notes** LB ⊗ No Children 12yrs Closed Nov-Feb

DENBIGHSHIRE

CORWEN　　　Map 15 SJ04

Bron-y-Graig

★★★★ ⊜ GUEST HOUSE

LL21 0DR
☎ **01490 413007**
e-mail: info@north-wales-hotel.co.uk
web: www.north-wales-hotel.co.uk
dir: *On A5 on E edge of Corwen*

A short walk from the town centre, this impressive Victorian house retains many original features including fireplaces, stained glass and a tiled floor in the entrance hall. Bedrooms, complemented by luxurious bathrooms, are thoughtfully furnished, and two are in a renovated coach house. Ground-floor areas include a traditionally furnished dining room and a comfortable lounge. A warm welcome, attentive service and imaginative food is assured.

Rooms 7 en suite 2 annexe en suite (34 fmly) S £39-£49; D £59-£68 **Facilities** STV FTV DVD Lounge tea/coffee Dinner available Direct Dial Cen ht Licensed Wi-fi ⊛ **Conf** Max 20 Class 20 Board 15 **Parking** 15 **Notes** LB

Plas Derwen Country House

★★★★ GUEST ACCOMMODATION

London Rd LL21 0DR
☎ **01490 412742 & 07773 965874**
e-mail: bandb@plasderwen.supanet.com
dir: *On A5 0.5m E of Corwen*

Set in four acres of mature gardens and fields in an elevated position with superb views of the River Dee, this elegant late 18th-century house has been restored to provide high levels of comfort and facilities. Quality furnishings and stylish decor highlight the many original features. A warm welcome is assured.

Rooms 3 rms (2 en suite) (1 pri facs) (2 fmly)
Facilities FTV TVL tea/coffee Cen ht Wi-fi **Parking** 6
Notes ⊗ Closed Dec-Jan

DENBIGH — Map 15 SJ06

Cayo Guest House

★★★ GUEST HOUSE

74 Vale St LL16 3BW
☎ 01745 812686
e-mail: stay@cayo.co.uk
dir: Off A525 into town, at lights turn up hill, supermarket on right. Guest house up hill on left

A warm welcome is assured at this Victorian house, which is situated on the main street, just a short walk from the town centre. Bedrooms are comfortably and thoughtfully furnished with lots of homely extras. Good home cooking is provided in a Victorian-themed dining room, and a cosy basement lounge is also available.

Rooms 4 en suite S £30-£32; D £60-£64* **Facilities** FTV TVL tea/coffee Cen ht Wi-fi 🔒 **Notes** Closed Xmas-New Year

---

LLANDRILLO — Map 15 SJ03

PREMIER COLLECTION

Tyddyn Llan Restaurant

★★★★★ ◉◉ 🍽 RESTAURANT WITH ROOMS

LL21 0ST
☎ 01490 440264 🖷 01490 440414
e-mail: info@tyddynllan.co.uk
web: www.tyddynllan.co.uk
dir: Off A4 at Corwen onto B4401, through villages of Cynwyd & Llandrillo. On right leaving village

Tyddyn Llan is a very well appointed property set in the Edeyrnion Valley at the gateway to Snowdonia. Whilst not all the individually styled bedrooms are spacious, they do offer many home comforts. The public areas are beautifully furnished and have open fires in the colder months. Susan runs the front of the house with friendly informed staff; service is formal and in keeping with the style of the establishment. Husband and chef Bryan sources ingredients as locally as possible and his cooking is sympathetic to the produce. An extensive breakfast menu is available.

Rooms 13 en suite (1 GF) S £120-£190; D £130-£200 **Facilities** STV FTV DVD iPod docking station Lounge tea/coffee Dinner available Direct Dial Cen ht Wi-fi 🔒 **Extras** Speciality toiletries **Conf** Max 30 Thtr 30 Class 10 Board 20 **Parking** 20 **Notes** LB Closed 2wks Jan No coaches Civ Wed

---

LLANDYRNOG — Map 15 SJ16

PREMIER COLLECTION

Pentre Mawr Country House

⬚ GUEST ACCOMMODATION

LL16 4LA
☎ 01824 790732 🖷 01824 790441
e-mail: info@pentremawrcountryhouse.co.uk
dir: From Denbigh follow Bodfari/Llandyrnog signs. Left at rdbt to Bodfari, 50yds, left into country lane, Pentre Mawr on left

Expect a warm welcome from Graham and Bre at this superb family country house set in nearly 200 acres of meadows, park and woodland. The property has been in Graham's family for over 400 years. Bedrooms are individually decorated, very spacious and each is thoughtfully equipped. Breakfast is served in either the morning room or, on warmer mornings, on the Georgian terrace. Dinner is served in the formal dining room. There is a salt water swimming pool in the walled garden.

Rooms 3 en suite 8 annexe en suite (7 GF) **Facilities** FTV TV5B tea/coffee Dinner available Cen ht Licensed Wi-fi ⬚ ⬚ ⬚ Fishing **Conf** Max 16 **Parking** 14 **Notes** No Children 13yrs

---

LLANGOLLEN — Map 15 SJ24

See also Corwen

Tyn Celyn Farmhouse

★★★★ BED AND BREAKFAST

Tyndwr LL20 8AR
☎ 01978 861117
e-mail: j.m.bather-tyncelyn@talk21.com
dir: A5 to Llangollen, pass golf club on right, next left signed Tyndwr outdoor centre, 0.5m sharp left onto Tyndwr Rd, past outdoor centre on left. Tyn Celyn 0.5m on left

This 300-year-old timber-framed farmhouse has stunning views over the Vale of Llangollen. Bedrooms, one of which is located on the ground floor, provide a range of thoughtful extras in addition to fine period furniture. Breakfast is served at a magnificent carved table in a spacious sitting-dining room.

Rooms 3 en suite (1 fmly) (1 GF) D £60-£65* **Facilities** DVD TVL tea/coffee Cen ht Wi-fi **Parking** 5 **Notes** LB ⊗ ⬚

RHYL — Map 14 SJ08

Barratt's at Ty'n Rhyl

★★★★ ◉◉ 🍽 RESTAURANT WITH ROOMS

Ty'n Rhyl, 167 Vale Rd LL18 2PH
☎ 01745 344138 & 0773 095 4994
e-mail: ebarratt5@aol.com
dir: A55 onto A525 to Rhyl, pass Sainsbury's & B&Q, pass Roger Jones on left, 50yds on right

This delightful 16th-century house lies in a secluded location surrounded by attractive gardens. The quality of the food reflects the skill of the owner-chef. Public areas are smartly furnished and include a panelled lounge, cosy library and an attractive conservatory. Bedrooms are comfortable and equipped with lots of thoughtful extras.

Rooms 3 en suite S £70; D £95* **Facilities** FTV DVD Lounge TVL tea/coffee Dinner available Cen ht Wi-fi ⬚ 🔒 **Extras** Sherry, sparking water, sweets, snacks **Parking** 20 **Notes** LB ⊗

RUTHIN   Map 15 SJ15

PREMIER COLLECTION

Firgrove Country House B&B

★★★★★ 🏆 ➾ BED AND BREAKFAST

Firgrove, Llanfwrog LL15 2LL
☎ 01824 702677 📠 01824 702677
e-mail: meadway@firgrovecountryhouse.co.uk
web: www.firgrovecountryhouse.co.uk
dir: 0.5m SW of Ruthin. A494 onto B5105, 0.25m past Llanfwrog church on right

Standing in immaculate mature gardens in a peaceful rural location, this well-proportioned house retains many original features, highlighted by the quality decor and furnishings throughout the interior. Bedrooms, complemented by smart modern bathrooms, are equipped with a wealth of thoughtful extras and memorable breakfasts, using home-made or local produce, are served in an elegant dining room. Imaginative dinners are also available by prior arrangement and a warm welcome is assured.

Rooms 2 en suite 1 annexe en suite (1 GF) S £60–£80; D £80–£110* **Facilities** FTV Lounge tea/coffee Dinner available Cen ht Wi-fi 🔒 **Extras** Fridge, mineral water, fresh milk - complimentary **Parking** 4 **Notes** ⊗ No Children Closed Dec-Jan

Tyddyn Chambers (SJ102543)

★★★★ FARMHOUSE

Pwllglas LL15 2LS
☎ 01824 750683 & 07745 589946 Mrs E Williams
e-mail: ella.williams@btconnect.com
web: www.tyddynchambers.co.uk
dir: 3m S of Ruthin. W from A494 after Fox & Hounds pub in Pwllglas, signed

This charming little farmhouse has been extended to provide carefully appointed, modern accommodation,

which includes a family room. The pleasant, traditionally furnished breakfast room has separate tables and a lounge is also available. The house stands in an elevated position with panoramic views.

Rooms 3 en suite (1 fmly) S £38–£42; D £60–£70* **Facilities** TVL tea/coffee Cen ht **Parking** 3 **Notes** ⊗ No Children 4yrs Closed Xmas & New Year ⊛ 180 acres beef/sheep

ST ASAPH   Map 15 SJ07

PREMIER COLLECTION

Tan-Yr-Onnen Guest House

━━━ GUEST HOUSE ━━━

Waen LL17 0DU
☎ 01745 583821 📠 01745 583821
e-mail: tanyronnenvisit@aol.com
web: www.northwalesbreaks.co.uk
dir: W on A55 junct 28, turn left in 300yds

A warm welcome is assured at Tan-Yr-Onnen, which is quietly located in six acres of gardens, yet conveniently close to the A55. The very well-equipped accommodation includes four ground-floor rooms with French windows opening onto the terrace which has tables and chairs. Upstairs there are two luxury suites with lounge areas. Hearty breakfasts are served in the dining room overlooking the gardens, and a conservatory lounge and Wi-fi access are also available.

Rooms 6 en suite (1 fmly) (4 GF) **Facilities** FTV tea/coffee Dinner available Cen ht Licensed Wi-fi **Parking** 8

Bach-Y-Graig (SJ075713)

★★★★ FARMHOUSE

Tremeirchion LL17 0UH
☎ 01745 730627 📠 01745 730627 Mrs A Roberts
e-mail: anwen@bachygraig.co.uk
dir: 3m SE of St Asaph. Exit A525 at Trefnant onto A541 to x-rds with white railings, left, down hill, over bridge, right

Dating from the 16th century, this listed building was the first brick-built house in Wales and retains many original features including a wealth of exposed beams and inglenook fireplaces. Bedrooms are furnished with fine period pieces and quality soft fabrics. Ground-floor areas include a quiet lounge and a combined sitting and dining room, featuring a superb Jacobean oak table.

Rooms 3 rms (2 en suite) (1 pri facs) (1 fmly) S £50–£55; D £80–£90* **Facilities** FTV DVD TVL tea/coffee Cen ht Wi-fi Fishing Woodland trail **Parking** 3 **Notes** LB ⊗ Closed Xmas & New Year 200 acres dairy/mixed

FLINTSHIRE

AXTON   Map 15 SJ18

Morgans Bed & Breakfast

★★★★ BED AND BREAKFAST

Pen y graig CH8 9DH
☎ 01745 570981
e-mail: info@morgansbedandbreakfast.co.uk
dir: A55 junct 31 follow signs for Prestatyn. Left at rdbt onto A5151 for 3m, turn sharp right at Total garage. After 0.5m left onto Axton Ln, sharp left at T-junct

A very warm welcome awaits guests at this hidden gem, where peace and quiet are guaranteed. Bedrooms are country cottage in style, equipped with every imaginable item you may need, including games and DVDs for wet weather. Hearty breakfasts feature home-grown produce and are served around one large table.

Rooms 3 en suite (2 fmly) S £40–£50; D £60–£70* **Facilities** FTV DVD TVL tea/coffee Dinner available Cen ht Wi-fi 🔒 **Parking** 3 **Notes** ⊗

NANNERCH Map 15 SJ16

The Old Mill Guest Accommodation

★★★★ GUEST ACCOMMODATION

Melin-Y-Wern, Denbigh Rd CH7 5RH
☎ 01352 741542
e-mail: mail@old-mill.co.uk
web: www.old-mill.co.uk
dir: A541, NW from Mold, 7m into Melin-Y-Wern, Old Mill on right

This converted stone stable block was once part of a Victorian watermill complex. Immediately adjacent is The Cherry Pie Inn where evening meals can be taken. The non-smoking guest accommodation offers modern, well-equipped bedrooms with en suite bathrooms.

Rooms 6 en suite (1 fmly) (2 GF) S £48-£62; D £64-£86*
Facilities FTV Lounge tea/coffee Direct Dial Cen ht Wi-fi ⓑ Parking 12 Notes LB ⊗ Closed Feb

GWYNEDD

BALA Map 14 SH93

Erw Feurig Guest House

★★★★ GUEST HOUSE

Cefnddwysarn LL23 7LL
☎ 01678 530262 & 07786 168399 ▤ 01678 530262
e-mail: erwfeurig@yahoo.com
web: www.erwfeurig.com
dir: 3m NE of Bala off A494. 2nd left after x-rds at Cefnddwysarn, turn at B&B sign

A warm welcome is assured at this delightful and peaceful farm cottage situated on a hillside with panoramic views of the Berwyn Mountains. The comfortable, individually styled bedrooms have a range of additional extras. A cosy lounge and a cheerful ground-floor breakfast room are available.

Rooms 4 rms (2 en suite) (2 pri facs) (1 GF) S £40-£45; D £60-£65* Facilities FTV Lounge tea/coffee Cen ht Wi-fi Fishing ⓑ Parking 6 Notes LB ⊗ No Children Closed Jan-Mar

BARMOUTH Map 14 SH61

See also Dyffryn Ardudwy

Richmond House

★★★★ GUEST HOUSE

High St LL42 1DW
☎ 01341 281366 & 07800 583815
e-mail: info@barmouthbedandbreakfast.co.uk
web: www.barmouthbedandbreakfast.co.uk
dir: In town centre. Car park at rear on Jubilee Rd

A warm welcome awaits at this lovely Victorian house, which has been modernised to provide good quality and thoughtfully equipped accommodation. Two of the bedrooms have sea views, as do the lounge and dining

room, where there are separate tables. There is also a pleasant garden.

Rooms 3 en suite (1 fmly) S £60; D £75-£85*
Facilities FTV DVD Lounge tea/coffee Cen ht Wi-fi ⓑ Parking 5 Notes LB ⊗

Llwyndu Farmhouse

★★★★ 🍴 GUEST ACCOMMODATION

Llanaber LL42 1RR
☎ 01341 280144
e-mail: intouch@llwyndu-farmhouse.co.uk
web: www.llwyndu-farmhouse.co.uk
dir: A496 towards Harlech where street lights end, on outskirts of Barmouth, take next right

This converted 16th-century farmhouse offers warm hospitality and traditional accommodation. Many original features are retained, including inglenook fireplaces, exposed beams and timbers. There is a cosy lounge and meals can be enjoyed in the licensed restaurant. Bedrooms are comfortable and well equipped, and some have four-poster beds. Four bedrooms are in the old dairy building.

Rooms 3 en suite 4 annexe en suite (2 fmly)
Facilities FTV TVL tea/coffee Dinner available Cen ht Licensed Wi-fi Conf Max 10 Parking 10 Notes Closed 25-26 Dec RS Sun no dinner

Morwendon House

★★★★ 🏠 🍴 GUEST ACCOMMODATION

Llanaber LL42 1RR
☎ 01341 280566 ▤ 07092 197785
e-mail: info@morwendon-house.co.uk
dir: A496 at Llanaber N of Barmouth. On seaward side 250yds past Llanaber Church

With its impressive location overlooking Cardigan Bay, Morwendon House is an ideal base for exploring the surrounding area and its many attractions. The bedrooms are well-equipped, and many rooms have sea views. Dinner is available by arrangement, and meals are taken in the attractive dining room overlooking the bay. There is also a comfortable lounge, again, with views over the bay.

Rooms 5 en suite 1 annexe en suite (1 GF)
S £52.50-£105; D £75-£105* Facilities FTV DVD Lounge tea/coffee Dinner available Cen ht Licensed Wi-fi ⚓ 18 ⓑ Parking 6 Notes LB ⊗ No Children 12yrs Closed 24-27 Dec

BEDDGELERT Map 14 SH54

Tanronnen Inn

★★★★ INN

LL55 4YB
☎ 01766 890347 ▤ 01766 890606
e-mail: tanbedd@12freeukisp.co.uk
dir: In village centre opposite river bridge

This delightful inn offers comfortable, well equipped and attractively appointed accommodation, including a family room. There is also a selection of pleasant and relaxing public areas. The wide range of bar food is popular with tourists, and more formal meals are served in the restaurant.

Rooms 7 en suite (3 fmly) S £50-£60; D £80-£100*
Facilities FTV tea/coffee Dinner available Direct Dial Cen ht Parking 15 Notes LB ⊗

BETHESDA Map 14 SH66

Snowdonia Mountain Lodge

★★ GUEST ACCOMMODATION

Nant Ffrancon LL57 3LX
☎ 01248 600500
e-mail: info@snowdoniamountainlodge.com

Located on the A5 south of Bethesda, and surrounded by mountains in a stunningly beautiful area, this establishment is very popular with walkers and climbers. A World Peace Flame monument is a feature on the attractive frontage. Bedrooms are located in chalet-style buildings. A comprehensive continental breakfast is served in an adjacent café. Specialist yoga and meditation classes are offered.

Rooms 19 en suite (19 GF) Facilities tea/coffee Wi-fi Riding Conf Max 30 Thtr 30 Class 30 Board 30 Parking 30 Notes ⊗ Closed 22 Dec-4 Jan

BETWS GARMON Map 14 SH55

Betws Inn

★★★★ 🍴 BED AND BREAKFAST

LL54 7YY
☎ 01286 650324
e-mail: stay@betws-inn.co.uk
dir: On A4085 (Caernarfon to Beddgelert), opposite Bryn Gloch Caravan Park

Set in the western foothills of the Snowdonia, this 17th-century former inn has been restored to create an establishment of immense charm. A warm welcome and caring service are assured. Bedrooms have a wealth of homely extras, and imaginative dinners feature local produce. Breakfast includes home-made bread and preserves.

Rooms 3 en suite Facilities FTV TVL tea/coffee Dinner available Cen ht Wi-fi Parking 3 Notes ⊗

Save on B&Bs and Hotels. Book at **theAA.com/hotel**

GWYNEDD 401 | WALES

CAERNARFON | Map 14 SH46

PREMIER COLLECTION

Plas Dinas Country House

★★★★★ 🛏 GUEST ACCOMMODATION

Bontnewydd LL54 7YF
☎ **01286 830214**
e-mail: info@plasdinas.co.uk
dir: *3m S of Caernarfon, off A487, 0.5m down private drive*

Situated in 15 acres of beautiful grounds in Snowdonia, this delightful Grade II listed building dates back to the mid-17th century, but had many Victorian additions. It was once the home of the Armstrong-Jones family, so there are many family portraits, memorabilia and original pieces of furniture on view. The bedrooms are individually decorated and include four-poster beds along with modern facilities. There is a stylish drawing room where a fire burns in the winter, and fresh local produce features on the dinner menu.

Rooms 10 en suite (1 GF) S £99-£225; D £129-£275* **Facilities** FTV iPod docking station Lounge tea/coffee Dinner available Direct Dial Cen ht Licensed Wi-fi ⚓ 18 ♨ **Conf** Max 20 Thtr 20 Class 20 Board 20 **Parking** 10 **Notes** LB No Children 13yrs Closed Xmas & New Year Civ Wed 60

Rhiwafallen Restaurant with Rooms

★★★★ ◉◉ 🛏 RESTAURANT WITH ROOMS

Rhiwafallen, LLandwrog LL54 5SW
☎ **01286 830172**
e-mail: ktandrobjohn@aol.com
dir: *A487 from Caernarfon. Right onto A499. Establishment signed*

Located south of Caernarfon on the Llyn Peninsula link, this former farmhouse is appointed to provide high levels of comfort and facilities. Quality bedrooms are furnished in minimalist style with a wealth of thoughtful extras. The original modern art in public areas adds vibrancy to the interior. Warm hospitality and imaginative cooking ensure a memorable stay at this owner-managed establishment.

Rooms 3 en suite D £100-£150* **Facilities** FTV DVD Lounge tea/coffee Dinner available Cen ht ⚓ ♨ **Parking** 10 **Notes** ⊗ No Children 12yrs Closed 25-26 Dec No coaches

---

Black Boy Inn

★★★★ INN

LL55 1RW
☎ **01286 673604** 📠 01286 674955
e-mail: office@black-boy-inn.com
dir: *A55 junct 9, A487, follow signs for Caernarfon. Inn within town walls between castle & Victoria Dock*

Located within Caernarfon's historic town walls, this fine 16th-century inn has low ceilings, narrow staircases and thick wooden beams from old ships. It is one of the oldest

inns in north Wales, and has a wealth of charm and character. The bedrooms provide modern accommodation, and hearty meals are available in both the restaurant and bar area. On-site parking is available.

Rooms 15 en suite **Facilities** FTV tea/coffee Dinner available Direct Dial Cen ht Wi-fi ⚓ 18 **Conf** Max 40 Thtr 40 Class 20 Board 30 **Parking** 20 **Notes** LB ⊗

The Stables

★★★★ GUEST ACCOMMODATION

Llanwnda LL54 5SD
☎ **01286 830711** 📠 01286 830413
dir: *3m S of Caernarfon on A499 towards Pwllheli*

This privately owned and personally run establishment is set in 15 acres of its own land, south of Caernarfon. The modern and comfortable en suite accommodation will suit all needs and budgets and is located in two motel-style buildings and two self-catering cottages. An optional, cooked buffet-style breakfast is taken in a spacious dining room decorated with a wealth of unusual memorabilia. The Stables also has a registered helipad, internet connection in the reception area and flat screen TV/DVD combo with Freeview in every room. Pets are welcome and there is also a fun and educational Pet's Corner for children.

Rooms 20 en suite (4 fmly) (20 GF) **Facilities** tea/coffee Direct Dial Cen ht Licensed **Conf** Max 50 Thtr 50 Class 30 Board 30 **Parking** 40

CRICCIETH | Map 14 SH43

Bron Rhiw

★★★★ GUEST ACCOMMODATION

Caernarfon Rd LL52 0AP
☎ **01766 522257**
e-mail: clairecriccieth@yahoo.co.uk
web: www.bronrhiwhotel.co.uk
dir: *From High St onto B4411*

A warm welcome and high standards of comfort and facilities are assured at this constantly improving Victorian property, just a short walk from the seafront. Bedrooms are equipped with lots of thoughtful extras and ground-floor areas include a sumptuous lounge, a cosy bar, and an elegant dining room, the setting for imaginative breakfasts.

Rooms 9 en suite (2 fmly) S £47-£60; D £74-£78* **Facilities** FTV Lounge tea/coffee Cen ht Licensed Wi-fi **Parking** 3 **Notes** LB ⊗ No Children 10yrs Closed Nov-Feb

---

Min Y Gaer

★★★★ GUEST HOUSE

Porthmadog Rd LL52 0HP
☎ **01766 522151**
e-mail: info@minygaer.co.uk
dir: *On A497 200yds E of junct with B4411*

The friendly, family-run Min Y Gaer has superb views from many of the rooms. Min Y Gaer is Welsh for "near

the fort", and so some of these fine views are of Criccieth Castle. Smart, modern bedrooms are furnished in pine, and the welcoming proprietors also provide a bar and a traditionally furnished lounge.

Rooms 10 en suite (1 fmly) S £40-£44; D £70-£80 **Facilities** FTV DVD Lounge tea/coffee Cen ht Licensed Wi-fi ♨ **Parking** 12 **Notes** Closed Nov-14 Mar

---

DOLGELLAU | Map 14 SH71

PREMIER COLLECTION

Tyddynmawr Farmhouse *(SH704159)*

★★★★★ FARMHOUSE

Cader Rd, Islawrdref LL40 1TL
☎ **01341 422331** Mrs Evans
e-mail: olwynevans@btconnect.com
web: www.wales-guesthouse.co.uk
dir: *From town centre left at top of square, left at garage into Cader Rd for 3m. 1st farm on left after Gwernan Lake*

A warm welcome is assured at this 18th-century farmhouse which lies at the foot of Cader Idris amidst breathtaking scenery. The bedrooms are spacious and have Welsh oak furniture; the upper room has a balcony and the ground-floor room has a patio area. The bathrooms are large and luxurious. The superb breakfasts offer an excellent choice of home-made items including bread, preserves, muesli or smoked fish. Self-catering cottages are also available. Tyddynmawr Farmhouse was a Finalist in the AA Friendliest B&B of the Year Award 2012-13.

Rooms 2 en suite (1 GF) S fr £55; D fr £78* **Facilities** Lounge TVL tea/coffee Cen ht Wi-fi Fishing ♨ **Parking** 8 **Notes** ⊗ No Children Closed Jan 🐄 800 acres beef/sheep

---

DOLGELLAU *continued*

Dolgun Uchaf Guesthouse

★★★★ GUEST HOUSE

Dolgun Uchaf LL40 2AB
☎ 01341 422269
e-mail: dolgunuchaf@aol.com
web: www.guesthousessnowdonia.com
dir: *Exit A470 at Little Chef just S of Dolgella. Dolgun Uchaf 1st property on right*

Located in a peaceful area with stunning views of the surrounding countryside, this 500-year-old, late medieval hall house retains many original features including exposed beams and open fireplaces. The bedrooms are equipped with thoughtful extras, and a lounge for guests is available.

Rooms 3 en suite 1 annexe en suite (1 GF) **Facilities** TVL tea/coffee Dinner available Cen ht Wi-fi **Parking** 6 **Notes** No Children 5yrs

Ivy House

★★★ GUEST HOUSE

Finsbury Square LL40 1RF
☎ 01341 422535 🗎 01341 422689
e-mail: marg.bamford@btconnect.com
web: www.ivyhouse-dolgellau.co.uk
dir: *In town centre. Straight across top of main square, house on left after bend*

Friendly hospitality is offered at this house, situated in the centre of Dolgellau at the foot of Cader Idris. Bedrooms are brightly decorated and thoughtfully equipped. Ground floor rooms include a comfortable lounge and a spacious dining room.

Rooms 6 rms (4 en suite) (1 fmly) S £45-£55; D £65-£75* **Facilities** FTV DVD TVL tea/coffee Cen ht Wi-fi 🔒 **Notes** ⊗

Royal Ship

★★★ INN

Queens Square LL40 1AR
☎ 01341 422209 🗎 01341 424693
e-mail: royalship.hotel@btconnect.com
dir: *In town centre*

The Royal Ship is very much at the centre of local activities and dates from 1813 when it was a coaching inn. There are three bars and several lounges, all comfortably furnished and attractively appointed. A wide range of food is offered, and the well-equipped bedrooms include family rooms. The property has a secure car park.

Rooms 24 en suite (4 fmly) **Facilities** FTV Wi-fi **Parking** 12

DYFFRYN ARDUDWY Map 14 SH52

Cadwgan Inn

★★★★ INN

LL44 2HA
☎ 01341 247240
e-mail: cadwgan.hotel@virgin.net
dir: *In Dyffryn Ardudwy into Station Rd, over railway crossing*

This very pleasant, privately-owned inn stands in grounds close to Dyffryn Ardudwy station, between Barmouth and Harlech, and the beach is just a short walk away. The good quality, well-equipped modern accommodation includes family rooms and a room with a four-poster bed. Public areas include an attractive dining room, popular bar and a beer garden.

Rooms 6 en suite (3 fmly) **Facilities** TVL tea/coffee Dinner available Cen ht Sauna Gym Pool table **Notes** ⊗ No coaches Civ Wed 60

HARLECH Map 14 SH53

Gwrach Ynys Country Guest House

★★★★ GUEST HOUSE

Talsarnau LL47 6TS
☎ 01766 780742
e-mail: deborah@gwrachynys.co.uk
web: www.gwrachynys.co.uk
dir: *2m N of Harlech on A496*

This delightful Edwardian house sits amid idyllic gardens with dramatic views of the surrounding mountains. The bedrooms are thoughtfully equipped and have modern facilities. Two comfortably furnished lounges have a home-from-home feel, and the hospitality is welcoming. Hearty breakfast can be enjoyed at separate tables in the dining room.

Rooms 7 rms (6 en suite) (1 pri facs) (3 fmly) S £35-£40; D £70-£85 **Facilities** FTV DVD iPod docking station Lounge TVL tea/coffee Cen ht Wi-fi 🔒 **Parking** 10 **Notes** LB ⊗ Closed mid Nov-mid Jan

LLANBEDR Map 14 SH52

Victoria Inn

★★★★ INN

LL45 2LD
☎ 01341 241213 🗎 01341 241644
e-mail: junevicinn@aol.com
web: www.victoriainnllanbedr.co.uk
dir: *In village centre*

This former coaching inn lies beside the River Artro in a very pretty village. Many original features remain, including the Settle bar with its flagstone floor, black polished fireplace and unusual circular wooden settle. The menu is extensive and is supplemented by blackboard specials. Bedrooms are spacious and thoughtfully furnished.

Rooms 5 en suite **Facilities** FTV tea/coffee Dinner available Cen ht 🔒 **Conf** Max 30 **Parking** 75 **Notes** LB

LLANDDEINIOLEN   Map 14 SH56

Ty'n-Rhos Country House & Restaurant
★★★★★ A GUEST ACCOMMODATION

Seion LL55 3AE
☎ 01248 670489 🖷 01248 671772
e-mail: enquiries@tynrhos.co.uk
web: www.tynrhos.co.uk
dir: *A55 junct 11, A5 for 50yds, right at mini-rdbt onto A4244. After 4m 2nd exit at rdbt, property signed in 0.5m*

Rooms 12 en suite 4 annexe en suite (3 fmly) (8 GF) **Facilities** FTV tea/coffee Dinner available Cen ht Licensed Wi-fi 🏊 🎣 18 Fishing **Conf** Max 60 Thtr 60 Class 40 Board 40 **Parking** 50 **Notes** Civ Wed 60

PORTHMADOG   Map 14 SH53

Tudor Lodge
★★★★ GUEST ACCOMMODATION

Tan-Yr-Onnen, Penamser Rd LL49 9NY
☎ 01766 515530
e-mail: info@tudor-lodge.co.uk
dir: *From main Porthmadog rdbt into Criccieth Rd, house 40mtrs on left*

This large property is conveniently situated within a short walk of the town centre. It has been considerably renovated to provide good quality modern accommodation, including family rooms. Separate tables are provided in the breakfast room, where a substantial self-service continental breakfast buffet is provided. There is also a pleasant garden for guests to use.

Rooms 13 en suite (3 fmly) (6 GF) S £48; D £74-£99 **Facilities** STV tea/coffee Cen ht Wi-fi 🎣 **Parking** 25 **Notes** LB 🐾

PWLLHELI   Map 14 SH33

Hendre Barns
★★★★ A BED AND BREAKFAST

Hendre Penprys, Pentre Uchaf LL53 8EZ
☎ 01758 750505
e-mail: enquiries@hendre-barns.co.uk
web: www.hendre-barns.co.uk
dir: *From A499 at Yffor onto B4354 to Nefyn. After 3.3m cross narrow bridge, then turn right onto single track road. On left after 0.3m*

Rooms 3 annexe en suite (1 fmly) (3 GF) S £55-£70; D £60-£75* **Facilities** FTV DVD tea/coffee Cen ht Wi-fi 🔒 **Extras** Bottled water, flowers - complimentary **Parking** 6 **Notes** LB 🐾

TYWYN   Map 14 SH50

Eisteddfa (SH651055)
★★★★ FARMHOUSE

Eisteddfa, Abergynolwyn LL36 9UP
☎ 01654 782385 🖷 01654 782385 Mrs G Pugh
e-mail: hugh.pugh01@btinternet.com
dir: *5m NE of Tywyn on B4405 nr Dolgoch Falls*

Eisteddfa is a modern stone bungalow situated less than a mile from Abergynolwyn, in a spot which is ideal for walking, and for visiting the local historic railway. The bedrooms are well equipped, and stunning views can be enjoyed from the attractive dining room.

Rooms 3 rms (2 en suite) (3 GF) S £35; D £60* **Facilities** STV FTV TVL tea/coffee Cen ht **Parking** 6 **Notes** LB Closed Dec-Feb 🐾 1200 acres mixed

MERTHYR TYDFIL

PONTSTICILL   Map 9 SO01

Penrhadw Farm
★★★★ GUEST HOUSE

CF48 2TU
☎ 01685 723481 & 722461 🖷 01685 722461
e-mail: treghotel@aol.com
web: www.penrhadwfarm.co.uk
dir: *5m N of Merthyr Tydfil. (Please see map on website)*

Expect a warm welcome at this 19th-century former farmhouse in the glorious Brecon Beacons National Park. The house is appointed to provide quality modern accommodation. The well-equipped, spacious bedrooms include two large suites in cottages adjacent to the main building. There is also a comfortable lounge. Separate tables are provided in the cosy breakfast room.

Rooms 5 en suite 5 annexe en suite (5 fmly) (1 GF) S £49-£55; D £75-£100* **Facilities** FTV TVL tea/coffee Dinner available Cen ht Wi-fi 🎣 18 ♨ **Conf** Max 10 Thtr 10 Class 10 **Parking** 22 **Notes** LB 🐾

MONMOUTHSHIRE

ABERGAVENNY   Map 9 SO21

Hardwick Farm (SO306115)
★★★★ FARMHOUSE

NP7 9BT
☎ 01873 853513 & 07773 775179
🖷 01873 854238 Mrs C Jones
e-mail: carol@hardwickfarm.co.uk
dir: *1m from Abergavenny, off A4042, farm sign on right*

Quietly located in the Usk Valley with wonderful views, this large family-run farmhouse provides warm hospitality. The spacious bedrooms are comfortably furnished, well equipped, and include one suitable for families. Farmhouse breakfasts are served at the communal table in the traditionally furnished dining room.

Rooms 3 rms (2 en suite) (1 pri facs) (1 fmly) S £45; D £60-£70 **Facilities** FTV tea/coffee Cen ht Wi-fi **Parking** 3 **Notes** LB Closed Xmas 230 acres dairy/mixed

Black Lion Guest House
★★★★ A GUEST HOUSE

43 Hereford Rd NP7 5PY
☎ 01873 851920 🖷 01873 857885
e-mail: blacklionaber@aol.com
Rooms 5 rms (2 en suite) (3 pri facs) (1 fmly) **Facilities** STV FTV tea/coffee Dinner available Cen ht **Parking** 3 **Notes** 🐾

LLANDOGO   Map 4 SO50

The Sloop Inn
★★★★ INN

NP25 4TW
☎ 01594 530291
e-mail: thesloopinn@btconnect.com
dir: *On A466 in village centre*

This welcoming inn is centrally located in the village of Llandogo, close to the River Wye in an outstandingly beautiful valley. It offers a selection of traditional food, as well as friendly hospitality. The dining room has delightful views over the valley, and the spacious bedrooms and bathrooms are equipped for both business and leisure guests.

Rooms 4 en suite (1 fmly) **Facilities** tea/coffee Dinner available Cen ht Pool table **Parking** 50 **Notes** RS Mon-Fri closed between 3-6

LLANTRISANT — Map 9 ST39

Greyhound Inn

★★★★ ⚠ INN

NP15 1LE
☎ 01291 673447 & 672505 🖹 01291 673255
e-mail: enquiry@greyhound-inn.com
web: www.greyhound-inn.com
dir: *M4 junct 24, A449, 1st exit for Usk, 2.5m from town square, follow Llantrisant signs*

Rooms 10 en suite (2 fmly) (5 GF) **Facilities** tea/coffee Direct Dial Cen ht Wi-fi **Parking** 75 **Notes** Closed 25-26 Dec RS Sun eve no food No coaches

MONMOUTH — Map 10 SO51

The Inn at Penallt

★★★★ ⚙ INN

Penallt NP25 4SE
☎ 01600 772765
e-mail: enquiries@theinnatpenallt.co.uk
web: www.theinnatpenallt.co.uk

This 17th-century farmhouse and inn underwent a renovation some two years ago when new owners Andrew and Jackie Murphy took over. Food is very much to the fore here, and fresh, local produce is sourced by head chef Peter Hulsmann. There are two bedrooms in the Barn, separate to the inn, and two bedrooms within the main building; all are smartly presented and comfortable. The bar, with beams and a wood-burner, offers a good selection of beers and spirits and a sound wine list. Guests can eat in the bar or the separate restaurant area. There is a conservatory lounge to relax in as well as a garden. The Inn at Penallt is the AA Pub of the Year for Wales 2012-13.

Rooms 2 en suite 2 annexe en suite (2 GF) S £57.50; D £75* **Facilities** STV FTV DVD iPod docking station Lounge tea/coffee Dinner available Cen ht Wi-fi **Extras** Bottled water **Parking** 26 **Notes** LB Closed 1-24 Jan No coaches

Penylan Farm

★★★★ ⚠ BED AND BREAKFAST

The Hendre NP25 5NL
☎ 01600 716435 🖹 01600 719391
e-mail: penylanfarm@gmail.com
web: www.penylanfarm.co.uk
dir: *5m NW of Monmouth. B4233 through Rockfield towards Hendre. 0.5m before Hendre turn right towards Newcastle. After 1.5m turn left, farm 0.5 m on right*

Rooms 3 en suite 3 annexe en suite (1 fmly) (2 GF) S £42-£48; D £65-£70* **Facilities** tea/coffee Dinner available Cen ht Wi-fi 🐾 🔒 **Parking** 10 **Notes** LB ⊗ Closed Xmas & New Year

Church Farm Guest House

★★★ GUEST HOUSE

Mitchel Troy NP25 4HZ
☎ 01600 712176
e-mail: info@churchfarmguesthouse.eclipse.co.uk
dir: *From A40 S, left onto B4293 for Trelleck before tunnel, 150yds turn left and follow signs to Mitchel Troy. Guest House on main road on left, 200yds beyond campsite*

Located in the village of Mitchel Troy, this 16th-century former farmhouse retains many original features including exposed beams and open fireplaces. There is a range of bedrooms and a spacious lounge, and breakfast is served in the traditionally furnished dining room. Dinner is available by prior arrangement.

Rooms 9 rms (7 en suite) (2 pri facs) (3 fmly) S £34-£36; D £68-£72* **Facilities** FTV TVL TV2B tea/coffee Dinner available Cen ht Wi-fi ch fac **Parking** 12 **Notes** LB Closed Xmas ⊛

ROCKFIELD — Map 9 SO41

The Stonemill & Steppes Farm Cottages

★★★★★ ⚙⚙ RESTAURANT WITH ROOMS

NP25 5SW
☎ 01600 775424
e-mail: bookings@thestonemill.co.uk
dir: *A48 to Monmouth, take B4233 to Rockfield. 2.6m*

Located in a small hamlet just west of Monmouth, close to the Forest of Dean and the Wye Valley, this operation offers six very well-appointed cottages. The comfortable rooms (for self-catering or on a B&B basis) are architect designed and has been lovingly restored to retain many original features. In a separate, converted 16th-century barn is Stonemill Restaurant with oak beams, vaulted ceilings and an old cider press. Breakfast is served in the cottages on request. This establishment's location proves handy for golfers with a choice of many courses in the area.

Rooms 6 en suite (6 fmly) (6 GF) S £70-£90; D £140-£180* **Facilities** FTV DVD TVL tea/coffee Dinner available Cen ht Wi-fi ♨ 18 🔒 Free golf **Conf** Max 60 Thtr 60 Class 56 Board 40 **Parking** 53 **Notes** LB ⊗ RS Sun eve & Mon closed No coaches Civ Wed 120

SKENFRITH — Map 9 SO42

PREMIER COLLECTION

The Bell at Skenfrith

★★★★★ ⚙⚙ 🍽 RESTAURANT WITH ROOMS

NP7 8UH
☎ 01600 750235 🖹 01600 750525
e-mail: enquiries@skenfrith.co.uk
web: www.skenfrith.co.uk
dir: *On B4521 in Skenfrith, opposite castle*

The Bell is a beautifully restored, 17th-century former coaching inn which still retains much original charm and character. It is peacefully situated on the banks of the Monnow, a tributary of the River Wye, and is ideally placed for exploring the numerous delights of the area. Natural materials have been used to create a relaxing atmosphere, while the bedrooms, which include full suites and rooms with four-poster beds, are stylish, luxurious and equipped with DVD players. The garden produces many of the fresh ingredients used in the kitchen where award-winning quality food is produced for relaxed dining in the welcoming restaurant.

Rooms 11 en suite (2 fmly) S £75-£110; D £110-£220 **Facilities** STV FTV tea/coffee Dinner available Direct Dial Cen ht Wi-fi 🔒 **Extras** Speciality toiletries, home-made shortbread **Conf** Max 20 Thtr 20 Board 16 **Parking** 36 **Notes** No Children 8yrs Closed last wk Jan-1st wk Feb RS Nov-Mar closed Tue No coaches

Parva Farmhouse Riverside Guest House & Restaurant

★★★★ 🍴 GUEST HOUSE

Monmouth Rd NP16 6SQ
☎ 01291 689411
e-mail: parvahoteltintern@fsmail.net
dir: On A466 at N edge of Tintern. Next to St Michael's Church on the riverside

This relaxed and friendly, family-run guest house is situated on a sweep of the River Wye with far-reaching views of the valley. Originally a farmhouse dating from the 17th century, many features have been retained, providing character and comfort in an informal atmosphere. The cosy Inglenook Restaurant is the place where quality ingredients are offered at breakfast and dinner. The individually designed bedrooms are tastefully decorated and enjoy pleasant views; one has a four-poster.

Rooms 8 en suite (2 fmly) S £50-£60; D £68-£90*
Facilities FTV Lounge tea/coffee Dinner available Cen ht Licensed 🔒 **Parking** 8 **Notes** No Children 12yrs

Newbridge on Usk

★★★★ ◉◉ 🍷 RESTAURANT WITH ROOMS

Tredunnock NP15 1LY
☎ 01633 451000 & 410262
e-mail: newbridgeonusk@celtic-manor.com
web: www.celtic-manor.com
dir: M4 junct 24, signed Newport, onto B4236. At Ship Inn turn right, over mini-rdbt onto Llangybi/Usk road. Turn right opposite Cwrt Bleddyn Hotel, signed Tredunnock, through village & down hill

This cosy, gastro-pub is tucked away in a beautiful village setting with the River Usk nearby. The well-equipped bedrooms, in a separate building, provide comfort and a good range of extras. Guests can eat at rustic tables around the bar or in the upstairs dining room where award-winning, seasonal food is served; there is also a small private dining room. Breakfast is one of the highlights of a stay with quality local ingredients offered in abundance.

Newbridge on Usk

Rooms 6 en suite (2 fmly) (4 GF) **Facilities** FTV DVD tea/coffee Dinner available Direct Dial Cen ht Wi-fi Facilities available at Celtic Manor Resort **Extras** Speciality toiletries - complimentary **Conf** Max 14 Thtr 14 Class 14 Board 14 **Parking** 60 **Notes** LB Civ Wed 80

PREMIER COLLECTION

The Crown at Whitebrook

☆☆☆☆☆ ◉◉◉ 🍷 RESTAURANT WITH ROOMS

NP25 4TX
☎ 01600 860254 🖹 01600 860607
e-mail: info@crownatwhitebrook.co.uk
dir: 4m from Monmouth on B4293, left at sign to Whitebrook, 2m on unclassified road, Crown on right

In a secluded spot in the wooded valley of the River Wye, this former drover's cottage dates back to the 17th century. Individually decorated bedrooms boast a contemporary feel with smart modern facilities. The restaurant and lounge combine many original features with a bright fresh look. The memorable cuisine features locally sourced ingredients, skilfully prepared; the dishes are marked by their clear, fresh flavours and razor-sharp timing.

Rooms 8 en suite S £100-£130; D £145-£180*
Facilities FTV DVD Lounge tea/coffee Dinner available Direct Dial Cen ht Wi-fi 🔒 Fishing, Shooting **Conf** Max 12 Board 12 **Parking** 20 **Notes** LB ⊗ No Children 12yrs Closed 22 Dec-4 Jan No coaches

NEATH PORT TALBOT

Cwmbach Cottages Guest House

★★★★ GUEST HOUSE

Cwmbach Rd, Cadoxton SA10 8AH
☎ 01639 639825
e-mail: l.morgan5@btinternet.com
web: www.cwmbachcottages.co.uk
dir: 1.5m NE of Neath. A465 onto A474 & A4230 towards Aberdulais, left opposite Cadoxton church, guest house signed

A terrace of former miners' cottages has been restored to provide a range of thoughtfully furnished bedrooms, with one on the ground floor for easier access. Spacious public areas include a comfortable lounge and a pleasant breakfast room with separate tables. A superb decked patio overlooks a wooded hillside rich with wildlife.

Rooms 5 en suite (2 fmly) (1 GF) S £40-£55; D £60-£75*
Facilities FTV DVD iPod docking station TVL tea/coffee Cen ht Wi-fi ⚓ 18 🔒 **Parking** 9 **Notes** LB ⊗

NEWPORT

Labuan Guest House

★★★★ GUEST HOUSE

464 Chepstow Rd NP19 8JF
☎ 01633 664533 🖹 01633 664533
e-mail: patricia.bees@ntlworld.com
dir: M4 junct 24, 1.5m on B4237

Expect a warm welcome from owners Pat and John at this delightful guest house which is set on the main road into Newport. The accommodation is comfortable and includes a ground-floor twin room; all bedrooms are of a good size and bathrooms feature a wide range of extras. The hearty breakfasts, with a good choice on the menu, are taken in the welcoming dining room at separate tables. Off-street parking is available.

Rooms 5 rms (3 en suite) (2 pri facs) (1 GF)
Facilities FTV TVL tea/coffee Dinner available Cen ht Wi-fi **Parking** 6 **Notes** LB ⊛

Kepe Lodge Guest House

★★★ GUEST HOUSE

46A Caerau Rd NP20 4HH
☎ 01633 262351 🖹 01633 262351
e-mail: kepelodge@hotmail.com
dir: 500yds W of town centre. M4 junct 27, town centre signs, 2nd lights left, premises on right

This attractive guest house in a quiet residential area is set back from the road in pleasant gardens. Guests can expect attentive service and comfortable homely bedrooms. Breakfast is served at individual tables in the well-appointed dining room. A comfortable lounge is also available.

Rooms 8 rms (3 en suite) **Facilities** FTV tea/coffee Cen ht **Parking** 12 **Notes** ⊗ No Children 10yrs ⊛

| REDWICK | Map 9 ST48 |

Brickhouse Country Guest House

★★★ GUEST HOUSE

North Row NP26 3DX
☎ 01633 880230 📠 01633 882441
e-mail: brickhouse@compuserve.com
dir: M4 junct 23A, follow steelworks road for 1.5m. Left after sign for Redwick, Brickhouse 1.5m on left

This impressive country house is in a peaceful location with attractive, well-tended gardens. The friendly hosts are most attentive and provide a relaxing atmosphere. Bedrooms are spacious and traditionally furnished, while the public areas include a choice of lounges. Dinners featuring home-grown produce are sometimes available by prior arrangement.

Rooms 7 rms (5 en suite) (2 pri facs) (1 fmly) S £40-£50; D £65* Facilities FTV Lounge TVL tea/coffee Dinner available Cen ht Licensed Wi-fi Parking 7 Notes ⊗

PEMBROKESHIRE

| FISHGUARD | Map 8 SM93 |

PREMIER COLLECTION

Erw-Lon Farm (SN028325)

★★★★★ 🏠 FARMHOUSE

Pontfaen SA65 9TS
☎ 01348 881297 Mrs L McAllister
e-mail: lilwenmcallister@btinternet.com
web: www.erwlonfarm.co.uk
dir: 5.5m SE of Fishguard on B4313

Located in the Pembrokeshire Coast National Park, with stunning views of the Gwaun Valley, this attractive farmhouse has been converted to provide modern well-equipped bedrooms with a wealth of homely extras. The McAllisters give the warmest of welcomes, and their memorable dinners feature the finest local produce.

Erw-Lon Farm

Rooms 3 en suite (3 smoking) Facilities FTV TVL tea/coffee Dinner available Cen ht Wi-fi Parking 5 Notes ⊗ No Children 10yrs Closed Dec-Mar 🐾 128 acres beef/sheep

| HAVERFORDWEST | Map 8 SM91 |

See also Narberth

College Guest House

★★★★ GUEST HOUSE

93 Hill St, St Thomas Green SA61 1QL
☎ 01437 763710
e-mail: colinlarby@aol.com
web: www.collegeguesthouse.com
dir: In town centre, along High St, pass church, keep in left lane. 1st exit by Stonemason Arms pub, follow signs for St Thomas Green/Leisure Centre/Police Station. 300mtrs on left by No Entry sign

Located in a mainly residential area within easy walking distance of the attractions, this impressive Georgian house has been upgraded to offer good levels of comfort and facilities. There is a range of practically equipped bedrooms, along with public areas that include a spacious lounge (with internet access) and an attractive pine-furnished dining room, the setting for comprehensive breakfasts.

Rooms 8 en suite (4 fmly) S £52-£60; D £75-£80
Facilities FTV DVD TVL tea/coffee Cen ht Wi-fi
Extras Water

| MANORBIER | Map 8 SS09 |

Castlemead

★★★★ RESTAURANT WITH ROOMS

SA70 7TA
☎ 01834 871358 📠 01834 871358
e-mail: castlemeadhotel@aol.com
web: www.castlemeadhotel.com
dir: A4139 towards Pembroke, B4585 into village, follow signs to beach & castle, establishment on left

Benefiting from a superb location with spectacular views of the bay, the Norman church and Manorbier Castle, this family-run business is friendly and welcoming. Bedrooms, which include some in a converted former coach house at ground floor level, are generally quite spacious and have modern facilities. Public areas include a sea-view residents' lounge and a restaurant accessed by stairs, which is available to non-residents, along with a cosy bar. There are extensive gardens to the rear of the property.

Rooms 5 en suite 3 annexe en suite (2 fmly) (3 GF) Facilities FTV Lounge tea/coffee Dinner available Direct Dial Cen ht Wi-fi Parking 20 Notes Closed Jan-Feb RS Nov maybe B&B only No coaches

| NARBERTH | Map 8 SN11 |

PREMIER COLLECTION

The Grove

★★★★★ ⊛⊛ 🏠 RESTAURANT WITH ROOMS

Molleston SA67 8BX
☎ 01834 860915
e-mail: info@thegrove-narberth.co.uk
web: www.thegrove-narberth.co.uk
dir: A48 to Carmarthen, A40 to Haverfordwest. At A478 rdbt 1st exit to Narberth, through town towards Tenby. At bottom of hill right, 1m, The Grove on right

The Grove is an elegant 18th-century country house set on a hillside in 24 acres of rolling countryside. The owners have lovingly restored this building with care, combining period features with excellent modern decor. There are bedrooms in the main house and additional rooms in separate buildings; all are appointed with quality and comfort. Some bedrooms are on the ground floor, and most have fantastic views out over the Preseli Hills. There are two sumptuous lounge areas, one with an open fire and a small bar, and two separate dining rooms that offer award-winning cuisine. Self-catering cottages are available.

Rooms 14 en suite 6 annexe en suite (3 fmly) (3 GF) S fr £135* Facilities FTV DVD Lounge tea/coffee Dinner available Direct Dial Cen ht Wi-fi Extras Speciality toiletries, Welsh cakes Conf Max 40 Thtr 40 Class 40 Board 40 Parking 45 Notes LB ⊗ Civ Wed 100

Highland Grange Farm (SN077154)

★★★ FARMHOUSE

Robeston Wathen SA67 8EP
☎ 01834 860952 & 07855 359919
📠 01834 860952 Mrs N Jones
e-mail: highlandgrange@hotmail.co.uk
web: www.highlandgrange.co.uk
dir: 2m NW of Narberth at Robeston Wathen, 400mtrs from A40 rdbt

Awake to birdsong in comfortable accommodation at this peaceful farmhouse property, with spacious bedrooms that are all on the ground floor. The property is set in the small hilltop village of Robeston Wathen, 400 metres from the A40, between Whitland and Haverfordwest, and enjoys wonderful panoramic views. The dining room has separate tables where a good hearty breakfast is provided. There is also a spacious and comfortable lounge.

Save on B&Bs and Hotels. Book at **theAA.com/hotel**

PEMBROKESHIRE 407 WALES

Rooms 3 rms (2 en suite) (1 pri facs) (1 fmly) (3 GF)
Facilities FTV TVL tea/coffee Dinner available Cen ht Wi-fi
ch fac ⅃ **Parking** 6 **Notes** ⊜ 150 acres mixed/sheep

Pinewood

★★★ BED AND BREAKFAST

Cliff Rd, Wiseman's Bridge SA67 8NU
☎ **01834 811082**
e-mail: info@pinewoodholidaypark.co.uk
dir: *A40 to St Clears onto A477 for Tenby. 2m past
Llanteg, left towards Wisemans Bridge. Left again after
1m. 0.75m turn left into Cliff Rd*

Close to the Pinewood Static Caravan Park, Pinewood
offers four en suite bedrooms; three doubles and a twin.
All have complimentary spring water and flat screen TV
with DVD players. (A small library of DVDs is available for
rent.) A wide choice is offered at breakfast, which is
taken in the large, bright conservatory. Guests can also
relax here and enjoy stunning views across Saundersfoot
Bay towards Monkstone Point and beyond to Caldy Island.
Pinewood is ideally situated for the Pembrokeshire
Coastal Footpath and the Celtic Way National Cycle Route
4. The beach is just 350yds away.

Rooms 4 en suite (3 GF) S £37.50-£42.50; D £55-£60*
Facilities FTV tea/coffee Cen ht **Parking** 12 **Notes** LB ⊗
No Children 8yrs Closed 5 Nov-2 Mar

NEVERN   Map 8 SN04

Trewern Arms

★★★★ INN

SA42 0NB
☎ **01239 820395** 🖷 **01239 820173**
e-mail: info@trewern-arms.co.uk
dir: *Off A48. Midway between Cardigan & Fishguard*

Set in a peaceful and picturesque village, this charming
16th-century inn is well positioned to offer a relaxing
stay. There are many original features to be seen in the
two character bars and attractive restaurant, and the
spacious bedrooms are appointed to a high standard and
include some family rooms.

Trewern Arms

Rooms 10 en suite (4 fmly) D £30-£59 (room only)
Facilities FTV Lounge tea/coffee Dinner available Cen ht
Wi-fi Fishing Riding Pool table 🛆 **Conf** Thtr 80 Class 40
Board 30 **Parking** 100 **Notes** ⊗

NEWPORT   Map 8 SN03

PREMIER COLLECTION

Y Garth Boutique B&B

★★★★★ 🏠 BED AND BREAKFAST

Dinas Cross SA42 0XR
☎ **01348 811777 & 07814 917920**
e-mail: aa@y-garth.co.uk
web: www.bedandbreakfast-pembrokeshire.co.uk
dir: *A487 from Fishguard, in Dinas Cross turn left after
tennis courts. 200yds on right*

A warm welcome can be expected from proprietor Joyce
Evans at this boutique-style B&B. The sea is close by
and the house is set in a quiet location some three
miles from Newport; St Davids and the Pembrokeshire
Coast National Park are also within easy driving
distance. The bedrooms offer quality soft furnishings
with sumptuous beds and many guest extras; two are
en suite and one has a luxury private bathroom. There
is a smart and cosy lounge plus a conservatory for
guests. An award-winning breakfast is provided.

Rooms 3 rms (2 en suite) (1 pri facs) S £40-£80;
D £80-£100 **Facilities** FTV DVD iPod docking station
TVL tea/coffee Cen ht Wi-fi ⅃ 18 🛆 **Extras** Robes,
chocolates, flowers - complimentary **Parking** 3
Notes LB ⊗ No Children 14yrs

Llysmeddyg

★★★★ ◎◎ RESTAURANT WITH ROOMS

East St SA42 0SY
☎ **01239 820008**
e-mail: contact@llysmeddyg.com
dir: *On A487 in centre of town*

Llysmeddyg is a Georgian townhouse offering a blend of
old and new, with elegant furnishings, deep sofas and a
welcoming fire. The owners of this property employed
local craftsmen to create a lovely interior that has an
eclectic style. The focus of the quality restaurant menu is
the use of fresh, seasonal, locally sourced ingredients.
The spacious bedrooms are comfortable and
contemporary in design; bathrooms vary in style.

Rooms 5 en suite 3 annexe en suite (3 fmly) (1 GF)
S £70-£135; D £100-£180* **Facilities** FTV DVD iPod
docking station Lounge tea/coffee Dinner available Cen ht
Wi-fi ch fac ⅃ 18 Riding 🛆 3/4 size snooker table (in
winter) **Extras** Speciality toiletries, mini-bar **Conf** Max 20
Class 20 Board 20 **Parking** 8 **Notes** LB No coaches Civ
Wed 90

Salutation Inn

★★★ Ⓐ INN

Filindre Farchog SA41 3UY
☎ **01239 820564 & 07793 488262** 🖷 **01239 820355**
e-mail: johndenley@aol.com
web: www.salutationcountryhotel.co.uk
dir: *On A487 between Cardigan & Fishguard. 3m N of
Newport*

Rooms 8 en suite (2 fmly) (8 GF) S £60; D £75*
Facilities FTV tea/coffee Dinner available Direct Dial
Cen ht Wi-fi ⅃ 18 Pool table **Conf** Max 25 Thtr 25 Class 12
Board 12 **Parking** 60 **Notes** LB

ST DAVIDS   Map 8 SM72

See also Solva

PREMIER COLLECTION

Ramsey House

★★★★ 🖥 🍽 GUEST HOUSE

Lower Moor SA62 6RP
☎ 01437 720321 & 07795 575005
e-mail: info@ramseyhouse.co.uk
web: www.ramseyhouse.co.uk
dir: From Cross Sq in St Davids towards Porthclais, house 0.25m on left

This pleasant guest house, under the ownership of Suzanne and Shaun Ellison, offers the ideal combination of professional management and the warmth of a family-run guest house. The property is quietly located on the outskirts of St Davids and surrounded by unspoilt countryside. It provides modern, well-equipped bedrooms and en suite bathrooms along with a good range of welcome extras. Carefully prepared dinners by chef Shaun feature quality local Welsh produce and breakfast provides a choice of home-made items including breads and preserves.

Rooms 6 rms (5 en suite) (1 pri facs) (3 GF) S £60-£110; D £100-£110* **Facilities** FTV Lounge tea/coffee Dinner available Cen ht Licensed Wi-fi **Extras** Speciality toiletries - complimentary **Parking** 10 **Notes** LB ⊗ No Children 16yrs Closed Nov-13 Feb

PREMIER COLLECTION

Lochmeyler Farm Guest House (SM855275)

★★★★★ FARMHOUSE

Llandeloy, Pen-y-Cwm SA62 6LL
☎ 01348 837724 📠 01348 837622 Mrs Margo Evans
e-mail: stay@lochmeyler.co.uk
web: www.lochmeyler.co.uk

(For full entry see SOLVA)

The Waterings

★★★★ BED AND BREAKFAST

Anchor Dr, High St SA62 6QH
☎ 01437 720876 📠 01437 720876
e-mail: enquiries@waterings.co.uk
web: www.waterings.co.uk
dir: On A487 on E edge of St Davids

Situated a short walk from the centre of St Davids, The Waterings offers spacious bedrooms that are accessed from a courtyard garden; most bedrooms have their own separate seating area. Breakfast, made from a good selection of local produce, is served in a smart dining room in the main house.

Rooms 5 annexe en suite (4 fmly) (5 GF) **Facilities** FTV tea/coffee Cen ht Licensed Wi-fi 🏌 ♿ 9 **Conf** Max 15 Board 15 **Parking** 20 **Notes** No Children 5yrs

SAUNDERSFOOT   Map 8 SN10

Vine Cottage

★★★★ GUEST HOUSE

The Ridgeway SA69 9LA
☎ 01834 814422
e-mail: enquiries@vinecottageguesthouse.co.uk
web: www.vinecottageguesthouse.co.uk
dir: A477 S onto A478, left onto B4316, after railway bridge right signed Saundersfoot, cottage 100yds beyond 30mph sign

A warm welcome awaits guests at this pleasant former farmhouse located on the outskirts of Saundersfoot, yet within easy walking distance of the village. Set in extensive, mature gardens which include some rare and exotic plants and a summer house where guests can sit and relax on warmer evenings. Bedrooms, including a ground-floor room, are modern and well equipped, and some are suitable for families. There is a comfortable, airy lounge. Breakfast is served in the cosy dining room.

Rooms 5 en suite (2 fmly) (1 GF) S £45-£50; D £70-£80* **Facilities** FTV Lounge tea/coffee Dinner available Cen ht 🔒 **Parking** 10 **Notes** LB No Children 6yrs ♿

SOLVA   Map 8 SM82

AA GUEST ACCOMMODATION OF THE YEAR FOR WALES

PREMIER COLLECTION

Crug-Glas Country House

★★★★★ 🖥 🍽 RESTAURANT WITH ROOMS

Abereiddy SA62 6XX
☎ 01348 831302
e-mail: janet@crugglas.plus.com
dir: From Solva to St Davids on A487. From St Davids take A487 towards Fishguard. 1st left after Carnhedryn, house signed

This house, on a dairy, beef and cereal farm of approximately 600 acres, is situated about a mile from the coast on the St Davids peninsula. Comfort, relaxation and flawless attention to detail are provided by the charming host, Janet Evans. Each spacious bedroom has the hallmarks of assured design plus a luxury bathroom with both bath and shower; one suite on the top floor has great views. In additional there are two suites in separate buildings. With AA Dinner and Breakfast awards, guests can be sure that dishes are prepared with the finest local produce. To top it all the sunsets can be stunning! Crug-Glas Country House is the AA Guest Accommodation of the Year for Wales 2012-13.

Rooms 7 en suite (1 fmly) (2 GF) **Facilities** FTV tea/coffee Dinner available Cen ht Wi-fi **Conf** Max 20 Thtr 20 Class 20 Board 20 **Parking** 10 **Notes** ⊗ No Children 12yrs Closed 24-27 Dec

PREMIER COLLECTION

Lochmeyler Farm Guest House (SM855275)

★★★★★ FARMHOUSE

Llandeloy, Pen-y-Cwm SA62 6LL
☎ 01348 837724 📠 01348 837622 Mrs Margo Evans
e-mail: stay@lochmeyler.co.uk
web: www.lochmeyler.co.uk
dir: *From Haverfordwest A487 (St Davids road) to Pen-y-Cwm, right to Llandeloy*

Located on a 220-acre dairy farm in a beautiful area, with easy access to the Pembrokeshire coast line, Lochmeyler provides high levels of comfort and excellent facilities. The spacious bedrooms, of which four are cottage style converted outbuildings, are equipped with a wealth of thoughtful extras and have private sitting rooms. Three are located in the main house which has its own separate entrance. Comprehensive breakfasts are served in the spacious dining room; a bar and pleasant lounge are also available.

Rooms 3 en suite 4 annexe en suite (6 fmly) (5 GF) S £45-£55; D £70-£80 **Facilities** FTV DVD Lounge tea/coffee Direct Dial Cen ht Licensed Wi-fi 🔋 **Extras** Speciality toiletries, robes, home-made Welsh cakes **Parking** 7 **Notes** LB 220 acres dairy

---

TENBY   Map 8 SN10

Esplanade

★★★★ GUEST ACCOMMODATION

1 The Esplanade SA70 7DU
☎ 01834 842760 & 843333 📠 01834 845633
e-mail: esplanadetenby@googlemail.com
web: www.esplanadetenby.co.uk
dir: *Follow signs to South Beach, exit South Parade into St Florence Parade. Premises on seafront adjacent to town walls*

Located beside the historic town walls of Tenby and with stunning views over the sea to Caldey Island, the Esplanade provides a range of standard and luxury bedrooms, some ideal for families. Breakfast is offered in the elegant front-facing dining room, which contains a comfortable lounge-bar area.

Rooms 14 en suite (4 fmly) (1 GF) **Facilities** tea/coffee Direct Dial Cen ht Licensed Wi-fi **Notes** Closed 15-27 Dec

Giltar Grove Country House

★★★ GUEST ACCOMMODATION

Penally SA70 7RY
☎ 01834 871568
e-mail: giltarbnb@aol.com
web: www.giltargrove.co.uk
dir: *2m SW of Tenby. Exit A4139, 2nd right after railway bridge*

Just a short walk from the spectacular Pembrokeshire Coastal Path, this impressive Victorian country house retains many original features. Some bedrooms have four-poster beds and some are on the ground floor; all are filled with homely extras. There is a cosy sitting room, an elegant dining room, and a spacious conservatory where breakfast is served.

Rooms 6 rms (5 en suite) (1 pri facs) (2 GF) S £30-£35; D £60-£65* **Facilities** FTV tea/coffee Cen ht **Parking** 10 **Notes** ⊗ No Children 8yrs Closed Dec-Feb 🐾

POWYS

BRECON   Map 9 SO02

See also Sennybridge

PREMIER COLLECTION

The Coach House

🏠 GUEST ACCOMMODATION

Orchard St LD3 8AN
☎ 01874 620043 & 07974 328437
e-mail: coachhousebrecon@gmail.com
dir: *From town centre W over bridge onto B4601. Coach House 200yds on right*

A warm welcome awaits at this former coach house that now provides contemporary accommodation; the friendly and enthusiastic proprietors ensure a memorable stay. The bedrooms are well equipped and extremely comfortable. A selection of imaginative Welsh home-cooked breakfast choices is served in the spacious dining room. The property has a lovely garden and is within easy walking distance of Brecon.

Rooms 7 en suite S £60-£85; D £70-£100 **Facilities** FTV DVD iPod docking station tea/coffee Direct Dial Cen ht Licensed Wi-fi 🔋 Resident holistic therapist, massage & reflexology **Extras** Speciality toiletries **Parking** 6 **Notes** LB ⊗ No Children 16yrs

PREMIER COLLECTION

Canal Bank

★★★★★ BED AND BREAKFAST

Ty Gardd, Canal Bank LD3 7HG
☎ 01874 623464 & 07929 369149
e-mail: enquiries@accommodation-breconbeacons.co.uk
dir: *B4601 signed Brecon, left over bridge before petrol station, turn right, continue to end of lane*

Expect a warm welcome at this delightful property, which was developed from a row of five 18th-century cottages. It provides very high quality, comfortable and well-equipped accommodation, and stands alongside the canal in a semi-rural area on the outskirts of Brecon, yet within walking distance of the town centre. Facilities here include a comfortable lounge, a very attractive breakfast room and a lovely garden.

Rooms 3 en suite S £50-£90; D £75-£98 **Facilities** FTV DVD iPod docking station Lounge tea/coffee Cen ht Wi-fi 🔋 **Parking** 5 **Notes** No Children 16yrs 🐾

BRECON *continued*

PREMIER COLLECTION

Peterstone Court

★★★★★ ⑳⑳ RESTAURANT WITH ROOMS

Llanhamlach LD3 7YB
☎ 01874 665387
e-mail: info@peterstone-court.com
dir: 3m from Brecon on A40 towards Abergavenny

Situated on the edge of the Brecon Beacons, this establishment affords stunning views overlooking the River Usk. The atmosphere is friendly and informal; without any unnecessary fuss. No two bedrooms are alike, but all share comparable levels of comfort, quality and elegance. Public areas reflect similar standards, eclectically styled with a blend of the contemporary and the traditional. Quality produce is cooked with care in a range of enjoyable dishes.

Rooms 8 en suite 4 annexe en suite (2 fmly) S £85-£145; D £95-£225* **Facilities** FTV DVD iPod docking station tea/coffee Dinner available Direct Dial Cen ht Wi-fi ↖ Fishing Riding Sauna Gym ♨ Pool open mid Apr-1 Oct Spa facilities **Conf** Max 100 Thtr 100 Class 100 Board 60 **Parking** 60 **Notes** LB Civ Wed

The Felin Fach Griffin

★★★★ ⑳⑳ INN

Felin Fach LD3 0UB
☎ 01874 620111
e-mail: enquiries@felinfachgriffin.co.uk
dir: 4m NE of Brecon on A470

This delightful inn stands in an extensive garden at the northern end of the village of Felin Fach. The public areas have a wealth of rustic charm and provide the setting for the excellent food that is served. The bedrooms are carefully appointed and have modern equipment and facilities. The service and hospitality are commendable here. The Felin Fach Griffin is the winner of AA Wine Award for Wales 2012-2013.

Rooms 7 en suite (1 fmly) S £97.50-£135; D £140-£210* (incl.dinner) **Facilities** tea/coffee Dinner available Direct Dial Cen ht ♨ ♨ **Conf** Max 15 Board 15 **Parking** 61 **Notes** LB Closed 24-25 Dec No coaches

Llanddetty Hall Farm *(SO124205)*

★★★★ FARMHOUSE

Talybont-on-Usk LD3 7YR
☎ 01874 676415 🖷 01874 676415 **Mrs H E Atkins**
dir: SE of Brecon. Off B4558

This impressive Grade II listed, 17th-century farmhouse in the beautiful Usk Valley is full of character, and the friendly proprietors ensure a comfortable stay. Bedrooms are very pleasant and feature traditional furnishings, exposed timbers and polished floorboards. Welcoming log fires are lit during cold weather in the comfortable lounge, and guests dine around one table in the dining room.

Rooms 3 rms (2 en suite) (1 pri facs) 1 annexe en suite (1 GF) S £45; D £65-£70 **Facilities** TVL TV1B tea/coffee Cen ht **Parking** 6 **Notes** ⊗ No Children 12yrs Closed 16 Dec-14 Jan RS Feb-Apr restricted service at lambing season ⊛ 48 acres sheep

The Usk Inn

★★★★ ➴ INN

Station Rd, Talybont-on-Usk LD3 7JE
☎ 01874 676251 🖷 01874 676392
e-mail: stay@uskinn.co.uk
dir: Off A40, 6m E of Brecon

This delightful inn is personally run in a friendly manner by the owners Jill and Andrew Felix, who have renovated the property to a high standard during their tenure. The thoughtfully equipped and well-appointed bedrooms include a family room, and one room has a four-poster bed. Public areas have a wealth of charm including a welcoming log fire on colder days. The inn has a well-deserved reputation for good food.

Rooms 10 en suite (1 fmly) **Facilities** TVL tea/coffee Dinner available Direct Dial Cen ht **Conf** Max 60 Thtr 60 Class 40 Board 20 **Parking** 30 **Notes** ⊗ Closed 25-27 Dec

The Beacons Guest House

★★★ GUEST HOUSE

16 Bridge St LD3 8AH
☎ 01874 623339 🖷 01874 623339
e-mail: guesthouse@thebreconbeacons.co.uk
dir: On B4601 opposite Christ College

Located west of the historic town centre over the bridge, this 17th-century former farmhouse by the river has been renovated to provide a range of homely bedrooms, some in converted barns and outbuildings. There is a guests' lounge and a cosy bar. This is a non-smoking establishment.

Rooms 11 rms (9 en suite) (2 pri facs) 3 annexe en suite (4 fmly) (3 GF) S £37-£64; D £58-£84* **Facilities** FTV TVL tea/coffee Cen ht Licensed Wi-fi ♨ **Conf** Max 30 Thtr 30 Class 25 Board 20 **Parking** 20 **Notes** LB ⊗

Borderers Guesthouse

★★★ GUEST ACCOMMODATION

47 The Watton LD3 7EG
☎ 01874 623559
e-mail: info@borderers.com
web: www.borderers.com
dir: 200yds SE of town centre on B4601, opposite church

This guest house was originally a 17th-century drovers' inn. The courtyard, now a car park, is surrounded by many of the bedrooms, and pretty hanging baskets can be seen everywhere. The bedrooms are attractively decorated with rich floral fabrics, and there is one room that has easier access.

Rooms 4 rms (3 en suite) (1 pri facs) 5 annexe en suite (2 fmly) (4 GF) S £40-£60; D £60-£70* **Facilities** FTV tea/coffee Cen ht Wi-fi **Parking** 6

Save on B&Bs and Hotels. Book at **theAA.com/hotel**

POWYS 411 WALES

The Lansdowne

★★★ GUEST ACCOMMODATION

The Watton LD3 7EG
☎ 01874 623321 📠 01874 610438
e-mail: reception@lansdownehotel.co.uk
dir: A40, A470 onto B4601

Privately-owned and personally-run, this Georgian house is conveniently located close to the town centre. The accommodation is well equipped and includes family rooms and a bedroom on ground-floor level. There is a comfortable lounge, a small bar and an attractive split-level dining room where dinner is available to residents.

Rooms 9 en suite (2 fmly) (1 GF) S £45; D £65*
Facilities FTV tea/coffee Dinner available Direct Dial Cen ht Licensed **Notes** LB No Children 5yrs

---

BUILTH WELLS   Map 9 SO05

Rhedyn Guest House

★★★★ 🍽 GUEST HOUSE

Rhedyn, Cilmery LD2 3LH
☎ 01982 551944 & 07703 209721
e-mail: info@rhedynguesthouse.co.uk
web: www.rhedynguesthouse.co.uk
dir: On A483 towards Garth

This detached property stands just off the main road outside Cilmery, which is a short drive from Builth Wells. Three comfortable bedrooms provide all the modern facilities including Wi-fi and a range of guest extras to enhance comfort. Two bedrooms are on the ground floor with their own entrances. Dinner, bookable at the time of reservation, offers imaginative menus. A hearty breakfast, including a selection of home-made preserves, is served in the delightful dining room around a communal table. Access to the guest house is via two gates through a field.

Rooms 1 en suite 2 annexe en suite (2 GF) D fr £80*
Facilities STV FTV DVD Lounge tea/coffee Dinner available Cen ht Wi-fi Riding 🐴 **Extras** Sherry - complimentary **Parking** 3 **Notes** ⊗

CAERSWS   Map 15 SO09

PREMIER COLLECTION

The Talkhouse

★★★★★ ⊛⊛ RESTAURANT WITH ROOMS

Pontdolgoch SY17 5JE
☎ 01686 688919 & 07876 086183
e-mail: info@talkhouse.co.uk
dir: 1.5m NW of Caersws on A470

A highlight of this delightful 19th-century restaurant with rooms is the food - home-made dishes make good use of local produce. The bedrooms offer luxury in every area and the cosy lounge, filled with sofas, is the place to while away some time with a glass of wine or a pot of tea. The bar features a large fireplace.

Rooms 3 en suite **Facilities** FTV Dinner available Cen ht **Conf** Max 20 **Parking** 50 **Notes** ⊗ No Children 12yrs Closed 1st 2wks Jan RS Mon & Tue open for group bookings only No coaches

---

CRICKHOWELL   Map 9 SO21

PREMIER COLLECTION

Glangrwyney Court

★★★★★ BED AND BREAKFAST

NP8 1ES
☎ 01873 811288 📠 01873 810317
e-mail: info@glancourt.co.uk
web: www.glancourt.co.uk
dir: 2m SE of Crickhowell on A40 (near county boundary)

Located in extensive mature grounds, this impressive Georgian house has been renovated to provide high standards of comfort and facilities. The spacious bedrooms are equipped with a range of homely extras, and bathrooms include a jacuzzi or steam shower. There are also comfortable bedrooms in an annexe; two have their own lounge and kitchen area. Comprehensive breakfasts are taken in the elegant dining room and a luxurious lounge is also provided.

Rooms 6 en suite 4 annexe en suite (1 fmly) (1 GF)
Facilities STV TVL tea/coffee Cen ht Licensed Wi-fi 🐾 🐾 Boules **Parking** 12 **Notes** No Children 12yrs Civ Wed 23

CRIGGION   Map 15 SJ21

Brimford House (SJ310150)

★★★★ FARMHOUSE

SY5 9AU
☎ 01938 570235 Mrs Dawson
e-mail: info@brimford.co.uk
dir: Exit B4393 after Crew Green left for Criggion, Brimford 1st on left after pub

This elegant Georgian house stands in lovely open countryside and is a good base for touring central Wales and the Marches. The bedrooms are spacious, and thoughtful extras enhance guest comfort. A cheery log fire burns in the lounge during colder weather; the hospitality is equally warm and creates a relaxing atmosphere throughout.

Rooms 3 en suite S £45-£60; D £60-£75* **Facilities** FTV TVL tea/coffee Cen ht Wi-fi Fishing **Parking** 4 **Notes** LB 250 acres arable/beef/sheep

Lane Farm (SJ305161)

★★★★ FARMHOUSE

SY5 9BG
☎ 01743 884288 Mrs L Burrowes
e-mail: lesley@lanefarmbedandbreakfast.co.uk
dir: On B4393 between Crew Green & Llandrinio

A warm welcome awaits at Lane Farm, a traditional 380-acre, organic, working beef and sheep farm, set beneath the tranquil Breidden Hills. Bedrooms are comfortably furnished with pine furniture and provide a good range of guest extras. There are two bedrooms at ground floor level. A substantial farmhouse breakfast is on offer and served in the beamed dining room around a communal table. Plenty of parking is available, free fishing on the Severn, and attractive gardens.

Rooms 4 en suite (2 GF) S £35-£40; D £54-£58 **Facilities** FTV Lounge tea/coffee Cen ht Fishing 🐾 **Parking** 8 **Notes** LB Closed 23-27 Dec 380 acres organic beef/sheep

ERWOOD   Map 9 SO04

Hafod-y-Garreg

★★★★ 🛏 BED AND BREAKFAST

LD2 3TQ
☎ **01982 560400**
e-mail: john-annie@hafod-y.wanadoo.co.uk
web: www.hafodygarreg.co.uk
dir: *1m S of Erwood. Off A470 at Trericket Mill, sharp right, up track past cream farmhouse towards pine forest, through gate*

This remote Grade II listed farmhouse dates in part from 1401 and has been confirmed, by dendrochronology, as the 'oldest dwelling in Wales'. As you would expect the house has tremendous character, and is decorated and furnished to befit its age; the bedrooms have all the modern facilities. There is an impressive dining room and a lounge with an open fireplace. Warm hospitality from John Marchant and Annie McKay is a major strength here.

Rooms 2 en suite D £86 **Facilities** STV iPod docking station tea/coffee Dinner available Cen ht Wi-fi 🔋 **Extras** Speciality toiletries, sherry, magazines, books **Parking** 6 **Notes** No Children Closed Xmas 🐾

HAY-ON-WYE   Map 9 SO24

See also Erwood

Old Black Lion Inn

★★★★ 🍴 INN

26 Lion St HR3 5AD
☎ **01497 820841** 📠 **01497 822960**
e-mail: info@oldblacklion.co.uk
web: www.oldblacklion.co.uk
dir: *From B4348 in Hay-on-Wye into Lion St. Inn on right*

This fine old coaching inn, with a history stretching back several centuries, has a wealth of charm and character. It was occupied by Oliver Cromwell during the siege of Hay Castle. Privately-owned and personally-run, it provides cosy and well-equipped bedrooms, some located in an adjacent building. A wide range of well-prepared food is provided, and the service is relaxed and friendly.

Old Black Lion Inn

Rooms 6 rms (5 en suite) (1 pri facs) 4 annexe en suite (2 GF) S fr £45; D fr £90* **Facilities** FTV tea/coffee Dinner available Direct Dial Cen ht Wi-fi **Parking** 12 **Notes** ⊗ No Children 8yrs Closed 24-26 Dec

LLANDRINDOD WELLS   Map 9 SO06

PREMIER COLLECTION

Guidfa House

★★★★★ 🏠 GUEST ACCOMMODATION

Crossgates LD1 6RF
☎ **01597 851241** 📠 **01597 737269**
e-mail: tony@guidfahouse.co.uk
web: www.guidfahouse.co.uk
dir: *3m N of Llandrindod Wells, at junct of A483 & A44*

Expect a relaxed and pampered stay at this elegant Georgian house just outside the town. Comfort is the keynote here, whether in the attractive and well-equipped bedrooms or in the homely lounge, where a real fire burns in cold weather. Breakfast is also a strength, due to the proprietor's skilful touch in the kitchen; a wide choice of expertly cooked options are offered.

Rooms 5 en suite 1 annexe en suite (1 GF) S £67.50-£93.50; D £87.50-£113.50* **Facilities** FTV DVD iPod docking station Lounge tea/coffee Cen ht Licensed Wi-fi 🔋 **Parking** 10 **Notes** LB ⊗ No Children 10yrs

Holly Farm *(SO045593)*

★★★★ FARMHOUSE

Holly Ln, Howey LD1 5PP
☎ **01597 822402** 📠 **01597 822402** **Mrs R Jones**
dir: *2m S on A483 of Llandrindod Wells near Howey*

This working farm dates from Tudor times. The bedrooms are homely and full of character, and the comfortable lounge has a warming log fire in cooler months. The traditional home cooking, using local produce, can be enjoyed in the dining room.

Rooms 3 en suite (1 fmly) S £36-£40; D £64-£76* **Facilities** FTV TVL tea/coffee Dinner available Cen ht Wi-fi **Parking** 4 **Notes** LB ⊗ 70 acres beef/sheep

LLANGAMMARCH WELLS   Map 9 SN94

The Cammarch

★★★★ GUEST ACCOMMODATION

LD4 4BY
☎ **01591 610802**
e-mail: mail@cammarch.com
web: www.cammarch.com
dir: *Exit A483 at Garth, signed Llangammarch Wells, opposite T-junct*

This property dates from the 1850s and was built as a hotel by the railway company. Owner Kathryn Dangerfield offers a warm welcome to all guests and the establishment provides modern, well-equipped bedrooms that are tastefully decorated. There is a comfortable spacious bar and lounge, with a log-burning fire, ideal for colder evenings. The conservatory dining room, overlooking the attractive gardens and pond, offers fresh local produce on the dinner menu and the hearty Welsh breakfast makes a good start to the day. Parking is provided at the side of the property. The Cammarch was a Finalist in the AA Friendliest B&B of the Year Award 2012-13.

Rooms 11 en suite (4 fmly) S £59-£69; D £79-£89* **Facilities** FTV DVD Lounge tea/coffee Dinner available Cen ht Licensed Wi-fi 🎣 Fishing 🔋 **Extras** Speciality toiletries **Conf** Max 20 Thtr 20 Class 15 Board 15 **Parking** 16 **Notes** LB RS Xmas-New Year Self catering only

LLANGEDWYN   Map 15 SJ12

Plas Uchaf Country House

★★★★ 🛏 GUEST HOUSE

SY10 9LD
☎ **01691 780588 & 07817 419747**
e-mail: info@plasuchaf.com
dir: *Mile End services Oswestry A483/Welshpool. After 2m right at White Lion public house, 4.5m Llangedwyn. 150yds after school on right*

Located in a superb elevated position amongst extensive mature parkland, this elegant Queen Anne house has been sympathetically renovated to provide high standards

Save on B&Bs and Hotels. Book at **theAA.com/hotel**

POWYS 413 WALES

of comfort and facilities. The interior flooring was created from recycled ship timbers from The Armada fleet of 1588, and furnishing styles highlight the many period features. Imaginative dinners are available, and a warm welcome is assured.

Rooms 6 en suite (1 fmly) (1 GF) S £52.50; D £90*
Facilities FTV iPod docking station Lounge tea/coffee Dinner available Cen ht Licensed Wi-fi 🐾 🎾 🛗
Conf Max 15 Thtr 15 Class 15 Board 15 **Parking** 30
Notes LB Civ Wed 50

LLANGURIG
Map 9 SN97

The Old Vicarage

★★★★ GUEST HOUSE

SY18 6RN
☎ 01686 440280 📠 01686 440280
e-mail: info@theoldvicaragellangurig.co.uk
web: www.theoldvicaragellangurig.co.uk
dir: *A470 onto A44, signed*

Located on pretty mature grounds, which feature a magnificent holly tree, this elegant Victorian house provides a range of thoughtfully furnished bedrooms, some with fine period items. Breakfast is served in a spacious dining room, and a comfortable guest lounge is also available. Afternoon tea is served in the garden during the warmer months.

Rooms 4 en suite (1 fmly) S £40; D £66* **Facilities** DVD TVL tea/coffee Dinner available Cen ht Licensed Wi-fi 🛗
Parking 6 **Notes** LB ♻

LLANIDLOES
Map 9 SN98

Mount Inn

★★★ INN

China St SY18 6AB
☎ 01686 412247
e-mail: mountllani@aol.com
dir: *In town centre*

Mount Inn is believed to occupy part of the site of an old motte and bailey castle, and started life as a coaching inn. The traditional bars are full of character, with exposed beams and timbers as well as cobbled flooring and log fires. Bedrooms, which include some in a separate building, are carefully furnished and equipped with practical and thoughtful extras.

Rooms 3 en suite 6 annexe en suite (3 fmly) (3 GF) S £47; D £70 **Facilities** FTV TVL tea/coffee Dinner available Cen ht ⚡ 🎱 Pool table **Conf** Max 20 Thtr 12 Class 20 Board 12 **Parking** 12

LLANWRTYD WELLS
Map 9 SN84

Carlton Riverside

★★★★ 🍴🍴 RESTAURANT WITH ROOMS

Irfon Crescent LD5 4SP
☎ 01591 610248
e-mail: info@carltonriverside.com
dir: *In town centre beside bridge*

Guests become part of the family at this character property, set beside the river in Wales's smallest town. Carlton Riverside offers award-winning cuisine which Mary Ann Gilchrist produces using the very best of local ingredients. The set menu is complemented by a well-chosen wine list and dinner is served in the stylish restaurant which offers a memorable blend of traditional comfort, modern design and river views. Four comfortable bedrooms have tasteful combinations of antique and contemporary furniture, along with welcome personal touches.

Rooms 4 en suite S £50; D £75-£100* **Facilities** Lounge tea/coffee Dinner available Cen ht Wi-fi 🛗 **Notes** LB Closed 20-30 Dec No coaches

---

Lasswade Country House

★★★★ 🍴🍴 RESTAURANT WITH ROOMS

Station Rd LD5 4RW
☎ 01591 610515 📠 01591 610611
e-mail: info@lasswadehotel.co.uk
dir: *Exit A483 into Irfon Terrace, right into Station Rd, 350yds on right*

This friendly establishment on the edge of the town has impressive views over the countryside. Bedrooms are comfortably furnished and well equipped, while the public areas consist of a tastefully decorated lounge, an elegant restaurant with a bar, and an airy conservatory which looks towards the neighbouring hills. The kitchen utilises fresh, local produce to provide an enjoyable dining experience.

Rooms 8 en suite S £55-£70; D £70-£115* **Facilities** TVL tea/coffee Dinner available Cen ht ⚡ Riding 🛗 **Conf** Max 18 Thtr 18 Class 14 Board 14 **Parking** 6 **Notes** LB No coaches

---

LLANYMYNECH
Map 15 SJ22

The Bradford Arms

★★★★ INN

SY22 6EJ
☎ 01691 830582 📠 01691 839009
e-mail: catelou@tesco.net
web: www.bradfordarmshotel.com

(For full entry see Oswestry (Shropshire))

MONTGOMERY
Map 15 SO29

The Dragon

★★★★ 🍴 INN

SY15 6PA
☎ 01686 668359 📠 0870 011 8227
e-mail: reception@dragonhotel.com
dir: *From A5 signed Montgomery, turn left then right onto Broad St, behind town hall*

This fine 17th-century coaching inn stands in the centre of Montgomery. Beams and timbers from the nearby castle, which was destroyed by Cromwell, are visible in the lounge and bar. A wide choice of soundly prepared, wholesome food is available in both the restaurant and bar. Bedrooms are well equipped and family rooms are available. There is a small indoor swimming pool in the grounds for guest use and ample parking to the rear of the property.

Rooms 20 en suite (5 fmly) (2 smoking) S £50-£60; D £65-£75 (room only)* **Facilities** FTV TVL tea/coffee Dinner available Direct Dial Cen ht Wi-fi 🏊 🎾 Sauna **Conf** Max 60 Thtr 60 Class 30 Board 25 **Parking** 22 **Notes** LB Civ Wed 100

SENNYBRIDGE   Map 9 SN92

Maeswalter

★★★★ GUEST ACCOMMODATION

Heol Senni LD3 8SU
☎ **01874 636629**
e-mail: bb@maeswalter.co.uk
web: www.maeswalter.co.uk
dir: *A470 onto A4215, 2.5m left for Heol Senni, 1.5m on right over cattle grid*

Set in a peaceful country location with splendid views of the Senni Valley, this 17th-century farmhouse offers a friendly and relaxing place to stay. The accommodation is well maintained and includes a suite on the ground floor of an adjacent building. A lounge-dining room is provided, and freshly cooked farmhouse breakfasts are a pleasure.

Rooms 4 en suite (1 fmly) (2 GF) **Facilities** STV FTV TVL tea/coffee Dinner available Cen ht **Parking** 12 **Notes** ⊗ No Children 5yrs

WELSHPOOL   Map 15 SJ20

See also Criggion

PREMIER COLLECTION

Moors Farm B&B

★★★★★ BED AND BREAKFAST

Oswestry Rd SY21 9JR
☎ **01938 553395 & 07957 882967**
e-mail: moorsfarm@tiscali.co.uk
web: www.moors-farm.com
dir: *1.5m NE of Welshpool on A483 on left*

A very warm welcome awaits guests at this impressive house, parts of which date from the early 18th century. It has a wealth of character, including exposed beams and log-burning fires, and the day rooms are spacious and tastefully furnished. The bedrooms feature smart, modern bathrooms and are equipped with a wealth of thoughtful extras.

Rooms 5 en suite (2 fmly) **Facilities** TVL tea/coffee Cen ht **Notes** ⊗

Heath Cottage *(SJ239023)*

★★★ 🏠 FARMHOUSE

Kingswood, Forden SY21 8LX
☎ 01938 580453 📠 01938 580453 Mr & Mrs M C Payne
e-mail: heathcottagewales@tiscali.co.uk
dir: *4m S of Welshpool. Off A490 behind Forden Old Post Office, opposite Parrys Garage*

The furnishings and decor highlight the original features of this early 18th-century farmhouse. Bedrooms have stunning country views, and a choice of lounges, one with a log fire, is available. Memorable breakfasts feature free-range eggs and home-made preserves.

Rooms 3 en suite (1 fmly) S £30; D £60* **Facilities** TVL tea/coffee Cen ht 🔒 **Parking** 4 **Notes** ⊗ Closed Oct-Etr 🐾 6 acres poultry/sheep

SWANSEA

LLANGENNITH   Map 8 SS49

Kings Head

★★★★ INN

Town House SA3 1HX
☎ 01792 386212 📠 01792 386477
e-mail: info@kingsheadgower.co.uk
dir: *M4 junct 47 follow signs for Gower A483. At next rdbt, 2nd left follow signs to Gowerton. At lights right onto B495, through old walls, keep left at fork. Kings Head on right*

This establishment is made up from three 17th-century buildings set behind a splendid rough stone wall; it stands opposite the church in this coastal village. In two of the buildings the comfortable, well-equipped bedrooms, including some on the ground floor, can be found. This is an ideal base for exploring the Gower Peninsula, whether for walking, cycling or surfing. Evening meals and breakfasts can be taken in the inn.

Rooms 27 en suite (3 fmly) (14 GF) D £85-£130* **Facilities** FTV tea/coffee Dinner available Direct Dial Cen ht Pool table **Parking** 35 **Notes** LB Closed 25 Dec RS 24 Dec closed for check-in

MUMBLES   Map 8 SS68

PREMIER COLLECTION

Little Langland

★★★★★ GUEST ACCOMMODATION

2 Rotherslade Rd, Langland SA3 4QN
☎ 01792 369696
e-mail: enquiries@littlelangland.co.uk
dir: *Exit A4067 in Mumbles onto Newton Rd, 4th left into Langland Rd, 2nd left into Rotherslade Rd*

Little Langland is only five miles from Swansea's city centre and within easy access of the stunning Gower Peninsula with its many coves and bays. The bedrooms are stylish, comfortable, and include free broadband. There is a café bar, ideal for a relaxing drink, and also a bar menu of freshly prepared snacks. Breakfast is served in the comfortable dining area.

Rooms 6 en suite **Facilities** FTV tea/coffee Direct Dial Cen ht Licensed Wi-fi **Parking** 6 **Notes** ⊗ No Children 8yrs

PARKMILL (NEAR SWANSEA)   Map 8 SS58

PREMIER COLLECTION

Maes-Yr-Haf Restaurant with Rooms

★★★★★ ⊛ RESTAURANT WITH ROOMS

SA3 2EH
☎ 01792 371000 📠 01792 234922
e-mail: enquiries@maes-yr-haf.com
dir: *A4118 W from Swansea*

Set in a peaceful location on The Gower in the small village of Parkmill, this property is well situated for easy access to Swansea and the coast. It offers contemporary, individually styled bedrooms with a very good range of guest extras, where comfort is the key. Bathrooms have both bath and shower. The food is created from high quality, locally sourced ingredients; dinner is a highlight, served in the modern restaurant, and breakfast provides a very good start to the day.

Rooms 5 en suite S £70-£100; D £80-£140* **Facilities** FTV DVD iPod docking station Lounge tea/coffee Dinner available Direct Dial Cen ht Wi-fi 🔒 **Parking** 20 **Notes** LB ⊗ No Children 6yrs Closed 11-31 Jan

Parc-le-Breos House (SS529896)

★★★★ FARMHOUSE

SA3 2HA
☎ 01792 371636 📠 01792 371287 Mrs O Edwards
e-mail: info@parclebreos.co.uk
dir: *On A4118, right 300yds after Shepherds shop, next left, signed*

This imposing early 19th-century house is at the end of a forest drive and set in 70 acres of delightful grounds. Many charming original features have been retained in the public rooms, which include a lounge and a games room. The bedrooms have comfortable furnishings, and many are suitable for families.

Rooms 10 en suite (7 fmly) (1 GF) **Facilities** FTV TVL tea/coffee Dinner available Cen ht Licensed Wi-fi Fishing Riding Pool table **Conf** Max 30 Thtr 30 **Parking** 12 **Notes** ⊗ Closed 25-26 Dec 65 acres arable/horses/pigs/chickens

---

REYNOLDSTON	Map 8 SS48

PREMIER COLLECTION

Fairyhill

★★★★★ ⑩⑩ ♨ RESTAURANT WITH ROOMS

SA3 1BS
☎ 01792 390139 📠 01792 391358
e-mail: postbox@fairyhill.net
web: www.fairyhill.net
dir: *M4 junct 47, A483, at next rdbt right onto A484. At Gowerton take B4295 for 10m*

Peace and tranquillity are never far away at this charming Georgian mansion set in the heart of the beautiful Gower peninsula. Bedrooms are furnished with care and are filled with many thoughtful extras. There is also a range of comfortable seating areas, with crackling log fires, to choose from, and the smart restaurant offers menus based on local produce and complemented by an excellent wine list.

Rooms 8 en suite S £160-£260; D £180-£280* **Facilities** FTV DVD iPod docking station Lounge TVL tea/coffee Dinner available Direct Dial Cen ht Wi-fi ♨ Holistic treatments **Conf** Max 32 Thtr 32 Board 16 **Parking** 50 **Notes** LB No Children 8yrs Closed 26 Dec & 1-27 Jan No coaches Civ Wed 40

SWANSEA	Map 9 SS69

The Alexander

★★★★ GUEST ACCOMMODATION

3 Sketty Rd, Uplands SA2 0EU
☎ 01792 470045 📠 01792 476012
e-mail: reception@alexander-hotel.co.uk

Located in fashionable Uplands between The Gower and the city centre, this Victorian house has been modernised to provide good levels of comfort and facilities. Bedrooms are comfortable with family rooms, doubles and twins available; all are filled with a very good range of practical extras, and some have marvellous views over Swansea Bay. Other areas include a cosy dining room where a hearty breakfast is served and a comfortably furnished lounge with a guest bar. The Alexander is very convenient for Swansea's Colleges and Universities.

Rooms 9 rms (8 en suite) (1 pri facs) (4 fmly) S £36-£50; D £75-£79* **Facilities** FTV Lounge tea/coffee Direct Dial Cen ht Licensed Wi-fi **Notes** ⊗

The White House

★★★★ GUEST ACCOMMODATION

4 Nyanza Ter SA1 4QQ
☎ 01792 473856 & 07729 414273 📠 01792 455300
e-mail: reception@thewhitehousehotel.co.uk
dir: *On A4118, 1m W of city centre at junct with Eaton Crescent*

Part of a short early-Victorian terrace in fashionable Uplands, this house retains many of its original features. It has been restored to provide thoughtfully furnished and equipped comfortable accommodation, with all bedrooms having en suite facilities. Breakfast offers a very good selection of hot and cold dishes including a cooked Welsh breakfast. On-road parking is available and there is easy access to local restaurants and shops.

Rooms 9 en suite (2 fmly) S £49; D £79* **Facilities** FTV Lounge tea/coffee Cen ht Wi-fi

---

Hurst Dene Guest House

★★★ GUEST HOUSE

10 Sketty Rd, Uplands SA2 0LJ
☎ 01792 280920 📠 01792 280920
e-mail: hurstdenehotel@yahoo.co.uk
web: www.hurstdene.co.uk
dir: *1m W of city centre. A4118 through Uplands shopping area into Sketty Rd, Hurst Dene on right*

This friendly guest house has a private car park and provides soundly maintained bedrooms with modern furnishings and equipment. Facilities include an attractive breakfast room with separate tables and there is a small comfortable lounge.

Rooms 10 rms (8 en suite) (3 fmly) (1 GF) S £38-£45; D £65* **Facilities** FTV TVL tea/coffee Cen ht Wi-fi **Parking** 7 **Notes** ⊗ Closed 22 Dec-1 Jan

See advert on page 416

WREXHAM

HANMER — Map 15 SJ43

The Hanmer Arms

★★★★ INN

SY13 3DE
☎ 01948 830532 & 830740 📠 01948 830740
e-mail: info@hanmerarms.co.uk
web: www.hanmerarms.co.uk
dir: On A539, just off A525 Whitchurch/Wrexham road

Located in the centre of Hanmer which is also home to the local crown-green bowling club, this former farm has been sympathetically renovated to provide a good range of facilities. Well equipped, comfortable bedrooms are situated in the former stables or barns. Rustic furniture styles highlight the many period features in the public areas including an attractive first-floor function room. Meals are available all day and use good quality ingredients. Ample parking is available.

Rooms 11 annexe en suite (2 fmly) (8 GF) Facilities FTV TVL tea/coffee Dinner available Cen ht Wi-fi Pool table Conf Max 100 Thtr 100 Class 60 Board 40 Parking 35

HORSEMAN'S GREEN — Map 15 SJ44

Murefield Bed & Breakfast

★★★★ BED AND BREAKFAST

Murefield SY13 3EA
☎ 01948 830790 📠 01948 830790
e-mail: enquiries@murefield.com
dir: Turn off A525 (Whitchurch to Wrexham road) to Horseman's Green, in centre of village turn left for Little Arowry. 350mtrs on right

Located in a peaceful rural setting between Whitchurch and Wrexham, this modern house provides very high standards throughout, along with well presented gardens and parking facilities. The thoughtfully furnished bedrooms are comfortable, well equipped with many extras, and both have modern efficient en suite bathrooms. One bedroom is on the ground floor for easy access and has a wet room en suite. Comprehensive breakfasts offer home-made and locally sourced produce.

Rooms 2 en suite (1 GF) S £40-£55; D £60-£85
Facilities FTV DVD tea/coffee Cen ht Wi-fi 🐾
Extras Sweets - complimentary Parking 2 Notes LB ⊗
No Children 8yrs Closed 22 Dec-3 Jan ⊗

LLANARMON DYFFRYN CEIRIOG — Map 15 SJ13

The Hand at Llanarmon

★★★★ ⊛ INN

LL20 7LD
☎ 01691 600666 📠 01691 600262
e-mail: reception@thehandhotel.co.uk
dir: Exit A5 at Chirk onto B4500 signed Ceiriog Valley, 11m to village

Appointed to a high standard, this owner-managed inn provides a range of thoughtfully furnished bedrooms, with smart modern bathrooms. Public areas retain many original features including exposed beams and open fires. Imaginative food utilises the finest of local produce. A warm welcome and attentive service ensure a memorable guest experience.

Rooms 13 en suite (4 GF) Facilities tea/coffee Dinner available Direct Dial Cen ht Wi-fi Pool table Conf Max 15 Thtr 10 Class 10 Board 15 Parking 19 Notes Civ Wed 60

West Arms

★★★★ ⊛ INN

LL20 7LD
☎ 01691 600665 & 600612 📠 01691 600622
e-mail: info@thewestarms.co.uk
dir: Off A483/A5 at Chirk, take B4500 to Ceiriog Valley

Set in the beautiful Ceiriog Valley, this delightful 17th-century inn has a wealth of charm and character. There is a comfortable lounge, a room for private dining and two bars, as well as an elegant, award-winning restaurant offering a set-price menu of imaginative dishes, utilising quality local produce. The attractive bedrooms have a mixture of modern and period furnishings.

Rooms 15 en suite (2 fmly) (3 GF) S £40-£110; D £67-£150* Facilities FTV tea/coffee Dinner available Direct Dial Cen ht Wi-fi ⚡ 18 Fishing 🐾 Conf Max 35 Thtr 35 Class 25 Board 20 Parking 22 Notes LB Civ Wed 50

Ireland

Giants Causeway, County Antrim

NORTHERN IRELAND

CO ANTRIM

BUSHMILLS
Map 1 C6

PREMIER COLLECTION

Whitepark House

☆☆☆☆☆ GUEST ACCOMMODATION

150 Whitepark Rd, Ballintoy BT54 6NH
☎ 028 2073 1482
e-mail: bob@whiteparkhouse.com
dir: On A2 at Whitepark Bay, 6m E of Bushmills

Whitepark House nestles above a sandy beach and has super views of the ocean and Scotland's Western Isles. The house features bijouterie gathered from Far Eastern travels, while the traditional bedrooms are homely. Breakfasts are served around a central table in the open-plan hallway, and hospitality is warm and memorable.

Rooms 3 en suite S £80; D £120 **Facilities** Lounge tea/coffee Cen ht Wi-fi **Extras** Bottled water, robes **Parking** 6 **Notes** ⊗ No Children 10yrs

PREMIER COLLECTION

Causeway Lodge

★★★★ GUEST HOUSE

52 Moycraig Rd, Dunseverick BT57 8TB
☎ 028 2073 0333 ▤ 0800 7565433
e-mail: stay@causewaylodge.com

Causeway Lodge offers high quality contemporary accommodation in an idyllic peaceful setting on the North Antrim Coast. Each of the individually designed bedrooms are thoughtfully presented and the Causeway Suite is very stylish. The house is close to the Giants Causeway, Carrick-A-Rede rope bridge and the famous Bushmills Distillery. Wi-fi is available and a warm welcome is assured from the friendly owners.

Rooms 4 rms (3 en suite) (1 pri facs) 1 annexe en suite (2 fmly) (1 GF) S £75; D £110 **Facilities** STV FTV iPod docking station TVL tea/coffee Cen ht Wi-fi ♨ **Extras** Speciality toiletries **Parking** 6 **Notes** ⊗

LARNE
Map 1 D5

Manor Guest House

★★★★ GUEST HOUSE

23 Older Fleet Rd, Harbour Highway BT40 1AS
☎ 028 2827 3305 ▤ 028 2826 0505
e-mail: welcome@themanorguesthouse.com
dir: Near Larne ferry terminal & harbour train station

This grand Victorian house continues to prove popular with travellers thanks to its convenient location next to the ferry terminal. There is an elegant sitting room and a separate cosy breakfast room. The well-equipped bedrooms vary in size and are furnished in modern or period style. Hospitality is especially good and ensures a real home-from-home experience.

Rooms 8 en suite (2 fmly) S £30-£35; D £55-£60* **Facilities** FTV Lounge tea/coffee Cen ht Wi-fi **Extras** Bottled water - complimentary **Parking** 6 **Notes** LB ⊗ Closed 25-26 Dec

BELFAST

BELFAST
Map 1 D5

Tara Lodge

☆☆☆☆ GUEST ACCOMMODATION

36 Cromwell Rd BT7 1JW
☎ 028 9059 0900 ▤ 028 9059 0901
e-mail: info@taralodge.com
web: www.taralodge.com
dir: M1 onto A55, left onto A1, right into Fitzwilliam St, left into University Rd, proceed to Botanic Av

Friendly staff and comfortable bedrooms make this new establishment popular for tourism and business. The stylish dining room is the scene for memorable breakfasts, while secure off-road parking is a bonus so close to the city centre.

Rooms 19 en suite 9 annexe en suite (3 GF) S £65-£75; D £75-£89* **Facilities** STV FTV DVD TVL tea/coffee Direct Dial Cen ht Lift Wi-fi **Parking** 19 **Notes** LB ⊗ Closed 24-28 Dec

CO DOWN

DONAGHADEE
Map 1 D5

Pier 36

★★★★ 🅰 GUEST HOUSE

36 The Parade BT21 0HE
☎ 028 9188 4466 ▤ 028 9188 4636
e-mail: info@pier36.co.uk
dir: A2 left onto flyover before Bangor, follow signs for Donaghadee (right across bridge). In 3m take 3rd exit at rdbt towards harbour. Pier 36 on right

Rooms 6 en suite (2 fmly) S £50-£70; D £70-£90* **Facilities** STV FTV TVL tea/coffee Dinner available Cen ht Licensed Wi-fi ♨ 18 ♨ **Conf** Max 14 Thtr 14 Class 14 Board 14 **Notes** ⊗

HOLYWOOD
Map 1 D5

PREMIER COLLECTION

Rayanne House

☆☆☆☆☆ ▤ GUEST HOUSE

60 Desmesne Rd BT18 9EX
☎ 028 9042 5859 ▤ 028 9042 5859
e-mail: info@rayannehouse.com
web: www.rayannehouse.com
dir: Exit A2 at Holywood, left into Jacksons Rd, pass golf club, 200yds on right

This elegant period house, set in its own grounds, is full of charm and enjoys a commanding position overlooking Belfast Lough and the Antrim Hills beyond. Bedrooms are all of a high standard and a host of thoughtful extras is provided. The house is a short drive from Belfast City centre and the George Best Belfast City Airport. Breakfasts are not to be missed and evening meals are served in the spacious dining room.

Rooms 10 en suite (2 fmly) (1 GF) S £70-£90; D £110-£130 **Facilities** FTV DVD iPod docking station Lounge tea/coffee Dinner available Direct Dial Cen ht Licensed Wi-fi ♨ 18 **Extras** Water **Conf** Max 17 Thtr 17 Class 17 Board 17 **Parking** 15 **Notes** LB ⊗ RS 25-26 Dec no breakfast service

CO FERMANAGH

ENNISKILLEN — Map 1 C5

Belmore Court & Motel

★★★★ GUEST ACCOMMODATION

Tempo Rd BT74 6HX
☎ 028 6632 6633 ▤ 028 6632 6362
e-mail: info@motel.co.uk
web: www.motel.co.uk
dir: On A4 (Belfast-Enniskillen road), opposite Tesco

Situated in the centre of Enniskillen, the Belmore Court offers an ideal location for visiting the North West and Fermanagh lakes. The accommodation offered has a range of styles from rooms with small kitchen areas to executive suites. These are stylish and have all the modern attractions of flat screen TVs and free Wi-fi. Some also come with espresso coffee makers. The public areas are also modern, and the breakfast room catches all the morning sun. Free parking.

Rooms 30 en suite 30 annexe en suite (17 fmly) (12 GF) S £70-£120; D £85-£135* Facilities FTV DVD iPod docking station TVL tea/coffee Direct Dial Cen ht Lift Wi-fi ⌛ 18 Conf Max 45 Thtr 45 Class 25 Board 16 Parking 60 Notes LB ⊗ Closed 24-27 Dec

CO LONDONDERRY

CASTLEDAWSON — Map 1 C5

The Inn Castledawson

★★★★★ ◉◉ INN

47 Main St BT45 8AA
☎ 028 7946 9777 ▤ 028 7946 9751
e-mail: info@theinncastledawson.com
web: www.theinncastledawson.com
dir: A6 at Magherafelt rdbt exit onto A54 into Castledawson. House next to post office on Main Street

Located in the heart of the pretty village of Castledawson, this inn offers a range of spacious comfortable bedrooms. Rear-facing rooms overlook both the garden and the tranquil River Moyola. The award-winning restaurant is very stylish and the cosy bar area is ideal for pre-dinner drinks. Business facilities are available and private parties are also catered for.

Rooms 10 en suite (3 fmly) (5 GF) S £68-£85; D £88-£120* Facilities FTV Lounge tea/coffee Dinner available Direct Dial Cen ht Wi-fi ⌛ 18 Extras Bottled water Conf Max 60 Thtr 60 Class 40 Board 40 Parking 6 Notes LB ⊗ Closed 25-26 Dec RS 2nd wk Jan Civ Wed 50

COLERAINE — Map 1 C6

PREMIER COLLECTION

Greenhill House (C849210)

★★★★★ ▤ FARMHOUSE

24 Greenhill Rd, Aghadowey BT51 4EU
☎ 028 7086 8241 & 07719 884103
▤ 028 7086 8365 Mrs E Hegarty
e-mail: greenhill.house@btinternet.com
web: www.greenhill-house.co.uk
dir: A29 from Coleraine, S for 7m, left onto B66 (Greenhill Rd) for 300yds. House on right (AA sign at front gate)

Located in the tranquil Bann Valley, overlooking the Antrim Hills, this delightful Georgian house nestles in well-tended gardens with views to open rolling countryside. Public rooms are traditionally styled and include a comfortable lounge and an elegant dining room. The pleasant bedrooms vary in size and style and have a host of thoughtful extras.

Rooms 6 en suite (2 fmly) S £45; D £70 Facilities FTV TVL tea/coffee Direct Dial Cen ht Wi-fi ⌂ Extras Snacks, bottled water Parking 10 Notes ⊗ Closed Nov-Feb RS Mar-Oct 150 acres beef

Heathfield (NW012782)

★★★★ FARMHOUSE

31 Drumcroone Rd, Killykergan BT51 4EB
☎ 028 2955 8245 & 07745 209296 Ms H Torrens
e-mail: relax@heathfieldfarm.com
dir: 8m S of Coleraine. On A29, 2m N of Garvagh

Heathfield is a delightful traditional farmhouse that is an integral part of a working farm. The house enjoys a rural setting and is a short drive from the towns of Garvagh and Coleraine making it an ideal base from which to explore the North Antrim Coast. Bedrooms are comfortable and all enjoy views of the surrounding countryside. Guests can enjoy a hearty breakfast in the dining room or relax in the lounge after a day's sightseeing.

Rooms 3 en suite S £40-£45; D £65-£70* Facilities FTV TVL tea/coffee Cen ht Wi-fi Parking 10 Notes ⊗ No Children 14yrs Closed Xmas & New Year beef

PORTSTEWART — Map 1 C6

Strandeen Bed & Breakfast

★★★★ BED AND BREAKFAST

63 Strand Rd BT55 7LU
☎ 028 7083 3159 & 07791 190964 ▤ 028 7083 3159
e-mail: strandeen@btinternet.com
web: www.strandeen.com
dir: A2 to Portstewart follow signs for The Strand, 400yds

This charming bed & breakfast enjoys a fabulous location with breathtaking views of the golden sandy beaches of Portstewart and the Atlantic Ocean. Close to the World Heritage Site of the Giants Causeway, the house makes an ideal base for exploring the beautiful Antrim coastline or playing golf at nearby Royal Portrush Golf Club. Bedrooms are very stylish and each is equipped with lots of thoughtful little extras. Guests can relax in the lounge with its real fire, enjoy the fabulous views or stretch their legs along the coastal walk. Breakfast is not to be missed. Strandeen B&B was a Finalist in the AA Friendliest B&B of the Year Award 2012-13.

Rooms 3 en suite (1 GF) S £60-£75; D £100-£135* Facilities FTV DVD iPod docking station TVL tea/coffee Dinner available Cen ht Wi-fi ⌛ 36 Riding ⌂ Extras Speciality toiletries - complimentary; robes/ slippers Parking 4 Notes LB ⊗ No Children 14yrs

CO TYRONE

DUNGANNON — Map 1 C5

PREMIER COLLECTION

Grange Lodge

★★★★★ ▥ ⌂ GUEST HOUSE

7 Grange Rd BT71 7EJ
☎ 028 8778 4212 & 07970 429965
▤ 028 8778 4313
e-mail: stay@grangelodgecountryhouse.com
web: www.grangelodgecountryhouse.com
dir: M1 junct 15, A29 towards Armagh, 1m Grange Lodge signed, 1st right & 1st white-walled entrance on right

Grange Lodge dates from 1698 and nestles in 20 acres of well-tended grounds. It continues to set high standards in hospitality and food, and excellent meals are served in the bright and airy extension. Home-baked afternoon teas can be enjoyed in the sumptuous drawing room.

Rooms 5 en suite Facilities STV FTV TVL tea/coffee Dinner available Direct Dial Cen ht Licensed Wi-fi ⌂ ⌛ 18 Snooker Conf Max 25 Parking 12 Notes ⊗ No Children 12yrs Closed 21 Dec-1 Feb

REPUBLIC OF IRELAND
CO CARLOW

CARLOW
Map 1 C3

Avlon House Bed & Breakfast

★★★★ BED AND BREAKFAST

Green Ln, Dublin Rd
☎ 059 9174222 ▤ 059 9173829
e-mail: avlonhouse@eircom.net
web: www.carlowbedandbreakfast.com
dir: N of town centre

Avlon House is a property built with visiting guests in mind. Located on the main approach from Dublin, there is secure car-parking and an attractively landscaped garden terrace. All of the bedrooms are comfortably appointed, and guests have the choice of two comfortable lounge areas. While it is a non-smoking house, there is a dedicated smoking lodge in the garden.

Rooms 5 en suite (1 fmly) **Facilities** STV FTV TVL tea/coffee Dinner available Direct Dial Cen ht Wi-fi **Parking** 7 **Notes** ⊗

Barrowville Town House

★★★★ GUEST HOUSE

Kilkenny Rd
☎ 059 9143324 & 086 2520013
e-mail: barrowvilletownhouse@eircom.net
dir: Carlow Town, N9 Kilkenny Rd near Institute of Technology

The Smyths are the friendly owners of this carefully maintained 18th-century town house. Many of the very comfortable bedrooms are spacious, and the public rooms are elegant and relaxing. The conservatory, with its fruiting vine, is where Barrowville's legendary breakfasts are served, overlooking well tended gardens. Ample car parking.

Rooms 7 en suite (3 fmly) **Facilities** STV TVL tea/coffee Direct Dial Cen ht Wi-fi **Parking** 11 **Notes** ⊗ No Children 10yrs Closed 24-26 Dec

CO CLARE

DOOLIN
Map 1 B3

Cullinan's Seafood Restaurant & Guest House

★★★ ◉ ▤ GUEST HOUSE

☎ 065 7074183
e-mail: cullinans@eircom.net
dir: In town centre at x-rds between McGanns Pub & O'Connors Pub

This charming guest house and restaurant is situated in the village of Doolin. Bedrooms are attractively decorated in a traditional style. Chef patron James Cullinan features locally caught fresh fish on his dinner menu which also includes steaks, lamb and vegetarian dishes, and there is a popular Early Bird menu. Dinner is served in the conservatory dining room overlooking the River Aille (closed Wed and Sun) in season. There is cosy guest lounge and ample off-street parking.

Rooms 8 en suite 2 annexe en suite (3 fmly) (3 GF) S €40-€70; D €60-€100 **Facilities** STV FTV Lounge TVL tea/coffee Dinner available Direct Dial Cen ht Wi-fi **Parking** 15 **Notes** ⊗ Closed mid Dec-mid Feb

LAHINCH
Map 1 B3

PREMIER COLLECTION

Moy House

★★★★★ ◉◉ ▤ GUEST HOUSE

☎ 065 7082800 ▤ 065 7082500
e-mail: moyhouse@eircom.net
web: www.moyhouse.com
dir: 1km from Lahinch on Miltown Malbay Rd, signed from Lahinch N67

This 18th-century former hunting lodge overlooks Lahinch Bay, the world-famous surfing beach and championship golf links. Individually designed bedrooms and suites are decorated with luxurious fabrics and fine antique furniture. The elegant drawing room has an open turf fire and guests can enjoy breathtaking views of the ocean while enjoying a pre-dinner drink from the honesty bar. The Conservatory Restaurant adjoins the elegant dining room and features award winning cookery. The menu is based on local seafood and seasonal produce from small independent farmers. A gourmet tasting menu is served on selected nights. Dinner must be pre-booked. Breakfast is also a treat, with a number of healthy options on offer together with the traditional Irish selection.

Rooms 9 en suite (2 fmly) (4 GF) **Facilities** STV FTV TVL Dinner available Direct Dial Cen ht Licensed Wi-fi Private access to beach **Conf** Max 16 Board 16 **Parking** 30 **Notes** LB ⊗ Closed Nov-Feb

LISCANNOR
Map 1 B3

Moher Lodge (R043917)

★★★★ FARMHOUSE

Cliffs of Moher
☎ 065 7081269 ▤ 065 7081589 Mr & Mrs Considine
e-mail: moherlodge@gmail.com
dir: 1m from Cliffs of Moher on R478

This very comfortable farmhouse is situated within walking distance of the world famous Cliffs of Moher. Three of the well appointed bedrooms are on the ground floor. There is a cosy sitting room with a turf fire and guests are greeted with tea and Mary's Guinness cake on arrival and there is a selection of dishes and freshly baked scones for breakfast. The locality offers restaurants, pubs with Irish music, ferries to the Aran Islands and the links golf course at Lahinch.

Rooms 4 en suite (1 fmly) (3 GF) **Facilities** FTV TVL tea/coffee Cen ht Wi-fi **Parking** 4 **Notes** ⊗ Closed Nov-Mar ⊕ 300 acres dairy/beef

LISDOONVARNA
Map 1 B3

Ballinsheen House

★★★★ BED AND BREAKFAST

Galway Rd
☎ 065 7074806 & 087 1241872
e-mail: ballinsheenhouse@hotmail.com
dir: On N67

Ballinsheen House is situated on an elevated site overlooking the spa town of Lisdoonvarna. Guests can enjoy the scenery from the lovely garden or relax in the cosy guest sitting room by the turf fire. A delicious breakfast is served in the conservatory dining room and includes Mary Gardiner's home baking and locally smoked salmon. The bedrooms offer good space and are attractively decorated, some are suitable for families. This is an ideal base for exploring the Burren region for walking or bicycle trips and secure off-street parking is available.

Rooms 4 en suite (2 fmly) S €40-€50; D €60-€80* **Facilities** STV Lounge TVL tea/coffee Cen ht Wi-fi ⌘ 18 ♠ **Parking** 9 **Notes** ⊗ Closed Nov-Feb

TUAMGRANEY
Map 1 B3

Clareville House

★★★★ ▤ BED AND BREAKFAST

☎ 061 922925 & 087 6867548 ▤ 061 922925
e-mail: clarevillehouse@ireland.com
web: www.clarevillehouse.net
dir: On R352 in village adjacent to Scarriff

Clareville House is attractively decorated and is situated in the pretty lakeside village of Tuamgraney. Bedrooms are furnished to a high standard and there is a cosy guest sitting room. Teresa's breakfast is a special treat. Walking tours are organised by Derek who has all the knowledge about fishing and golf in the area, and also offers a taxi service and airport collection.

Rooms 4 en suite (4 fmly) S €45-€50; D €75*
Facilities FTV TVL tea/coffee Cen ht Wi-fi ♨ 18 Riding ⚓
Extras Bottled water, magazines **Parking** 8 **Notes** LB ⊗

CO CORK

BALTIMORE   Map 1 B1

Rolfs Country House

★★★ ❀ RESTAURANT WITH ROOMS

Baltimore Hill
☎ 028 20289 📠 028 20930
e-mail: info@rolfscountryhouse.com
dir: *Before village turn sharp left up hill. House signed*

Situated on a hill above the fishing village of Baltimore, are the 400-year-old stone buildings that the Haffner family converted into accommodation. Available are ten traditionally furnished en suite bedrooms in annexe building, a cosy bar with an open fire, and a rustic restaurant on two levels. Dinner is served nightly during the high season and at weekends in the winter months; the menu features quality meats, artisan cheeses and fish landed at the busy pier. This is a lovely place to stay and the hosts are very friendly.

Rooms 10 annexe en suite S €40-€60; D €80-€100
Facilities tea/coffee Dinner available Cen ht Wi-fi
Parking 60 **Notes** LB Closed 20-26 Dec No coaches

BANDON   Map 1 B2

Glebe Country House

★★★★ 🏠 BED AND BREAKFAST

Ballinadee
☎ 021 4778294 & 086 3680202 📠 021 4778456
e-mail: info@glebecountryhouse.ie
dir: *Exit N71 at Innishannon Bridge signed Ballinadee, 8km (along river bank), left after village sign*

Situated in the charming village of Ballinadee this lovely bed and breakfast stands in well-kept gardens, and is run with great attention to detail. Antique furnishings predominate throughout this comfortable house, which has an elegant, lounge and dining room. Bedrooms are spacious and well appointed; the ground-floor room has access to the lovely garden. There is an interesting breakfast menu featuring local and garden produce. A country-house style dinner is available by arrangement.

Rooms 4 en suite (2 fmly) S €50-€55; D €80-€100*
Facilities TVL tea/coffee Dinner available Direct Dial Cen ht Wi-fi ch fac ⚓ **Parking** 10 **Notes** LB Closed 21 Dec-3 Jan

BLARNEY   Map 1 B2

PREMIER COLLECTION

Ashlee Lodge

★★★★★ GUEST HOUSE

Tower
☎ 021 4385346 📠 021 4385726
e-mail: info@ashleelodge.com
dir: *4km from Blarney on R617*

Ashlee Lodge is a purpose-built contemporary guest house, situated in the village of Tower, close to Blarney village and local pubs and restaurants. Bedrooms and suites are decorated with comfort and elegance in mind, some with whirlpool baths; one room has its own entrance. The extensive breakfast menu is memorable and includes home baking and quality local produce. Guests can unwind in the sauna or the outdoor hot tub. Transfers to the nearest airport and railway station can be arranged, and tee times can be booked at many of the nearby golf courses.

Rooms 10 en suite (2 fmly) (6 GF) **Facilities** STV FTV TVL tea/coffee Dinner available Direct Dial Cen ht Licensed Wi-fi Sauna Hot tub **Parking** 12

CLONAKILTY   Map 1 B2

Duvane House (W349405)

★★★★ 🏠 FARMHOUSE

Ballyduvane
☎ 023 8833129 Mrs N McCarthy
e-mail: duvanefarm@eircom.net
dir: *1km SW from Clonakilty on N71*

This Georgian farmhouse is on the N71 Skibbereen road. Bedrooms are comfortable and include four-poster and brass beds. There is a lovely sitting room and dining room, and a wide choice is available at breakfast (dinner is available by arrangement). Local amenities include Blue Flag beaches, riding and golf.

Rooms 4 en suite (1 fmly) **Facilities** TVL tea/coffee Dinner available Cen ht Wi-fi ♨ 9 Fishing Pool table ⚓ **Parking** 20 **Notes** LB ⊗ Closed Nov-Mar ⊕ 100 acres beef/dairy/mixed/sheep/horses

Springfield House (W330342)

★★★★ FARMHOUSE

Kilkern, Rathbarry, Castlefreke
☎ 023 8840622 📠 023 8840622 Mr & Mrs J Callanan
e-mail: jandmcallanan@eircom.net
dir: *N71 from Clonakilty for Skibbereen, 0.5km left after Pike Bar & signed for 5km*

A Georgian-style farmhouse in a picturesque rural setting. Maureen and John Callanan are genuine and welcoming hosts, and their comfortable home has well-appointed bedrooms and lovely gardens. You are welcome to watch the cows being milked. Home cooking is a speciality.

Rooms 4 rms (3 en suite) (2 fmly) **Facilities** TVL TV3B Cen ht **Parking** 8 **Notes** ⊗ Closed 20-27 Dec ⊕ 130 acres dairy/beef

An Sugan Guesthouse

★★★ GUEST HOUSE

Long Quay
☎ 023 8833719 & 023 8833498 📠 023 8833825
e-mail: info@ansugan.com
dir: *N71 Cork to Clonakilty, in Clonakilty straight over rdbt, take 1st left*

This historic house was built in the late 1800s and has been recently refurbished to a good standard. Bedrooms are attractively decorated and the dining room and guest sitting room are comfortably furnished. Breakfast is a real treat with Mrs O'Crowley's home baking and quality local produce. Guests check in at An Sugan Restaurant and bar next door where seafood and steaks are available throughout the day and evening.

Rooms 7 en suite (1 fmly) (1 GF) S €30-€40; D €70-€100 **Facilities** FTV iPod docking station Lounge tea/coffee Direct Dial Cen ht Wi-fi **Notes** ⊗ Closed 23-26 Dec RS 9-27 Jan

CORK | Map 1 B2

Crawford House

★ ★ ★ ★ GUEST HOUSE

Western Rd
☎ 021 4279000 📠 021 4279927
e-mail: info@crawfordguesthouse.com
dir: *0.8km from city on N22 (Cork-Killarney road), opposite University College*

Two adjoining Victorian houses form this friendly guest house, close to the university and city centre. Appointed in a contemporary style, the bedrooms have refreshing natural colour schemes featuring oak and marble furniture. Bathrooms are in the main spacious, some featuring power showers and jacuzzi baths. The attractive dining room and conservatory overlook a colourful patio. An interesting breakfast menu is available and there is ample secure parking to the rear.

Rooms 12 en suite (2 fmly) (2 GF) **Facilities** STV tea/coffee Direct Dial Cen ht Wi-fi **Parking** 12 **Notes** ⊗ Closed 22 Dec-15 Jan

Garnish House

★ ★ ★ ★ GUEST HOUSE

1 Aldergrove, Western Rd
☎ 021 4275111 📠 021 4273872
e-mail: garnish@iol.ie
web: www.garnish.ie
dir: *Opposite Cork University College*

Garnish House is a very welcoming house, and tea and scones are offered on arrival. Bedrooms vary in size and are furnished with guest comfort in mind, some with jacuzzi baths, fridges and safes. There is a cosy guest sitting room and a spacious bright dining room where breakfast is served. Expect a wide choice of dishes including home baked breads and preserves. Situated close to UCC and the city centre and convenient for the ferry and airport. Off-street car parking available.

Rooms 21 en suite (4 fmly) (1 GF) (10 smoking) **Facilities** STV FTV TVL tea/coffee Direct Dial Cen ht Wi-fi **Parking** 20 **Notes** ⊗

Killarney Guest House

★ ★ ★ ★ GUEST HOUSE

Western Rd
☎ 021 4270290 📠 021 4271010
e-mail: killarneyhouse@iol.ie
dir: *On N22 (Cork-Killarney) opposite University College*

Mrs O'Leary is the welcoming owner of this long-established guest house, which stands near Cork University and within walking distance of the city centre. Bedrooms are all comfortably furnished and brightly decorated. There is a comfortable lounge, and a spacious dining room with Wi-fi facilities. The spacious parking to the rear of the house can accommodate vans and trailers. Breakfast is a special treat cooked to order, including delicious freshly-baked scones and breads.

Rooms 19 en suite (3 fmly) **Facilities** STV TVL tea/coffee Direct Dial Cen ht Wi-fi **Parking** 15 **Notes** ⊗ Closed 24-26 Dec

DURRUS | Map 1 B2

Blairscove House & Restaurant

★ ★ ★ ★ ★ ◉ ◉ RESTAURANT WITH ROOMS

☎ 027 61127 📠 027 61487
e-mail: mail@blairscove.ie
dir: *From Durrus on R591 towards Crookhaven, 2.4km, house (blue gate) on right*

Blairscove comprises four elegant suites located in the courtyard of a Georgian country house outside the pretty village of Durrus near Bantry; each room is individually decorated in a contemporary style and has stunning views over Dunmanus Bay and the mountains. The restaurant is renowned for its wide range of hors d'oeuvres and its open wood-fire grill. The piano playing and candle light add to a unique dining experience.

Rooms 4 annexe en suite (1 fmly) (4 smoking) S €105-€160; D €150-€260* **Facilities** STV DVD tea/coffee Dinner available Direct Dial Cen ht 🛁 **Extras** Sherry - complimentary; wine - chargeable **Parking** 30 **Notes** ⊗ Closed Nov, Jan & Feb RS Dec wknds only No coaches Civ Wed 30

GOLEEN | Map 1 A1

AA GUEST ACCOMMODATION OF THE YEAR FOR IRELAND

The Heron's Cove

★ ★ ★ ★ ◉ 🛏 BED AND BREAKFAST

The Harbour
☎ 028 35225 & 0868 073072 📠 028 35422
e-mail: suehill@eircom.net
web: www.heronscove.com
dir: *By harbour in Goleen*

There are charming views of the harbour, fast-flowing stream and inland hills from Heron's Cove, at Ireland's most south-westerly point, near Mizen Head. Bedrooms are comfortably furnished, some with balconies. The restaurant and wine bar is run by chef-patron Sue Hill, where the freshest fish and local produce feature and guests can choose their own wines from the cocktail bar shelves. Breakfast is a special treat and the best of West Cork ingredients can be enjoyed while watching the herons on the cove. Heron's Cove is the AA Ireland's Guest Accommodation of the Year 2012-13.

Rooms 5 en suite (2 fmly) S €45-€60; D €70-€80 **Facilities** STV tea/coffee Dinner available Direct Dial Cen ht Licensed Wi-fi **Parking** 10 **Notes** LB ⊗ Closed Xmas & New Year RS Oct-Mar bookings essential

KINSALE | Map 1 B2

PREMIER COLLECTION

Friar's Lodge

★ ★ ★ ★ ★ GUEST HOUSE

5 Friars St
☎ 086 2895075 & 021 4777384 📠 021 4774363
e-mail: mtierney@indigo.ie
dir: *In town centre next to parish church*

This family-run and owned lodge was purpose-built and is situated near the Friary on a quiet street just a short walk from the historic town of Kinsale, renowned for its restaurants and bars. Bedrooms and suites are particularly spacious and furnished with guest comfort in mind. Being close to The Old Head Golf Club, and many others, there is storage for clubs and a drying room available with secure parking to the rear. There is a cosy lounge where a wine and snack menu is available. The elegant dining room is the setting for imaginative Irish breakfasts.

Rooms 18 en suite (2 fmly) (4 GF) **Facilities** STV tea/coffee Direct Dial Cen ht Lift Wi-fi **Parking** 20 **Notes** Closed Xmas ⊜

Save on B&Bs and Hotels. Book at **theAA.com/hotel**

CO CORK 425 IRELAND

The Old Bank House

★★★★★ GUEST HOUSE

11 Pearse St
☎ 021 4774075 📠 021 4774296
e-mail: info@oldbankhousekinsale.com
dir: *On main road into Kinsale from Cork Airport (R600). House on right at start of Kinsale, next to Post Office*

The Fitzgerald family has restored this delightful Georgian house to its former elegance. The en suite bedrooms, with period furniture and attractive decor, combine charm with modern comforts. Sailing, deep-sea fishing and horse riding can be arranged. Dinner is available at the sister Blue Haven Hotel.

Rooms 17 en suite (3 fmly) S €59-€95; D €70-€170*
Facilities FTV TVL tea/coffee Direct Dial Cen ht Lift Wi-fi **Conf** Max 15 Thtr 15 Class 10 Board 12 **Notes** LB ⊗ Closed 23-28 Dec

Rivermount House

★★★★★ BED AND BREAKFAST

Knocknabinny, Barrells Cross
☎ 021 4778033 📠 021 4778225
e-mail: info@rivermount.com
dir: *3km from Kinsale. R600 W towards Old Head of Kinsale, right at Barrells Cross*

There are spectacular views over the Bandon River from this charming modern family home which is close to the Old Head Golf links and a five minute drive from the bustling town of Kinsale. The smartly decorated range of bedrooms is furnished to a high standard with many thoughtful extras. Guests can relax in the contemporary conservatory lounge where an interesting snack menu is available; Claire's breakfast buffet is generous with speciality items cooked to order. Packed lunches can be arranged.

Rooms 6 en suite (3 fmly) (2 GF) **Facilities** TVL tea/coffee Direct Dial Cen ht Wi-fi **Parking** 10 **Notes** ⊗ Closed Dec-Jan

The White House

★★★★ ⊛ RESTAURANT WITH ROOMS

Pearse St, The Glen
☎ 021 4772125 📠 021 4772045
e-mail: whitehse@indigo.ie
dir: *In town centre*

Centrally located among the narrow, twisting streets of the charming town of Kinsale, this restaurant with rooms dates from 1850, and is a welcoming hostelry with modern, smart, comfortable bedrooms. The bar and bistro are open for lunch and dinner, and the varied menu features local fish and beef. The courtyard makes a perfect setting in summer and there is traditional music in the bar most nights.

Rooms 10 en suite (2 fmly) **Facilities** STV tea/coffee Dinner available Direct Dial Cen ht Wi-fi **Notes** LB ⊗ Closed 24-25 Dec

Woodlands House B&B

★★★★ BED AND BREAKFAST

Cappagh
☎ 021 4772633 📠 021 4772649
e-mail: info@woodlandskinsale.com
dir: *R605 NW from Kinsale, pass St Multose's Church, 0.5km on left*

Situated on a height overlooking the town, about a 10-minute walk away on the Bandon road, this new house offers great comfort and the personal attention of Brian and Valerie Hosford. Rooms are individually decorated, some with views towards the harbour. Breakfast is a particular pleasure, featuring home-made breads and preserves. Free Wi-fi is also available.

Rooms 6 en suite (1 fmly) (2 GF) S €50-€80; D €70-€100 **Facilities** FTV TVL tea/coffee Direct Dial Cen ht Wi-fi ♿ 18 **Parking** 8 **Notes** ⊗ Closed 16 Nov-Feb

MALLOW — Map 1 B2

Greenfield House B&B

★★★★ BED AND BREAKFAST

Navigation Rd
☎ 022 50231 & 08723 63535
e-mail: greenfieldhouse@hotmail.com
dir: *Exit N20 at Mallow rdbt onto N72 (Killarney road), last house, 300mtrs on left*

This purpose-built bed and breakfast is situated within walking distance of the town centre of Mallow, the railway station and Cork Racecourse. The bedrooms offer good space and are well appointed. There is a cosy guest sitting room and the breakfast menu includes gluten-free and vegetarian dishes as well as the full Irish breakfast. There is ample off-street car parking available.

Rooms 6 en suite (1 GF) S €40-€45; D €60-€70*
Facilities STV Lounge TVL tea/coffee Cen ht Wi-fi **Parking** 10 **Notes** ⊗

SHANAGARRY — Map 1 C2

Ballymaloe House

★★★★★ ⊛⊛ GUEST HOUSE

☎ 021 4652531 📠 021 4652021
e-mail: res@ballymaloe.ie
dir: *N25 onto R630 at Midleton rdbt. After 0.5m, left onto R631 to Cloyne. 2m after Cloyne on Ballycotton road*

This charming country house is on a 400-acre farm, part of the Geraldine estate in east Cork. Bedrooms upstairs in the main house retain many original features, and the ground floor and courtyard rooms have garden patios. The relaxing drawing room and dining rooms have enchanting old-world charm. Ballymaloe is renowned for excellent meals, many of which are created using ingredients produced on the farm. There are a craft shop, café, tennis and small golf course on the estate.

Rooms 21 en suite 9 annexe en suite (2 fmly) (3 GF) **Facilities** TVL Dinner available Direct Dial Cen ht Licensed Wi-fi ♦ ♿ ⚒ ♪ 9 Fishing Children's sand pit/slide **Conf** Max 200 Thtr 200 Class 50 Board 50 **Parking** 50 **Notes** Closed 23-26 Dec, 8-28 Jan Civ Wed 170

SKIBBEREEN — Map 1 B2

Ilenroy House

★★★ BED AND BREAKFAST

10 North St
☎ 028 22751 & 22193 📠 028 23228
e-mail: ilenroyhouse@gmail.com
dir: *90mtrs from main street on N71 (Clonakilty road)*

Conveniently situated in the centre of Skibbereen this well maintained house has comfortable bedrooms that are equipped to a high standard. This is an excellent base from which to tour South West Cork and the Islands.

Rooms 5 en suite (2 smoking) S €35-€40; D €70-€75*
Facilities STV tea/coffee Direct Dial Cen ht **Notes** ⊗

YOUGHAL — Map 1 C2

PREMIER COLLECTION

Ahernes

★★★★★ ⊛ ⬛ GUEST HOUSE

163 North Main St
☎ 024 92424 ▤ 024 93633
e-mail: ahernes@eircom.net

This property has been run by the Fitzgibbon family for almost 80 years. Located at the edge of the walled town of which Sir Walter Raleigh was once Mayor. It is a warm and friendly house, offering high quality accommodation in the original townhouse on the quiet main street and in more recently built spacious rooms to the rear. Ahernes is also home to a renowned bar and restaurant, specialising in seafood. Resident guests also have the use of a cosy fire-lit lounge. The breakfast menu is varied, certain to set one up for the day, perhaps in preparation for a round of golf on the many courses in the region. Good secure car-parking is available nearby.

Rooms 12 en suite (2 fmly) (3 GF) **Facilities** FTV tea/coffee Dinner available Direct Dial Cen ht Licensed Wi-fi **Conf** Max 20 Thtr 20 Class 20 Board 12 **Parking** 20 **Notes** Closed 23-26 Dec

CO DONEGAL

CARRIGANS — Map 1 C5

Mount Royd Country Home

★★★★ ⬛ BED AND BREAKFAST

☎ 074 914 0163 ▤ 074 914 0400
e-mail: jmartin@mountroyd.com
dir: From Letterkenny on N14. At Dry Arch rdbt 2nd exit onto N13. At next rdbt 2nd exit onto N14 towards Lifford. Left at R236 to Carrigans. Or from Derry take A40 to Carrigans

Mount Royd is a creeper-clad house with lovely gardens in the pretty village of Carrigans a short distance from Derry. The friendly Martins have brought hospitality to new heights - nothing is too much trouble for them. Breakfast is a feast of choices including home baking and eggs from their own hens. Bedrooms are very comfortable, with lots of personal touches.

Rooms 4 en suite (1 fmly) (1 GF) D €65-€75 **Facilities** FTV TVL tea/coffee Cen ht Wi-fi **Parking** 7 **Notes** LB ⊗ No Children 12yrs RS Nov-Feb ⊠

DONEGAL — Map 1 B5

The Arches Country House

★★★★ BED AND BREAKFAST

Lough Eske
☎ 074 972 2029
e-mail: archescountryhse@eircom.net
dir: 5km from Donegal. Signed off N15, 300mtrs past garage turn left

This family-run guest house is set in an idyllic location on an elevated site overlooking Lough Eske, and is a ten minute drive from Donegal town. Bedrooms are very comfortable, some with seating areas making the most of the views. A guest lounge is available, perfect for a relaxing read or surfing the web. The breakfast menu includes the traditional Irish Fry, but other lighter options are also available. Noreen is a very hospitable and welcoming hostess.

Rooms 6 en suite (3 fmly) (2 GF) **Facilities** STV FTV TVL tea/coffee Cen ht Wi-fi **Parking** 10 **Notes** ⊗

Ardeevin

★★★★ BED AND BREAKFAST

Lough Eske, Barnesmore
☎ 074 972 1790 & 0868 229753 ▤ 074 972 1790
e-mail: seanmcginty@eircom.net
dir: N15 Derry road from Donegal for 5km, left at junct after garage for Ardeevin & Lough Eske & signs for Ardeevin

Enjoying commanding views over Lough Eske, Ardeevin has been welcoming guests for over four decades. Recently refurbished, this is a very comfortable home with individually designed and decorated bedrooms that have many thoughtful additional touches. Some are quite spacious, but they are all very comfortable. The varied breakfast is tempting and features Mary McGinty's home baking. This house is set in beautifully landscaped gardens.

Rooms 6 en suite (2 fmly) (2 GF) S €45-€50; D €65-€70 **Facilities** STV FTV TVL tea/coffee Cen ht Wi-fi **Parking** 10 **Notes** ⊗ Closed Dec-mid Mar

Ard Na Breatha

★★★★ ⬛ GUEST HOUSE

Drumrooske Middle
☎ 074 972 2288 & 086 842 1330 ▤ 074 974 0720
e-mail: info@ardnabreatha.com
web: www.ardnabreatha.com
dir: From Donegal onto N56 (Killybegs road), 200yds, 1st right, signed Ard na Breatha & Lough Eske. To mini-rdbt, right at XL Shop, 0.5m, under bypass, Ard na Breatha at top of hill

This family-run guest house is just a short drive from the town centre. Bedrooms are all well-appointed and very comfortable, with a relaxing lounge for residents. Evening meals are served in the popular restaurant at weekends and during high season, but can be arranged for

residents at other times. The menu features much of the produce from the family farm which surrounds the house.

Rooms 6 en suite (1 fmly) (3 GF) S €40-€69; D €70-€110 **Facilities** FTV Lounge TVL tea/coffee Dinner available Direct Dial Cen ht Licensed Wi-fi ⅃ ♿ Swimming pool & gym available at local hotel **Conf** Thtr 20 Class 30 Board 20 **Parking** 16 **Notes** LB Closed Nov-Jan

DUNKINEELY — Map 1 B5

Castle Murray House and Restaurant

★★★★ ⊛ RESTAURANT WITH ROOMS

St Johns Point
☎ 074 973 7022 ▤ 074 973 7330
e-mail: info@castlemurray.com
dir: From Donegal take N56 towards Killybegs. Left to Dunkineely

Situated on the coast road of St Johns Point, this charming family-run restaurant with rooms overlooks McSwynes Bay and the castle. The bedrooms are individually decorated and appointed with guest comfort very much in mind, as is the cosy bar and sun lounge. There is a strong French influence in the cooking; locally landed fish, and prime lamb and beef are featured on the menus. Closed dates are subject to change, please telephone for details.

Rooms 10 en suite (2 fmly) S €60-€70; D €110-€130* **Facilities** FTV DVD tea/coffee Dinner available Direct Dial Cen ht Wi-fi ♿ **Extras** Home-made cookies **Parking** 40 **Notes** LB RS wknds Oct-Mar, 5 days May/Jun/Sep, 7 days Jul/Aug Civ Wed 80

DUBLIN

DUBLIN — Map 1 D4

PREMIER COLLECTION

Butlers Town House

★★★★★ GUEST HOUSE

44 Lansdowne Rd, Ballsbridge
☎ 01 6674022 ▤ 01 6673960
e-mail: reservations@butlers-hotel.com

This fine Victorian house, in the heart of Dublin's Embassy belt, has been restored and retains the charm of a gracious family home. Bedrooms are air-conditioned and individually furnished and decorated. The public areas are particularly relaxing and there is a charming and comfortable drawing room and conservatory style breakfast room. Limited off-street parking is available.

Rooms 20 en suite **Facilities** STV FTV Direct Dial Licensed Wi-fi **Parking** 14 **Notes** ⊗ Closed 22-28 Dec

Save on B&Bs and Hotels. Book at **theAA.com/hotel**

DUBLIN 427 **IRELAND**

PREMIER COLLECTION

Glenogra Town House

★★★★★ GUEST HOUSE

64 Merrion Rd, Ballsbridge
☎ 01 6683661 ⬚ 01 6683698
e-mail: info@glenogra.com
web: www.glenogra.com
dir: *Opposite Royal Dublin Showgrounds & Four Seasons Hotel*

This fine 19th-century red brick house is situated across from the RDS and close to the Aviva Stadium. The bedrooms are comfortably appointed and include many thoughtful extras; three bedrooms are on the ground floor. There is an elegant drawing room and dining room, and the interesting breakfast menu offers a range of dishes. Secure parking is available, and The Aircoach and city-centre buses stop in Merrion Road; the DART rail is around the corner.

Rooms 13 en suite (1 fmly) (3 GF) S €59-€109;
D €69-€199* **Facilities** STV TVL tea/coffee Direct Dial
Cen ht Wi-fi **Parking** 10 **Notes** LB ⊗ Closed 23-28 Dec

PREMIER COLLECTION

Harrington Hall

★★★★★ GUEST HOUSE

69-70 Harcourt St
☎ 01 4753497 ⬚ 01 4754544
e-mail: harringtonhall@eircom.net
web: www.harringtonhall.com
dir: *St Stephen's Green via O'Connell St, in Earlsfort Ter pass National Concert Hall & right onto Hatch St, right onto Harcourt St*

This restored Georgian house is on a one-way street system, just off the south west corner of St Stephen's Green in the centre of the city. The spacious bedrooms are well appointed and include comfortable suites. A lovely plasterwork ceiling adorns the relaxing drawing room. An extensive breakfast menu is served in the basement dining room. A lift, porter service and limited off-street parking is available.

Rooms 28 en suite (3 fmly) (3 GF) **Facilities** STV tea/coffee Direct Dial Cen ht Lift **Conf** Max 20 Thtr 20 Class 6 Board 12 **Parking** 8 **Notes** ⊗

Charleville Lodge Guest House

★★★★ GUEST HOUSE

268/272 North Circular Rd, Phibsborough
☎ 01 8386633 ⬚ 01 8385854
e-mail: info@charlevillelodge.ie
web: www.charlevillelodge.ie
dir: *N from O'Connell St to Phibsborough, left fork at St Peter's Church, house 250mtrs on left*

Situated close to the city centre near Phoenix Park, this elegant terrace of Victorian houses has been restored to a high standard. The two interconnecting lounges are welcoming, and the smart dining room offers a choice of breakfasts. Bedrooms are very comfortable with pleasant decor, and there is a secure car park.

Rooms 30 en suite (2 fmly) (4 GF) S €25-€90;
D €55-€150 (room only)* **Facilities** STV FTV TVL Direct Dial Cen ht Licensed Wi-fi ↧ 18 **Conf** Max 10 Thtr 10 Class 10 Board 10 **Parking** 18 **Notes** LB ⊗ Closed 21-26 Dec

Glenshandan Lodge

★★★★ GUEST ACCOMMODATION

Dublin Rd, Swords
☎ 01 8408838 & 0765 92114 ⬚ 01 8408838
e-mail: glenshandan@eircom.net
dir: *Beside Topaz on airport side of Swords Main St*

Glenshandan Lodge is a warm and friendly family-run guest accommodation with hospitable proprietors and good facilities. Bedrooms come in a number of sizes, and are particularly suited to large family groups. They are comfortable and well appointed, with a relaxing seating area on the mezzanine, together with a limited kitchen area. Located on the south side of Swords, Dublin Airport is easily accessible. There is ample parking available, and buses to the airport and the city pass the front door. Facilities for dogs can be arranged.

Rooms 9 en suite (5 fmly) (5 GF) **Facilities** FTV TVL tea/coffee Cen ht Wi-fi ch fac ↧ 36 **Conf** Max 20 **Parking** 10 **Notes** Closed Xmas & New Year

Ardagh House

★★★ GUEST HOUSE

1 Highfield Rd, Rathgar
☎ 01 4977068 ⬚ 01 4973991
e-mail: enquiries@ardahouse.com
dir: *S of city centre through Rathmines*

Ardagh House is an early 19th-century house with modern additions, and stands in a premier residential area on the outskirts of the city close to local restaurants and pubs. It retains many original features and has a relaxing lounge that overlooks a delightful garden. There is an attractive dining room where hearty breakfasts are served at the individual tables. The comfortable bedrooms vary in size. Ample off-street parking is available.

Rooms 19 en suite (4 fmly) (1 GF) S €55-€95;
D €70-€150 **Facilities** FTV TVL tea/coffee Direct Dial Cen ht Wi-fi **Parking** 20 **Notes** ⊗ Closed 22 Dec-3 Jan

DUBLIN *continued*

Leeson Bridge Guest House

★★★ GUEST HOUSE

1 Upper Leeson St
☎ 01 6681000 & 6682255 ▤ 01 6681444
e-mail: info@leesonbridgehouse.ie
dir: *At junct of N11 & N7, Leeson St*

This guest house is located right by Leeson Street Bridge, close to the city centre and easily accessible from the ferry ports. Centred around a Georgian house, many of its original architectural features are retained. It offers a range of en suite bedroom styles, some with spa baths, sauna or galley kitchenette. Residents have access to ample car parking at the rear. A take-away breakfast is offered to early morning departing guests.

Rooms 20 en suite (1 fmly) (2 GF) (10 smoking) Facilities STV FTV TVL tea/coffee Direct Dial Cen ht Lift Wi-fi Fishing Parking 18 Notes ⊗

CO DUBLIN

RUSH   Map 1 D4

Sandyhills Bed & Breakfast

★★★★ ⬢ BED AND BREAKFAST

Sandyhills
☎ 01 8437148 & 086 242 3660 ▤ 01 8437148
e-mail: mary@sandyhills.ie
dir: *Exit M1 onto N1, right to Lusk on R127. 3rd exit at rdbt in Lusk to Rush. Right towards church car park, right to Corrs Ln, then 2nd right*

Set just a stroll from the sea and the village of Rush, within easy reach of Dublin Airport, Sandyhills has spacious bedrooms, well equipped with thoughtful extra facilities. Breakfast is a special treat featuring local produce along with Mary Buckley's preserves, freshly baked cakes and breads. There is a cosy sitting room and a lovely garden with secure car parking.

Rooms 5 en suite (2 fmly) Facilities Direct Dial Cen ht Wi-fi Parking 20 Notes ⊗ No Children 12yrs

CO GALWAY

CLIFDEN   Map 1 A4

Ardmore House (L589523)

★★★★ FARMHOUSE

Sky Rd
☎ 095 21221 & 076 6030227 Mr & Mrs J Mullen
e-mail: info@ardmore-house.com
web: www.ardmore-house.com
dir: *N59 from Galway to Clifden. Just N of Clifden centre follow signs on left for 'Sky Road', 5km, house on left*

Ardmore is set among the wild scenery of Connemara between hills and the sea on the Sky Road. Bedrooms are attractively decorated and the house is very comfortable throughout. A pathway leads from the house to the coast.

A good hearty breakfast is provided featuring Kathy's home baking.

Rooms 6 en suite (3 fmly) (6 GF) D €70-€80*
Facilities STV FTV TVL tea/coffee Cen ht Wi-fi Parking 8
Notes LB ⊗ Closed Oct-Mar ⊜ 25 acres non-working

Faul House (L650475)

★★★★ FARMHOUSE

Ballyconneely Rd
☎ 095 21239 ▤ 095 21998 Mrs K Conneely
e-mail: info@ireland.com
dir: *1.5km from town right at rugby pitch signed Rockglen Hotel*

A fine modern farmhouse stands on a quiet and secluded road overlooking Clifden Bay. It is smart and comfortable with large bedrooms, all well furnished and with good views. Kathleen offers a hearty breakfast with home baking. There are Connemara ponies available for trekking.

Rooms 6 en suite (3 fmly) (3 GF) Facilities FTV TVL tea/coffee Cen ht Wi-fi Parking 10 Notes Closed Nov-26 Mar ⊜ 35 acres sheep/ponies/hens/ducks

Mallmore House

★★★★ BED AND BREAKFAST

Ballyconneely Rd
☎ 095 21460
e-mail: info@mallmore.com
dir: *1.5km from Clifden towards Ballyconneely take 1st right*

A charming Georgian-style house built in the 17th century and lovingly restored by Alan and Kathleen. It is situated close to the town and has a beautiful garden and mature woodland, and overlooks Clifden Bay. Bedrooms are spacious and very well appointed with antique furniture. The drawing room is delightfully relaxing with a turf fire. There is a wide choice available at breakfast including home baking and locally smoked fish. Mallmore is a lovely place to stay and enjoy peace and quiet in the heart of Connemara.

Rooms 6 en suite (2 fmly) (6 GF) D €60-€80*
Facilities FTV DVD Lounge tea/coffee Cen ht Wi-fi
Parking 15 Notes ⊗ Closed Nov-1 Mar ⊜

Ben View House

★★★ GUEST HOUSE

Bridge St
☎ 095 21256 ▤ 095 21226
e-mail: benviewhouse@ireland.com
dir: *Enter town on N59, opposite Esso fuel station*

This house is well located in the centre of the town with ample on-street parking. Dating from 1824, it offers good quality accommodation at a moderate cost. The breakfast room and lounge feature an old world atmosphere, with antique furniture and sparkling silverware in everyday use.

Rooms 10 rms (9 en suite) (3 fmly) Facilities TVL TV9B tea/coffee Cen ht Notes ⊗

GALWAY   Map 1 B3

Marian Lodge Guest House

★★★★ GUEST HOUSE

Knocknacarra Rd, Salthill Upper
☎ 091 521678 ▤ 091 528103
e-mail: celine@iol.ie
dir: *From Galway to Salthill on R336, through Salthill, 1st right after Spinnaker Hotel into Knocknacarra Rd*

This large modern house is only 50 metres from the seafront. The fully equipped bedrooms have orthopaedic beds and en suite facilities. There is also a lounge and separate breakfast room available.

Rooms 6 en suite (4 fmly) Facilities STV TVL tea/coffee Direct Dial Cen ht Parking 10 Notes ⊗ No Children 3yrs Closed 23-28 Dec

Clochard Bed & Breakfast

★★★ BED AND BREAKFAST

4 Spires Gardens, Shantalla Rd
☎ 091 521533 & 086 0523132 ▤ 091 522536
e-mail: clochard@eircom.net
dir: *N59 (Galway ring road) after Quincentennial Bridge, left at 4th lights, right into Shantalla Rd. Spires Gdns opposite school*

Clochard is part of a small development in the Galway City Council award-winning Spires Gardens which is located within walking distance from the Galway University College and Hospital and close to the city centre and Salthill. Bedrooms, guest sitting and dining room are attractively decorated and comfortably furnished. Freshly-baked scones and barm brack loaf are included with a substantial breakfast. Guests can be dropped off at the shuttle bus for the Aran Island Ferry, and routes for day trips are organised with maps supplied by the Hanlon family.

Rooms 4 en suite (2 fmly) (1 GF) Facilities FTV TVL tea/coffee Cen ht Wi-fi Parking 4 Notes ⊗ No Children Closed Dec-Feb

SPIDDAL (AN SPIDÉAL)   Map 1 B3

Ardmor Country House

★★★★ BED AND BREAKFAST

Greenhill
☎ 091 553145
e-mail: ardmorcountryhouse@yahoo.com
dir: *On R336 (coast road) from Galway, 1km W of Spiddal*

There are superb views of Galway Bay and the Aran Islands from this beautifully appointed luxury home. Bedrooms are spacious and there are relaxing lounges, a well-stocked library and delightful gardens.

Rooms 5 en suite (2 fmly) (5 GF) **Facilities** TVL tea/coffee Cen ht Wi-fi ch fac **Parking** 20 **Notes** ⊗ Closed Dec-Feb RS Mar-Nov ⊜

Ard Aoibhinn

★★★ BED AND BREAKFAST

☎ 091 553179
e-mail: aoibhinn@gofree.indigo.ie
dir: *500mtrs W of Spiddal village on right hand side of R336 Coast road*

This long established bed and breakfast is a modern bungalow set back from the road in a lovely garden. It is a five minute walk from the Gaeltacht village (Irish language speaking area) of An Spidéal, and it has benefited from a recent renovation and refurbishment programme. The lounge features a picture window with panoramic views of Galway Bay towards the Aran Islands. Bedrooms are well appointed and comfortable, with beverage making facilities. This is an ideal base for touring Connemara or a day trip to the islands.

Rooms 5 en suite (1 fmly) (5 GF) D €60-€70*
Facilities FTV TVL tea/coffee Cen ht Wi-fi **Parking** 5
Notes LB ⊗ Closed Xmas wk

CO KERRY

DINGLE (AN DAINGEAN)   Map 1 A2

PREMIER COLLECTION

Emlagh House

★★★★★ GUEST ACCOMMODATION

☎ 066 9152345 📠 066 9152369
e-mail: info@emlaghhouse.com
web: www.emlaghhouse.com
dir: *Pass rdbt at entrance to town, turn left. House ahead*

An impressive Georgian-style house, on the outskirts of Dingle, where attention to detail and luxury combine to make a stay memorable. The stylish drawing room, conservatory and dining room overlook the harbour. Bedrooms and bathrooms are individually decorated to a high standard with antique furniture, with ground floor rooms having private patios. Breakfasts are very special here and make good use of fresh local produce.

Rooms 10 en suite (1 fmly) (4 GF) S €95-€125;
D €160-€220 **Facilities** STV Direct Dial Cen ht Lift
Licensed Wi-fi ♨ 18 **Extras** Fruit - complimentary
Parking 20 **Notes** LB ⊗ No Children 8yrs Closed 5
Nov-10 Mar Civ Wed 35

PREMIER COLLECTION

Gormans Clifftop House & Restaurant

★★★★★ ⊛ GUEST HOUSE

Glaise Bheag, Ballydavid
☎ 066 9155162 & 083 0033133 📠 066 9155003
e-mail: info@gormans-clifftophouse.com
dir: *R559 to An Mhuirioch, turn right at T-junct, N for 3km*

Sile and Vincent Gorman's guest house and restaurant is perched over the cliffs on the western tip of the Slea Head Peninsula near Ballydavid village. The beauty of the rugged coastline, rhythm of the sea and the sun going down on Smerwick Harbour can be enjoyed over a delicious dinner in the smart dining room. The menu includes produce from the garden, local seafood and lamb. Bedrooms are comfortably proportioned and thoughtfully equipped and have breathtaking views of the ocean or mountains, the ground floor rooms are adapted for the less mobile. Bracing cliff walks can be accessed across from the house. Gormans was last year's AA Guest Accommodation of the Year for Ireland (2011-2012).

Rooms 8 en suite (2 fmly) (4 GF) **Facilities** tea/coffee
Dinner available Direct Dial Cen ht Licensed Wi-fi
Bicycles for hire **Parking** 15 **Notes** LB ⊗ Closed 24-26
Dec RS Oct-Mar reservation only Civ Wed 25

An Bothar Pub

★★★ GUEST HOUSE

Cuas, Ballydavid
☎ 066 9155342
e-mail: botharpub@eircom.net

This traditional guest house and pub is located close to the town of Dingle on the Slea Head Drive at the foot of Mount Brandon. The Walsh family has been welcoming guests for three generations and the pub is famous for music and dancing. Fresh fish, their own farm produce and home baking are included on the daily menu. Walking, cycling, horse riding, golf, swimming and windsurfing are all locally available activities. The comfortable bedrooms are attractively decorated and furnished, some suitable for families.

Rooms 7 en suite (2 fmly) **Facilities** STV FTV TVL Dinner available Direct Dial Cen ht Licensed Pool table **Parking** 30 **Notes** ⊗ Closed 24-25 Dec RS Oct-Mar No evening meals available

Barr na Sraide Inn

★★★ GUEST HOUSE

Upper Main St
☎ 066 9151331 & 9151446 📠 066 9151446
e-mail: barrnasraide@eircom.net

Barr na Sraide Inn is a family-run guest house which has its very own traditional pub on site and free car parking at the rear. It is situated in the heart of Dingle town and just a stroll from many restaurants, traditional music venues and shops. The en suite bedrooms are attractively decorated and comfortably furnished. There is a cosy guest sitting room and a hearty breakfast can be chosen from the breakfast menu which includes Patricia's home-baked breads.

Rooms 26 en suite (7 fmly) (4 GF) S €35-€60;
D €70-€110 **Facilities** STV FTV TVL tea/coffee Direct Dial
Cen ht Licensed Wi-fi ♨ 18 Riding 🅿 **Parking** 18
Notes ⊗ Closed 19-25 Dec

Hurleys Farm *(Q392080)*

★★★ FARMHOUSE

An Dooneen, Kilcooley
☎ 066 9155112 & 0862 142580   Ms Hurley
e-mail: andooneen@eircom.net
dir: *11km W of Dingle town on Ballydavid-Muirioch road*

Hurleys Farm is tucked away behind the church in Kilcooley, 1.5 kilometres from the beach and sheltered by Mount Brandon, a popular place for hill walkers. Accommodation includes a cosy TV room, dining room and comfortable en suite bedrooms, graced by some special pieces of high quality furniture. The whole area is rich in early historic and prehistoric relics: ogham stones, ring forts and the famous dry-stone masonry 'beehive' huts.

Rooms 5 en suite (2 GF) **Facilities** TVL Cen ht **Parking** 6
Notes ⊗ Closed Nov-Mar ⊜ 38 acres non-working

GLENBEIGH   Map 1 A2

Mountain View

★★★ BED AND BREAKFAST

Droum West
☎ 066 9768541 & 087 6241658 📠 066 9768541
e-mail: mountainstage@eircom.net
dir: *4km W of Glenbeigh, 200mtrs off N70*

The O'Riordan's bed and breakfast is an ideal place to stay when touring the Ring of Kerry; it is located just off the N70 road between Glenbeigh and Kells. There is a lovely large garden and ample car parking. The bedrooms are well appointed, three of them are on the ground floor and there are spacious rooms to accommodate families. There are lovely views of the mountains from the comfortable guest sitting room and Anne serves a substantial breakfast.

Rooms 4 en suite (4 fmly) (3 GF) S €40; D €60-€70
Facilities STV FTV TVL Dinner available Cen ht Wi-fi 🅿
Parking 8 **Notes** LB ⊗ Closed Nov-Feb RS Mar

KENMARE — Map 1 B2

Shelburne Lodge

★★★★ GUEST HOUSE

Cork Rd
☎ 064 6641013 ◫ 064 6642135
e-mail: shelburnekenmare@eircom.net
dir: On Cork road (R569), 500mtrs from Kenmare centre

Dating from the mid 18th century, this long established guest house is well deserving of its reputation. Located within easy walking distance of the town, it offers a range of individually decorated bedrooms, together with reception rooms that ooze comfort and relaxation. Breakfast is a highlight of a stay, with a wide selection of fruits, preserves and home bakery, complementing a menu of cooked items that feature carefully selected local and artisan foods.

Rooms 8 en suite 2 annexe en suite (1 fmly) S €70-€95; D €100-€165* **Facilities** STV Direct Dial Cen ht Wi-fi ☕ **Parking** 20 **Notes** ⊗ Closed 16 Nov-15 Mar

Davitts

★★★★ GUEST HOUSE

Henry St
☎ 064 6642741 ◫ 064 6642757
e-mail: info@davitts-kenmare.com
dir: On N22 (Cork-Killarney rd) at Kenmare junct (R569). In town centre

This family-run guest house is situated in the centre of the heritage town of Kenmare. With the popular Davitts Bar Bistro at street level serving excellent food, it is the perfect location for an enjoyable holiday all under the one roof. The spacious, well-appointed bedrooms are decorated in a contemporary style, and there is a cosy sitting room available on the first floor, with secure parking to the rear.

Rooms 11 en suite (1 fmly) **Facilities** STV TVL Dinner available Direct Dial Cen ht Licensed Wi-fi **Parking** 4 **Notes** ⊗ Closed 1-14 Nov & 24-26 Dec

Harbour View

★★★★ BED AND BREAKFAST

Castletownbere Rd, Dauros
☎ 064 6641755 & 087 7684564
e-mail: maureenmccarthy@eircom.net
dir: From Kenmare on N71 towards Glengarriffe, right onto Castletownbere Haven road (R571), 1st right after bridge. Harbour View 6.5km on left

This charming house is situated on the seashore, with lovely views of Kenmare Bay and the mountains beyond. Maureen McCarthy is a cheerful, caring hostess with infectious enthusiasm, and her attention to detail is evident throughout the comfortable bedrooms. The breakfast menu includes fresh and smoked seafood and the home baking is excellent.

Rooms 4 en suite (1 fmly) (4 GF) **Facilities** STV TVL tea/coffee Cen ht Wi-fi **Parking** 6 **Notes** ⊗ Closed Oct-Apr ⊜

Kenmare House B&B

★★★★ BED AND BREAKFAST

Sneem Rd
☎ 064 6641283 ◫ 064 6642765
e-mail: info@kenmarehousebandb.com
dir: From Kenmare left onto N70 towards Sneem & Ring of Kerry. House 500mtrs on right

Annagry House is owned and run by the O'Sullivan family; it is situated on the Ring of Kerry road (N70) only minutes from Kenmare town. Bedrooms are spacious and comfortably furnished to accommodate families and there are two ground floor rooms. The relaxing guest sitting room has books, maps and information on the area. The extensive breakfast menu includes Fionnuala's home baking, and Danny will advise on tours and activities available

Rooms 6 en suite (3 fmly) (2 GF) **Facilities** FTV TVL tea/coffee Cen ht Wi-fi **Parking** 11 **Notes** ⊗ Closed 26 Oct-Apr ⊜

Muxnaw Lodge

★★★★ BED AND BREAKFAST

Casletownbere Rd
☎ 064 6641252 & 087 2922895
e-mail: muxnaw@eircom.net

Located on the Castletownbere Road, within easy walking distance of Kenmare Town, this warm and friendly house is a former hunting lodge dating from the early 19th century. It is set on an elevated site in mature gardens. Bedrooms and en suites are individually decorated and have benefited from recent refurbishment, with some enjoying views of the Kenmare River. The guest lounge retains much of its original character, with a bright and airy sun room recently added. Ample parking available to the rear.

Rooms 5 en suite (1 fmly) S €40; D €70-€90* **Facilities** STV TVL tea/coffee Cen ht Wi-fi ☕ **Parking** 5 **Notes** ⊗ Closed 24-25 Dec ⊜

Sea Shore Farm Guest House

★★★★ GUEST HOUSE

Tubrid
☎ 064 6641270 & 6641675 ◫ 064 6641270
e-mail: seashore@eircom.net
dir: 1.6km from Kenmare off N70 Ring of Kerry road. Signed at junct N70 & N71

Overlooking Kenmare Bay on the Ring of Kerry road, this modern farm guest house is close to town and has spacious bedrooms. Ground-floor rooms open onto the patio and have easier access. Guests are welcome to enjoy the farm walks through the fields to the shore, and salmon and trout fishing on the Roughty River. There is a comfortable sitting room and dining room and a delightful garden.

Rooms 6 en suite (2 fmly) (2 GF) S €55-€80; D €90-€120* **Facilities** FTV Lounge tea/coffee Direct Dial Cen ht Wi-fi **Extras** Speciality toiletries, snacks - complimentary **Parking** 10 **Notes** ⊗ Closed Nov-19 Mar

Whispering Pines

Ⓤ

Bell Height
☎ 064 6641194 & 087 2861183
e-mail: wpines@eircom.net
dir: S of town on N71

Currently the rating for this establishment is not confirmed. This may be due to a change of ownership or because it has only recently joined the AA rating scheme.

Rooms 4 en suite (3 fmly) (4 GF) **Facilities** TVL tea/coffee Cen ht Wi-fi **Parking** 8 **Notes** ⊗ No Children 5yrs Closed Oct-Mar ⊜

KILGARVAN — Map 1 B2

Birchwood

★★★★ BED AND BREAKFAST

Church Ground
☎ 064 6685473 ◫ 064 6685570
e-mail: birchwood1@eircom.net
dir: 500mtrs E of Kilgarvan on R569

Birchwood stands in extensive gardens facing a natural forest and backed by the Mangerton Mountains, an area ideal for hill-walking and touring. The MacDonnells are caring hosts in this tranquil location, and offer comfortable and attractively decorated bedrooms. The nearby Rivers Roughty and Slaheny provide good salmon and trout fishing.

Rooms 5 en suite (3 fmly) **Facilities** FTV TVL tea/coffee Cen ht **Parking** 6 **Notes** ⊗ ⊜

KILLARNEY — Map 1 B2

PREMIER COLLECTION

Fairview Guest House

★★★★★ GUEST HOUSE

College St
☎ 064 6634164 ◫ 064 6671777
e-mail: info@fairviewkillarney.com
dir: In town centre off College St

This smart guest house is situated in the town centre and close to the bus/railway station. Great attention to detail has been taken in the furnishing and design of the property. Bedrooms come in a range of types including some with air conditioning and jacuzzi baths. They all ensure guest comfort with quality furnishings and fittings. There is a lift to all floors and the impressive penthouse suite enjoys views over the town towards the Kerry mountains. There is a relaxing guest sitting area and the breakfast menu offers a selection of dishes cooked to order. Local activities and excursions include lake cruises, championship golf courses and the Killarney National Park.

Rooms 29 en suite (1 GF) (2 smoking) **Facilities** STV TVL tea/coffee Dinner available Direct Dial Cen ht Lift Licensed Wi-fi Jacuzzi suites available **Parking** 11

Foleys Town House

★★★★★ GUEST HOUSE

22/23 High St
☎ 064 6631217 ▤ 064 6634683
e-mail: info@foleystownhouse.com
dir: In town centre

Charming, individually-designed bedrooms are a feature of this well-established townhouse right in the centre of the town. They are all well appointed and decorated with elegance. A warm welcome is assured at this property which is family-owned and run by Carol Hartnett who is also the chef in the adjoining popular bar and restaurant that specialises in seafood. There is a relaxing first floor lounge reserved for guests, together with secure off-street parking to the rear.

Rooms 28 en suite **Facilities** STV TVL tea/coffee Dinner available Direct Dial Cen ht Lift Licensed Wi-fi **Parking** 60 **Notes** LB ⊗ Closed 6 Nov-16 Mar

Old Weir Lodge

★★★★★ GUEST HOUSE

Muckross Rd
☎ 064 6635593 ▤ 064 6635583
e-mail: oldweirlodge@eircom.net
web: www.oldweirlodge.com
dir: On N71 (Muckross Rd), 500mtrs from Killarney

This purpose-built Tudor-style guest house is situated within walking distance of the town on the road to the National Park and the INEC Centre. There are two relaxing lounges, and the dining room is a lovely bright area with a conservatory that overlooks the rear garden. The spacious and comfortable bedrooms are equipped to a high standard; those upstairs can be accessed by lift. A varied range of tasty options is available at breakfast including Maureen's freshly baked breads, and special dietary requirements can be facilitated with notice. Dermot will help with boat trips on the Killarney Lakes, golf, fishing and walking tours. There is also a drying room and ample off-road parking.

Rooms 30 en suite (2 fmly) (6 GF) **Facilities** STV TVL tea/coffee Dinner available Direct Dial Cen ht Lift Licensed Wi-fi ⌁ 18 **Parking** 30 **Notes** ⊗ Closed 23-26 Dec

Ashville House

★★★★ GUEST HOUSE

Rock Rd
☎ 064 6636405 ▤ 064 6636778
e-mail: info@ashvillekillarney.com
dir: In town centre. Exit at N end of High St into Rock Rd

This inviting house is just a stroll from the town centre and near the N22 (Tralee road). Bedrooms are comfortably furnished, and there is a pleasant sitting room and dining room. There is a private car park, and tours can be arranged.

Rooms 12 en suite (4 fmly) (4 GF) S €50-€100; D €70-€110* **Facilities** STV FTV TVL tea/coffee Direct Dial Cen ht Wi-fi **Parking** 13 **Notes** LB ⊗ Closed Nov-1 Mar

Killarney Villa Country House & Gardens

★★★★ BED AND BREAKFAST

Mallow Rd
☎ 064 6631878 ▤ 064 6631878
web: www.killarneyvilla.com
dir: From Killarney take N22 E towards Macroom & Cork. At 2nd rdbt left onto N72 signed Mallow. Villa 300mtrs on right

This luxurious country home has a rooftop conservatory where complimentary beverages are available. It is situated on the outskirts of the town within easy reach of the beautiful Killarney lakes and mountains. Bedrooms are very comfortable and well equipped, and there is a lovely dining room where a variety of dishes are available at breakfast.

Rooms 6 en suite (3 fmly) (1 GF) S €30-€40; D €60-€70 **Facilities** STV Lounge TVL tea/coffee Cen ht Wi-fi **Parking** 20 **Notes** LB ⊗ No Children 6yrs Closed Nov-Apr

Kingfisher Lodge

★★★★ GUEST HOUSE

Lewis Rd
☎ 064 6637131 & 087 2580351 ▤ 064 6639871
e-mail: info@kingfisherlodgekillarney.com
dir: Dublin link straight through 1st rdbt. Right at next rdbt towards town centre, Lodge on left

This welcoming, modern guest house is home to the Carroll family. It is situated within walking distance of the town centre, and has comfortable and well-appointed bedrooms, all of which are en suite. A delicious breakfast is served in the attractively decorated dining room and there is also a relaxing lounge and conservatory with Wi-fi. A drying room is available for fishing and wet gear. Golf, walking and fishing trips can be arranged. There is ample car parking, and complimentary pick-up from the bus and train station are offered.

Rooms 10 en suite (1 fmly) (2 GF) **Facilities** STV FTV Lounge TVL tea/coffee Direct Dial Cen ht Wi-fi ch fac ⌁ 18 Walking Fishing Horseriding Golf can be booked **Parking** 11 **Notes** LB Closed 15 Dec-13 Feb

KILLORGLIN   Map 1 A2

Carrig House Country House & Restaurant

★★★★★ ⊚ ▥ GUEST HOUSE

Caragh Lake
☎ 066 9769100 ▤ 066 9769166
e-mail: info@carrighouse.com

Located on the shores of Lake Caragh a short drive from Killorglin, amid natural green woodlands, this family-run house is the perfect retreat for a relaxing break. There is a range of room styles on offer, with some having lake views. Each is decorated to a high standard, with guest comfort in mind. Public rooms include elegant drawing rooms and cosy nooks. There is a true passion for food in evidence at dinner, where local seafood and seasonal produce is cooked and presented with care in the Lakeshore Restaurant. With over fifteen golf courses and a range of other outdoor pursuits available, there is something to suit all tastes.

Rooms 16 en suite **Facilities** TVL Dinner available Direct Dial Cen ht Licensed ⅂ Fishing **Parking** 20 **Notes** No Children 8yrs Closed Oct-Feb

The Grove Lodge

★★★★ GUEST HOUSE

Killarney Rd
☎ 066 9761157 & 08720 73238 ▤ 066 9762726
e-mail: info@grovelodge.com
dir: 800mtrs from Killorglin Bridge on N72 (Killarney road)

A lovely riverside house extended and developed to a high standard, with all the rooms en suite and fully equipped. Mrs Foley is an enthusiastic host who likes to please her guests and for those who just want to relax there is a patio seating area in the garden by the river.

Rooms 10 en suite (4 fmly) (4 GF) **Facilities** STV FTV tea/coffee Direct Dial Cen ht Wi-fi Fishing **Parking** 15 **Notes** ⊗ Closed 22-30 Dec

KILLORGLIN *continued*

O'Regan's Country Home & Gardens

★★★★ BED AND BREAKFAST

Bansha
☎ 066 9761200 & 087 8651333 ▤ 066 9761200
e-mail: jeromeoregan@eircom.net
dir: *1.6km from Killorglin on N70, turn right at sign for An Bainseach*

The O'Regan family have been welcoming guests to their family home for many years, with some returning regularly. Set in beautifully kept gardens overlooking the Kerry Mountains, the house is particularly comfortable and welcoming. The lounge and breakfast room overlook the gardens. The bedrooms have benefited from recent refurbishment and are well appointed. Breakfast features a wide selection, including Christina's delicious home baking.

Rooms 4 en suite (1 fmly) (4 GF) **Facilities** TVL tea/coffee Cen ht Wi-fi ⅃ 18 **Parking** 8 **Notes** ⊗ Closed Nov-Feb

Torine House

★★★ BED AND BREAKFAST

Sunhill Rd
☎ 066 9761352 & 087 9297329 ▤ 066 9761352
e-mail: torinehouse@eircom.net
dir: *Entering town from Tralee at rdbt take Sunhill Rd to top of hill. 1st right, 3rd house on left*

This welcoming family home is located high over the town of Killorglin, the home of the annual Puck Fair. It is an ideal base for climbers enjoying the challenges of Mcgillycuddy's Reeks or golfers, who have a choice of eight golf courses in the region. Bedrooms are comfortably appointed with orthopaedic beds. There is an extensive choice offered at breakfast. Guests are welcome to use the relaxing lounge which overlooks the well tended gardens and patio. Arrangements can be made for evening meals for groups.

Rooms 6 rms (5 en suite) (1 pri facs) (3 fmly) (4 GF) S €35; D €60* **Facilities** FTV TVL tea/coffee Dinner available Cen ht Wi-fi ⅃ 18 ♿ **Parking** 20 **Notes** LB ⊗ No Children 5yrs Closed Dec-Feb

---

ATHY Map 1 C3

PREMIER COLLECTION

Coursetown Country House

★★★★★ ≋ BED AND BREAKFAST

Stradbally Rd
☎ 059 8631101 ▤ 059 8632740
dir: *M7 exit to M9, then exit at Ballitore onto N78 to Athy, take R428*

This charming Victorian country house stands on a 100-hectare tillage farm and bird sanctuary. All bedrooms are furnished to the highest standards, with a comfortable lounge and bright airy breakfast room. Convalescent or disabled guests are especially welcome, and Iris and Jim Fox are happy to share their knowledge of the Irish countryside and its wildlife. Breakfast is a highlight of a visit to this welcoming house.

Rooms 5 en suite (1 GF) **Facilities** TVL tea/coffee Direct Dial Cen ht **Parking** 22 **Notes** No Children 12yrs Closed 15 Nov-15 Mar

---

KILKENNY Map 1 C3

Rosquil House

★★★★ GUEST HOUSE

Castlecomer Rd
☎ 056 7721419 ▤ 056 7750398
e-mail: info@rosquilhouse.com
dir: *From N: exit N77 into Castlecomer Rd, house on right. From S: exit N77 into Dublin Rd. At light right into Castlecomer Rd. At rdbt left (Castlecomer Rd), house on left*

Just a few minutes from the Kilkenny town centre, Rosquil House is furnished with great attention to design and detail. Bedrooms are stylishly furnished, as are the guest sitting and breakfast rooms. There is a real treat in store at breakfast where stewed fruits and a choice of hot dishes are complemented by Rhoda Nolan's home baking. There is ample off-street parking available.

Rooms 7 en suite (1 fmly) (3 GF) **Facilities** STV tea/coffee Direct Dial Cen ht Wi-fi **Parking** 10 **Notes** ⊗

Butler House

★★★★ GUEST HOUSE

Patrick St
☎ 056 7765707 & 7722828 ▤ 056 7765626
e-mail: res@butler.ie
web: www.butler.ie
dir: *In centre near Kilkenny Castle*

Once the dower house of Kilkenny Castle, this fine Georgian building fronts onto the main street with secluded gardens at the rear, through which you stroll to

---

have full breakfast in Kilkenny Design Centre. A continental breakfast is served in bedrooms, which feature contemporary decor. There is a comfortable foyer lounge and conference-banqueting suites.

Rooms 13 en suite (4 fmly) **Facilities** STV FTV tea/coffee Direct Dial Cen ht Wi-fi **Conf** Max 120 Thtr 120 Class 40 Board 40 **Parking** 24 **Notes** ⊗ Closed 24-29 Dec Civ Wed 70

PORTLAOISE Map 1 C3

O'Sullivan

★★★ BED AND BREAKFAST

8 Kelly Ville Park
☎ 0502 22774
dir: *In town centre opposite County Hall car park*

This family-run semi-detached house on the edge of the town offers a homely atmosphere. The en suite bedrooms are comfortable and secure parking is available.

Rooms 4 en suite (1 fmly) (2 GF) **Facilities** STV TVL Cen ht **Parking** 8 **Notes** ⊗ ⊜

ADARE Map 1 B3

Berkeley Lodge

★★★★ BED AND BREAKFAST

Station Rd
☎ 061 396857 ▤ 061 396857
e-mail: berlodge@iol.ie
dir: *N21, at rdbt turn to village centre*

Situated in the pretty village of Adare this homely bed and breakfast has very comfortably furnished and attractively decorated bedrooms. The lounge leads on to an attractive conservatory-style breakfast room, which offers Bridie's home baking and a choice of hot dishes. Adare Manor and many other golf courses and horse riding stables are close by.

Rooms 6 en suite (2 fmly) (1 GF) S €50; D €65-€70* **Facilities** iPod docking station TVL tea/coffee Cen ht Wi-fi ♿ **Parking** 6 **Notes** ⊗

CARLINGFORD Map 1 D4

Ghan House

★★★★ ⊛⊛ ≋ GUEST ACCOMMODATION

☎ 042 9373682 & 086 6000399 ▤ 042 9373772
e-mail: info@ghanhouse.com
dir: *M1 junct 18 signed Carlingford, 5mtrs on left after 50kph speed sign*

Dating from 1727, Ghan House has been restored to a high standard and oozes charm and comfort. Set in two acres of walled gardens, the house is within 50 metres of the centre of the medieval village of Carlingford, making it an ideal base for walking and touring the Cooley peninsula. Bedrooms are warm and well appointed, either in the house itself or in a converted barn in the grounds. The public rooms are comfortable, featuring log fires and relaxing armchairs; perfect for getting lost in a good book. Food is an important element of the business, with a successful cookery school operating here for many years. Dinner is a highlight of a visit, with an emphasis on artisan produce and, given its location the renowned Cooley Lamb. Breakfast is a real treat with a great choice of fruit compôtes and preserves.

Rooms 4 en suite 8 annexe en suite (3 fmly) (4 GF) S €65-€95; D €130-€220 **Facilities** iPod docking station Lounge tea/coffee Dinner available Cen ht Licensed Wi-fi ch fac Riding ♨ **Extras** Home-made biscuits **Conf** Max 50 Thtr 50 Class 26 Board 32 **Parking** 35 **Notes** LB ⊗ Civ Wed 45

DROGHEDA   Map 1 D4

Windsor Lodge

★★★★ BED AND BREAKFAST

1 The Court
☎ 041 9841966 🖷 041 9841966
e-mail: unagarvey@eircom.net
dir: From M1 take exit 10 (Drogheda N). Through 3 rdbts & lights, driveway 60mtrs

The home of Olive Murphy is delightfully furnished and decorated with guest comfort in mind. Two of the bedrooms are on the ground floor and the guest lounge is very relaxing and comfortable. A hearty breakfast is served in the conservatory style dining room. Windsor Lodge is situated just off the M1 on the north road and within walking distance of the hospital and Drogheda town centre. Close to Newgrange and many historical sites and golf courses.

Rooms 7 en suite (2 fmly) (2 GF) S €45-€55; D €70-€80 **Facilities** STV FTV Lounge TVL tea/coffee Cen ht Wi-fi ♿ 18 ♨ **Parking** 12 **Notes** ⊗

CO MAYO

ACHILL ISLAND   Map 1 A4

Lavelle's Seaside House

★★★ GUEST ACCOMMODATION

Dooega
☎ 098 45116 & 085 2330026
e-mail: lavellesseasidehouse@gmail.com
web: www.lavellesseasidehouse.com
dir: R319, NW from Achill Sound, Gob an Choire. In 3.8km left onto L1405 (Dooega/Dumha Eige junct). 3.8km to house

Friendliness and good food are offered at this comfortable house close to the beach. Facilities include a lounge, breakfast room, and a traditional pub where seafood is available during the high season. The more-spacious bedrooms are in the new wing.

Rooms 14 en suite (5 fmly) (14 GF) S €45; D €70 **Facilities** TVL tea/coffee Dinner available Cen ht Licensed Pool table ♨ **Parking** 20 **Notes** LB ⊗ Closed 2 Nov-mid Mar RS Dinner served Jul/Aug only

BALLINA   Map 1 B4

Red River Lodge B&B

★★★★ BED AND BREAKFAST

Iceford, The Quay Rd
☎ 096 22841
e-mail: redriverlodge@eircom.net
dir: 3km from quay

Located on the N59 just five miles from Ballina Town, Red River Lodge is a very comfortable family home set in half an acre of beautifully landscaped gardens. Bedrooms are very well appointed in a contemporary style, with many of them having spectacular views of the estuary of the River Moy. Dolores and Mark are perfect hosts, and are renowned for the quality of their breakfasts, served in the bright and airy conservatory. This house is an ideal location for visitors touring the counties of Mayo and Sligo.

Rooms 4 en suite (2 fmly) (1 GF) S €35; D €60 **Facilities** STV FTV Lounge Cen ht Wi-fi ♿ 18 **Parking** 6 **Notes** ⊗ Closed 30 Sep-1 May

CASTLEBAR   Map 1 B4

Lough Lannagh Lodge

★★★ GUEST ACCOMMODATION

Old Westport Rd
☎ 094 9027111 🖷 094 9027295
e-mail: info@loughlannagh.ie
web: www.loughlannagh.ie
dir: N5 around Castlebar. 3rd rdbt, 2nd exit. Next left, past playground, 1st building on right

Lough Lannagh is in a delightful wooded area within walking distance of Castlebar. There is a conference centre, fitness centre, tennis, table tennis, laundry and drying facilities, a private kitchen, and many activities for children. Bedrooms are well appointed and breakfast is served in the café. Dinner is available by appointment for groups.

Rooms 24 en suite (24 fmly) (12 GF) **Facilities** FTV TVL Dinner available Direct Dial Cen ht Wi-fi ch fac ♨ Sauna Gym Steam room Table tennis **Conf** Max 100 Thtr 100 Class 54 Board 34 **Parking** 24 **Notes** ⊗ Closed 8 Dec-11 Jan

WESTPORT   Map 1 B4

Carrabaun House

★★★★ BED AND BREAKFAST

Carrabaun, Leenane Rd
☎ 098 26196 🖷 098 28466
e-mail: carrabaun@anu.ie
dir: On N59 S. Leave Westport town, 1.6km pass Maxol station on left, house 200mtrs

This elevated house has stunning views of Croagh Patrick and Clew Bay, situated on the outskirts of Westport town. The Gavin family are friendly hosts and serve a hearty breakfast. Bedrooms are attractively furnished and there is a comfortable guest sitting room and dining room. There is private parking, and lovely gardens surround the house.

Rooms 6 en suite (6 fmly) (1 GF) **Facilities** TVL tea/coffee Cen ht **Parking** 12 **Notes** ⊗ Closed 16-31 Dec

Bertra House (L903823)

★★★ FARMHOUSE

Thornhill, Murrisk
☎ 098 64833 🖷 098 64833 **Mrs M Gill**
e-mail: bertrahse@eircom.net
web: www.bertrahse.com
dir: W of Westport off R335, near Croagh Patrick on L1833

This attractive bungalow overlooks the Blue Flag Bertra beach. Four bedrooms are en suite and the fifth has its own bathroom. Breakfast is generous and Mrs Gill offers tea and home-baked cakes on arrival in the cosy lounge.

Rooms 5 rms (4 en suite) (1 pri facs) (3 fmly) (5 GF) **Facilities** FTV TVL tea/coffee Cen ht **Parking** 7 **Notes** ⊗ No Children 6yrs Closed 15 Nov-15 Mar ⊜ 40 acres beef

CO MEATH

NAVAN
Map 1 C4

Killyon

★★★★ GUEST ACCOMMODATION

Dublin Rd
☎ 046 9071224 & 08681 71061 ▤ 046 9072766
e-mail: info@killyonguesthouse.ie
dir: On N3, River Boyne side, opposite Ardboyne Hotel

This luxurious house has fine views over the River Boyne from the balcony and cosy guest lounge. The comfortable bedrooms are individually decorated with antique beds and quality soft furnishings. Sheila Fogarty's breakfast is a special treat which includes home baking, jams and local products, and is served in the sun lounge or on the balcony. There is off-street parking at the front of the house in the colourfully planted garden.

Rooms 6 en suite (1 fmly) (1 GF) **Facilities** STV TVL Direct Dial Cen ht Wi-fi ch fac Fishing **Parking** 10 **Notes** ⊗ Closed 23-25 Dec

Dalys B&B

★★★ BED AND BREAKFAST

R153, Mooretown
☎ 046 9023219 & 085 7089813
e-mail: info@dalysbandb.com
web: www.dalysbandb.com
dir: Take R153 from Navan, B&B is 2km on the right

The Daly family provide a home-from-home atmosphere in this lovely house which is on a sheep farm two kilometres from Navan town. Brian gives advice on the many historical sights and the Hill of Tara can been seen from the comfortable bedrooms. There is a combined sitting/dining room and breakfast is served at a communal table set with lovely china and includes Pauline's bread and preserves. There is ample car parking and a lovely garden to relax in.

Rooms 3 en suite (1 fmly) **Facilities** STV FTV TVL tea/coffee Cen ht Wi-fi ⌿ 27 **Parking** 8 **Notes** ⊗

SLANE
Map 1 D4

PREMIER COLLECTION

Tankardstown

★★★★★ ⊛ ▤ GUEST ACCOMMODATION

☎ 041 9824621
e-mail: info@tankardstown.ie
dir: N51 (Navan-Slane road), take turn directly opposite main entrance to Slane Castle, signed Kells. Continue for 5km

Tankardstown is a magical place. Set in 80 acres of parkland, it has many strings to its bow. The main house is host to elegant heritage rooms, with others in cottages in the converted stable yard. Each is individually decorated to a very high standard, luxury and comfort exudes from all areas. The cottages have the benefit of spacious kitchens and living areas, ideal for longer stays. The property is also host to Brabazon, a fine dining restaurant and a bistro for more casual fare. Excellent breakfasts are served in the main house, with an option of having it delivered to the cottages. This fine property is ideal for family gatherings and intimate wedding celebrations. There is a small gym in the grounds, together with a hot tub and all-weather tennis court.

Rooms 6 rms (5 en suite) (1 pri facs) 10 annexe en suite (6 fmly) **Facilities** STV FTV DVD Lounge TVL tea/coffee Dinner available Direct Dial Cen ht Licensed Wi-fi ch fac ⌘ Fishing Gym 🔒 Hot tub **Extras** Still water - complimentary; mini-bar - chargeable **Conf** Max 150 Thtr 150 Class 80 Board 50 **Notes** Civ Wed 200

TRIM
Map 1 C4

Brogans

★★★ GUEST HOUSE

High St
☎ 046 9431237 ▤ 046 9437648
e-mail: info@brogans.ie
web: www.brogans.ie
dir: M50 junct 6. At rdbt 1st exit to Blanchardstown. N3 at rdbt 2nd exit, 1st left, left again onto R154. Continue to High St

Brogans is situated in the designated heritage town of Trim, and was built nearly two centuries ago using much of the original stone from Trim Castle. There are bedrooms in the main house and newer rooms in the courtyard. There is a cosy traditional bar where food is served throughout the day and at weekends in the Beacon Restaurant. It is convenient for New Grange, the Hill of Tara and many championship golf courses.

Rooms 18 en suite (3 fmly) (4 GF) S €40-€70; D €50-€140* **Facilities** TVL tea/coffee Dinner available Direct Dial Cen ht Licensed 🔒 **Notes** LB Closed 24-25 Dec

CO MONAGHAN

EMYVALE
Map 1 C5

An Teach Bán

★★★★ BED AND BREAKFAST

Main St
☎ 047 87198 & 086 6072996 ▤ 047 87198
e-mail: anteachban@eircom.net
dir: On N2, 11km N of Monaghan town

An Teach Bán bed and breakfast is situated in the picturesque village of Emyvale where there is a selection of traditional pubs and restaurants as well as fishing, golf and equestrian centre. The area is ideal for walking and cycling enthusiasts. The house is attractively decorated throughout and bedrooms are comfortably furnished and well appointed. Two ground floor rooms have the added benefit of access to the garden and car park and one is fitted to accommodate the less able. The garden is available for guests to relax and listen to the birds in. A hearty breakfast is cooked to order and includes the local mushrooms and freshly baked breads.

Rooms 5 en suite (3 fmly) (3 GF) **Facilities** FTV TVL tea/coffee Cen ht Wi-fi ch fac Fishing Riding **Parking** 7 **Notes** ⊗ Closed Dec-Jan

GLASLOUGH
Map 1 C5

PREMIER COLLECTION

The Castle at Castle Leslie Estate

★★★★★ GUEST HOUSE

☎ 047 88100 ▤ 047 88256
e-mail: info@castleleslie.com
dir: M1 junct 14, N2 to Monaghan then N12 onto N185 for Glaslough

Set in 1000 acres of rolling countryside, The Castle is the centre of the Leslie Estate which has been in the family since the 1660s. Bedrooms are all decorated in keeping with the age and style of the period, and are ideal for relaxing breaks where guests enjoy the peace and tranquillity of the property without any interference from televisions or other distractions. With a successful equestrian centre and a private fishing lake, this is an ideal location for those who enjoy country pursuits.

Rooms 20 rms (19 en suite) (1 pri facs) **Facilities** Dinner available Direct Dial Cen ht Lift Licensed Wi-fi ⌘ ⌿ 18 Fishing Riding Snooker Spa treatment rooms Private cinema **Extras** Speciality toiletries **Conf** Max 280 Thtr 280 Class 150 Board 150 **Parking** 100 **Notes** LB ⊗ Closed 22-27 Dec Civ Wed 80

CO SLIGO

BALLYSADARE   Map 1 B5

Seashore House

★ ★ ★ BED AND BREAKFAST

Lisduff
☎ 071 9167827 📄 071 9167827
e-mail: seashore@oceanfree.net
dir: *N4 onto N59 W at Ballisadore, in 4km Seashore signed on right. Turn down road, 600mtrs on right*

Seashore House is an attractive dormer bungalow in a quiet seashore location. A comfortable lounge with open turf fire and sunny conservatory dining room look out over attractive landscaped gardens to sea and mountain scenery. Bedrooms are attractively appointed and comfortable, and there is also a tennis court and bicycle storage. Credit cards only accepted during high season.

Rooms 5 rms (4 en suite) (2 fmly) (3 GF) S €35-€45; D €70* **Facilities** STV FTV TVL Cen ht Wi-fi ⌣ Fishing ⬥ **Parking** 6 **Notes** LB ⊗ No Children

BELTRA   Map 1 B5

Rafter's Woodfield Inn

★ ★ ★ ★ GUEST ACCOMMODATION

Larkhill
☎ 071 9166610 📄 071 9166610
dir: *On N59*

This delightful property is attached to a cosy traditional pub, established in 1775, that serves bar food in the evening. Guests can relax in the conservatory lounge while enjoying the views of the Ox Mountains. Three of the bedrooms are on the ground floor and are fitted to accommodate less able guests; all bedrooms are well furnished, individually decorated and identified by names from the local area. Breakfast menu includes Carol's brown bread, spotted dog scones and preserves.

Rooms 5 en suite (3 fmly) (3 GF) **Facilities** FTV TVL Cen ht Licensed Wi-fi **Parking** 25 **Notes** ⊗ 🖃

GRANGE   Map 1 B5

Rowanville Lodge

★ ★ ★ ★ BED AND BREAKFAST

Moneygold
☎ 071 9163958 📄 071 9163958
e-mail: rowanville@hotmail.com
dir: *On N15, 1km N of Grange village*

This smart bed and breakfast is just five minutes from the town centre. It is part of Manor West retail park which has many shopping opportunities. Spacious well-appointed bedrooms are matched by comfortable public areas, including the Bar and Bistro where food is served throughout the day, with fine dining available in the Walnut Room. There is a high spec Leisure Club, and a variety of treatments are offered in the Harmony Wellness suites. A range of meeting and banqueting rooms are also available.

Rooms 4 en suite (4 fmly) (2 GF) **Facilities** STV FTV TVL tea/coffee Dinner available Cen ht Wi-fi ⌁ 18 **Parking** 9 **Notes** Closed 20-27 Dec

STRANDHILL   Map 1 B5

Strandhill Lodge and Suites

★ ★ ★ ★ GUEST HOUSE

Top Rd
☎ 071 9122122 📄 071 9122795
e-mail: info@strandhilllodgeandsuites.com
dir: *From Sligo onto R292 for Strandhill*

Located in the centre of Strandhill village, just five kilometres from Sligo town, this recently built property offers particularly spacious accommodation finished to a very high standard. Many of the rooms have stunning views of the bay. Public areas are open-plan in design, with a bright and airy breakfast room where complimentary continental breakfast is served. This is an ideal property for those playing golf or participating in the many other adventure pursuits that are available in the region. There is a meeting room on the first floor, and ample parking to the rear. A number of cosy pubs and quality restaurants are located in the village.

Rooms 21 en suite 1 annexe en suite (7 fmly) (8 GF) S €59-€99; D €69-€149* **Facilities** STV FTV DVD iPod docking station Lounge TVL tea/coffee Direct Dial Cen ht Lift Wi-fi ⌣ ⌁ 18 Fishing Riding ⬥ **Extras** Water **Conf** Max 20 Thtr 20 Class 10 Board 8 **Parking** 22 **Notes** LB ⊗ Closed Jan-5 Feb

CO TIPPERARY

CASHEL   Map 1 C3

Ard Ri House

★ ★ ★ ★ BED AND BREAKFAST

Dualla Rd
☎ 062 63143 📄 062 63037
e-mail: ardrihouse@gmail.com
dir: *From town centre, 1st right after Information Office onto R688, left after church onto R691, 1km on right*

A warm welcome awaits you at this non-smoking house, only a short distance from the town on the Kilkenny Road. All of the bedrooms are comfortably furnished with thoughtful extras, and are on the ground floor. The breakfast served by Eileen features locally sourced ingredients from a varied menu. Facilities are available for children.

Rooms 4 en suite (1 fmly) (4 GF) D €70-€90 **Facilities** TVL tea/coffee Cen ht Wi-fi **Parking** 8 **Notes** ⊗ Closed Nov-Feb

Ashmore House

★ ★ ★ BED AND BREAKFAST

John St
☎ 062 61286 & 0861 037010 📄 062 62789
e-mail: info@ashmorehouse.ie
dir: *Exit N8 in town centre, into John St, house 100mtrs on right*

Ashmore House is a Georgian building set in a colourfully planted walled garden, right in the centre of the town. There is secure car parking at the rear. It is within walking distance of the Rock of Cashel. Guests have use of a large sitting and dining room, and bedrooms come in a variety of sizes from big family rooms to a more compact double. Children are welcome and guests have Wi-fi access.

Rooms 5 en suite (2 fmly) **Facilities** STV FTV TVL tea/coffee Dinner available Cen ht Wi-fi **Parking** 10 **Notes** ⊗

THURLES Map 1 C3

PREMIER COLLECTION

The Castle
★★★★★ BED AND BREAKFAST

Twomileborris
☎ 0504 44324 ⬛ 0504 44352
e-mail: bandb@thecastletmb.com
web: www.thecastletmb.com
dir: *7km E of Thurles. On N75 200mtrs W of Twomileborris at Castle*

Pierce and Joan are very welcoming hosts. Their fascinating house, sheltered by a 16th-century tower house, has been in the Duggan family for 200 years. Bedrooms are comfortable and spacious, there is a relaxing lounge, and the dining room overlooks the delightful garden. Golf, fishing, hill walking, and traditional pubs and restaurants are all nearby. Dinner is available by arrangement.

Rooms 4 en suite (3 fmly) S €50-€60; D €70-€100 **Facilities** STV FTV TVL tea/coffee Dinner available Cen ht Wi-fi 🐾 🦢 ♨ 18 Fishing Pool table ⚓ **Conf** Max 40 Board 20 **Parking** 30 **Notes** LB ⊗

PREMIER COLLECTION

Inch House Country House & Restaurant
★★★★★ ◉ GUEST HOUSE

☎ 0504 51348 & 51261 ⬛ 0504 51754
e-mail: mairin@inchhouse.ie
dir: *6.5km NE of Thurles on R498*

This lovely Georgian house, at the heart of a working farm, was built in 1720 and has been carefully restored by the Egan family. The elegant drawing room ceiling is particularly outstanding among the grand public rooms, and the five spacious bedrooms are delightfully appointed. Reservations are essential in the fine restaurant, where an imaginative choice of freshly prepared dishes is on offer, with an emphasis on local produce. Some of the produce from the kitchen is available in a number of specialist outlets throughout the country.

Rooms 5 en suite (1 fmly) **Facilities** TVL tea/coffee Dinner available Direct Dial Cen ht Licensed Wi-fi **Parking** 40 **Notes** LB ⊗ Closed 2wks Xmas RS Sun & Mon Restaurant closed evening Civ Wed 30

TIPPERARY Map 1 C3

Ach-na-Sheen House
★★★ GUEST HOUSE

Clonmel Rd
☎ 062 51298 ⬛ 062 80467
e-mail: gernoonan@eircom.net
dir: *In town centre*

This large, modern bungalow, set in a lovely garden, is only five minutes walk from the main street of Tipperary town, on the N24 road to Clonmel. This is a family-run house where guests are made feel very much at home. The public areas include a spacious guest sitting room and bright and airy breakfast room. The bedrooms are comfortably appointed and there is good off-street parking available.

Rooms 8 en suite (5 fmly) (6 GF) **Facilities** STV tea/coffee Cen ht **Parking** 13 **Notes** ⊗ Closed 11 Dec-8 Jan

Aisling
★★★ BED AND BREAKFAST

Glen of Aherlow
☎ 062 33307 & 087 2278230 ⬛ 062 82955
e-mail: ladygreg@oceanfree.net
web: www.aislingbedandbreakfast.com
dir: *From town centre R664 for 2.4km, past golf club*

Aisling is close to Tipperary on the R664, Glen of Aherlow road. The bedrooms are well furnished and attractively decorated. There is a comfortable guest sitting room and a delightful garden with patio seating. Marian and Bob will arrange day trips and have maps and good information on the locality.

Rooms 5 rms (4 en suite) (1 pri facs) (2 fmly) (5 GF) (2 smoking) S €30-€40; D €70-€80 **Facilities** FTV Lounge TVL Dinner available Cen ht Wi-fi ch fac ♨ ⚓ **Extras** Wine, chocolate, water - complimentary **Conf** Max 6 Class 6 **Parking** 5 **Notes** LB

CO WATERFORD

BALLYMACARBRY Map 1 C2

PREMIER COLLECTION

Hanoras Cottage
★★★★★ ◉ GUEST HOUSE

Nire Valley
☎ 052 6136134 & 6136442
e-mail: hanorascottage@eircom.net
dir: *From Clonmel or Dungarvan R672 to Ballymacarbry, at Melodys Bar turn into Nire Valley, establishment by bridge beside church*

Nestling in the beautiful Nire Valley, Hanoras Cottage is very popular with hill and forest walkers, bird watchers and nature lovers. Run by two generations of the Wall family, it offers spacious bedrooms that are comfortably appointed and beautifully decorated. There are cosy lounge areas and the award-winning restaurant serves dinner from an interesting menu that features local produce. Those with special dietary needs are well cared for. Breakfast is a particular treat, with home baking and a range of hearty and healthy options. It deserves to be savoured at leisure.

Rooms 10 en suite S €75-€95; D €150-€190 (incl. dinner) **Facilities** STV FTV Lounge TVL tea/coffee Dinner available Direct Dial Cen ht Licensed ♨ 18 Fishing ⚓ Jacuzzi in all rooms **Conf** Class 40 **Parking** 15 **Notes** LB ⊗ No Children 12yrs Closed Xmas wk RS Sun Restaurant closed Civ Wed 40

TRAMORE — Map 1 C2

Cloneen

★★★★ BED AND BREAKFAST

Love Ln
☎ 051 381264 🖷 051 381264
e-mail: cloneen@iol.ie
dir: N25 onto R675 to Tramore, Majestic Hotel on right, continue up hill until road bears left, take 1st left

This pleasant family home is situated on a quiet residential area off the coast road and within walking distance of the seaside town of Tramore. Bedrooms are stylishly furnished with guest comfort in mind; some of the ground floor rooms have their own patio overlooking the lovely garden. Guests can relax in the conservatory-style sitting room and enjoy a hearty breakfast in the bright dining room.

Rooms 6 en suite (2 fmly) (4 GF) S €45-€50; D €70-€80* Facilities STV TVL tea/coffee Cen ht Wi-fi Parking 8

Seacourt

★★★★ BED AND BREAKFAST

Tivoli Rd
☎ 051 386244 🖷 051 386244
e-mail: seacourthouse@gmail.com
dir: Leave Waterford City on R675 to Tramore. Over 2 rdbts, at 3rd rdbt (boat in middle) straight over, 1st B&B on left

Seacourt is a very comfortable house situated in the seaside town close to Splashworld, the beach and Tramore Race Course and many other tourist attractions available locally. Bedrooms are comfortably furnished with a spacious family room on the ground floor. There is a cosy guest sitting room, a wide choice of cooked breakfast served in the dining room and ample off-street parking available.

Rooms 5 rms (5 pri facs) (1 fmly) (1 GF) S €40-€45; D €60-€80 Facilities STV TVL tea/coffee Cen ht Wi-fi ⚿ 18 🔒 Parking 10 Notes No Children 6yrs Closed Oct-2 Apr

WATERFORD — Map 1 C2

PREMIER COLLECTION

Sion Hill House & Gardens

★★★★★ GUEST ACCOMMODATION

Sion Hill, Ferrybank
☎ 051 851558
e-mail: sionhill@eircom.net
dir: Near city centre on R711, 300mtrs from Rice Bridge & railway station

Situated on a hill overlooking the river and the city, this 18th-century residence has extensive peaceful gardens, which include a walled garden, a meadow and woodlands. Flanked by two pavilions, the house provides two fine reception rooms and comfortable en suite bedrooms. The hospitable proprietors take a keen interest in their guests, as the visitors' book shows. The house is within easy walking distance to the city and all its hidden treasures.

Rooms 4 en suite (2 fmly) S €30-€50; D €60-€96 Facilities STV FTV TVL tea/coffee Cen ht 🔒 Parking 16 Notes LB ⊗ Closed 23-28 Dec

Belmont House

★★★ BED AND BREAKFAST

Belmont Rd, Rosslare Rd, Ferrybank
☎ 051 832174 🖷 051 832174
e-mail: belmonthouse@eircom.net
dir: Exit N25 at Luffany rdbt, follow R711 (Waterford N). Belmont House 4km from junct, 2nd B&B on left after service station

This comfortable bed and breakfast is within walking distance of the city centre. A hospitality tray is available in the relaxing guest sitting room and a hearty breakfast is served in the dining room at separate tables. Bedrooms are well appointed and offer good quality and space.

Rooms 6 rms (4 en suite) (2 pri facs) (3 fmly) S €40-€55; D €60-€76 Facilities TVL Cen ht Wi-fi Parking 6 Notes ⊗ No Children 7yrs Closed Nov-Apr 🏵

Claddagh Bed & Breakfast

★★★ BED AND BREAKFAST

Lower Newrath, Mullinabro, Ferrybank
☎ 051 854797 & 087 2792069
e-mail: mashacorcoran@yahoo.com

Claddagh B&B is a lovely house with five attractively decorated bedrooms all on the ground floor and furnished with guest comfort in mind. There is a cosy guest sitting room where tea is offered on arrival and Miriam's hearty breakfast is a treat. It has the added advantage of being situated close to Waterford Golf Club where green fees can be arranged and the bar and restaurant is within walking distance. There is ample private car parking available. Waterford City is close by and the house is just a few minutes' drive from the new bridge and N25/N9 motorway.

Rooms 5 rms (5 pri facs) (3 fmly) (5 GF) S €35-€40; D €65-€70* Facilities STV FTV TVL tea/coffee Cen ht Wi-fi ⚿ 18 Riding Parking 12 Notes ⊗ No Children Closed Nov-17 Mar

CO WESTMEATH

HORSELEAP — Map 1 C4

Woodlands Farm House (N286426)

★★★★ FARMHOUSE

Streamstown
☎ 044 9226414 Mrs M Maxwell
e-mail: maxwells.woodlandsfarm@gmail.com
dir: From N6 N onto R391 at Horseleap, farm signed 4km

This very comfortable and charming house has a delightful setting on a farm. The spacious sitting and dining rooms are very relaxing, and there is a hospitality kitchen where tea and coffee are available at all times.

Rooms 5 rms (4 en suite) (1 pri facs) (2 fmly) (2 GF) Facilities TVL Cen ht Parking Notes Closed Nov-Feb 🏵 120 acres mixed

CO WEXFORD

CAMPILE — Map 1 C2

PREMIER COLLECTION

Kilmokea Country Manor & Gardens

★★★★★ GUEST ACCOMMODATION

Great Island
☎ 051 388109 🖷 051 388776
e-mail: stay@kilmokea.com
dir: R733 from New Ross to Campile, right before village for Great Island & Kilmokea Gardens

This fine property is an 18th-century former rectory, lovingly restored to its original glory by the hospitable Emma Hewlett and her husband Mark. It is located in wooded and beautifully landscaped gardens that are in themselves a popular visitor attraction. The bedrooms are richly furnished in a mix of styles, but all have particularly comfortable beds. The drawing and reading rooms all retain the style and proportions of the era, with an honesty bar for those tempted to have a night-cap. Dinner is available by prior arrangement, in what was the original dining room of the house, or in summer, in the conservatory, where a hearty and delicious breakfast is also served. In the grounds there is a spa building which contains an indoor heated swimming pool, and offers an aromatherapy service.

Rooms 4 en suite 2 annexe en suite (1 fmly) (2 GF) S fr €75; D €160-€240* Facilities STV Lounge TVL TV2B tea/coffee Dinner available Direct Dial Cen ht Licensed Wi-fi ch fac 🏊 🌿 Fishing Riding Sauna Gym 🔒 Aromatherapy treatments Meditation room Jacuzzi Conf Max 75 Thtr 40 Class 30 Board 25 Parking 23 Notes LB RS Nov-end Jan Civ Wed 60

NEW ROSS — Map 1 C3

Woodlands House

★★★ BED AND BREAKFAST

Carrigbyrne
☎ 051 428287 ▤ 051 428287
e-mail: woodwex@eircom.net
dir: On N25 (New Ross-Wexford route), 0.4km from Cedar Lodge Hotel towards New Ross

Commanding panoramic views and only a 30-minute drive from Rosslare Harbour, this is a bungalow with pretty gardens. The bedrooms vary in size, though all are very comfortable, and there is a guest sitting room. Snacks are available, and dinner is on offer by prior arrangement.

Rooms 4 en suite (4 GF) **Facilities** tea/coffee Dinner available Cen ht Licensed **Parking** 6 **Notes** ⊗ No Children 5yrs

WEXFORD — Map 1 D3

Killiane Castle (T058168)

★★★★ 🏠 FARMHOUSE

Drinagh
☎ 053 9158885 ▤ 053 9158885 Mr & Mrs J Mernagh
e-mail: killianecastle@yahoo.com
dir: Off N25 between Wexford and Rosslare

This 17th-century house is part of a 13th-century Norman castle where the Mernagh family run a charming house on a dairy farm close to Wexford town. The comfortable reception rooms and bedrooms are beautifully furnished. Breakfast is a real treat and includes farm produce and Kathleen's baking and preserves. There is a hard tennis court, croquet lawn, a golf driving range and walks to wander through the farm.

Rooms 8 en suite (2 fmly) S €60-€70; D €90-€100* **Facilities** TVL Cen ht Wi-fi 🎱 ⛳ Driving range 18 hole pitch & putt **Parking** 8 **Notes** ⊗ Closed Dec-Feb 230 acres dairy

Maple Lodge

★★★★ BED AND BREAKFAST

Castlebridge
☎ 053 9159195 ▤ 053 9159195
e-mail: sreenan@eircom.net
dir: 5km N of Wexford. On R741, N on outskirts of Castlebridge, pink house on left

This imposing house, set in extensive mature gardens, is in a peaceful location close to Curracloe Beach. Eamonn and Margaret Sreenan offer warm hospitality in their comfortable home. There is a varied breakfast menu offered and secure parking in the grounds.

Rooms 4 en suite (2 fmly) **Facilities** STV TVL Cen ht Wi-fi **Parking** 5 **Notes** ⊗ No Children 10yrs Closed mid Nov-mid Mar

Slaney Manor

★★★★ GUEST ACCOMMODATION

☎ 053 9120051 ▤ 053 9120510
e-mail: info@slaneymanor.ie
dir: On N25, 0.8km W of N11 junct

This attractive manor house stands in 24 hectares of woodland overlooking the River Slaney. Restored by the owners, the house retains many fine features. The elegant, high-ceilinged drawing room and dining room have views of the river, and four-poster beds feature in all bedrooms. The rooms in the converted coach house can be reserved on a room only basis for those travelling on the Rosslare ferry.

Rooms 9 en suite (2 fmly) (4 GF) S €55-€105; D €90-€170* **Facilities** FTV DVD Lounge TVL tea/coffee Dinner available Direct Dial Cen ht Lift Licensed Wi-fi **Conf** Max 250 Thtr 250 Class 100 Board 100 **Parking** 30 **Notes** LB Civ Wed 250

CO WICKLOW

AUGHRIM — Map 1 D3

Clone House

★★★★ BED AND BREAKFAST

☎ 0402 36121 & 087 2517587
e-mail: stay@clonehouse.com
dir: N11 from Dublin to Ashford, right at Texaco station signed Gleneally, right signed Rathdrum, to Aughrim, 2m S to house

Clone House dates from the 16th and 17th centuries, and is located between Arklow and Aughrim. The house has been refurbished with care and attention by Liam, who has created a truly comfortable retreat. There is a drawing room, library, parlour and dining room for guest use, each with open log fireplaces and a wonderful range of Irish art and literature to enjoy. The bedrooms have been beautifully decorated and furnished with guest comfort in mind; Aine is responsible for the home baking, and the delicious dinners which are available by prior arrangement.

Rooms 4 en suite **Facilities** TVL Dinner available Cen ht Wi-fi ⚓ 18 Fishing Riding **Parking** 10 **Notes** ⊗

DUNLAVIN — Map 1 C3

Tynte House (N870015)

★★★★ FARMHOUSE

☎ 045 401561 ▤ 045 401586 Mr & Mrs J Lawler
e-mail: info@tyntehouse.com
web: www.tyntehouse.com
dir: N81 at Hollywood Cross, right at Dunlavin, follow finger signs for Tynte House, past market house in town centre

This 19th-century farmhouse stands in the square of the quiet country village of Dunlavin in the west of County Wicklow. The friendly hosts have carried out a lot of restoration resulting in cosy bedrooms and a relaxing guest sitting room. Breakfast, featuring Caroline's home baking, is a highlight of a visit to this house. An all-weather tennis court is located in the grounds, together with an indoor games room. This house is an ideal base for touring the Wicklow and Kildare areas with their many sporting attractions.

Rooms 7 en suite (2 fmly) S €40-€50; D €70-€80 **Facilities** Lounge TVL tea/coffee Direct Dial Cen ht Wi-fi ch fac 🎱 ⚓ 18 Playground Games room **Parking** 16 **Notes** LB Closed 16 Dec-9 Jan 200 acres beef/tillage

COUNTY MAPS

Londonderry
Donegal
Antrim
NORTHERN
Tyrone
IRELAND
Fermanagh
Down
Armagh
Monaghan
Sligo
Leitrim
Cavan
Mayo
REPUBLIC
Louth
Roscommon
Longford
OF
Meath
Westmeath
Galway
Dublin
Offaly
Kildare
IRELAND
Laois
Wicklow
Clare
Carlow
Tipperary
Kilkenny
Limerick
Wexford
Kerry
Waterford
Cork

```
0        20       40       60       80     100 miles
0   20   40   60   80   100   120   140  160 kilometres
```

England

 1 Bedfordshire
 2 Berkshire
 3 Bristol
 4 Buckinghamshire
 5 Cambridgeshire
 6 Greater Manchester
 7 Herefordshire
 8 Hertfordshire
 9 Leicestershire
10 Northamptonshire
11 Nottinghamshire
12 Rutland
13 Staffordshire
14 Warwickshire
15 West Midlands
16 Worcestershire

Scotland

17 City of Glasgow
18 Clackmannanshire
19 East Ayrshire
20 East Dunbartonshire
21 East Renfrewshire
22 Perth & Kinross
23 Renfrewshire
24 South Lanarkshire
25 West Dunbartonshire

Wales

26 Blaenau Gwent
27 Bridgend
28 Caerphilly
29 Denbighshire
30 Flintshire
31 Merthyr Tydfil
32 Monmouthshire
33 Neath Port Talbot
34 Newport
35 Rhondda Cynon Taff
36 Torfaen
37 Vale of Glamorgan
38 Wrexham

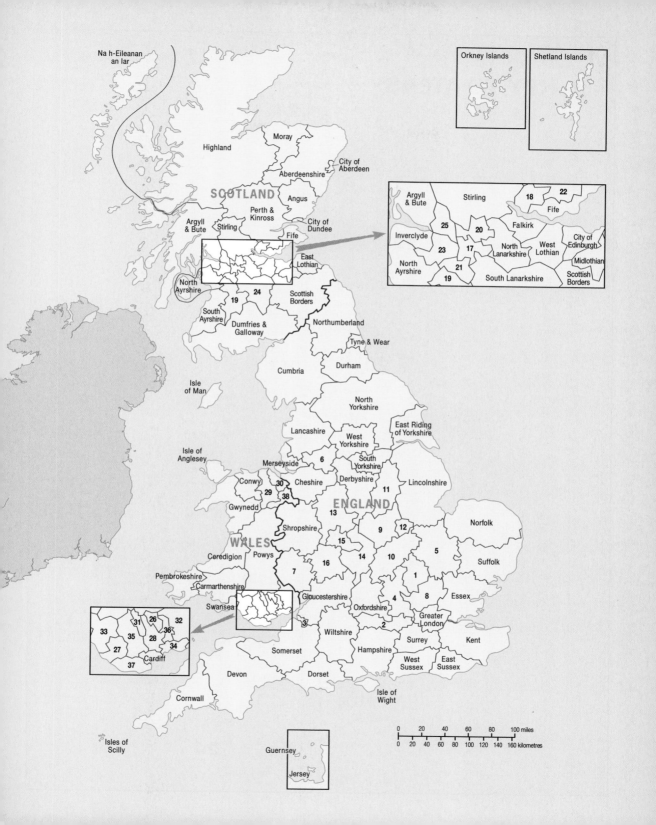

Na h-Eileanan
an Iar

Highland

Moray

Aberdeenshire

City of
Aberdeen

SCOTLAND

Angus

Perth &
Kinross

City of
Dundee

Argyll & Bute

Stirling

Fife

East
Lothian

North
Ayrshire

24

19

Scottish
Borders

South
Ayrshire

Dumfries &
Galloway

Northumberland

Tyne & Wear

Cumbria

Durham

Isle
of Man

North
Yorkshire

Lancashire

East Riding
of Yorkshire

West
Yorkshire

Isle of
Anglesey

Merseyside

6

South
Yorkshire

Lincolnshire

Conwy

30

Cheshire

Derbyshire

11

29

38

Gwynedd

13

ENGLAND

Shropshire

9

12

Norfolk

Ceredigion

WALES

15

Powys

16

14

10

5

Suffolk

Pembrokeshire

7

1

Carmarthenshire

Gloucestershire

Swansea

4

8

Essex

3

Oxfordshire

Greater
London

2

Wiltshire

Surrey

Kent

Somerset

Hampshire

West
Sussex

East
Sussex

Devon

Dorset

Isle of
Wight

Cornwall

Isles of
Scilly

Guernsey

Jersey

Orkney Islands

Shetland Islands

Argyll
& Bute

Stirling

18

22

Fife

Inverclyde

25

20

Falkirk

23

17

North
Lanarkshire

West
Lothian

City of
Edinburgh

North
Ayrshire

21

Midlothian

19

South Lanarkshire

Scottish
Borders

31

26

32

33

35

36

27

28

34

37

Cardiff

0   20   40   60   80   100 miles

0   20   40   60   80 100 120 140 160 kilometres

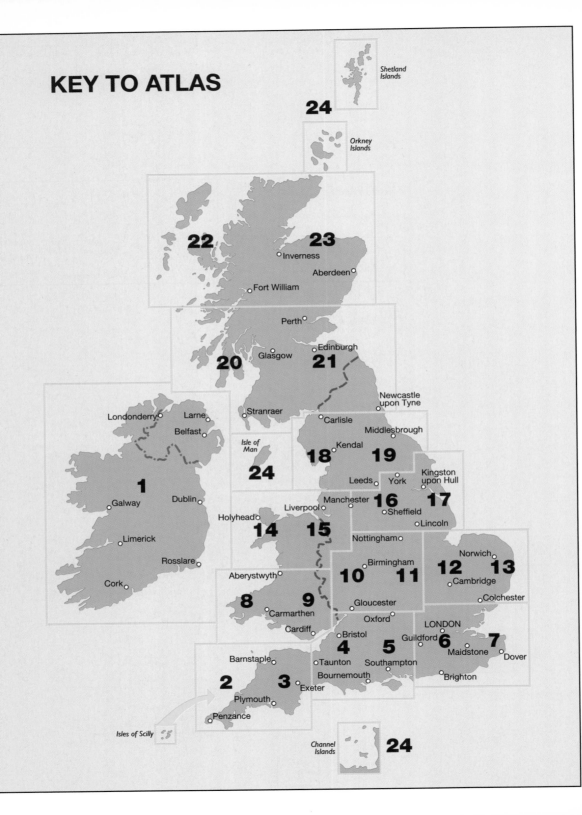

KEY TO ATLAS

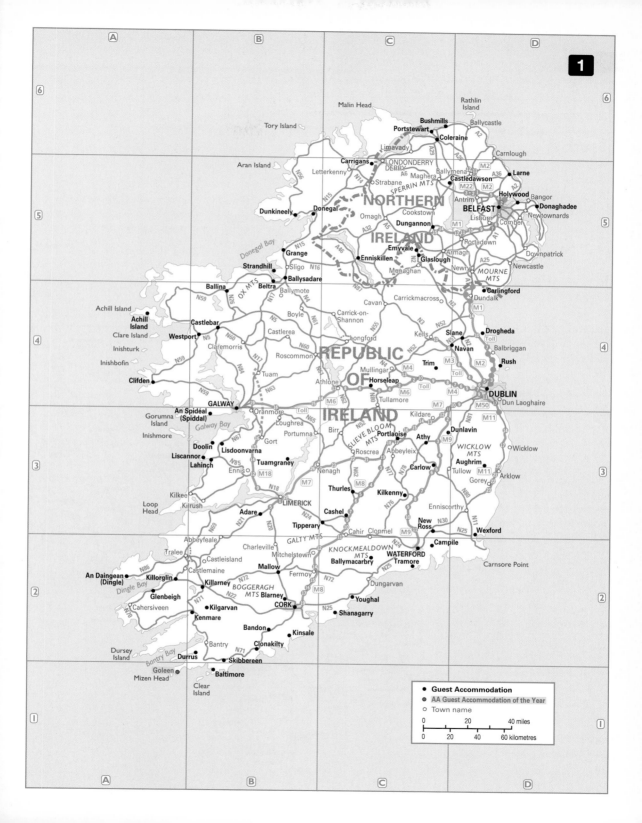

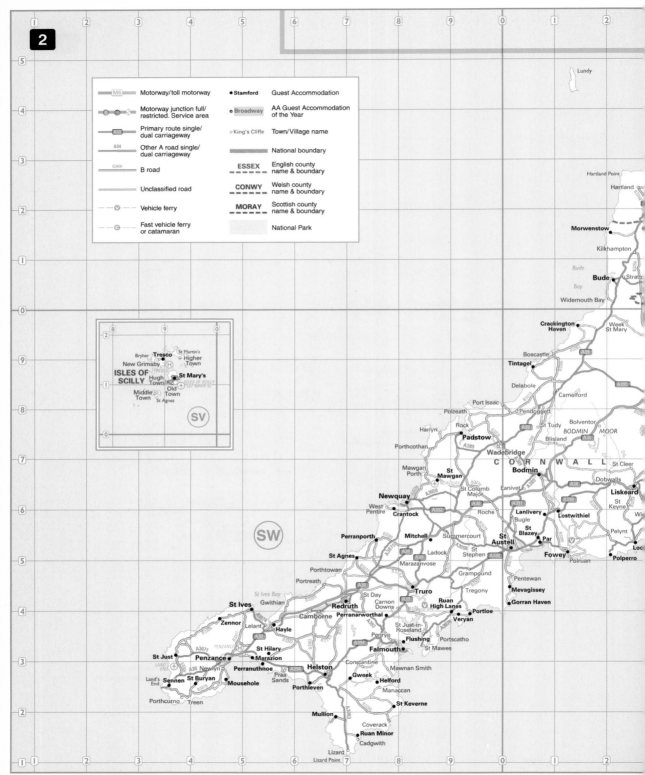

2

Motorway/toll motorway
Motorway junction full/ restricted. Service area
Primary route single/ dual carriageway
Other A road single/ dual carriageway
B road
Unclassified road
Vehicle ferry
Fast vehicle ferry or catamaran

● **Stamford** Guest Accommodation
● **Broadway** AA Guest Accommodation of the Year
○ King's Cliffe Town/Village name
National boundary
ESSEX English county name & boundary
CONWY Welsh county name & boundary
MORAY Scottish county name & boundary
National Park

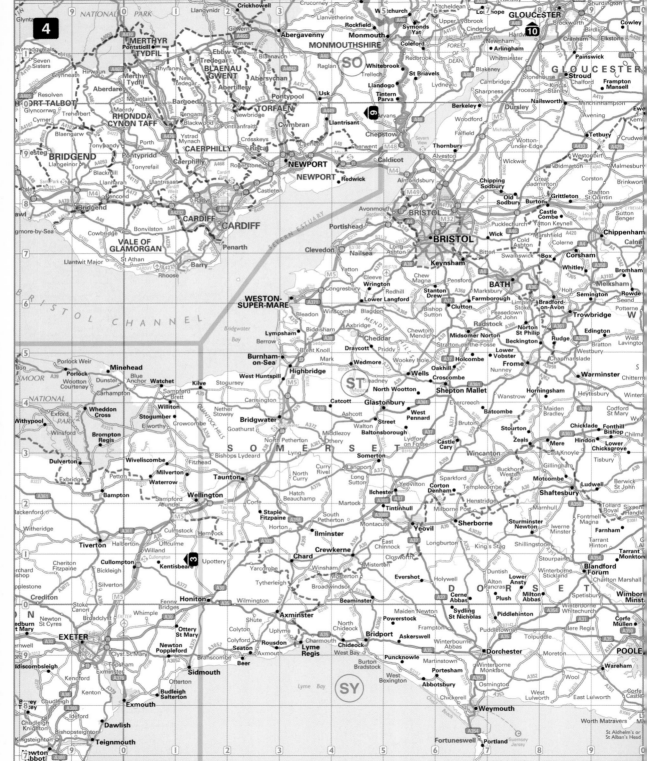

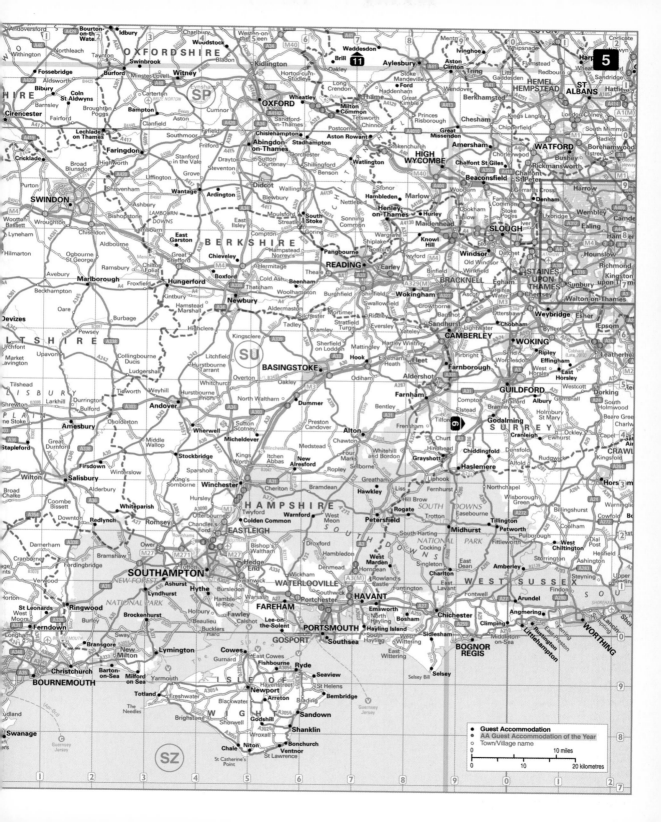

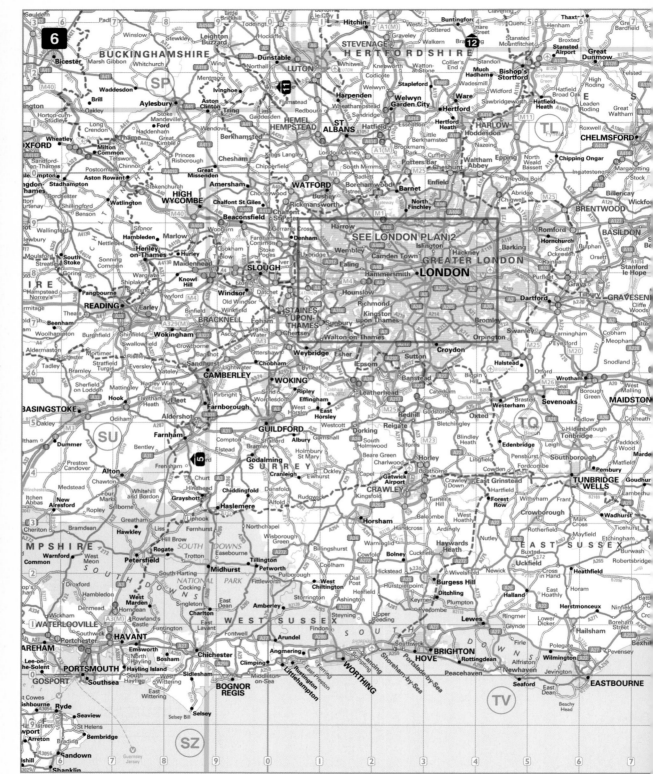

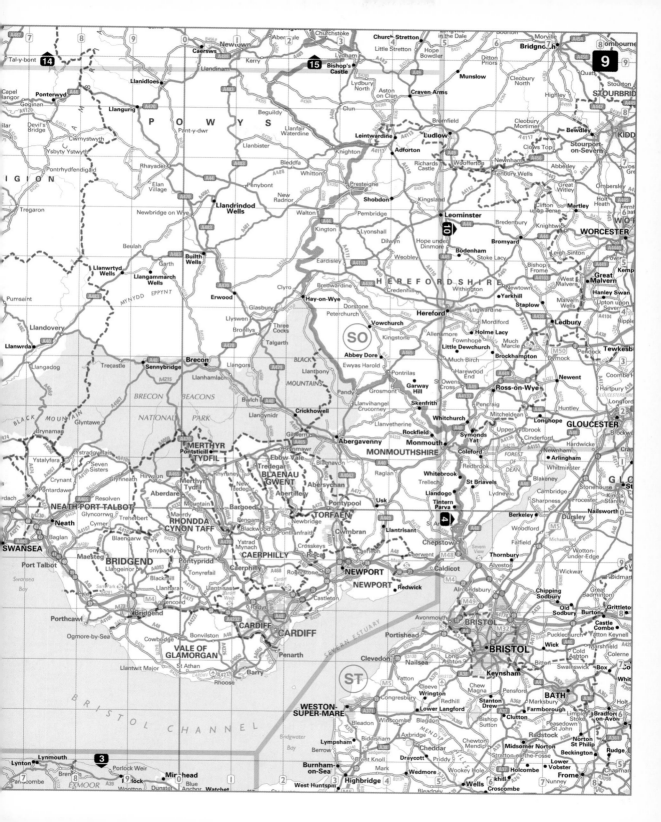

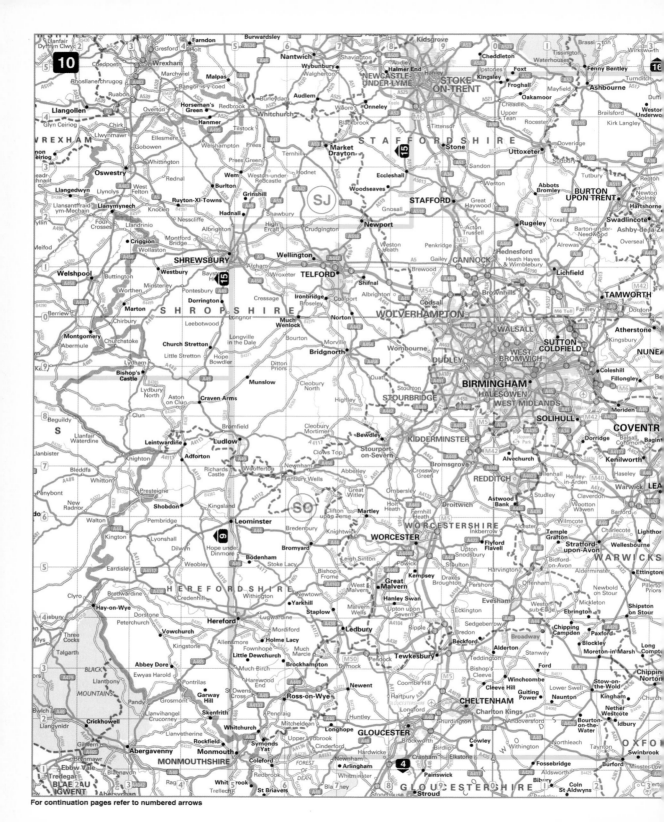

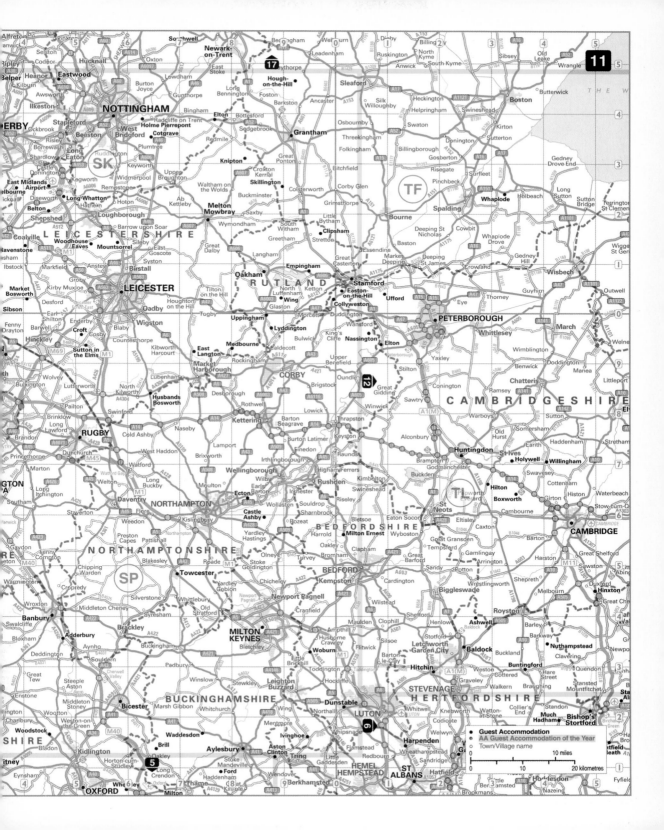

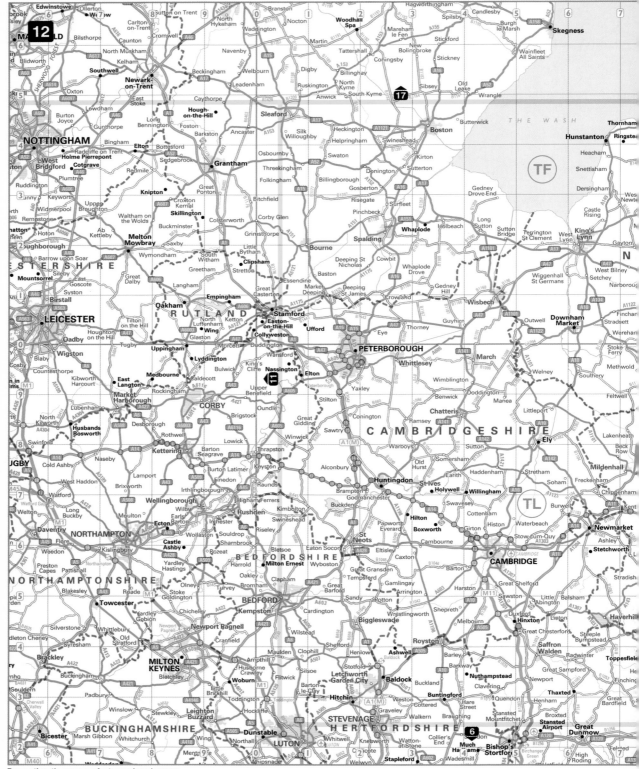

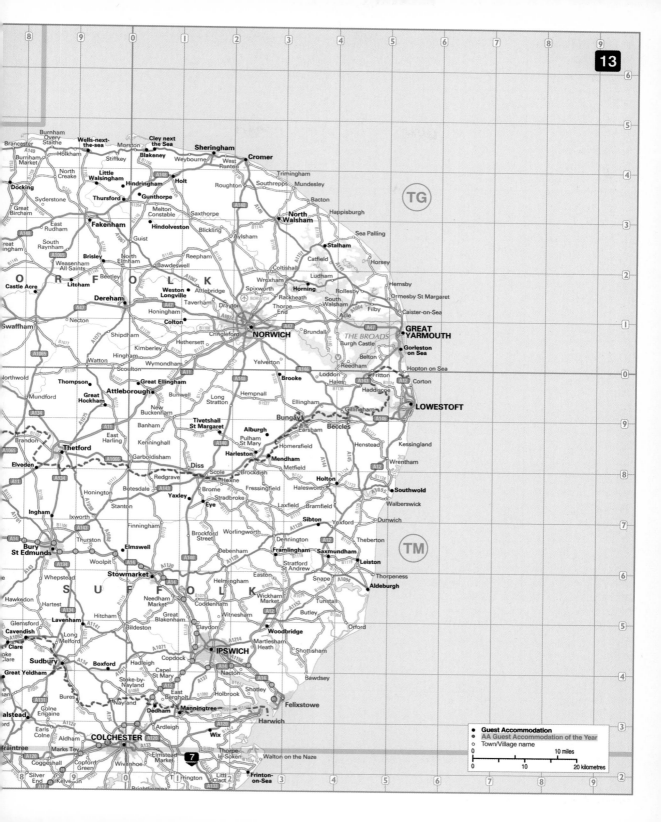

ISLE OF
ANGLESEY

Cemaes
Amlwch
Llanerchymedd
Llanfachraeth
Holyhead
Benllech
Red Wharf Bay
Llangoed
Pentraeth
Trearddur Bay
Holy Island
Llangefni
Rhosneigr
Menai Bridge Bangor
Beaumaris
Llanfairfechan
Llandudno
Rhôs-on-Sea
Rhy
Deganwy
Colwyn Bay
Aberge
Dwygyfylchi Conwy
Penmaenmawr
Llanddulas
Aberffraw
Llanfair PG
Llansanffraid Glan Conwy
Betws-yn-Rhos
Newborough
Y Felinheli
Llanllechid
Tal-y-Cafn
Llanfair Talhaiarn
Llansannan
Caernarfon
Bethesda
Tal-y-Bont
Llangernyw
Bontnewydd
Llanddeiniolen
Trefriw
Llanrwst
Llanrug
Llanberis
CONWY
Bylchau
Caernarfon
Bay
Llandwrog
Llanwnda
Betws Garmon
Capel Curig
Penygroes
Rhyd-Ddu
Dolwyddelan
Betws-y-Coed
Pentrefoelas
Clynnog-fawr
S N O W D O N I A
Penmachno
Cerrigydrudion
SH
Beddgelert
Blaenau Ffestiniog
Y Maer
Llanaelhaearn
Prenteg
Ffestiniog
Morfa Nefyn
Nefyn
PENINSULA
Tremadog
Maentwrog
Llandder
Bodfuan
Llanystumdwy
Porthmadog
Penrhyndeudraeth
N A T I O N A L
Bala
LLEYN
Criccieth
Borth-y-Gest
Talsarnau
Trawsfynydd
Sarn
Pwllheli
G W Y N E D D
Llanuwchllyn
Llanbedrog
Harlech
PARK
Llanw
Aberdaron
Y Rhiw
Abersoch
Llanbedr
Ganllwyd
L
Dyffryn Ardudwy
Bardsey Island
Tal-y-bont
Llanwd
Dolgellau
Dinas-Mawddwy
Barmouth
Llangadfa
Fairbourne
Mallwyd
M O U N T A I N
Corris
Llwyngwril
Cemmaes Road
Llanbrynmair
Bryncrug
SN
Tywyn
Pennal
Machynlleth
Carno
Aberdyfi
Borth
Tal-y-bont
Llandre
CARDIGAN BAY
Llanidloes
9
Aberystwyth
Capel Bangor
Ponterwyd

Guest Accommodation
AA Guest Accommodation of the Year
Town/Village name

0   10 miles
0   10   20 kilometres

For continuation pages refer to numbered arrows

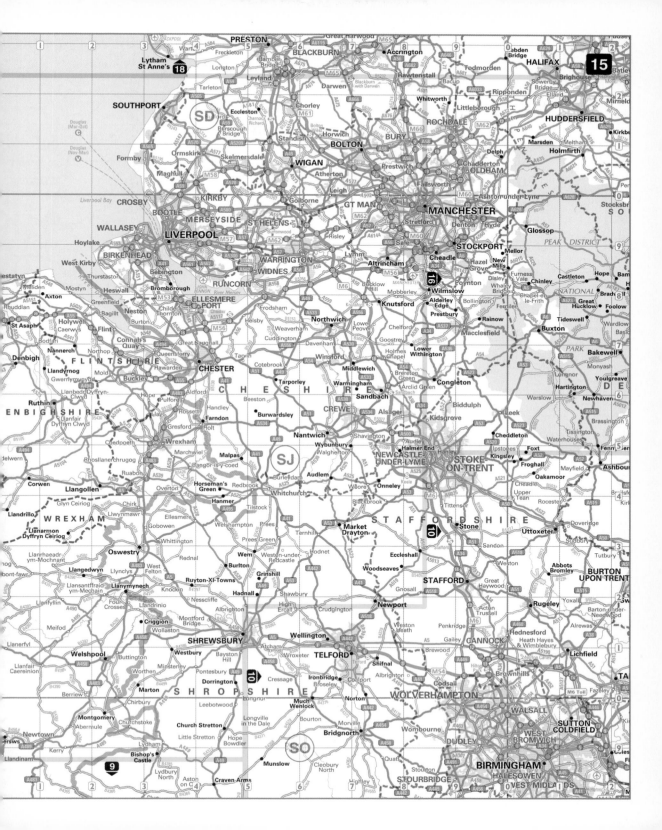

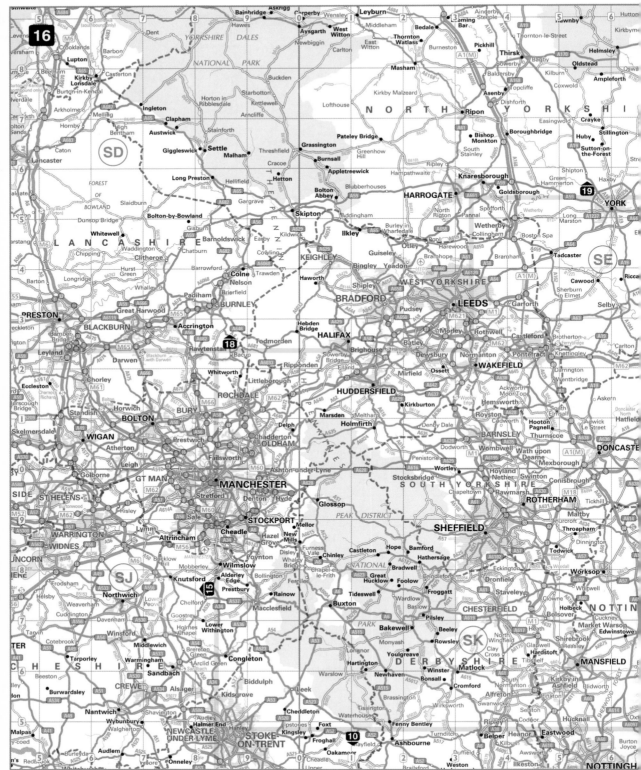

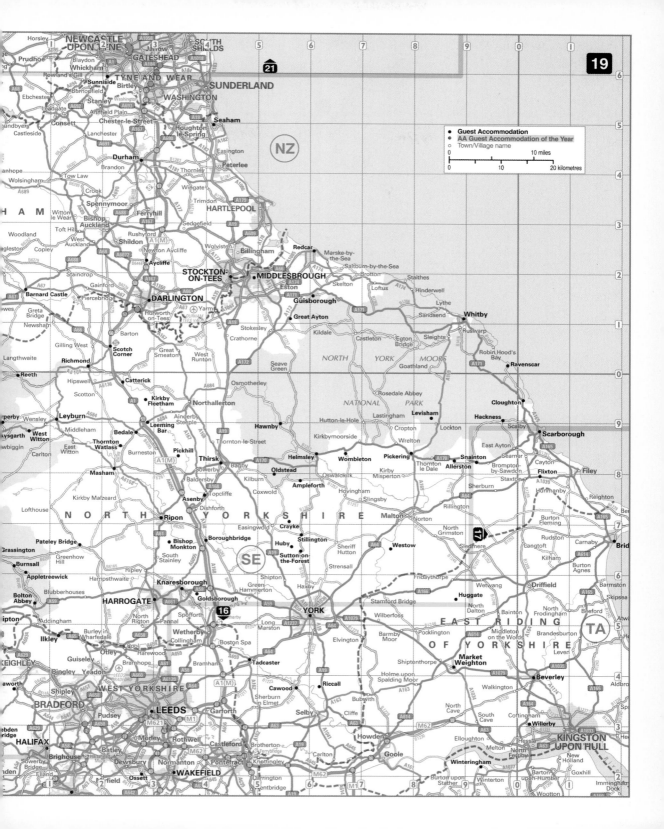

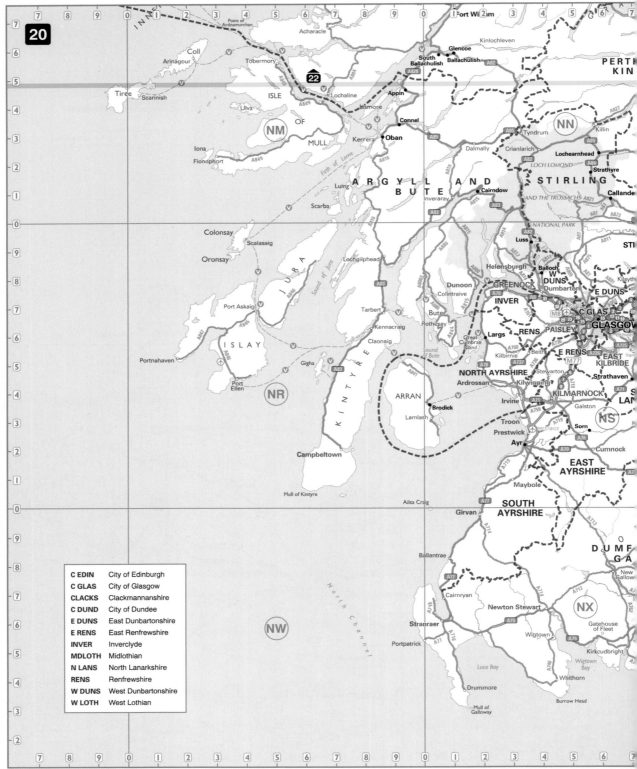

PERTH
KIN

Fort Wi?iam
Kinlochleven
Glencoe
South Ballachulish
Ballachulish
A82

NN

Acharacle

Point of Ardnamurchan

Coll
Arinagour
Tobermory
ISLE OF MULL

22

Lochaline
Lismore
Appin
Connel
Kerrera
Oban
A85
Dalmally
Tyndrum
Killin
Lochearnhead
Crianlarich
Strathyre
LOCH LOMOND
STIRLING
Callande
AND THE TROSSACHS

Tiree
Scarinish

Ulva
Iona
Fionnphort
A849
A816

NM

ARGYLL AND BUTE

Luing
Scarba
Inveraray
Cairndow

Colonsay
Scalasaig
Oronsay

Lochgilphead

JURA

Sound of Jura

Port Askaig

ISLAY

Portnahaven

Port Ellen

NR

KINTYRE

Gigha
A83

Tarbert
Kennacraig
Claonaig

Sound of Bute

ARRAN
Brodick
Lamlash

Campbeltown

Mull of Kintyre

Ailsa Craig

NATIONAL PARK
Luss
A82
STI

Helensburgh
Balloch
W DUNS
Kilsyth
Dunoon
GREENOCK
Dumbarton
E DUNS
Colintraive
INVER
Bute
M8
C GLAS
GLASGOW
Rothesay
RENS
PAISLEY
Great Cumbrae Island
Largs
E RENS
EAST KILBRIDE
M77
Kilbirnie
NORTH AYRSHIRE
Stewarton
Ardrossan
Kilwinning
Strathaven
LAN
Irvine
KILMARNOCK
Galston
NS
Troon
Sorn
PRESTWICK
Prestwick
Ayr
Cumnock
EAST AYRSHIRE
Maybole
SOUTH AYRSHIRE
Girvan

Ballantrae

North Channel

Cairnryan
Newton Stewart
Stranraer
NX
Wigtown
Gatehouse of Fleet
Portpatrick
A75
Kirkcudbright
Luce Bay
Wigtown Bay
Whithorn
Drummore
Burrow Head
Mull of Galloway

DUMF
GA

New Gallow

NW

C EDIN	City of Edinburgh
C GLAS	City of Glasgow
CLACKS	Clackmannanshire
C DUND	City of Dundee
E DUNS	East Dunbartonshire
E RENS	East Renfrewshire
INVER	Inverclyde
MDLOTH	Midlothian
N LANS	North Lanarkshire
RENS	Renfrewshire
W DUNS	West Dunbartonshire
W LOTH	West Lothian

For continuation pages refer to numbered arrows

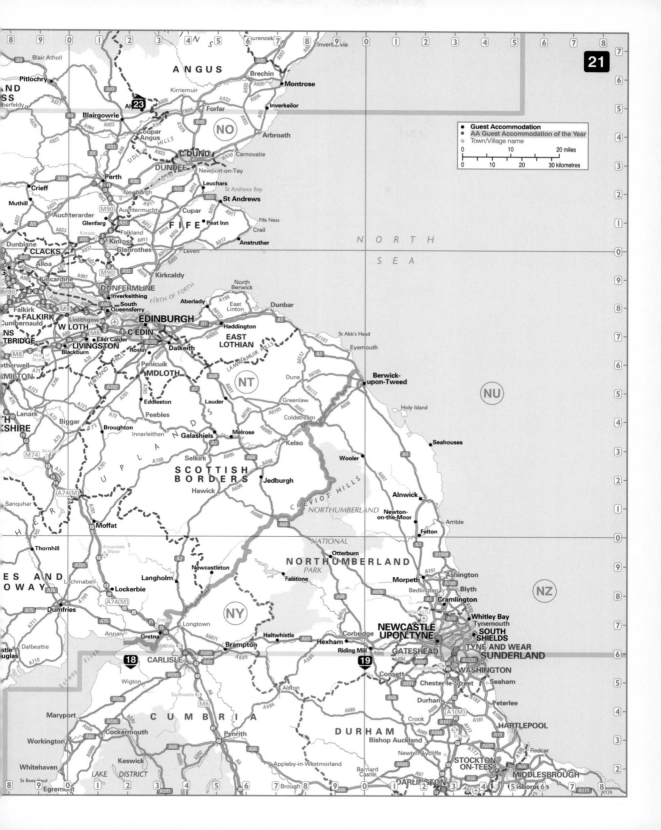

Cape Wrath

Rudha Rhobhanais
(Butt of Lewis)
Port Nis
(Port of Ness)
Cellar
Head

Handa Island

Scourie

NA

Great
Bernera

Carlabhagh
(Carloway)

LEWIS

Tiumpan
Head

NB

OF

Inchnadam

Steornabhagh
(Stornoway)

STORNOWAY

Lochinver

ISLE

NA H-EILEANAN
AN IAR

THE MINCH

Scarp

Taransay

Tairbeart
(Tarbert)

Scalpay

Gruinord
Bay

Ullapool

Sgarasta Bheag
(Scarista)

HARRIS

THE LITTLE MINCH

Poolewe

Pabbay

Gairloch

Boreray

Berneray

NORTH UIST

Loch nam Madadh
(Lochmaddy)

Staffin

Kinlochewe

Achnasheen

Uig

Torridon

Ronay

NF

Benbecula

Wiay

NG

Edinbane

Portree

ISLE

Dunvegan

Raasay

SOUTH
UIST

Struan

OF

Cannich

Loch Baghasdail
(Lochboisdale)

Drynoch

Scalpay

SKYE

Kyle of
Lochalsh

Ardelve

Eriskay

Soay

Shiel
Bridge

BARRA

Canna

A888

Bagh a Chaisteil
(Castlebay)

Rùm

Ardvasar

Invergarry

Sandray

Mallaig

Eigg

Mingulay

NORTH

Spean
Bridge

INNER HEBRIDES

Muck

Fort William

Point of
Ardnamurchan

NM

Kinlochleven

Acharacle

Glencoe

NL

Coll

Tobermory

South
Ballachulish

Ballachulish

Arinagour

Tiree

Scarinish

20

ISLE

Lochaline

Appin

WEST
HIGHLANDS

Connel

Ulva

OF

Lismore

Iona
Fionnphort

MULL

Kerrera

Oban

Dalmally

Crianla

OUTER HEBRIDES

For continuation pages refer to numbered arrows

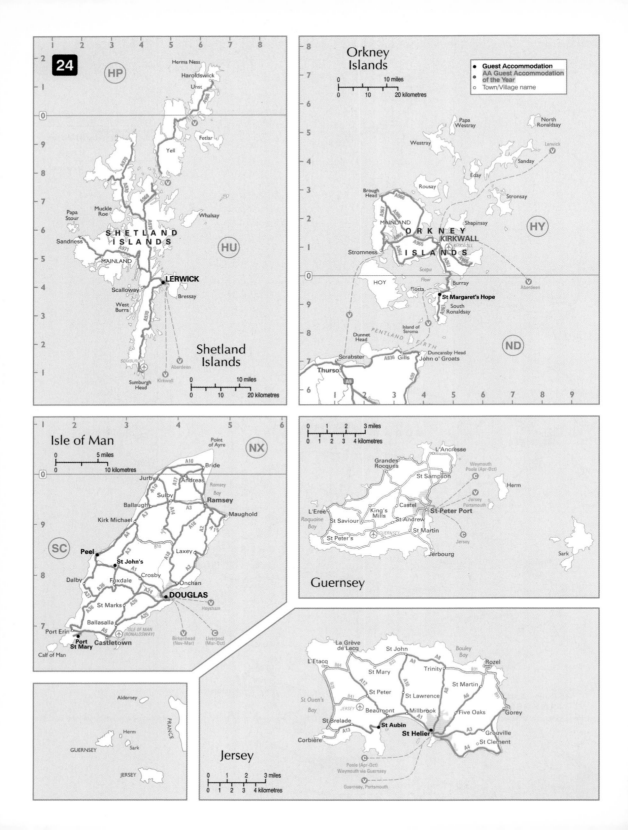

24

HP

Herma Ness
Haroldswick
Unst

Fetlar

Yell

Papa
Stour
Muckle
Roe

Whalsay

**S H E T L A N D
I S L A N D S**

Sandness

HU

MAINLAND

LERWICK

Scalloway

Bressay

West
Burra

SUMBURGH

Aberdeen

Kirkwall

**Shetland
Islands**

Sumburgh
Head

10 miles

0   10   20 kilometres

Orkney
Islands

- Guest Accommodation
- AA Guest Accommodation
  of the Year
○ Town/Village name

0   10 miles

0   10   20 kilometres

Papa
Westray

North
Ronaldsay

Westray

Sanday

Lerwick

Rousay

Eday

Stronsay

Brough
Head

MAINLAND

O R K N E Y

Shapinsay

KIRKWALL

Stromness

I S L A N D S

KIRKWALL

HOY

Scapa
Flow

Burray

Aberdeen

Flotta

St Margaret's Hope

HY

South
Ronaldsay

PENTLAND

Dunnet
Head

Island of
Stroma

FIRTH

Duncansby Head
John o' Groats

ND

Scrabster

Gills

Thurso

A9

Isle of Man

0   5 miles

0   10 kilometres

Point
of Ayre

NX

A10

Bride

Jurby

Andreas

Ramsey
Bay

Ballaugh

Sulby

Ramsey

Kirk Michael

Maughold

SC

Peel

St John's

Laxey

Dalby

Foxdale

Crosby

Onchan

St Marks

DOUGLAS

Heysham

Ballasalla

*ISLE OF MAN
(RONALDSWAY)*

Port Erin

**Port
St Mary**

Castletown

Birkenhead
(Nov-Mar)

Liverpool
(Mar-Oct)

Calf of Man

---

0   1   2   3 miles

0   1   2   3   4 kilometres

L'Ancresse

Grandes
Rocques

St Sampson

Weymouth
Poole (Apr-Oct)

Herm

L'Eree

King's
Mills

Castel

St Peter Port

Jersey
Portsmouth

St Saviour

St Andrew

Roquaine
Bay

St Peter's

GUERNSEY

St Martin

Jersey

Guernsey

Jerbourg

Sark

Alderney

Herm

FRANCE

GUERNSEY

Sark

JERSEY

La Grève
de Lecq

St John

Bouley
Bay

L'Etacq

B64

St Mary

A9

Trinity

Rozel
B31

St Peter

St Lawrence

A8

St Martin

A6

St Ouen's
Bay

JERSEY

B41

Beaumont

Millbrook

Five Oaks

Gorey

St Brelade

St Aubin

A1

St Helier

Grouville

Corbière

A13

A4

St Clement

Jersey

Poole (Apr-Oct)
Weymouth via Guernsey

Guernsey, Portsmouth

0   1   2   3 miles

0   1   2   3   4 kilometres

Central London

Plan 1

KEY TO B & B LOCATIONS

Each B & B in London has a map reference, eg C2. The letter 'C' refers to the grid square located at the bottom of the map. The figure '2' refers to the grid square located at the left hand edge of the map. For example, where these two intersect, Buckingham Palace can be found. Due to the scale of the map, only a rough guide to the location of a B & B can be given. A more detailed map will be necessary to be precise.

■ Congestion Charging Zone boundary

London Plan 2

Central London Congestion Charging Zone

Guest Accommodation

Index of Bed & Breakfasts

Acknowledgements

The Automobile Association would like to thank the following photographers, companies and picture libraries for their assistance in the preparation of this book.

Abbreviations for the picture credits are as follows – (t) top; (b) bottom; (c) centre; (l) left; (r) right; (AA) AA World Travel Library

England Opener AA/John Miller; Scotland Opener AA/Stephen Whitehorne; Wales Opener AA/Mark Bauer; Ireland Opener AA/Christopher Hill; 001b Miles-Flashpoint Pictures/Alamy; 002l Rob Cousins/Alamy; 003tl Elizabeth Whiting & Associates/Alamy; 005tl Courtesy Rains Farm; 006bl AA/Kit Fanner; 007br MBI/Alamy; 009t Seapix/Alamy; 010br Loop Images/Craig Holmes/Images of Birmingham; 011 AA/Mike Kipling Photography; 012t AA/Kit Fanner; 013t Courtesy Dragonfly; 013b Courtesy Marble Arch by Montcalm; 014t Courtesy East House; 014b Courtesy Arden Country House; 015t Courtesy Crug-Glas Country House; 015b Courtesy The Heron's Cove; 016 Courtesy Rains Farm; 018t Courtesy Rains Farm; 019t Courtesy Rains Farm; 019b Courtesy Rains Farm; 020/021l Courtesy Dragonfly; 022t Courtesy Dragonfly; 023t Courtesy Dragonfly; 188b AA/Michael Busselle; 356b Peter Cain/4Corners; 357 AA/AA; 417 AA/Stephen Lewis; 439 AA/Caroline Jones

Every effort has been made to trace the copyright holders, and we apologise in advance for any unintentional omissions or errors. We would be pleased to apply any corrections in a following edition of this publication.

Readers' Report Form

Please send this form to:–
Editor, The B&B Guide,
Lifestyle Guides,
AA Media,
Fanum House,
Basingstoke RG21 4EA

e-mail: lifestyleguides@theAA.com

Please use this form to recommend any guest house, farmhouse or inn where you have stayed, that is not currently listed in the guide. If you have any comments about your stay at an establishment listed in the guide, please let us know, as feedback from readers helps to keep our Guide accurate and up to date. If you have a complaint during your stay, we recommend that you discuss the matter with the establishment.

Please note that the AA does not undertake to arbitrate between you and the establishment, or to obtain compensation or engage in protracted correspondence.

Date

Your name (BLOCK CAPITALS)

Your address (BLOCK CAPITALS)

Post code

E-mail address

Name of establishment

Location

Comments

(please attach a separate sheet if necessary)

Please tick here ☐ if you DO NOT wish to receive details of AA offers or products

PTO

Readers' Report Form *continued*

Have you bought this guide before? ☐ YES ☐ NO

Do you regularly use any other accommodation, restaurant, pub or food guides? ☐ YES ☐ NO
If YES, which ones?

....

....

Why did you buy this guide? (tick all that apply)

Holiday ☐   Short break ☐   Business travel ☐   Special occasion ☐
Overnight stop ☐   Find a venue for an event e.g. conference ☐
Other (please state)

How often do you stay in B&Bs? (tick one choice)

More than once a month ☐   Once a month ☐   Once in 2-3 months ☐
Once in six months ☐   Once a year ☐   Less than once a year ☐
Other (please state)

Please answer these questions to help us make improvements to the guide:

Which of these factors are the most important when choosing a B&B? (tick all that apply)

Price ☐   Location ☐   Awards/ratings ☐   Service ☐
Decor/surroundings ☐   Previous experience ☐   Recommendation ☐
Other (please state)

Do you read the editorial features in the guide? ☐ YES ☐ NO

Do you use the location atlas?   ☐ YES ☐ NO

What elements of the guide do you find most useful when choosing somewhere to stay? (tick all that apply)

Description ☐   Photo ☐   Advertisement ☐   Star rating ☐

Is there any other information you would like to see added to this guide?

....

....

....

....

....